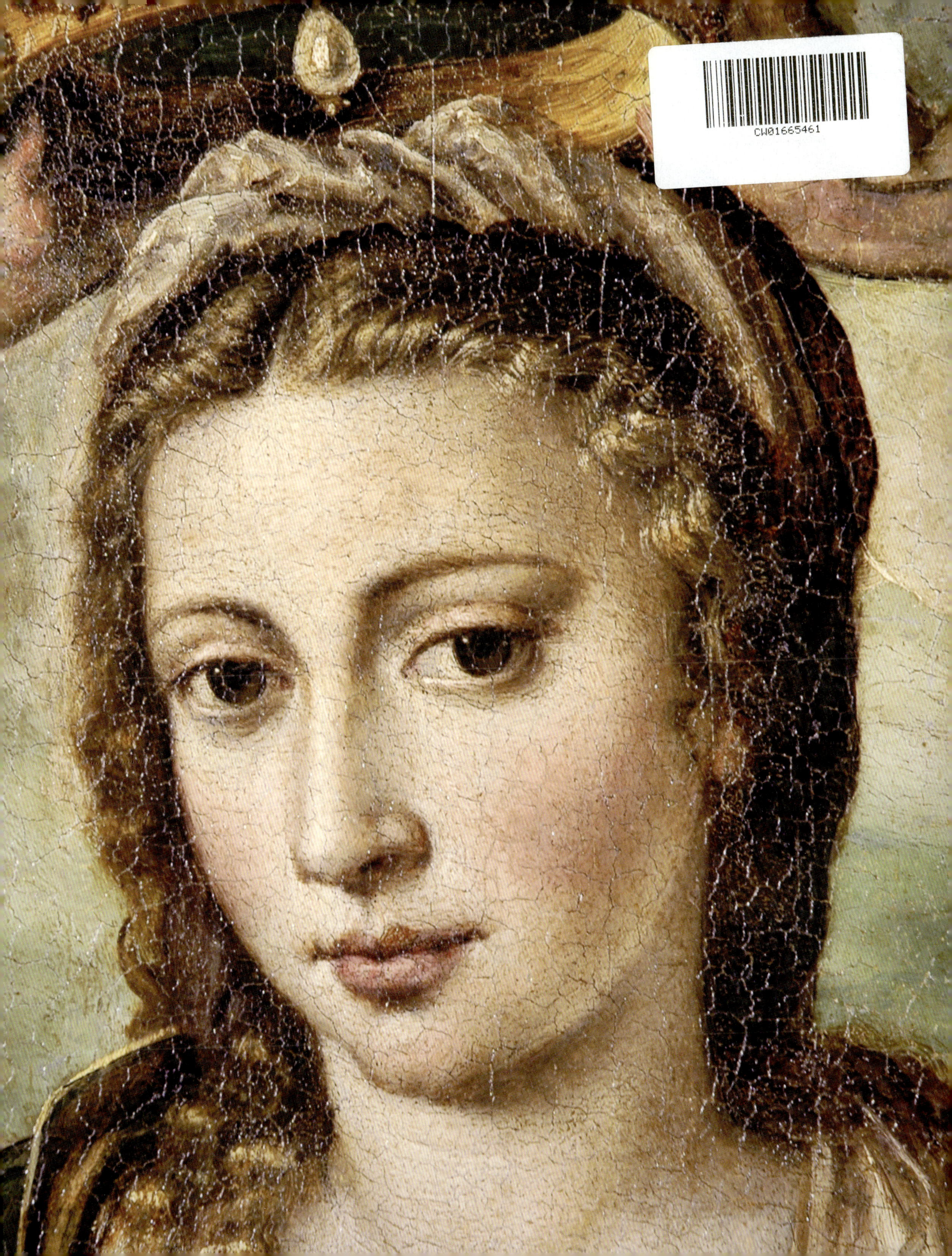

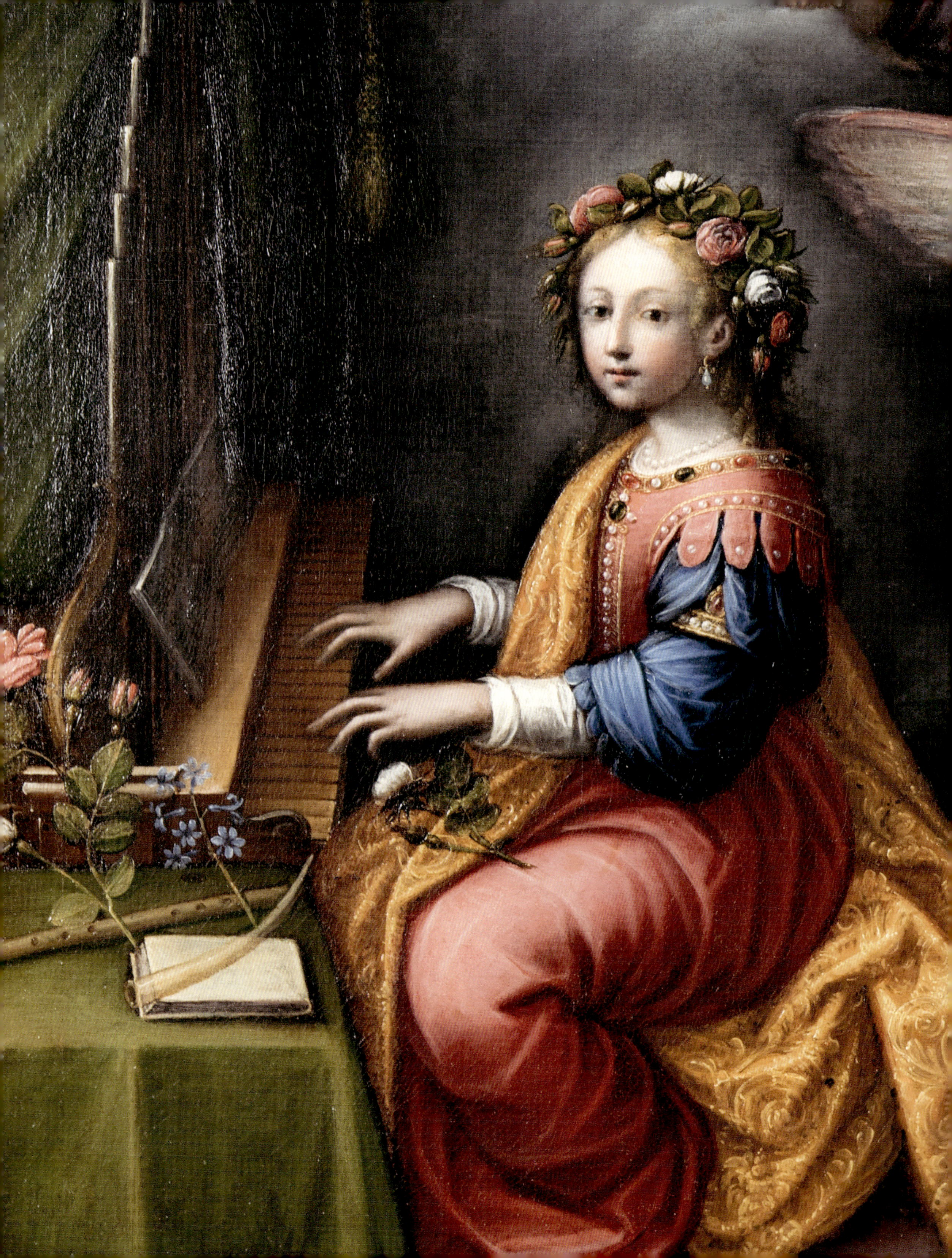

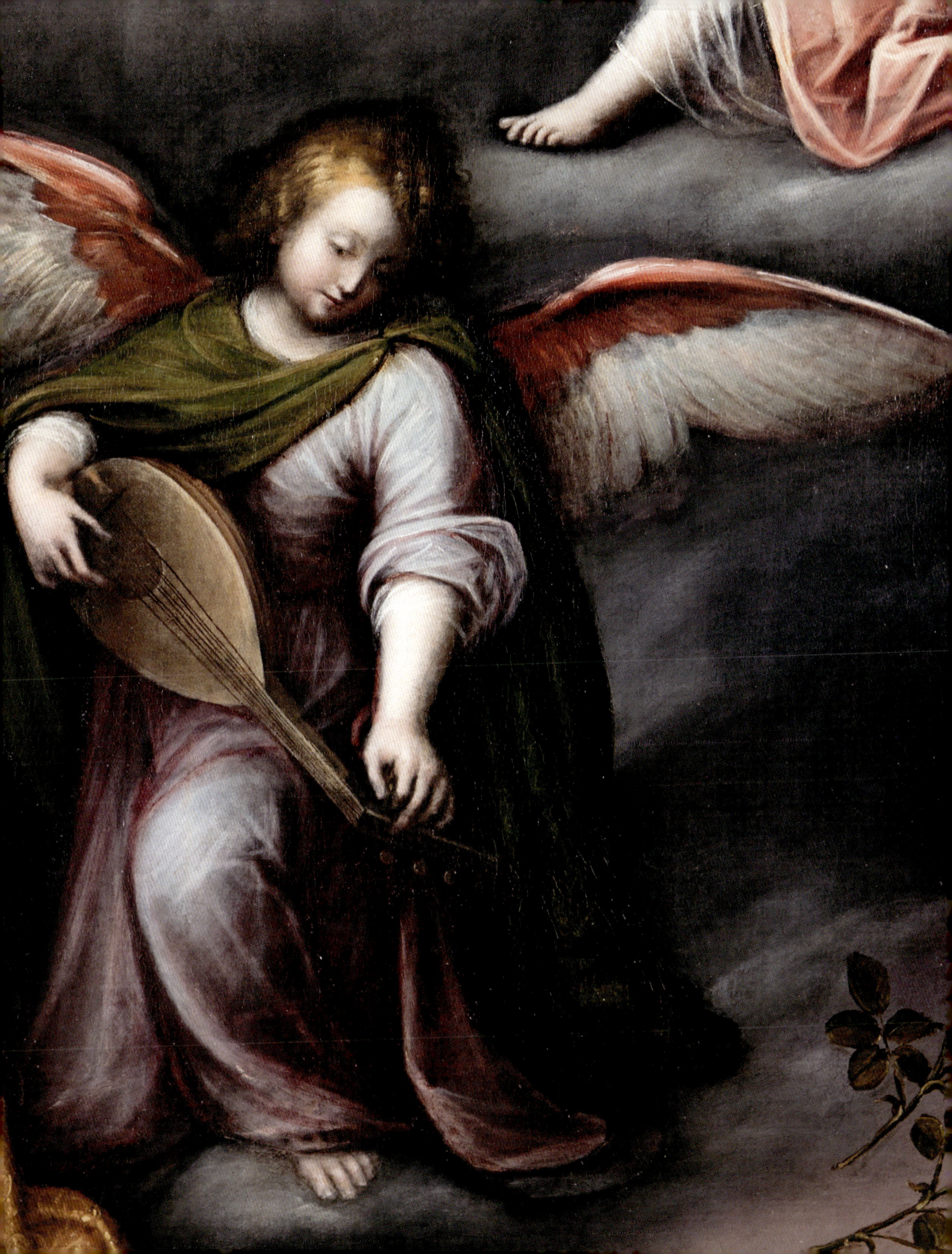

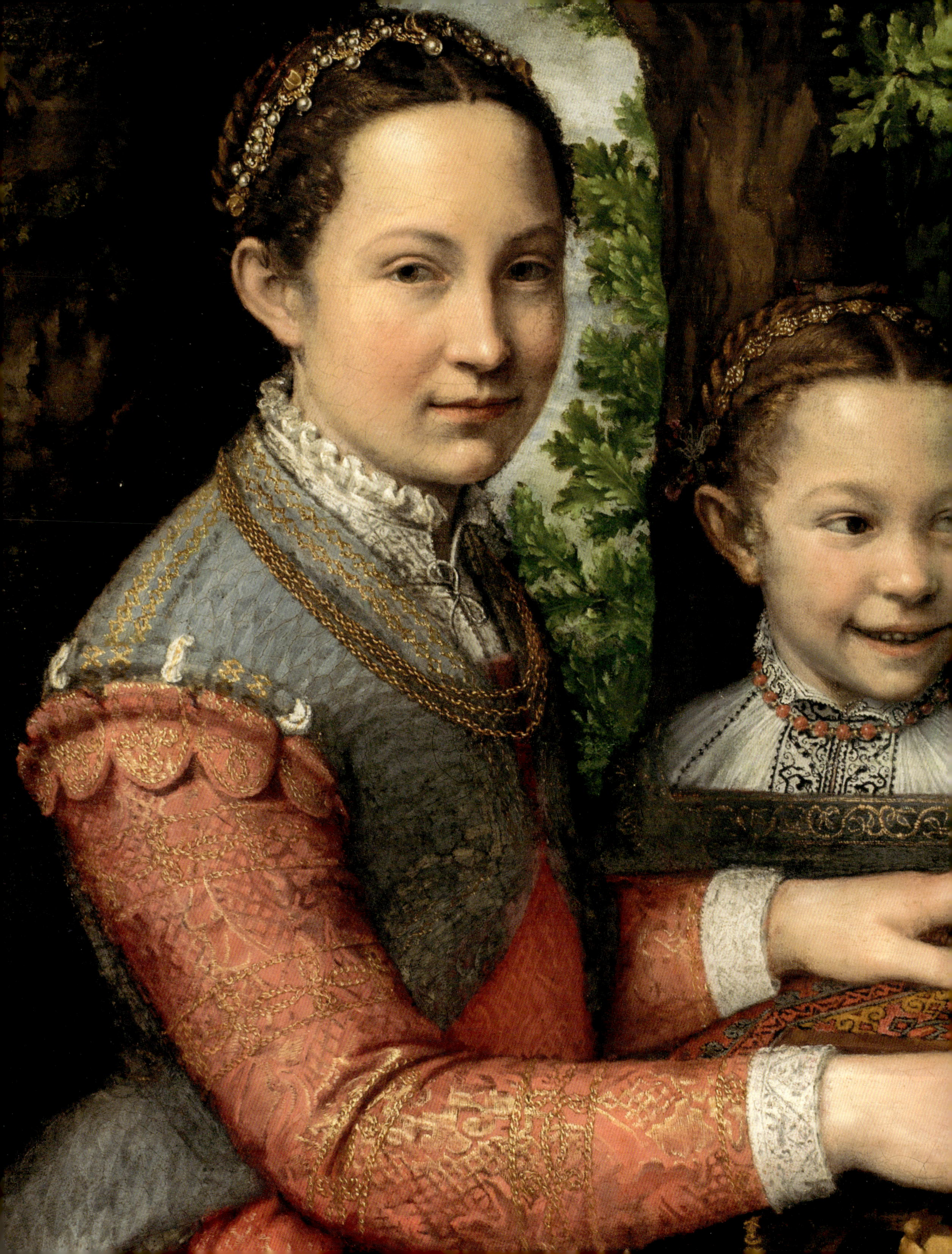

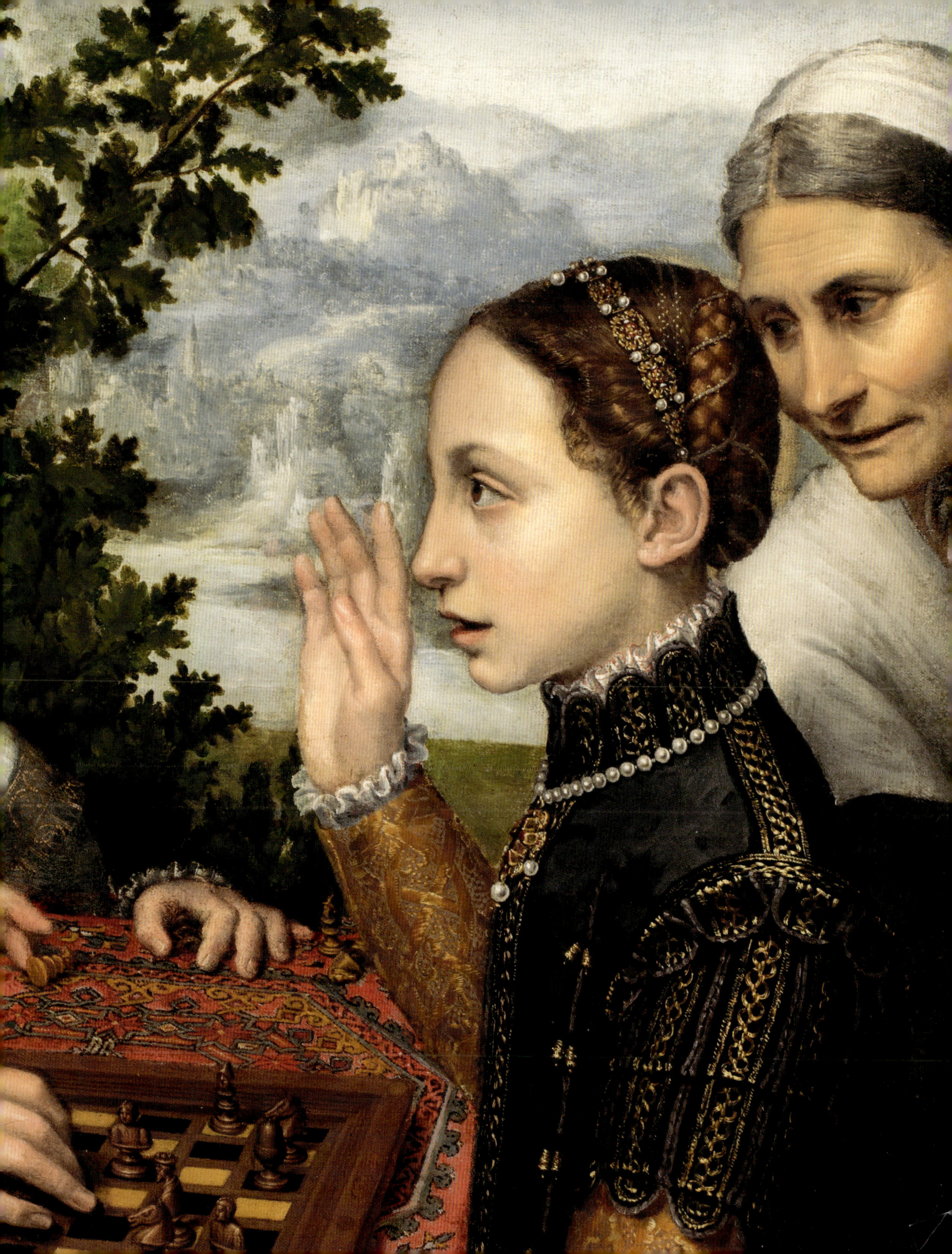

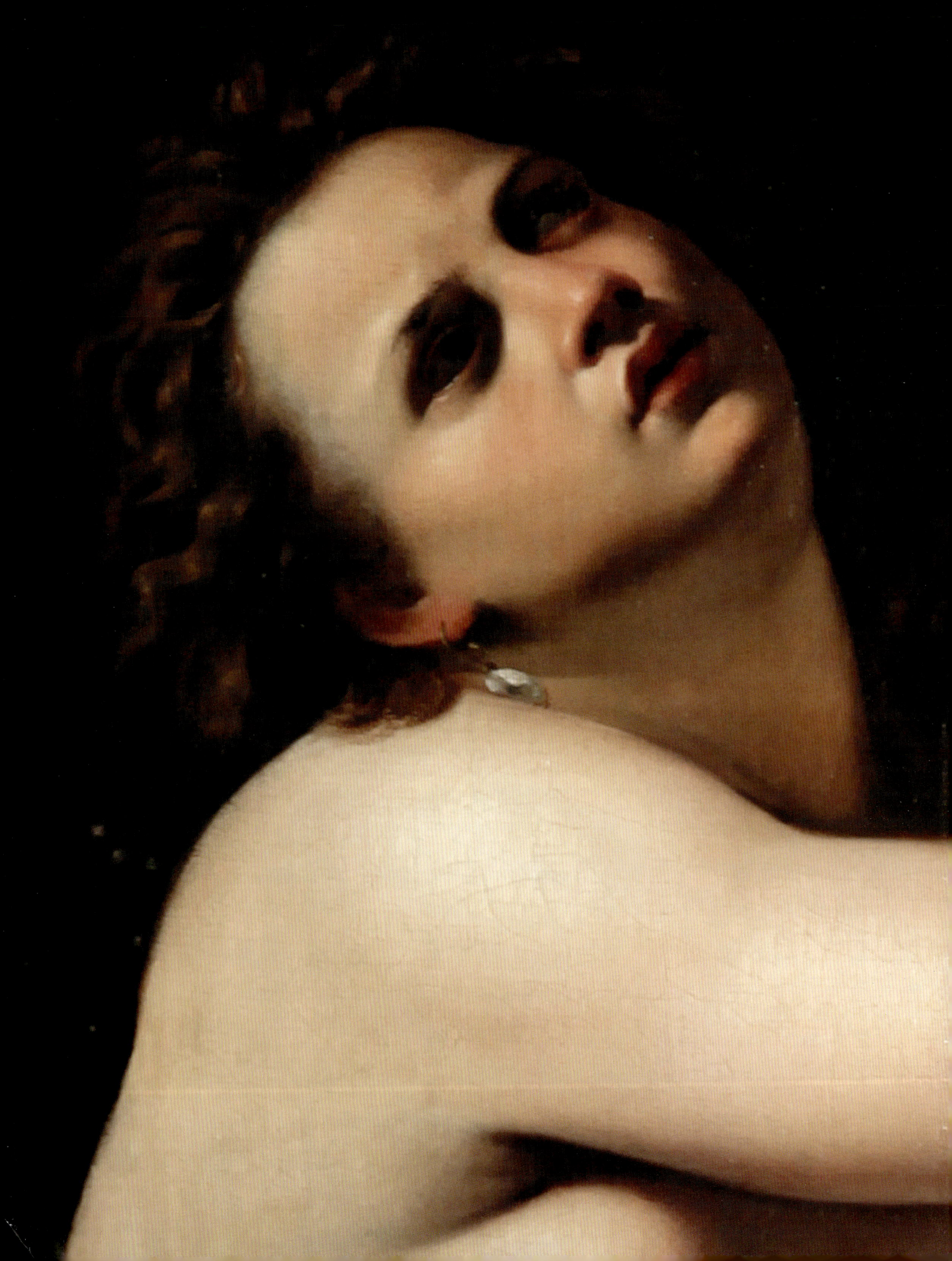

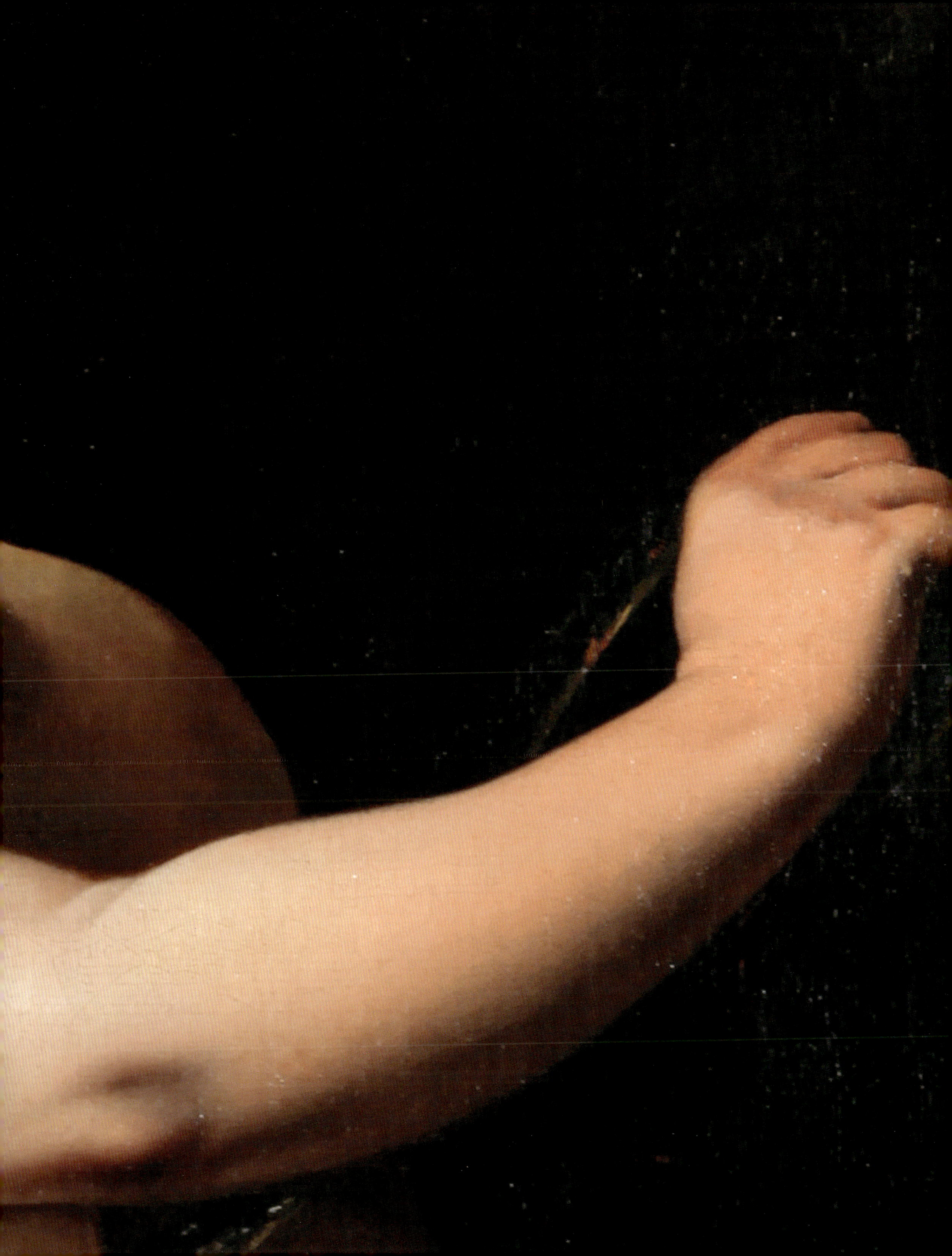

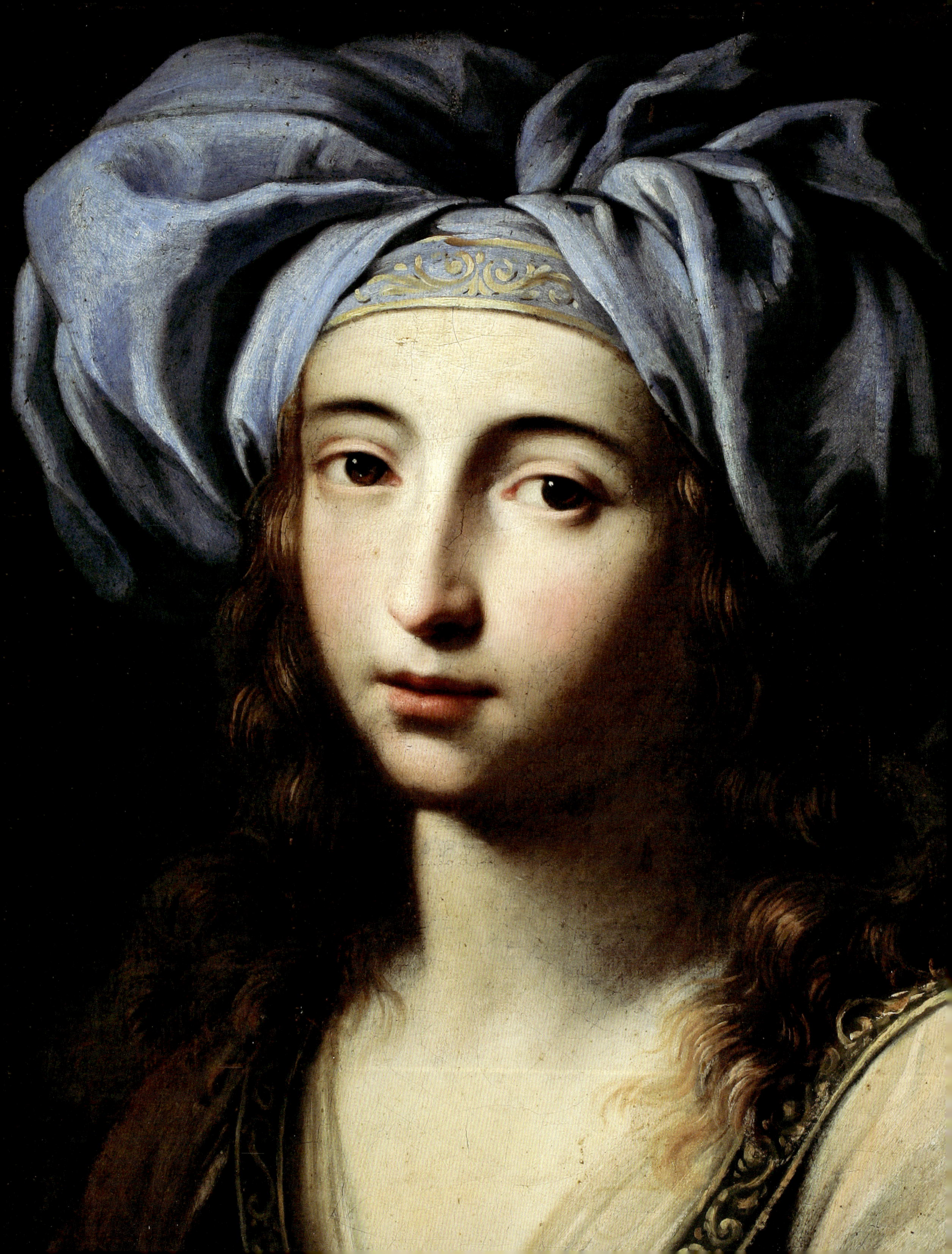

The Ladies of Art

Stories of Women in the 16th and 17th Centuries

edited by Annamaria Bava, Gioia Mori, Alain Tapié

SKIRA

Cover
Fede Galizia
Judith with the Head of Holofernes, detail
1601
(cat. 3.48)

Page 1
Sofonisba Anguissola
Madonna dell'Itria, detail
1578–1579
(cat. 1.12)

Pages 2–3
Orsola Maddalena Caccia
Saint Cecilia Playing a Positive Organ and Musician Angels, detail
c. 1620–1630
(cat. 2.7)

Pages 4–5
Sofonisba Anguissola
Chess Game, detail
1555
(cat. 1.8)

Pages 6–7
Artemisia Gentileschi
Cleopatra, detail
c. 1620
(cat. 5.3)

Page 8
Ginevra Cantofoli
Young Woman (Sibyl), detail
c. 1650
(cat. 3.22)

Design
Marcello Francone

Editorial Coordination
Eva Vanzella

Copy Editor
Sara Tedesco

Layout
Marina Boer
Paola Ranzini

Translations
Ben Bazalgette (pp. 81–89)
Gordon Fisher, Liquid Translations (prelims, pp. 92–149, 266–295, 346–349)
Catherine Frost (pp. 24–53)
Patricia B. Garvin (pp. 66–80, 150–177, 192–231, 296–333 except Adelina Modesti's texts)
Carol Lee Rathman (pp. 54–65, 232–265, 334–345)

Iconographic Research
Paola Lamanna

First published in Italy in 2021 by
Skira editore S.p.A.
Palazzo Casati Stampa
via Torino 61
20123 Milano
Italy
www.skira.net

Printed and bound in Italy.
First edition

ISBN: 978-88-572-4682-6

Distributed in USA, Canada, Central & South America by ARTBOOK | D.A.P., 75 Broad Street, Suite 630, New York, NY 10004, USA.
Distributed elsewhere in the world by Thames and Hudson Ltd., 181A High Holborn, London WC1V 7QX, United Kingdom.

This book was published on the occasion of the exhibition "The Ladies of Art: Stories of Women in the 16th and 17th Centuries", curated by Annamaria Bava, Gioia Mori, Alain Tapié
Palazzo Reale, Milan,
2 March – 25 July 2021

Contents

“IF PABLO HAD BEEN PABLITA”

ITALIAN WOMEN ARTISTS OF THE RENAISSANCE AND BAROQUE ERAS, FACT AND FICTION

Gioia Mori

To my mother Biancamaria, in gratitude

"A" as in Amilcare, "B" as in Bianca, "C" as in Cremona; it all seemed so easy to the young woman trying to teach the alphabet to the sumptuously dressed old lady seated in the Dante chair, who struggled to link those signs she saw in the copybook to the familiar names of the Anguissola family. The girl laughed; and Michelangelo too may have smiled too when, at about the age of eighty, he received the "most bizarre drawing" from the hand of Sofonisba Anguissola, a girl of around twenty from Cremona.[1] He may have remembered other women of his time who had practiced art passionately and competently, all of them dead by now: Giovanna di Montefeltro, Duchess of Urbino, the "prefetessa of Rome", who had backed Raphael; Isabella d'Este, who had tenaciously managed to obtain his *Sleeping Cupid* passed off as ancient, and as a true connoisseur had proclaimed "among modern works it has no equal"; and Vittoria Colonna, "a man in a woman, and even a god".

A few women artists were active, and Michelangelo's friend Vasari, whose *Lifes* had already been published by Lorenzo Torrentino, had praised the sculptress Properzia de' Rossi from Bologna, who died in 1530. This determined woman was often involved in lawsuits, some due to a temper that led her so far as to attack with her nails, others to her will to impose her presence on the all-male construction site of San Petronio. In Florence there was a successful workshop headed by a Dominican nun, Plautilla Nelli; and a few great Flemish women miniaturists, some of whom worked at the court of England, were known in Michelangelo's day. The girl from Cremona showed a certain "inclination", causing Michelangelo to reply with a challenge, as told by Tommaso Cavalieri: "He said he would have thought a weeping boy something much harder to depict, and [...] she sent him [...] a portrait of her brother whom she had purposely reduced to tears".[2]

As to the drawings discussed in the correspondence between Michelangelo and Sofonisba's father, the nobleman Amilcare, eager to promote his daughter's talent, the first was probably the model for an etching done in Rome by Jacob Bos[3] (fig. 1); the latter, the one donated by Tommaso Cavalieri to Cosimo I in 1562[4] (fig. 2). The relationship between Michelangelo and Amilcare Anguissola culminated in a refined, deferential letter dated 7 May 1557, where the girl's father, in thanking the artist for the "loving affection he has shown to Sofonisba", asks him to send "one of your drawings so that she can colour it in oil, promising to send it back faithfully finished by her own hand".[5]

It may have been Michelangelo, who had made the talented girl his *protégée*, to call her to Vasari's attention, and when he went to Cremona in May 1566 he visited the Anguissola family, who were friends of many intellectuals, among them Annibal Caro and Girolamo Vida. Although Sofonisba was already in Madrid, at the strict court of Philip II, Vasari saw some of her paintings and conversed at length with her little sister Europa, she too an artist. In the second edition of his *Lifes*, published by Giunti in 1568, Sofonisba has no chapter of her own, but is mentioned in various contexts. In the "Life of Madonna Properzia" he sings her praises, but fails to mention any of her works.[6] After haven seen the *Portrait of the Artist's Family* now at Nivå and the *Chess Game* (cat. 1.8), and having read the correspondence between the

1. Jacob Bos
(after Sofonisba Anguissola)
Girl Laughing at a Silly Old Woman
1560–1564
London, The British Museum

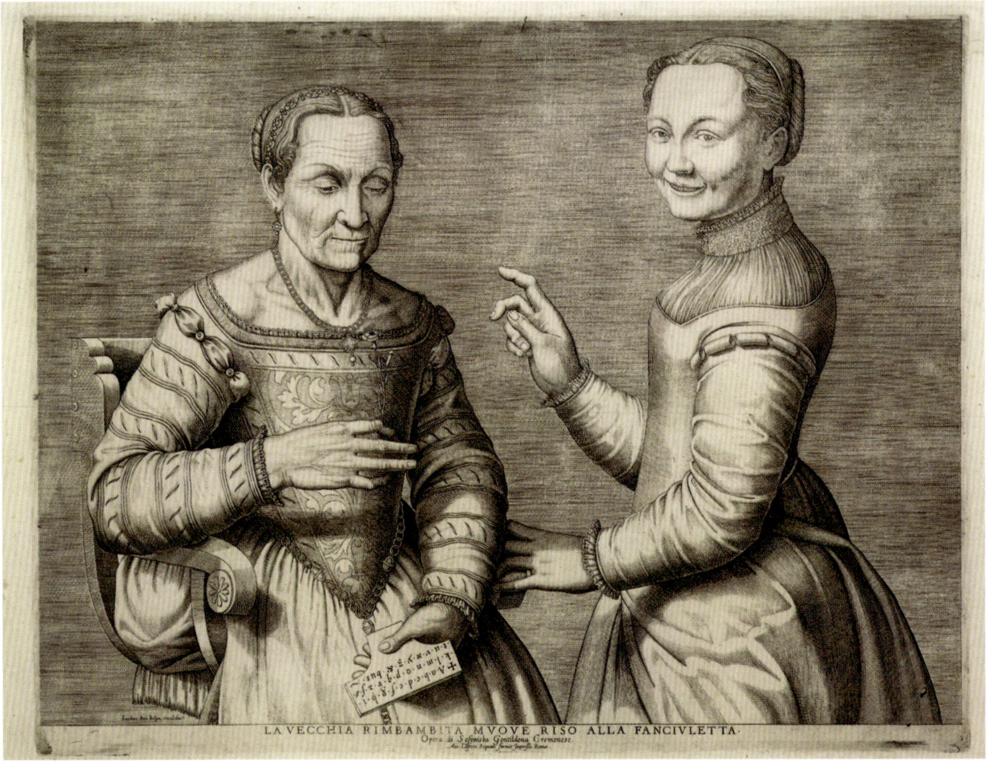

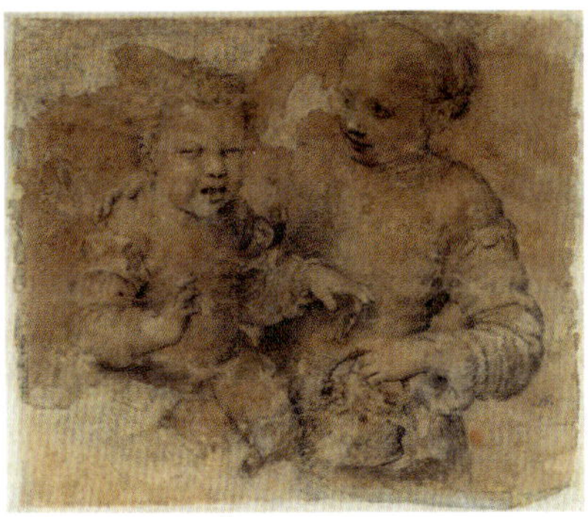

2. Sofonisba Anguissola
Asdrubale Bitten by a Shrimp
1555–1558
Naples, Museo e Real Bosco di Capodimonte, Gabinetto Disegni e Stampe

young artist and Pope Pius IV in 1561 concerning a portrait of Isabella di Valois, he inserts a more detailed account in the “Life of Benvenuto Garofalo and Girolamo da Carpi and Other Lombards”. In the “Life of Taddeo Zuccari” he mentions a self-portrait then in Rome, at the home of Cardinal Innocenzo Ciocchi del Monte, which Sofonisba had donated to Pope Julius III.[7]

In 1568, just when her fame had received Vasari’s placet, Sofonisba met with tragic events at the court in Madrid. In July came the death of mad prince Carlos – Verdi’s tragic *Don Carlos*. She had painted a portrait of him that Philip II had ordered the court painter Alonso Sánchez Coello to make thirteen copies of, even though his son had plotted against him. Then in October came the death of Isabella of Valois. This daughter of Catherine de’ Medici, who had become Philip’s third wife at the age of fourteen, succumbed to the complications of a pregnancy. Bernardo Maschi, Ambassador of Urbino to the court, reported on Sofonisba’s grief: “Signora Sofonisba says that she no longer wants to live”.[8] But Sofonisba remained at the Madrid court, where she had enjoyed the prestigious friendship of Joanna of Hapsburg, the highly cultivated sister of Philip II, a Jesuit follower who was to retire to a convent, a melancholy widow deprived for political reasons of her son left in Portugal. At the Madrid court Sofonisba painfully adhered to the strict etiquette governing every moment in the Queen’s Residence, stated in writing by Philip II with the arrival of his fourth wife Anne of Austria. In 1571 these rules provoked a nocturnal revolution that involved even the placid Sofonisba, with the destruction of the barricades and partitions that had restricted contact with the outer world.[9] From that exclusive viewpoint, she witnessed the preparations for the great Battle of Lepanto, won by Don John of Austria, half-brother of Philip II. The memory of those events, fortified by recitation of the rosary demanded by the Pope of all Christianity and all the

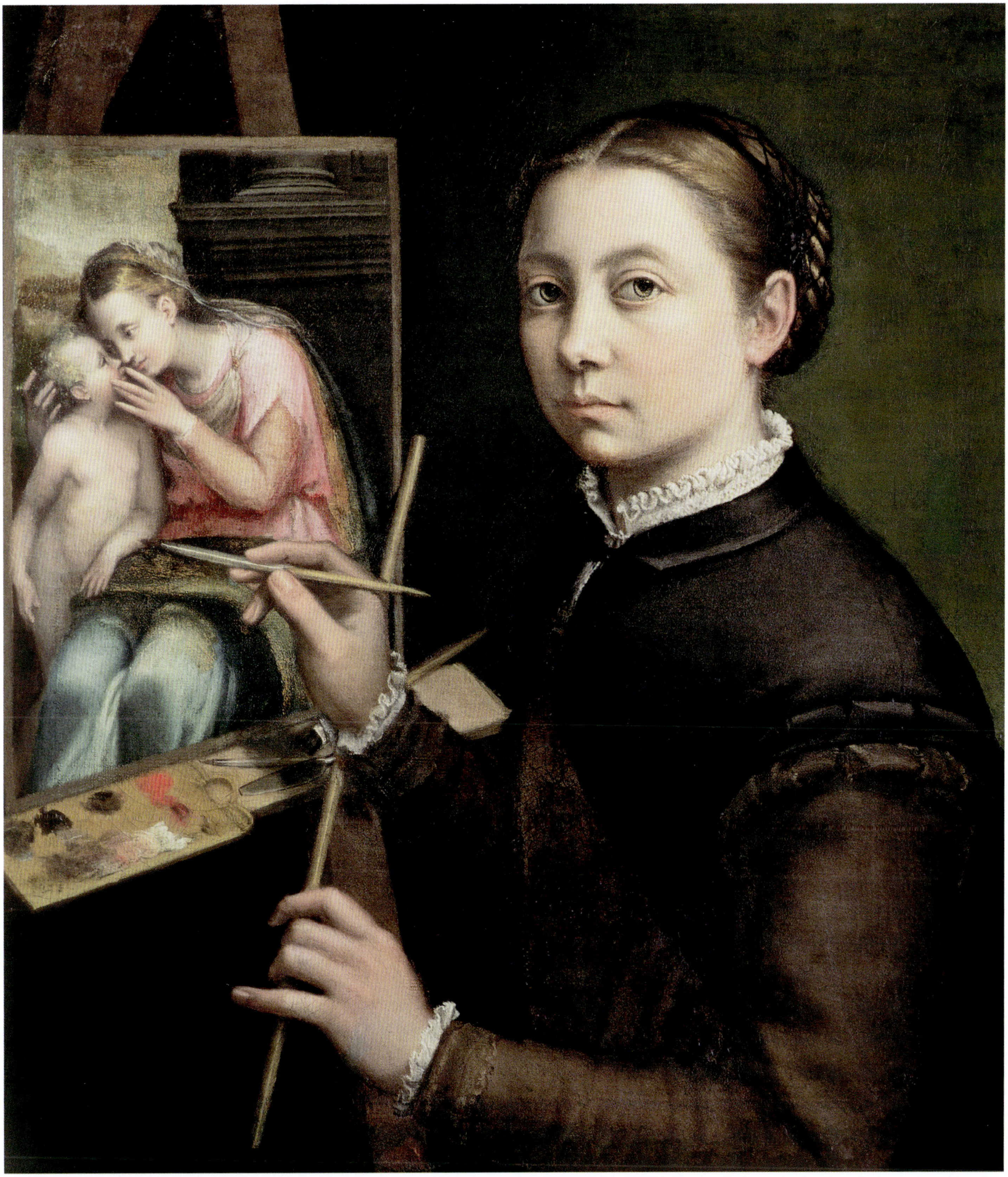

3. Sofonisba Anguissola
Self-Portrait at the Easel
1556
Łańcut, Muzeum Zamek

soldiers of the Holy League, clearly emerges in the portrait of Philip II, grasping the beads in his hand like a weapon.

Sofonisba received several marriage proposals, which had to be approved by the king. Among her suitors were two Italian diplomats, Count Broccardo Persico and Girolamo Negri. She chose instead Fabrizio Moncada, whom she had met at the court of Madrid, perhaps in 1571, the year when Cesare Moncada died, and Fabrizio requested, but without success, the custody of his child nephew. The wedding took place only in 1573, and Sofonisba arrived in Sicily with a generous dowry provided by the king: twelve thousand *scudi* and a trousseau of jewels and clothing, with "a gown adorned with pearls". The Moncada court was governed with "a truly masculine spirit", according to Lengueglia,[10] by his sister-in-law Aloisia Luna, a woman imbued with Jesuit spirituality, the descendent of a powerful family related to the highest European nobility. Sofonisba, welcomed with all honours, lived at Paternò, where Fabrizio served as governor. This Norman fortress overlooked a vast plain resembling the Spanish plateau, when viewed at a distance from the profile of Mount Etna. The lady from Cremona, well versed in Spanish etiquette, managed to resolve complicated family matters while still finding some time for painting.

Her artistic *corpus*, duly signed during her years in Cremona, anonymous while in Spain, since her duties at court were not connected with art, anonymous during her Sicilian period as the wife of a nobleman, is still awaiting detailed analysis, despite the recent attempt of Cole.[11] Crucially important for understanding her Sicilian period was the discovery of an altarpiece with ancient iconography, the *Madonna dell'Itria* (cat. 1.12), left at Paternò after the death of her beloved Fabrizio, who drowned along the coast of Capri in 1578 while fleeing from Algerian pirates. Still unclear is Sofonisba's production during her years in Genoa with her second husband, Orazio Lomellini, married without the approval of Philip II. In Genoa she became the diplomatic link sought by all the artists intent on reaching the Spanish court. Still to be investigated is her relationship with the Savoy court, where the Infanta Catalina Micaela arrived in 1585 as the bride of Charles Emmanuel I of Savoy. Like her mother, Catalina was destined to die in premature childbirth when barely thirty. Sofonisba's ties to the House of Savoy did not end even when she moved to Palermo in 1615, where her husband Lomellini had gone for business reasons. The Viceroy of Sicily starting in 1622 was in fact Emmanuel Philibert of Savoy, third-born child of Infanta Catalina Micaela, who was to die in Palermo during the plague of 1624. Anthony van Dyck, arriving in Sicily to paint his portrait, met Sofonisba. Now over the age of ninety, she was an artist who had been admired by his master Pieter Paul Rubens, who had painted a portrait of the Infanta Isabella Clara Eugenia (cat. 1.11), now a Poor Clare and Governor of the Netherlands.[12]

The destiny of Sofonisba, coming from a family related to several noble houses in Northern Italy,[13] was perhaps greater than her father had expected when he allowed her to attend Bernardino Campi's studio, perhaps mindful of the Flemish women artists at the English court, Levina Bening Teerlinc and Susanna Horenbout. The latter was known in Northern Italy for having, with her father Gerard, illuminated parts of the *Grimani Breviary*, a masterpiece that had been in Venice at the home of Cardinal Domenico Grimani since 1520; and then there was Catharina van Hemessen, summoned to the Spanish court by Charles V's sister, Mary Queen of Hungary and Bohemia. In 1548 Catharina had painted a *Self-Portrait at the Easel,* deemed the prototype of the modern era's female self-portrait,[14] very similar in composition to Sofonisba's youthful *Self-Portrait* now in Łańcut (fig. 3).

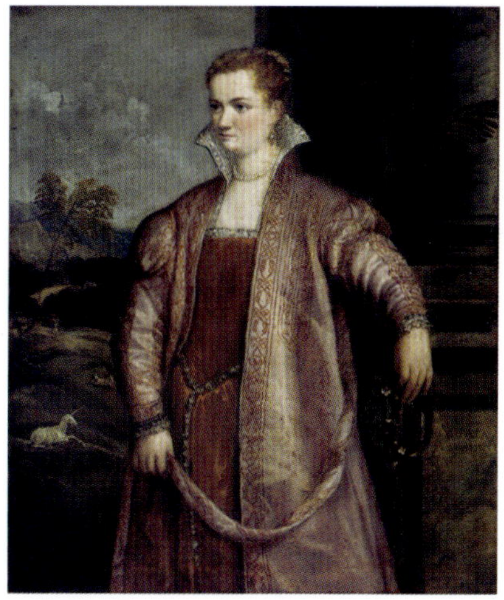

4. Giovan Paolo Pace
and Titian
Irene di Spilimbergo
c. 1560
Washington, The National
Gallery of Art

Noblewomen and Female Artists

When Vasari explored the narrow confines of female art, he traced a series of careers with locales and styles differing from those of male artists, that form the investigative theme of this exhibition. Few indeed, and mainly of noble birth, were the women given the chance to study with a renowned master. More often instead, women practiced their art behind the walls of a convent, or in a family workshop.

In discussing the four Anguissola sisters, Vasari stresses the exceptional nature of their case, with a highly privileged *status* allowing natural talent to be enhanced by study: "it is necessary to have by nature an inclination for art, and then to add to that study and practice, as has been done by those four noble and gifted sisters, so much enamoured of every rare art, and in particular of the matters of design, insomuch that the house of Signor Amilcare Anguisciuola, most happy father of a fair and honourable family, appeared to me the home of painting, or rather, of all the arts".[15] Even centuries later, in 1877, Marco Minghetti, author of a book on Italian Renaissance and Baroque women artists, noted how education, literature and the arts were the prerogative of high-born girls. "Anyone who carefully studies the histories of Italy in the 15th and 16th centuries must see how women (especially those of the nobility) were educated with the utmost care, and how greatly they profited by such education".[16] The final goal for these girls, educated in accordance with Baldassarre Castiglione's *Cortegiano* (1528) and Archbishop Giovanni Della Casa's *Galateo* (1558), was the figure of the "virtuosa" young woman.[17]

Among the noblewomen, Vasari includes the Florentine Lucrezia Quistelli (cat. 1.16), wife of Count Clemente Pietra, whose brief career in art has been recently studied by Sheila Barker,[18] and the Friulian Contessina Irene di Spilimbergo, heroine of the sad legend that her death at the age of only twenty-one had been caused by art. By the time the second edition of the *Lifes* was published, her fame as a "virtuosa" noblewoman, devoted to art, a highly cultivated person who annotated and transcribed texts, was already consolidated. It had in fact been praised in a book published in Venice in 1561, *Rime di diuersi nobilissimi et eccellentissimi autori, in morte della signora Irene delle signore di Spilimbergo. Alle quali si sono aggiunti uersi latini di diuersi egregij poeti in morte della medesima signora.*[19] The laudatory collection was edited by Dionigi Atanagi da Cagli (1504–1573), at the time Secretary of the Accademia della Fama. Although he had in the past been closely involved with the Curia in Rome, this had not prevented his work *De le lettere di tredici huomini illustri libri tredici* from being put on the Index in 1554. The client for the *Rime di diuersi nobilissimi et eccellentissimi autori, in morte della signora Irene delle signore di Spilimbergo* was the Venetian nobleman Giorgio Gradenigo, who held important administrative posts.[20] To the collection for Irene – 279 poems in the vernacular and 102 in Latin –

contributed both anonymous authors and 143 who signed their work.[21] Among these, some bore the taint of reformist ideas, such as Bernardo Tasso[22] and Giovan Francesco Alois, soon to be beheaded and burned at the stake for heresy in Naples. Irene's father, Count Adriano, was in fact sympathetic to reformist circles, as shown by some of the texts in his library.[23] Moreover, the Accademia di Spilimbergo, founded by him, had been entrusted to such figures as Bernardino Partenio and Francesco Stancaro, who had already been arrested for preaching unorthodox doctrines. Interestingly enough, several women poets were included – Bianca Aurora da Este, Cassandra Giovia, Diamante Dolfi, Dianora Sanseverina, Costanza d'Avalos Duchess of Amalfi, the Duchess of Mondragone Ippolita Gonzaga, Laura Battiferri, Laura Terracina, and Lucia Albana Avogadra. They were appreciated in Venice, where two anthologies of poetry by women had already been published, *Lettere di molte degne Signore* (1548) and *Versi vari di alcune nobili e valenti dame* (1559), followed in 1620 by the *Teatro delle dame di Cultura*.

The book published in 1561 elaborates on the legend of Irene, dying for love of art, glorious in her virginity as shown by the symbols of the unicorn and the crown of fame appearing in the portrait in the Washington National Gallery (fig. 4). Family tradition attributes this work to Titian, who may have been had a hand in finishing a work by Giovan Paolo Pace.[24] In this portrait, it is hard to detect the fascinating young woman with "magic eyes".[25] Her elegant composure and noble origins are instead clearly indicated in the precious gown adorned with a gold chain given her by the Queen of Poland, Bona Sforza during a visit to the castle of Spilimbergo.

Vasari may have been told her life story directly, since he was acquainted with Titian, who had painted a portrait, around 1534, of Irene's grandfather, the erudite Giovanni Paolo Da Ponte. In this recently rediscovered painting, in the Scarpa collection, the merchant wears a luxurious wolf-skin coat and holds a book adorned with cords, perhaps the very memorial in which he was to note precisely, a few years later, the moment of Irene's birth, on October 17, 1538.[26] "Dal divin Titiano et immortale / l'arte imparò già di ritrar altrui / Irene…" ["From Titian, divine and immortal / the art of portraying others / learned Irene…"]; while Diamante Dolfi and Ippolita Gonzaga merely say that Irene painted, and Laura Terracina hypothesizes that "che se dipinto / Havesse ella il bel volto; nel ritratto / Proprio mirando, in quel punto, e 'n quell'atto" ["If she had painted / Her lovely face, in the portrait / Gazing at herself, at that point and in that act"], she would have met with the fate of Narcissus.

As was indeed to happen, since Irene died after twenty-two days of fever brought about by excessive zeal in painting a copy. The fault, we might say, was of Sofonisba Anguissola, totally unaware and already in Madrid. Because – states Atanagi – when Irene was shown "a portrait of Sofonisba Anguisciola done by her own hand, and shown to King Philip, and hearing marvellous praise of her in the art of painting; moved by generous emulation, she was seized with ardent desire to equal that noble and valorous young woman. And so with the advice of Signor Titian she set to painting […]. Hence in the time of a month and a half she made copies of some paintings by the said Titian, with special attention to gradations of light and shade, as well as the glimpses of nerves and bones in the soft, tender flesh, and no less to the drapery of the clothing".[27]

Here then is the model: Sofonisba, artist at the strictest Counter-Reformation court in Europe, sister of a nun, descendent through her mother of the Dominican Saint Peter the Martyr. The perfect model for the story of the life of Irene, which takes the form of hagiography, insistently describing virtues and manners in keeping with the rules of aristocratic behaviour set forth in Monsignor Della Casa's *Galateo*, published posthumously at Treviso in 1558. This text was indispensable in the Veneto territory, where the Venetian nunciature of the Florentine archbishop had been marked by intense Inquisitional activity and by the trial of the Bishop of Capodistria, Paolo Vergerio. Viewed within this context, the defence of Irene, published in 1561, a few years before the Council of Trent (1564), may perhaps be interpreted as a mode of redemption for a family deeply sympathetic to reform, a declaration of compliance required by the growing embitterment of the religious debate.

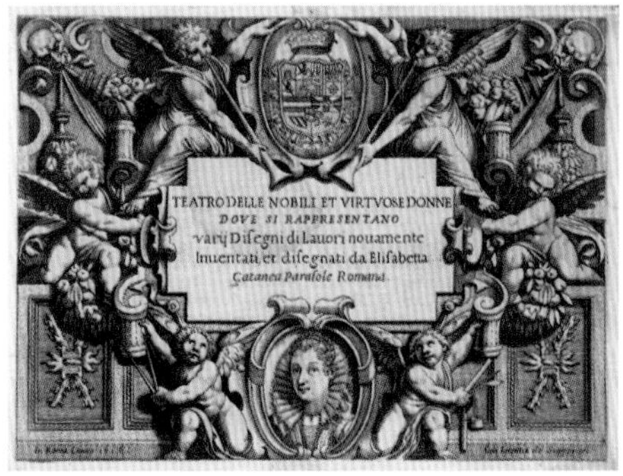

5. Elisabetta Parasole
Teatro delle nobili et virtvose donne dove si rappresentano varij Disegni di Lauori nouamente Inuentati, et disegnati da Elisabetta Catanea Parasole Romana
Rome, 1616
Paris, Bibliothèque Nationale de France

In this brief review of aristocratic female artists and their education, an interesting theme consists of embroidery, considered by the historiography of the time as parallel to and often preparatory to the activity of painting. This tradition was still prevailing in the seventeenth century, as shown by the story of Elisabetta Parasole (1580–1617), a young noblewoman from Bergamo who was to be admitted to the Accademia di San Luca, the author of two volumes of drawings for embroidery published in Rome, *Studio delle virtvose dame* (1597) and the *Teatro delle nobili et virtvose donne* (1616) (fig. 5). Among the many arts practiced by Irene was embroidery which, says Atanagi, was useful to her in approaching painting.[28] The poetess Girolama Corsi compares her to Arachne, who had dared to challenge Minerva in weaving and filled her canvas with the ineffable loves of the gods. An anonymous sonnet describes a veil embroidered by her with a sense of colour and composition, her needle bringing to life the scene of a landscape inhabited by nymphs and animals.[29]

This same principle was expressed by Lomazzo and Morigia in regard to Caterina "of the de Leuco family, most noble, & ancient in Milan",[30] who had married the nobleman Bartolomeo Cantoni in 1559. She had learned to embroider in fulfilment of a vow, as states Morigia in texts dating from 1592 and 1595, made to protect her from some danger, either childbirth or the plague.[31] In 1587 Lomazzo, in his *Rime*, places her beside the women artists active in painting and sculpture, such as Properzia and Sofonisba.[32] Morigia, in *La Nobiltà di Milano* (1595), is even more explicit in stating the equivalence of the arts of embroidery and of painting, when he writes of Barbara Cantoni,[33] Caterina's daughter, and in the chapter "Delli Huomini, e Donne, che nella virtù del ricamare sono eccellenti", where, in mentioning Caterina, he states that embroidery consists of "painting with a needle". "Hence this honoured Gentlewoman with the Needle, and with colours of Silk & Gold, amazingly imitates whenever she wants more famous paintings, or miniatures".[34] The life story of Caterina Cantoni also intersects with that of Sofonisba Anguissola. Both of them worked for Philip II, for whom Caterina created with a stitch of her own invention a filmy embroidered fruit-bowl cover with a complicated allegorical design, described by Lomazzo in 1590.[35] Both of these artists numbered

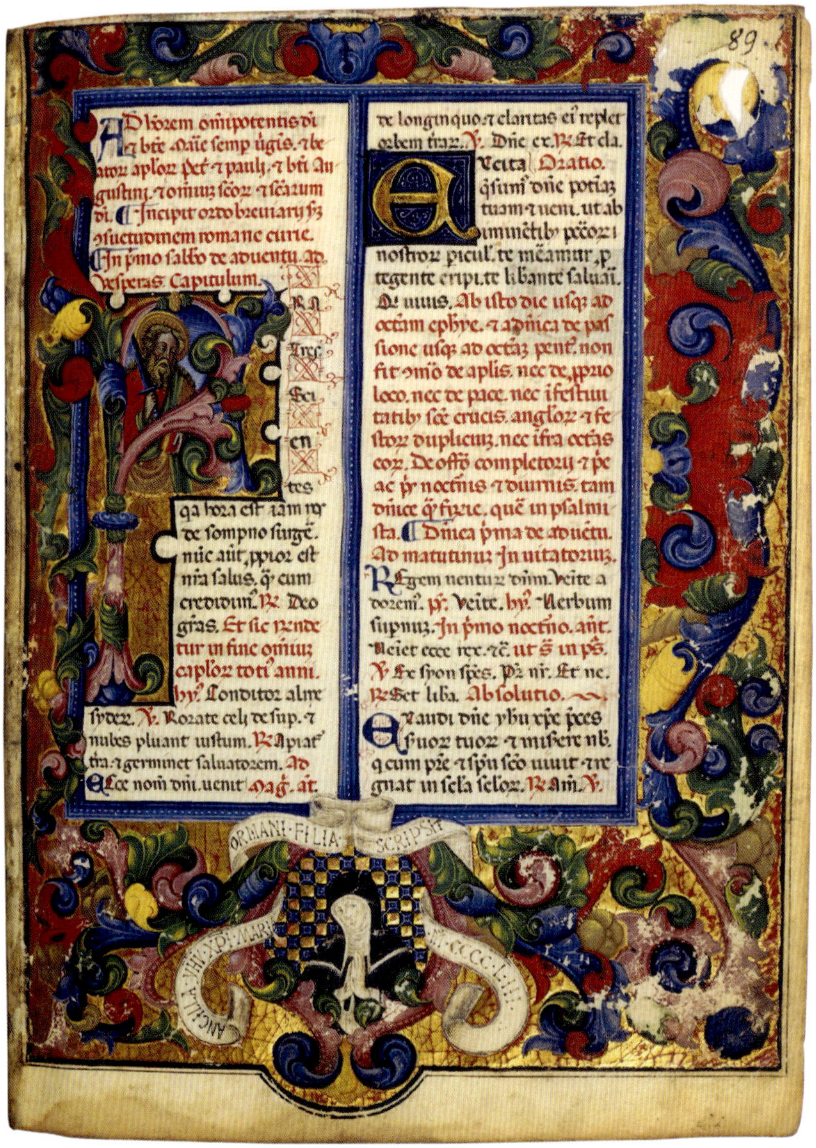

6. Maria Ormani degli Albizi
Breviarium cum calendario parthenonis ordinis s. Agustini in ditione
1453
Vienna, Österreichische Nationalbibliothek, Sammlung von Handschriften und alten Drucken, Cod. 1923, fol. 89*r*

among their admirers the Infanta Catalina Duchess of Savoy. They even became distantly related, when Caterina's firstborn son Pietro, jurist and man of letters, married Agata Ponzoni, a cousin of Sofonisba.

Women Artists in the Convent

At the time of Vasari, Caterina Vigri, founder of the Corpus Domini convent in Bologna, a miracle-worker and promoter of mystical spirituality, had been dead for a century, and her work as illuminator may already have been known. Vasari, however, fails to mention her among the women artists, probably deeming her work exclusively devotional in nature. It was Malvasia who recognised Caterina Vigri as an artist,[36] the acknowledged forerunner of the Bolognese line that was to culminate in the work of Lavinia Fontana – who retired to a convent in her old age – and Elisabetta Sirani.[37] And the artistic nature of Caterina's work was confirmed again by the dedication of the Accademia Clementina in 1710, two years before she was proclaimed a saint (cat. 2.1). Catarina Vigri's work was typical of a centuries-long secular tradition of producing embroidered goods enclosed within the walls of convents. This production included embroidered articles, liturgical vestments and reliquaries made of cheap materials or even the ground-up bones of saints, in a practice where the creation of an object coincided with an inner journey of intense reflection on Christ's sacrifice. The art of illuminating was pursued just as intensely by such figures as the Tuscan Maria Ormani degli Albizi, an Augustinian nun, who in 1453 signed her name to a self-portrait in one of the miniatures in the *Breviarium* now at the Österreichische Nationalbibliothek in Vienna (fig. 6), and Eufrasia Burlamacchi (1482–1548), active in Vasari's lifetime. Women often entered these convents, places parallel to civic society, for reasons of inheritance or the impossibility of a suitable marriage. Here they lived in real centres of culture, paradoxically freer to express their artistic talent, as shown by many studies conducted on the cloistered world.[38]

Among the artist-nuns, Vasari mentions the Carmelite Antonia Doni (1456–1491), "who had knowledge of drawing",[39] daughter of Paolo Uccello, and the Dominican Plautilla Nelli, "now Prioress in the Convent of S. Caterina da Siena, on the Piazza di S. Marco in Florence". Of her he writes in the "Life of Fra Bartolomeo della Porta" without giving her name, but declaring that many of his drawings were in that monastery, "in the possession of a nun who paints", from which copies were made. More explicit mention appears in the "Life of Madonna Properzia de' Rossi", where he describes Plautilla's career, starting as illuminator and continuing as copyist, "beginning little by little to draw and to imitate in colours pictures and paintings by excellent masters", and going on to make marvellous things, within the bounds of the female condition. Study of the human body was in fact prohibited, so that "in her works the faces and features of women, whom she has been able to see as much as she pleased, are no little better than the heads of men, and much nearer to the reality".[40] Inspired by the strict spirituality of Savonarola,[41] from devotional works of small format Plautilla went on to produce, in 1550–1568, the largest work yet created by a woman, the canvas nearly seven meters long, now in the Museo di Santa Maria Novella, originally painted for the monastery's refectory, depicting the *Last Supper*.[42] Vasari's observation that she was good at painting women's faces, being deprived of suitable anatomical knowledge, is disproven by the thirteen life-size male figures seated around a table displaying a meal served by Plautilla and her team of nuns that reflected, through the humble fare of convent tradition, the peasant food of the territory.

While Plautilla was an artist-nun who had learned by copying the paintings in the convent, a better chance was offered to two seventeenth-century nuns, Orsola Maddalena Caccia, daughter of the painter Guglielmo, and Lucrina Fetti, sister of Domenico. Orsola lived in a "domestic" convent, built by their father for his daughters at Moncalvo. Here she taught painting to other young Ursuline nuns, among them Angelica Bottero; her work expresses a sophisticated, erudite baroque mysticism (cats. 2.7–8) in elaborate symbolic rebuses, with a lighter touch of floral and ornithological insertions revealing a knowledge of modern treatises on botany and wild-life.[43] The other nun, Lucrina, from Rome, was a real court artist. Confined to the Mantua convent under the protection of the Gonzagas and guided by the family's noblewomen, she had sponsors of the highest rank, as shown by the fact that Duke Ferdinand paid her nun's dowry, and by the place where her talent was expressed.[44]

From the Workshop to the Academy

Among the many Flemish artists mentioned by Vasari, only two worked in miniature without having professional forebears: Anna Seghers, who died in 1566, the "daughter of Meister Segher, a physician",[45] and Clara de Keysere (c. 1470–1545) from Gand, described by Guicciardini as a "great painter and great illuminator",[46] an opinion confirmed by Antoon Sanders[47]. On the other hand, the list of women artists whose years spent in workshops had provided tools for learning the technique and dealing with clients is a long one: Susanna Horenbout (c. 1503 – c. 1554), daughter of Gerard of Gand, the first woman artist taken into the service of Henry VIII around 1522;[48] Levina Bening (1510/1520–1576), coming from the "Athenas Belgicas", Bruges, the daughter of Simon Bening, illuminator and painter, also worked at the English court, moving there in 1545 with her husband Georg Teerling of Blakenberge;[49] Catharina van Hemessen (1520 – post 1587), daughter of Giovanni, wife of a musician, both *protégées* of Charles V's sister, Mary of Hungary, governor of the Netherlands from 1531.[50] Among the Italians, Vasari notes, in addition to Antonia Doni, the "marvellous" Diana Scultori,[51] daughter of Giovan Battista and wife of the architect Francesco Capriani; and the gracious Barbara Longhi,[52] whose life shows how women artists often conducted their careers without emerging from the family circle.

Escaping the pattern of strict dependency on their father's career was Lavinia Fontana, born in 1552, at a time when her father Prospero was in contact with such acquaintances of Amilcare Anguissola as Michelangelo, Vasari and Annibal Caro, engaged with him in the creation of Villa Giulia in Roma, commissioned by Pope Julius III.

Malvasia in *Felsina pittrice* (1678), published over sixty years after the death of Lavinia, emphatically relates the story of Prospero's daughter. He was a painter who "preferred speed to diligence", an artist "determined and hasty", able to complete demanding tasks quickly, a talent that allowed him to live with "great pomp and splendour", "in a grand manner", but "although he earned treasures, he died as a pauper & unhappily".[53] Acquainted with the leading intellectuals of Bologna, such as the scientist Ulisse Aldrovandi and the humanist Achille Bocchi, perpetuator of old fables, allegories and emblems, Prospero educated his daughter Lavinia to art; and "under her father's discipline she approached drawing, in which she became expert, and delicate in colouring". It was she to acquire the fame and honours that had been squandered by Prospero, in his last years almost entirely barred from important commissions due to his rejection of the new Carracci style. We thus find Lavinia received with regal honours, as may never have been the case before: "She was received like a Princess, granting her a formal reception, & lining the streets with the usual Militias on parade upon her arrival",[54] and besought by wealthy clients, who loved to see exhibited in their portraits those elements of pomp and splendour so familiar to Lavinia: gowns made of precious fabric, jewellery, hair adorned with lace; embroidery, trimming and accessories, meticulously portrayed by the artist (with the aid of her husband, according to Malvasia) with the gaze of an entomologist, exercised in frequenting Aldrovandi's studio and the *Wunderkammern* of Bologna.

Alert and intelligent – according to Malvasia – her professional revolution was accompanied by an unusual "private" revolution. Well aware of her own capability and of the pressing need to exercise her talent, proud of her status as a highly educated woman, she depicts her condition in little self-portraits where she emulates Sofonisba, seated at the spinet or before her easel (cats. 3.2–3).

And she chooses as her life's companion a man who will allow her to work, to develop her natural talent. "It also seemed to the wise young woman that she could be quite sure of the naivety, and rather simplicity of her future husband; and this because, having become his wife on condition that he would not only allow her to paint, but also help her, working hard; and if unsuccessful in this, she would ridicule him; and requiring him to make at least a bust for those portraits, which she finished, & only to dress them, she added that he should be glad to be at least a Tailor, since Heaven would not let him be a Painter".[55] Rather than living in the shadow of a man, she herself seems to have cast a shadow over a man. An anomaly for the times, which however did not deprive him of his legal power as husband to sign and guarantee contracts for his wife; and that remained within the bounds of the Counter-Reformation family order that was to lead the couple to join the Capuchin Fathers' Figliolanza della Religione[56] in Rome.

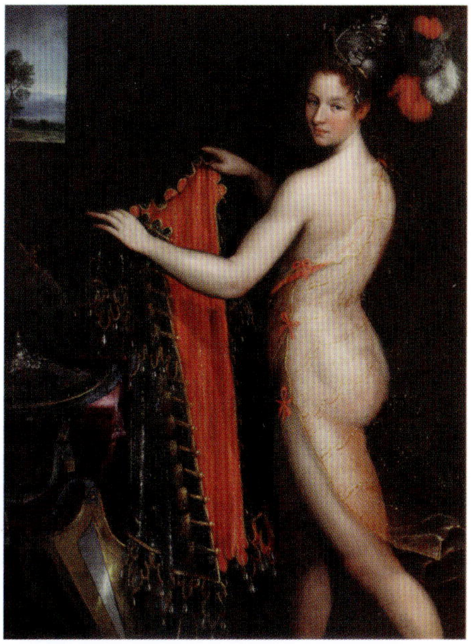

7. Lavinia Fontana
Nude Minerva
c. 1604–1605
Private collection

Unlike her father Prospero, Lavinia always managed to update her style and to harmonize the complex symbolism of her paintings with a swift, light *ductus*, both pleasing and accurate. Lavinia, then, competed with the male painters of her day not only in producing very large altarpieces, according to the iconographic dictates of Gabriele Paleotti's *Discorso intorno alle immagini sacre e profane* (1582), compiled by the Cardinal with some advice from Prospero Fontana, but also in producing paintings to be kept in "secret rooms". She clothes her Venuses in precious jewellery and flimsy veils (cat. 3.15) in a seductive game of false concealment, and accompanies Galatea with sea monsters that seem to emerge from the pages of "mirabilia", innocuous "stage props" as light as *papier mâché* (cat. 3.14). The erudite references of her "fables", staged as for the theatre, with lighting effects borrowed from stagecraft, aroused the poetic comments of many contemporary writers.[57] Dating from 1605 are the words of Ottaviano Rabasco, referring to the *Nude Minerva* (c. 1604–1605) in a private collection (fig. 7). Here the goddess of wisdom is transformed into a lady surprised in the privacy of her bedchamber, wearing a fetching plumed helmet and a gossamer tunic revealing the shape of her body beneath. It is an original conception, with Minerva appearing as Venus, in a clever dual deceit – "Ma Venere figuri, / Se Palla fingi, e doppio appar l'inganno" ["But Venus appears / If Pallas feigns, and the trickery is doubled"][58] – that suggests the dual power of the feminine, where acquired knowledge coexists with natural wisdom, with the art of seduction, in a new reconciliation of opposites.

Over twenty years after Lavinia's death (1614), and ten years after Fede Galizia died, perhaps in the 1630 epidemic of plague in Milan, another artist's daughter was born in Bologna in 1638. This was Elisabetta Sirani, who in a decade of activity produced nearly two hundred canvases, surpassing the fame of her father. He, Giovanni Andrea Sirani, was initially reluctant to make her a painter, says Carlo

Cesare Malvasia, who convinced him instead to let her "risk with the brushes".[59] The profile he traces is that of a dynamic young woman, who "was excessively eager to venture beyond the Paternal Walls",[60] possessing traits deemed at the negative and typical time of the woman artist, a view disproven by the impact of the stories transposed onto canvas, taken from the books in her father's vast library. Hence the "womanly grace" and "womanly patience", terms often used to describe a style that was meticulous but considered veined with sentimentality, ceases to exist in Elisabetta. And for Malvasia, the fact that her work was "virile" is deemed a point of arrival: "Elisabetta [...] at the cost of blood and sweat acquired for herself the Virile Sex. Though she was born Female, she possessed nothing of effeminate but the Name", and "not only did she never work as a woman, but even more than as a man".[61]

Averse to frilly feminine attire, devoted solely to her work and to caring for her sick father, Elisabetta offers examples of courageous women, ready to challenge male authority, showing unaffected pride.[62] Although her images remain scrupulously true to the sources, her aim of revealing unexpected sides of femininity clearly emerges. Of Circe, for example (cat. 3.33), it is not the effects of enchantment, or the vulnerability of falling in love, that we see, but instead the origin of her power, the study of books handing down magical practices. Her Circe, possessor of ancient knowledge, is an ancestor of the Alexandrine Hypatia, endowed with philosophical wisdom. She takes her place beside the more common iconography of Saint Catherine of Alexandria, the Christian martyr who challenged men on their own terrain, that of knowledge, in whose guise the women artists of the time often depicted themselves. Unusual and highly personal, a kind of manifesto addressed to all the "virile" women endowed with fortitude appears the image of Timoclea (1659) (cat. 3.27), shrewd avenger of the rape she has endured. The scene, not set in the protective darkness where Judith acts, is devoid of the heroic aura surrounding the Biblical figure, who beheads a man to save her homeland. Timoclea instead, in broad daylight, renders justice for a personal affront. Elisabetta's invention appears as a trial and condemnation almost concerning known facts, episodes involving women whose names have not been forgotten. She may have been aware of the rape of Artemisia, occurring nearly fifty years before, which had not concluded with the slaying of the rapist. Ending in homicide was instead the rape of Beatrice Cenci, executed in Rome in 1599 for having killed her father, a scandalous event. And perhaps another female artist, Onorata Rodiani known as "Amazzone", was still spoken of. She was the daughter of the painter Ilario and the author of frescoes in Gabrino Fondulo's palazzo at Castelleone, near Cremona. In 1422–1423, at about the age of twenty, while she was painting in a room in the palazzo, a courtier tried to rape her. She killed him by sticking a compass into his throat, causing him to fall from the scaffolding. The girl escaped disguised as a man, turning to a military life "in Oldrado Lampugnan's mercenary cavalry".[63] Some thirty years later, she died in defending Castelleone from the Venetians. Onorata, Beatrice, and Timoclea are all heroines worthy of the admiration of Elisabetta, *femme forte*, as is Omphale, who taunts Hercules in one of

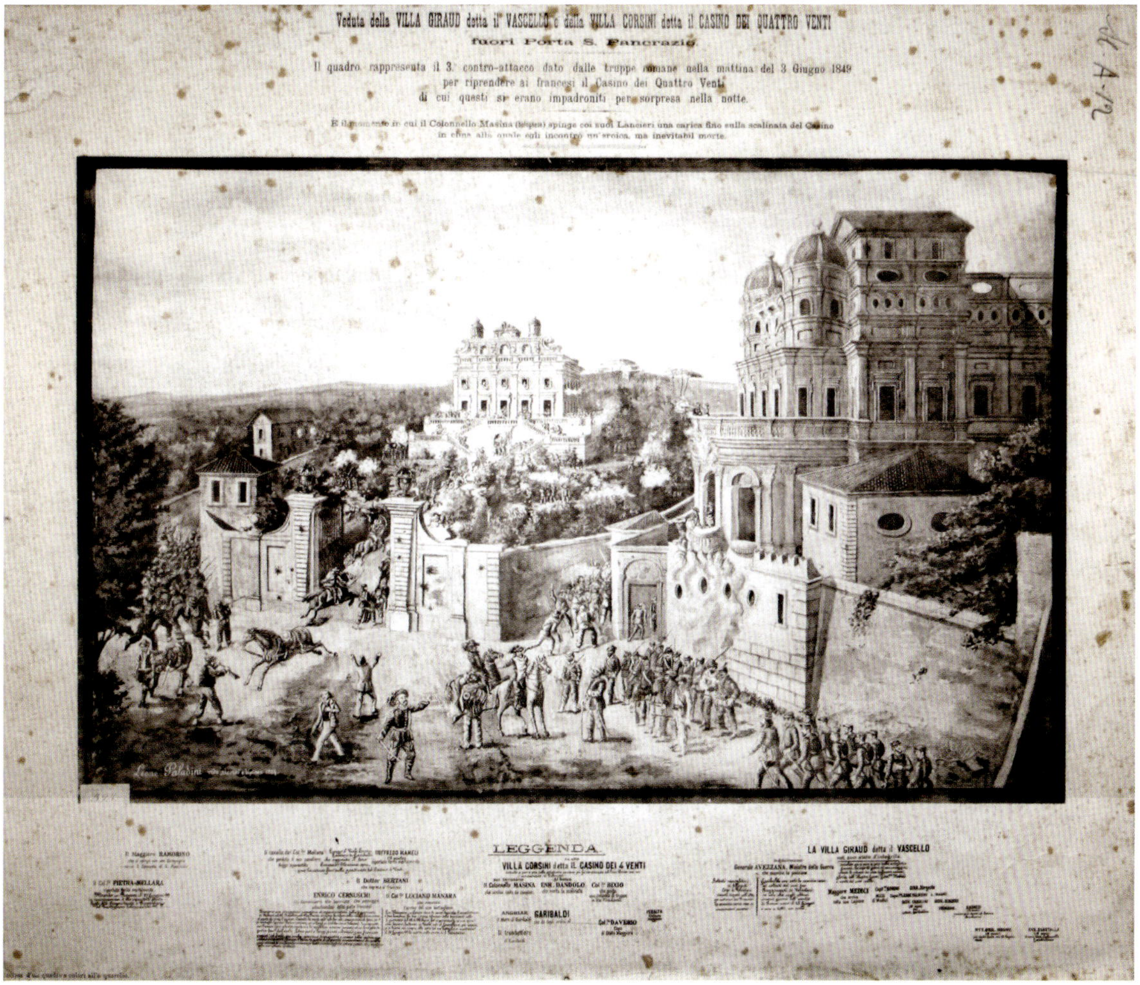

8. From Leone Paladini
View of Villa Giraud, Known as Il Vascello, and of Villa Corsini, Called the Casino dei Quattro Venti
1884
Rome, Istituto per la storia del Risorgimento italiano

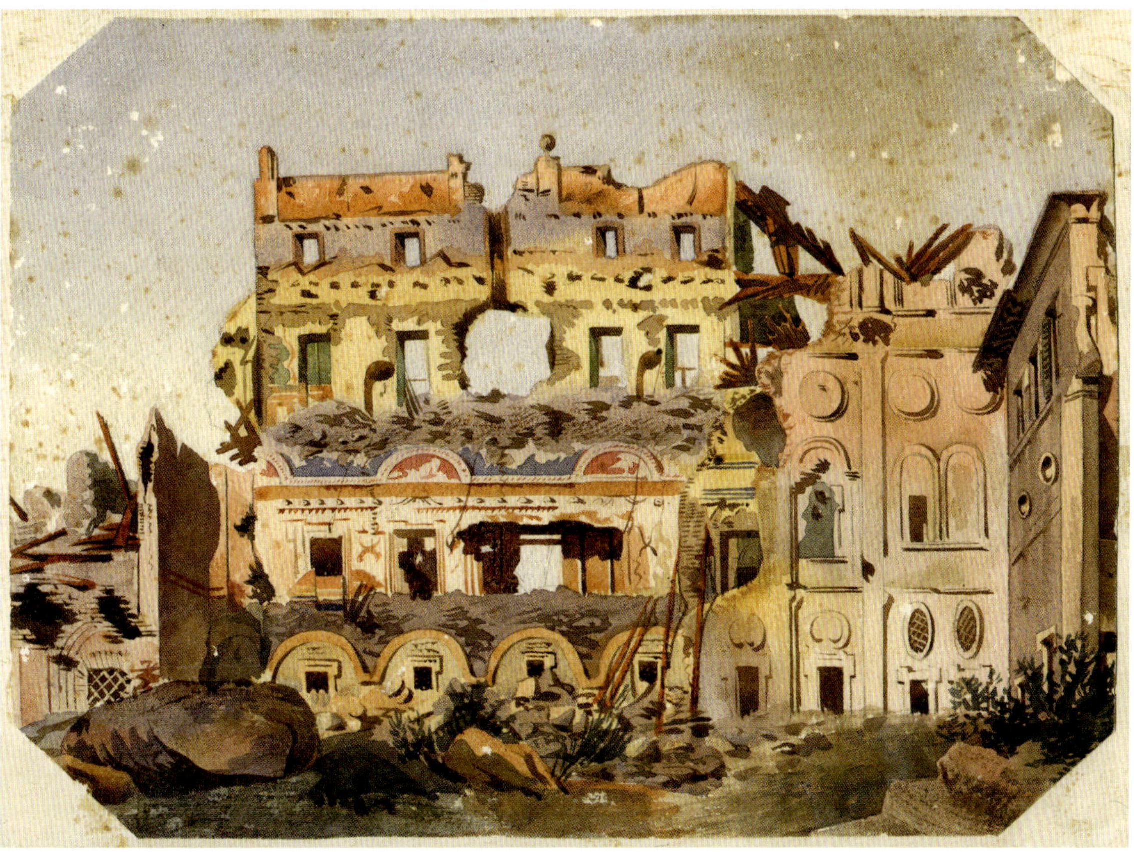

9. Anonymous
Ruins of the Vascello
Post 1849
Rome, Istituto per la Storia del Risorgimento italiano

her paintings, or Portia who wounds herself, emulating the mutilation practiced by the Amazons.

In Elisabetta's brief life she attained, along with Lavinia Fontana, the glory of becoming an "academic", admitted to the prestigious Accademia di San Luca in Rome. The times had changed. Diana Scultori had been the forerunner, admitted to the Accademia dei Virtuosi al Pantheon in 1580. Then in 1607 the Accademia di San Luca had changed its statute, opening to women on the basis of their fame and on condition that they donate one of their works to the institution, but barring them from presiding at executive sessions and thus depriving them of any decisional voice. In the list of their names, along with Elisabetta and Lavinia appear Giovanna Garzoni, Maddalena Corvina, and Virginia Vezzi, among others.[64] Another of the "academics" was Plautilla Bricci, painter and "female architect", an independent woman who rejected marriage, daughter of the versatile artist Giovanni Bricci. The chief promoter of her talent was Abbot Elpidio Benedetti, secretary to Cardinal Mazzarino, agent of the King of France in Rome, weaver of artistic and political dialogue between these two contexts, designer of temporary architectural decorations and art dealer. For him Plautilla created the visionary project of Villa Benedetta outside of Porta San Pancrazio, on the Via Aurelia Antica, designed like a ship run aground on a reef, an extravagance described by its client – under the pseudonym of Matteo Mayer – in a booklet published in 1677.[65] Built by a Francophile ecclesiastic, the villa met with an amazing destiny. It was destroyed less than two centuries after being built, during the battle between French troops and the defenders of the Roman Republic in June 1849. A print taken from a painting by Sergeant Leone Paladini illustrating moments of the battle, including the wounded and dying Goffredo Mameli, author of the Italian national anthem text, shows the astounding architecture of the still intact villa (fig. 8), while an unpublished watercolour now at the Istituto per la Storia del Risorgimento Italiano documents its destruction. Through a broken wall appear the colours of the interior, along with a decorative fresco in tones of red and blue (fig. 9). Are they perhaps fragments of paintings by Pietro da Cortona, or Francesco Allegrini or Giovan Francesco Grimaldi, on which the enterprising Plautilla had also worked?

The Case of Artemisia

Artemisia Gentileschi, born in 1593, was active around the same time as Orsola Maddalena Caccia, Fede Galizia, Chiara Varotari, Virginia Vezzi and the pious Giovanna Garzoni, with whom she shared friendship and travels between Venice and Naples. But Artemisia soon became a case, a scandalous legend interweaving art and life, nourished by salacious sonnets popularised a few years after her death by Charles Alphonse Du Fresnoy, who wrote that she was by now famous "all over Europe for her Amours, and Love-Intrigues, as for her talent in paintings".[66]

A spotlight has been trained on the traumatic events of her life: her rape at the age of eighteen by Agostino Tassi and her father's delay in denouncing him, perhaps more interested in Tassi's theft of one of his paintings than in his daughter's shame; the trial held in 1612 where she was subjected to torture, the conviction of the rapist, the marriage to Pierantonio Stiattesi, and her move – a kind of exile – to Florence. These events have been studied since the publication in 1981, edited by Eva Menzio, of some of the proceedings of the trial, to which new materials have since been added.[67]

Victimized and dishonoured, her name besmirched by men who hurled at her infamous slander, she defended herself in the trial with tenacity and composure. In her repertoire, fragile heroes such as David and fearless heroines such as Judith, Susannah, Jael, and Dalilah blaze victorious in duels with seemingly unconquerable giants, primarily through intelligence and trickery, with the aid of various weapons. These are some of the elements that have made her, Artemisia, a heroine. Studies by the American Mary Garrard, then, starting with the piece published in 1980,[68] have led to a re-interpretation of her career from a modern viewpoint that sees Artemisia as a manifest proto-feminist, demanding recognition of a professional *status* far above the misogynous stereotype of the time, and proclaiming her resentment of the violent masculine world. To the image of proud rejection of the vulgar Roman world she had lived in, the publication by Francesco Solinas in 2011 of part of her correspondence with the Florentine Francesco Maria Maringhi, her lover and financial backer, has added new aspects: a touch of passionate, sentimental impetuosity – "my precious darling heart", implores Artemisia – of ungrammatical verbal violence, of surprising tenderness along with a striving for upward social mobility, an ambitious desire for wealth and the reckless financial management of her affairs. In Florence, all this was to lead to the humiliation of sequestration, of seeing official seals affixed to her belongings, her home and her study, and to her own precipitous flight.[69]

Within the framework of Vasari's scheme (noblewomen artists, convent artists, daughters of artists), Artemisia may be classed among those who grew up in their father's studio. A descendent of the prominent Lomi family from Pisa, boasting many artists, she was honoured by admission to the Florence Academy of Drawing in 1616. However, such a complex personality as hers arouses many questions: how Artemisia was seen by her contemporaries and even more, how she wished to be seen. The pictorial documents, her self-portraits, show her appearance and her vehement attitude, her fiery, dominating nature. More deeply revealing is the *Self-Portrait as the Allegory of Painting* (fig. 10), where the allegory is painted as described by Cesare Ripa, with the same attributes, in his *Iconologia.* Artemisia does not depict herself as her male colleagues usually did, seated before the canvas elegantly dressed, but appears instead with dark, dishevelled hair, caught at the moment of inspiration, of creative "fury", of the "blank page", the empty canvas that must be filled with composition, drawing, colour and narrative, where natural talent is governed and organised by study.[70]

This is an image of proudly proclaimed professional *status,* where the artist prevails over the great lady in sumptuous attire depicted by Vouet (fig. 11), certainly at the request of Artemisia herself, eager to identify with the canons of the time. This portrait is the one that most closely fits a document recently published by Sheila Barker, a fictional biography of Artemisia compiled by Cristofano di

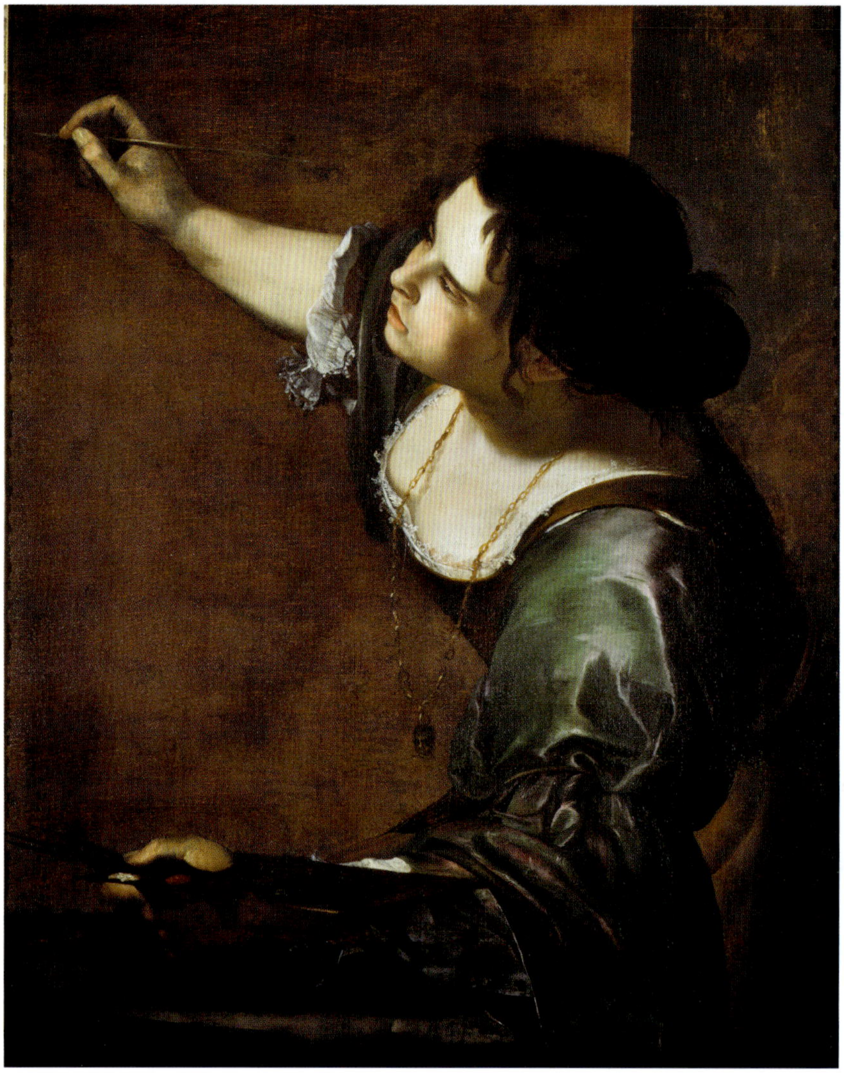

10. Artemisia Gentileschi
Self-Portrait as the Allegory of Painting
1638–1639
The Royal Collection / Her Majesty Queen Elizabeth II

Ottaviano Bronzini.[71] Born in Ancona around 1580, he had moved to Florence from Rome in 1615, following Cardinal Carlo de' Medici. The author of four volumes entitled *Della dignità & nobiltà delle donne* (Florence 1622–1632), Bronzini knew several women artists: Lavinia Fontana, when he was in Rome, with whom he saw the altarpiece she had painted for San Paolo fuori le Mura; Diana Scultori, from whom he had purchased two prints; in Florence, Giovanna Garzoni, whose musical talent, miniatures and calligraphy he appreciated; and Arcangela Paladini, the *protégée* of Maria Maddalena of Austria. Among the fifty manuscript pages found by Barker appears the first biography of Artemisia, written between 1615, the year of Bronzini's arrival in Florence, and 1620, the year of Artemisia's departure. She would thus have been between twenty-two and twenty-seven years old when that text was written, and in fact it deals with her youth, her training and her life in Rome. No mention is made of the rape and the trial. Since it is plausible to suppose that the text was written under Artemisia's supervision, it shows clearly how she wished to appear. It is a re-writing of her story, wholly idealised to comply with a model that was entirely foreign to her.

Hence Artemisia, who could never have signed a work with the attribute used by Sofonisba and Lavinia, "virgo", makes up for this by attributing her father with the desire to make her a pious nun and above all an honourable woman, and by inventing years spent in the Convent of Santa Apollonia in Trastevere prior to marriage. To become an artist-nun would have been her destiny, like Orsola Maddalena Caccia, who around that time, in 1620, had entered a convent. And as the convent had been the training ground for Plautilla Nelli, so it would have been for Artemisia, who in Bronzini's text states that the Abbess introduced her to Caravaggio's art, showing her a Susanna, and to develop her innate talent encouraged her to make copies of it, some of which were sold at high prices. She thus appears as a self-taught artist, possessing that natural "inclination" to which she assigns her own image in 1615, in the painting for the ceiling of Casa Buonarroti. A talent she seems to have discovered around the age of twelve when, to lengthen an apron, she made "di suo capriccio, un nuovo disegno di ricamo; il quale veduto da persone esperte, et pratiche [...] nel Dissegno et nella Pittura appresso posero in consideratione al Padre che la dovesse applicare alla Pittura" ["of her own capriccio, a new embroidery design; which, when seen by persons expert and experienced [...] in Drawing and Painting immediately advised her Father that she should engage in Painting"]. And Artemisia is here transformed into a "virtuosa" young girl who practices the noble art of embroidery preparatory to painting, and equally important, as Bronzini insists. In his view, drawing, painting and embroidery are all on the same level. He notes the inventor's *bravura*, in composing and colouring with her needle, of Arcangela Paladini, the wife of "mastro Giovanni Ricamatore", that is Jan Broomans, of "Francesca di Giesù da Toledo" and of "three sisters from Ferrara".

Educated to the strict, sober life of the convent, "virtuosa" noblewoman such as Sofonisba and Irene, great lady as she appears in Vouet's portrait, daughter of an artist *malgré lui*, member of the Academy: Artemisia – with her imaginary and real traits – shows a complex identity that includes all possible categories of women artists of the time.

The reality concealed by Artemisia was instead that of the crime-ridden, degraded Rome she had grown up in, with a father described by Baglione as animal-like and aggressive. "If Horatio Gentileschi had been of more amiable temperament, he would have been quite successful in life; but his nature was more bestial than human; taking no account of any subject, however eminent, that he portrayed. He had his own opinions, and with his satirical tongue he offended everyone. By the grace of God we must hope for the pardon of all his faults".[72] A father who had failed to protect his daughter from Agostino Tassi, a man accustomed to "ride out with his sword", who "was a close friend of Orazio Gentileschi [...] and, resembling him in both spirit and behaviour, they cordially liked each other", notes Passeri, who rendered Artemisia twice a victim, in words casting doubt on her conduct: "and she would have been worthy of great esteem, had she been more honest, and honoured".[73] Admired and requested all over Europe, Artemisia shrewdly rewrote her own life, through allegorical self-portraits and contacts that brought her far indeed from her origins. She appears in a scene in a musical drama held at the Medici court, as was customary for literary noblewomen. In Venice, she was in contact with erudite women's circles as well as the intellectuals of the Accademia de'

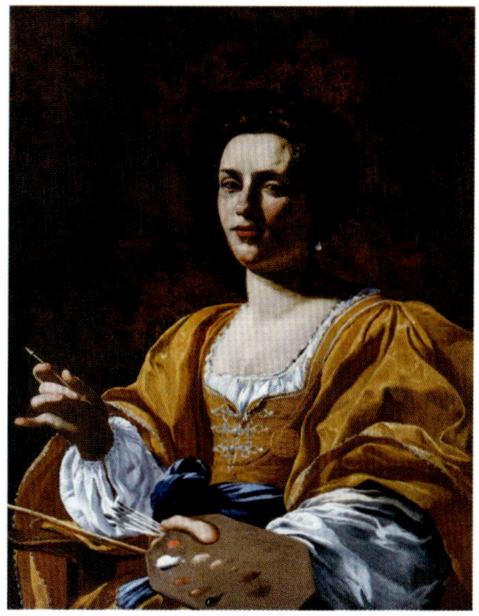

11. Simon Vouet
Portrait of Artemisia Gentileschi
1623–1626
Fondazione Pisa – Palazzo Blu

Desiosi, and in Naples with the members of the Accademia degli Oziosi.[74] In her Neapolitan studio she welcomed artists, diplomats and foreign authors, such as the German Joachim von Sandrart and the Englishmen Bullen Reymes and Nicholas Lanier.[75] Filippo Baldinucci speaks of her as a "virtuosa woman". In 1795, Marco Lastri, in *Etruria pittrice*, called her the most representative artist of the seventeenth century in Pisa – where she had "matriculated" by entering the Accademia delle Arti del Disegno – but also one of the two women artists most representative of Tuscany at any time, along with Suor Plautilla Nelli. The twentieth century has seen her as a proto-feminist. In recent decades, studies have revealed a more complex picture of her many-sided activity, exploring every stage, from her life in Rome with Orazio to her fertile Florentine period, her brief stay in Venice, her activity in London, up to the Neapolitan years and the establishing of the atelier she managed with energetic determination even during the financial crisis occurring both before and after the revolt of Masaniello in 1647.[76]

She was undoubtedly a "condottiero", a "virile" spirit, as she herself explained to Don Antonio Ruffo in 1649: "Ritrovera uno animo di Cesare nell'anima duna donna" ["You will find the spirit of Caesar in the soul of a woman"].

Legendary Women Artists: The Talk of the Nineteenth Century

One of the first pictorial documents to comment on a woman artist in the style of a fable was presented in Paris at the Salon of 1822 by Louis Ducis, a pupil of David. It depicts Properzia de' Rossi (fig. 12), known at the time more as a woman disappointed in love than as a famous artist. The painting formed part of the collection of the Duchess of Berry, that is, Carolina of Bourbon Princess of the Two Sicilies, whose life was filled with tragic events, both political and emotional. At the time, Charles Ferdinand d'Artois Duke of Berry, married in 1816, had just been assassinated (1820), and the duchess, perhaps in memory of their union, grouped within a single frame four works by Ducis illustrating unhappy loves, under the title of *Les Arts sous l'empire de l'Amour*, now at the Musée des Beaux-Arts in Limoges. In a publication from 1823, illustrated with prints of the duchesses' contemporary collection, the scene is described as follows: "Properzia de Rossi, artist from Bologna, shows to a young man she loves, but who does not love her, a bas-relief whose subject is linked to the story of her life and unhappy loves".[77] The whole scene presents elements for describing Properzia as artist and as woman, based on the earliest historiographical sources and those that had accentuated her love story. She is represented, according to Vasari, as a woman "with a beautiful body who played and sang [...] better than any other woman in her city", who put her "little hands, so tender and so white, [...] to manual labours, braving the the roughness of marble and the unkindly chisels", applying her "intellect both capricious and very ready".[78] Her studio is strewn with tools of work, some of which appear in the etching by Nicolas de Larmessin that illustrates Isaac Bullart's text dated 1682 (cat. 1.3), which attributes Properzia with a good knowledge of the rules of architecture and perspective, the ability to paint and etch on copper, along with her-well known talent as sculptress. The allusion to Properzia's skill at practicing all of the arts is

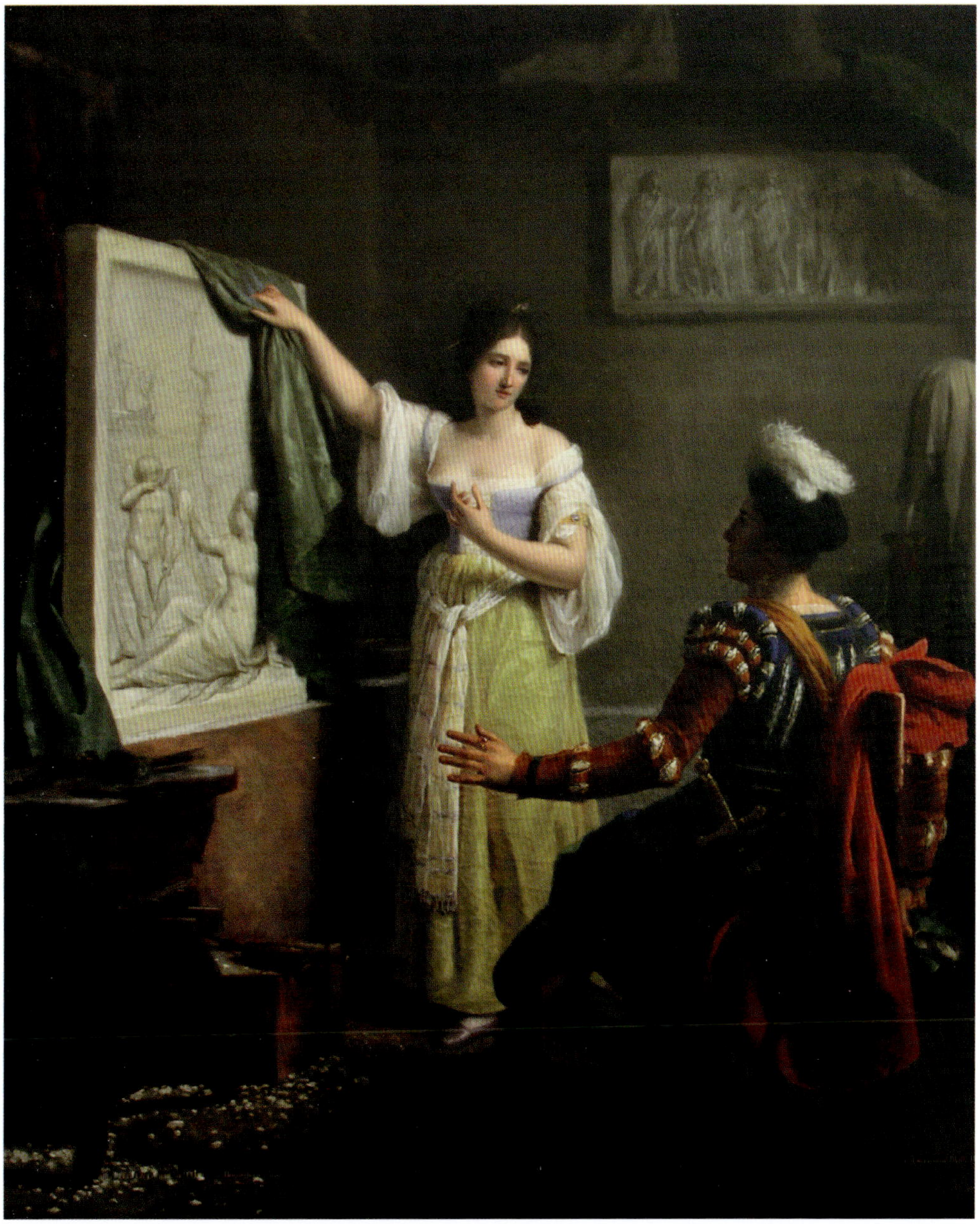

12. Louis Ducis
Properzia de' Rossi Showing her Bas-Relief to a Gentleman
1822
Limoges, Musée des Beaux-Arts, in storage by the Musée du Louvre since 1876

emphasized by the bas-relief Ducis places behind her, a citation of the Roman sarcophagus of the Muses dating from the second century A.D., coming from the Albani collection and displayed at the Louvre since 1815. Having shown Properzia's devotion to art, Ducis fills the scene with elements alluding to her legendary misfortune in love, barely hinted at by Vasari ("Finalmente alla povera innamorata giovane ogni cosa riuscì perfettissimamente, eccetto il suo infelicissimo amore", "In the end, everything turned out perfectly for the poor enamoured girl, except her unhappy love") but amply described by Bullart, who sees in Properzia's vain attempts to conquer her beloved – like Potiphar's wife, who pursues the unwilling Joseph in her sculpture for San Petronio – the cause of her death, which occurred a few days before Pope Clement VII's arrival in Bologna.[79] Properzia's unhappiness is evoked by hints appearing in her studio: emblematic of the abandoned woman is Ariadne, deserted on the island of Naxos by Theseus; and on a shelf stands a little copy of the statue of *Ariadne* in the Musei Vaticani. In 1822 – the year of Ducis's painting – the statue had only recently been returned to Rome after having been in Paris for several years. There it had been exhibited in Napoleon's triumphal procession of July 1798, then placed in the Musée Central des Arts in 1800, removed in 1815 and finally transferred to the Museo Pio Clementino a year later. And the bas-relief that Properzia shows to the elegant young man, as if to reveal her thoughts, also refers to Ariadne. To the right she stands in a grotto, while in the background Theseus' ship is setting sail. Before her Cupid weeps, sharing in her suffering, in the guilty pose he often takes when scolded by Venus for having missed the target with his arrows of love. But the young Properzia is seen placing her hand over her heart in a hopeful gesture, perhaps desiring an end as triumphant as that of Ariadne, set in the sky by the god Bacchus.

Ducis's painting and the bas-relief depicting Ariadne served as inspiration to a young English poetess, Felicia Hemans, who personally experienced the torment of abandonment, as shown by her poem *Properzia Rossi*, published in 1828 in a larger collection.[80] In a consolingly romantic affinity of status and emotion – both are artists and abandoned women – she shares her suffering with the sculptress from Bologna, appealing in a play of mirrors to the ancestral myth of Ariadne to commemorate her unhappy love: "Speak to him of me, / Thou, deserted by the lonely sea, / With the soft sadness of thine earnest eye, / Speak to him, forlorn one! deeply, mournfully, / Of all my love and grief!". The painting by Ducis, the bas-relief of Ariadne, and the history of Properzia are transformed into a visual letter that, accompanied by her verses, will reach her distant husband in a different form, becoming part of the abundant correspondence exchanged with her man, who had preferred the exciting life of Rome to the dreary English moors.[81] And fate was to stress again the similarity of Properzia and Felicia, who both died when barely forty. In that same year, 1828, Properzia, the icon of unhappy love, was the heroine of the tragedy *Properzia de' Rossi*, Paolo Costa's theatrical work inspired by *Stella*, Goethe's "play for lovers".

Another favourite legend in the Romantic age was that of Irene di Spilimbergo. In 1840 it inspired the Scottish artist William Dyce to paint *Titian and Irene da Spilimbergo*, displayed at the annual exhibition of the Royal Academy and described in a brief, ironical note in a review published by *Blackwood's Edinburgh Magazine* in September 1840.[82] The painting, now lost, portrayed Titian reclining in a garden while conversing with Irene, a subject recalling that of Eugenio Moretti-Larese in 1856 (Trieste, Civici Musei di Storia ed Arte di Trieste). But this theme serves as inspiration mainly to the Friuli artists. In 1852 Domenico Fabris depicts Irene intent on portraying Titian in a fresco in Palazzo Mangilli-Del Torso at Udine (fig. 13); Antonio Rotta participates in the Esposizione di Belle Arti held in Milan in 1853 with the painting *Titian Instructs Irene di Spilimbergo in the Art of Painting*; in 1856 Jacopo D'Andrea paints *Titian Teaches Painting to Irene di Spilimbergo*, presented at the Esposizione Friulana di Belle Arti of Udine, and in 1857, commissioned by the Counts of Maniago, *Queen Bona of Poland Gives Irene di Spilimbergo a Gemstone Tiara*. The Swiss artist Antonio Barzaghi Cattaneo, who had attended the Accademia di Brera, portrays Irene seated at the spinet in 1877. Also inspired by the legend of the

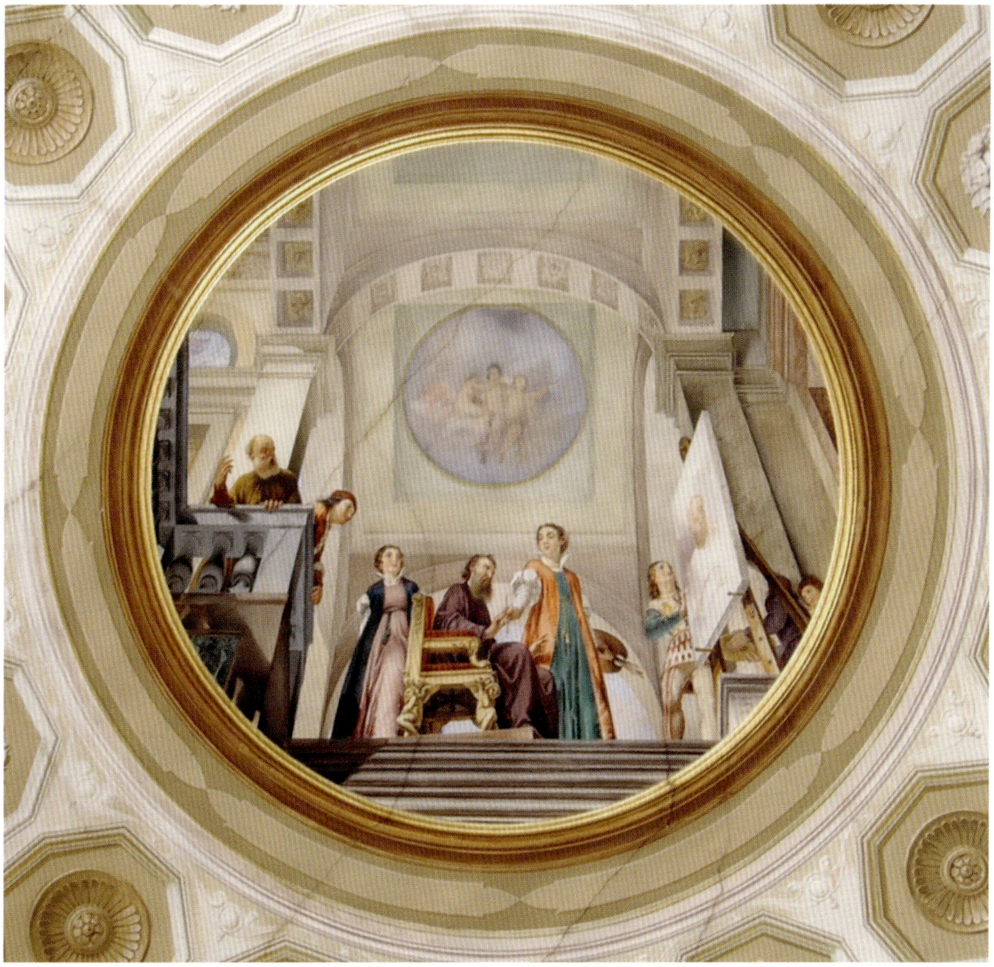

13. Domenico Fabris
Irene di Spilimbergo Painting Titian's Portrait
1852
Udine, Palazzo Mangilli-Del Torso

young artist from Spilimbergo was Ippolito Nievo (1831–1861), who dedicated to her a poem published posthumously in *Canti del Friuli*.[83]

Emblematic of passionate paternal love was the story of Marietta Robusti, Tintoretto's daughter, who as a girl is said to have frequented his studio dressed as a man to avoid arousing scandal. In nineteenth-century mythography she appears grieving, portrayed by her father at the moment of his untimely death. The Aversan playwright Luigi Marta, who had published in 1830 *La dama pittrice*, the story of a woman artist set in Paris at the time of Henry III, was the author of *Il Tintoretto e sua figlia*, staged in Milan on 7 March 1845, and in 1859 Ferdinand Dugué wrote the drama *La Fille de Tintoret.* Along with these plays were canvases by such artists as Léon Cogniet (1843, Bordeaux, Musée des Beaux-Arts), Philippe-Auguste Jeanron (1857, Le Mans, Musée de Tessé), Henry Nelson O'Neill (1873, Wolverhampton Art Gallery and Museum), and the Italians Eleuterio Pagliano (1861, Milan, Galleria d'Arte Moderna) and Guglielmo De Martino (ante 1881, Catanzaro, MARCA; cat. 3.40).

Elisabetta Sirani was only twenty-seven when she died. Malvasia had hinted at homicide committed by a servant girl who "did not deny having dissolved a powder in her soup",[84] and that death became a detective story in nineteenth-century current affairs, inspiring the text *Di Elisabetta Sirani pittrice bolognese e del supposto veneficio* by Ottavio Mazzoni Toselli (1833). And in 1854 Ulisse Guidi analysed the *Prove legali sull'avvelenamento della celebre pittrice Elisabetta Sirani emergenti dal relativo processo.*[85]

Women's Art as Presented in Manuals and Exhibitions

The same century that freely interpreted the lives of some female artists under a romantic light also saw the first systematic studies of women's art and the first exhibitions devoted exclusively to their creativity.

The first historicizing attempt dates from 1858, with the publishing in Berlin of the work by Ernst Guhl (1819–1862) titled *Die Frauen in der Kunstgeschichte*. Divided into nine chapters, it is the first analytical study devoted to women outstanding in literature, visual arts and architecture, ranging from names lost in the byways of Greek and Roman history to artists active in the first decades of the nineteenth century. In those two hundred and eighty-eight pages are condensed names, life stories and works of women artists, many of them labelled today as "rediscovered", in a work compiled by investigating an enormous amount of information found in the essays and historiography of the individual cities and regions of Europe. Guhl's historic approach was applied by the American Elizabeth Fries Lummis Ellet (1818–1877), who had begun her investigation of the female world by rediscovering the heroines of the American revolution, narrated in three volumes published in 1845. In 1859 she published in London *Women Artists in All Ages and Countries*, with the objective of studying the social conditions of women artists of the past, who were often unable to sign contracts or receive payment, activities delegated to their fathers or husbands.

Starting from the mid-nineteenth century, several attempts to compile a history of women's art were made. Near the end of the century, in 1893, the gigantic achievement of Marius Vachon (1850–1928), *La Femme dans l'Art*, was published in Paris. Its stated objective was "The glorifying of woman [...] As inspirer of great geniuses, As model for masterpieces, As protector of masters, As artist". This last aspect is perhaps the one least investigated by the author in over six hundred pages enriched with abundant illustrations. In the early twentieth century, in 1904, the American Clara Erskine Clement Waters (1834–1916) published *Women in the Fine Arts*, the first dictionary devoted to female artists, from the "A" of the Norwegian Marie Helene Aarestrup to the "W" of the German Margarethe Waldau. Next came the volume of Walter Shaw Sparrow (1862–1940), *Women Painters of the World*, published in London in 1905, which analyzed "from the time of Caterina de' Vigri" to that of Rosa Bonheur, while the book by Hans Hildebrandt (1878–1957) *Die Frau als Künstlerin*, published in Berlin in 1928, illustrated with over three hundred reproductions, stresses the importance of feminine creativity ranging from the production of ceramics and textiles to the artists of the Russian avant-garde and the Twenties, from marionette makers to sculptresses, painters and architects.

At the end of the nineteenth century, women were still not admitted to academies in many European countries. This gave rise to the first associations of women artists who, being barred from most major expositions, began to hold showings of their own. In Paris in 1881, the Union des Femmes Peintres et Sculpteurs (UFPS), was founded by the sculptress Hélène Bertaux (1825–1909), a combative group that struggled to affirm the concept that their art, like that of men, was a profession. Their exhibitions, held annually starting in 1882[86] were the first

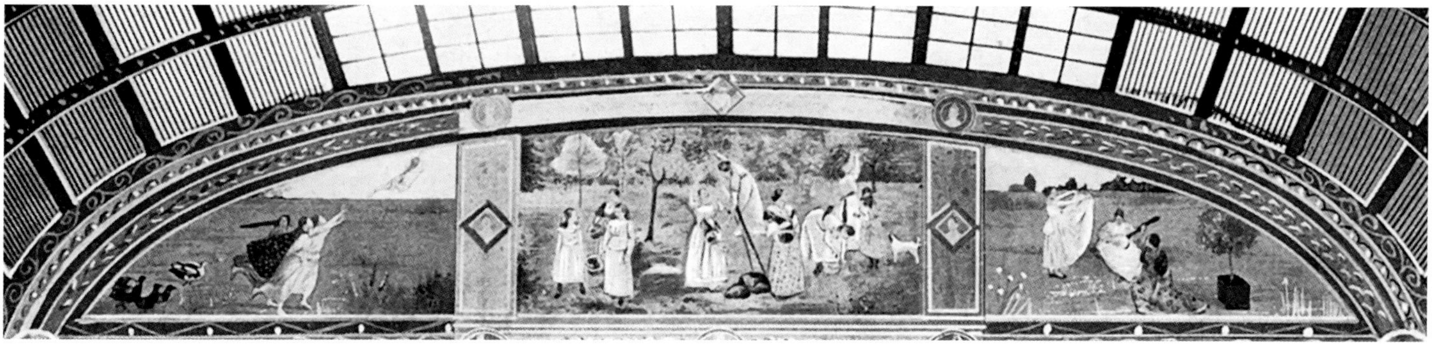

14. Mary Cassatt
Modern Woman
1893
Work installed in Sophia Hayden's Woman's Building during the World's Columbian Exposition, Chicago, 1893, lost

designed to explore, exhibit and study feminine creativity, limited however to contemporary activity. Berteaux won important recognition in 1893, when she represented France – along with other women artists, among them Sarah Bernhardt appearing as a sculptress – at the World's Columbian Exposition, held in Chicago in 1893 to celebrate the four hundredth anniversary of the discovery of America.

For this occasion, the Woman's Building was constructed, designed by Sophia Hayden, the first woman awarded a degree in architecture, in 1890, from the Massachusetts Institute of Technology in Boston. The building, in the form of a neo-Renaissance villa, was described as "essentially feminine in character; it has the qualities of reserve, delicacy, and refinement".[87] Adorned by sculptural groups celebrating Virtue, Sacrifice and Charity – the traditional qualities required of a woman – it presented at the entrance a long list of names inscribed in gold letters: women artists, mystics, pioneers and businesswomen were recalled along with the great female rulers of all time.[88] The pictorial decoration at the entrance was the work of several women artists among them Mary Fairchild MacMonnies and Mary Cassatt, who had been living for years in Paris, where they prepared their panels. Bertha Palmer, who coordinated the event, easily persuaded the Board of Lady Managers to include MacMonnies, known in her homeland mainly as the wife of the sculptor Frederick MacMonnies, who designed the monumental fountain at the centre of the exposition and was supported in the creation of his panel, *Primitive Woman*, by Puvis de Chavannes. There were instead problems in accepting the project of Mary Cassatt. Born in Philadelphia and now a well-established artist in the Impressionist enclave but unknown in her homeland, she had met Palmer through the merchant Durand-Ruel, from whom she had bought a Degas. Cassatt produced her work in 1892–1893,[89] after managing to overcome the reluctance of the board, doubtful that, being almost fifty at the time, she could complete such a demanding task. With difficulty, she managed to be paid as well as a man, and to overcome the disappointment caused by an article published in New York that saw her work as an illustration of a woman dressed by the most famous stylist of the time ("The Modern Woman as Glorified by Worth"). The work arrived from Paris in April[90] and was installed on the south gable of the entrance hall. On the white walls trimmed in gold, the play of greens and blue in the panel called *Modern Woman* (fig. 14) stood out for its narrative modernity devoid of any rhetorical or declamatory notes. Her allegory of women's activities, shown in the central part harvesting the fruit of the Tree of Knowledge, in the right-hand scene, of the Arts, with a designer seated, a

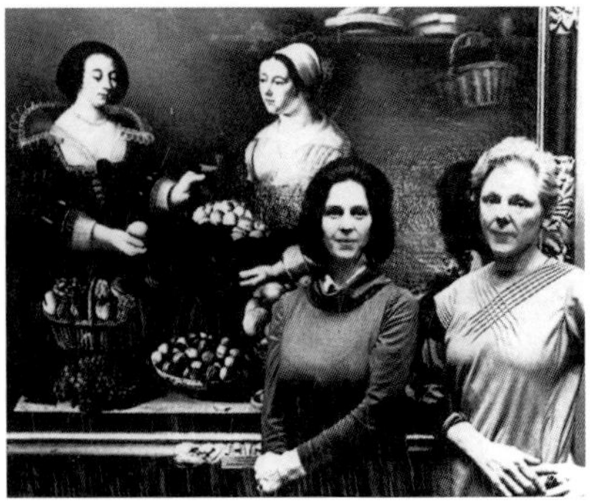

15. Marianna Diamos
Ann Sutherland Harris and Linda Nochlin at the Exhibition "Women Artists 1550–1950", Los Angeles, County Museum, December 1976
In *Los Angeles Times*, 27 December 1976, p. IV/1

banjo player with Japanese features and a ballerina dancing the skirt-dance, a popular version of the can-can; on the left appears the Fame rising upward, followed by three "little women". The entire scene evokes the everyday routine of a modern woman's life, like the one depicted thirty years before in the coming-of-age novels by Louisa May Alcott, where ancestral domestic duties exist alongside more modern artistic aspirations. The joyful tone of Cassatt's paintings, devoid of rhetorical emphasis, met with negative criticism from the Chicago press, which went so far as to label her work "cynical".[91]

The exhibitions held at the Woman's Building should be considered embryonic examples of investigation conducted through centuries of art. In the building decorated with peacocks' feathers were displayed purely artisan activities alongside works of academic discipline. As concerns Italy, the official catalogue lists prints by Elisabetta Sirani, Diana Scultori, Teresa Del Po and Caterina Piotti displayed in various parts of the building;[92] while the national pavilion, placed under the patronage of Queen Margherita, held a precious collection of items produced by the artisans' schools promoted by the queen herself, along with the priceless collection of Burano lace belonging to the royal family, and embroidery by noblewomen of the court, in keeping with ancient Renaissance and Baroque tradition.

The nineteenth century then, which had seen the first global studies of women's art, closed with this Chicago exhibition, and by now the idea of giving feminine talent the consideration reserved to men for centuries had become a reality. When UFPS in 1932 celebrated the fiftieth anniversary of the first exhibition with a show held at the Grand Palais, it shared its mission with another group, formed in 1930 as the Syndicat des Femmes Artistes, then called Femmes Artistes Modernes (FAM), headed by the painter Marie-Anne Camax-Zoegger (1881–1952). Its first exposition, held in Paris at the Galerie Pleyel, with eighty participants, produced a certain uneasiness in the press, which asked why women's art, by now fully accepted, should be organised. However, in reading the comments of the time, it appears clear that women's painting was still considered weak, accomplished by that "womanly hand" of ancient memory.[93]

The foundational event of modern studies was the exhibition "Women Artists: 1550–1950", held in 1976 in Los Angeles, at the County Museum, curated by Ann Sutherland Harris and Linda Nochlin (fig. 15). In it, eighty-three women artists spanning four centuries brought to the attention of the world and of scholars a reality hidden among the folds of art history.[94] In an interview published by the *Los Angeles Times*, Nochlin answered, to the question that then became the title of her famous pamphlet, *Why Have There Been No Great Women Artists?*, "That women do not have genius – that genius is restricted to men – is obviously untrue. But genius does have to do with access to art education. Take Picasso. His father was an artist who saw to it that Pablo Picasso got art education. The question is would Pabblita [*sic*] – a girl – have gotten it?".[95] If Pablo had been Pablita, would she have received the same education in art?

Basically, the reply is the same as the one given by Vasari in speaking of Plautilla Nelli, talented, but unable to study, except within the walls of a convent.

[1] F. Baldinucci, *Notizie de' professori del disegno da Cimabue in qua* (1681–1728), edited by F. Ranalli, Florence 1846, II, p. 80: "a most bizarre drawing, in which she depicted a young girl laughing at an old woman who, with great care, is studying the alphabet board. Laughing heartily, she points a finger at her" ("bizzarissimo disegno, nel quale fece vedere una fanciulla, che burlandosi d'una vecchierella, che con grand'attenzione studia l'abbicì, sopra una tavola da fanciulli con allegro riso la sta mostrando a dito").

[2] "Disse che harebbe voluto vedere un putto che piangesse come cosa molto più difficile, et [...] lei li mandò [...] un ritratto di un suo fratello fatto piangere studiosamente", letter from Tommaso Cavalieri to Cosimo I de' Medici, 20 January 1562, in R. Sacchi (edited by), "Regesto", in *Sofonisba Anguissola e le sue sorelle*, exhibition catalogue (Cremona, Centro culturale "Città di Cremona" Santa Maria della Pietà, 17 September – 11 December 1994), Milan 1994, p. 370.

[3] Entry by B. W. Meijr, in *Sofonisba Anguissola e le sue sorelle* cit. (note 2), p. 272. The drawing now in the Uffizi is thought to be a variation of it, see entry by G. Bora, ivi, p. 270.

[4] G. Vasari, "Vita di M<adonna> Properzia de' Rossi scultrice Bolognese", in Id., *Le Vite de' più eccellenti pittori scultori e architettori* (1568), edited by P. Della Pergola, L. Grassi, G. Previtali, Novara 1967, IV, p. 341; English edition: "Life of Madonna Properzia de' Rossi Sculptor of Bologna", in Id., *Lives of the Most Eminent Painters, Sculptors and Architects*, trans. G. du C. De Vere, London 1912–1915, V, p. 128: "And it is no long time since Messer Tommaso Cavalieri, a Roman gentleman, sent to the Lord Duke Cosimo (in addition to a drawing by the hand of the divine Michelagnolo, wherein is a Cleopatra) another drawing by the hand of Sofonisba, containing a little girl laughing at a boy who is weeping because one of the cray-fish out of a basket full of them, which she has placed in front of him, is biting his finger; and there is nothing more graceful to be seen than that drawing, or more true to nature" ("Tommaso Cavalieri, gentiluomo romano, mandò al s<ignor> duca Cosimo (oltre a una carta di mano del divino Michelangelo dove è una Cleopatra) un'altra carta di mano di Sofonisba, nella quale è una fanciullina che si ride di un putto che piagne; perché avendogli ella messo inanzi un canestrino pieno di gambari, uno d'essi gli morde un dito").

[5] "uno vostro disegno perché lei lo collerisse in olio, con obligo de rimandarlo di propria mano fidelmente finito", letter from Amilcare Anguissola to Michelangelo, 7 May 1557, in R. Sacchi (edited by), "Regesto", in *Sofonisba Anguissola e le sue sorelle* cit. (note 2), pp. 364–365.

[6] G. Vasari, "Vita di M<adonna> Properzia de' Rossi scultrice bolognese", in Id., *Le Vite* cit. (note 4), IV, p. 341; English edition: "Life of Madonna Properzia de' Rossi Sculptor of Bologna", in Id., *Lives* cit. (note 4), V, p. 124: "as did, in our own day, Properzia de' Rossi of Bologna, a young woman excellent not only in household matters, like the rest of them, but also in sciences without number" ("ha con più studio e con miglior grazia che altra donna de' tempi nostri faticato dietro alle cose del disegno, percioché ha saputo non pure disegnare, colorire e ritrarre di naturale e copiare eccellentemente cose d'altri, ma da sé sola ha fatto cose rarissime e bellissime di pittura").

[7] G. Vasari, "Vita di Benvenuto Garofalo e di Girolamo da Carpi pittori ferraresi e d'altri lombardi", in Id., *Le Vite* cit. VI, pp. 353-355; Id., "Vita di Taddeo Zuccari", ivi, VII, p. 95; English edition: "Benvenuto Garofalo and Girolamo da Carpi and Other Lombards", in *Lifes* cit., VIII, p. 47; Id., "Taddeo Zucchero", ivi, VIII, p. 261.

[8] "la signora Sofonisba dice che non vuole più vivere", letter from Bernardo Maschi to Francesco Maria della Rovere dated 4 October 1568, in R. Sacchi (edited by), "Regesto", in *Sofonisba Anguissola e le sue sorelle* cit. (note 2), p. 373.

[9] The violent nocturnal reaction of the ladies in the Queen's House is documented in J. S. Lozano, "'Quella Cremonese che dipinge': Sofonisba Anguissola in Spagna", in *Sofonisba Anguissola,* proceedings of the international study day (Catania, Università degli Studi di Catania, 13 October 2019), *Archivio Storico per la Sicilia Orientale*, III, 2, 2019, pp. 67–74. By the same author is the contribution "Entre publicidad y virtud. Sofonisba Anguissola, autorretratista", in *Me veo luego existo. Mujeres que representan, mujeres representadas,* proceedings of international congress (València, Universitat de València, 5–7 November 2013), edited by E. Alba Pagán, L. Pérez Ochando, Madrid 2015, pp. 523–537.

[10] "con sì maschile spirito", G. A. della Lengueglia, *Ritratti della prosapia et heroi Moncadi nella Sicilia,* Vicenza 1657, p. 570. A thorough examination, based on previously unpublished sources, of the Moncadas and the period spent by Sofonisba in the family is provided by L. Scalisi, "Sofonisba Anguissola alla corte dei Moncada. Tra potere, arte e cultura", in *Sofonisba Anguissola,* proceedings cit. (note 9), pp. 105–117.

[11] M. W. Cole, *Sofonisba's Lesson. A Renaissance Artist and her Work*, Princeton 2019. This accurate record is a point of arrival – and of departure – which fails however to resolve intricate questions of attribution, emerging also from the work carried out in *Historia de dos pintoras: Sofonisba Anguissola y Lavinia Fontana,* exhibition catalogue (Madrid, Museo Nacional del Prado, 22 October 2019 – 2 February 2020), edited by L. Ruiz Gómez, Madrid 2019, pp. 15–37. On her Spanish period, see the contributions of Maria Kusche, "Sofonisba Anguissola en España", in *Archivo Español de Arte*, LXII, 248, 1989, pp. 391–420; "Sofonisba Anguissola al servizio dei re di Spagna", in *Sofonisba Anguissola e le sue sorelle* cit. (note 2), pp. 89–116; "Sofonisba e il ritratto di rappresentanza ufficiale nella corte spagnola", ivi, pp. 117–152, up to "Comentarios sobre las atribuciones a Sofonisba Anguissola por el doctor Alfio Nicotra", in *Archivo Español de Arte*, LXXXII, 327, 2009, pp. 285–295.

[12] *Van Dyck in Sicily 1624–1625. Painting and the Plague,* exhibition catalogue (London, Dulwich Picture Gallery, 15 February – 27 May 2012), edited by X. F. Salomon, Cinisello Balsamo 2012.

[13] Important are the documents discovered by C. Gamberini, "Sofonisba Anguissola at the Court of Philip II", in *Women Artists in Early Modern Italy. Careers, Fame, and Collectors*, edited by S. Barker, Turnhout 2016, pp. 29–38.

[14] Fundamentally important for an analysis of women's self-portraits in the modern age is the article by C. King, "Looking a Sight: Sixteenth-Century Portraits of Woman Artists", in *Zeitschrift für Kunstgeschichte*, 58, 3, 1995, pp. 381–406.

[15] "bisogna avere da natura inclinazione alla virtù, e poi a quella aggiugnere l'esercizio e lo studio come hanno fatto queste quattro nobili e virtuose sorelle, tanto innamorate d'ogni più rara virtù et in particolare delle cose del disegno, che la casa del signor Amilcare Angosciuola (perciò felicissimo padre d'onesta

et onorata famiglia) mi parve l'albergo della pittura, anzi di tutte le virtù", their names are mentioned in G. Vasari, "Vita di M<adonna> Properzia de' Rossi scultrice bolognese", in Id., *Le Vite* cit. (note 4), IV, pp. 335–339; Enghish edition: "Life of Madonna Properzia de' Rossi Sculptor of Bologna", in Id., *Lives* cit. (note 4), V, pp. 127–128; more detailed information in "Vita di Benvenuto Garofalo e di Girolamo da Carpi pittori ferraresi e d'altri lombardi", ivi, VI, pp. 355–356; "Benvenuto Garofalo and Girolamo da Carpi and Other Lombard", ivi, VIII, pp. 47–48: "A sister of hers, called Lucia, left at her death fame no less than that of Sofonisba, by means of some pictures by her hand [...] The third of the sisters Anguisciuola, called Europa, who is still a child in age, yet full of grace and virtue, and to whom I spoke this year, will be [...] in no way inferior to Sofonisba and Lucia, her sisters. [...] And because Anna, the fourth sister, although but a little girl, is also giving her attention with much profit to design" ("Una sorella della quale, chiamata Lucia, morendo ha lasciato di sé non minor fama che si sia quella di Sofonisba, mediante alcune pitture di sua mano [...] La terza sorella Angosciola, chiamata Europa, che ancora è in età puerile et alla quale, che è tutta grazia e virtù, ho parlato questo anno, non sarà [...] inferiore né a Sofonisba, né a Lucia sue sorelle. [...] E perché Anna, quarta sorella, ancora piccola fanciulletta, attende anch'ella con molto profitto al disegno").

[16] "Chiunque prenda a considerare attentamente le istorie d'Italia nel XV e nel XVI secolo, dovrà persuadersi come le donne (specialmente se di case signorili) si educassero con grandissima cura, e come gran profitto della educazione sapessero trarre", M. Minghetti, *Le donne italiane nelle Belle Arti al secolo XV e XVI*, Florence 1877, p. 3.

[17] An analysis of the concept of "giovane donna virtuosa" and its various meanings, examining many sources in the treatises and poetry of the epoch, is found in F. H. Jacobs, *Defining the Renaissance Virtuosa. Women Artists and the Language of Art history and Criticism*, Cambridge 1997.

[18] G. Vasari, "Vita di M<adonna> Properzia de' Rossi scultrice bolognese", in Id., *Le Vite* cit. (note 4), IV, p. 340; English edition: "Life of Madonna Properzia de' Rossi Sculptor of Bologna", in Id., *Lives* cit. (note 4), V, p. 127; S. Barker, "Lucrezia Quistelli (1541–94). A Woman Artist in Vasari's Florence", in *Women Artists in Early Modern Italy* cit. (note 13), pp. 47–80.

[19] The volume was printed by the brothers Domenico and Giovan Battista Guerra, from Valvasone (Friuli), who moved to Venice in 1560, see G. Comelli, "Irene di Spilimbergo in una prestigiosa edizione del Cinquecento con un carme latino di Tiziano", in *Spilimbèrc*, edited by N. Cantarutti, C. Bergamini, Udine 1984, pp. 223–236. The most recent study on Irene di Spilimbergo is by E. van Kessel, "A Martyr of Painting: Irene di Spilimbergo, Titian, and Venetian Portraiture between Life and Death", in *The Lives of Paintings: Presence, Agency and Likeness in Venetian Art of the Sixteenth Century*, Boston-Berlin 2017, pp. 131–179.

[20] Giorgio Gradenigo (1522–1600) was the Mayor of Portogruaro (1552–1553); as Senator of the Venetian Republic he held the posts of Senior Auditor (1557–1559), Overseer of Acts and Things of the Kingdom of Cyprus, fiscal advocate (1570), Conservator of Laws and Superintendent of Fortifications (1592).

[21] A. Jacobson Schutte, "Irene di Spilimbergo. The Image of a Creative Woman in Late Renaissance Italy", in *Renaissance Quarterly*, 44, 1, 1991, pp. 42–61. The collection was studied also by Benedetto Croce, "Scrittori del pieno e del tardo Rinascimento. XIX, Irene di Spilimbergo", in *La Critica*, 41, 1943, pp. 123–131, in particular pp. 126–127.

[22] Also contributing to the collection was the young Torquato Tasso with three sonnets, see A. Corsaro, "Dionigi Atanagi e la silloge per Irene di Spilimbergo (Intorno alla formazione del giovane Tasso)", in *Italica*, 75, 1, 1998, pp. 41–61.

[23] C. Scalon, *La biblioteca di Adriano di Spilimbergo (1542)*, Spilimbergo 1988.

[24] The family tradition was accepted by J. A. Crowe and G. B. Cavalcaselle, *Titian: His Life and Times*, London 1877, II, p. 302. On this basis the painting and the *pendant* with the portrait of Emilia, Irene's sister, were included in 1904 in the *Catalogo degli oggetti di sommo pregio*, Rome 1904, p. 8, published by the Ministry of Public Education. But, states C. Ricci, "Ritratti 'tizianeschi' di G. Paolo Pace", in *Rivista del R. Istituto d'archeologia e storia dell'arte di Roma*", I, fasc. II, 1929, pp. 249–265, in particular 257–265: "On 31 October 1908 Count Enrico D'Attimis Maniago, heir to the late Pietro Antonio, requested that the objects of 'highest value' be removed from the list, and consequently left free for exportation. The matter was, according to law, submitted to the Upper Council of Antiquities and Fine Arts, which instructed two of its members to report on it. It was following their report and direct examination of the works that the above-mentioned Council, on 27 January 1909, consented to 'the request for cancellation from the catalogue and revocation of the declaration'. The decision was unanimous. Present were Marchese Emilio Visconti Venosta, Camillo Boito, Alfredo d'Andrade, Luigi Cavenaghi, Pompeo Molmenti, Primo Levi, Adolfo Venturi, Giulio Cantalamessa, Domenico Gnoli and the undersigned". The paintings went to London, purchased by the antique dealer Duveen, returned to Italy to be restored by Elia Volpi in the summer of 1909, and on 30 October 1909 the *Illustrated London News* announced they had been sold to Pierpont Morgan. For the attribution, H. Tietze, E. Tietze-Conrat, "I ritratti Spilimbergo a Washington", in *Emporium*, CXVII, 699, 1953, pp. 99–107, refer to an extract from Giovanni Paolo Da Ponte's memorial: "June 28, 1560: I called for Messer Tutian for the work made by him, the portrait of our blessed Irene, rather badly sketched by Ser Zuan Paolo de Pase and left unfinished for the two years remaining before the poor lady passed on to better life. But thankfully Messer Tutian carried out the task of finishing it and it can now be said for certain that a greater likeness could not have been achieved even had she been present. I sent him six Venetian ducats and he was content, although deserving much more" ("Giugno 28, 1560: mandai a messer Tutian per l'opera per lui fata nel retrato della nostra già benedetta memoria d'Irene abozata assai malamente da Ser Zuan Paolo de Pase et lassata imperfetta per dui anni si che rimase ben che la poverina andò a miglior vita. Ma Messer Tutian per me gratia si tolse il cargo di volerlo finir et conzata talmente che si può dir per certo che se fusse sta presente meglio si non poteva desiderare. Gli mandai ducati 6 viniziani et per sua cortesia se à contenta che merita assai più").

[25] D. Atanagi, "Vita della Signora Irene", in Id., *Rime di diversi nobilissimi et eccellentissimi autori in morte della Signora Irene delle Signore di Spilimbergo* (Venice 1561), republished by P. Giordani, "In omaggio 'A Madama Adelaide Calderara Butti'", in *Fiori d'arti e di lettere italiane per l'anno 1839*, edited by F. Ambrosoli, Milan 1839, pp. 128–153, in particular p. 153: "She had enchanting eyes. And she was well aware if the effect of those eyes, keeping them almost always wide open; and accompanying them with a sweet laugh from her beautiful mouth, she directed her gaze majestically, both honestly and charmingly; taking the freedom of turning her gaze on everyone, with a grave bearing of the person and dressed with propriety; and at the same time showing herself to be a beautiful woman, most gracious and most proper" ("aveva gli occhi maghi. Questa forza degli occhi suoi era molto ben conosciuta da lei: perchè quasi sempre li teneva ben aperti; e accompagnandoli con certo suo dolce riso procedente da bellissima bocca, li reggeva con maestà insieme onesta e soave; usando la libertà del volgerli verso ciascuno, con portamento della persona grave e con l'abito onesto; che ad un tempo istesso la facevano conoscere per donzella bellissima, graziosissima, onestissima").

[26] O. Ulm, "I ritratti d'Irene ed Emilia di Spilimbergo erroneamente attribuiti a Tiziano", in *Emporium*, XXXI, 182, 1910, pp. 126–135, in particular p. 128.

[27] "un ritratto di Sofonisba Anguisciola fatto di sua mano, e rappresentato al re Filippo, e sentendo meravigliose lodi di lei nell'arte della pittura; mossa da generosa emulazione s'accese tutta d'un caldo desiderio di pareggiar quella nobile e valorosa donzella. Laonde coll'indirizzo del signor Tiziano si pose al colorito [...]. Perciocchè in ispazio d'un mese e mezzo trasse copia d'alcune pitture del detto signor Tiziano, con tanti particolari avvertimenti alle misure a' lumi alle ombre, e così agli scorci a' nervi alle ossature alla tenerezza e dolcezza delle carni, e non meno alle pieghe de' panni", D. Atanagi, "Vita della Signora Irene", in Id., *Rime di diversi nobilissimi et eccellentissimi autori* cit. (note 25), p. 149.

[28] Ivi, p. 148: "and receiving help in the art of embroidery, at which she excelled over all others; she applied herself with such diligent study and so much patience, that in a few days she accomplished what no man, nor woman, would perhaps have done in many years" ("e ricevendo aiuto dall'arte del ricamare, nella quale valeva sopra ogni altra; attese con sì diligente studio e con tanta pazienza, che in pochi giorni fece quello che uomo, non che donna, non avrebbe fatto forse in molti anni").

[29] The sonet is published in B. Croce, "Scrittori del pieno e del tardo Rinascimento" cit. (note 21), pp. 123–131, in particular pp. 126–127: "A nymph here with the breeze has parted / her hair, and with her plectrum and lyre / she plays, singing with admirable skill. / Apollo, who listens to her and looks on, / from the sweet glow and the gentle song / overcome by envy and love, sighs with her. / Far from this beautiful nymph / there are many children, who let their flocks / wander where they will. / And while they are intent on other things, / some plucking beautiful flowers, others weaving / cages, singing in sweet new tones, / the cunning fox from the grove comes out / and towards the place where their pockets are hidden / does creep around. / He seems to approach his prey ever closer / and well you might say, Daphnis, that she is alive, / aiming a little at her distant arts..." ("Una ninfa qui presso a l'aura sparte / ha le chiome, e col plettro e con la lira / suona cantando con mirabil arte. / Apollo, che vicin l'ascolta e mira, / dai dolci lumi e dal soave canto / vinto d'invidia e amor, seco sospira. / Lunge da questa bella ninfa alquanto / molti fanciulli son ch'i loro armenti / lasciano errando andar per

ogni canto. / E mentre stanno ad altre cose intenti, / altri a coglier bei fiori, altri ad ordire / gabbie, cantando in dolci e novi accenti, / l'astuta volpe dal boschetto uscire / si vede e verso il luogo ove riposte / hanno le tasche lor, serpendo gire. / Par che alla preda più sempre s'accoste / e ben diresti, Dafni, ch'ella è viva, / mirando un poco l'arti sue discoste…").

[30] P. Morigia, *Historia dell'antichità di Milano*, Milan 1592, p. 674.

[31] Ivi, p. 675: "for the fear that she had of childbirth in the year 1577" ("per timore ch'ella ebbe del parto l'anno 1577"); Id., *La Nobiltà di Milano*, Milan 1595, p. 299: "for the fear that she felt at the time when the Plague struck Milan in the year 1576" ("per timor ch'ella hebbe al tempo della Peste che fù in Milano l'anno 1576").

[32] G. P. Lomazzo, *Rime*, Milan 1587, p. 115: "Of Propertia, sculptress in our day, / of Europa; Sofonisba, and their sisters, / Painters of Kings and Noblemen. / But to the great Cantona the noblest honours, / In embroidering ornate and beautiful effigies, / Lie beyond what any ink can say" ("Di Propertia scoltrice à tempo nostro, d'Europa; Sofonisba, e lor sorelle, / Lessi di Rè pittrici et di Signori. / Ma de la gran Cantona i chiari honori, / In ricamar effigie ornate e belle, / Auanza ciò che può dirne ogni inchiostro").

[33] P. Morigia, *La Nobiltà di Milano* cit. (note 31), p. 282: "Full praiseworthy is the noble & virtuous Barbara Cantona; This girl is stupendous, and miraculous in drawing, & and if she persists, I judge that she will become an outstanding painter. Moreover, with the Needle (at this tender age) she is imitating her famous and most expert mother" ("Degna di lode è la nobile & virtuosa Barbara Cantona; Questa fanciulla è stupenda, e miracolosa nel disegno, & s'ella perseuera, giudico ch'ella debba riuscire un eccellente pitrrice. Oltre che con l'Ago (in questa sua tenera età) va imitando diuinamente la virtuosissima, e celebre sua madre").

[34] "Questa dunque honorata Gentildonna con l'Ago, e con i colorii di Seda & Oro, imita con stupore ogni qual si voglia più notabile pittura, ò miniatura", ivi, p. 299.

[35] G. P. Lomazzo, *Idea del Tempio della Pittura*, Milan 1590, pp. 166–167: "And now this singular woman is occupied in furnishing a fruit-bowl cover representing the Coronation of His Catholic Majesty King Philip the Second of Spain, with the renunciation of the States made to him by the Caesarean Majesty of Emperor Charles V his father, wherein appear depicted the States of His Majesty, with their Imprese, & Queen Maria with many Knights, & all around appear the figures of Religion, Justice, Fortitude, Prudence, Peace, Happiness and Fame, with some Imprese representing these virtues. And all of these Princes are portrayed realistically, & can be seen equally well from both sides. It will also, at the same time, represent the contrast between Pallas & Aragne, & the excellences, & the weaknesses of the Gods. But it would take too long to describe her works one by one, & to praise them as they deserve. And so I leave this to Tasso, & to many other fine minds of these days, who are praising her in their poems" ("Et hora è occupata questa singolar donna in fornire vn fruttiero doue rappresenta la Coronatione della Catholica Maestà del Rè Filippo Secondo di Spagna, con la rinuncia de gli Stati fattagli dalla Cesarea Maestà dell'Imperatore Carlo Quinto suo padre, oue si vedono gli Stati di S. Maestà in figure, con le Imprese loro, & la Regina Maria co molti Caualieri, & all'intorno sono in figure, la Religione, la Giustitia, la Fortezza, la Prudenza, la Pace, la Felicità, la Fama, con alcune Imprese che conformano con dette virtù. E sono tutti questi Principi ritratti al naturale, & si veggono da tutte due le parti egualmente. Attende ancora nell'istesso tempo à rappresentare il contrasto tra Pallade, & Aragne, & l'eccellenze, & i vituperi de i Dei. Mà troppo lungo farebbe il raccontar aduna aduna l'opere sue, & degnamente lodarle. Si che ne lascio cura al Tasso, & à molti altri begl'ingegni di questi tempi, che la vanno celebrando ne i loro poemi").

[36] C. C. Malvasia, *Felsina Pittrice, vite de pittori bolognesi*, Bologna 1678, I, pp. 33–34. For a studio of Caterina Vigri's production, see *Pregare con le immagini. Il breviario di Caterina Vigri*, V. edited by Fortunati, C. Leonardi, Bologna 2004.

[37] An analysis of the presence of women artists in the territory, from the Bolognese Caterina Vigri to the Ravenna-born Barbara Longhi, is found in I. Graziani, "La leggenda dell'artista donna", in *La pittura in Emilia e in Romagna. Il Cinquecento*, edited by V. Fortunati, Bologna 1994, pp. 129–147.

[38] One of the first studies, dedicated to the Germanic world, is by A. Weil Carr, "Women Artists in the Middle Ages", in *The Feminist Art Journal*, 5, 1, 1976, pp. 5–9, 26. An analysis of convent activity is found in the volume *Vita artistica nel monastero femminile. Exempla*, edited by V. Fortunati, Bologna 2002: in particular, the problem is examined by V. Fortunati, "Ruolo e funzione dell'immagine nei monasteri femminili", ivi, pp. 11–42. A thorough analysis of convent life and the production of artist-nuns is in G. Zarri, "Culture nel chiostro. Tra arte e vita", in *Artiste nel chiostro. Produzione artistica nei monasteri femminili in età moderna*, edited by S. Barker, Florence 2015, pp. 19–29. Dealing with Florentine convents are the texts by S. Barker, "Painting and Humanism in Early Modern Florentine Convents", ivi, pp. 105–139, and M. D. Garrard, "The Cloister and the Square: Gender Dynamics in Renaissance Florence", in *Early Modern Women*, 11, 1, 2016, pp. 5–44. Recently held in Florence was an international symposium devoted to miniaturist nuns, Biblioteca di San Marco (11 and 12 October 2018), "The Colors of Paradise. Painting Miniatures in Italian Convents, c. 1300–1700".

[39] "che sapeva disegnare", G. Vasari, "Vita di Paolo Uccello", in Id., *Le Vite* cit. (note 4), I, p. 167; English edition: "Paolo Uccello", in Id., *Lives* cit. (note 4), II, p. 140.

[40] "nelle sue opere i volti e fattezze delle donne, per averne veduto a suo piacimento, sono assai migliori che le teste degli uomini non sono e più simili al vero", G. Vasari, "Vita di Fra Bartolomeo della Porta", in Id., *Le Vite* cit., III, p. 493; Id. *Vita di M<adonna> Properzia de' Rossi scultrice bolognese*, ivi, IV, pp. 339–340; English edition: "Fra Bartolomeo di San Marco [Baccio della Porta]", in Id., *Lives* cit., IV, p. 161; "Life of Madonna Properzia de' Rossi Sculptor of Bologna", ivi, V, pp. 126–127.

[41] M. G. D'Apuzzo, "Le monache di Savonarola tra arte e committenza", in *Vita artistica nel monastero femminile* cit. (note 38), pp. 131–145; see also: C. Turrill Lupi, "Biografia e fortuna critica di Plautilla Nelli: una rilettura", in *Plautilla Nelli. Arte e devozione sulle orme di Savonarola*, exhibition catalogue (Florence, Gallerie degli Uffizi, 8 March – 4 June 2017), F. Navarro, Livorno 2017, pp. 19–33 and F. Navarro, "'Semplice lecto, semplice studio, semplici figure'. Suor Plautilla Nelli 'dipintora' per Santa Caterina de' Ricci tra Firenze e Prato", ivi, pp. 34–59.

[42] This work measures 192 × 671 cm and was moved from the Convent of Santa Caterina to that of Santa Maria Novella in 1817, subsequent to Napoleon's suppression of the religious orders. It underwent restoration, concluded in 2019, as part of the Advancing Women Artists project.

[43] A. Ghirardi, "Dipingere in onore del Cielo: suor Orsola Maddalena Caccia e la vocazione artistica delle Orsoline di Moncalvo", in *Vita artistica nel monastero femminile* cit. (note 38), pp. 115–129; P. Caretta, "Orizzonti figurativi e riferimenti culturali nell'opera di Orsola Maddalena Caccia", in *Artiste nel chiostro* cit. (note 38), pp. 179–190.

[44] C. A. Gladen, "Suor Lucrina Fetti: pittrice in una corte monastica seicentesca", in *I monasteri femminili come centri di cultura fra Rinascimento e Barocco*, proceedings of the international historical symposium (Bologna, 8–10 December 2000), edited by G. Pomata, G. Zarri, Rome 2005, pp. 123–141; M. Bourne, "From Court to Cloister and Back Again: Margherita Gonzaga, Caterina de' Medici and Lucrina Fetti at the Convent of Sant'Orsola in Mantua", in *Domestic Institutional Interiors in Early Modern Europe*, edited by S. Cavallo, S. Evangelisti, Farnham 2009, pp. 153–179

[45] G. Vasari, "Di diversi artefici fiaminghi", in Id., *Le Vite* cit. (note 4), VII, pp. 472–473; English edition: "Divers Flemings", in Id., *Lives* cit. (note 4), IX, pp. 269–270, containing all of the notations on the Flemish artists mentioned here.

[46] L. Guicciardini, *Descrittione di tutti i Paesi Bassi*, Antwerp 1567, p. 99, calls her "Clara Skeysers".

[47] A. Sandero, *Flandria Illustrata*, Cologne 1641, p. 163.

[48] L. Guicciardini, *Descrittione* cit. (note 46), pp. 38–39, says she is from Antwerp: "Susanna […] who was excellent at painting, the greatest at producing minute works, & most excellent at illuminating, so that the great King Henry VIII by way of splendid gifts & great recompense, attracted her to England, where she lived for many years in great favour, & appreciated by all of the Court, & and where she finally died rich & honoured" ("Susanna […] la quale fu eccellente nella pittura, massime nel fare opere minutissime oltre a ogni credere, & eccellentissima nell'alluminare, in tanto che il gran' Re Henrico ottauo con gran' doni & gran' prouuisione, la tirò in Inghilterra, doue visse molti anni in gran' fauore, & gratia di tutta la Corte, & iui finalmente si mori ricca, & honorata"); A. Sandero, *Flandria Illustrata* cit. (note 47), p. 164.

[49] L. Guicciardini, *Descrittione* cit. (note 46), p. 100: "Levina, the daughter of Master Simone di Bruggia […], was greatly beloved by Queen Mary, & and now much loved by Queen Elizabeth" ("Leuina, figliuola di maestro Simone di Bruggia […], fu molto amata dalla Regina Maria, & hora è amatissima dalla Regina Elisabetta"); A. Sandero, *Flandria Illustrata* cit. (note 47), p. 210.

[50] L. Guicciardini, *Descrittione* cit. (note 46), p. 100: "Caterina daughter of Master Giouanni d'Hemssen […], wife of Christiano most excellent player of cord instruments among others, such that given their rare qualities, the Queen of Hungary brought them both with her to Spain, where at her death she left them a life-time provision" ("Caterina figliuola di maestro Giouanni d'Hemssen […], moglie di Christiano eccellentissimo Sonatore di buon' accordo, & d'altri strumenti talche la Regina d'Vngheria per la loro rara virtu li condusse seco ambedue in Hispagna, oue poi alla sua morte, lasciò ancor' loro prouuisione a vita").

[51] G. Vasari, "Vita di Benvenuto Garofalo e di Girolamo da Carpi pittori ferraresi e d'altri lombardi", in Id., *Le Vite* cit. (note 4), VI, pp. 347–348; English

edition: "Benvenuto Garofalo and Girolamo da Carpi and Other Lombards", in Id., *Lives* cit. (note 4), VIII, p. 42: "Thus, to that Giovan Battista Mantovano, an excellent sculptor and engraver of prints, [...], have been born two sons, who engrave copper-plates divinely well, and, what is even more astonishing, a daughter, called Diana, who also engraves so well that it is a thing to marvel at; and I who saw her, a very gentle and gracious girl, and her works, which are most beautiful, was struck with amazement" ("Con ciò sia che di Giovambattista mantoano, intagliator di stampe e scultore eccellente, [...] sono nati due figliuoli che intagliano stampe di rame divinamente; e che è cosa più maravigliosa, una figliuola, chiamata Diana, intaglia anch'ella tanto bene, che è cosa maravigliosa, et io che ho veduto lei, che è molto gentile e graziosa fanciulla, e l'opere sue che sono bellissime, ne sono restato stupefatto").

[52] G. Vasari, "Vita del Primaticcio", in Id., *Le Vite*, cit. (note 4), VII, p. 298; English edition: "Francesco Primaticcio", in Id., *Lives* cit., IX, p. 155.

[53] C. C. Malvasia, "Di Prospero Fontana e di Lavinia sva figlivola", in *Felsina pittrice* cit. (note 36), I, pp. 213–224, in particular p. 216 ("nonostante che guadagnasse tesori, ebbe quasi a morir pezzente, & infelice").

[54] Ivi, p. 219 ("fù riceuuta come vna Principessa, facendosele formale incontro, & armandosi le strade delle solite Milizie in fila, e in ordinanza al suo arrivo").

[55] Ivi, p. 220 ("Parue in oltre alla sagace giouane potersi francamente assicurare della dabbenaggine, anzi semplicità del futuro sposo; il perche, diuenutale poscia consorte, con condizione non solo di permetterle, che proseguire potess'ella il dipingere, mà lei ancora aiutar douesse, e in ciò affaticarsi, nulla riuscendo, solea burlarlo; e ponendolo a fare almeno il busto a que' ritratti, ch'ella ricauaua, & a vestirli solamente, soggiongere, che in tal guisa si contentasse fare almeno il Sartore, già che il Cielo non lo volea Pittore").

[56] On Lavinia Fontana's stay in Rome, M. T. Cantaro, *Lavinia Fontana "pittora singolare" (1552-1614)*, Milan-Rome 1989, pp. 15–19.

[57] Among the many is Rinaldi, who dedicates a sonnet to Lavinia and one to Fede Galizia (in *Delle Rime di Cesare Rinaldi Bolognese*, Bologna 1598, pp. 98–99) and the poem *Herodiade con la testa di S. Gio. Battista di Lauinia Fontana* by G. B. Marino (in *La Galeria del cavalier Marino distinta in pitture & sculture*, Ancona 1620, p. 56).

[58] On this invention by Lavinia, L. De Girolami Cheney, "Lavinia Fontana's Nude Minervas", in *Woman's Art Journal*, 36, 2, 2015, pp. 30–40, and P. Tosini, "Ottaviano Rabasco, un letterato dimenticato nella Roma di Caravaggio, e la *Pallade ignuda* di Lavinia Fontana per Marco Sittico Altemps IV", in *Caravaggio e i letterati*, edited by S. Ebert-Schifferer, L. Tezza, Todi 2020, pp. 125–140.

[59] C. C. Malvasia, "Di Gio. Andrea Sirani e di Elisabetta sva figlivola", in Id., *Felsina pittrice* cit. (note 36), II, pp. 452–487, in particular p. 454. This chapter contains the "Nota delle pitture fatte da me Elisabetta Sirani", a catalogue of paintings accomplished from 1655 to 1665; on p. 487 some lines are devoted to Ginevra Cantofoli.

[60] "ebbe oltramodo l'animo inclinato à viaggiar fuori dalle Mura Paterne", ivi, pp. 458–459.

[61] "Elisabetta [...] à prezzo di sangue, non che di sudori s'acquistò il Sesso Virile. Nacque Femmina, ma d'effemminato altro non ritenne, che la corteccia del Nome", e "non solo non oprò mai da donna, e più che da huomo", ivi, pp. 458, 478.

[62] B. Bohn, "The Antique Heroines of Elisabetta Sirani", in *Renaissance Studies*, XVI, 1, 2002, pp. 52–79; A. Modesti, "'Il Pennello Virile': Elisabetta Sirani and Artemisia Gentileschi as Masculinized Painters?", in *Artemisia Gentileschi in a Changing Light*, edited by S. Barker, Turnhout 2017, pp. 131–146.

[63] F. Odorici, "Dello spirito di associazione di alcune città lombarde nel medio evo", in *Archivio Storico Italiano*, XI, I, 21, 1860, pp. 73–108, in particular p. 91. The story can be traced to the late eighteenth-century text by G. Biffi, *Memorie per servire alla storia degli artisti cremonesi*, edited by L. Bandera Gregori, Cremona 1989, pp. 33–34; and given as an *exemplum* of chastity in J. K. Dabbs, "Sex, Lies and Anecdotes: Gender Relations in the Life Stories of Italian Women Artists, 1550–1800", in *Aurora: The Journal of the History of Art*, 6, 2005, pp. 17–37, in particular pp. 26–27.

[64] The manner of their presence, sound documentation and the lists of their names have recently been analysed by P. M. Lukehart, "Giovanna Garzoni, 'Accademica'", in *La grandezza dell'universo nell'arte di Giovanna Garzoni*, exhibition catalogue (Florence, Gallerie degli Uffizi – Palazzo Pitti, 28 May – 28 June 2020), edited by S. Barker, Livorno 2020, pp. 96–105.

[65] For the Villa del Vascello, M. Mayer, *Villa Benedetta*, Rome, for Mascardi, 1677; on the Abbot Elpidio Benedetti, see Y. Primarosa, *Elpidio Benedetti (1609-1690). Committenza e relazioni artistiche di un agente del re di Francia nella Roma del Seicento*, preface by A. Zuccari, Turin 2018; the life-story and work of Plautilla Bricci have been studied by Y. Primarosa, "Nuova luce su Plautilla Bricci pittrice e 'architettrice'", in *Studi di Storia dell'arte*, no. 25, 2014, pp. 145–161, and by C. Lollobrigida, *Plautilla Bricci. Pictura et Architectura Celebris. L'architettrice del Barocco Romano*, Rome 2017. The artist is the subject of a good historical novel by M. Mazzucco, *L'architettrice*, Turin 2019.

[66] C. A. Du Fresnoy, *De Arte Graphica. The Art of Painting* (1668), London 1695, p. 320.

[67] *Artemisia Gentileschi / Agostino Tassi. Atti di un processo per stupro*, edited by E. Menzio, Milan 1981, republished in 2004 in *Artemisia Gentileschi. Lettere precedute da Atti di un processo per stupro*, with the addition of an essay by A. Boetti and a text by R. Barthes. On her marriage to Pierantonio Stiattesi, see S. Barker, "A New Document Concerning Artemisia Gentileschi's Marriage", in *The Burlington Magazine*, CLVI, 1341, 2014, pp. 803–804.

[68] M. D. Garrard, "Artemisia Gentileschi's Self-Portrait as the Allegory of Painting", in *The Art Bulletin*, LXII, 1, 1980, pp. 97–112; Ead., "Artemisia and Susanna", in *Feminism and Art History. Questioning the Litany*, edited by N. Broude, M. D. Garrard, New York 1982, pp. 146–171; Ead., *Artemisia Gentileschi: The Image of the Female Hero in Italian Baroque Art*, Princeton 1989; Ead., *Artemisia Gentileschi Around 1622. The Shaping and Reshaping of an Artistic Identity*, Berkeley 2001; Ead., *Artemisia Gentileschi*, Princeton 2008; Ead., "Identifying Artemisia: The Archive and the Eye", in *Artemisia Gentileschi in a Changing Light* cit. (note 62), pp. 11–40; Ead., *Artemisia Gentileschi and Feminism in Early Modern Europe*, London 2020.

[69] *Lettere di Artemisia*, edited by F. Solinas, Rome 2011, collection of over seventy letters, including her correspondence with Francesco Maria Maringhi (1593-after 1653), the letters sent from Naples to her friend Cavalier Cassiano dal Pozzo (1588–1657), to Don Antonio Ruffo (1610–1678), aristocratic collector from Messina, the letters sent to Grand Dukes Cosimo II (1620) and Ferdinando II de' Medici (1635), to the Minister Andrea Cioli, to Galileo Galilei and to Duke Francesco I d'Este (1635, 1637). See also F. Solinas, "'Bella, pulita, e senza macchia': Artemisia and Her Letters" in *Artemisia*, exhibition catalogue (London, National Gallery, 20 October 2020 – 21 January 2021), edited by L. Treves, London 2020, pp. 46–63.

[70] C. Ripa, *Iconologia* (1618), Turin 1986, II, p. 121: "Painting. Woman, with thick black hair, dishevelled and twisted in various manner, with arched brows that reveal fantastic thoughts, covering her mouth with a band tied behind her ears, a gold chain around her neck, from which hangs a mask bearing the word *imitatio*. She will hold in one hand a brush, & in the other the palette, with a gown of shimmering fabric that covers her feet, & at the end of the table, some painting tools may be seen, to show that painting is a noble practice, since it cannot be done without great application of the intellect" ("Pittura. Donna bella, con capelli negri, & grossi, sparsi, & ritorti in diverse maniere, con le ciglia inarcate, che mostrino pensieri fantastichi, si cuopre la bocca con una fascia legata dietro à gli orecchi, con una catena d'oro al collo, dalla quale penda una maschera, & abbia scritto nella fronte, *imitatio*. Terrà in una mano il pennello, & nell'altra la tavola, con la veste di drappo cangiante, la quale le cuopra li piedi, & a' piedi di essa si potranno fare alcuni istromenti della pittura, per mostrare che la pittura è essercitio nobile, non si potendo fare senza molta applicatione dell'intelletto").

[71] C. Bronzini, *Della dignita et della nobiltà delle donne*, Biblioteca Nazionale Centrale di Firenze, Magl. Cl. VIII, 1525, I, fol. 102*r*, in S. Barker, "The First Biography of Artemisia Gentileschi: Self-Fashioning and Proto-Feminist Art History in Cristofano Bronzini's Notes on Women Artists", in *Mitteilungen Kunsthistorischen Institutes in Florenz*, LX, 3, 2018, pp. 405–435, in particular p. 433.

[72] "Se Horatio Gentileschi fusse stato di humore più patticabile hauerebbe fatto assai buon profitto nella virtù, ma più nel bestiale, che nell'humano egli daua; e di qualsiuoglia soggetto per eminente, ch'egli fusse, conto non faceua; era di sua opinione, e con la sua Satirica lingua ciascheduno offendeua, e dalla benignità di Dio habbiamo da sperare il perdono d'ogni suo fallo", G. Baglione, "Vita di Horatio Gentileschi, Pittore", in Id., *Le Vite de' Pittori scultori et architetti. Dal pontificato di Gregorio XIII del 1572. In fino a' tempi di Papa Vrbano Ottauo nel 1642*, Rome 1642, pp. 359–360.

[73] "e sarebbe stata degna d'ogni stima, se fosse stata di qualità più onesta, ed onorata", G. B. Passeri, *Vite de' pittori, scultori ed architetti che hanno lavorato in Roma, e che son morti dal 1641 al 1673*, Bologna 1772, p. 105.

[74] J. Locker, "Artemisia Gentileschi: The Literary Formation of an Unlearned Artist", in *Artemisia Gentileschi in a Changing Light* cit. (note 62), pp. 89–102.

[75] On Artemisia's complicated years in Naples: R. Lattuada, "Unknown Paintings by Artemisia in Naples, and New Points Regarding her Daily Life and *Bottega*", in *Artemisia Gentileschi in a Changing Light* cit. (note 62), pp. 187–216.

[76] The "Artemisia case", biographical and artistic, has become iconic, fuelled by major exhibitions such as: *Artemisia*, exhibition catalogue (Florence, Casa Buonarroti, 18 June – 4 November 1991), edited by R. Contini, G. Papi, Rome 1991; *Orazio e Artemisia Gentileschi*, exhibition catalogue (Rome, Palazzo Venezia, 20 October 2001 – 20 January 2002; New York, The Metropolitan Museum of Art, 14 February – 12 May 2002; Saint Louis, The Saint Louis Art Museum,

15 June – 15 September 2002), edited by K. Christiansen, J. W. Mann, Milan 2001; *Artemisia. Storia di una passione,* exhibition catalogue (Milan, Palazzo Reale, 22 September 2011 – 30 January 2012), edited by R. Contini, F. Solinas, Milan 2011; *Artemisia. La musa Clio e gli anni napoletani*, exhibition catalogue (Pisa, Palazzo Blu, 23 March – 30 June 2013), edited by R. Contini, F. Solinas, Rome 2013; *Artemisia Gentileschi e il suo tempo*, exhibition catalogue (Rome, Palazzo Braschi, 30 November 2016 – 7 May 2017), edited by F. Baldassari, J. Mann, N. Spinosa, Milan 2016; *Artemisia* cit. (note 69).

[77] "Properzia de Rossi, artiste bolonaise, fait voir à un jeune homme dont elle est éprise, mais qui ne la paie pas de retour, un bas-relief dont le sujet est lié à l'histoire de sa vie et des tristes amour", this is the description given by the Conservator of the royal museum, the painter and Cavalier C. P. Landon, *Choix de tableaux modernes de la Galerie de son Altesse Royale M.me la Duchesse de Berry*, Paris 1823, p. 5. The three works by Louis Ducis (1775–1847) placed together to tell the love stories of artists and poets were *Le Tasse lisant ses vers à la princesse*, *Van Dyck faisant le portrait d'une jeune paysanne*, exhibited at the Salon in 1819, and *Marie Stuart jouant du clavecin est accompagnée par David Rizzo, musician attaché au service de son palais*, 1822, destined to be assassinated in the queen's presence.

[78] "Del corpo bellissima e sonò e cantò [...] meglio che femmina della sua città", "mise le tenere e bianchissime mani nelle cose mecaniche e fra la ruvidezza de' marmi e l'asprezza del ferro", applicando il suo "capriccioso e destrissimo ingegno", G. Vasari, "Vita di M<adonna> Properzia de' Rossi scultrice bolognese", in Id., *Le Vite* cit. (note 4), IV, p. 336; English edition: "Life of Madonna Properzia de' Rossi Sculptor of Bologna", in Id., *Lives* cit. (note 4), V, p. 124.

[79] I. Bullart, *Academie des Sciences et des Arts, Contenant les Vie, & les Eloges Historiques des Hommes Illustres, Qui ont excellé en ces Professions depuis environ quatre Siécles parmy diverses Nations de l'Europe*, Paris 1682, I, pp. 375–377: "Il n'y a point d'artifice dont elle n'usast pour luy donner de l'amour, ny d'attraits qu'elle n'employast pour gaigner sur son Coeur les mesmes avantages qu'il avoit remportez sur le sien. Mais ses efforts furent impuissans: cét homme altier fut pour elle tout de glace, pendant qu'elle estoit pour luy toute de feu; & ses froideurs affligerent tellement l'amoureuse Propertia, que cedant à la violence de sa douleur, & de sa passion; elle s'abandonna à une vie languissante [...], negligea sa santé jusqu'au point, qu'aprés avoir languy quelque temps, elle cessa de vivre en la fleur de ses années". On the portraits of Properzia de' Rossi, I. Graziani, "Ritratto di Madonna Properzia de' Rossi, scultrice", in V. Fortunati, I. Graziani, *Properzia de' Rossi. Una scultrice a Bologna nell'età di Carlo V*, Bologna 2008, pp. 29–43.

[80] F. Hemans, *Records of Woman: With Other Poems*, Edinburgh-London 1828; the poem *Properzia Rossi* is on pp. 46–54. Felicia Dorothea Browne Hemans (1793–1835) was born in Liverpool, lived in Wales as an adolescent and then moved to Dublin, where she died.

[81] "The bright work grows / Beneath my hand, unfolding, as a rose, / Leaf after leaf, to beauty; line by line, / I fix my thought, heart, soul, to burn, to shine, / Thro' the pale marble's veins. It grows – and now / I give my own life's history to thy brow / Forsaken Ariadne! thou shalt wear / My form, my lineaments...", ivi, p. 49.

[82] "Royal Academy Exhibition", in *Blackwood's Edinburgh Magazine*, XLVIII, CCXCIX, 1840, pp. 374–386, in particular p. 380: "No. 197. Titian and Irene da Spilimbergo. W. Dyce – This represents Titian reclining on the grass in the grounds of a villa, enjoying the conversation of the beautiful Irene. There is something so odd in this picture, that you are at first more disposed to laugh at it than to admire. It is, however, a clean picture, though in many parts affected, as in the whiteness of Irene's face; and certainly poor Titian, whom we never think of but with respect, is here too much of the sprawling Scaramouch or Jackpudding. There is an audacity in the picture, which, subdued, may make a painter".

[83] I. Nievo, *Canti del Friuli*, Udine 1912, pp. 73–74: "On the great black wall shone / the wide triforium, like a joyful / triptych of radiant spring, / and above the young blond head / of Irene, all absorbed in her usual / work, lingered the dying / May sun. It was a quiet sunset / full of flight. Saint Daniel high up / in the great light, down in the shadows the shore / of the river, in the middle, like a stage / salient and green, the plain, and the sky / was above it, as clear as enamel. / And Irene raised her eyes: Oh that true / and vivid light of sunset, oh that / diffused serenity of the evening, / that so sweet to the soul does speak, / may it be fixed on the canvas! Painting the enchantment, / that at every moment in heaven is renewed! / The brush laid down. Her brow was wet with tears, her heart yearned for it, a song throbbed with beauty, while the sky lit up with stars" ("Splendeva su la gran parete nera / l'ampia trifora, simile a giocondo / trittico di raggiante primavera, / e sopra il giovanile capo biondo / d'Irene, tutta assorta nel consueto / lavoro, indugiava il moribondo / sole di maggio. Era un tramonto quieto / pieno di voli. San Daniele in alto / nella gran luce, giù nell'ombra il greto / del fiume, in mezzo, simile a uno spalto saliente e verde, la pianura, ed era sovr'essa il cielo terso come smalto. / E levò gli occhi Irene: O quella vera / e viva luce di tramonto, o quella / serenità diffusa della sera, / che così dolce all'anima favella, / su la tela fissar! Pinger l'incanto, / che ad ogni istante in ciel si rinnovella! / Il pennello depose. Avea di pianto / umido il ciglio, dentro al cuore anelo / le palpitava di bellezza un canto, / mentre di stelle si accendeva il cielo").

[84] "non negò auer posto nella di lei minestra vna poluere", C. C. Malvasia, "Di Gio. Andrea Sirani e di Elisabetta sva figlivola", in Id., *Felsina pittrice* cit. (note 36), II, p. 479.

[85] The legend of Elisabetta Sirani is told by V. Roncuzzi Roversi-Monaco, "Il 'personaggio' Elisabetta Sirani nella produzione editoriale bolognese dell'Ottocento", in *Elisabetta Sirani "pittrice eroina" 1638-1665*, exhibition catalogue (Bologna, Museo Civico Archeologico, 4 December 2004 – 27 February 2005), edited by J. Bentini, V. Fortunati, Bologna 2004, pp. 153–163.

[86] The group's first exhibition was held from 25 January to 14 February 1882 in a hall at the Cercle des Arts Libéraux in Rue Vivienne 49 with fifty or so works by thirty-eight artists, see "Union des Femmes peintres et sculpteurs", in *La Gazette des Femmes*, 25 January 1882, p. 1, which also states some declarations of intent: "les artistes hommes s'arrogent la part du lion et traitent les travaux de femmes avec trop de dédain. Mais, au lieu de se répandre en lamentations inutiles, elles ont fièrement réclamé leur droit à la critique raisonnée, impartiale, et se son dit: 'Nous aurons *notre* exposition !'". A detailed presentation of the works displayed is found in J. A., "La première exposition de L'Union des Femmes peintres et sculpteurs", in *La Gazette des Femmes*, 10 February 1882, pp. 1–3.

[87] M. Howe Elliott, *Art and Handicraft in the Woman's Building of the World's Columbian Exposition*, Paris-New York 1893, p. 25. The World's Columbian Exposition was inaugurated on 1 May 1893. The construction of the Woman's Building and the display of artistic works and handicraft was managed by a board of women alone, chaired by Bertha Honoré Potter Palmer, a collector and philanthropist from Chicago.

[88] Ivi, p. 31: "side by side with the sovereigns of Europe – Isabella, Elizabeth, and Victoria – are the names of the workers, the seers, the pioneers". The building also housed a library with over eight thousand books by women authors, S. Wadsworth, W. A. Wiegand, *Right Here I See My Own Books. The Woman's Building Library at the World's Columbian Exposition*, Amherst 2013.

[89] For the story of the organisation of the Woman's Building and for a thorough analysis of the related events, J. M. Weimann, *The Fair Women. The Story of The Woman's Building World's Columbian Exposition Chicago 1893*, Chicago 1981.

[90] The panels arrived from Paris on 3 April, see "Miss Cassatt's Painting Arrives", in *Chicago Tribune*, 4 April 1893, p. 6.

[91] The artist herself in a letter to Palmer specifies that her work represented a woman in contemporary dress, and she had tried to convey "a general effect as bright, as gay, as amusing as possible", J. M. Weimann, *The Fair Women* cit. (note 89), p. 200. The work was accused of having been done in a spirit of derision, deemed "cynical" by E. M. Henrotin, "An Outsider's View of the Woman's Exhibit", in *The Cosmopolitan*, XV, 5, 1893, pp. 560–566, in particular p. 561.

[92] *Official Catalogue of Exhibits. World's Columbian Exposition. Woman's Building*, Chicago 1893, pp. 57, 58, 59.

[93] E. T., "On expose", in *L'Intransigéant*, 26 May 1930, p. 5. In the following year, the group abandoned its vindictive tone, inaugurating on 27 January the first official exhibition of the Femmes Artistes Modernes, at the Galerie du Théâtre Pigalle, with seventy participants. The debate within the group, during the months elapsed from the first initiative, must have been heated. It is not so much the change of name to indicate a different direction, as the establishing of a committee – all male, perhaps not for the irony of fate but for tactical reasons – composed of members of institutions, such as Paul Léon, Count F. d'Andagne, Anatole de Monzie, Raymond Koechlin and critics from the leading newspapers, ranging from Arsène Alexandre to Gustave Kahn and Louis Vauxcelles.

[94] The exhibition was held in America at several different venues: Los Angeles, Los Angeles County Museum of Art (23 December 1976 – 13 March 1977), Austin (Texas), University Art Museum (12 April – 12 June 1977), Pittsburgh, Pennsylvania, Carnegie Museum of Art (14 July – 4 September 1977), New York, Brooklyn Museum (4 October – 27 November 1977). Since then, several expositions have focussed on specific periods in women's art. As concerns Italian women artists of the sixteenth and seventeenth centuries, the forerunner is the very thorough *Italian Women Artists from Renaissance to Baroque*, exhibition catalogue (Washington, The National Museum of Women in Arts, 16 March – 15 July 2007), edited by V. Fortunati, J. Pomeroy, C. Strinati, Milan 2007.

[95] U. Vils, "A Tribute to Women Artists", in *Los Angeles Times*, 27 December 1976, pp. IV/1, 6.

THE LADIES OF BAROQUE, BETWEEN PORTRAIT AND SELF-PORTRAIT

THE TRANSGRESSION OF GENRES*

Alain Tapié

An astonishing historic continuum links Sofonisba Anguissola's first self-portraits with those of Lavinia Fontana, Artemisia Gentileschi, and Elisabetta Sirani. The intense relations among the idea, nature, and the illusion of reality construct a complex and near-invisible unity around these likenesses, upset only by the gradual rise of an ever more heroic expressiveness in each of these artists, owed to the lessons of their Venetian models. It is the same plasticism that characterizes Titian's later work, and that lies at the root of impressionism's naturalist modernism. Artemisia knew to turn towards Venice at the end of her stay in Florence and before her return to Rome. Her brushwork, which highlights the *impasto* and the colour, works well with the more illusionistic optical techniques typical of Lombard culture. The sense of illusion allows itself to be contaminated by the decorum of fabrics and flesh, while the real, just as present in the painted space, obeys the principles of a conceptualised space. The descriptive finesse, the realism of the rapports are supported by the abstraction of the symbols. The iconic pose, in its fixity, is in no way disturbed by the harmonious and decorative profusion of these fabrics that envelop the figures.
In these portraits and self-portraits, rarely have the possibilities of painting – reality, naturalness, concept, illusion – been the object of a synthesis, at once simple and complex, which eludes banal wonder and plastic conformity, in order to create the sensations of measured infinity, acute interrogation, intermediary and suspended temporality in a stoic calm. Giorgio Vasari called this manner of painting – which was in keeping with both the spirit of the times and the various milieux frequented, and different in its continuity of the staging – from the interior towards the exterior – *donnesca mano*,[1] an unconscious invention in the manner of painting which characterized the territory of women painters – though not exclusively. Between the enclosure of the room and the opening of the window, the *mise en abyme* is elaborated.

The styles that one encounters in the art of these women originate for the most part in the workshops of their masters, often a close relative. The identification of the artistic and family environment is reinforced by the collaboration on works which were often considered a common asset. As for the subject, a means of transmitting the value of virtue and the shunning of vice, *donnesca mano*, through the evocation of similar reactions to social and stylistic constraints, establishes a perfectly identifiable singularity. In the elaboration of these portraits and self-portraits, mirrors play an essential role: to tame reality, thus contributing to the *mélange* of austere or intense concentrations, endowed with harmonious sensations. The restrained violence is thus a source of delight. The spirit of Mannerism still flows in these portraits and self-portraits. The emergence of life in the artifices of pictorial construction stimulates the rhetoric of the composition. The artist's *maniera* remains unencumbered by such stylistic devices as the exploitation of chromatic dissonance or the clever use of *contrapposto*.

In terms of *maniera*, the work of Fede Galizia is also noteworthy. A renowned portraitist as of the age of twenty, but more appreciated as a painter of still lifes with fruits and flowers, Fede Galizia painted a Judith and her maid in 1596 – two years

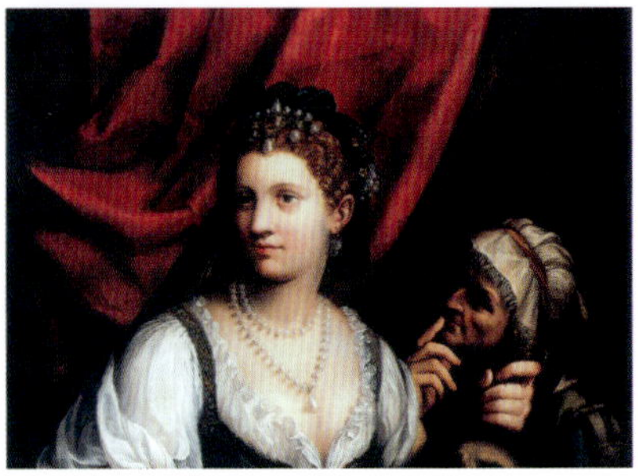

1. Fede Galizia
Judith with the Head of Holofernes, detail
1596
Sarasota, The John & Mable Ringling Museum of Art

before Caravaggio's interpretation. Among her versions of *Judith with the Head of Holofernes*, two stand out, one in the Ringling Museum of Art in Sarasota (fig. 1) and the other, signed, in the Galleria Borghese in Rome (fig. 2). The two versions seem to respond to the preferences of a clientele that esteemed luxury and ostentation as evidenced by the opulence of the fabrics and jewellery.
The meticulous and precious execution is typical of this mannerist culture, which combines an abundance of detail with a monumental grandeur. The subject is enriched by the balance obtained by drawing from these two elements.
We encounter the quest for harmonious decorum dear to the concept of *ut pictura poesis*. The static pose invites the delectation of an elegant image of ostentation. While Judith's gaze is lost in the distance in the Sarasota version, it is focused in the one in Rome. The illusionistic appearance fits in perfectly with the realistic fragments, visually more imposing in the Rome painting. Beyond the portrait and self-representation, the moral example is the key to interpretation here. Judith, the beautiful widow from Bethulia, delivers her people from oppression by seducing and then killing the Assyrian General Holofernes, with the help of her maid. Rather than the clamour of the beheading, Fede Galizia chooses to represent the return to silence after the struggle and the conspiratorial whispering of the maid, Abra, who has just placed the victim's head in a basin. Unlike Caravaggio, who envisions Judith throwing herself into the violence of the act, Galizia conjures up an image of Salome resolutely carrying out her plan. The version conserved in the Galleria Borghese, made more incisive by the focus of the gaze on what is to come, and in the heightened suspensive gestures, fully engages in a new approach to the allegory introduced by Titian, taken up by Tintoretto, and climaxing in Rome under Caravaggio's brush. It is characterised by a gesturality of heroic magnitude, nourished by realistic accents and supported by a powerfully illusionist modelling. The more penetrating, spontaneous, formally compelling execution of the Roman version suggests that it predates that of Sarasota. This is already a "Caravaggesque" vision that Fede Galizia worked towards two years before her illustrious contemporary, and for which she should be given wider recognition. In this new form of allegorical exemplarity, Fede Galizia shows outstanding inventiveness, as does her still life with apricots, a pear and flowers, painted in 1602, today lost, the copies of which make us think it could rival Caravaggio's legendary basket of fruit.

Denied access to academic training, these women painters, in the absence of a theoretical harbour, cultivated a freedom in the construction of the image that extended with surprising similarities from one artist to the other. The lack of references to the statues of antiquity led them to work from live models, often themselves. Sofonisba Anguissola practised her art as a dilettante, given her social status and prestigious position as lady-in-waiting and court painter, notably in the court of Philip II. Lavinia Fontana also eluded the spirit of academic tradition. It was not until 1604, when she was fifty-two years old, that she was admitted to the Accademia San Luca in Rome. This late recognition in no way interfered with her business sense and her commercial success. As for Artemisia, her admittance to the

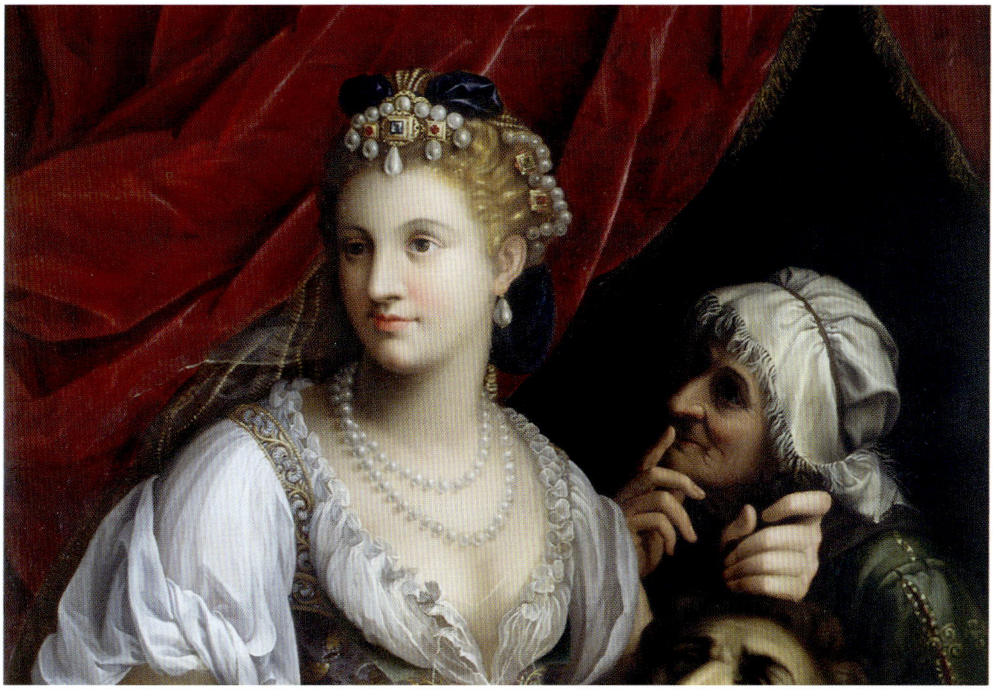

2. Fede Galizia
Judith with the Head of Holofernes, detail
1601
Rome, Galleria Borghese

Accademia di Disegno of Florence in 1616, at the start of her career, was nothing short of an epic conquest. The charm and *sprezzatura* in the purest mannerist tradition are present in the work of Sofonisba and Lavinia. They are instead metamorphosized in Artemisia, where the border between culture and intimate spaces disappears. Artemisia seems to implement fully what Vasari writes about Titian: "for greater delicacy and texture, while continuing to copy nature to the best of his ability, he worked directly with colour, proceeding with raw and soft hues according to what he saw in his model".[2]

Artemisia grazes an illusionist manner through a plastic equivalence practised in Venice throughout the sixteenth century: unctuous and natural brushstrokes shaping the colours – which, in actuality, is their essence. Caravaggio's influence can also be seen in the play of light, though the contrasts are contained. In this abundance of physical expression, passion becomes the natural link between the profane and the sacred. Artemisia follows the committed vision of women artists who preceded her, that of a behind-closed-doors theatricality. But, in the intimacy of place, and the rapport between the subjects, she goes beyond the pose and even the action. Emblematic in this sense is the figure of Judith, the different versions of which represented by Artemisia become a symbol of woman's struggle against male dominance. The exploits of this heroine are celebrated in western literature starting in the third century, reaching a peak at the end of the sixteenth, as a result of the emergence of the figure of woman in the context of the propagation of the faith and an expression of virtue. From pose to action, increasingly expressive and inventive, this feminine dynamic is based on the persistent legend according to which Judith, who, transcending herself, represents the Hebrew people; the Bible's Book of Judith may have, in fact, been written by a woman.[3] In the episode of Holofernes' beheading, the focus would henceforth be the glorification of the heroine, Judith, in the defined space of the scene – open and closed, private and historical at the same time – concealing and revealing the feminine sensuality that Giorgione and Titian had already placed at the epicentre of the image.

Caravaggio joins in the play on this female continuum. He paints from life, using models, an expedient already employed in popular image-based theatre promoted by the Jesuits. He is responsible for the transition from pose to action, with a progressive emphasis on violence. Artemisia undoubtedly follows in Caravaggio's footsteps, but in the story underpinning her life, she dispenses with the theatrical scene, going beyond the action to focus on the act. The staging of the decisive moment in the murder of Holofernes, characteristic of Caravaggio's vision, is scattered across Artemisia's closed spaces, multiplying itself in all instances of the composition. The framing captures the complexity of gestures, reaching a degree of intimacy not seen before in paintings at the time. Artemisia seems to forsake history to be but a painter. The *donnesca mano* no longer fears the suggestion of a political message, and focuses on sex and violence which it assumes. Moving away from the social and political message, Artemisia does not deny herself the jubilation of the folds of satin dresses, of those silky fabrics rolled up at the cuffs, those flamboyant jewels made to be admired close up in detail and in the illusion of truth. She effectively develops an art of proximity that Elisabetta Sirani would adopt as her model, fully embracing these gestural transgression. With Artemisia, it is no longer politics that is the focus of heroic female acts, but an eternal self-portrait where the woman makes the painting her allegory.

While Mannerism and the Baroque usually shared the same aesthetic content – theatrical mood, fusion of genres and themes, intensification of affects and plastic effects, universalisation of symbols – with the Baroque came expansion, qualification, mission and conquest. The fondness for portraits and self-portraits probably permitted, in this narrow space, the imperceptible shift from the concept to the natural and the real, thanks to a more radical approach to illusion, often attributed to Caravaggio, overlooking to what point it should have been extended to and shared with these women painters. Thanks to the blurred line between portrait and self-portrait, a consistent feature of all these artists, allegory plays a leading role. The construction of the space is the means that conveys the idea, the message, which can, without distinction, have a moral and educational tenor as well as a meditative and sensual one. The representation of inanimate things, with an accurate and meticulous description of their nature, transforms the works into receptacles of messages with an obvious moral and symbolic dimension. In this regard, the work of Giovanna Garzoni stands out. She is best known and appreciated for her compositions of fruit and flowers painted on vellum, defying reality in their conceptual veracity, surpassing the natural by their illusionist quality. The symbolic dimension attached to them, far from creating links between the objects, far from the harmony of decorum, implements an element of astonishment that has no need for dramatic staging.

Giovanna Garzoni was born in Ascoli Piceno in 1600, into a family of artists and craftsmen. She is said to have been a pupil of Palma il Giovane from whom she acquired a knowledge of the representation of religious figures. However, most of her commissions involved the accurate depiction of botanical species, arising from the flourishing market for scientific knowledge of the natural things of the world. Giovanna was passionate about her work and never considered her artistic and economic interests separate. She dedicated the same attention to her production of commissioned portraits. A vow of chastity taken very early on cut short her marriage with the Venetian portrait painter Tiberio Tinelli. She was taken under her brother's protective wing, and the independence thus acquired in terms of her private life translated into greater freedom in her choice of subjects and clients. When she settled in Rome in 1631, her earliest contacts were with prominent figures of the intellectual circles, members of Pope Urban IV Barberini's family, as well as scholars associated with his patronage of the arts, such as the poet Cassiano del Pozzo. She established ties with the scientific Accademia dei Lincei in her eagerness to deepen her knowledge of botany, her first love, without losing a sense of the ideal form that she wished to create for each species. On the small scale of miniature illustration, as in that of the anatomical details showing fruits, flowers and vegetables, Garzoni's art launched a new craze.

In 1632, Giovanna entered into the service of the Duchess of Savoy, Christine of France. Religious and naturalistic compositions were now treated with a cloistered purity breathing of spirituality. Other artistic scenes of this sort can be found in the Lombard milieu, in particular that of the Caccia family in Moncalvo, but Giovanna's style remains unmatched for its gravity-defying visual richness.

After a probable stay in Paris, we find her back in Florence in 1642. Her creations, in their apparent modesty, are based on an unprecedented scheme in which two complete opposites are reconciled: a spirituality sublimated by the truth of nature, and an ideal form inhabited by a charm bordering on sensuality. Her art is understated but extraordinary, going beyond the purely decorative and scientific functions usually assigned to this type of subject. Far from becoming scattered in the diversity of techniques and supports – miniatures, vellum, parchment, and *pietra dura* – after approaching the subject in a quasi-conceptual way, her questing spirit settled on the fine texture of fruit skins, the transparency of the peelings. She kept her distance from the culture of illusionist models presenting themselves as better than the real thing, proposed in Florence by two newcomers from Amsterdam, Otto Marseus van Schrieck and his brilliant pupil, Willem van Aelst. Followers of Jacopo Ligozzi, these artists were in the service of the Medici court, which favoured an objective approach to the wonders of nature. Willem contributed chromatic harmony, while Marseus stood out for the almost savage vital force of his plan and animals.

It is this same force that we find in the fruit that Giovanna painted – so ripe it is about to split open, arranged on plates that are often chipped, suggesting the passage of time. These compositions harbour a persistent interest in the symbolism of colour. At times the symbology is explicit: the rare shells alongside vases of flowers recalling the vanity of precious goods, or the insistence on placing red fruits alongside cups – cherries and strawberries as well as nuts, walnuts and hazelnuts – referring to the supreme importance of Christ's sacrifice. The birds,

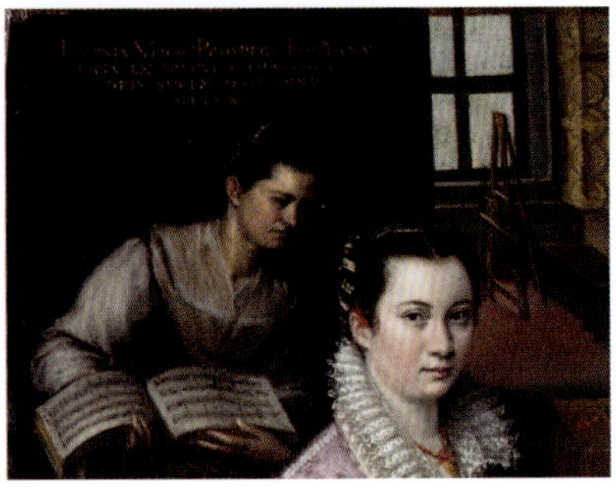

3. Lavinia Fontana
Self-Portrait at the Spinet, detail
1577
Rome, Accademia
Nazionale di San Luca

the fly, the snails, the morning glory, the tulip – all of them speak of the breath of life, decay, the passing of life, vanity, death. They offer contexts for meditation available to the contemplator, like an optional accompaniment to the poetic atmosphere. In Rome, where she arrived in 1651, Giovanna Garzoni unflaggingly pursued this line of work, very successfully. She resumed her contact with the Accademia di San Luca, but was not in any way influenced by it, neither in terms of her style nor her inspiration.

The clear relationship between the figure and the object promotes spatial syntheses of great visual impact. The *donnesca mano* accentuates the feeling of intimacy throughout the pictorial space. As in Albrecht Dürer's self-portrait, the figure is more than ever divine, at once heroic and human. The Council of Trent would promote this strategy of convergence to enhance divine or epic grace through a poignant feminine domesticity. In this respect, Sofonisba's 1561 self-portrait is exemplary. In it, any semantic shift seems possible, from sacred music to profane seduction, the passage of time from youth to an old age indicated by the blurry figure of the maid, and on through to the manifestation of a beauty that is entirely conceptual but caught up in reality when the pose expresses an action. In her self- portrait of 1577, Lavinia brings her maid into the picture, in the act of handing the book of madrigals to the artist. The setting expands, opening up in the space outside the window. A genre scene seems to unfold, but the real breakthrough is the subject's gaze straight into the observer's eyes (fig. 3). If the anatomy of the body can be reduced to a few succinct contours and the pale, absorbed face (fig. 4), the seduction must come about through the fabrics and the jewels. Thanks to the mirror, a preliminary, pre-composition tool, the details stop floating and find their place, while the self-representation is free in the choice of pose. The figure is not painted directly, the reflection is a stand-in for it, legitimising the use of the nude for mythological scenes. This is a giant step forward in the quest for truth, which does without copies and models of ancient statuary. As for the objects, the musical instruments (the spinet for Sofonisba and Lavinia, the lute for Artemisia) capture the basics of a proper female education in the image, while the act of playing represents the decisive moment – often used by Caravaggio to create astonishment. When the subject prepares to play, her action is "foiled" because it only produces an air as intangible, as imperceptible as an idea can be. Sofonisba, Lavinia, and Artemisia use this device to reveal the "decisive moment", injecting the allegorical situation with the weight of reality. It is a procedure typical of Caravaggio that was clearly shared by these contemporary artists, but which Sofonisba and Lavinia adopted in complete independence. This sense of the decisive moment that catches the observer by surprise and allegorizes reality already appears in a drawing of 1554, where Sofonisba captures a child's grimace of horror and pain when nipped by a crayfish.[4] This may have been a fine lesson for Caravaggio in his future portrayals of Bacchus. Some art historians, ever eager to draw conclusions, go so far as to suggest that Michelangelo Merisi saw this drawing in Cavalier d'Arpino's workshop.

The *donnesca mano* rediscovered the significance of the gesture suspended at the decisive instant, delaying indefinitely the moment when the instrument will be

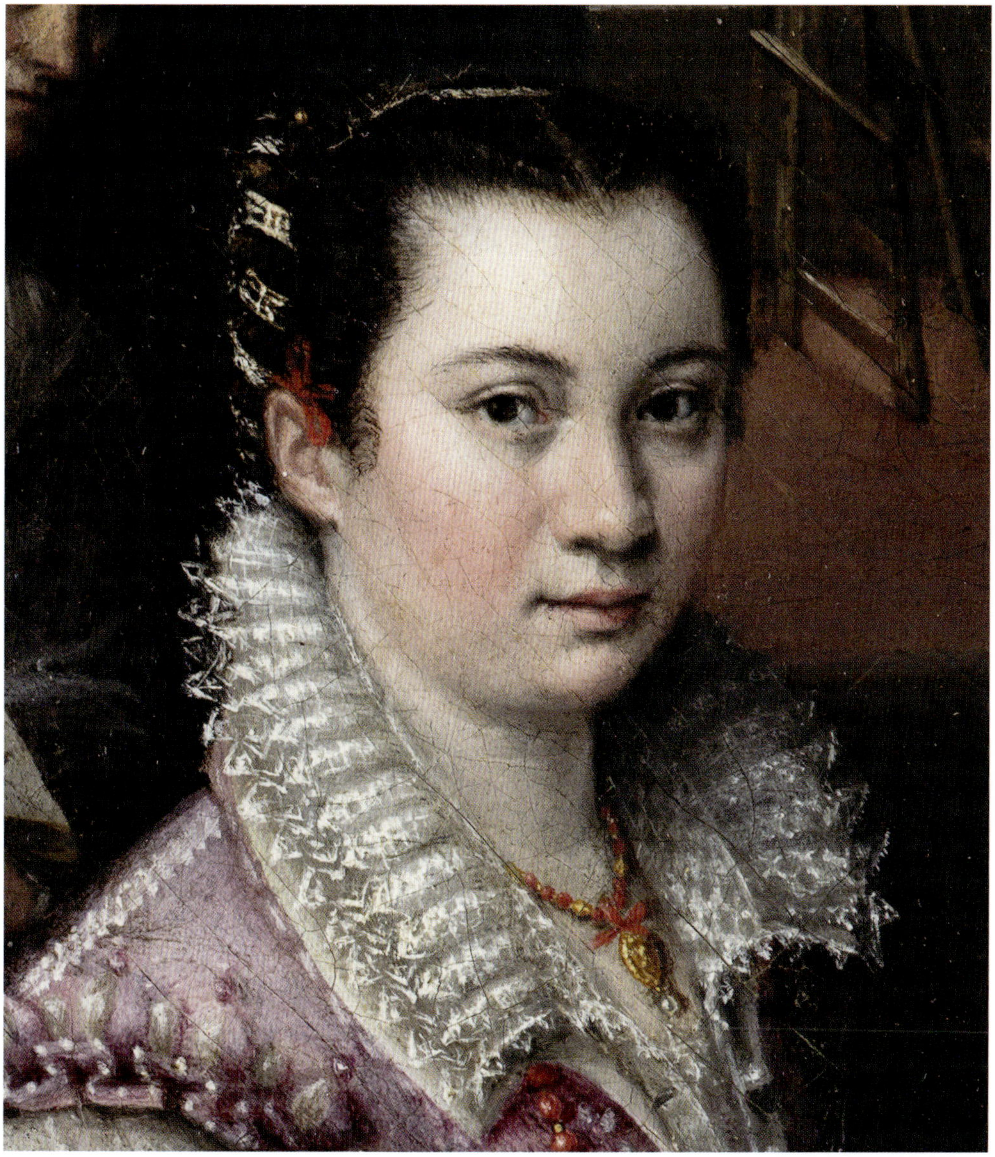

4. Lavinia Fontana
Self-Portrait at the Spinet, detail
1577
Rome, Accademia
Nazionale di San Luca

heard. Titian had already introduced it in 1550 with *Salome* presenting the head of John the Baptist on a platter. The rhetoric of the wedding portrait or formal representation made way for a placid heroism, a sensual epiphany. Martine Lacas recounts an anecdote about Marietta Robusti, known as "la Tintoretta" – whose biography is more familiar to us than her work. It offers us a glimpse of the artist's compositional freedom: "The keyboard of the spinet that Marietta depicts has a strange layout of the black and white keys which, far from being a misrepresentation, could be due to the common practice of disassembling and reassembling instruments, sometimes according to personal preferences".[5] Marietta thus would have depicted not just any spinet, but her own (fig. 5).

Between 1550 and 1680 the portraits and self-portraits painted by these artists appear to share an identical vision of space, defined simply in its depth and not through stylistic imitation. This is a distinguishing characteristic that took hold in Venice, Florence, and Rome, all artistic crossroads. When the market opened up to painting with a predominantly spiritual and moral scope, these artists were obliged to produce, in the limited field of the figure, transcendent effects on both the

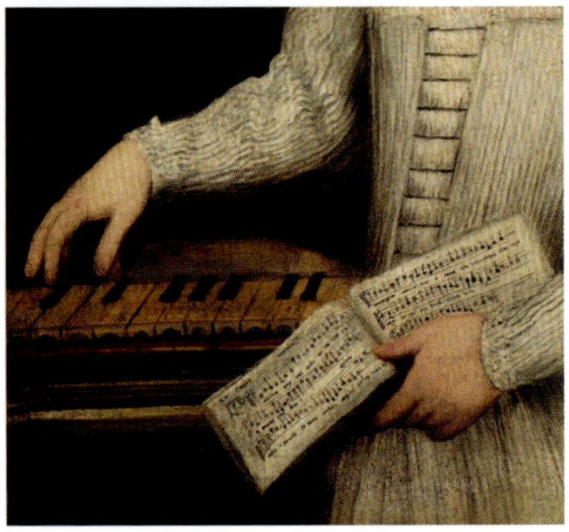

5. Marietta Robusti,
known as Tintoretta
Self-Portrait with Madrigal, detail
c. 1580
Florence, Gallerie degli Uffizi

natural and the divine levels. As the mannerist artifices tended to disappear, along with the playful attitude and intellectual conceits, the painted image acquired transparency. Sensibilities became palpable, like an early foreshadowing of *Cézannesque* sensation, as if a musical paradigm wakened to favour unity and polyphony.

In their by-now baroque vision, rarely do these women, who portray themselves at the spinet, the lute, or the virginal, succumb to the great rhetoric of the flux of Baroque. The self-image compromises neither the primordial sacred nor the real ordinary. A theatre of life, an essential theatre, stripped of that embellishment of spaces that would come to subvert the highest spiritual and moral principles. "The accomplished acts are carried out in a troubling association of distance and energy, requiring a new compositional mode believed to have its roots in a luminist culture found in Venice and in Lombardy, which comes to graft onto first-hand experiences and a familiarity with popular theatricalized scenes".[6] The solidity of the attributes dear to the Lombard culture corresponds to the inner strength of the figures. Over time, thanks to Artemisia's gracefulness, an ecstasy, just as restrained but more violent, heroic, will, through the free movement of the fabrics, triumph over the lovely iconic *minéralisé*. It is worthwhile to insist on the visual rendering in the art of these women. In their compositions, the association of high-definition fragments suggests, by their juxtaposition, the use of mirrors and camera obscuras. They served less in the quest for resemblance than in the reconstruction of rapports between figures and the effects of presence, insisting on illusion through descriptive processes close to northern culture, while in other parts of the composition, the Venetian manner, the spirit of flux and plastic equivalents verging on eloquence prevail. Once again, it is Artemisia who leads the transition. This sweeping unity is fully Baroque, while a pathetic interiority is exalted or restrained. Herein is a movement responsible for the aesthetic mutation of Lavinia's manner towards that of Artemisia, with no loss of its dark melancholy. In the transition from one to the other, the action must not hinder the search for a particular and mysterious ideal. The "real allegory" associated with Caravaggio's compositions actually seems to have been conceived two decades earlier and would enjoy popularity for some years to come. As of Sofonisba's first portraits and self-portraits, the imperceptible play of transgression focuses on the mysteries of symbolic interpretation.

In this economy of metaphor, they do not deviate from the rapports, forms, and drawings, which must maintain all their legibility in order to ultimately preserve transcendence – to let emotion surface, without altering the message so sought-after in classical thought. If there is theatre, it is that of virtue, if there is a message, it is that of asceticism, a condition of freedom for the woman painter. This stoic attitude denotes a self-mastery that is clearly reflected in the geometric perspectives, once again, restrained in Sofonisba and Lavinia, open to fluidity in Artemisia and Elisabetta. If natural forms are at the service of virtue and educational purposes, nothing prevents the observer from going beyond the face value of these musical instruments, and perceiving them, in shared amazement, as an invitation to sensual admiration. Symbolism is like a scent that some can pick up and some cannot, then comes interpretation.

The *Self- Portrait at the Spinet* from 1577 invites us to consider the beauty of the female gender as a platonic homage, an idea not lacking in support from authors who pay homage to women: Boccaccio in his *De Mulieribus Claris*, Baldassare Castiglione in *The Book of the Courtier*, or even Giorgio Vasari in his *Lives*. It is a principle of recognition presiding over any examination of feminine pursuits. This consideration is immediately followed by one of good education, and then seduction. These are all the virtual realities which music evokes. But there is another, much more compelling power, one mainly attributed to the world of men: access to *ut pictura poesis*, in its intense path through invention, expression, instruction, decorum. The easel in the background shows that the woman painter finally has access and that "the strategy of conquest is at work".[7]

According to the writings of Linda Nochlin and Ann Sutherland Harris,[8] to which Consuelo Lollobrigida's recent treatises[9] and Martine Lacas' work refer,[10] the study of art by these women, between 1560 and 1680, follows the classic profile that seeks to discard the principles of transmission through the apprenticeships and that they, who belong to the baroque era, received.

Their academic apprenticeship, or lack thereof, would tend to lend a strong classic orientation to the analysis of their artistic status. The contexts of a mannerist and baroque aesthetic would instead allow a more empirical approach to their training. In fact, when addressing feminine art, the history of art looks toward Leon Battista Alberti's treatise *De Familia* which defines the rules of access to the painter's profession: a restricted circle which does not authorize direct access to historical paintings whose principal purpose is major moral instruction.[11]

The systematic evocation, in the foreword, of the qualities and character of the feminine differs even more in their artistic practice. Rather than focus on the major transgressions committed by Lavinia and Artemisia in their history painting, portraits, social scenes, the symbolic composition of objects in their works, as well as their possible combinations, are a narrow but infinite opening onto the realm of invention of expression and symbolic transmission. Much has been made of their academic deprivation of the study of the male nude and of classic models, as if to infer that the ateliers, or even the observation of admired masters – Dürer, Correggio, Caravaggio – afforded no opportunities to scheme a way around these anatomical canons.

We see figures posed as in daily situations. The objects composing the atmosphere are familiar. At the heart of these peaceful lives, penetrating gazes open the foreground of the image toward the viewer whereas the window in the background is the eye that looks towards the other exterior. An intimate but open world, it leans on the constructive schema whose scope is as universal as the feminine element in these unique portraits. Allegory – impregnated with religious sentiment, the notion of virtue from a mythological image – pervades these open-ended spaces, in portraits as well as genre scenes. It was customary, in this fine *mélange* of allegorized reality, to take as a model for the path towards virtue a figure of a courtisan turned respectable through the sublimation of the gift of self. The faces of these women painters, captured in self-portraits, have a similar transfigurative function. They distance both physiognomy and anatomy. The gestures and actions they contain stop at the margins of the description. Impassive in Sofonisba and Lavinia, these faces open to a pathetic fixity with Artemisia and Elisabetta. The interiorized energy of the *maniera* is transformed into a baroque fluidity. The Platonic message has its place through Petrarch's vision where physical beauty carries moral beauty. A universal message in the spirit of the Renaissance, an individual manner of the *donnesca mano* establishes its construction. In *Self-Portrait at the Spinet,* Lavinia is accompanied by her maidservant. The painting is reminiscent of a miniature. Its format is that which offers women painters the gentle impression of everyday life, in order to preserve without description the silence of expressions.

In her *Madonna and Child,* Lavinia gives us the impression that portrait, self-portrait, genre scene are conflated in order to contribute to the imperceptible ascension of the sacred image as if the Flemish lesson of *devotio moderna* had been heard. The presence of the divine can be manifested in every instant.

The convergence of these elements making for *donnesca mano* evokes the style of Rembrandt where painting acts in a similar transgression of the classic aesthetic. We find a same sense of improvised anatomies which allow historical images to be read in everyday language. The social status of these women had nevertheless protected their painted images from the *rembranesque* excesses of promiscuity. A fine example of this balance can be seen in Lavinia's *Noli Me Tangere,* where Christ, disguised as a gardener, extends towards Mary Magdalene, a pure gesture of familiar seduction, devoid of all sensuality, as is always the case when the sensible intention has been achieved. The female figures painted by these artists are self-portraits, most often in the omnipresence of features which open onto universal feminism. "Rembrandt lends his likeness to the expression of every sentiment, every attitude, every role".[12] As Hoogstraten points out, the painter, like an actor, tends to represent himself in the place of another. He is successively prince and beggar, executioner and victim, a living incarnation of both joy and despair. The omnipresence of Rembrandt's features is less an expression of the artist's self-absorption than the dissolution of self into universal humanity: "Becoming everyone, one is no longer anyone".[13]

Between 1550 and 1680, these ladies of the Baroque, through their portraits and self-portraits, painted the feminine – in the intimacy of the home. They painted familiar objects, symbolic objects. They painted nature – bouquets, flowers, fruit; they painted musical instruments – the spinet, virginal, lute. Their works included mirrors, and at times the tools of their art – brushes and easels – which served to open up the interior space towards the fiction of the outside world. In this spatial intensity, happiness lies in the act of painting. The interiorized exaltation pierces through the painting, drawing in the viewer. The simplicity and essentiality produce – and herein lies the paradox – a complexity of situation bathed in Aristotelian mimesis. The imagination travels in the idea, in nature, as in reality. The act of painting makes thought a physical state, kept in silence but animated in its insistence upon calling attention towards what "painting in the feminine" would be – inviting the reflection on the migration of "painting in the feminine" towards painters who happen to be men.

**This essay resumes and expands upon reflections on "Les Dames du Baroque", an exhibition held at the Musée des Beaux-Arts in Ghent, autumn 2018.*

[1] G. Vasari, *Le vite de' più eccellenti architetti, pittori, et scultori italiani, da Cimabue insino a' tempi nostri*, Florence 1550.
[2] G. Vasari, *The Lives of the Artists*, Translated with an Introduction and Notes by J. Conaway Bondanella and P. Bondanella, Oxford-New York 1998, p. 489.
[3] J. Anderson, *Judith*, Paris 1997, p. 12.
[4] C. d'Orazio, *Caravaggio secreto*, Milan 2013, fig. p. 44.
[5] M. Lacas, *Des femmes peintres, du XVe à l'aube du XIXe siècle*, Paris 2015, p. 29.
[6] A. Tapié, "Postface", in *Artemisia 1593-1654. Pouvoir, gloire et passions d'une femme peintre*, exhibition catalogue (Paris, Musée Maillol, 14 March – 15 July 2012), edited by R. Contini, F. Solinas, Paris 2012, p. 223.
[7] M. Lacas, *Des femmes peintres* cit. (note 5), p. 29.
[8] L. Nochlin and A. Sutherland Harris, *Femmes peintres. 1550-1950*, Paris 1976.
[9] *Di mano donnesca. Donne artiste dal XVI al XVII secolo*, exhibition catalogue (Rome, Palazzo Venezia, 4–14 October 2012), edited by C. Lollobrigida, Rome 2012; C. Lollobrigida, *Artiste a Roma tra Controriforma e Barocco*, in Ead., *Plautilla Bricci. Pictura et Architectura Celebris. L'architettrice del Barocco Romano*, Rome 2018, pp. 30–38.
[10] M. Lacas, *Des femmes peintres* cit. (note 5).
[11] *Di mano donnesca* cit. (note 9), p. 5.
[12] T. Todorov, *L'art ou la vie! Le cas Rembrandt. Suivi d'Art et morale*, Paris 2015, p. 39.
[13] Ivi, p. 47.

GIOVANNA GARZONI AT THE HOUSE OF SAVOY: DIAGNOSTIC IMAGING APPLIED TO THE PORTRAITS OF EMMANUEL PHILIBERT AND CHARLES EMMANUEL I

GIOVANNA GARZONI IN TURIN

Annamaria Bava

In the summer of 1632, Giovanna Garzoni arrived at the Savoy court accompanied by her fame as a skilled portraitist.[1] By the early 1630s, Turin had achieved the appearance of an entirely renewed city. This was due to the artistic and cultural policy implemented first by Emmanuel Philibert, who transferred the duchy capital from Chambéry to Turin in 1563 after the reacquisition of the Savoy territories, and subsequently by Charles Emmanuel I, who ascended the throne at the age of eighteen on 30 August 1580 and ruled as duke for fifty years until 1630.[2] The city had been enhanced by the construction of important new buildings and the restoration of ancient ones, among them the ducal residence and the old Castello degli Acaja, for which a wide range of artists had been summoned from every corner of Italy and across Europe to ensure that Turin might compare equally with any of the other great international courts.

Contemporaneously, the Savoys had painstakingly constructed a consolidated image of the dynasty by implementing a detailed programme of genealogical exaltation in order to legitimise its noble origins.[3] As at all international courts, portraiture at the Turin court constituted an aspect of major interest within the field of figurative art, both for its symbolic value and because it represented the sole medium for the exchange of images over distance. During the years around the turn of the seventeenth century, dynastic portraiture was entrusted to artists specialised in the genre, among them Giacomo Vighi from Ferrara, known as "l'Argenta", Alessandro Ardente from Faenza and Antonino Parentani from Lombardy, as well as local painters such as Giorgio Solcri from Alessandria and Giacomo Rossignolo from Vercelli. Yet despite the ample documentation of their work by the sources, little evidence of it remains. Far more fully chronicled is the fortuitous production of Flemish artist Jan Kraeck, employed as court painter and author of the official portraits of Charles Emmanuel I and his consort, Catalina Micaela of Spain, daughter of King Philip II of Spain, and their children.[4]

For the creation of paintings, engravings and precious miniature portraits set in rare jewels, the court selected Flemish artists, who were distinguished by their mastery in rendering realistic images. However, from the mid-1500s on, refined pencil portraits of Emmanuel Philibert and his wife Margaret of Valois, daughter of Francis I and sister of Henry II of France, reveal how the diffusion of the ducal image was also assigned to drawings and miniatures by the French circle of artists, following the tradition disseminated by Jean and François Clouet's sketchbooks of *drawings* in pastel. Subsequently, beginning in the 1610s, the intimate realism of Ottavio Leoni's work in coloured pencil for a time attracted the attention of Charles Emmanuel I and his sons, Prince Thomas and Cardinal Maurice of Savoy.[5] In 1620, a breath of novelty was brought by the arrival in Turin of Christine of France, wife of Prince Victor Amadeus, the future duke of Savoy who ruled from 1630 until 1637. In the field of portraiture, a more contemporary international style was introduced by Flemish-Parisian painter Ferdinand Elle, who made numerous portraits of members

1. Giovanna Garzoni
Catalina Micaola, Duchess of Savoy
1646–1648 (?)
Florence, Gallerie degli Uffizi, Galleria delle Statue e delle Pitture

2. Giovanna Garzoni
Victor Amadeus I of Savoy
1646–1648 (?)
Florence, Gallerie degli Uffizi, Galleria delle Statue e delle Pitture

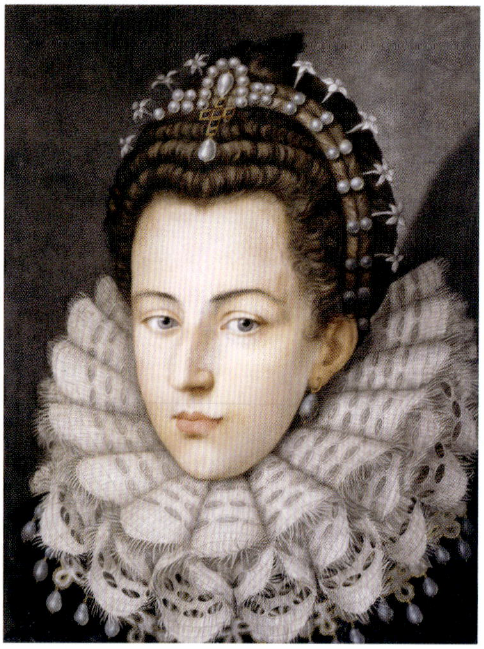

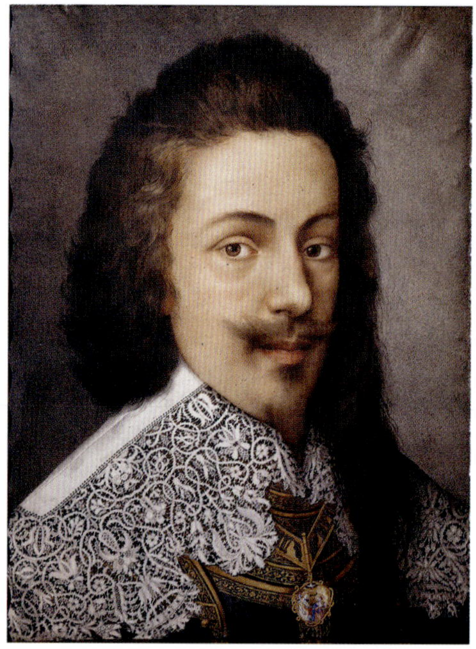

of the ducal family, while September 1626 saw the arrival from Paris of Philibert Torret, known as "il Narciso", who was nominated court painter with an annual stipend of two hundred ducats.[6]

At the start of the 1630s, the new duke inherited a number of carefully assembled collections, documented in the 1631 ducal palace and castle inventory, which catalogues antique and modern sculptures, more than eight hundred paintings, including works by famous sixteenth-century masters, paintings from the Venetian school, paintings influenced by Caravaggesque naturalism and Bolognese classicism, examples of work by contemporary Lombard painters, and also still lifes, landscapes, battles, portraits and genre paintings, interspersed with a significant collection of graphic works, maps and *Wunderkammer* curiosities.[7] As a symbolic location for his collections, Charles Emmanuel I chose the Grande Galleria, which connected the palace and castle. The gallery walls were embellished with a succession of Savoy genealogy, the ceiling displayed the celestial constellations, and the mosaic floor had images of fish and sea creatures. The gallery also housed the duke's vast library, where books covering every discipline were arranged in twenty-two bookcases, each divided into three sections.[8] The choice of figurative art is reflected in the 1635 inventory compiled by Antonio Della Cornia, which describes the images displayed in the rooms of Palazzo di San Giovanni, located next to the cathedral. In 1619 Victor Amadeus chose the palazzo as the residence for himself and his newlywed wife, Christine of France, transferring to it a considerable part of his father's picture gallery, which was catalogued and exhibited in the latest manner and further augmented by prestigious commissions and purchases.[9]

This is the context into which Giovanna Garzoni entered Turin, summoned by Madame Christine, who on 28 April 1632 wrote to Ludovico d'Aglié, the Savoy Ambassador to Rome: "Since we are exceedingly desirous to have the miniaturist Giovanna Garzoni here at our service as promptly as can be, we have decided to strictly urge you to assist her using all your authority in anything that needs to be done to send her here to us as swiftly and safely as possible. To this end we are sending you our passport for her so that it may be of use". The Savoy treasury advanced the sum of two hundred *doppie* to cover the artist's travel expenses. Her departure, however, was delayed by a few months, and on 24 June the Savoy correspondent informed the court that Garzoni "impatient with the lengthening delay, and despite the great heat, wished to set out immediately, knowing that the intensity of her most vivid colours could not be more worthily employed than in portraits of the royal and immortal features of Your Most Serene Highness".[10] Contact between the court and the young painter must have relied on the intermediary Cassiano dal Pozzo, a learned collector from Biella with whom Giovanna Garzoni had forged close ties during her two stays in Rome, before and after her time in Naples in the service of the Duke of Alcalá between 1630 and 1631.[11]

On her arrival in Turin, Giovanna was thirty-two and Christine six years younger. It is not hard to imagine the closeness that would develop between the two women, linked not only by their feminine sensibility but also by their similar interests and a particular artistic taste for rare, precious and refined objects. In 1633, Garzoni joined the ranks of artists salaried by the Savoy court and in the exclusive service of the duchess. This is confirmed by the fact that on 10 January, Victor Amadeus I ordered the treasurer general to pay her a fixed annual sum of one thousand golden *scudi*, the equivalent of three thousand *lire*, for her work as "miniaturist to the Madame Royale", an amount she received for five years, until the end of 1637, when she left the Turin court. This was a considerable sum, given that it was the same annual salary that would also be paid to Lombardy artist Cavalier Francesco Cairo, who was named painter to the Savoy court a year after Garzoni.[12] Moreover, in all likelihood Cairo and Garzoni were each given the use of a house near the ducal residence, or Garzoni may have more probably been housed in Palazzo di San Giovanni itself, where Madame Royale had her apartments, and where Garzoni possibly had her studio.[13]

Despite the five years Garzoni spent in the Savoy capital, very little of her work remains. Evidence of her production in Turin still seems incomplete, first and foremost because of the difficulty in tracing any image of Madame Royale, whom Giovanna must have been required to portray on many occasions. What does remain as a record of her depiction of the members of the House of Savoy are four same size miniatures in tempera on parchment. Two of them, portraits of dukes Emmanuel Philibert and Charles Emmanuel I (cats. 4.10–11), are conserved in the collections of the Palazzo Reale in Turin, while the two others, a portrait of Catalina Micaela of Spain, wife of Charles Emmanuel, and one of Duke Victor Amadeus I, are held in the Uffizi collections (figs. 1–2).[14] Despite the fact that documentary sources attribute the four works to two different periods in the artist's career, linking the first two miniatures to her time in Turin and the other two to her subsequent work for Cardinal Leopoldo de' Medici, prior to 1648, we may suppose that the portraits were originally part of a single cycle, probably commissioned by Christine with the desire to once again emphasise, through a series of dynastic miniature portraits, the

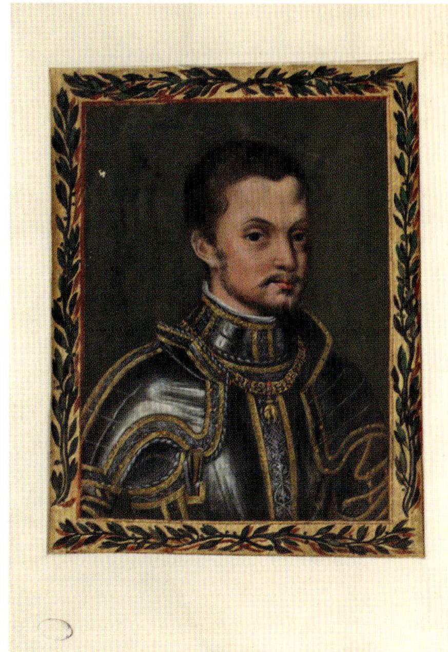

3. Miniaturist working at the House of Savoy
Emmanuel Philibert
c. 1550
Turin, Archivio di Stato (Sezioni Riunite, *Camera dei conti di Savoia*, inv. 1, fol. 1, register 14 bis)

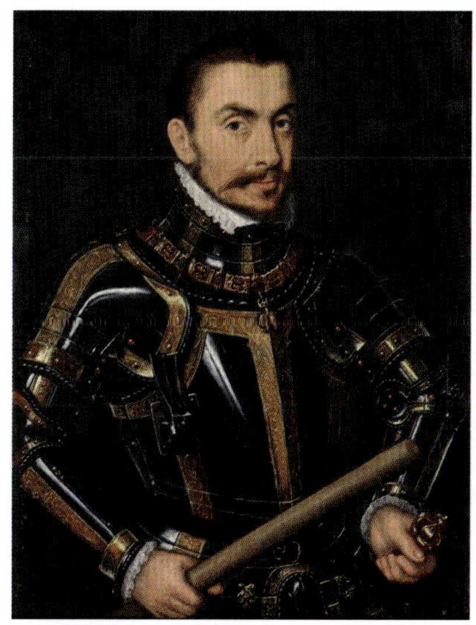

4. Antonio Moro (attributed)
Emmanuel Philibert
c. 1560
Private collection

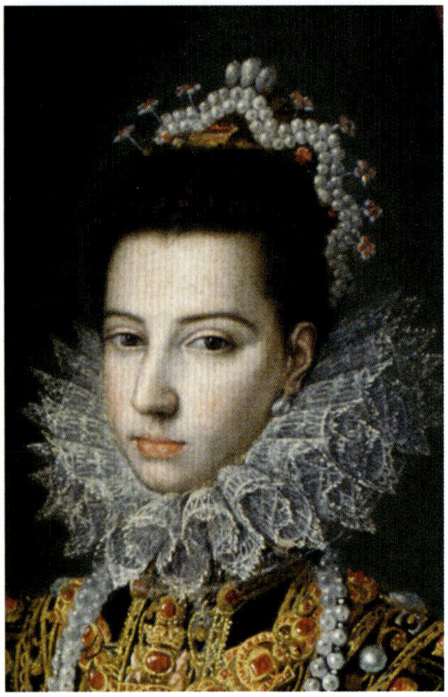

5. Jan Kraeck
Catalina Micaela Duchess of Savoy, detail
c. 1585
Saluzzo, Museo Civico
Casa Cavassa

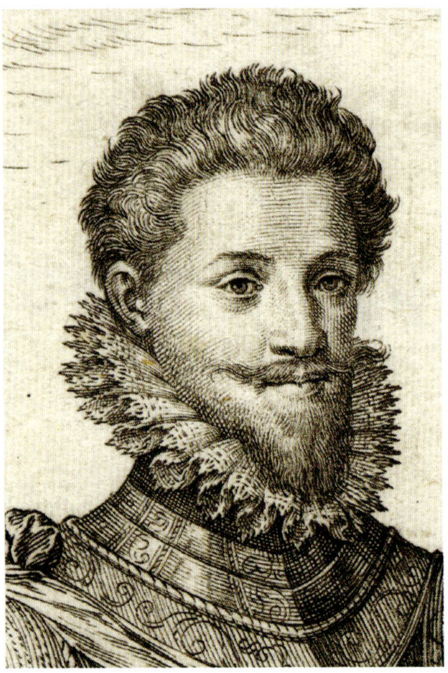

6. Jan Kraeck and Raphael Sadeler
Charles Emmanuel I of Savoy, detail
c. 1590–1600
Chambéry, Musée Savoisien,
Inv. PS 108

prestige of the members and consorts of the House of Savoy. The cycle may have been partially replicated during Garzoni's years in Florence, or it may have arrived in Tuscany sometime later.[15] The four figures, portrayed in the immediate foreground in a barely perceptible three-quarter view, emerge from a dark, shaded background, with the two Turin miniatures bearing the artist's signature.

For the posthumous portraits of illustrious rulers, Giovanna Garzoni had several examples she was able to turn to for inspiration in the form of courtly portraits reproduced not only as paintings but also as drawings and engravings. For Emmanuel Philibert, portrayed with heavy eyebrows, a short beard and thick moustache, and dressed in shiny laminar armour from which the collar of the Santissima Annunziata emerges, Garzoni may have studied as a model a portrait of the duke by l'Argenta, similar to one now in the Galleria Sabauda, datable to around 1570.[16] However, the duke's vivid gaze and the style of composition leave no doubt that she had access to the collections of pastel works and miniatures in the ducal collections. Indeed, the portrait in tempera on parchment among the pages of the so-called *Libro dei giuramenti* of the Turin Archivio di Stato (fig. 3), which immortalises the duke in his youth, seems almost an earlier photogram of Garzoni's portrait from his mature years.[17] It is also opportune to place in this sequence a very fine small panel portrait of the duke attributed to Antonio Moro, held in a private collection (fig. 4). For the image of Catalina and Charles Emmanuel I, Garzoni turned to various portraits by Flemish artist Jan Kraeck. Apart from the rendering of the gaze and features, which are more delicate and subtle in Garzoni's parchment, there are remarkable similarities between Catalina's face depicted by Garzoni and the severe, regal image immortalised in the full-length portrait in the Museo Civico Casa Cavassa in Saluzzo (fig. 5). In both, the wide ruff collar frames the face, but in Garzoni's parchment the tightly woven lace leaves gaps that reveal a perforated fabric, embellished along the hem with a row of pendant pearls.[18] Even closer similarities appear in the half-length portrait of the duchess conserved at the Castello di Racconigi. Here, Garzoni has replicated the same set of jewels that adorn the elegant hairstyle: from the charming earring poised on the collar, to the lustrous spherical pearls and small flowers entwined in her hair, with at the centre a delightful group of precious stones bearing yet another large hanging pearl.[19]

Among the many notable portraits of Charles Emmanuel I, an evocative likeness of the duke's face is taken from an idea by Kraeck for an elaborate equestrian portrait based on the image that was to be displayed on the walls of the Grande Galleria and was made into an engraving by Raphael Sadeler[20] (fig. 6). In it, Charles Emmanuel, wearing a proud expression, has a trimmed beard, a pointed goatee and an upturned moustache. His neck is enveloped in a ruff that rises above his cuirass, which in Garzoni's miniature is an example of the superlative Milanese armour, complete with grotesque-style decorative motifs and Savoy knots, that on several occasions arrived in Turin.[21]

For her portrait of Victor Amadeus I, either depicted from life or from memory, Garzoni seems to have studied the classic image of the duke, namely the full-length portrait in the Quirinale collections (fig. 7), which also exists in other varying versions. This ceremonial portrait, which immortalises Victor Amadeus in his armour, is probably based on a prototype by Van Dyck, executed when the Flemish artist visited Turin in 1622. It became the essential model for every artist commissioned to portray the Savoy duke: from Pellegrino Brocardo from Nice to Francesco Cairo from Lombardy, and also Giovenale Boetto from Fossano, whose finely executed engravings disseminated the duke's official image.[22] In the painting, Victor Amadeus has an English hairstyle with a lock of hair falling onto his left shoulder and a lace collar of the latest fashion, which in Garzoni's miniature is even more meticulous in its exceptionally precise execution of the floral details. However, a notable distance exists between Garzoni's work and earlier models, notably in the way she has captured the intimacy of the characters and the more delicate and refined depiction of the faces, characterised by their intense, penetrating gazes, which seem to stare directly at the viewer.

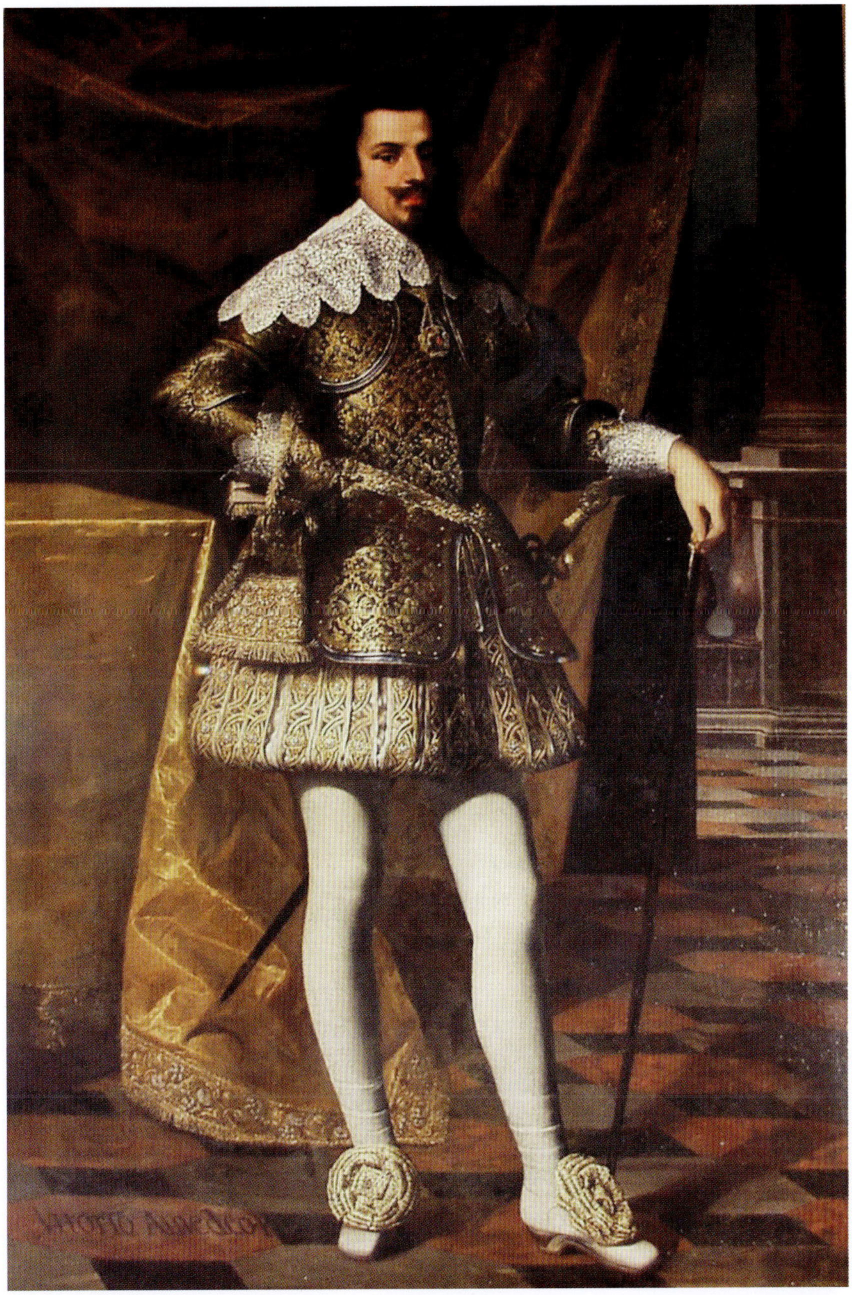

7. Painter active at the House of Savoy
(after Anthony van Dyck)
Portrait of Victor Amadeus I of Savoy
c. 1632–1635
Rome, Segretariato Generale della Repubblica, Palazzo del Quirinale

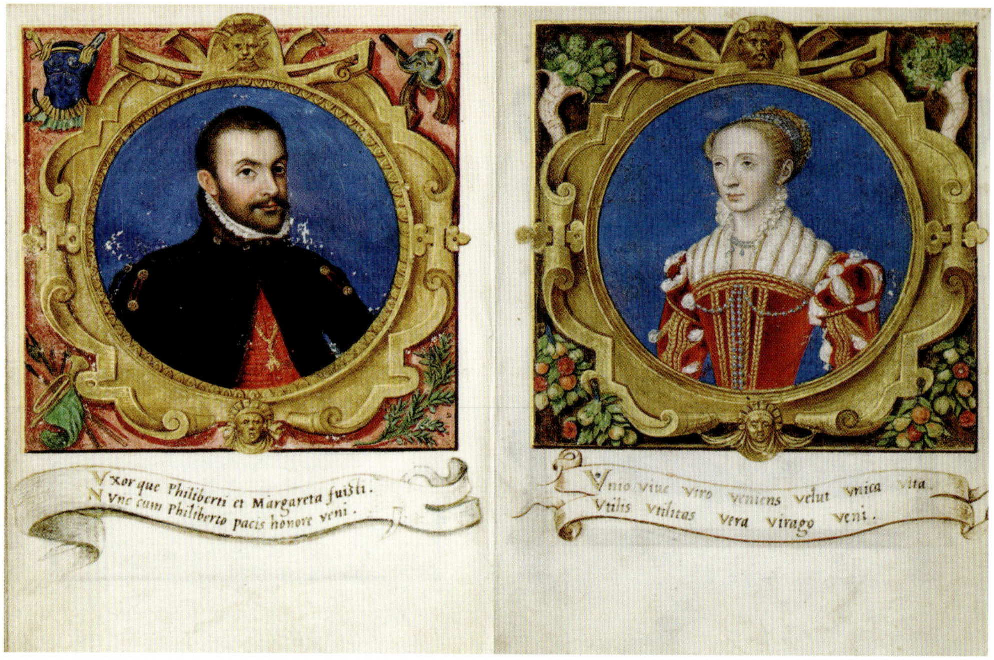

8–9. François Clouet (?) and French miniaturists
Portraits of Emmanuel Philibert of Savoy and Margaret of Valois, from the *Libro di preghiere offerto a Margherita di Valois*
1559
Turin, Biblioteca Reale, Varia 84, fols. 21*v* and 22*r*

Assuming that this was a single series composed of images of the three ducal couples, and that those of Charles Emmanuel and Catalina are the only pair remaining, implies that the spouses had to be portrayed in the customary way, namely in a mirror image facing each other. This means that the portrait of Margaret of Valois, wife of Emmanuel Philibert, is missing. For this image, Garzoni would have been able to refer to the various pre-existing mid-sixteenth-century French models made in the Clouet style, depicting the duchess with her husband. Among these are the beautiful portrait in the *Libro di preghiera,* donated by Cristoforo Duc and now in the Biblioteca Reale (Varia 84) (figs. 8–9); the refined drawing conserved in the Bibliothèque du Conservatoire National des Arts et Métiers (Me, vol. I, nos. 21 and 22); and the half-length panel portrait of Margaret, attributed to the workshop of François Clouet, now in the Galleria Sabauda (inv. 190).[23] An accurate idea of Madame Royale's portrait is provided by the official image of the duchess that was circulated before 1637 in an engraving by Giovenale Boetto. It was a pendant to the portrait of Victor Amadeus I (figs. 10–11) and bears more than a resemblance to Garzoni's radiant pointillist style.[24]

The mid-1630s at the Turin court marked a period of great artistic vitality in the field of portraiture, not only because of the concurrent presence in Turin of Giovanna Garzoni and Francesco Cairo, but also the addition to the Savoy picture gallery of an absolute masterpiece by Anthony van Dyck, *The Three Eldest Children of Charles I,* now in the Galleria Sabauda. Gifted by Queen Henrietta to her beloved sister Christine so that she could see images of her niece and nephews, it arrived a dozen years after Van Dyck's time at the Turin court, where he had painted portraits of the duke and princes, documented in various sources but now lost.[25]

Van Dyck's example and the experiments of the Lombardy painter Cairo marked a watershed in court portraiture and the obligatory reference models, and effectively influenced entire future generations of painters. However, Garzoni's

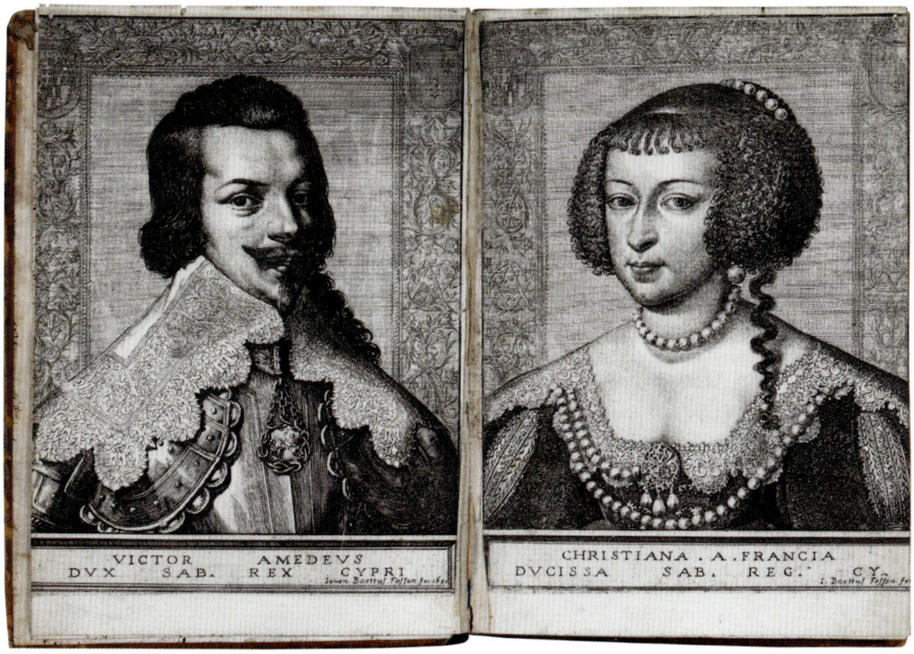

10–11. Giovenale Boetto
Victor Amadeus I, Duke of Savoy, King of Cyprus and Christine of France, Duchess of Savoy, Queen of Cyprus, 1635–1637, from Gabriel Le Meschinière, *Le chariot d'honneur de S.A.R. Victor Amedée...*, Turin, printed by Iean Michel Barella 1638
Turin, Biblioteca Nazionale Universitaria, Ris. 46.25

approach was different. Her aim was not so much to create new compositions as to use her highly refined technique to transform official and codified portraits into timeless images, symbols of a young but ambitious court: masterpieces of elegance and refinement that would fully satisfy the expectations of its rulers. For this reason, it seemed especially relevant on the occasion of the exhibition dedicated to sixteenth- and seventeenth-century female artists to focus on the two miniatures depicting Emmanuel Philibert and Charles Emmanuel I in the collections of the Musei Reali in Turin. By undertaking a comprehensive campaign of diagnostic investigations, conducted and financed by Fondazione Bracco, we have been able to analyse in detail Giovanna Garzoni's extraordinary technique. The results reported in the following pages illustrate her process from the initial elegant drafting of the underlying drawing made with a thin, continuous line, probably in silverpoint – to the painting itself, executed in thick, rapid brushstrokes capable of capturing the most minute details and exploiting the potential of the parchment support, and to her use of a rich palette of colours and particularly precious pigments, such as silver, gold, lapis lazuli and red lake.

The two paintings were identified for the first time in the 1682 inventory of the Savoy collections, which registers a "picture ten inches high and eight wide depicting the Portrait of Charles Emmanuel, first made in Miniature with Glass in front and a small black Frame. Plus another Picture of Similar size with a similar Frame, painted in miniature with Glass in front, depicting the Portrait of Emmanuel Philibert of Savoy".[26] The paintings do not appear in the inventory compiled in 1635 by Antonio Della Cornia, who only partially recorded the artefacts located in Christine of France's apartments. What is surprising, however, is that by the start of the nineteenth century the identity of the two figures appears to have been lost, assuming that they were, in fact, the two miniatures of the same size portraying warriors that were recorded in the list of the Palazzo Reale "Objects of Painting and Sculpture consigned to Sig. Giacomo Spalla" in 1803, together with a "large miniature of a warrior by Giovanna Garzoni", which, however, has been lost without trace.[27]

On the other hand, the 1635 inventory informs us of the presence of five miniatures attributed to Garzoni, all of which the compiler judged to be of good quality: a "Life-Size Head of Apollo"; a "Saint Sebastian Bound to a Column"; a "Venus with Time Carrying Love Away"; a "Young Hare with Fruit"; and "A Bowl with Various Fruits", which testify to the artist's diversified production during her stay in Turin.[28] In the subsequent inventory of the Palazzo Reale from 1682, the miniature depicting Apollo is found again and described in greater detail as "Portrait of the Miniaturist Crowned with Leaves, ten inches high and eight wide with Glass in front and an undulating black Ebony frame",[29] namely a self-portrait of the artist in the guise of the sacred guardian of the arts, which has been thought to correspond to the *Self-Portrait as Apollo* crowned with laurel leaves, holding a six-stringed viola, signed by Giovanna Garzoni on the musical instrument and located in the collections of the Palazzo del Quirinale[30] (fig. 12). However, the age of the young woman depicted – no more than twenty – suggests an earlier date for the Roman miniature, namely the years of Garzoni's first stay in Florence between 1618 and 1621, thus linking it to her love of singing and music and her performances at that time for the Grand Duchess Maria Magdalena of Austria. It also aligns with the common practice of female painters representing themselves in the act of playing a musical instrument, as Garzoni's colleague and friend Artemisia Gentileschi had done a few years earlier in her *Self-Portrait as a Lute Player*, conserved in the Wadsworth Atheneum Museum of Art.[31] Yet a reconstruction of the inventories indicates the Quirinale miniature came from the Savoy collections, and the similarities of composition and style between the miniature and the Savoy portraits, which are also the same size, suggest that the thirty-year-old artist wanted to portray herself with a more youthful appearance, better suited to the idealised features of the god – unless she perhaps brought some of her earlier works with her to Turin as gifts for Madame Royale, as was customary.

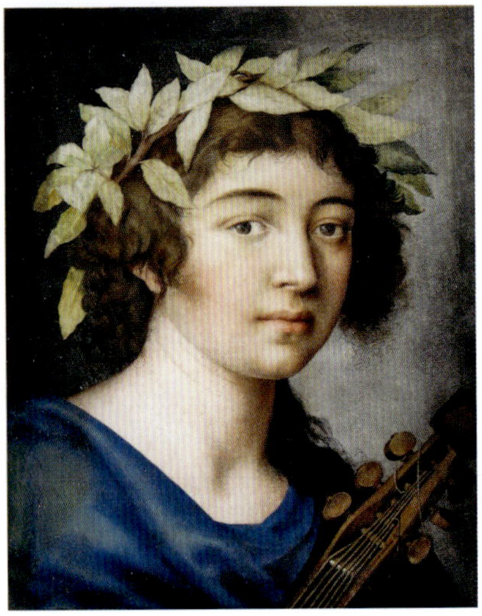

12. Giovanna Garzoni
Self-Portrait as Apollo
1632–1635
Rome, Segretariato Generale della Repubblica, Palazzo del Quirinale

Listed but still untraced are the sacred and mythological miniatures and the two still lifes that were immediately transferred to Christine's apartments in the Castello del Valentino. Registered in the 1644 inventory of Madame Royale's bedroom are "time who steals Love from Venus, a Miniature by Sig. ra Garzoni that has an Ebony Frame", and, in the first-floor study, next to paintings of flowers and fruit, "two others above the Bergamina fruits Miniature by Sig.ra Giovanna Garzoni, which have Ebony Frames". Perhaps the same works, differently framed to suit the new fashion, are better described in the following inventory from 1677 as "A small painting in miniature of a blue bowl filled with a cedro, flowers and Citrons, with a Frame decorated with gold leaf by Giovanna Garzoni" and "another small painting by Giovanna the Miniaturist of a plate of fruit, Shrimps and snails on Parchment in a frame decorated with gold leaf".[32] The works verify that also during her earlier years in Turin, Garzoni had successfully tackled the still life genre, associated with her greatest fame and a major part of her successful production. Indeed, thanks to her connections with Cassiano dal Pozzo, during her time in Rome she had even been granted entrance to the scientific circle of the Accademia dei Lincei.[33]

The large number of works available at the Turin court may have provided her with many other stimuli.[34] The naturalistic interests of Duke Charles Emmanuel I, developed over the course of his long reign, had greatly enriched Turin's collections in this field due to the Savoy ambassadors' painstaking search for books, paintings and curiosities, and also court invitations to artists specialising in the genre.[35] Ambrogio Figino's presence in Turin must have been influential, given that contemporary sources record him as a skilled still life painter, while art critic Carlo Malvasia recalls that Carlo Antonio Procaccini, whose finest work was in this genre, made several paintings for the Duke of Savoy. Miniaturist Nunzio Galizia, who came from Lombardy to Turin, is documented at the Savoy court from the years 1620 to 1621 for various paintings and for rare works using musk and amber. Perhaps his daughter Fede accompanied him: three of her works appear in the 1635 Savoy picture gallery inventory, which also lists three paintings by Panfilo Nuvolone.[36] Numerous paintings of fruit, flowers, animals and genre scenes, both Italian and Flemish, are listed in the inventories from the 1630s, where in addition to the canvas depicting *The Big Market* by Jacopo Bassano, now in the Galleria Sabauda, worthy of note are several paintings with animals by the Genoese artist Sinibaldo Scorza; fine paintings of birds by Carlo Battaglia (known as Paieur, chamberlain to the Duke of Savoy); miniatures by Pellegrino Brocardo and Carlo Conti; and still lifes with symbolic meanings linked to nature and time, such as those by Flemish painters Ludovico Susio and Guglielmo Nef, or by the German artists Peter Binoit and Isaak Soreau.[37] One can only imagine Giovanna Garzoni's curiosity as she strolled through the Regio Parco, designed by Emmanuel Philibert and extensively enriched by Charles Emmanuel I, which not only boasted marvellous gardens, with indigenous and exotic flowers and plants of the rarest species, but also woods populated by all sorts of game and by animals from distant lands.[38] Or her admiration as she leafed through the precious albums of flowers, birds and fish now preserved in the Biblioteca Reale in Turin (Varia 225, 229, 230). And again, how her interest much have been captured by the embellishment of the new rooms in the Palazzo di San Giovanni, which Christine of France had decorated with precious silk fabrics adorned with flowers and birds; or the Valentino residence's private rooms, whose walls were ornamented with garlands of flowers and collections of small paintings, along with a variety of other precious objects.[39]

Among the works of particular distinction that Garzoni realised during her years in Turin is certainly the refined *Portrait of Zaga Christ* (fig. 13): a very small parchment signed on the back in Latin and Ethiopian letters and dated 1635, depicting the African prince whom the painter met at the Turin court. Zaga Christ wears a red jacket topped by an elaborate lace collar, similar to the one worn by Victor Amadeus I. The prince had come to Turin to recover from a serious illness, and Garzoni's affectionate, intimate portrayal reflects the prince's state of mind.[40] The sky-blue background against which the figure stands out is the same colour Garzoni used ten years earlier for her *Portrait of a Gentleman*, now in The Hague.[41]

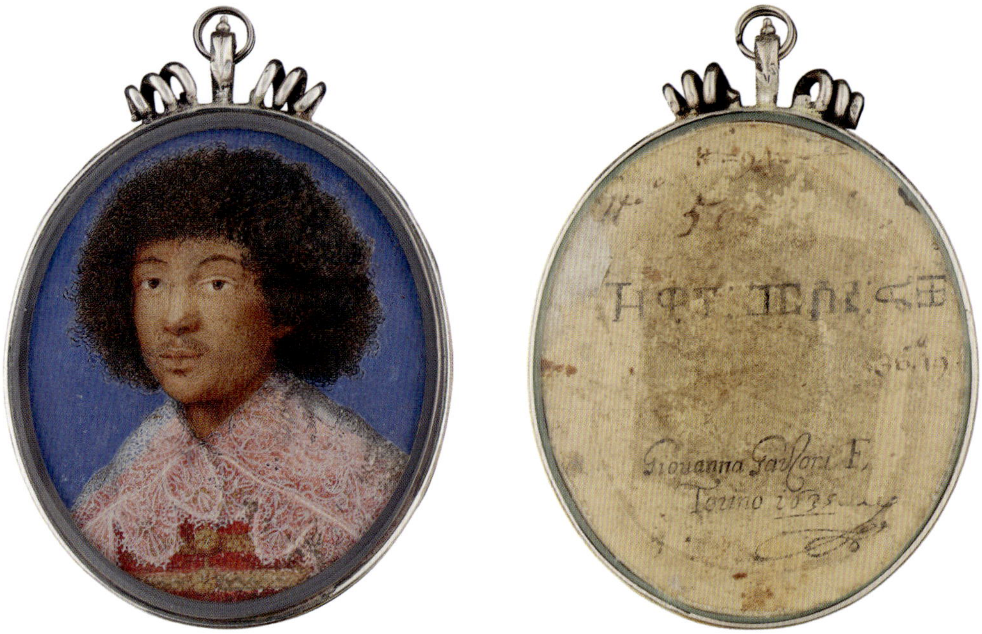

13. Giovanna Garzoni
Portrait of Zaga Christ,
recto and *verso*
1635
London, Philip Mould
& Company

Precious miniature portraits, either worn as jewels or commissioned from artists to be given away as signs of affection or as diplomatic gifts, circulated widely, including at the Savoy court. Garzoni would have had the opportunity to carefully study the various repertoires, such as two elegant French portraits on a blue background, depicting Emmanuel Philibert and Margaret of Valois. Set in circular medallions with frames decorated with grotesques, military trophies and garlands of fruit and flowers, the portraits were inserted into the small prayer book that Count Cristoforo Duc presented to the duchess in 1559 (figs. 8–9).[42]

Sources from the period also mention Garzoni's miniature portrait of the Abbot Filiberto Amedeo Scaglia di Verrua, a member of a prestigious noble Piedmont family who played a strategic role in Savoy diplomacy.[43] Following in the footsteps of his uncle Alessandro Cesare, a great patron and collector of Van Dyck's work, the Savoy ambassador also had to conduct relations with the artists who circulated at the court. In 1648 he requested the assistance of his diplomatic acquaintances to search in Florence at Garzoni's workshop for a portrait she had made of him several years earlier in Turin, or perhaps in England, when his appearance was still that of "a blond-haired young man, dressed in the French style with the frilled cuffs that were worn at the time".[44] We can therefore suppose that over the years Garzoni not only compiled examples of the flowers and fruits she drew from life, but also took pains to assemble albums of drawings of the people she encountered in the course of her travels and sojourns at various courts, either drawn from life or copied from famous prototypes. In this way she continued the established tradition of gathering drawings and miniatures in notebooks that was also widely practised at the Savoy court.

Among the various examples of these in the ducal collections, ideas and inspiration for the young painter might have come from two late-sixteenth-century notebooks containing pencil portraits of individuals linked to the Savoy family and subdivided into male and female. These were later destroyed in the fire of 1904 that also damaged the Biblioteca Nazionale in Turin. Nonetheless, some are known from the discovery of a series of photos of drawings from the album featuring the ladies at Charles Emmanuel's court, which opens with two portraits of Duchess Catalina that are not unlike Garzoni's own painting of her.[45] Moreover, like other artists working at the Turin court, Garzoni also had to satisfy the requests of the members of the Piedmontese nobility who were present there. And so it is no surprise to find "a small painting with three miniature flowers on parchment, a meticulous work by Sig. ra. Giovanna Garsona" in the impressive collection of Amedeo dal Pozzo, Marquis of Voghera, not only because of the close ties between the Piedmontese and Savoy families but also because of the mutual esteem between Garzoni and Cassiano dal Pozzo, who would have undoubtedly recommended her works to his cousin.[46]

On 7 October 1637 Duke Victor Amadeus I died. Tension at the Savoy court soon became palpable due to the heightened political differences between Madame Royale and her brothers-in-law over the regency of the throne. In this stormy climate, Giovanna Garzoni concluded her five-year stay in the city of Turin, never to return. She most certainly took with her the memory of a rich experience and the support of the brilliant and strong-willed Christine of France, who paved her way to new horizons: first to London, where Madame Royale's sister Queen Henrietta of England awaited Giovanna's arrival, and subsequently to Paris, where her brother Louis XIII would also open his doors to the miniaturist.[47]

[1] For Giovanna Garzoni's invitation to the House of Savoy, see: A. Griseri, "La pittura", in *Mostra del Barocco piemontese*, exhibition catalogue (Turin, Palazzo Madama, Palazzo Reale, Palazzina di Stupinigi, 22 June – 10 November 1963), edited by V. Viale, Turin 1963, III, p. 67; A. Baudi di Vesme, *Schede Vesme. L'arte in Piemonte dal XVI al XVIII secolo*, 4 vols., Turin 1963–1982, II, 1966, pp. 516–517; M. Rosci, "Giovanna Garzoni dal Palazzo Reale di Torino a Superga", in *Scritti di Storia dell'Arte in onore di Federico Zeri*, Milan 1984, II, pp. 565–567; A. Griseri, "Ritratti sabaudi di Giovanna Garzoni", in *Studi Piemontesi*, XIV, 2, 1985, pp. 355–357; M. Di Macco, "Quadreria di Palazzo e pittori di corte. Le scelte ducali dal 1630 al 1684", in *Figure del Barocco in Piemonte. La corte, la città, i cantieri, le province*, edited by G. Romano, Turin 1988, pp. 52–53; S. Pettenati, in *Diana trionfatrice. Arte di Corte nel Piemonte del Seicento*, exhibition catalogue (Turin, 27 May – 24 September 1989), edited by M. Di Macco, G. Romano, Turin 1989, p. 140, no. 145; G. Casale, *Giovanna Garzoni, "insigne miniatrice" 1600–1670*, Milan-Rome 1991, pp. 18–20, 52–53, 57–58; *Gli incanti dell'iride. Giovanna Garzoni pittrice nel Seicento*, exhibition catalogue (San Severino Marche, 1996), edited by G. Casale, Cinisello Balsamo 1996, pp. 18–19; M. B. Failla, in *La reggia di Venaria e i Savoia. Arte, magnificenza e storia di una corte europea*, exhibition catalogue (Reggia di Venaria Reale, 12 October 2007 – 30 March 2008), edited by E. Castelnuovo, 2 vols., Turin 2007, II, pp. 41–42, nos. 2.26–2.29; S. Barker, "L'universo di Giovanna Garzoni. L'arte, i viaggi e un immaginario geografico senza confini", in *"La grandezza dell'universo" nell'arte di Giovanna Garzoni*, exhibition catalogue (Florence, Gallerie degli Uffizi – Palazzo Pitti, 10 March – 24 May 2020), edited by S. Barker, Livorno 2020, pp. 21–22; S. Ffolliott, "'La Miniatrice di Madama Reale': Giovanna Garzoni in Savoia", in ivi, pp. 46–53.

[2] On the years of Emmanuel Philibert: P. Astrua, "Gli anni di Emanuele Filiberto", in *"Il nostro pittore fiamengo". Giovanni Caracca alla corte dei Savoia (1568–1607)*, exhibition catalogue (Turin, Galleria Sabauda, 21 September 2005 – 8 January 2006), edited by P. Astrua, A. M. Bava, C. E. Spantigati, Turin 2005, pp. 9–26; on the years of Charles Emmanuel I, see *Le collezioni di Carlo Emanuele I di Savoia*, edited by G. Romano, Turin 1995, and *Le meraviglie del mondo. Le collezioni di Carlo Emanuele I di Savoia*, exhibition catalogue (Turin, Musei Reali, 16 December 2016 – 2 April 2017), edited by A. M. Bava, E. Pagella, Genoa 2016, together with extensive previous bibliography.

[3] A. M. Bava, in *Blu, rosso e oro. Segni e colori dell'araldica in carte, codici e oggetti d'arte*, exhibition catalogue (Turin, Archivio di Stato, 29 September – 30 November 1998), edited by I. Massabò Ricci, M. Carassi, L. C. Gentile, Milan 1998, pp. 190–194, nos. 184–188; C. Maritano, "Filiberto Pingone e la storia dinastica di Casa Savoia", in *Le meraviglie del mondo* cit. (note 2), pp. 75–77.

[4] On Jan Kraeck and the portraitists working in Turin between the sixteenth and seventeenth centuries, see the volume *"Il nostro pittore fiamengo"* cit. (note 2).

[5] G. Romano, "Artisti alla corte di Carlo Emanuele I: la costruzione di una nuova tradizione figurativa", in *Le collezioni di Carlo Emanuele I di Savoia* cit. (note 2), pp. 18–22, 36–40; M. B. Failla, "L'immagine della Corte sabauda: taccuini di disegni e ritratti incisi", in *"Il nostro*

pittore fiamengo" cit. (note 2), pp. 57–68; M. B. Failla, in *La reggia di Venaria* cit. (note 1), II, p. 33, nos. 2.3–2.4.

[6] A. Baudi di Vesme, *Schede Vesme* cit. (note 1), III, 1968, pp. 1050–1052; M. Di Macco, "Quadreria di Palazzo e pittori di corte. Le scelte ducali dal 1630 al 1684", in *Figure del Barocco in Piemonte* cit. (note 1), p. 50; A. Griseri, *Il Diamante. La villa di Madama Reale Cristina di Francia*, Turin 1988, pp. 53–86; M. Di Macco, "Il ritratto e l'omaggio simbolico", in *Diana trionfatrice* cit. (note 1), pp. 18–19; M. B. Failla, in *La reggia di Venaria* cit. (note 1), II, p. 51, no. 2.39; A. Giovannini Luca, "Femmes fortes e cultura del ritratto nell'epoca delle Reggenti", in *Madame Reali. Cultura e potere da Parigi a Torino. Cristina di Francia e Giovanna Battista di Savoia Nemours*, exhibition catalogue (Turin, Palazzo Madama, 20 December 2018 – 6 May 2019), edited by C. Arnaldi di Balme, M. P. Ruffino, Genoa 2019, pp. 51–57.

[7] The 1631 inventory was published by G. Campori, *Raccolta di cataloghi ed inventarii inediti di quadri, statue, disegni, bronzi, dorerie, smalti, medaglie, avorii, ecc. dal secolo XV al secolo XIX*, Modena 1870, pp. 76–104, republished and edited by A. M. Bava, in *Le collezioni di Carlo Emanuele I* cit. (note 2), pp. 53–62.

[8] On the Grande Galleria of Charles Emmanuel I: A. Baudi di Vesme, *Schede Vesme* cit. (note 1), III, 1968, under the entry for "Zuccari Federico", pp. 1111–1129; G. Romano, "Le origini dell'armeria sabauda e la Grande Galleria di Carlo Emanuele I", in *L'Armeria Reale di Torino*, edited by F. Mazzini, Busto Arsizio 1982, pp. 15–30; J. Kliemann, *Gesta dipinte. La grande decorazione nelle dimore italiane dal Quattrocento al Seicento*, Cinisello Balsamo 1993, pp. 203–208; A. M. Bava, "La collezione di pittura e i grandi progetti decorativi", in *Le collezioni di Carlo Emanuele I di Savoia* cit. (note 2), pp. 224–236; G. Dardanello, "Memoria professionale nei disegni degli Album Valperga. Allestimenti decorativi e collezionismo di mestiere", in ivi, pp. 64–112; S. Mamino, *Reimagining the Grande Galleria of Carlo Emanuele I of Savoy*, in "Res, Anthropology and Aesthetics", 27, 1995, pp. 70–88; G. Romano, "Artisti alla corte di Carlo Emanuele I: la costruzione di una nuova tradizione figurativa", in *Le collezioni di Carlo Emanuele I di Savoia* cit. (note 2), pp. 47–52; J. Kliemann, "Federico Zuccari e la Grande Galleria di Torino", in *Der Maler Federico Zuccari*, international congress proceedings of the Bibliotheca Hertziana (Rome–Florence, 23–26 February 1993), edited by M. Winner, D. Heikamp, Munich 1999, pp. 317–346; S. Mamino, "La Grande Galleria come 'Tipocosmo'. Interessi naturalistici e enciclopedismo in Carlo Emanuele I", in *Le magnificenze del XVII–XVIII secolo alla Biblioteca Reale di Torino*, exhibition catalogue (Turin, Biblioteca Reale, 28 October – 15 December 1999), edited by G. Giacobello Bernard, A. Griseri, Milan–Turin 1999, pp. 47–67; F. Varallo, "Dal Theatro alla Grande Galleria. La biblioteca ducale tra Cinque e Seicento", in *Il Teatro di tutte le scienze e le arti. Raccogliere libri per coltivare idee in una capitale di età moderna. Torino 1559–1861*, exhibition catalogue (Turin, Archivio di Stato, 22 November 2011 – 27 February 2012), edited by M. Carassi, I. Massabò Ricci, S. Pettenati, Turin 2011, pp. 25–34; P. Tosini, "La Grande Galleria di Federico Zuccari a Torino: il capolavoro mancato", in *Le meraviglie del mondo* cit. (note 2), pp. 65–73; F. Varallo, "Il luogo del sapere: la Grande Galleria di Carlo Emanuele I", in ivi, pp. 117–127.

[9] The inventory of the Savoy collections of 1635 is published in A. Baudi di Vesme, "La Regia Pinacoteca di Torino", in *Le Gallerie Nazionali Italiane*, Rome 1897, III, pp. 35–68, republished with corrections in *Musei d'Arte a Torino. Cataloghi e inventari delle collezioni sabaude*, edited by S. Pinto, undated [1994], file I.

[10] A. Baudi di Vesme, *Schede Vesme* cit. (note 1), II, 1966, pp. 516–517.

[11] G. Casale, *Giovanna Garzoni* cit. (note 1), pp. 7–8; S. Barker, "L'universo di Giovanna Garzoni" cit. (note 1), pp. 18–19.

[12] A. Baudi di Vesme, *Schede Vesme* cit. (note 1), I, 1963, pp. 233–239. On the economic conditions of the artists at the House of Savoy between the sixteenth and seventeenth centuries, see A. M. Bava, C. Goria, "Artists Working for the House of Savoy in the Seventeenth Century", in *The Court Artist in Seventeenth-Century Italy*, edited by E. Fumagalli, R. Morselli, Rome 2014, pp. 199–235.

[13] In his day, Jan Kraeck has also been a guest at the Ducal Palace, where he had a studio: A. M. Bava, "Giovanni Caracca alla corte dei Savoia", in *"Il nostro pittore fiamengo"* cit. (note 2), pp. 27–44.

[14] Turin, Musei Reali – Palazzo Reale, inv. 1966, nos. 5206 and 5246; Florence, Uffizi, inv. 1870, nos. 814 and 817 (the parchment with Emmanuel Philibert was featured in the exhibition following the restoration work carried out by Filippo Capellaro with the supervision of Tiziana Sandri, thanks to the support received as part of the "Rivelazioni" project promoted by Borsa Italiana; at the same time, the maintenance of the climaframe of both Turinese works was carried out). The four Savoy miniatures measure around 43 × 33 cm each, with a difference between them of no more than a centimetre. On the miniatures, see: A. Griseri, "La pittura", in *Mostra del Barocco piemontese* cit. (note 1), p. 47; S. Meloni Trkulja, in "Omaggio a Leopoldo de' Medici", part II: *Ritrattini*, exhibition catalogue (Florence, Gabinetto Disegni e Stampe degli Uffizi, February–April 1976), edited by A. Forlani Tempesti, A. M. Petroli Tofani, S. Meloni Trkulja, Florence 1976, p. 48; A. Griseri, "Ritratti sabaudi di Giovanna Garzoni" cit. (note 1), pp. 356–357; S. Meloni Trkulja, "Garzoni Giovanna", in *Il Seicento fiorentino: arte a Firenze da Ferdinando I a Cosimo III*, exhibition catalogue (Florence, Palazzo Strozzi, 21 December 1986 – 4 May 1987), edited by G. Guidi, D. Marcucci, Florence 1986, III, pp. 97–98; A. Griseri, *Il Diamante* cit. (note 6), pp. 62–69; S. Pettenati, in *Diana trionfatrice* cit. (note 1), p. 140, no. 145; C. Piglione, "Giovanna Garzoni", in *La pittura in Italia. Il Seicento*, edited by M. Gregori, E. Schleier, 2 vols., Milan 1989, II, p. 755; G. Casale, *Giovanna Garzoni* cit. (note 1), pp. 18–19, 52–57; G. Casale, "Sul rapporto 'Arte-Scienza' nel sec. XVII: Giovanna Garzoni Pittrice Ascolana (1600–1670)", in *Il Seicento nelle Marche. Profilo di una civiltà*, edited by C. Costanza, M. Massa, Ancona 1994, p. 237; *Gli incanti dell'iride* cit. (note 1), pp. 38–41; F. Bottacin, "Giovanna Garzoni pittrice di ritratti 'amorevoli': una proposta per il soggiorno veneziano", in *Donne a Venezia: vicende femminili fra Trecento e Settecento*, edited by S. Winter, Rome 2004, pp. 71–83; L. Calzona, in *"Il nostro pittore fiamengo"* cit. (note 2), pp. 126–127, no. 26; M. B. Failla, in *La reggia di Venaria* cit. (note 1), II, pp. 41–43, nos. 2.26–2.29; F. Panero, in *Le meraviglie del mondo* cit. (note 2), pp. 36–37, no. 21; F. Solinas, in *De dames van de barok. Vrouwelijke schilders in het Italië van de 16de en 17de eeuw / Les dames du baroque. Femmes peintres dans l'Italie du XVIe et XVIIe siècle*, exhibition catalogue (Gand, Museum voor Schone Kunsten, 20 October 2018 – 20 January 2019), edited by V. De Beir, F. Solinas, A. Tapié, Gand 2018, pp. 181–183, no. 46; M. Betti, in *Madame Reali* cit. (note 6), p. 126, no. 7; S. Ffolliott, in *"La grandezza dell'universo"* cit. (note 1), pp. 130–131, no. 6.

[15] For the hypothesis that the two Florentine miniatures might be replicas of prototypes already made in Turin,

also supported by the original presence in the album of Garzoni's models left at the Accademia di San Luca of sheets with Savoy portraits that later disappeared (including one of Victor Amadeus I), see A. Cipani. Cipriani, "Giovanna Garzoni miniatrice", in Ricerche di Storia dell'Arte, I, 1–2, 1976, pp. 242 and 245, note 12; S. Pettenati, in *Diana trionfatrice* cit. (note 1), p. 140, no. 145; M. B. Failla, in *La reggia di Venaria* cit. (note 1), II, pp. 41–42, nos. 2.26–2.29. For the hypothesis that they are instead early versions carried out in Piedmont and which later reached Tuscany: M. Betti, in *Madame Reali* cit. (note 6), p. 126, no. 7.

[16] C. Lanzi, in *"Il nostro pittore fiamengo"* cit. (note 2), p. 84, no. 8; A. M. Bava, in *De Van Dyck à Bellotto. Splendeurs à la cour de Savoie*, exhibition catalogue (Brussels, Palais des Beaux-Arts, 20 February – 24 May 2009), edited by P. Astrua, A. M. Bava, S. Damiano, C. E. Spantigati, Turin 2009, p. 80, no. 1.1; F. Panero, in *Le meraviglie del mondo* cit. (note 2), p. 32, no. 8.

[17] Turin, Archivio di Stato, Sezioni Riunite, Camera dei conti di Savoia, inv. 1, fol. 1, *Inventaire des titres et registres concernans la jurisdiction et droit des souvrains et reglemens de la Chambre des comptes de Savoie*, register 14 bis: M. B. Failla, "L'immagine della Corte sabauda: taccuini di disegni e ritratti incisi", in *"Il nostro pittore fiamengo"* cit. (note 2), p. 61.

[18] The official images handed down by the portraits of the ducal consorts held at the Museo Civico Casa Cavassa in Saluzzo constitute prototypes of reference for numerous replicas: E. Pianea, in *La reggia di Venaria* cit. (note 1), II, p. 35, nos. 2.12–2.13; F. Panero, in *Le meraviglie del mondo* cit. (note 2), p. 33, no. 11.

[19] A. Griseri, *Il Diamante* cit. (note 6), p. 23. On the Duchess of Savoy: *L'infanta Caterina d'Austria, duchessa di Savoia (1567–1597)*, edited by B. A. Raviola, F. Varallo, Rome 2013. Among the various images of reference, we must also remember the splendid little portraits of Charles Emmanuel and Catalina of Spain, at their wedding, produced by Johannes Wierix and to be found today in the Lugt collection in Paris: M. B. Failla, "L'immagine della Corte sabauda: taccuini di disegni e ritratti incisi", in *"Il nostro pittore fiamengo"* cit. (note 2), p. 61 and figs. 5–6.

[20] For the engraving housed at the Musée Savoisien of Chambéry inv. PS 108: M. B. Failla, in *"Il nostro pittore fiamengo"* cit. (note 2), pp. 152–153, no. 37. For a later variation engraved by Hans Hogenbergh, now in Turin, Palazzo Madama – Museo Civico d'Arte Antica (inv. 5760/SILA): C. Arnaldi di Balme, in *Le meraviglie del mondo* cit. (note 2), p. 35, no. 17.

[21] M. Epifani, "La collezione di armi di Carlo Emanuele I", in *Le meraviglie del mondo* cit. (note 2), pp. 321–323.

[22] M. Di Macco, in *Diana trionfatrice* cit. (note 1), p. 20, no. 20 with a hypothetical attribution to Pellegrino Brocardo; M. B. Failla, in *La reggia di Venaria* cit. (note 1), II, pp. 43–44, no. 2.31; M. B. Failla, in *De Van Dyck à Bellotto* cit. (note 16), pp. 84–85, no. 1.4; S. Ffolliott, in *"La grandezza dell'universo"* cit. (note 1), pp. 130–131, no. 6. For the engravings by Boetto: A. Griseri, "Giovenale Boetto incisore", in N. Carboneri, A. Griseri, C. Morra, *Giovenale Boetto. Architetto e incisore*, Fossano 1966, pp. 33–62, figs. 111–236; A. Griseri, *Il Diamante* cit. (note 6), p. 30; C. Goria, G. Spione, "Cultura figurativa nell'età delle Madame Reali", in *Madame Reali* cit. (note 6), pp. 67–68.

[23] G. Romano, "Artisti alla corte di Carlo Emanuele I: la costruzione di una nuova tradizione figurativa", in *Le collezioni di Carlo Emanuele I di Savoia* cit. (note 2), pp. 36–37; M. B. Failla, "L'immagine della Corte sabauda: taccuini di disegni e ritratti incisi", in *"Il nostro pittore fiamengo"* cit. (note 2), pp. 57–58; M. B. Failla, in ivi, pp. 132–133, no. 29; F. Panero, in *Le meraviglie del mondo* cit. (note 2), pp. 30–31, no. 3.

[24] The portraits of the rulers appear in the volume by Gabriel Le Meschinière titled *Le chariot d'honneur de S.A.R. Victor Amedée* published in Turin in 1638 by Iean Michel Barella; for the relationship between Garzoni's miniatures and Boetto's engravings: A. Griseri, *Il Diamante* cit. (note 6), p. 43; C. Goria, G. Spione, "Cultura figurativa nell'età delle Madame Reali", in *Madame Reali* cit. (note 6), pp. 67–70.

[25] A. M. Bava, M. B. Failla, "Antoon Van Dyck e i Savoia", in *Van Dyck pittore di corte*, exhibition catalogue (Turin, Galleria Sabauda, 16 November 2018 – 3 March 2019), edited by A. M. Bava, M. G. Bernardini, Rome 2018, pp. 61–67; A. M. Bava, in ivi, pp. 237–238, nos. 40–41.

[26] *Musei d'arte a Torino* cit. (note 9), file II, pp. 13–14, nos. 270–271.

[27] S. Pettenati, in *Diana trionfatrice* cit. (note 1), p. 140, no. 145. In the Palazzo Reale inventory of 1822, three miniatures by Garzoni are still listed in the cabinet adjacent to the Porcelain Chamber: L. Levi Momigliano, "Per la storia delle collezioni sabaude: due inventari del 1822", in *Conoscere la Galleria Sabauda. Documenti sulla storia delle sue collezioni*, Turin 1982, pp. 87–100.

[28] *Musei d'arte a Torino* cit. (note 9), file I, p. 14, nos. 239 and 241; p. 21, nos. 390, 391, 392.

[29] *Musei d'arte a Torino* cit. (note 9), file II, p. 13, no. 263. In the inventory of 1754, the work is registered as featuring "a poetess": ivi, file III, p. 9, no. 366.

[30] On the passage of the work from the Savoy collections to those of the Quirinale: L. Laureati, L. Trezzani, *Il patrimonio artistico del Quirinale. Pittura antica. La quadreria*, Rome–Milan 1993, p. 38, no. 23; L. Morozzi, in *La reggia di Venaria* cit. (note 1), II, p. 177, no. 9.22.

[31] S. Barker, "'Marvellously Gifted': Giovanna Garzoni's First Visit to the Medici Court", in The Burlington Magazine, CLX, 1385, 2018, pp. 654–659; S. Barker, in *"La grandezza dell'universo"* cit. (note 1), pp. 124–125, no. 3.

[32] *Il Castello del Valentino*, edited by M. Bernardi, Turin 1949, pp. 350 and 356; S. Pettenati, in *Diana trionfatrice* cit. (note 1), pp. 145–146, no. 152.

[33] On the production of Giovanna Garzoni's still lifes: S. Meloni Trkulja, "Le miniature degli Uffizi", in *Gli Uffizi. Catalogo generale*, Florence 1979, pp. 1167–1172; S. Meloni Trkulja, "Giovanna Garzoni miniatora medicea", in FMR, 15, 1983, pp. 77–96; E. Fumagalli, *Giovanna Garzoni*, in *La natura morta in Italia*, edited by F. Porzio, F. Zeri, Milan 1989, II, pp. 568–571; G. Casale, *Giovanna Garzoni* cit. (note 1); G. Casale, "Sul rapporto 'Arte-Scienza' nel sec. XVII: Giovanna Garzoni Pittrice Ascolana (1600–1670)", in *Il Seicento nelle Marche* cit. (note 14), pp. 234–256; *Gli incanti dell'iride* cit. (note 1); E. Fumagalli, "Il granducato di Ferdinando II (1628–1670). Il cardinale Leopoldo (1617–1675)", in *Il Giardino del Granduca. Natura morta nelle collezioni medicee*, edited by M. Chiarini, Turin 1997, pp. 141–153; *Natures mortes. Giovanna Garzoni*, edited by S. Meloni Trkulja, E. Fumagalli, Paris 2000; S. Barker, "Marvellously Gifted" cit. (note 31); *"La grandezza dell'universo"* cit. (note 1).

[34] Three still lifes have been attributed to Garzoni's activity in Turin, now found in private collections in Asolo and Turin: M. Rosci, "Octavianus Monfort e la miniatura su pergamena nel XVII secolo", in P. Chiapatti, M. Rosci, *Octavianus Monfort*, Turin 1985, pp. 10–12; E. Fumagalli, "Giovanna Garzoni", in *La natura morta in Italia* cit. (note 33), p. 568; S. Pettenati, in *Diana trionfatrice* cit. (note 1), pp. 145–146, no. 152; G. Casale, *Giovanna Garzoni* cit. (note 1), pp. 19–20, 86–87, 174–175; G. Casale, "Sul rapporto 'Arte-Scienza' nel sec. XVII: Giovanna Garzoni

Pittrice Ascolana (1600–1670)", in *Il Seicento nelle Marche* cit. (note 14), pp. 238, 241; *Gli incanti dell'iride* cit. (note 1), pp. 42–47, nos. 8–9–10; M. D. Garrard, "Le nature 'non proprio morte' di Giovanna Garzoni", in *"La grandezza dell'universo"* cit. (note 1), pp. 63–65.

[35] In 1618, Abbot Alessandro Scaglia di Verrua, Savoy ambassador to Rome, procured for the Duke of Savoy the volume of the *Aquatilium animalium historiae* by Ippolito Salviani, now at the Biblioteca Nazionale of Turin (O.II.142), and at the same time he sent him an *Herbarium* by Mattioli: A. M. Bava, "La collezione di oggetti preziosi", in *Le collezioni di Carlo Emanuele I di Savoia* cit. (note 2), p. 325.

[36] *Musei d'arte a Torino* cit. (note 9), file I: of the three works by Fede Galizia, two (p. 24 no. 470 and p. 25 no. 488) appear to be variations, judged to be of mediocre quality (one of which is still found in the deposits of Palazzo Reale) of the painting portraying *Judith with the Head of Holofernes*, painted by the artist on several occasions; while the third, featuring "a cup of cherries with a butterfly" is believed to be of good quality (p. 28, no. 588), and has apparently been traced to a private collection: S. Ffolliott, "'La Miniatrice di Madama Reale'" cit. (note 1), pp. 47–48. Regarding the hypothesis that two other works cited in the 1635 inventory (of which one referred to Nuvolone) may be identified with paintings by Fede Galizia now in Cremona, see the profiles by Mario Marubbi in this catalogue.

[37] A. M. Bava, "La collezione di pittura e i grandi progetti decorativi", in *Le collezioni di Carlo Emanuele I di Savoia* cit. (note 2), pp. 222–224; A. M. Bava, "Pittura e scultura: scelte figurative e committenze di corte", in *Le meraviglie del mondo* cit. (note 2), p. 261.

[38] The diplomatic correspondence documents the arrival in Turin on several occasions of large citrus plants and a range of flower bulbs; parrots and other rare animals of all kinds, such as tigers, leopards, lions, dogs of all breeds and even elephants were sent from France, Spain, England and Holland: A. M. Bava, "La collezione di oggetti preziosi", in *Le collezioni di Carlo Emanuele I di Savoia* cit. (note 2), pp. 323–325. On Charles Emmanuel I's naturalist collections, see also S. Mamino, "Quarantotto immagini naturalistiche per la 'Grande Galleria' di Carlo Emanuele I di Savoia", in *Politica e cultura nell'età di Carlo Emanuele I. Torino, Parigi, Madrid*, conference proceedings (Turin 1995), edited by M. Masoero, S. Mamino, C. Rosso, Turin 1999, pp. 289–309; P. Passerin d'Entrèves, "Album di pesci, molluschi, crostacei, rettili e cetacei", in *Le magnificenze del XVII–XVIII secolo* cit. (note 8), pp. 69–71; P. Passerin d'Entrèves, "Atlante degli uccelli", in ivi, pp. 71–72; P. Passerin d'Entrèves, "Le meraviglie della natura", in *Le meraviglie del mondo* cit. (note 2), pp. 129–135, with previous bibliography.

[39] On the tastes of Christine of France: *Il Castello del Valentino* cit. (note 32); A. Griseri, *Il Diamante*, cit. (note 6); M. Di Macco, "Quadreria di Palazzo e pittori di corte. Le scelte ducali dal 1630 al 1684", in *Figure del Barocco in Piemonte* cit. (note 1), pp. 48–61; M. Di Macco, "'Critica occhiuta': la cultura figurativa (1630–1678)", in *Storia di Torino*, IV: *La città fra crisi e ripresa (1630–1730)*, edited by G. Ricuperati, Turin 2002, pp. 352–353; M. Di Macco, "Duchi, Madame Reali e Re sabaudi: forme d'arte di corte a Torino dal Cinquecento al Settecento", in *La reggia di Venaria* cit. (note 1), I, pp. 248–252; M. B. Failla, P. Cornaglia, "Il palazzo di San Giovanni per i duchi Vittorio Amedeo di Savoia e Cristina di Francia", in *Carlo e Amedeo di Castellamonte 1571–1683. Ingegneri e architetti per i Duchi di Savoia*, convention proceedings (Venaria, Turin, 2013), edited by A. Merlotti, Rome 2016, pp. 97–115; A. Griseri, "Cristina di Francia e Filippo d'Agliè. La scacchiera del Potere", in *Madame Reali* cit. (note 6), pp. 15–23 and the other contributions to the volume *Madame Reali* cit. (note 6), with extensive previous bibliography.

[40] H. Groen, in *"La grandezza dell'universo"* cit. (note 1), pp. 128–129, no. 5.

[41] A. Cosgrove, "'E scrittrice, e pittrice': Giovanna Garzoni e l'arte della calligrafia", in *"La grandezza dell'universo"* cit. (note 1), p. 34.

[42] M. B. Failla, in *"Il nostro pittore fiamengo"* cit. (note 2), pp. 132–133, no. 29. The production of small portraits to be set in jewellery or included in small volumes was, for example, one of the tasks of Jan Kraeck, author of the rare miniature portraying Charles Emmanuel I at around eighteen years of age, now in the Museo Nazionale del Bargello: M. B. Failla, in *"Il nostro pittore fiamengo"* cit. (note 2), pp. 120–121, no. 23.

[43] A. Pennini, under the entry for "Verrua, Filiberto Amedeo Scaglia di", in *Dizionario Biografico degli Italiani*, vol. 99, Rome 2020.

[44] A. Baudi di Vesme, *Schede Vesme* cit. (note 1), II, 1966, pp. 516–517.

[45] M. B. Failla, "Il 'cahier' delle dame di Caterina Micaela", in *L'infanta Caterina d'Austria* cit. (note 19), pp. 329–340.

[46] The collections of Amedeo dal Pozzo were carefully investigated by A. Cifani and F. Monetti, "'L'illustrissimo cugino': Cassiano e Amedeo dal Pozzo. Le relazioni artistiche del Marchese di Voghera e la storia della sua quadreria", in *I segreti di un collezionista. Le straordinarie raccolte di Cassiano dal Pozzo (1588–1657)*, exhibition catalogue (Biella, Museo del Territorio Biellese, 16 December 2001 – 16 March 2002), edited by F. Solinas, Rome 2001, pp. 29–52.

[47] Giovanna went to England probably as early as 1638, perhaps together with the painter Artemisia Gentileschi: S. Meloni Trkulja, "Garzoni Giovanna", in *Il Seicento fiorentino: arte a Firenze da Ferdinando I a Cosimo III* cit. (note 14), p. 98; S. Barker, "L'universo di Giovanna Garzoni" cit. (note 1), p. 22; for her stay in France: G. Casale, *Giovanna Garzoni* cit. (note 1), p. 9; E. Fumagalli, "Giovanna Garzoni in Paris", in *Natures mortes*, cit. (note 33), pp. 11–12; S. Barker, "L'universo di Giovanna Garzoni" cit. (note 1), p. 23.

A READING OF IMAGES THROUGH DIAGNOSTIC ANALYSIS: THE PORTRAITS OF DUKES EMMANUEL PHILIBERT AND CHARLES EMMANUEL I

Marco Gargano, Matteo Interlenghi, Tiziana Cavaleri, Christian Salvatore and Isabella Castiglioni

For the study of the work on parchment by Giovanna Garzoni featuring Charles Emmanuel I of Savoy, now held at the Royal Palace of Turin, non-invasive high-resolution diagnostic imaging techniques – multi-band and hyperspectral – were employed, including very high-resolution optical microscope images, coupled with non-invasive point spectroscopic techniques such as fibre-optic reflectance (FORS) and characteristic X-ray fluorescence (XRF) analyses (a brief description of the instrumentation used is given at the end of the paper). This multi-modal approach allowed us to characterise the work from a material-organic point of view, from the most superficial visible layers to the underdrawing and the background preparation, offering a visual representation through images that are particularly effective at representing the material characteristics present in the painted areas, in the underdrawing and their spatial distribution. The work carried out on the work was then compared with the results of the investigations carried out on a similar portrait of Duke Emmanuel Philibert, also held in the Musei Reali of Turin.

FORS, XRF Analyses, Microscope Photography, Yperspectral Imaging in Vis/NIR

The parchment with the portrait of Duke Charles Emmanuel I was analysed entirely with hyperspectral imaging in Vis/NIR, and with FORS and XRF point spectroscopy in representative specific points, as indicated in figure 14A, for the area of the

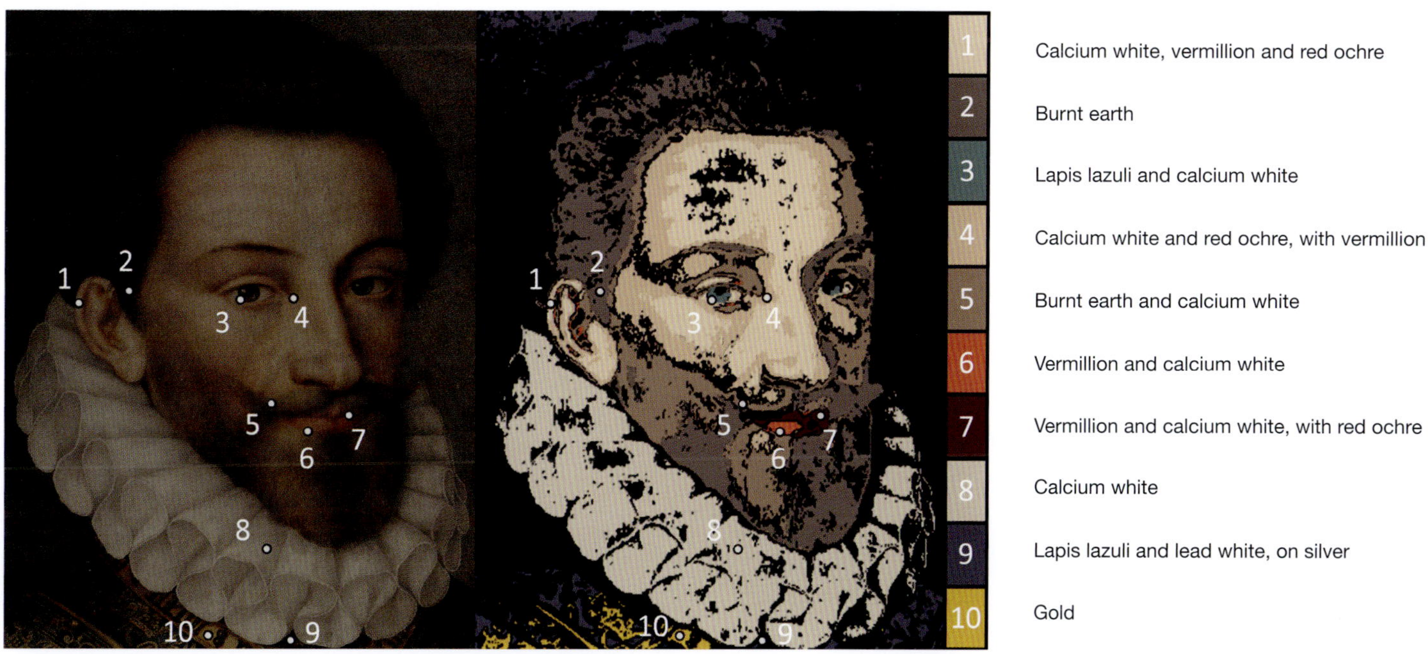

14. Portrait of Charles Emmanuel I: A) visible light image of the work with analysis points for material investigation; B) map of areas with similar pigments and pigment mixtures

15. Portrait of Charles Emmanuel I: A) visible light image of the detail of the Annunziata medal with analysis points for material investigation; B) map of areas with similar pigments and pigment mixtures

16. Maps of areas with similar pigments and pigment mixtures in the portrait of Charles Emmanuel I (A) and that of Emmanuel Philibert (B)

17. Maps of areas with similar pigments and pigment mixtures of the details of the medals in the portrait of Charles Emmanuel I (A) and that of Emmanuel Philibert (B)

duke's face and collar, and in figure 15A, concerning the region of the Annunziata medal the duke wears around his neck.

Figure 14B shows the map of areas found to have similar pigments as a result of a comparison of FORS and Vis/NIR hyperspectral imaging results, obtained using specific processing algorithms (Spectral Angle Mapper – SAM). The table adjacent to the figures shows the hypothesized mixtures obtained by cross-referencing the hyperspectral imaging data in the Vis/NIR, FORS and XRF analyses.

As can be seen in figure 14, the material analyses revealed the presence of calcium even in the darkest backgrounds, indicating a preparation with a calcium carbonate base. The dark colours in the background of the portrait are characterised by carbon based/organic materials.

The elements found in the skin tones of Duke Charles Emmanuel I combined to FORS spectra show the presence of vermillion and ochre/red earth, in various concentrations, mixed with lead white to lighten the skin. The brown of the beard and hair are made with burnt earth, while the blue eyes were painted with dotted brushstrokes of lapis lazuli. The pigments used for the armour and gold decorations reveal again the presence of lapis lazuli but with the combined use of precious metals: silver and gold.

Similarly to figure 14, figure 15A shows the points of analysis with FORS and XRF spot analyses in correspondence of the Santissima Annunziata medal – a symbol of the highest honour in the House of Savoy. Figure 15B shows a map of the areas that seems to have similar pigments as a result of the comparison of the FORS and Vis-NIR hyperspectral imaging results, obtained through specific SAM processing. Again, the table adjacent to the figures shows the mixtures that make up the pigments identified in the mapped areas of the medal, obtained by cross-referencing the Vis-NIR hyperspectral imaging with the FORS and XRF data.

Despite the small size of the detail, the use of a rich palette emerges for the Annunziata medal: gold for the frame and aureoles, lead white for the dove, ochres and red lake for the Virgin's dress, lapis lazuli and lead white for the angel's dress, lapis lazuli for the Virgin's mantle, and finally green earth for the curtain in the background, with the presence of lead white in some areas to lighten the colour.

A comparison between the pigments used in the portrait of Charles Emmanuel I and those used in the portrait of Emmanuel Philibert is shown in figure 16. The figure compares areas with similar pigments: in figure 16A for the portrait of Charles Emmanuel and in figure 16B for the portrait of Emmanuel Philibert, following a SAM analysis of the corresponding hyperspectral images. As can be seen, the use of similar pigment recipes for the execution of the two works is confirmed. In particular, the collars were made with the same white (calcium-based) pigment, as were the armours and gold decorations. The different distribution of colour for the face in the portrait of Emmanuel Philibert shows a greater use of vermillion to create darker shades in certain areas of the forehead and cheeks.

Like figure 16, figure 17 also shows a comparison of the areas with similar pigments used for the realization of the medals in the two works through a SAM analysis of hyperspectral images: figure 17A refers to the portrait of Charles

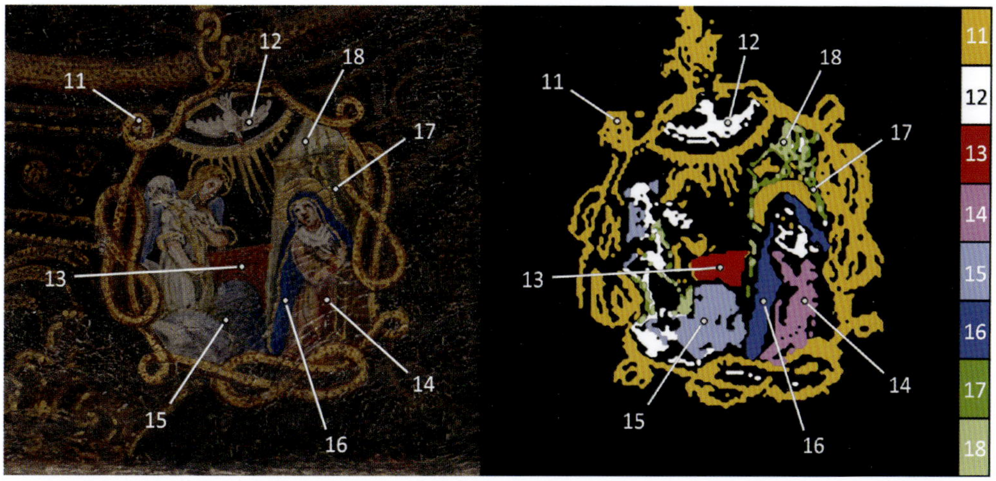

- 11 Gold
- 12 Lead white
- 13 Red ochre
- 14 Red lake
- 15 Lapis lazuli and lead white
- 16 Lapis lazuli
- 17 Green earth
- 18 Green earth and lead white

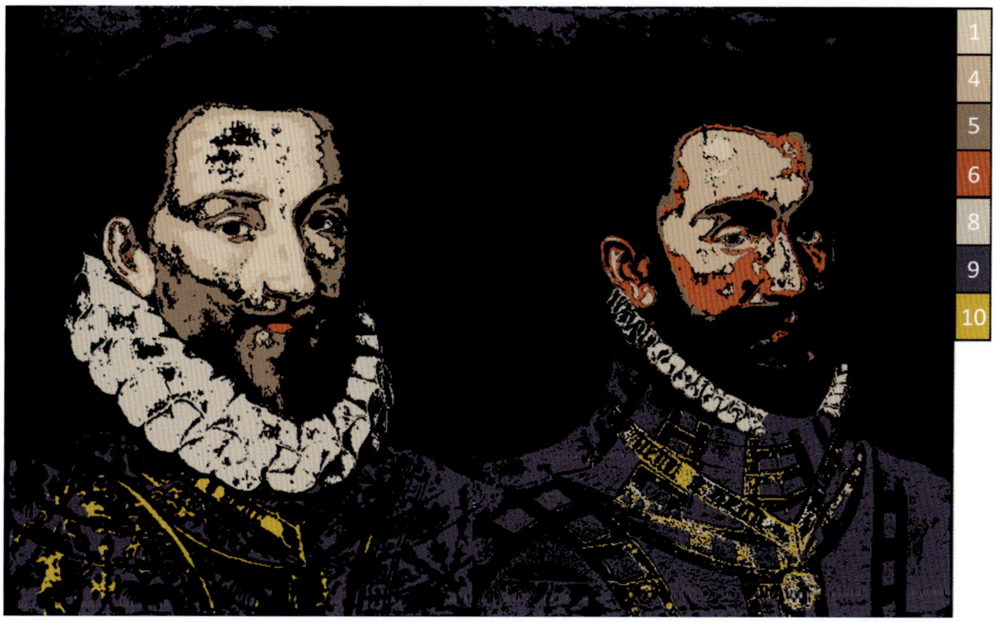

- 1 Calcium white, vermillion and red ochre
- 4 Calcium white and red ochre, with vermillion
- 5 Burnt earth and calcium white
- 6 Vermillion and calcium white
- 8 Calcium white
- 9 Lapis lazuli and lead white, on silver
- 10 Gold

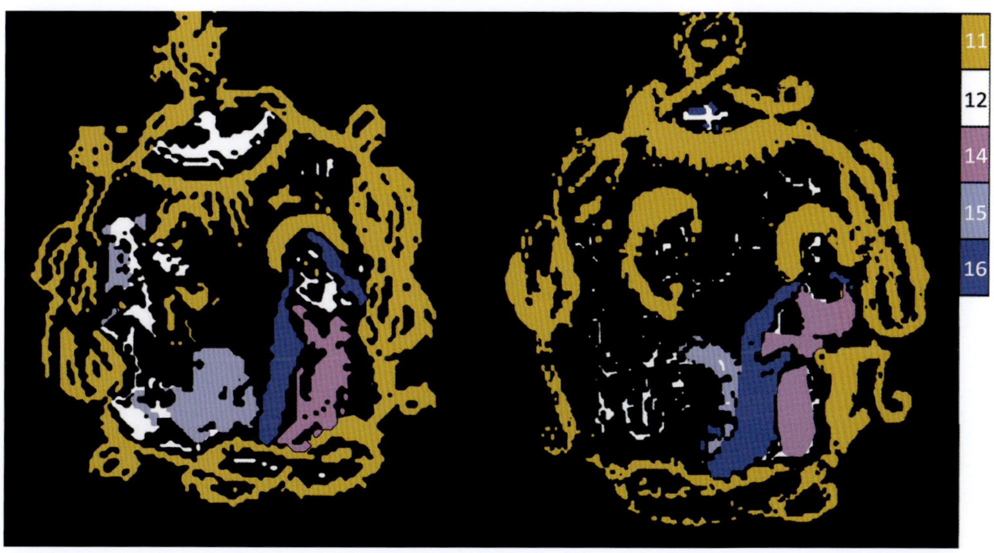

- 11 Gold
- 12 Lead white
- 14 Red lake
- 15 Lapis lazuli and lead white
- 16 Lapis lazuli

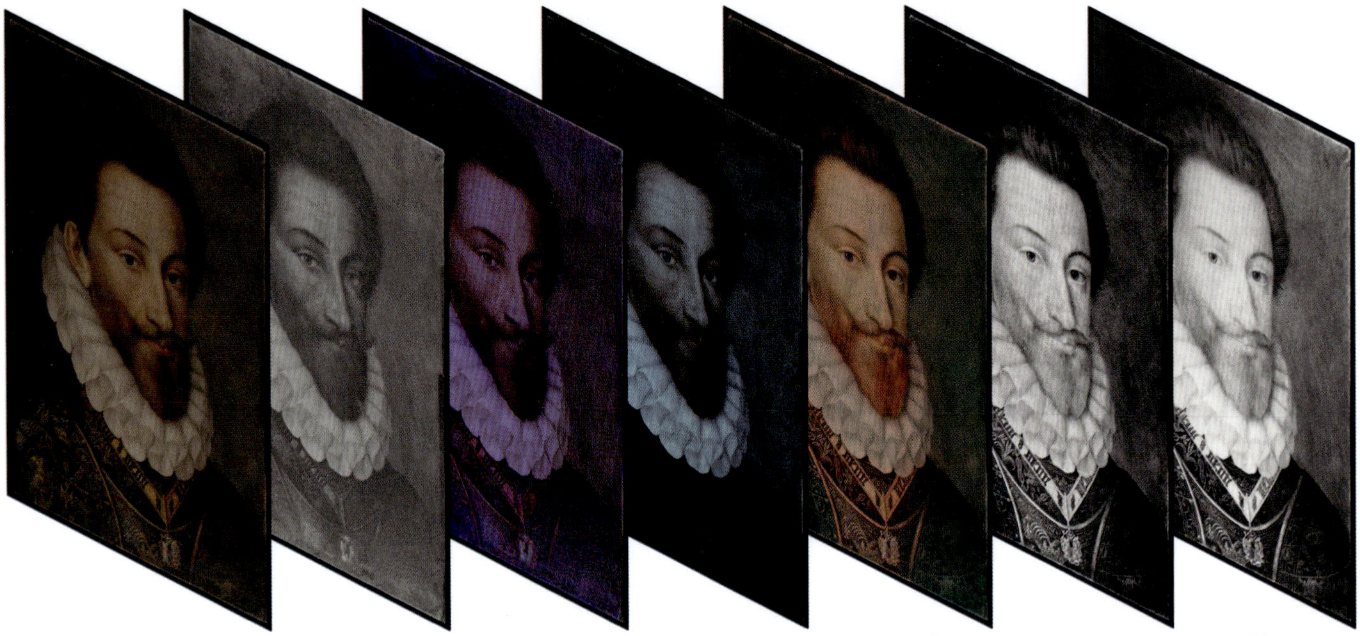

18. Portrait of Charles Emmanuel I, multispectral imaging sequence in visible light (Vis), ultraviolet reflected (UVR), ultraviolet false-colour (UVFC), UV-induced visible fluorescence (UVIF), infrared false-colour (IRFC), infrared between 850 and 1000 nm (IR1) and infrared between 1000 and 1700 nm (IR2)

Emmanuel I, while figure 17B refers to the portrait of Emmanuel Philibert. The comparison shows the use of the same precious pigments such as gold and lapis lazuli, the latter in both paintings with the addition of lead white in order to obtain the lighter blue of the angel's robe.

High-Resolution Multispectral Imaging in UV, Visible and Near Infrared Light

High-resolution imaging provided a series of images in various spectral bands that allowed for the identification of important information on the portrait of Charles Emmanuel I, both from a conservational and historical-artistic point of view. Images of the portrait were acquired in the visible, ultraviolet reflected, UV-induced visible fluorescence spectrum and in two bands of reflectographic infrared (850–1000 nm and 1000–1700 nm), as shown in the sequence in figure 18.

The initial outcome of the results of this analysis is shown in figure 19 in relation to the region of the duke's eyes, where we may appreciate the great ability to detect the very smallest details, such as the peculiar brushstrokes used for the eyes.

Again, in figure 19, in the detail acquired in UV-induced fluorescence, we see the limited previous conservation interventions that demonstrates the extraordinary state of conservation of the painting, even though it was painted on parchment, which is one of the most fragile and perishable materials, subject to particularly high thermo-hygrometric, radiative and mechanical stress. The infrared false-colour images, on the other hand, offer an initial representation of the various painting materials used. For example, the blue of the iris is rendered with the false colour of red, which corresponds to the precious pigment lapis lazuli. In this detail, it is also possible to visually appreciate the thin brush strokes of vermillion, which appear yellow in false colour.

Infrared reflectography, on the other hand, allows us to visualise the extraordinary underdrawing created. From the analysis of the thin, continuous and uniform trace without interruptions, we can hypothesise the use of a tool consisting of a metal point. This material is also the most suitable for working on a rigid support such as parchment.

Figure 20 shows another detail of the work, in correspondence with the lips and nose, where the underdrawing is particularly evident. It can also be noted in the light edges delimiting the parts of the armour between the shoulders and neck. The use of near-infrared imaging technique was essential to highlight its presence, as the pigments hide it to the naked eye in the visible range.

However, in some parts, where the brushstrokes are less dense, the underdrawing can be seen even in the visible image, but only by means of macro- and microphotographs, as illustrated on the left of figure 21 for the detail of the ear, and in figure 22 for the detail of the right eye. In correspondence with these areas, it was also possible to visualise the artist's painting and execution technique using

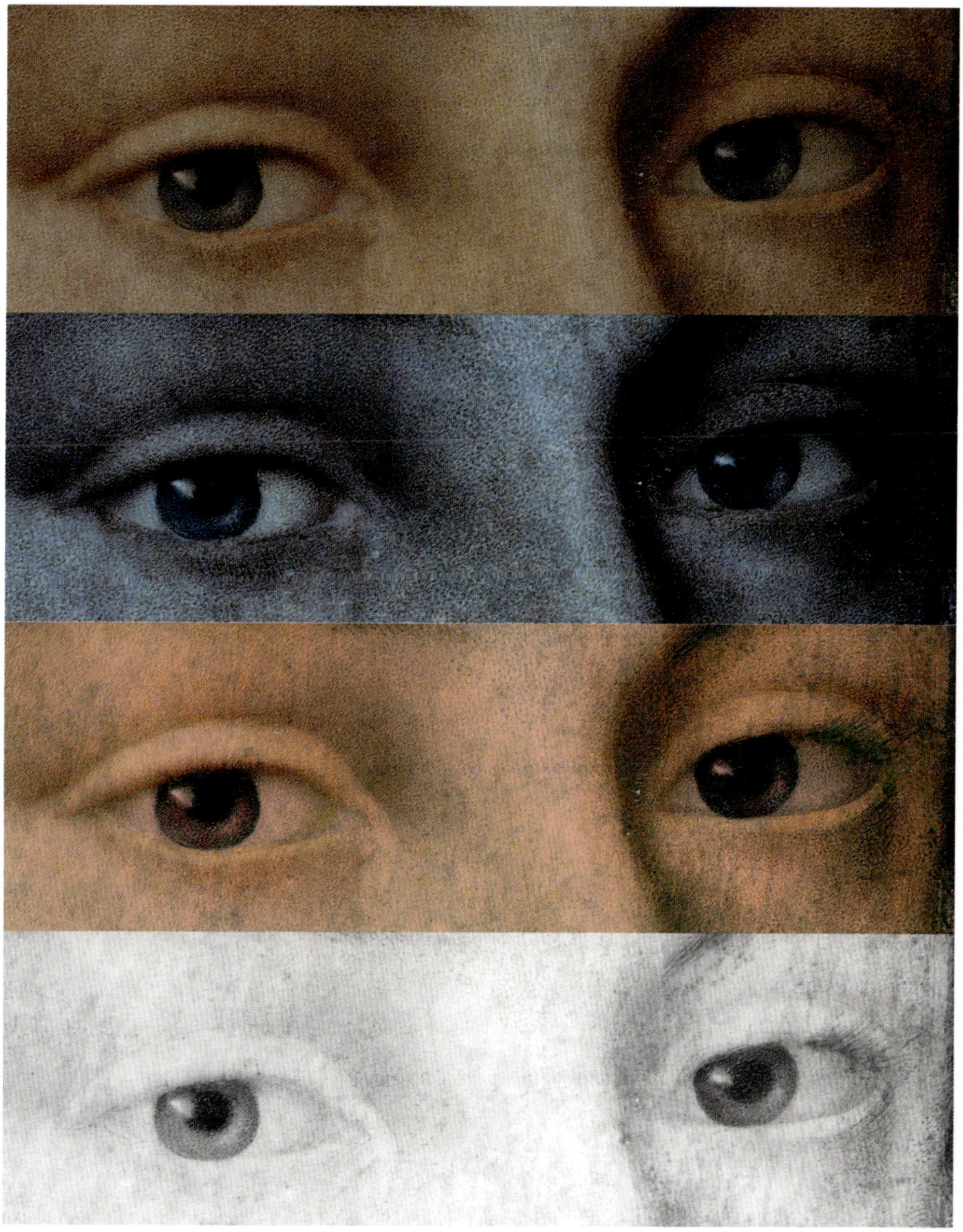

19. Portrait of Charles Emmanuel I, detail of the eyes: sequence of multispectral images in visible light, UV-induced visible fluorescence, infrared false-colour and infrared between 1000 and 1700 nm

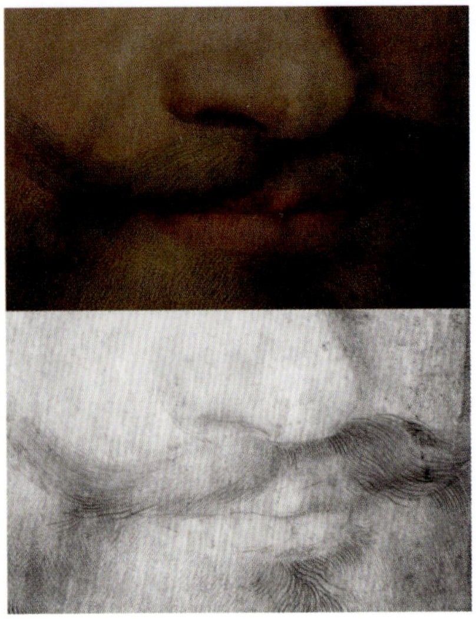

20. Portrait of Charles Emmanuel I, detail of moustache and lips: comparison between visible light and infrared reflectography (1000–1700 nm)

thin, light brushstrokes, as documented by high-magnification images (55x and 220x) shot using polarized microscope. In this group of details, it is in fact possible to see the shape of the brushstrokes in correspondence with the ear and the right eye; in the latter it is possible to see the blue of the lapis lazuli for the iris, the red of the ochre for the skin tones and the vermillion for the lacrimal caruncle. Finally, in infrared reflectography, it is possible to appreciate the underdrawing.

Comparing the portrait of Charles Emmanuel I with the portrait of Emmanuel Philibert, we notice in the latter an underdrawing made with technique and materials similar to the former. For this purpose, we present the comparison with the detail of the ear on the right of figure 21, acquired in the same spectral bands.

Again, with the aim of comparing the two works, the central detail of Emmanuel Philibert's face is shown in infrared reflectography (1000–1700 nm; fig. 23), where it is possible to see the drawing line that defines the eyes, nose, mouth and the contour of the face. Analysing the right eye in particular, we notice in fig. 24 a more descriptive line outlining the anatomy of this part of the face, which is somewhat more detailed than what the artist applied for the portrait of Charles Emmanuel I. In the detail of the neck of the armour (fig. 25), infrared reflectography also shows the presence of underdrawing in correspondence of the gilded decorations. This result proves the presence of an underdrawing also in areas different than the face, probably used by the artist as a precise reference for the graphic positioning of the decorations to be painted.

The pendant with the image of the Santissima Annunziata deserves a special mention, as it reveals even more minute and precious details in the painting (fig. 26). Thanks to the multispectral macro-photographs, it is possible to appreciate the complex execution process. Figure 27 shows the results of the analysis in the various spectral bands, where it is possible to see both the underdrawing, in this case made with a brush and a fluid opaque material in infrared such as a carbon ink, and the distribution of pigments in infrared false-colour and UV-induced fluorescence. The mantle of the Virgin of the Annunciation, as shown by imaging and spectroscopic techniques for the characterisation of pictorial materials (hyperspectral imaging in Vis/NIR, FORS and XRF), is made of lapis lazuli, which appears purplish-red in infrared false-colour, while the red region in the background is made of vermillion – yellow in false colour. The Virgin's red dress, on the other hand, as already indicated by FORS analysis, appears to be made of a lake, with its typical orange

21. Portrait of Charles Emmanuel I (left), detail of ear: microscope photograph and comparison between visible light and infrared images (1000–1700 nm). Portrait of Emmanuel Philibert (right), detail of ear: comparison between visible light and infrared images (1000–1700 nm)

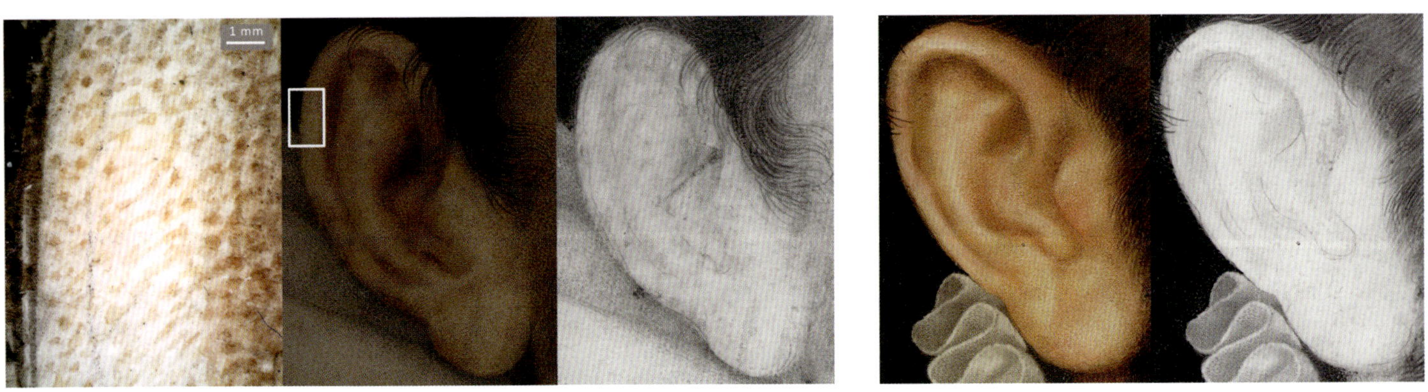

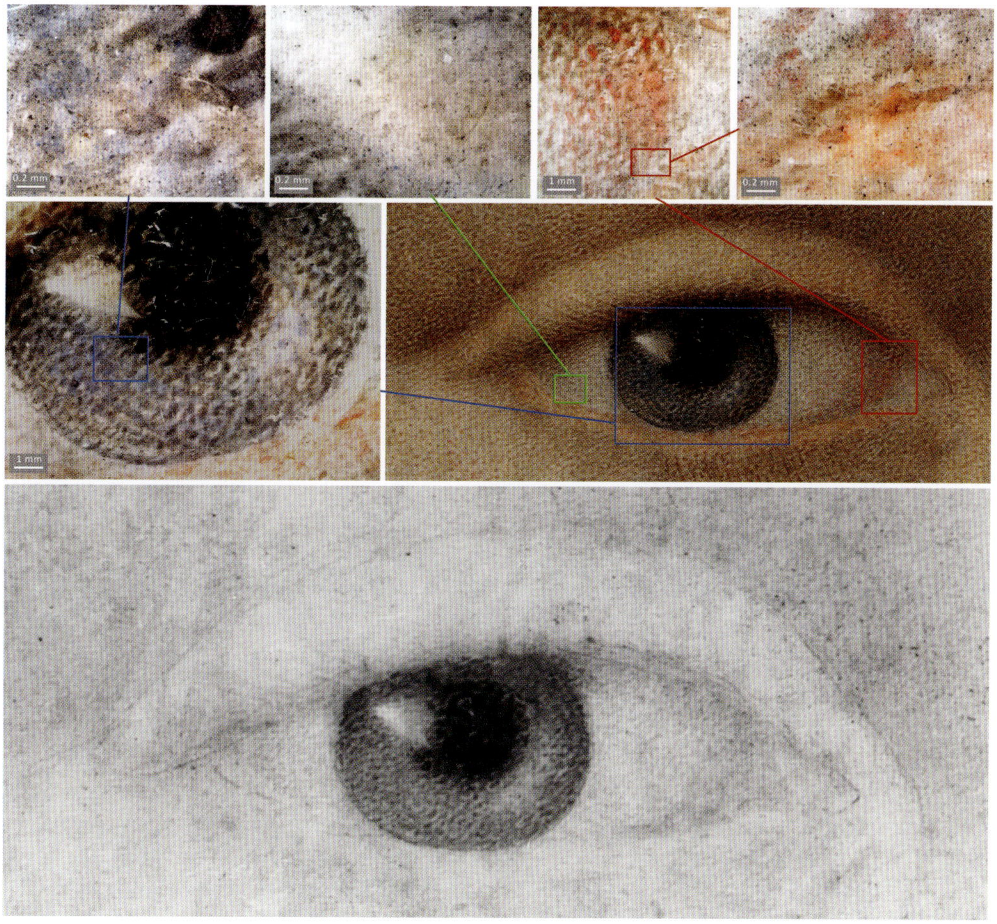

22. Portrait of Charles Emmanuel I, detail of the right eye: microscope photographs at different magnifications (55x and 200x), detail of visible light and infrared photography (1000–1700 nm)

response in UV fluorescence. The comparison with the same decorations in the portrait of Emmanuel Philibert shows more material and pictorial differences both in the visible (fig. 29) and multispectral imaging (fig. 28). It is interesting to note and confirm what the hyperspectral imaging showed for this detail, namely the use of a more limited colour palette. However, as with the pendant in the portrait of Charles Emmanuel I, the investigation shows the use of lapis lazuli pigment and red lake in the Virgin's mantle, of which the former appears purplish-red in infrared false-colour, while the latter seems orangey in UV-induced fluorescence.

Technical Characteristics of the Instrumentation Deployed

Two halogen lamps were used for lighting, max 150 W, with Lenses condenser to optimise the beam on the works and reduce surface heating.

Images in visible light were acquired with Phase One XF camera system with IQ3 digital back and "Trichomatic" detector (100 MP), Schneider Kreuznach 120 mm LS f/4.0 Macro optics.

Microscope images were acquired in visible light with Dino-Lite AM4013MZ digital optical microscope (5 MP with 55x and 220x magnification).

UV-induced visible fluorescence images were acquired using the Phase One XF photo system with IQ3 digital back and "Trichomatic" detector (100 MP), Schneider Kreuznach 120 mm LSf/4.0 Macro optics with low-pass filter at 415 nm to eliminate the visible blue-violet component present in LED emission. Two 3 W

23. Portrait of Emmanuel Philibert, detail of the central part of the face in infrared light

24. Portrait of Emmanuel Philibert, detail of right eye in visible light and infrared reflectography (1000–1700 nm)

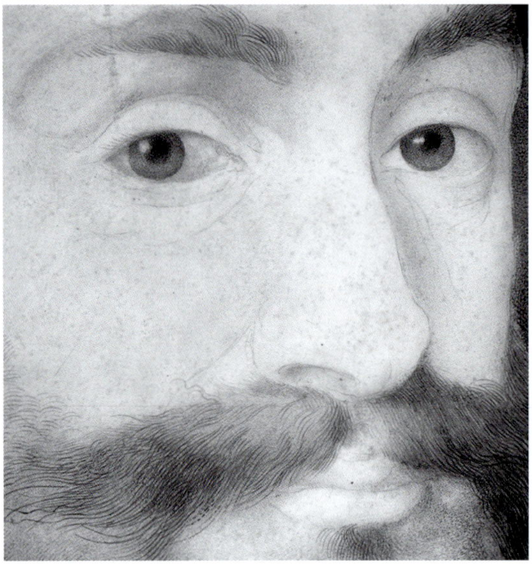

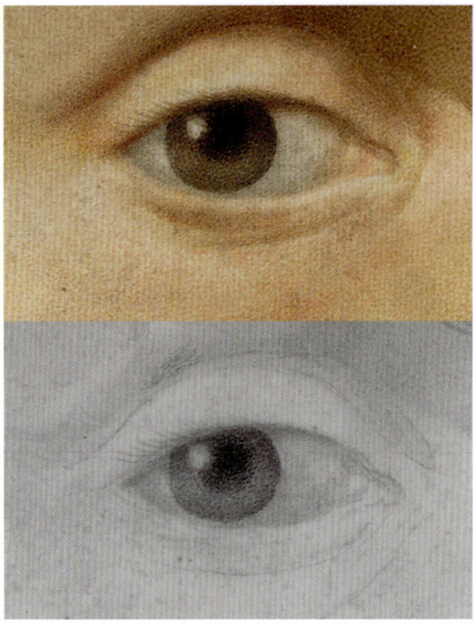

LED lamps (365 nm emission) were used for UV illumination, shielding other light sources.

Infrared reflectography in the 850–1000 nm band images were acquired using the Phase One XF photo system with IQ3 digital back and "Trichomatic" detector (100 MP), modified to acquire images up to 1000 nm and Schneider Kreuznach 120 mm LS f/4.0 Macro optics with high-pass filter in wavelengths to select infrared radiation in the 850–1000 nm range.

Infrared reflectographic images were acquired in the 1000–1700 nm band using a prototype that exploits spherical scanning by means of a motorised head and a solid-state camera with InGaAs detector, detector size 512 × 640 pixels.

All images were acquired with a camera-object distance of 45 cm, obtaining a spatial resolution of 50 points/mm.

Hyperspectral imaging shots in the visible, near-infrared range. Hyperspectral camera (204 bands), 400–1000 nm. These images were taken with a work-subject distance of 50 to 20 cm, resulting in a sampling rate of 0.49 to 0.09 mm^2.

X-ray fluorescence spectroscopy (XRF) was made using Micro-EDXRF Bruker ARTAX 200 with fine focus X-ray source with molybdenum anode, ADC with 4,096 channels, spot variable between 0.65–1.5 mm; anode voltage adjustable to between 0–50 kV, anode current adjustable to between 0–1500 A (max power 50 W).

Fiber optic reflectance spectrophotometry (FORS) was realized using Ocean Optics HR2000+ES spectrophotometer with a spectral range of 200 nm–1100 nm and a spectral resolution of about 2.5 nm, an Ocean Optics HL2000-FHSA halogen lamp and optical fibres with a diameter of 400 µm, in 2 × 45°/0° optical geometry with an ad hoc probe holder.

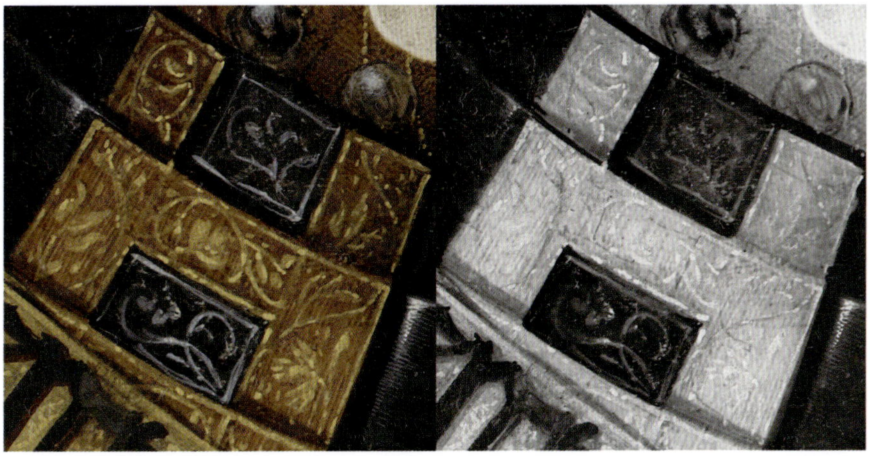

25. Portrait of Emmanuel Philibert, detail in visible light and infrared reflectography (1000–1700 nm) of gilded decorations around the neck of the armour

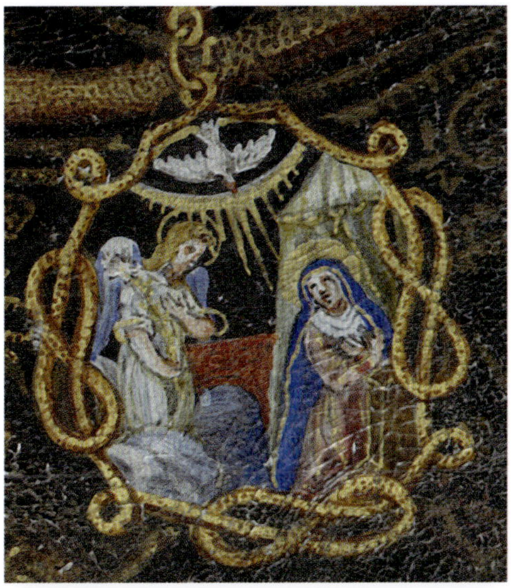

26. Portrait of Charles Emmanuel I, detail of the Annunziata medal in visible light

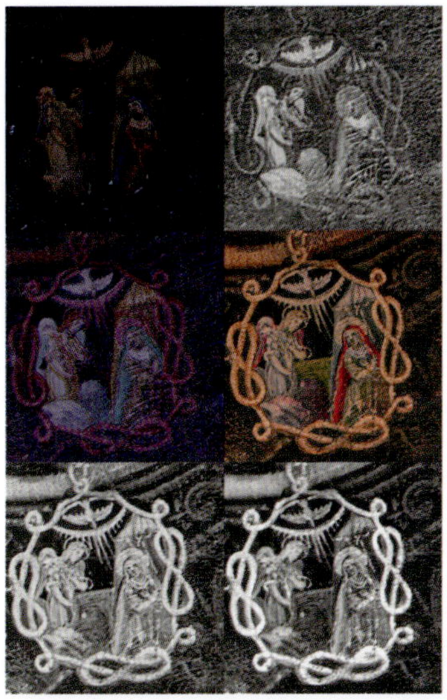

27. Portrait of Charles Emmanuel I, detail of the Annunziata medal: sequence of multispectral images in UV-induced visible fluorescence, ultraviolet reflected, ultraviolet false-colour, infrared false-colour, infrared between 850 and 1000 nm and infrared between 1000 and 1700 nm

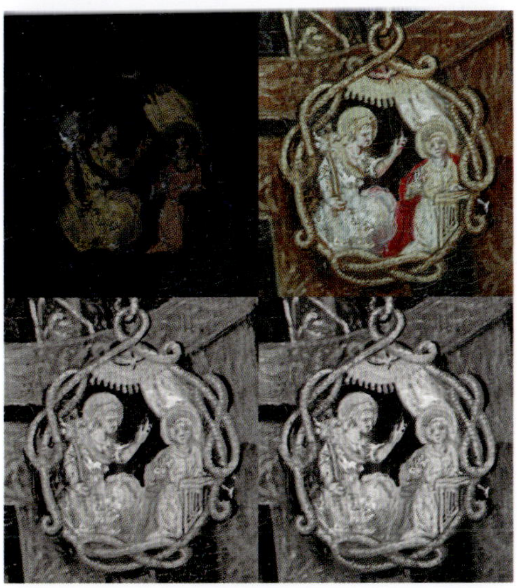

28. Portrait of Emmanuel Philibert, detail of the Annunziata medal: sequence of multispectral images in UV-induced visible fluorescence, infrared false-colour, infrared between 850 and 1000 nm and infrared between 1000 and 1700 nm

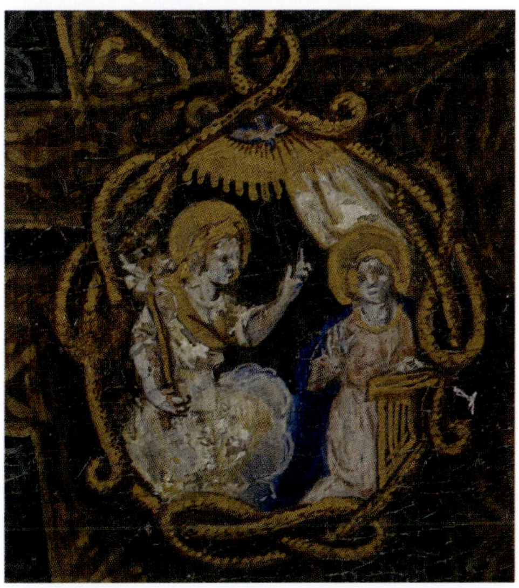

29. Portrait of Emmanuel Philibert, detail of the Annunziata medal in visible light

ARTWORKS IN EXHIBITION

VASARI'S FEMALE ARTISTS

In the first edition (1550) of the *Vite de' più eccellenti pittori scultori et architettori* (*The Lives of the Most Eminent Painters, Sculptors and Architects*), Vasari included just one biography of a woman: the Bolognese sculptress Properzia de' Rossi, who had worked at the male-dominated construction site of the Basilica of San Petronio, where she strenuously defended her own output.

More female artists appear in the second edition of the *Lives* (1568). The epistolary relationship between the Cremonese nobleman Amilcare Anguissola and Michelangelo concerning two esteemed drawings by Amilcare's daughter Sofonisba led Vasari to visit the Anguissola household in 1566. Sofonisba had been at the court of Madrid for years, but he spoke at length with Europa, a painter in her own right, as had also been their sister Lucia. The Arezzo-born biographer then wrote extensive notes on the Anguissola sisters, underlining the exceptional nature of their case, which arose out of their privileged status and which enabled them to study in order to develop their natural inclination.

Other female artists are cited by Vasari as examples of women endowed with natural talent duly fostered through a solid education – at that time, the preserve of children from high-ranking families – encompassing song, music, dance, literature, and painting.

These were all arts practised by the young countess, Irene di Spilimbergo, who according to family legend had been a student of Titian. While her identity as an artist was elusive, her early death at the age of twenty-one made her a favourite subject in the nineteenth century. Equally noble was the Florentine, Lucrezia Quistelli, who had been raised in the ambit of the Medici and was not only a student of Alessandro Allori but also the wife of Count Clemente Pietra; only one of her works has survived into the modern day. For her part, in the early seventeenth century, Claudia del Bufalo, who belonged to a Roman family noted for its interest in antiques, had a sophisticated educational background. In her only signed work to have come down to us, a portrait of her sister, the richness of the jewellery betrays a patent sense of family pride.

Another activity practised by noblewomen was the art of embroidery, considered an introductory art form equivalent to painting: the most renowned embroideress of the late sixteenth century was the Lombard Caterina Cantoni – the wife of a Milanese noble – who was lauded by several European courts. The early seventeenth century saw the emergence of Antonia Pellegrini, a Milanese artist who is celebrated above all for the embroidery she produced for the canonisation of Saint Charles Borromeo.

PROPERZIA DE' ROSSI

Bologna, c. 1490 – Bologna, 1530

Just one biography is dedicated to a female artist in Giorgio Vasari's *Lives*: right from the first edition of 1550, the shining star of Bolognese *schultora* (sculptress) Properzia de' Rossi could not be passed over by the storiographer, who found himself constrained to take account of the unusual female presence on the construction site for the Basilica of San Petronio in Bologna. The historical identity of the sculptress appears to be confirmed by a number of archival documents, which state that she was the daughter of a certain Girolamo de' Rossi, putting her year of birth at around 1490.[1] That she led a rather transgressive life is evinced by the criminal archives, which include information on two trials in which she was embroiled: the first in 1520 for "contested possession" – i.e. for having "tossed", in the company of Anton Galeazzo Malvasia, of whom she was stated to be the "concubine", twenty-four feet of vines and a marasca cheery tree into the vegetable garden of their neighbour, the velvet-maker Francesco da Milano; the second, 1525, for having assaulted and "scratched" the face of the painter Vincenzo Miola alongside the painter Domenico Francia.[2] But the most serious transgression highlighted by Vasari concerns her dedication to the art of sculpture, whereby she "[dared to put her] tender and lily-white hands [...] between the roughness of marble and the harshness of iron", as the historiographer comments.[3] Incredible audacity, then, led Properzia to enter the city's greatest construction site – one that was extremely prestigious in the Europe of the time, given that Bologna was the second most important city in the Papal States – on which de' Rossi (referred to as "de Rubeis") is documented as having spent the period between January 1525 and July 1526.[4] The cash books and ledgers of the *Fabbriceria* (administrative body) record payments to the so-called *madona* Properzia for the creation of sibyls, angels and "one picture" intended for the portals of the facade. The vagueness of the notes and the collective nature of the activities of the artists at San Petronio make it difficult to identify which reliefs are by the sculptress out of the numerous examples that come thick and fast in the arches of the side doors of the church.[5] Alongside the work she did in translating models supplied by colleagues (Bernardino da Carrara, Niccolò Tribolo, Alfonso Lombardi), Properzia also accumulated an oeuvre of reliefs that she conceived and produced directly. The "one picture" entirely of her own invention (1526), cited in the archive documents of the *Fabbriceria*, is a panel with *Joseph Tempted by Potiphar's Wife* (Bologna, Basilica of San Petronio, museum); it is the only marble piece that can be attributed with any certainty to the sculptress thanks to Vasari's biography, according to which Properzia is said to have "expressed" the "most burning passion" she felt for a young man who did not reciprocate her affections, by casting herself as the main character in the Bible story.[6] In the "picture" of the chaste Joseph, the sculptress shows herself to have been a shrewd interpreter of the "modern manner", reworking the styles of Giulio Romano, Michelangelo, Alfonso Lombardi and Correggio with intelligence and originality, evoking Parmigianino in the process.[7]

In addition to her output as a sculptress at San Petronio – other works were dubiously attributed to her on a stylistic basis, such as *Potiphar's Wife Accuses Joseph* in the museum of the Basilica,[8] and a *Sibyl* in the right-hand portal[9] – it was once again Vasari who bore witness to Properzia's ability both in the unusual technique of *intaglio* in miniatures,[10] and in the graphic arts; her copper etchings have not thus far been traced.

Properzia's tumultuous life had a tragic epilogue: in the hospital of San Giobbe, where those suffering from syphilis were treated, she wrote her will in April 1529.[11] She died in 1530, and was buried in the *Ospedale della Morte*, before Pope Clement VII, in the city for the coronation of Charles V and "anxious to see her", had the opportunity to meet her.[12]

Irene Graziani

1 Fortunati, Graziani 2008, pp. 76, 78 note 2; Giansante 2017.
2 Mazzoni Toselli 1868, II, pp. 66–159.
3 Vasari 1550, English ed. 1998, p. 340.
4 Lullini, in Fortunati, Graziani 2008, pp. 80–83.
5 Fortunati 1981; Brugnoli 1984; Fortunati 2008.
6 Vasari 1550, English ed. 1998, p. 341.
7 Fortunati 2008, p. 21.
8 Fortunati 2008, pp. 23–24.
9 Sarchi 2015, p. 96.
10 Graziani 2008b.
11 Supino 1914, p. 106, no. 82.
12 Vasari 1550, English ed. 1998, p. 341.

1.1
Properzia de' Rossi
Crest of the Grassi Family
c. 1520
Silver filigree, cast sections, rock crystal, boxwood, stones, 39 × 22 cm
Bologna, Museo Civico Medievale, inv. 2135

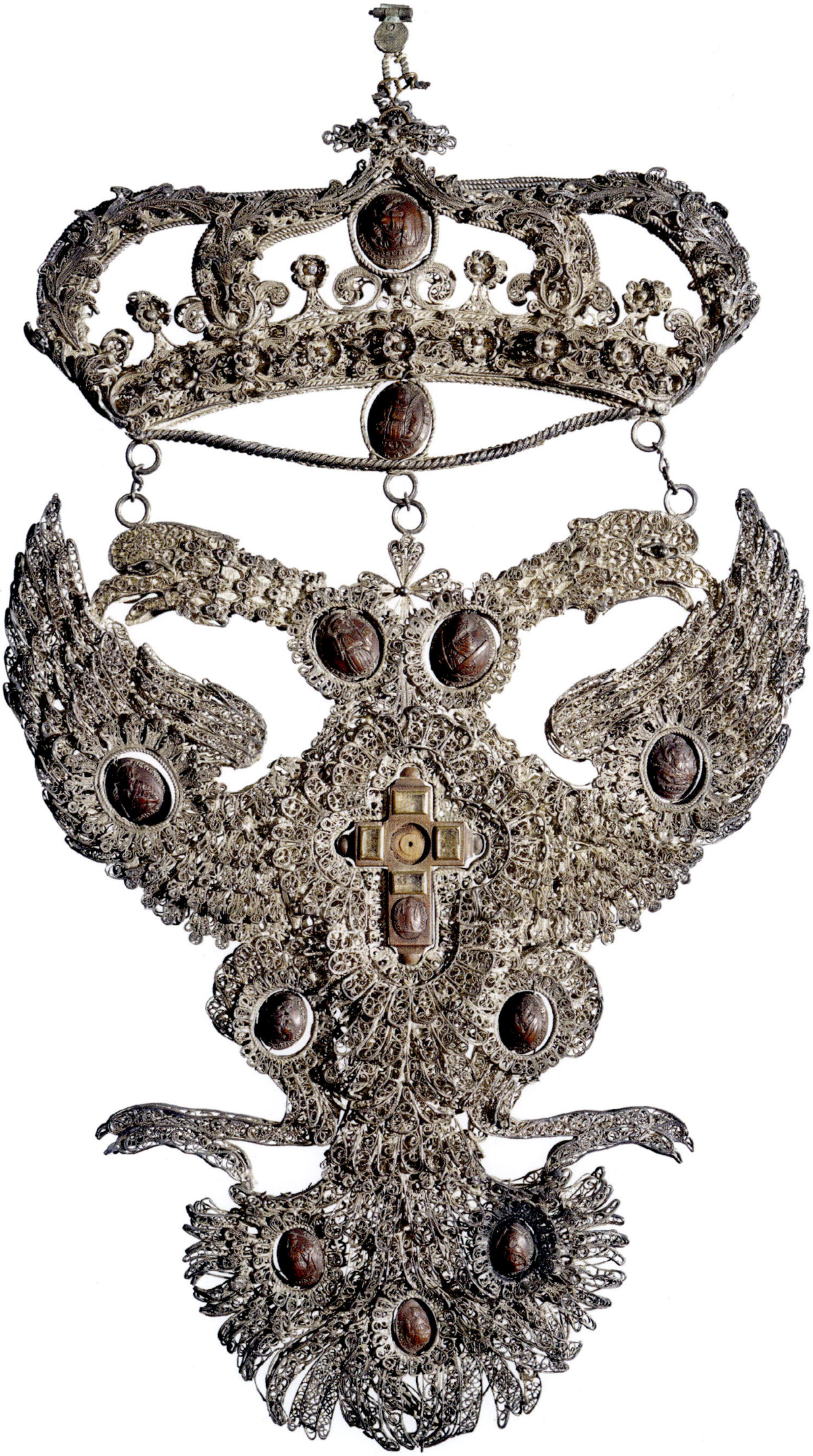

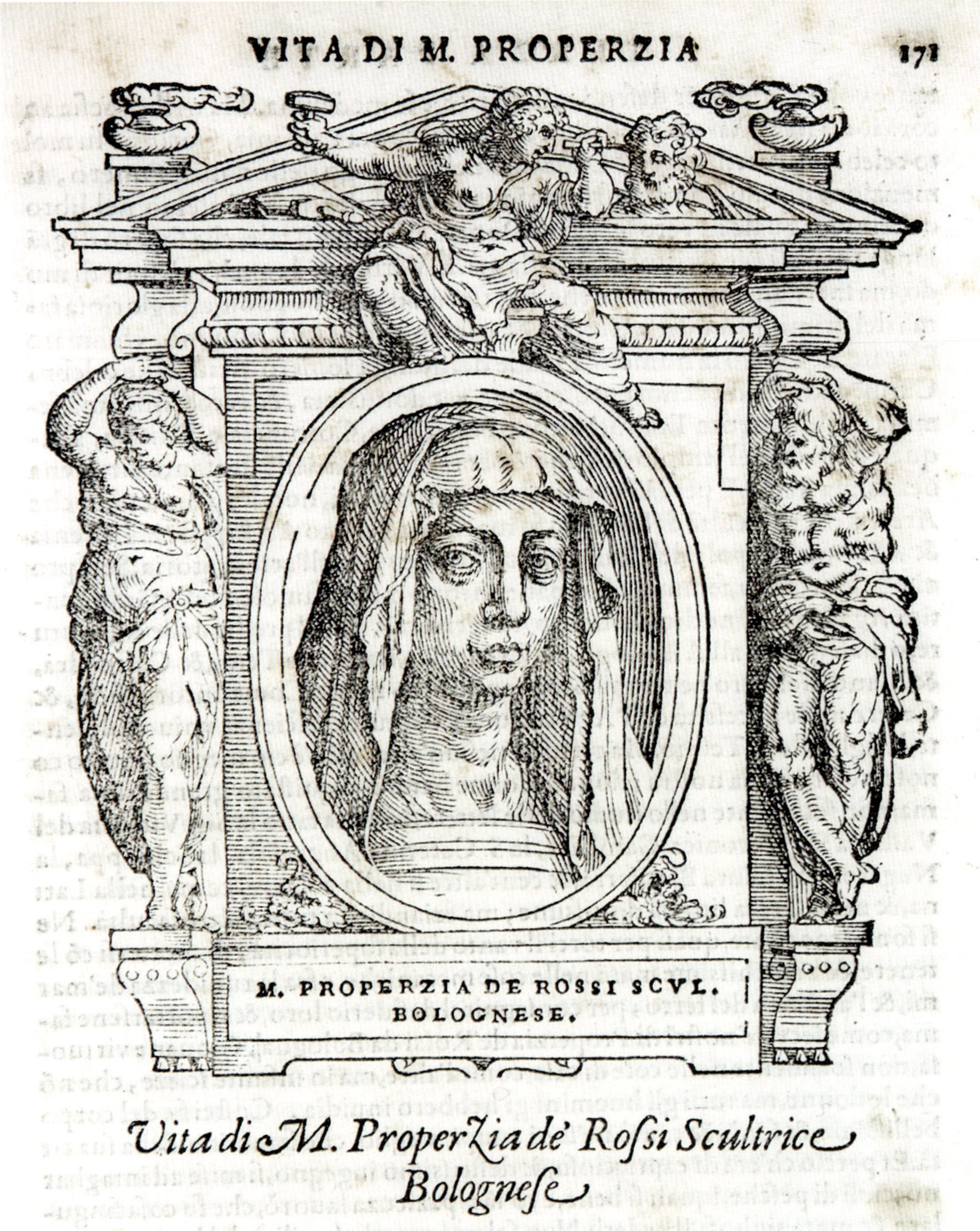
VITA DI M. PROPERZIA 171

M. PROPERZIA DE ROSSI SCVL.
BOLOGNESE.

Vita di M. Properzia de' Rossi Scultrice Bolognese

1.2
Giorgio Vasari
Le vite de' più eccellenti pittori scultori e architettori
In Fiorenza: appresso i Giunti, 1568, vol. 3
Printed book with etchings, 245 × 175 mm
Milan, Pinacoteca di Brera and Biblioteca Nazionale Braidense, ZNN.IV.41

1.3
Isaac Bullart
Academie des sciences et des arts, contenant les vies, & les éloges historiques des hommes illustres, qui ont excellé en ces professions depuis environ quatre siècles
Amsterdam: Elzevier, 1682
Printed book with etchings, 345 × 220 mm
Rome, Biblioteca Angelica, L.22.42

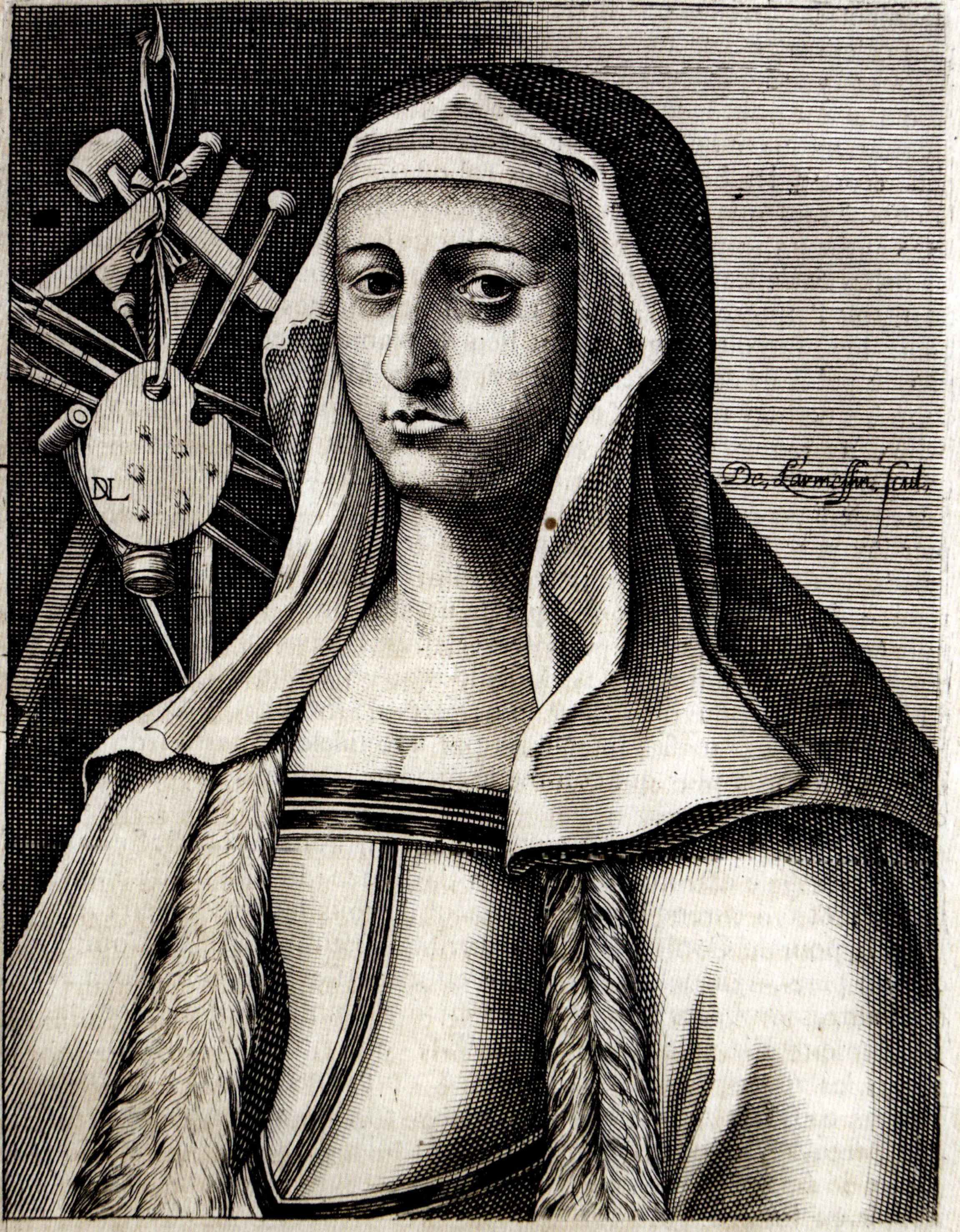

PROPERTIA, DE, ROSSI, SCVLT,

PROPERTIA DE ROSSI.

SOFONISBA ANGUISSOLA

Cremona, c. 1532/1535 – Palermo, 1625

The first of seven children, Sofonisba was born in Cremona around 1532.[1] As a daughter of the noble decurion Amilcare Anguissola and Bianca Ponzoni, she was educated in the arts, literature and painting along with her sisters.[2] She trained under Bernardino Campi (1522–1591) between 1546 and 1549, and even though it is not entirely clear where she served her apprenticeship, it was probably in the Anguissola home.

In 1549, Sofonisba became a student of Bernardino Gatti (1495/1496–1576), completing her artistic education, which had been concerned mostly with portraiture and small devotional works.[3] In the meantime, her father Amilcare created a rich network with the Italian courts, in order to promote her artistic talents sending out of self-portraits.[4] Her father's strategies brought her to being chosen in 1559 as a lady-in-waiting and painting teacher of Elisabeth of Valois, third wife of Philip II of Spain.[5] The letters addressed to the courts of Mantua,[6] Ferrara[7] and Parma,[8] along with her portraits, bear witness to Sofonisba's skill in constructing a public image for herself, demonstrating that she was in possession of a comprehensive education, and was capable of reading, writing and playing an instrument, as well as painting,[9] on the model proposed by Baldassarre Castiglione.

Amilcare addressed two letters to King Philip,[10] in which he identified the Duke of Alba, Fernando Álvarez de Toledo, the Duke of Sessa, Gonzalo Fernández de Córdoba, and Count Broccardo Persico – recently recognised as a relative of Sofonisba[11] – as being responsible for calling Sofonisba to the court. The Anguissola family had also already developed relations with the Habsburgs over previous years, and the court itself was populated by numerous members of the Cremonese family.[12]

Sofonisba left Lombardy in the autumn of 1559, heading for Guadalajara, accompanied by two of her relatives – as De Ribera notes –, probably Count Broccardo Persico[13] and Ferrante Gonzaga di Castiglione.[14] Having reached the court of Spain as a lady-in-waiting to the Queen, she continued to paint: Vasari recalls the portrait of Joanna of Austria, sister of Philip II, for Pope Pius IV and the portrait of Elisabeth of Valois.[15]

The attribution of the court portraits remains an open issue: a number of scholars have tried to discern the hand of Sofonisba in paintings previously attributed to Alonso Sánchez Coello, without reaching a unanimous agreement, both due to the works not being signed and due to the absence of documentation,[16] although recent technical and radiographical analyses have endeavoured to shed light on Sofonisba's pictorial oeuvre.[17]

In 1568, Elisabeth of Valois died, signalling the dissolution of the Household of the Queen, to which Sofonisba belonged.[18] At this point, it seems that the artist entered the service of the Household of the Infantas, Isabella Clara Eugenia and Catalina Micaela, as she awaited marriage to a man worthy of her standing. After various failed attempts,[19] in May 1573 "Lady Sofonisba finally saw that day, so desired by her, of her blessed wedding"[20] and got married to the Sicilian nobleman Fabrizio Moncada. Sofonisba would live for five years between Palermo and Paternò. In relation to her artistic output during this period, it is probable that her works came to be scattered for the most part across private collections, given that she remained artistically active. In this regard, we should cite the *Madonna dell'Itria* (cat. 1.12), the authorship of which is confirmed by a document discovered in the Catania archive.[21]

Unfortunately, it seems that her dowry and the annual pension given to her by the king, including the income from customs duties, were insufficient. Indeed, driven by the necessity, in 1578 Fabrizio Moncada set out to reach the court of Philip II with the intention of requesting help on matters of inheritance. Sadly, following an attack launched by pirates off Capri, Moncada drowned.[22] Sofonisba, now a widow, had to face numerous expenses and attempted to regain her dowry. Since her father Amilcare had been dead for a few years, it was her brother Asdrubale who came to Sicily to help her, taking on power of attorney for his sister and administering her finances.

The two set sail in Palermo around 1580 on the *Patrona*, captained by Orazio Lomellini and headed for Genoa. Lomellini was the illegitimate son of a noble Genoese family, and it was easy to imagine that he and the painter already knew each other, given that within a short time they were married without the consent of

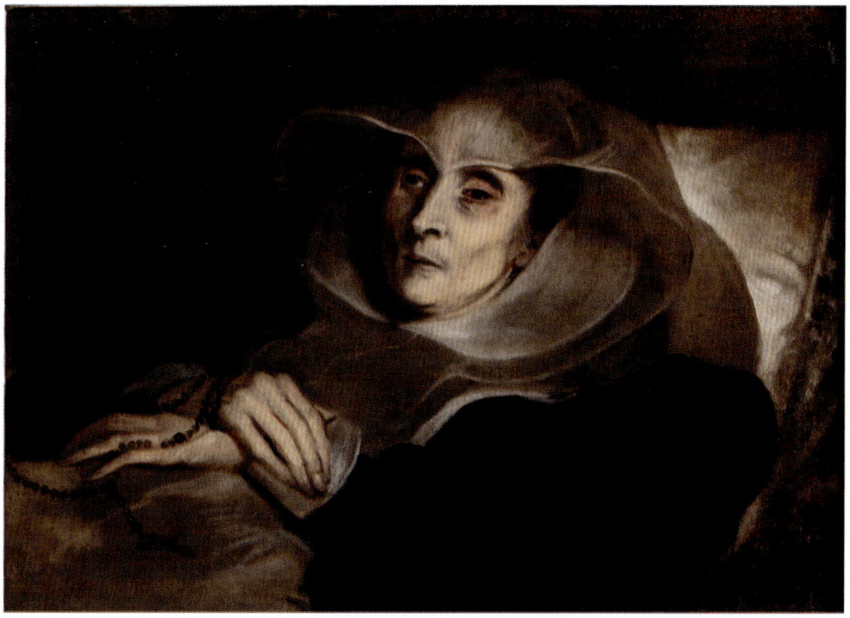

1.4
Anthony van Dyck (?)
Sofonisba Anguissola on her Deathbed
c. 1625
Oil on canvas, 52 × 72 cm
Turin, Musei Reali – Galleria Sabauda, inv. 304, cat. 686

Sofonisba's brother or even that of the King of Spain.[23] Noteworthy in this regard is her correspondence with the Grand Duke of Tuscany, Francesco I de' Medici, who was well-known at the court of Spain and who, having been informed in December 1579 that Sofonisba wanted to marry "against her brother's wishes",[24] strove to dissuade her from doing so.[25] But Sofonisba, by now married to Lomellini, responded that "the letter from Your Most Serene Highness arrived late", commenting moreover that "marriages are made in heaven and then on earth".[26]

After a year or so in Pisa, Sofonisba moved with her husband to Genoa, staying in various aristocratic residences.[27] The city was the base for several of the most important painters of the time, including Luca Cambiaso, Giovan Battista Castello and Pietro Francesco Piola, who not only influenced Sofonisba's art but also established relationships with her.[28] Myriad figures associated with the court of Spain had to pass through Genoa, including Philip II's sister Maria of Austria, and the Infantas. It is also important to bear in mind the period that Sofonisba spent at the court of Turin, after the marriage of the Infanta Catalina Micaela to Charles Emmanuel I, Duke of Savoy, in 1585.

Sofonisba and Orazio, as a result of the latter's trading operations, left Genoa in 1615 to return to Palermo.[29] We do not have any validated information about the artist's production in this period, but we do know that she was gradually losing her sight.[30] The young Anthony van Dyck, having made his way to Palermo in 1624, depicted Sofonisba in a page of his travel diary. During their meeting, Sofonisba gave him "valuable information" on the practice of painting, and advised him "not to place the lamp too high, so that the shadows of the wrinkles do not become too large".[31]

Shortly after, on 16 November 1625, Sofonisba died. Her husband Orazio had a stone laid to commemorate forever the virtues of his late wife in the church of San Giorgio dei Genovesi in Palermo.[32]

Cecilia Gamberini

[1] Bonetti 1928, p. 289.
[2] Gilardi 1994.
[3] Bora 1994.
[4] Ghirardi 1994a.
[5] Sacchi 1988, pp. 73–76.
[6] Tellini Perina 1992.
[7] Venturi 1885.
[8] Caro 1574–1575, II, pp. 182–183.
[9] Ghirardi 1994a.
[10] Archivo General de Simancas, Estado-Milan, leg. 1210, fol. 190, fol. 153; 6 September 1559, 26 November 1559, cit. in Sacchi 1988, pp. 77–78, 87.
[11] Pérez de Tudela 2019, p. 67, no. 29.
[12] Gamberini 2016, pp. 32–33.
[13] De Ribera 1609, pp. 313–316.
[14] Ferrante Gonzaga would lead the dances during the celebrations of the wedding of Philip II of Spain and Elisabeth of Valois in 1560, dancing the galliard with Sofonisba; Archivio di Stato di Mantova, Gonzaga, Esteri 590, 29 January 1560, cit. in Justi 1909, p. 12; Gamberini 2016.
[15] Vasari 1568, ed. 1878–1885, VI, pp. 498–502.
[16] Kusche 1989; Pinessi 1998, pp. 43–70.
[17] Jover de Celis, Gayo García, Carcelén 2019.
[18] Archivio di Stato di Firenze (from now on: ASFi), Ducato di Urbino, cl. I, Division G, string 184, fol. 54. Gronau 1936, pp. 268-269.
[19] Kusche 1989, p. 413.
[20] ASFi, Ducato di Urbino, cl. I, Division G, string 184, fol. 619; Gronau 1936, pp. 268–269. Toledo, Archivo Histórico Nacional, Sección Nobleza, CP.410, D.8, in Gamberini 2018, p. 197; Gronau 1936, p. 269.
[21] Iozzia 2012, pp. 12–15; Nicotra 2019.
[22] Sacchi 1994b, pp. 153–159.
[23] Soprani 1674, I, pp. 414–415.
[24] ASFi, Mediceo del Principato 252, fol. 104*v*–105, 24 December 1579. Perlingieri 1992, p. 170.
[25] Sacchi 1994d, p. 385.
[26] ASFi, Mediceo del Principato 730, fol. 120*r-v*, 27 December 1579. Perlingieri 1992, p. 170.
[27] Barone 2019, pp. 147–154.
[28] Sacchi 1994a, p. 73.
[29] Sacchi 1994b, p. 153.
[30] Sacchi 1994a, p. 74.
[31] Anthony van Dyck, *Taccuino italiano*, 1621–1627, London, British Museum, acc.no. 1957, 1214.207.110: "Portrait of Mrs. Sofonisba Anguissola, painter, painted from life in Palermo in the year 1624 on the 12th day of July: she was aged 96 having her memory and mind still very much alive, very polite and although due to her advanced age her eyesight was failing, she still wished to place the pictures before her and with great effort placing her nose above the picture succeeded in discerning part of it and still received great pleasure in that way, making the portrait of herself, she gave me various recommendations telling me not to place the lamp too high, so that the shadows of the wrinkles of her old age would not become too large, offering him useful advice and stating that she realised she was a naturally talented painter and the greatest sorrow she felt was from her lack of sight which prevented her from painting any more; her hand was still steady without the slightest tremble". See Tramelli 2016.
[32] Sacchi 1994a, p. 74.

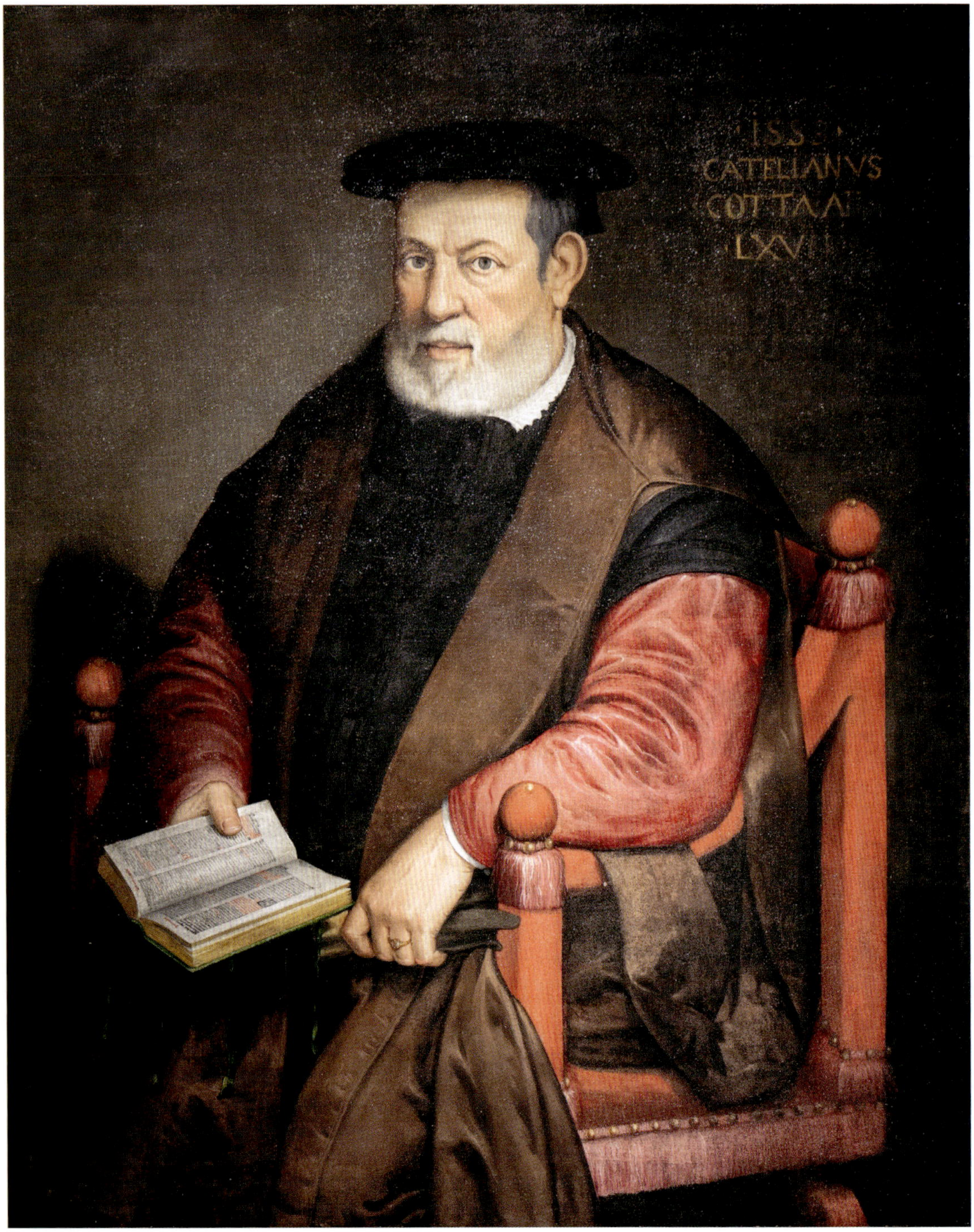

1.5
Bernardino Campi
Portrait of Catellano Cotta
1553
Oil on canvas, 103.5 × 82.5 cm
Cremona, Museo Civico
Ala Ponzone, inv. 118

1.6
Sofonisba Anguissola
Portrait of Lateran Canon
1556
Oil on canvas, 57 × 53 cm
Brescia, Pinacoteca Tosio
Martinengo, inv. DI137

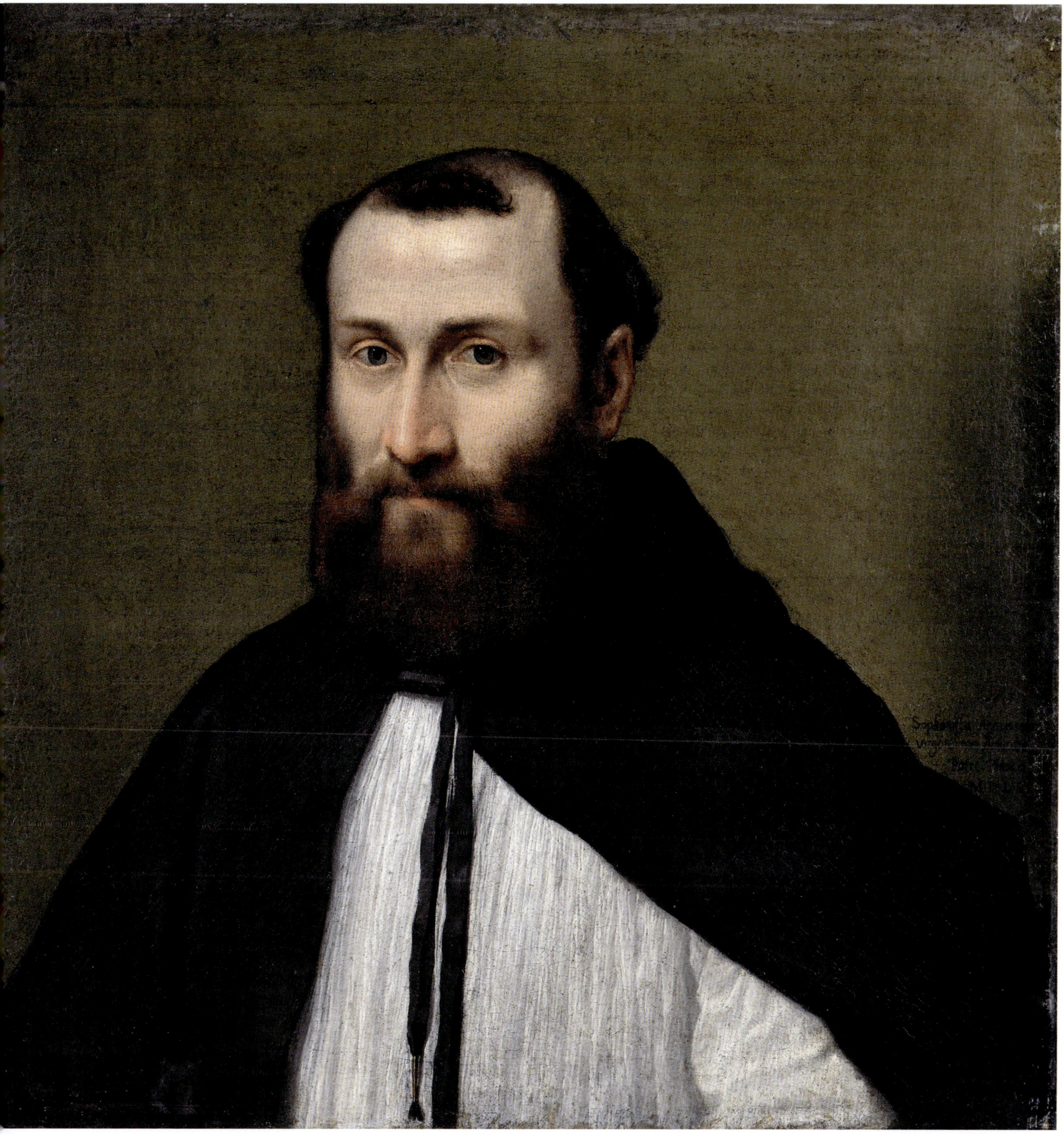

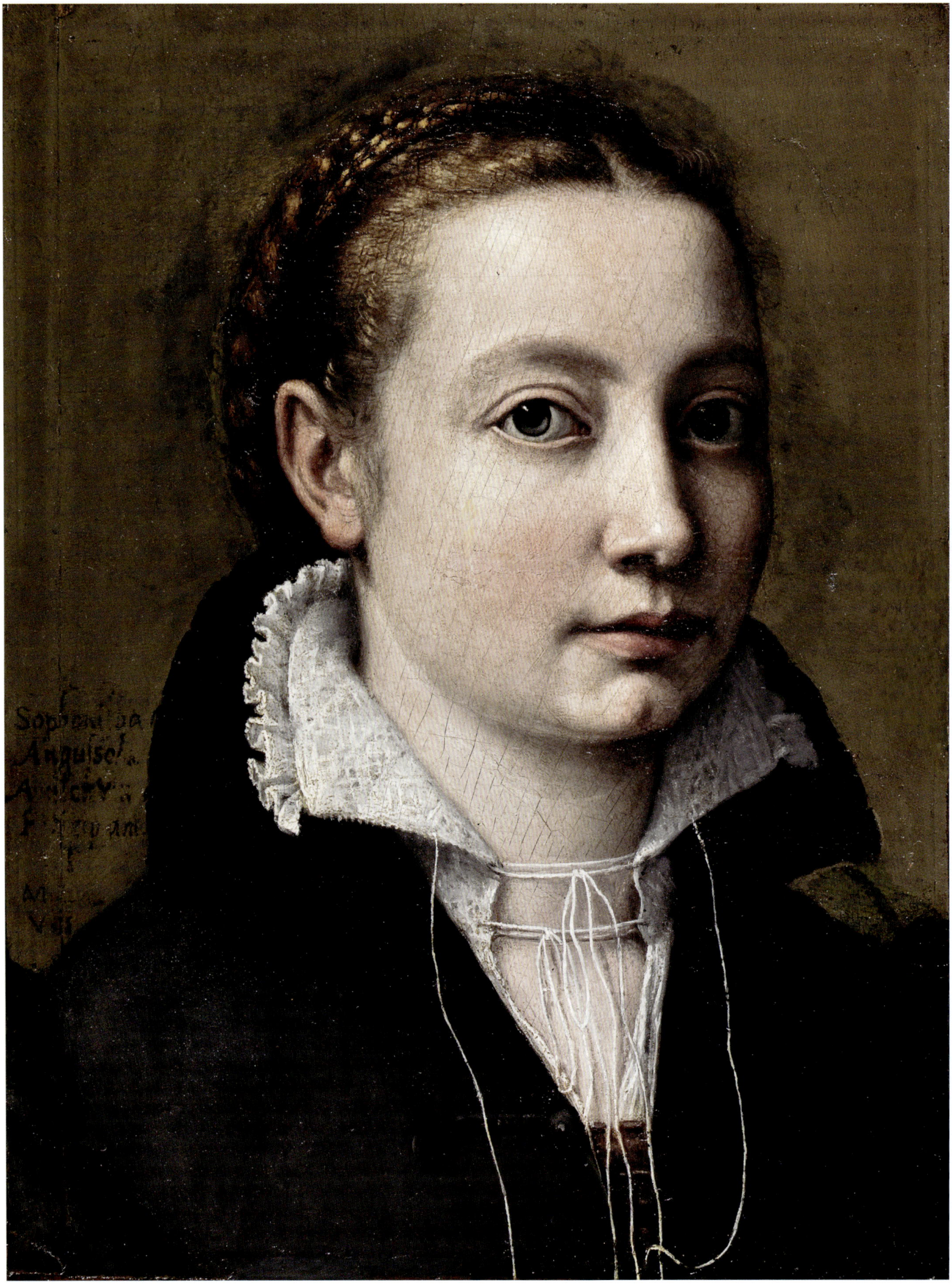

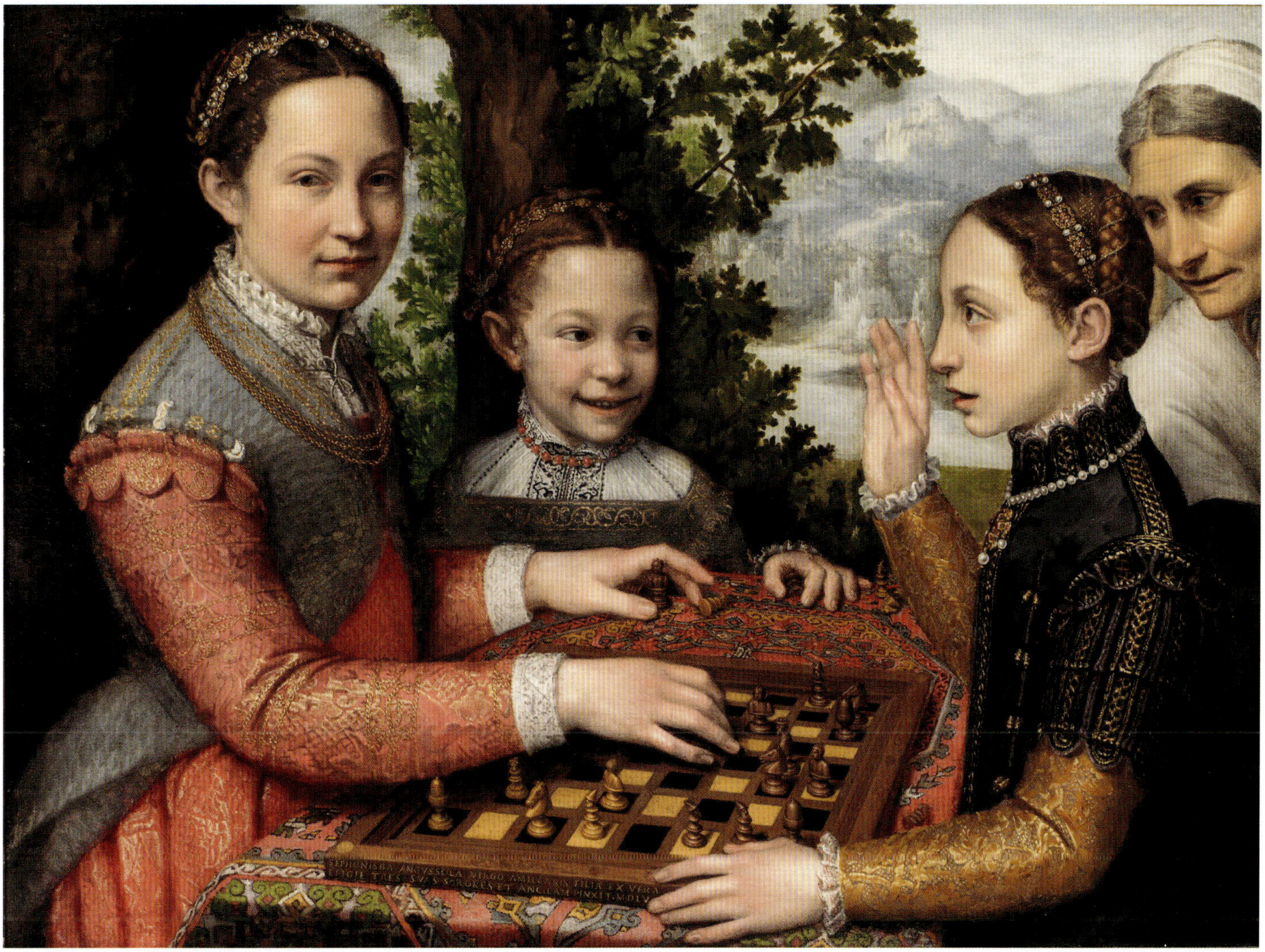

1.7
Sofonisba Anguissola
Self-Portrait
1558
Oil on paper mounted on panel, 26.6 × 19.3 cm
Rome, Principi Colonna collection, fidecommissum no. 578

1.8
Sofonisba Anguissola
Chess Game
1555
Oil on canvas, 70 × 94 cm
Poznań (Poland), Fundacja im. Raczyński przy Muzeum Narodowym w Poznaniu, MNP FR 434

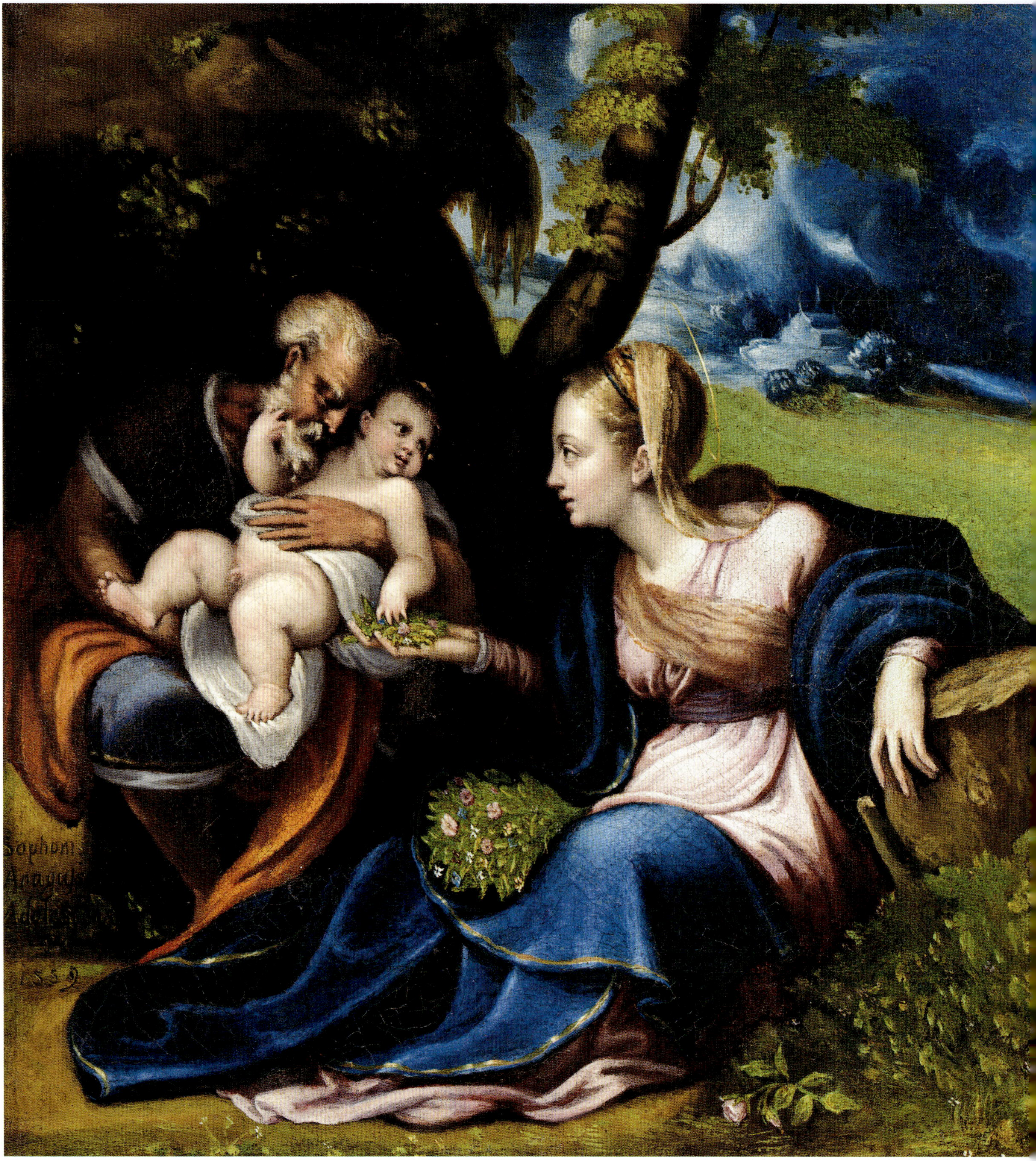
Sophonis
1559

1.9
Sofonisba Anguissola
Holy Family
1559
Oil on canvas, 36.7 × 31.9 cm
Bergamo, Accademia Carrara,
inv. 58MR00050

1.10
Sofonisba Anguissola
Pietà
1574–1585
Oil on panel, 46.5 × 32.5 cm
Milan, Pinacoteca di Brera,
inv. Reg. Cron. 1283

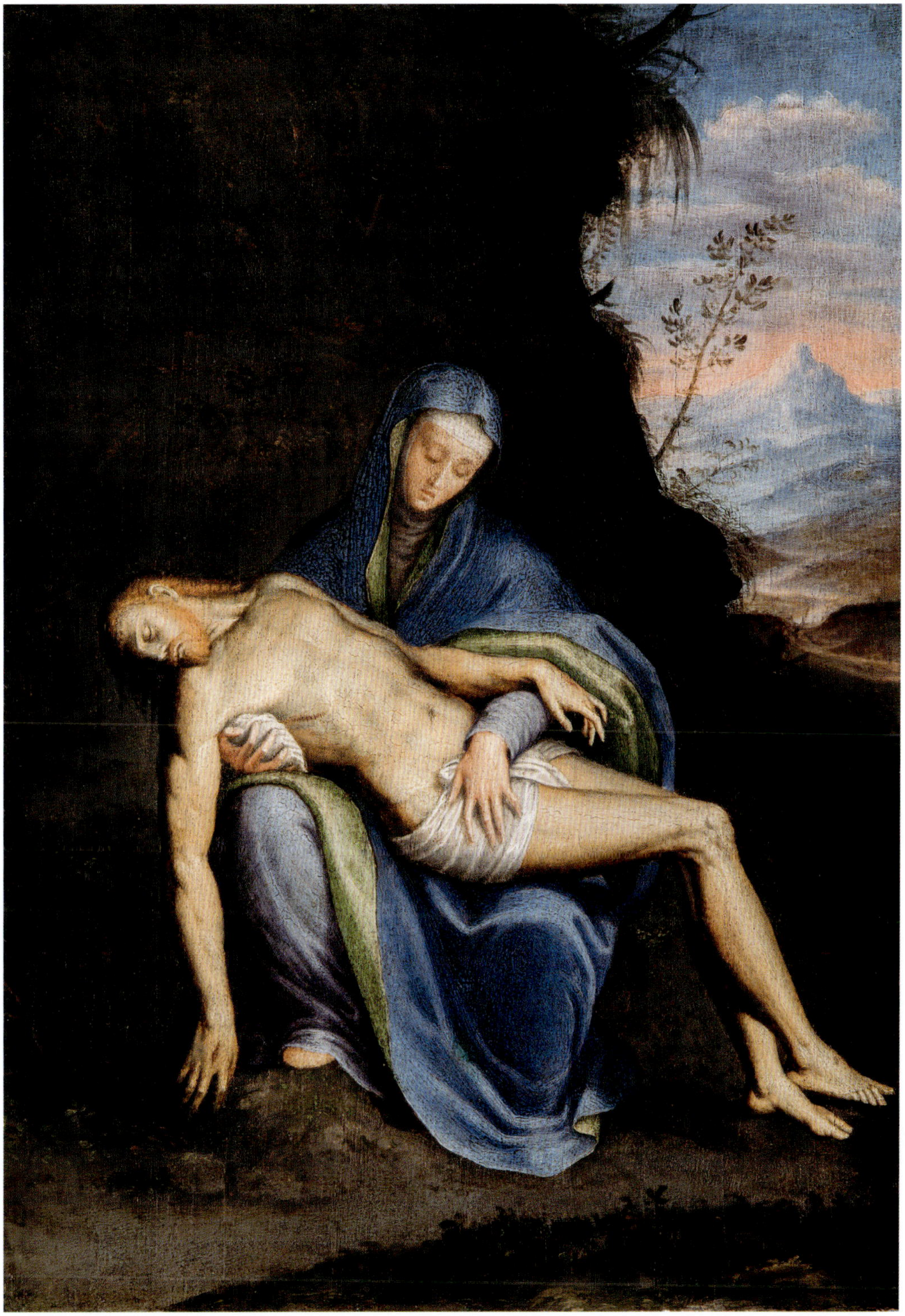

1.11
Sofonisba Anguissola
Portrait of the Infanta
Isabella Clara Eugenia
c. 1573
Oil on canvas, 57 × 48.5 cm
Turin, Musei Reali – Galleria
Sabauda, inv. 755, cat. 328

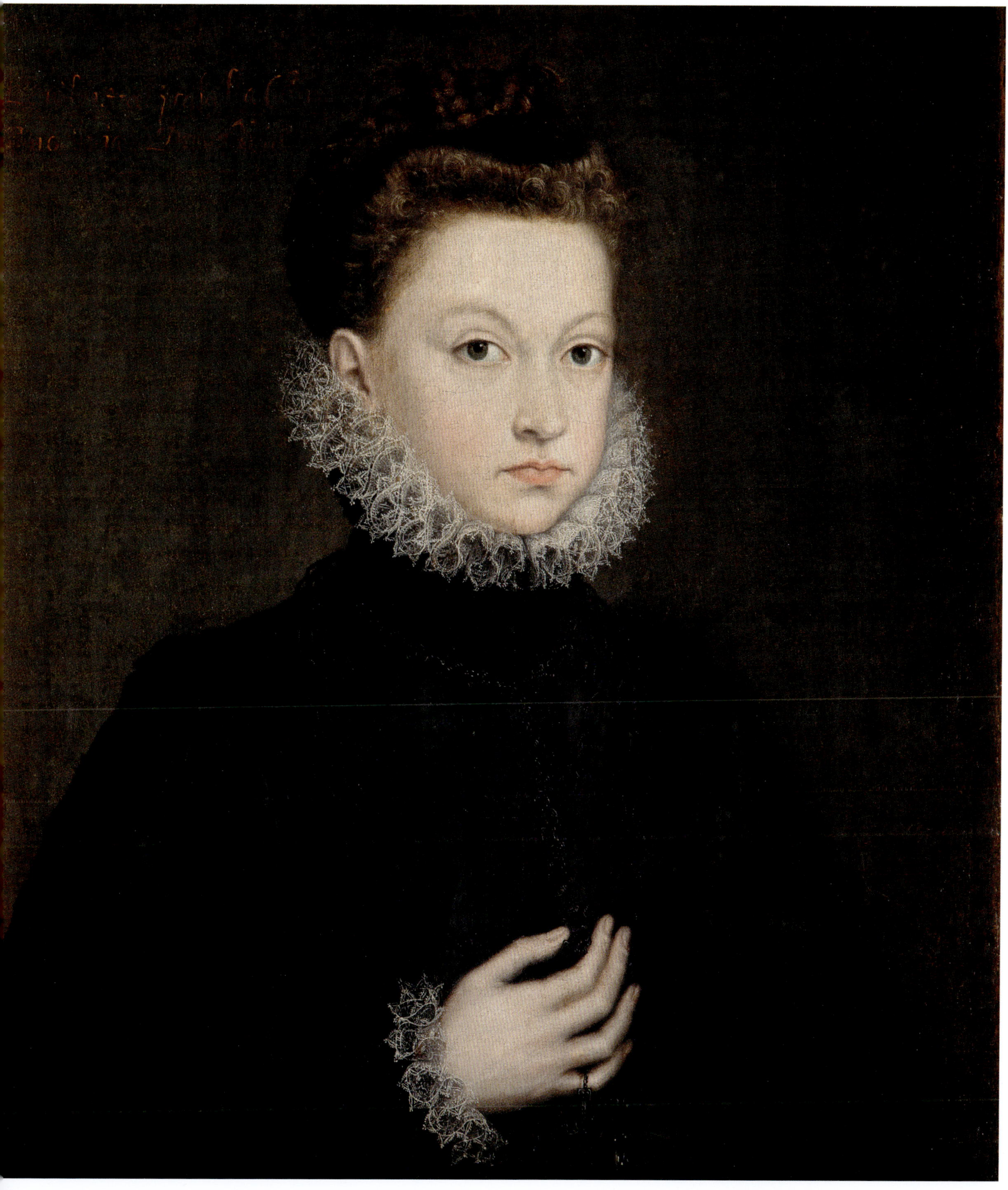

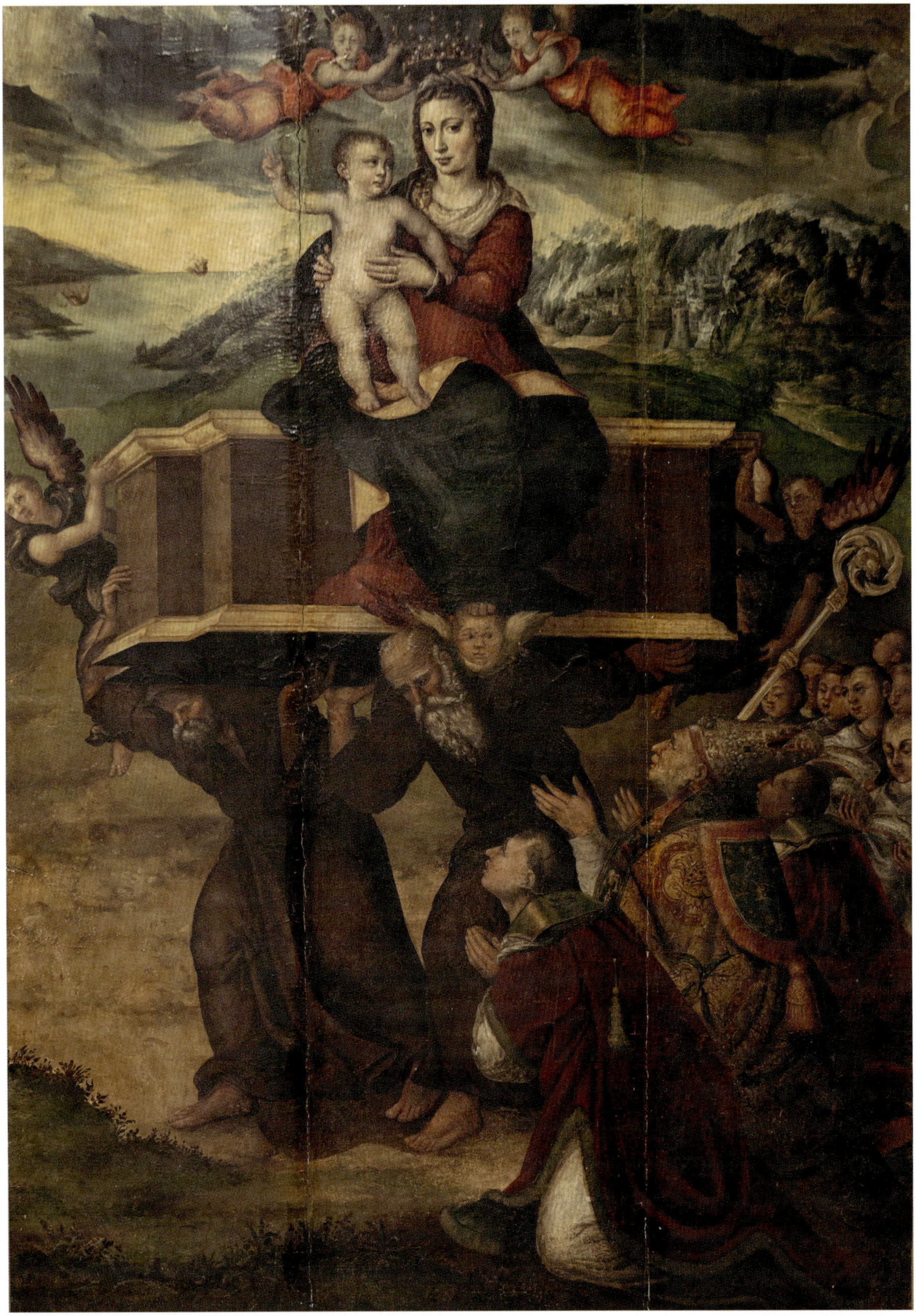

1.12
Sofonisba Anguissola
Madonna dell'Itria, before and after restoration (2020–2021)
1578–1579
Oil on panel, 239.5 × 170 cm
Paternò (Catania), parish of Santa Maria dell'Alto, church of the former convent of the Santissima Annunziata, inv. 131231

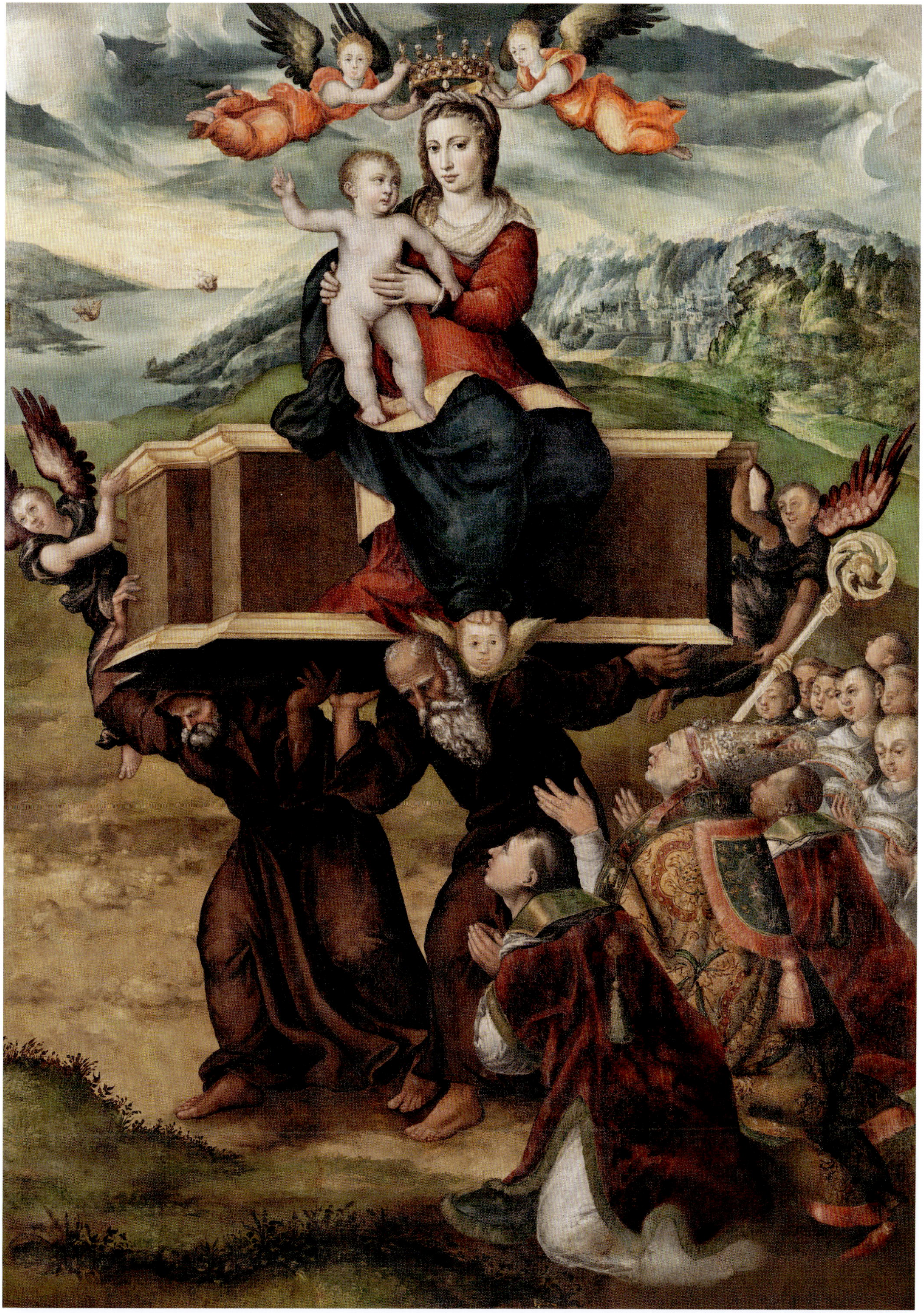

LUCIA ANGUISSOLA

Cremona, c. 1537/1542 – Cremona, 1565

Lucia was the third-born of the Anguissola sisters. Her date of birth is uncertain, but has been estimated to around 1540, with a minimal margin of error based on her supposed age in the paintings in which she is portrayed: in the oldest of these, the *Chess Game* by Sofonisba, now in Poznań, dated 1555 (cat. 1.8), where she is seen on the left, moving the pawns on the chessboard, she appears to be aged between fifteen and eighteen.[1] In contrast to her two elder sisters (Sofonisba and Elena), who were students of Bernardino Campi between 1546 and 1549, and then of Bernardino Gatti,[2] Lucia had to learn the basics of art directly from Sofonisba.[3] The first work of hers of which there remains any trace is a *Madonna with Child*, previously in a private collection in Ravenna, signed and dated 1555,[4] unfortunately now lost and no longer verifiable, which the reproductions lead us to believe was a very early work. This phase may also have included the *Portrait of a Virtuoso*, previously in the Melzi d'Eril Barbò collection in Milan, which may be a rather immature self-portrait.[5] The renowned *Self-Portrait* in the Picture Gallery of the Castello Sforzesco dates from 1557, and the *tondo* with the *Portrait of Europa* in the Pinacoteca Tosio Martinengo in Brescia is likely to have been produced around the same time.[6] The Cremonese sources all make mention also of her talents for music and singing[7] – so much so that attempts would have been made to identify her, aged around twenty and with the same clothing as seen in the self-portrait in the Castello Sforzesco, in the canvas by Sofonisba in the Spencer collection at Althorp, were it not for the ancient inscription, documented since 1766, claiming it to be a self-portrait of her older sister.[8] Lucia's signature can also be seen on the attractive *Portrait of Pietro Manna* at the Prado,[9] which constitutes perhaps her most painstaking artwork and which betrays the influence of the paintings of Bernardino Campi upon her. The picture is not dated, but given that it displays a greater maturity with respect to the *Self-Portrait* in the Castello Sforzesco, it must date from between 1558 and 1560, the year of Manna's death. The portrait was admired by Vasari when he visited the Anguissola home in 1566, together with the – in his opinion – even more successful portrait of the Duke of Sessa, Gonzalo II Fernández of Cordoba, governor of Milan, commenting that Lucia "left at her death fame no less than that of Sofonisba".[10] The premature death of the painter must have occurred prior to Vasari's visit to Cremona, perhaps in 1565, even though it was recorded only in a later source.[11] In 1569, the Cremonese humanist Francesco Zava had lauded her marvellous and almost divine ingenuity (*mirum propeque divinum artificis ingenium*) in his description of the portrait of the military architect Benedetto Ala, which at the time could be seen in the home of Canon Pietro Antonio Lanzoni, known as Tolentino.[12] Lucia's final output, subsequent to Sofonisba's departure for Spain, remains nebulous and subject purely to reconstruction by scholars. There do exist, however, Anguissola portraits such as the three presumed to have been painted by her sister Minerva and currently displayed in the Milwaukee Art Museum, in the Museo Poldi Pezzoli in Milan and in a private Cremonese collection,[13] which may well date from between 1560 and 1564, the year of Minerva's death.[14]

Mario Marubbi

[1] In this regard, see Gilardi 1994, p. 75 and now Miscioscia 2019, pp. 28–36.
[2] The first to make the claim was Lamo 1584, ed. 1774, pp. 35–36.
[3] Zaist 1774, I, pp. 233 and 234.
[4] Caroli 1973, p. 70.
[5] Carotti 1901, p. 63. See the reproduction in Gregori 1994, p. 35, fig. 7.
[6] See Gilardi's profile, in *Sofonisba Anguissola* 1994, pp. 286–287.
[7] Arisi 1715–1720, I, p. 60: "Not content with painting, she also studied and became very accomplished in music, with the subtlety of her song and the sweetness of her voice being no less graceful than her paintings".
[8] On this question, see the considerations of Gilardi, in *Sofonisba Anguissola* 1994, p. 212, and a comprehensive discussion of the opinions of the scholars in Cole 2019a, pp. 168–169. See the image reproduced in *Sofonisba Anguissola* 1994, p. 27.
[9] Gilardi, in *Sofonisba Anguissola* 1994, pp. 284–285 and Ruiz Gómez, in *Historia* 2019, pp. 124–125.
[10] Vasari 1568, English ed. 1912–1915, VIII, p. 47. Note, however, that neither Vasari nor Antonio Campi (in contrast to the statements made in Ghirardi 1992, pp. 35–36) date Lucia's death to 1565.
[11] Arisi 1715–1720, I, p. 59.
[12] Zava 1569, fol. 85*r*. The information reappears in Guazzoni 1994, pp. 65–66, whereas the passage of the oration of Zava is transcribed in Sacchi 1994e, pp. 405–406.
[13] Reproduced respectively in *Sofonisba Anguissola* 1994, pp. 229, 291 and 301. On the iconographic question relating to the portraiture of Minerva, see Ghirardi 1992.
[14] Arisi 1702–1706, II, p. 300.

1.13
Lucia Anguissola
Self-Portrait
1557
Oil on panel, 28 × 20 cm
Milan, Castello Sforzesco, Pinacoteca, inv. 562

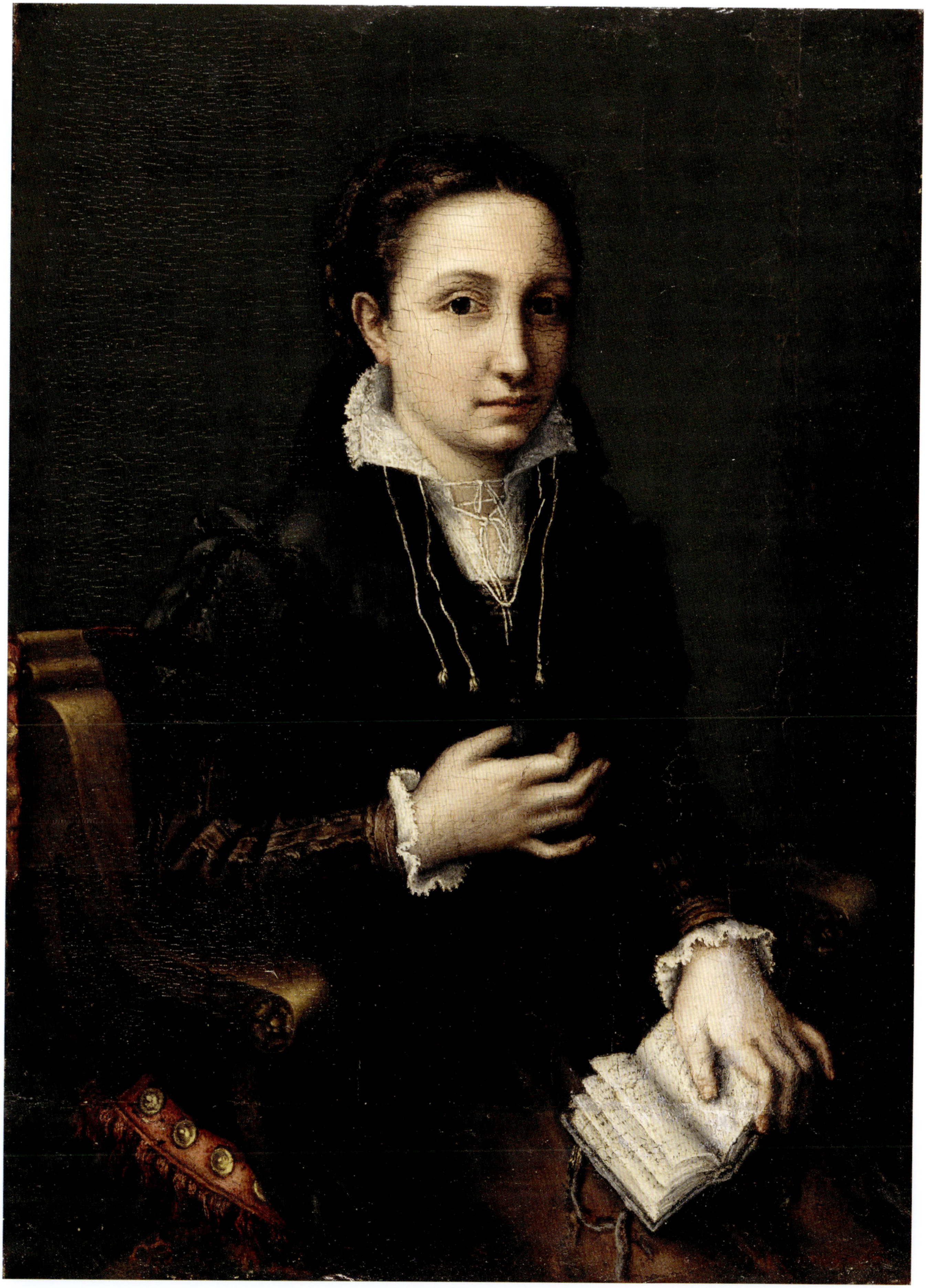

EUROPA ANGUISSOLA

Cremona, 1548/1549 – Cremona, 1578

The fifth of the sisters, Europa was born in Cremona around 1548–1549. As a child, she was portrayed by Sofonisba at the centre of the *Chess Game* (1555), now in Poznań, where she appears to be aged five or six (cat. 1.8). A couple of years later, she was portrayed by Lucia in a *tondo* now in the Pinacoteca Tosio Martinengo in Brescia. She must have begun painting when very young with her older sisters' encouragement, and by 1557 her father Amilcare, writing to the Duchess of Mantua, Margherita Paleologa, in a letter to accompany a little painting by Sofonisba, acclaimed her precocious talent, and declared that she "may surpass in virtue and goodness all of my other daughters".[1] At the age of thirteen, around 1560–1561, Europa painted what was perhaps her first work (*primum suae virtutis lumen*, according to the dedicatory inscription): an *Annunciation*, based on the fresco by Bernardino Gatti at the Basilica of Santa Maria di Campagna in Piacenza, offered as a gift to her sister Minerva.[2] When in 1566 Vasari came to Cremona, he met Europa along with the others at home, referring to her as "the third of the sisters Anguisciuola", as Lucia and Minerva had by then passed away. He stated that she was young but "in so far as one can see from her works and drawings, she will be in no way inferior to Sofonisba and Lucia, her sisters".[3] In 1569, she married Carlo Schinchinelli, with whom she had several children: only Bianca survived. For the Schinchinelli chapel in the church of Sant'Elena, she also painted the *Vocation of Peter and Andrew* – now in the parish church of Vidiceto, no longer a small-scale portrait but an actual altarpiece – which betrays the fact that she did not benefit from a discipleship as her sisters had done. Her art was discussed by Antonio Campi ("most excellent in painting"),[4] an opinion that is perhaps not validated by the surviving works, leading us to imagine some form of relationship between the most intellectual of the Campi brothers and the young Anguissola. Perhaps, some of the historiography claims that Europa may have used sketches by Campi for her compositions;[5] a conjecture verified at least by the *Saint Francis Receiving the Stigmata* formerly in the church of Sant'Elena (still in Cremona, but now at Sant'Agata), which would seem to derive from a Campi innovation, but one first arrived at by Giulio.[6] The painting was a commission from Angela Fossa, the wife of one of her husband's cousins, whose portrait "in abysso" is akin to the sisters' traditional speciality.[7] The two "family" altarpieces (early 1580s) reveal an evident awkwardness *vis-à-vis* history painting, which not even the recourse to authoritative models could mitigate. These did not remain Europa's only attempts to work within this genre of painting, given that another version of the *Saint Francis Receiving the Stigmata* was sited at the convent of the Friars Minor in Casalbuttano,[8] a fiefdom of the Schinchinelli family, and a *Saint John* of hers is cited in the inventory of assets of the notary Sebastiano Ferrari in 1649.[9] However, it is in the details – as in the portrait of Angela Fossa – that Europa is at her best, and from here we must begin to reconstruct her oeuvre of portraiture, as lauded both by Vasari and by Francesco Zava,[10] which included a portrait of her mother, Bianca Ponzoni, sent to Sofonisba in Madrid to document her progress;[11] a self-portrait, part of the Cremonese collection of Pietro Antonio Lanzoni (Tolentino);[12] and a work owned by Count Broccardo Persico, displayed in his Milanese residence.[13] Out of the portraits attributed to her sisters, those that are most closely related to Europa's style seem to be the *Portrait of an Old Woman* in the Nivå Museum,[14] and the *Portrait of a Lady* in a private collection.[15]

Mario Marubbi

[1] Sacchi 1994d, p. 364, doc. dated 12 March 1557.
[2] The painting, in a private collection, is mentioned by Olivato 2016, and then again by Tanzi 2017, pp. 75–76.
[3] Vasari 1568, English ed. 1912–1915, VIII, p. 48.
[4] Campi 1585, p. L.
[5] The sources, though, are late: Orlandi 1753, p. 160; Grasselli 1827, p. 19.
[6] Now in the Museo Civico Ala Ponzone, see reproduction in *La Pinacoteca* 2003, p. 93.
[7] Europa's autograph is revealed by Baldinucci 1681–1728, ed. 1768–1820, VI, p. 106 and later by 1762, p. 82.
[8] Panni 1762, pp. 82–83.
[9] Sacchi 1994c, p. 350.
[10] Zava 1569, fol. 85*r*.
[11] Vasari 1568, English ed. 1912–1915, VIII, p. 48.
[12] The painting then changed hands, and in 1615 it was to be found in the inventory of Angelerio Barbò (Sacchi 1994d, p. 400, doc. dated 1615, 27 November).
[13] Sacchi 1994d, p. 376, doc. dated 1570, 25 February.
[14] Sacchi, in *Sofonisba Anguissola* 1994, pp. 306–307.
[15] Caroli, in *Sofonisba Anguissola* 1994, pp. 298–299, who however attributes the painting to Anna Maria Anguissola. On the identity of the subject, see Miscioscia 2019, p. 44.

1.14
Europa Anguissola
or
Lucia Anguissola
Portrait of Livia de Zanchi
1560–1565
Oil on canvas, 98 × 73 cm
Milan, Castello Sforzesco, Pinacoteca, inv. 590

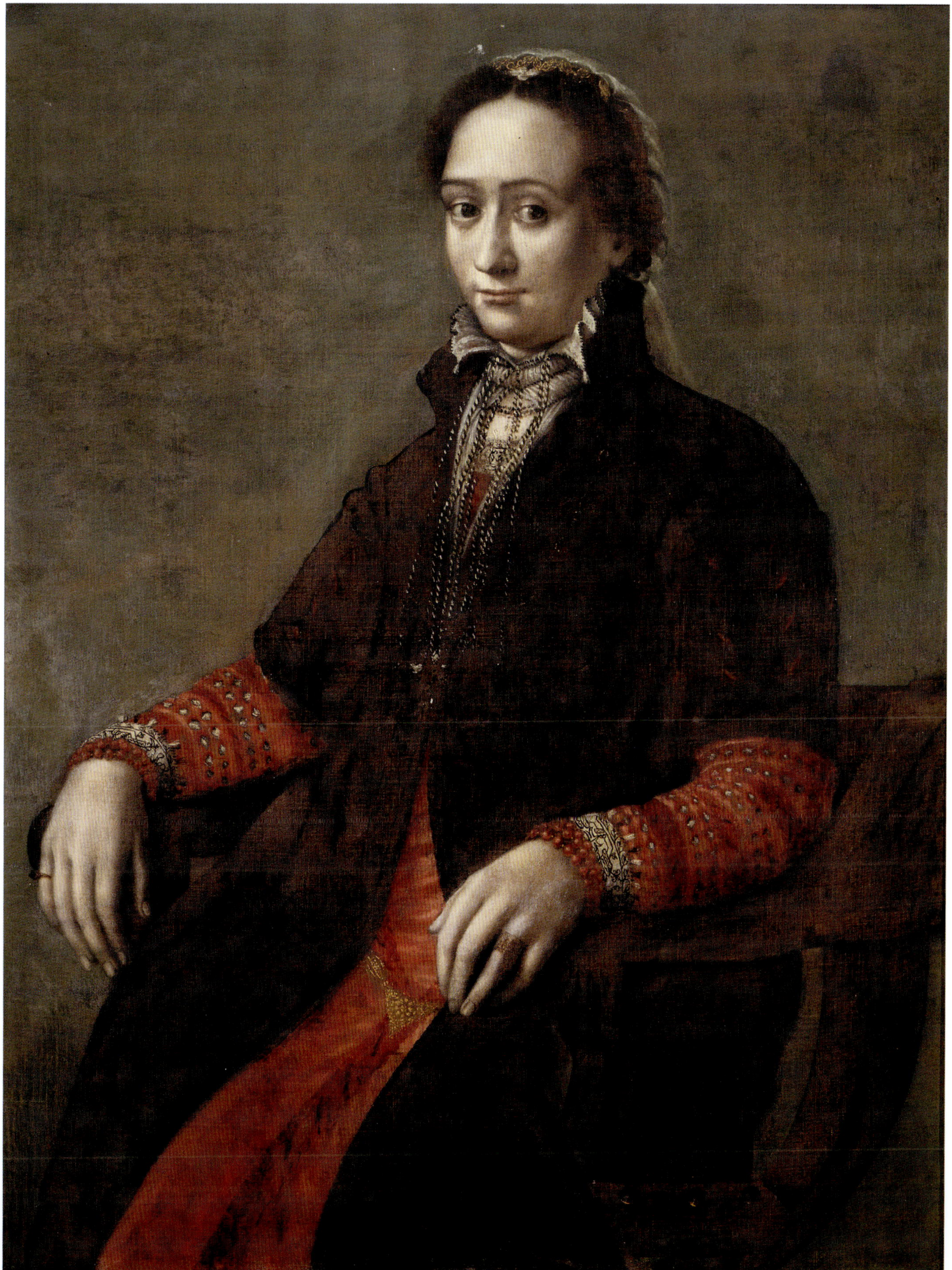

IRENE DI SPILIMBERGO

Spilimbergo (Pordenone), 1538 – Venice, 1559

We have detailed information both about the birth of Irene di Spilimbergo on 17 October 1538, as reported in the family biography written by her maternal grandfather, the Venetian merchant Giovanni Paolo Da Ponte,[1] and about her death in Venice on 17 December 1559,[2] after twenty-two days of fever, caused by her excessive zeal for painting: "not having paused from morning 'til night in her steadfast intention to copy certain things, in order that the example would in no way be far from the exemplar, she became weak with a raging fever accompanied by an acute headache".[3] Her early death was the reason behind a celebratory collection conceived by the nobleman Francesco Gradenigo and curated by Dionigi Atanagi, *Rime di diuersi nobilissimi et eccellentissimi autori, in morte della signora Irene delle signore di Spilimbergo. Alle quali si sono aggiunti uersi latini di diuersi egregij poeti in morte della medesima signora*, published in Venice in 1561. The biography by Dionigi Atanagi that opens the volume is the primary source of information on Irene's output, along with a number of poems published therein. Irene's father was the nobleman Adriano (c. 1511–1541) of the house of Spilimbergo and Zuccola, son of Susanna di Valvasone and of Ercole, who is recorded as being in Padua in 1530. It was there that he received the training that allowed him to become a "highly literate gentleman, both in languages and in the sciences, who in his studies of moral theology and mathematics made great progress. He spoke Arabic, Greek and Latin".[4] On 5 July 1535, he married Giulia Da Ponte, who had a dowry of two thousand ducats, with the senator Niccolò Zeno serving as ring bearer. The couple would live for a time in Venice, before moving to Spilimbergo, where Adriano, attracted by the ideas of the Reformation, subsidised the academy run by Bernardino Partenio, where Latin, Greek and Hebrew were studied. The marriage saw the birth of three daughters: Emilia in 1536, who would go on to become a musician, Irene in 1538 and Isabella in 1541. Adriano's premature death in 1541 led Giulia to marry again, in 1543, to a relative of her first husband, Gian Francesco di Spilimbergo, a knight of Charles V, with whom she would have ten children. Family disputes caused Irene to move in with her grandfather in Venice in 1554. Here, according to Atanagi's biography, she met Campaspe Giancarli,[5] and having learned the basics of drawing, "with guidance from Titian she moved on to painting; [...]. And so within the space of one and a half months she completed copies of a number of paintings by Titian, learning a great deal about measurements, light and shade, and perspectives, sinews, bones, and softness and smoothness of flesh, and also about the folds of clothing".[6] In addition to this information provided by Atanagi, there is also an anonymous poem in the same collection: "From the divine and immortal Titian / learned the art of portraying others / Irene...", as well as allusions in other poems, including those by Diamante Dolfi, Ippolita Gonzaga and Laura Terracina. In his "Life of Titian", Vasari describes her as a "very lovely maiden, skilled in letters and music and a student of design",[7] but he makes no mention of her having been a regular visitor to the studio run by Titian, who had portrayed both her grandfather and her mother. In relation to the paintings produced by Irene, Atanagi confirms that these included copies of works by Titian, whereas Fabio di Maniago, in his *Storia delle Belle Arti friulane* (1819), refers to a number of works held "in Maniago with the family of that name, having come to it as the heirs of a branch of the Spilimbergo family" and described as follows: "three small paintings that represent the flight into Egypt, Noah entering the ark and the flood; compositions rich in figures, carried out with honesty of brushstroke, intelligence of design, taste and power in the use of colour, and which seem to emerge from the hands of an experienced artist, not those of a young damsel who only picked up the brushes a matter of months ago. Beautiful and new is the singular innovation of the flight into Egypt, where she depicts the holy family, which sets out on its path in the darkness of the night, while an angel with a bright face scatters the shadows and escorts the family on its way".[8] This information then reappears in Bonturini,[9] Crowe and Cavalcaselle,[10] and Zotti, who states that the work is located "in a study on the ground floor of the Amminis-Maniago palace in Maniago".[11] Recently, Kessel has partially confirmed the findings of Ronchi, who had considered a painting held in the Musei Civici in Padua attributed to Padovanino as a copy of the *Portrait of Irene di Spilimbergo* by Titian.[12] The scholar proposes that the painting is a copy of a self-portrait by Irene[13]. The similarity of the work to various almost identical versions, including that in the Galleria

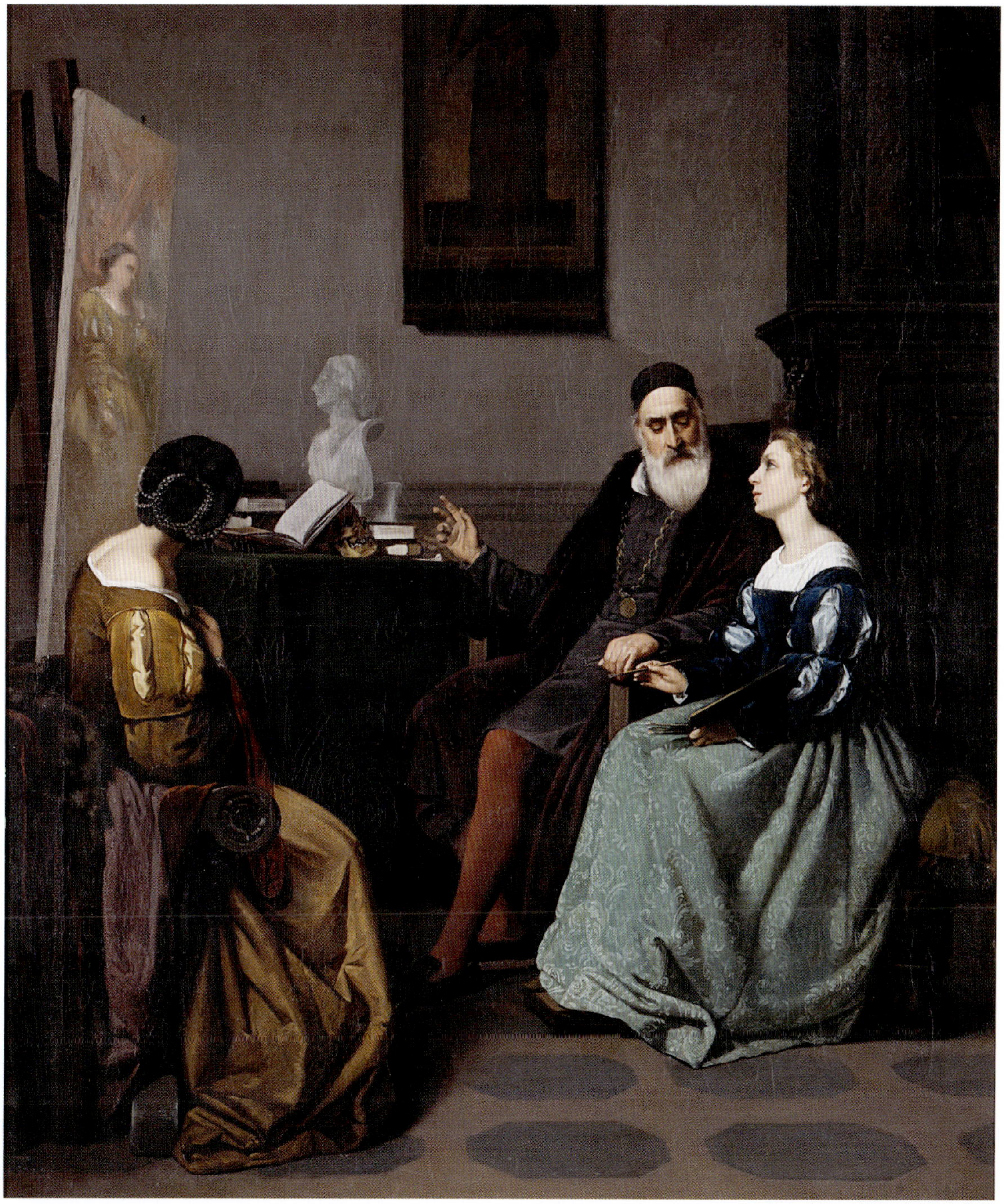

1.15
Silvestro Lega
Titian and Irene di Spilimbergo
1859
Oil on canvas, 97.5 × 81 cm
Carpi (Modena), Palazzo Foresti collection

Borghese attributed to Marietta Robusti, makes it difficult to arrive at a definitive identification of the subject and of the prototype.[14] While, therefore, Irene's artistic profile remains rather vague in historical terms, her reputation nevertheless gave rise in the nineteenth century to a substantial series of paintings celebrating her apprenticeship with Titian.
Gioia Mori

[1] The text appears in Ulm 1910, p. 128.
[2] Riga 2018, in particular p. 606; Kessel 2017, p. 137, in contrast, has her passing away on 19 December 1559.
[3] Atanagi 1561, ed. 1839, p. 150: "This infirmity was diagnosed by certain doctors as petechia, by others as simple fever, and by some as abscesses generated by the head. Whatever the pestiferous nature of her illness, within twenty-two days, as she had virtuously lived, so she religiously died".
[4] Atanagi 1561, ed. 1839, p. 139.
[5] A Venetian female painter with this name was cited by Gratiano 1636, ed. 1997, pp. 175–177.
[6] Atanagi 1561, ed. 1839, p. 149.
[7] Vasari 1568, English ed. 1912–1915, IX, p. 175.
[8] Di Maniago 1819, pp. 89, 173.
[9] Bonturini 1869, p. 7.
[10] Crowe, Cavalcaselle 1877, II, p. 302.
[11] Zotti 1914, p. 35.
[12] Ronchi 1922, p. 149. For an analysis of the work and the various proposals for attribution and identification, refer to the profile by Banzato, in *Lo spirito* 2009, pp. 63, 99, no. 34.
[13] Kessel 2017, pp. 167–168.
[14] See the profile of the work by C. Terribile cat. 3.38.

LUCREZIA QUISTELLI

Florence, 1541 – Florence?, 1594

Lucrezia Quistelli was born in Florence on 11 January 1541[1] to a noble family, which did not originally hail from Tuscany but had gone there to enter the service of the Medici. As the daughter of Giulia Santi and Alfonso Quistelli della Mirandola, she was raised in what was a very culturally stimulating environment, which strongly influenced her inclinations. Vasari's first reference to Lucrezia comes in his biography of Properzia de' Rossi, placing her between Sister Plautilla Nelli and Sofonisba Anguissola: "Likewise, Madonna Lucrezia, the daughter of Messer Alfonso Quistelli della Mirandola and now the wife of Count Clemente Pietra, has to her great praise studied design and painting and is still doing so, having learned from Alessandro Allori, the student of Bronzino, as we can see in her many paintings and portraits, which are worthy of being praised by everyone".[2] Despite the approbation recognising her as a student of Allori, we cannot as yet attribute to her a definite *corpus* of works, whereas we can do so for Sofonisba and Plautilla, whose artistic output is widely known.

Certainly, though, there are shared reference points with the background of the Cremonese artist: both noblewoman, they received an education commensurate with their standing that, together with the study of literature, music and dance, also included painting.[3] Her mother came from an esteemed family of humanists and *literati*, while her father had been honoured with the role of magistrate and then *podestà* (chief magistrate).[4] Subsequently, he became Cosimo de' Medici's fiscal auditor, a role created in 1543 that involved supervising the interests of the sovereign, collecting fines, and seizing the assets of bandits, assassins and those who died without heirs. He was also entitled to intervene in all criminal cases in which the interests of the treasury were at stake. He was, therefore, a figure of great primacy at court.[5] Although the Quistelli family never fostered direct relationships with the world of art, Alfonso would dedicate himself to the profitable world of literary patronage to imbue his descendants with greater prestige. It was no accident, then, that in 1557 the humanist and man of letters Benedetto Varchi dedicated to him a sonnet alluding to the marriage of his daughter Lucrezia.[6] It was probably through Varchi that the Quistelli family became close to Alessandro Allori, a student of Bronzino and painter of the Medici, who would become Lucrezia's teacher.

Lucrezia must also have known the work of the city's most famous artists, given that through her father she had access to the output of Pontormo – of whom he owned a painting – Bronzino and Allori. By the same token, we can imagine her strolling through Florentine churches and being dazzled by the frescoed marvels, with easy access to the paintings of Botticelli in the church of San Barnaba, where her sister and daughter would take their vows. It is thought that her first lessons in drawing under the guidance of Allori began in 1555, when Lucrezia was aged around fourteen, whereas by 1568, the year of publication of Vasari's *Lives*, her education in painting must have been complete.

Sofonisba would certainly have influenced Lucrezia's development, especially in light of the fact that the works of the Cremonese artist were circulating through various courts, and the presence of her drawings in Florence is confirmed by archival documents.[7] In 1557, aged sixteen, Lucrezia married Clemente Pietra, son of Count Brunoro and Caterina Bianca Stampa.[8] Her husband was something of a promoter of the intellectual qualities of "dames", given that he served as a patron of the 1549 publication of Ludovico Domenichi's *La nobiltà delle donne*.[9] Due, no doubt, to the "philogyny" of her husband, Lucrezia continued to paint even after her marriage.

Count Pietra was fully inserted within the Medicean court: a trusted confidant of Cosimo I de' Medici, for whom he carried out diplomatic missions, he had fought alongside him in the battle against Siena between 1554 and 1556. Upon Cosimo's death, his son Francesco I de' Medici called Clemente "my beloved gentleman",[10] and continued to afford the count a pre-eminent role within the court, maintaining a relationship based on trust.

In 1568, Lucrezia and Clemente moved to Palazzo Pandolfini,[11] an exceptionally rich building designed by Raphael, paying rent to the Salviati family. Theirs was a happy marriage, which produced eight children. Their destiny, though, changed in 1574, when Clemente was attacked by Francesco Somma, who wounded him with a poisoned blade.[12] Lucrezia, now widowed, attempted to demonstrate the premeditation of the homicide, abetted by the input of the Gran Duke himself, who – together with the physicians – stated with conviction that the strange clotting of the blood resulting from the wound had been caused by a poisonous herb. Cardinal Borromeo sought to dissuade Lucrezia from the undertaking through the intercession of the Grand Duchess of Tuscany, Joanna of Austria,[13] to whom Lucrezia was very close, even going so far as to have Lucrezia's daughter Giulia enter into her service.

Another daughter, Porzia Pietra, was introduced to the court of the Medici as a lady-in-waiting of Bianca Cappello in 1580, and in 1581 of Francesca Eleonora Virginia Orsini, while in 1584 she would become the governess of Maria de' Medici. It can be said that her position of prestige derived from the role of her family and from their closeness to the Medicean court, but her special aptitude for the arts should not be overlooked, nor should the excellent education that her mother must certainly have ensured she receive.

Her son Alfonso Pietra married Fausta di Ottavio Visconti, who commissioned the only original work signed by his mother appearing in the exhibition (cat. 1.16). According to the Archivio dell'Opera del Duomo,[14] Lucrezia was also the godmother of Fulvia Striggi at her baptism. The daughter of Alessandro Striggi, an esteemed musician at the Medici court with a Europe-wide reputation, was placed under Lucrezia's guardianship, indicating not only a closeness to the Striggi family but also an interest in music as well as the arts in general.[15]

Another four daughters became nuns: Lucrezia ensured, however, that they were assigned to convents located close to Palazzo Pandolfini, demonstrating her strong attachment to them. Accordingly, in 1587 Lucrezia went to Milan in order to ensure their rights to the feudal titles of their late father.

Lucrezia Quistelli died in 1594 at the age of fifty-three. To commemorate their mother, her children laid a commemorative stone in the church of San Barnaba: "LUCRETIAE QUISTELLIAE INSIGNIS PRUDENTIAE SANCTITATIS ET PUDICITIAE MILIERI ALFONSUS PETRA COMES SILVANI ET CLEMENS FILII CARISSIMAE ET BENEMERENTI MATRI POSUERE AN. MDXCIV. VIXIT AN. LIII. M. III. D. XIV."[16]

Cecilia Gamberini

[1] My thanks go to Dr Sheila Barker for her advice on the drafting of this biography, which is based essentially on the data compiled in Barker 2016.

[2] Vasari 1568, English ed. 1912–1915, V, pp. 127–128.

[3] Guazzoni 1994.

[4] From the Middle Ages onwards, the chief magistrate had to hail from another town, specifically to avoid the risk of corruption.

[5] Archivio di Stato di Firenze (from now on: ASFi), Camera e auditore fiscale, row 3001. See references in Barker 2016, p. 47.

[6] *Al Sig. Conte Clemente Pietra*, published in Varchi 1821, p. 17.

[7] Sacchi 1994c.

[8] The link with Sofonisba is confirmed by the painting of Massimiliano II Stampa, now in Baltimore, which was one of her first official commissions. See also Sacchi 2008.

[9] Domenichi 1549.

[10] ASFi, Mediceo del Principato, 5927a, fol. 22*r*. See Barker 2016, p. 77 note 81.

[11] Bucci, Bencini 1973, p. 79.

[12] ASFi, Mediceo del Principato, 5047, foll. 140*r*, 145*v*. See Barker 2016, p. 78 note 107.

[13] See Barker 2016, p. 79 note 109.

[14] Florence, Archivio dell'Opera del Duomo, Registri battesimali, Battesimi Femmine, Reg. 234, c. 94*r*. See Butchart, forthcoming.

[15] I would like to thank Dr Barker for this information, and Dr David Butchart for allowing me to read the draft of his forthcoming article on the Striggi family.

[16] Richa 1758, p. 67.

1.16
Lucrezia Quistelli
Mystical Marriage of Saint Catherine
1576
Oil on canvas, 180 × 120 cm
Silvano Pietra (Pavia),
parish church of Santa Maria and San Pietro

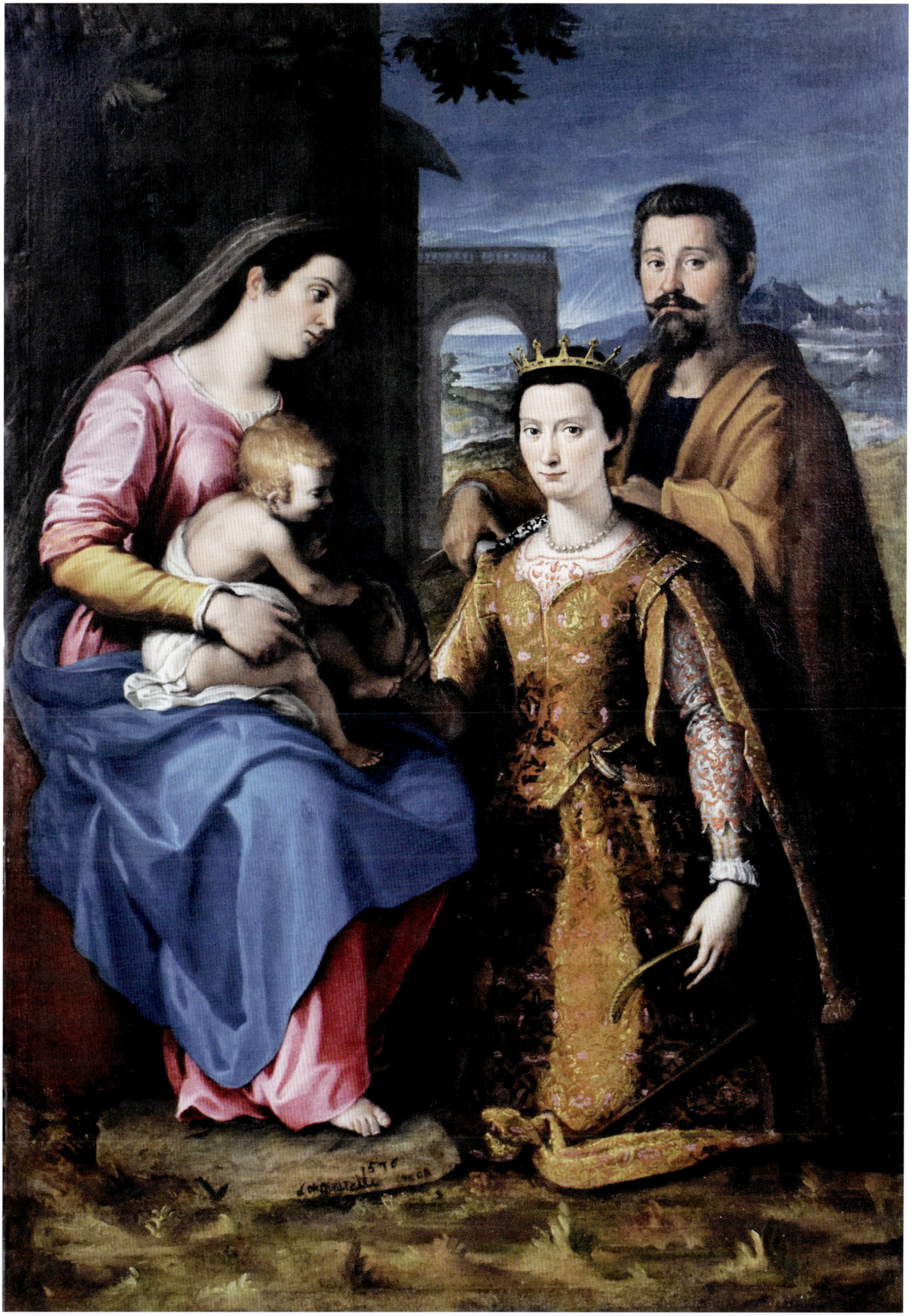

CLAUDIA DEL BUFALO

Active in Rome in the late sixteenth and early seventeenth centuries

At present, the painting on display constitutes the only remaining example of the artistic output of this Roman noblewoman, who belonged to the extensive del Bufalo family. Around the time at which this work was produced, the prestige of the house had reached its apex thanks to Innocenzo del Bufalo (1565/1566–1610), the apostolic nuncio in France from 1601 to 1604. Prior to his return to Rome, Innocenzo was appointed as a cardinal and, in taking part in the two conclaves that followed the death of Clement VIII, he contributed to the election of Pope Leo XI (Alessandro de' Medici) and, later, Pope Paul V (Camillo Borghese), both candidates of the French party.

Claudia's work falls into that category of paintings produced by female painters but erroneously attributed to male artists, despite her (female) name being clearly visible at the base of the column. As far back as 1650, the inventory drafted by Giacomo Manilli at the painting's former home of Villa Borghese states that the artist was male, Claudio rather than Claudia,[1] and the same error was then repeated by Paola Della Pergola in her 1954 essay, even though the artist's signature is clearly visible on the painting.[2]

Claudia was perhaps an amateur artist, but this sole signed painting embodies a refined, erudite personality. Both her biography and her artistic output should be enriched by further, in-depth study.

Silvia Malaguzzi

[1] Manilli 1650, p. 115.

[2] Della Pergola 1954, pp. 139–140: in the main body of the article, the author mistakenly refers to the essay by "Domenico Manilli", when it should be Giacomo Manilli, and she also makes the same Claudio/Claudia mistake. She states that at the time the work was in "the Hercolani-Borghese house, at Palazzo Borghese, and I am grateful to Princess Santa Hercolani for the photograph reproduced here", but the erroneous reading of the signature indicates that she had not seen the painting in the flesh.

1.17
Claudia del Bufalo
Portrait of Faustina del Bufalo
1604
Oil on canvas, 105 × 88 cm
Rome, Dario del Bufalo
collection, inv. P127

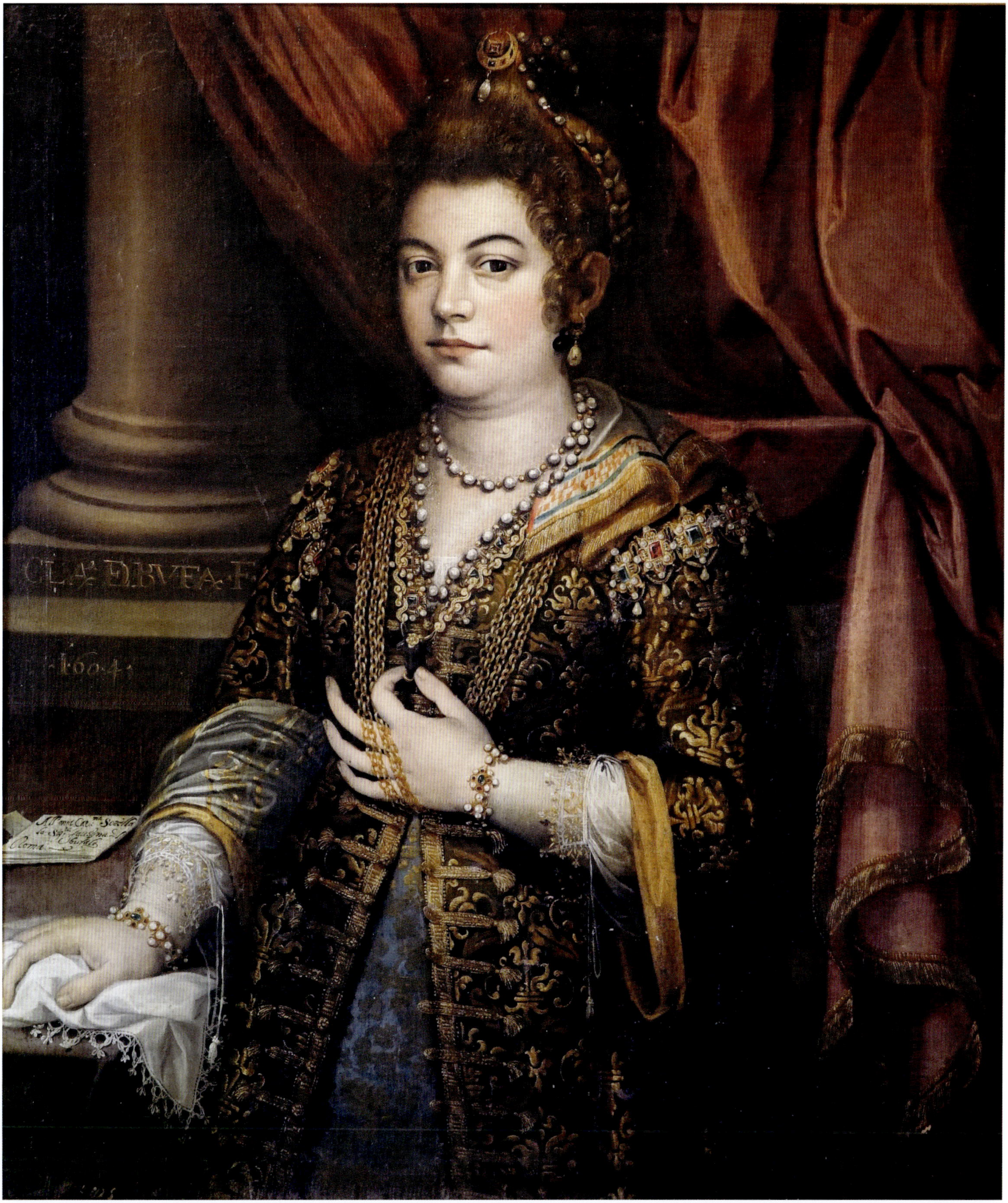
1604

CATERINA CANTONI

Milan, 1542 – Milan, 1601

The "famous Catarina Cantone, noblewoman of the city of Milan, but more noble for her exceptionally rare genius, and for the excellence of her art of embroidering on canvas and netting; in which she has never had any equal nor will she ever have [...]. Indeed, aside from her other areas of expertise, she sews with such mastery that the stitch appears the same on both sides. When excellence is required, the stitch of the great Cantona's needle is called for".[1] This acclaim from Giovanni Paolo Lomazzo is an exemplary validation of the esteem in which the embroideress was held, her works, as the writer himself states, being in demand at the European courts. Her artistry was admired by the *literati* and the aristocracy, but her reputation fluctuated in that, from the second half of the eighteenth century, she became "a name without works", one of the numerous artists cited by the sources to which no specific pieces could be attributed.

Through her research, Silvia Mausoli has reconstructed Caterina's biography.[2] She was born in Milan in 1542 to Giovanni Ambrogio Leuco, a leading Milanese goldsmith, and Anna da Ponte. In 1559, she married the Milanese nobleman Bartolomeo Cantoni, with whom she had four children: the first-born, Pietro, would become a jurist and man of letters, going on to marry Agata Ponzoni, a cousin of Sofonisba Anguissola; Giovan Francesco, who would enter into the service of the Duke of Parma as a knight; Angelo, an aficionado of ancient literature, who died aged just over eighteen in 1594; and last of all, Barbara. As Paolo Morigia states in reference to her in the section dedicated to painters, the young Barbara must have been skilled and talented both in painting and in embroidery, a technique with which she emulated "divinely her virtuous and celebrated mother".[3] Unfortunately, thus far no information has emerged on her. Caterina herself died in 1601, as evinced by her funerary epigraph, now destroyed, sited in the Basilica of San Nazaro in Brolo, in Milan.

Nothing is known for certain about her training or her output. According to Morigia "[...] she learned this virtue herself, having vowed to make a cover for a goblet at the Sacrestia de' Padri Cappuccini, out of the fear that she had at the time of the plague that was in Milan in 1576. Those Fathers still have that cover or veil, which they conserve as something very precious, using it only on the most solemn occasions throughout the year".[4] While embroidery may have been an unusual part of a woman's education, Caterina benefited from an extremely rich, stimulating environment, since she was involved with the Academy of the Val di Blenio, which was also frequented by another well-known embroiderer, Scipione Delfinone.[5] Equally unresolved is the question of the studio from which Caterina may have worked. The sources often refer to gifts, such as the cloth given to Catalina Micaela, Duchess of Savoy, and used for the baptism of her first-born child,[6] as well as those found in "many churches in Milan and outside it", mentioned by Morigia in his *Historia dall'antichità di Milano*.[7] In all likelihood, these precious gifts may have formed part of the "stupendous works made by this divine hand" conserved in "more than thirty churches both in this city and elsewhere" cited once more by the Milanese historian.[8] It would appear that the sources want to underline how Cantoni worked not for profit but for pleasure and amusement.[9] She certainly did not embroider alone: in a letter of 1614, Giovan Battista Solaro encourages Philip III of Spain to purchase a "set of drapes" made over the course of twelve years by Caterina "with the help of a number of damsels".[10] Over and above these doubts, Caterina must have been relatively prolific, as indicated by the numerous works cited in the sources, which are often quite demanding both iconographically and technically, resulting in very protracted completion times. One example is provided by the drape for a bed or table, entirely embroidered with flowers, birds and almost one hundred "Greek and Roman histories" accompanied by an inscription in Latin, offered to the Duke of Mantua, which was more than four years in the making.[11]

A small but precious *corpus* remains of Caterina's works. Maria Teresa Binaghi was responsible for identifying "Ariadne's Embroidery", cited both by Morigia and by Lomazzo, as the cloth now shared by Vienna and Frankfurt, positing that Camillo Procaccini was responsible for the cartoons.[12] On the basis of this work, it is possible to attribute to her the cloth found at the Museo Civico in Turin, with its as-yet-undeciphered iconography, the models of which derive partially from prints by Adriaen Collaert taken from drawings by

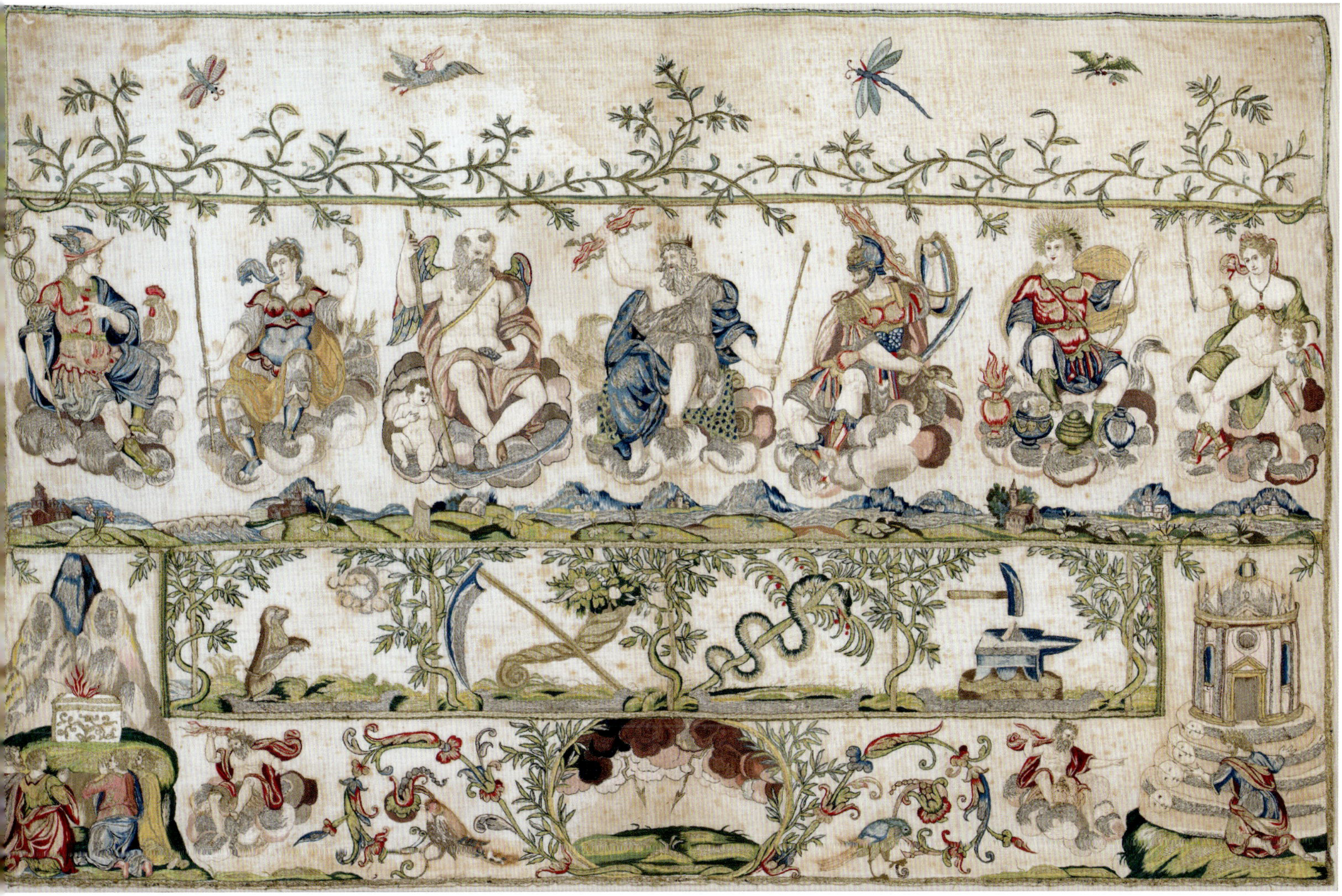

1.18
Caterina Cantoni (attributed)
Cloth embroidered with planetary divinities, emblems and religious scenes
c. 1590
Linen cloth embroidered in silk, gold and silver yarn with point painting, straight stitch, split stitch, couching, 62 × 94 cm
Moshe Tabibnia Gallery, inv. 133526

Maarten de Vos,[13] as well as the border on display at the exhibition (see cat. 1.18).

All of the works are marked out by a complex, multi-layered pictorial scheme, by their highly refined technical rendering and above all by the use of the so-called *Cantona stitch*, lauded by Lomazzo and Morigia, who also attribute its invention to her.[14] It is a stitch that did not remain the exclusive preserve of the embroideress, and went on to be used also by other female artists, such as Pellegrini,[15] and by "amateur" nobles such as Catalina Micaela, wife of Charles Emmanuel I, Duke of Savoy.[16]

Gian Luca Bovenzi

1 Lomazzo 1590, p. 166.
2 Mausoli 2015; Mausoli 2020.
3 Morigia 1595, p. 282.
4 Morigia 1595, p. 299.
5 On the Academy of the Val di Blenio, see *Rabisch* 1998.
6 Morigia 1595, p. 299.
7 Morigia 1592, p. 675.
8 Morigia 1595, p. 299.
9 Mausoli 2020, pp. 116–117.
10 Mausoli 2020, p. 127.
11 See Piccinelli 2003, pp. 306–307.
12 Binaghi 1994, pp. 102–105.
13 Bovenzi, in *Tessuti, ricami, merletti* 2008, pp. 75–77, no. 4; Bovenzi 2016, pp. 283–288.
14 Lomazzo 1590, p. 166; Morigia 1592, p. 675.
15 Rizzini 2011, p. 92.
16 Binaghi Olivari 2013, pp. 362–363.

ANTONIA PELLEGRINI

Milan, 1583 – Milan, after 1635

Antonia Pellegrini was one of the Milanese embroideresses operating in Milan in the late sixteenth and early seventeenth centuries who is most cited in the bibliographies and critical literature of the eighteenth century. She is associated above all with the embroidery produced between 1609 and 1610 for the canonisation of Saint Charles Borromeo (see cat. 1.19). Already in the nineteenth-century texts, doubts had begun to emerge on the identity of Antonia and Ludovica Pellegrini, to such an extent that they were fused into a single person, Ludovica Antonia, thus creating a sort of "two-headed mythological creature". Recent research by Alba Osimo has accurately identified the two embroideresses.[1]

Born Antonia dell'Oro in 1583 in Milan, she married the painter Gian Domenico Pellegrini. We do not know what training she received, but she must have acquired a certain level of renown given that she was entrusted with the silk embroidery of the drapes for Saint Charles, working alongside the celebrated Pompeo Berlusconi. It may have been her husband, who was also her manager and agent, who put her forward – he was in contact with the Fabbrica del Duomo, for which he produced, in 1603, one of the large paintings of the *Stories of Saint Charles* featuring the *Transfer of the Holy Relics and Remains*.[2] From the *Status animarum* it emerged that, in 1611, she had two daughters – Angela, aged four, and Anna Maria, aged three – with a third, Marta, arriving in 1614. No information is provided by the documents *vis-à-vis* her output or her presence in any studio. Osimo has her as still alive in 1635. The researcher was also responsible for the discovery of another document, which makes clear that on 13 July 1635 Ludovica (or "Ludovina") Pellegrini, daughter of Gian Domenico Pellegrini and wife of Carlo Antonio Locatelli, received from the convent of Sant'Eustorgio in Milan the commission to embroider "by stitching, with the finest Neapolitan silks, with fine gold and silver yarn, which must be stitched well, placing them appropriately, with beautiful colours" a banner "of white crimson, beautiful and good", depicting Saint Peter Martyr and an angel, according to the sketch provided by a certain Daniele. The embroideress cited in the document is, then, Antonia's daughter, born after 1614.

This important statement has made it possible to identify clearly "the two Pellegrine [*sic*]": the mother, Antonia, and the daughter, Ludovica. The latter can be identified with certainty as the person responsible for the embroidery of an altar cloth, which has been subject to a major modern overhaul and which features the signature, applied by brush, "LIDOVINA PE" on the central medallion, depicting the birth of the Virgin Mary. The hypothesis that Ludovica was responsible for the embroidery is confirmed in an inventory of the cathedral, drafted in 1653, where there is an entry for a "cloth [...] in the shield of the nativity of the Blessed Virgin worked by Lidovica Pellegrini".[3]

Far more complex is the *corpus* of her mother, defined by Lanzi as the "Minerva of her day".[4] Together with the embroidery for the beatification of Saint Charles (see cat. 1.19), there are numerous objects conserved in Milan that the historiographer attributed to Antonia, often on the exclusive basis of their high technical quality.[5] Her name also appears in relation to works held outside Lombardy, such as an altar frontal in the chapel of the Santissima Sindone in Turin,[6] based on a cartoon by Giulio Cesare Procaccini, which has extraordinarily survived to the present day.[7] Last but not least, the only work signed by Antonia, the so-called "Farnese chasuble", was neglected by the critical establishment but is to be found in the church of Gesù in Rome. Bearing the signature "Peregrina", it was produced – probably between 1610 and 1620 – for Cardinal Odoardo Farnese, who was associated with the Borromeo and Sfondrati families.[8]

Gian Luca Bovenzi

[1] Osimo 2011.
[2] Rizzini 2001, p. 92.
[3] Bovenzi 2011a, pp. 156–157, no. 40.
[4] Lanzi 1815-1817, IV, p. 217.
[5] See Bovenzi 2011a, pp. 133–135, 139–141.
[6] Bovenzi 2016, pp. 281-289; Vanoli, in *Le meraviglie* 2016, pp. 278–279, no. 163.
[7] Brigstocke, D'Albo 2020, pp. 366–367.
[8] Tassinari 2015, pp. 119–126.

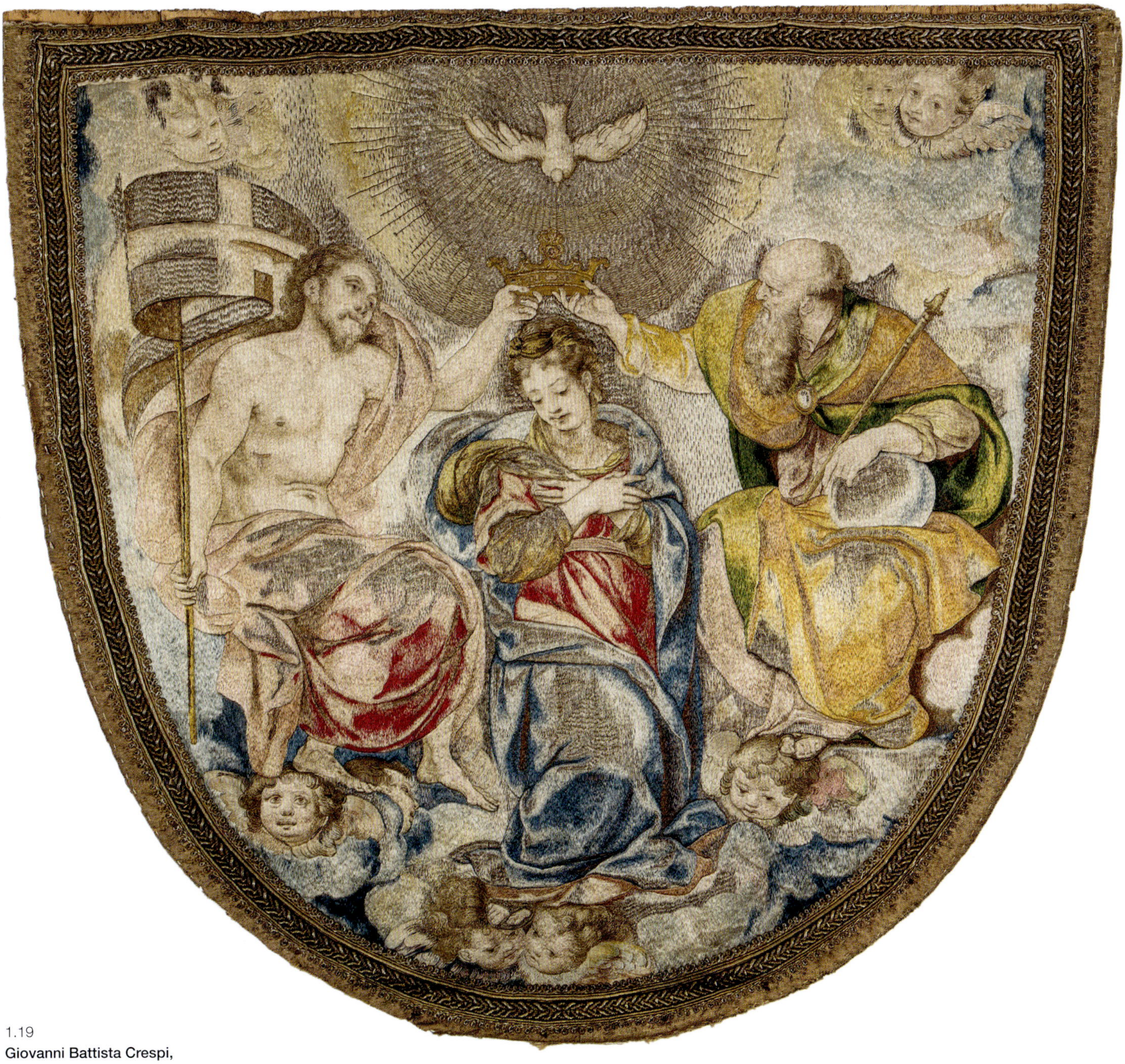

1.19
Giovanni Battista Crespi, known as Il Cerano (drawing)
Antonia Pellegrini (embroidery)
Cope Hood with Coronation of the Virgin
1609–1610
Taffeta embroidered with silk, gold yarn and silver yarn, embroidered gold bullion,
51 × 53 cm
Milan, Veneranda Fabbrica del Duomo di Milano, inv. TSR 3

ARTISTS IN THE CONVENT

In his *Lives*, Vasari cites two artists who were also nuns: the Carmelite Antonia Doni, who died in 1491 and was the daughter of the painter Paolo Uccello; and the Dominican Plautilla Nelli, who at the time was prioress of the convent of Santa Caterina da Siena in Florence.

Plautilla, who had trained by copying the drawings of Fra Bartolomeo, was an adherent of the strict spirituality of Savonarola; with her fellow nuns, she had set up a workshop in which she produced devotional works, some of which were traded. One illustrious predecessor of hers was Caterina Vigri of Bologna: already on the path towards sainthood upon her death in 1463, she was recognised as an artist by Malvasia in the seventeenth century – a factor that would lead, in 1710, two years before she was indeed canonised, to the dedication of the Accademia Clementina to her.

Two seventeenth-century nuns underwent more extensive training: Lucrina Fetti and Orsola Maddalena Caccia. The former, who was the sister of the famous painter Domenico, was active in the Mantuan convent of Sant'Orsola – a highly prestigious site for the Gonzaga dynasty – and produced not only religious paintings but also wonderful court portraits. For her part, the latter was educated by her father Guglielmo, known as "Il Moncalvo", who had worked in Turin with Federico Zuccari on the decoration of the Great Gallery of Charles Emmanuel I and in Milan with the artists of Federico Borromeo. In 1620, at the age of twenty-four, alongside her sisters Orsola entered Ursuline convent in Bianzè; in 1625, her father established a "domestic" convent in Moncalvo, near Asti, out of a desire to have his daughters close to him once again and to "benefit from the labours of Sister Orsola Maddalena". Abbess from 1627 until around 1652, she continued to produce work until at least 1670, catalysing the life of the Moncalvo community around her painting studio, transforming the cloister into an artistic and cultural hub. Her paintings ranged from altarpieces to chamber pictures, and also included a number of valuable still lifes.

CATERINA VIGRI

Bologna, 1413 – Bologna, 1463

Daughter of Giovanni Vigri,[1] a jurist of Ferrara in the service of Nicolò III d'Este, and Benvenuta Mammolini, a Bolognese noblewoman, Caterina spent her early years in Bologna. Having moved to Ferrara around 1420, she was educated in the Humanities by dint of living at the Este court as a companion of Margherita, daughter of the seigneur of the city. However, the devotional component was to prove fundamental to her background and to her work as a writer and miniaturist. Having left the court in 1426, Vigri entered the lay community that led a life of devotion inspired by the rule of Saint Augustine, without the requirement for vows, founded by Bernardina Sedazzari, but at that time under the guidance of Lucia Mascheroni. Upon the dissolution of the community following an internal conflict between two different spiritual orientations, Caterina, allying herself with the group of pious women bound to Franciscan observance, participated in the establishment – with the support of the Poor Clares of Mantua – of the convent of Corpus Domini in Ferrara, which adopted the rule of Saint Clare (1431). As a professed nun, her roles included being in charge of the bakery and then teaching novices. Much of her literary and artistic output dates from this period: she wrote *Le Sette armi spirituali* (*The Seven Spiritual Weapons)*, a treatise on perfection intended for her fellow nuns;[2] she also wrote religious works in verse;[3] and she copied and decorated the *Breviary* (Bologna, convent of the Corpus Domini, the saint's own chapel),[4] in which the acts of transcribing and illuminating are inseparably intertwined and meet the need to carry out an "exerticio mentale" to keep the mind fixed on God, stopping the mind from "wandering".[5] Her oeuvre has been subject to in-depth philological analysis, geared towards reconstructing her cultural make-up, interpreted in close conjunction with the historical context in which she lived and with the purposes that she had set herself – to teach the sisters but also to communicate relentlessly, and sometimes impetuously, the mystical gifts with which she had been blessed.[6] Indeed, in her *Breviary* there are recurring hieratic images awash with symbolism – the pared-back physiognomy of Christ with his enigmatic, beady eyes, emerging amid the exhortations; the swaddled Child floating in the void on the border of the page as if in the mystical abyss of the soul – that offer dazzling insights into the Absolute.[7] Caterina's artistic creativity should, then, be interpreted in relation to the practices of the religious life and the specific paths taken towards spirituality within the conventual community, which served as the springboard for her extraordinary charismatic energy.

Caterina's reputation for sanctity led her to be sent to Bologna in July 1456 to establish a new convent, also named Corpus Domini, which under her inspired and enlightened stewardship became a centre of spirituality and a frame of reference for the entire life of the city: Giovanni II Bentivoglio himself and his family would become devout followers. Caterina was a "living saint", to whom prophetic and magical properties were attributed.[8] Upon her death in 1463, her body was buried and after eighteen days exhumed and found to be untainted: displayed publicly in the convent, she became the first icon venerated by the piety of the faithful. This and other miracles fed into the cult of Saint Catherine, who obtained the concession of her own office and mass in 1524. In 1594, following the interest taken by Cardinal Gabriele Paleotti, her name was inscribed in the *Roman Martyrology*. The process of canonisation was very drawn out, coming to an end only in 1712 with her proclamation as a saint by Pope Clement XI.[9]

Irene Graziani

[1] Spanò Martinelli 1979; Spanò Martinelli 1998; Serventi 2018.
[2] Vegri 1985; Vigri 2000b.
[3] Vigri 2000a.
[4] Biancani 2002; *Pregare con le immagini* 2004.
[5] Bembo 2001.
[6] Leonardi 1988; Leonardi 2004.
[7] Fortunati 2004b, pp. 7–81.
[8] Zarri 1990.
[9] *Il processo* 2003.

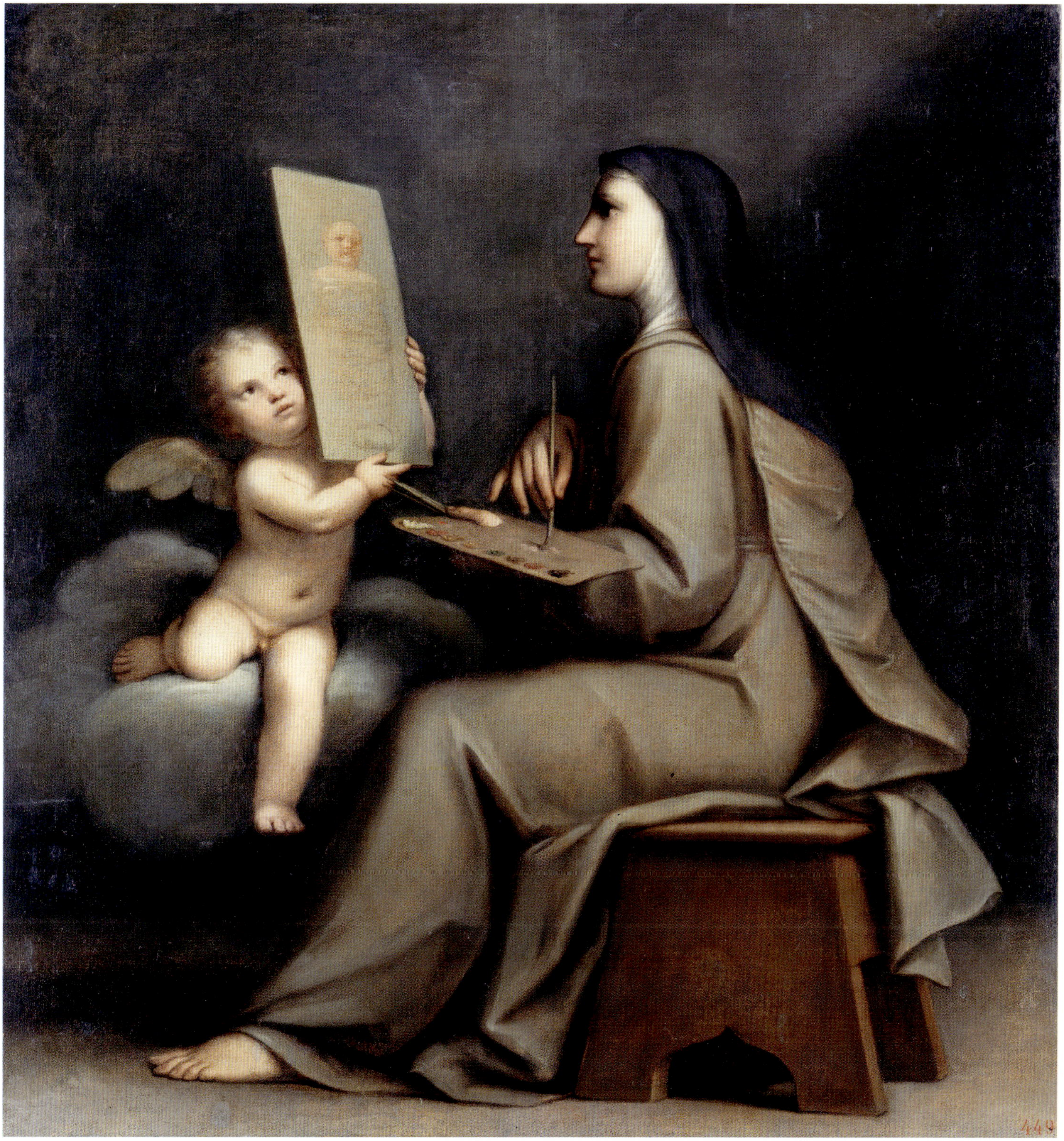

2.1
Marcantonio Franceschini
Saint Catherine Vigri Paints the Christ Child
1723
Oil on canvas,
141.8 × 129.5 cm
Bologna, Pinacoteca Nazionale, inv. 843

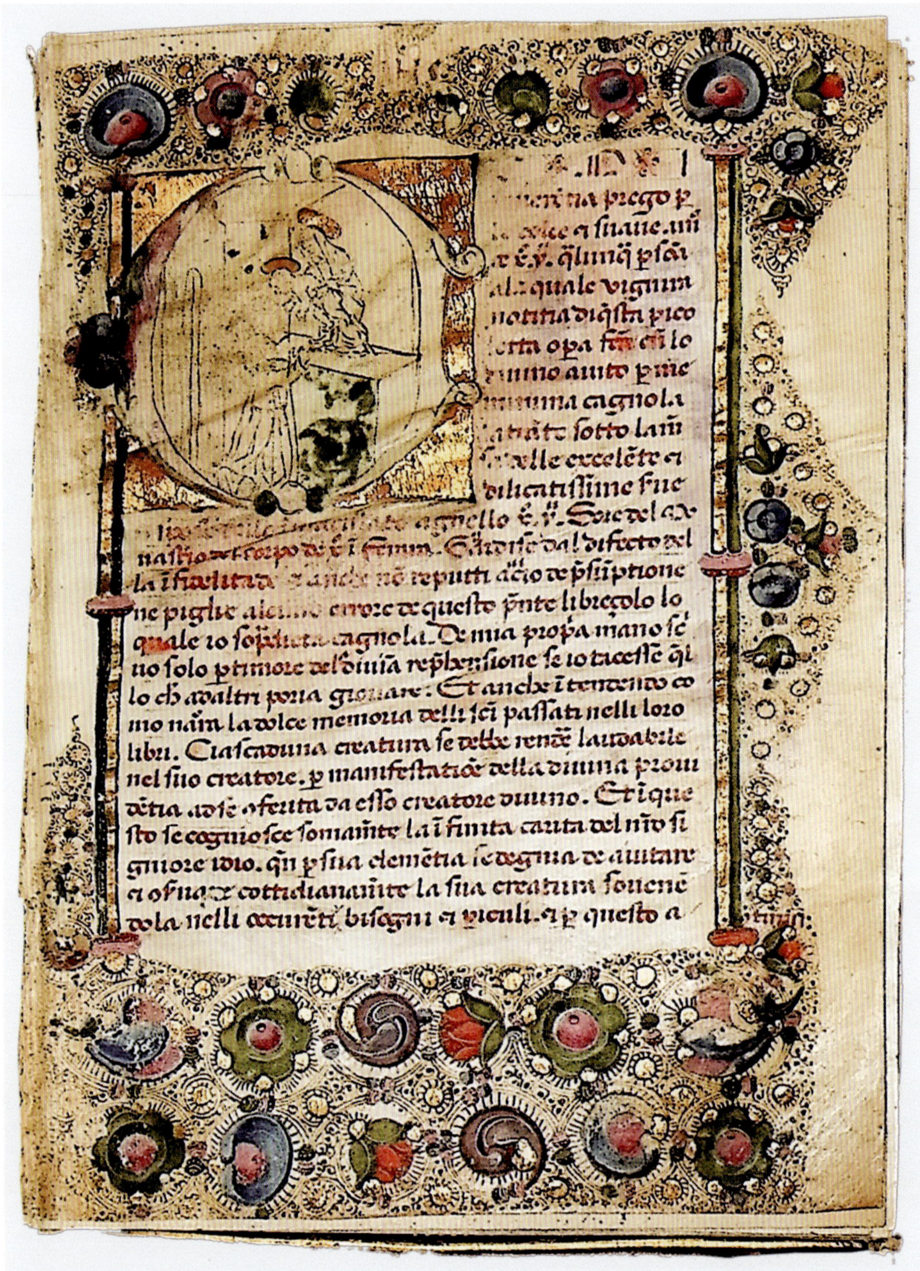

2.2
Unknown miniaturist (copy after Caterina Vigri)
The Seven Spiritual Weapons – Initial C with the Virgin Passing the Christ Child to a Nun (*Caterina Vigri's Vision of Christmas Night*), fol. 1*r*
c. 1463

Parchment codex, fols. 40;
167 × 115 mm
Ferrara, Biblioteca Comunale Ariostea, BCAFE, MS Classe I.354

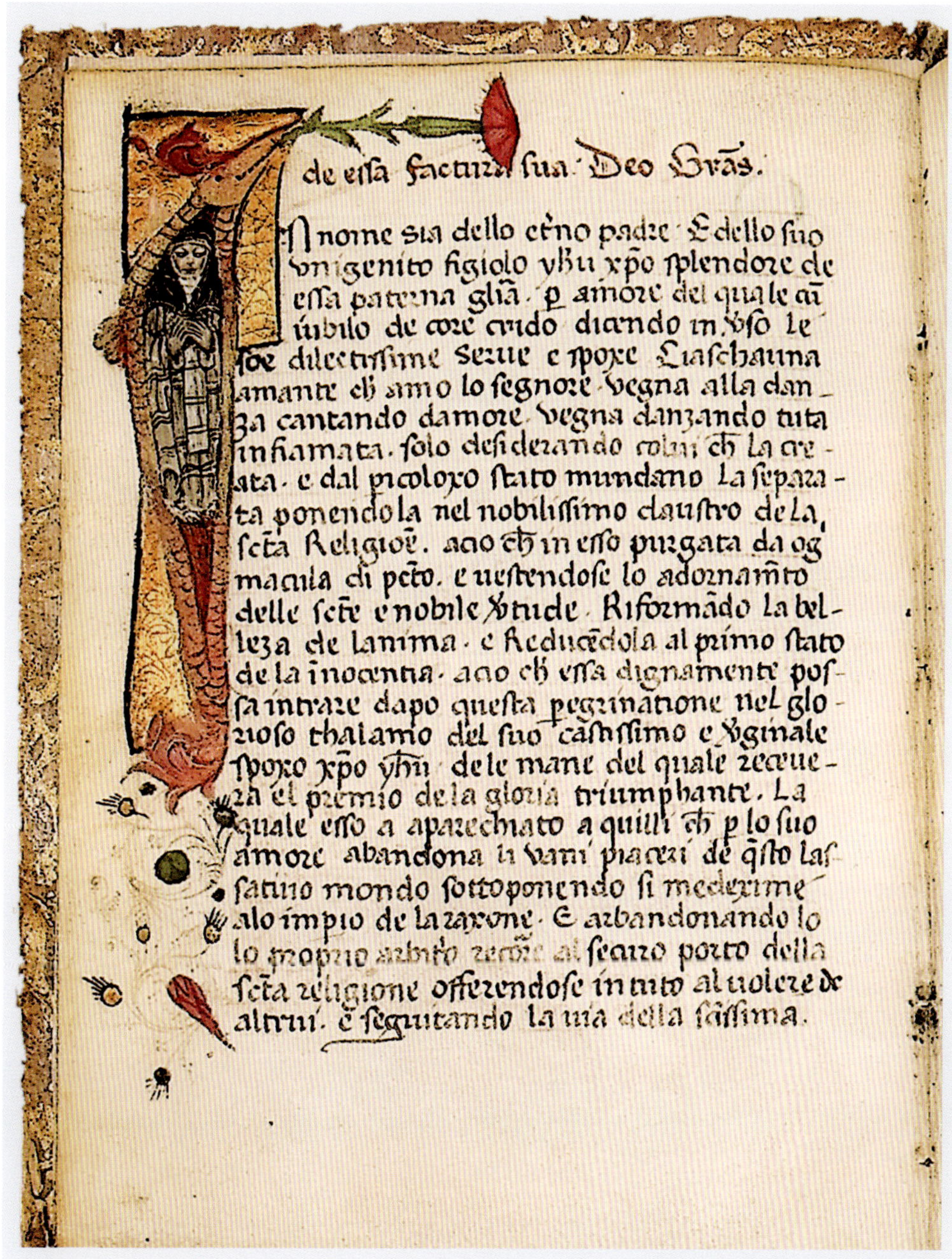

2.3
Unknown miniaturist (copy after Caterina Vigri)
The Seven Spiritual Weapons – Initial I with the Figure of a Nun with Hands Clasped, within a Fish, fol. 1*r*
c. 1463

Parchment codex, fols. 59;
165 × 120 mm
Ferrara, Biblioteca Comunale Ariostea, BCAFE, MS Classe I.356

PLAUTILLA NELLI

Florence, 1524 – Florence, 1588

Pulissena Margherita Nelli was born in Florence, where she was baptised in 1524; in 1538, she would take her vows with the name of Sister Plautilla. The Dominican convent of Santa Caterina in Cafaggio was affiliated to the nearby monastery of San Marco, and as such was linked to the figure of Girolamo Savonarola. In his preaching, the friar had stressed the importance of art in the spiritual and cultural life, recommending that religious people above all should engage with art to elevate the soul and the intellect and to allow religious communities to support themselves autonomously.

As at the monastery of San Marco, where Beato Angelico and Fra Bartolomeo had worked, the sources state that art and culture flourished at the convent of Santa Caterina. As a woman and a nun, Plautilla had not served a proper apprenticeship in an artist's studio but had trained herself by making miniatures and drawings. She would copy the works of other masters, including Fra Bartolomeo, whose collection of sketches, cartoons, engravings and models had reached the convent. Once she had become a master, she went on to run an important "sacred workshop".

For a long time, the only paintings known to have been produced by Plautilla were the *Lamentation* (Museo di San Marco), *The Last Supper* (convent of Santa Maria Novella) – both sourced from the convent of Santa Caterina – and the Pentecost (church of San Domenico in Perugia).[1] Vasari, who writes of the "paintress" in the second edition of the *Lives*,[2] cites the various works in the convent, the large-format paintings made for public commission and "so many paintings" of private devotion produced for "the houses of gentlemen throughout Florence".[3] Among them, are the several images of Saint Catherine of Siena that Plautilla realized in an entrepreneurial spirit geared towards the dissemination of certain "standards" of decorum and moderation of the images in the wake of Savonarola's precepts, associated with *simplicitas* and the educational function of art.[4]

The studio's collective approach to work explains the stylistic and qualitative differences in the paintings and the difficulty of reconstructing the artist's oeuvre, which has been researched over the past twenty years, leading to numerous publications,[5] restoration campaigns and conventions,[6] as well as to the first exhibition of her output,[7] for which an updated catalogue of her works was compiled, including the series of paintings with Saint Catherine of Siena/de' Ricci, the drawings in the Uffizi and the two *Annunciations* in the Uffizi and the Musei Civici in Florence.

Prioress of the convent in the periods 1563–1565, 1571–1573 and 1583–1585, the authoritative, pro-active Sister Plautilla was not just an excellent painter but also an exemplary, venerable and devout nun. She spent around fifty years in the convent of Santa Caterina, animating its spiritual and artistic life, and she died there in 1588.

Carla Scagliosi

1 For possible dates and more detail, see Muzzi 2008, pp. 33–36.
2 Vasari 1568, English ed. 1912–1915, V, pp. 123–128.
3 Vasari 1568, English ed. 1912–1915, V, p. 126.
4 In her paintings, Plautilla uses the formula *orate pro pictora* (in its feminine version) as used by Fra Bartolomeo and by the painters associated with the so-called School of San Marco (Albertinelli, Sogliani, Tosini, etc.) to stress her affiliation with that artistic tradition.
5 See, amongst others, *Plautilla Nelli* 2008, *Artiste nel chiostro* 2015, *Fra Bartolomeo* 2019.
6 "Suor Plautilla Nelli (1523–1588). The First Woman Painter of Florence", curated by J. Nelson (Fiesole, 27 May, 1998); "Fra Bartolomeo 1517", curated by J. A. Assonitis, L. Cinelli, M. Tamassia (Florence, 26–28 October, 2017).
7 "Plautilla Nelli: arte e devozione sulle orme di Savonarola / Art and Devotion in Savonarola's Footsteps", curated by J. F. Navarro, Florence, Gallerie degli Uffizi, 8 March–4 June, 2017.

2.4
Plautilla Nelli
Saint Catherine of Siena / Caterina de' Ricci
1560–1580
Oil on canvas, glued on panel, 57 × 41 cm
Perugia, Galleria Nazionale dell'Umbria, inv. 533 (I.M. 148)

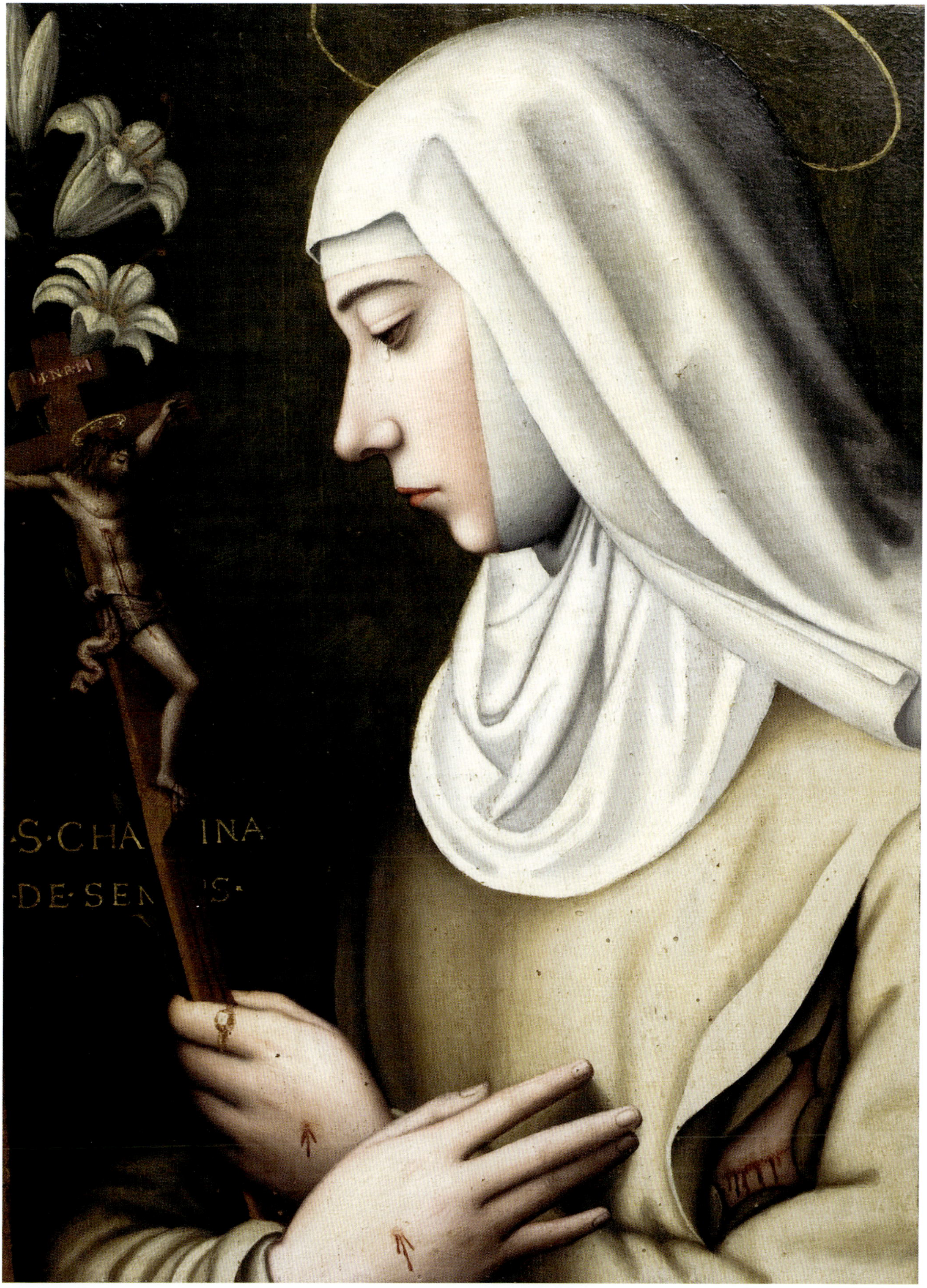

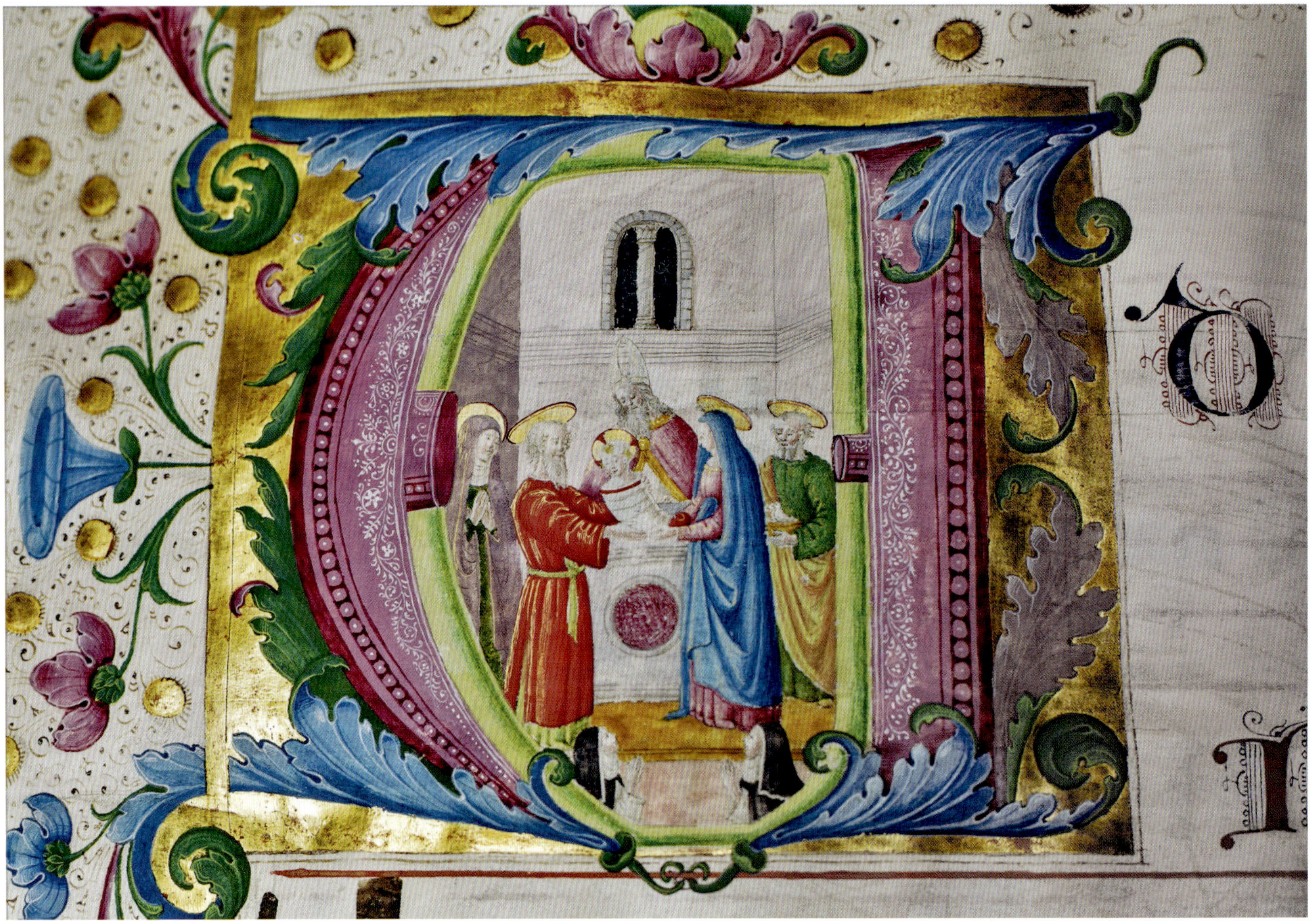

2.5
Plautilla Nelli (attributed)
Antiphonary E – Initial A with the Presentation of Jesus at the Temple with Two Nuns, fol. 233*v*
c. 1545–1557
Tempera, gold leaf and ink on parchment, 587 × 414 mm
Florence, Museo di San Marco – Direzione Regionale Musei della Toscana, Ms San Marco 565

2.6
Plautilla Nelli (attributed)
Antiphonary C – Initial A with Adoration of the Child and the Virgin Mary, Joseph and Two Nuns, fol. 2*v*
1558
Tempera, gold leaf and ink on parchment, 584 × 422 mm
Florence, Museo di San Marco – Direzione Regionale Musei della Toscana, Ms San Marco 566

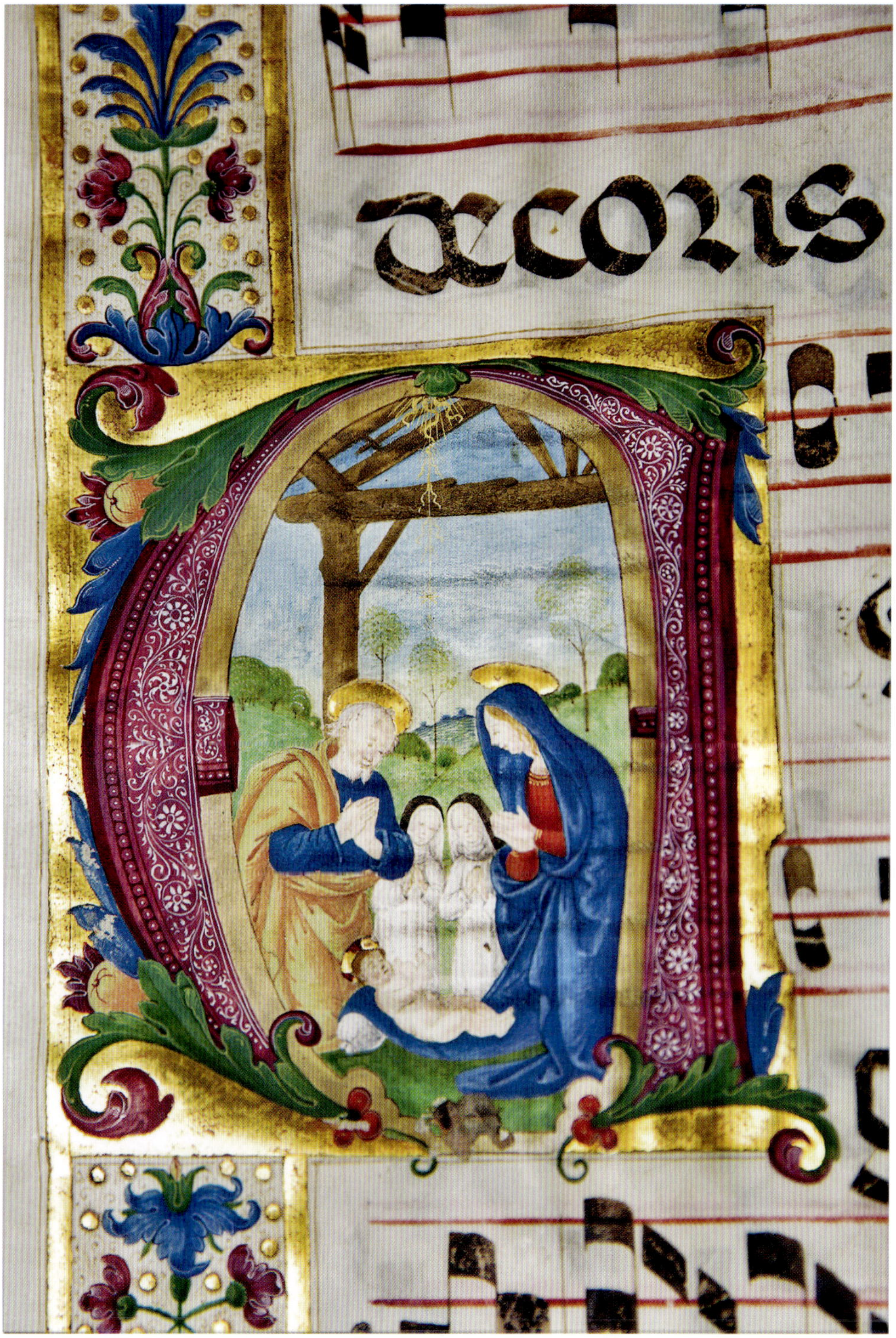
decoris

ORSOLA MADDALENA CACCIA

Moncalvo (Asti), 1596 – Moncalvo (Asti), 1676

Orsola Maddalena Caccia was born towards the end of 1596 in Moncalvo, at that time part of the duchy of Mantua and Monferrato, to Guglielmo Caccia and Laura Oliva.[1] Theodora – her given name – grew up in an artistic milieu. Her father, known as "Il Moncalvo" was the most celebrated painter in this area; he had worked with Federico Zuccari on the Great Gallery of Charles Emmanuel I in Turin, and in Milan with the artists of Federico Borromeo.[2] His mother's side of the family also included various painters working in Casale Monferrato.[3] Theodora and her sister Francesca – who died at the age of twenty in 1628 – followed in their father's footsteps, becoming "le Gentilesche o le Fontane del Monferrato".[4] Like Lavinia and Artemisia, Theodora was "educated in painting" by her father, learning from him and from the masters of the Renaissance,[5] who they studied via the prints in the studio, as evinced by her youthful *Holy Family* (Cavallini Sgarbi collection) inspired by Raphael's *Madonna of Divine Love*.

The house-studio was the fulcrum of the life of the painter who, in the second decade of the seventeenth century, became the trusted pupil and collaborator of il Moncalvo to the extent that she would stand in for him as and when required, doing so on numerous works. In 1620, at the age of twenty-four, along with her sisters Theodora entered the Ursuline monastery in Bianzè, where she lived for five years, taking the name of Orsola Maddalena. Of that period there remain three *Capilettera* (Vercelli, Archivio di Stato), significant traces of a graphic oeuvre that also includes the *Holy Family and Saint Anne* (Frankfurt, Städel Museum, inv. 438 Z).[6]

In the spring of 1625, il Moncalvo established within the walls of his home "a new Congregation or Monastery" of Ursuline nuns, out of a desire to have his daughters, who had by now become nuns, close to him once again and to "benefit from the labours of Sister Orsola Maddalena" until his death, which came in the November of the same year. The monastery represents a singular case, having been established, at least in part, for artistic purposes. Within it, Guglielmo had set aside a room "where painting is done" and, through his will, he ensured that his two daughters would have access to his drawings, equipment and incomplete works on a usufruct basis. Orsola, abbess of the monastery from 1627 until around 1652, continued painting until at least 1670, the date of the handover of the Bianzè altarpiece.[7] Heir to the Moncalvo tradition, her output encompassed altarpieces – which made her one of the most prolific female artists of the early modern era – and chamber pictures, as well as a very small but highly valuable set of poetic still lifes.[8]

The painter's works, suspended between devotion and contemplation, had an exceptionally strong influence. The closest relationships she established during her career included that with Scipione Agnelli, Bishop of Casale and courtier of the Gonzaga family. Orsola shared the prelate's sensitivity towards the mysticism of the time, as evinced by the *Mystical Marriage of Osanna Andreasi* (1648; Mantua, Museo Diocesano) and by the presence in his collection of versions of the *Child Sleeping on the Cross*, a theme very dear to the artist.[9] Her interest in this type of spirituality reverberates through highly imaginative works such as the oneiric *Vision of Saint John*, recently rediscovered in the sanctuary of Crea.

Far from the world of the courts – which to some extent she yearned to enter, as revealed in a 1643 letter to Cristine of France – Orsola succeeded, for fifty years, in catalysing the life of the Moncalvo community around her painting studio, transforming her cloistered enclosure into a place where arts and culture were put centre stage, making it a frame of reference for the educated young women of the nobility and the notability of Monferrato.

The commemoration of herself as an individual, and of her status as a painter, was entrusted by Orsola to a painted image: a *Saint Anthony*, now lost, but on the title block of which it was still possible, in the late nineteenth century, to read the testament of her soul.[10]

Antonella Chiodo

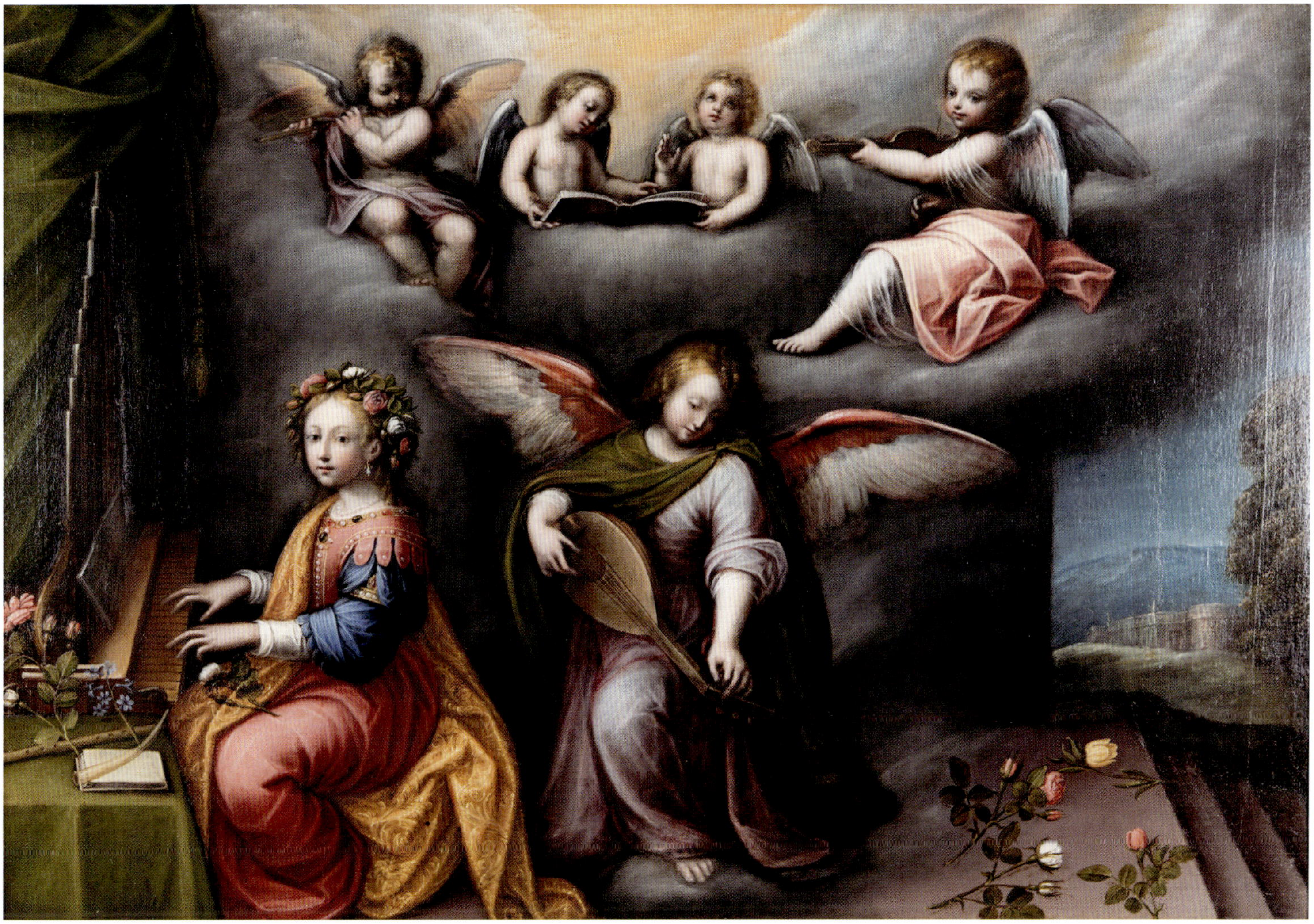

2.7
Orsola Maddalena Caccia
Saint Cecilia Playing a Positive Organ and Musician Angels
c. 1620–1630
Oil on canvas, 114 × 148 cm
Turin, Musei Reali – Galleria Sabauda, inv. 141

[1] Romano 1972; Ghirardi 2002; Chiodo 2003; *Orsola* 2012; Chiodo 2015, pp. 11-14.
[2] Bava 1997; *Seicento* 2013.
[3] Ambrogio Oliva, Orsola's grandfather, had married Maria Elisabetta Luzaga of Brescia (Prosperi 2019, pp. 310-344), which implies contact between the family and that city, and supports the Brescian tangents highlighted in Oliva's painting (Romano 1970, p. 72; Chiodo 2008, pp. 87-95).
[4] Lanzi 1809, ed. 1968-1974, III, p. 243.
[5] Morandotti 2005, p. 258.
[6] Chiodo 2003; Chiodo 2012, p. 103.
[7] Chiodo 2003, p. 197; Chiodo 2007, p. 44 before the restoration.
[8] Cottino 2012; cf. Chiodo 2012; Ferro 2012; Morandotti 2015, pp. 63–65.
[9] Lorenzoni 2018, p. 197; D'Albo 2012, p. 48.
[10] Baudi di Vesme 1963-1982, I, pp. 230–231.

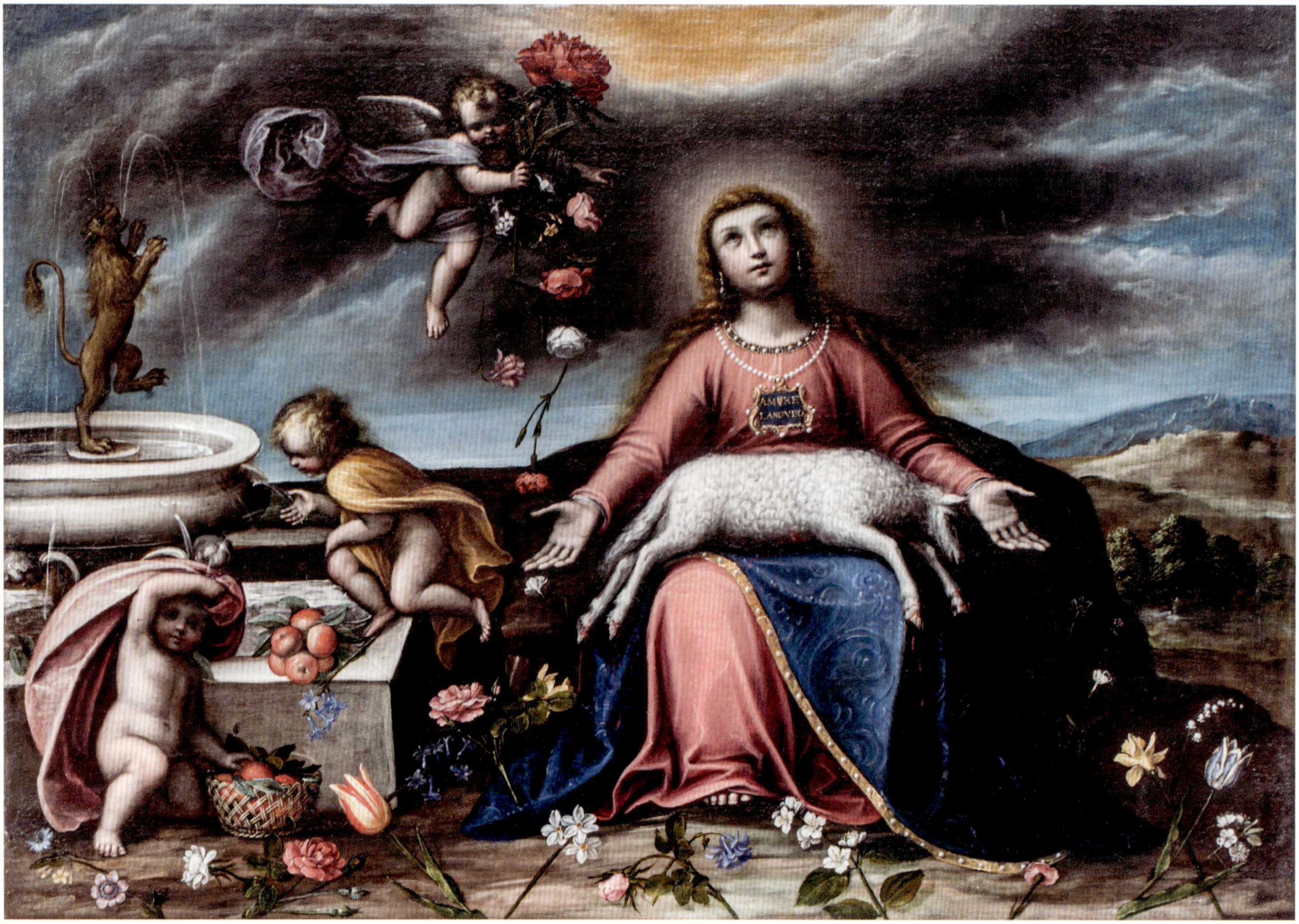

2.8
Orsola Maddalena Caccia
Mystical Allegory
(Amore langueo)
c. 1635
Oil on canvas, 84 × 118 cm
Curtatone (Mantua),
sanctuary of the Beata Vergine
delle Grazie

2.9
Orsola Maddalena Caccia
Nativity of Saint John
the Baptist
c. 1630–1640
Oil on canvas, 290 × 200 cm
Moncalvo (Asti),
parish of Sant'Antonio
di Padova – Diocese of Casale
Monferrato (Alessandria)

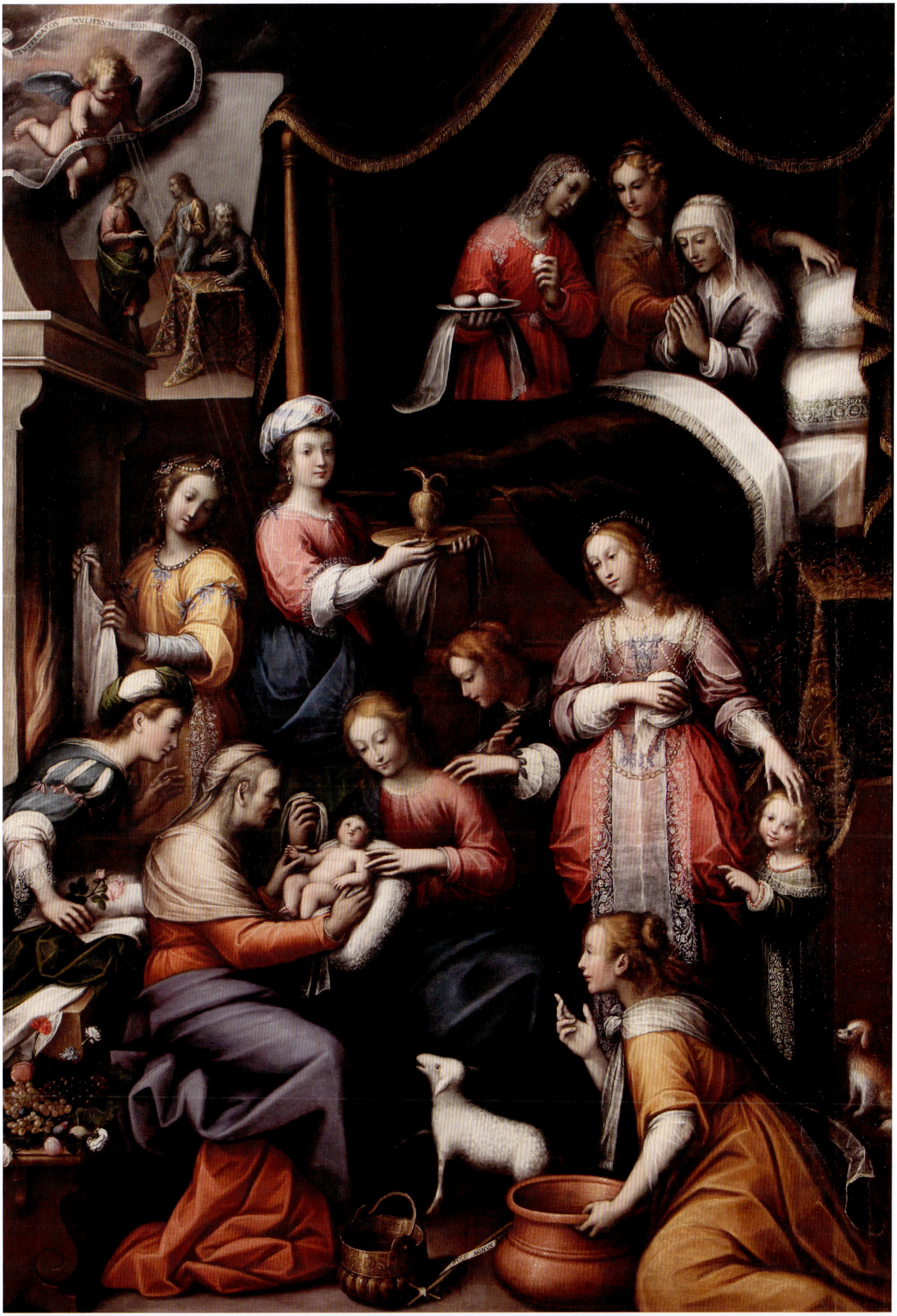
INTER NATOS MVLIERVM NON SVRREXIT

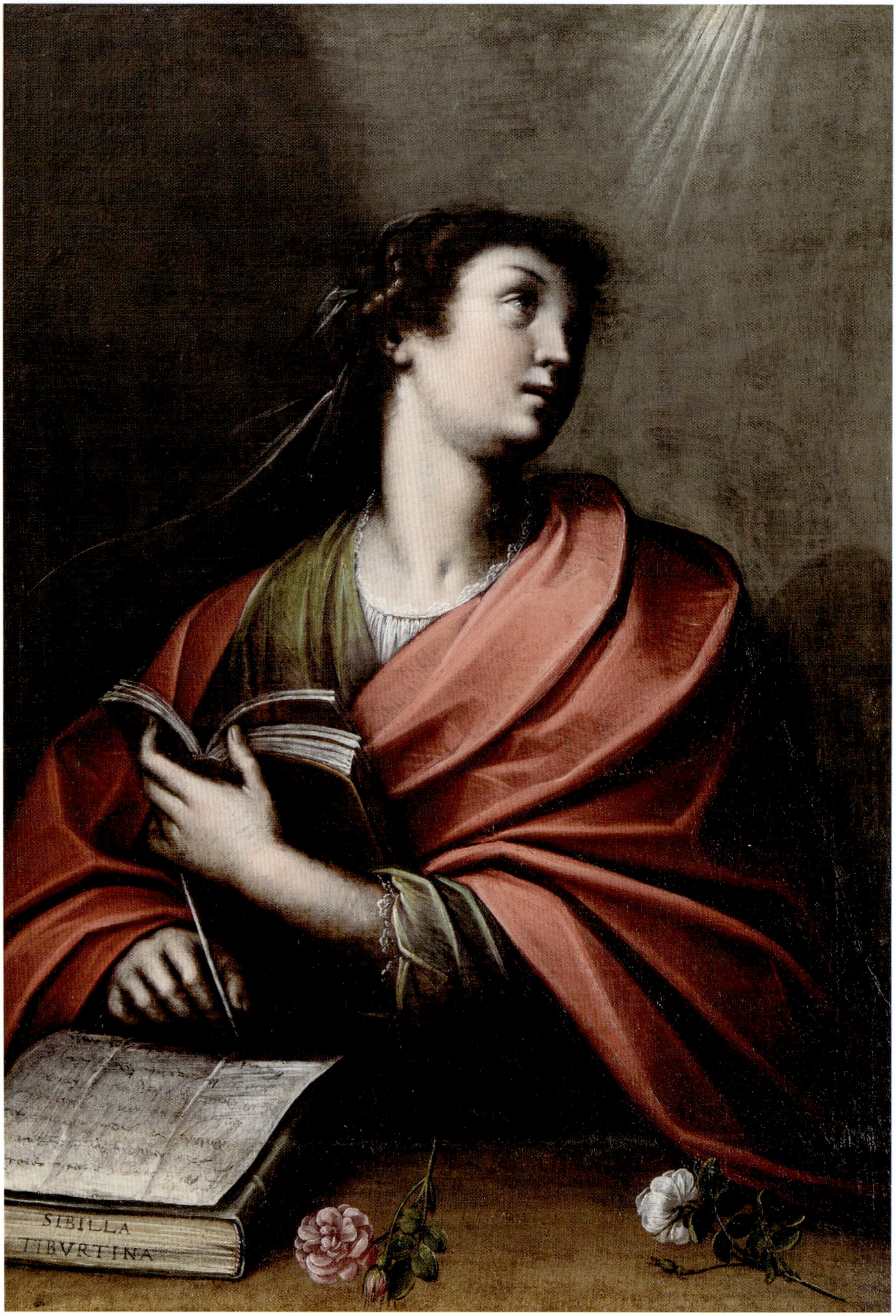
SIBILLA
TIBVRTINA

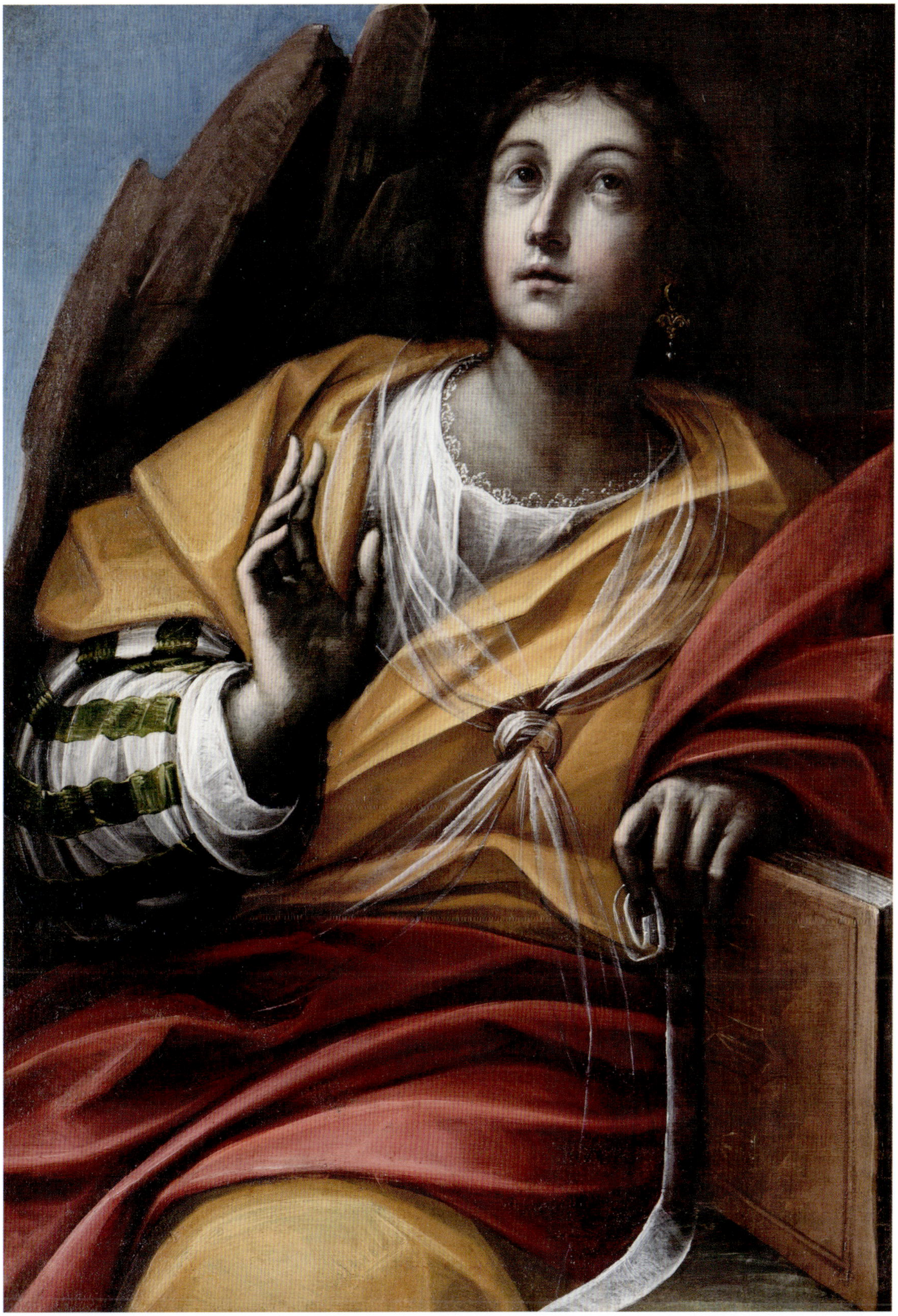

2.10
Orsola Maddalena Caccia
Tiburtine Sibyl
c. 1640–1650
Oil on canvas, 110 × 76.5 cm
Asti, Fondazione Cassa
di Risparmio di Asti collection

2.11
Orsola Maddalena Caccia
Cumaean Sibyl
c. 1640–1650
Oil on canvas,
106.5 × 77.5 cm
Asti, Fondazione Cassa
di Risparmio di Asti collection

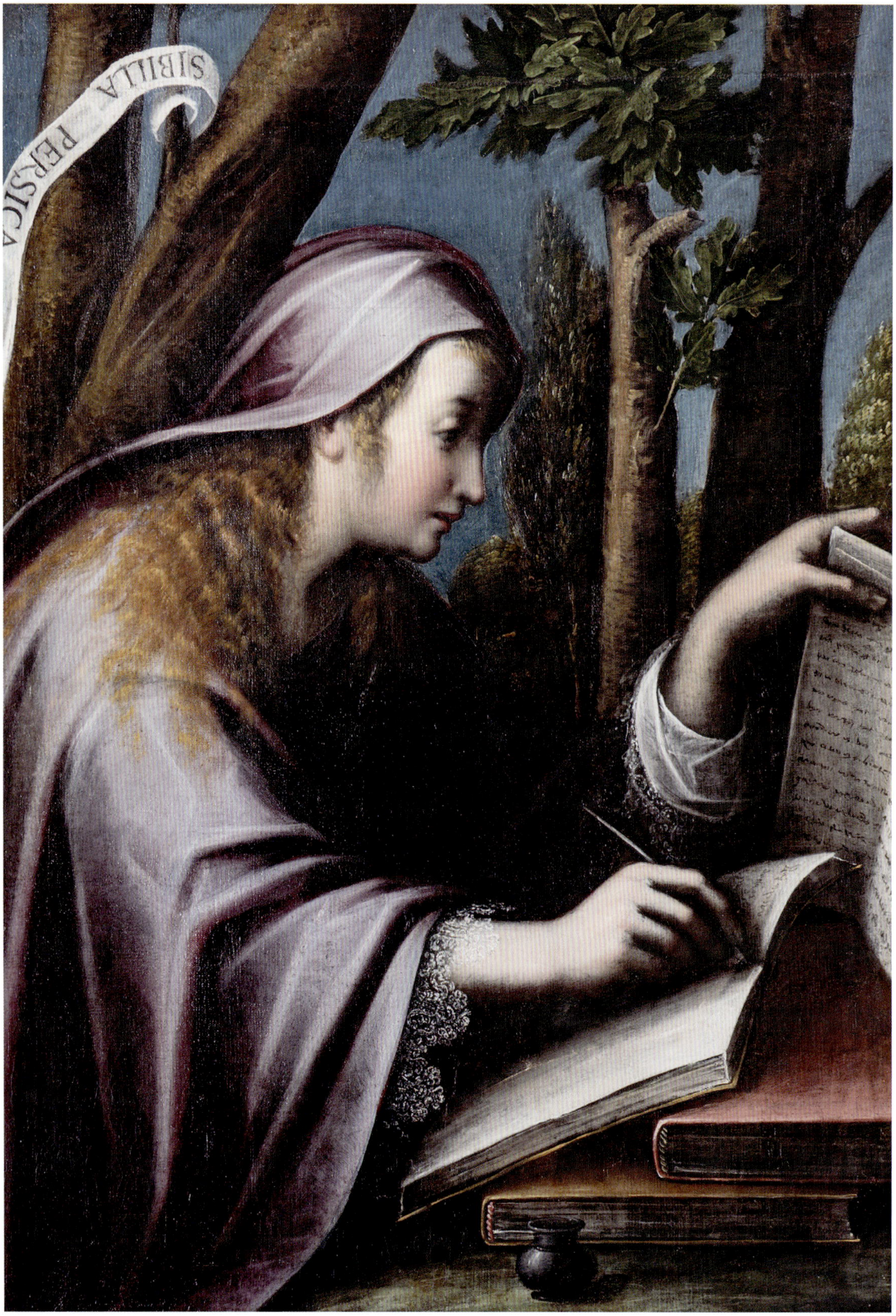

2.12
Orsola Maddalena Caccia
Persian Sibyl
c. 1640–1650
Oil on canvas, 110 × 78.5 cm
Asti, Fondazione Cassa
di Risparmio di Asti collection

2.13
Orsola Maddalena Caccia
Delphic Sibyl
c. 1640–1650
Oil on canvas, 110.5 × 78 cm
Asti, Fondazione Cassa
di Risparmio di Asti collection

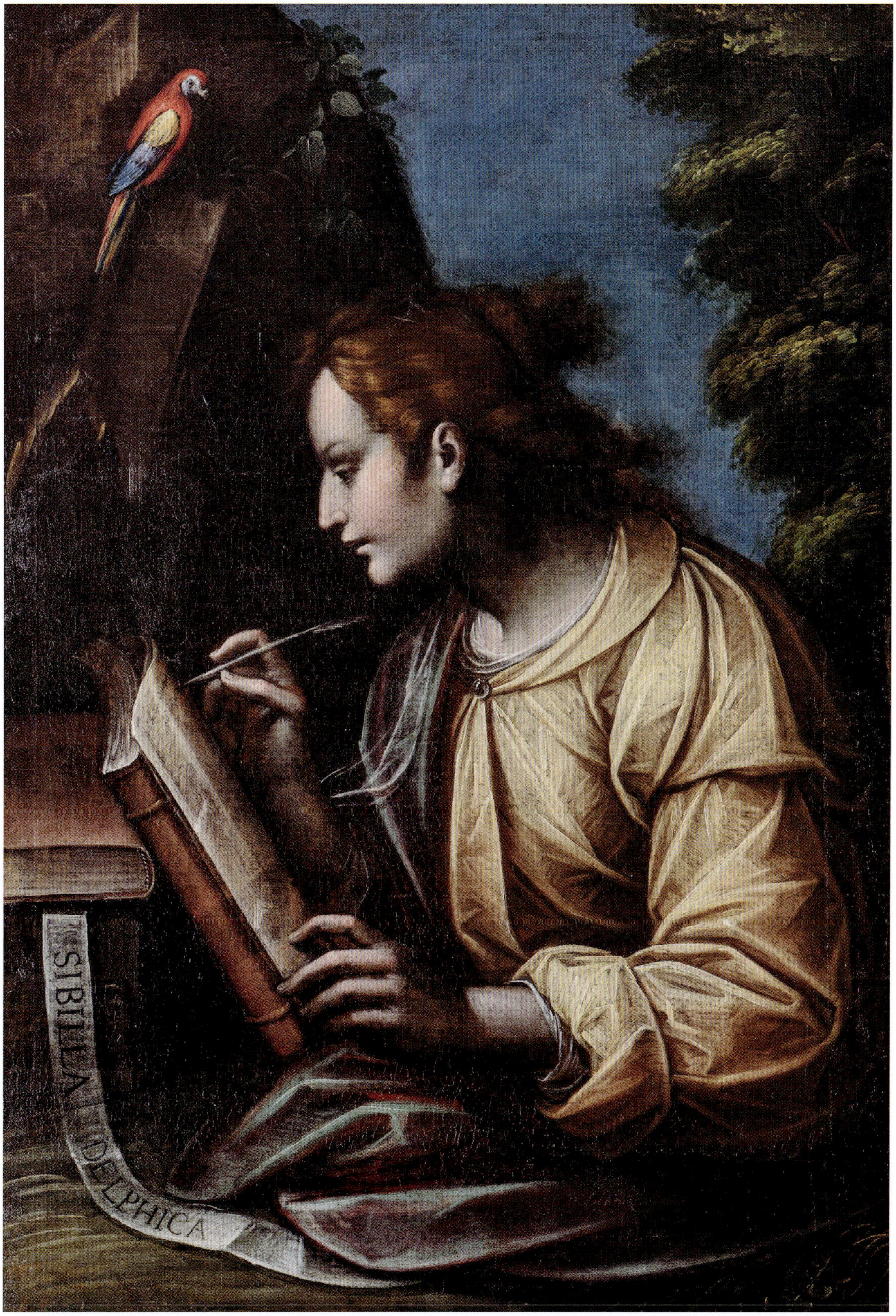
SIBILLA DELPHICA

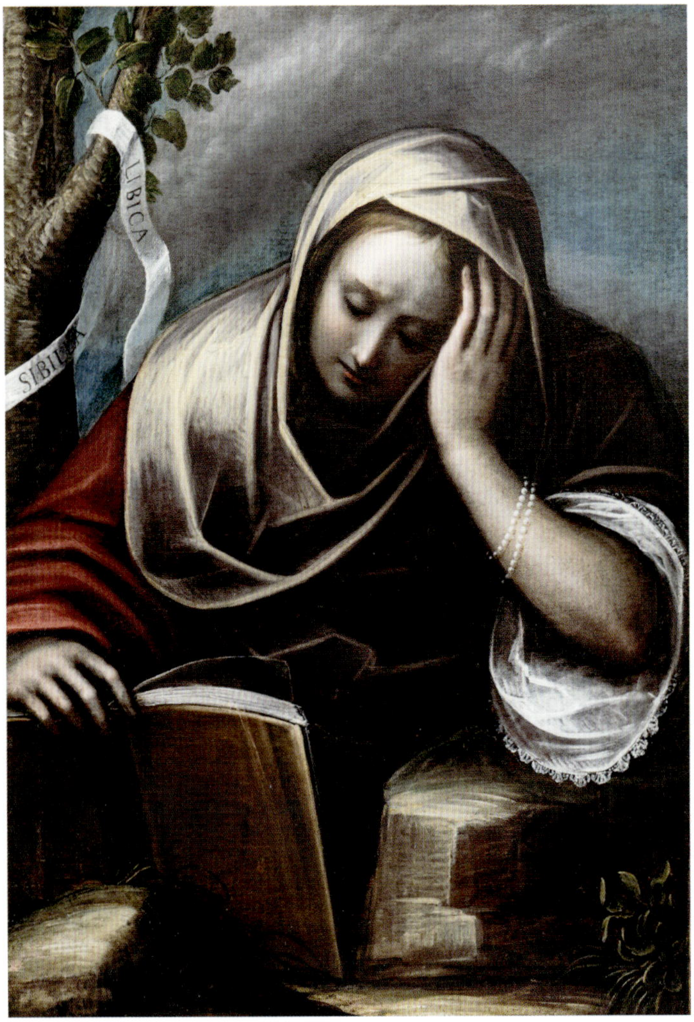

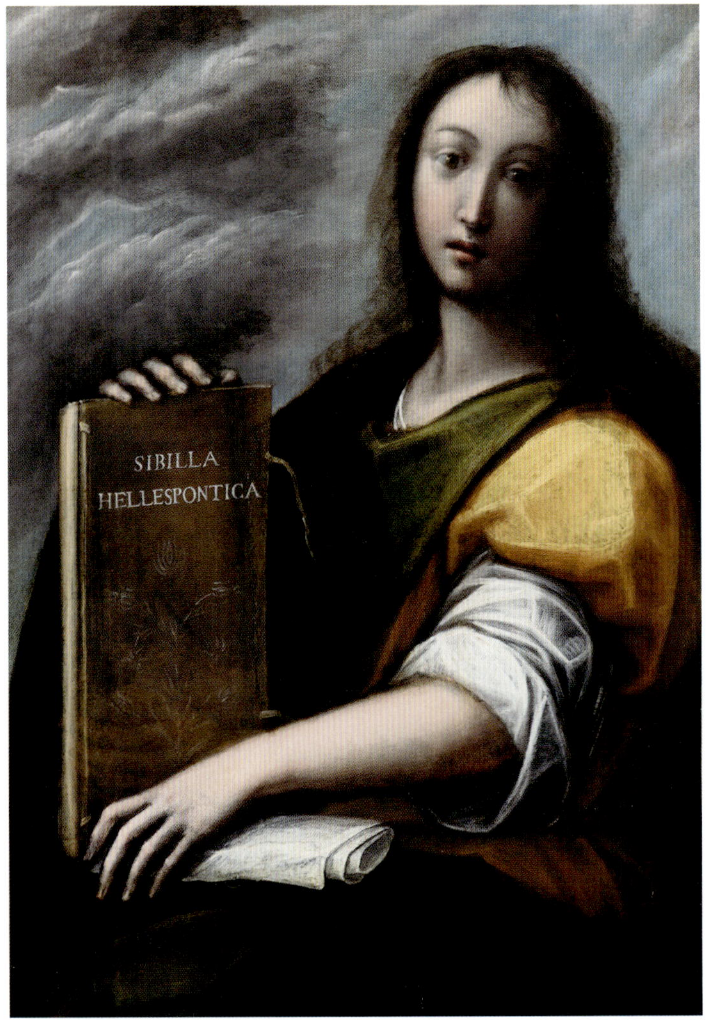

2.14
Orsola Maddalena Caccia
Libyan Sibyl
c. 1640–1650
Oil on canvas,
106.5 × 77.5 cm
Asti, Fondazione Cassa
di Risparmio di Asti collection

2.15
Orsola Maddalena Caccia
Hellespontine Sibyl
c. 1640–1650
Oil on canvas,
106.5 × 77.5 cm
Asti, Fondazione Cassa
di Risparmio di Asti collection

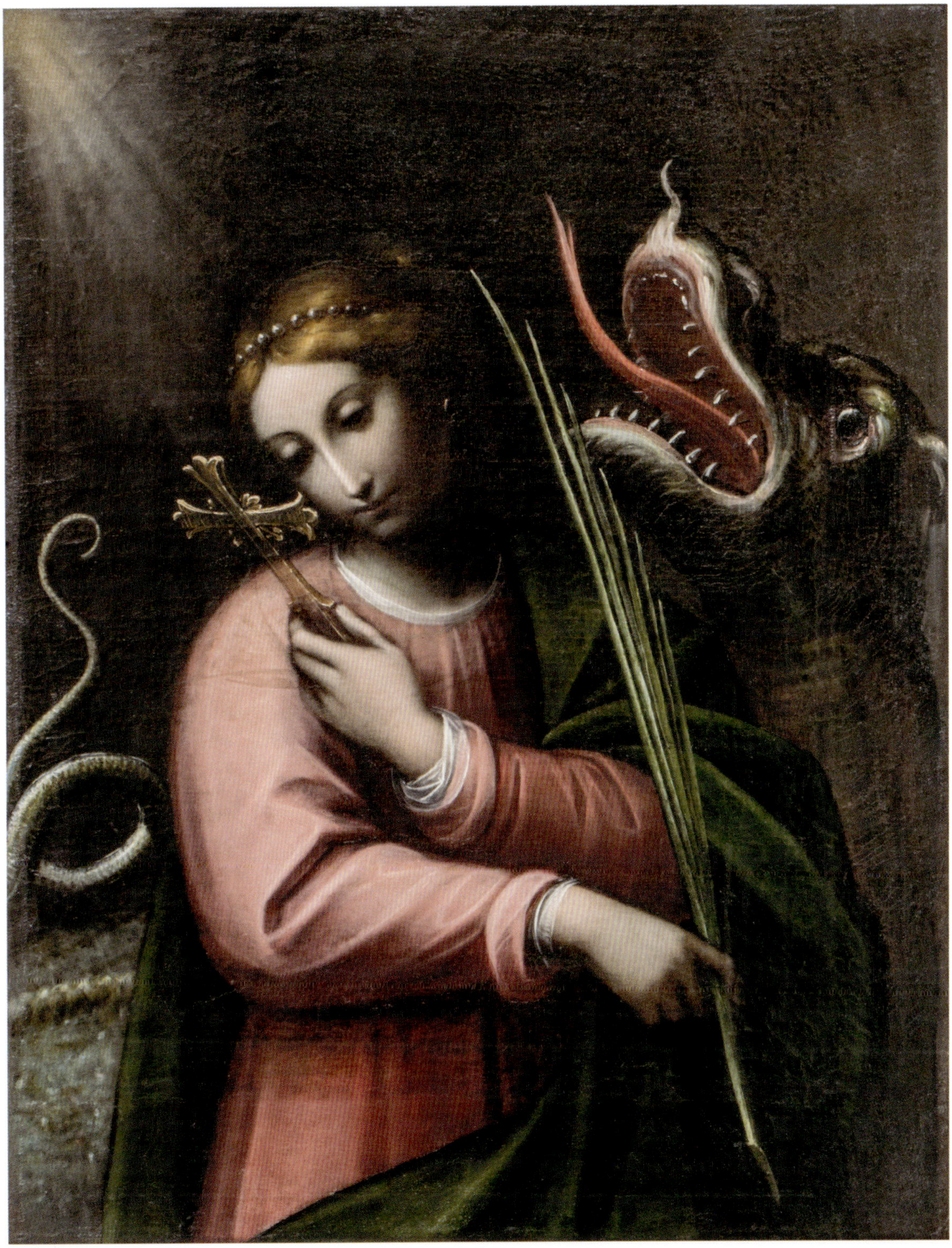

2.16
Orsola Maddalena Caccia
Saint Margaret of Antioch
c. 1640–1650
Oil on canvas, 95 × 73 cm
Curtatone (Mantua),
sanctuary of the Beata Vergine
delle Grazie

LUCRINA FETTI

Rome, c. 1595 – Mantua, 1651

Although the exact date of birth of Giustina Fetti has yet to be confirmed (she was certainly born in Rome, probably around 1595),[1] the life of Sister Lucrina, the name she chose and by which she was known since 1614, came to an end in Mantua in 1651, in the convent of Sant'Orsola, where she would take her vows and would spend her adult life.[2] The importance of making these details clear runs far deeper than simple biography: the conventual dimension was crucial in enabling her to produce paintings for extremely prestigious clients (without the anxiety of financial need, and far removed from the jealousies of the court), and the reputation and, indeed, the flourishing of the convent of Sant'Orsola were, for the sister of the great Domenico Fetti,[3] her life's mission. Like her brother, she learned the rudiments of painting in the Roman studio of her father, Pietro, but without doubt Domenico was crucial in allowing her to develop her skills, especially in light of the training offered to the male sibling alone at the studio of the academic Ludovico Cardi, known as Cigoli. In 1614, Domenico was called upon by Ferdinando Gonzaga to become his main court painter.[4] He was accompanied to Mantua by his father and sisters, including Giustina, who due to her laudable talent entered the convent of Sant'Orsola, a key site of prestige for the Gonzaga dynasty, as well as an important place of worship, second only to the Palazzo Ducale. The convent had been founded in 1599 by Margherita Gonzaga,[5] daughter of the sixth Duke of Mantua, having returned to her home town after the death of her husband Alfonso d'Este,[6] the Seigneur of Ferrara.[7] Entry into the convent, to which she was entitled as a lady-in-waiting, was reserved for young women from the upper echelons of society. For Lucrina, the spiritual dowry, which every aspiring nun had to pay to cover their living expenses, was settled by Ferdinando Gonzaga, who on 3 December 1614 gave 1500 *scudi* on her behalf.[8] She is not known to have produced any paintings prior to entering the convent but, when her brother was appointed court painter, Lucrina immediately became the celebrated female painter of the second institution of the Gonzagas' power.[9] Lucrina's artistic output can be divided into two categories: religious paintings and portraits – the execution of works in both genres reflected the diplomatic and power requirements of the convent.[10] In terms of her religious paintings, a total of eleven works are recorded: in the church adjacent to the convent, but external to it (for public services),[11] the sides of the high altar were decorated by the full-figure portraits of *Saint Mary Magdalene* (lost) and *Saint Barbara* (previously in a private collection in Rome);[12] the same location also featured an image of *Saint Margaret* in honour of the founder of the convent (previously in a private collection in New York). In the church within the convent, reserved for the nuns' own services, the sides of the high altar were adorned with a *Deposition* on the left and an *Adoration of the Shepherds* on the right, whereas on the opposite side of the church there was an *Agony in the Garden*;[13] an *Archangel Gabriel* and an *Annunciation* embellished the marble staircase leading to the upper floor of the convent.[14] Together with this latter painting, another three are still found in Mantua (*Crowning with Thorns*, *Adoration of the Magi*, *Visitation*), which were painted in 1629 and are signed.[15] In terms of the portraits, we know of seven carried out by Sister Lucrina, all depicting women from the House of Gonzaga who lived in the convent:[16] two of Margherita Gonzaga, produced between 1614 and 1618, when the duchess and the painter lived together in the convent;[17] a portrait of Caterina de' Medici, wife of Duke Ferdinando from 1617, who lived in the convent for a few months in 1626, as a widow, before returning to Florence;[18] one of Eleonora Gonzaga I, signed and dated 1622 on the occasion of the marriage of the subject to Emperor Ferdinand II; one of Eleonora Gonzaga II as a youngster (lost);[19] one of Maria Gonzaga (lost), daughter of Francesco Gonzaga IV and Margaret of Savoy; and a final painting identified as a portrait either of Eleonora Gonzaga II (perhaps painted in 1651 on the occasion of her marriage to Emperor Ferdinand III) or of Anne of Austria, sister of the founder Margaret, who in 1611 married Emperor Matthias.[20] The artistic output of Sister Lucrina was, then, closely associated with the political strategies of the convent of Sant'Orsola, but the link that the painter established with the convent had more deeply personal aspects that became even stronger after the death of Margherita Gonzaga: in 1632, Sister Lucrina financed, to the tune of one hundred *scudi*, the transfer to Sant'Orsola of her sister Giuliana Ferdinanda, a nun at the convent of Santa Chiara;[21] but above all, following the death of her brother Domenico – and, subsequently, of her other brothers (Tommaso, Clemente and Vincenzo) who had initially inherited his assets – Lucrina laid claim to the estate of the illustrious painter, not for herself but for the convent of Sant'Orsola, within which she found social dignity and artistic celebrity.[22]

Cecilia Paolini

[1] Bourne 2009, p. 166.

[2] The convent of Sant'Orsola, founded by Margherita Gonzaga, followed the Rule of Saint Francis, but was entitled to own moveable and immoveable assets (on condition that they were exclusively under the auspices of the convent) and to host laypersons. These exceptions had been requested by the founder and approved by Pope Clement VIII in 1604, see Gladen 2005, pp. 127–128.

[3] Domenico Fetti (Rome, 1589 – Venice, 1623).

[4] Ferdinando Gonzaga, Sixth Duke of Mantua (Mantua, 1587 – Mantua, 1626).

[5] Initially in the *contrada delle Borre*, but she was transferred in 1603 to the Pradella district following the acquisition of a number of buildings, see Gladen 2005, p. 127.

[6] Alfonso d'Este, Third Duke of Ferrara (Ferrara, 1476 – Ferrara, 1534).

[7] Although she had her own apartments within the convent she had founded, Margherita Gonzaga (Mantua, 1564 – Mantua, 1618) would never take her vows.

[8] Archivio di Stato di Mantova (from now on: ASMn), Magistrato Camerale Antico, P. V Donazioni (1600–1619). Gladen 2005, p. 129.

[9] Giovanni Baglione, who stayed in Mantua in 1621 and 1622, was the first to highlight her artistic reputation (Baglione 1642, p. 155); her posthumous fame is cited in many sources, including the entry in Orlandi 1753.

[10] The list of paintings produced by Lucrina Fetti can be deduced not only from the signed works that are already known but also from two documentary sources: Cadioli 1763 and the inventory of assets of the convent compiled by Giovanni Bottani in 1786, the year of its closure (ASMn, Notarial Archive, notary Angelo Pescatori, b. 7110).

[11] The external church was constructed by Antonio Maria Viani, an architect of the Gonzaga court, between 1608 and 1613.

[12] Signed and dated 1619 "Lucrina Fetti feci l'anno 1619 / in S.ta Orsola".

[13] The *Deposition* and the *Agony in the Garden* are held at the Palazzo Ducale in Mantua.

[14] Circa 1620, oil on canvas, 226.4 × 173.7 cm, Mantua, Palazzo Ducale (inv. no. 708). For stylistic reasons, the painting, depicting the Announced Virgin, was attributed by Sanguineti to the German Karl Santner; this attribution was subsequently confirmed by Stefano L'Occaso (Sanguineti, in *Dipinti* 2002, pp. 78–81; L'Occaso 2004, p. 54; L'Occaso 2011, p. 312, no. 369).

[15] Gladen 2005, p. 137.

[16] Except the half-figure portrait of Margherita Gonzaga (held at the Museo di Castelvecchio in Verona), the portrait of Maria Gonzaga and that of Eleonora II as a youngster (both lost), the others are held at the Palazzo Ducale.

[17] One is a half-figure portrait of the duchess and bears the inscription "Margherita Gonzaga / Abadessa di s. Orsola e Fondatrice di detto convento / di Lucrina Fetti"; the other is a full-figure portrait that is found in the Palazzo Ducale in Mantua.

[18] This portrait is cited in the 1786 inventory as *Sant'Elena*; it was attributed to Lucrina da Ozzòla and identified as Caterina de' Medici in the guise of Saint Helen by Askew: Ozzòla 1949, p. 4, no. 18; Askew 1976, p. 127; Gladen 2005, p. 140.

[19] Intra 1895, p. 24.

[20] The identification of the subject as Eleonora Gonzaga II was posited by Askew, and was then supported by Zerbi Fanna and Gladen (Askew 1976, p. 126, no. 22; Zerbi Fanna 1989, p. 39; Gladen 2005, p. 139). For the exhibition "Splendours of the Gonzaga", Chambers and Somers Cocks posited that the painting could be a copy of the *Portrait of Anne of Austria* painted in 1613 by Jeremias Günter and held at the Kunsthistorisches in Vienna; this hypothesis is also supported by Molly Bourne (*Splendours of the Gonzaga* 1981, p. 242, no. 273; Bourne 2009, p. 167). In this regard, Intra states that the elderly Lucrina produced two portraits of Eleonora Gonzaga II, see Intra 1895, p. 24.

[21] The convent of Santa Chiara was home to two sisters of Domenico and Lucrina Fetti – Giuliana Ferdinanda and Lucrezia Vittoria. Their dowries (of 400 *scudi* each) were paid by their brother Domenico: ASMn, Notarial Archive, Notary A. Dall'Oglio, June-December 1619, b. 3972 bis, fols. 239*v*-240*r*; Gladen 2005, p. 131.

[22] This inheritance consisted, in the main, of the Zuccaro Tower, granted by Duke Ferdinando to Domenico and returned to the Gonzaga court after the death of the last Fetti brother; in 1633, alongside the assignment to the convent of said building, Sister Lucrina, together with her fellow nuns, requested the assignment of the income from other buildings that had belonged to her brother; Gladen 2005, pp. 132–133.

2.17
Lucrina Fetti
Portrait of Eleonora Gonzaga I
1622
Oil on canvas, 201.8 × 119.9 cm
Mantua, Complesso Museale
Palazzo Ducale, inv. 6832

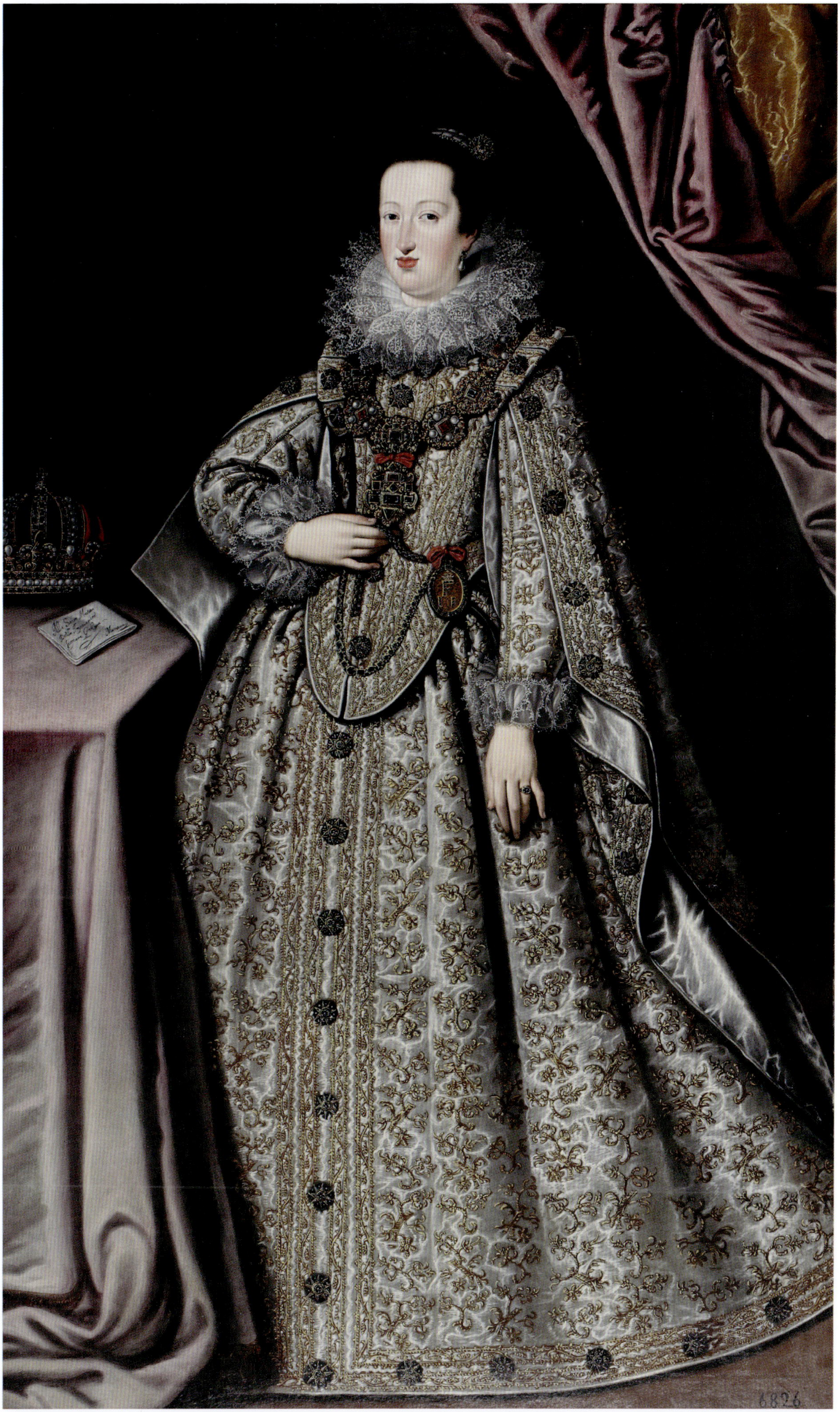
6826

FAMILY STORIES

Since it was almost impossible for a woman who was not of noble birth to study painting methods and techniques, this meant that, for most Italian and foreign female artists, the paternal workshop became a place of privileged training. From northern to southern Italy, many women made art their profession by inheriting not only the occupation from a family member, but frequently the workshop and clients as well. This was true from Milan, the birthplace of Fede Galizia, daughter of the Trentino miniaturist Nunzio, to as far as Palermo, where Rosalia Novelli, daughter of the painter Pietro, became an enterprising female figure who played an important social role.

Alongside stories of work carried out entirely under paternal guidance, as occurred with Barbara Longhi from Ravenna, daughter of Luca, and remembered by Vasari for her grace, or Maddalena Natali from Cremona, who followed her father Giovanni Battista to Rome, there are also examples of women artists who sought independence from the paternal model, surpassing their familial teachers in both social status and critical appreciation. This was true of the celebrated Lavinia Fontana from Bologna, who acquired the fame and honours her father had squandered, and also Elisabetta Sirani, a painter who died at twenty-seven, yet who in a mere ten years of activity eclipsed her father, the painter Giovan Andrea (school of Guido Reni), who also taught Ginevra Cantofoli. In the Veneto there is the legend of the intense love that bound Tintoretto to his daughter Marietta, who grew up in his workshop but died in her mid-thirties, and the story of the painter Chiara Varotari's dedication to her famous brother Alessandro, known as Il Padovanino.

An unusual case from the second half of the seventeenth century is that of the three Milanese daughters of the Burgundian painter Vincent Voulot (Italianised as Vincenzo Volò): Margherita, Francesca Vicenzina and Giovanna Vicenzina, who all specialised in painting flowers. The most renowned was the eldest daughter Margherita, who honed her skills at her father's side, yet left home at the age of nineteen to follow her husband Ludovico Caffi. From that moment she began an independent career, gaining the international fame that eluded her two sisters. Around the middle of the seventeenth century other female artists also distinguished themselves as skilled flower painters: Anna Stanchi from Rome (probably a relative of the well-known painter Giovanni), whose only surviving works are two signed canvases, and the mysterious Elisabetta Marchioni from Rovigo, wife of the goldsmith Sante Marchioni.

LAVINIA FONTANA

Bologna, 1552 – Rome, 1614

Born in Bologna, Lavinia was baptised on 24 August 1552.[1] Her parents are Prospero Fontana, engaged in the service of Pope Julius III from Bologna to Rome, and Antonia de' Bonardis, who came from a family of printers and booksellers. Taught by her father, Lavinia grew up in a cultured *milieu*, her education enhanced by Prospero's travels to fulfil commissions in Genoa, Fontainebleau, Rome, Florence, and other sites throughout Italy, and the contact she had with visitors he received at his Bologna studio, including artists, distinguished scientists, as the naturalist Ulisse Aldrovandi, and educated writers, as the humanist Achille Bocchi. Lavinia's first *Self-Portrait at the Spinet* from 1575 (private collection) is a theme she repeated several times (cats. 3.2–3) and reflects her education. In an ambitious comparison with Sofonisba Anguissola, whose self-portraits placed her on a par with the mythical female painters of antiquity praised by Pliny the Elder and Boccaccio, Lavinia portrayed herself as a refined "court lady", who desired "news of literature, music and painting", as Baldassar Castiglione suggests in the *The Book of the Courtier* (1528).[2] On 14 February 1577, Prospero Fontana signed Lavinia's marriage contract with Giovan Paolo, son of the merchant Severo Zappi from Imola. The marriage and resulting eleven children, born between 1578 and 1595, did not interrupt Lavinia's artistic career, promoted by her husband, whose surname she included in her signature. During those years Fontana's success grew rapidly. In 1579 she signed and dated her *Self-Portrait in the Studio* (Florence, Uffizi; cat. 3.1), which was intended to be copied and engraved as a complement to the one by Sofonisba in the famous Rome portrait gallery belonging to the Dominican father Alfonso Chacón. The painting confirms the professional level achieved by Fontana, who chose to portray herself as she practises her art by drawing models from antiquity. Erudition and art accompany the fame of other illustrious women who preceded Lavinia in Bologna: besides the notable presence of women at the university Studio, other female figures included the abbess-painter Caterina Vigri and the sculptress Properzia de' Rossi.[3] The learned, aristocratic world made haste to be portrayed by the new Bolognese celebrity painter. Members of a family of physicians (*Portrait of Girolamo Mercuriale*, Baltimore, The Walters Art Museum); humanists (*Portrait of Carlo Sigonio*, Modena, Museo Civico d'Arte; cat. 3.4) and scholars (*Portrait of the So-Called Senator Orsini*, Bordeaux, Musée des Beaux-Arts; *Portrait of a Scholar*, Bologna, Pinacoteca Nazionale; cat. 3.5) are depicted while intent on their intellectual activities in a rhetorical representation Fontana constructed by combining her father's teaching with that of Bartolomeo Passerotti.[4] The 1584 was important for Fontana, who completed *Our Lady of the Assumption of Ponte Santo and Saints Cassiano and Pier Crisologo* (Imola, Pinacoteca Comunale). The altarpiece was requested by the city of Imola for the Magistrate's Chapel in the Town Hall. With Lavinia, the status of the female artist rose to the height of important public commissions. She had already addressed the theme of the sacred, softening her father's lessons with her own melancholic atmospheres, influenced by Tasso[5] (*Saint Francis Receives the Stigmata*, Bologna, Seminario Arcivescovile, cat. 3.10; *Noli Me Tangere*, Florence, Uffizi), and by incorporating the Carracci family's new approach to naturalism. The *Portrait of the Gozzadini Family* is also from 1584 (Bologna, Pinacoteca Nazionale), "a sort of domestic altarpiece dedicated to the cult of the 'Lares'",[6] where the solemn composition eternalises the continuity of lineage between the living and the dead. These themes are encountered again in the portrait of childhood.[7] Later on, another *Family Portrait* (Milan, Pinacoteca di Brera; cat. 3.6) animated the world of affections in the style of Ludovico Carracci. In the 1590s Fontana achieved great success with her portraiture of Bolognese noblewomen, and from there went on to paint the monumental *Visit of the Queen of Sheba to Solomon* (Dublin, National Gallery). Her success is confirmed by her altar paintings: in 1589, King Philip II of Spain received *The Holy Family with the Sleeping Child and Saint John the Baptist* (El Escorial, Real Monasterio de San Lorenzo; see cat. 3.11); in 1593, *The Assumption* in Pieve di Cento; in 1599 the Gnetti family altarpiece for the church of Santa Maria dei Servi (Marseille, Musée des Beaux-Arts; cat. 3.9) and the *Vision of Saint Hyacinth* (Rome, Santa Sabina), which led to new commissions in the eternal city, where she moved in 1603, at the age of almost fifty, in order to paint the now lost *Martyrdom of Saint Stephen* for the church of San Paolo fuori le Mura (see cat. 3.7).[8]

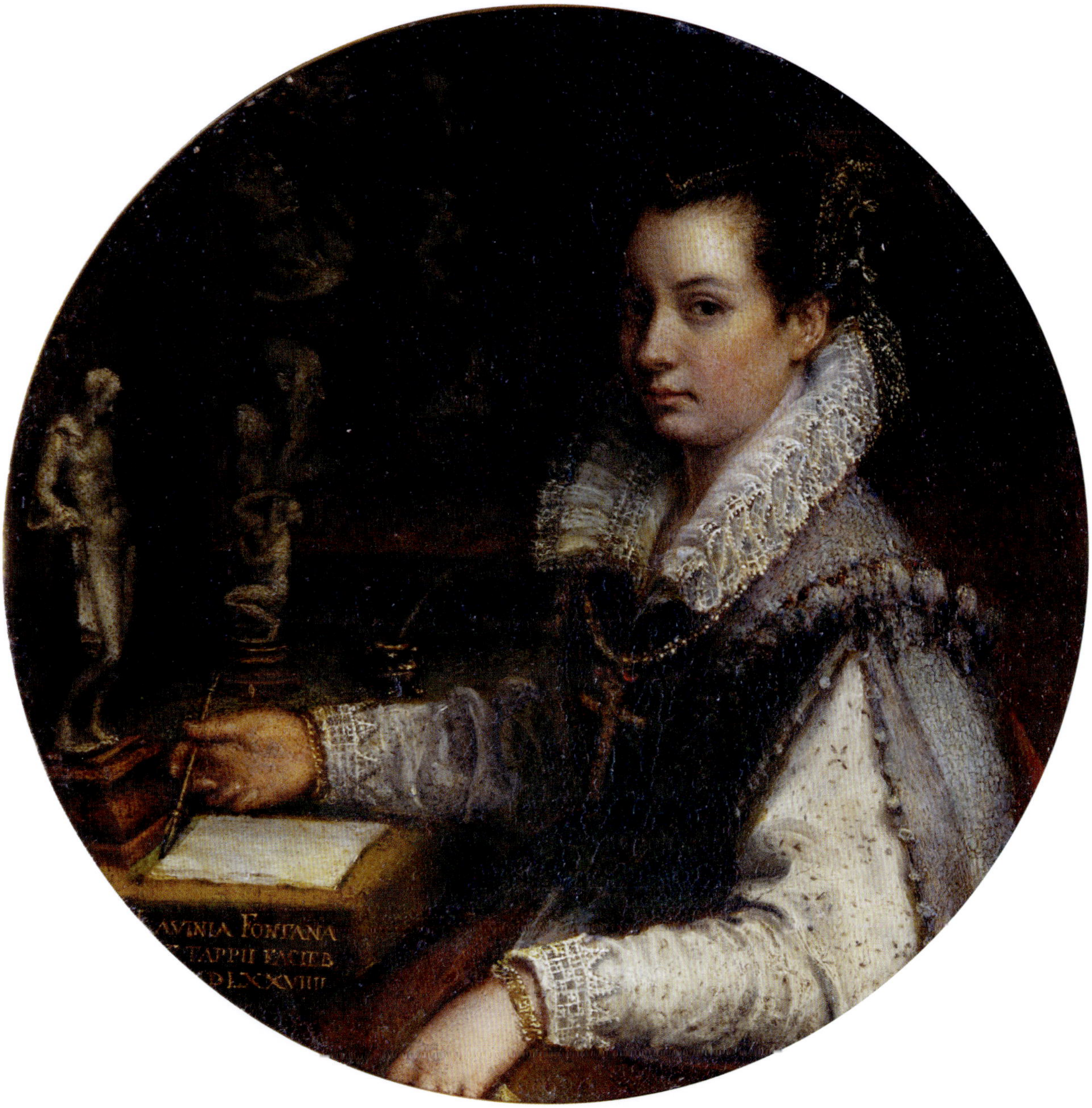

3.1
Lavinia Fontana
Self-Portrait in the Studio
1579
Oil on copper, Ø 16 cm
Florence, Gallerie degli Uffizi, 1890, inv. 4013

Sacred themes return again *Christ and the Samaritan Woman* (1607, Naples, Museo e Real Bosco di Capodimonte), in the cycle of saints for Santa Maria della Pace (from 1611), and in the altarpiece for the Santissima Trinità di Piano in Sorrento (1612). However, Lavinia Fontana's true spiritual testament is a painting of a profane subject: *Minerva Dressing*, executed for Scipione Borghese in 1613. Given the examples on the market in recent years (cats. 3.14–15), the work demonstrates confident with erotic subjects, combining both international influences (Fontainebleau and the Rudolfini painters) and Italian ones (from Tiziano to Carracci).[9] Lavinia died in Rome on 11 August 1614 and is buried in the church of Santa Maria sopra Minerva.
Stefania Biancani

[1] The first documentary reconstruction of the artist's life was made by Romeo Galli (1940) and updated in the principal monographic surveys: Ghirardi 1984; Fortunati Pietrantonio 1986; Cantaro 1989; *Lavinia Fontana* 1994; Fortunati 1997; *Lavinia Fontana* 1998; Murphy 2003. International attention was confirmed by *Italian Women Artists* 2007; *De dames* 2018; *Historia* 2019.
[2] Ghirardi's 1994a account remains fundamental.
[3] See Graziani, 1994.
[4] Concerning the portrait in Emilia Romagna, see Ghirardi's 2013 summary with bibliography.
[5] Fortunati 1994, pp. 22–23.
[6] Fortunati 1994, p. 29.
[7] See Ghirardi 1993–1994 and Ghirardi 2003, now in Ghirardi 2019a, pp. 9–86.
[8] According to Karel van Mander, Lavinia was in Rome in 1603 (Ghirardi 2019b, p. 251).
[9] For a final summary, see *Amor è vivo* 2002, Dal Pozzolo 2019, and most recently De Girolami Cheney 2020a and Tosini 2020.

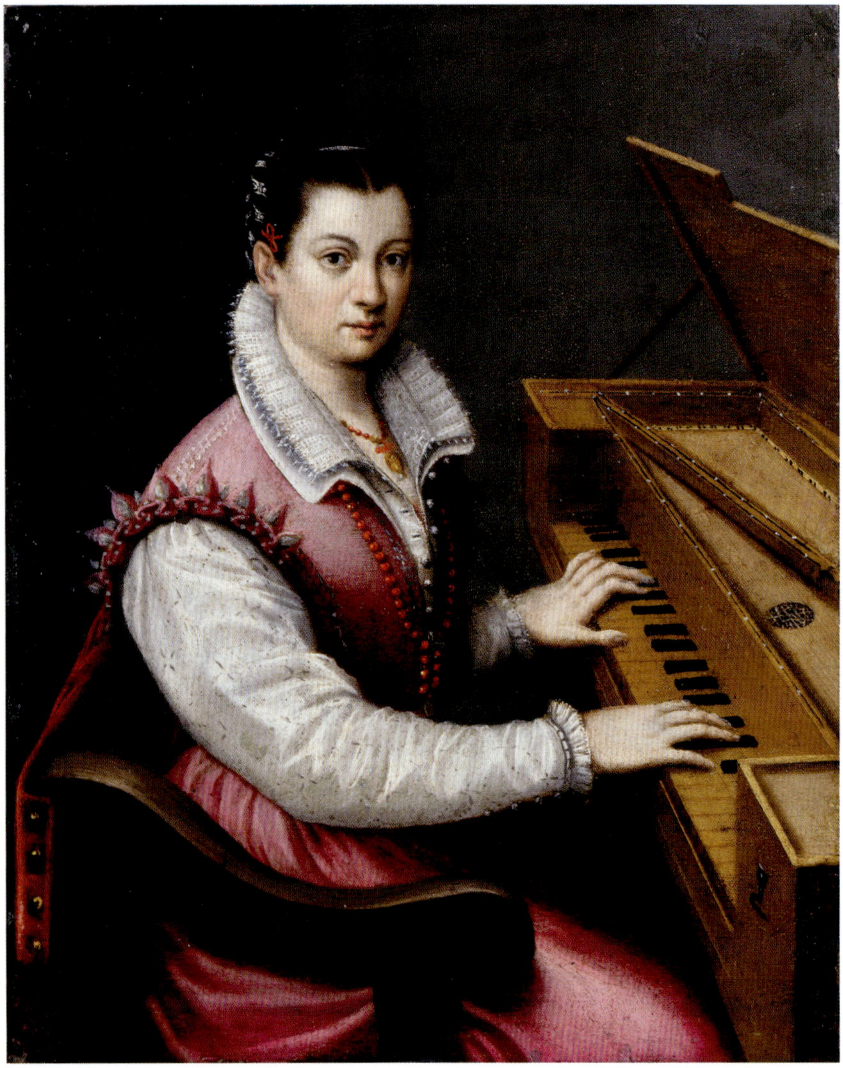

3.2
Lavinia Fontana
Self-Portrait at the Spinet
c. 1595
Oil on copper, 13.7 × 10.6 cm
Mario Scaglia collection,
inv. D 25

3.3
Lavinia Fontana
Self-Portrait at the Spinet
1577
Oil on canvas, 27 × 23.8 cm
Rome, Accademia Nazionale
di San Luca

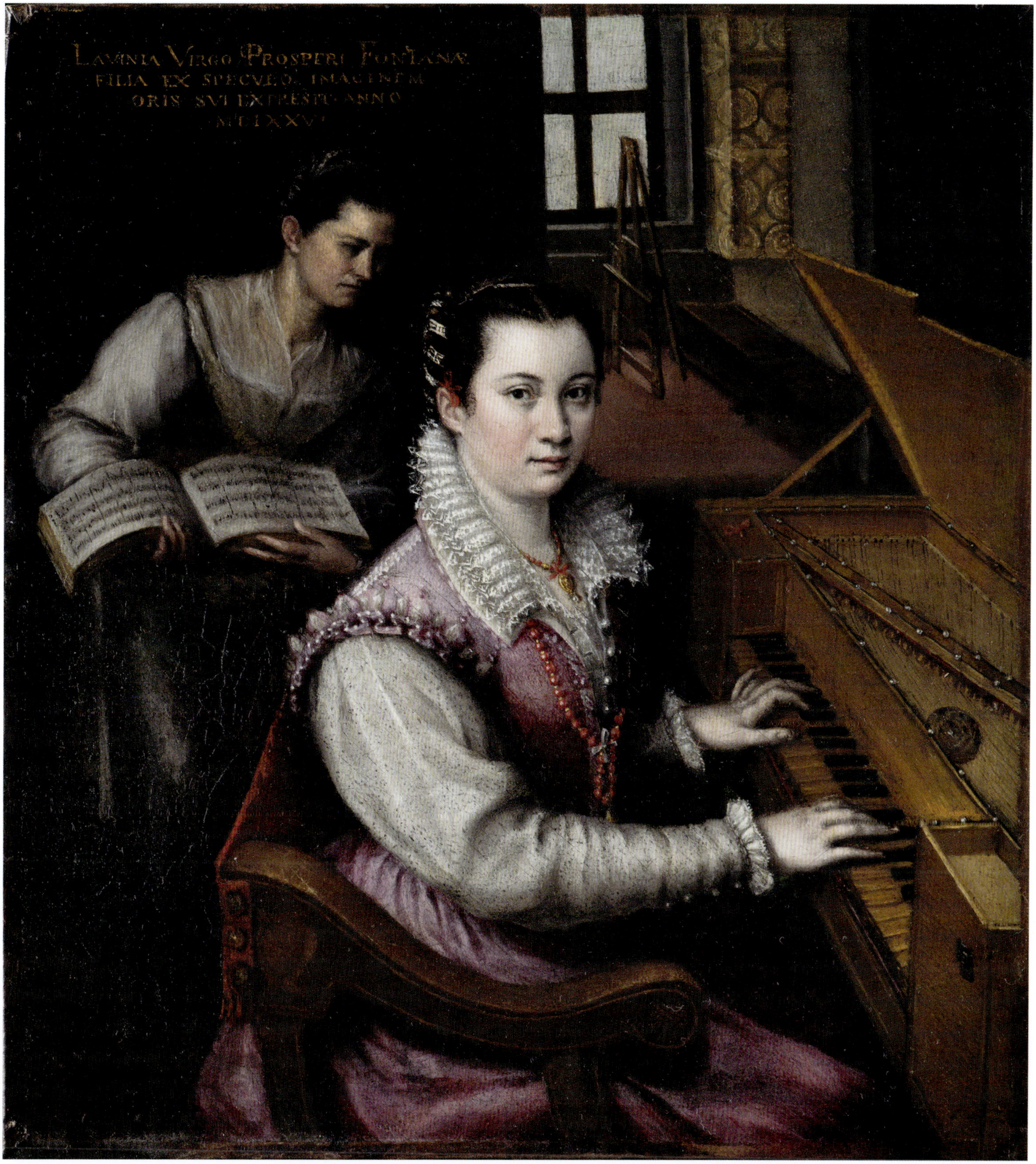
LAVINIA VIRGO PROSPERI FONTANÆ
FILIA EX SPECVLO IMAGINEM
ORIS SVI EXPRESSIT ANNO
MDLXXVI

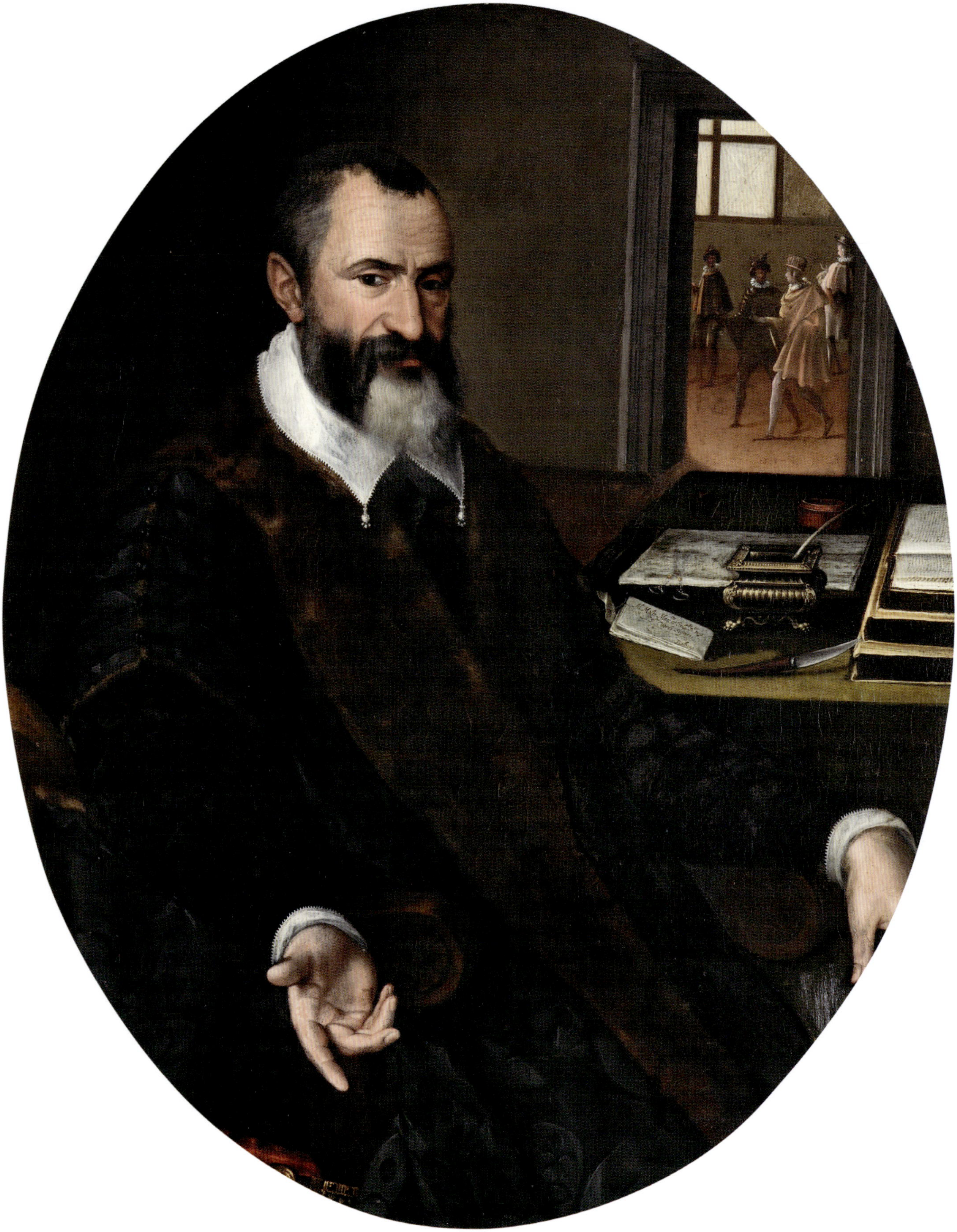

3.4
Lavinia Fontana
Portrait of Carlo Sigonio
c. 1578
Oil on canvas, 125.5 × 98 cm
Modena, Museo Civico d'Arte, inv. 85

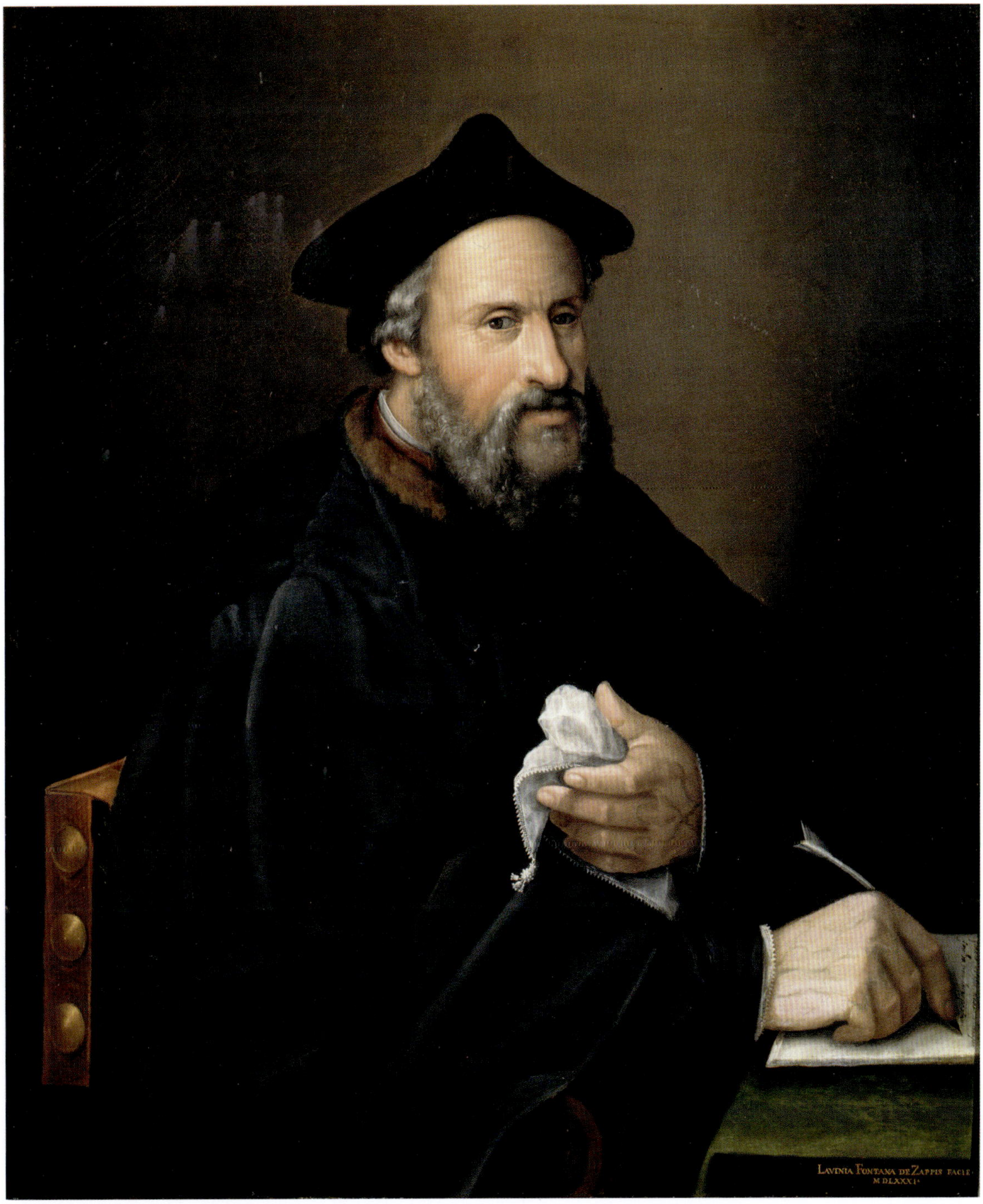

3.5
Lavinia Fontana
Portrait of a Scholar
1581
Oil on canvas, 87 × 72 cm
Bologna, Pinacoteca Nazionale, inv. 6472

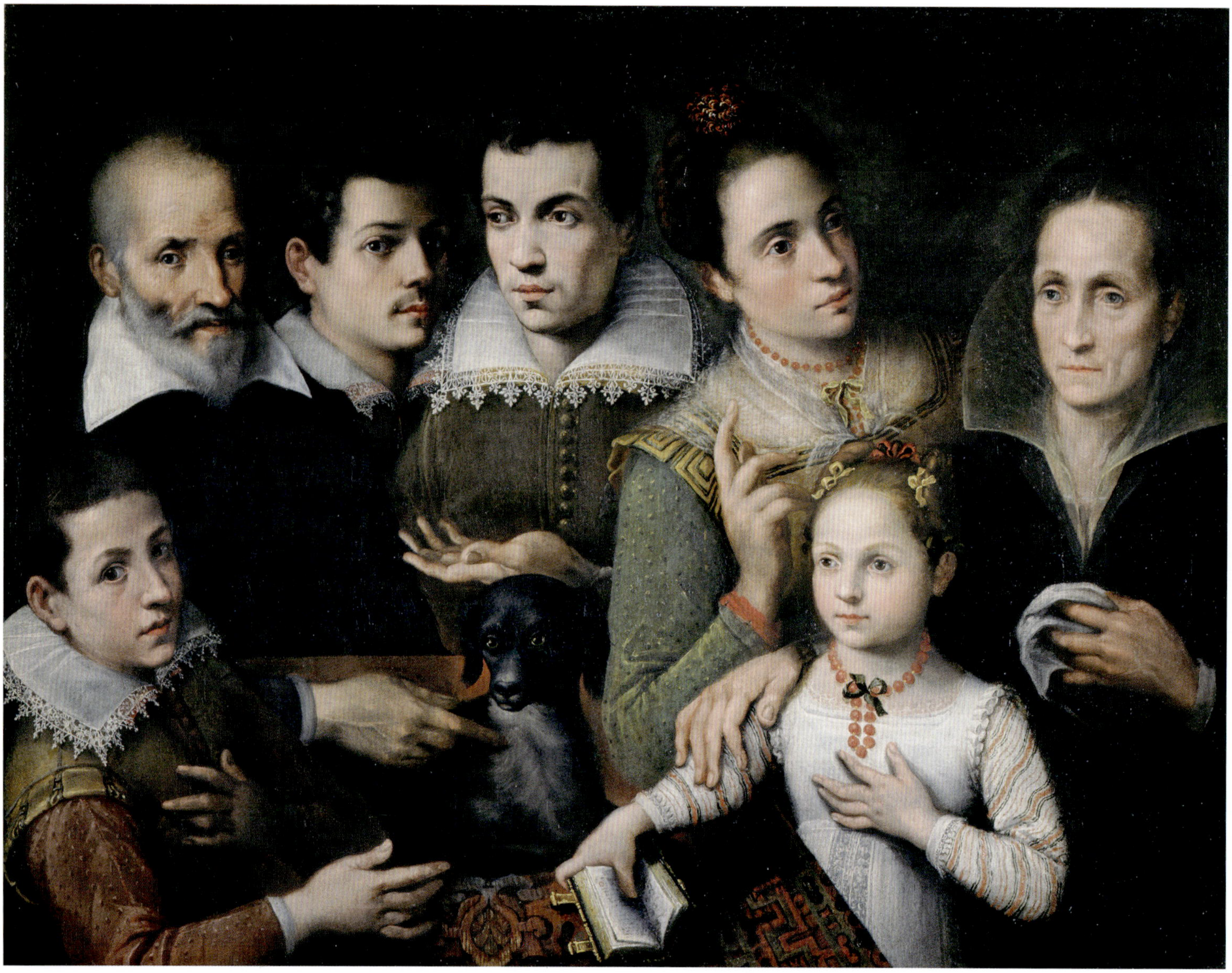

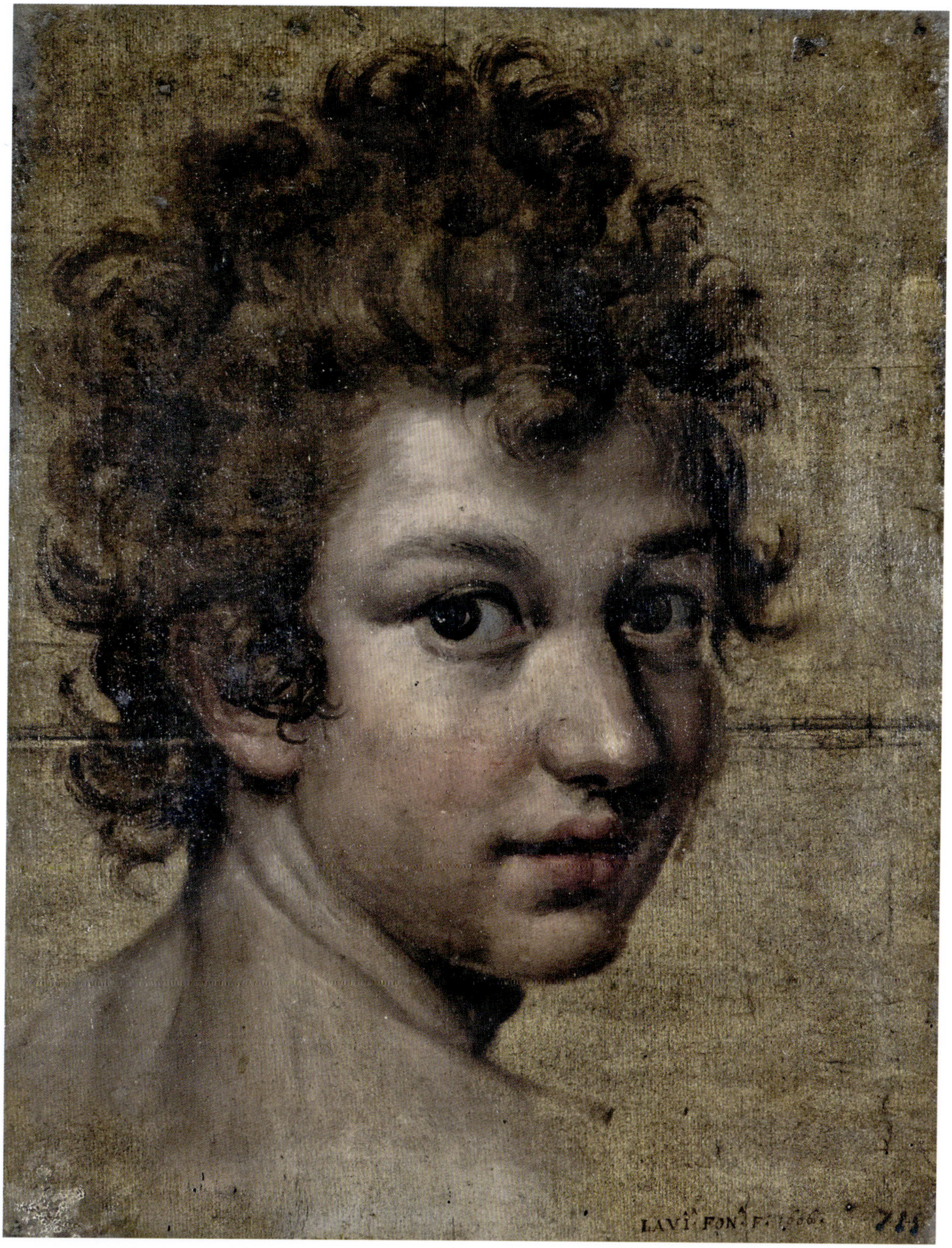

3.6
Lavinia Fontana
Family Portrait
c. 1595–1600
Oil on canvas, 85 × 105 cm
Milan, Pinacoteca di Brera,
inv. Reg. Cron. 382

3.7
Lavinia Fontana
Head of a Young Boy
1606
Grease pencil, tempera and
white lead on brown paper,
475 × 355 mm
Rome, Galleria Borghese,
inv. 81

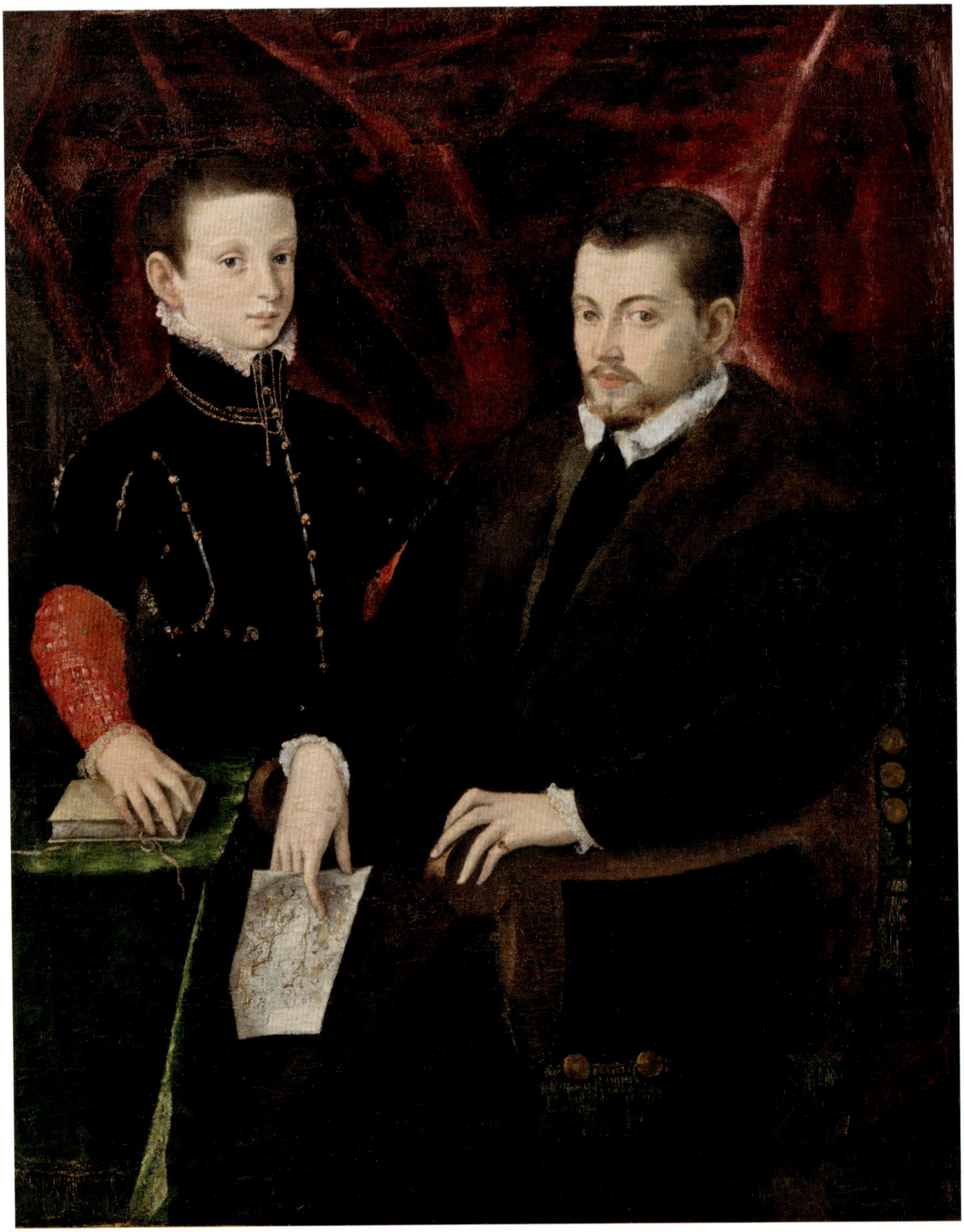

3.8
Lavinia Fontana
Portrait of a Gentleman with a Young Boy
1575–1578
Oil on canvas, 133 × 105.5 cm
Cremona, Museo Civico Ala Ponzone, inv. 192

3.9
Lavinia Fontana
Consecration of the Virgin Mary (*Gnetti Altarpiece*)
1599
Oil on canvas, 281 × 185 cm
Marseilles (France), Musée des Beaux-Arts, inv. BA16

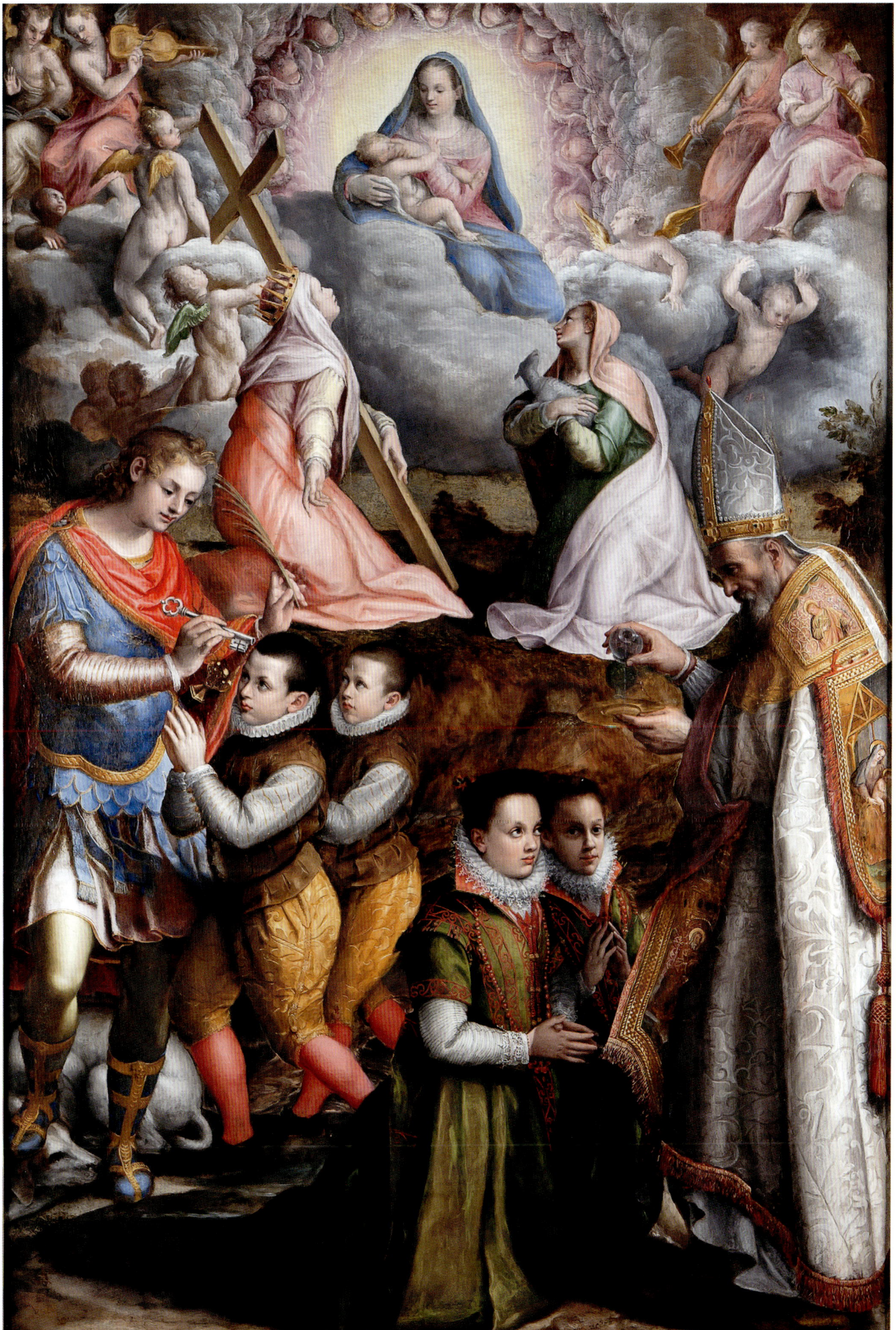

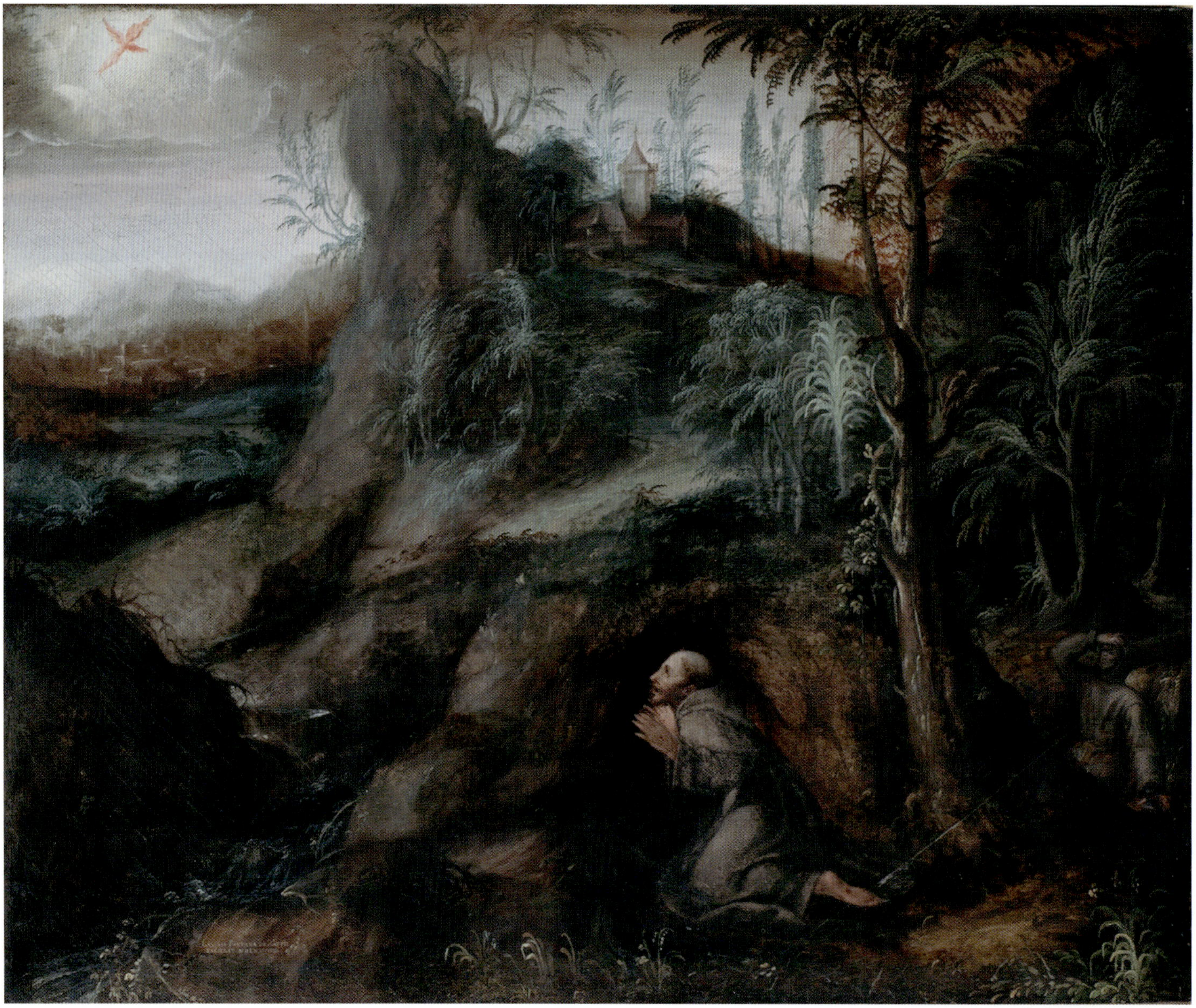

3.10
Lavinia Fontana
Saint Francis Receives the Stigmata
1579
Oil on canvas, 63 × 75 cm
Bologna, Seminario Arcivescovile, F7Z0068–F7Z0069

3.11
Lavinia Fontana
Sleeping Jesus (*Our Lady of Silence*)
1591
Oil on copper, 43 × 33 cm
Rome, Galleria Borghese, inv. 437

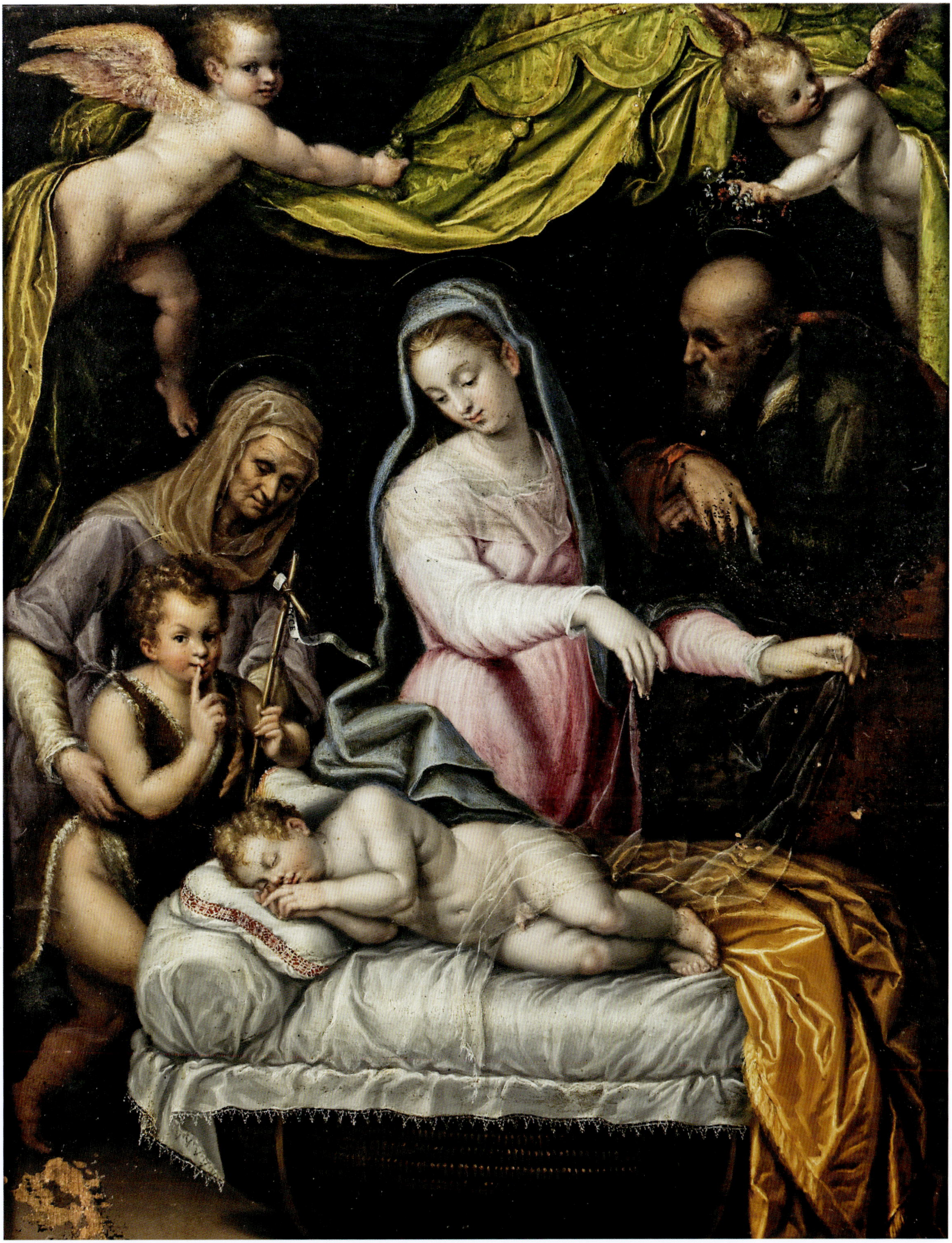

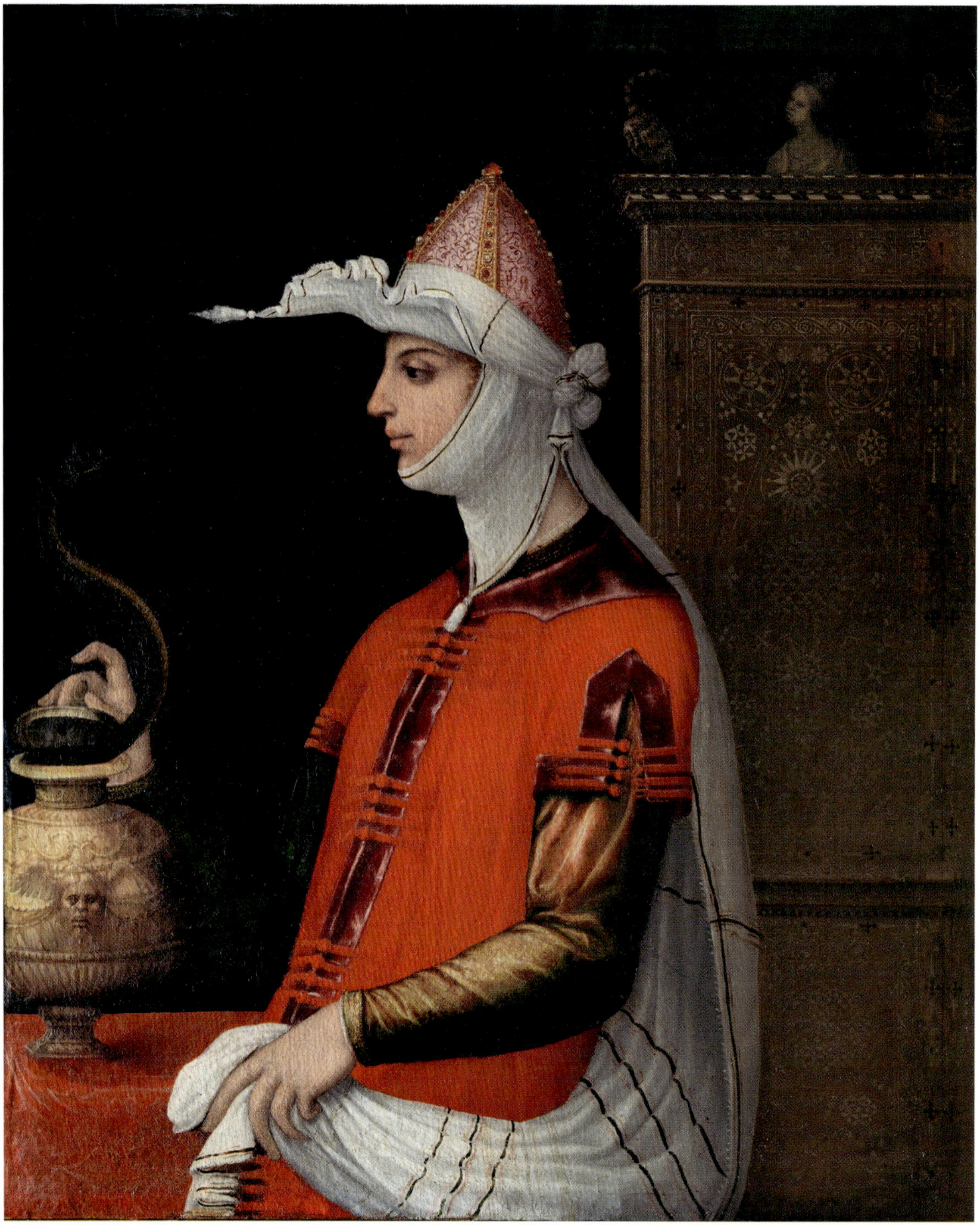

3.12
Lavinia Fontana
Cleopatra
c. 1595
Oil on canvas, 87.5 × 71 cm
Rome, Galleria Spada – Direzione dei Musei Statali della Città di Roma, inv. 245

3.13
Lavinia Fontana
Judith and Holofernes
c. 1595
Oil on canvas, 120 × 93 cm
Bologna, Fondazione Ritiro San Pellegrino

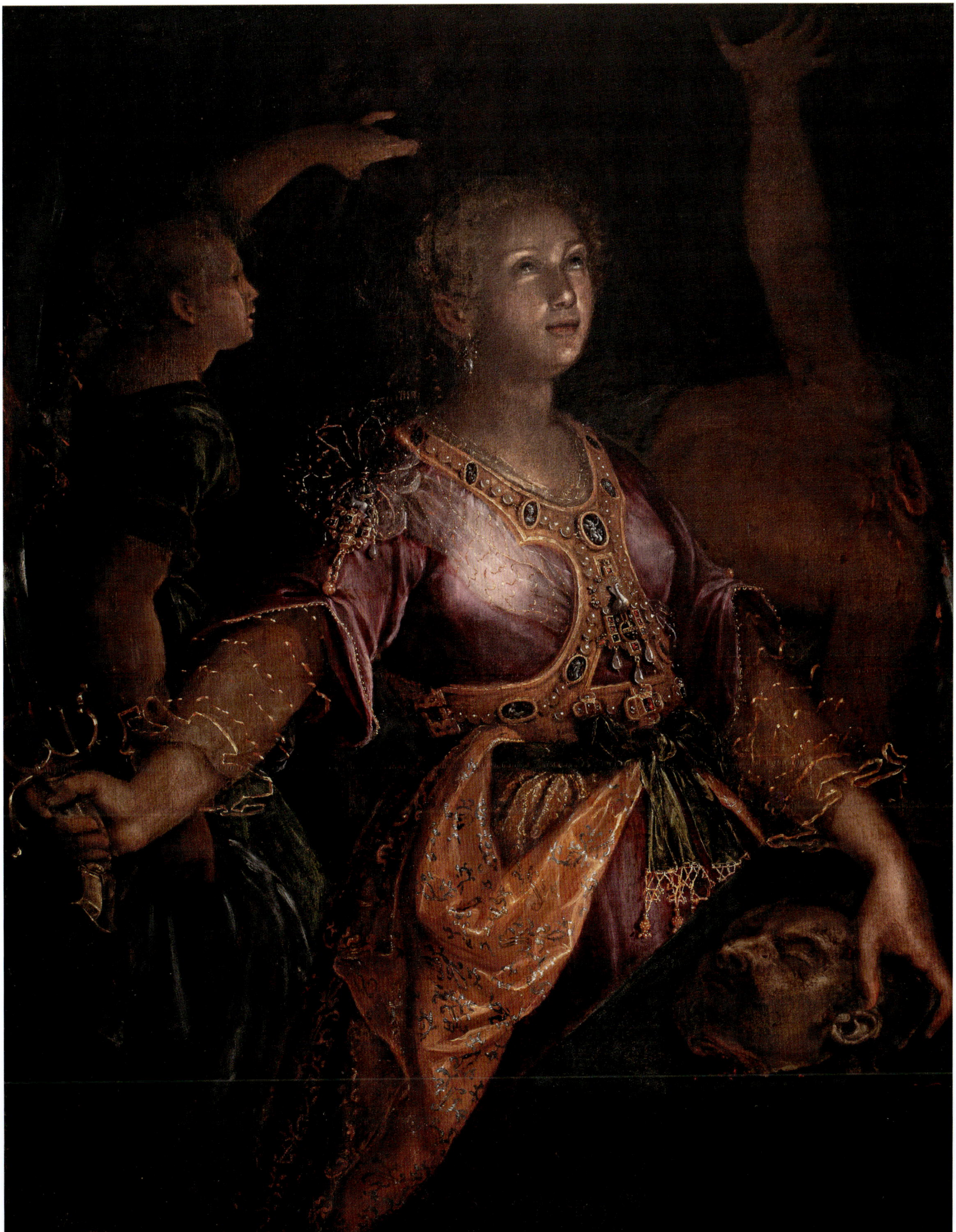

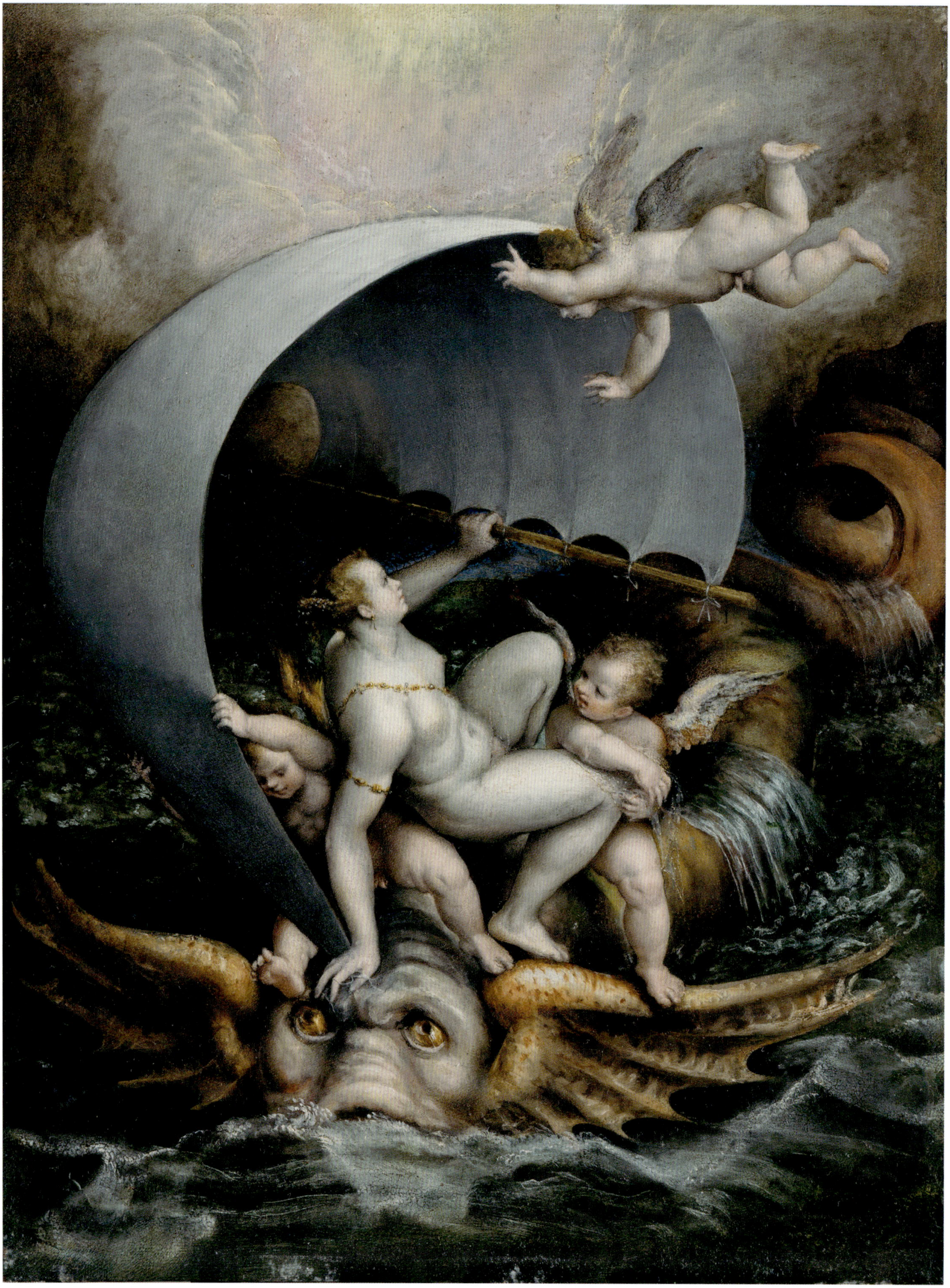

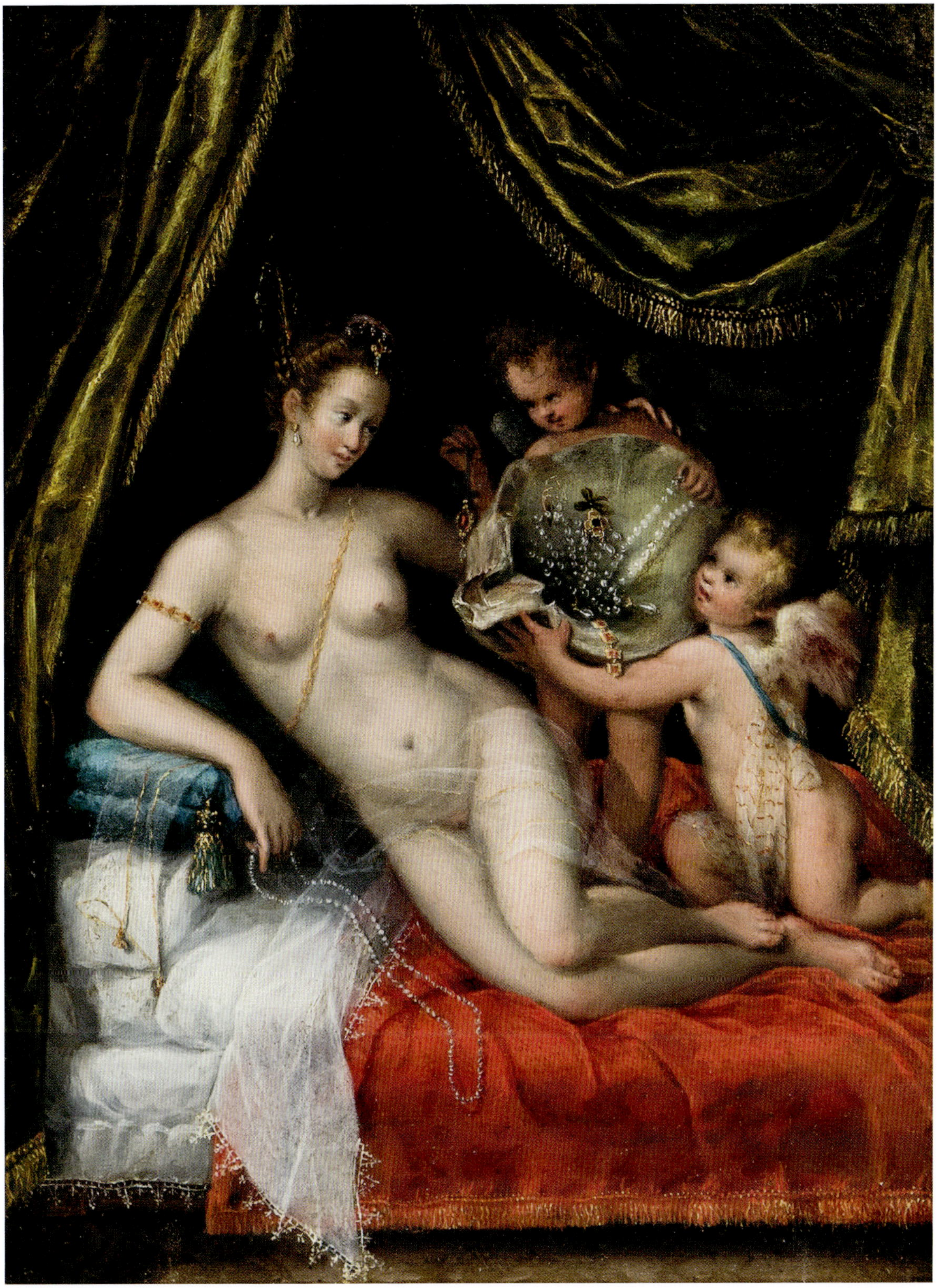

3.14
Lavinia Fontana
Galatea and Cherubs Riding the Stormy Waves on a Sea Monster
c. 1590
Oil on copper, 48 × 36.5 cm
Private collection

3.15
Lavinia Fontana
Venus Receives Homage from Two Cherubs
c. 1590
Oil on copper, 38.5 × 28 cm
Private collection

BARBARA LONGHI

Ravenna, 1552 – Ravenna, 1638

Barbara Longhi was born in Ravenna on 21 September 1552, daughter of the established local painter Luca and Bernardina Baronzelli.[1] Barbara had several siblings, about whom little is known except for Francesco (1544–1618), who was also a painter.

Barbara was the same age as another much more famous female painter, Lavinia Fontana, born in Bologna on 24 August 1552, the youngest child of Prospero Fontana and one of the most important and prolific artists of sixteenth-century Emilia Romagna. Barbara, like her future fellow artist, also took her first steps as a painter in her father's workshop. However, unlike Lavinia, who certainly enjoyed the privileged position of being able to fully exploit the fame and influential contacts of her father, Prospero, Barbara's career never went beyond the city of Ravenna where her father had strong ties. Indeed her work was limited to a purely domestic sphere, characterised by a pleasant but mostly serial art produced for private local clients.

Unfortunately, there is very little biographical information about Barbara. In the Giuntina edition of Vasari's *Lives* (1568), in which he briefly mentions Luca Longhi, he also refers to the promising gifts of "a daughter of his, still but a little girl, called Barbara", who "draws very well, and has begun to do some work in colour with no little grace and excellence of manner".[2] Some time later, the scholar and academic Muzio Manfredi (1535?–1609), a native of Cesena but a naturalised Ravenna citizen, also dedicated admiring lines to Barbara, "who is so marvellous at this art that her father himself begins to marvel at her, especially where portraiture is concerned".[3] However, the only portrait unanimously authenticated by scholars as the work of Barbara is one on copper in a less than optimal state of conservation, depicting an unknown Camaldolese monk. Preserved in the Museo d'Arte della Città di Ravenna (inv. QA 0143), it bears a poorly legible date, transposed as 1570 or 1573.[4]

Compared to the unmistakable and very personal style of her father, Luca, "who by nature was inclined to produce what was graceful and tender"[5] Barbara's painting, by using soft colours and fine finishing, has a humbler tone and is generally simpler in execution.[6] Yet despite being inevitably indebted to her father's style, which she closely observed in every respect, her works manage to find their own distinctive dimension and are perhaps even more intimate and charming.

The death of Luca Longhi in 1580 coincided with a professional hiatus for his daughter Barbara. The running of the workshop was assumed by her brother Francesco, whose style Barbara appears to have initially drawn closer to.

Although most of Barbara's early production comprises a pleasant series of female half-busts portraying in particular Saints Catherine and Barbara, plus a number of Madonnas and Holy Families executed in full adherance to her father's style, notable among her mature work is the 1618[7] *Our Lady of Mount Carmel with Saints Charles Borromeo and Simone Stock, and the Blessed Margherita Molli and Gentile Giusti* in the Ravenna church of Carmine di Russi, and also the monumental (and therefore unusual) *Immaculate Conception* in Ravenna's archiepiscopal seminary, influenced by the more illustrious version of the same subject by Flemish painter Denijs Calvaert (1540?–1619) for the Bolognese church of Sant'Antonio Abate.[8]

On 6 August 1624 "Barbara Lunghi [*sic*], Painter of Ravenna, daughter of the former Messer Luca of that City, a very famous Painter", deposited her first will,[9] stating that she should be buried beside her father in the local church of San Domenico and that, having no direct heirs, her possessions should go to her siblings' children. On 30 June 1630 she made a second will, similar to the first, but containing a more detailed list of her personal effects. Barbara died in Ravenna on 23 December 1638 at the age of eighty-six, although her death certificate gives her age as ninety-five.[10]

Giulia Daniele

[1] Bernicoli 1914, p. 636; Viroli 2005, p. 638. For the birth certificate, see Simoni 2000, p. 213.
[2] Vasari 1568, English ed. 1912–1915, IX, p. 155.
[3] Cappi 1853, p. 152.
[4] Ceroni 1993, p. 28; Simoni 1999, p. 67, fig. 4; Viroli 2000, p. 191; Ceroni 2007; Simoni 2011, p. 15, fig. 12.
[5] Cappi 1853, p. 8.
[6] Viroli 2000, p. 34.
[7] Simoni 1999, p. 68, fig. 5; Viroli 2000, pp. 216–217.
[8] Viroli 2000, pp. 215–216.
[9] Simoni 1999, pp. 68–69.
[10] Simoni 1999, p. 72.

3.16
Barbara Longhi
Saint Catherine of Alexandria
c. 1580
Oil on canvas, 70 × 53.5 cm
Bologna, Pinacoteca Nazionale, inv. 1097

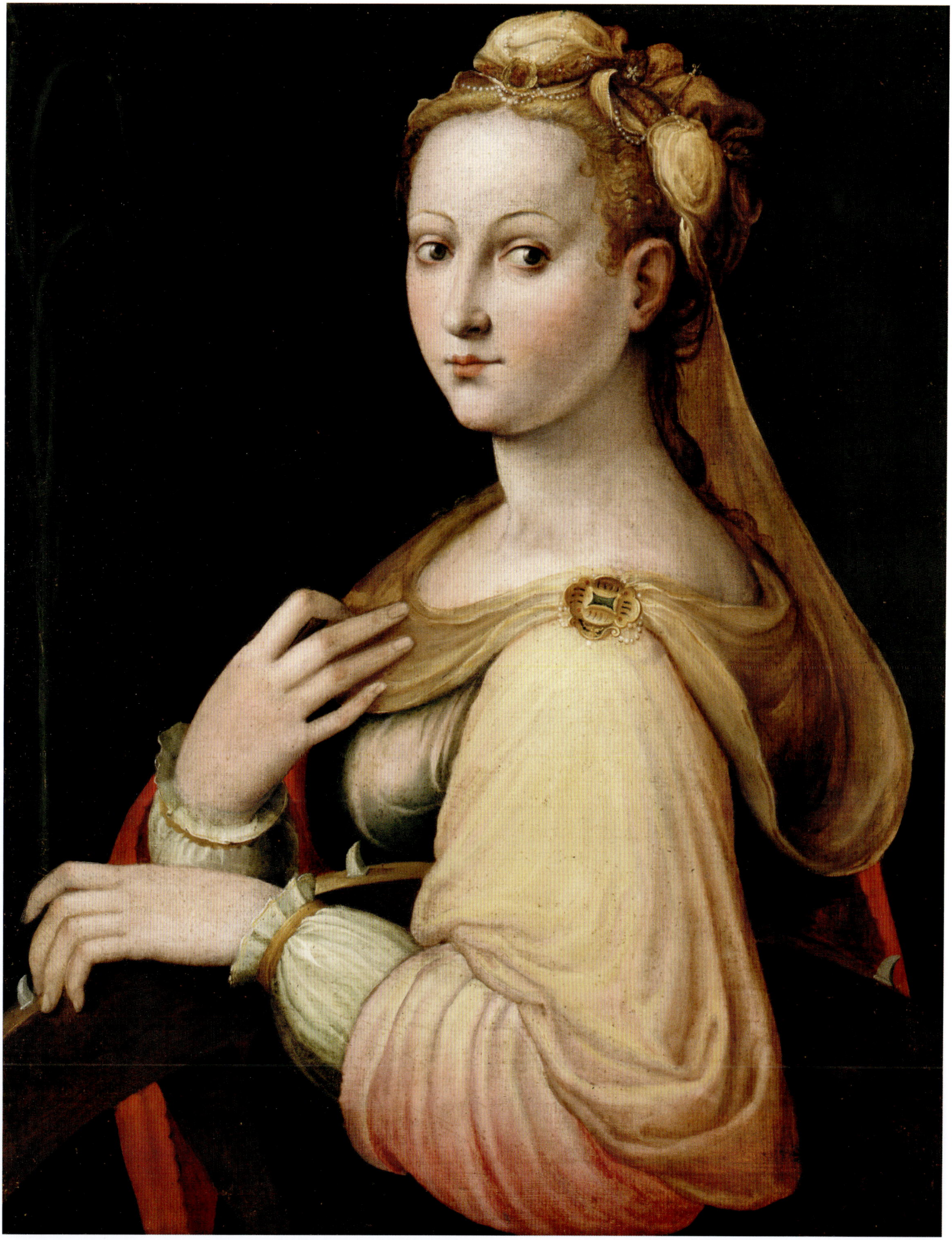

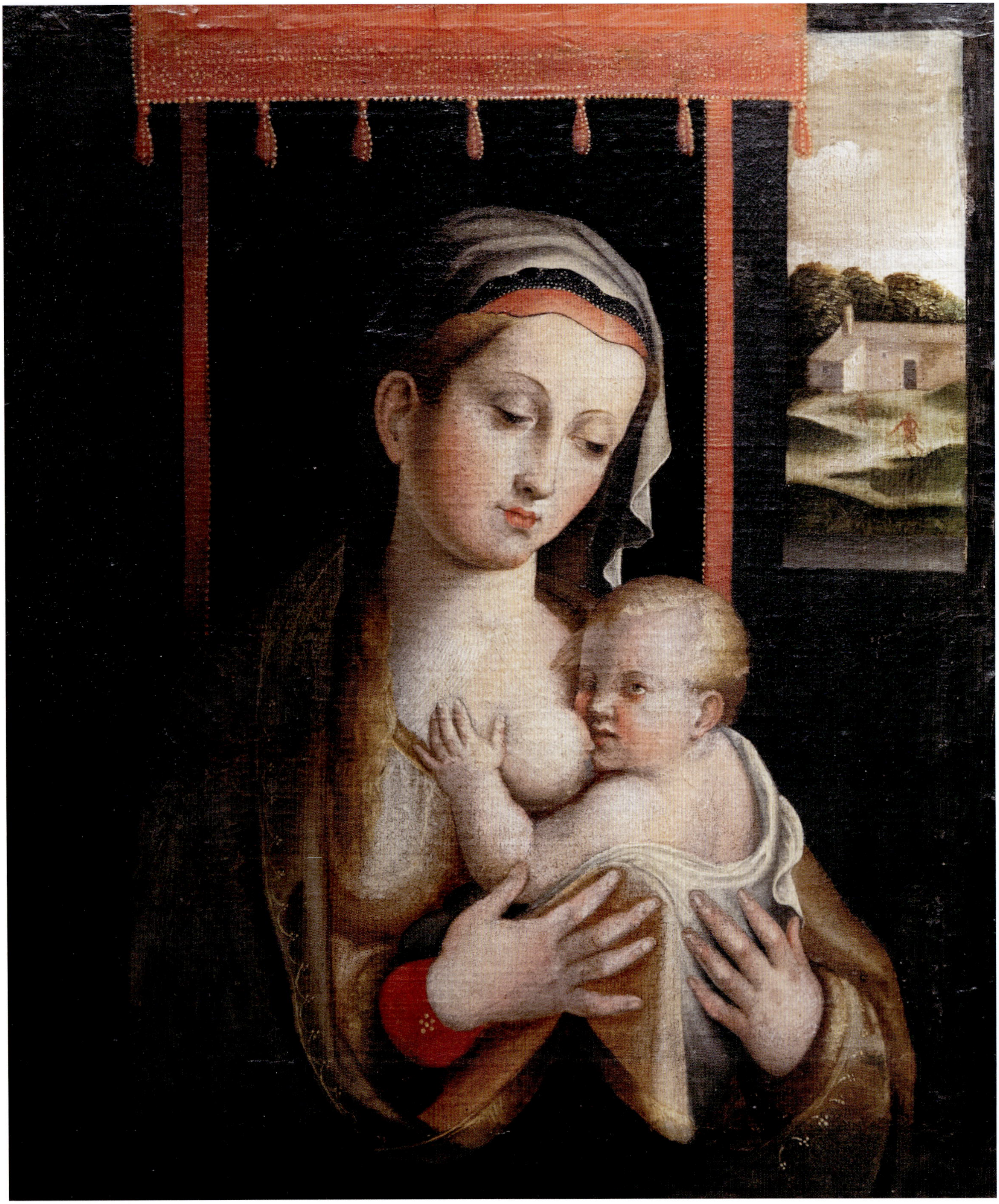

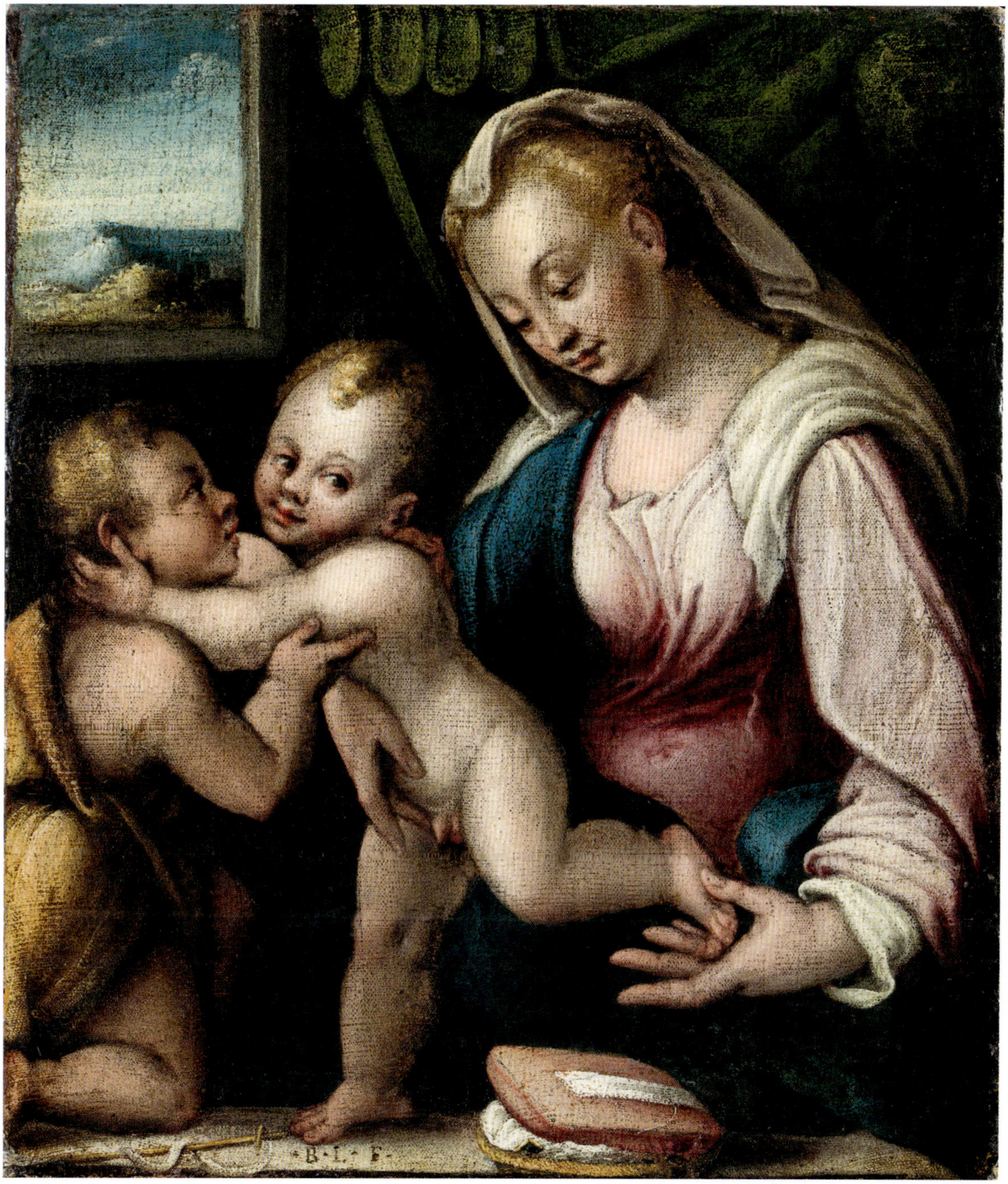

3.17
Barbara Longhi
Madonna of the Milk
c. 1580
Oil on canvas, 41 × 34 cm
Cremona, Museo Civico
Ala Ponzone, inv. 188

3.18
Barbara Longhi
Madonna and Child with Saint John the Baptist
1580–1590
Oil on canvas, 37 × 31.5 cm
Ravenna, MAR – Museo d'Arte della Città di Ravenna, inv. QA 89 (1994–)

GINEVRA CANTOFOLI

Bologna, 1618 – Bologna, 1672

Little is known about the life of this singular painter who has only recently become a subject of study. The fact that Ginevra was born in Bologna in 1618 can be calculated from her death certificate, which gives her age as fifty-four when she died in 1672. Her parents were Francesco Cantofoli and Ottavia Buldrini, and it can be hypothesised that the young Ginevra already demonstrated self-taught talent before her acquaintance with Giovanni Andrea Sirani (school of Guido Reni), who it seems became her teacher.

The first certain date is 11 May 1653, when Ginevra Cantofoli married Francesco di Michele Facchini of Mantua at San Tommaso's church in Bologna. On 27 August that same year she bought a property from the sisters of the Bologna church of Santi Vitale e Agricola. In 1656 she gave birth to a daughter, Orsola Catterina Facchini, and the then eighteen-year-old artist Elisabetta Sirani notes in her diary that she had painted a *Portrait of Signora Ginevra Cantofoli, Painter*. This painting, lost today, is one of the very first created by the young daughter of Giovanni Andrea Sirani, and the fact that she already defines Ginevra as a "painter" confirms the latter's consolidated activity, and perhaps her role as a teacher during Elisabetta's early days as a painter. Ginevra must certainly have been an example for Elisabetta, and only a few years later in 1658, Ginevra saw her work recognised when she received a commission for an altarpiece for the important Bolognese church of San Giacomo Maggiore. In a European painting capital, which Bologna was at the time, crowded with local painters and newcomers who came to study there, it was not easy for a woman to win commissions for altarpieces, and Ginevra was to accomplish six in the course of her career. The only other one we know of is the beautiful *Immaculate Conception with the Christ Child Presenting the Rosary*, held by Bologna's Pinacoteca Nazionale and now in the church of the Franciscan sisters. The public consecration of her work *Saint Thomas of Villanova* was a great success, and the event was recorded by an engraving made from it.

Records show that in 1659 three paintings were commissioned by Nicolò Girolamo Fracassati.

On 4 October 1668 her husband Francesco died, and a few days later she drew up a tutelary inventory in favour of her daughter Orsola Catterina. This document, published by Stefania Sabbatini in 1995, constitutes the most important and richest source concerning Cantofoli's activity and her private life. Among the fifty-one paintings listed, there are also paintings on crystal, thus confirming earlier references to her small-format works, which Malvasia also mentions, informing us that it was Elisabetta Sirani who urged Cantofoli to devote herself to works of larger scope, which led to her greater success. The inventory also mentions a "copperplate etching with the image of Saint Thomas of Villanova carved by the aforementioned lady" (a print of this work is conserved at the Metropolitan Museum in New York). Among her other works is a *Portrait of Carlo II Gonzaga, Duke of Nevers*, several allegories and the myth of Calypso, as well as a number of religious paintings and some unfinished works. Records from the years that followed show sales of properties and land that demonstrate Ginevra's economic and professional independence up until 29 March 1672, when she drew up her will, leaving several paintings to her servant, Giovanna Zanetti, and to her sister Caterina Zambonini. The rest of her assets were to pass to her daughter, whom she entrusted into the care of Clementia Ercolani Leoni. In her will, she requested that next to her tomb in the church of San Giacomo Maggiore "a stone headstone should be installed in a convenient place to be seen by all".[1] Ginevra died on the 10 or 11 May 1672 and was buried in the altar of San Tommaso, which she herself had painted.

After centuries of oblivion, renewed interest in Elisabetta Sirani's work and style paved the way for studies on Ginevra. The monograph on Ginevra Cantofoli, published by this writer in 2006, is only a starting point for future research.

Massimo Pulini

[1] Bologna, Archivio di Stato, Notarile Camillo Felini, row 4, no. 22.

3.19
Ginevra Cantofoli
Allegory of Painting
c. 1650
Oil on canvas, 66.1 × 49.9 cm
Milan, Pinacoteca di Brera,
inv. Reg. Cron. 101

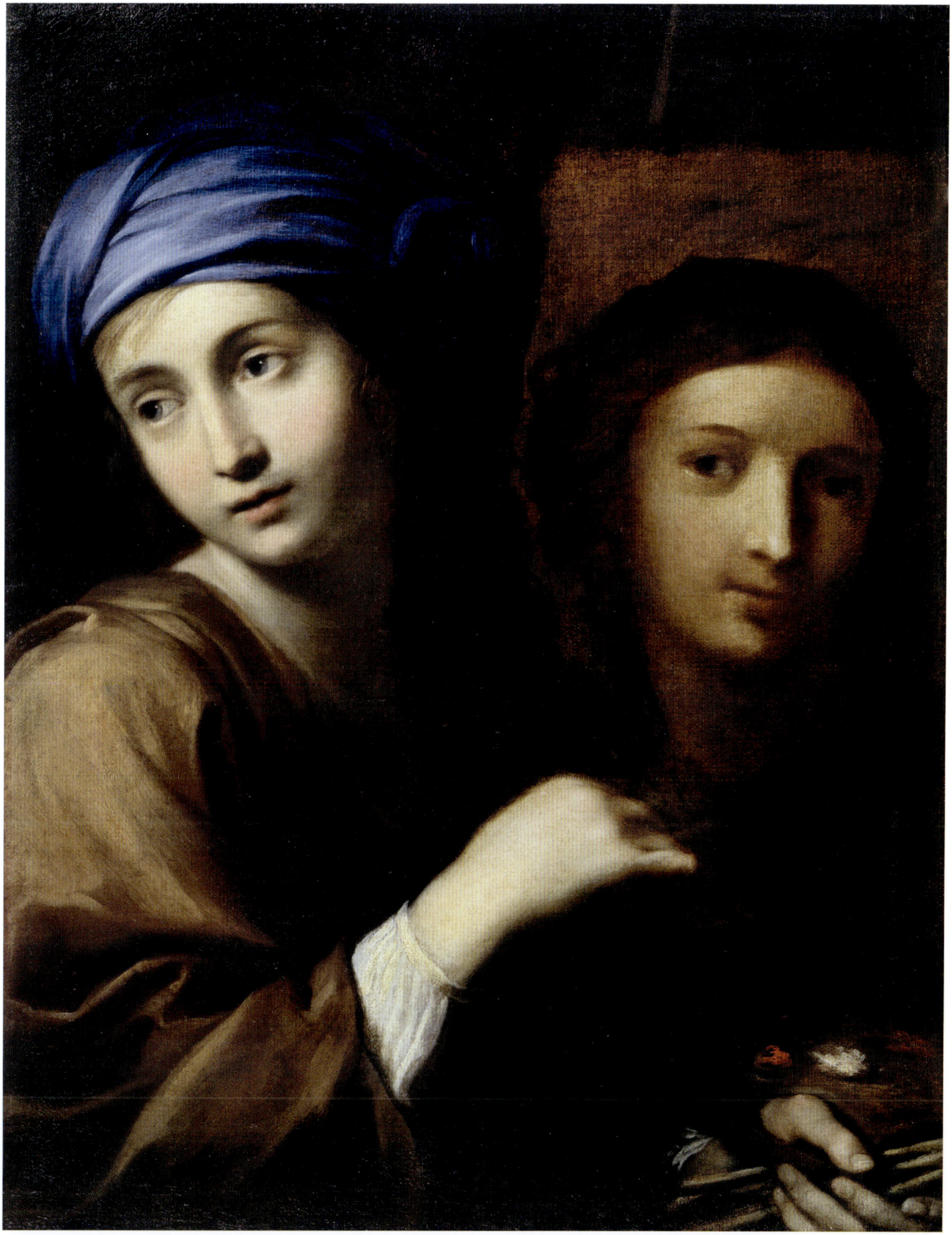

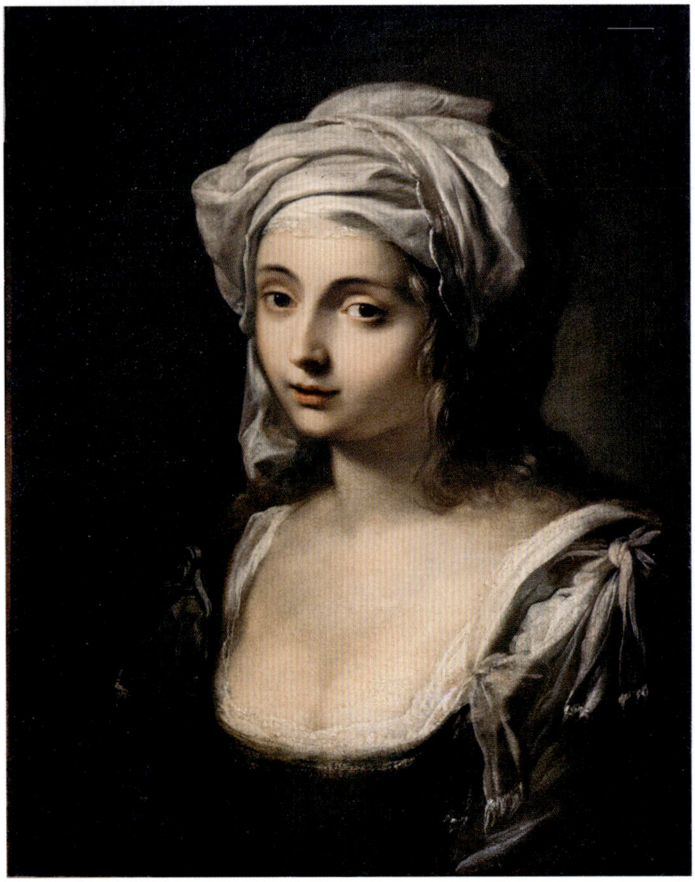

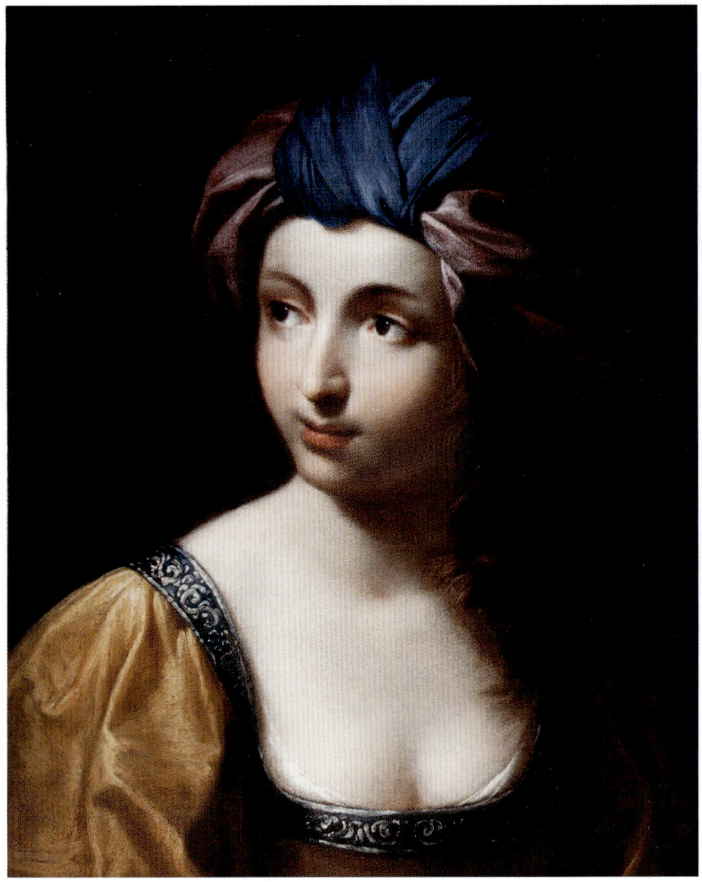

3.20
Ginevra Cantofoli
Young Woman (*Sibyl*)
c. 1660
Oil on canvas, 65.5 × 51 cm
Cremona, Museo Civico Ala Ponzone, inv. 2139

3.21
Ginevra Cantofoli
Sibyl
c. 1650
Oil on canvas, 63 × 46 cm
Private collection, courtesy of Cantore Galleria Antiquaria

3.22
Ginevra Cantofoli
Young Woman (*Sibyl*)
c. 1650
Oil on canvas, 65 × 50 cm
Padua, Museo d'Arte Medioevale e Moderna, legacy of Count Leonardo Emo Capodilista, 1864, inv. 132

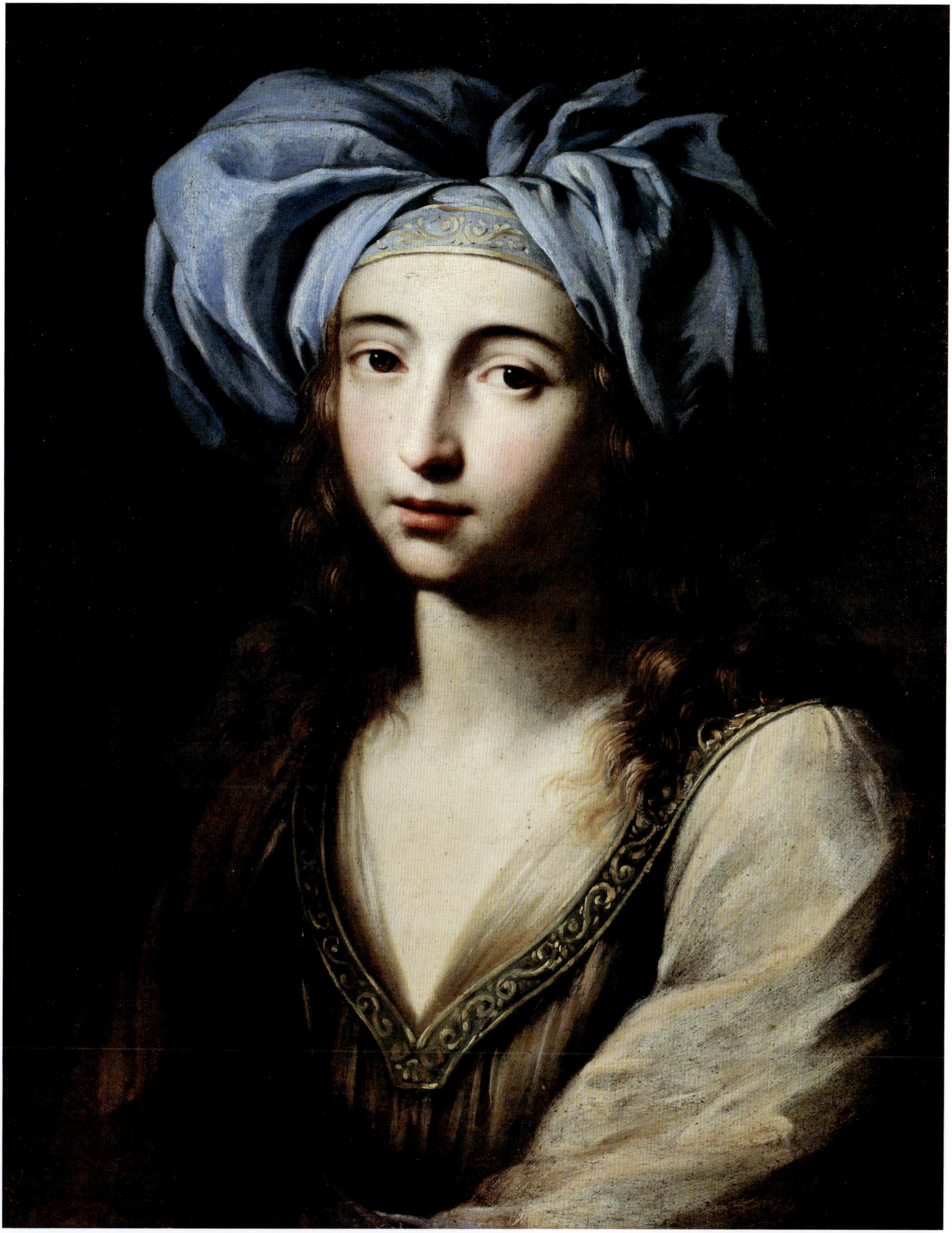

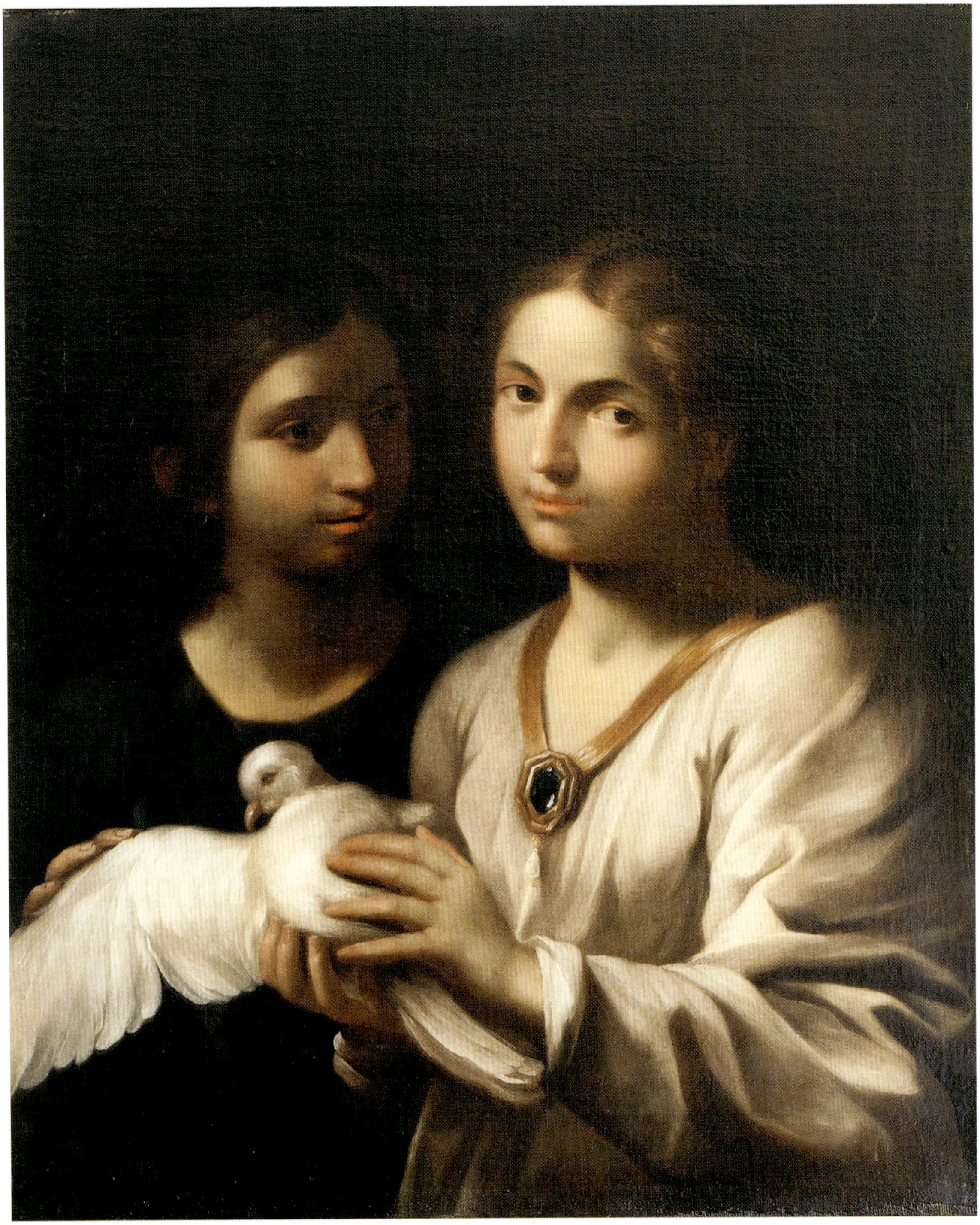

3.23
Ginevra Cantofoli
Allegory of Sincerity
c. 1650
Oil on canvas, 71 × 59 cm
Private collection

3.24
Ginevra Cantofoli
Berenice
c. 1660
Oil on canvas, 76 × 59 cm
Rome, Galleria Borghese, inv. 99

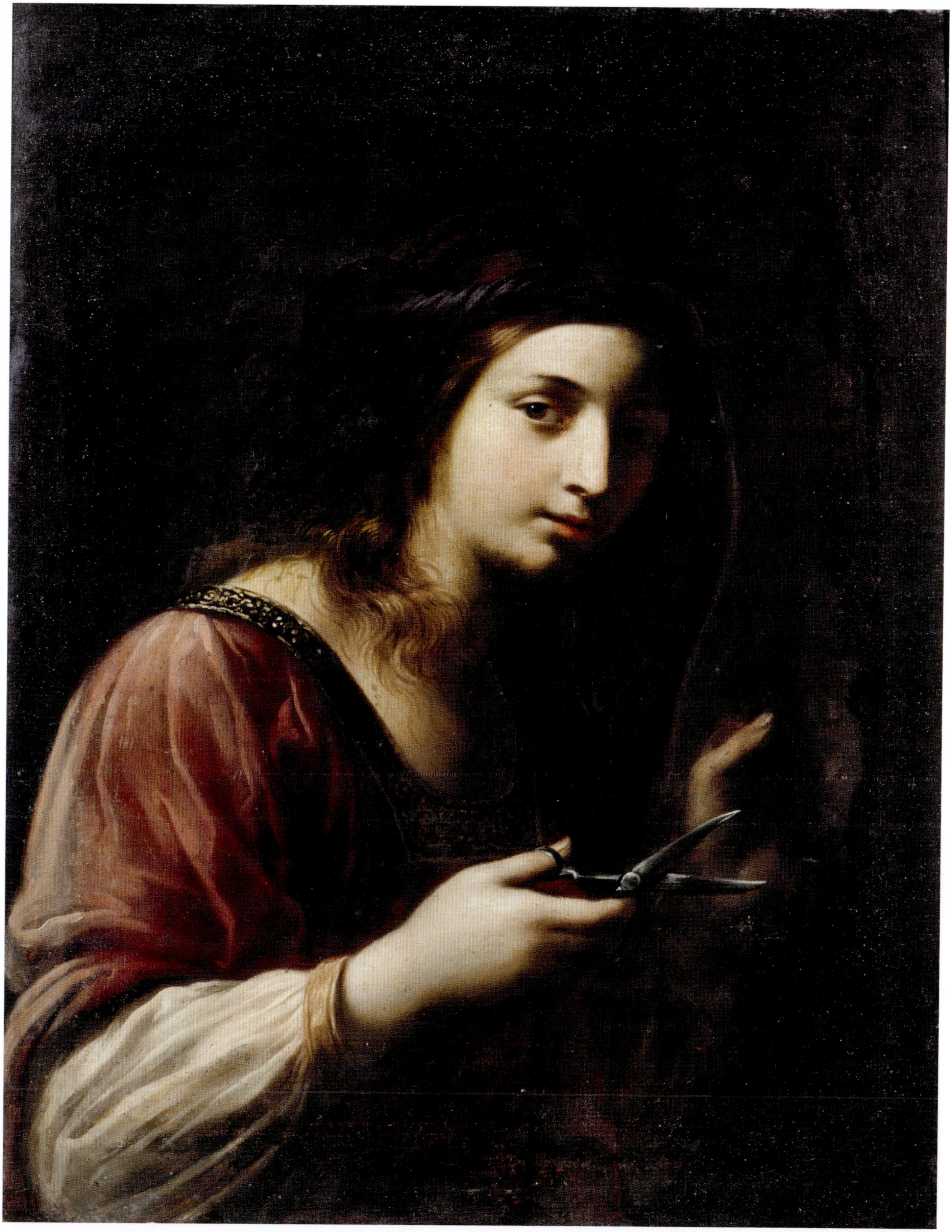

ELISABETTA SIRANI

Bologna, 1638 – Bologna, 1665

Elisabetta Sirani was born on Friday 8 January 1638 in Counter-Reformation Bologna, the most important papal state after Rome with a culturally rich artistic and university environment. She died on 28 August 1665 from peritonitis as a result of a ruptured peptic ulcer, at the age of 27.[1] Remaining unmarried, she was able to pursue her chosen career with ambition and professional success.[2]

The eldest of five children, four girls and a boy, Elisabetta was the daughter of Margherita Masini della Mano and Giovanni Andrea Sirani (1610–1670), an established Bolognese artist and art merchant who had been Guido Reni's prime assistant, and who taught her painting, draughtsmanship and printmaking.[3] Around 1662 Elisabetta became head of the Sirani family workshop, one of the most successful and productive artist studios in Bologna, after Giovanni Andrea could no longer paint due to gout (*chiragra*) crippling his hands.[4] Elisabetta was soon supporting the entire family through her work,[5] eclipsing her father in quality, output and popularity. As a professional artist she was documented as a member of the Accademia di San Luca, Rome, though, being a woman, she was not able to attend the academy's meetings, as had been stipulated in the 1607 statutes,[6] and confirmed by recent studies.[7]

Elisabetta was one of the most innovative and influential artists of the Bolognese school, especially on the women artists of the city. Bologna boasted a flourishing school of women artists, with Elisabetta its brightest star, and she imparted her deep technical and theoretical knowledge on the next generation of professional women painters and printmakers by opening up her studio to them. She is known to have taught her two younger sisters Barbara and Anna Maria, as well as collaborating with Ginevra Cantofoli.[8] Elisabetta's biographer and protector, the influential art critic Count Carlo Cesare Malvasia further listed a number of other "women and young girls" who "follow the example of this most worthy painter".[9] Despite her early death and the brevity of her career (1654-1665), Elisabetta was also instrumental in transmitting Guido Reni's Baroque Classicism to the following generations of Bolognese artists, making sure, however, to develop her own distinct expressive and bold manner. Renowned for her technical brilliance, Elisabetta's canvases, with their broad painterly brushwork and fluid impasto, express an elegant *sprezzatura,* combined with rich neo-venetian *colorito* and caravagesque *chiaroscuro*, evident also in her brush and ink-wash drawings.[10] Contemporaries gendered her style as masculine, with Malvasia claiming that Elisabetta "had something virile and great" about her,[11] whilst Padre Bonaventura Bisi wrote that she "paints as a man, with great readiness and invention".[12]

Archival documentation confirms that Elisabetta was one of the most talented, erudite, prolific and successful Bolognese artists of the mid-seventeenth century. Her extraordinary speed of execution saw her completing some 200 canvases, 11 prints and innumerable drawings and wash sketches in a career that barely spanned more than a decade. She gained many public commissions and provided devotional *quadretti da letto* representing beautiful Madonnas, the Holy Family or Saints for her many private patrons.[13] Elisabetta in particular specialised in images of heroic women, courageous, proud and intelligent.[14] She also painted classical and religious narratives (*Istoria*) – quite unusual for women who were prevented from studying life drawing – as well as allegories and portraits, achieving critical acclaim and respect in a profession traditionally the preserve of men. In this she was following the example and successes of her Bolognese predecessor Lavinia Fontana (1552 –1614).[15]

The artist recorded her paintings in a work diary, *Nota delle pitture fatte da me Elisabetta Sirani*, begun in 1655 and later published by Malvasia in his *Felsina pittrice* of 1678.[16] Via this important document we can trace the range and breadth of the artist's production and patronage networks as she carefully describes each commission and its subject matter over a period of 10 years, identifying the client for whom each work was painted. Elisabetta here lists close to 200 commissions from 100 different patrons from all social levels: artists, merchants and professionals, as well as the intellectual, aristocratic, ecclesiastical and political elite of Bologna. Royalty and diplomatic leaders throughout Italy and the Continent, such as the Medici and the King of Poland, also sought the artist's work, so that her paintings, prints and drawings were represented in major European collections even in her own short lifetime. Elisabetta's extensive patronage networks, developed through self-fashioning, display and marketing strategies such as the diplomatic gifting of her work, were aided by her father's entrepreneurial management as well as by agents from Bologna's senatorial families who actively promoted the young artist.[17] Elisabetta subsequently became one of the most sought-after and collected Bolognese artists in the seventeenth and eighteenth centuries.[18]

Elisabetta was working on commissions for two important royal women[19] when she took ill in mid 1665, complaining of severe stomach pains. Following her death, Bologna's "Pittrice Eroina" (Malvasia) was given an elaborately staged civic funeral by the city's elders in the church of San Domenico, where she was laid to rest in the Guidotti Chapel of the Rosary, next to the tomb of Guido Reni, Bologna's other cultural hero.[20]

Adelina Modesti

[1] On the pharmacology of Elisabetta's treatment and cause of death see Baldi 1958; Baron 1998.

[2] For an introduction to the life and art of Elisabetta Sirani see the pioneering work of Fiorella Frisoni: Frisoni 1978; Frisoni 1992a; Frisoni 2004; and also Modesti 1995; Modesti 2004; *Elisabetta Sirani* 2004; Modesti 2014; Modesti 2018a.

[3] For Elisabetta's print production see Modesti 2001b; for her drawings, see note 10 below; for her artistic training, Modesti 2004, chap. 4; for Reni and the Sirani, Bohn 2011.

[4] On the Sirani bottega see Modesti 2013; for Elisabetta as head of the Sirani studio, Modesti 2018b pp. 89-91. For Giovanni Andrea's illness, which had started to manifest itself as early as 1649, see the letter from Pietro Antonio Davia in Bologna to Antonio Ruffo in Messina, dated 19 June 1649; letters from Marquis Ferdinando Cospi in Bologna to Prince Leopoldo de' Medici in Florence, dated 19 August 1662, and September 1663, in Archivio di Stato di Firenze, Catalogo degli Artisti (from now on ASFi, CDA), XVI, fols. 348*r* and 140r-41*r*; and Malvasia 1678, ed. 1841, II, p. 402. Giovanni Andrea Sirani himself referred to his "infirmità" in two letters to the Medici Prince, dated 29 October 1663 and 29 April 1667, in ASFi, CDA, IX, fols. 215*r*, 241*r*.

[5] As Cospi reported to Cardinal Leopoldo de' Medici, letter dated 19 August 1662, ASFi, CDA, XVI, fol. 348*r*: "the daughter who is now a maestra here supports all her numerous family with her work".

[6] Modesti 2004, pp. 11, 108.

[7] Lukehart 2020, in examining the Academy's papers, has found no evidence to suggest that women actively participated in the institutional meetings or classes in the seventeenth century.

[8] For Barbara and Anna Maria Sirani and Ginevra Cantofoli see Sabbatini 1995; Modesti 2004, pp. 77, 108–14, 300; Graziani 2004a; Pulini 2008; Bohn 2019, pp. 85–90.

[9] Malvasia 1678, ed. 1841, II, p. 407.

[10] For Elisabetta's draughtsmanship see Bohn 2004b.

[11] Malvasia 1678, ed. 1841, II, p. 386.

[12] Letter from Bisi to Leopoldo de' Medici dated 22 January 1658, in ASFi, CDA III, folder 30, fol. 493.

[13] Malvasia considered Elisabetta's Madonnas to be the most beautiful since those of Guido Reni (ed. 1841, II, pp. 340–341). On the sacred and maternal in Elisabetta's art see Fortunati 2004a, pp. 26–29.

[14] Sutherland Harris, in *Women Artists* 1976, pp. 401-2; Modesti 2001a, pp. 401–402; Bohn 2002; Modesti 2004, chap. 5.

[15] See Cantaro 1989; *Lavinia Fontana* 1994; Murphy 2003; Rocco 2017, pp. 30–91.

[16] Malvasia 1678, ed. 1841, II, pp. 393–400.

[17] Such as the Sirani patrons and Medici agents Marquis Ferdinando Cospi and Count Annibale Ranuzzi. See Goldberg 1983, chap. 2; Carapelli 1984; Carapelli 1988; Modesti 2003; Bohn 2013a.

[18] As the archival studies of Morselli 1998a and Morselli 1998b; Bonfait 2000; Modesti 1995, pp. 750–754; Modesti 2004; Modesti 2014; Bohn 2013b; Bohn 2019.

[19] The Grand Duchess of Tuscany Vittoria della Rovere and Empress Palatine Eleonora Gonzaga. See Modesti 2003, p. 373 and note 70; Modesti 2020, p. 167.

[20] For the artist's funeral see Modesti 2001a, p. 402; Modesti 2004, Epilogo; Merkel 2011.

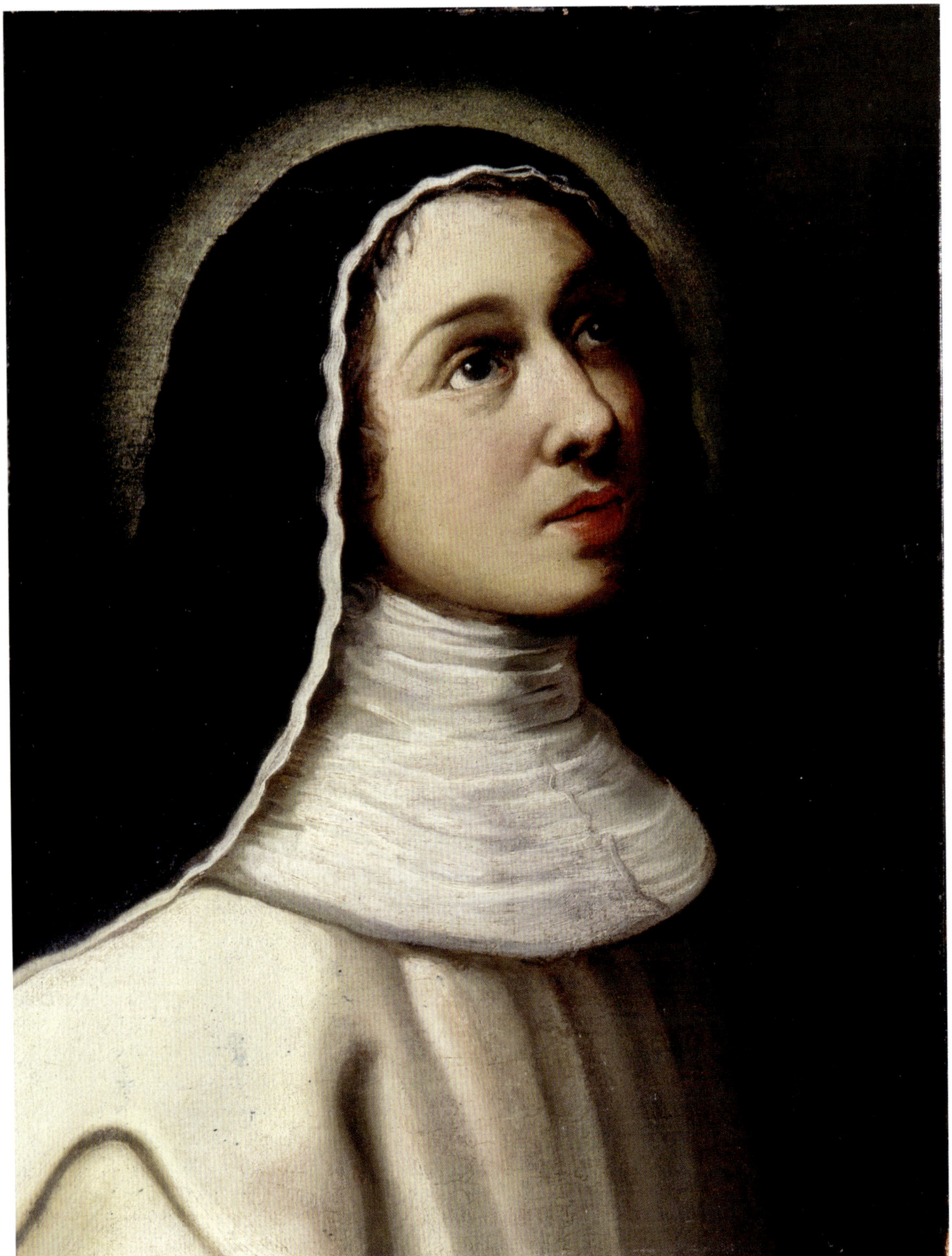

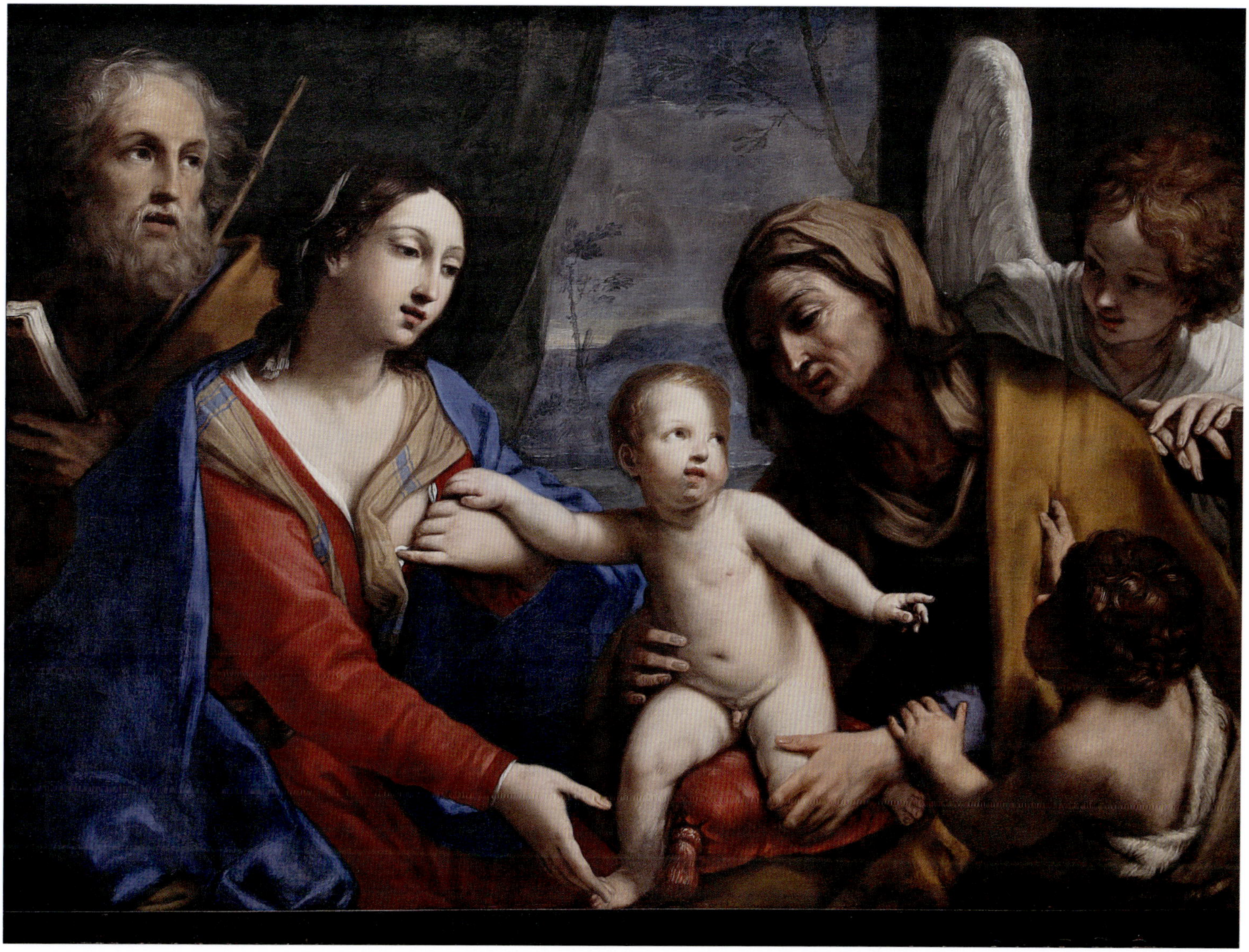

3.25
Elisabetta Sirani
Self-Portrait as a Saint (Certosina)
1658
Oil on canvas, 50.5 × 38 cm
Bologna, Pinacoteca Nazionale, inv. 57

3.26
Elisabetta Sirani
The Holy Family, Saint Anne, Saint John the Baptist and an Angel
1660
Oil on canvas, 100.5 × 131 cm
Vercelli, Fondazione Museo Francesco Borgogna, inv. 1906, IV, 113

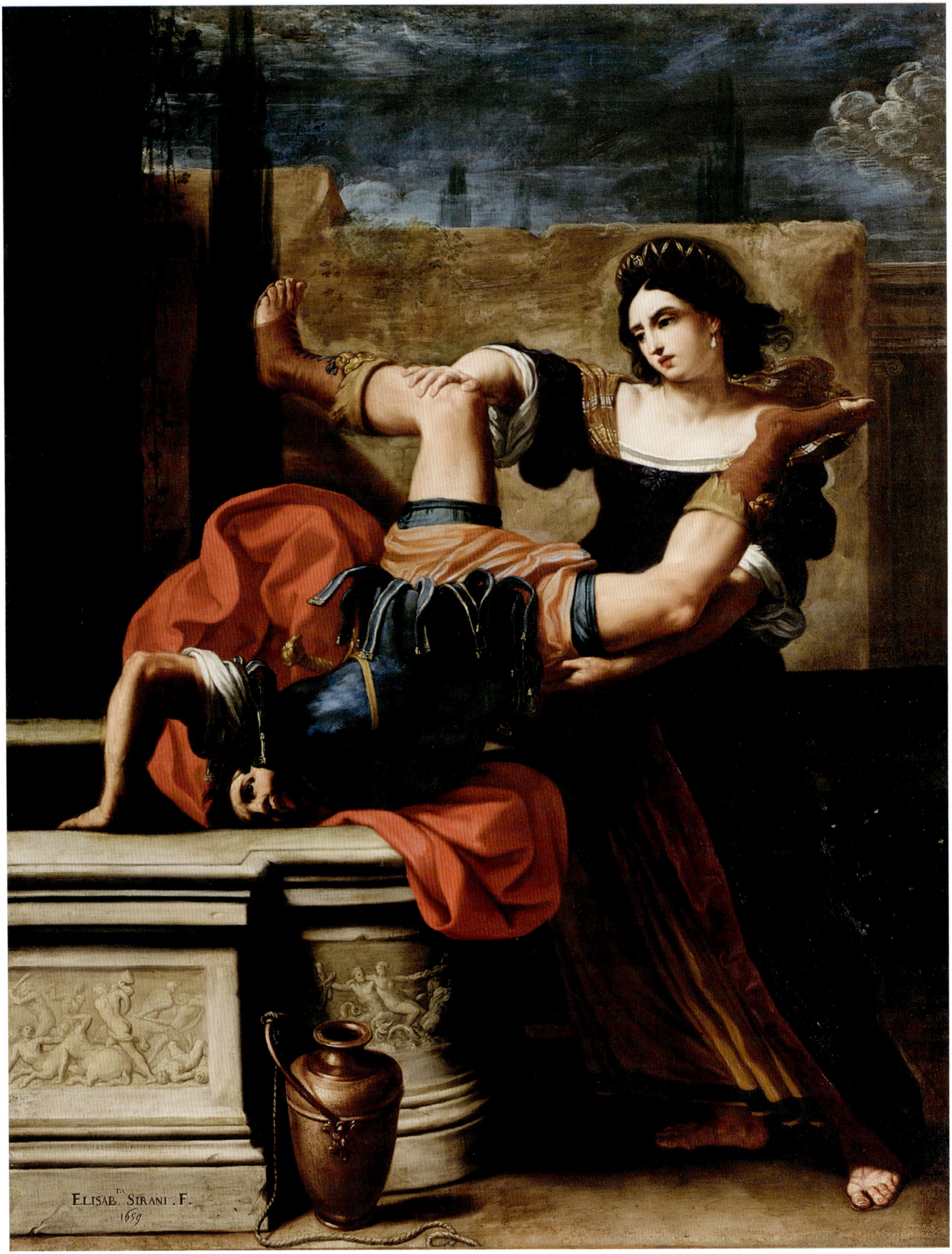
ELISAB.TA SIRANI . F.
1659

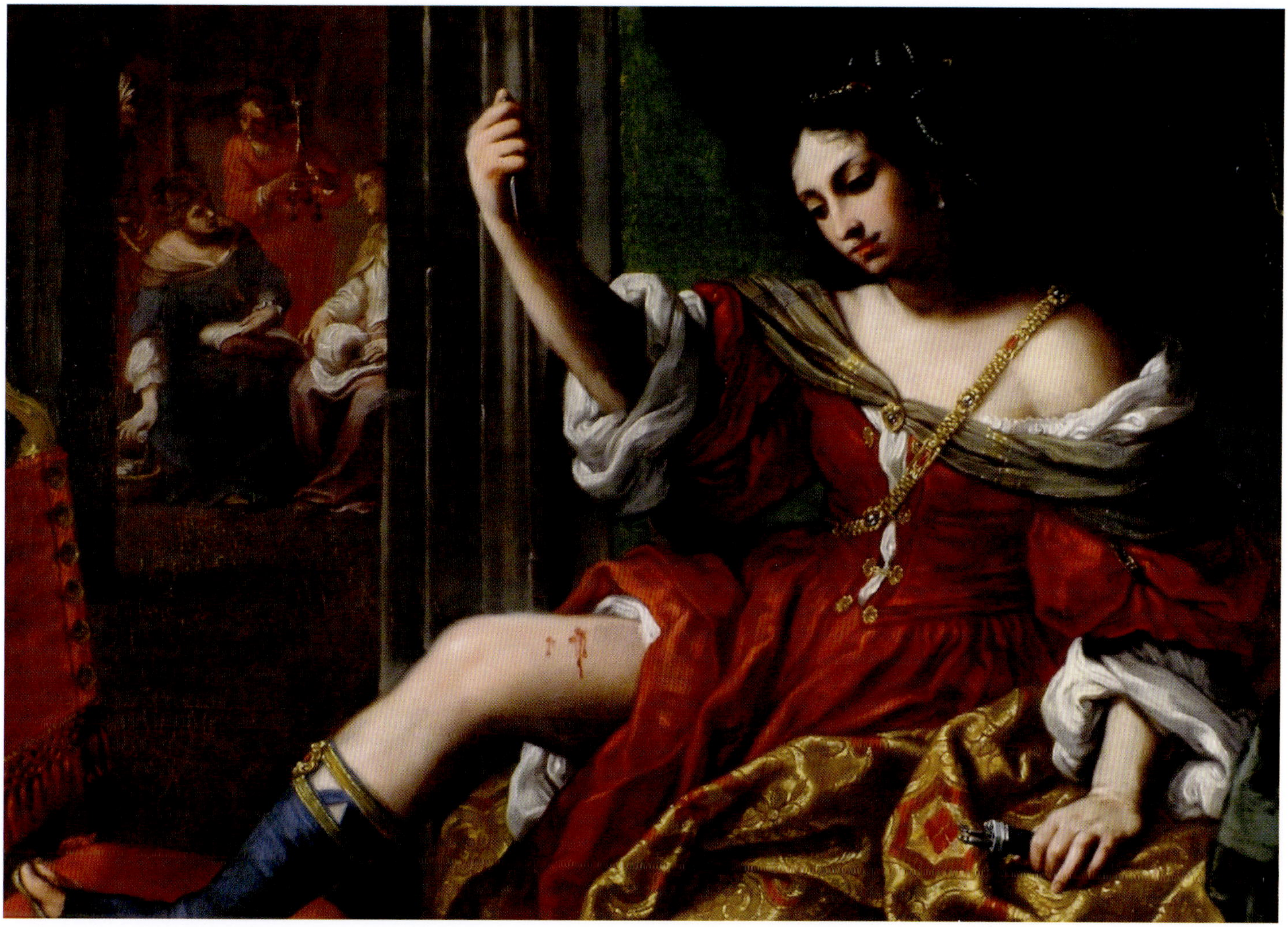

3.27
Elisabetta Sirani
Timoclea Kills the Captain of Alexander the Great
1659
Oil on canvas, 228 × 174.5 cm
Naples, Museo e Real Bosco di Capodimonte, inv. Q633

3.28
Elisabetta Sirani
Portia Wounding her Thigh
1664
Oil on canvas, 101 × 138 cm
Bologna, Collezione d'Arte e di Storia della Fondazione Cassa di Risparmio in Bologna, inv. M32228

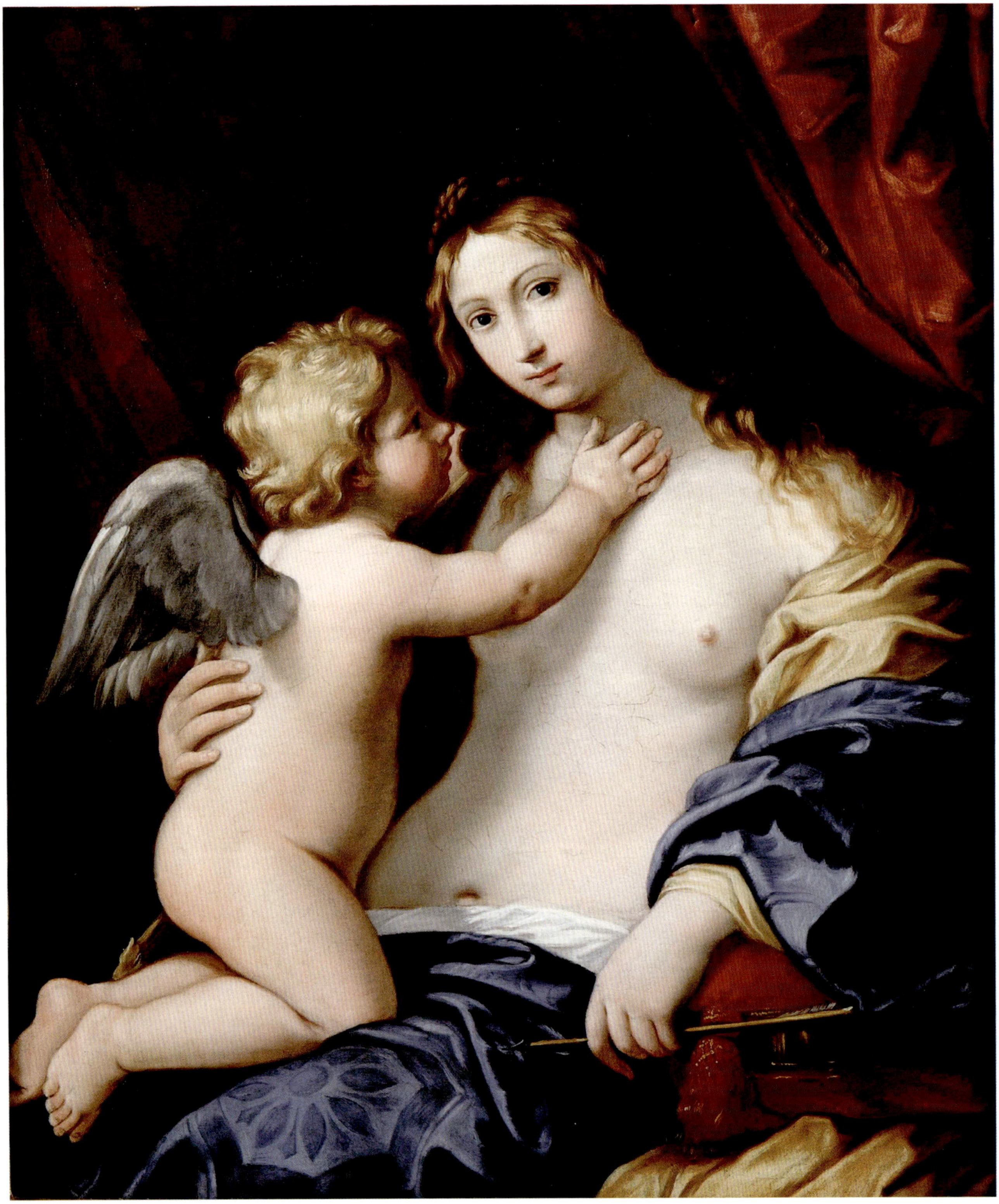

3.29
Giovanni Andrea Sirani
Venus and Cupid
c. 1645
Oil on canvas, 112 × 93 cm
Bologna, Collezione d'Arte
e di Storia della Fondazione
Cassa di Risparmio
in Bologna, inv. F32243

3.30
Elisabetta Sirani
Venus and Cupid
1664
Oil on canvas, 101 × 85 cm
Private collection

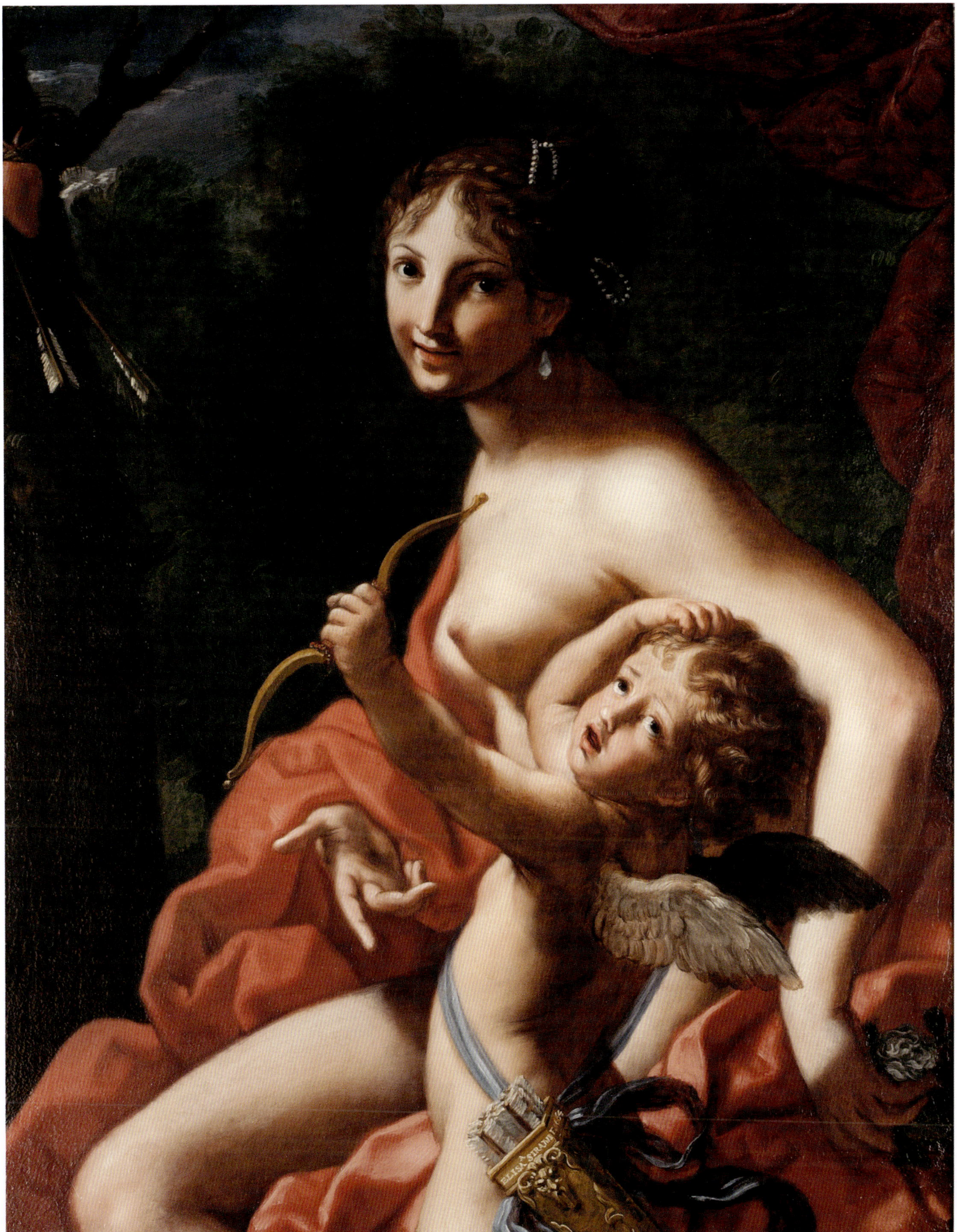
ELISA SIRANI F.

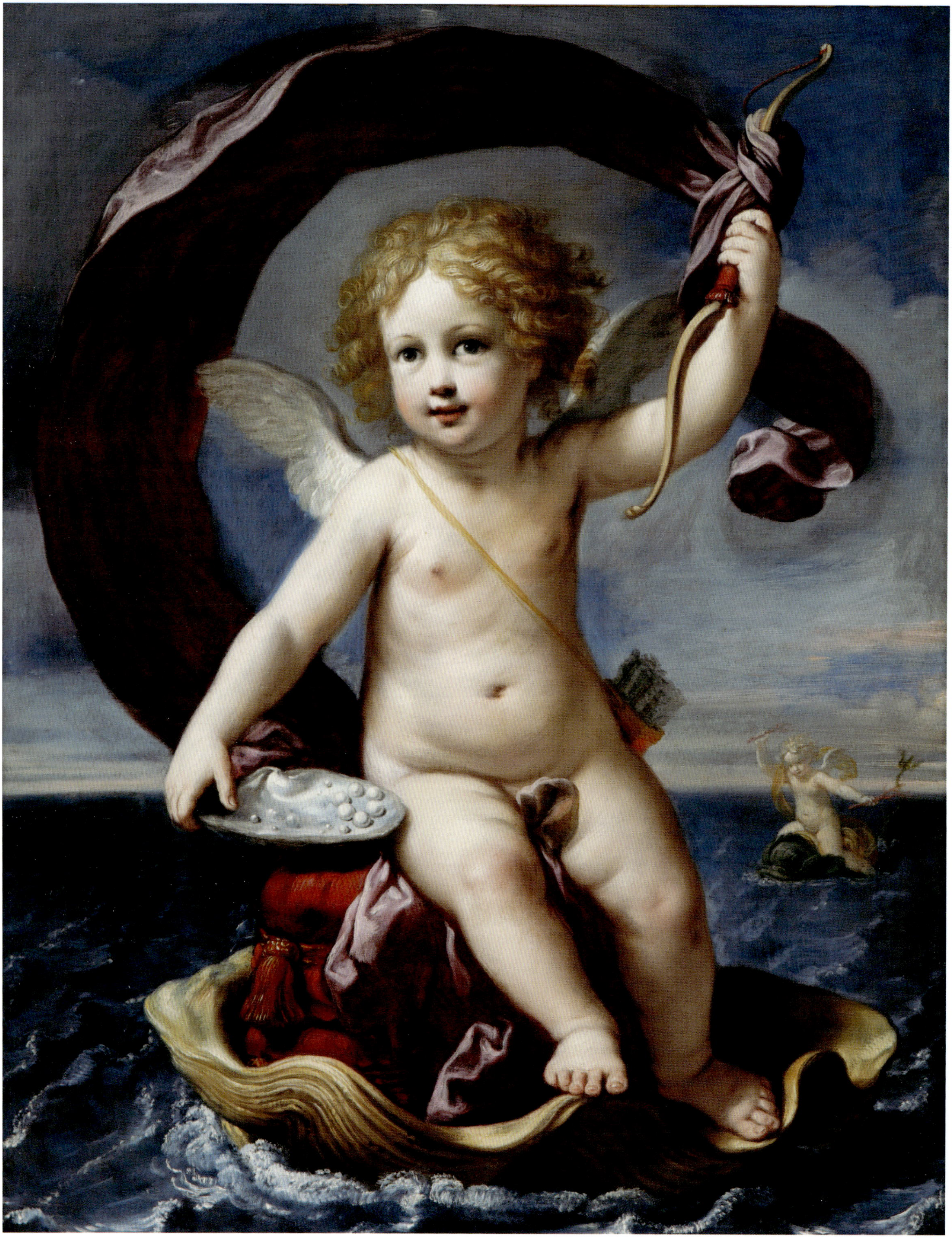

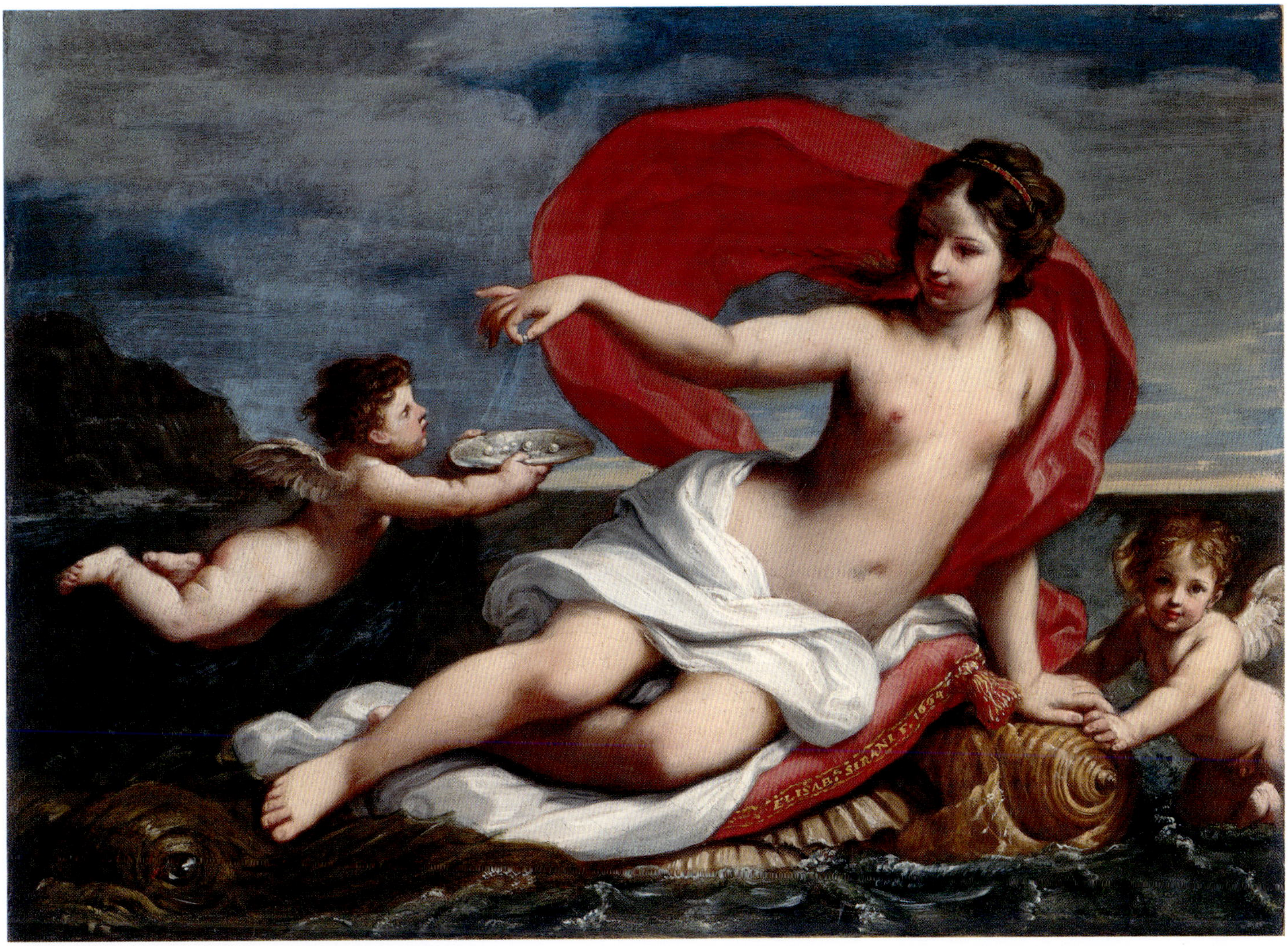

3.31
Elisabetta Sirani
Triumphant Cupid
(*Medici Cupid*)
1661
Oil on canvas, 89 × 70 cm
Bologna, private collection

3.32
Elisabetta Sirani
Galatea
1664
Oil on canvas, 43 × 58.5 cm
Modena, Museo Civico d'Arte,
inv. Ser. 8

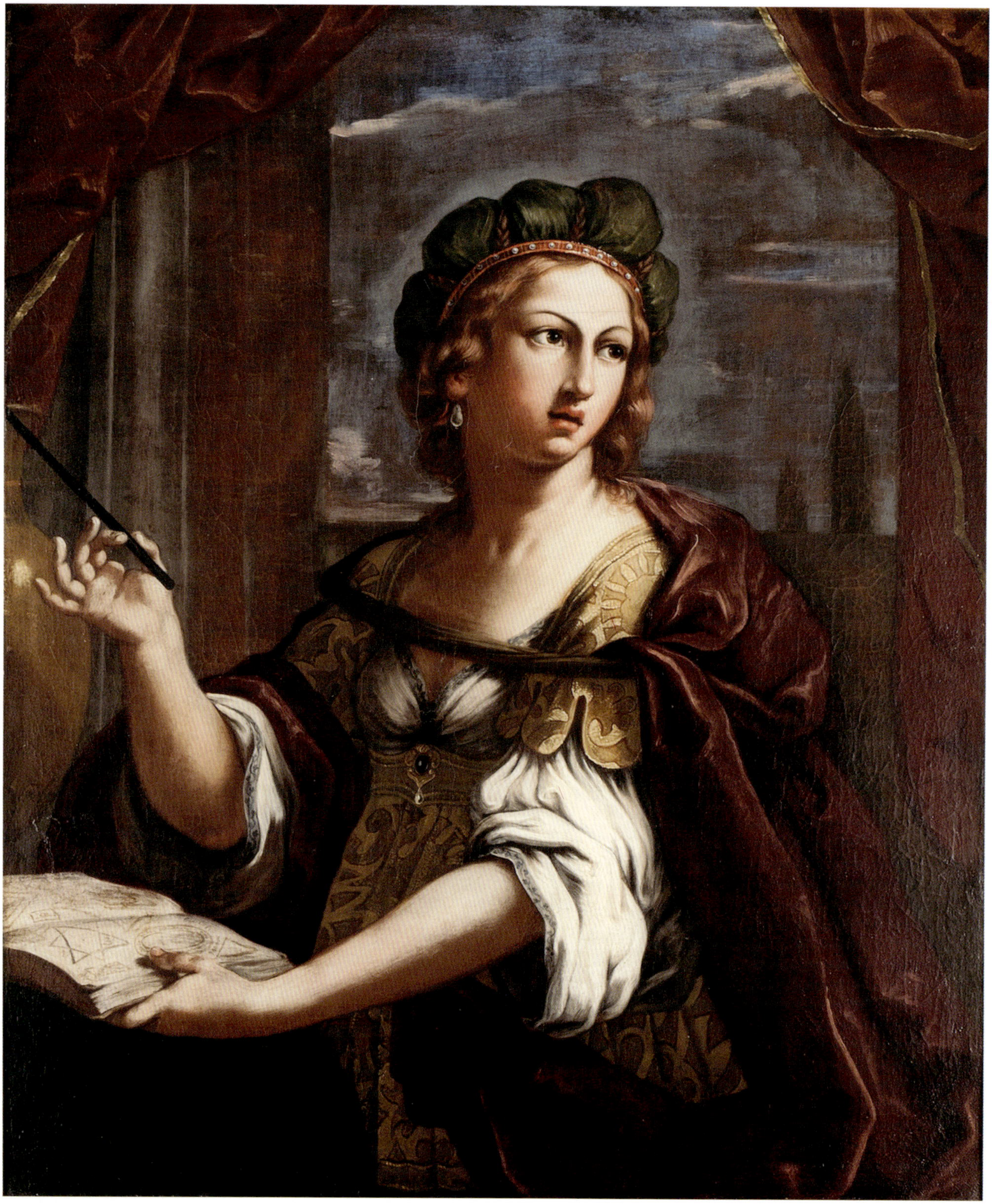

3.33
Elisabetta Sirani
Circe
c. 1664
Oil on canvas, 112 × 92 cm
Private collection

3.34
Elisabetta Sirani
Cleopatra
c. 1664
Oil on canvas, 110 × 91 cm
Private collection

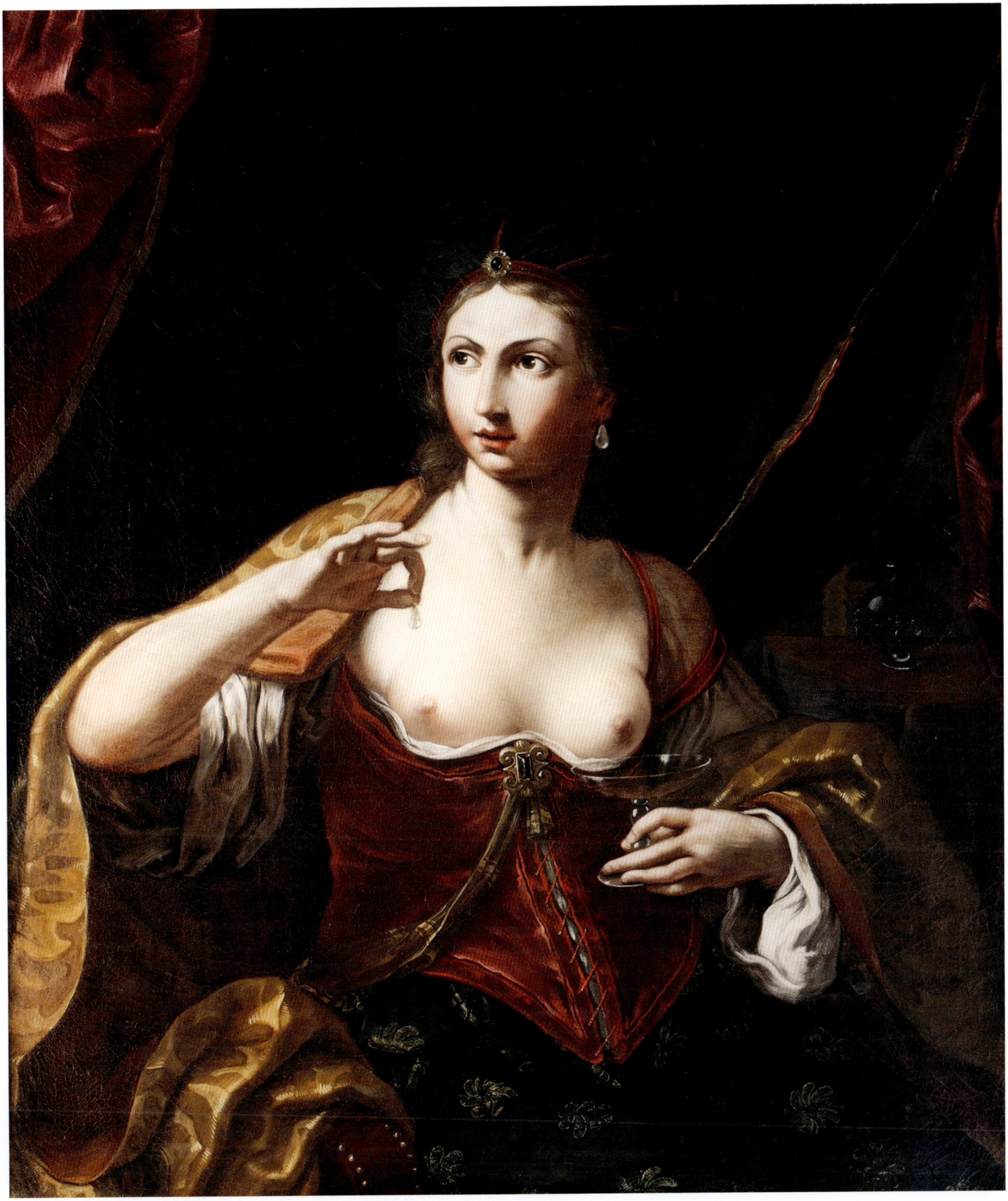

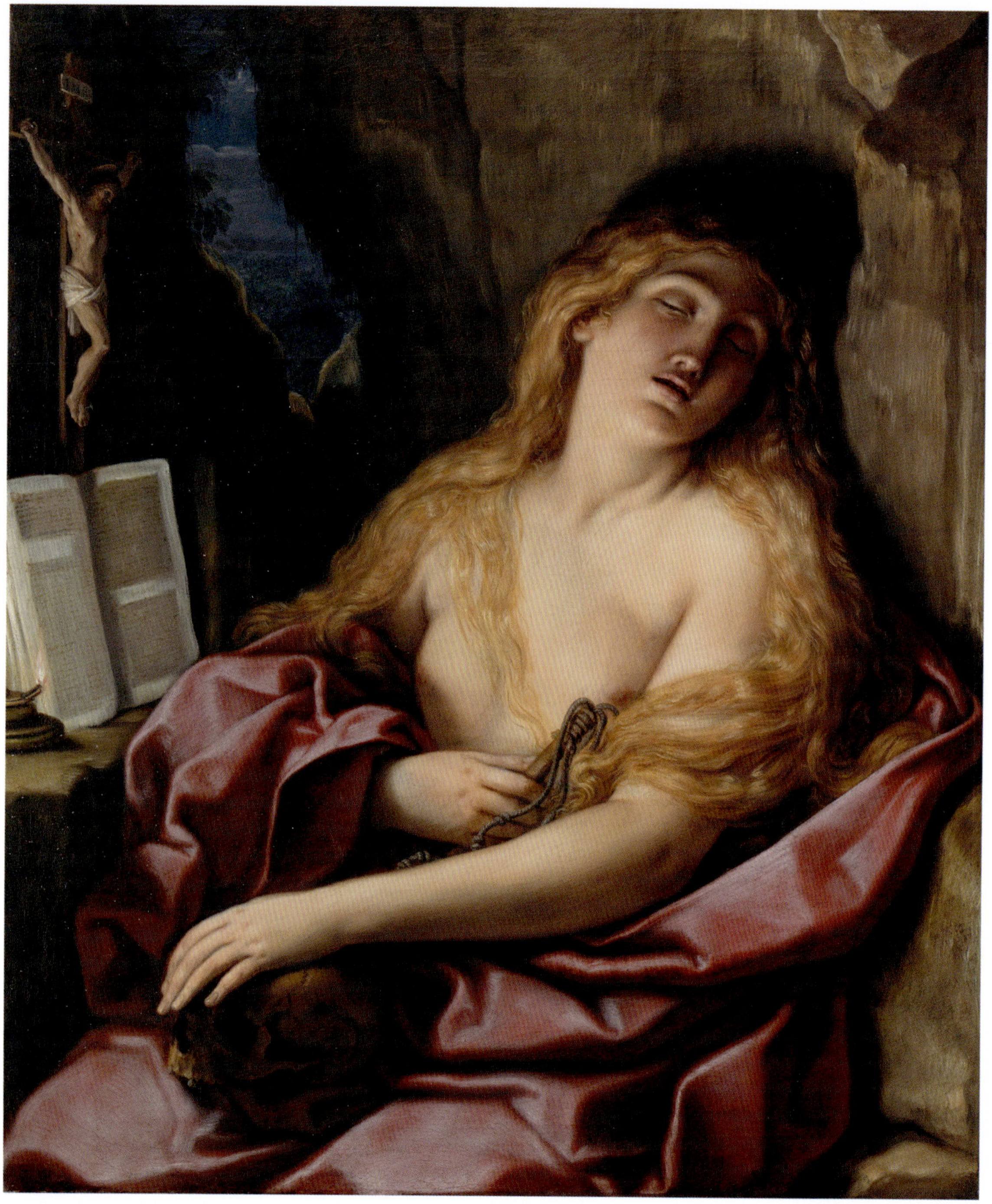

3.35
Elisabetta Sirani
Penitent Mary Magdalene
1663
Oil on canvas, 113.5 × 94 cm
Paris, Musée du Louvre,
in deposit in Besançon,
Musée des Beaux-Arts
et d'Archéologie,
inv. D.864.1.3/569

3.36
Elisabetta Sirani
Anna Maria Ranuzzi
Portrayed as Charity
1665
Oil on canvas, 96 × 78 cm
Bologna, Collezione d'Arte
e di Storia della Fondazione
Cassa di Risparmio
in Bologna, inv. M3085

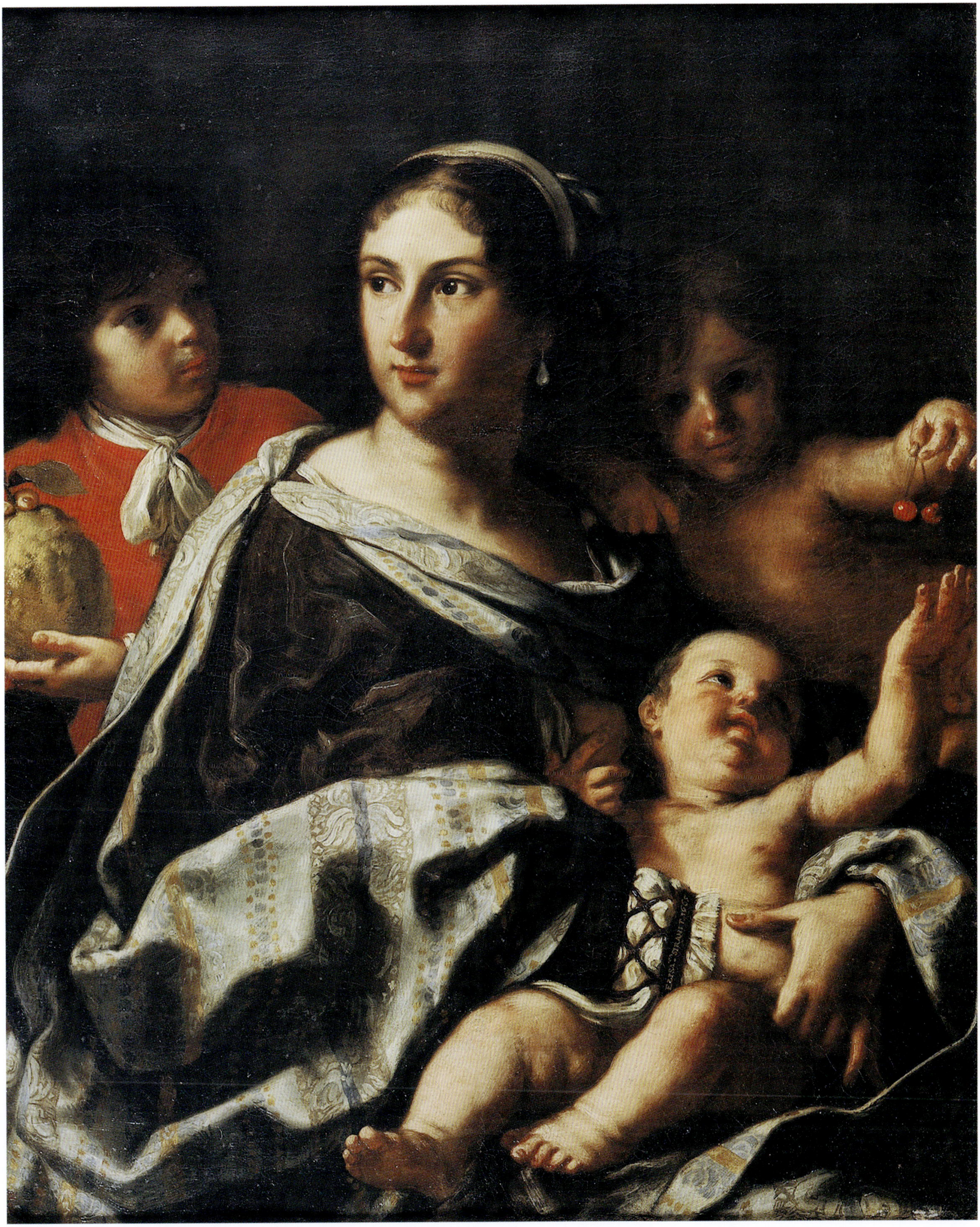

MARIETTA ROBUSTI, KNOWN AS TINTORETTA

Venice, c. 1554 – Venice, 1590

Marietta Robusti, known as Tintoretta, was the eldest daughter of Jacopo Tintoretto (1518–1594), a master of Venetian painting in the post-Tridentine era. According to an apocryphal genealogy of the artist's family,[1] Marietta was the child of a premarital relationship between the painter and "a German woman" with whom he was very much in love.[2] After Marietta's birth, the artist married Faustina Episcopi (or de' Vescovi), a woman of higher social rank, with whom he had four sons and four daughters. Like Marietta, some of her brothers also worked in the paternal workshop, among whom the most talented was Domenico. At that time the profession of painter was almost exclusively the prerogative of men; for most female artists the only path was to join their father's workshop, as Marietta did at a very young age.

We know little about her life: we do not know the exact dates of her birth and death, nor the cause of her death, which is generally given as around 1590, four years before her father died. The considerable research, interpretations and legends concerning the artistic identity of Tintoretta have only fuelled the mystery. One of the main sources is a 1584 monograph entitled *Il riposo* by Raffaello Borghini (1537–1588), a Florentine scholar who was a contemporary of Robusti.[3] The other, from about fifty years later, is a biography of Tintoretto published by Venetian Carlo Ridolfi (1594–1658) in 1642.[4] Both texts refer to a very intense relationship between the painter and his eldest daughter. Borghini relates that Tintoretto had a daughter whom everyone called Tintoretta, and who "in addition to beauty and grace, and the ability to play the harpsichord, lute and other instruments, paints very well and has made many beautiful works", which include the *Portrait of Jacopo Strada*, Emperor Maximilian II's antiquarian, and a *Self-Portrait* of the emperor kept in his room as "a rare thing".[5] Like his predecessor, Ridolfi also praises Marietta's qualities as a portraitist and commends her musical education, attributing several portraits to her, notably that of Marco Episcopi (the father of Tintoretto's wife, Faustina) together with his son Piero, in addition to the one of the famous imperial antiquarian and others portraying her husband's friends. He also adds that Marietta worked on "other works of invention" and made copies of her father's work.[6] The search for Tintoretta's paintings has so far failed to yield satisfactory results. Despite her biographers and the inventories citing numerous portraits by her hand, such as the painting in the Galleria Borghese of unknown provenance mentioned since 1790 (cat. 3.38), the only that is generally attributed to her is the Uffizi *Self-Portrait* (cat. 3.39). According to Ridolfi, Tintoretto was asked to send Marietta to the court of King Philip II of Spain and to Archduke Ferdinand of Habsburg. However, "Tintoretto, was instead pleased to see her married to Mario Augusta, a jeweller, so as to have her always close by, since he loved her dearly, rather than to be without her, although she was favoured by princes". In this way her father was never separated from his daughter and she never stopped painting.[7] Marietta remained in Venice and continued to work in her father's workshop, compelled in those years to take on an ever-increasing number of orders for the aristocracy and for the various institutions of the Serenissima.

However, since she never signed her works, Tintoretta was destined to remain buried in the maze of her father's production, where she soon became a character lost in the myth, brought to light only by the efforts of researchers.

Valentine De Beir

[1] Checa 2004.
[2] Checa 2004, p. 205.
[3] *Il riposo in cui della pittura e della scultura si favella, dei più illustri pittori, e scultori, e delle più famose opere loro si fa menzione; E le cose principali appartenenti a detti arti si insegnano.*
[4] *Vita di Giacomo Robusti*, later included in the two-volume work *Le meraviglie dell'arte. Le vite degl'illustri pittori veneti e dello stato* published in 1648.
[5] Borghini 1584, pp. 558–559.
[6] Ridolfi 1648, p. 260; Tietze-Conrat 1934, p. 259.
[7] Ridolfi 1648, p. 260.

3.37
Jacopo Robusti, known as Tintoretto
Portrait of Jacopo Soranzo
c. 1550–1551
Oil on canvas, 75 × 60 cm
Milan, Castello Sforzesco, Pinacoteca, inv. 64

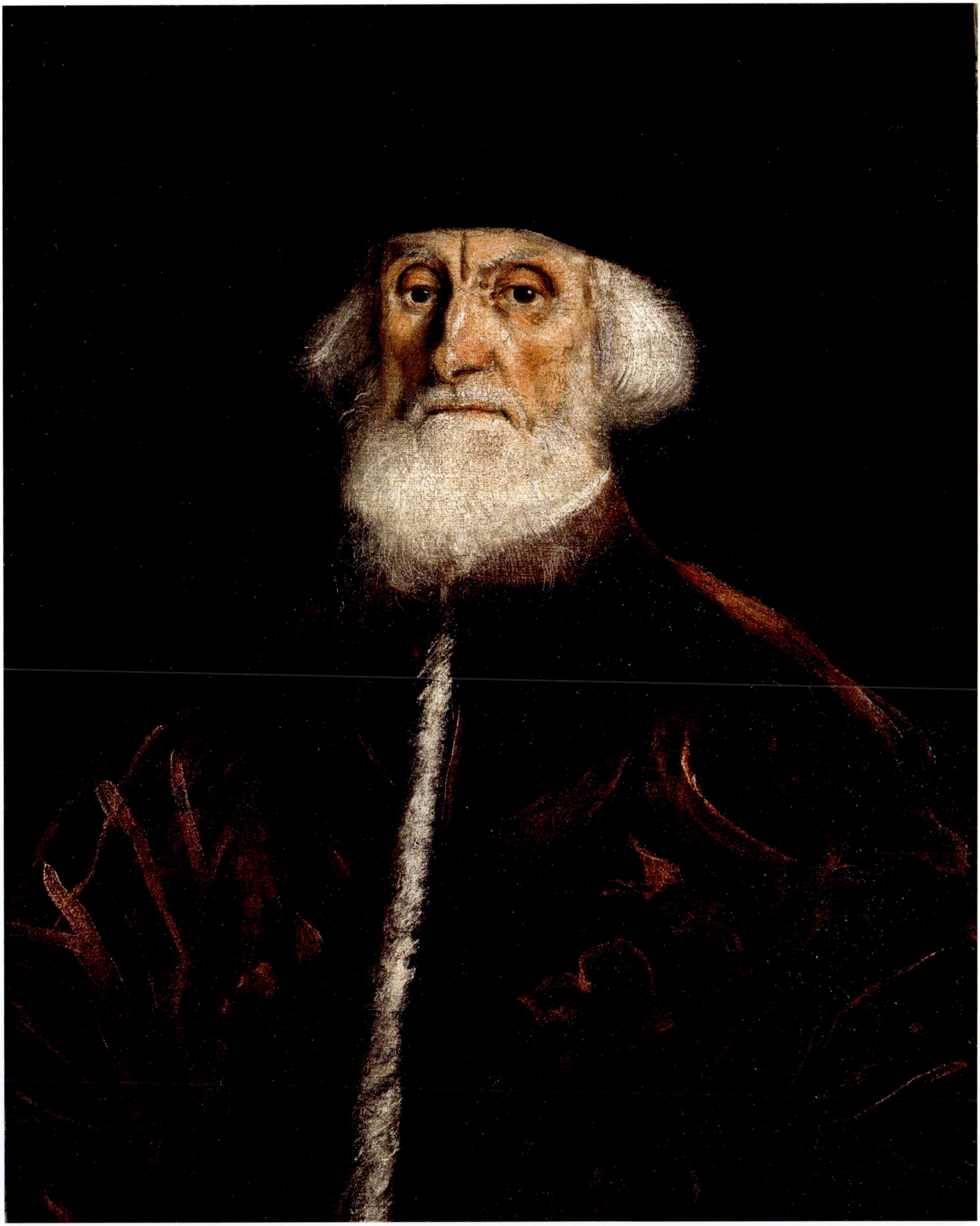

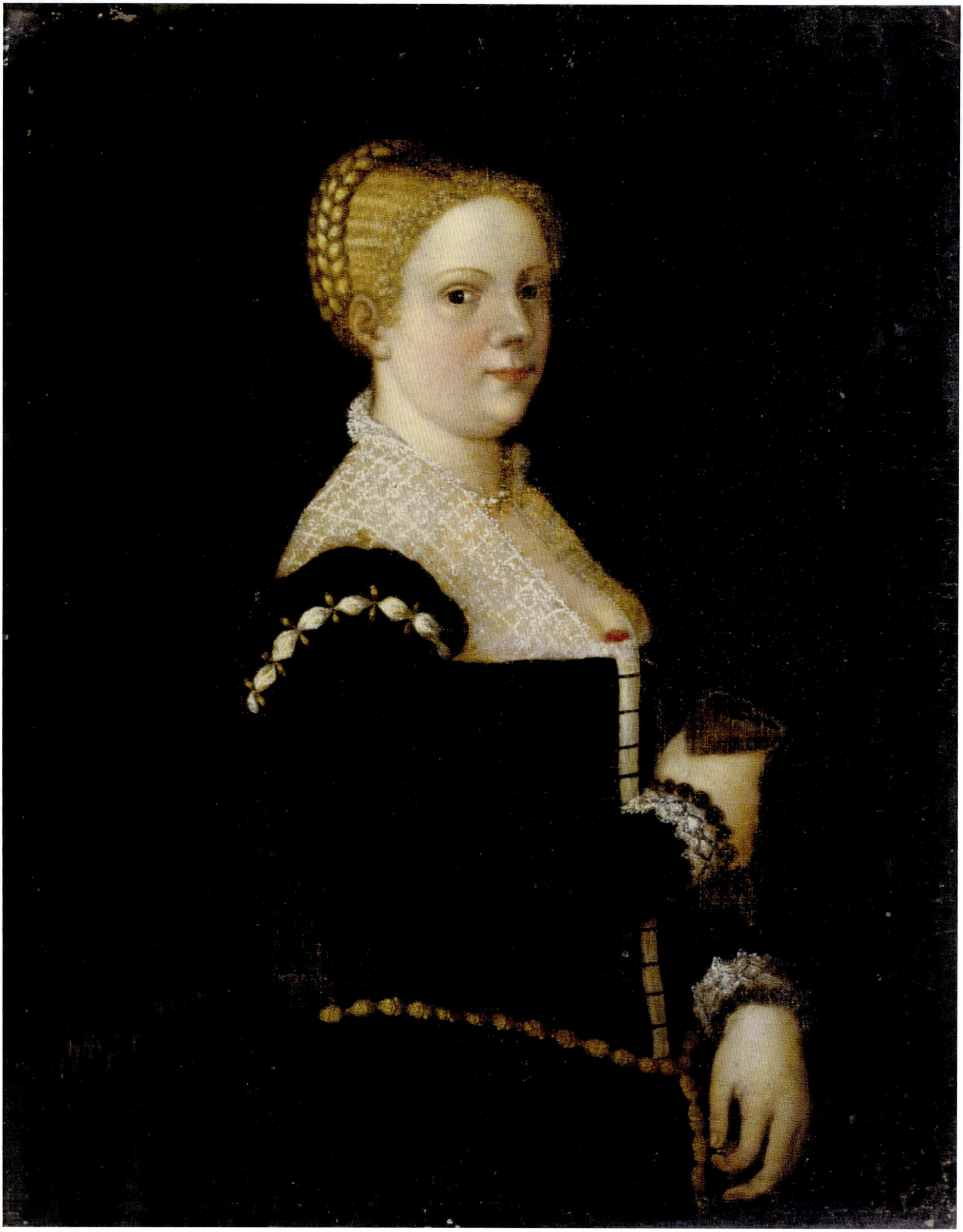

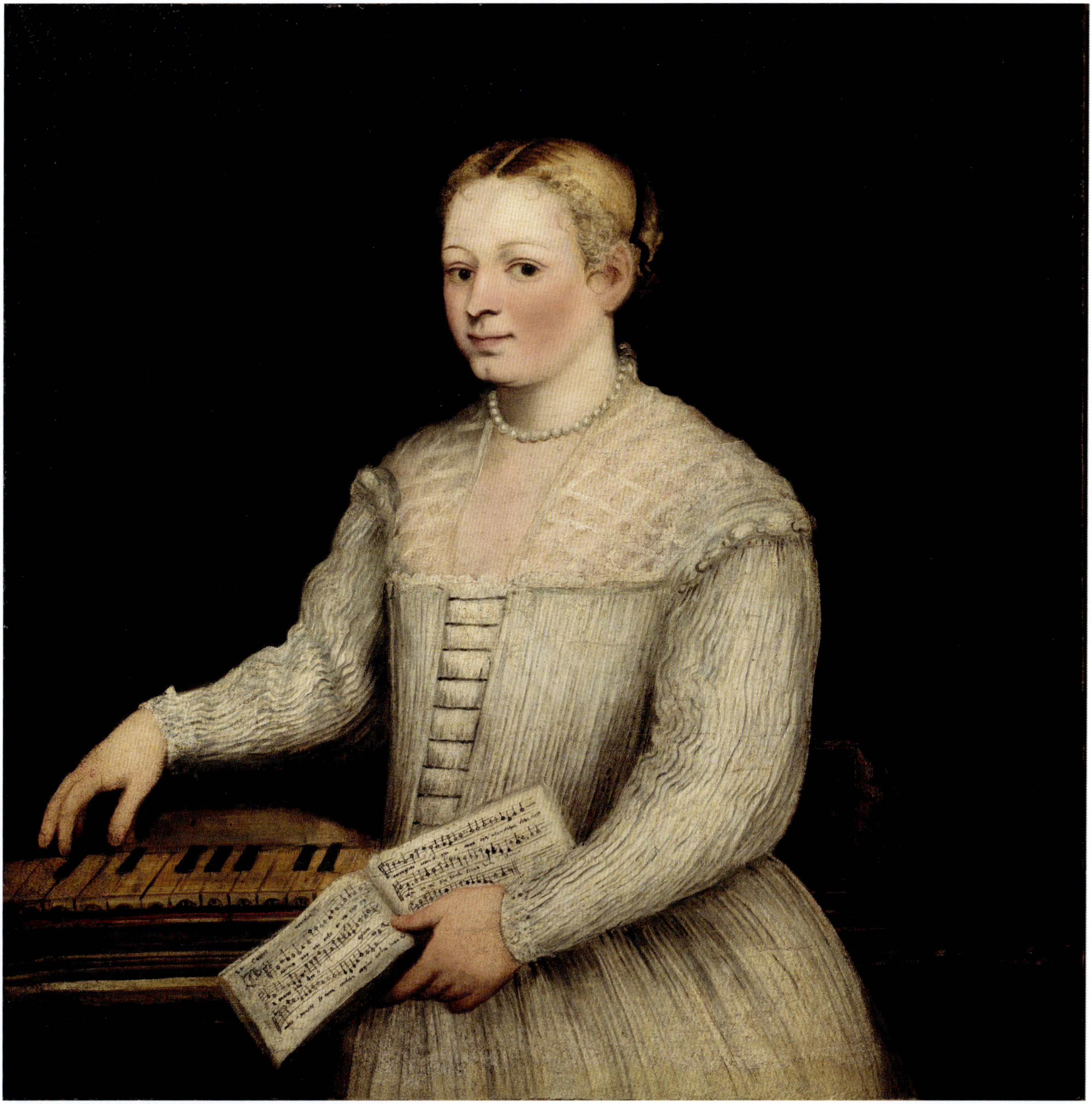

3.38
Marietta Robusti, known as Tintoretta (attributed)
Self-Portrait (?)
Before 1590
Oil on canvas, 101 × 78 cm
Rome, Galleria Borghese, inv. 93

3.39
Marietta Robusti, known as Tintoretta
Self-Portrait with Madrigal
c. 1580
Oil on canvas, 93.5 × 91.5 cm
Florence, Gallerie degli Uffizi, 1890, inv. 1898

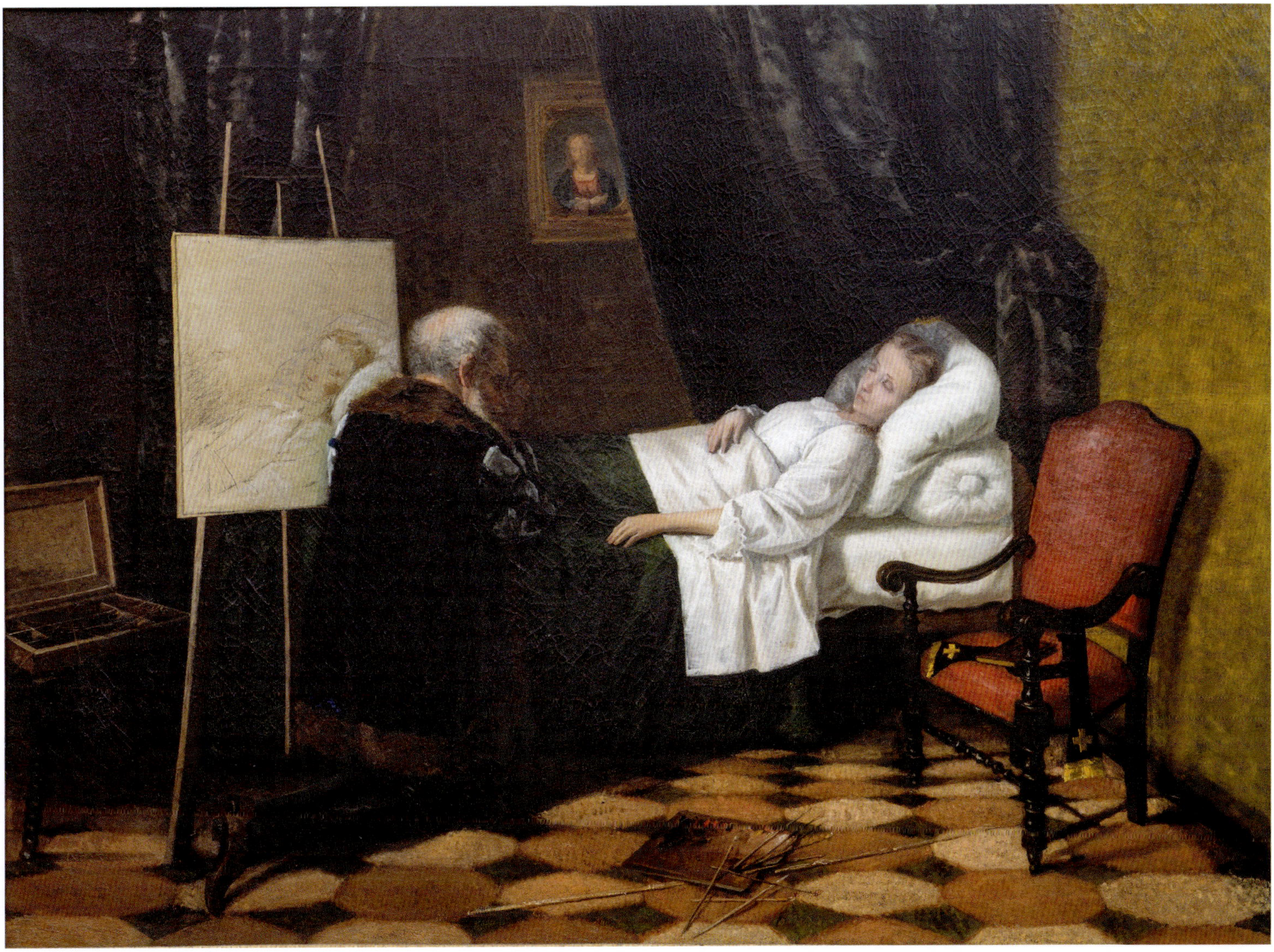

3.40
Guglielmo De Martino
Tintoretto Portraying his Dying Daughter
Before 1881
Oil on canvas, 77.5 × 103.5 cm
Catanzaro, MARCA – Museo delle Arti di Catanzaro, inv. 0011345

CHIARA VAROTARI

Padua, 1584 – Venice, post 1663

Chiara Varotari was born in Padua in 1584. Her parents were Dario, a painter and architect of Veronese origin, and Samaritana, daughter of Giovanni Battista Ponchini, an artist from Castelfranco.[1] Her father probably moved to Padua in the 1570s, where in addition to painting he also created frescoes for clients from both secular and religious backgrounds.

In his *Vita di Marietta Tintoretta*, Carlo Ridolfi cites Chiara among examples that demonstrate "the recognition accessible today to a perspicacious woman who has been educated",[2] and describes her in *Vita di Dario Varotari* as an "able woman" dedicated to the paternal home, having refused "every honourable position", and whose work includes "many beautiful and faithful portraits".[3] Marco Boschini also praises her, describing her as "unique (if that can be said) in making portraits", and suggests that she ran a painting school whose pupils included Lucia Scaligeri and Caterina Tarabotti,[4] although Luigi Lanzi[5] questions its existence.

Varotari's date of death is established as post 1663, given that Giustiniano Martinioni, in his appendage to Francesco Sansovino's *Venetia città nobilissima et singolare*, mentions her among the painters living in Venice in that year, defining her as "skilful at painting".[6]

As mentioned above, Chiara learned to paint within the family. In addition to her father, her four-year younger brother Alessandro, known as Padovanino, was also a painter. In 1614[7] he moved to Venice, where she probably followed him. Giannantonio Moschini reserves a few pages in his history of Paduan painting to the Varotari family (Dario, Alessandro, Chiara, and Dario, Padovanino's son), noting that their father's fame was even greater due to Alessandro and Chiara, and recalling that the three were depicted together in a painting at the Muneghin house in Ca' Lando.[8]

Sources agree in pointing out Varotari's ability as a portraitist. Her skill in meticulously depicting clothes, jewels and hairstyles, and in emphasising the social status of the person portrayed must have been particularly appreciated and requested in Padua and Venice (Boschini writes that many of her portraits were to be seen of "Venetian Ladies, Paduan Ladies and others").[9]

We learn from Giovambattista Rossetti that her works were kept in private Paduan collections, among them an *Annunciation* at the home of Count Camposampiero in San Leonardo and other paintings at Palazzo Sala in San Biagio.[10] Moreover, Antonio Meneghelli[11] notes that the art collection of the lawyer Antonio Piazza in Vanzo contained, among others, paintings by Dario and Chiara.

Not many of Chiara Varotari's works are extant. Among them is a *Portrait of a Lady*, dated 1621, in a private collection, which might have depicted a member of the Buzzaccarini family, given that its pendant is the *Portrait of Ottavia Vitaliani Buzzaccarini* (1620), according to the inscription at the top right. However, due to the difference in pictorial quality,[12] this latter work is attributed to an imitator of Chiara's work. The *Portrait of a Lady* is an example of Varotari's impressively elegant production. The three-quarter portrait of the gentlewoman, depicted full figure, together with the elaborate refinement of the clothing and the position of the arm along her body, are among the characteristic touches dear to Varotari.

Another work, dated 1624 and signed on the back, is the *Portrait of Schinella Conti*, also held in a private collection. Born in Padua in 1572 to Alberto and to Giulia Speroni, daughter of the famous scholar and jurist Sperone Speroni, and died in 1627, Schinella was a philosopher and naturalist. Among other siblings he also had a twin brother, Ingolfo.[13]

Padua's art museum holds an important nucleus of works by Varotari that formerly belonged to the Emo Capodilista picture gallery, which in 1864 Count Leonardo left as a legacy to the Municipality of Padua.[14]

In addition to the paintings on display in this exhibition (cats. 3.41–43) is the *Portrait of a Lady*, signed at the bottom right, which Botter considers may depict Piera, daughter of Pio Capodilista and Pantasilea Dotto, who in her turn, still according to Botter, is depicted in the portrait inv. 138,[15] and the one depicting Anzola Muneghina, once believed to be a self-portrait by Chiara. Unlike the others, which are ceremonial portraits, the last-mentioned has an intimate character and has been compared by some to two portraits of young women in the Museo Correr, with the proposal to also attribute these Venetian paintings to Varotari.[16]

Two other portraits attributable to Chiara have been reported: one in the art collections of the Ospedale Maggiore in Milan and the other (in 1987) at Leasarte in Milan.[17]

According to sources, Varotari also painted the portrait of a female friend of Venetian Giovan Francesco Sagredo,[18] that of Rizzarda and other works that were in the studio of the Gualdo home in Vicenza,[19] and a profile portrait of her brother Alessandro (Padovanino), which Boschini saw at the home of Dario, Chiara's nephew.[20]

Elisabetta Gastaldi

[1] For Varotari's biography see: Pietrucci 1853, pp. 64–65; Pietrucci 1858, pp. 279–280; *Varotari, Chiara*, in Thieme, Becker 1940, p. 117 (mentioned here are works by Varotari in Hannover and in Naples); Donzelli, ad vocem *Varotari, Chiara,* in Donzelli, Pilo 1967, p. 408; Fantelli 1973; *Varotari, Chiara*, in *Dizionario* 1976, p. 254; Pallucchini 1981, I, p. 106; Ericani 1995, pp. 75–76; Ericani 1996, pp. 64–75; Banzato 2000, pp. 129, 136, 149, 153; Banzato 2001; Pedrocco 2003, pp. 75–76; Rubbi 2007; Lamon 2013, pp. 47–49.

[2] Ridolfi 1648, part II, p. 71.

[3] Ridolfi 1648, part II, p. 83.

[4] Boschini 1660, p. 525 and following.

[5] Lanzi 1823, III, p. 245.

[6] Sansovino, Martinioni 1663, p. 23.

[7] Ridolfi 1648, part II, pp. 83–84.

[8] Moschini 1826, pp. 85, 90 (Chiara).

[9] See L. Procacci, U. Procacci 1965, p. 100.

[10] Banzato, in *Lo spirito e il corpo* 2009, pp. 99–100, cat. 36, p. 100, cat. 37 (with bibliography).

[11] Meneghelli 1842, p. 85 (where "Marietta" should be read as "Chiaretta").

[12] Banzato, in *Lo spirito e il corpo* 2009, pp. 99–100, cat. 36, p. 100, cat. 37 (with bibliography).

[13] Banzato, in *Lo spirito e il corpo* 2009, p. 100, cat. 39 (with bibliography).

[14] Banzato, in *La Quadreria* 1988, pp. 113–116, cat. 172–178. Ericani (1996, p. 74) suggests including in Varotari's catalogue the *Portrait of a Gentleman* from the Emo Capodilista collection (inv. 12), a proposal accepted by Bottacin 2004a, pp. 165–166.

[15] Botter 1967, pp. 25–26, note 28.

[16] Fossaluzza 1977 [1994], p. 129. Fossaluzza's proposal was accepted by Banzato 2000, pp. 149–150, note 32.

[17] Bottacin 2004a, pp. 162–164.

[18] In a letter from 11 May 1619, Giovan Francesco Sagredo tells his friend Galileo Galilei that he has made friends with il Padovanino, who has arranged that Chiara will paint the portrait of Sagredo's female friend (Pallucchini 1981, I, p. 106).

[19] Gualdo jr. 1972, pp. 88–89.

[20] Boschini wrote this in a letter of 18 May 1675, addressed to Cardinal Leopoldo de' Medici (L. Procacci, U. Procacci 1965, p. 100).

3.41
Chiara Varotari
Portrait of a Lady
c. 1620–1629
Oil on canvas, 205 × 120 cm
Padua, Museo d'Arte Medioevale e Moderna, legacy of Count Leonardo Emo Capodilista, 1864, inv. 138

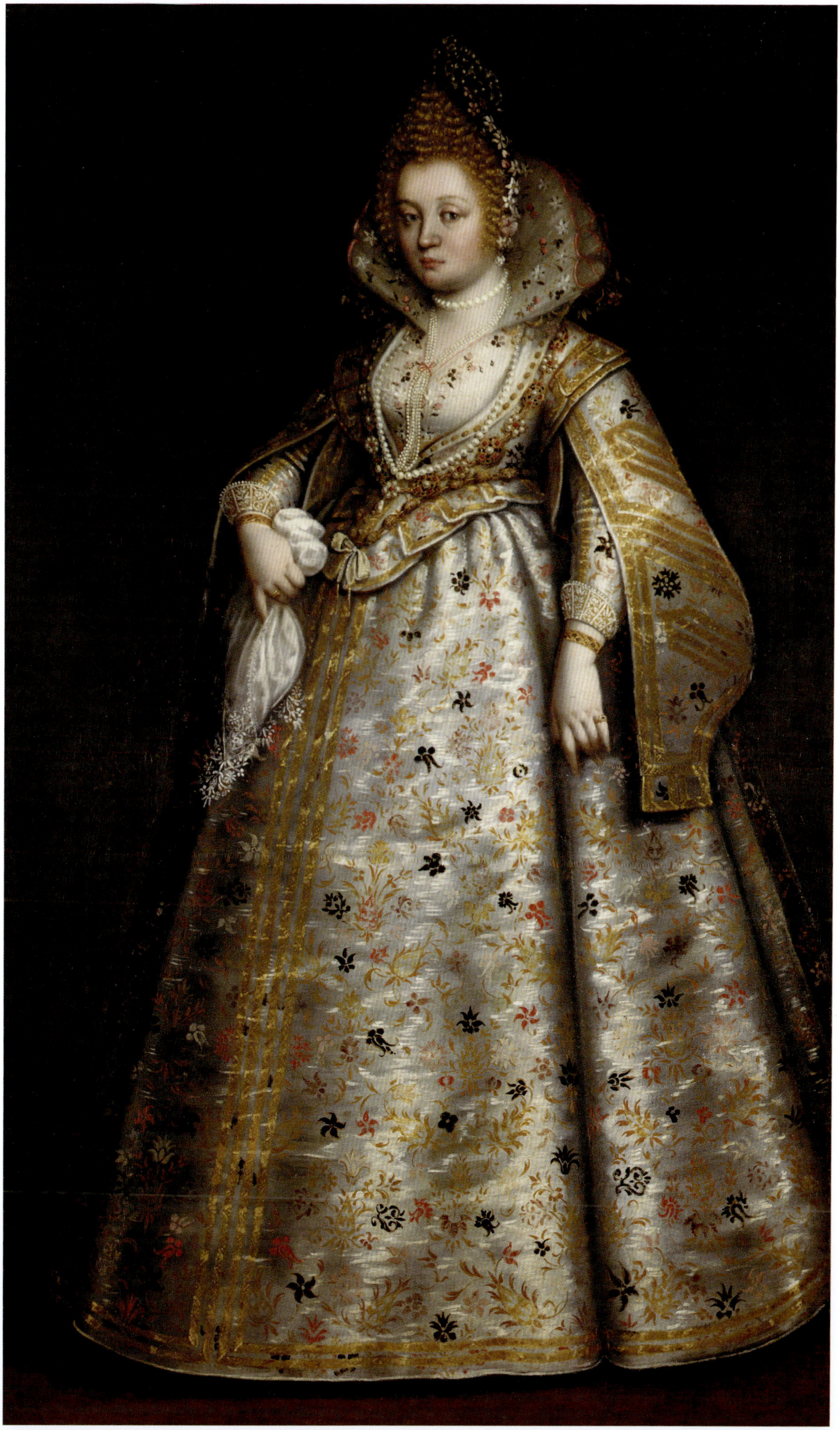

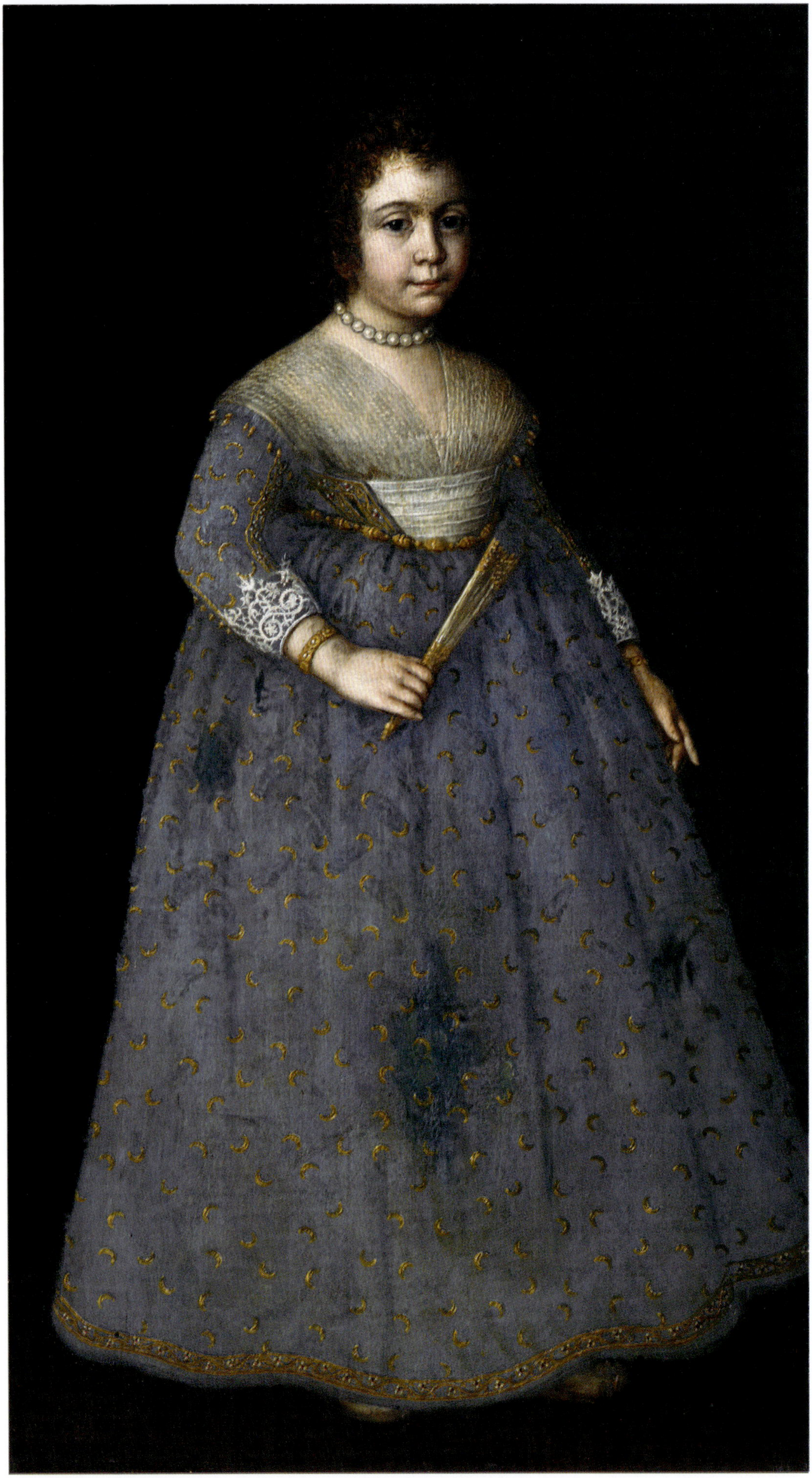

3.42
Chiara Varotari
Portrait of a Girl
c. 1620–1629
Oil on canvas, 122 × 70 cm
Padua, Museo d'Arte Medioevale e Moderna, legacy of Count Leonardo Emo Capodilista, 1864, inv. 134

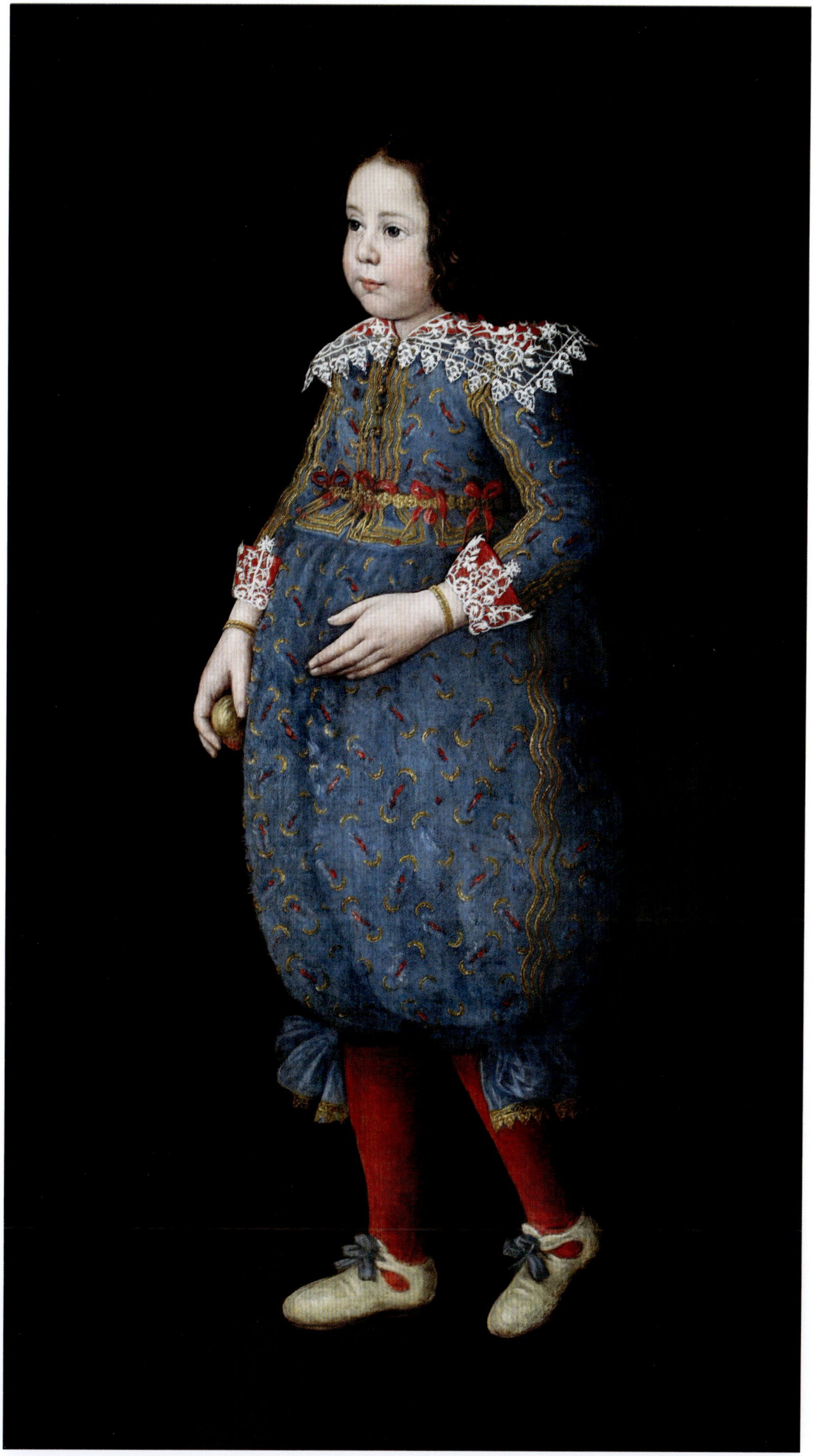

3.43
Chiara Varotari
Portrait of a Boy
c. 1620–1629
Oil on canvas, 122 × 70 cm
Padua, Museo d'Arte Medioevale e Moderna, legacy of Count Leonardo Emo Capodilista, 1864, inv. 140

FEDE GALIZIA

Milan?, 1574/1578 – Milan, post 21 June 1630

Fede was the daughter of Nunzio Galizia, a versatile Trentino artist active in the Lombardy capital since at least 1573.[1] She was probably born in Milan towards the middle of the 1580s.[2] Since no baptismal certificate has been discovered, her date of birth remains uncertain and can only be inferred from what is most likely an apocryphal inscription accompanying the *Portrait of Paolo Morigia* in the Pinacoteca Ambrosiana, in which she gives her age as eighteen.[3] Trained in her father's workshop, she soon began to study contemporary Milanese portraiture, with particular interest in the works of Lomazzo, Figino and Peterzano. Lomazzo himself confirms her precocious artistic talent as early as the *Rime* (1587),[4] whereas in the *Idea* (1590) he remembers her as a copyist who "undertook the imitation of the most excellent of our art",[5] practising in particular the works of Correggio. This is substantiated by her extant works,[6] by the testimony to this effect in her will[7] and by testimonies documented in the Settala collection.[8] In 1592 the poet Gherardo Borgogni wrote a sonnet in praise of her portrait of him: a wood engraving reproduced on the back of the title page, and used again in later editions.[9] The *Borgogni Portrait* is therefore Fede's oldest work and can be linked to her father's practice of engraving, such as his 1578 execution of a copperplate *View of Milan*.[10]

In 1595 her mentor, Paolo Morigia, was able to celebrate her recognised work as a portraitist, which by this point also included his own portrait (conserved today in the Ambrosiana), those of his parents, and ones of Maria Giron de Velasco, Duchess of Frias, and the Milanese noblewoman Camilla Ferraro. Morigia also confirms: "Her fame had even flown to his Supreme Majesty, Emperor Rudolph II, who was pleased to have things from the hand of this virtuous Fede".[11] Again we learn from Borgogni that works by Galizia reached the court in Prague via the artist Giuseppe Arcimboldo.[12] The relationship between the two painters may indeed have stimulated Fede's interest in still lifes.[13] Her fame also reached the Savoy court, where her father was active between 1620 and 1621.[14] One of Fede's commissions for the Dukes of Savoy is indirectly confirmed by Fede herself, who in 1630 was still owed payments from Duke Charles Emmanuel and his son Victor Amadeus.[15]

In the 1635 inventory of the Savoy collection there are at least three still lifes by Galizia, probably made in Turin (or brought there from Milan), and two *Judith and Holofernes*.[16] The oldest version of this subject is one dated 1596, conserved in the Ringling Museum in Sarasota, but others followed, with only one bearing a date (1601), now in the Galleria Borghese (cat. 3.48). On the other hand, the oldest still life with a signature is from 1602, a painting of a *Metal Fruit Stand with Plums, Pears and a Rose*, formerly in the Anhalt collection, Amsterdam, and very similar to another previously in the Lodi collection.[17] The metal fruit stand is the same one that appears in other compositions, although the identical formal construction of the image does not guarantee their chronology. In fact, dating Fede's still lifes remains a complex topic, also because until now we know of only one other dated work (1607), a version of the *Crystal Fruit Stand with Peaches, Quinces and Jasmine Flowers* illustrated in this exhibition by the Cremona example (cat. 3.45). Among the creations that must have enjoyed great success are the *Ceramic Fruit Dish with Grapes* known in four examples with variants,[18] and the *Perforated Ceramic Fruit Bowl*, also in different versions,[19] one of which is on display (cat. 3.44).

Added to these are the inventory records that further expand her catalogue.[20] Dating from the 1610s is a series of portraits of famous figures (Ludovico Settala, Federico Zuccari),[21] as well as of lesser-known notables, among them the spouses Giacomo Menochio and Caterina Candiana, painted in miniature within an architectural composition created by Nunzio.[22] Fede's portraiture continued to develop in the following years, as documented by the *Portrait of Pietro Martire Mascheroni* from 1622 in Ca' Granda.[23] In the 1610s Fede began to undertake sacred painting, producing important altarpieces: *Saint Charles in Ecstasy*, signed and dated 1611, now in Naples,[24] the *Noli Me Tangere* in the Brera from 1616;[25] *Saint Charles Adoring the Holy Nail* for the Theatines religious order of Sant'Antonio Abate in Milan (cat. 3.47); and the two semi-lunettes with Saint Anthony and Saint Paul the Hermit in the choir of the same church, probably painted between 1617 and 1619, the same years Moncalvo was decorating the choir.[26] Galizia's connection with the Theatines must have continued, since in her will, drawn up in June 1630, they were the recipients of several paintings. In all likelihood, Fede Galizia did not survive the plague.

Mario Marubbi

[1] Fogolari 1898, p. 295; Massimi 1998, pp. 499–500.

[2] Bottari 1965, p. 9 and p. 27 note 8.

[3] The painting bears an inscription with the date 1596, but Giacomo Berra ably argues that in reality the portrait in the Ambrosiana was painted some time earlier, between 1592 and 1595 (Berra 1989, pp. 18–23; Berra, in *Pinacoteca Ambrosiana* 2006, pp. 149–153 note 234). This would place Fede's date of birth to between 1574 and 1577, assuming the age stated in the inscription is reliable, but which we know to be apocryphal. These arguments do not agree with the probably inaccurate date in the 1610 *Status animarum* of the Galizia family, which assigns Fede the age of thirty (Besta 1933, p. 460).

[4] Lomazzo 1587, p. 335.

[5] Lomazzo 1590, p. 163.

[6] Massimi 1998, p. 501; Bona Castellotti 1978; Geddo, in *Museo d'Arte Antica* 1999, pp. 89–91 note 313.

[7] Milan, Archivio di Stato, Fondo di Religione, folder 972, dated 21 June 1630. See Valsecchi 1971, also transcribed in Caroli 1989a, pp. 20–21.

[8] Terzago 1664, pp. 143–144, transcribe in Caroli 1989a, p. 21.

[9] Borgogni 1592, p. 176; Berra 1989, pp. 15–16, p. 25 note 6 and pl. 5b. Regarding the wood engraving of the *Portrait of Gherardo Borgogni*, see Colombo, in *Il ritratto in Lombardia* 2002, p. 130.

[10] Massimi 1998, p. 499.

[11] Morigia 1595, p. 282.

[12] Borgogni 1598, cc. 39v-40r; Berra 1989, pp. 16–17.

[13] See a first approach to the problem in Berra 1990.

[14] Baudi di Vesme 1963–1982, II, p. 490.

[15] The Savoy debts still due to Fede were designated in favour of her nephew Carlo Enrico in her will.

[16] The still lifes are a "Bowl of Cherries with a Butterfly" "By Fede Galicia" (*Musei d'Arte* [1994], I, p. 28, no. 558), and a "Glass Bowl with Peaches, and Quinces 2 ½" (*Musei d'Arte* [1994], I, p. 33, no. 656, attributed, however, to Panfilo Nuvolone), and a "Basket of Chestnuts, Apples and a Rabbit" (*Musei d'Arte* [1994], I, p. 25 note 480) (displayed here are the two panels of the Museo Civico Ala Ponzone pertaining to the last two subjects (cats. 3.45–46). For *Judith and Holofernes* see cat. 3.48.

[17] These are reproduced in Caroli 1989a, pls. 5 and 6. Variations of this type are the still lifes already in the Campagnano and Lazarus collections (Caroli 1989a, pls. 7 and 8) and the *Fruit Stand with Figs and Melon* known in two copies (Caroli 1989a, pls. 29 and 47). Similar in concept is the *Fruit Stand with Cherries and Butterfly* from a private collection (see *Italian Women Artists* 2007, p. 181; Ffolliott 2020, p. 47). However, due to the type of support, it does not seem identifiable as the "Bowl of Cherries with a Butterfly" described in the Savoy inventory. A different metal stand is published by Ferro 2018, p. 79.

[18] The first known example in this series appeared at Sotheby's London in 1984 (reproduced in *Forma vera* 1985, p. 138, pl. 24 and Caroli 1989a, pl. 35). Fede must have rethought the composition for the second version, as can be seen from the still life formerly in the Safra collection (Sotheby's, New York, 1 February 2018, lot 20) and the almost identical one in the Milanese collection (Caroli 1989a, pl. 62). The most elaborated version of this composition was recently auctioned in Zurich (Koller, 19 June 2020, lot 3018).

[19] The ceramic bowl appears in a version with peaches and in one with cherries (Caroli 1989a, pls. 25 and 26), the composition of the latter resembles the Savoy "bowl of cherries", but without the butterfly. A slightly different bowl contains pears in the former Griseri specimen (Caroli 1989a, pl. 16) while two examples are also known of a version with a deeper bowl holding pears, grapes and plums (Caroli 1989a, pls. 32 and 34), one of which is on display.

[20] For the results of this, see Berra 2016, pp. 70–73.

[21] Berra 1992, pp. 40–44; Terzaghi, in *Il ritratto in Lombardia* 2002, pp. 104–107, nos. 31 and 32 where the *Portrait with Skull* in the Koelliker collection is already described around 1738 in the collection of Gian Matteo Pertusati (Bona Castellotti 1991, pp. 72–73 note 23).

[22] Morandotti 2004–2005.

[23] Caroli 1989a, p. 87, no. 27 and pl. 27.

[24] Ruotolo 1968.

[25] Strada 2013, pp. 46–49.

[26] Strada 2013, pp. 49–50.

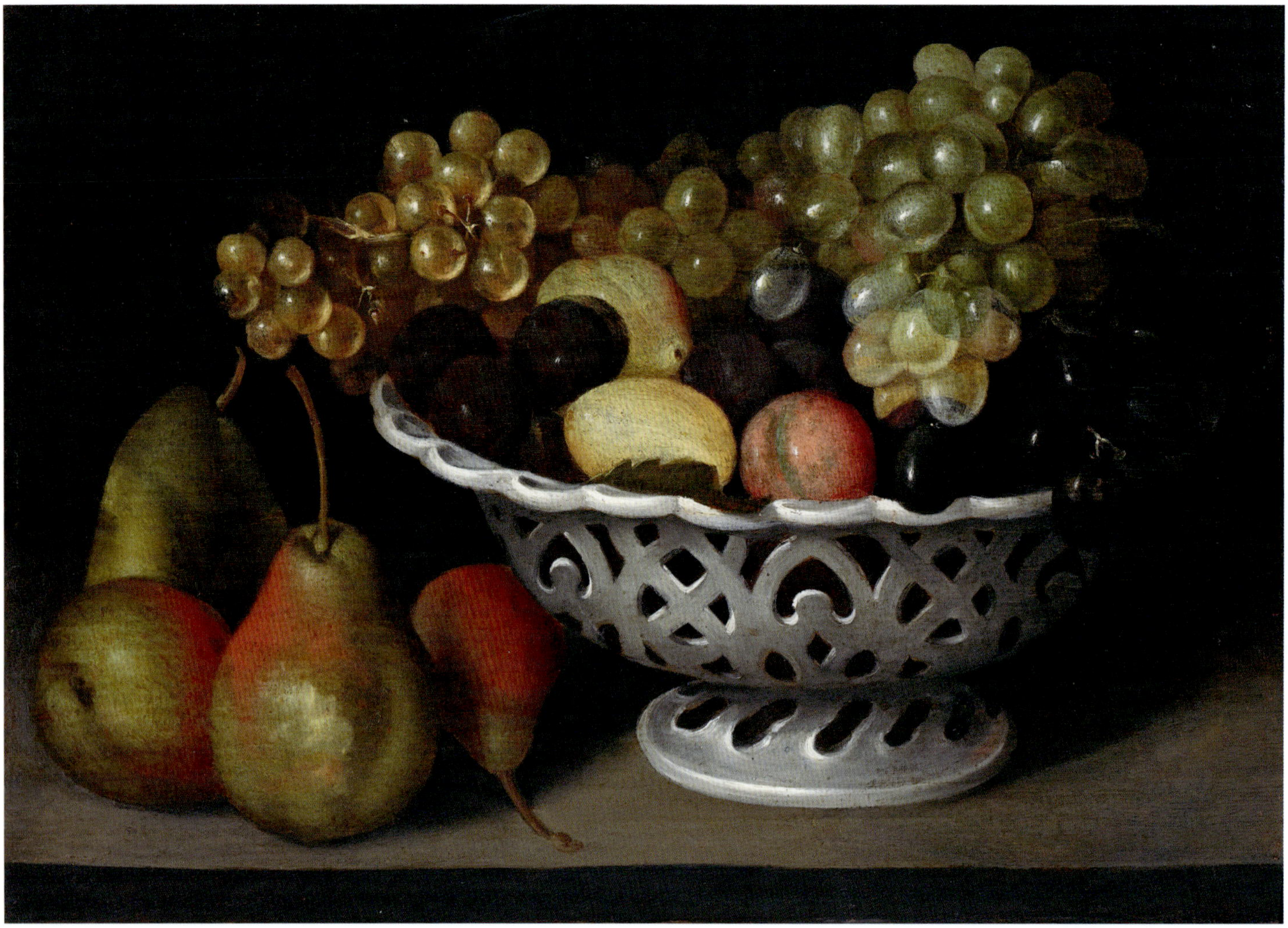

3.44
Fede Galizia
Pears and a Majolica Fruit Bowl with Grapes and Plums
c. 1610
Oil on panel, 27.5 × 38 cm
Private collection

3.45
Fede Galizia
Crystal Fruit Stand with Peaches, Quinces and Jasmine Flowers
c. 1607
Oil on poplar wood panel, 28.8 × 41 cm
Cremona, Museo Civico Ala Ponzone, inv. 217

3.46
Fede Galizia
Basket of Chestnuts with Apples and a Rabbit
c. 1607–1610
Oil on poplar wood panel, 28.8 × 41 cm
Cremona, Museo Civico Ala Ponzone, inv. 218

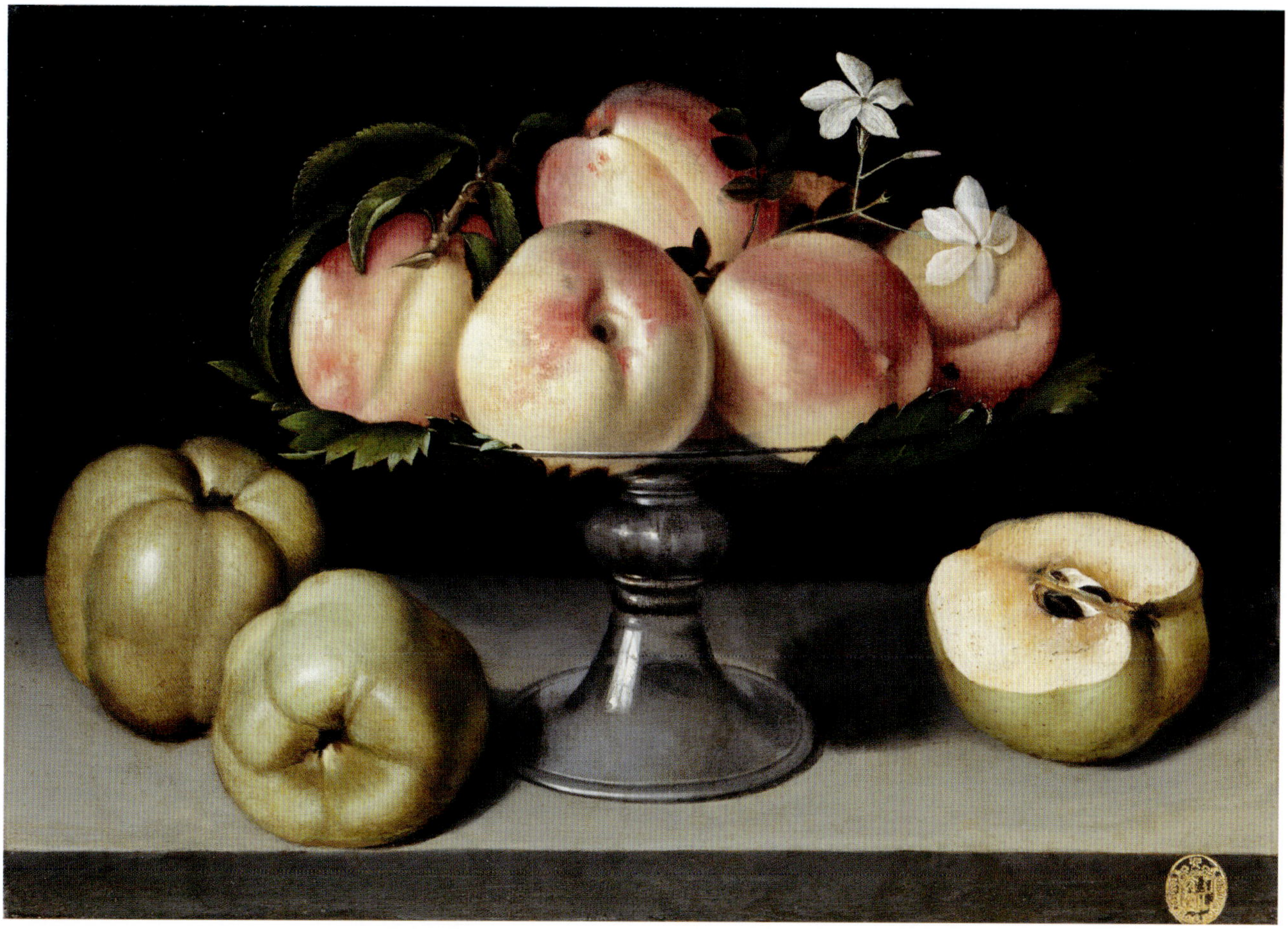

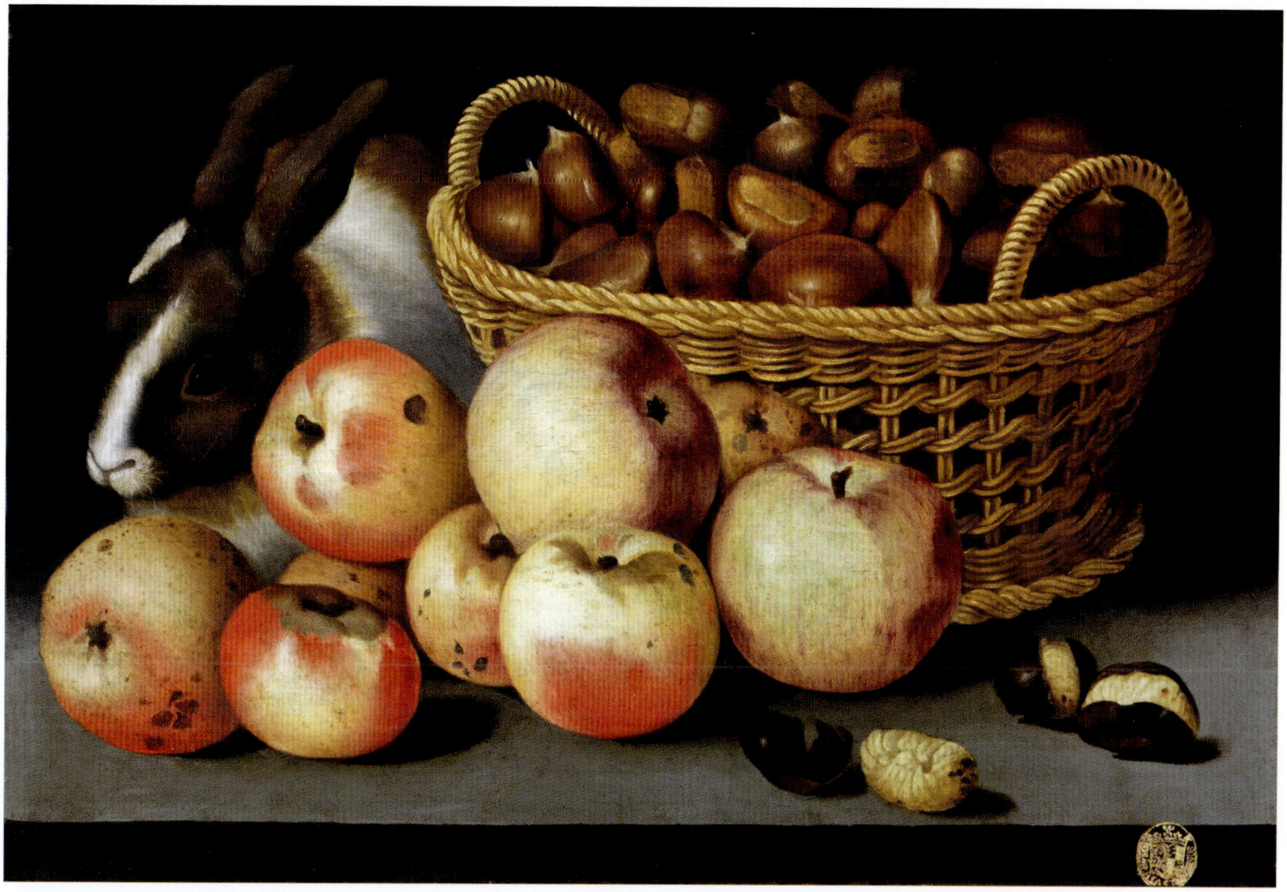

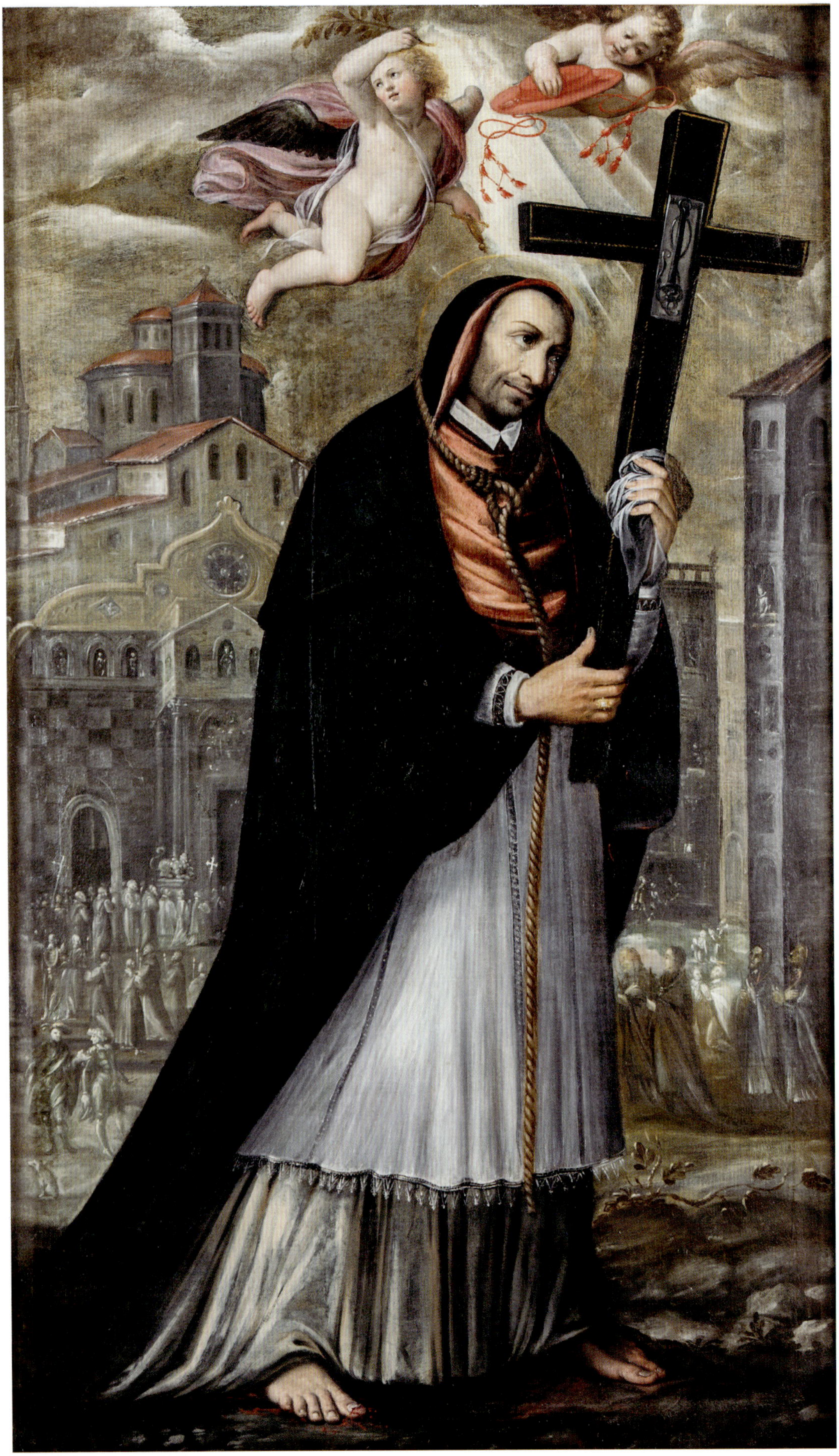

3.47
Fede Galizia
Saint Charles in a Penitential Robe with the Cross and the Holy Nail
c. 1615
Oil on canvas, 216 × 121 cm
Milan, Veneranda Fabbrica del Duomo di Milano, inv. D10

3.48
Fede Galizia
Judith with the Head of Holofernes
1601
Oil on canvas, 123 × 92 cm
Rome, Galleria Borghese, inv. 165

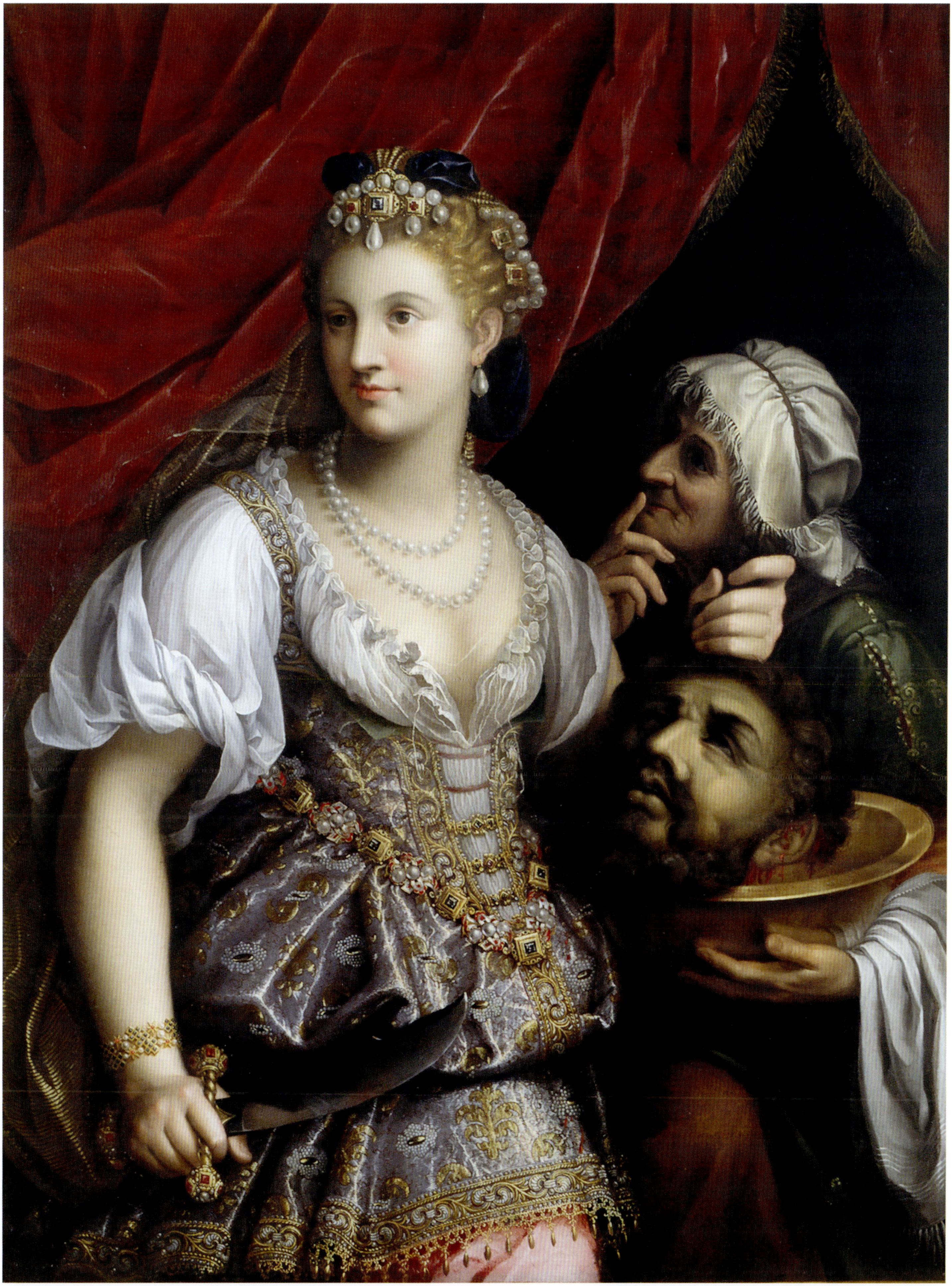

MADDALENA NATALI

Cremona, 1654 – Cremona or Rome, documented until 1675

The only historic source that mentions Maddalena Natali is Giambattista Zaist's *Notizie istoriche*, which suggests she was born in 1657 and that her father was Carlo Natali.[1] In actual fact, Maddalena Teodora Natali was born in Cremona on 3 August 1654, first of the many children of painter Giovanni Battista Natali (the son of Carlo) and Prudenzia Vincenzi from Rome, whom Giovanni Battista met during his first visit there from 1649 to 1654. The couple then returned to his home city of Cremona.[2] Maddalena was therefore the granddaughter and daughter of artists: her grandfather Carlo, her father, and later her brother Giuseppe, were members of an ancient trading family who had developed interests in the fields of architecture and painting, at times even filling the coveted role of engineer at the cathedral building site.[3]

We know nothing of her training in painting, but it is most likely that it took place in her father's workshop, together with her brother Giuseppe, born in 1661, and Francesco Boccaccino. Her early production comprised as yet unidentified local portraiture, until her father, in a 1674 letter to Cardinal Leopoldo de' Medici, sought an introduction to the reigning pope's household and attempted to promote Maddalena's career by claiming how "very able she is in portraying Ladies, however distinguished they may be".[4]

The Natali family had by then moved back to Rome, where the letter to the cardinal was written, and where in 1675 the family was registered in the census records of the parish of Santi Celso e Giuliano in the Ponte district as Giovanni Battista, Prudenzia, and five children: Maddalena (said to be eighteen but who in reality must have been twenty), Sofonisba (seventeen), Giuseppe (fifteen), Margherita (one) and Catherine (five months).[5] The two infants must have been born after the return to Rome. However, excluding two who had died, five other children born in Cremona are missing. We know that two of these reached marriageable age and at least one had children. Presumably a part of the family remained in Cremona, perhaps under the responsibility of the third child Marco Antonio (born in 1658) and of their grandfather Carlo, who resided there until his death in 1687 at almost 100 years of age. Perhaps Giovanni Battista brought with him the children who were most promising and eager to continue his business. Giuseppe entered the workshop of Ciro Ferri and became a member of the Compagnia dei Virtuosi at the Pantheon from 1685 to 1697.[6] Nothing is known of Sofonisba; whose given name was that of Giovanni Battista's paternal grandmother, Sofonisba Pesenti, daughter of a painter. Certainly, for a woman from Cremona, and above all for the father who had chosen it, the name might have augured a destiny with reference to a famous Sofonisba Anguissola. Maddalena was perhaps the only one who had already validated her artistic skill. Her only currently identified work, the *Portrait of a Prelate* (cat. 3.49), is dated 1675. According to Zaist, Maddalena later returned to Cremona with her father and was there in the summer of 1676, but an in-depth analysis of the records of their home parish of Sant'Elena has revealed no evidence.[7]

From that moment, all traces of her are lost, but it is not unlikely that she had returned to Rome where the presence of her father and brother Giuseppe are again recorded from 1685.

Mario Marubbi

[1] Zaist 1774, II, pp. 86–87.
[2] The baptismal certificate from the parish of Sant'Elena was published by Maccabelli in 2015, pp. 43–44, 51 note 32.
[3] Regarding the many activities of the family, which made its name in the production and trade of moleskin before focusing on the arts, see Maccabelli 2015, pp. 19–21.
[4] Bandera 1979, p. 104.
[5] Maccabelli 2015, pp. 171–172, doc. 7.
[6] Maccabelli 2006, pp. 254–255 and 259–261.
[7] Maccabelli, in *La Pinacoteca* 2007, p. 225.

3.49
Maddalena Natali
Portrait of a Prelate
1675
Oil on canvas, 69.5 × 57 cm
Cremona, Museo Civico
Ala Ponzone, inv. 1220

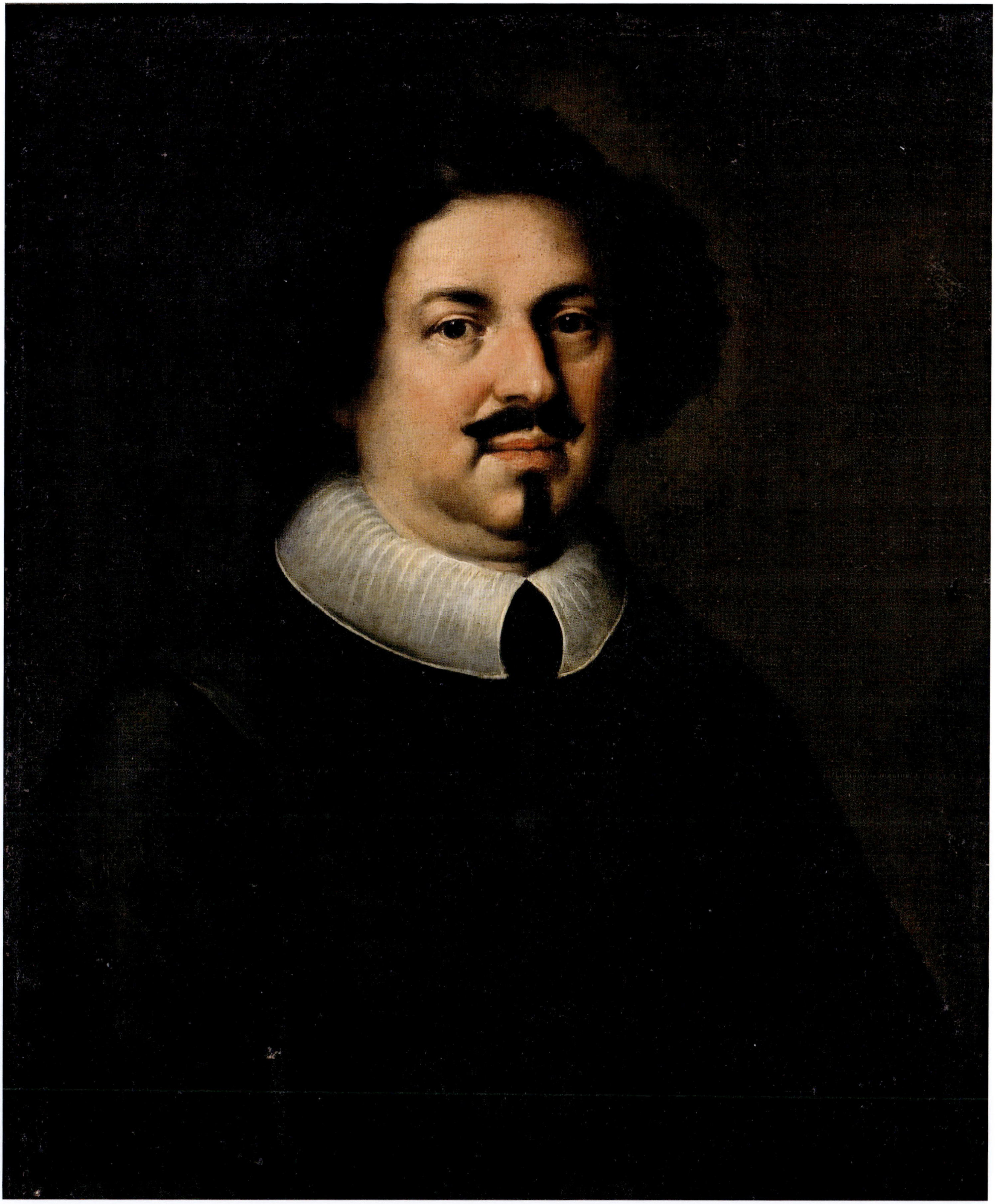

ROSALIA NOVELLI

Palermo, 1628 – Palermo, documented until 1689

Rosalia Novelli was born in Palermo on 1 February 1628. Her parents were the painter Pietro (Monreale, 1603 – Palermo, 1647) and Costanza Adamo. The following day she was baptised at the cathedral. Her godparents were the parish priest, Don Marco Gezio, an admirer of her father's work and a collector of his paintings, and Laura La Motta, wife of the notary Cesare, both prominent figures in local society.[1]

Rosalia's early years and her education are shrouded in mystery. It is likely that the young woman received a good education, as her graceful handwriting suggests, although her mother, Costanza, was illiterate like most women of the time. Rosalia was the last of a line of artists that began with her grandfather Pietro Antonio, and, in addition to her father, included her uncle Vincenzo and her elder brother Pietro Antonio. She probably began learning her profession in her father's workshop at an early age. "The transmission of the art of painting from father to son or daughter" was in fact part of a "corporate and professional conception of art",[2] even if it is fair to ask whether her father's intention was to prepare Rosalia for the profession of artist or whether her training in art was solely part a particular cultural education. It is also possible that Rosalia and her older brother collaborated with their father in executing his paintings, especially in the last hectic phase of his life, when he divided his time between painting commissions and the work of a royal engineer, which often took him far from Palermo.

Beyond the hypotheses, the only documented reference to Rosalia's work is the execution of a painting for the church of Gesù in Palermo between 1662 and 1663, and it is not known if she continued the family workshop after the death of her father (1647), followed one year later by that of her brother (1648).

If what has been presented so far is a rather hypothetical biographical path, the history of the painter's mature years is supported to some degree by documentary evidence that mainly concerns the most unusual aspect of her life: her three marriages. On 8 June 1647, at the age of nineteen, Rosalia married twenty-eight-year-old Carlo Maria Durante Poerio, an *utriusque juris doctor* (a doctor in both civil and canon law), son of Don Giovanni Paolo, one of the six royal secretaries and *referendari regi*.[3] Through this union – certainly the result of her father's relations with administrative and upper-middle-class circles – Rosalia became a member of the dominant social class, directly linked to the viceroyalty. In his turn, Novelli gave his daughter a substantial dowry, but a few months later, on 27 August, Novelli died from a wound received during the anti-Spanish revolt led by Giuseppe d'Alesi. This left his son and heir Pietro Antonio in the difficult situation of paying the contracted debt without the previous generous contribution from his father's profitable work as a painter and architect.[4] However, what seemed to be an irresolvable situation for the Novelli family took an unexpected turn in less than a year.

Rosalia's husband was also destined to succeed his own father in the prestigious position of secretary, thanks to a privilege (the so-called "extension") which, upon payment of a large sum, gave Durante senior the right to appoint to his own position either his heir or another person of his choice.[5] However, somewhere between 17 February and 28 May 1648 his son died before being able to receive this legacy, the victim of an epidemic of "malignant fevers" that decimated Palermo.[6] His father followed him shortly after, but in his will, dictated on 28 May 1648, with a codicil on June 1, he made his daughter-in-law Rosalia universal heir to the family assets and established that the office of secretary would be entrusted to whomever she married. Finally, he requested that Rosalia herself should choose for this purpose a person whom she esteemed.[7] She chose Don Diego Bono, a forty-seven-year-old widower who possessed the necessary legal expertise. Rosalia married him within a few months, on 15 July of the same year, and on 20 August she appointed him secretary and *referendario regi*.[8] It was a marriage of mutual interest, a pure and simple contract concluded in the shortest possible time in order to replace the deceased official. The same situation repeated itself eighteen years later, when her second husband died on 15 December 1666.[9] On 12 April 1667, Rosalia again married another doctor *in utroque jure*, Don Lorenzo Ferretti,[10] who began to serve as secretary the following July.[11]

3.50
Giuseppe Patania
The Benedictine Fathers of Monreale Visit Pietro Novelli in his Studio
1835–1840
Pen, dark ink and grey watercolour on ivory paper, 290 × 450 mm
Palermo, Galleria Regionale della Sicilia – Palazzo Abatellis, inv. S.L.M. Patania tav. 42

3.51
Rosalia Novelli
Saint Prassede
c. 1648–1667
Black pencil and grey watercolour on ivory paper, 270 × 220 mm
Palermo, Galleria Regionale della Sicilia – Palazzo Abatellis, inv. 1565/1

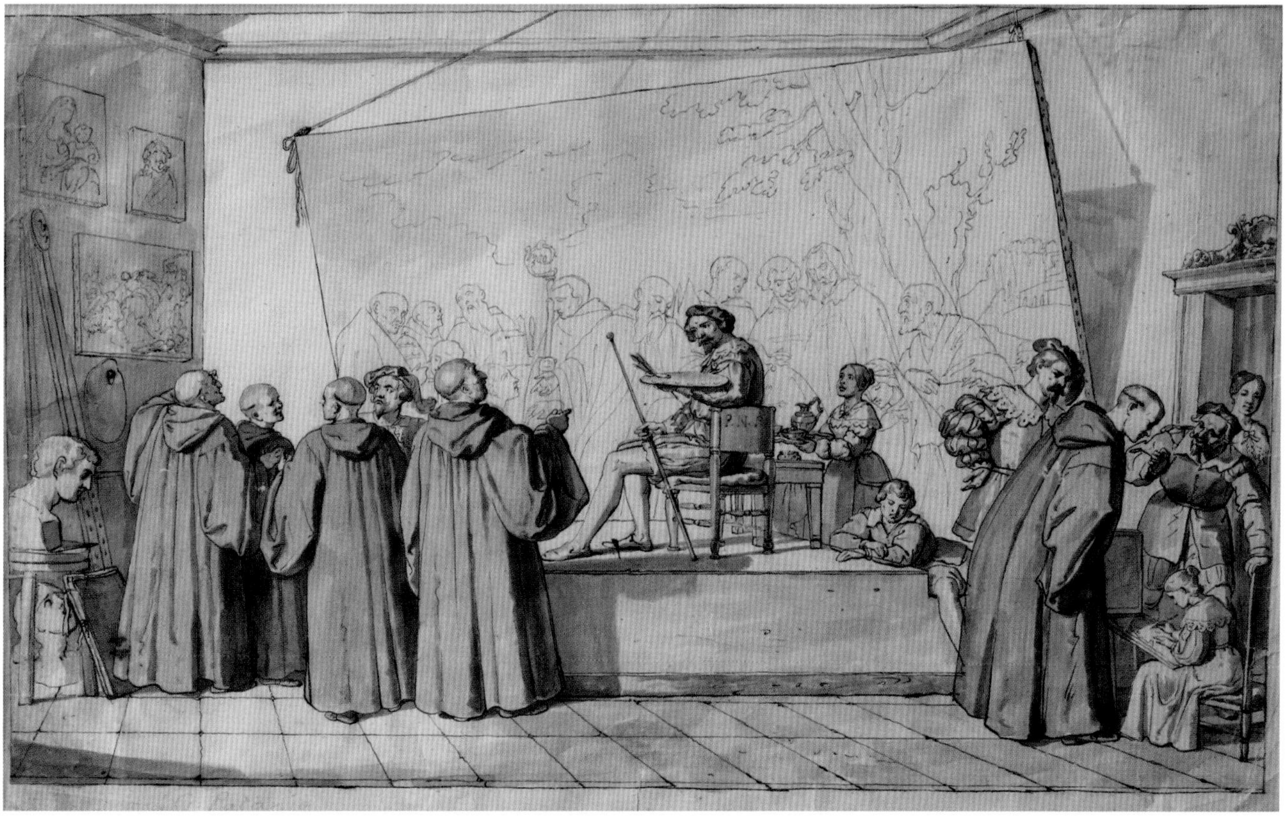

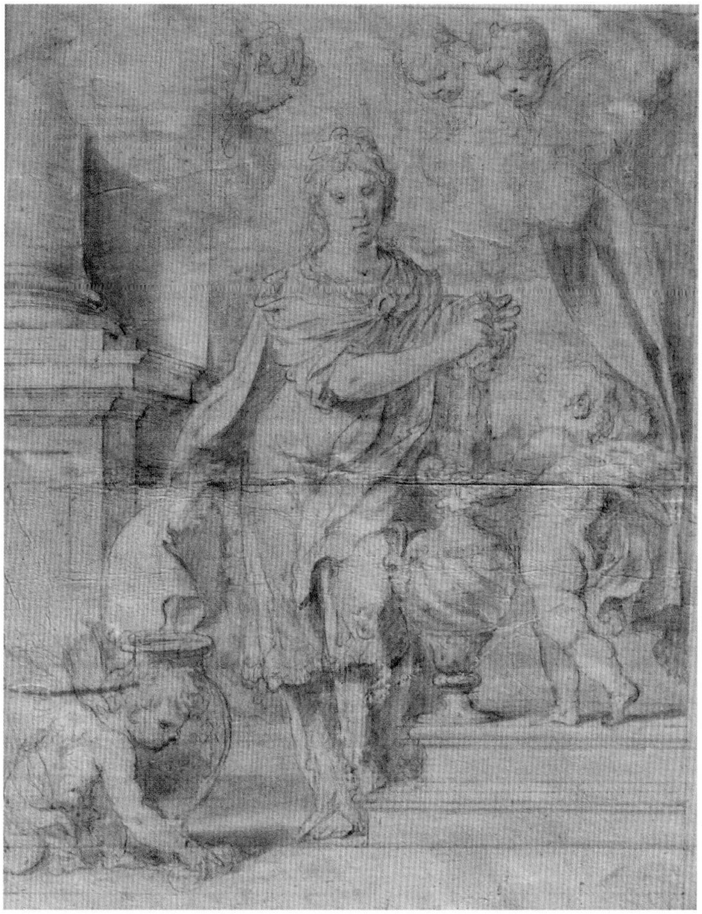

Rosalia was now thirty-nine, which at that time was considered late for marriage. Yet once again it was an essential requisite for the conferral of the public office she controlled. Rosalia also survived her third husband, who died at on unspecified date after August 1675, when his service as secretary was interrupted.[12] Other traces of the painter, found in archival papers in relation to the *domus magna* in which she lived between 1684 and 1689,[13] confirm that Rosalia, thanks to the social rank of her spouses, led a comfortable life and had a privileged role that allowed her as a woman to follow the difficult road of painting in an age when social conventions made such a choice extremely difficult.

Santina Grasso

[1] Millunzi 1911, p. 368, doc. no. XXX.
[2] Guazzoni 1994, p. 62.
[3] Millunzi 1911, p. 368, doc. no. XXXI.
[4] Millunzi 1911, p. 368, doc. no. XXXI and pp. 369–372, no. XXXII.
[5] Millunzi 1911, pp. 327–330.
[6] Grasso 2017, p. 44.
[7] Millunzi 1911, p. 330. Grasso 2017, p. 45.
[8] Grasso 2017 p. 45.
[9] Grasso 2017, p. 46.
[10] Cuccia 1993, p. 379.
[11] Grasso 2017, p. 46.
[12] Grasso 2017, p. 46.
[13] Grasso 2017, pp. 47–48.

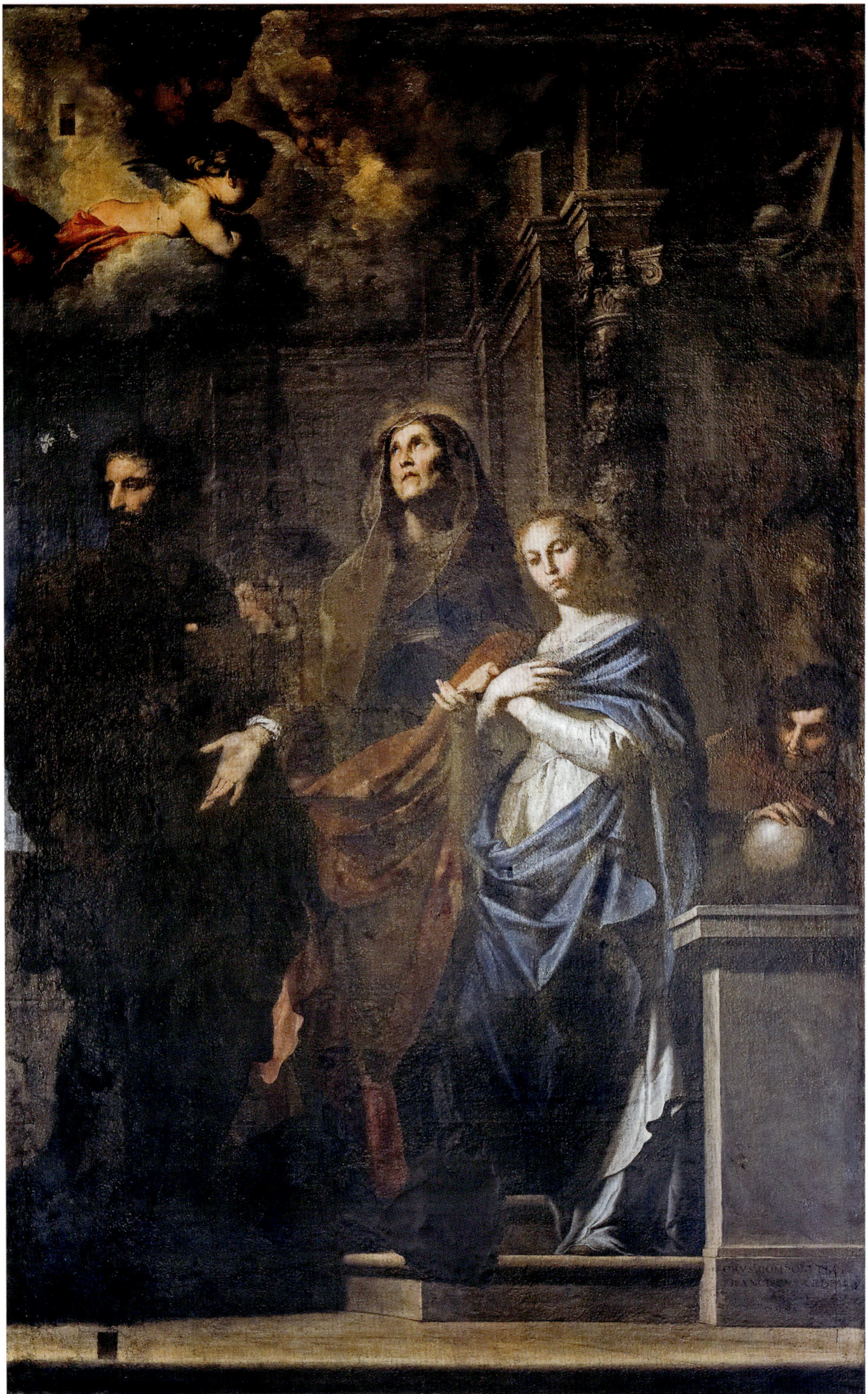

3.52
Pietro Novelli
Marriage of the Virgin
1647
Oil on canvas, 305 × 185 cm
Palermo, Arcidiocesi
di Palermo, church of San
Matteo al Cassaro, inv. 7

3.53
Rosalia Novelli
The Immaculate Virgin Mary and Saint Francesco Borgia
1663
Oil on canvas, 200 × 160 cm
Palermo, church of the Gesù,
Casa Professa – Direzione
centrale degli Affari dei culti
e per l'amministrazione
del Fondo Edifici di Culto
del Ministero dell'Interno

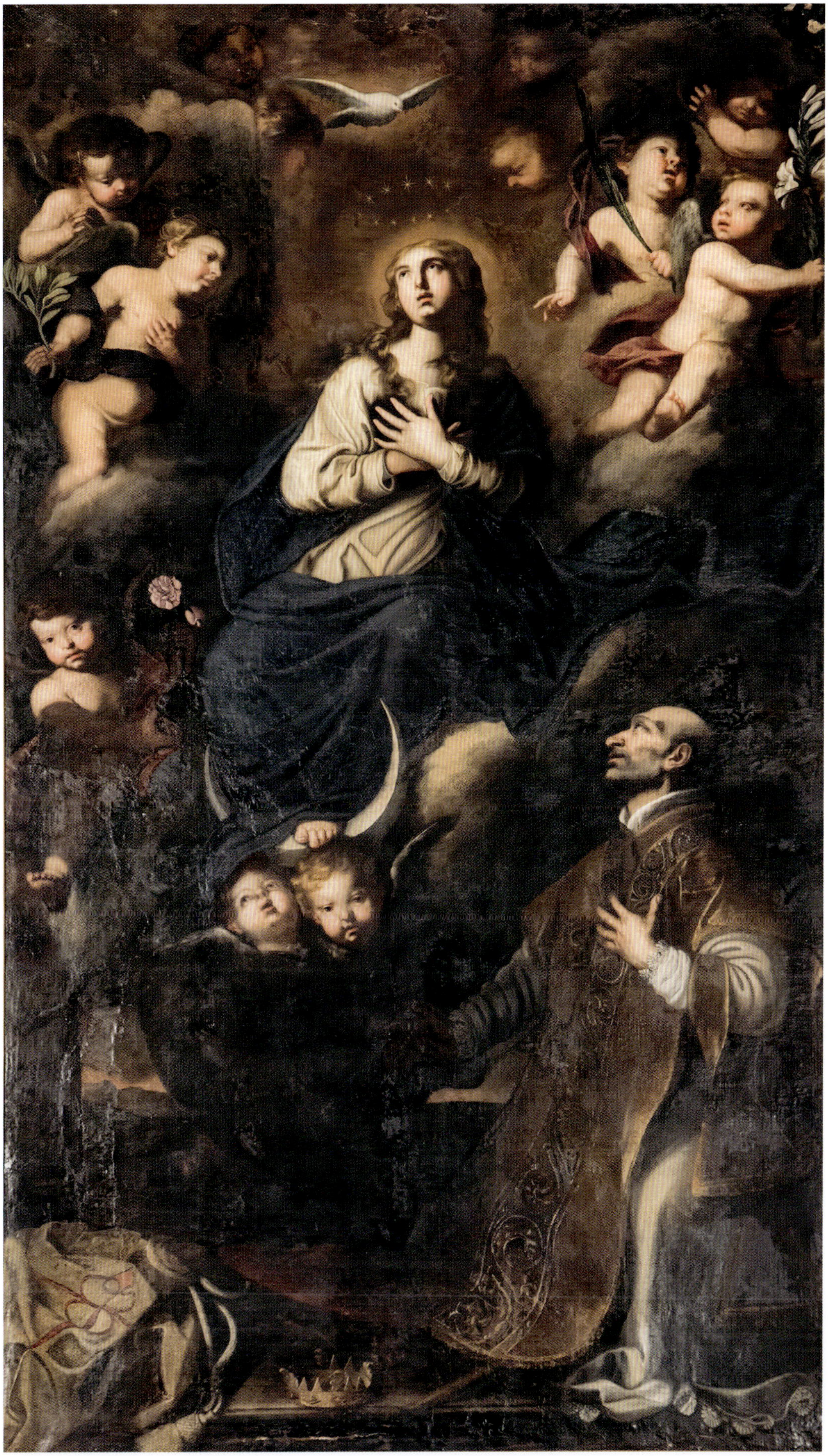

MARGHERITA VOLÒ CAFFI

Milan, 1648 – Milan, 1710

Margherita Volò, known in art and literature as Margherita Caffi, was the eldest daughter of the Burgundy-born painter Vincent Voulot (Vincenzo Volò) and Veronica Masoli from Milan.

Born in Milan on 26 March 1648,[1] her artistic development took place working beside her father, nicknamed *Vincenzino dei Fiori*. Margherita left home at a young age in order to accompany her husband Ludovico Caffi, who wanted to return to his hometown, Cremona. The couple married on 15 October 1667.

From that time on, aged only nineteen, Margherita began to progress in complete artistic autonomy, experimenting with new techniques and gaining a reputation that her two sisters Francesca and Giovanna were unable to equal.

Unlike her family, whose activities gravitated around Milan, Margherita became known in many Italian and European cities and courts, maintaining her reputation as a painter of exclusively flora, excluding in her work additional subjects such as fruit or small animals, which were a specialisation her father passed on, however, to her sisters and her brother Giuseppe.

After her husband and his brother murdered a certain Giuseppe Gattoni from Cremona, their compromised legal situation led Margherita to flee the city after little more than two years of residence there, taking refuge with her husband and two small daughters across the Po in nearby Piacenza, where they arrived in the spring of 1670. There the Caffi family counted on the presence of Cristoforo, Ludovico's eldest brother, and on the protection ensured by several aristocrats, such as the Pallavicino, whose families had estates north and south of the river. The support of the Piacenza nobility is also evidenced by the presence of Marquis Felice Landi as a witness to the baptism of their third child Carlo Francesco.

Having gained a reputation in Cremona by working for illustrious families such as the Picenardi, Margherita expanded her professional life in Piacenza, arousing the interest of local clients. Her fame spread rapidly, and, after only two years, in the autumn of 1672 she moved to Bologna.

Her stay in the Emilian capital, mentioned by two eighteenth-century historical sources – the Bolognese Marcello Oretti and the Cremonese biographer Desiderio Arisi – lasted about five years, until the spring of 1676. Both writers praise Margherita's talent, leaving her husband rightly in the shade, although there is evidence of the couple's collaboration on paintings from the start of their time in Bologna. Oretti quotes Giampietro Zanotti from the latter's *Storia dell'Accademia Clementina*: "At painting flowers she was the very best, as her fame demonstrates; moreover, her works are much sought after and purchased at a high price".[2]

The period in Bologna, which came to light only a few years ago,[3] was a turning point in Margherita's career. She began to receive her first important commissions, among them the creation of twenty-nine floral canvases for the Duke of Modena Francesco II d'Este, and paintings for her cousin, Prince Cesare Ignazio d'Este, mentioned by Marquis Giuseppe Campori in 1870. Oretti saw examples of Caffi's work in the Malvasia home, but others too at the homes of Count Girolamo Leoni in 1691, Senator Annibale Ranuzzi in 1698, and Countess Angelica Teresa Zanchini Zambeccari in 1783. Caffi's paintings are registered in the collection of Countess Eleonora Strozzi Sacrati from nearby Ferrara (1801) and in the Piazza collection in Forlì (1788). A possible contact with fellow artist Elisabetta Marchioni in Rovigo dates to these years, as does the commencement of commercial ties with her brother-in-law Francesco, who after fleeing Cremona had settled in Venice. It was he who in the second half of the 1680s facilitated the sale of the paintings for the Medici court.

On returning to Piacenza with her family, Margherita remained there until 1682, when, on receiving assurances that her husband would no longer be prosecuted in the Duchy of Milan, she moved back to Cremona. Of particular importance was the renewal of her relationship with her sisters Francesca and Giovanna. At Margherita's request, between 1678 and 1679 the sisters had moved to Piacenza to work with her on a commission from the Counts Scotti of Agazzano: a cycle of six canvases destined for their house in the city. Between the end of 1684 and the beginning of 1685, Margherita moved permanently to Milan, where she became fully involved in the Vicenzini workshop along-

3.54
Vincenzo Volò, known as Vincenzino dei fiori
Two-Handled Metal Vase with Roses, Tulips, Lilies, Bluebells and Other Flowers
1667
Oil on panel, 36 × 33 cm
Cremona, Museo Civico Ala Ponzone, inv. 1038

3.55
Vincenzo Volò, known as Vincenzino dei fiori
Two-Handled Ceramic Vase with Anemones, Roses, Tulips, Jasmine and Other Flowers
1667
Oil on panel, 36.5 × 33 cm
Cremona, Museo Civico Ala Ponzone, inv. 1039

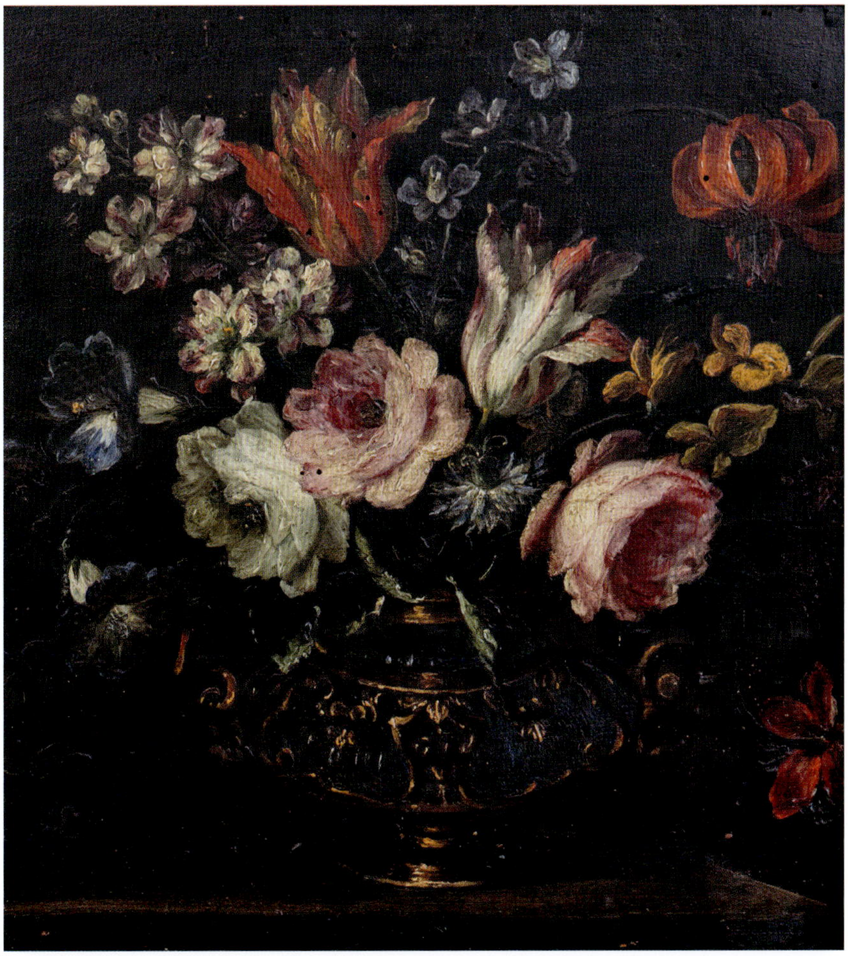

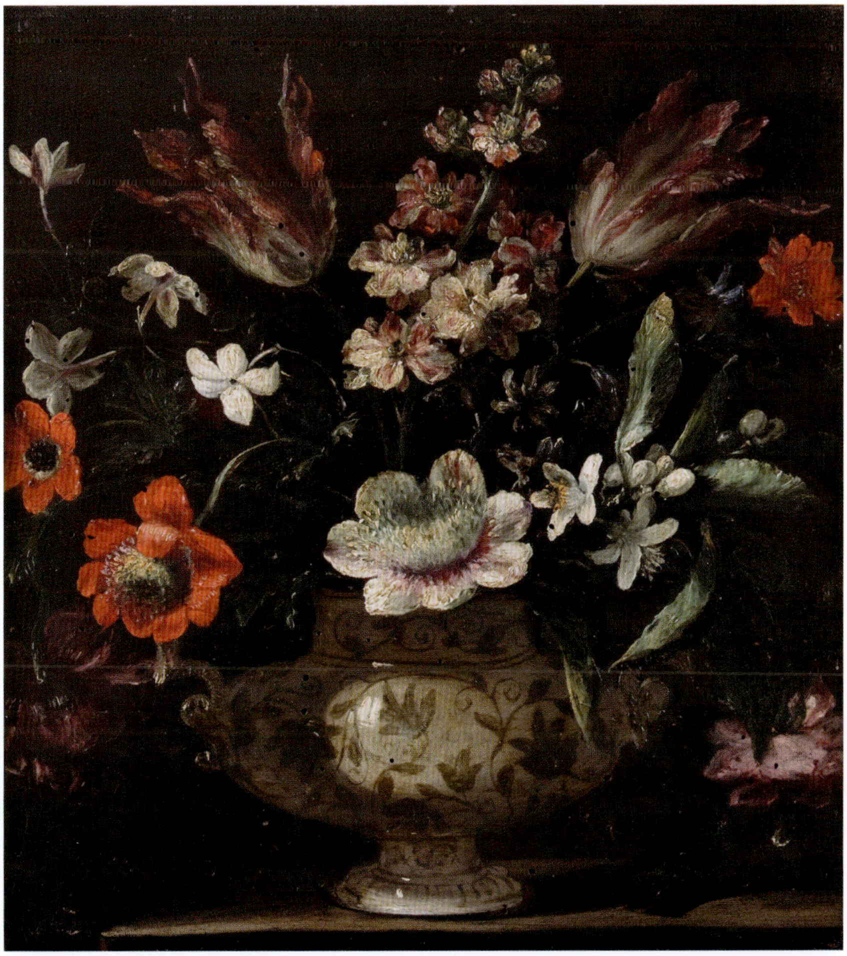

side her siblings Francesca and Giuseppe and began to sign her paintings with the patronymic "Vicenzina". Her paintings are listed in the eighteenth-century inventories of numerous Milanese families, but always under the name of Caffi. Among her works are those of Captain Gerolamo d'Adda (1704–1705), Marquis Cesare Pagani (1707), Duke Tolomeo Saverio Gallio Trivulzio (1711), General Giovan Francesco Arese (post-1749), Count Luigi Caroelli (1720), Marquis Giovanni Francesco Stoppani (1722), Marquis Giacinto Orrigoni (1728), Marquis Tiberio II Crivelli (1731), Count Giovanni Battista Durini (1734), Count Costanzo Taverna (1736), Marquis Giorgio Clerici (1738) and Count Filippo Maria Stampa (1756).
Between 1693 and 1694 she worked with her brother Giuseppe on Giberto Borromeo's villa in Senago, creating a pictorial cycle inspired by ones designed by Giovanni Saglier in the palace on Isola Bella.
On 2 February 1697 she was admitted to the Milanese Academy of San Luca, together with her sister Francesca and an otherwise unknown artist Lucrezia Ferrari, the first and only women to receive this privilege.
Margherita Caffi died on 20 September 1710. Her husband Ludovico had preceded her on 18 October 1691.
Gianluca Bocchi

[1] Bocchi 2015, pp. 49–50.
[2] Oretti 1760–1780, mss. B. 123–135.
[3] Bocchi 2013.

3.56
Margherita Volò Caffi
Vase with Flowers
and a Garland of Flowers
1685
Oil on canvas,
116 × 106.5 cm
Varallo (Vercelli), Palazzo
dei Musei, Pinacoteca,
inv. 3424-2014

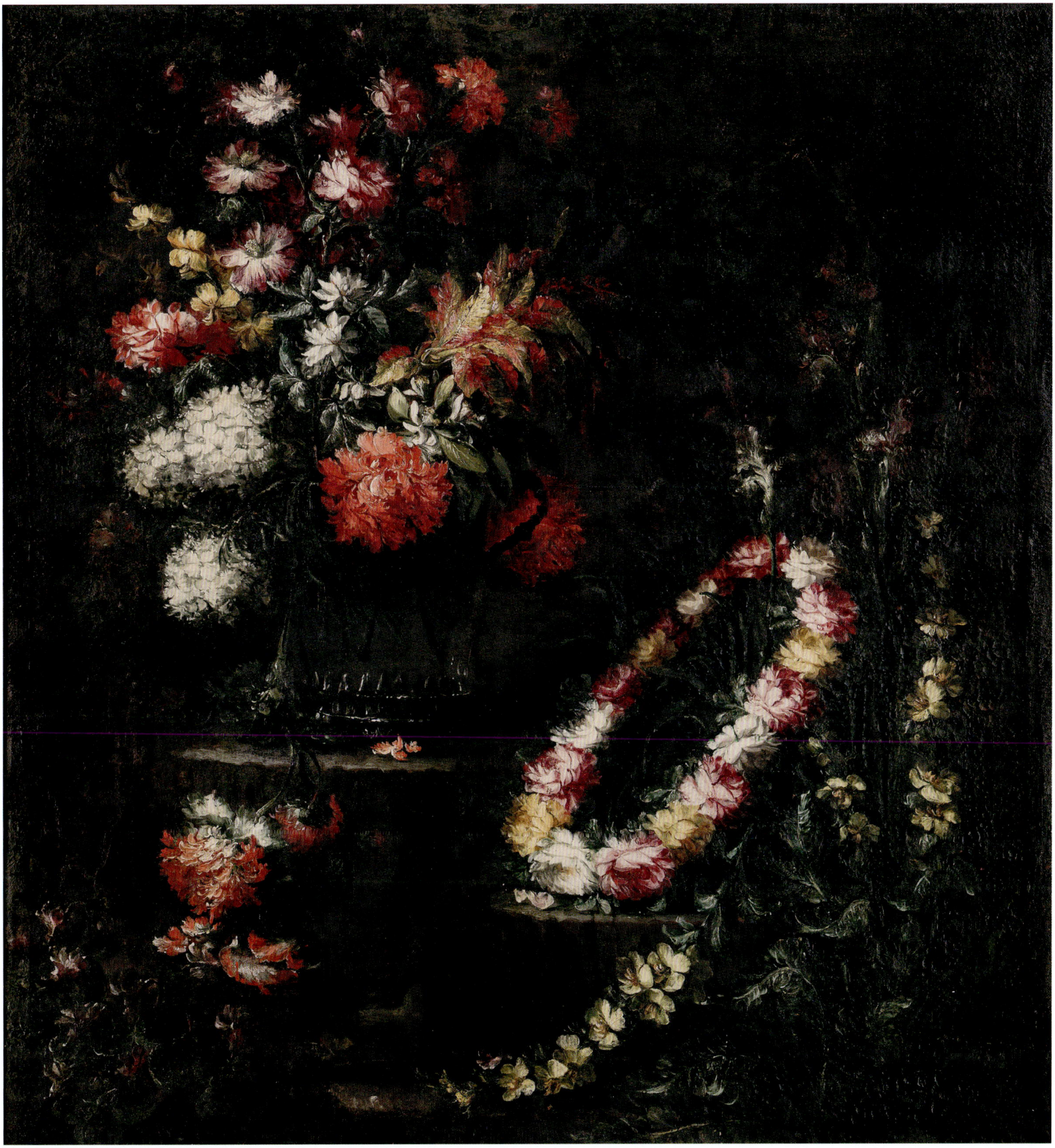

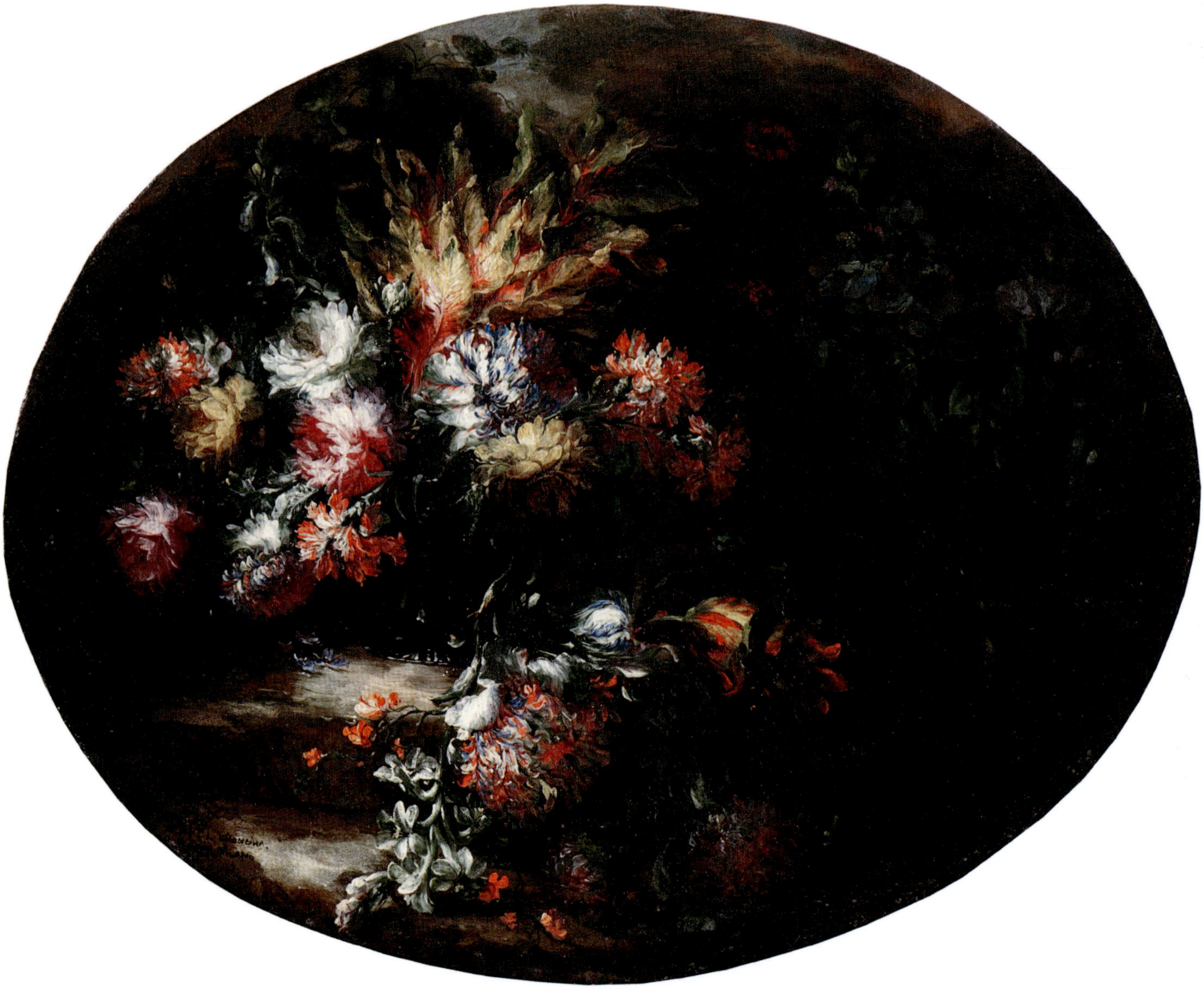

3.57
Margherita Volò Caffi
Vase with Flowers Outdoors
1694
Oil on oval canvas,
63 × 83 cm
Private collection

3.58
Margherita Volò Caffi
Still Life with Flowers
1697
Oil on canvas, 72 × 98 cm
Milan, Castello Sforzesco,
Pinacoteca, inv. 1010

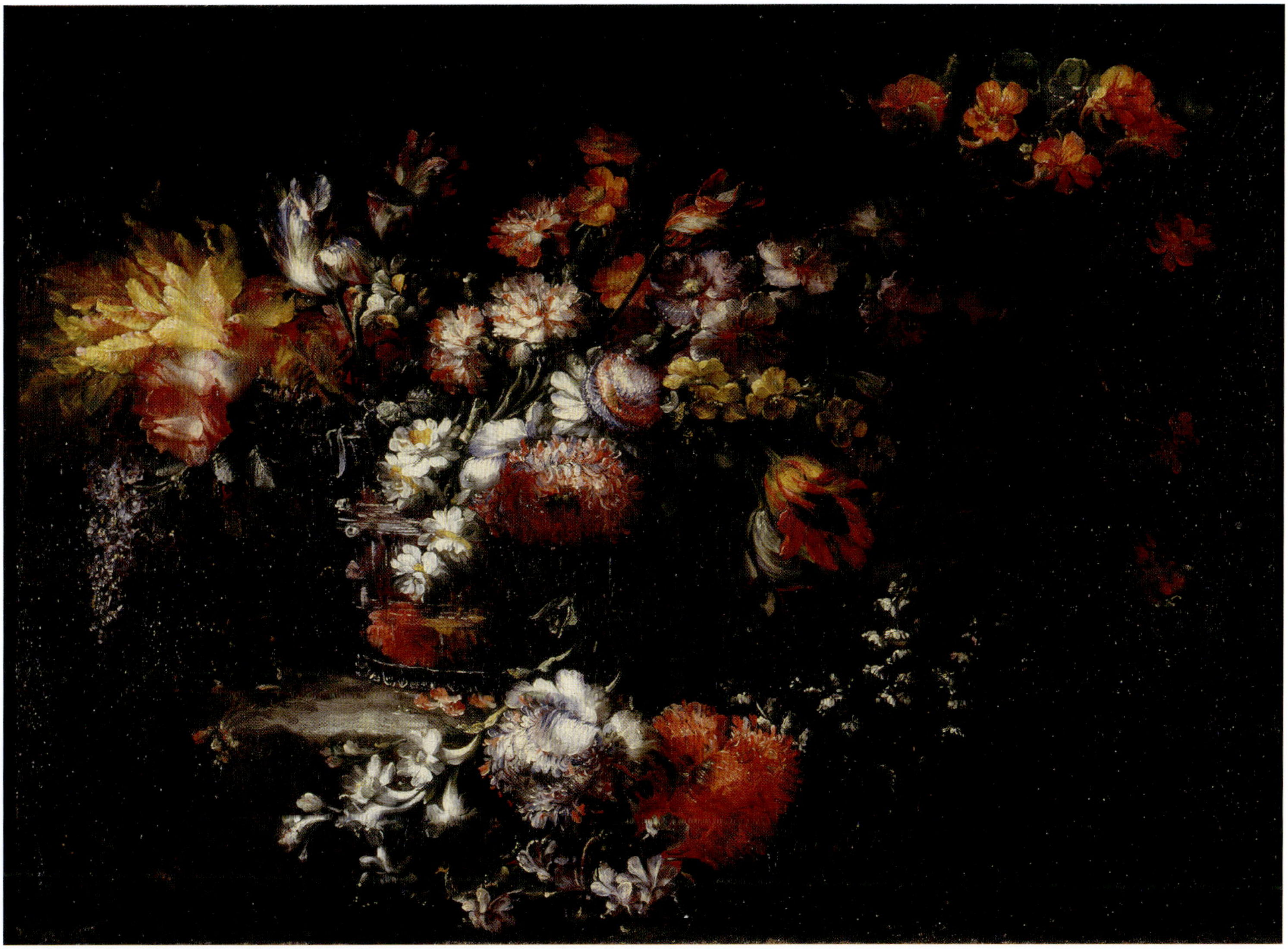

FRANCESCA VOLÒ, KNOWN AS FRANCESCA VICENZINA

Milan, 1650 – Milan?, 1700

Only rediscovered in 1998 with the publication of some previously unknown signed canvases,[1] Francesca Vicenzina has benefited in the last twenty years from a series of recently established biographical data that enable the reconstruction of a broader, more definitive historical and artistic record of her contribution within the Vicenzini workshop in Milan.[2]

Born on 15 November 1650 in the parish of San Pietro in Caminadella, Francesca Antonia Maria Volò was the second child of Vincenzo Volò and his most faithful pupil, devoting herself, as he had done, to the illustration of flowers, fruits, vegetables and small birds, produced equally on stone, wood panel and canvas supports.

The death of her father at the end of 1671 left Francesca with no male relative to assist her, yet she demonstrated excellent management skills by successfully taking charge of the family studio for at least fifteen years, assisted by her nineteen-year-old sister Giovanna, until the latter's death in 1680 left Francesca completely alone to run the firm. However, in 1689, at the age of thirty-nine, she married a soldier, Nicolaus Miller, probably of Swiss origin, with whom she had a daughter, Barbara Maria, born 27 June 1691.

Protected by Vitaliano VI Borromeo who had employed her father Vincenzo, during the 1670s the two sisters gradually acquired independence and unusual respect in an era when women painters were still very few. The inventory of the assets of the Isola Bella palace drawn up in 1690 on the death of Vitaliano VI Borromeo lists as many as forty floral paintings in their name. Although several other inventories mention collaborative works produced by the Vicenzine sisters with painters such as Scaramuccia, Federico Bianchi and Giorgio Bonola, very few paintings with their identifiable contribution have been found.

After Giovanna's death, Francesca began to train her fourteen-year-old brother Antonio and to perfect the skills of eighteen-year-old Giuseppe, a task the latter successfully achieved, as demonstrated by the collaborative paintings the siblings made in the 1680s.

Giuseppe's rapid professional growth, plus the return to Milan of their older sister Margherita at the beginning of 1685, greatly consolidated the capacity of the Vicenzini atelier and enabled the family to accept demanding commissions, also due to the earlier experience of collaboration between Francesca, Giovanna, Margherita and Ludovico Caffi, which had produced excellent results in Piacenza between 1678 and 1679, and did again in 1680 for the Barbiano princes of Belgioioso.

The period between 1685 and the end of the century marks the greatest splendour of the Vicenzini workshop, but also the last phase of Francesca's life. She died aged only fifty in 1700.

Francesca's known signed works are all from this fifteen-year period and were a consequence of the arrival of her sister Margherita, whose individuality and charisma influenced a considerable number of canvases which she signed with her own name, leading her siblings to do the same and so ending the family tradition of uniform identity dating from the early 1670s.

Francesca reduced or perhaps interrupted her art work for some time before and after the birth of Barbara Maria, indicated by her absence during the commission at the Villa Borromeo at Senago between 1693 and 1694, on which Margherita and Giuseppe worked alone.

It was probably in 1695 that Francesca returned in strength to the Milanese art scene: in December, she, Margherita and Lucrezia Ferrari asked to participate in donating artworks to the Accademia di San Luca, a prelude to their membership candidacy in December 1696.

On 2 February 1697, the admission of the three artists was made official, with Francesca and Margherita both named "Vicenzina Pittrice Milanese", in recognition of the Vicenzini workshop, already known by that title in Milan. Their admittance, the first and only women in the history of the Academy of San Luca, was a tangible sign of the protection granted to them by Andrea Lanzani, prince of the Academy, and by their brother-in-law, councillor Federico Macagni, both decisive figures in modifying the statute which had previously allowed access only to male artists.

The work Francesca produced in the 1690s marked a departure from the stylistic canons previously shared with Giuseppe and reflected Margherita's progressive

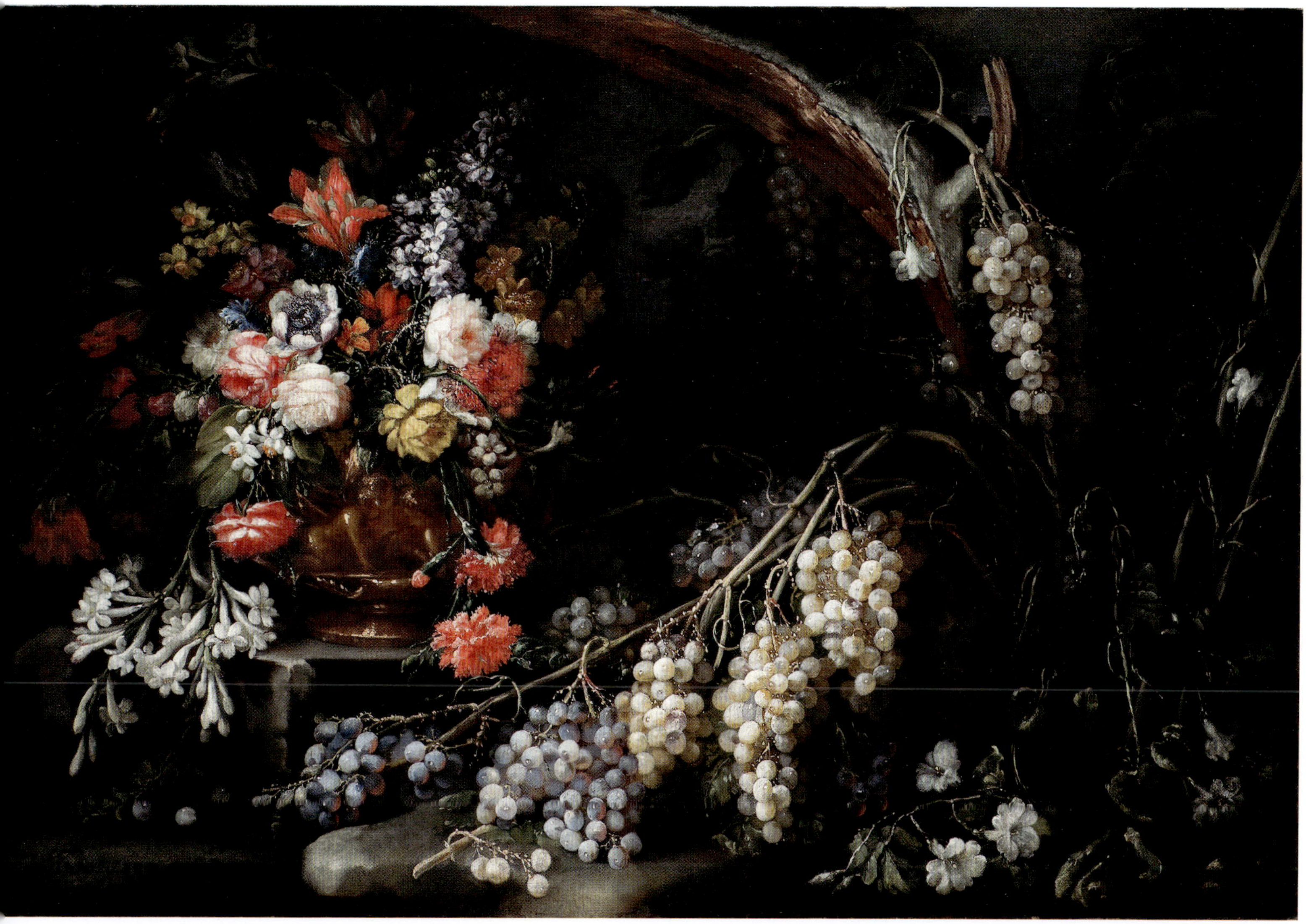

3.59
Francesca Volò, known as Francesca Vicenzina
Still Life Outdoors with Flowers and Grapes
1680–1685
Oil on canvas, 84.5 × 122.5 cm
Private collection

influence. Her painting became less planned and more instinctive, composed of strokes, darts and flashes of light.

Although records exist for the Miller family residing in the parish of San Babila, where their daughter was born (1691) and Francesca's husband died (1704), no certificate relating to the death of Francesca Vicenzina has ever been found, perhaps because she occasionally worked away from home and may have been buried elsewhere. Her death in the year 1700 is known only from the registration of her name in the annual minutes of the Accademia di San Luca.

Gianluca Bocchi

[1] G. Bocchi, U. Bocchi 1998c.
[2] Bocchi 2015.

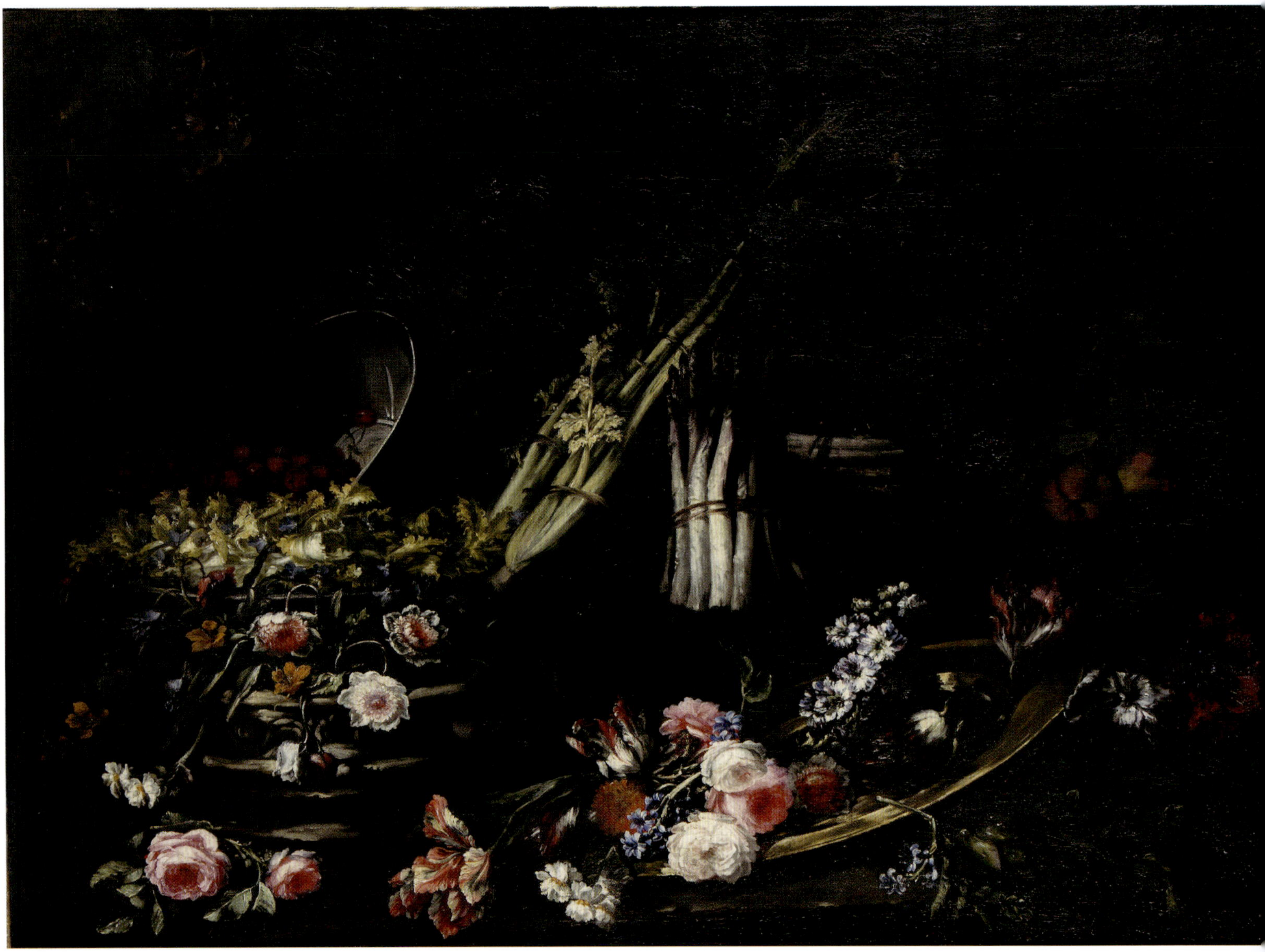

3.60
Francesca Volò, known as Francesca Vicenzina
Still Life Outdoors with Flowers, Fruit and Vegetables
1694–1696
Oil on canvas, 90 × 118 cm
Private collection

3.61
Francesca Volò, known as Francesca Vicenzina
Still Life Outdoors with Flowers, Frisee Salad, Oysters and Strawberries in a Fruit Bowl
1697–1700
Oil on canvas, 88 × 111 cm
Private collection

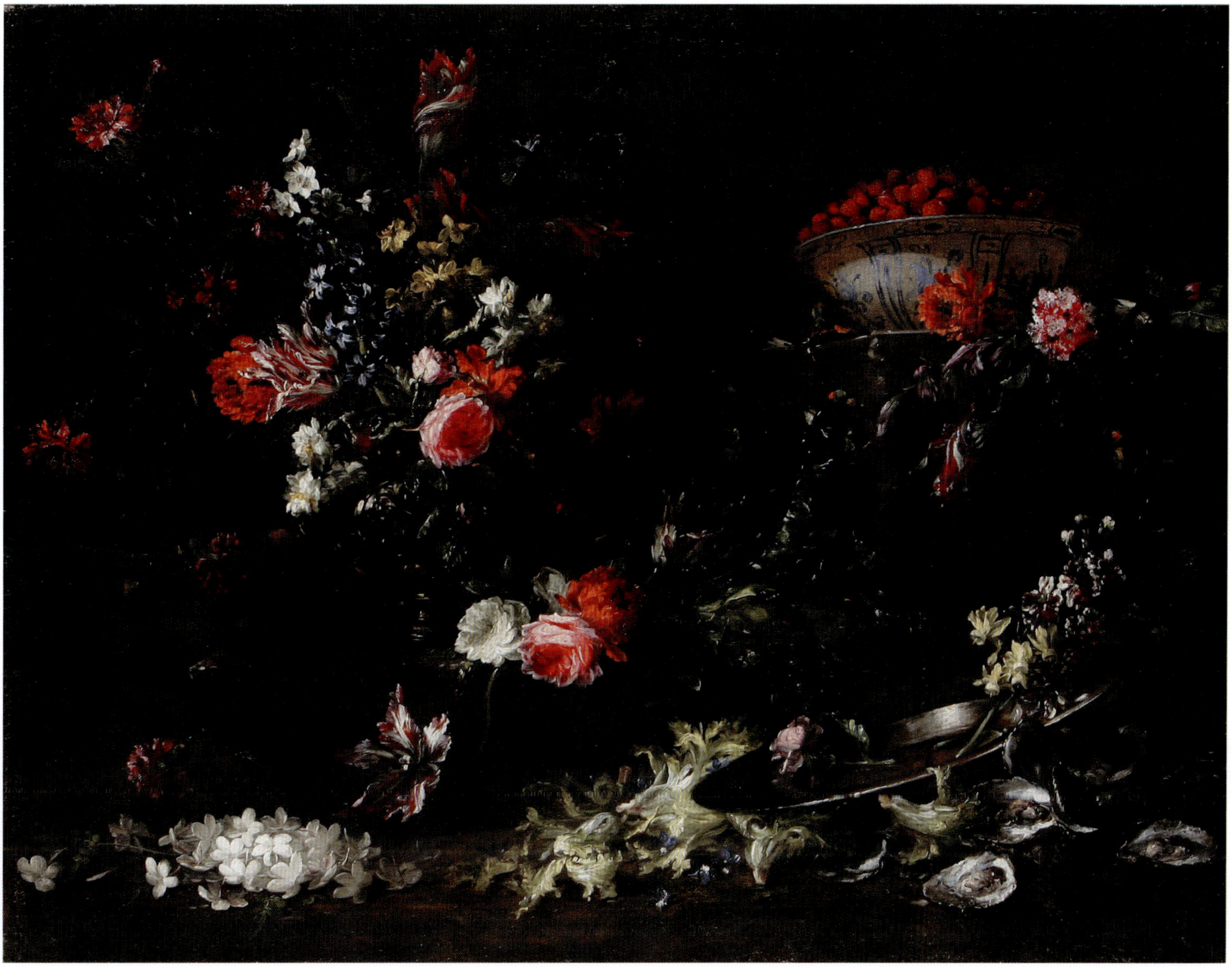

GIOVANNA VOLÒ, KNOWN AS GIOVANNA VICENZINA

Milan, 1652 – Milan, 1680

Giovanna, the third child of Vincenzo Volò and Veronica Masoli, is certainly the least known of the three Vicenzine sisters: no signed works have been found and, until now, art literature has never attempted to distinguish her work from that of her older sisters Margherita and Francesca.

Historical and personal data searches in recent years have made it possible to trace a fairly comprehensive biographical profile that has enabled a better evaluation of her art.

Giovanna had a short life: she was born in Milan in the parish of San Pietro in Caminadella on 24 June 1652 and died of puerperal sepsis at the age of twenty-eight on 13 October 1680, eighteen days after the birth of her first child, Giuseppe Maria Carlo.

Growing up in her father's workshop like her two older sisters, she had just begun her apprenticeship when in 1667 her sister Margherita left Milan for Cremona to accompany her husband Ludovico Caffi. This very early separation prevented her from adopting the style of her eldest sister's works as a model, so her production was based solely on her father's, mainly floral illustration in all its variants, including garlands and fruits.

On her father's death in 1671 she found herself assisting Francesca in the arduous task of continuing the activity of their father's workshop and, at the same time, of maintaining the large family consisting of her mother and ten siblings. So began a decade during which the two sisters managed to impose their own style, often working in symbiosis and calling themselves the "Vicenzine", a recurring name in seventeenth-century Milanese inventories.

Francesca and Giovanna skilfully put their father's acquaintanceship to good use by inheriting the favour and protection of an important patron, Vitaliano VI Borromeo. Strengthened by his support and under the artistic direction of Giovanni Saglier, who had been their father's first pupil, between 1672 and 1678 Francesca and Giovanna worked hard to decorate the Isola Bella palace. In the inventory drawn up on death of the count in 1690, forty works are credited to the "Vicenzine", without making any distinction made those painted by Francesca or Giovanna.

When in the second half of 1678 renovation work of the building began and commissions were interrupted for about three years, the two sisters accepted an invitation from their sister Margherita to go to Piacenza, where she worked and lived with her family.

Between 1678 and 1679 Margherita, Francesca and Giovanna began a fruitful collaboration that initially resulted in a painting cycle for the Counts Scotti of Agazzano at their city palace and continued in 1680 with a similar commission from the Barbiano princes of Belgioioso.

During their stay in Piacenza, Giovanna proved her versatility by painting flowers, fruits and sweets to embellish several of her brother-in-law Ludovico Caffi's paintings featuring carpets, commissioned by important local families such as the Marquises Casati.

The collaborative relationships Vincenzo Volò had established with notable artists in the circle of the new Accademia Ambrosiana led the two Vicenzine to work with various painters: sources mention Luigi Scaramuccia, Giorgio Bonola, Andrea Pozzo, Federico Macagni and Federico Bianchi.

Particularly interesting in this exhibition is Federico Bianchi's *Garland of Flowers with a Religious Scene* belonging to the Fondazione Molina in Varese (cat. 3.62). The garland of flowers that surrounds this octagonal painting is a fairly early example of Giovanna's work. The most important figure in the last phases of Giovanna's life and who, after her death, offered the greatest support to the Vicenzini workshop was her husband Federico Macagni, who married Giovanna in the church of San Maurilio on 21 September 1679. An able painter but above all a skilled and ambitious promoter of social and professional relationships, Macagni had spent time Rome with Ambrogio Besozzi and had been admitted to the select "Virtuosi al Pantheon", an institution that also included Carlo Manieri, a prolific and ambitious still life painter active in Rome and a keen advocate of models derived from the work of Michelangelo Pace, known as Il Campidoglio, and of Benedetto Fioravanti. Federico Macagni introduced these new models to the Volò workshop, as well as popular Roman-style elements, such as historiated vases and classical architectural inserts, which appear in Giovanna's final works.

Although never found, this phase of Giovanna's work

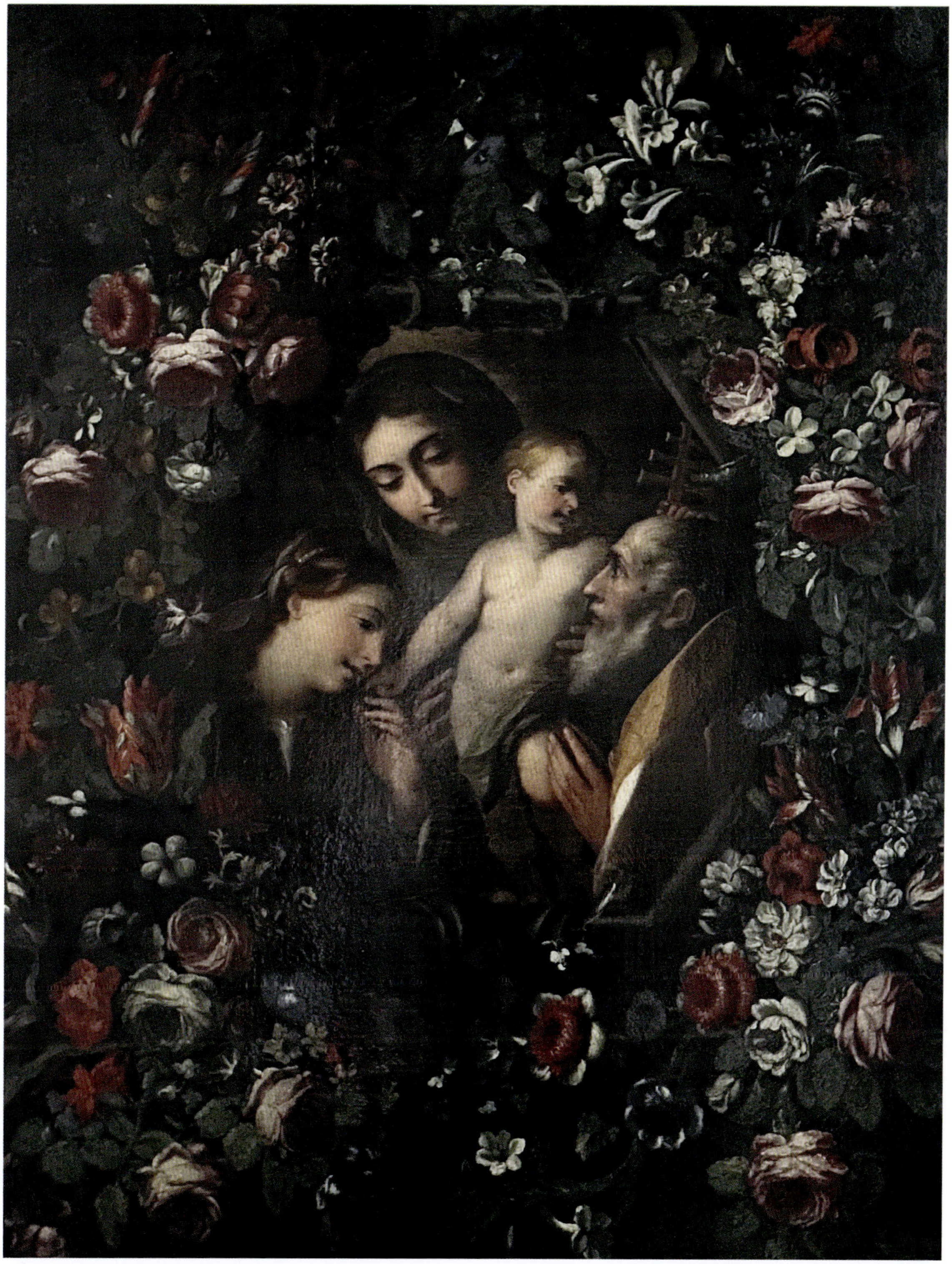

3.62
Giovanna Volò, known as Giovanna Vicenzina
Federico Bianchi
Garland of Flowers with a Religious Scene
1670–1675
Oil on canvas, 120 × 90 cm
Varese, Fondazione F.lli Paolo e Tito Molina

also included "Two paintings of fruits and flowers by the hand of a Milanese woman, called Macagna, the wife of Federico Macagni painter, and daughter of Vincenzino de' fiori, measuring 5 palms and 4", registered in the inventory of the painting collection of Gaspar de Haro y Guzmán, seventh marquis del Carpio, compiled between 7 September 1682 and 1 January 1683. Giovanna became pregnant immediately after her marriage and spent the last year of her life mainly devoting herself to the artistic education of her eighteen-year-old brother Giuseppe.

Giovanna's influence on Giuseppe is evident in some stylistic features her brother inherited from her, and also the Roman references, especially those of Campidoglio, which can be seen in his paintings.

Gianluca Bocchi

ANNA STANCHI

Active in Rome in the mid-seventeenth century

Roman historical sources are silent on the existence of a flower painter called Anna Stanchi, and even the most complete studies on the Stanchi family of painters conducted at the beginning of this century[1] has shed no light on her. Research only began due to the discovery of two canvases signed "Anna Stangui": a fragment of a garland dated 1643 and a splendid garland of flowers with Venus and Adonis in the centre dated 1647.[2]

The only known seventeenth-century document where there is a partial reference to Anna is a mention in a 1692 inventory relating to the assets of Cardinal Flavio Chigi in the palace in Piazza Santi Apostoli, namely a picture of "painted flowers and fruits by Stanghi". The same collection contained seventeen paintings by Giovanni Stanchi, two of which consisted of garlands of flowers with religious scenes in the centre: in one was a "Holy Saviour with the world in his hand", and in the other, the "Holy Madonna with her hands folded on her chest".

The simultaneous presence in the same collection of works painted by two artists sharing the same surname, plus the knowledge that Giovanni Stanchi was a prolific and very able painter of floral wreaths, strongly suggest that Anna was a member of the same family, perhaps Giovanni's wife or a younger sister, born after his birth in 1608 but before his two brothers Niccolò and Angelo, whose births are recorded with a reasonable degree of reliability as 1623 and 1626.

The notion of considering "Anna Stangui" a close relative of Giovanni Stanchi is supported by unequivocal stylistic reliefs and botanical models that only an artist active in his workshop could have reproduced with such fidelity.

Gianluca Bocchi

[1] Ravelli 2005; Proni 2005.

[2] Crispo 2013.

3.63
Anna Stanchi
Garland of Flowers with Venus and Adonis
1647
Oil on canvas,
125 × 111.5 cm
Private collection

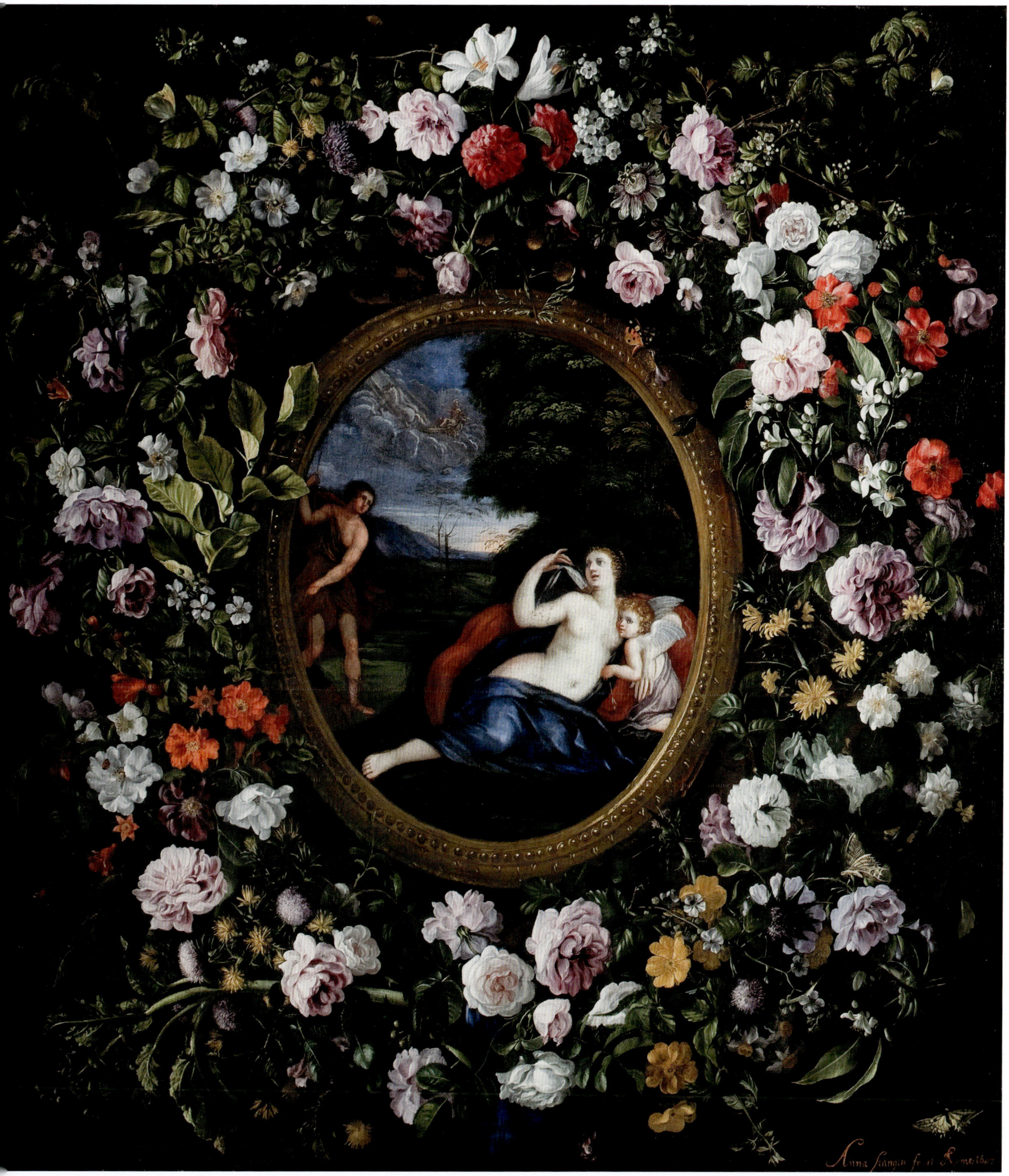

ELISABETTA MARCHIONI

Active in Rovigo in the second half of the seventeenth century

More than two centuries after the mention of a painter called Marchioni active in Rovigo in the second half of the seventeenth century, it is still very difficult to trace an adequate biographical profile.

No one has so far discovered either the year of her birth, or her death, which Bartoli has suggested was "around 1700". This lack of information also makes any details of her professional life uncertain. A stylistic examination of the paintings attributed to her suggests she lived until the beginning of the 1700s, which would make Elisabetta Marchioni a contemporary of Margherita Caffi, an artist with whom she was repeatedly confused during the last century, and whose works she may well have been acquainted with when Caffi was living in nearby Bologna (1672–1676). Or she may have known of her through the paintings Caffi sent to her brother-in-law in Venice, the merchant Francesco Caffi, during the commercial relationship the two shared until at least the end of the 1680s.

Biographical information regarding Marchioni is quite scarce: the first historical source to research her life was Francesco Bartoli, who mentions a "Marchioni, renowned flower painter" as the "wife of Sante Marchioni, a goldsmith by profession".[1]

Luigi Lanzi records a "Marchioni Rodigina, who is almost the Bernasconi of the Venetian school in her mastery of floristry, although she does not share the same renown as the Roman artist".[2] This brief information from Bartoli and Lanzi refers to her married name, leaving us without her maiden name, which might have told us something more about her artistic training and if she benefited from professional examples from other family members.

More recent news relating to her comes from nineteenth and twentieth-century art historians who have not however revealed their sources, thus removing the possibility of adequate verification.

Her baptismal name is also undocumented. It was proposed by Vincenzo De Vit only at the end of the nineteenth century,[3] yet despite a lack of proof, De Vit's information has been accepted as valid by art historians and subsequent commentators, so that the name "Elisabetta" appears in all later literature, with the evident risk that a possibly mistaken identity has been generated which might prove difficult to eradicate.

Perhaps Giuseppe Fiocco could have provided further information. He alone has stated her Forlì origin, yet also neglecting to indicate his source.[4]

News of the existence of a flower painter from the Venetian province active in the second half of the seventeenth century, and the simultaneous presence in Venice of a second specialist, an artist even less known, namely the mysterious Madama Duramano recorded by Pietro Zani in the early nineteenth century,[5] poses serious questions about the true origin and training of Elisabetta Marchioni, who may well have followed an apprenticeship in the same Venetian cultural milieu, which was much more enriching than Rovigo.

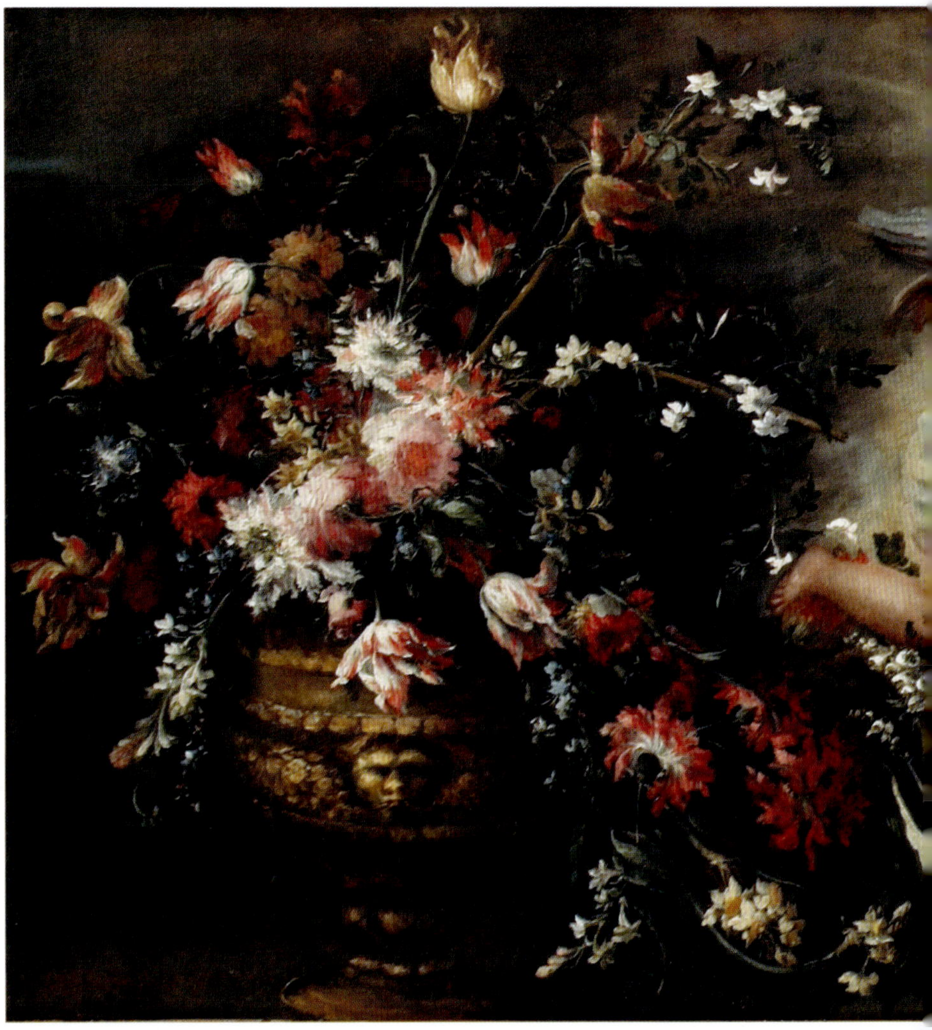

3.64
Elisabetta Marchioni
Frontal for the Holy Eucharist
End of the seventeenth century
Oil on canvas, 94 × 234 cm
Rovigo, Pinacoteca dell'Accademia dei Concordi, inv. 387

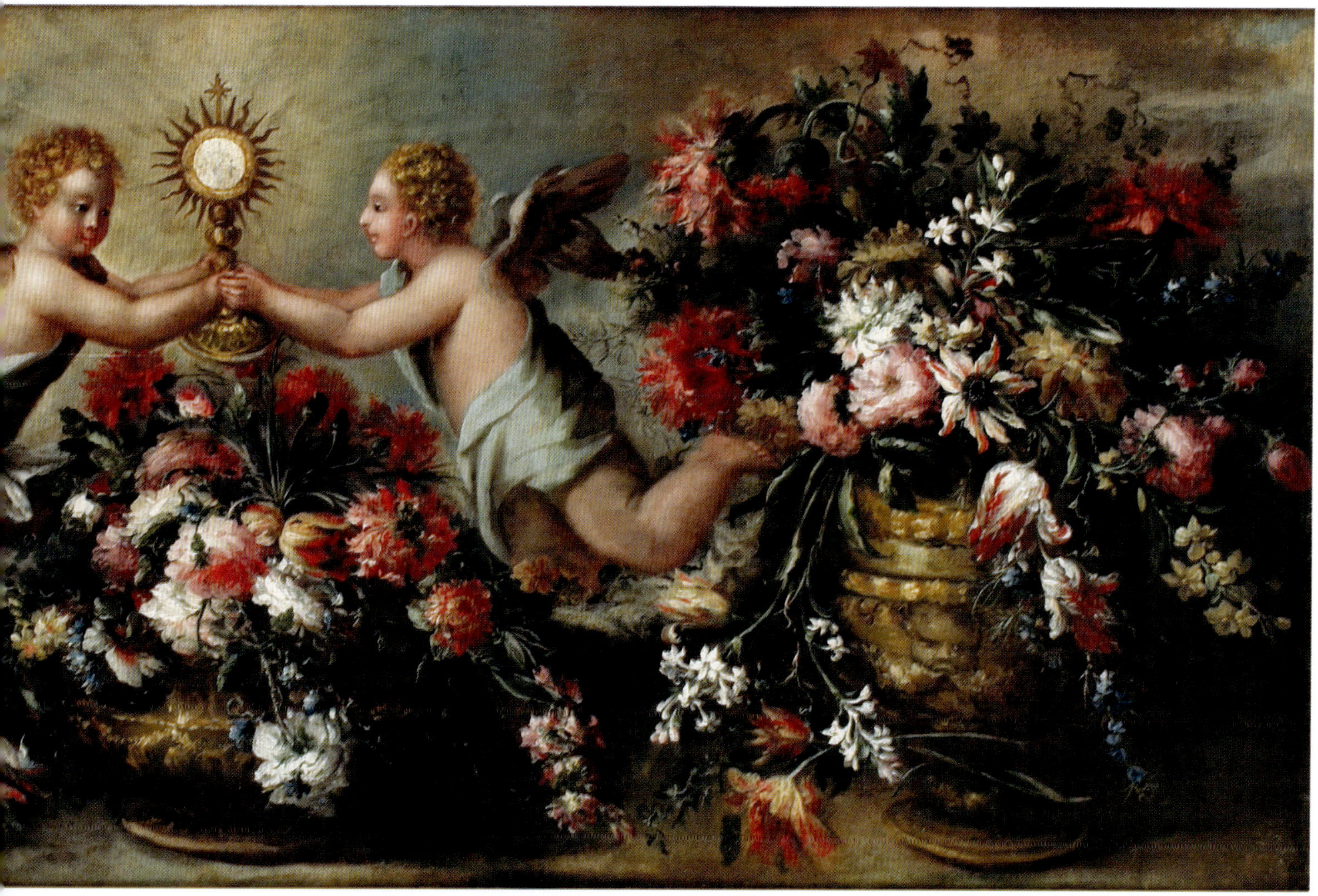

The fact that no other historical source mentions Elisabetta Marchioni provides reassurance in the belief that she was a painter with a strong local value whose fame did not go far beyond the borders of Rovigo. This is supported by the absence of any paintings bearing her name in the inventories of collections in the most important nearby cities of Venice, Padua, Bologna, Ferrara and Mantua.
In all likelihood, her marriage to the goldsmith Sante Marchioni guaranteed her a comfortable life and good connections with the Rovigo aristocracy, clergy and upper middle class, without any need to seek work elsewhere.
According to the comment made by Francesco Bartoli at the end of the eighteenth century, Elisabetta Marchioni "had a great deal of fame with this kind of painting". Indeed, even in his own day Bartoli was able to confirm this appreciation by declaring that "almost all the houses in Rovigo have four, six, eight pieces by this painter" even if "perhaps their overabundance has made them less valuable".[6]
Gianluca Bocchi

[1] Bartoli 1793, pp. 318–319.
[2] Lanzi 1823, III, pp. 278–279.
[3] De Vit 1885, p. 9.
[4] Fiocco 1955, p. 205 note 2.
[5] Zani 1817–1824, part I, vol. VIII, p. 30.
[6] Bartoli 1793, pp. 318–319.

THE ACADEMICS

The first woman to be admitted to an association of artists was Diana Scultori from Mantua. She moved to Rome in 1575, and in 1580 she was accepted in the Compagnia di San Giuseppe di Terrasanta – Saint Joseph being the dedicatee of the chapel in the Pantheon that Paul III assigned in patronage to the association in 1542. The Congregation, exclusive to painters, sculptors, and architects, had mutual aid activities as its primary purpose, and Giovanni Baglione called it the Accademia dei Virtuosi.

Giorgio Vasari founded the Accademia delle Arti del Disegno in 1563 with the approval of Cosimo I de' Medici. The academy had various purposes and goals: to recognise the excellence of the artists and to ensure the transmission of their knowledge through teaching. Artemisia Gentileschi was admitted to the Florentine Academy in 1616.

In Rome, there was the Università dei Pittori, Miniatori e Ricamatori that in 1577, on the initiative of the painter Girolamo Muziano, became the

Accademia delle Arti della Pittura, della Scultura e del Disegno, an institution that would later merge into the Accademia di San Luca, founded by Federico Zuccari in 1593 with the same intentions as Vasari's academy. In 1607, the statute was modified to accept women, but without the right to participate in executive sessions. Each woman artist, admitted due to the reputation she had earned, had to donate one of her works to the institution. The lists show the names of women specialised in various techniques: some of them are more or less famous, such as Lavinia Fontana, Giovanna Garzoni, Elisabetta Sirani, Virginia Vezzi, Plautilla Bricci, Anna Maria Vaiani, Maddalena Corvina, Isabella Parasole. Others are still completely unknown, or nearly so, such as Teresa Del Po, Lucia Neri, Ippolita De Biagi, Giustiniana Guidotti, and Caterina Ginnasi.

DIANA SCULTORI, KNOWN AS DIANA MANTOVANA

Mantua, c. 1547 – Rome, 1612

Diana Scultori, known as Mantovana (especially in the English-language publications), and erroneously Ghisi,[1] was born in Mantua in around 1547, daughter of the sculptor, plasterer and engraver Giovanni Battista de Spinchieris,[2] native Verona. The surname Scultori is descriptive of Giovanni Battista's profession, and is the same by which Diana's elder brother Adamo was known, he, too, a well-regarded engraver, while Ghisi is the surname of Giorgio, another pupil of Giovanni Battista. She was initiated into the engraving profession by her father, who had been a collaborator of Giulio Romano, working as sculptor and plasterer in the construction sites of Mantua. She later specialised in reproductive engravings of other artists' work. By reason of her age, the theory she trained under Giulio Romano himself, who died in Mantua in 1546, is to be excluded, but in the first period of her activity, apart from subjects provided by her father, Diana engraved many inventions by Raphael's pupil, demonstration of the enduring popularity of his style in the Mantua milieu. Although presumably she did not have any specific training in drawing, and as a woman she was precluded from the study from life of anatomy,[3] in her reproduction prints of Giulio's models, Diana shows freedom in compositional choices, making variations and adjustments to the graphic sources she was preparing to translate, in particular by adding natural settings and landscapes. The testimony of Giorgio Vasari, who met her in 1566 during a brief visit to Mantua, is important in identifying Diana's skills in the art of engraving. In his second edition of his *Lives* from 1568, Vasari writes of her in flattering terms, contributing to her fame.[4] In the 1560s, she met the architect Francesco Capriani da Volterra, in those years in the service of Cesare Gonzaga, Count of Guastalla. The date of their marriage is not known but was certainly before 1575, the year in which Diana moved to Rome to be with her spouse, who had been living there since 1570. On 5 June 1575, shortly after her arrival in Rome, Pope Gregory XIII granted her the privilege to sign her creations with her own name and to sell them exclusively for a period of ten years.[5] 1575 was also the year of the Jubilee, and Diana hoped that her engravings would be as widely circulated as possible in Rome; of the five subjects named in the privilege, three were inventions by Giulio Romano in Mantua (*Jesus Christ and the Adulteress*, cat. 4.4, the *Banquet of Cupid and Psyche*, the *Procession of the Horsemen*), and therefore had already been made before her arrival in the papal city, while the other two, a *Nativity* after Giulio Clovio[6] and a *Saint Jerome* after Daniele da Volterra[7] were obviously made that year. Evidence of the quality of her production can be found in a letter addressed to Francesco Capriani from Ottavio Rossi.[8] Diana's engraving activity continued successfully in Rome, where the artist dedicated herself to promoting the professional pursuits of her husband, engaged in important commissions, by printing architectural studies he produced.[9] In the same period, she accompanied her engravings with long dedications to illustrious personages who orbited between Mantua, Rome and her husband's birthplace Volterra, of which Diana too was a recognised citizen (among the dedicatees were Claudio Gonzaga, *Marriage of Psyche*, Scipione Gonzaga, the *Procession of the Horsemen*, Livia Massimo, the *Infant Saviour*). In 1580, she was admitted to the Accademia dei Virtuosi del Pantheon, of which her husband and her brother Adamo were already members.

Diana also made engravings from classical models, and her version of *Hercules with the Golden Apples*, after the gilded bronze *Forum Boarium Hercules* preserved at the Musei Capitolini, was included in a late edition of the *Speculum Romanae Magnificentiae* (1581). Diana's subjects range from mythology to sacred images, in addition to a *Lunario*, an almanac engraved in 1584 in collaboration with her architect husband and reprinted in the following two years.[10] Her catalogue, reconstructed by Paolo Bellini, counts sixty-three certain engravings, and some dubious ones; the last dated one, the *Visitation*, after an invention by Giorgio Vasari, shows the year 1588. Diana's late activity is not documented, and her biographers believe that she no longer practised the profession of engraver. After the death of her husband in 1594, Diana remained in Rome near Via della Scrofa, but in 1596, after her second marriage, to the architect Giorgio Pelosi, she moved to Via del Corso, where she died in 1612.[11]

Rita Bernini

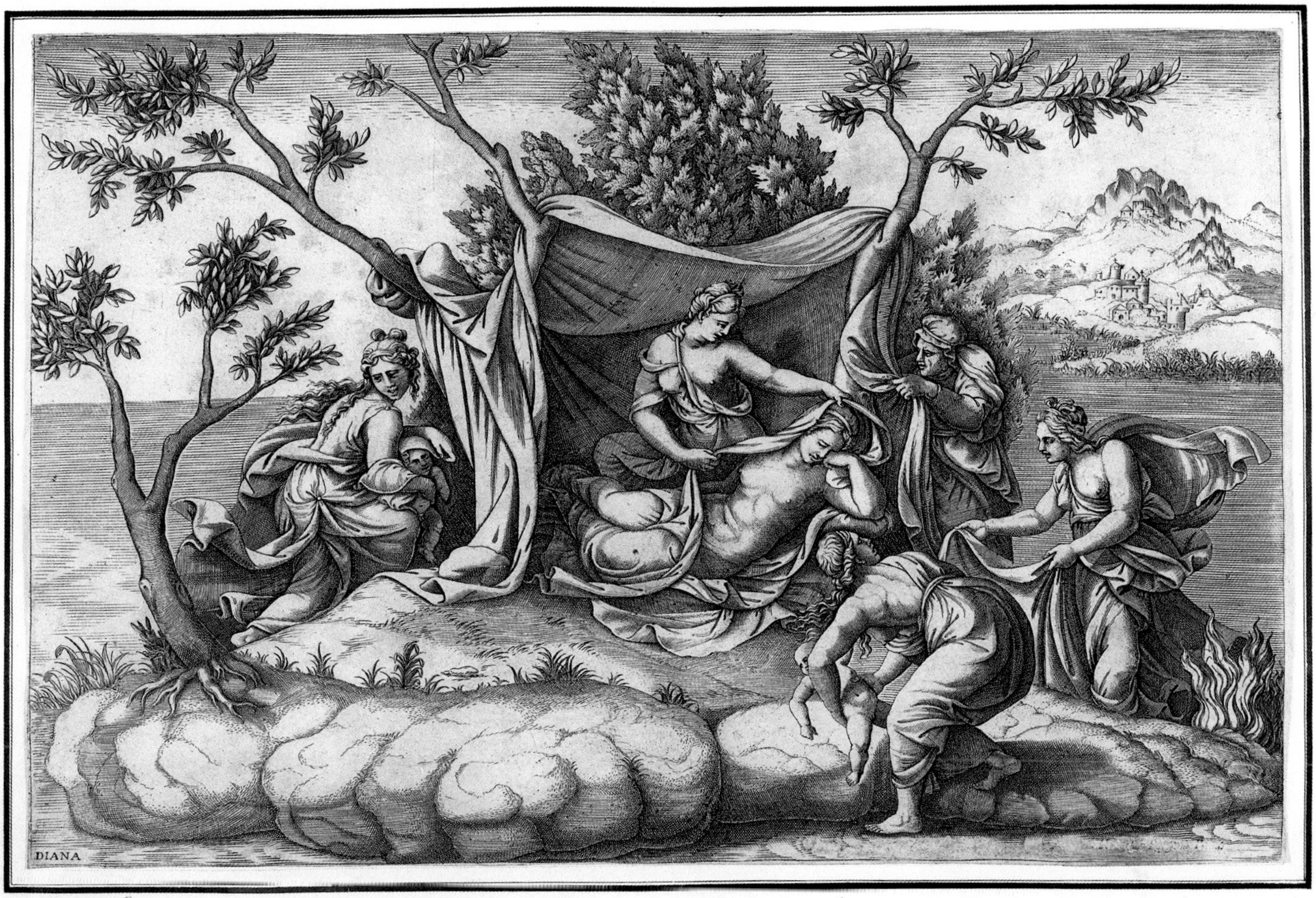

4.1
Diana Scultori, known as Diana Mantovana
Latona Giving Birth to Apollo and Diana on the Island of Delos
1565–1572
Burin, trimmed sheet
257 × 384 mm
Rome, Istituto centrale per la grafica, inv. FC50748 (property of the Accademia Nazionale dei Lincei)

[1] Vasari 1568, ed. 1966–1987, V, p. 424.
[2] Rebecchini 2002, p. 73.
[3] Furlotti 2018.
[4] "[...] and what is more remarkable, a daughter called Diana, a gentle and graceful child whom I have seen, who also engraves remarkably, her beautiful works amazing me": Vasari 1568, English ed. 1963, 3, p. 316. https://archive.org/details/livesofpainterss0000unse_a2c1/page/316/mode/2up?q=Diana
[5] Lincoln 2000, pp. 123 f., p. 189 for the transcription of the document; Witcombe 2004, p. 183.
[6] Not identified, but, translated by Giulio Clovio himself, the line engraving depicting the *Sacrifice of Abraham* is reported in Diana's catalogue with indication of Gregory XIII's concession, Bellini 1991, pp. 193–194, n. 19.
[7] Bellini 1991, pp. 208–209, n. 25.
[8] "The works by your Lady Diana are quite wonderful and that feast of the gods is stupendous": Bottari, Ticozzi 1822–1825, IV, p. 87, referring to the *Marriage of Psyche*, a striking three-sheet engraving.
[9] *Ionic Volute of a Composite Capital*, dated 1576, in Bellini 1991, p. 214, n. 29; Pagani 1992, p. 83; Lincoln 2000, pp. 112–116. Two other engravings with architectonic motifs designed by her architect husband Francesco da Volterra are pointed out by Bellini 1991, pp. 218–219, nos. 32-33.
[10] Pagani 1991.
[11] Pagani 1992.

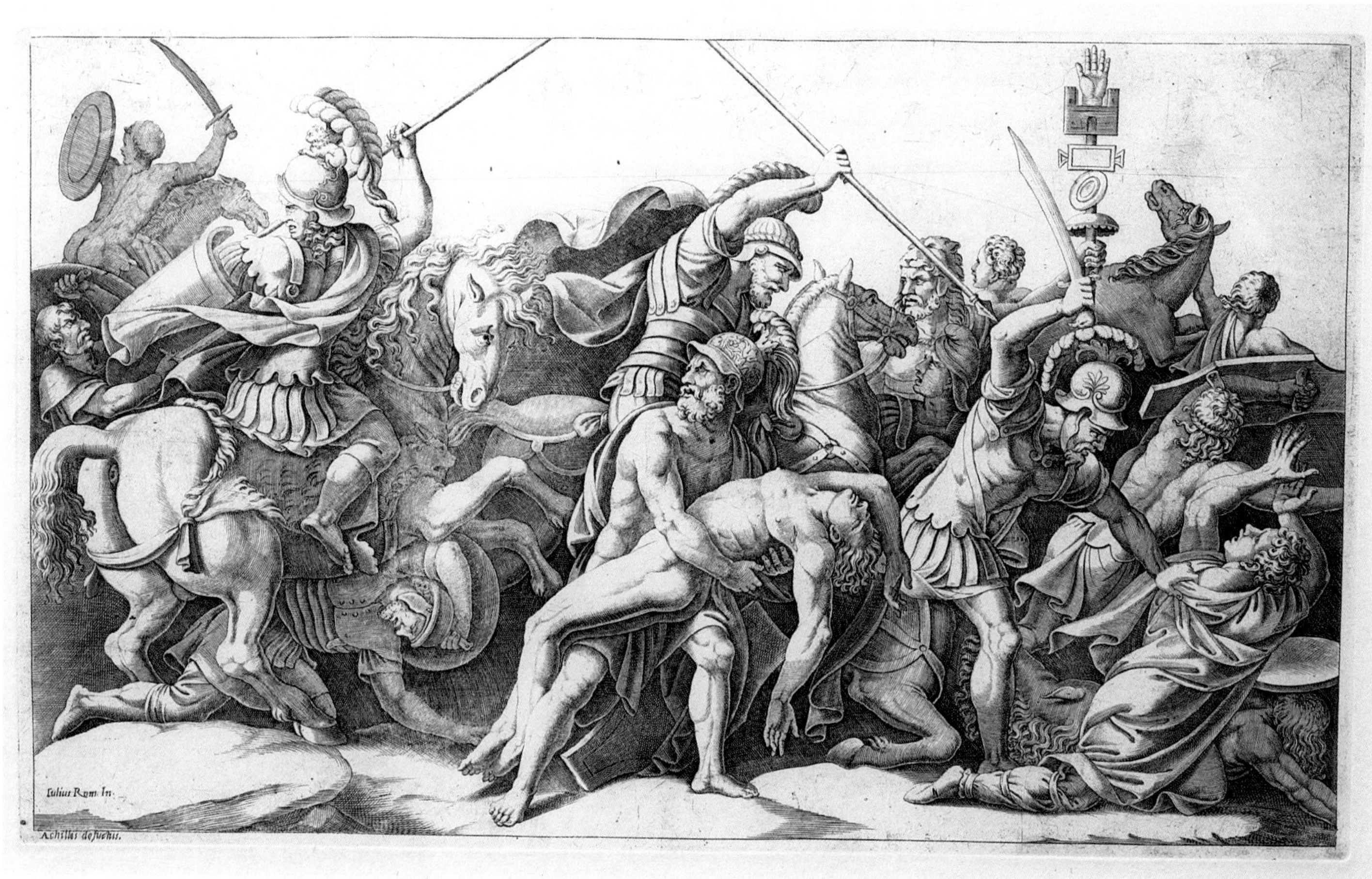

4.2
Diana Scultori,
known as Diana Mantovana
Achilles Defuctus, Battle around the Body of Patroclus
c. 1570
Burin, sheet 456 × 654 mm, impression 244 × 398 mm
Rome, Istituto centrale per la grafica, inv. CL2452/746

4.3
Diana Scultori,
known as Diana Mantovana
The Continence of Scipio
Before 1575
Burin, sheet 370 × 478 mm, impression 207 × 255 mm
Rome, Istituto centrale per la grafica, inv. CL2452/752

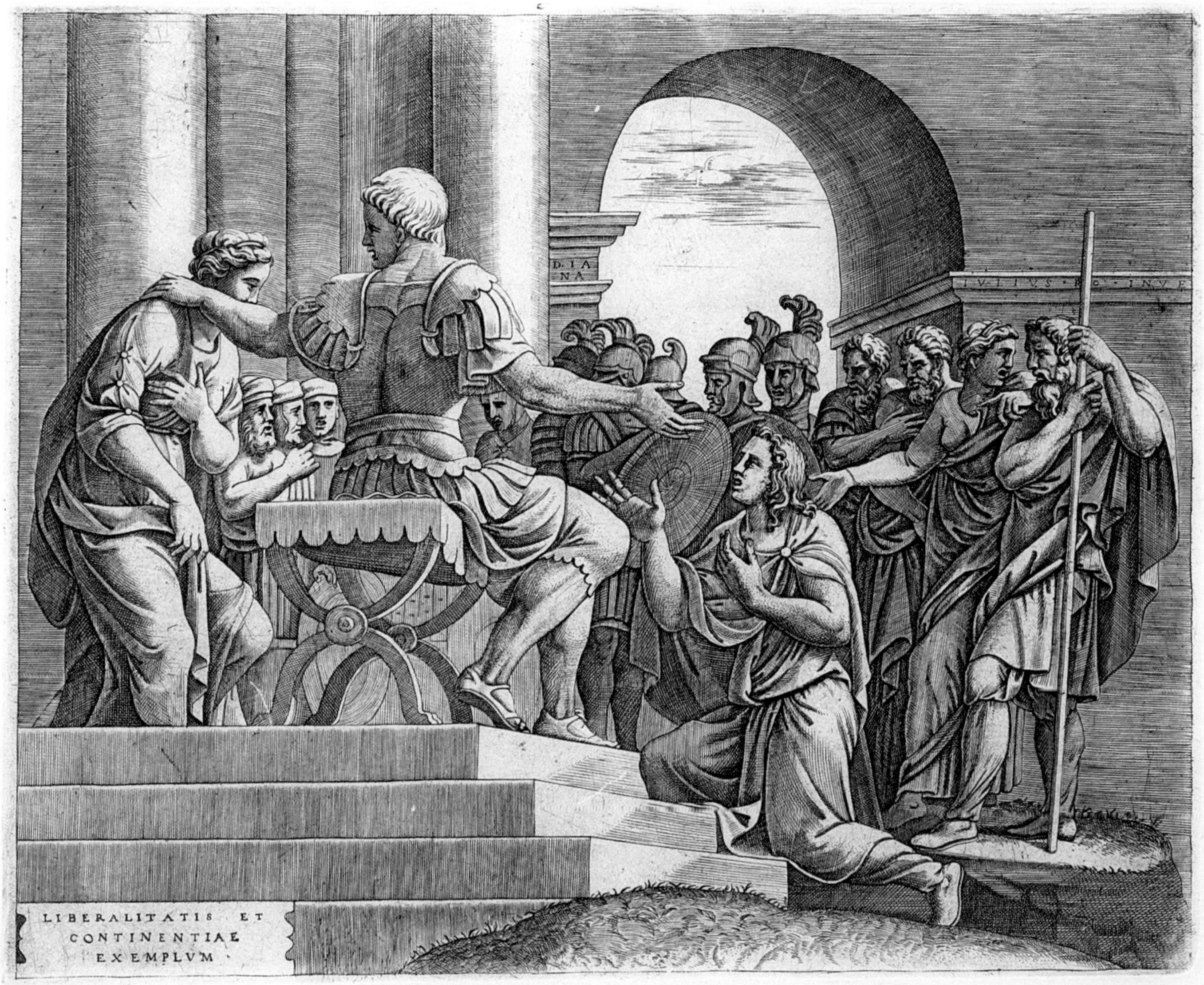
D.IA
NA
IVLIVS RO. INVE
LIBERALITATIS ET
CONTINENTIAE
EXEMPLVM

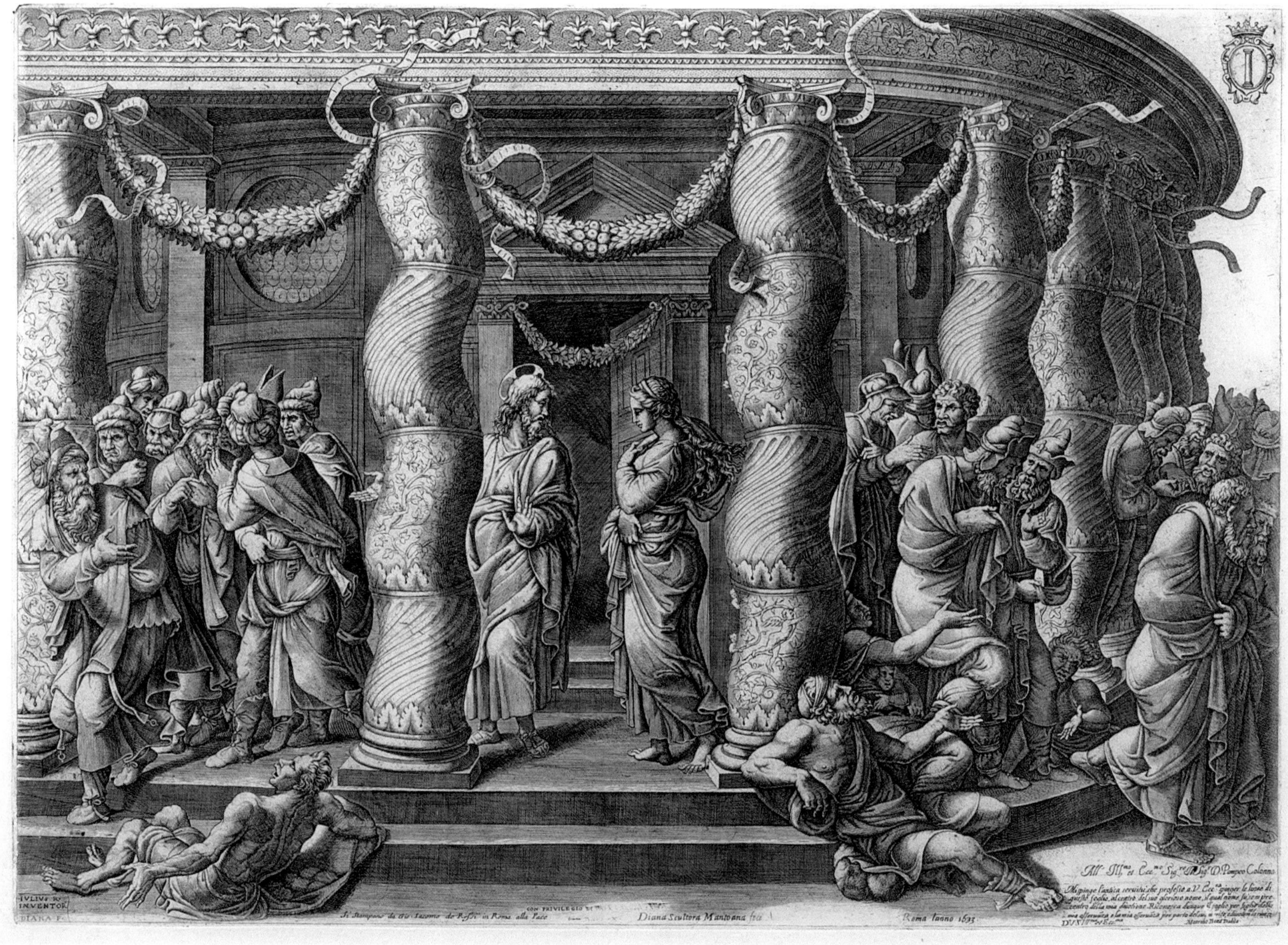

4.4
Diana Scultori,
known as Diana Mantovana
Jesus Christ and the Adulteress
By 1575
Burin, sheet 610 × 871 mm, impression 423 × 583 mm
Rome, Istituto centrale per la grafica, inv. CL2452/744

4.5
Diana Scultori,
known as Diana Mantovana
Madonna and Child with the Archangels Michael, Gabriel and Raphael
Before 1572–1575
Burin, sheet 646 × 469 mm, impression 361 × 272 mm
Rome, Istituto centrale per la grafica, inv. CL2496/2392

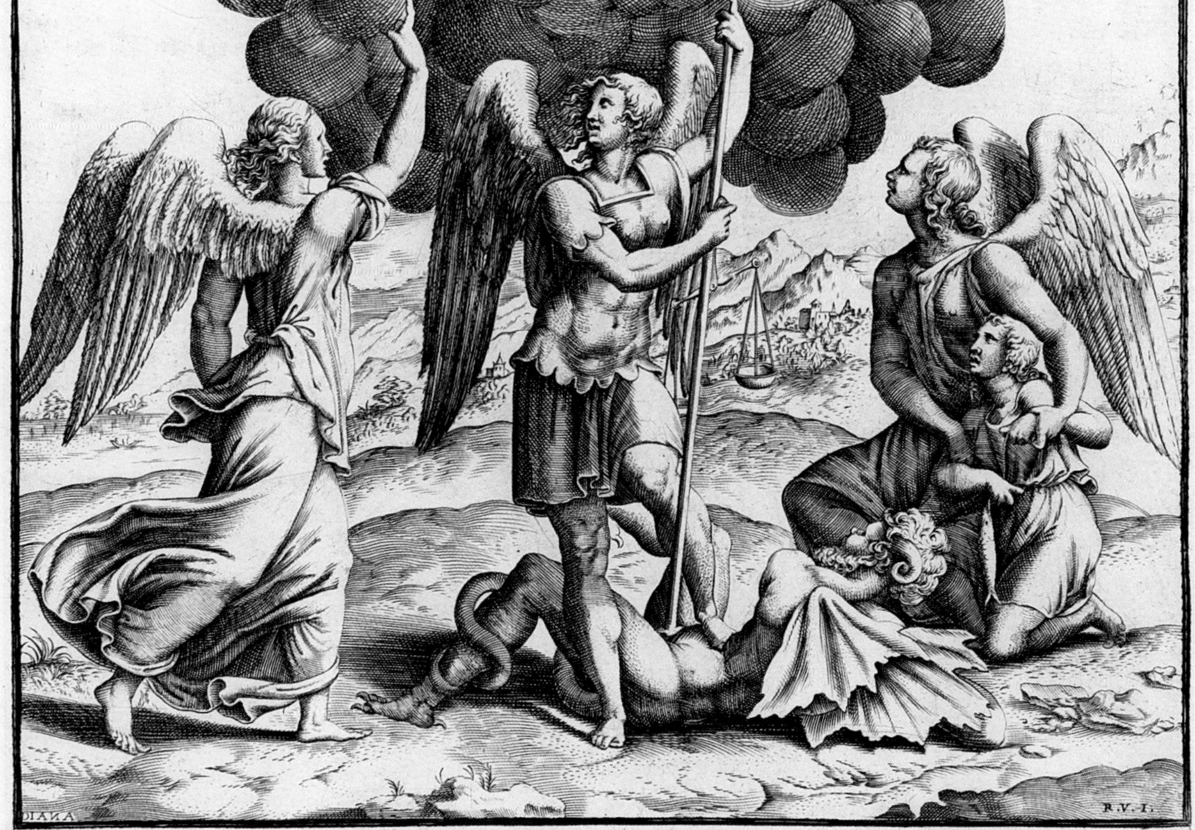
DIANA
R.V.I.
REGINA ANGELORVM
CVM TRIBVS ARCHANGELIS, MICHAELE, GABRIELE, RAPHAELE.
Romę ex Chalcographia Dominici de Rubeis Heredis Io. Iacobi de Rubeis ad Templum S. Marię de Pace cum Priu. S. Pont.

ANNA MARIA VAIANI

Milan, c. 1604? – Rome, 1654

Anna Maria Vaiani was born in Milan around 1604 to the Florentine painter Alessandro Vaiani and Angela Scelpia of Milan. The family is documented in the parish of San Babila from 1610 to 1617. Before 1626, the Vaiani family moved to Rome. Anna Maria, like her brother Sebastiano, learned the rudiments of the trade from her father. We have a half-length portrait of her engraved by Claude Mellan (1626–1627) in which she is elegantly dressed.[1] Her first known work dates from 1627, an etching showing Saint Mary Magdelene (cat. 4.6) The accounts of her contemporaries render an image of a talented young woman, versatile and "virtuous", worthy of the protection of important personalities, the likes of Caterina Riccardi Niccolini, the wife of the Grand Ducal ambassador in Rome. It was Galileo who, in 1630, recommended her to Michelangelo Buonarroti the Younger due to her "very great merit", so that he could introduce her to the artistic milieu of the Barberini court. The relationship between the scientist and Anna Maria was characterised by mutual esteem and affection, feelings that would continue unchanged over the years.[2] In Rome, she received her first commissions: the Barberinis bought her copy of a work after Titian and a painting of a coral, both lost.[3] In this scholarly milieu, Vaiani came into contact with Cassiano dal Pozzo: some drawings from antiquity for his *Museo Cartaceo* have been attributed to her hand.[4] In June 1632, she was assigned three illustrations for the *Galleria Giustiniana*: the *Pallas* and the portrait busts of Homer and Pindar, and of Sappho and the Young Cleopatra.[5] She was also involved in the Giovan Battista Ferrari's *De Florum Cultura* (1633), for which she engraved an elegant vase filled with rare flowers.[6] After the death of her father in 1631, the artist completed the fresco decoration of the chapel of Urban VIII in the Vatican and the altar painting with a *Lamentation over the Dead Christ*. Unfortunately, the appraisal for the payment of the balance of 348 scudi, drawn up by Gian Lorenzo Bernini in March 1632, does not distinguish the parts executed by Anna Maria from those by Alessandro.[7] Towards the close of 1636, the illuminator Giovanni Battista Stefaneschi wrote to Galileo from Rome, asking him to introduce her to the Grand Duchess, recalling that Anna Maria "does so well in painting and drawing, playing musical instruments and better than average singing, [that] she would gladly leave this city".[8] Later, she sent two pictures of flowers to Carlo de' Medici, for which she was not paid adequately.[9] In 1651, in some documents of the Accademia di San Luca, she was registered as present at a meeting of female academic painters: Giustiniana Guidotti, Caterina Ginnasi and Giovanna Garzoni.[10] In the last years of the artist's life, she was afflicted by personal problems, while her career was now on a downward spiral. In 1647, she married the painter Jacques Courtois (1621–1676), who was seventeen years younger than her. It soon proved to be a difficult union: after running away and threatening to reveal very serious things about her husband, she was arrested for spousal desertion, but quickly released.[11] The separation culminated with the restitution of her dowry (1653). By now unwell, Anna Maria Vaiani dictated her will and died at her home in Strada Felice on 21 January 1654, at the age of around fifty. She was buried in the church of San Carlo alle Quattro Fontane.[12]

Isabella Rossi

[1] For the biographical profile of the artist, see Guerrieri Borsoi 2010, Lollobrigida 2017b, p. 124. For the portrait, see the entry for Brejon de Lavergnée, in *Claude Mellan* 1989, p. 259, no. 66.

[2] Bredekamp 2019, pp. 275–283.

[3] Guerrieri Borsoi 2010, pp. 247-–248.

[4] See the entry for V. Carpita, in *I segreti di un collezionista* 2000, p. 144, no. 160 (*Two Views of a Charioteer's Head*), p. 148, no. 164 (*Head of a Satyr*).

[5] See the entries for Fusconi, in *I Giustiniani* 2001, pp. 181–183, no. 3, pp. 295–297, no. 32, p. 580, no. II.56.

[6] See Tomasi Tongiorgi 2008, pp. 164–166. Guerrieri Borsoi 2010, p. 250 note 21. In 1630 the artist received payment of 5 scudi "down payment for the flower and vase that she depicted (and to be carved in copper)", see Merz 1991, p. 326. On the genesis of Ferrari's treatise, see Serafini 2003–2004, available on-line at www.academia.edu, especially pp. 149–162. On Vaiani's involvement, ivi, pp. 155–156.

[7] Guerrieri Borsoi 2010, pp. 251–259.

[8] Bredekamp 2019, p. 282. Letter to Galileo dated 22 December 1636. The correspondence is available on-line (Galileo//Thek@).

[9] Guerrieri Borsoi 2010, p. 260. The news of a trip to England in 1637–1638 is reported in Solinas 2000, p. 38. Guerrieri Borsoi 2010, p. 260, points out that on 3 January 1638, Anna Maria was in Rome, and from there wrote to Galileo Galilei. On 3 July that same year, she is mentioned in a letter from Antonio Nardi to Galileo.

[10] Melasecchi 2001, p. 22. Lollobrigida (2017b, p. 124 and note 9, p. 129) points out her name in the registries of the mandates of the Accademia di San Luca (1630 and 1655). See also Guerrieri Borsoi 2010, p. 259.

[11] See Guerrieri Borsoi 2010, p. 262.

[12] The inheritance was divided between the sisters and Canon Giovanni Gismanni who drew up the inventory of the assets: the list includes sacred and profane paintings, none of which is identifiable. See Guerrieri Borsoi 2010, p. 263.

4.6
Anna Maria Vaiani
Saint Mary Magdalene
1627
Etching, sheet 252 × 203 mm, impression 184 × 144 mm
Rome, Istituto centrale per la grafica, inv. FC76527 (property of the Accademia Nazionale dei Lincei)

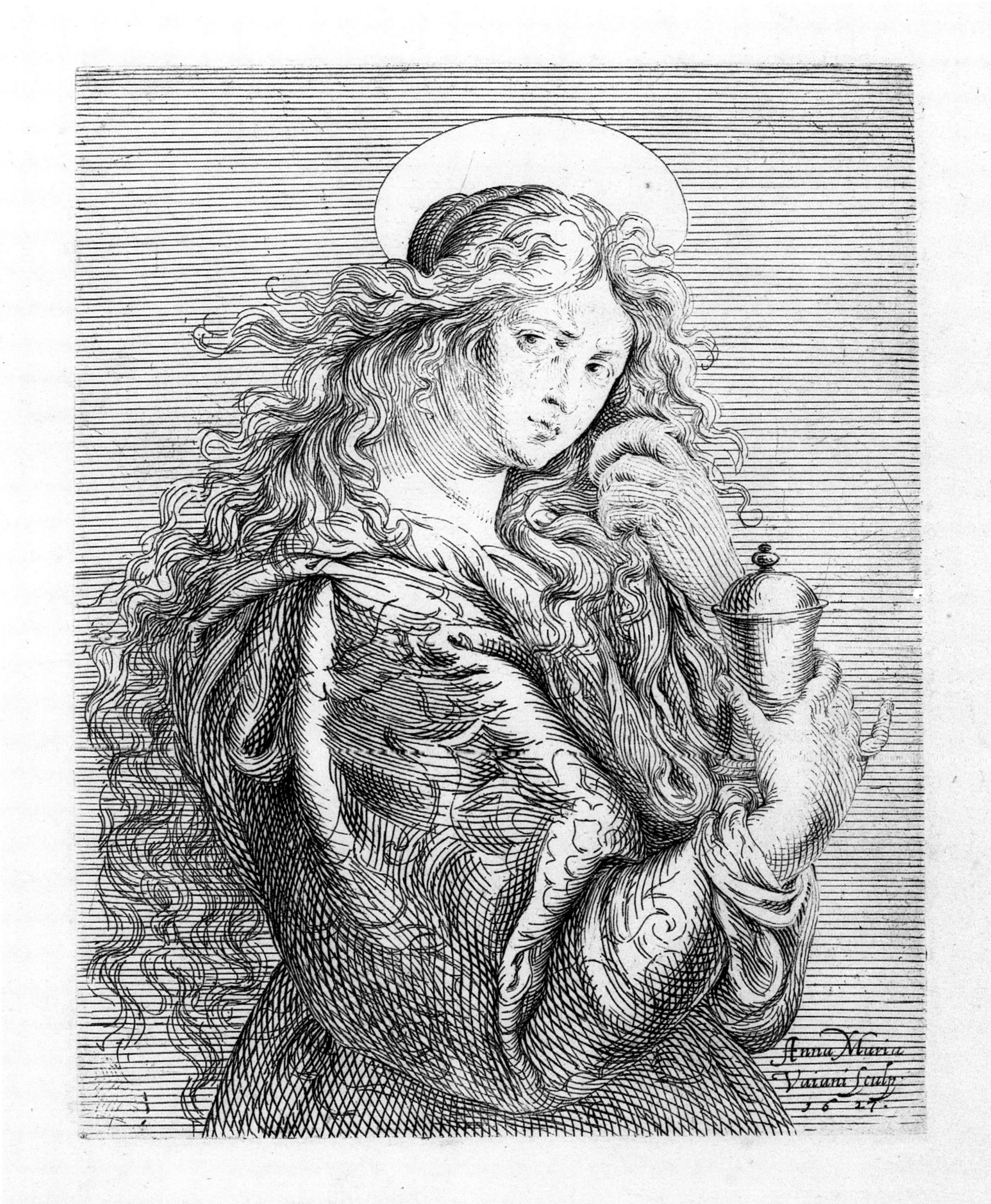
Anna Maria
Vaiani Sculp.
1 6 2 7.

MADDALENA CORVINA

Rome, 1607 – Rome, 1664

Maddalena Corvina was born in Rome on 17 October 1607, the daughter of Caterina Castelli († 1641) and Hendrik De Raef (c. 1565–1639), apothecary of Delft who moved to Rome at the close of the sixteenth century, changing his name to Enrico Corvino. During that period the papal capital was frequented by many foreign intellectuals and artists who played a fundamental role in the definition of an international cultural identity that developed both in adherence and in antithesis to the Baroque, in the avant-garde of art as well as of science. Enrico Corvino's pharmacy[1] became one of the places where this cultural ferment was spreading. In her years of training, Maddalena was indirectly exposed to many stimuli through her father's circle of acquaintances, who were central in the evolution of her career; her maternal grandfather, Frans van de Casteele (c. 1541–1621), famous miniaturist from Brussels, contributed in equal measure. The artist carried out her apprenticeship with Guido Reni, though we have yet to determine exactly when this took place.[2] The sensitive portrait that Claude Mellan engraved in 1636 indicates that Corvina was already recognised as a painter and illuminator in that year. She chose not to marry, probably so as not to be subjected to marriage contracts that would have curtailed her independence. Her activity started around 1630 and continued through the papacies of Urban VIII and Alexander VII. Her hand has been recognised in some cuttings and the illuminated Sistine Chapel missals, created for the popes.[3] Maddalena has been mentioned in connection with a fragment of a liturgical book in the Bodleian Library at Oxford "formerly of the Sistine Chapel, Lat. Liturg. A. 8, fol. 2 (no. 1029), with Alexander VII's coat of arms attributed with reservations to the papal miniaturist Maddalena Corvina, perhaps used at the Pope's first mass at Christmas 1655, when Christine of Sweden was confirmed".[4] Also attributed to her was the parchment depicting *Pope Urban VIII Celebrating Mass*, auctioned in 1935 in London and now lost.[5] It is highly likely that she did the illustrations for Federico Cesi's *Syntaxis Plantaria*,[6] which constituted a novelty in the field of botanical representation for their detailed description of the reproductive parts of plants, necessary for a correct classification. Many of her drawings are recalled in an album also containing prints, donated to the artist by Domenico Avvantaggi in 1634 and then passed into the Biblioteca Albani, where it remained until the nineteenth century.[7] The volume may have been part of a collection begun as a part of Cassiano dal Pozzo's *Museo Cartaceo*, considering the artist's involvement in the initiatives promoted by the Barberini court's famous patron of art.[8]

Continuing in our attempt to reconstruct Corvina's career, her name is mentioned in the *Studiolo di pittura nella Galleria della Ricchezza* by Antonio degli Effetti, the description of a large piece of collector's furniture decorated by sixty-six artists all of whom were her contemporaries. In the list of the one hundred paintings of Prince Antonio Ruffo's primogeniture, a *Small Madonna with Putto* set in a "silver bolster frame made by Innocenzo Mangani" is cited.[9] Other works, not identified today, appear in the inventories of Italian and foreign collections. In 1664, Giovan Pietro Bellori described the Corvini family estate, inherited by Maddalena's brother following their father's passing, in the "Museo di cose naturali et di varie curiosità antiche e peregrine", pointing out some "delightful miniatures by Signora Maddalena Corvini, famous in this art".[10] Many of her works have not been traced, while the miniature with the portrait of her father, made on the occasion of his death, has come down to us thanks to the engraved translation by Johannes Valdor.[11]

In recent years, the *corpus* of Corvina's works has expanded with new attributions: *The Young Gentleman Holding Gloves* of 1639 in the Fondazione Cavallini Sgarbi is one such addition.[12] The decorative strip of Pope Urban VIII's Benedictional conserved in Toledo (Archivio e Biblioteca Capitulares, ms. 312, fol. 4*v*), with floral decoration made up of anemones, tulips, and carnations, is now also included in the Roman artist's ouput.[13] The miniature of the *Madonna and Child*, dated 1640 – perhaps her best-known work exhibited in the Sala delle Vetrine of the Galleria Palatina, Palazzo Pitti (inv. 1890, no. 5574) – has recently been pointed out by Elena de Laurentis as a touchstone for attributing to Maddalena Corvina a portrait of Artemisia Gentileschi as Saint Catherine of Alexandra identified on the antiques market.[14]

In 1655, she appears in the list of artists of the Accademia di San Luca: at that time, it was not considered

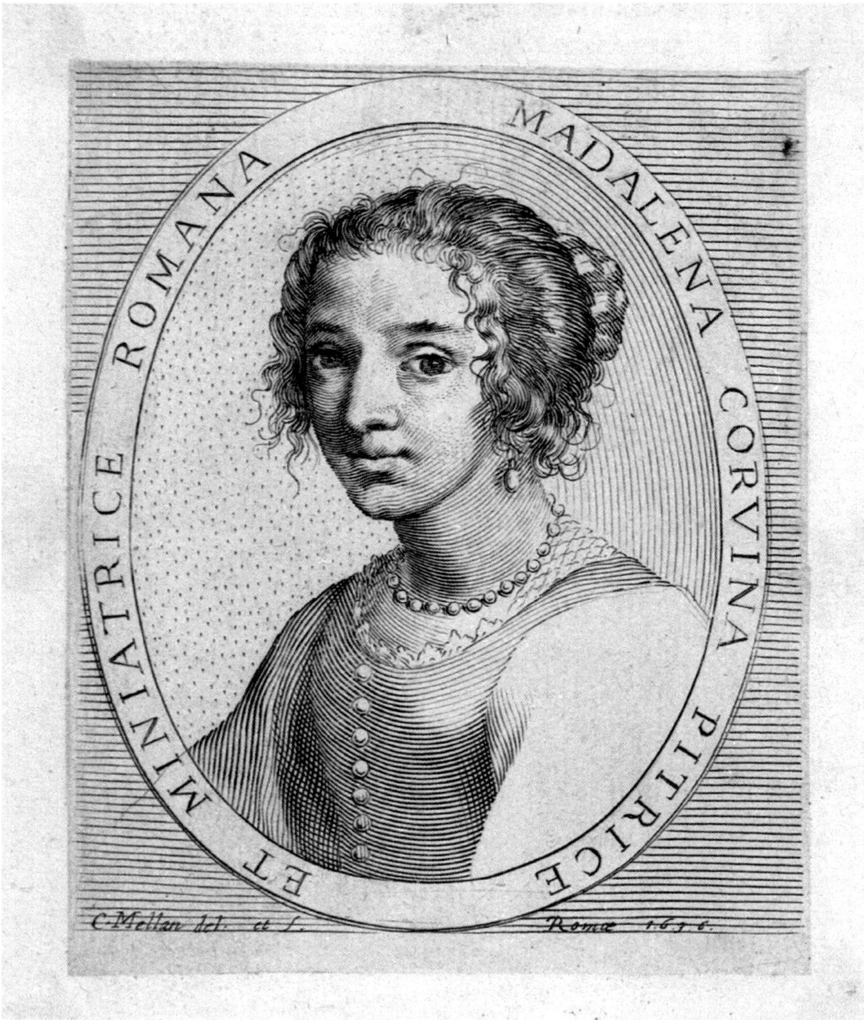

4.7
Claude Mellan
Portrait of Maddalena Corvina
1636
Burin, trimmed sheet
117 × 85 mm
Rome, Istituto centrale per la grafica, inv. FC32050 (property of the Accademia Nazionale dei Lincei)

appropriate for women to paint the male nude figure from life, a restriction that in fact excluded women from practicing history painting, and relegating them with few exceptions to the spheres of decoration and the portrait. Maddalena's activity as a "minor" painter did not prevent her from attaining a certain renown, and the Tuscan scholar Filippo Baldinucci described her as an "excellent illuminator" in his chapter on Francesco Allegrini, whom he mistakenly believed was the brother of her pupil Anna Angelica, and not her father.[15] She died on 3 February 1664.[16]

Gabriella Bocconi

[1] Michel (1995, p. 398) mentions Corvino's pharmacy as having opened in around 1595, under the sign of the Black Eagle. Belloni Speciale 1993 and Lollobrigida (2017b, p. 123) instead mention it as the Imperial Eagle, indicating respectively two parallel Roman roads, Via Monte Giordano and Via del Governo Vecchio, which could refer to the same building. It is not to be excluded that Corvino's laboratory changed location over time and the term "Imperial" was adopted following the pharmacist's appointment as officer "for the nation of Flanders", received together with Paul Bril in 1614.

[2] See cat. 4.7.

[3] Biblioteca Apostolica Vaticana, *Mss. Cappella Sistina* 8 and 41 (Meloni Trkulja 1983a).

[4] Daneu Lattanzi 1972, p. 54.

[5] Christie's, 29 March 1935, lot. 143; Bénézit 1999; Lollobrigida 2017b, p. 123.

[6] Barker 2020, p. 18.

[7] Pietro Zani mentions it, 1817–1824, part I, vol. VII, pp. 71, 179–180 no. 239.

[8] As proof of the relationship with the famous collector, it should be recalled that Maddalena's mother named Cassiano dal Pozzo as the executor of her will, calling him the "very peculiar master" of her house. It is reasonable to interpret the term "master" as client.

[9] In this list, the artist is registered as "Madalena Corvino nephiew of the Roman Doctor Pietro Castelli". Pietro Castelli (1574–1662) was an important intermediary for the commissions received from the Sicilian city: Ruffo 1916, p. 181 note 3.

[10] Bellori 1664, ed. 1976, pp. 27–28; Mazzetti di Pietralata 2010, p. 95.

[11] See cat. 4.8.

[12] See cat. 4.9; Sgarbi, in *L'arte delle donne* 2007, p. 341; Petrucci 2008, p. 542; De Laurentiis 2010b, p. 67, fig. 101.

[13] Mazzetti di Pietralata 2010, p. 95; *The Lost Manuscripts* 2010; De Laurentiis 2011, p. 43, fig. 21.

[14] https://wannenesgroup.com/lots/397-70-maddalena-corvina/.

[15] Baldinucci 1681–1728, ed. 1767-–1774, XIX, pp. 163–165.

[16] In a letter addressed to Prince Antonio Ruffo, dated 10 July 1666, Abraham Brueghel communicated the death of Maddalena with the following words: "About the illuminated things, Signora Madalena Corvini has died, and her brother has a few of her small pieces, but he highly values them, apart from any sense of duty; and in that Profession, here there is only occasional work and they get well paid", Ruffo 1916, pp. 181–182.

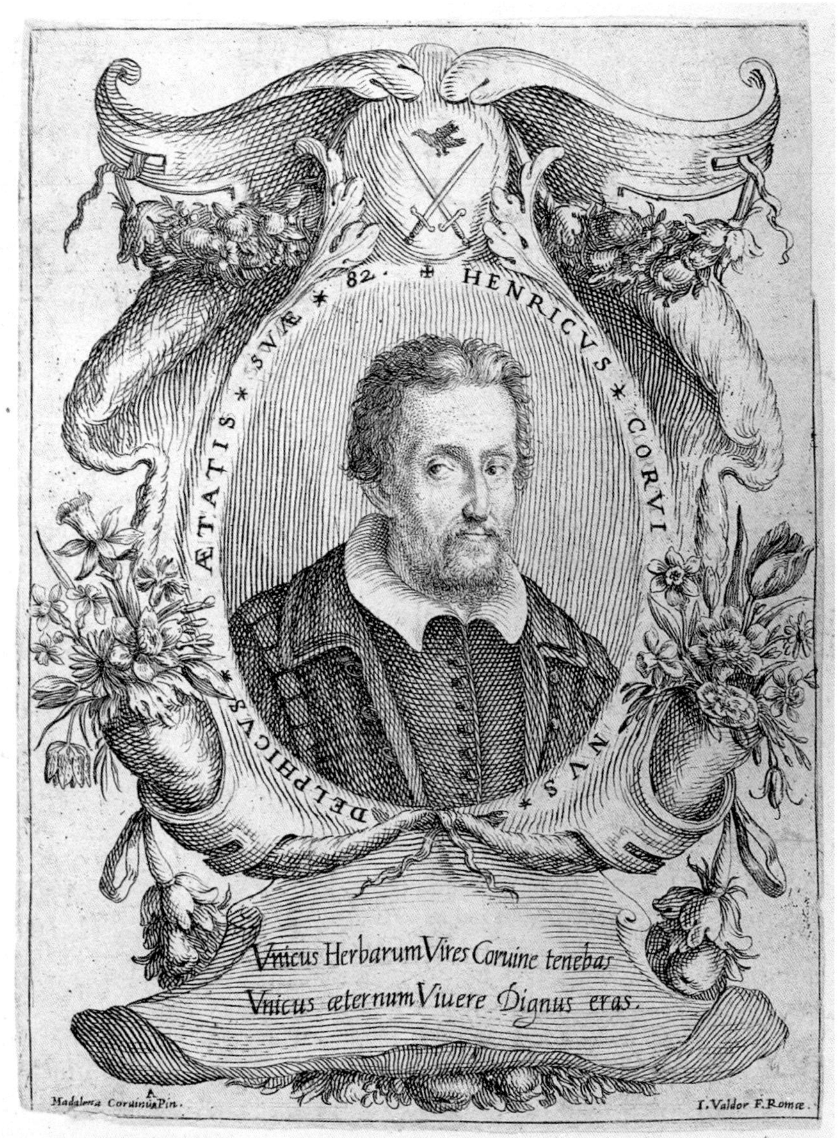

4.8
Johannes Valdor II
(after Maddalena Corvina)
Portrait of Enrico Corvino
1639–1640
Etching and burin, trimmed sheet 148 × 112 mm
Rome, Istituto centrale per la grafica, inv. FC41062 (property of the Accademia Nazionale dei Lincei)

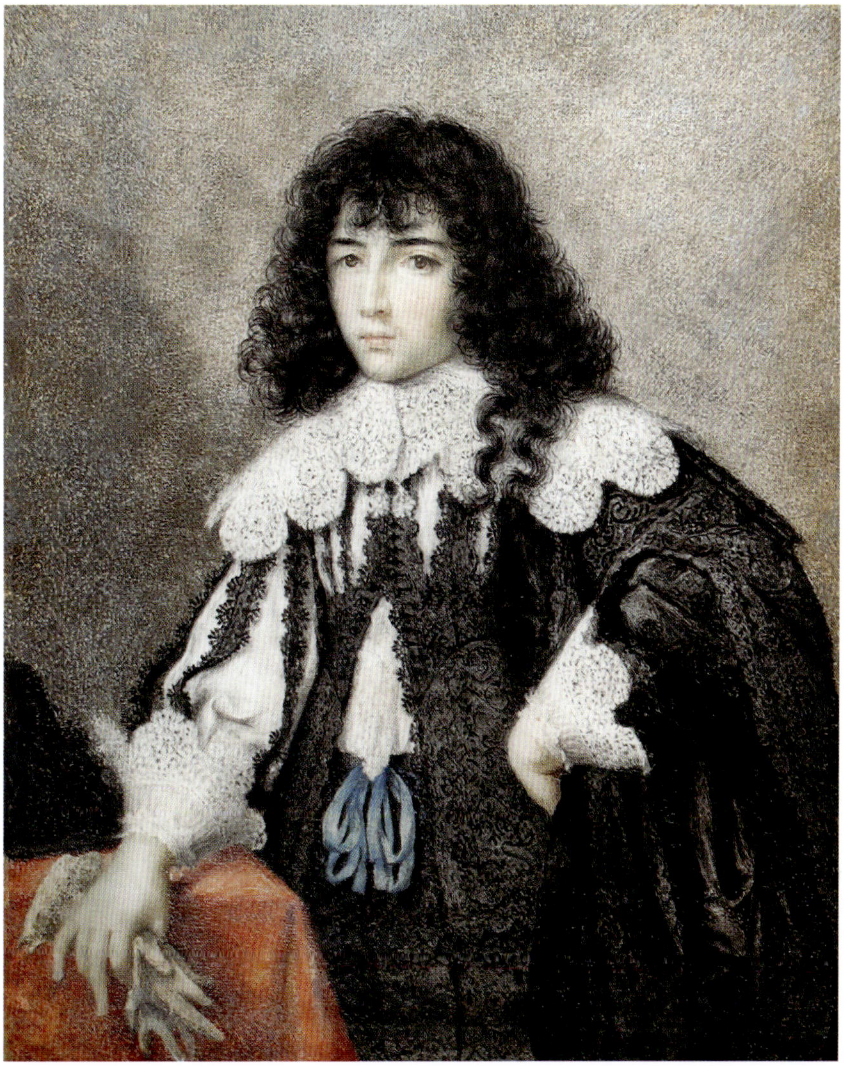

4.9
Maddalena Corvina
Young Gentleman Holding Gloves
1639
Gouache on parchment,
140 × 110 mm
Fondazione Cavallini Sgarbi

GIOVANNA GARZONI

Ascoli Piceno, 1600 – Rome, 1670

Giovanna Garzoni is considered the most important Italian miniaturist of the Baroque era. The main nucleus of her work consists of numerous gouache paintings on parchment, gouache being a variety of tempera characterised by a certain lightness of body and rapidness of execution, requiring exceptional technical ability, used both in portraiture and in studies of nature. The latter, in particular, showing clever compositions of different types of plants, flowers, fruits, vegetables, animals and insects, were widely appreciated in her own time[1] for the peculiar illusionist sensitivity with which the painter seems to challenge the given reality, while still allowing the observer to perceive its profound symbolic dimension[2] (cat. 4.19). She was born in Ascoli Piceno (Marches) in 1600 to a family of craftsmen of Venetian origin. Her early artistic training was probably in Venice, where she spent her young adulthood with her older brother Mattio. She probably started out by studying the paintings of Jacopo Palma the Younger, attending Giacomo Rogni's school of calligraphy between 1617 and 1622.[3] In fact, her first predilection towards this practice of lettering and later on towards the art of illumination would clinch her definitive abandonment of the traditional pictorial genres, an expression of the curious cultural climate that took hold in early seventeenth-century society, when the "minor" arts tended to be seen as particularly suited to female artists.[4] At an unspecified time between 1618 and 1621, the painter stayed in Florence for the first time, while she sought to obtain a prestigious position at the court of Maria Maddalena of Austria, Grand Duchess of Tuscany.[5] During this stay, Garzoni may have bonded with Artemisia Gentileschi, who enjoyed the favour of the Medici and with whom she shared subsequent visits to Venice, Naples, and London.[6] In 1630, together with Artemisia, Garzoni moved to Naples in the service of the viceroy Fernando Afán de Ribera, Duke of Alcalá. During the journey, she stopped for some time in Rome, where she was able to establish a relationship with the erudite collector Cassiano dal Pozzo and from him learn about the naturalistic studies of the Accademia dei Lincei, founded by Federico Cesi in 1603.[7] About a year after her arrival in Naples, the Duke of Alcalá was recalled to his homeland and Garzoni, finding herself without a fixed salary, turned to Dal Pozzo, asking him to find a place in Rome, where she moved again towards the end of 1631. It was her fame as a portraitist that led Christine of France, Duchess of Savoy, to request her services in Turin. In the summer of 1632, Garzoni thus arrived at the Savoy court, where she carried out an intense artistic activity: in fact, the inventories of the House of Savoy hold references to some miniatures of a sacred and mythological character, as well as to portraits, including those of the Dukes Emmanuel Philibert (cat. 4.10) and Charles Emmanuel I (cat. 4.11), still conserved in the Palazzo Reale collections (inv. 1966, nos. 5206-5246), which Garzoni modelled on the examples of late Mannerist artists active at court, such as Giacomo Vighi, called L'Argenta, and the Flemish artist Jan Kraeck.[8] During the period in Turin, Garzoni must have developed the art of nature studies, being in a position to take advantage of the lively cultural climate animated by the masters of the Lombard school, such as Fede Galizia and Panfilo Nuvolone, and Nordic ones, such as Lodewijck Susi, Isaak Soreau and Peter Benoit.[9] In 1637, due to the death of Victor Amadeus of Savoy, the artist left the capital of the Duchy, inaugurating a series of visits North of the Alps: it appears that in 1638 she went to England, perhaps again in the company of Artemisia,[10] attracted by the contemporary portraiture work of John Hoskins; a letter dating from the start of the 1640s instead attests to her presence in Paris,[11] where she was active for Cardinal Richelieu and the highest dignitaries of the court of Louis XIII of France.

Following the transalpine interlude, Garzoni, by now a successful artist thanks to her personal style, unique in the panorama of seventeenth-century Europe, she returned to Rome, to then be newly summoned to Florence, in 1642, in the service of the court of the Grand Dukes of Tuscany. During this second stay in Florence, the artist was not only able to deepen her knowledge of Jacopo Ligozzi's scientific illustrations, but also to gain direct access to the Medici collections, composed of *naturalia et mirabilia* from every corner of the world.[12] Various members of the family were among Garzoni's main clients and admirers of her work, starting with the Grand Duke Ferdinando II and his wife Vittoria Della Rovere, with whom a deep bond of artistic and cultural understanding arose.[13] Proof of this are many miniatures left to the Grand Duchess as a gift, including the faithful *Lapdog* (cat. 4.12) and the *Glass Vase with Flowers* (cat. 4.13), as well as other parchments probably meant for the decoration of handheld fans (cats. 4.15–16) and the series of twenty plates of fruit, made before 1662 on commission by Ferdinando II himself.[14] Only in recent times it has been possible to trace a further nucleus of miniatures to a private collection, which in terms of size and subject are linked to the well-known series created for the Grand Duke (cats. 4.14, 4.17-18). Such compositions, which stand out for their skilful drawing, soft and appealing colours, and highly refined technique, were executed partly in Florence and partly in Rome, where the artist settled permanently in 1651. In this year, Garzoni forged relations with the Accademia di San Luca, making regular donations to the institution from 1654; however, as was the fate of all the women of her time, she was probably never admitted to the meetings and the lectures held there.[15] Still, despite these prohibitions, she must have been esteemed within the institution, since Carlo Maratti himself, elected *principe* for the first time in 1654, dedicated an evocative portrait to her in old age (cat. 4.20). Garzoni died in Rome, at that point ailing and almost completely blind, between the 10 and the 15 February 1670. She was buried in the church of Santi Luca e Martina where, respecting her last wishes, the Academy had a funerary monument erected, not completed until 1698. In her will, dating from 1666, the artist had arranged for all her possessions to be donated to the Accademia di San Luca, including the precious *Libro di miniature e disegni*,[16] which holds only a few of the masterful expressions of her life and career.

Matteo Procaccini

[1] The miniaturist's career has enjoyed a varied historiographic tradition, starting with the lengthy mention about her by the Medici biographer Cristofano Bronzini, recently published in Barker 2018a, p. 658, followed by that of Ridolfi 1648, p. 71, and reproposed by Baldinucci 1681–1728, VI, pp. 619–620. Between the eighteenth and nineteenth centuries, see also the medallions dedicated to her by Orlandi 1719, p. 206; Pascoli 1736, pp. 451–452; Lanzi 1823, II, pp. 229–230, and the research on her illustrious correspondence published by Bottari 1754, pp. 342–348 and Baudi di Vesme 1963–1982, II, pp. 516–517, as well as the pioneering studies of Cantalamessa Carboni 1830, pp. 202–204 and Ricci 1834, pp. 293–295.

[2] Tapié 2018, p. 176.

[3] Cosgrove 2020, pp. 30–35 (with previous bibliography).

[4] Between 1622 and 1624 in Venice Garzoni married the portraitist Tiberio Tinelli though she later requested annulment of the marriage due to a vow of celibacy made as a girl to escape the prophecy that she would die in childbirth. See Bottacin 1998, p. 142.

[5] Barker 2018a, pp. 654–659.

[6] Barker 2020, pp. 16–18, 22–23.

[7] Casale 1991, p. 21.

[8] Failla, in *La reggia* 2007, II, pp. 41–43, cats. 2.26–2.29; Panero, in *Le meraviglie* 2016, pp. 36–37, cat. 21 (with previous bibliography).

[9] In this regard, see *Mostra* 1963, p. 47 and Casale 1991, pp. 17–20.

[10] Barker 2020, p. 22; Hogan, in *La grandezza* 2020, p. 133, cat. 7.

[11] Fumagalli 2000, p. 11.

[12] Morena 2020, pp. 88–95. On the *Stanza dell'Aurora*, an example of a Medici *Wunderkammer* set up in the villa of Poggio Imperiale, see Focarile 2020, pp. 106–115.

[13] Fumagalli 2020.

[14] Barker, in *La grandezza* 2020, pp. 196–211, cats. 41-60 (with previous bibliography).

[15] Lukehart 2020.

[16] Cipriani 1976; Policicchio 2018.

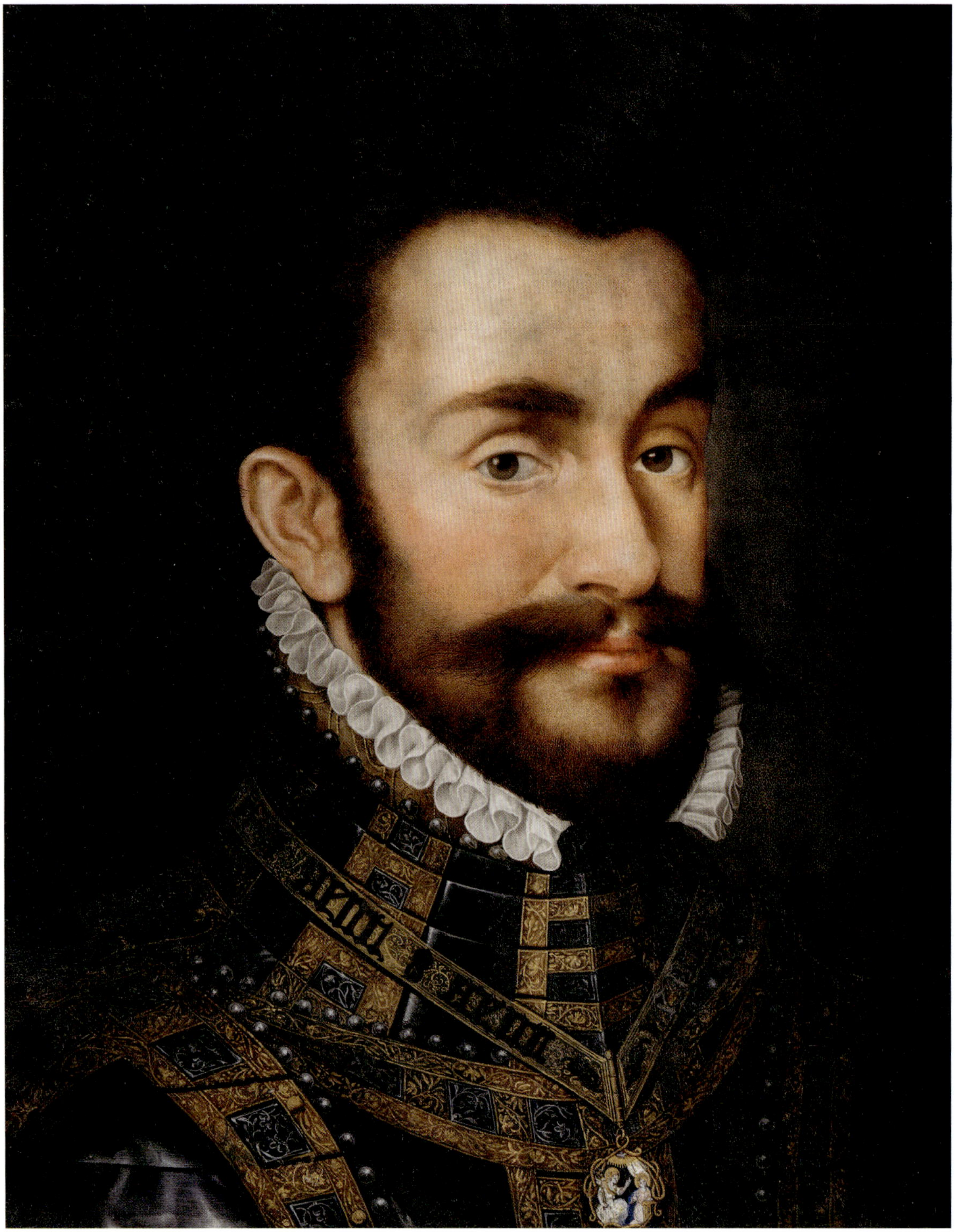

4.10
Giovanna Garzoni
Emmanuel Philibert of Savoy
c. 1632–1637
Tempera on parchment,
425 × 330 mm
Turin, Musei Reali – Palazzo
Reale, inv. 1966, no. 5206

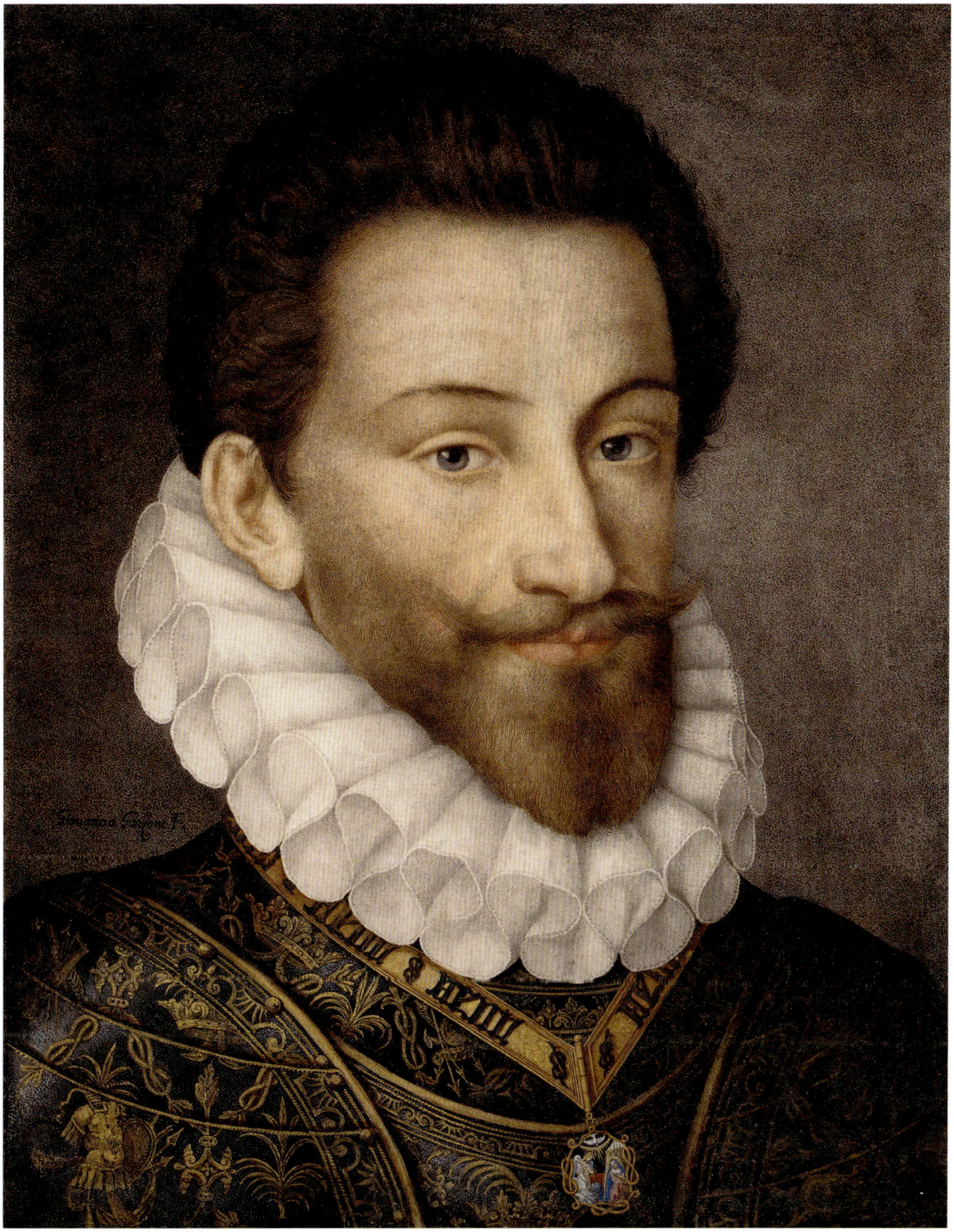

4.11
Giovanna Garzoni
Charles Emmanuel I of Savoy
c. 1632–1637
Tempera on parchment,
430 × 330 mm
Turin, Musei Reali – Palazzo
Reale, inv. 1966, no. 5246

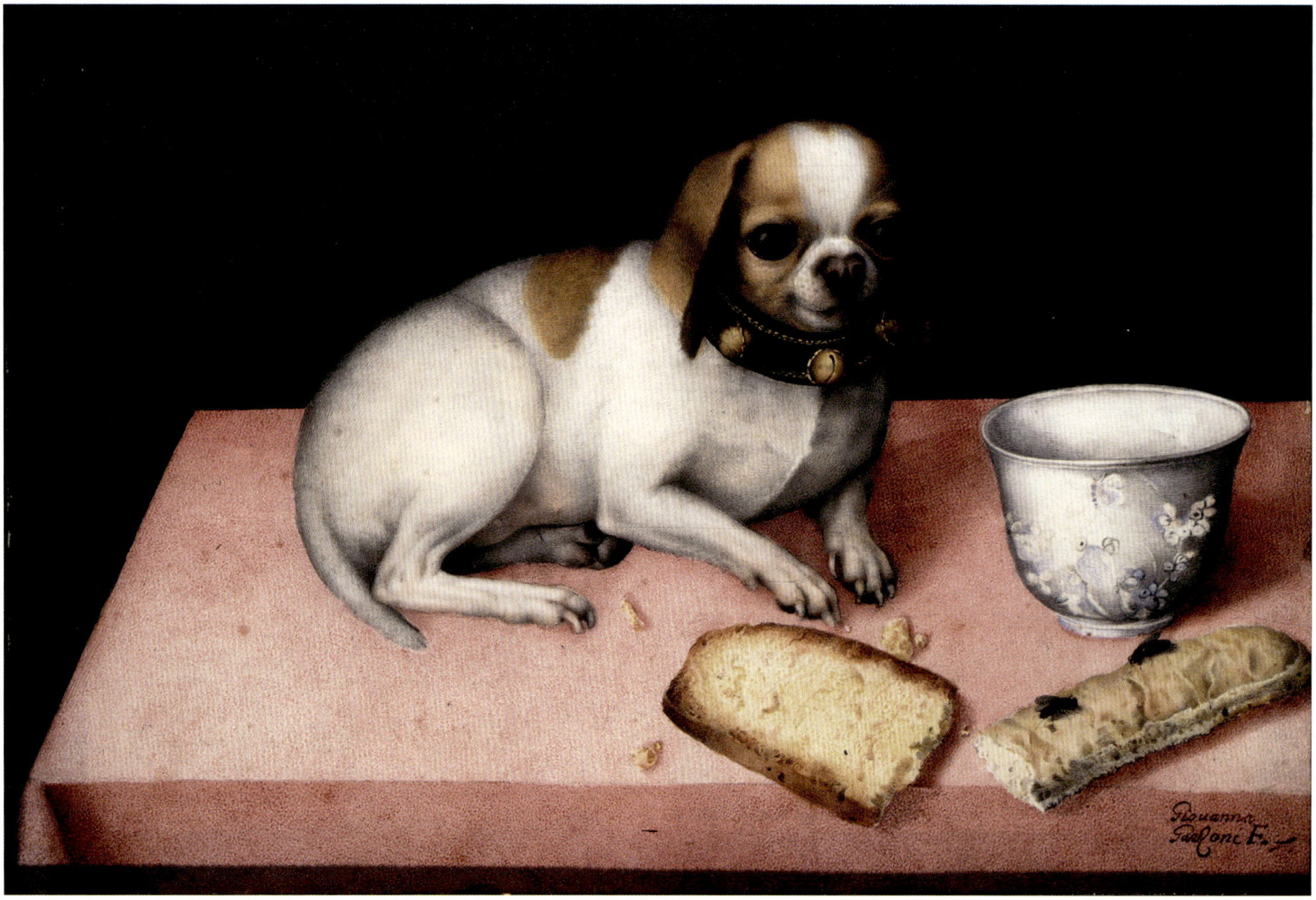

4.12
Giovanna Garzoni
Lapdog with Biscotti and a Chinese Cup
1648
Tempera on parchment, 275 × 395 mm
Florence, Gallerie degli Uffizi, inv. Pal. 4770

4.13
Giovanna Garzoni
Glass Vase with Flowers
1648
Tempera on parchment, 330 × 230 mm
Private collection, inv. 650

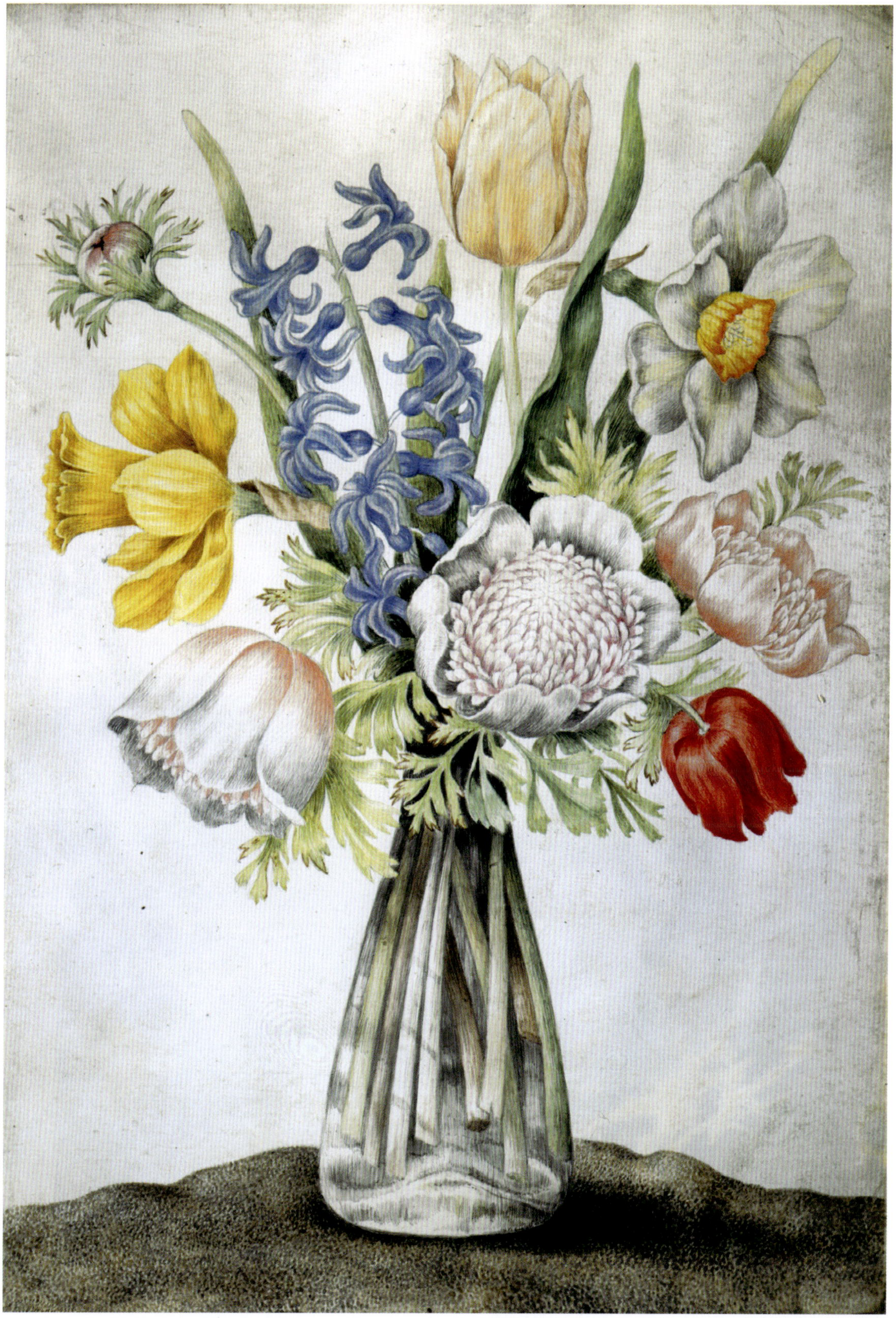

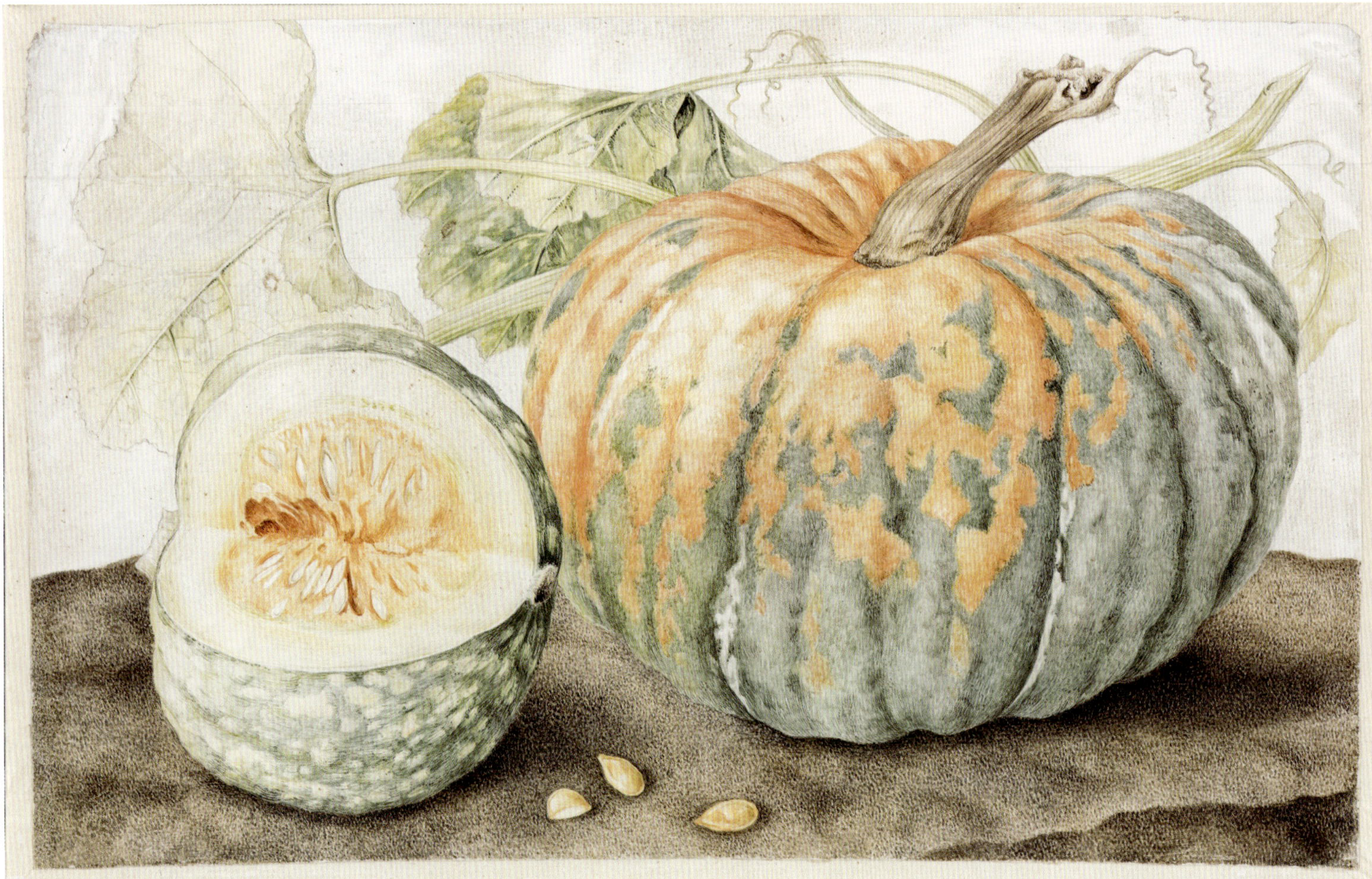

4.14
Giovanna Garzoni
Still Life with Squash
c. 1650
Tempera on parchment,
222 × 343 mm
Private collection, inv. 488

4.15
Giovanna Garzoni
Figs with a Beetle
c. 1650
Tempera on parchment,
152 × 184 mm
Private collection, inv. 957

4.16
Giovanna Garzoni
Quince with a Lizard
c. 1650
Tempera on parchment,
154 × 187 mm
Private collection, inv. 956

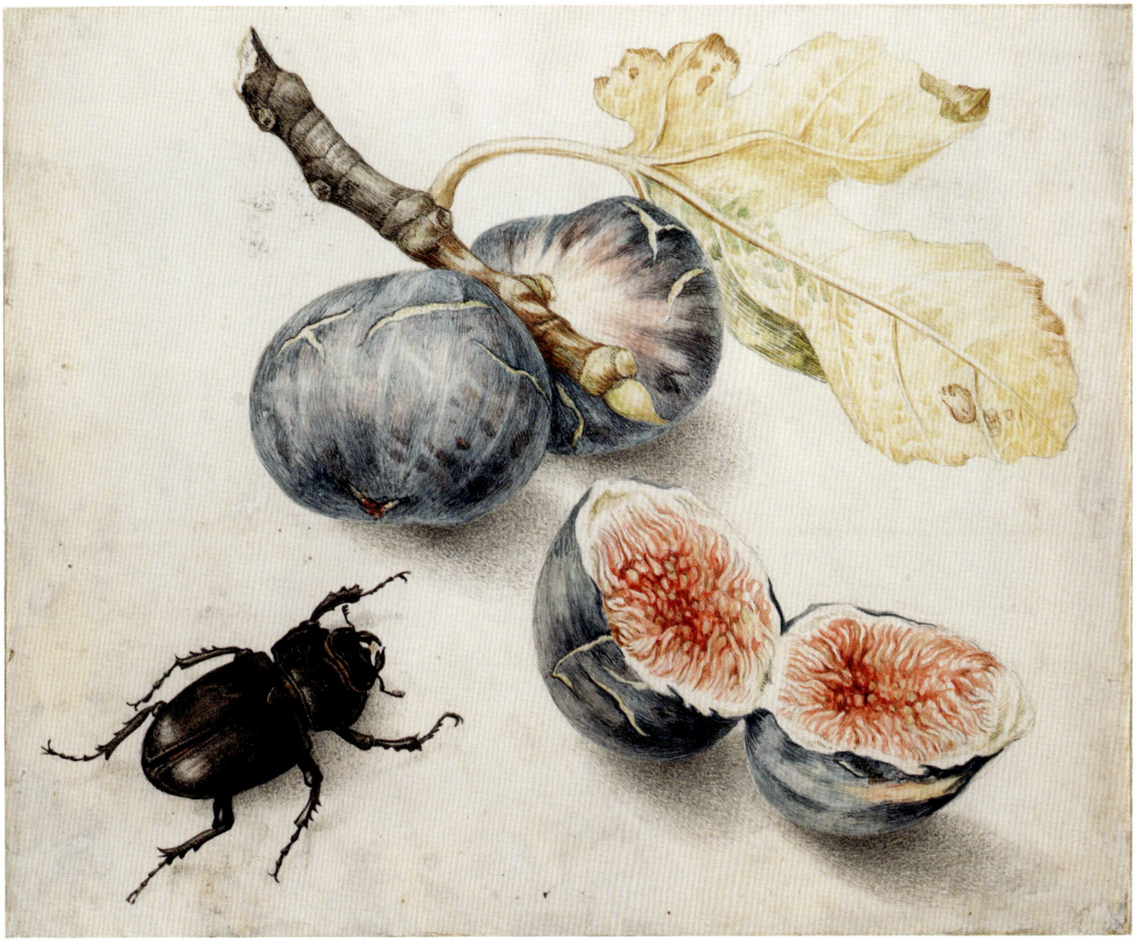

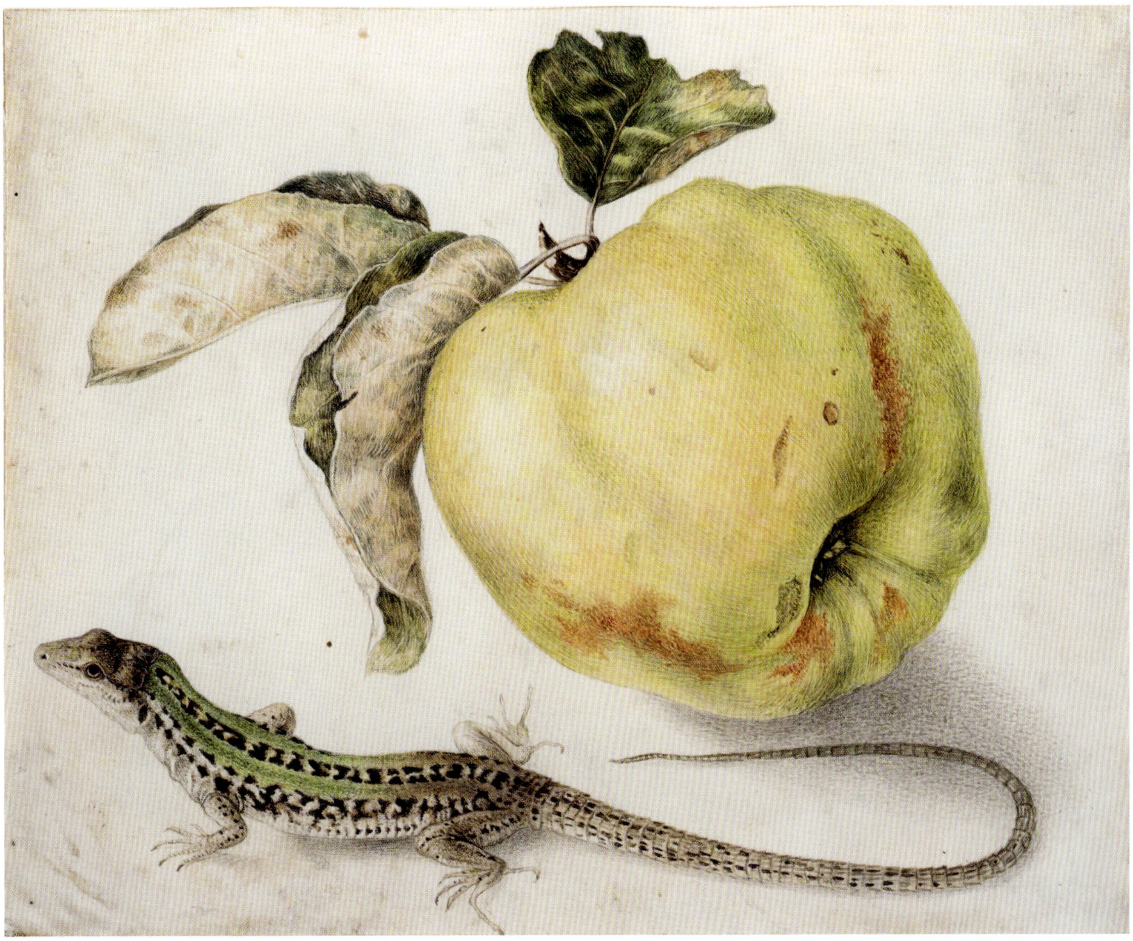

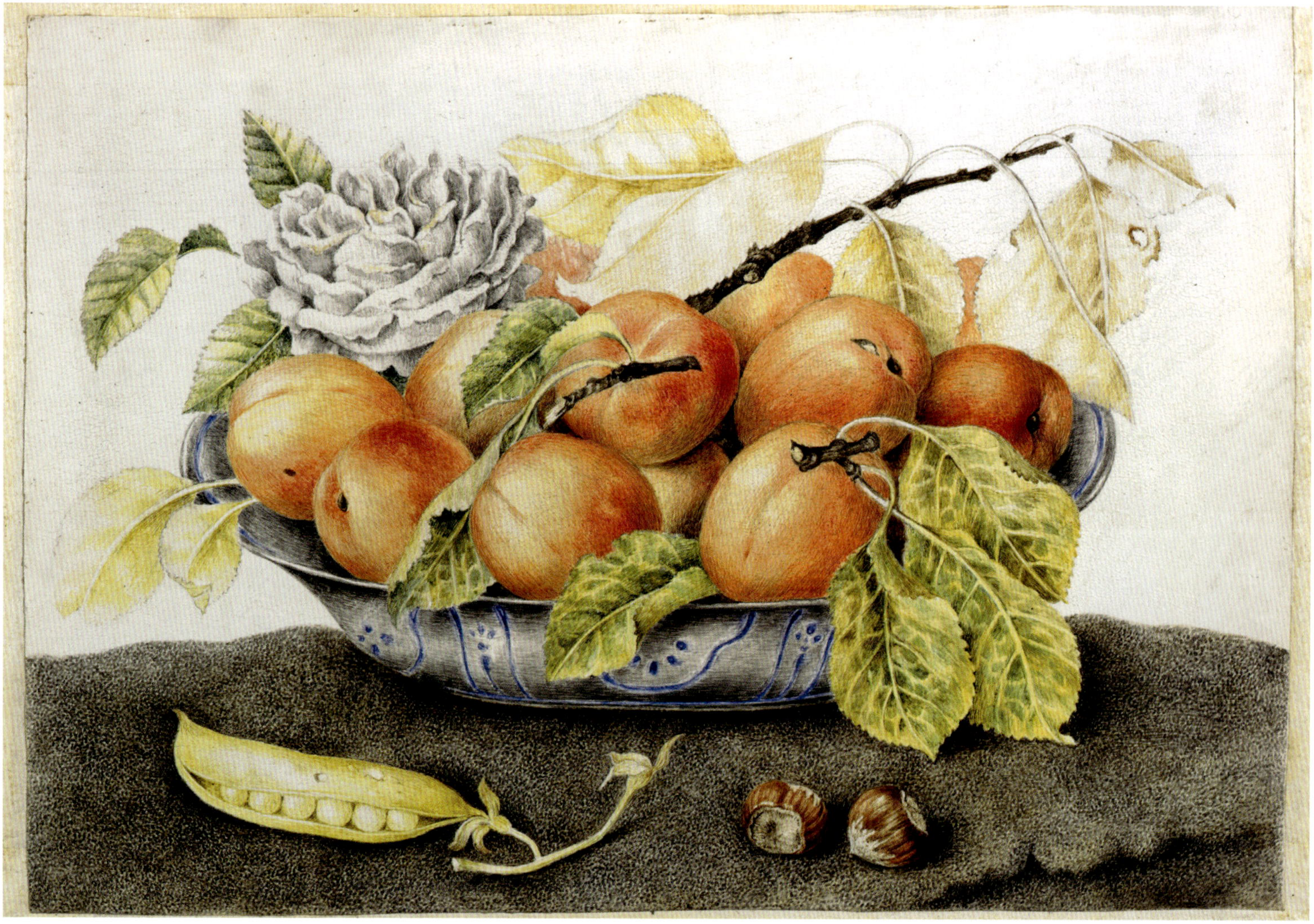

4.17
Giovanna Garzoni
Plate of Apricots with a Rose
c. 1655–1662
Tempera on parchment,
260 × 365 mm
Private collection, inv. 516

4.18
Giovanna Garzoni
Still Life with Lemons
c. 1655–1662
Tempera on parchment,
225 × 335 mm
Private collection, inv. 550

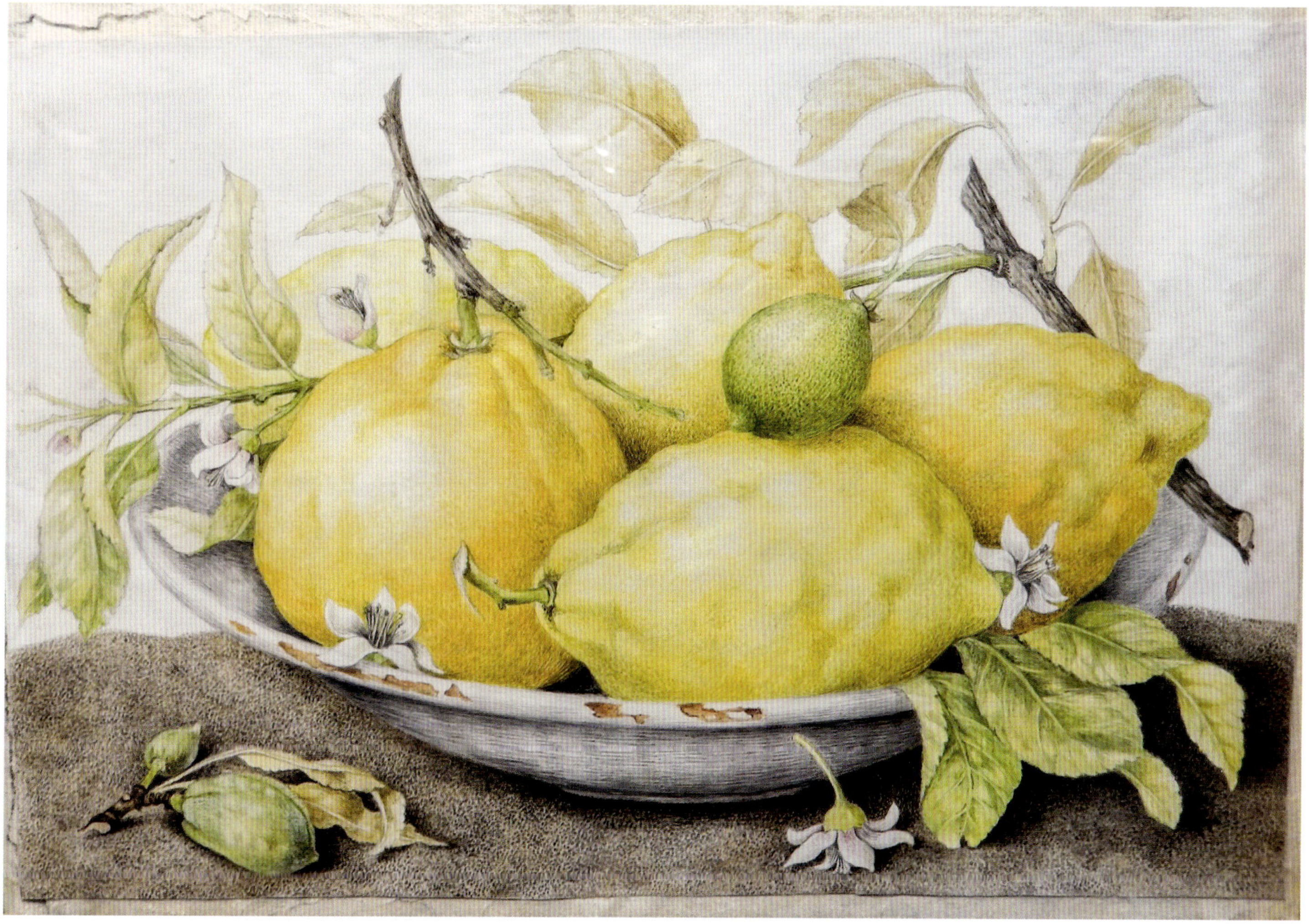

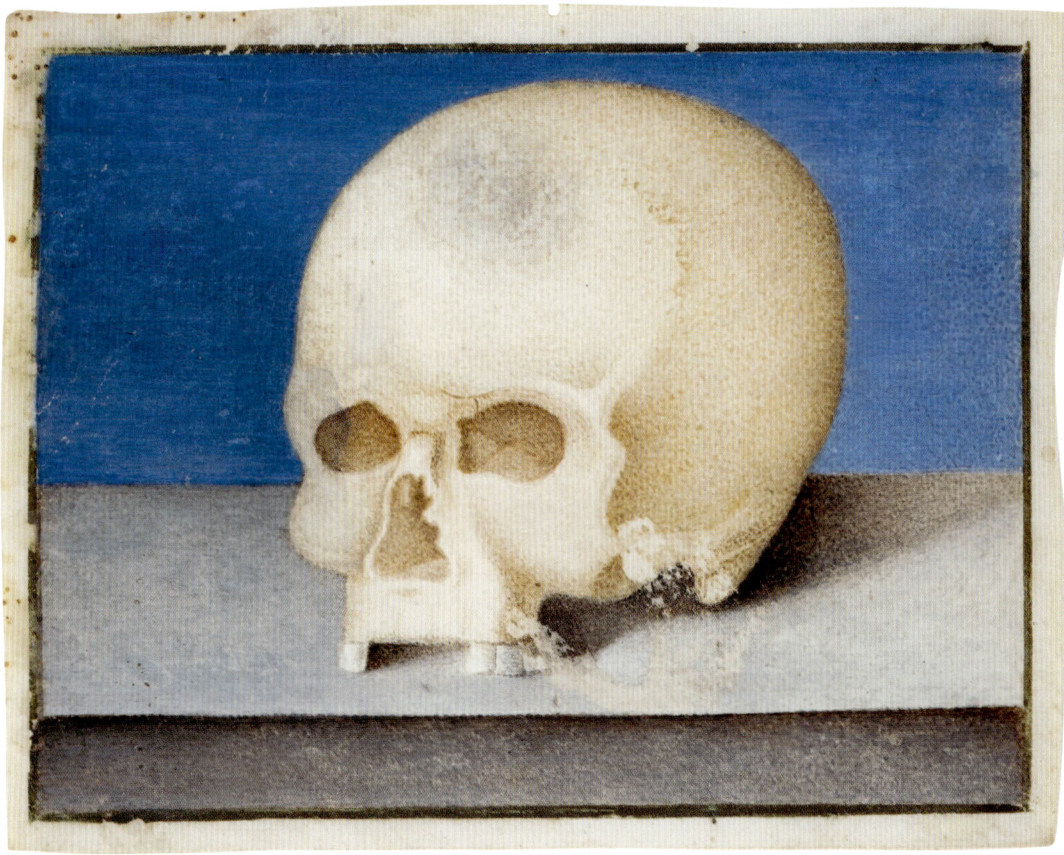

4.19
Giovanna Garzoni (attributed)
Memento mori
c. 1665–1670
Tempera on parchment, 110 × 135 mm
Ascoli Piceno, Pinacoteca Civica, inv. 121

4.20
Carlo Maratti
Portrait of Giovanna Garzoni
c. 1665
Oil on canvas, 64 × 49 cm
Ascoli Piceno, Pinacoteca Civica, inv. 364

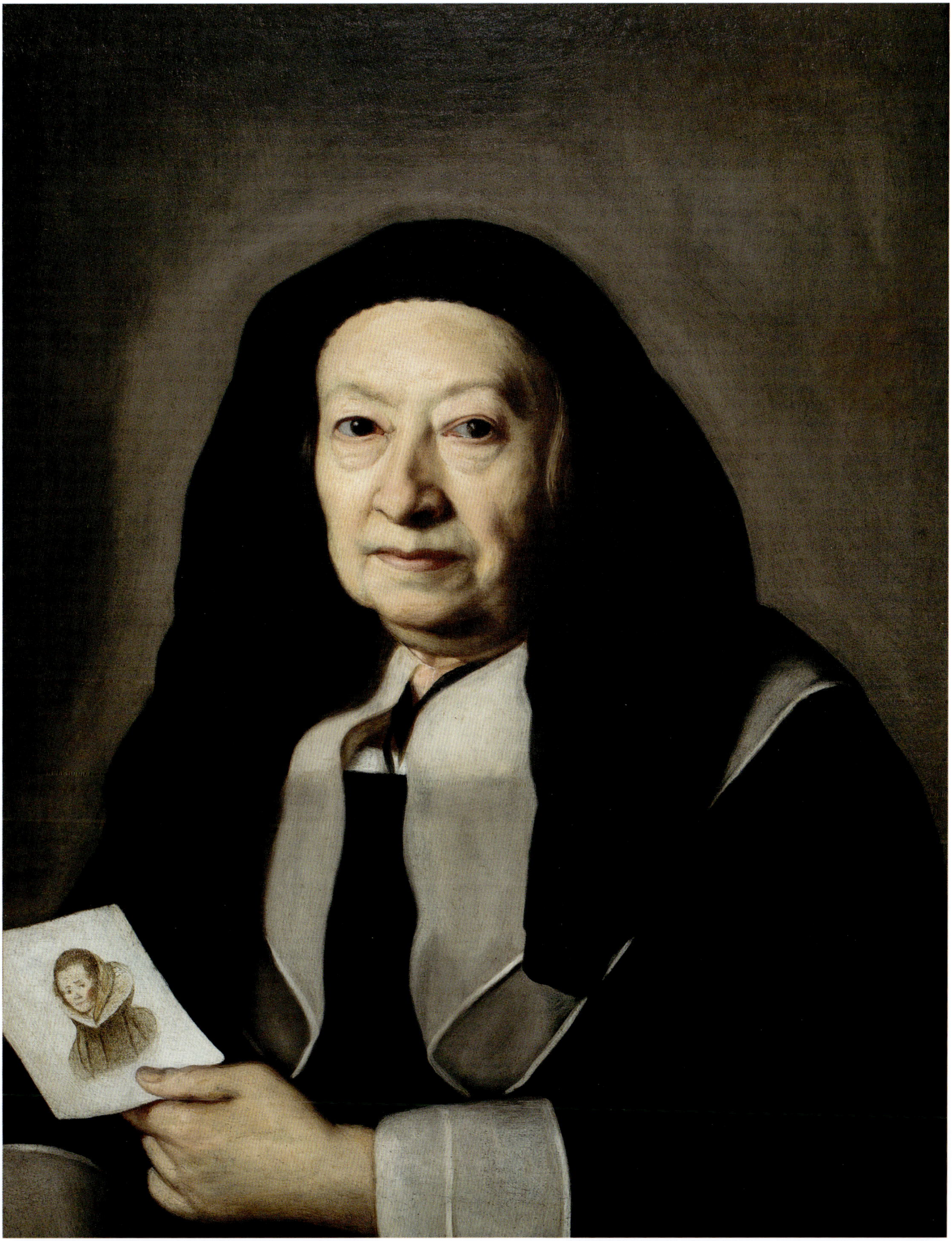

VIRGINIA VEZZI

Velletri (Rome), 1600 – Paris, 1638

Virginia Vezzi (or Da Vezzo or Del Vezzo) was born in Velletri on 24 June 1600 to Pompeo Vezzi, a large landowner of Velletri and Plinia Ferri, a midwife.[1] From 1611 she lived in Rome near the church of San Nicola in Archione.[2] The sources report that Virginia showed promise as a painter at an early age, and her father decided to move to Rome to allow the child to study. In her early years in Velletri, Virginia probably came into contact with the *maestro* Antonio Vezzi, perhaps a relative of Pompeo.[3] When she was in Rome, it is quite possible that she frequented Marco Tullio Montagna, a painter of Velletri who arrived in Rome before 1616, the Cavalier d'Arpino, Gaspare Celio, and Lanfranco, all of whom at the time had busy and well-organised workshops that also trained women.

It can be assumed that the Vezzi family had residence in the area of San Nicola in Arcione from 1611 to 1622, while from 1622 to 1626 documents show they were in Via Ferratina (Via Frattina), near San Lorenzo in Lucina, where from 1623 to 1627 Simon Vouet also lived.[4]

When Vouet arrived in Via Frattina, Virginia was twenty-three years old and probably knew how to wield a paintbrush rather well, if that same year the painter fell in love with her "seeing her beautiful works and her very beautiful self".[5]

From 1623 Virginia attended the workshop of her future husband to improve her technique, as reported by various people, first among whom Cassiano dal Pozzo, who calls her a disciple of Vouet.[6]

In 1624, Vezzi was admitted to the Accademia di San Luca and was therefore unanimously recognised as a painter. The presentation tableau for acceptance at the academy may be the only work attributed to her with certainty, a *Judith* conserved at the Nantes Musée des Beaux-Arts that displays the maturity and talent of the artist.[7] That same year, Vouet was elected *principe* of the Accademia di San Luca.[8]

In 1626 Simon Vouet and Virginia were married in San Lorenzo in Lucina, the parish where they resided and the church around which French painters in Rome gravitated.[9]

Vouet made the decorations for the Aleleoni chapel in the same church,[10] and it seems likely that his future wife helped him, especially in the execution of the figures of the angels.

In 1626, a book of poems by the poet Marcello Giovannetti, a friend of the couple, was published in Rome, including a sonnet dedicated to the *Danae* painting by Virginia, perhaps traceable to the work in the Blanton Museum of Art in Austin, in which the poet recognises the painter's talent.[11]

During these years, the couple met and frequented the leading painters and scholars in Rome, until 1627 when Vouet was forced by King Louis XIII to leave Rome and the Accademia di San Luca and return to Paris.[12]

Simon organised a workshop in Paris capable of satisfying all the demands of the king, Maria de' Medici, and Cardinal Richelieu, and his wife worked alongside him as a model, painter, and drawing instructor.

Virginia died prematurely in Paris on 17 October 1638.

Sara Bruno

[1] Archivio Storico Diocesano di Velletri, Register of Baptisms, cathedral of San Clemente, years 1592–1604, fol. 88*r*.

[2] Archivio Storico Diocesano di Roma (henceforth ASDR), San Giovanni in Laterano, Confirmation Register, year 1611, fol. 81*r*.

[3] Tersenghi 1926, p. 59.

[4] ASDR, San Lorenzo in Lucina, *Status animarum*, years 1622 fol. 15*v*, 1623 fol. 18*r*, 1624 fol. 19*r*, 1625 fol. 17*v*.

[5] Magni 1875, p. 111.

[6] Anselmi 2004, p. 267.

[7] Michel 1992, p. 127.

[8] Lafranconi 2000, pp. 211–216.

[9] ASDR, San Lorenzo in Lucina, Register of Marriages, 1607–1641, fol. 155*r*, 21 April 1626.

[10] Marini 1974.

[11] Crelly 1992, pp. 177–180.

[12] Bousquet 1952, p. 299.

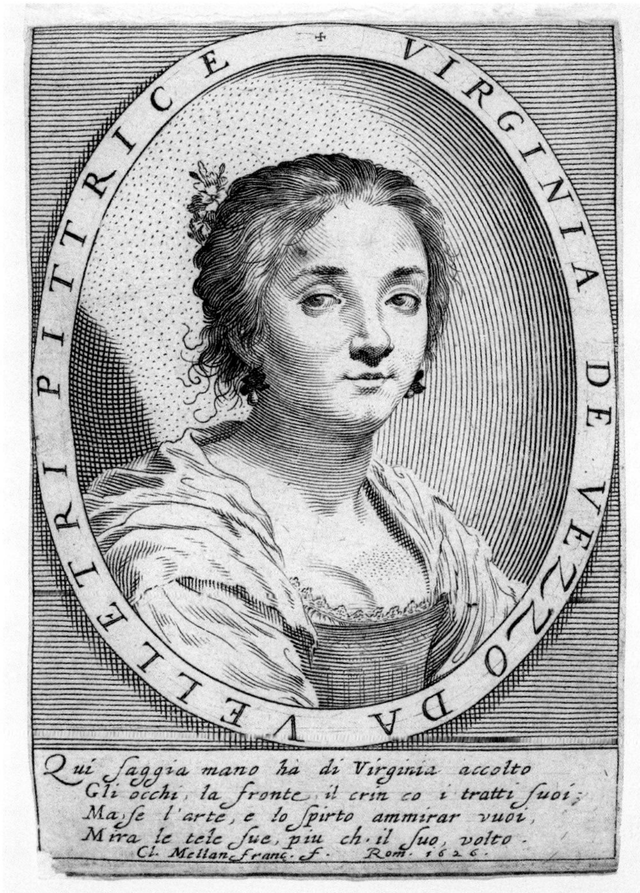

4.21
Claude Mellan
Portrait of Virginia Vezzi
1626
Burin, 113 × 78 mm
Rome, Istituto centrale per la grafica, Gabinetto Stampe, inv. FC32049 (property of the Accademia Nazionale dei Lincei)

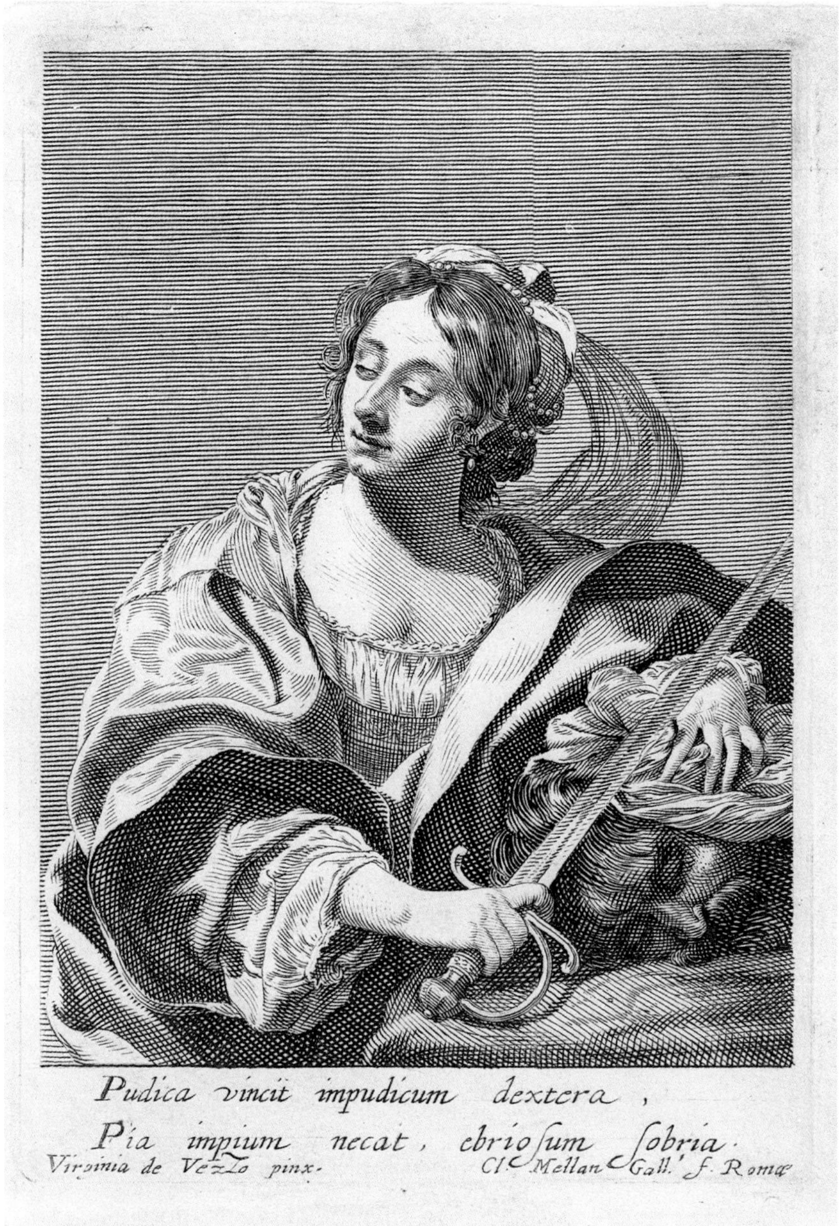

4.22
Claude Mellan
(after Virginia Vezzi)
Judith with the Head of Holofernes
c. 1626
Burin, 163 × 114 mm
Rome, Istituto centrale per la grafica, inv. FC43866 (property of the Accademia Nazionale dei Lincei)

4.23
Simon Vouet
Madonna and Child
(*Madonna of the Basket*)
1625–1626
Oil on panel, 132 × 98 cm
Florence, Gallerie degli Uffizi, inv. 1890, no. 984

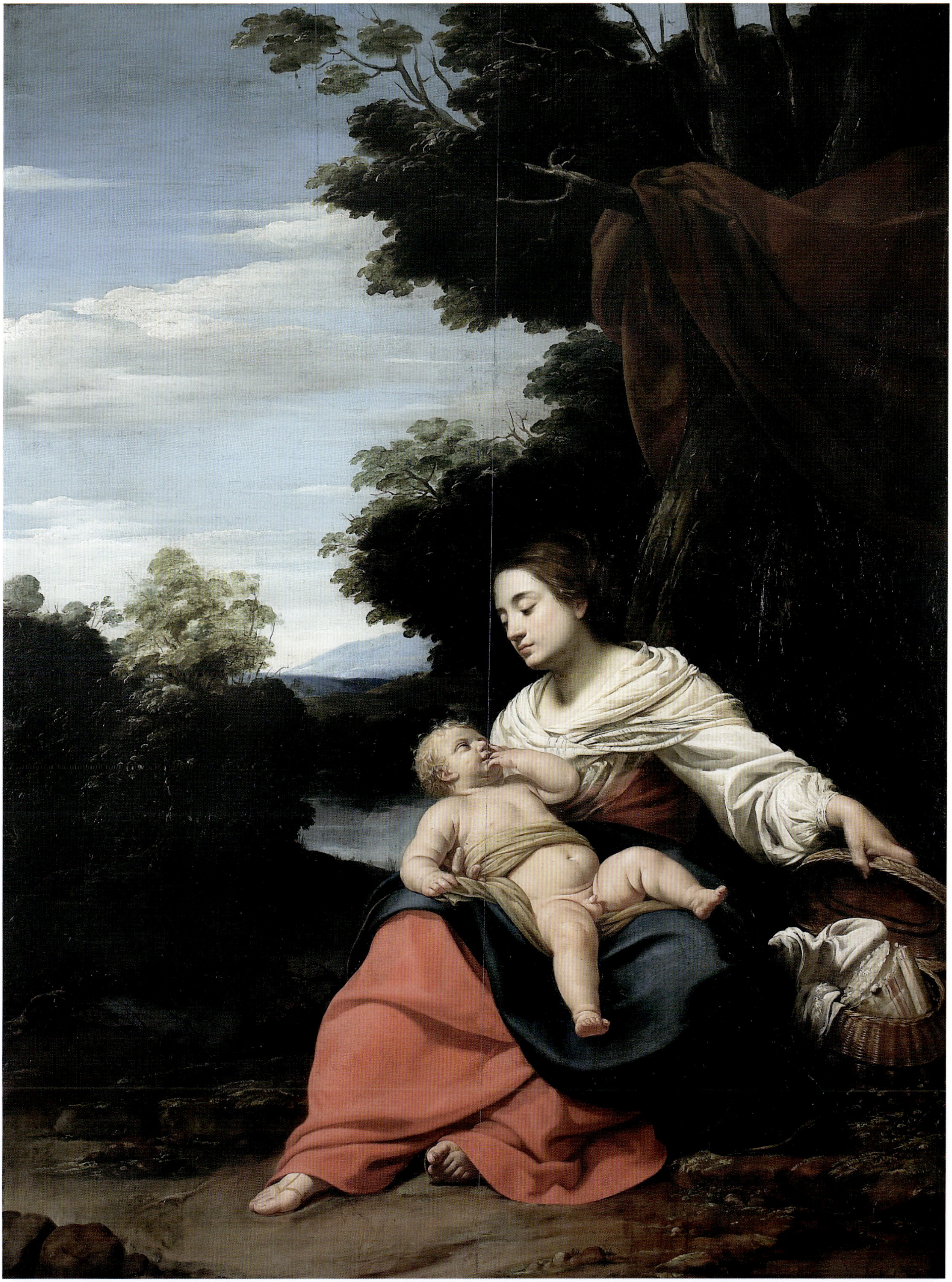

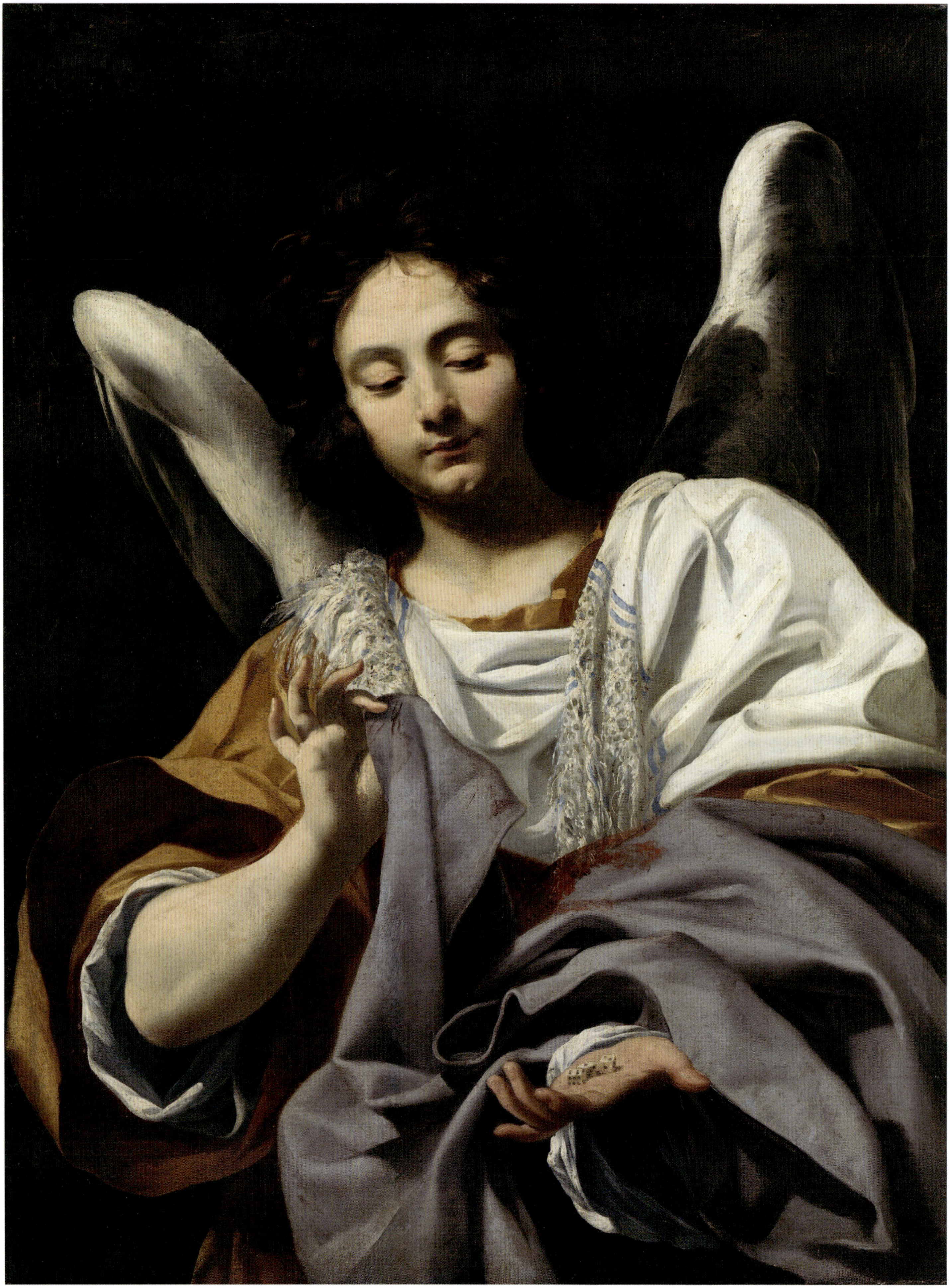

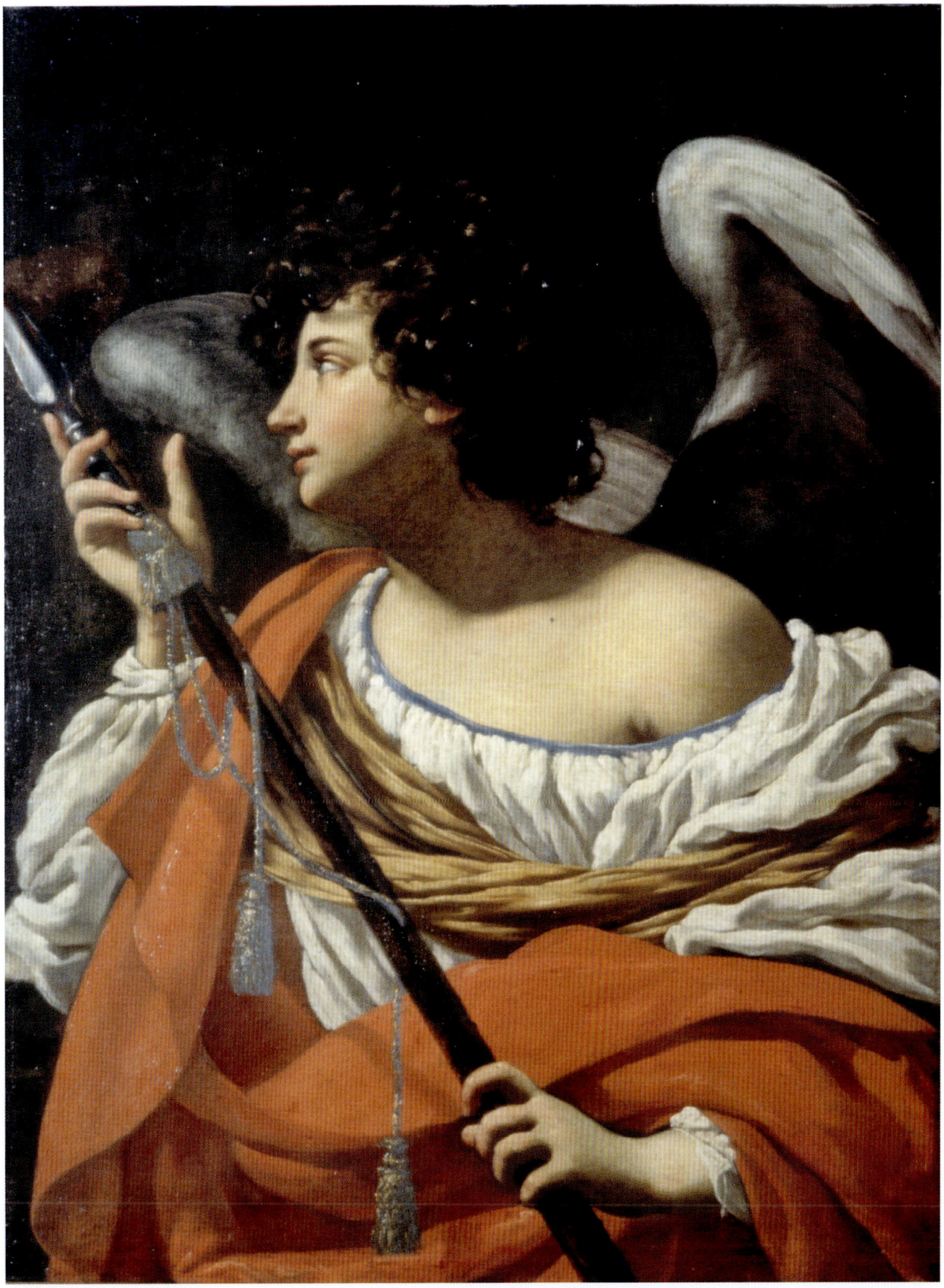

4.24
Simon Vouet
with the collaboration
of Virginia Vezzi
Angel with Tunic and Dice
1627
Oil on canvas, 104 × 77 cm
Naples, Museo e Real Bosco
di Capodimonte, inv. Q1141

4.25
Simon Vouet
Angel with Sponge and Spear
1627
Oil on canvas, 105 × 80 cm
Naples, Museo e Real Bosco
di Capodimonte, inv. Q1142

PLAUTILLA BRICCI

Rome, 1616 – Rome, post 1690

A multi-faceted and very long-lived artist,[1] a talented painter, a member of the Accademia di San Luca, and expert creator of decorative apparatuses and "noteworthy works of art",[2] Plautilla Bricci is the only woman architect of the seventeenth century whose memory has come down to us: it is an exceptional case that occurred thanks to the encounter between a rare artistic talent and a powerful patron prepared to offer constant protection to the one who became, as early as 1655, her "house artist".

Like nearly all her colleagues, Plautilla was born into an artistic family, even if in the Roman workshop of her father, the still undiscovered Giovanni Bricci (1579–1645), who was active in the Cavaliere d'Arpino's entourage, she acquired much more than just the rudiments of drawing and colouring. In fact, in addition to painting shop signs, erudite family crests, and "some oil paintings for altars outside of Rome", Giovanni was also an amateur musician and composer, poet and an eclectic writer. The special artistic and literary education received in the family certainly laid the foundations for Palutilla's creative versatility, although her success on the Roman art scene came only belatedly, and thanks to the decisive meeting with Abbot Elpidio Benedetti and his sister Flavia, another "amateur painter", who were among the first to encourage the artist's talent: Elpidio as a refined and wealthy client, Flavia (alias Sister Maria Eufrasia della Croce) as a "pupil' and a connection with the Carmelite order. Bricci's first public work was the altarpiece in the Roman church of Santa Maria in Montesanto, datable between 1635 and 1640.[3]

The year 1663 marked the start of the construction of her most famous work, Abbot Benedetti's suburban villa outside the southern city gate of Porta San Pancrazio; "built to look like a ship thrown on the rocks"[4] it was unfortunately destroyed in 1849 during the French siege of Rome. In addition to being responsible, together with her brother Basilio, for the highly inventive design, Bricci worked with the elderly Pietro da Cortona, Francesco Allegrini, and Giovan Francesco Grimaldi on the realisation of the painted decoration of the "country house", with the fresco of *Happiness Surrounded by Allegorical Figures* in the gallery and the oil painting of an *Assumption of the Virgin* for the chapel altar.

There followed, in terms of paintings, the large lunette of the Lateran canons, the banner for the church of San Giovanni Battista in Poggio Mirteto (1675), and the *Madonna of the Rosary* for the cathedral in the same Sabine village (1683–1687), which was the birthplace of Elipidio's father, Andrea Benedetti, papal embroiderer.[5] The abbot even commissioned from the artist an entire chapel in the Roman church of San Luigi dei Francesi (1673–1680), the pictorial decoration of which was carried out between 1676 and 1680,[6] the year that Bricci's altar was solemnly inaugurated with a great crowd of people, receiving the admiration of the most "knowledgeable".

Yuri Primarosa

[1] The rediscovery of the figure of Plautilla Bricci has only begun in recent times: Michel 1972, XIV; Primarosa 2012; Primarosa 2014; Lollobrigida 2017a; Primarosa 2018; Mazzucco 2019.
Consuelo Lollobrigida (2017a, p. 133) has placed Bricci's death in December 1705. The death certificate published by the scholar, relating to a certain "Plautilla Sig.ra q[uondam] nihil" residing in Trastevere, in my opinion has little to do with the artist, whose death would have been recorded in the same parish registers accompanied by her surname or an indication of the name of her father. The last documentary trace of Bricci still in life therefore remains the will of Elpidio Benedetti, drawn up in September 1690.

[2] Benedetti 1677, pp. 5, 62.

[3] Primarosa 2018, pp. 42–44.

[4] Roisecco 1750, I, p. 156. About the villa, see Benocci 2007.

[5] Primarosa 2014.

[6] Primarosa 2018, pp. 56–59.

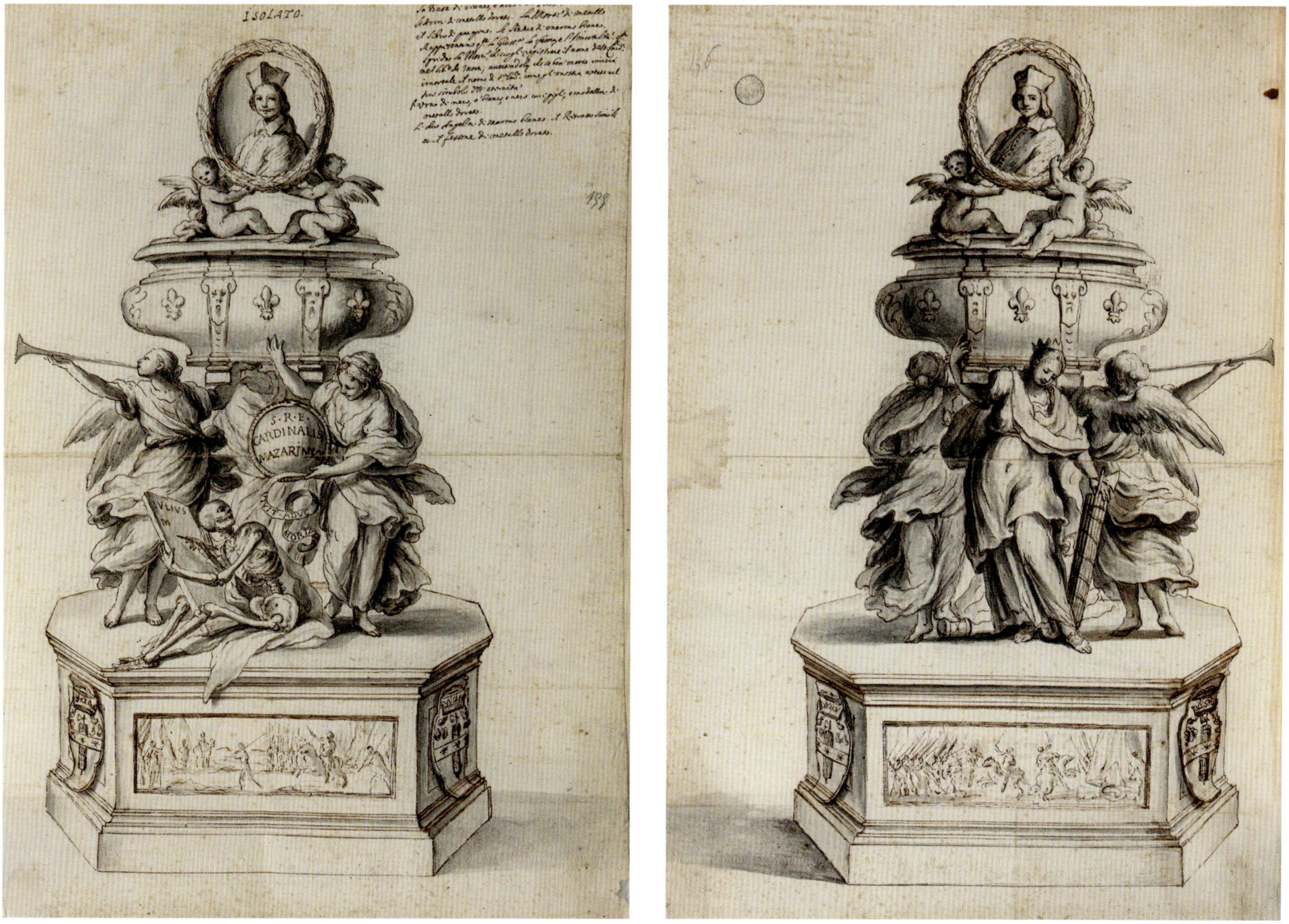

4.26
Plautilla Bricci (execution)
Elpidio Benedetti (concept)
Design of the Funeral Monument of Cardinal Giulio Mazzarino
1657

Pen and brown ink, grey watercolour on light-coloured paper, 512 × 391 mm
Turin, Biblioteca Nazionale Universitaria, *Album Valperga*, q.I.65, nos. 155–156

ARTEMISIA GENTILESCHI "THAT MOST TALENTED OF FEMALE PAINTERS"

In his *Notizie del disegno da Cimabue in qua*, an important work published from 1681 onwards, the Florentine biographer and painter Filippo Baldinucci deems Artemisia Gentileschi to be superior to the other female artists, defining her as the most gifted of all. In the twentieth century, her story as a woman and her artistic talent became emblematic. Due to her tormented unconventional life, Artemisia was a legendary rebel, and as a painter she is very much the poster girl for having an awareness of one's own professional identity.

Raped at the age of eighteen by the painter Agostino Tassi and subjected to torture at the subsequent trial, she reacted with great strength of character, overcoming the portrayal of her as a "disgraced" woman through her marriage to Pierantonio Stiattesi, and engaging in a longstanding affair with the Florentine aristocrat Francesco Maringhi, with whom she was associated for most of her life – conduct that at the time generated a great scandal.

Her biblical heroines, such as Judith, Delilah and Jael – the protagonists of heinous episodes in which men become victims – are embodiments of revolt and vendetta, just as the diminutive David vanquishes the giant Goliath, in a role-reversal in which the strength of the weak comes to the fore. Her historical heroines, like Cleopatra and Lucretia, make their presence felt with a monumental, vibrant corporality in the dramatic moment of suicide – a choice taken in preference to subjugation. Her saints, from Mary Magdalene to Catherine of Alexandria, are women who aspired to salvation, through repentance or knowledge.

Born in Rome in 1593, Artemisia was the daughter of the painter Orazio Lomi Gentileschi, and soon, from the second decade of the seventeenth century on, her art rivalled that of the most well-established painters, and she was sought out by prestigious clients. Blessed with ambition and determination, she spent time with scholars and *literati*, blossoming from an illiterate painter into a member of the academy in Florence, welcomed into the most elite cultural circles in Venice and Naples. Restless and forever in search of success, her painting would take her to London before she settled in Naples, where she set up a dynamic studio with a number of male partners. There is no further trace of her in Naples or elsewhere after August of 1654.

ARTEMISIA LOMI GENTILESCHI

Rome, 1593 – Naples, after August 1654

The daughter of the painter Orazio Lomi Gentileschi and Prudenzia di Ottaviano Montoni, Artemisia lost her mother on 26 December 1605. She certainly trained in her father's workshop, and in a letter of 3 July 1612 to the Grand Duchess of Tuscany he stated that she had reached artistic maturity three years previously. The *Susanna and the Elders* in the Pommersfelden Museum, signed and dated 1610, is considered Artemisia's first work, perhaps produced under her father's supervision. Her early output in Rome included the *Madonna and Child* in the Galleria Spada in Rome and the canvas of the same name in Palazzo Pitti in Florence. *Judith Slaying Holofernes*, held at the Museo di Capodimonte in Naples, is one of the most dramatic interpretations of the Bible story following the trail blazed by Caravaggio. In March 1612, Orazio Gentileschi pressed charges against the painter Agostino Tassi, who had been his partner, accusing him of raping his daughter. It was claimed that the rapes had continued for more than a year, starting in May 1611, with the young woman being taken in by false promises of marriage. Tassi's trial was one of the darkest and most ambiguous sources of the anthropological and juridical literature of the early seventeenth century. Without any doubt, Artemisia's life was forever scarred by the experience. Two days after Tassi was sentenced to exile from Rome, on 29 November 1612 Artemisia married the Florentine Pierantonio Stiattesi in Rome; at the beginning of the next year, the two of them moved to Florence. The marriage, clearly geared towards the social rehabilitation of the bride, produced a son, Giovanni Battista, born on 20 September 1613, followed by another, Cristofano, on 8 November 1615, and then by two daughters: Prudenzia (or Palmira), born on 1 August 1617, and Lisabella, on 13 October 1618 (died on 9 June 1619). On 19 July 1616, Artemisia was admitted to the Accademia del Disegno in Florence, with which she would be associated until 1620, and developed relationships with people such as Galileo Galilei and Michelangelo Buonarroti the Younger, who commissioned from her the *Allegory of Inclination* for the Buonarroti home, paid for in 1616. During this period, she also produced works of clear Tuscan inspiration including the *Saint Cecilia* in the Galleria Spada (Rome); *Judith and her Maidservant* and *Mary Magdalene*, in the Galleria Palatina in Florence (signed); the *Self-Portrait as a Lute Player* in the Wadsworth Atheneum Museum of Art, in Hartford (Connecticut); and *Saint Catherine of Alexandria*, now at the Uffizi in Florence. Also dating from the end of the Florentine period are *Judith Slaying Holofernes*, signed, at the Uffizi, and *Jael and Sisara*, at the Szépművészeti Múzeum in Budapest, a work dated 1620. Having returned to Rome in March 1620 with her husband and daughter, Artemisia produced works such as the *Portrait of a Gonfaloniere* (1622; Bologna, Collezioni Comunali d'Arte) and *Susanna and the Elders* dating from the same year (Stamford, Lincolnshire, Burghley House). Shortly thereafter, her husband Pierantonio Stiattesi disappeared from her life. In 1627–1628 she was in Venice, and while evidence does exist of her success in that city, there are no extant works to validate her reputation. The *Sleeping Venus* at the Piasecka Johnson Foundation in Princeton, which has been seen as a tribute to Titian, may date from this period. From 1630 to around 1638, Artemisia lived in Naples. Dating from shortly before or shortly after her move to the viceregal capital is *Christ Blessing the Children* (Rome, church of San Carlo al Corso, sacristy); moreover, the *Annunciation* in the Museo di Capodimonte is signed and dated 1630. Even before that year, and indeed throughout her life, Artemisia engaged in frequent correspondence with high-profile Italian intellectuals, collectors and power-brokers including Cassiano dal Pozzo, Galileo Galilei, Andrea Cioli, Antonio Ruffo and Francesco I d'Este. The commission for the *Birth of John the Baptist* for a chapel dedicated to the saint in the Buen Retiro Park in Madrid, the decoration of which was co-ordinated by Massimo Stanzione (who produced several paintings), was received at almost the same time as that for *Clio, the Muse of History* (Pisa, Palazzo Blu), signed and dated 1632. This initial stay in Naples also saw the creation of a number of major works, including *Ester before Ahasuerus* (New York, Metropolitan Museum) and *Corisca and the Satyr*, signed (private collection). The other public works produced in Naples were the three paintings for the choir of the cathedral of Pozzuoli, commissioned by Bishop Martín de León y Cárdenas, presumably conceived between 1635 and 1638. The three paintings, of varying quality and states of conservation, depict *Saints Procu-*

lus and Nicea and *Saint Januarius in the Amphitheatre at Pozzuoli* (both today at the Museo di Capodimonte) and the *Adoration of the Magi* (currently in the Museo Nazionale di San Martino in Naples). Even though she constantly declared herself to be dissatisfied by her life and work in Naples, Artemisia remained there until her death, with the exception of a sojourn in England from 1638 to 1640, during which she finished off commissions from King Charles I initially given to her father Orazio (who died in London on 7 February 1639). *The Allegory of Painting*, at Hampton Court Palace in London (perhaps a self-portrait, and perhaps incomplete), is one of the paintings on which she can confidently be said to have worked during this period. The current thinking is that Artemisia may also have completed the pictorial cycle begun by her father at the Queen's House in Greenwich. Having returned to Naples, Artemisia became one of the leading lights of the city's art scene, collaborating with Massimo Stanzione, Bernardo Cavallino, Domenico Gargiulo and other renowned masters; during the years of her physical decline she was assisted by Onofrio Palumbo, with whom she must have worked on the paintings that were most demanding in terms of their format and execution. The years between the first and second Neapolitan phase saw the production of challenging works such as *Lot and his Daughters* (Toledo, Museum of Arts) and *David and Bathsheba* (Columbus, Columbus Museum of Art, Ohio); it is not clear whether the two versions of *Judith and her Maidservant* (Cannes, Musée des Beaux-Arts, and Naples, Museo di Capodimonte) belong to the first Neapolitan period or were in fact produced in her final years; the unimpressive *Susanna and the Elders* in the Moravian Gallery in Brno, signed and dated 1649, and the more accomplished *Susanna and the Elders* in the Pinacoteca Nazionale in Bologna, signed and dated 1652, are amongst the last of her large-scale works. Small-scale works on copper, still produced entirely by the artist and with notable formal input, such as the *Madonna and Child* (El Escorial, Casita del príncipe), signed, and the luminous *Judgement of Paris* in Vienna at Akademie der Bildenden Künste – not by accident long-attributed to Pacecco de Rosa) – can probably be dated to the fifth decade of the seventeenth century. A key figure for female artistic historiography, Artemisia cut a very particular dash from the moment of her entry onto the Roman art scene. Her rape at the hands of Tassi was, in large part, a case of perverse seduction and circumvention onto which were grafted the immorality and venal interest of the man who really raped her – her father Orazio. An experience of the sort would have destroyed just about any woman living in the early seventeenth century, but Artemisia was able to transform her trauma – which she faced up to as an illiterate nineteen-year-old, coping moreover with interrogation under torture – into great success. Artemisia's intellectual and creative development is impressive in every sense. All of the elements of her training can be traced back to her father Orazio, a horrible man but a sublime teacher and shrewd businessman, who did not, however, exert any durable influence over her. Discoveries, some made recently, confirm Artemisia as the author of one of the largest epistolaries in the history of Italian art, and this was despite her aforementioned illiteracy as recorded in the trial documents. A noteworthy aspect of her proclivity for writing letters was that, out of those found thus far, not one was addressed to her father. Artemisia was the sole artifice of her career also in terms of her ability – so crucial for any seventeenth-century artist – to come into contact and ingratiate herself with buyers, clients, protectors and mediators, even having recourse to the mechanisms of flattery and of grumbling about her precarious finances. She was also capable of producing reasonably priced versions – painted by assistants under her supervision – of her most sought-after works. Artemisia's modernity does not lie only in her flexible, chameleon-like ability to meet market demand – a skill that she developed within an aggressive, patriarchal society, marked by the almost total absence of opportunities to climb the social ladder. From her recently rediscovered letters we know that she also succeeded in creating for herself a genuinely passionate love life, into which she threw herself with a quite extraordinary sense of freedom. It was in Francesco Maria Maringhi, a Florentine aristocrat she met during her Tuscan years and forever by her side from then on, that she found a true, lasting love – an island of passion and serenity where she could take shelter from the violent and complicated world in which she had to live and work.

Riccardo Lattuada

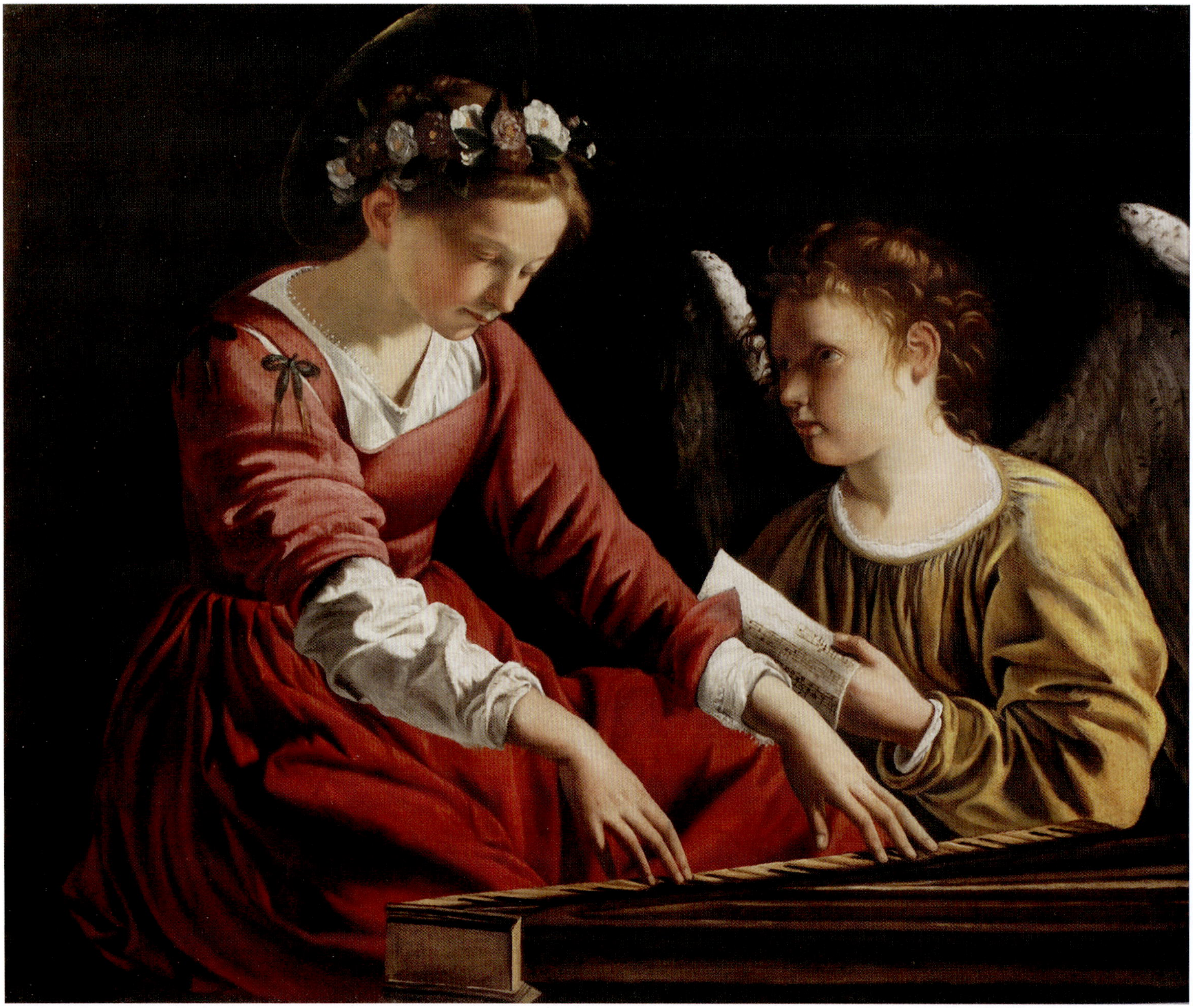

5.1
Orazio Lomi Gentileschi
Saint Cecilia Playing the Spinet
1615–1620
Oil on canvas, 90 × 105 cm
Perugia, Galleria Nazionale dell'Umbria, inv. 1083

5.2
Artemisia Gentileschi (attributed)
Nursing Madonna
1617–1620
Oil on canvas, 123.5 × 86 cm
Private collection

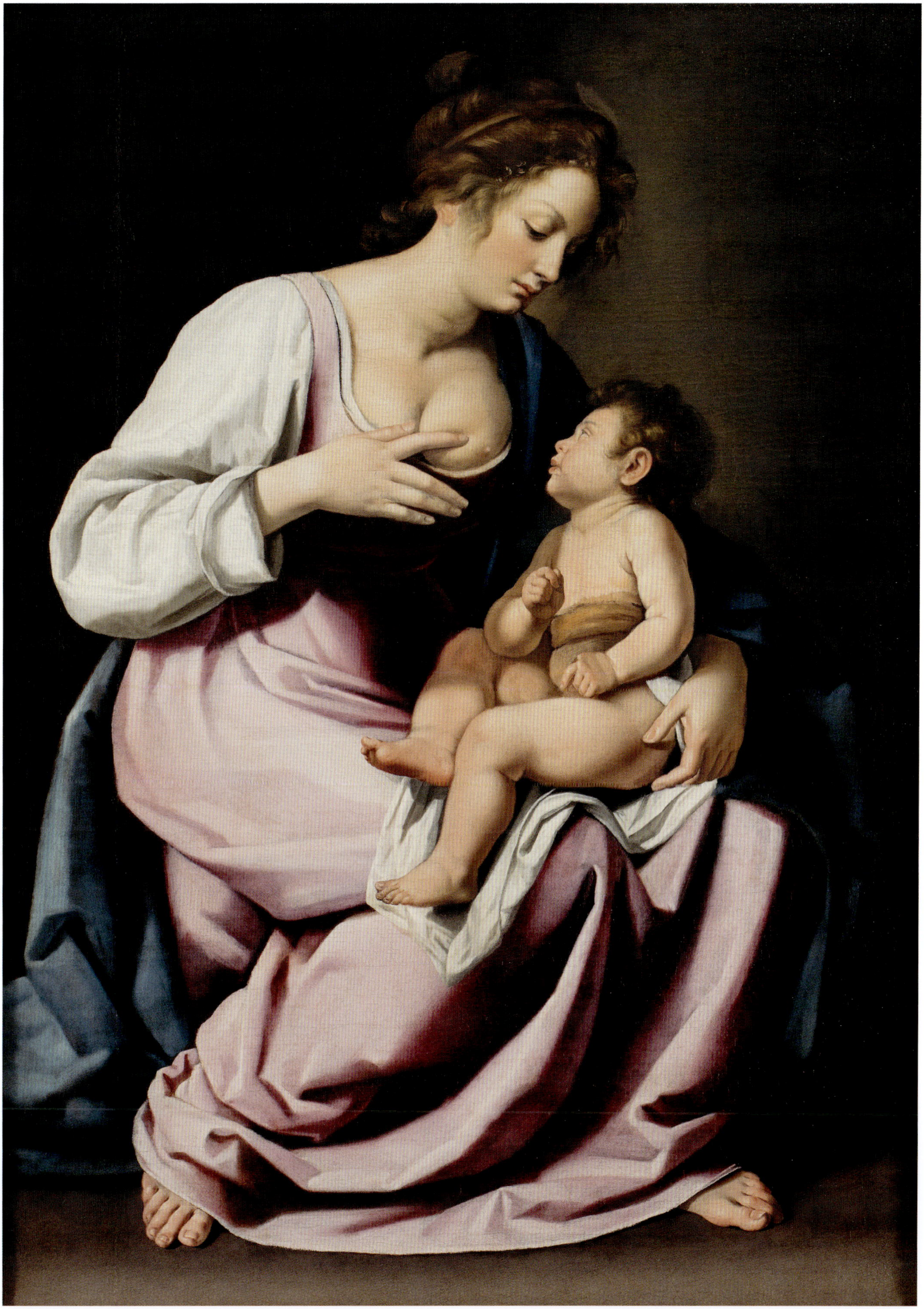

5.3
Artemisia Gentileschi
Cleopatra
c. 1620
Oil on canvas, 97.5 × 71.5 cm
Fondazione Cavallini Sgarbi,
inv. 215

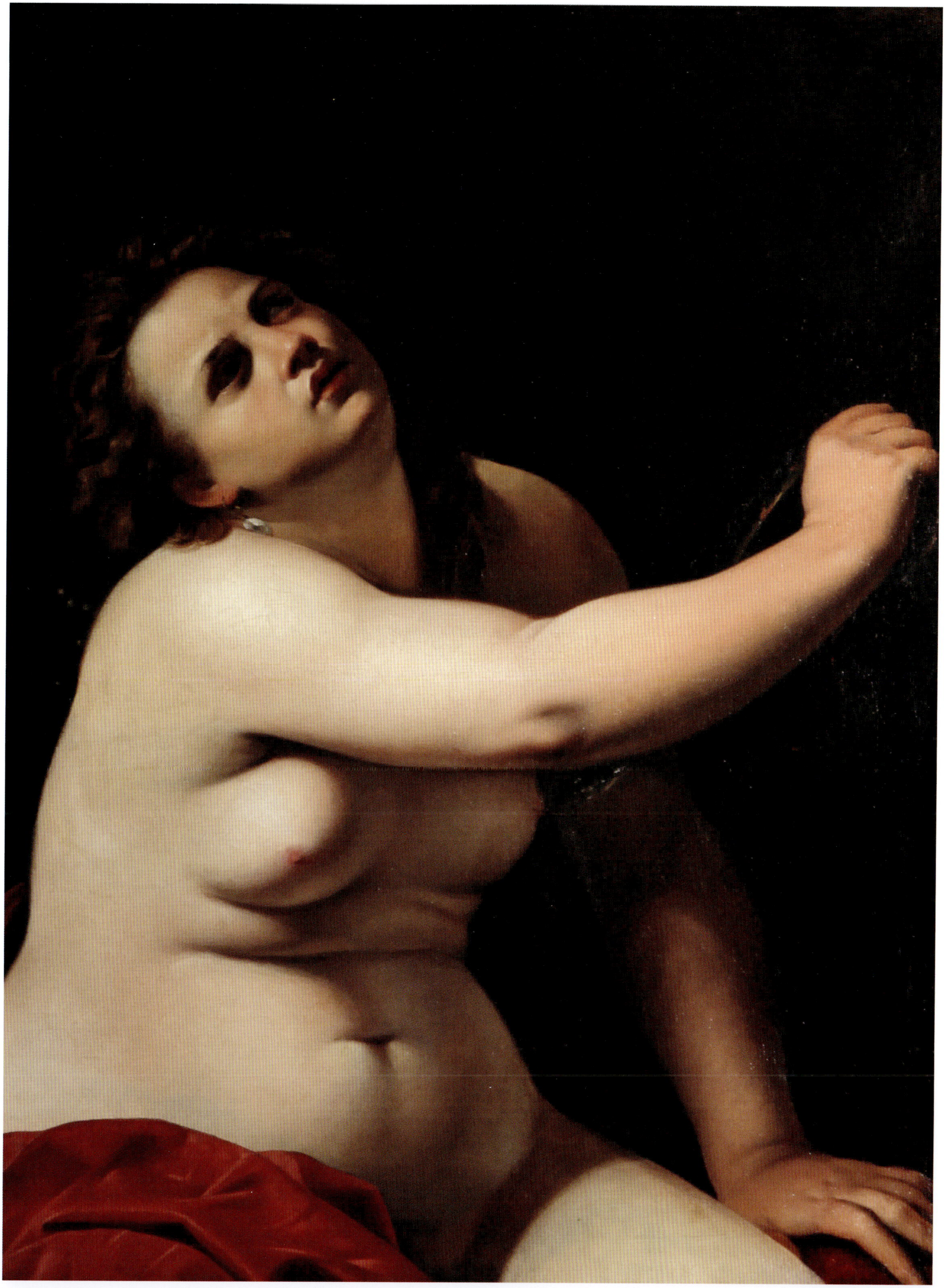

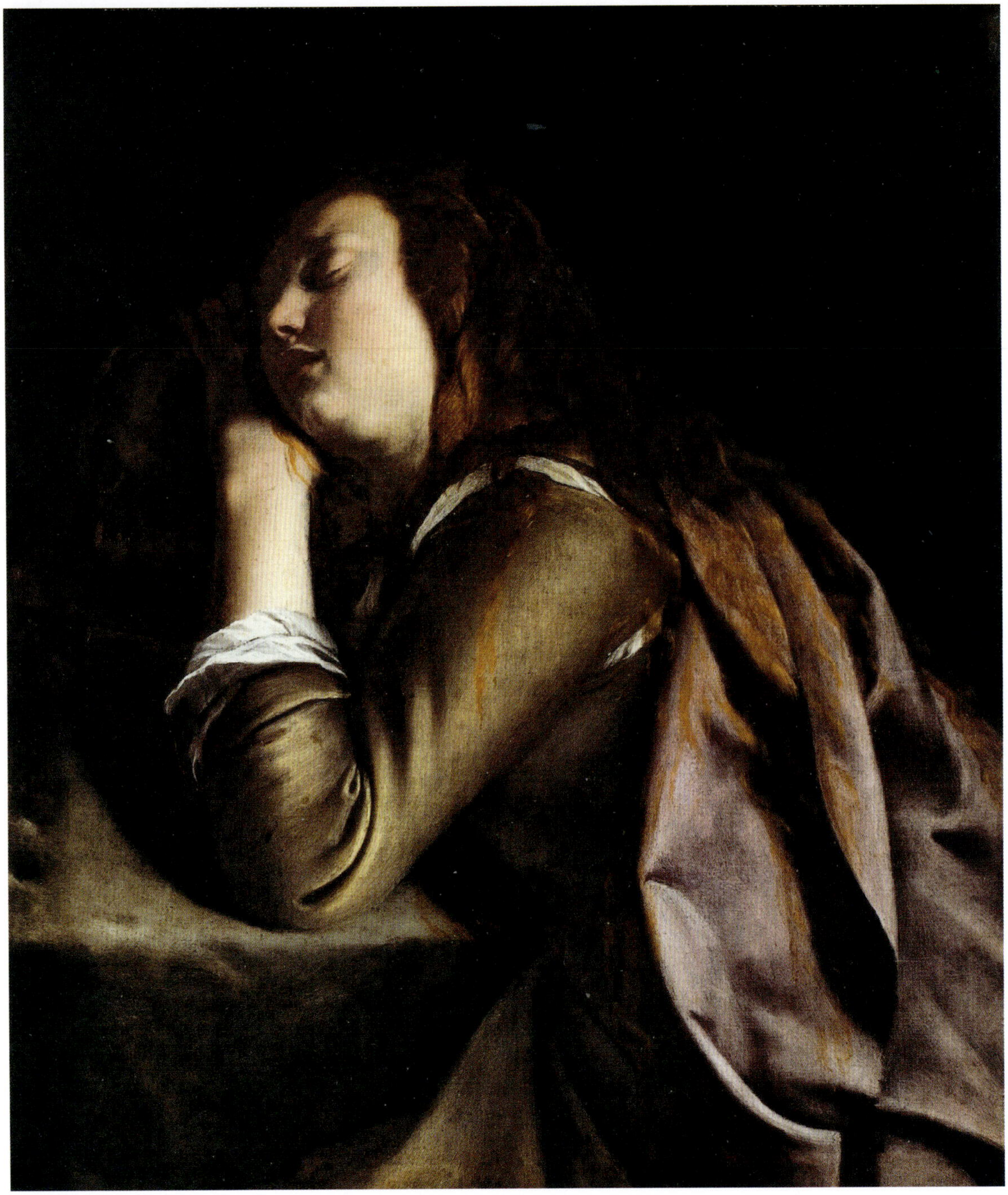

5.4
Artemisia Gentileschi
Mary Magdalene in Meditation
c. 1630–1631
Oil on canvas, 100 × 73 cm
Sorrento (Naples), Museo Correale di Terranova, inv. 2925

5.5
Artemisia Gentileschi
David with the Head of Goliath
1630–1631
Oil on canvas, 203.5 × 152 cm
Private collection

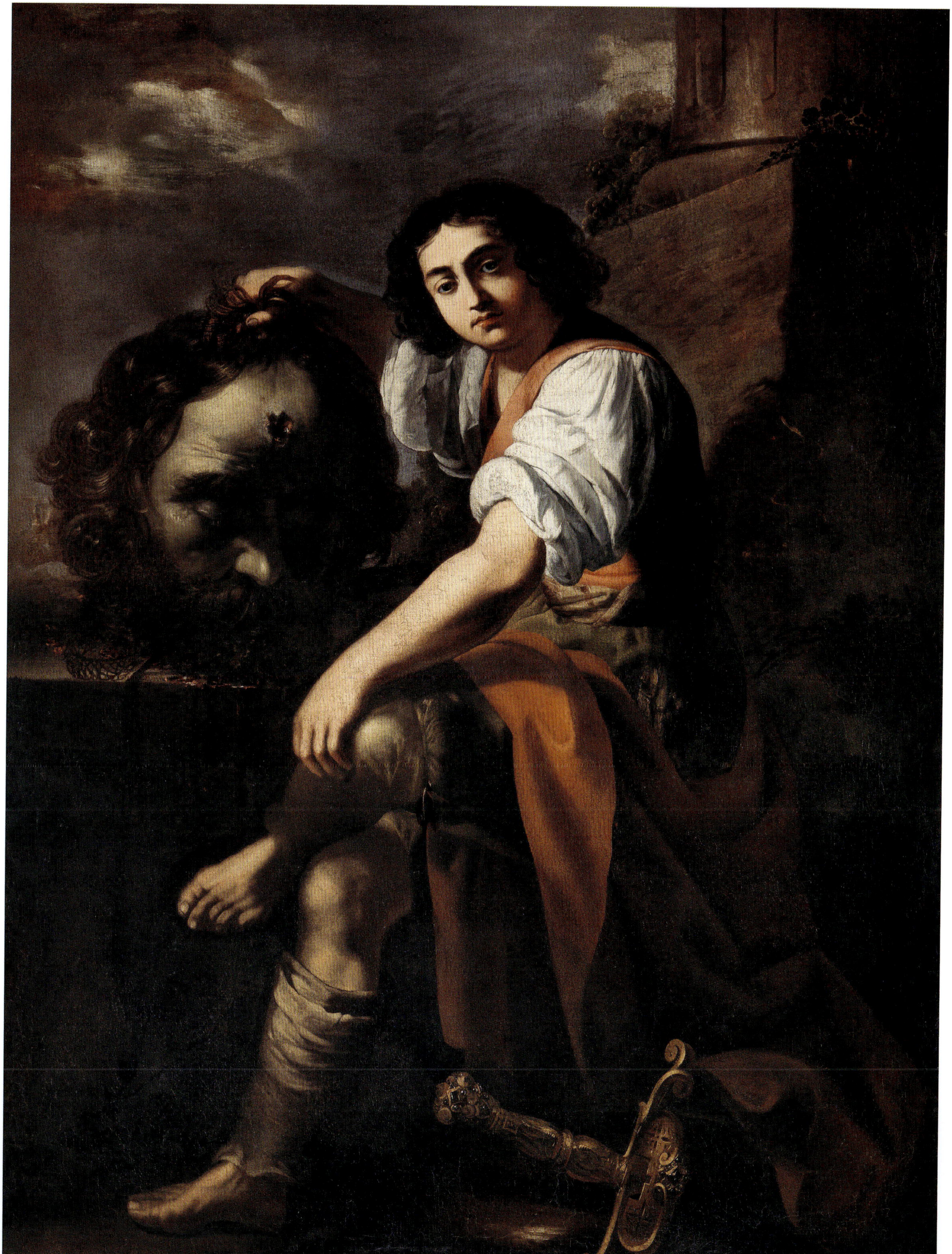

5.6
Artemisia Gentileschi
Mary Magdalene
1630–1631
Oil on canvas, 102 × 118 cm
Beirut, Sursock Palace
Collection

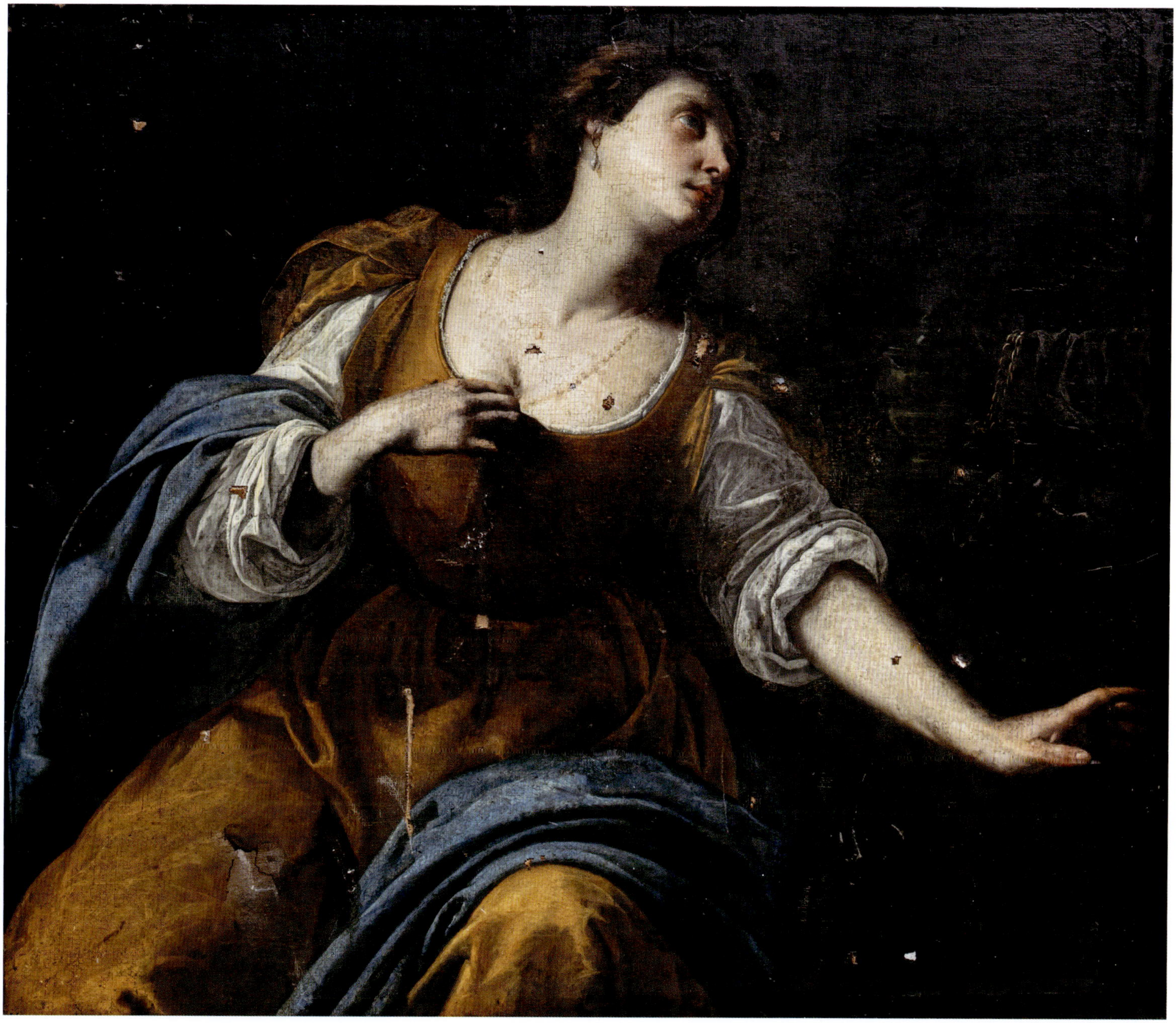

1.1
Properzia de' Rossi
Bologna, c. 1490 – Bologna, 1530
Crest of the Grassi Family
c. 1520
Silver filigree, cast sections, rock crystal, boxwood, stones, 39 × 22 cm
Bologna, Museo Civico Medievale, inv. 2135

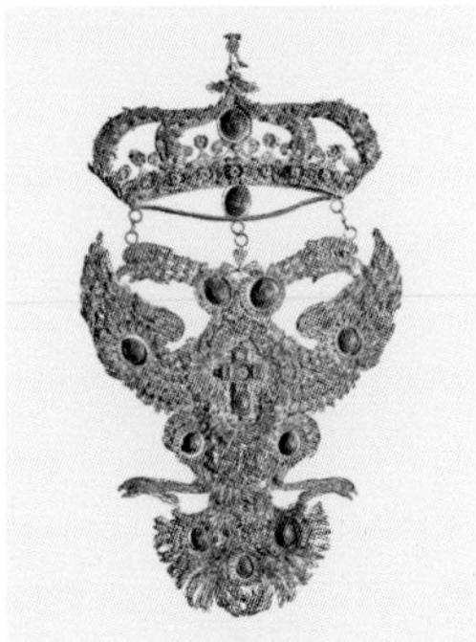

Alongside her rare works of marble sculpture – the technique considered the most difficult and ambitious by certain theorists of the time when attempting to rank the various artistic disciplines – Giorgio Vasari recalls Properzia's curious inlay work: "And because she had a ready and inventive wit, she began to carve peach-stones, which she did so well and with such patience that they were most unusual and marvellous to see" (Vasari 1550, English ed. 1998, p. 341). The Arezzo-born historiographer was most won over by the "miracle" of "a stones", today lost but in the nineteenth century believed to be part of the collection of Count Domenico Bonamini Pepoli di Pesaro (Cerboni Baiardi 2014), into the tiny surface of which she had carved "the entire Passion of Christ [...] with countless characters besides the crucifiers and the Apostles" (Vasari 1550, English ed. 1998, p. 340). Probably on the basis of this information from Vasari, the carving of eleven stones (if not peach then possibly plum or apricot) was attributed to Properzia, all visibly set within the silver filigree frame of the crest of the Grassi family, which had as its crest a two-headed eagle (Graziani, in Fortunati, Graziani 2008, pp. 64–67). Having been discovered in 1704 and immediately assigned to the sculptress (Orlandi 1704, p. 329), the coat of arms features small shrines with relics of saints in the central cross, thus serving a religious function while also celebrating the Bolognese senatorial family. The use of a non-precious material – in contrast to the approach customarily taken by the ancient art of glyptics – constitutes an extravagance, indicative of Properzia's "ready and inventive wit", but also of the sophisticated tastes of the client. One cautious hypothesis posits that it was Achille Grassi who requested the crest, the laborious creation of which may have been the work of the goldsmiths Giacomo and Andrea Gessi, who were working for the Bolognese nobleman at the time of his appointment to the cardinalship in 1511 (Corelli Grappadelli 2004, pp. 328–329). Within the wonderful artifice of the plumage of the eagle, we can make out figures of martyr saints and virgin martyrs carved into the two faces of the stones, with identifying inscriptions based on a method derived from ancient numismatics. Through the very minimal relief, the hagiographic attributes and the palms of martyrdom are brought to the fore, facilitating the immediate identification of the characters, presented with a formal composure in line with those figurative solutions of the sixteenth century most indebted to "sweet" Bolognese humanism.
A sense of more artificial theatricality seems to be expressed only in the image on the stone at the apex, in which Saint Peter appears in the magnificence of his draped figure, with the keys held protectively in the foreground by his hands. Her ability in the calligraphic subtleties of intaglio – which Properzia flaunts in the Alexandrian cameo grace of the head of Potiphar's wife – gives perhaps some indication of her background, which is still open to conjecture. The deployment of the microtechnique may, in fact, bring her *schultora* (sculpture) into the orbit of the studio of Francesco Francia, whose brother Domenico seems to have been her accomplice in one of the raids documented in the criminal archive (trial of 1525). But to arrive at an assessment of the professional quality of Properzia, it is necessary to return to the only work for which it is known beyond doubt that she was responsible. Engaging in a dialogue with the iconographic model of Giulio Romano, disseminated via a print by Marcantonio Raimondi, the marble in San Petronio with *Joseph Tempted by Potiphar's Wife* makes reference to the tenderness of Alfonso Lombardi and the sensuality of Correggio to confer naturalness and seductiveness to the female body. The energetic conspicuousness of the arm with which the biblical protagonist grasps the clothing of the chaste Joseph seems, in contrast, to translate the anatomical vigour of Michelangelo, almost out of a desire to signify women's desire to decide their own love lives for themselves, alluding to the life of the sculptress herself, who was rejected by the young man with whom she had fallen in love, as narrated by Vasari (Fortunati 1981; Fortunati 2008, p. 20).
Irene Graziani

1.2
Giorgio Vasari
Arezzo, 1511 – Florence, 1574
Le vite de' più eccellenti pittori scultori e architettori
In Fiorenza: appresso i Giunti, 1568, vol. 3
Printed book with etchings, 245 × 175 mm
Milan, Pinacoteca di Brera and Biblioteca Nazionale Braidense, ZNN.IV.41

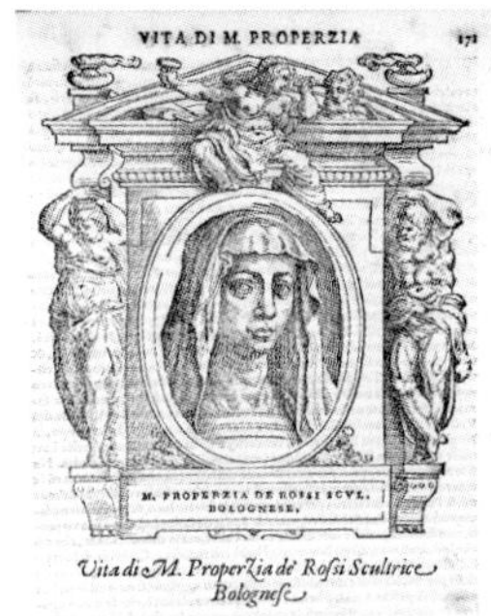

1.3
Isaac Bullart
Rotterdam (Holland), 1599 – Arras (France), 1672
Academie des sciences et des arts, contenant les vies, & les éloges historiques des hommes illustres, qui ont excellé en ces professions depuis environ quatre siècles
Amsterdam: Elzevier, 1682
Printed book with etchings, 345 × 220 mm
Rome, Biblioteca Angelica, L.22.42

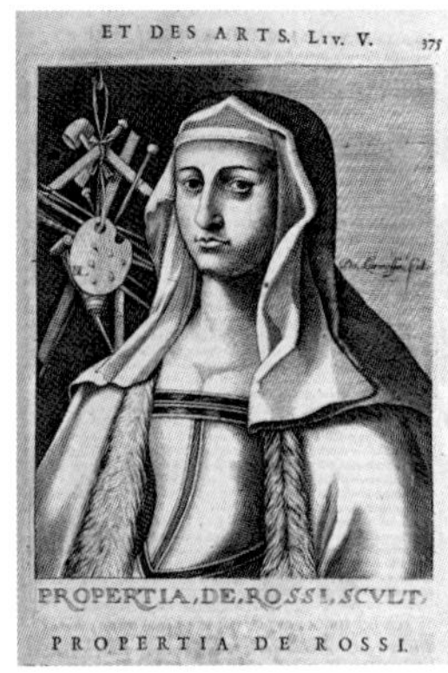

1.4
Anthony van Dyck (?)
Antwerp (Belgium), 1599 – London, 1641
Sofonisba Anguissola on her Deathbed
c. 1625
Oil on canvas, 52 × 72 cm
Turin, Musei Reali – Galleria Sabauda, inv. 304, cat. 686

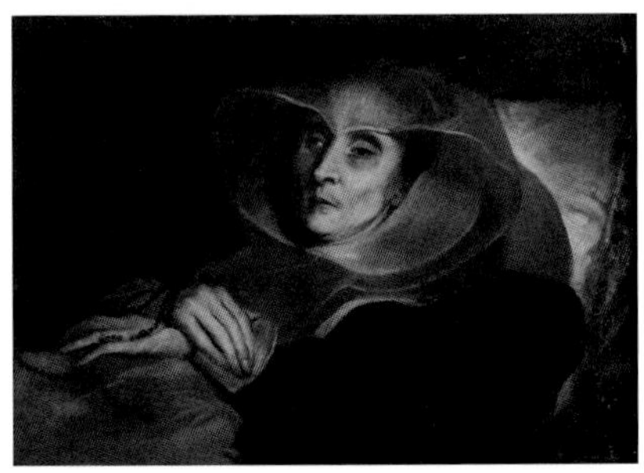

On 12 July 1624, while the plague was raging in Palermo, a very young and already established Anthony van Dyck, having gone to the Sicilian city at the request of the viceroy, Emmanuel Philibert of Savoy paid a visit to Sofonisba Anguissola, the noblewoman now in

her nineties who had given her life to painting and had been living in Palermo since at least 1615, with her second husband Orazio Lomellini. This was an extraordinary meeting between two individuals who were highly unusual in terms not just of their exceptional artistic ability but also their strong, determined characters. On that occasion, the Flemish painter drew – in his Italian sketchbook, now held at the British Museum – the three-quarter portrait of the old woman, depicted at a slight angle, sitting in a chair with her hands resting on her arms and her head covered by a long veil. She is by now almost blind, but her gaze remains alert and attentive, intrigued by what is going on. In his brief report on that happy meeting, van Dyck describes her as having "her memory and mind both very much alive", "her hand was still steady without the slightest tremble". Sofonisba asked her younger colleague, so distant from her in terms of background and culture, not to portray her with "the lamp too high, so that the shadows of the wrinkles of her old age would not become too large", offering him useful advice and stating that she realised she was a naturally talented painter and the greatest sorrow she felt was from her lack of sight which prevented her from painting any more". Sofonisba had reached the end of a life full of honours and successes. She was the leading light – albeit in the traditional position of wife and lady-in-waiting – of an initial female affirmation and emancipation, achieved thanks to her talent, her tenacity and her unconventional choices, overcoming the prejudices of her time in relation to female artists. She died the next year, on 16 November 1625, unanimously lauded by her contemporaries.
Critics have long debated the question of which work or works van Dyck describes having put before the painter on that day to allow her to see as much as she possibly could given her compromised vision, and whether "the portrait of herself" to which van Dyck refers is the drawing in his sketchbook or a painted image, establishing a relationship between the Antwerp-born painter's stay in Palermo and a group of works including the *Portrait of Sofonisba Anguissola* previously in the Nauta collection in Amsterdam and today lost, the canvas in the Galleria Sabauda (Larsen 1980, p. 118, cat. 455; Larsen 1988, II, no. 321) and the portrait in the Sackville collection at Knole House in England (Millar 1969, p. 417; Salomon, in *Van Dyck* 2012, p. 74, no. 6).
The Turin painting, which came from the collections of the Piedmontese entrepreneur and collector Riccardo Gualino, was identified by Lionello Venturi (1926, pl. XLV) as the portrait "recently discovered in Palermo, and attributed to Van Dyck" cited by Lionel Cust (1902, p. 25) in his essay on van Dyck's sketchbook, which was then transferred, according to the scholar, to the Simonetti collection in Rome before being acquired by Gualino. Venturi stressed its similarity – which can now be discounted – to the presumed *Self-Portrait* by the painter held at the Nivå Museum in Denmark. Documented as being in the hall of Cereseto Castle in a photograph taken during a shoot by Gian Carlo Dall'Armi in the Gualino residence between 1918 and 1919, the painting was declared to be of cultural interest and protected as part of the national heritage on 6 November, 1921, by what was then Soprintendenza dell'Arte Medievale e Moderna of Turin, together with other paintings from the same collection, and in 1930 it was given by Gualino free of charge to the State, along with his remaining group of works of ancient art in response to the bankruptcy in which his companies found themselves (Bava 2019, p. 93 and photo B14). Produced, according to Larsen, in Genoa, after the passing of the old artist and van Dyck's re-entry to the Ligurian city, the portrait in the Galleria Sabauda has been more recently dated to a time prior to the departure of the artist from Palermo (Viscuso, in *Pietro Novelli* 1990, pp. 148–149, no. 1.4), taking account of the documentary discoveries that have seen van Dyck's stay in Sicily extended to September 1625 (Abbate 2004, pp. 70–71). A certain similarity with the female figure illustrated in the sketchbook does indeed make it possible to identify the subject as Sofonisba Anguissola. The woman is portrayed lying on her deathbed with her head resting on a pillow, her hands with their tapered fingers rest on her stomach and hold the rosary, her eyes appearing veiled and inward-looking. The close framing and diagonal orientation highlight her gaunt, suffering face. This is an image that, while materially compromised by inappropriate cleaning and interventions, still captures the artist's emotional reaction to the woman now at the end of her days, together with the desire to render realistically the ravages of time and the pain of her face and hands. However, we cannot fail to take account of the latest ideas of the critics, which have thrown into question the authorship of the painting both for stylistic reasons (Salomon, in *Van Dyck* 2012, p. 76, no. 7; Meijer, Sluiter, Squellati Brizio 2011, I, no. 306) and due to the less-than-adequate state of conservation, which makes it difficult to read the pictorial surface, complicating any efforts to attribute the work with any certainty to the Flemish painter (Failla, in *Van Dyck* 2018, pp. 218–219, cat. 10).
Sofia Villano

1.5
Bernardino Campi
Cremona, 1522 – Reggio Emilia, 1591
Portrait of Catellano Cotta
1553
Inscriptions: "[155]3 ME[N]SE AGVS. EXEMPLAR ISTVD FACTVM / E[ST?] CATELLIANO AGENTE [AN]NVM [69]) / ET MENSES DVO", at top right "1553 / CATELIANVS / COTTA A[N] / LXVII[I]", at top right, apocryphal "Bernardinus / Campus / Cremon.s f."
Oil on canvas, 103.5 × 82.5 cm
Cremona, Museo Civico Ala Ponzone, inv. 118

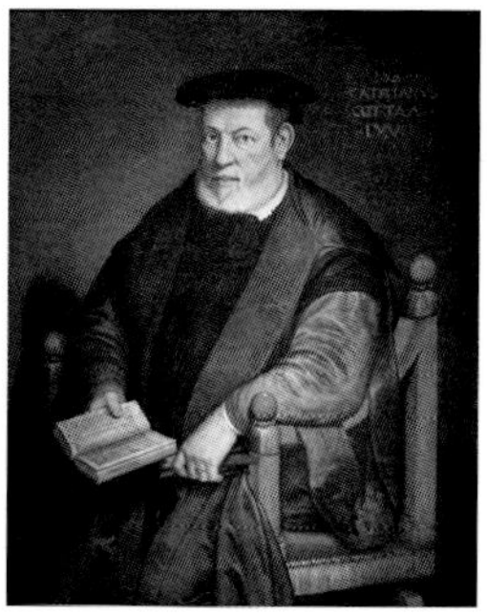

Paolo Michele Cotta, known as Catellano (Milan, 1484–1553), as he preferred to be called in memory of his father, was an important jurist and a member of the College of Jurisconsults of Milan in 1512. During his lifetime, he carried out a significant *cursus honorum* that led to him being appointed Deputy Magistrate in the years 1529, 1548 and 1549. While filling that role, he ordered the erecting of a monument surmounted by a lion in Milan's Piazza San Babila, to commemorate the wars against Venice, which was later transformed (1628) into the column we see today. He produced texts that were exclusively concerned with legal matters, including an annotated edition of the *Statuta Mediolani* of 1552 (Vittori 1984). The biographer of Bernardino Campi, Alessandro Lamo, recalls that he "made the Portrait of Mr Catelano Cotta" (Lamo 1584, ed. 1774, p. 46), which in all likelihood is the painting on display, which entered the Cremona museum collection through acquisition in 1957 (Miller, in *I Campi* 1985, p. 159).
Cotta is seated on a chair, in a three-quarter portrait, with a cap on his head; he wears a heavy cloak over a black garment with red sleeves and holds an open book that evinces his work as a jurist (Ghirardi 1994c, p. 79). The soft, almost frontal light lingers on the folds of the clothing, the knobs and the fringes of the chair, caressing his time-worn face and hints of grey in his beard before fading out to the greenish-brown so beloved of Sofonisba. The careful pictorial handling flagged up by the critics (Guazzoni, in *Sofonisba* 1994, p. 316) and a sort of stylistic archaism with respect to the more penetrating capacity of observation found in the subsequent portraits (Miller, in *I Campi* 1985, p. 159) have always been read as his signature style, albeit somewhat detached from the more mature portraiture starting from the *Prospero Quintavalle* dating from 1556. In truth, the propensity for squared-off shapes and for the anecdotal naturalism in the minute rendering of the details, not yet sublimated by that "great elegance" that the critics of the time would soon attribute to him (Lamo 1584, ed. 1774, p. 49), seems to have originated during an earlier phase of his output, as seen in the portrait of Facio Trezzi inserted into the *Assumption* now in the church of Sant'Agata in Cremona (see more detail with a reproduction of the portrait in Marubbi 1999, p. 111) dated 1542 or 1544 (Miller, in *I Campi* 1985, pp. 157–158). While the most obvious inscription is to be considered apocryphal and added later,

the date of 1553 is, however, confirmed by the original epigraph, albeit partially abraded (Tanzi 1981, p. 74; Tanzi 2016, p. 12), but now explored in more detail by Mario Lazzari, whose reading allows us to confirm Cattelano's age, 69, at the time of the creation of the portrait, meaning it was produced in the last year of his life. Lamo, too, who does not specify the dating of the portrait, inserts Cotta's painting into the events described as taking place between June 1551 and early 1554 (Marubbi 1999, p. 48 note 40). Bernardino must therefore have painted it in Milan, to which he had moved in 1549, making it very difficult that Sofonisba could have seen it, even when it was under development. In the absence of other portraits by the painter datable to the 1540s, it is in any case correct to assume that Campi's portraiture in that period was expressed precisely through the disillusioned naturalism that comes across clearly in the *Portrait of Catellano Cotta*. This, then, would have been the stylistic approach that Sofonisba would have learned in the painter's studio and which is very evident in her portrait of her father Amilcare in the Nivå painting.
Mario Marubbi

1.6
Sofonisba Anguissola
Cremona, c. 1532/1535 – Palermo, 1625
Portrait of Lateran Canon
1556
Oil on canvas, 57 × 53 cm
Inscriptions: on the canvas, next to the canon's left shoulder: "Sophonisba Anguissola Virgo Coram Amilcare Patre[m] pinxit MDLVI"
Brescia, Pinacoteca Tosio Martinengo, inv. DI137

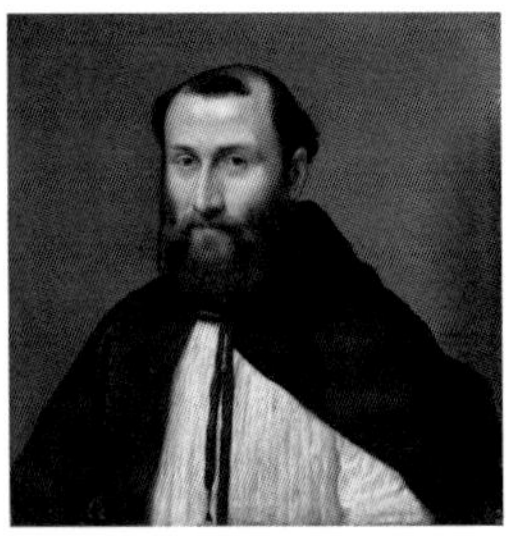

The painting, identifiable thanks to the still-visible text on the bottom right, was inventoried in the Paolo Brognoli collection in 1823 as a portrait of Ippolito Chizzola. The attribution to Anguissola and the identity of the subject are based on the description by Rossi, who stated "we enjoy his portrait [of Chizzola], painted by Sofonisba the Cremonese Painter, who produced it while he was preaching, some say in Cremona, & others in Genoa" (Rossi 1620, pp. 350–351). Subsequently, in 1853, described as the "portrait of Ippolito Chizzola, by the female painter Anguissola" (Odorici 1853, p. 194), it appeared in the collection of Camillo Brozzoni of Brescia, and was then donated to the city of Brescia in 1863. According to Marchetti, Chizzola was in Cremona to preach and had developed close relations with the Gonzaga family (Marchetti 1981, pp. 67–72), and in particular with Ferrante and Francesco. For its part, the Anguissola family also had strong links with the Gonzagas, stretching back to before Sofonisba's arrival in Spain (Gamberini 2016, p. 39). In light of this, the choice of the painted subject – as part of what we could call a "family" circle within which Sofonisba would find herself daily – would not seem to have been random. This interpretation is bolstered by the habit worn by the monk, of the order of the Lateran canons, to which Chizzola did indeed belong (Sacchi, in *Sofonisba Anguissola* 1994, p. 192). Mina Gregori also states that the subject "is likely to be the preacher Ippolito Chizzola" (Gregori 1994, pp. 22–23).
This painting patently demonstrates Sofonisba's ability to paint from life, by now fully developed, deploying smooth colour modulations. She achieves a Leonardesque *sfumato* infused with the influence of Moroni that transmits the canon's austere intensity. Nicodemi observes that the "gravity of the figure eliminates from the painting the exquisite effortlessness of other works by the same artist" (Nicodemi 1927, p. 54). The viewer's attention is attracted by the face of the believer, whose intense gaze stands out against a green background. His beard and hair frame the face of a man who is still relatively young but steadfast in his expression, with thin lips clamped shut. Sofonisba succeeds in making the figure less static thanks to a slight contortion of the face, together with the asymmetry of the cloak shifted slightly onto the left shoulder. The painting was subject to numerous conservation issues – a coat of paint prevented the full legibility of the inscription and the layering, while the white garment was generally in very poor condition – which were restored in 2017.
The canvas was compared and contrasted with the *Portrait of the Dominican Astronomer* – previously in the Calligaris collection and now lost, dated 1555 – for the physiognomic definition of the face with a hint of a smile; on the table are his working papers, where amongst the mathematical calculations there appears Sofonisba's signature (Gregori 1994, p. 36). There is also another portrait of a Lateran canon, probably once again Ippolito Chizzola, which was sold at auction by Dorotheum on 15 October 2013 and had previously belonged to Alfio Nicotra, a Sicilian doctor and academic. This painting is similar to that in the Martinengo Picture Gallery in terms not only of the format but also of the technique and conception of the work, to such an extent that Maria Kusche has posited the idea that they may have been conceived in pairs to be displayed opposite each other, which would explain why the latter painting may not have been signed (Kusche 2009, p. 292). In light of the above, and reconsidering the text found on the painting, in which the letter "I" of the surname Anguissola is highlighted differently from the portraits of the 1550s, this may be a later addition, as previously stated by Rossana Sacchi (Sacchi, in *Sofonisba Anguissola* 1994, p. 192).
Cecilia Gamberini

1.7
Sofonisba Anguissola
Cremona, c. 1532/1535 – Palermo, 1625
Self-Portrait
1558
Oil on paper mounted on panel, 26.6 × 19.3 cm
Inscriptions: signed lower left "Sophonisba / Anguisola / Amilc... [Amilcaris?] / F[ecit] o P[inxit] /...p.am [seipsam?]. / M. / VIII"
Rome, Principi Colonna collection, fidecommissum no. 578

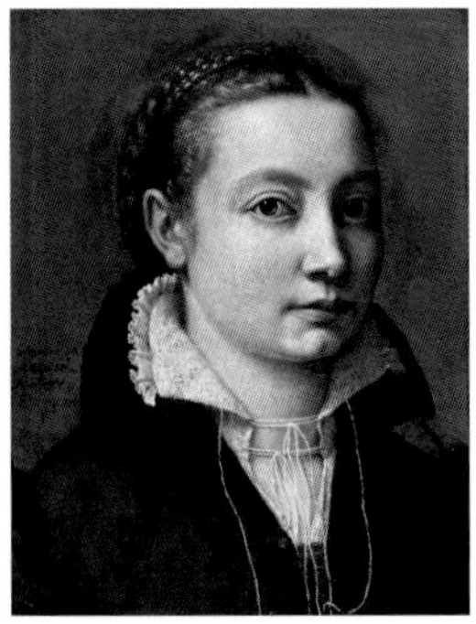

This work remained unseen until 1996, when a descriptive account of the inventories of the Colonna collection was published for the first time by Eduard Safarik (Safarik 1996, pp. 6, 46, 61); appearing in the catalogue of paintings in the apartment of Princess Isabelle at Palazzo Colonna in 1998 and 1999, we also find it amongst the masterpieces of portraiture in the Colonna collection (*Galleria Colonna* 1998, p. 13, no. 9; Safarik 1999, p. 208, fig. 366; Piergiovanni, in *Palazzo Colonna* 2019, pp. 320–322, no. 150). In addition, Patrizia Piergiovanni stresses "that the painting, centuries on, has continued to engender the admiration of the descendants of the Family, and was selected by Donna Isabelle Sursock Colonna (1889–1984) to be immortalised at her side" (Colonna 2010, p. 242).
The self-portrait of the Cremonese painter Sofonisba Anguissola is probably the only work on paper by the artist, together with the miniature self-portrait held at the Museum of Fine Arts in Boston (Sacchi, in *Sofonisba Anguissola* 1994, p. 196) for which, though, parchment glued onto panel was used. This type of surface could perhaps be associated with Sofonisba's formative years, and at the same time to her activity as a painting teacher, first to her sisters and later to Queen Elisabeth of Valois.
At the lower left we can read the signature of the artist "Sofonisba Anguisola" and the year of execution, 1558. According to the aforementioned hypothesis posited by Patrizia Piergiovanni, the word on the third line could refer to the name of the painter's father, the nobleman Amilcare (Piergiovanni, in *Historia* 2019, p. 102, no. 6). This

methodology of execution is aligned with that of the other inscriptions found on the self-portraits produced in this first phase of her training, when her father was sent his daughter's works as gifts to nobles and "princes", as Annibal Caro stated after his request was rejected.
The portrait is recorded from 1611 as "A little picture of an old lady with a walnut frame" (Safarik 1999, p. 208), but as stressed by Piergiovanni, its entry into the collection may have occurred previously, since the document in which it appears refers to the assets inherited by Prince Filippo I Colonna (1578–1639) and by his nephew Marcantonio IV Colonna (1595–1611) in the early seventeenth century.
In the inventory of 1613, again concerning the assets of Prince Filippo I Colonna, it is described once more as "A little picture of an old lady with a walnut frame" but this time with the addition of the name of the painter "by Sofonisba", thus confirming the recognised value of the painting (Gozzano 2004, p. 27). In the 1639 inventory it is described as being in "Hall no. 10. Two portraits of heads and busts of Women in walnut frame, one-and-a-quarter palms tall, one of which is suffonisba Anguissola [*sic*] marked no. 124, the other no. 128" (Safarik 1996, p. 704).
It is likely that this self-portrait can be associated chronologically with those held in Łáncut and Naples and with the Brera *Self-Portrait*, datable, according to Rossana Sacchi and Mina Gregori, to around 1559 (Sacchi, in *Sofonisba Anguissola* 1994, pp. 224–225), before the painter's departure for Madrid. We can discern in this work the reaching of Sofonisba's artistic maturity, encapsulated by Alessandro Lamo (1584, ed. 1774, pp. 34, 47) as "resemblance to life" alongside "great elegance", as well as a certain influence from Moroni in the desire to make the profile stand out against a light background, along with a confident, smooth plasticity. The spatial arrangement of the Colonna work is similar to that of the Milanese portrait, with the face shown in three-quarter view, the same hairstyle with the braid around the head and the large, prominent pale blue eyes that look towards the outside of the canvas. What certainly differentiates the two works is the different purpose of the representation: while in the Brera painting Sofonisba is depicted as a lady, with a purple dress and jewellery to complement her hairstyle, in the self-portrait in the Colonna Gallery, artificiality gives way to rigour, and the painter is depicted as virtuous, with a dark bustier under which we can see a white blouse.
Cecilia Gamberini

1.8
Sofonisba Anguissola
Cremona, c. 1532/1535 – Palermo, 1625
Chess Game
1555
Oil on canvas, 70 × 94 cm
Inscriptions: on the base of the chessboard "SEPHONISBA ANGUSSOLA VIRGO AMILCARIS FILIA EX VERA EFIGIE TRES SUAS SORORES ET ANCILAM PINXIT MDLV"
Poznań (Poland), Fundacja im. Raczyńskich przy Muzeum Narodowym w Poznaniu, MNP FR 434

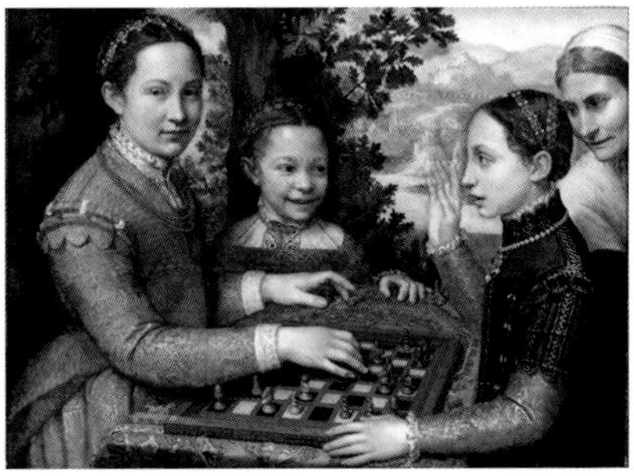

This painting was reported for the first time by Vasari: "I saw this year in the house of her father at Cremona, in a picture executed with great diligence by her hand, portraits of her three sisters in the act of playing chess, and with them an old woman of the household, all done with such care and such spirit, that they have all the appearance of life" (Vasari 1568, English ed. 1912–1915, VIII, p. 45).
Exhibited for a long time in the reception room at the Anguissola home, together with the *Family Portrait* now in Nivå, the painting is a testament to the inventive ambitions of the young Sofonisba, which she most likely shared with her father. According to Sacchi (in *Sofonisba Anguissola* 1994, p. 190), the painting was in Rome in 1600, appearing in the inventory of Fulvio Orsini together with the *Self-Portrait at a Spinet* now held in the Museum of Capodimonte in Naples, both inherited by Odoardo Farnese: "No. 3: Painting framed in walnut, of games of chess, painted by Sophonisba" (De Nolhac 1884, p. 431). It still features in the Farnese inventories of 1653 and 1662 – "A canvas painting with carved walnut frame showing a chess game with four half figures of women, garden perspective, painted by Sophonisba Piacentina, and in it is the portrait of her" – in which reference is made to the Piacentine origins of the Anguissola family, at least as far as the main branch is concerned.
Subsequently, the painting moved from Rome to Parma and finally to Naples, together with the rest of the Farnese collection (Bertini 1987, pp. 136 et seq.). Acquired by Luciano Bonaparte (Haskell 1982, p. 75), it was sold once again in 1815 (Fredericksen 1993, p. 114), whereas in 1823 Count Athanasius Raczyński purchased it for three thousand francs, before it ended up in the picture gallery in Berlin. Its final move was to the museum in Poznań along with a large part of the count's collection.
In the inscription the painter curiously signed her name as "SEPHONISBA" (Cole 2019a, p. 162, no. 10), which probably offers us a clue about the method used to produce the work: "EX VERA EFIGIE" – an indication of the existence of a preparatory sketch, on which the artist must have worked (Cole 2019a, p. 110).
Sofonisba's three sisters, who according to the identification provided by De Ribera (1609, p. 313) were Lucia, Minerva and Europa, were portrayed in a family scene as they concern themselves with the chess game, while the maid – probably Cornelia Appiani, who would also accompany Sofonisba to Spain and appears in the Simancas payments (Pinessi 1998, p. 51) – observes the scene with a vigilant gaze.
As noted by Garrard (1994, p. 600), in that very period the rules were changing within the chess game for the queen, who could now move diagonally across the board, gaining new options for attack (Leoncini 2016, p. 55). It was a change that reflected a renewed female status, with greater importance afforded to women in society and the arts; in Sofonisba's case, the education made available to her by her father was indicative of the new cultural models (Guazzoni 1994, p. 57).
The canvas thus represents various expressions and attributes that aim to engage the viewer in its dynamism. To the left, Lucia, richly dressed and with her hair adorned by a headdress, the same as those also worn by her sisters, turns her head towards the viewer. To her left, little Europa smiles while Minerva, donning the pearl necklace already seen in the portrait of her mother held in Berlin, raises her hand to attract the attention of her older sister. Everything takes place under the watchful eye of the maid, Cornelia. Despite the expressive power of the faces, Sofonisba's difficulty in representing the proportions of the bodies is clear: the figures appear profoundly mannered, with the limbs often too long an unnatural, but while in Parmigianino the mannerism of the proportions imbues the figures with a certain grace, in Sofonisba it betrays a hand that has not been fully developed. Nor are the rules of perspective afforded sufficient respect: at that angle, the table would not be able to support the chessboard, which is perilously oriented towards the outside of the canvas. The setting for the scene is a lush garden, probably the same one that can be admired in Cremona from the indoor patio of the house that was at one time the Anguissola home and has recently been restored. The blue-tinted landscape recalls the Flemish tradition (Sacchi, in *Sofonisba Anguissola* 1994, p. 190).
Cecilia Gamberini

1.9
Sofonisba Anguissola
Cremona, c. 1532/1535 – Palermo, 1625
Holy Family
1559
Oil on canvas, 36.7 × 31.9 cm
Inscriptions: "SOPHONISBA / ANAGUSSOLA / ADOLESCENS / F. 1559"
Bergamo, Accademia Carrara, inv. 58MR00050

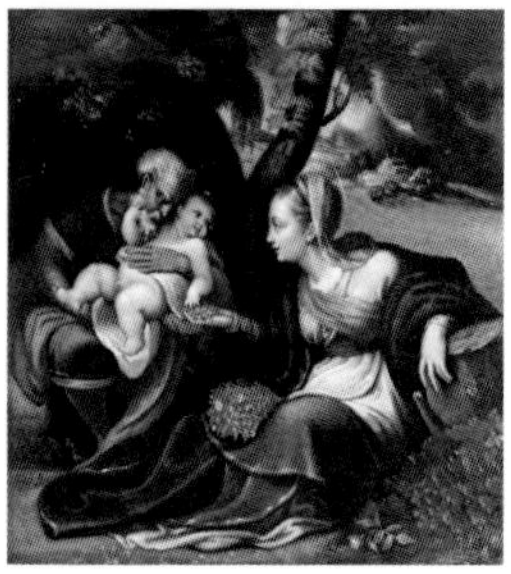

Having entered the collection of Giovanni Morelli in 1872 (Sacchi 1872, p. 349), the work probably belonged to the Bresciani collection in Bergamo from as far back as the nineteenth century, reaching the Carrara Academy in 1891 with the Morelli bequest (Zeri, Rossi 1986, pp. 201–202; Guazzoni 1994, in *Sofonisba Anguissola* 1994, p. 262). The theme to which the composition refers is the Flight into Egypt; nature is seen as an allusion to the brevity of life and to the transience of worldly goods, as symbolised also by the cut flowers. It is, however, evident that this is not an original invention, but rather a composition based on a model by Camillo Boccaccino, now found in Glasgow (Di Giampaolo 1978), or, as is the case for the *Pietà* in Brera (cat. 1.10), it may be based on a model by Bernardino Campi (Guazzoni, in *Sofonisba Anguissola* 1994, p. 262). A drawing by Boccaccino with the same subject is held in the Biblioteca Ambrosiana in Milan (Bora 1971, pp. 25–26, no. 14), even though the version by the Cremonese artists is associated in chromatic terms with the small oil painting in Glasgow (García-Frías Checa, in *Historia* 2019, p. 190). The painting refers back in any case to models originating in Lombardy, above all in relation to the landscape and the use of light. Sofonisba's brushstrokes and style are recognisable from the soft *sfumato* and the expressiveness of the faces, albeit that the work betrays a certain stylistic immaturity.
The lack of creative impetus in compositional terms had already been highlighted by Sofonisba's father, Amilcare, who had requested a drawing from Michelangelo so that his daughter could paint it; Mina Gregori has also underlined the limited predisposition of the Lombard painters to themes of this type, since they were trained, in contrast, to paint from life (Gregori, in *I Campi* 1985, p. 173). Alessandro Lamo states that Sofonisba had learned early on "to copy any sort of drawing, always choosing her templates from the most excellent and the best" (Lamo 1584, pp. 37–38).
The painter showed herself capable of adapting to the precepts of the Council of Trent and to the rigid, dogmatic schemes that required the saints, and the Virgin Mary, to be represented in accordance with a pre-determined model: for example, Saint Joseph in the guise of an old man, who holds the Child affectionately, or Mary seated on a trunk that seems to allude to the wood of the cross (García-Frías Checa, in *Historia* 2019, p. 190). The painting is signed and dated on the rock at the foot of Saint Joseph "SOPHONISBA / ANAGUSSOLA / ADOLESCENS / 1559" with an evident spelling error that would lead us to believe that the inscription is apocryphal and was not added by the painter herself (Cole 2019a, p. 170). There is a replica of the work, signed in this case "Sophonisba Angussola", with compositional differences that concern above all the addition of Saint Francis and the young Saint John – possibly in response to a request by the client (García-Frías Checa, in *Historia* 2019, p. 191). This latter painting is today in a private collection in Milan, but its whereabouts had remained unknown from 1914 onwards. It was displayed alongside the version in the Carrara Academy in Bergamo on the occasion of the exhibition on the painter at the Prado Museum in 2019.
Cecilia Gamberini

1.10
Sofonisba Anguissola
Cremona, c. 1532/1535 – Palermo, 1625
Pietà
1574–1585
Oil on panel, 46.5 × 32.5 cm
Milan, Pinacoteca di Brera,
inv. Reg. Cron. 1283

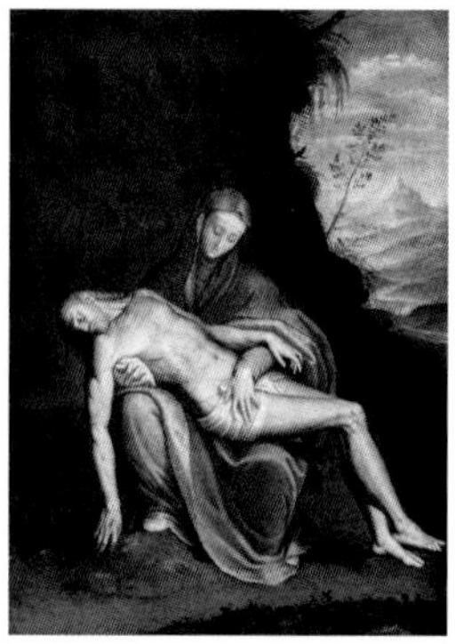

Initially considered to have been painted by Bernardino Campi, the work was acquired by the Pinacoteca in 1909. As previously highlighted by Venturi (Venturi 1933, pp. 924–926), it may be, in truth, a painting by Sofonisba, perhaps a reduced-scale copy of the central part of Campi's *Pietà*, again held in the Brera gallery, created around 1574. Sofonisba must then have taken her inspiration from this painting after her time spent in Madrid, around 1574, rendering the atmosphere less dramatic and more intimate, based on its probable devotional and private use.
For his part, Valerio Guazzoni does not reject the idea that it may be a copy by Campi himself, who subsequently painted two versions of the *Pietà* on slate for Marcantonio Arese and for the Marquis of Ayamonte. The scholar adds, moreover, that the possibility of Sofonisba having had access to a copy (perhaps just a drawn version) of Campi's work during her Spanish sojourn should not be ruled out, in light of the frequent contacts with and dispatches of his works (Guazzoni, in *Sofonisba Anguissola* 1994, p. 264). Sofonisba's little painting is, in any case, an *unicum* in her pictorial output. More recently, the idea has emerged that it should be considered a small-scale version of the central part of the *Pietà* by her first teacher, Bernardino Campi, produced between 1572 and 1574 and found in the church of Santa Caterina da Crema (García-Frías Checa, in *Historia* 2019, p. 195). Another version of Campi's work, held at the church of San Lorenzo in Lodi and dating from around 1574, is cited by Alessandro Lamo (1584, ed. 1774, p. 81).
The reference to Michelangelo and to his 1499 sculptural composition in San Pietro Basilica's is, however, evident – providing the source for the pyramidal composition and the suffering expression of the Virgin Mary as she presents the body of her dead son to the world.
The chromatic tones chosen by the painter are earthy and characterised by subtle modulations; the drapery of the Virgin is, however, less convincing. The light fades against the backdrop, creating a suffused atmosphere typical of the silent and meditative composure of prayer. There is no lack of natural elements, which seem to emerge cautiously from the darkness, creating a sort of niche that encapsulates the pathos of the central scene.
This intimacy can be traced back to a later reworking of an older painting, almost a reflection on the trail blazed by the teacher, which is here rendered in a more spiritual key (Guazzoni, in *Sofonisba Anguissola* 1994, p. 264).
Cecilia Gamberini

1.11
Sofonisba Anguissola
Cremona, c. 1532/1535 – Palermo, 1625
Portrait of the Infanta Isabella Clara Eugenia
c. 1573
Oil on canvas, 57 × 48.5 cm
Inscriptions: top left "L'Infantta Isabella Clara Eughenia Daustria"
Turin, Musei Reali – Galleria Sabauda,
inv. 755, cat. 328

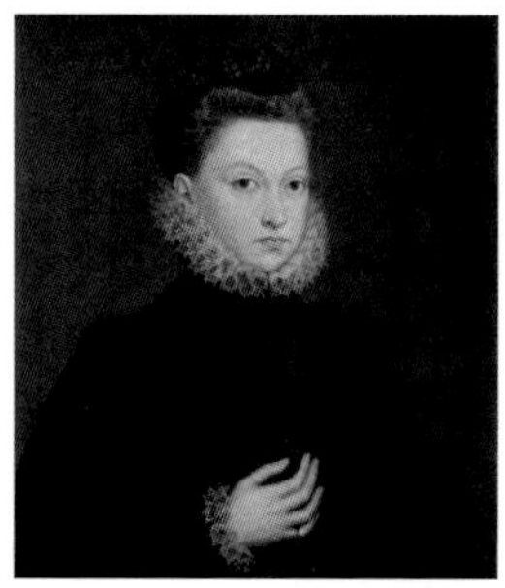

When she painted this portrait, Sofonisba had already been at the court of Philip II of Spain for many years, and was about to return to Italy. Queen Elisabeth of Valois, for whom she had been a lady-in-waiting, was now dead, and the painter, in light of her closeness to the deceased, had consented to remain in Madrid at the request of the king to take care of the two orphaned infantas: Isabella Clara Eugenia – the first-born and future regent of the Low Countries together with her husband Albert, Archduke of Austria – and Catalina Micaela,

who was destined to marry Charles Emmanuel I and to become Duchess of Savoy. Sofonisba had developed a portraiture of great formal intelligence and communicative efficacy, with the capacity to align the physiognomical and psychological exploration of the subject with the representational needs of the royal family, receiving not just honours and recognition from the sovereigns, but also the enthusiastic admiration of many contemporary painters.
The identity of the subject was unknown for many years, and only in the final decades of the nineteenth century was the young girl depicted identified as Princess Isabella Clara Eugenia, as stated for the first time in the catalogue of the Regia Pinacoteca of Turin, published in 1884 (Villano, in *Van Dyck* 2018, pp. 224–225, cat. 19). The infanta, born in 1566, is depicted in a slight three-quarter, half-length portrait, wearing a black dress with a high ruff, with her right hand on her chest, grasping between her thumb and index finger the long necklace that embellishes the dress. Recent infra-red reflectology carried out on the painting has made it possible to appreciate in particular the detailed design of the white lace, exceptionally refined in its almost impalpable transparency, as well as the subtlety of the rendering of her face and hand, and the minute strokes used to delineate the short curls escaping from her elegant coiffure.
The portrait, which is not identifiable with any certainty in the ancient inventories of the Savoy collections, was attributed in the past to the Spaniard Alonso Sánchez Coello, a court painter of Philip II (Villano, in *Van Dyck* 2018, pp. 224–225, cat. 19, with previous bibliography). Only over recent years have the critics questioned the veracity of that claim, and in particular Maria Kusche (1992, p. 28; Kusche, in *Sofonisba* 1994, pp. 136–137 and p. 250, no. 28; Kusche 2003, p. 233, figs. 203, 209) has attributed the work to Sofonisba Anguissola, recognising in it close stylistic, technical and compositional similarities with the portrait of Queen Anna of Austria, fourth wife of Philip II and stepmother to the young girl, and with the portrait of the Spanish sovereign, both at the Prado in Madrid. According to the scholar, the dark, austere clothes worn by the subjects would be perfectly suited to the proposed dating of 1573, this being the year that saw the establishment of the feast of the Rosary – which the king holds in his hands – and the funeral of Elisabeth of Valois, along with the transfer of her remains to the convent of the Escorial. The painting in the Galleria Sabauda also displays a close similarity to a beautiful *Portrait of Catalina Micaela* in a private collection, in which the child, who holds a little monkey to her chest, is similarly depicted in a half-figure portrait, again wearing a black dress against a dark backdrop, with the light lingering on her face and delicate hands, making it possible to suppose both that the two paintings had been produced *en pendant* and perhaps kept by the infantas amongst their personal belongings – although there is no trace of them in the post-mortem inventories of their estates – and also that the portrait of Isabella had been brought by Catalina Micaela to Turin to remember her beloved older sister and their childhood spent together in Spain (Kusche, in *Sofonisba* 1994, pp. 136–137 and p. 250, no. 28). Recently, this group of works has been expanded to include another portrait with the same dimensions and iconographic arrangement, now at the San Diego Museum of Art, depicting a young prince at the Spanish court; the subject is probably Ferdinando, the royal couple's first child, who was born in 1571. The painting features an inscription at the top left similar to that appearing on our painting (Pérez de Toleda, in *Historia* 2019, pp. 156–157, nos. 30–31).
Isabella seems here to be older than seven, which is the age she would have been if the painting had been produced in 1573, but perhaps the rigidity of her pose, the seriousness of her rather melancholic gaze and the mourning costume make her seem older than she actually was. What is certain is that, even in her still-youthful face, we can make out the strong, resolute character of a woman who, from 1598 onwards, together with her husband Alberto, would be in charge until her death of the governing of the Spanish Low Countries, the sovereignty of which – in contrast to the strict rules imposed by the Salic Law – had been transferred by her father to her and to Catherine out of his deep love for them. Sofonisba chose a small format and a close-up depiction, offering an image that is intimate and imbued with loving sensitivity, but also with intensity, featuring careful observations of Isabella's limpid, penetrating eyes, her closed mouth, the position of her hand and the details of her dress and ornamentation. The painting embodies a silent dialogue between the painter-teacher and the child-princess – two female figures that, albeit with different statuses, constrained within the social conventions of the time, succeeded in breaking down the barriers imposed upon women by the prejudices of a still-patriarchal Europe.
Sofia Villano

1.12
Sofonisba Anguissola
Cremona, c. 1532/1535 – Palermo, 1625
Madonna dell'Itria
1578–1579
Oil on panel, 239.5 × 170 cm
Paternò (Catania), parish of Santa Maria dell'Alto, church of the former convent of the Santissima Annunziata, inv. 131231

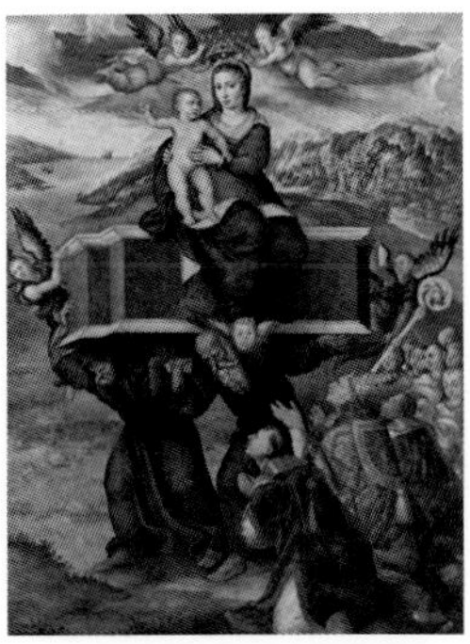

This panel is one of the most recent and most important additions to the catalogue of the Cremonese painter. Flagged up in 1995 by Alfio Nicotra on a stylistic basis (Fallica 1995), only since the rediscovery of a document the proves her authorship beyond any doubt (Marotta Rizzo 2002; transcribed by A.M. Iozzia in Kusche 2009, pp. 294–295, and now also in Iozzia 2019, pp. 100–102) has it been unreservedly accepted onto the list of confidently attributed works (Kusche 2009, pp. 285–287; Cole 2019a, p. 146 and p. 200, no. 51; Ruiz Gómez 2019, pp. 24–25), constituting an important reference point for the reconstruction of Sofonisba's activity in Sicily. The painting is now fully legible thanks to Domenico Cretti's restoration.
The curious iconography refers to the ancient Byzantine icon of the Virgin Hodegetria ("she who points the way"), shortened in Italian to "Itria" from "Odighítria". In contrast, though, to the original icon, which included solely the depiction of the Virgin with Child, the figurative tradition that would take root in Sicily, Sardinia and certain areas of the southern mainland derived from a figurative eclecticism interpreted, in part, through specific local cults. Sofonisba's panel illustrates the legend according to which, at the time of the iconoclasm, a number of Basilian monks hid a panel depicting Hodegetria inside a wooden chest and let it float out to sea; it eventually reached the southern coasts of Italy (Porcella 2012, pp. 687–690). As such, in the painting we see the two Caloyer monks carrying the chest on their shoulders, the Virgin sitting atop it crowned by two angels and depicted as holding the blessing Child. Below, a bishop accompanied by two deacons and a number of clerical cantors constitutes a variable element of the iconography, at times replaced by local saints. The two monks may allude either to those who entrusted the precious painting to the sea, or to the orthodox monks fleeing the Balkans and Greece who, following the Islamic conquest, headed westwards with their images and cults. Emblematic in this regard is the case of the Palermitan icon from Piana degli Albanesi, which reached there in 1488, brought by a group of refugees (Mariani 1966, p. 92). As had already been the case for the Hodegetria of Constantinople, which soon became a palladium for Byzantium in the effort to defend against the Turks, so the *Madonna dell'Itria* was elected protectress against pirate raids, with stories of the liberation of Christian slaves and the conversion of infidels being woven around it; moreover, it was soon invoked against the plague. In the late sixteenth century, its cult was very widespread across the island, and to this day it can still be seen in significant works of figurative art, both in sculpture (Corleone, Piazza Armerina) and in painting. Those paintings include the altarpieces by Riccio in Santa Maria in Valverde, Messina, that by Alessandro Allori in the museum in Messina, that by Zoppo di Gangi in Carini, that by

Alvino in Monreale and that by Filippo Jannelli in Barcellona.
The rediscovery of the act of donation of the panel by Sofonisba has made it possible to investigate the genesis of the painting in more detail. It was on 25 June 1579, that Sofonisba – now widowed and preparing to leave the island to return to Cremona together with her brother Asdrubale, who had gone to meet her with the express intention of accompanying her back home – signed a public deed of donation, in which she left, to the conventuals of the church of San Francesco in Paternò, the painting of the Madonna dell'Itria "constructum et factum in tabula per eandem dominam donatricem et dittum quondam dominum don Fabricium eius virum et participio de eorum manibus". The unusual formula whereby the painter also extended to her husband the ownership of the painting – an involvement based more on love than on necessity – leads us to posit that he may also have participated in the creation of the painting. While unprecedented, this practice may be discerned in certain areas marked out by anatomical uncertainties, an excess of graphical elements and the laboured conquest of forms reworked time and again, as apparently indicated by the two angels that hold aloft the crown, those that support the chest, the cherubim in the centre and even the rather awkward and caricatured faces of the bishop, the deacons and the clerics. While these details cannot confidently be attributed to someone else, by the same token they do not embody Sofonisba's steady, precise hand, thus opening up the possibility that her husband may well have been involved. At the time of the donation, the panel was, however, no longer located in the palace of the Moncada family, which was about to be abandoned, but in the church of San Giovanni Evangelista, where it had probably been sited in the expectation that the Franciscans would prepare the altar for which the panel was destined. The friars would have been working tirelessly with a view to celebrating a mass on the date of the anniversary of Fabrizio Moncada's death, but since this obligation was no longer applicable, Sofonisba arranged for the *Madonna dell'Itria* to be moved to the parish church, and if here too the vicar was no longer in a position to respect the requirement to celebrate mass, then it would fall to the Carmelites of Santa Maria della Catena.
It is patently obvious that Sofonisba was worried that, in her absence, the memory of her husband would no longer be honoured. The panel must have remained in the church of San Francesco for only a little over a century, since the building was badly damaged by the earthquake of 1693, as was clear from the signs of fallen rubble left on the surface of the painting. Perhaps following the cataclysm it was then moved to the ancient mother church (Santa Maria dell'Alto) and from there to its current site. Although the ambiguity concerning the chest carried on the shoulders of the caloyers, which had been thought in some way to allude to the tragic end of Fabrizio Moncada, has since been resolved (given that the chest has been shown to be an integral part of the iconography of the Virgin Hodegetria), it remains difficult to claim that the painting does not conceal some autobiographical allusions, starting with the face of the Madonna, which appears to all intents and purposes to be a secret self-portrait. In relation to the Flemish-style landscape – like many that Sofonisba would have been able to admire in Madrid – it does not offer any topographical clues, though in the portion of the sea at the top left we can glimpse two ships that, while apparently insignificant, cannot fail to bring to mind the final moments of Fabrizio's life. The events that led to him losing his life are well-known: having embarked on the galley *Capitana* on 25 April 1578 in Palermo, with the intention of going to Madrid to claim from the king his rights to the inheritance of the fiefdom, he drowned off Capri in an attempt to reach the coast after being attacked by a flotilla of Barbary pirates (Tornamira 1674; Kusche 1992, p. 13; Sacchi 1994d, pp. 382–383).
The report of the events (recently published in a critical edition) that the artillery captain, Baltasar Gago – an occasional passenger on the *Capitana* – submitted a few days later to the viceroy of Sicily, Marc'Antonio Colonna, is so precise that it is hard not to grasp the affinities with the scene painted by Sofonisba. In that narrow sea crossing, two boats can be seen: one with its sails billowing, which seems to be sailing away, and one with its sails lowered, which has released the lifeboat on which a number of men have been saved. From Gago's account, we know that the *San Ángel*, having left Palermo together with the *Capitana* to sail to Genoa, managed to avoid the first attack but was then intercepted later by the pirates off Sardinia. For its part, the *Capitana*, in an attempt to make emergency landfall on the island, got trapped on the rocks. Gago describes how he worried about safeguarding his most illustrious passenger, the Duke of Terranova, Carlo Aragona Tagliavia. Many men had already gone overboard and were trying to swim to shore, but Don Fabrizio Moncada drowned as he tried to cross a small gulf ("ya la galera estaba encallada en un escollo, y de ella a tierra había un golfillo algo hondo adonde, según me pareçe, se ahogó don Fabricio de Moncada, y otros", see Gago 2020, p. 96). The Sicilian nobleman's end did not go unnoticed on the small island: in the record of deaths for the parish of Capri in 1578, his death is duly registered as having taken place at Punta di Mulo ("don Fabricio Mongada [*immersed*?] with the galley taken at Mulj, galley of Sicily"; see *Libro dei morti 1392-1614* in the Capri parish archive; modern copy in the Library of the Centro Caprense Ignazio Cerio, Archivio Carelli, file 329). The two boats and the lifeboat appearing in the background of the painting are so consistent with Gago's description that it is highly unlikely that Sofonisba did not want in some sense to refer to the event, as it would have been recounted to her by one of the survivors. Indeed, the painting, on which work certainly began prior to Fabrizio's departure, must have taken a long time to complete, and perhaps was only finished shortly before the painter began preparing to leave Sicily. After the years spent at court, where her output was exclusively focused on portraiture, Sofonisba seems here to return to an approach interrupted in Lombardy at the end of the 1550s: the tonal succession of the planes that fade into the musky greens and azures of the background retraces the layout of the Nivå *Family Portrait*, just as in the *Madonna* the memory of the Correggesque stylings of Bernardino Gatti is still fresh.
The spatial construction of a large altarpiece was, though, a complex undertaking, the like of which she had perhaps never attempted before. To overcome the challenge, Sofonisba was required to force the perspective from below – a necessary move in order to present the chest with the Virgin Mary above, with a bird's eye view. This must have been very difficult to achieve: the influence of Northern Italian Mannerism being enriched with elements taken from the international milieu of the court of Madrid to match the island tradition. Despite the ambiguity of the construction and the numerous anatomical imperfections, it is in the background that the painting is at its best, with the curved, infinite horizon seeming to refer back to Patinir, and the sky streaked with menacing clouds that in Spanish painting (even before El Greco) is to be found in certain works by Luis de Morales, such as the *Holy Family* of the Hispanic Society in New York. Having brought to fruition this sort of cenotaph, and having imparted to the Franciscan friar Vincenzo Caruso the necessary instructions for the religious services to be celebrated for all eternity, Sofonisba could now leave her little court of Paternò and head back out to sea.
Mario Marubbi

1.13
Lucia Anguissola
Cremona, c. 1537/1542 – Cremona, 1565
Self-Portrait
1557
Oil on panel, 28 × 20 cm
Inscriptions: "MD / LVII / Lucia / Anguisola / virgo Amilca / ris filia se ip / sam pinxit"
Milan, Castello Sforzesco, Pinacoteca, inv. 562

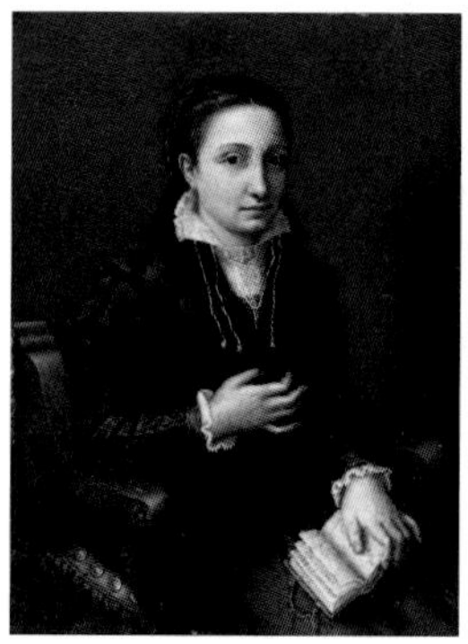

No light has been shed on the ancient vicissitudes of the painting, which entered the Milanese civic collections through acquisition in 1937. It is, though, a highly significant work within the output of Lucia Anguissola, since it is the only self-portrait of her that we are aware of today (signed and dated 1557), made all the more precious by the use of panel as the surface. Within the Anguissola family, this technique was reserved for artworks intended to be displayed within the family circuit; in this case, its deployment seems to have arisen from a clear desire for emulation – and not just in formal terms – of the youthful *Self-Portrait* by Sofonisba dating from 1554 today in the Kunsthistorisches Museum in Vienna, so much so as to replicate its rather self-satisfied signature (*virgo se ipsam fecit*), changing only the verb. With respect to the icon of her sister, which portrays her from the waist up, Lucia enlarges the visual field to a three-quarter view that portrays her seated, like that of *Bianca Ponzoni* by Sofonisba at the Gemäldegalerie in Berlin dating from the same year. But in Lucia's little painting, the posture of the figure in the chair is more effectively resolved, albeit within the artifice of an empirically accurate perspective. With respect to her sister's auroral image, which is challenging in the magnetic flow that emanates from her large eyes, Lucia reveals here her virginal demureness in her veiled and discrete gaze, "true mirror of her inner qualities" (Rodeschini Galati, in *Pittura a Cremona* 1990, p. 275), and in that gesture of shyness betrayed by the thumb that seeks shelter under her blouse, as if to keep in check her poorly concealed nervousness about not succeeding in the endeavour (Gilardi, in *Sofonisba Anguissola* 1994, p. 282). What comes across is a sort of existential restlessness under investigation, achieving a more acute synthesis, also seen in the attractive sketch in the Uffizi (inv. 13248F), this time produced by Sofonisba, which for its part portrays her seated, with the book open and her right hand raised to her chest (see the reproduction in *Sofonisba Anguissola* 1994, p. 279). The youngster depicts herself here in the moment in which she raises her eyes towards the viewer after having rested on her knee a book, perhaps a poetry book, which she appears intent upon reading. Her coiffure is understated, her hair tied back, a black surcoat placed over a plum-coloured garment from which emerge the cuffs and collar of her blouse with its little ties, the only whim permitted by a costume that is highly suited to Lucia's reserved nature and to the construction of that image of virtuousness that their father Amilcare wished for his daughters. A creative intelligence is unleashed that seems to reveal, on Lucia's part, that same commitment towards nature and towards the emotions already seen in the work of her sister Sofonisba (Geddo, in *Museo d'Arte Antica* 1999, p. 21). In light of the pictorial quality of this painting, Vasari's appreciation does not appear exaggerated (1568, ed. 1966–1987, II, pp. 562–563); that said, having visited the Anguissola family home in Cremona in 1566, when he would have been able to admire a number of her pictures, he did not then go on to cite this particular *Self-Portrait*.
Mario Marubbi

1.14
Europa Anguissola
Cremona, 1548/1549 – Cremona, 1578
or
Lucia Anguissola
Cremona, c. 1537/1542 – Cremona, 1565
Portrait of Livia de Zanchi
1560–1565
Oil on canvas, 98 × 73 cm
Inscriptions: in the background on the left, now no longer visible "LIVIA DE ZANCHIS / ANNO AE [...] 8"
Milan, Castello Sforzesco, Pinacoteca, inv. 590

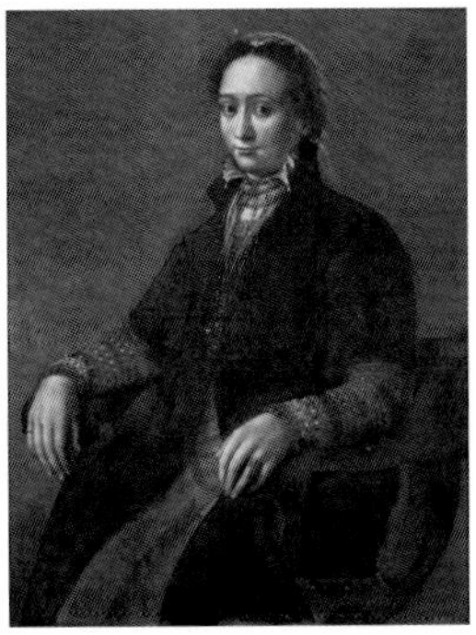

The portrait, bearing a generic attribution to the Cremonese school, was received by Milan City Council as a bequest in 1864. We know nothing of its previous history, but its Cremonese origin has never been questioned and is manifested at first sight through the style of the composition, with its pleasing naturalism, which harks back to the world of Bernardino Campi, and its light green background so typical of Sofonisba. The painting was then in a poor state of conservation, having been subject to cuts, excessive cleaning and fading of the colour, all of which greatly compromised the painted surface, so much so that it was highly abraded in certain dark areas (chair, surcoat, hair). A 1975 restoration attempted to repair this damage, but ended up concealing the inscription on the left side of the painting, which stated the woman's name and age. The traditional reading from an old photograph taken at the time of that restoration indicated that her name was Livia de "Lanchi", though a new inspection here proposes that the surname is in fact "Zanchi". The Zanchi were a notable family in Bergamo, of which there were no known branches in Cremona – nevertheless, it must have been the family of the painter Alessandro Zanchi, who was active in the late sixteenth century in Bergamo (Guazzoni 1990, p. 57) and Piacenza, in the ambit of Campi and Malosso. The youngster, perhaps aged twenty-eight, as the only legible number of the inscription may indicate, is portrayed in three-quarter view, seated and with her arms on the armrests of the chair, set against a green background. She wears a brown surcoat over a bright red dress with finely worked sleeves, from which emerge the embroidered cuffs of her blouse, which features a collar decorated with hanging cords. Her tied-back hair is held in place by a veil with a golden chain. Other pieces of jewellery displayed with care confirm that she belongs to a high-ranking family: a chain round her neck, a gold belt around her waist, and two coral bracelets. Cristina Geddo was the first to investigate the painting, bringing it into the orbit of the Anguissola sisters and cautiously putting forward the name of Europa (Geddo, in *Museo d'Arte Antica* 1999, pp. 22–24). Based on more recent studies, it is worth considering the recent proposal to insert the portrait into the catalogue of Lucia Anguissola (Miscioscia 2019, p. 33). If we compare Livia's face with the *Portrait of Minerva* in the Museo Poldi Pezzoli, unanimously attributed to Lucia (see the reproduction in *Sofonisba Anguissola* 1994, p. 282), we are struck by the same meticulous descriptive exploration – in the Castello Sforzesco painting perhaps rendered with less effectiveness due to the unfortunate vicissitudes of conservation – but in the more readable parts, such as the face, the painting seems to be aligned with the approach taken by Lucia in her mature phase. While a specific distinction between the youngest of the Anguissola sisters is far from easy, the *Portrait of Livia de Zanchi* may quite possibly be one of the final works by Lucia, datable to between 1560 and 1565.
Mario Marubbi

1.15
Silvestro Lega
Modigliana (Forlì-Cesena), 1826 – Florence, 1895
Titian and Irene di Spilimbergo
1859
Oil on canvas, 97.5 × 81 cm
Inscriptions: on the rear, handwritten in ink "Firenze / Silvestro Lega inventò e dip. / Anno 1859"
Carpi (Modena), Palazzo Foresti collection

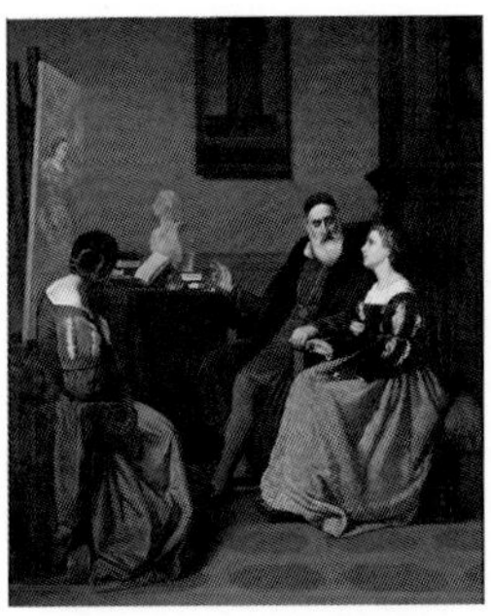

Lega's art "until 1859 remained ostentatiously academic" (Martelli 1895), and this painting – the last among the ones with a historical-romantic theme which he made before going "with some friends to the countryside to study" (*Lettere dei Macchiaioli* 1953, p. 127)

– is dated 1859, the year when the practice of painting *en plein air* had already become a habit for the Macchiaioli. The work, which is of fundamental importance, must be considered the culmination of Lega's academic training, since it defines a delicate evolutionary moment in the development of his painting and serves as an essential key to understand the specific quality of the leap he makes from the purist tradition towards the embracing of a very personal domestic realism marked out by subtle intimist inflections, similar to the one of Piagentina. This painting – with its tone of serene, descriptive softness that is integrative and supplementary in its slow focus on the details, observed within an ensemble of balanced analytical rigour – stands as a direct antecedent of the painted interiors of the Batelli house, of which it already intones the gentle whispering, and confirms how in them Lega keeps alive the lesson of Nazarene purism, mitigated by a smooth, Ingres-style fluidity. In this way, Lega combines an evocation of antiquity that is far-removed from the bombastic, celebratory richness normally *de rigueur* in the canons of historical romanticism, intensified in the dialogue with the Verdian drama, but modulated by a faint, sweet narrative cadence of Nordic inspiration, not only with the purpose of eulogising the ethical and civil implications of an event but in order to evoke with abundance of details, its "atmosphere", describing the environment in an accurate, wide-ranging way, speckling it with velvet colours, as already noted by the critics in 1926: "*Titian and Irene di Spilimbergo* offers a pleasing array of grey, cold green, dark azure and warm brown, swiftly touched" (Tarchiani 1926, p. 199).
Silvio Balloni, Giuliano Matteucci

1.16
Lucrezia Quistelli
Florence, 1541 – Florence?, 1594
Mystical Marriage of Saint Catherine
1576
Oil on canvas, 180 × 120 cm
Inscriptions: signed "L. de Quistelli 1576"
Silvano Pietra (Pavia), parish church
of Santa Maria and San Pietro

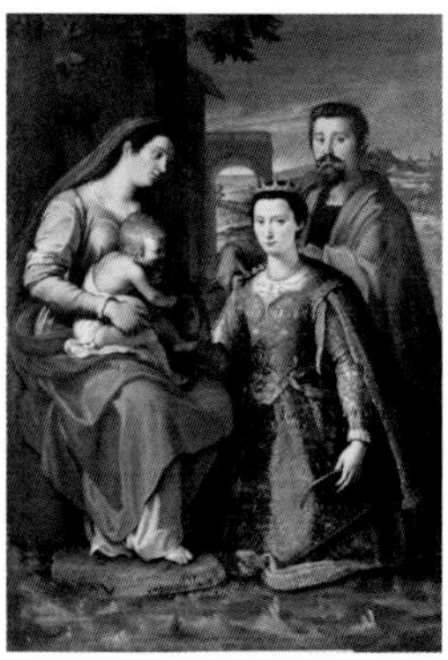

According to the report on the restoration carried out in 2015 by Gabbantichità, the first certain piece of information relating to the painting is found in the decrees of the parish of Silvano Pietra. In particular, in the period 1572–1576 Monsignor Girolamo Regazzoni, a right-hand man of Pope Paul IV and Pope Pius V, was responsible for visiting the diocese of Tortona, and his detailed report is held in the historical archive of the diocese (Archivio Storico Diocesano, Tortona, Visita Apostolica Mons. Regazzoni e Gambara, 1 [B 209]).
Specifically, the decrees for the parish of Silvano Pietra are dated 16 March 1576 and state: "in the Altar of the church of Santa Caterina there is a beautiful altarpiece and a beautiful iron keystone", indicating that four months had been set aside for the realisation of the work, on pain of prohibition of celebrations at the altar itself (Archivio Storico Diocesano, Tortona, Visite Pastorali 1, Visita Apostolica Mons. Regazzoni [B 209], p. 111). Subsequently, on 30 June 1596, Bishop Cesare Gambara decreed that "the altarpiece is in place" – i.e. within a marble or stone frame, where it remains to this day (Archivio Storico Diocesano, Tortona, Visita Apostolica Mons. Cesare e Maffeo Gambara [B 183], 4, file 11).
The timescale that dates the creation of the painting to between March and June of 1576 is confirmed, together with the name of the painter, in the inscription discovered thanks to the restoration. The work was commissioned by Alfonso Pietra, son of Lucrezia Quistelli and third Count of Silvano, who was at the service of and in contact with the Medici of Florence, like his father Clemente before him. The commission is celebratory in nature, the intention being to commemorate the ancestors Brunoro and Caterina Bianca Stampa; Alfonso asked his mother, a student of Alessandro Allori and someone who was deeply embedded in the art scene of the time, to paint the work.
Despite the various reworkings, as revealed by technical and radiographic studies, and the poor state of conservation in which the painting and the altar itself were languishing, they have now had their original splendour reinstated. Quistelli represents on the canvas the Virgin with Child surrounded by soft drapery in bright colours, in the wake of the indications issued by the Council of Trent. Opposite her there kneel the two ancestors: Caterina Bianca Stampa, in the damask garments of Saint Catherine, recognisable by the instrument of martyrdom, and Brunoro, who stare out at the viewer. Appearing in the background are Leonardesque landscapes in bright blue tones that render the atmosphere muted and delineate ancient pieces of architecture and a remote glow, while lush vegetation frames the sacredness of the representation. Sheila Barker has recently studied Lucrezia Quistelli and her artistic output, bringing to light a patchy and fragmented history (Barker 2016). In relation to this painting, Barker proposes that it should be post-dated for stylistic reasons, given that the naturalism of the work has its roots in the 1580s, and specifically in the output of Cigoli, Passignano and Santi di Tito. Quistelli may have painted it around 1587, when she is recorded as having been in Lombardy. For its part, nor does the inscription that should certify its authorship actually provide clarification; indeed, there is no evidence that the Quistelli family would customarily sign their name with "de" preceding the surname (Barker 2016, p. 65). In any case, as previously affirmed, the documents indicate 1596 as the *terminus ante quem* for the production of the painting. The scholar rejects the possibility that the two people praying in the picture may represent Count Alfonso Pietra and his wife Fausta Visconti, claiming instead – with reference to a late sixteenth-century portrait – that there are no matching somatic traits between the countess and Saint Catherine. If the subject were in fact the same individual, the Silvano altarpiece would be dated to the second decade of the seventeenth century, meaning that Quistelli could not have painted it (Barker 2016, p. 80 note 140).
Cecilia Gamberini

1.17
Claudia del Bufalo
Active in Rome in the late sixteenth and early seventeenth centuries
Portrait of Faustina del Bufalo
1604
Oil on canvas, 105 × 88 cm
Inscriptions: on the base of the column "CLA[UDI]^A E [L] BVFA [LO] F / 1604";
on the letter resting on the table "All'mia Car:ma Sorella / La Sig:ra Faustina DI / bufalo / Roma"; lower left "6005"
Rome, Dario del Bufalo collection, inv. P127

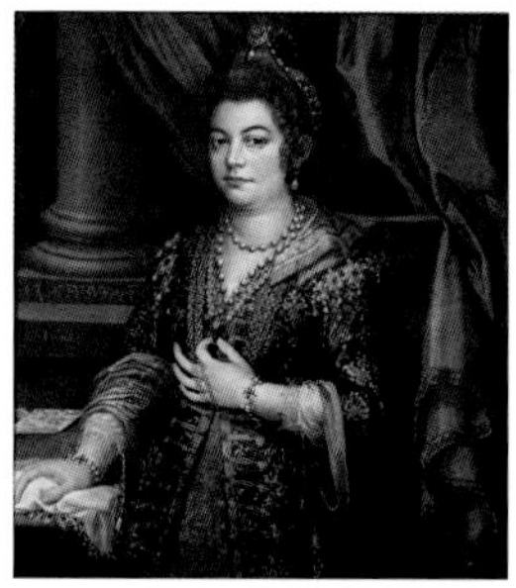

The painting constitutes the only known output of this aristocratic female painter, who belonged to the patrician del Bufalo family, whose signature appears at the base of the column in elegant epigraphic capital letters, in which the noble "del" section is resolved with an interwoven Roman style. This specific feature had an authoritative precedent in the miniature *Self-Portrait* by Sofonisba Anguissola (1556), today in the Museum of Fine Arts in Boston. Although there is no information on the artist's training, the spelling and the decision to intertwine the characters represent a clear indication of her antiquarian skills and of her interests in the environment in which she operated. Nevertheless, it is worth recalling the existence of a treatise entitled *Nel qual*

s'insegna à Scriuer ogni sorte lettera, Antica, & Moderna, di qualunque natione, con le sue regole, & misure, & esempi, written by the Roman citizen M. Giovanbattista Palatino and published in Rome in 1545 as clear evidence of the renewed interest in that genre of graphics.
Alongside the signature, the work also features a dedication – easy to read on the surface under the column – by the painter to her sister Faustina del Bufalo, who is most likely to be the subject of the portrait. However, despite the apparent abundance of information on the identity of the artist and the subject, and on their family connections and the date of the work (1604, on the plinth of the column), the family tree does not seem to confirm the information which we have in our possession. According to the family's memoires, Claudia was the daughter of Quinzio del Bufalo, the younger brother of Innocenzo del Bufalo, a legal scholar who enjoyed a brilliant ecclesiastical career during the pontificate of Clement VIII. Quinzio had married Cassandra di Lorenzo Strozzi, and after her death he had undertaken his ecclesiastical career, assuming – among his various roles as a canon – the post of deputy castellan of Castel Sant'Angelo from 1625 and that of governor of the Fabbrica dell'Università della Sapienza from 1629, until his death in 1647. Quinzio and Cassandra had five children: Innocenzo, Silvia, Virginia, Dianora and Ottavio Giacinto, but no Claudia or Faustina are documented. The explanation may be that the two sisters, as was common practice amongst the *literati* of the time, had adopted pseudonyms carefully chosen from the repertoire of proper names of Roman origin; alternatively, Claudia and Faustina belonged to another branch of the family, yet to be identified.
Moreover, although the signature on the painting is clearly that of a female name, it is cited as a work by Claudio del Bufalo in the inventory of Villa Borghese (to which the number 6005 at the bottom of the canvas probably refers) compiled by Giacomo Manilli in 1650 (Manilli 1650, p. 115) and repeated by Giovanni Giorgio Grevio in the *Thesaurus Antiquitatum et historiarum Italiae* published in 1723 (Graevius 1723, t. VIII, part IV, col. 43). Despite the treacherous nature of the terrain of historical certainties, the portrait of Faustina is fascinating. Stylistically, it can be traced back to the sixteenth-century models of official portraiture, where the opulent fashions and refined jewellery form part of a codified lexicon of dynastic references. The gesture of the lady's left hand attracts the viewer's attention to the heraldic pendant wherein the buffalo's head on the family's coat-of-arms is presented as a pendant in the shape of a bovine protome. Hanging from a chain with eye-catching links, the object takes on the characteristic appearance of a knightly collar, an unusual privilege for a woman, betraying an obvious sense of family pride. Her hairstyle is embellished by numerous pearls and by a central jewel: a crescent moon with a red gem (a type of spinel called a balas, or a ruby or garnet) and a pendant drip pearl. Seemingly modern, the jewel in reality returns to the form of the *lunula*, a female pendant/amulet worn by Roman women in antiquity, a detail that, drawing its inspiration from archaeology, stresses the antiquarian interests of the painter and her family. Worn as a piece of head jewellery, however, the *lunula* evokes the iconography of the goddess Diana, often portrayed with a diadem adorned with a crescent moon (see Titian, *Diana and Actaeon*, Edinburgh, National Gallery), linking her mythological chastity with that of Faustina. The red precious stone and the pearl add a symbolic connotation entirely in keeping with the evocative shape of the necklace, given that red gemstones symbolise charity and love (D'Ascoli 1327, ed. 2011, v. 3045, p. 304; Leonardi 1502, ed. 1516, pp. 25*v*, 26*r*; Dolce 1565, p. 35*r*), whereas the pearl, emerging from the shell fertilised by the heavenly dew (Pliny, 9, 107), is an emblem of fertile chastity (Leonardi 1502, ed. 1516, p. 37*r*). Alongside the bracelets, of which the subject wears a pair, and the ostentatious ornaments on the sleeves that, at shoulder height, simulate the presence of opulent *armillae*, there are rubies, pearls and emeralds, the gems of Venus, which according to astrological lapidaries lead to both fertility (Ficino 1480–1489, ed. 1995, p. 203) and chastity (Leonardi 1502, ed. 1516, p. 43*r-v*; Dolce 1565, p. 61*r*). The pearl, that great feature of fashions in the sixteenth and seventeenth centuries, has a significant role in Faustina's ear as a memento of purity, according to the prescriptions of Marco Antonio Altieri in his treatise on marriage, written shortly after 1500 (Altieri 1500, ed. 1833, p. 68). In contrast, the black sphere (perhaps jet, a fossil variety of lignite, symbol of chastity), next to the earring, is enigmatic in terms of both its material and its ornamental function, since it is neither a little bow (Della Pergola 1954, pp. 139–140) nor a second earring, given that it is too distant from the lobe.
In the sixteenth and seventeenth centuries, chastity, fertility and generosity, as fundamental virtues for a young patrician women, were frequently underlined by accessories and jewellery, above all in the portraits intended to document the features of the *inamorata* for the benefit of her fiancé. The dedication by the painter to her sister seems to indicate that said sister would be the intended recipient of the portrait (rather than anyone else), and in any case the pearl necklace and the chain, probably added later, would appear to suggest a potential matrimonial destination of the work, at least in a subsequent phase. The fact that the left hand is ring-less – a clear indication that the subject was unmarried – but woven several times in gold chain seems to confirm the presence of a sentimental relationship. In the *Mundus Symbolicus*, a treatise on heraldry by Filippo Picinelli, the chain is described as the ornament that weighs down and adorns at the same time, like the bonds of marriage that, in imposing a linkage, ennoble the bride (Picinelli 1653, ed. 1669, p. 674). A similar value can be attributed to the pearl necklace with small golden beads used as spacers. One eloquent detail is the handkerchief, a refined lace-trimmed accessory, the colour of which is a reference to chastity, while its symbolism is bound up with court rituals as an engagement and wedding gift (Dickey 1995). Therefore, in contrast to the Roman Faustina, the "improper" wife of Marcus Aurelius, Faustina del Bufalo is most probably an anxious fiancée portrayed by her sister at the moment in which she is about to leave the paternal home – of which she bears the insignia – to enter that of her husband.
Silvia Malaguzzi

1.18
Caterina Cantoni (attributed)
Milan, 1542 – Milan, 1601
Cloth embroidered with planetary divinities, emblems and religious scenes
c. 1590
Linen cloth embroidered in silk, gold and silver yarn with point painting, straight stitch, split stitch, couching, 62 × 94 cm
Moshe Tabibnia Gallery, inv. 133526

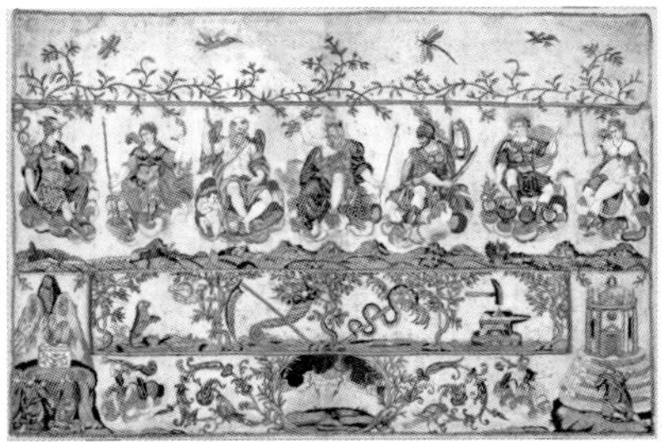

"There is no human figure, fair, bird, buildings, landscape, hill, mountain, atmosphere, river, lake, tree, grass, fruit or flower that she cannot represent with the most natural colours, to the amazement of those who see her paintings" (Morigia 1592, pp. 674–675). Paolo Morigia used these words to praise Caterina Cantoni, one of the most renowned embroideresses of the late sixteenth century, often referenced by contemporary sources but only recently subject to a rediscovery in both art-historical (Binaghi 1994, pp. 96–123) and biographical terms (Mausoli 2015; Mausoli 2020).
Two works have been attributed to the embroideress, whose output was in demand at the most prominent European dynasties: the so-called "Ariadne's Embroidery", split into two cloths held at the Angewandte Kunst Museum in Frankfurt and the Österreichisches Museum für angewandte Kunst in Vienna, with the altar cloth being held at the Museo Civico in Turin (Bovenzi 2011a, pp. 152–155, no. 38). This small but precious oeuvre can be expanded to include the fragment in question, which entered the antiques market as an eighteenth-century French or Italian work (*Sotheby's* 2016, lot no. 250). The embroidery actually features a very large number of elements shared with Cantoni's needle painting: the same figurative culture of the graphical models, attributable to the Lombard ambit (specifically to the Procaccini)

and to engravings and prints, the same arrangement and the same taste for extremely complex, multi-layered iconography that is often difficult to decipher. The four cloths also share the same technique of execution: a satin stitch with reverse, invented, according to the sixteenth-century literature, by the embroideress herself and defined as the "Cantona stitch" (Lomazzo 1590, p. 166; Morigia 1592, p. 675). In the cloth in question, the decoration is structured into three bands. Above, seated on clouds, are seven divinities, identifiable through their attributes: Mercury, Diana, Saturn, Jove, Mars, Apollo and Venus, which may symbolise the planets with the Moon and the Sun; under them there is a depiction of a mountainous landscape, with various buildings. The intermediate band features four scenes, the meaning of one of which is not clear, separated by shrubs enveloping a post: the first scene shows an unidentifiable rampant animal facing the Moon, followed by a sickle crossed over a cornucopia full of flowers, a snake wrapped around a palm tree full of red fruit and, last of all, an anvil and a hammer. In the third and final section, in the centre, there is an emblem bearing two flashes darting through clouds, inserted within a phytomorphic frame, from which originate plant volutes animated by birds, along with two representations of Jove sitting on the clouds and two scenes in which praying male figures are kneeling opposite, respectively, an altar and a circular-plan temple. The embroidery is completed by birds, both real and fantastical, butterflies and fireflies in flight. For this object the embroideress uses two emblems already found in the Turin altar cloth: the scythe crossing the cornucopia, and the flashes that, in the Turinese work, strike the sea. In chronological terms, its similarity to "Ariadne's Embroidery", datable to around 1590, indicates that it may date from the late sixteenth century. The fragmentary state of the cloth does not allow us to understand its use – a difficulty that we face in all of Cantoni's extant works. Are they precious altar cloths, or the still-mysterious "fruit bowls", the richness of which must have been considerable, as implied by their descriptions in the texts of the sixteenth and seventeenth centuries? For example, Giovanni Paolo Lomazzo describes a "fruit bowl where [Cantoni] represents the Coronation of the Catholic Majesty of King Philip Second of Spain, with the transfer of the States to him by the Caesarean Majesty of Emperor Charles V his father, wherein can be seen the States of His Majesty in figures, with their Exploits, and Queen Mary with many Knights, and around them are, in figures, Religion, Justice, Strength, Prudence, Peace, Happiness, Reputation, with certain Exploits that conform to these virtues. And all of these Principles are portrayed *au naturale* (Lomazzo 1590, p. 166). They may even be refined baptismal cloths, which would often feature a similar layout (Grönwoldt 1993, pp. 78–81, nos. 23–26). In referring to the "much praised" Cantoni, Morigia cites the "marvellous cloths that she gifted to the infanta Catalina Micaela, Duchess of Savoy, which were used in the Solemn Baptism of the Prince her first-born child" (Morigia 1595, p. 299; see also Binaghi Olivari 2013, p. 336). Beyond these doubts, the work appears to be an additional important element in defining the career of one of the most highly appreciated female artists of her day, in a period in which the professional embroidery scene was dominated by men – out of the 350 or so embroiderers cited in the documents and operating in Milan between 1580 and around 1620, no mention is made of any woman whatsoever (Rizzini 2001, pp. 132–143).
Gian Luca Bovenzi

1.19
Giovanni Battista Crespi, known as Il Cerano
(drawing)
Cerano (Novara), 1573 – Milan, 1632
Antonia Pellegrini (embroidery)
Milan, 1583 – Milan, after 1635
Cope Hood with Coronation of the Virgin
1609–1610
Taffeta embroidered with silk, gold yarn and silver yarn, embroidered gold bullion, 51 × 53 cm
Milan, Veneranda Fabbrica del Duomo di Milano, inv. TSR 3

The cope hood depicting the *Coronation of the Virgin*, together with an altar frontal also found at the Museo del Duomo in Milan (inv. TSR 2), is all that remains of the rich and sumptuous tapestries commissioned by the Fabbrica del Duomo in 1609 for the two solemn masses celebrated at the same time in Rome and in Milan on 4 November 1610, at the conclusion of the process of canonisation of Saint Charles Borromeo, which began in 1601. The critics had assigned to this group a corporal case – again held at the same museum (inv. TSR 4), but in reality traceable back to a commission from Sister Angelica Agata Sfondrata – identifying it as that donated by the illustrious nun in 1613 to the tomb of Saint Charles and cited the following year by Marco Aurelio Grattarola (1614, pp. 499–500; Bovenzi 2011a, p. 150, no. 36). While the tapestries have been more or less destroyed (those in Milan were burned, since they were threadbare, in 1765), fortunately the extensive documentation has been conserved, through which it is possible to reconstruct the process of their design and production (see Rizzini 2001, pp. 87–97; Buss, in *Milano* 2017, pp. 290–293, nos. 220-221). From these documents it emerges that the embroidery was entrusted to Pompeo Berlusconi for the metal part and to Antonia Pellegrini for the parts in polychrome silk. The embroideress is represented by her husband, Domenico Pellegrini, who served as her agent. It is very probable that the Fabbrica del Duomo entered into contact with the artist – chosen in part for her affordability – thanks to her husband, to whom one of the large paintings of the *Stories of Saint Charles* was entrusted and produced in 1603.
Unfortunately, the documents do not cite the clipeus, the quality of which was not lost on Marco Aurelio Grattarola who, in describing the canonisation ceremony of Saint Charles, lingered on the hood "so brilliantly worked, with coloured silk stitching in which, with illustrious design and delicate manner, the Coronation of the Most Holy Virgin was embodied" (Grattarola 1614, p. 289). It was initially attributed to Antonia Pellegrini in an extensive inventory of 1775, in which it is described as being within a frame (Biblioteca e Archivio del Capitolo Metropolitano, Milan, Fondo Sacrestia Meridionale, folder 4, file 2, *Inventario di tutti gli Arredi e Sacri Suppellettili della Ven. Sacrestia Meridionale…1775*, fol. 85); this attribution was welcomed unanimously by the critical establishment, in part due to the similarity with the medallion of the altar frontal, the authorship of which is certain (Buss, in *Milano* 2017, pp. 290–292, no. 220). The documents underline that Pellegrini is capable of creating "innovations the *quondam* Cantona", meaning the double-faced satin stitch (Rizzini 2001, p. 92; on Caterina Cantona see cat. 1.18), but the impossibility of seeing the rear does not allow us to confirm the use of this particular technique. Over and above this doubt, the embroideress has succeeded in translating, with exceptional expertise, the graphical and chromatic model of the *Coronation of the Virgin*, the authorship of which is not specified, although the name of Cerano is indicated for the cartoons entrusted to Pompeo Berlusconi. The critical literature has posited, on a stylistic basis and taking account of the role played in the canonisation, the intervention of the painter also in the silk embroidery both for the medallion of the altar frontal (Terzaghi, in *Il Cerano* 2005, pp. 164–165, no. 33), and for the hood (Rosci 2000, p. 107).
Pellegrini's work for the canonisation of Saint Charles must not have come to an end with the embroidery of the tapestries. An extant document of 1610, relating to the artists who produced the paintings with the miracles of Saint Charles, refers to "a painting made by Signora Pelegrina", which may be the embroidered portrait previously displayed in the saint's crypt (Milan, Sacrestia Capitolare del Duomo, inv. 1202). If this hypothesis were correct, it would illustrate her capacity to adapt her technique to meet different sets of requirements; indeed, in this panel, the execution seems more rapid and cursive (Bovenzi 2011a, p. 151, no. 37).
Gian Luca Bovenzi

2.1
Marcantonio Franceschini
Bologna, 1648 – Bologna, 1729
Saint Catherine Vigri Paints the Christ Child
1723
Oil on canvas, 141.8 × 129.5 cm
Bologna, Pinacoteca Nazionale, inv. 843

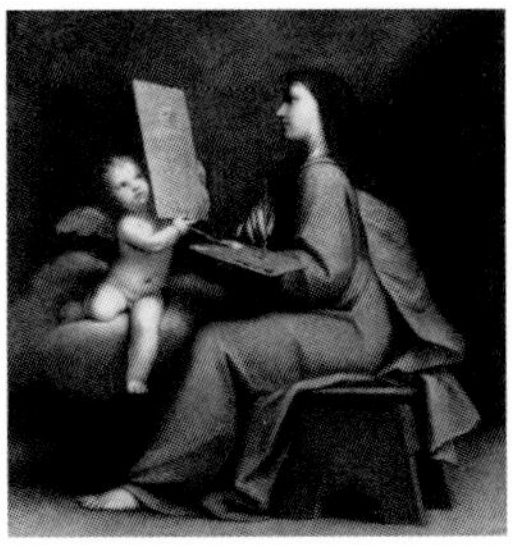

Donated in 1723 by the painter himself to the Accademia Clementina, as noted by Giampietro Zanotti, secretary of the illustrious Bolognese institution (*Atti* 2005, p. 72), the icon of the artist-nun was located in the Meeting Room of the residence (Ghirardi 1998, p. 32; Graziani 2002, pp. 233–241; Graziani 2004b, pp. 29–39; Chiodini, Miller, in *Pinacoteca Nazionale* 2011, pp. 96–97, no. 55). Recently sanctified through the solemn proclamation of Pope Clement XI (1712), Vigri was cited as a patron of the academy in Bologna from its foundation in 1710 by virtue of the reputation she had garnered as a miniaturist and painter. Her artistic output, today radically re-scaled thanks to the work of scholars (Biancani 2002), included at the time not only the *Breviary*, the only book for which she was responsible, but also paintings, including the miraculous portrait of the *Swaddled Christ Child*, brought to visit the sick "for spiritual consolation" (Masini 1666, p. 118), still conserved like a relic in the sanctuary at the convent of the Corpus Domini in Bologna. This work would seem to be that referenced in the "painting within a painting" held aloft by the angel, introduced by the painter to endow the image with plausibility. Depicting the Poor Clare and Bolognese mystic in an emblematic and celebratory mode, she is deliberately portrayed in profile. Staring into his eyes, Catherine is actually contemplating Jesus as she paints him. Her hand holding the brush has come to a stop over the palette; every sound is silenced in the cell, even the light avoids generating contrast or junctures. Everything appears motionless: "contemplating connotes a stasis of the mind and a specific exercise: absolute concentration on the object and the slow passage from one part to the other of that object" (Pozzi 1999, p. 55). This was precisely the action chosen by Franceschini to express the saint's profound identity. Closely connected to the convent of the Poor Clares in Bologna, into which a daughter of his, Felicita, entered as a nun in 1709, the painter was also the preferred artist of the convent to which Catherine had belonged, which entrusted him with the project of decorating her church (1689–1696; Miller 2001, 135–161; De Fanti 2002), in view of the canonisation of their founder.
The "customs" of the painter, "sincere", "honest", "angelic", as they would be defined by Giampietro Zanotti (1739, II, pp. 219, 233, 245; Graziani 2016, pp. 205–209), are fully aligned with the stylistic choices made in the frescoes of the church of the Corpus Domini – evincing a pure, precise, elegant and clean approach – and they were also deemed by the other teachers at the Clementina Academy to be very well-suited with the subject of the painting. Indeed, the innovation of depicting Catherine as she concentrates on the act of painting, already deployed by Franceschini in a *grisaille* of the lost decoration of the church and today documented by the preparatory cartoon at the Museo dell'Opera del Duomo in Orvieto, is simplified through the reduction to a minimum of the appearance of the attending angels. The pared-back setting – which evokes the austerity of the cloistered life, inspired by the vow of poverty of the Poor Clares – marks the completion of the undertaking to perfect the official iconography of the new saint.
Catherine is the progenitor of a tradition of female artists who were well-represented in the pontifical city, which welcomed them into the Clementina Academy as honorary members. The renowned Venetian expert in the use of pastels Rosalba Carriera was appointed in 1720 (*Atti* 2005, p. 63), followed by the Bolognese Lucia Casalini Torelli in 1729 (*Atti* 2005, p. 94). In the meantime, in the city other accolades were received by Maria Vittoria Delfini Dosi, who was awarded her doctorate with a thesis on legal matters (1722), and Laura Maria Caterina Bassi Veratti, who was awarded a PhD in philosophy in (1732), justifiably earning Bologna the epithet of "women's paradise" given to it by Anton Francesco Ghiselli (before 1730, c. 517).
Irene Graziani

2.2
Unknown miniaturist
(copy after Caterina Vigri)
The Seven Spiritual Weapons – Initial C with the Virgin Passing the Christ Child to a Nun (Caterina Vigri's Vision of Christmas Night), fol. 1*r*
c. 1463
Parchment codex, fols. 40; 167 × 115 mm
Ferrara, Biblioteca Comunale Ariostea, BCAFE, MS Classe I.354

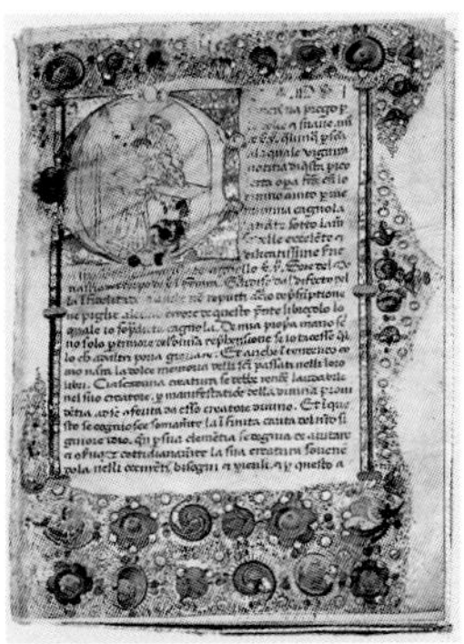

The manuscript contains the transcription of *The Seven Spiritual Weapons* by Caterina Vigri, a treatise on spiritual perfection written in 1438 and probably revised between 1450 and 1456 by the author (Vegri 1985, pp. 108–111; Degl'Innocenti, in Vigri 2000b, p. XV), whose original manuscript is held at the convent of the Corpus Domini in Bologna. *The Seven Weapons* is an academic work dedicated by Catherine to her fellow nuns so that they could acquire the "weapons" necessary for the spiritual battle. At the same time, it is a sort of inner autobiography, with the author drawing on her own spiritual and mystical experience, as demonstrated by the recounting of the episode illustrated in the illuminated folio in which, within a floral-motif frieze, we see the Virgin in the act of entrusting the Christ Child to the outstretched arms of a nun kneeling next to an altar. The scene, which is contained within the letter "C", the *incipit* of the preface to *The Seven Spiritual Weapons* ("With reverence I pray for the sweet and gentle Christ Jesus"), actually portrays the vision of Christmas night – an episode that entered the iconography of the saint and is described by her within the treatise on perfection: while still a nun in Ferrara, she had retreated into the church to pray on Christmas night, and at the time of Jesus's birth the Virgin appeared to Catherine, offering her the Child in her arms. Catherine brought her own face close to that of the "most sweet baby Christ Jesus" and sensed the "pleasing aroma" of his "pure flesh" (Vigri 2000b, pp. 41–42, no. 117). The encounter would remain indelibly impressed on the memory of the Poor Clare, as stated by her first biographer and sister, Illuminata Bembo, in the *Specchio d'illuminazione* (1469): after that night, Catherine "would happily paint the little Christ Child in his swaddling clothes, and in many places in the convent in Ferrara and in books she portrayed him so young" (Bembo 1469, ed. 2001, I, 9). Indeed, the image can be found scattered across the pages of the saint's *Breviary* (Bologna, convent of the Corpus Domini, saint's chapel), which was transcribed by Catherine herself, "with great effort", and also illuminated by her, for the use of the community of nuns and specifically "to assist those who lacked it, such was her charity" (Bembo 1469, ed. 2001, V, 8).
Closely associated, then, with the life of the convent, Catherine's output as a copyist and writer seems to have subsequently inspired in-house production at the Corpus Domini (Serventi, in Vigri 2000a, p. CXIV). Indeed, the nuns themselves, in a letter dated 4 July1463, state that they have "copied, and had copied" the "book" of *The Seven Weapons*, to fulfil the numerous requests submitted to the convent after Catherine's death (Degl'Innocenti, in Vigri 2000b, p. XVI). This was the context for the transcription of the Ariostea codex, the opening page of which betrays in any case the expert hand of a professional miniaturist. The frieze and the scene around it should be attributed to an as yet unidentified master miniaturist operating around 1463 in Bologna or Ferrara. The decoration – not coloured in, except for the

gold leaf of the foreshortened halos – illustrates the saint's tender meeting with Jesus, who is affectionally proffered to her within the perspectivally constructed space of the convent church (Degl'Innocenti, in Vigri 2000b, pp. XX–XXI, no. 8, with previous bibliography; Biancani 2002, pp. 218–219; Graziani, in Spanò Martinelli, Graziani 2015, pp. 361–362, figs. 9.3).
Irene Graziani

2.3
Unknown miniaturist (copy after Caterina Vigri)
The Seven Spiritual Weapons – Initial I with the Figure of a Nun with Hands Clasped, within a Fish, fol. 1*r*
c. 1463
Parchment codex, fols. 59; 165 × 120 mm
Ferrara, Biblioteca Comunale Ariostea, BCAFE, MS Classe I.356

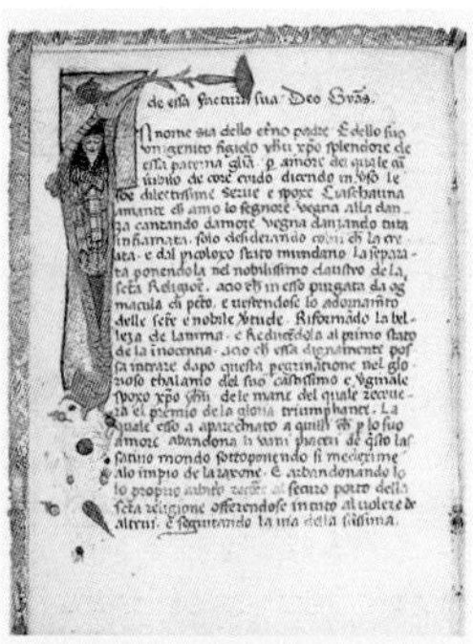

Originating from the dissemination of the autograph of Caterina Vigri's *Seven Spiritual Weapons*, on which the sisters of the church of the Corpus Domini in Bologna worked immediately after the founder's death (1463), codex MS. Cl. I.356 of the Ariostea library would indeed appear to date from the 1460s. The circulation of the treatise was carried out by means of manuscripts up until the year of the first printed edition (*Incomenza uno libretto* 1475). In contrast to manuscript MS Cl. I354, held in the same library in Ferrara (cat. 2.2), in which on the opening page there is a depiction of the episode of the vision of Christmas night, here there is a decorated "I" at the beginning of the first paragraph of the text ("In the name of the eternal Father and of his only begotten Son Christ Jesus") with the figure of a nun with clasped hands, fully enveloped within the outline of a fish, from the mouth of which there emerges a flower (Degl'Innocenti, in Vigri 2000b, p. XXI, no. 9, with previous bibliography; Biancani 2002, pp. 218–219; Graziani, in Spanò Martinelli, Graziani 2015, p. 361, fig. 9.2). The evident allusion to the acronym used to indicate Jesus Christ, transliterated from the Greek into Latin characters (Iēsus Christos Theou Yios Sōtēr, *ichthys*, meaning "fish" in Greek), seems to indicate the nun's intention to share the will of God as fully as possible, wearing the dress of the *sponsa Christi* together with the nun's habit. This is, then, a reference to the following of Christ, embraced by the nun through the leading of a cloistered life, awash with difficult challenges, but also with precious gifts offered by the Bridegroom – the argument of the treatise written by Caterina herself.
The decorative quality of the folio, which is indicative of the input of an author schooled in the art of illumination, betrays no connection to the "primordial", "naïve" style adopted by Caterina in her *Breviary* (Fortunati 2002), in which the images with the face of Christ the Bridegroom and of the "swaddled" Jesus are accompanied by myriad glosses through which Caterina invokes, but also chants and exalts, the love of God that she felt in her mystical visions, allowing her fellow nuns to participate in those experiences (Leonardi 2004).
The codified, expert language of the art of illumination as evinced by the Ariostea manuscript leads us to believe that the artist responsible had a canonical background, which Caterina certainly lacked, meaning that she could not have passed it on to her companions. If the production of this codex can be attributed to the Poor Clares of the church of the Corpus Domini, the actual artist was certainly a professional miniaturist, as yet unidentified, who was entrusted with the task of adding suitable decoration to the first page of the "book" of *The Seven Weapons*. The possibility of attributing the copying of the manuscript to someone outside the convent was also pursued by the nuns in relation to the transcription of the text, as demonstrated by the letter of 4 July 1463 – written in the name of the entire college, albeit probably drafted by Illuminata Bembo – in which the Bolognese nuns declare not only that they have "copied" the treatise but also that they have "had it copied" (Degl'Innocenti, in Vigri 2000b, p. XVI). This latter commitment must have in some way derived from the wishes of Caterina herself, who in a letter delivered to the confessor, Fra Battista da Modena, had asked him to correct the book (referred to as the "liberzolo"), transcribe ("re-write") it and furnish the sisters of the "Corpo de Christo in Ferrara" with a copy (Degl'Innocenti, in Vigri 2000b, pp. 61–62), envisaging however a circulation of the volume specifically to benefit the monastic communities with which she was associated.
A similar fruition within the cloister was behind the production of the miniature accompanying the *Breviary*, which was the source of the "legend", greatly amplified by later historiography, of Caterina the painter (Biancani 2002).
Irene Graziani

2.4
Plautilla Nelli
Florence, 1524 – Florence, 1588
Saint Catherine of Siena / Caterina de' Ricci
1560–1580
Oil on canvas, glued on panel,
57 × 41 cm
Perugia, Galleria Nazionale dell'Umbria,
inv. 533 (I.M. 148)

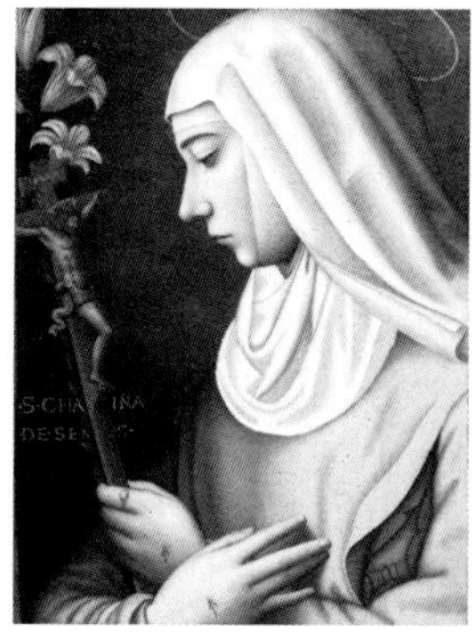

Having reached the museum's collections through the Napoleonic suppression of 1810, the work – which on the rear bears an inscription applied by paintbrush ("Gio. Batta. 1779"), the name of a possible owner or restorer – was attributed to an unknown artist and dated between 1580 and 1610. It was then ascribed to Plautilla Nelli based on research following the discovery of a painting with the same iconography preserved in the Museum of the Last Supper by Andrea del Sarto. Other versions have been identified, similar in dimensions but with small variations and differing levels of quality, datable to the 1560s and 1570s (see Navarro 2017, pp. 34–59). The two paintings in Siena (convent of San Marco) and Perugia have different sizes and are of better quality. They may, then, be attributed to Plautilla and considered the prototypes for the others, produced in her studio (Navarro, in *Plautilla Nelli* 2017, p. 86, no. 7).
Infra-red reflectography and the graphical analysis based on it have shown the presence of a preparatory drawing carried out using the *spolvero* or pouncing techniques, subsequently covered with charcoal. The drawings, which can be overlaid, confirmed the derivation from a single cartoon or from copies of it (re-scaled thanks to the use of *quadrettatura* or "gridding"), which made it possible to work faster (Lari 2017). This is the same cartoon that Plautilla used for the figure of the sorrowful Virgin in the *Lamentation* (Museo di San Marco). It probably derived in turn from a drawing or a cartoon by Fra Bartolomeo, as demonstrated by a number of female profiles in his works (Navarro 2017, pp. 54–55).
This revealed the technique and organisation used by Plautilla's studio, which was like a modern "workshop" in which the serial production of devotional works was arranged as a shared, collective undertaking, guaranteeing the adherence of the images to official Dominican and Tridentine precepts, and the moral and spiritual rigour of the women who made them. In the Perugian version, the underlying drawing comes through clearly in the nose hairline and the upper part of the head. The gesso and glue preparation has not been entirely smoothed down, causing irregularities on the surface. The paint was added with broad brushstrokes, showing its application and direction. The half-bust figure of Saint Catherine, with her

"Neoquattrocentesque" profile, stands out against a green background. She has her hands crossed on her chest and an engrossed expression, contemplating the cross. Her purity and innocence are underlined by the white shades of her Dominican gown, of which Plautilla deliberately excluded the black cap of the Mantellate nuns (Navarro 2015, p. 148). From the saint's swollen, reddened eye, two large tears fall which, with the blood that gushes from the stigmata, represent the evidence of the union and identification with Christ.
This concept derived from the writings of Saint Catherine, for whom tears indicated the divine presence in the human body, since they arise directly from the heart (Webb 2011, p. 102). The wounds and the Passion of Christ are clear references to Savonarola, who had found in those years his most fervent interpreter in Caterina de' Ricci, the "sainted nun" of Prato, to whom Christ had given visions, prophesies and the signs of stigmata. The traditional iconography of Saint Catherine of Siena is, then, deliberately re-read by Plautilla in an ambiguous way, to enable another identification – that with the "living saint" Caterina de' Ricci – thus visually and spiritually combining the two figures. The creation of this new, potent "official" iconography of the saint would be popularised in Dominican and Neosavonarolan contexts.
Carla Scagliosi

2.5
Plautilla Nelli (attributed)
Florence, 1524 – Florence, 1588
Antiphonary E – Initial A with the Presentation of Jesus at the Temple with Two Nuns, fol. 233v
c. 1545–1557
Tempera, gold leaf and ink on parchment,
587 × 414 mm
Florence, Museo di San Marco – Direzione Regionale Musei della Toscana,
Ms San Marco 565

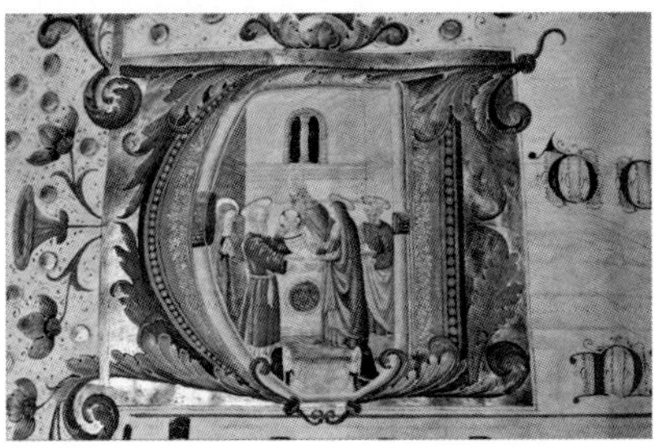

As confirmed by Vasari, Razzi and Rucellai, who defines Plautilla Nelli a "most excellent oil painter, highly esteemed, and laudable in illumination" (*Memorie Istoriche del Monasterio di Santa Caterina…*, cited in *Plautilla Nelli* 2017, p. 78), the artist was self-taught, copying the drawings and works of masters. Before producing oil painting and large-scale works, the artist made miniatures for private worship. In this period, she created the two miniatures which are described here and in the next entry (see cat. 2.6), definitively attributed to the painter at the Uffizi exhibition (Barker, in *Plautilla Nelli* 2017, pp. 70–77).
Previous research had helped to attribute the two works to the ambit of Plautilla Nelli's workshop. In compiling the 2008 list, Turrill had classed them as "possible attributions" (Turrill 2008, pp. 128–129). The nineteenth-century sources indicated that the miniatures in the Antiphonaries E and C, respectively, should be ascribed to an "Unknown Dominican Miniaturist. Possibly School of Sister Plautilla Nelli. 16th Century" and to the "Manner of Sister Plautilla Nelli" (Rondoni 1872, pp. 70–71, nos. 51–52).
The reason for thinking that the two decorations had not been carried out by the same artist lie in the fact that those of Antiphonary E demonstrate an uncertain *ductus*, not highly accomplished technically, which determines a lower quality than those of the other illuminated code.
The scene painted with the initial "A", the only decorated letter of Ms 565, depicts the interior of the Temple of Jerusalem, where the figures of Mary and Joseph, who has brought two doves as an offering, are arranged symmetrically in relation to the two figures: Simeon, who receives the Child from the arms of his Mother, and of the prophetess Anna, represented in a meditative attitude with her hands clasped to her chest. Centrally, behind the altar, the rabbi officiates at the ceremony.
In the foreground, two nuns in profile pray, contemplating the vision of the sacred event. The gilded highlighting on the figures' clothes, the shining halos outlined in red and the whiteness of the back wall of the temple all refer to the presence of a divine light, the origin of and reason for the revelation of the Messiah to Simeon, and of the miraculous purification of Mary. These two episodes are fused into a single iconography. In the twentieth century, the attribution to Nelli's school was rejected in favour of an earlier dating of the two miniatures, thought to have been produced at the end of the fifteenth century (D'Ancona 1914, nos. 534–535), due to the affinities with the decoration of the works of the so-called "Maestro del Lattanzio Riccardiano" (Barker, in *Plautilla Nelli* 2017, p. 70).
If we accept the attribution of the work to Plautilla, the uncertainties and hesitations that diminish the quality of the miniature and of the decoration of the folio can be traced back, as said, to a certain naivety, these being the artist's first experiments using the medium of tempera on parchment. We can, then, locate the work within an early phase: the timeframe proposed by Barker is based on these considerations and on the higher quality of the decorations found in Ms 566.
The supposed date of execution of those decorations (1558) would thus become the *terminus ante quem* for the dating of Ms 565. In the absence, however, of certain dates and documentary evidence for both works, their chronology will most likely be subject to additional investigation.
Carla Scagliosi

2.6
Plautilla Nelli (attributed)
Florence, 1524 – Florence, 1588
Antiphonary C – Initial A with Adoration of the Child and the Virgin Mary, Joseph and Two Nuns, fol. 2v
1558
Tempera, gold leaf and ink on parchment,
584 × 422 mm
Florence, Museo di San Marco – Direzione Regionale Musei della Toscana,
Ms San Marco 566

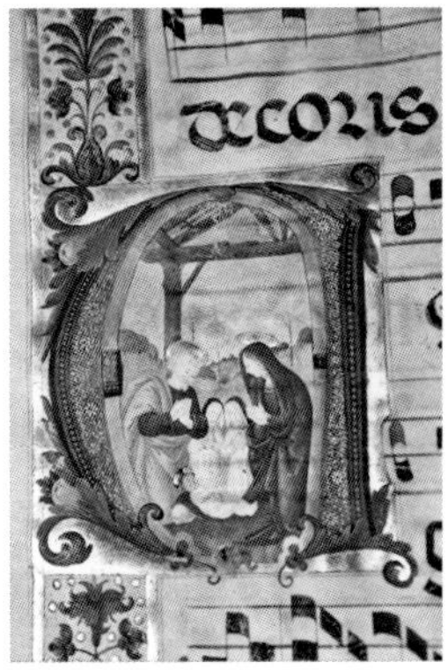

Like Ms 565, Antiphonary C also comes from the convent of Santa Maria Novella and reached the Museo di San Marco in 1867. The quality of its decorations embodied the talents celebrated by the first biographers of Plautilla Nelli. In a landscape with delicate tones of green and blue, featuring gentle slopes and trees studded with golden leaves, the divine light illuminates the Child. The Virgin and Saint Joseph are portrayed as worshipping the Son. Behind them, kneeling, two Dominican nuns contemplate the miracle of the Incarnation. As in the frescoes by Beato Angelico in the convent of San Marco, inserting the figures of the nuns into the sacred episode facilitates the contemplation and meditation through the identification with the two painted figures. Thus, historical time is dissolved in an eternal present in which the holy stories become actual.
The initial, enriched by an intricate decoration at the tip of the brush, is enclosed in a lush vegetal ornamentation with acanthus leaves, fruits and flowers. The pigments used are the same as those found in the main scene, which is indicative of a single authorship (Barker, in *Plautilla Nelli* 2017, p. 76). Even if Plautilla did not have a true apprenticeship, the convent of Santa Caterina was already known for its artistic and culture fervour thanks to personalities associated with the world of art and the proximity of the monastery of San Marco, where the acclaimed miniaturist Fra Eustachio di Baldassarre was based. While it's not possible to assume an apprenticeship, there would undoubtedly have been contact between them. Plautilla's *Adoration of the Child* betrays affinities with Fra Eustachio's *Nativity* (Antiphonary B, fol. 7, Museo dell'Opera del Duomo, Florence) (Turrill 2017, pp. 20–21). From the *Nativity*, Plautilla re-uses Joseph's kneeling pose, with the hands clasped, and his

clothing (the puffed sleeve of the cloak over the right shoulder), the element of the hut with the uncovered roof and the theme of the Child lying out on his Mother's mantle. Other similarities can be found with the two versions of the *Adoration of the Shepherds* attributed to Giovanni Antonio Sogliani (previously in Kassel) and Lorenzo di Credi (Uffizi), from which Nelli takes the pose of the Child who, with his arms raised and crossed, brings the index finger of his left hand to his mouth. In terms of Plautilla's *corpus*, however, the San Marco illuminated initials can be placed in relation to the two devotional works attributed to her recently: a small painting depicting the *Virgin with Child, Saint Dominic and Saint Catherine of Siena* (Museum Catharijneconvent, Utrecht) and a small-scale *Saint Catherine of Siena* painted on copper and held in the Uffizi (Turrill 2015, pp. 160–161). All the faces have minute, delicate features and similar physiognomies. The profiles of the female figures (those of the Virgin in both miniatures and of the two nuns in Ms 565) have a receding, undefined chin, and a continuous line that joins the forehead to the nose. The physiognomies of the figures depicted in three-quarter view also show clear similarities: the round heads with their infantile features, the eyes with their rounded pupils and upper eyelashes only, and the mouth with a more pronounced lower lip (see the nuns praying in this *Adoration*).
For these reasons, all of these works can be attributed to the intermediate phase of Plautilla's output, when she focused on the creation of miniatures and "works of illumination" (Vasari 1568, ed. 1966–1987, IV, p. 404). The chronology proposed by Barker is 1558, based on the presence of the date appearing on fol. 150r of the antiphonary (Barker, in *Plautilla Nelli* 2017, p. 74).
Carla Scagliosi

2.7
Orsola Maddalena Caccia
Moncalvo (Asti), 1596 – Moncalvo (Asti), 1676
Saint Cecilia Playing a Positive Organ and Musician Angels
c. 1620–1630
Oil on canvas, 114 × 148 cm
Turin, Musei Reali – Galleria Sabauda, inv. 141

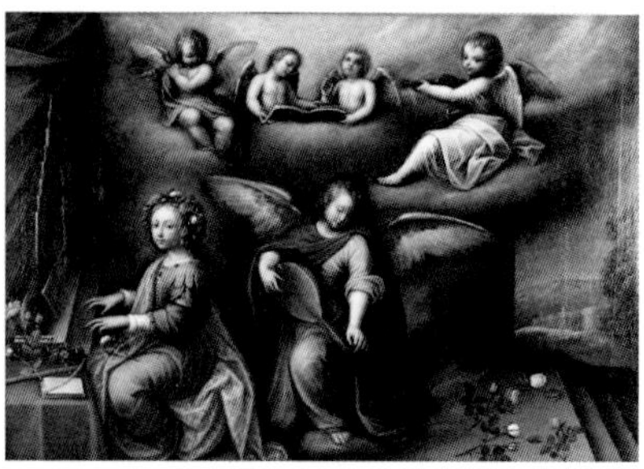

"Just as the wind is in the habit of blowing the clouds away [...] so from the words that came from this burning ray of superhuman and incomprehensible sun I saw clearly the melting of cold hearts in the saintly heat". These verses by Sister Cherubina Venturelli in the *Representation of Saint Cecilia Virgin and Martyr* (first edition 1612) provide a commentary on the vision depicted by the painter. The *Representation* is a celebrated work of the nuns' theatre (Weaver 2002, p. 261), a sub-genre of the sacred theatre of the seventeenth century, into which the Bishop of Casale, Scipione Agnelli (1624–1653), protector of the monastery of Moncalvo and patron of Orsola (*Osanna e Orsola* 2018), immersed himself.
As if it were a stage suspended between the real and the divine, infant figures emerge from a dense layer of clouds, like dispersing fog, affording glimpses of Saint Cecilia (patron of music) seated at the organ, immobile, listening to the heavenly melodies played by musician angels and singers (one seems to be keeping the beat), while an angel appearing at her shoulder tunes a lute before playing it. A grazing light brings out the brightness and warmth of the red clothing and the gold-colour damask fabric, and the preciousness of the jewels worn by the saint, breaking up the cold tones that dominate the composition.
There must have been an inclination towards musical culture in the Caccia household. We know that over the course of his career Orsola's father, Guglielmo, produced iconography associated with music. Orsola's evocative painting in the Galleria Sabauda (acquired by Bertinelli in 1863) and dating from her early years in the monastery of Moncalvo, was a work intended for the family. When the painter's brother, the physician Gerolamo Caccia, died in 1651, his children received the paintings in house of Moncalvo (adjacent to the monastery) appraised by Orsola herself; the first on the list is "My Painting of Saint Cecilia, which is worth at least double 12" (Prosperi 2019, p. 549; Chiodo, forthcoming), which we find again, in 1681, in the possession of one of Gerolamo's children, Angelo Francesco, and identified as the Turinese work (Romano, in *Diana* 1989, p. 109, no. 117).
Music constitutes a recurring theme in Orsola's output, in terms of both altarpieces, such as the *Trinity and Concert of Angels* (Biella, San Sebastiano; Chiodo, in *Arti figurative* 2009, p. 66), and chamber pictures such as the *Heavenly concert* (Casale Monferrato, Museo Civico; Romano, in *Le collezioni del Museo* 1995, p. 55, no. 6) where there is an evident focus on the shape of the instruments and the gestures of angel musicians and singers, who hold up scrolls and partbooks (like the one on the table of Saint Cecilia) with scores taken from pieces of religious music.
These elements allude to the degree of erudition that Orsola and her fellow nuns had attained within their monastery, and to their education. Highly evocative in this regard is the *Allegory of Music* (Casale Monferrato, Museo Civico; Ghirardi 2002, pp. 124–125) by Angelica Bottero, one of the two nun painters, originally from Casale, who were welcomed into the Moncalvo monastery (Laura in 1665, Angelica in 1667) to assist Orsola on the commissions, having established their skills in painting. In the Casale painting, the young artist includes her signature and a date, 1666, on the score next to the organ, whereas the female figure – who can be interpreted as a self-portrait in the guise of Saint Cecilia – turns towards the viewer, indicating her awareness of the *topos* of the self-portrait of a woman artist in the guise of a musician (most recently, Cole 2019b) and of her being *au fait* with the latest seventeenth-century models, such as the solutions proposed by Sirani and Carlo Dolci (Baldassari 2015, pp. 230–233) on the theme of Saint Cecilia at the organ. At the moment of the declaration (6 September 1668) Angelica was given on a usufruct basis by her paternal uncle, Filippo Bottero, a substantial *corpus* of 530 engravings, 216 drawings by "various gifted men", 25 heads on paper and paintings with "Saint Thomas of Vilanova with various figures, a full-figure Saint Laurence *al naturale*, a half-figure crying Saint Peter, and a full-figure Our Lady of the Annunciation" (Chiodo, forthcoming) which must have been instrumental in the education of the Bottero sisters and keeping the monastery up to date.
Antonella Chiodo

2.8
Orsola Maddalena Caccia
Moncalvo (Asti), 1596 – Moncalvo (Asti), 1676
Mystical Allegory (Amore langueo)
c. 1635
Oil on canvas, 84 × 118 cm
Curtatone (Mantua), sanctuary of the Beata Vergine delle Grazie

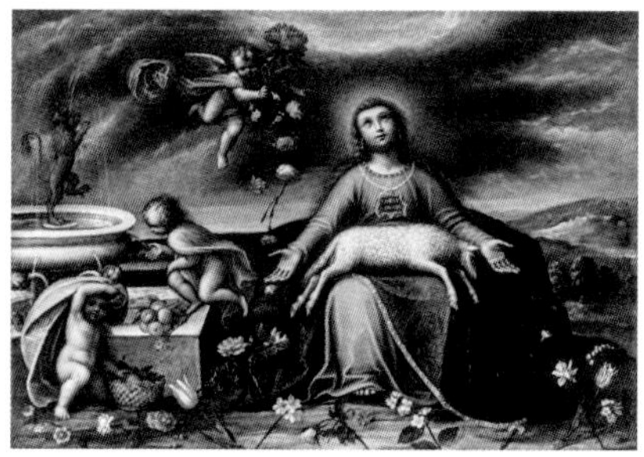

We discovered this refined painting on 7 October 2011, together with the *Saint Margaret of Antioch* (cat. 2.16, also shown here) in a depository of the sanctuary of the Beata Vergine delle Grazie in Curtatone, near Mantua, thus confirming yet further the presence of Orsola in the Mantua area and sealing an intense bond with this essential place of worship. The application of the paint is of an exceptionally high quality; the composition is fascinating and enigmatic, betraying subtle textual and iconographic knowledge. On the right, a female figure, her hair untied, carries on her knee a dead lamb, an evident allusion to the *Vesperbilder* (literally "images of the Vespers", being those fourteenth-century devotional sculptures created in the German ambit and depicting the Pietà, with Christ lying horizontally on his mother's knees). And indeed, the hooves and the rib cage of the mystical lamb are indicative of the bleeding wounds of the torture on the cross. For an accurate

interpretation of the allegory, it is important to pay attention to a number of elements of the painting, starting from the monumental medallion hanging around the woman's neck and bearing the text "AM♥RE | LANGUEO" (with the "o" of "amore" represented by a heart). Taking the form of a puzzle, together with other elements of the painting, it refers to the fifth verse of the second poem of the *Song of Songs*, which states (in Latin): "Fulcite me floribus, stipate me malis, quia amore langueo", meaning "Stay ye me with raisin cakes, comfort me with apples: for I am lovesick". Although "raisin cakes" is the term used as the translation of the Latin "floribus", it is clear that the Latin term refers immediately to "flowers" (which are abundant in the painting, scattered from above by a cherub, and which are a signature element in Orsola's output). Similarly, the *putti* on the fountain have apples next to them. As such, the painting is a visual description of that passage, and the female figure is, then, a reference both to the Virgin and to Shulamite (the woman to whom Solomon dedicates the song). On the left of the composition there is a fountain that jets water from various parts, as well as from the centre of the rampant lion's mouth. Beyond the entertainment value of the child positioned on the edge of the lower basin who splashes water on the other child (who, in turn, protects himself with his cape), it is worth asking whether the reference may once again be to the *Song of Songs* (4:15 "You are a garden fountain, a well of fresh water flowing down from Lebanon", perhaps with an allusion to both the lion and to the River Litani (Leonte, in Italian), aka the Nahr al-Līṭānī, which flows from the city of Baalbek along the Beqaa Valley before flowing out into the Mediterranean north of Tyre). The figures appear in an open landscape, with hills, woods and mountains in the distance, while in the sky the clouds gather, opening up in the centre to allow the divine light to shine through. The narrative is reflected in the cascade of flowers that are scattered from above, right across the foreground of the painting. These are for the most part inflorescences that, in floriography, are associated with meanings relating to love, grace, purity and innocence (roses of different colours, carnations, tulips, perhaps a shrub rose and others). Antonella Chiodo makes a valid proposal of correspondences between the painting and the *Mariale* (Agnelli 1633) by Scipione Agnelli (Mantua, 1593 – Casale Monferrato, 1653) in which the image of *amore langueo*, also with reference to Mary, recurs in various passages of the text. Unfortunately, it has not been possible to trace the ancient line of ownership of the painting, but the iconography is significantly linked with the spirituality of Agnelli, who was Bishop of Casale Monferrato and a refined theologian, as well as a client of the painter and a highly cultured critic (Nigrelli 2018). From a technical point of view, at the moment of its discovery it was unlined, without evident damage. The entire surface was affected by a general clouding, but the restoration – carried out by Monica Marino in 2016 and 2017 under the supervision of Emanuela Scaravelli – reinstated the full legibility of the work, which reveals itself to be one of Orsola's masterpieces, and forms part of a multi-year project of recovery and enhancement of the artistic heritage of the sanctuary of Beata Vergine delle Grazie near Mantua.
Paolo Bertelli, Paola Artoni

2.9
Orsola Maddalena Caccia
Moncalvo (Asti), 1596 – Moncalvo (Asti), 1676
Nativity of Saint John the Baptist
c. 1630–1640
Oil on canvas, 290 × 200 cm
Moncalvo (Asti), parish of Sant'Antonio di Padova – Diocese of Casale Monferrato (Alessandria)

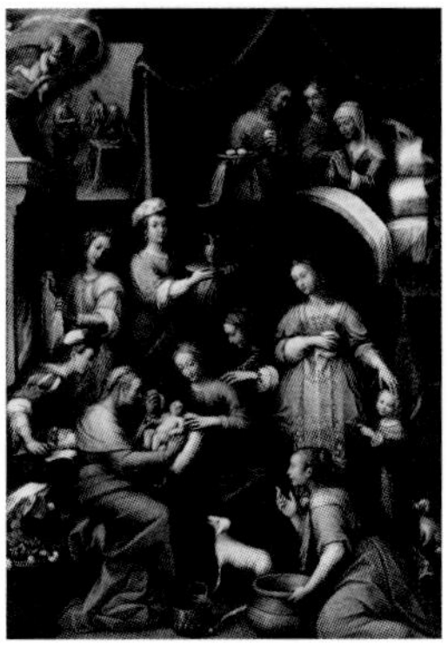

This is one of the most enchanting and fascinating works produced by Orsola during her long and prolific career, and is representative of her output of altarpieces. The painting had been conceived by the artist for her own worship and that of her fellow nuns since it was intended to be displayed in the church of the Ursuline monastery in Moncalvo, founded in 1625 at the behest of her father, Guglielmo Caccia, for his nun daughters and in which she spent fifty years of her life. The altarpiece, housed within the altar dedicated to Saint John the Baptist until the closure of the monastery, was transported following the Napoleonic suppression (1802) – together with others produced by the painter and her father for other convents in the city – to the church of San Francesco, within the parish of Sant'Antonio di Padova (Chiodo 2013; Monti, Bertola, Vaglio 2015).
During Orsola's career, she drew on illustrated material that she received on a usufruct basis from her father for the creation of her own compositional solutions: the altarpiece on display – which displays similarities to the painting intended for private worship depicting the *Nativity of the Virgin* (Pavia, Musei Civici) – derives from paternal models such as the extant folios in the Szépművészeti Múzeum in Budapest, the Gabinetto dei Disegni in the Pinacoteca di Brera (Chiodo, in *Seicento* 2013, p. 138, no. 1) and also, in terms of the figure of the maid next to the crib, the drawing in the Staatliche Kunstsammlungen in Dresden (inv. C 1937-775). However, the inventions of Il Moncalvo are reinterpreted and recomposed by the painter, who succeeds in infusing her own works with a personal interpretation and, as in the case of the work in question, an elaborate symbolic reading of the narrated episode.
Indeed, a female universe is imagined by Orsola in the birth of John the Baptist in Moncalvo: in the intimacy of a domestic interior, in the bedroom of the woman who has just given birth – where only women, albeit of different ages, may enter including a gracious young girl, a furtive spectator who turns to us and guides our gaze to the saint – we witness the ritual of the gestures and actions associated with birth. The painting is endowed with an all-encompassing, tangible, everyday dimension.
In an equilibrium between impalpable naturalness and sophisticated spirituality, the scene is awash with symbolic references and veiled allusions: from the appearance and ternary arrangement of the figures to the objects in the foreground, evoking the destiny of John the Baptist and the pre-figuring of Christ. We note in particular the element of still life demonstrating the painter's skills in this genre, with lush bunches of grapes side-by-side with flowers, such as the red carnation that stands out against a bright white cloth (Verdon 2013, pp. 27–30; Monti, Bertola, Vaglio 2015, p. 52).
The Moncalvese altarpiece, which is reminiscent of the *Christ in the Desert Comforted by the Angels* (Asti, sacristy of the cathedral) and the *Miracles of the Blessed Salvatore d'Horta* (Trino, San Francesco; Chiodo 2007, pp. 24–25), is a prime example of the pictorial style of her artistic maturity (c. 1630–1650) and of the typical inclinations of her approach. First and foremost, there is a lenticular rendering of detail, as can be observed in the sumptuous jewellery, inspired perhaps by that of her own family, which she and her sisters had to renounce upon their entry into the monastery, as confirmed by the sale in Milan for one hundred *scudi* of the gold chain that had belonged to her sister Caterina (Prosperi 2019, p. 531). Moreover, the reinstatement of the chromatic combinations and the material preciousness of the fabrics, in particular of the elegant dresses embellished with bows and lofty lacework, denotes an "understanding of the issues involved in textile design" (Bovenzi 2011b, p. 78) and draws attention towards the embroidery being produced in convents (see Strocchia 2015), as well as highlighting her propensity to depict young women and saints – in works such as *Saint Margaret* (Crea, sanctuary) and *Saints Catherine, Agatha and Apollonia* for the Cathedral Company of Textile Workers in Casale (today Lu Monferrato, Museum; Palmieri 2011, pp. 17–19; Pecchenini 2011) – as refined, fashionably dressed ladies-in-waiting.
Antonella Chiodo

2.10
Orsola Maddalena Caccia
Moncalvo (Asti), 1596 – Moncalvo (Asti), 1676
Tiburtine Sibyl
c. 1640–1650
Oil on canvas, 110 × 76.5 cm
Asti, Fondazione Cassa di Risparmio
di Asti collection

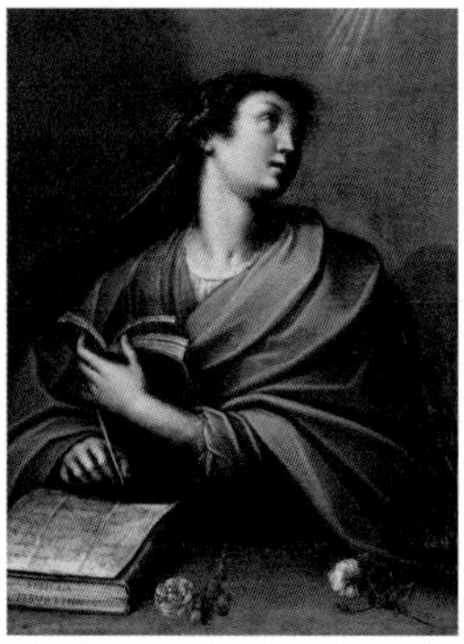

2.11
Orsola Maddalena Caccia
Moncalvo (Asti), 1596 – Moncalvo (Asti), 1676
Cumaean Sibyl
c. 1640–1650
Oil on canvas, 106.5 × 77.5 cm
Asti, Fondazione Cassa di Risparmio
di Asti collection

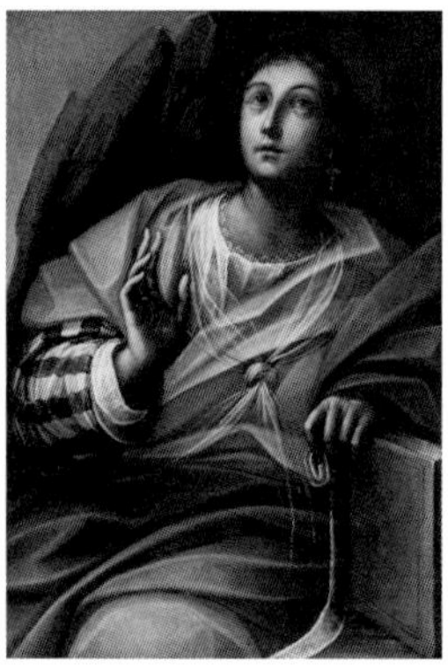

2.12
Orsola Maddalena Caccia
Moncalvo (Asti), 1596 – Moncalvo (Asti),
1676
Persian Sibyl
c. 1640–1650
Oil on canvas, 110 × 78.5 cm
Asti, Fondazione Cassa di Risparmio
di Asti collection

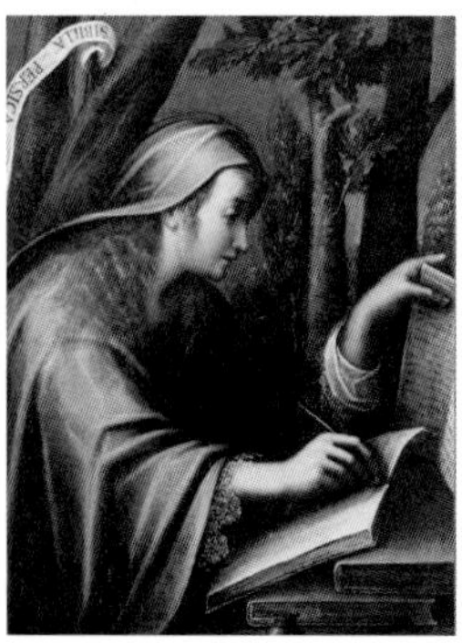

2.13
Orsola Maddalena Caccia
Moncalvo (Asti), 1596 – Moncalvo (Asti), 1676
Delphic Sibyl
c. 1640–1650
Oil on canvas, 110.5 × 78 cm
Asti, Fondazione Cassa di Risparmio
di Asti collection

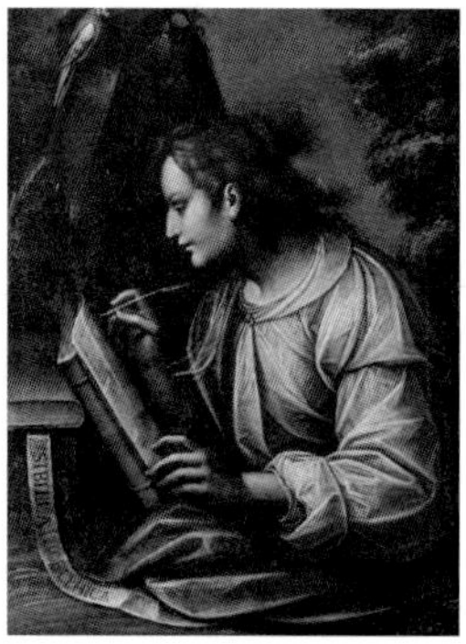

2.14
Orsola Maddalena Caccia
Moncalvo (Asti), 1596 – Moncalvo (Asti), 1676
Libyan Sibyl
c. 1640–1650
Oil on canvas, 106.5 × 77.5 cm
Asti, Fondazione Cassa di Risparmio
di Asti collection

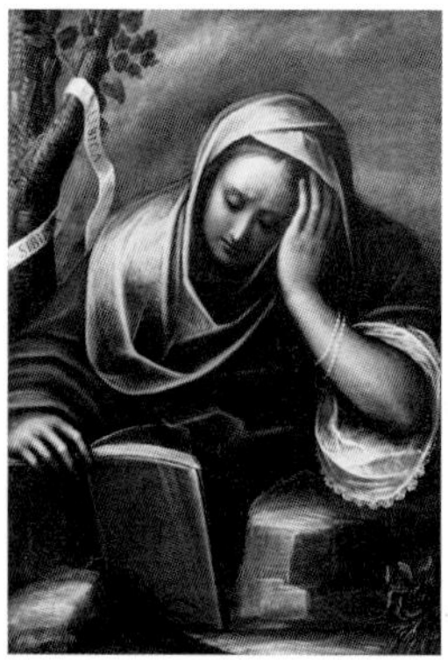

2.15
Orsola Maddalena Caccia
Moncalvo (Asti), 1596 – Moncalvo (Asti),
1676
Hellespontine Sibyl
c. 1640–1650
Oil on canvas, 106.5 × 77.5 cm
Asti, Fondazione Cassa di Risparmio
di Asti collection

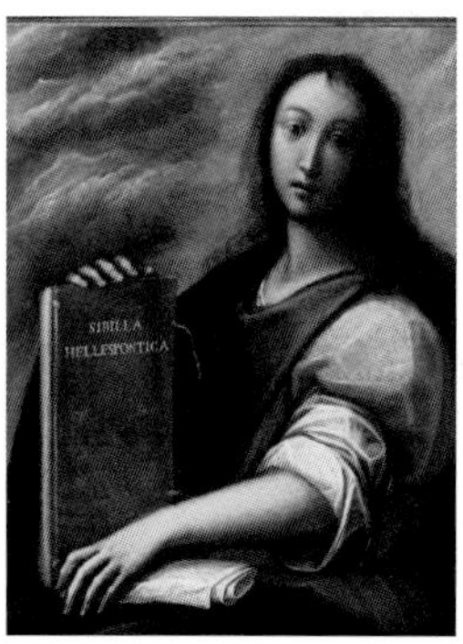

The *Sibyls* series was acquired in 1998 by the Fondazione Cassa di Risparmio di Asti at the auction for the sale of the Dal Pozzo collection in Montebello della Battaglia (Pavia). During the Napoleonic period, Count Ferdinando Dal Pozzo di Castellino (1768–1843) accumulated in his Moncalvo palazzo a noteworthy group of works by Guglielmo and Orsola Maddalena Caccia – today, partially channelled into the collection of the foundation and into that housed at Casa Zuccala in Marentino. In 1813, in Alessandria, the count acquired "four of the famous Sibyls" attributed to Il Moncalvo, accounting for four of the six works in the exhibition.
The *Sibyls*, which portray female figures devoted to the contemplative life, present a number of compositional differences. Four of the paintings feature scrolls with the sibyls' names on them, whereas the *Hellespontine* points to hers on the cover of the book facing the viewer; the last of them lacks any such designation. This figure, identified as the *Cumaean Sibyl*, is dressed in different garb and strikes a wider, diagonal pose. The *Libyan*, *Persian* and *Delphic Sibyls* are immersed in nature, intent on writing or reading, whereas the *Tiburtine Sibyl* is shown inside a room, with the book on a surface next to two roses. Pictured in a more affected, slightly curved pose, she is captured by divine illumination, symbolised by the ray of light that penetrates through the space of the painting (Chiodo 2013). Books in various shapes and sizes take centre stage alongside the six prophetesses, as evinced by the volume held up by the *Hellespontine Sibyl*. On its cover, Orsola used the tip of her brush to paint a weightless twig with flowers, composed in the same way as her still lifes or in florilegia dating from the same period. As indicated in the autobiographical *Saint Luke in the Study* (Chiodo 2012, pp. 103–104; Solinas, in *De dames* 2018, pp. 126-127, cat. 28), circulating within the family were books on various subjects, of different dimensions: on his death in 1651, Gerolamo, her physician brother, had amassed a library of 687 titles, in formats ranging from the *folio* to the *sexto decimo* (Prosperi 2019, p. 549).
The *Sibyls* document the painter's continued interest in her father's models many more years down the line: in the list of March 1626, out of the works left on a usufruct basis by Guglielmo to his daughters Orsola Maddalena and Francesca, there appear "Two Sibyls from the waist up" (the same "Two Sibyls writing, bodies from the waist up, by the same artist [Il Moncalvo]" appearing in the inventory of the grandson Angelo Francesco, dated 1681) and "Two heads of Sibyls large on canvas". In the *Delphic* and in the *Tiburtine*, the painter reworks two *Sibyls* by Il Moncalvo, which have been traced to private collections (Caretta 2015, pp. 182, 316).
The series finds parallels with works dating from the fifth decade of the seventeenth century. The *Delphic Sibyl* is transfigured to become the 1643 *Saint John the Evangelist* (Marentino, Casa Zuccala; Caretta, in *Orsola* 2012, pp. 62–63), while the Montemagno *Saint John the Baptist* (1644; Bava, in *Acquisizioni* 2000, pp. 72–73) can be matched with the *Hellespontine Sibyl* through the use of the same model for the faces.

In this artistic phase, the warm playfulness demonstrated by the painter in the works of the 1630s is tempered, making way for scenes dominated by cold colours, languid figures with livid, ruddy flesh, and dense, deep shadows, in line with contemporary Lombard painting, as encapsulated by the *Saint Charles in Adoration of the Name of Jesus* in Susa (1649; Ghirardi 2018, pp. 45–46) and the *Presentation of Jesus at the Temple* produced around 1648 (Trino Vercellese; Chiodo 2007, pp. 25–28). Attention has been drawn, for example, to the influence of the Milanese Francesco Cairo, in the service of Christine of France in Turin in the 1630s and '40s (Bava, in *Acquisizioni* 2000, pp. 26–29). In 1643, Orsola Maddalena entered briefly into correspondence with the duchess to draw attention to her paintings and to send her a gift of a *Madonna with Saint Christine*. Commissions were forthcoming shortly thereafter for a *Nativity of Jesus* and a *Saint John the Baptist* with uncertain iconography. All have been lost (Baudi di Vesme 1963–1982, I, p. 230).
Antonella Chiodo

2.16
Orsola Maddalena Caccia
Moncalvo (Asti), 1596 – Moncalvo (Asti), 1676
Saint Margaret of Antioch
c. 1640–1650
Oil on canvas, 95 × 73 cm
Curtatone (Mantua), sanctuary of the Beata Vergine delle Grazie

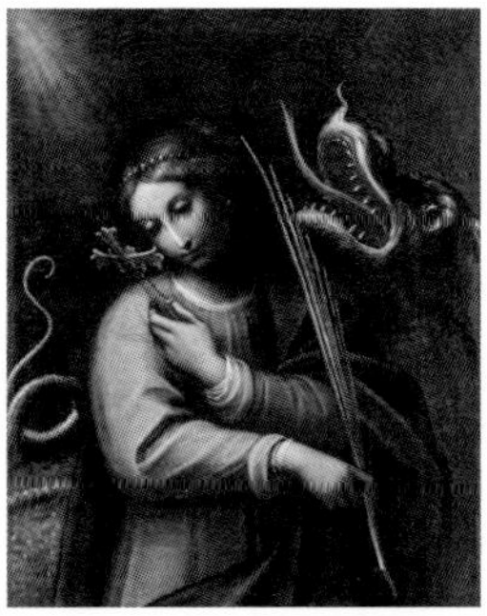

The rediscovery of not one but two easel paintings (the painting profiled here and the *Allegory* also on show, cat. 2.8), unseen and evidently by Orsola Maddalena Caccia, uncovered during the exploration of a number of closed areas of the sanctuary of the Beata Vergine delle Grazie in Curtatone, near Mantua, almost ten years ago now, was a moment of unadulterated joy for those who appreciate the nun's artistic output. It also afforded an opportunity to explore in more depth the links between the painter and the city of Mantua, adding a place until then disconnected from her oeuvre – the aforementioned sanctuary. The painting, laudable for its design, technique and composition, bears comparison with other high-quality works painted by Orsola and intended for private worship, such as the *Saint Catherine of Alexandria* (Pavia, Musei Civici). The saint is positioned on the left side of the painting, juxtaposed against the dragon rearing up with its face pointing upwards. Margaret is blonde, her hair held in place by a string of pearls (naturally); the features of her face – oval-shaped, elongated and illuminated by a ray of light falling from above – embody close-up the typical physiognomy used by the nun-painter in works such as the altarpiece with the *Saint Liberata, Saint Agatha and Saint Lucy*, signed and dated 1637 (Moncalvo, church of Sant'Antonio di Padova). I feel, then, that the work in question can be dated to the 1640s – around ten years later than another of Orsola's paintings found at the sanctuary in Mantua. It is characterised once again by a brighter palette and by a vibrant passion for flowers. In relation to the subject, the saint holds in her left hand a semi-transparent cross, apparently made of crystal, whereas her right hand, positioned lower down, holds the palm of martyrdom. Particularly remarkable are the flesh tones, the refinement of the facial features, the folds of the dress (a triumph of lacquering) and of the blouse, and the intensity of the green of the cloak that falls over her left shoulder. Alongside her is the dragon, the coils of which move from the far left of the canvas up to its head. This imposing character occupies the right side of the painting, its face appearing less vicious than that in the altarpiece with *Saint Margaret* in the Crea sanctuary, in Monferrato (Caretta, in *Orsola* 2012, pp. 98–101, 106–107; Chiodo 2012, p. 104) and recalling perhaps the snout of some pet with its features augmented, or even (if this is a legitimate comparison) the dragons of the Chinese popular tradition. In any case, the dragon is fascinating, with its dark-green mantle, rounded, wide-open eye and its gaping jaws revealing its teeth and its long, forked tongue. From a technical perspective, at the time of its rediscovery the work was unlined, properly tensioned on a non-extendable frame. The pictorial film was rather dull, but fortunately had never been cut. The restoration, carried out by Monica Marino under the expert supervision of Emanuela Scaravelli, has reinstated the full legibility of the work, and is part of a wider project to make the most of the artistic heritage of the sanctuary of the Beata Vergine delle Grazie.
Paolo Bertelli, Paola Artoni

2.17
Lucrina Fetti
Rome, c. 1595 – Mantua, 1651
Portrait of Eleonora Gonzaga I
1622
Oil on canvas, 201.8 × 119.9 cm
Mantua, Complesso Museale Palazzo Ducale, inv. 6832

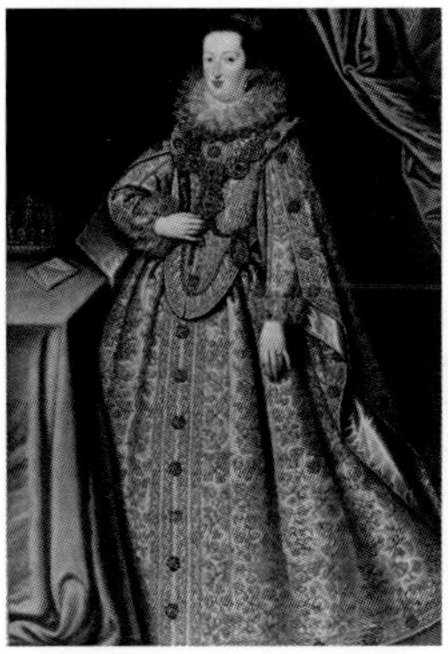

Out of the seven portraits of women of the Gonzaga family produced by Sister Lucrina Fetti, that of Eleonora Gonzaga I (Mantua, 1598 – Vienna, 1655) is the only one to have been signed and dated: "Suor Lucrina Fetti romana in S. Orsola, Mantova, ha fatto, 1622". The subject was the youngest daughter of Duke Vincenzo Gonzaga I (Mantua, 1562–1612) and Eleonora de' Medici (Florence, 1567 – Cavriana, 1611). At the age of ten, after her mother's death, Eleonora I lived in the convent of Sant'Orsola, having been entrusted to the care of her aunt Margaret, the founder of the monastery. She was introduced to Giustina Fetti (later renamed Sister Lucrina) in 1614, when the Roman painter decided to take her vows in that same convent. The date shown on the painting is particularly significant: 1622 witnessed the wedding of Eleonora I and Ferdinand II, Holy Roman Emperor (Graz, 1578 – Vienna, 1637). Since her father had died ten years before, his brother Ferdinand, Duke of Mantua, paid the dowry of 150,000 *scudi* (Gladen 2005, p. 139). Her imperial dignity is carefully highlighted in this portrait, not only through the pendant with the Habsburg monogram on the left side of the bustier and the crown resting on the table to her right, but above all through the letter in front of the crown, on which we can read: "Alla sacra Maesta dell'Imperatrice Gonzaga". In the catalogue of the 1981 exhibition, Chambers and Somers Cocks (in *Splendours of the Gonzaga* 1981, p. 242, no. 273) defined this portrait as a copy of an original painting by Justus Sustermans held at the Kunsthistorisches in Vienna (no. inv. GG_7146). The *raison d'être* of the earlier portrait is cited by Baldinucci (1681–1728, ed. 1845–1847, IV, pp. 479f.) who mentions the permit granted in 1620 to Sustermans to leave the Florentine court (where he served as the principal portraitist) to paint the portrait of Eleonora I in Mantua (permission being given by the Grand Duke Cosimo de' Medici II, whose father, Ferdinando I, was Eleonora I's great uncle). In reality, though the two portraits may have the same layout (undoubtedly Flemish, as evinced by the curtain in the background), there are also clear differences: in the Viennese portrait, on the table, in place of the crown and the letter, there sits a small dog being stroked by Eleonora; in the Lucrina version, her arm is bent, while in the other hand she holds a lace handkerchief. The clothing, too, is not the same: while the corset, the imperial pendant and the Venetian ruff are identical, the skirt and the dress coat are different. Moreover, in the Sustermans portrait, the skirt has two rows of sequins rather than one, and the lining of the dress coat is red rather than gold.
Cecilia Paolini

3.1
Lavinia Fontana
Bologna, 1552 – Rome, 1614
Self-Portrait in the Studio
1579
Oil on copper, Ø 16 cm
Inscriptions: signed and dated "[L]AVINIA FONTANA / [DE] TAPPII FACIEB / [M] DLXXVIIII"
Florence, Gallerie degli Uffizi, 1890, inv. 4013

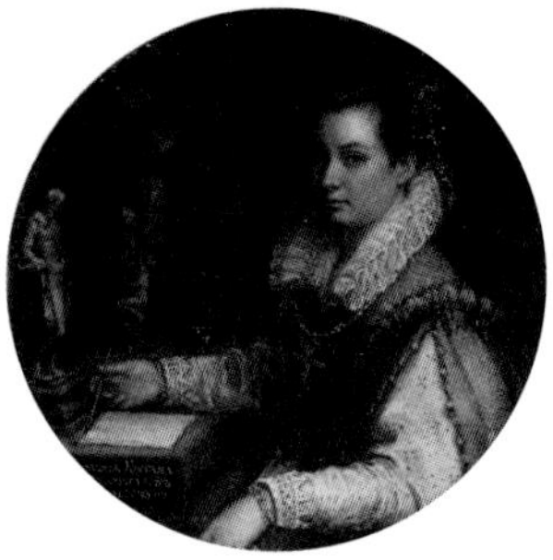

Romeo Galli (1940, pp. 78–81, 115–116; Cantaro 1989, pp. 305–306) was responsible for the publication of documents related to the prestigious commission of the small tondo, which re-emerged in 1713 in the collections of Grand Prince Ferdinando de' Medici and was then transferred to the Uffizi in 1773 (Strocchi 1976, pp. 103–104).
On 17 October 1578, the Spanish Dominican father Alfonso Chacón, who had already received from Lavinia three small portraits of Carlo Sigonio, Alessandro Achillini and Ludovico Boccadiferro, wrote to the painter from Rome inviting her to send him "a small self-portrait the size of the other three, in order to make a life-size painting of you to accompany the one of *Sophonisba*". Like the previous paintings, the self-portrait was to serve as a model for a reproduction in large format, and would also appear in the form of an engraving in a collection of five hundred images of illustrious men and women, printed at the expense of Ferdinand, Archduke of Austria. The Chacón gallery became part of the humanistic tradition of iconographic collections of famous historical and cultural personalities, led by the example of the Museo di Paolo Giovio in Como, but what distinguished it was its section on women's portraits, thirty-four in total, including queens and noblewomen, exceptional women of Roman history, wives and daughters of Ottoman sultans and literary figures. Among the list are the names of two contemporary painters: Sofonisba Anguissola and Lavinia Fontana (Herklotz 2009, pp. 119, 142).
The opportunity was unmissable. Lavinia sent the painting on 3 May 1579, accompanied by a letter that was "shrewd, embellished and sinuous with similes and metaphors" (Ghirardi 1994a, pp. 43–45). Self-confident, and gifted in rhetoric, Fontana presented herself with false modesty. According to her letter, the self-portrait had been requested solely to highlight the talents of Sofonisba and the other painters ("You have thought that by means of the imperfection and darkness of my portrait to illustrate your very noble Museum all the more").
In reality, the work reflects the self-assurance Lavinia had achieved. By then a married woman, she signed herself with a double surname: her father's and that of her husband Giovan Paolo Zappi ("[L]AVINIA FONTANA / [DE] TAPPII"), with whom she was perhaps expecting at the time their third child Orazio (born on 4 November 1579; most recently Cantaro, in *Historia* 2019, pp. 106–107, 232–233). Lavinia was wealthy and is depicted wearing elegant clothes and jewels, notable among which is the large cross on her chest. Observing this, the cultured Dominican client would have identified her as a devout artist, a female equivalent to the model of the "Christian artist" whom Cardinal Gabriele Paleotti had been theorising in Bologna during those years (Fortunati 1994, pp. 27, 29).
As in the portraiture by Prospero Fontana and Bartolomeo Passerotti, setting and gesture contribute to delineate the image. Lavinia is seated in a study full of antiques, perhaps the study in her father's house – "for all the virtuosos of that century, the lobby and the emporium" (Malvasia 1678, I, p. 174; Fortunati Pietrantonio 1986, p. 728). Certain pieces among the plaster casts on display are identifiable: the foot of the Constantine *Colossus*, a version of *Aphrodite Removing Her Sandal* and a bust of a philosopher. On the table in the foreground is a version of Doidalsas's *Crouching Venus* and a reverse image of *Mercury*, formerly in the Sassi collection in Rome and probably derived from an engraving (De Girolami Cheney 2001, specified by Giordani, in *Volti* 2011, p. 152). Heir to the estate of her elderly father or by then a collector herself (Ghirardi, in *Lavinia Fontana* 1994, p. 182; De Girolami Cheney 2001; Murphy 2003, p. 73; Matthiews-Grieco 2017, p. 37), Lavinia portrays herself preparing to practise her drawing and copy models from antiquity. Compared to the *Self-Portrait* of 1575 (replicated in 1577, cat. 3.3), the former girl who had received the education prescribed by Baldassar Castiglione's *The Book of Courtier* had by this point become a cultured and confident artist who was able to converse with her erudite patron.
Stefania Biancani

3.2
Lavinia Fontana
Bologna, 1552 – Rome, 1614
Self-Portrait at the Spinet
c. 1595
Oil on copper, 13.7 × 10.6 cm
Mario Scaglia collection, inv. D 25

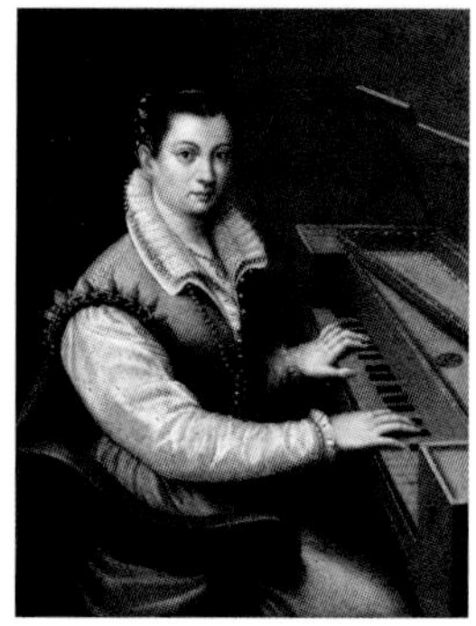

First seen on the antiques market in 1988, the painting was released for the exhibition devoted to the Mario Scaglia collection (Di Lorenzo, in *La raccolta* 2007, pp. 182–185). It is a small painting on copper derived from Lavinia Fontana's famous *Self-Portrait at the Spinet*, known through the signed exemplars of 1575 (private collection) and of 1577 (Rome, Accademia Nazionale di San Luca, cat. 3.3), as well as through subsequent copies. Examples of the success of the original during antiquity are a canvas that bears the date 1578 (Florence, Gallerie degli Uffizi) and a copper painting dated 1575, which appeared at a Christie's auction in New York in 2013. Neither is autograph, but both are datable to the seventeenth century (Cantaro 2014, in particular pp. 99–102).
The iconographic interpretation of the prototype – in which Lavinia is depicted elegantly dressed while playing the spinet, with the score held by the maid, an easel in the background and a Latin inscription which identifies her – is linked to the spread of the model of refined female education proposed for "the lady of the house" in Baldassar Castiglione's *The Book of Courtier* (1528). Compared to the model, the copper version in the Scaglia collection, which is more or less the size of a miniature, has a neutral background and focuses only on the figure of Lavinia intent on playing. The architectural setting, the easel, the figure of the maid and the inscription are missing.
In 2016, the Scaglia *Self-Portrait* was the subject of an interesting attribution debate between Andrea Di Lorenzo and Maria Teresa Cantaro (Di Lorenzo, Cantaro 2016). Although Cantaro (pp. 131–132) acknowledges the excellent quality of the painting, she refutes the authorship and justifies her opinion on the basis of the reduced iconographic composition, the face appearing inconsistent with Lavinia's physiognomy, especially the eyes, and the lack of softness in the colour and use of chiaroscuro. In contrast, Di Lorenzo (pp. 129–130) supports the attribution to Fontana, noting that the quality conforms to her production, and justifies the iconographic simplification as due to the smaller dimensions of the support, while attributing the less smooth face and dark circles under the eyes to an updating of her self-portrait after observing herself in the mirror a decade after the original work of 1575. Di Lorenzo's opinion is plausible.

In at least one other instance Lavinia made changes when returning to a face. She did so for the two known versions of the *Portrait of Costanza Alidosi*: one in Washington (National Museum of Women in the Arts), the other in a private collection. To date, the two paintings have been considered chronologically close, from around 1595, but considering the heavier face in the second version, the two portraits should perhaps be spaced a few years apart (the second should not, however, be dated after 1597, the year of Costanza's death, aged forty (most recently Biancani, in *Historia* 2019, pp. 180–181; Cantaro 1989, pp. 172–173). Moreover, Lavinia returns to her own mature face in the drawing on fol. 2 of the sketchbook held by the Morgan Library in New York, which Cantaro (2014, pp. 105–106, p. 110, no. 23) currently dates to the mid-1590s.
Compared to the examples of 1575 and 1577, in the Scaglia *Self-Portrait* Lavinia focuses on the gaze. A similar study of the face can be seen in the girl turned toward the viewer in the Gnetti altarpiece (Marseilles, Musée des Beaux-Arts), signed and dated 1599 (cat. 3.9), in which Fontana demonstrates her knowledge of the Carracci cousins' new naturalism. Indeed, in those years Annibale Carracci also reflected on his own image, which can be observed in his small *Self-Portrait* in the Galleria Nazionale di Parma, dated 1593, "imminent and unadorned" (Ghirardi, in *Galleria Nazionale* 1998, p. 162). Certainly, Lavinia did not reach such psychological depth, but the exploration of the Self reveals her attention to the naturalistic innovations of the Carracci cousins and dates the small copper painting from the Scaglia collection to the 1590s.
Stefania Biancani

3.3
Lavinia Fontana
Bologna, 1552 – Rome, 1614
Self-Portrait at the Spinet
1577
Oil on canvas, 27 × 23.8 cm
Inscriptions: signed and dated "LAVINIA VIRGO PROSPERI FONTANAE / FILIA EX SPECVLO IMAGINEM / ORIS SVI EXPRESIT ANNO / MDLXXVII"
Rome, Accademia Nazionale di San Luca

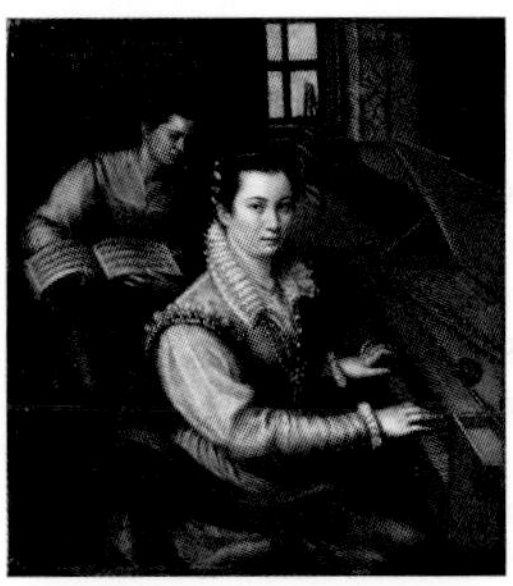

The painting entered the Accademia di San Luca after 1940 as a gift from academician Giulio Navone. Previously, it had been in private collections in Florence, Paris and Rome (Cantaro 1989, pp. 72–74). The work is an autographed replica of a *Self-Portrait at the Spinet* on copper, signed and dated 1575 and recorded in the collection of Archduke Leopold William of Austria in 1659 (Galli 1940, p. 73; Cantaro 1989, p. 64). It reappeared on the market in 2005 (Di Lorenzo, in *La raccolta* 2007, pp. 182–185).
Romeo Galli, followed by subsequent studies, is the first to associate the work with the marriage of Lavinia Fontana to Giovan Paolo, son of the Imola merchant Severo Zappi (Galli 1940, pp. 17–23, 78, 107–110; Cantaro 1989, pp. 302–303). On 13 February 1577, Lavinia's future father-in-law wrote to his wife and son stating that he had been informed by painter Orazio Samacchini and others that Lavinia was a promising painter, and that she was "God-fearing, very honest, of fine character [...] and endowed with virtue". Severo Zappi also mentions that he owns "two portraits by her hand which please me greatly". The correspondence between date and subject has identified one of the two self-portraits as belonging to the Accademia di San Luca. Maria Teresa Cantaro (2014, p. 103) proposes that the second painting Zappi mentions is the prototype from 1575. Whatever the genesis of the model, the iconography is perfectly suited to planning a wedding. The painting not only introduced Lavinia to her future father-in-law, self-portraits also served as a means of becoming known. An immediate precedent exists in Sofonisba Anguissola's numerous self-portraits, which were an agreed advertising strategy promoted by her father, Amilcare, and paved the way to her success. Sofonisba also made a *Self-Portrait at the Spinet* (Naples, Museo di Capodimonte), which she repeated with the inclusion of a maidservant (perhaps a portrait of her sister Lucia), now in the Spencer collection at Althorp. Before her, the Flemish painter Catharina van Hemessen had produced the image of a *Young Woman at the Virginal* dated 1548, held by the Wallraf-Richartz-Museum in Cologne.
Like Sofonisba, Lavinia was inspired by Baldassar Castiglione's model of female education in *The Book of Courtier*: the court lady had to know how to "paint, play and sing, write poetry and hold a witty and intelligent conversation" (Sutherland Harris 1979, pp. 24–25). Lavinia, well dressed and accompanied by a maid in servant's clothes, indicates her future social status.
Angela Ghirardi (1994a, pp. 37–43) points out the skilful construction that underpins the work. As in Sofonisba's self-portraits (Vienna, Kunsthistorisches Museum; Boston, Museum of Fine Arts), Lavinia accompanies the work with a Latin inscription, namely the language of culture, introducing herself as *virgo Prosperi Fontanae filia*, and, like Sofonisba, she uses a mirror. These features are courtly references to the mythical female painters of antiquity, described in the legendary biographies Pliny the Elder included in his *Naturalis Historia*, and later by Boccaccio in *De Claris Mulieribus*. Notably, Boccaccio expands the profile of Iaia di Cizico, who becomes Marzia di Varrone, and focuses on her virtuous virginity and on the self-portrait she made with the help of a mirror.
In Lavinia's painting, the inscription, a guarantee of her education, also plays on the ancient theme of the father-teacher. Prospero Fontana's art instruction is evident in the painting's spatial construction: in the background, illuminated by the window, the easel dominates. As Vera Fortunati has noted so well, the easel "directly relates to the figure of Lavinia; indeed it is linked to her hands which are playing" (Fortunati, in *Da Cimabue* 2015, p. 142). They are hands that know how to write and how to play, but above all they are hands that know how to paint.
Stefania Biancani

3.4
Lavinia Fontana
Bologna, 1552 – Rome, 1614
Portrait of Carlo Sigonio
c. 1578
Oil on canvas, 125.5 × 98 cm
Inscriptions: signed "LAVINI [...] / FON [...]"
Modena, Museo Civico d'Arte, inv. 85

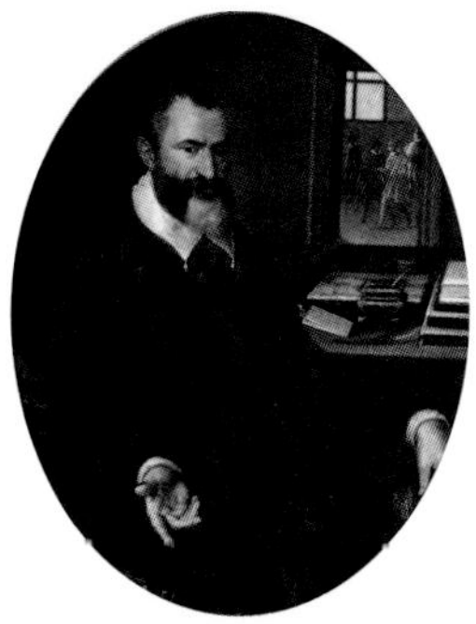

The portrait entered the Modena Town Hall in 1655 as the bequest of Antonio Guarini (Galli 1940, p. 71, no. 106, fig. 11). When restored between 1978 and 1980 by M. Parlatore Melega, the artist's signature came to light, damaged when the canvas was transformed into an oval format (Benati, in *Mostra* 1980, pp. 28–30).
The writing on the letter lying on the table: "Al Molto Mag.co et Ecel.te mio / il S.or Carolo Sigonio / Bologna", enable the sitter to be identified: the historian Carlo Sigonio (1520/1523–1584) from Modena, who had come to Bologna from Padua in October 1563 to take up the Vespers Chair of Humanity. His position had been supported by the naturalist Ulisse Aldrovandi, professor at the city's Studio. Sigonio was already the author of several books on Roman history and law, including a famous commented edition of Tito Livy's *Historiarum ab Urbe condita libri* (1555). In Bologna he had been commissioned by the Senate to draft a *Historia Bononiensis* and had contributed to the founding of a city printing company (Lavenia 2018). By the time Lavinia Fontana portrayed him, Sigonio was already a well-known author, a renowned teacher and a prominent figure in Bologna's cultural milieu.

The work is from around 1578, a time when Lavinia also painted two other portraits of the historian, unknown today. The first is mentioned by the Spanish Dominican father Alfonso Chacón on 17 October 1578, when he wrote to Lavinia from Rome to ask her to make "a small portrait of herself" (cat. 3.1), the same size as three paintings he had already received from her: "the three portraits of Carolo Sigonio Alexandro Aquilino, bocca di ferro". Sigonio himself was to act as intermediary in the request (Cantaro 1989, p. 305). Destined to be copied in large format for Chacón's gallery of portraits of illustrious personalities, the painting was small in size and cannot be the Modena painting. A second example by Lavinia was sent by Sigonio himself to Fulvio Orsini in Rome, as reported in Sigonio's letters of 3 November and 12 December 1579 (Cantaro 1989, pp. 306–307). Neither can this painting be identified as the portrait in the Musei Civici, for although the 1600 inventory drawn up on Orsini's death describes it as oval, it is on copper (De Nolhac 1884, p. 435).
To depict the scholar, Lavinia Fontana used the setting learned from her father, Prospero. In the foreground, Carlo Sigonio is seated at a table where the tools of his work are presented with Flemish precision: papers, inkwell, letter opener, glasses and the parchment binding of the books. The background reveals another room with a group of animated young people. According to S. Urbini (in *Lavinia Fontana* 1994, p. 170) they are in all likelihood members of the "Compagnia della Perseveranza", an association of students strongly supported by Cardinal Gabriele Paleotti "to renew the religious life of the Studio" (Prodi 1959–1967, II, p. 215), and whose manifesto was written by Sigonio himself. Sigonio's relationship with Paleotti, who in those years was writing his *Discorso intorno alle immagini sacre e profane*, with advice from Prospero Fontana (Fortunati Pietrantonio 1982), is confirmed by his words to Orsini about the portrait, expressing his fear of being considered "the vainest man in the world" (Cantaro 1989; Ghirardi 2019b, pp. 249–250). For the cardinal, the portrait was to be in fact a model of virtue and not an occasion for pride. To respond to the need for decorum requested by Paleotti, Lavinia used artist Bartolomeo Passerotti's "talking portrait" approach, comprised of gestures that underscored the social role of the subject portrayed. In the painting, the professor holds his hand out with the fingers open, signalling his "exacting mode of speech, conducted on the basis of a cogent argument" (Ghirardi 2019b, p. 247).
Stefania Biancani

3.5
Lavinia Fontana
Bologna, 1552 – Rome, 1614
Portrait of a Scholar
1581
Oil on canvas, 87 × 72 cm
Inscriptions: signed and dated "LAVINIA FONTANA DE ZAPPIS FACIE / MDLXXXI"
Bologna, Pinacoteca Nazionale, inv. 6472

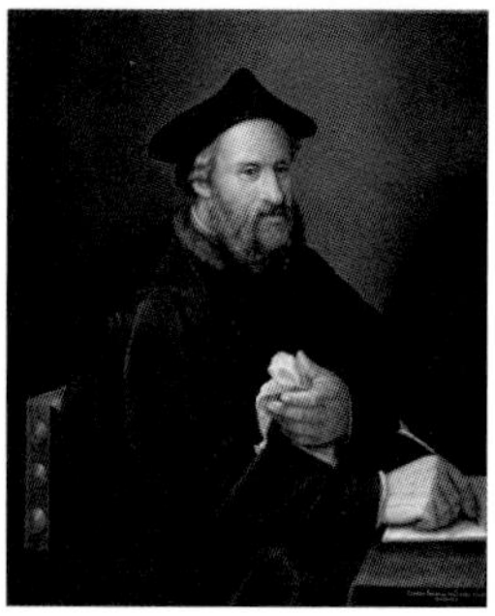

The first mention of the work is from 1922 (Borenius 1922, plate I), when it was part of Sir Leonel Earle's English collection. After passing through the Bukowsky (Stockholm, 1952) and Dorotheum (Vienna, 1969) auction houses, in 1970 the painting was purchased by the Italian State from the Austrian collection of Fernanda Stecker in Weidling, Klosterneuburg, and brought to the Pinacoteca Nazionale of Bologna, where it underwent restoration (Cantaro 1989, pp. 106–107; Graziani, in *Pinacoteca Nazionale* 2006, II, p. 206, no. 146). No information is available to identify the subject, who can be described as a scholar since he is portrayed writing, and because his clothing is characterised by the "four-sided black hat", a prerogative of university doctors (Sabbatini, in *Lavinia Fontana* 1994, p. 195). Portraying scholars was a successful genre in the university city of Bologna (Ghirardi 1994b, pp. 148–152) and had already been tackled by Lavinia in the *Portrait of So-Called Senator Orsini* (Bordeaux, Musée des Beaux-Arts) and the *Portrait of Carlo Sigonio* (Modena, Musei Civici; cat. 3.4), both referrable to between 1578 and 1579. Compared to these, which have detailed settings and staged compositions divided into several rooms as she had learned from her father's teaching, the Bologna painting, in common with other portraits from 1581, is a close-up (Fortunati Pietrantonio 1986, p. 730). Although Lavinia investigates the few details with optical precision, among them the lace border on the cuffs and handkerchief, or the regular handwriting of the letter on the table, sobriety dominates the portrait, notably in the neutral background, the absence of accessory elements and the elderly scholar's dark robe. The light that enters from the left encounters nothing to stop its path, so that it falls directly on to the man's greying visage and aged hands, his calm character and his slow and tired gesture.
There is no allowance for celebration and self-satisfaction: the severity of the setting corresponds to the man's composed attitude. The painting was a clear response to the precepts of Cardinal Gabriele Paleotti, with whom Prospero Fontana collaborated in the realisation of the *Discorso intorno alle immagini sacre e profane* (1582), in which artists are warned about "the dangers of going beyond 'decorum' in displays of vanity" (Fortunati 1994, p. 32). In this work Lavinia and her client show that they are committed to the new path of Tridentine morality.
Stefania Biancani

3.6
Lavinia Fontana
Bologna, 1552 – Rome, 1614
Family Portrait
c. 1595–1600
Oil on canvas, 85 × 105 cm
Milan, Pinacoteca di Brera, inv. Reg. Cron. 382

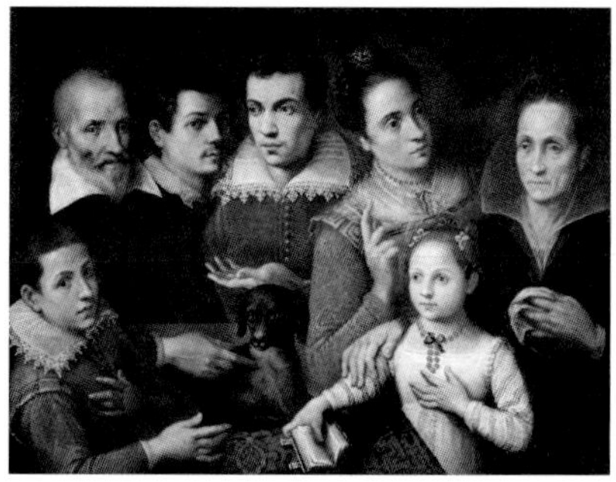

The painting was purchased on 29 July 1808 by the government of the Kingdom of Italy along with other works from the Ravenna collection of Giovanni Battista Pio. On 11 August it entered the Pinacoteca del Reale Palazzo delle Scienze ed Arti di Brera as "Seven portraits on canvas by Lavinia Fontana" (Centanni 1939, p. 317; Noè 1993, pp. 23–26; Sabbatini, in *Lavinia Fontana* 1994, pp. 193–194; Simoni 2018, pp. 103–111). The attribution to Fontana, which has accompanied the work ever since, was definitively confirmed by Vera Fortunati and Maria Teresa Cantaro (Fortunati Pietrantonio 1986, p. 733; Cantaro 1989, p. 196; Fortunati Pietrantonio, in *Pinacoteca di Brera* 1991, pp. 190–192).
Lavinia Fontana had addressed the theme of the family on at least one other occasion, in the large ceremonial *Portrait of the Gozzadini Family* (Bologna, Pinacoteca Nazionale, signed and dated 1584), "a sort of domestic altarpiece dedicated to 'the cult of the Lares', where next to the living there are also the dead" (Fortunati 1994, p. 29), which was repeated at least four times, "in a similar way to copies of a 'family book', destined for the different branches of the extended family" (Ghirardi 2003, now in Ghirardi 2019a, pp. 40–41).
Although lacking the courtly tone of the Bolognese painting, the Brera *Portrait of a Family* also illustrates the link between the living and the dead. On the left, the elderly deceased head of the family indicates the black dog of the afterlife (Murphy 1996, pp. 195–197), while on the right, the widow, whom Murphy (1996, p. 200) believes commissioned the work, has "her eyes still wet with tears" (Ghirardi 2003, now in Ghirardi 2019a, p. 41). Compared to the *Famiglia Gozzadini,* this portrait is set in a middle-class context. The suggestion of a reference to Ludovico Carracci's *Famiglia Tacconi* (Bologna, Pinacoteca Nazionale) is inevitable: through the simplified space, the construction of a theatre of gestures and affections (the grandmother's hand on the shoulder of her granddaughter, the mother's

head inclined towards her husband's) and the Venetian-style chromatic matrix, Lavinia demonstrates her awareness of the new naturalism approach of the Carracci artists. The work can therefore be located towards the end of the sixteenth century, between 1595 (Ghirardi 2003, now in Ghirardi 2019a, p. 41) and 1598 to 1600, according to Vera Fortunati Pietrantonio (1986, p. 733, followed by Graziani, in *Italian Women Artists* 2007, p. 156. However, Cantaro 1989, p. 196 and Cantaro, in *Historia* 2019, p. 182 dates it as late as the early seventeenth century). Compared with Ludovico Carracci's painting, intended for his sister Prudenza and brother-in-law Francesco Tacconi, Lavinia Fontana's family portrait seems to have been composed according to a precise scheme. On the left is the group of men, on the right the women; the elderly are at each end and the children in front. The gestures follow an evident pattern: the grandfather points to the dog, the father to the grandfather, the grandmother hugs the little girl who holds the prayer book, and both children place their hand on their chest with their fingers open (according to Zanchi 2016, taken from Cantaro, in *Historia* 2019, p. 182, this is the apotropaic sign of the "V"). Lastly, the mother points to the sky. This is the regulated world of the post-Tridentine age, where men have "the task of guiding the family order, as Tasso writes" (*Il padre di famiglia* was published in 1582). Meanwhile, the female triad presents "the family as a model of the domestic church, a space more sacred to the affections than to rites" (Fortunati 1994, p. 30).
Stefania Biancani

3.7
Lavinia Fontana
Bologna, 1552 – Rome, 1614
Head of a Young Boy
1606
Grease pencil, tempera and white lead on brown paper, 475 × 355 mm
Inscriptions: signed and dated "LAVI.^ FON.^F . 1606 ."
Rome, Galleria Borghese, inv. 81

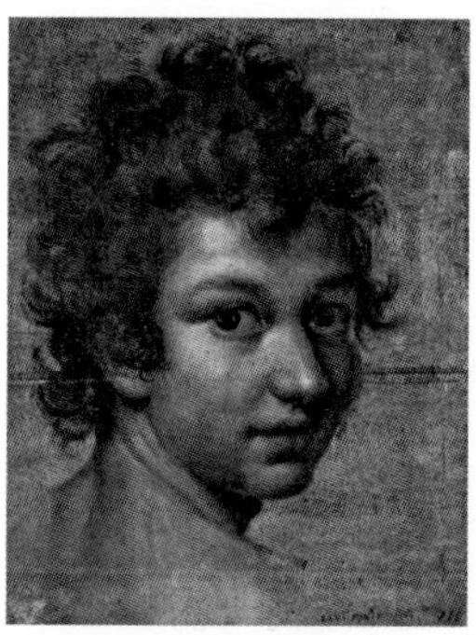

The work, signed and dated 1606, is mentioned from 1650 onward in the inventories of the Galleria Borghese, where it perhaps arrived as a purchase made by Cardinal Scipione, nephew of Pope Paul V (Della Pergola 1955–1959, I, p. 36).
In 1606 Lavinia Fontana was in Rome, where according to Van Mander she arrived in 1603 (Vaes 1931, pp. 195, 204, 208; Ghirardi 2019b, p. 251 note 63) to paint the altarpiece depicting the *Stoning of Saint Stephen* for the church of San Paolo fuori le Mura.
Lavinia had preciously sent from Bologna the altarpiece of *The Vision of Saint Hyacinth* (signed and dated 1599, Rome, Santa Sabina). The client was Girolamo Bernerio, prior of the convent of Santa Sabina, a native of Correggio and cardinal of Ascoli (Ghirardi 1984, pp. 150–151). The Saint Hyacinth painting had encountered great success and had paved the way for Lavinia to move to Rome. The definitive occasion for the move was therefore the commission of the *Stoning of Saint Stephen*. The contract was signed by Giovan Paolo Zappi and Angelo da Genova, abbot of San Paolo fuori le Mura, on 19 February 1603 in Cardinal Bernerio's Rome palace (Ghirardi 1984, p. 154). Fontana subsequently continued to work in Rome until her death (1614). She painted different genres: portraits, sacred subjects, such as the four saints in oil on blackboard for the Rivaldi Chapel in Santa Maria della Pace (1611–1614), and profane works, such as *Minerva Dressing* for Cardinal Scipione Borghese (1613, Rome, Galleria Borghese). Within this broad panorama it is difficult to assign a precise place to this *Head of a Young Boy*. Observing the lively character of the face, Paola Della Pergola (1955, p. 36) thinks it is a study for a portrait. However, the cut of the figure, painted from behind with his head turned, refutes this possibility and tends to suggest a preliminary drawing for a subject destined for another context. Angela Ghirardi believes him to be the character in the left foreground of the *Stoning of Saint Stephen* altarpiece (1603–1604), destroyed in 1823 in the disastrous fire at the Basilica of San Paolo, but known through an engraving by Jacques Callot made around 1611. If this is the case, the date 1606 accompanying the signature would not refer to the date of execution but would have been attached at the time of the sale (Ghirardi 1984, pp. 154–155). Maria Teresa Cantaro (1989, p. 212) considers the tempera work representative of Fontana's iconography and believes the figure to be Saint John the Baptist in the lost *Mystical Marriage of Saint Catherine* (formerly in the collection of the Duke of Leuchtenberg).
Since "Fontana's education was not exactly Carraccesque", Roberto Longhi (1928, p. 185) considered the head "a derivation from a Raphaelesque form", thus contradicting Adolfo Venturi (1893, p. 75), who believed it to be linked to a study by the Carracci painters. Yet Venturi was right. On several occasions Lavinia shows interest in the Carraccis' return to nature, and in this study she is particularly attentive to Annibale Carracci. As Angela Ghirardi ably notes, the work is similar in approach to studies of character heads by Annibale, the youngest of the three Bolognese painters and in those years a successful artist in Rome (Ghirardi, in *Historia* 2019, p. 162). And it was Annibale who was influenced for more than twenty years by the softness and affection in Correggio's work: in Annibale's *Baptism of Christ* altarpiece (Bologna, Santi Gregorio e Siro, dated 1585), the figure of the young man below left, who is indicating the central action, anticipates Lavinia's magnificent head.
Stefania Biancani

3.8
Lavinia Fontana
Bologna, 1552 – Rome, 1614
Portrait of a Gentleman with a Young Boy
1575–1578
Oil on canvas, 133 × 105.5 cm
Cremona, Museo Civico Ala Ponzone, inv. 192

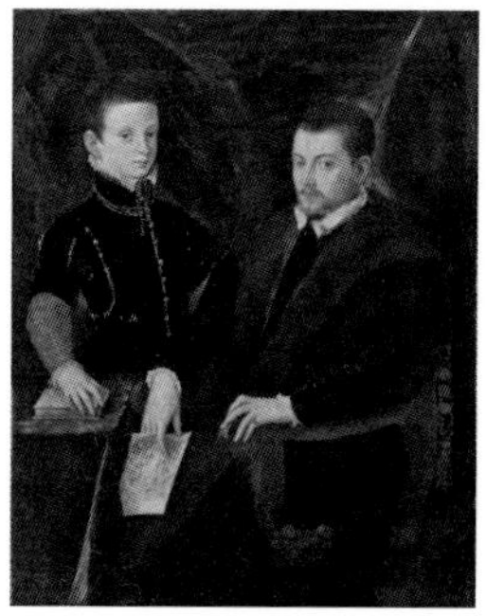

The double portrait in the Pinacoteca of Cremona is part of a well-documented production in the Fontana workshop, starting from the cleric *Giovanni Fagnani Pecori with Assistant* painted by Prospero around 1560 and now in the Galleria Nazionale di Palazzo Barberini in Rome. Lavinia herself later experimented several times with the theme (*Portrait of a Gentlewoman with a Child*, Bologna, Pinacoteca Nazionale; *Self-Portrait at the Virginal with Handmaid*, Rome, Accademia di San Luca, to mention just two of the best known and here in exhibition).
In the Cremona canvas, a young gentleman is seated in a pose that recurs in Lavinia's portraiture: one hand rests on the arm of a chair while with the other hand he holds a drawing of *Hercules and the Hydra* (Benati, in *La Pinacoteca* 2003, pp. 107–108). The man wears a cloak with a wide fur collar over a black suit. Next to him stands a child, almost certainly his son, leaning his hand on a leather-bound book lying on a table. The boy is decked out in a black doublet from which the embroidered collar of his shirt and layered red sleeves protrude. Both have their eyes turned toward the viewer. The total absence of inscriptions or coats of arms prevents their identification, but the man's suit and bearing present the typical image of the scholar, and as such it was included in the gallery of Bolognese academics and notables who often appear in portraits by Prospero and Lavinia Fontana. The only significant element to suggest the man's profession is the drawing he holds in his hand: perhaps he was a collector or a lover of antiquities, or maybe

the subject of the drawing alludes to his name (Ercole). Roberto Longhi attributed the painting to Lavinia (Puerari 1951, p. 149) and also proposed the date as around 1584, finding similarities with the *Portrait of the Gozzadini Family* from that year.
Alfredo Puerari points out that the painting was already much restored and far from its original state. In fact, the canvas arrived in the Cremona art gallery in 1894 as part of the bequest of art dealer Vincenzo Favenza, and like all the works received by the museum from that donation, it had been heavily repainted, perhaps to conceal the abrasions that had made it hard to sell at the time. As verified from the old photographs, the background had been completely reworked; the man wore a three-horned cap and his suit had been embellished with invented decorative elements, such as lapels with fur linings that bore no resemblance to the original painting. The work had been subjected to a promotional restoration that had ended up altering the canvas to give it a romantic aura. The work is now on display after Michele Bernardi's restoration, which removed the heavy nineteenth-century repainting, revealing what remains of the original version, at times still characterised by a chromatic tone and lightness of touch compatible with Lavinia's juvenile production, as already suggested by critics who saw similarities with other works dating to around 1575 (Cantaro 1989, p. 79).
Mario Marubbi

3.9
Lavinia Fontana
Bologna, 1552 – Rome, 1614
Consecration of the Virgin Mary
(Gnetti Altarpiece)
1599
Oil on canvas, 281 × 185 cm
Inscriptions: signed and dated "LAVINIA FONT. D. Z. MDLXXXXIX"
Marseilles (France), Musée des Beaux-Arts, inv. BA16

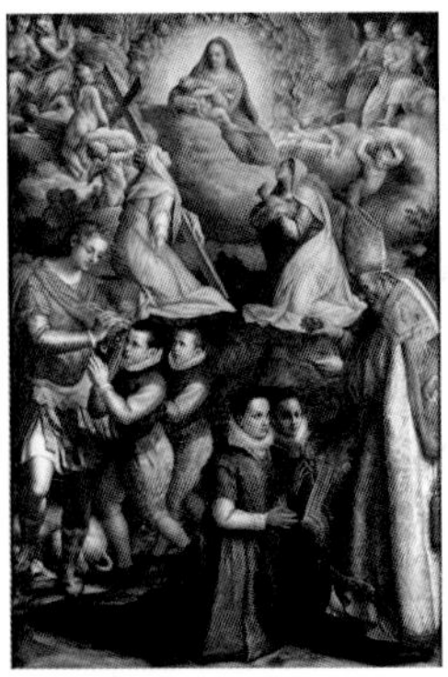

The painting was originally located on the Gnetti family altar in the Bologna church of Santa Maria dei Servi. In 1662 patronage of the altar was assumed by the Bonazzi family, who removed the altarpiece when they ceded the altar in 1739. Subsequently it entered the Hercolani collection in Bologna, followed by the Campana collection in Rome, before being donated to the Marseilles museum (Cantaro 1989, pp. 192–193).
In the centre of the lower part of the canvas is the artist's signature, accompanied by the date. The state of the painting in this extremely damaged area has led to various interpretations: at the end of the eighteenth century the date was deciphered as 1591 (Oretti 1760–1780, ms B. 104, fols. 60, 135; Calvi 1780, p. 38), or 1592 (Oretti 1760–1780, ms B. 124, fol. 10); while at the beginning of the twentieth century it was read as 1599 (Auquier 1908, pp. 359–360; Ghirardi 1984, p. 160, no. 27; Fortunati Pietrantonio, in *Nell'età di Correggio* 1986, pp. 133–134).
The altarpiece has a pyramidal composition. At the top, surrounded by a halo of light and angelic choirs, the Virgin is seated on clouds, lovingly touching the face of the child she holds in her arms. Below her, Saints Elena and Agnes kneel and turn towards her, mediators between celestial and earthly space. Lower still, the painting ends with Saints Donnino and Pier Crisologo, who make protective gestures as they look at the children of the Gnetti family, portrayed in a devout attitude before them. The saints' gestures link the separated spaces of heaven and earth into a single narrative: on the right, Saint Pier Crisologo bends his head towards the two girls kneeling in front of him and pours the liquid from an ampoule. The hands that perform the rite are connected to those of Saint Donnino, who on the left raises the key and the palm above the heads of the two children praying. From above, the hand of Saint Elena is lowered to point at the young Gnetti boys while turning her gaze to the Virgin, invoking her protection of them.
In the work's controlled organisation, Lavinia Fontana re-proposes "the archetype of the Catholic reform altarpiece invented by her father Prospero" in the *Alms of Saint Alexis* (1573, Bologna, San Giacomo Maggiore): "a circular, harmonious cosmos, where everyone, with strict composure, maintains the role consonant with his status" (Fortunati 1994, p. 29). The children's respectful behaviour corresponds to Tridentine precepts: "Lavinia's library cannot lack books or discourses on how to raise children in a Christian manner" (Fortunati 1994, p. 35). The Gnetti family heirs thus embody a virtuous example for future Bolognese society (Murphy 2003, pp. 191–193; Fortunati, in *Historia* 2019, p. 210).
In the Gnetti family painting Lavinia Fontana continues to reflect on the theme of the altarpiece, which began in 1584 with her first public commission, the *Our Lady of the Assumption of Ponte Santo and Saints Cassiano and Pier Crisologo* (Imola, Pinacoteca Comunale), and which she now returns to through the two-level structure and the use of quotations, such as in the figure of the angel with the violin on the left. As Vera Fortunati notes, Lavinia's heavenly vision moves away from her father's Mannerism to create her own neo-Correggio sweetness, similar to examples of Guido Reni's early work (Fortunati, in *Historia* 2019, p. 210).
In the lower part of the canvas, the Venetian lighting exemplifies Lavinia's adhesion to the Carraccis' reformed naturalism, notably in the figures of the holy bishop and the four children. Here the faces of the girls reflect Lavinia's interest in the new Lombard-style psychological portrait, with which the Bolognese cousins were experimenting (cat. 3.2).
Stefania Biancani

3.10
Lavinia Fontana
Bologna, 1552 – Rome, 1614
Saint Francis Receives the Stigmata
1579
Oil on canvas, 63 × 75 cm
Inscriptions: signed and dated "LAVINIA FONTANA DE ZAPPIS / FACIEBAT MDLXXVIIII"
Bologna, Seminario Arcivescovile, F7Z0068–F7Z0069

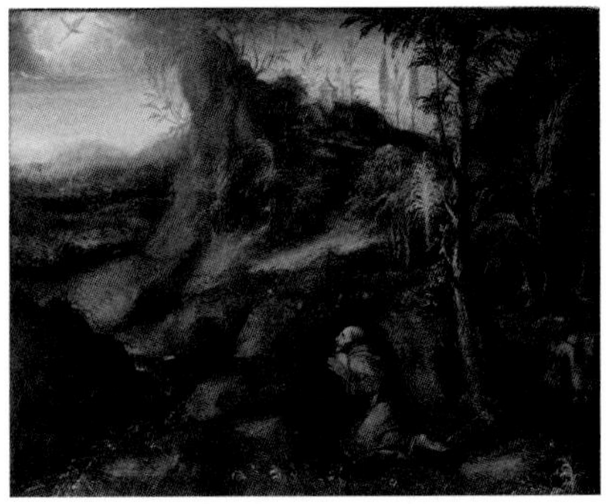

The circumstances that link this work, intended for private devotion, to its current location at the Bologna Archiepiscopal Seminary in Villa Revedin are unknown. Signed and dated 1579 on a rock in the lower left corner, the painting was recorded for the first time in 1936 on the occasion of the publication of a copy in the Pinacoteca Civica di Budrio, and in 1988 it was restored by Katia Ronzani (Mauceri 1936, pp. 16–17; Giudici, in *Dall'avanguardia* 1988, p. 171).
The landscape dominates the composition. Below, in front of a cave, Saint Francis kneels, small and alone. Behind him is a dense forest (Mauceri 1936, p. 16 mentions the name of Altdorfer), in the centre is a great cliff, while in the distance to the left a city lies at the foot of white mountains. The light of the celestial apparition breaks through from above.
Lavinia mediates between past and present: although the urban view is still influenced by Nicolò dell'Abate's dreamlike landscapes, filtered through examples of her father's work (Prospero Fontana, *Christ Praying in the Garden*, Bologna, Museo Davia Bargellini), the taste for botanical analysis recalls the scientific classifications of Ulisse Aldrovandi, a Fontana family friend. The autonomy of the landscape reflects recent Roman experiments in the genre, in particular the manner of

Girolamo Muziano, which, through the prints of Cornelis Cort, Lavinia may have known due to the presence of the Bolognese workshop of Flemish painter Denys Calvaert (Cantaro 1989, pp. 92–93; Biancani, in *Lavinia Fontana* 1994, p. 186). Compared to the models, however, "In Lavinia's vision the static universe of the Aldrovandian encyclopaedia or of the Flemish landscape is transformed into the poignant charm of more mysterious natural beauties, Tasso-like, similar to Tintoretto: 'Beauty will be transmutable and, chameleon-like, will take different colours, different shapes and different images and appearances' (Tasso)" (Fortunati 1994, p. 23). It is a "predilection for cloudy leaden skies, ornate vegetation, the melancholy of sunsets" (Fortunati 1994, p. 23) which is found in the landscape inserts of other works by Lavinia, from *Noli Me Tangere* in the Uffizi (1581) to *Christ and the Samaritan* in the Museo di Capodimonte (1607), via the *Assumption of the Virgin* in Pieve di Cento (1593).
Due to the expansion of the Lavinia's catalogue, in recent years her interest in the landscape has been seen in a new light. In fact, by comparison with her *Saint Francis* in Villa Revedin, as early as 1976 Giovanni Godi attributed Fontana with two fragments from *Views of the Bolognese Countryside* of unknown location (Godi 1976, p. 89). On the strength of this report, Angelo Mazza revisited the comparison with the *Saint Francis* and assigned three large canvases with views of the Bolognese countryside to Lavinia (private collection, 230 × 190 cm, the third slightly reduced), which in 1939 Alberto Graziani, admiring them in Palazzo Bianconcini, mentioned to Bartolomeo Cesi. Restored in 1993 by Ottorino Nonfarmale, the paintings reveal Lavinia's treatment of nature and confirm her interest in Nordic prints, evoked in the cartographic precision, consistent with what was happening in Rome, where Bolognese Pope Gregory XIII Boncompagni (1572–1585) commissioned the decoration of the Gallery of Geographic Maps. Comparing the *Saint Francis* in the seminary, Mazza believes he can suggest the date of the three canvases as 1583 due to "the more nuanced portrayal of the landscape" (Mazza 2002).
Oscillating between the Aldrovandian scientific description, Flemish-style topographical accuracy and Tasso-like atmospheric touches, Lavinia showed a constant interest in the landscape from her youth to maturity. Further confirmation of this is the discovery of *Parnassus*, datable to between 1598 and 1600 (Fortunati, in *La gloria* 2006, pp. 33–40).
Stefania Biancani

3.11
Lavinia Fontana
Bologna, 1552 – Rome, 1614
Sleeping Jesus (*Our Lady of Silence*)
1591
Oil on copper, 43 × 33 cm
Inscriptions: signed "LAVI... FACIE... MDLXXXXI"
Rome, Galleria Borghese, inv. 437

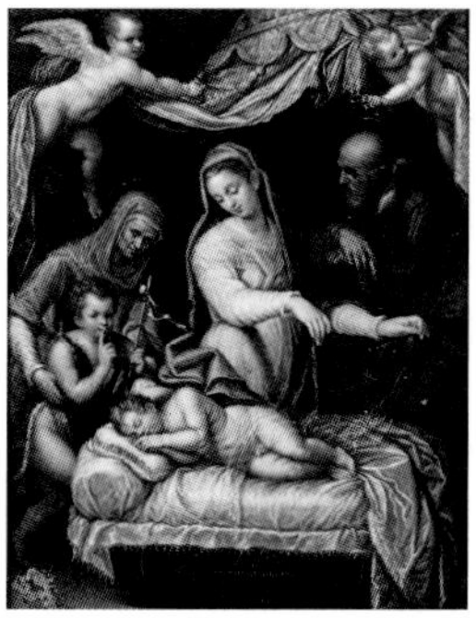

The first citation of the work is from 1693, when the Borghese inventory mentions "A picture on wood panel measuring two palms, the Madonna with Saint Joseph, Saint John and Saint Anna with the Child sleeping on a bed, no. 198 marked on the back, with a silver frame with the engraved arms of Sign. Cardinal Borghese, by Lavinia Fontana" (Cantaro 1989, p. 156). The circumstances of the commission are unknown. Caroline Murphy speculates that the painting, dated 1591, may have been made for Camillo Borghese, the future Pope Paul V, who was vice-delegate in Bologna that year (Murphy 2003, pp. 170–171).
The work on copper is derived from the altarpiece with *Our Lady of Silence* (El Escorial, Real Monasterio de San Lorenzo), signed and dated 1589. Through the mediation of the Dominican father Alfonso Chacón, for whom Lavinia had previously made some works (cat. 3.1), the altarpiece was sent to Philip II of Spain, for which she received payment of one thousand ducats, as Francisco Pacheco recalls (1649, ed. 1990, p. 94). When the painting arrived at the Escorial monastery in 1593, Philip II hung it in the Capítulo Vicarial. In 1667 it was documented in the area of the altar of the Iglesia Vieja, where it remained until 1813, when it was moved to the Real Academia de San Fernando in Madrid. It returned to the Escorial shortly after and was deposited in the sacristy, as reported in descriptions from 1820 and 1857. Finally, Queen Isabella II, exiled in 1868, decided to move it to its current location on the Mausoleo de Párvulos altar to protect the eternal sleep of the royal children (Pérez de Tudela, in *Historia* 2019, pp. 206–207).
In 1602, friar José de Sigüenza (later reported by Ilario Mazzolari: Malvasia 1678, I, p. 224), told of the existence of ten copies of the Escorial altarpiece of varying quality (Sigüenza 1602, ed. 1988, p. 535; Pérez de Tudela, in *Historia* 2019, p. 206). This group might also include the Borghese copper, which differs from the prototype in some significant ways, such as the insertion of Elizabeth, the reflective attitude of Joseph, the entire figure of John the Baptist and a more distanced setting to allow for the presence of the canopy supported by angels (Cantaro 1989, pp. 156–157). The iconography of the Virgin drawing the veil over Jesus derives from Raphael's *Madonna of the Veil*, and in particular from the version by Sebastiano del Piombo, faithfully reproduced in the group of the Madonna and Child. The invitation to silence by Saint John is from Michelangelo's *Our Lady of Silence*, a work destined for Vittoria Colonna reproposed by Lavinia in a painting now in the Walker Art Gallery, attributed to her in 1959 by Roberto Longhi (Cantaro 1993, pp. 95–99). Lavinia may have known this work by Michelangelo from an engraving by Giulio Bonasone, which was known in Bologna and had already inspired Orazio Samacchini (Winkelmann 1986, p. 656). In the fusion between the two archetypes of Raphael and Michelangelo, the iconography is enriched with symbolic meanings: in the Spanish altarpiece the inscription "COR MEUM VIGILAT" on the couch of the Christ Child explains – as in symbol "LXIIII" of Achille Bocchi's *Symbolicae Quaestiones*, which reads *Silentio Deum cole*, "worship God in silence" – the importance of silent contemplation in order to arrive at the truth (Urbini, in *Lavinia Fontana* 1994, pp. 184–185; Fortunati 1998, pp. 20–21).
The replica of the Escorial painting in the form of the small Borghese copper *Sleeping Jesus*, which Roberto Longhi (1928, p. 221) defined as "an excellent representation by this painter", is a symbol of Fontana's formal and imaginative ability, as well as of the success she achieved. Philip II had brought international recognition to Sofonisba Anguissola's portraiture: it was up to Lavinia to demonstrate the ability of a female artist to also tackle the altarpiece genre.
Stefania Biancani

3.12
Lavinia Fontana
Bologna, 1552 – Rome, 1614
Cleopatra
c. 1595
Oil on canvas, 87.5 × 71 cm
Rome, Galleria Spada – Direzione dei Musei Statali della Città di Roma, inv. 245

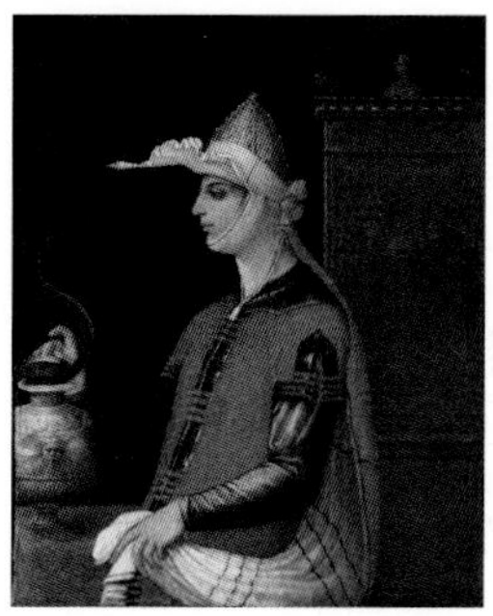

The work can be recognised with certainty from the description: "the Turkish woman dressed in red with a vase in her hand", mentioned in the 1759 Spada inventory (Zeri 1954, pp. 80–81, no. 92). However, it has been speculated that a previous reference to the painting may also be found in a seventeenth-century inventory, in which a "portrait of a woman with a crest" appears (Vicini, in *Cléopâtre* 2004, p. 106; Vicini, in

Kleopatra 2013, p. 172). Whatever the case, the evocative painting, which was only given the documented title *Cleopatra* towards the mid-nineteenth century, has been attributed not only to Andrea del Sarto and generically to the "Florentine" school, but also to the eighteenth-century Venetian school.
It was while Federico Zeri was personally compiling the legendary Gallery Spada catalogue he had restored that he proposed the name of the Bolognese painter, a convincing attribution that has been consolidated since the first studies on Fontana (confirmed in Zeri 1957, p. 44; then Ghirardi 1984, p. 159; Fortunati Pietrantonio 1986, p. 731; Cantaro 1989, pp. 201–211). Less agreed upon is the date of the painting, considered by some to be a manifestation of the archaic, neo-Gothic painting style favoured at the end of the sixteenth century and so datable to the 1590s (Zeri, Ghirardi, Fortunati Pietrantonio); others see it as a cultural effect of the intense contact with the East that occurred during the pontificate of Paul V Borghese, and therefore posit the date as post-1605, the last decade of Lavinia's work (Cantaro). This is not the only question the painting leaves open: it is a highly mysterious and inventive image where several iconographies intersect in what was probably a deliberate stratification for portraying one of the most famous women from antiquity.
Portrayed half-length and in profile, the flamboyant figure, whose authority is accentuated by exotic clothing and slow gestures, is represented in the act of uncovering a precious carved metal vase from which a snake is emerging. Half warrior, half priestess, Cleopatra stares at the reptile which slowly uncoils before her, while with her left hand she is holding the large embroidered veil that descends from the back of her headdress to her hip. In the background, an inlaid cupboard is surmounted by three objects: an ibis, a female bust and a three-footed vessel with a handle. The preciousness of the furnishings, the richness of the fabrics, the posture of the figure and the pose of the snake, together with the secluded setting beyond a dark green curtain that can be seen to the left, give the scene a singular, ritualistic character that has provoked the interest of a wide cross section of scholars (see for example Montanari 2019, pp. 2–3).
Vera Fortunati Pietrantonio (in *Lavinia Fontana* 1994, pp. 202–203) suggested a combination of Cleopatra, Queen of Egypt, and a second, lesser-known Cleopatra, namely an alchemist from antiquity who lived in Egypt around the third century BCE, while reference to the iconography of the "Grand Countess" Matilda di Canossa was also spreading, due to the hat, which is certainly the most characteristic detail of the picture: a conical headdress complete with wimple and finished by a fluttering veil over the forehead (see a summary in Giovannini Luca, *Le raccolte del Principe* 2012, pp. 214–215).
There is no doubt that the influence of what became known as "Matildic iconography" is very strong in the figure, whereas a Cleopatra in warrior and priestly guise seems to be an invention destined to remain unique. Recently, Liana De Girolami Cheney (2018; 2020a, pp. 155–171) returned to the question of identifying the ephemeral alchemist Cleopatra, famous for a page of symbols and diagrams for turning matter into gold. Gathering together the various details of the painting, such as the starry decoration on the cupboard, the face with wings that embellishes the golden vase, and the motif of the snake presents in numerous alchemical texts, De Girolami Cheney proposed newly identifying this iconography as that of the alchemist Cleopatra.
Even if certain comparisons objectively contribute to a better interpretation of the painting, the genesis of this invention remains to be further explored, also in relation to Matilda in her original shadowy version by Parmigianino. For example, the influence on Lavinia Fontana of a previous image is quite possible in her reconstruction of the effigy of one of the "famous women" from antiquity.
The painting was restored in 1953, and further maintenance occurred between 2001 and 2002. An X-ray conducted in 2019 showed no significant modifications. The original frame, lost during external storage during the 1930s, has been replaced by a period frame.
Adriana Capriotti

3.13
Lavinia Fontana
Bologna, 1552 – Rome, 1614
Judith and Holofernes
c. 1595
Oil on canvas, 120 × 93 cm
Inscriptions: signed "LAVI.FONT."
Bologna, Fondazione Ritiro San Pellegrino

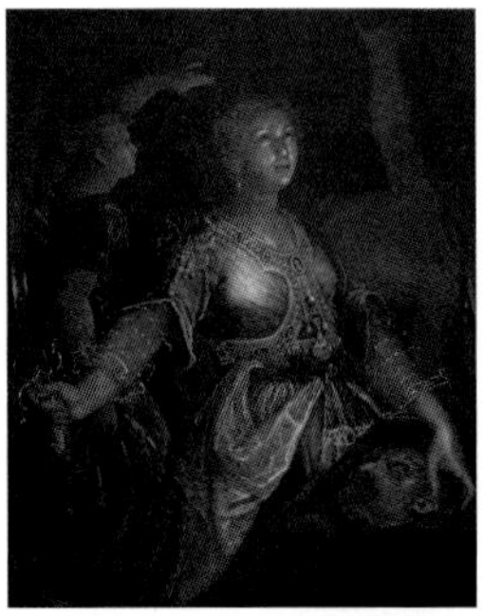

Malvasia was the first to record Lavinia's *Judith*, which he saw in the Ratta family home, together with her portrait of Monsignor Dionisio: "that of Monsig. Ratta, to whom a Cleric is proffering the Breviary, in the house of Signor Gioseffo Carlo of the same address, and in the same house a half-length Judith seen by torchlight" (Malvasia 1678, I, p. 220). The work is later mentioned in the 13 March 1707 *Inventario delle robbe di casa Ratta*, and again by Oretti at the end of the century (Urbini, in *Lavinia Fontana* 1994, p. 204; Cantaro, in *Historia* 2019, p. 209). Although not referable with any certainty to these two works, several documents testify that Lavinia Fontana painted for Dionisio Ratta in the 1590s. The name of the painter is briefly mentioned in a letter dated 4 December 1593, in which Pompeo Vizzani talks to the monsignor, then in Rome, about relations with the artists consulted for the Bolognese commissions: "I have not spoken to you about Madonna Lavinia" (Malvasia 1678, I, p. 217). A few years later the *Giornale* di Dionisio Ratta (1596–1597) reports a commitment to pay Lavinia "for a rosary to be painted for the church of Vedana" and registers the expenditure "for a casing for the Fontana painting" (Urbini, in *Lavinia Fontana* 1994, p. 204).
The Judith theme belongs to post-Tridentine imagery, which through texts and images proposed the stories of biblical heroines as models of virtuous behaviour. Emblematic are those in Tomaso Garzoni's 1586 *Le vite delle donne illustri della Scrittura Sacra* (Urbini, in *Lavinia Fontana* 1994, p. 204). The success of the subject is confirmed by the presence of another painting by Lavinia of *Judith and Holofernes* (Bologna, Museo Davia Bargellini), signed and dated 1600, where the widow from Bethulia is represented after the beheading, her face turned towards the viewer, victorious and cognisant of her role. Silvia Urbini notes the pendant with the peacock that Judith wears in both versions and links it to Girolamo Ruscelli's description of the *Imprese illustri* (1566): "The peacock [...] was a recurring image in sixteenth-century imagery as a symbol of 'generosity and loyalty of soul, since the peacock displaying its feathers loyally shows all its richness and beauty'", and it was also associated with vigilance (Urbini, in *Lavinia Fontana* 1994, p. 205). Vigilant, loyal and generous of heart, the Ratta *Judith* is also depicted after the deed is done, but with her gaze turned upward, full of the divine inspiration that guided her. Judith's own widowhood leads Murphy to speculate that the client is Laerzia Rossi Ratta, wife of the deceased Carlo Ratta and mother of Lorenzo, Monsignor Dionisio's heir (Murphy 2003, p. 152).
As Vera Fortunati Pietrantonio (1986, p. 728) notes, this *Judith,* with her open arms that guide the gaze to the opposite ends of the raised sword and to the decapitated head of Holofernes, has adopted the iconography of *Judith with the Head of Holofernes* (Bologna, Quadreria di Palazzo Magnani), formerly attributed to Lorenzo Sabatini and today reassigned by Benati to Agostino Carracci, but perhaps derived from a prototype that was by Sabatini (Benati 1999, pp. 51–53, 59–60). Agostino's engraving based on the painting defines the shadows more strongly, in particular around Judith's face, where the upper part is lit and the cheek and neck are obscured by thick cross-hatching. Experimentation with light by Venetian and Lombard painters, already typical of Lavinia's *Nativity of the Virgin* (Bologna, church of Santissima Trinità), is also the basis for this *Judith* who, as Maria Teresa Cantaro correctly

points out (in *Historia* 2019, p. 209), should be dated to the 1590s. With delicate touches, the brush creates strands of light on the heroine's sumptuous robes, while her face emerges sculpturally from among the reflections of the "light of the torch" and, with a touch of realism, Holofernes' blood coagulates on the sword.
Stefania Biancani

3.14
Lavinia Fontana
Bologna, 1552 – Rome, 1614
Galatea and Cherubs Riding the Stormy Waves on a Sea Monster
c. 1590
Oil on copper, 48 × 36.5 cm
Private collection

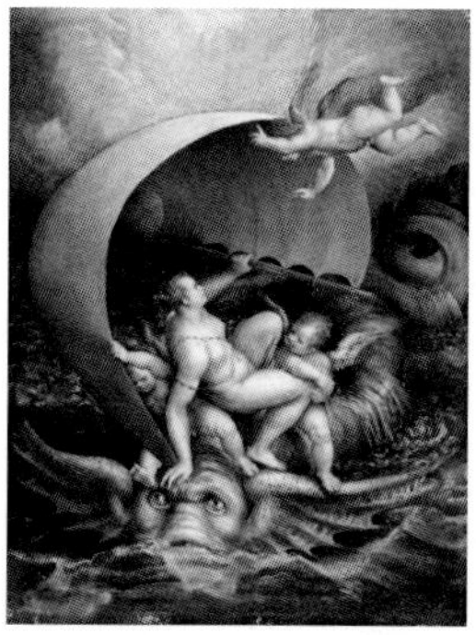

As Vera Fortunati notes, in recent years the arrival on the market of new works by Lavinia Fontana has led to a reconsideration of her role during the Counter-Reformation. For a long time, major studies on the artist (Fortunati, Ghirardi, Cantaro, Graziani, Murphy) saw her success in relation to her having embodied the female version of the "Christian artist" as proposed by Cardinal Gabriele Paleotti in his book *Discorso intorno alle immagini sacre e profane* (1582). Protected by Paleotti and by Pope Gregory XIII, Lavinia was the first female painter from Catholic Europe to have received and systematically executed public commissions for altarpieces, often linked to the Marian theme. Yet alongside her official paintings, a more secret production emerged, in which Lavinia explored myth and the erotic nude, in response to the sophisticated requests of prestigious clients who kept these paintings in private rooms in their homes (Fortunati 2007, p. 43).
The oil on copper titled *Galatea and Cherubs Riding the Stormy Waves on a Sea Monster* belongs to this nucleus from Lavinia's mature phase, which follows the earlier *Venus and Cupid* (Venice, private collection), signed and dated 1585. Transferred from a private collection in Bergamo to the current owner, the work was published by Daniele Benati in 2009 and was recently shown at the Prado Museum in Madrid in the exhibition of works by Sofonisba Anguissola and Lavinia Fontana (Benati 2009, p. 119; Gozzi, in *Historia* 2019, pp. 214–215).
Fausto Gozzi correctly associates the iconography of the painting with *Symbol CVIII* in *Book IV* of the *Symbolicae Quaestiones* by Achille Bocchi, an erudite client of Lavinia's father Prospero Fontana, who was "very dear" to him (Malvasia 1678, I, p. 216; Gozzi, in *Historia* 2019, p. 214. De Girolami Cheney 2020b, however, sees a link with the image of Fortune). Engraved by Giulio Bonasone, the symbol that Lavinia chose to show in the pose, now reversed, is a female figure, her legs bent and arms outstretched: a naked woman riding a dolphin in the storm; namely *Prudentia circumspecta*, accompanied by the motto "CONOSCE, ELIGE, MATVRA". Compared to the original symbol, the complex symbology is freer in the painting and concentrates on the sensuality of the female figure accompanied by cupids, which makes her more easily identifiable as the naiad Galatea. The erotic power of the young woman, emphasised by her pose and the way the playful cupid slips a light veil of transparent silk over her thighs, vibrates with the tenderness of the flesh, thus departing from the Fontainebleau artists' idea of "cold beauty" (Chastel 1966) and inclining towards the seductive figures of contemporary Rudolfine painters.
Borne by a sea monster moving forward the agitated water, Galatea struggles to control the wind-swollen sail as the foam hits the monster's snout and the waves burst against its snakelike body before collapsing into the sea. The fantastic imagery of the monster, combined with the visual detail of natural elements, reflects the influence of the Bologna Studio where the naturalist Ulisse Aldrovandi, a close friend of the Fontana family, classified with encyclopaedic scrupulousness real and imaginary animal species. Poised between science and myth, nature and symbol, Lavinia constructed a polished image that would have intrigued the eye of any cultured client and led Dal Pozzolo to suggest the presence of an international milieu (Dal Pozzolo 2019, p. 36).
Stefania Biancani

3.15
Lavinia Fontana
Bologna, 1552 – Rome, 1614
Venus Receives Homage from Two Cherubs
c. 1590
Oil on copper, 38.5 × 28 cm
Private collection

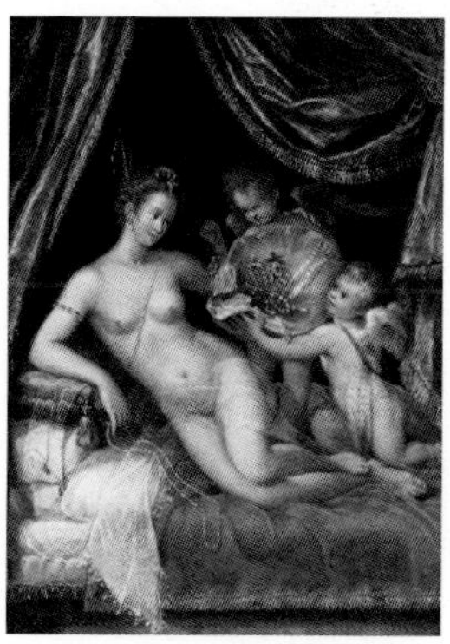

Lavinia Fontana's mythological and erotic catalogue of paintings has been expanding in recent years with the rediscovery of paintings, some in small format, intended for select viewing in the seclusion of private rooms in aristocratic palazzi. Fontana's production of profane works unfolded over a broad arc of time: from the *Venus and Cupid* (Venice, private collection) signed and dated 1585, to the *Minerva Dressing* (Rome, Galleria Borghese), created for Cardinal Scipione Borghese in 1613, a year before her death. This painting on copper was presented by Daniele Benati, together with the first version of *Minerva Dressing* (Bologna, private collection), in April 2002 at the Milanese exhibition "Amor è vivo" (Benati, in *Amor è vivo* 2002, and subsequently in *Percorsi* 2002, pp. 46–48).
The painting depicts Venus lying sensually on a bed with lace-trimmed sheets as she receives homage from two cupids who offer a large seashell valve containing jewels. The scene is framed by sumptuous drapery, which opens like a stage curtain to reveal the goddess's nakedness, covered only by a transparent silk veil. Benati (in *Amor è vivo* 2002, and in *Percorsi* 2002, p. 46; most recently in *Historia* 2019, pp. 216–217) recognises a close similarity with Lavinia's painting on copper of *Sleeping Jesus* in the Galleria Borghese, signed and dated 1591 (cat. 3.11), especially in the disposition of the bed and in the cupids, who become angels in the sacred painting. During the 1590s, Lavinia was influenced by the international painting being cultivated in major European courts from Fontainebleau to Prague under Rudolph II of Habsburg. In this work, the sumptuousness of the ambience combined with a certain solidity of the body, and the feminine roundness highlighted by soft shading, is decidedly more inclined towards Rudolfine imperial painting, although the play of transparency created by the fine veil across the body has its roots in the Fontainebleau court, which since the time of Francis I had been a source of fruitful exchange between Italian, Flemish and French artists. It is still not clear how Lavinia came to know these models of international Mannerism. Her father, Prospero, had been to Fontainebleau in the late 1550s but had returned to his homeland very soon afterwards, and his experience at the Valois court is unknown. Whatever the circumstances, traits of the international repertoire of erotic subjects are evident in Lavinia's painting.
Maria Teresa Cantaro links another of Lavinia's paintings with a highly erotic mythological theme to the School of Fontainebleau female portrait style: the *Venus and Cupid* in the Musée des Beaux-Arts in Rouen, signed and dated 1592, which is probably an allegorical portrait of Isabella Ruini. This link is due to the likeness the Venus shares with Ruini's portrait in the Galleria Palatina in Florence (Cantaro 1989, pp. 161–164; most recently Fortunati, in *Historia* 2019, pp. 218–221). While rejecting

the relationship with Fontainebleau in favour of a knowledge of Prague models, on the basis of this interpretation Daniele Benati (in *Amor è vivo* 2002, n.p., and in *Percorsi* 2002, pp. 46–48) sees a resemblance between the faces of Venus in *Venus Receives Homage from Two Cherubs* and in the private collection version of *Minerva Dressing Up*, and believes them to be portraits of the same person. Vera Fortunati also accepts this plausible notion regarding the Minerva as a portrait (Fortunati, in *Italian Women Artists* 2007, p. 164). It remains to be seen who the lady portrayed might have been. Benati leaves all the hypotheses open, from a young bride to a courtesan, while Patrizia Tosini considers the face of Lavinia's daughter, Laudomia, who died aged sixteen in 1605 (Tosini, in *Historia* 2019, p. 227). If this were the case, which remains to be verified, it would also date the *Venus* to 1604–1605.
Stefania Biancani

3.16
Barbara Longhi
Ravenna, 1552 – Ravenna, 1638
Saint Catherine of Alexandria
c. 1580
Oil on canvas, 70 × 53.5 cm
Bologna, Pinacoteca Nazionale, inv. 1097

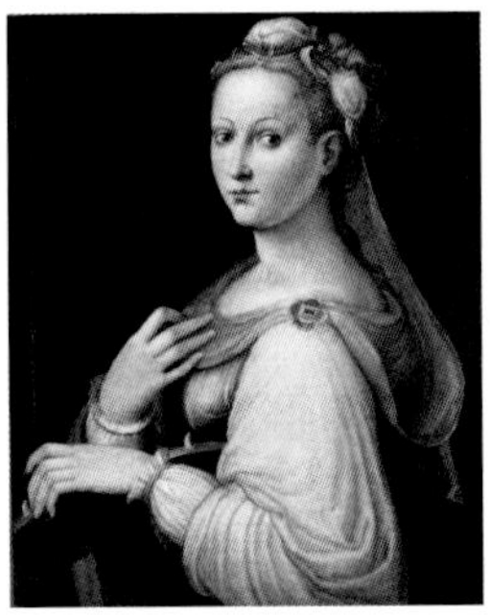

The painting portrays the saint, a virgin martyr, who according to tradition was beheaded in the fourth century CE in Alexandria, Egypt. The young woman is depicted half-length, in a three-quarter pose with her gaze turned toward the viewer. She rests her left arm on the toothed wheel, alluding to the torture inflicted on her before her beheading, and holds her martyrial palm in her hand.
The dark backdrop of the canvas accentuates the iridescent yellow, orange and pink of her gown and her elaborate hairstyle embellished with strings of pearls and a veil held on her shoulder with a gold brooch.
The painting is typical of the Luca Longhi (1507–1580) family workshop in Ravenna. Luca often gave his son Francesco, and Barbara in particular, models to copy, and the work is undoubtedly configured as a chamber painting without a specific devotional use (Graziani 1994; Viroli 2000; Viroli, in *Pinacoteca Nazionale* 2006, pp. 214–215, cat. 153). Although part of a series of works on the same subject, each is distinct in its facial features and in other slight variations, showing the qualitative intention to make each version unique. In addition to this painting, four other examples are known so far: two in the Pinacoteca Comunale, Ravenna, one sharper and more detailed, generally attributed to Luca Longhi (inv. QA334; Simoni 2011 suggests Barbara), the second is attributed to Barbara (inv. QA226). A third, held by the Muzeul Național de Artă al României in Bucharest (inv. 8047/81), is also by Barbara, while the last was sold at a Christie's auction in London (5 December 1997, lot 50) with a generic reference to the "circle of Lavinia Fontana". The Bologna canvas's portrayal of an elegant woman with a slender, elongated face finds a direct comparison in the Bucharest example, which has, however, a simpler rendering of the saint's clothing and hairstyle. The remaining versions are characterised by fuller, shapelier faces and, once again, less refined hairstyles. Moreover, the Bologna painting is the largest in size, and although it was part of the Zambeccari legacy, it does not appear in the inventory of the collection drawn up in 1796 (Cammarota 2000, pp. 393–394). Without drawing any hasty conclusions, it is nevertheless interesting to point out that its measurements are the same as those mentioned by the Ravenna Count Alessandro Cappi, author of an extensive book dedicated to Luca Longhi and his family business (Cappi 1853, p. 166). One of the examples of the same subject known to him was held at the time by "Signor Don Giovanni Rayn", a Jesuit abbot and collector in Fano, who owned a valuable collection of paintings that was divided up after his death (1855).
The saint's pose, with her direct and questioning gaze that captures the viewer's attention, is well suited to the portrait genre, and it is not surprising that art critics have unanimously considered the unknown model in the series of five paintings to be the painter herself. This assumption is based on the comparison with a female figure seated on the right in the foreground of *The Wedding at Cana*, a large wall painting in oils by Luca Longhi (completed after his death by his son Francesco) in the former refectory of the convent of Classe in Ravenna (1579–1580). In fact, it is believed that in the painting he depicted not only the client but also himself, seen from behind, seated between Francesco and Barbara. Indeed Barbara's appearance, clothing and pose bear a notable similarity to those of Saint Catherine, especially in the two Ravenna versions.
As studies on the subject already illustrate (Graziani 1994, p. 144), the practice of self-portraiture has been very popular among female artists from every era as a validation of their status, and therefore a tool for self-affirmation and professional recognition. Moreover, Catherine was the quintessential aristocratic saint, cultured and refined, and also the protector of girls, therefore embodying the ideal alter ego for young, talented women. Barbara Longhi's habit of portraying herself in the guise of exemplary female figures is seen again in two paintings portraying a *Lady with a Unicorn*, one in the Museo Nazionale di Castel Sant'Angelo in Rome (inv. III / 51), the other in a private collection (Daniele 2013a). The painting in Rome, attributed to Luca Longhi and taken from a prototype by Leonardo da Vinci, certainly constituted the model for the second, attributed to Barbara, where the face is very similar to the Bolognese Saint Catherine. Although the idealised portrait of Giulia Farnese (1475–1524) is perhaps the essence of her father's painting, Barbara must still have enjoyed its prestige and found the allegorical meaning of the unicorn, a symbol of purity and moderation, particularly suited to her.
Giulia Daniele

3.17
Barbara Longhi
Ravenna, 1552 – Ravenna, 1638
Madonna of the Milk
c. 1580
Oil on canvas, 41 × 34 cm
Cremona, Museo Civico Ala Ponzone, inv. 188

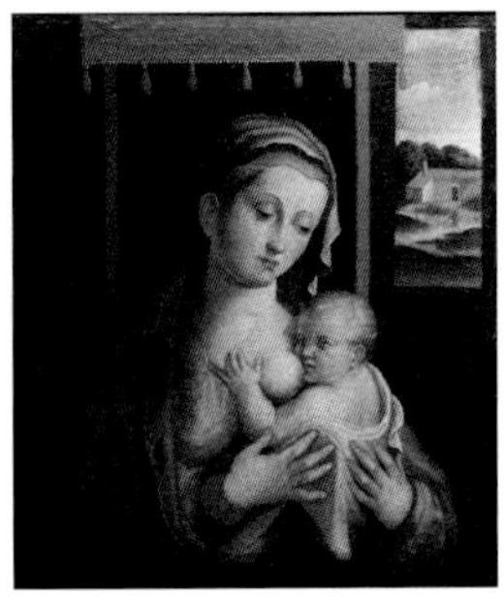

Against the background of a dark wall illuminated by a single window, beyond which lies a hilly landscape, a farmhouse and the silhouette of a human figure, a half-length image of the Virgin is seated under a canopy, intent on breastfeeding the infant Jesus, who turns his face to the viewer. The mother's gaze is absorbed and thoughtful, perhaps already presaging the child's tragic fate.
This small canvas, about which very little was known before its arrival at the Cremona museum at the beginning of the twentieth century, has been the subject of a rather intricate story over the decades. At the time of the Federici gift to the museum, the work bore an attribution to Sofonisba Anguissola, based on an inscription that accompanied a nineteenth-century engraving made by Giovanni Ceresa from Pavia for the book by Count Bartolomeo di Soresina Vidoni, *La pittura cremonese* (Milan 1824). However the reproduction in the book was of a different painting, albeit the same subject (Sambo, in *La Pinacoteca* 2003, p. 101, no. 66). This latter work, slightly smaller (37 × 28.5 cm) than the version examined here, was owned at the time by Count Folchino Dodici Schizzi and exhibited in Cremona in 1899. It, too, was attributed to Anguissola, which in turn

created confusion among art scholars. In fact, although Schweitzer (1900, p. 70) was the first to correctly assign the smaller work to Luca Longhi, Alfredo Puerari (1951, pp. 147–148) confused it with the painting in the Museo Civico Ala Ponzone, and on the strength of an oral communication by Roberto Longhi, also attributed its origin to the Longhi workshop while suggesting Barbara as the artist. In more recent years, Ada Foschini (in Viroli 2000, pp. 191–192, no. 109), while confirming the attribution of the Ala Ponzone painting to Barbara Longhi, still failed to distinguish it from its Dodici Schizzi counterpart, which Flavio Caroli (1989b) identified in a private collection in 1989 but mistook it for the engraving and so returned the attribution once again to Sofonisba.
In an attempt to create order from the historical succession of names and attributions, it should be stated that the Dodici Schizzi canvas, both stylistically and qualitatively, is unequivocally a work by Luca Longhi, as is a second version with the addition of Mary Magdalene behind the Virgin, which appeared on the British antiques market (41.7 × 34.7 cm; Christie's London, 7 July 2000, lot 199; see Daniele 2013b, p. 68). Compared with these two specimens, the painting in the Ala Ponzone collection in Cremona, despite its overall satisfying finish, is more routine in its execution and less precise in the rendering of details, thus more in the style of Barbara (Sambo, in *La Pinacoteca* 2003, p. 102, no. 66). It is just one of the many serial productions intended for private devotion and typifies the output of the Longhi workshop. This is confirmed by a further series of replicas, all attributed to Luca. One, formerly at Villa Canera di Salasco in Arcugnano (Vicenza) then sold at auction (Finarte, 3 March 1987, lot 69) and now in a private collection, is more likely the work of Barbara. A second was formerly in the church of Sain Silvestro e Valentino in Cividale del Friuli (Foschini, in Viroli 2000, p. 192). And finally a third, which was offered for sale in 2003 (42.4 × 34 cm; Sotheby's New York, 23 January 2003, lot 173) and recently reappeared on the antiques market (41 × 33 cm; Stair Hudson, New York, 9 October 2020, lot 13).
The prototype of the *Virgo lactans* on which the composition is based is a rather widespread model in northern European art from the fifteenth and sixteenth centuries, variously traced to the Dutch artist Dieric Bouts (1415–1475; see Foschini, in Viroli 2000, pp. 64, 192). Bouts painted a series of versions of the Madonna and Child, which although comparable in conception to the Longhi typology, do not seem to constitute its direct and immediate antecedent. On the other hand, several works by Flemish Joos van Cleve (1485–1541) share a greater similarity, and paintings attributed to his circle match the composition of the Longhi series, thus confirming that the Ravenna versions were the result of the circulation of engravings: for example the *Madonna and Child* in the Nelson-Atkins Museum of Art in Kansas City (inv. 31–115), several similar versions of which have appeared on the antiques market, most notably among them a panel painting sold by Bonhams, New York, on 4 May 2011 (lot 6), which in turn is a replica of a more famous model in a private collection that has identical scenery, including the canopy and the window open in the background.
Finally, regarding the date of the work, although Barbara's catalogue is chronologically uncertain, around the 1580s has been proposed for the Cremona canvas (Zama 2001, pp. 81, 83), which seems likely.
Giulia Daniele

3.18
Barbara Longhi
Ravenna, 1552 – Ravenna, 1638
Madonna and Child with Saint John the Baptist
1580–1590
Oil on canvas, 37 × 31.5 cm
Inscriptions: initialled at lower "B.L.F."
Ravenna, MAR – Museo d'Arte della Città di Ravenna, inv. QA 89 (1994–)

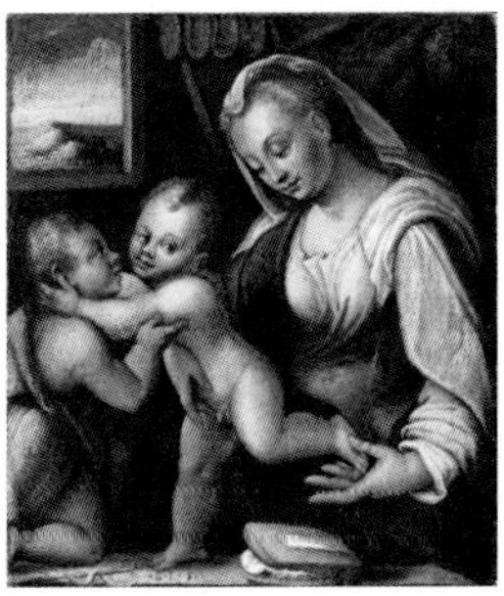

This painting of unknown provenance was first published by Corrado Ricci, who attributed it to Barbara Longhi based on the initials on the edge of the balustrade (Ricci 1897, p. 132). For Giordano Viroli, the 1580s seems a plausible date, since at that time Barbara could still count on the protection of her father, Luca, who owned a workshop until his death in 1580 (Viroli, in *Pinacoteca comunale di Ravenna* 2001, p. 98). The exceptional sign of authorship, which is anything but consolidated, makes this small canvas a fixed point in Barbara Longhi's production, which is not always easy to catalogue, especially when it comes to series of compositionally standard chamber paintings. The workshop had an assorted repertoire of models, starting with Raphael, mostly copied by Marco Dente or Marcantonio Raimondi, with the gradual addition of works by Emilian masters Correggio and Parmigianino, and later those of central Italian artist-writers: the Zuccaro brothers, Marco Pino and Ludovico Dolce. The late years of Mannerism included Bolognese variations by Lorenzo Sabatini and Orazio Samacchini. It was among these congeries that Barbara began her internship, possibly influenced by Lavinia Fontana who was the same age. It is not to be excluded that the two knew one another, and that it was Lavinia's father, Prospero, who pointed out Barbara's precocious talent to Vasari, subsequent to conversations in Ravenna, when the Bolognese painter collaborated in the *Lamentation over Christ Deposed from the Cross* that the abbey at Classe had commissioned from Vasari (Fabbri 2011, pp. 50–51). In fact, Vasari (1568) was responsible for Barbara's first historiographic mention, writing that she takes her first steps "with very good grace and manner", as an aside during his brief nod to Luca Longhi within his description of the life of Francesco Primaticcio.
The iconography of Barbara's *Madonna and Child with Saint John the Baptist* in Ravenna is a variant of the *Madonna of Divine Love*, and similar to that of Fra Bartolomeo's *Madonna and Child and Saint John*, now in the National Gallery in London. Moreover, Barbara adds a Leonardesque embrace between the children as a starting point for breaking free of her father's icy, and at times even captious classicism, in her search for a more intimate voice. Indeed, in the era of the Counter-Reformation, the discussion of affectivity had become central in the debate around the representation of sacred images. For Barbara, the rhetorical exercise concerns the theme of tenderness, which the iconography of the *Mater amabilis* seeks to exalt. The cursive brushstroke combines with a succession of gestures and glances that create their own evolutions around the rose madder gown, the true centre of gravity for the many counterpoints. A comparison with the version by Barbara in the Gemäldegalerie, Dresden, based on Correggio's painting of the same theme in the Prado, allows us to trace the stylistic development. The softness of the modelling, accompanied by a skilful use of colour, makes this painting a work at the height of a classicist trajectory, albeit still under the paternal aegis, produced no later than the end of the 1570s (Viroli 2000, p. 194).
The Ravenna canvas seems to anticipate a Mannerist impulse, notable in gestures pushed to an extreme of contortionism in order to establish the devotional climax in the web of emotions. The apportioning of the abbreviated passages of colour that form the shapely oval of the Madonna make this painting a precursor of innovation in late sixteenth-century Bolognese painting, namely when workshops could no longer count on the prestige of the father, and the theme of reform, albeit delayed, appeared to be unstoppable. If this juncture is assumed, then the date can be attributed to around the 1590s.
Alberta Fabbri

3.19
Ginevra Cantofoli
Bologna, 1618 – Bologna, 1672
Allegory of Painting
c. 1650

Oil on canvas, 66.1 × 49.9 cm
Milan, Pinacoteca di Brera, inv. Reg. Cron. 101

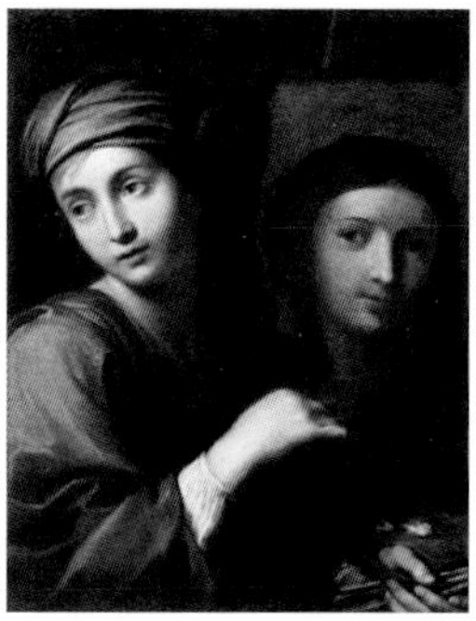

She turns her gaze in the direction of the light beyond her right shoulder but at the same time seems lost in thought, this painter with her head wrapped in a blue turban and her body enveloped in a rust and dark green iridescent mantle. Propped on her easel is a painting in which a woman's face is clearly delineated, a face similar to her own but not enough to consider it a self-portrait.
Below, in a heavily shadowed scene in the right-hand corner of the image, we see the painter's left hand holding the palette with her thumb while her right hand is suspended in mid-air, still in the act of holding a brush.
This *Allegory of Painting* seems to be interpreted by ideal figures whose physical features appear rendered to embody an aesthetic idea that is both a model of calm and languor.
The canvas is conserved in the Pinacoteca di Brera depository, where it entered in 1813 along with many works from the Napoleonic suppression of religious orders. There is no history of its previous location, and since it does not depict a sacred subject, the idea of its origin in a church or convent is improbable. Instead, it should be noted that in the inventories of the vast Milanese collection, in the early twentieth century the painting came to be associated with the name of the Bolognese painter Ginevra Cantofoli, who at the time was relatively unknown.
It is now difficult to discover the reasons or sources for the attribution, but it is conceivable that before the painting was recanvased in the nineteenth century, the name Cantofoli was on the back of the original canvas or frame. Usually the most well-known names are suggested when identifying anonymous works, so it is unlikely that a painting of this quality would be traced to a name that no one remembered unless there was due reason. Yet despite this uncertainty in its identification, subsequent literature has maintained the attribution. As Anna Maria Degli Angeli records in an essay (Degli Angeli 1987), Renzo Grandi was the first to express the opinion that the *Sibyl* in Palazzo Barberini, a very famous work formerly but incorrectly considered a portrait of Beatrice Cenci, was linked to the canvas in the Pinoteca di Brera.
This was the moment that the second life of Ginevra Cantofoli can be said to have begun, and in 2006 this writer published the first monograph (Pulini 2006, pp. 99–102), in which Cantofoli's work is largely reconstructed on the stylistic basis of these two paintings. The book was the result of intense research which led to the location of at least two of the six altarpieces that ancient sources ascribe to Ginevra, thus confirming other attributions made on the basis of their similarities.
In the book, I propose the hypothesis that in the Brera painting – generally interpreted as a self-portrait on an easel – Cantofoli was recalling an episode that had taken place several years earlier, when a very young Elisabetta Sirani had painted her portrait. Indeed Sirani notes in her diary, still preserved, that in 1656 she painted a *Portrait of Signora Ginevra Cantofoli Painter* (Malvasia 1678, II, p. 393). With Elisabetta's violent death aged only twenty-seven, Ginevra, who was twenty years older and considered her like a daughter, perhaps intended to recall that episode by imagining an *Allegory of Painting* as if the late Elisabetta were creating it.
Ginevra had been a pupil of Elisabetta's father, Giovanni Andrea Sirani, and was already considered a "painter" by that time, so she may have played a role as an artist-tutor to Elisabetta herself, and perhaps also helped her when she wanted to set up a school for painters in her rooms.
It is known that Sirani senior refused to allow his daughter to complete her studies in Florence and Rome, and that in response Elisabetta refused to leave the house, gathering around her instead a group of female artists from Bologna and the countryside. It was this opposition to her father's veto on travel that prompted the creation of the first female painting academy in the history of European art.
Ginevra's *Allegory of Painting* should therefore be seen as a symbolic reminder of that exciting, albeit very brief, artistic event.
Massimo Pulini

3.20
Ginevra Cantofoli
Bologna, 1618 – Bologna, 1672
Young Woman (*Sibyl*)
c. 1660
Oil on canvas, 65.5 × 51 cm
Cremona, Museo Civico Ala Ponzone, inv. 2139

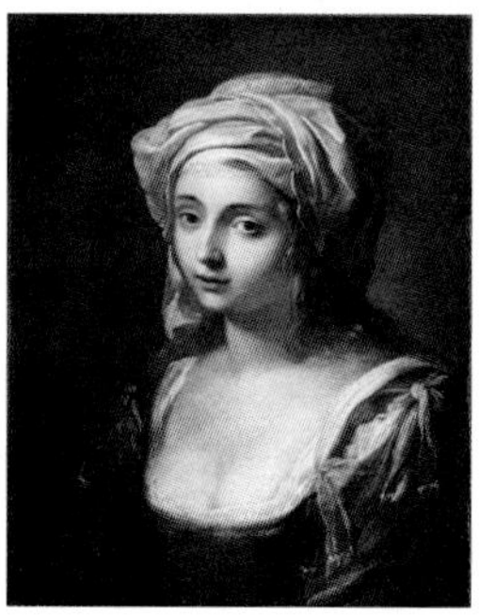

A young woman depicted in a three-quarter pose observes us with discreet smile and a look that might be described as modest were it not for her low-cut gown, daring for her time. However, this is not a portrait or a painting from life, instead we are looking at an ideal interpretation of the exotic and archaic theme of the Sibyl.
Ginevra Cantofoli repeatedly returned to this genre, which enabled her to explore a line between modesty and sensuality, and clarity and mystery. On this occasion, however, the folding of the turban, which in other works signals the oriental origin of the subject, seems more casually arranged, and her dress, with the bows hanging from the shoulders, gives the figure a decidedly more countryside air. In the monograph on Cantofoli (Pulini 2006, pp. 113–115) I described her dress as "Saturday in the village" style, referring to the three similar versions of the same image I presented on that occasion. This one, which recently re-emerged at the Cremona museum, is definitely the most refined example and perhaps the prototype, although the other versions are also her work. Two of these have appeared on the antiques market, while the third is in the Burghley House Collections at Stamford, England.
Interestingly, the version auctioned at Christie's in London on 29 June 1951 bore the title *Portrait of Beatrice Cenci*, an appellation traditionally attached to the work in question, which was a bequest to the Brera museum from Carla Antonioli Bodini. The reference to "a seventeenth-century Bolognese school" and to a possible *Portrait of Beatrice Cenci* suggests that the style and physical resemblance to the *Sibyl* in Palazzo Barberini had been noted. This famous painting had long been mistakenly identified as a portrait by Guido Reni of the young Roman parricide beheaded in the public square in 1599.
Aside from the sadness and hesitancy so masterly expressed in the Barberini *Sibyl*, which made it one of the most famous and replicated paintings in the nineteenth-century world, in this work the physical as well as expressive qualities appear the same and are in fact consistent with the purist classicism that imagined them.
I believe, however, that the Cremona canvas is from a later phase in Ginevra Cantofoli's stylistic parabola than it has been possible to verify until now. In fact the painting has a livelier, more Baroque and international flavour, which also attempts to bring a more secular and natural emphasis to the Sibylline subject.
Massimo Pulini

3.21
Ginevra Cantofoli
Bologna, 1618 – Bologna, 1672
Sibyl
c. 1650
Oil on canvas, 63 × 46 cm
Private collection, courtesy of Cantore Galleria Antiquaria

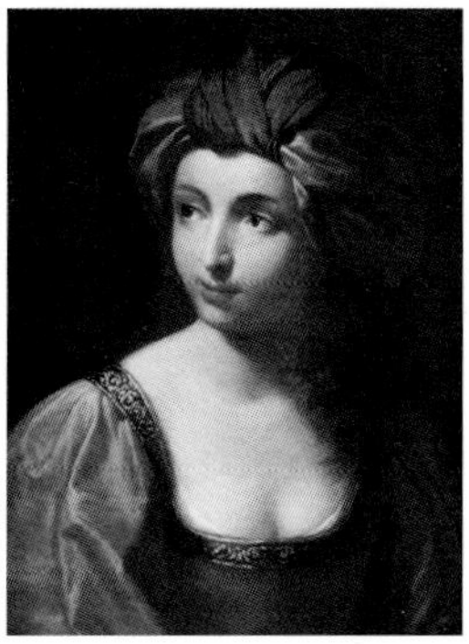

Closely linked to a painting of a similar subject and size conserved in Galleria Rizzi, Sestri Levante, this *Sibyl* was presented at the Pandolfini auction house in Florence on 15 October 2013 as an anonymous work of the Bolognese school. It was published by this writer as the work of Ginevra Cantofoli in the catalogue of the exhibition held in Cesena, devoted to Galleria Cantore (Pulini, in *Il Visibile Narrare* 2013, p. 40).
Compared to the Ligurian painting, this canvas shows greater sophistication, with more elegant period clothes and a turban tied in two different coloured fabrics. However, apart from the oriental nature of the costume, the refined model, whether imagined or portrayed from life, is the same.
The indirect gaze, turned toward the light source, silhouettes and defines the facial features and gives the young woman a lively expression. Charm and grace, exoticism and sensuality, discretion and mystery are the ingredients of a work that in a single, motionless figure combines geographical and temporal distances.
These brief descriptions indicate the expressive and stylistic coordinates of a painter who made the sibyl her signature theme. The folds in the fabric and the flash of light in a well-studied turban were enough for Ginevra to create a nest of enigmatic thoughts, and sufficient to frame a reserved and at the same time resolute face.
Whereas in other larger canvases, such as those in the Cassa di Risparmio di Spoleto, scrolls and inscriptions appear that enable us to identify Samia of Eritrea, or elsewhere Cumana of Delphi, in small compositions like this the theme of the Sibyl becomes an unspecific genre that anticipates the orientalist taste that was to come into vogue throughout Europe two centuries later.
Yet as early as the seventeenth century, the theme had spread to lands far from Italy, perhaps even due to the notoriety of works similar to this one. Jan Vermeer's so-called *Girl with a Pearl Earring*, for example, which also falls within the genre of the Sibyl and seems to have been inspired by a version of the Palazzo Barberini *Sibyl*, attributed to Ginevra Cantofoli herself. This reiteration, which has a white-painted turban and dress, was copied and replicated since the 1640s, and based on a misunderstanding that identified it as a *Portrait of Beatrice Cenci* by Guido Reni it became one of the most famous faces in Europe until at least the beginning of the twentieth century. The Sestri Levante version, which again adopts a monochrome mantle and head covering, was perhaps attempting to replicate the former's unsurpassed success.
Although there is no chronological certainty, compared to the first model in London's National Gallery, the present *Sibyl* seems to have been painted a decade later, around the middle of the 1600s.
Massimo Pulini

3.22
Ginevra Cantofoli
Bologna, 1618 – Bologna, 1672
Young Woman (Sibyl)
c. 1650
Oil on canvas, 65 × 50 cm
Padua, Museo d'Arte Medioevale e Moderna, legacy of Count Leonardo Emo Capodilista, 1864, inv. 132

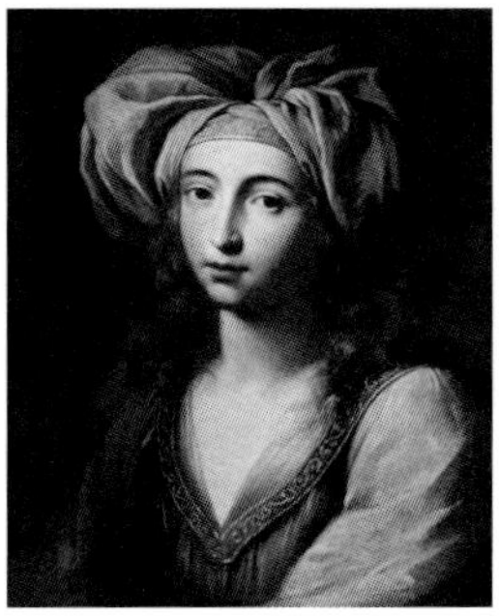

Under a blue turban shaped like a large pumpkin emerges the sweet face of a young woman with a melancholy, meditative look. Her features are regular, and, although idealised, by no means diminish the sincere humanity in girl's sad expression. Despite the lack of the usual attribute of a book or cartouche, her oriental garments lead us to identify her as a Sibyl.
In the early seventeenth century, several Bolognese artists, among them Domenichino, Reni and later Guercino, were the innovators of the reform and the vast success of this iconographic theme, which combines prophetic enigma with youthful beauty. Previously, this ancient and exotic theme had been interpreted by images of grim elderly female figures, such as the fearful, frowning presences that populate the vault of the Sistine Chapel, far removed from the thoughts and features of this young woman, who merges mystery with a certain introversion. Until about fifteen years ago the painting was attributed to the Umbrian painter Giandomenico Cerrini, a former pupil of Domenichino in Rome, yet neither the features nor the depiction of the draped fabrics correspond to the well-known style of the so-called "Cavalier perugino". In 2006, after a brief mention two years earlier, this writer included the work in the monograph on Ginevra Cantofoli, a pupil of Giovanni Andrea Sirani and an associate of his daughter Elisabetta (Pulini 2006, pp. 94–96). The evident stylistic similarities that link the Padua canvas to the *Sibyl* in Palazzo Barberini (formerly known as the *Portrait of Beatrice Cenci*) and to the *Allegory of Painting* in the Pinoteca di Brera are determining. Indeed the Milan painting provided the name and documentary evidence on which the entire artistic trajectory of Ginevra Cantofoli has been reconstructed.
Among the first forty works gathered in the monograph are three other canvases preserved in the same Padua museum, all from the Count Emo Capodilista collection, although the *Sibyl* in question is certainly superior in terms of pictorial quality and beauty. It shares a close relationship with another *Sibyl* conserved in the Hermitage in St. Petersburg (inv. GE192 – 2859), and together these two works are the pinnacle of Cantofoli's currently known production and should be dated to the end of the 1640s. This first group, linked by evident affinities in style, theme and composition, has grown in number in recent years, finding consensus and contributions from various other scholars, though not all are shared. As I state several times in the pioneering monograph, one signed painting is still missing, and documents of the period so far record only two Bolognese altarpieces.
The characteristics that emerge from the *corpus* of her work, particularly successful in this painting, reflect a classical ideal pushed to the limits of purism, while at the same time avoiding any sense of detachment or alterity and displaying a grace that is congenial and at the same time disarming. Languor was the expressive keynote of a painter who should be seen to have played a more important role than Malvasia presents in his book *Felsina pittrice*. Ginevra was twenty years older than Elisabetta Sirani, and given the quality of her aesthetic sensitivity, it seems likely that in Giovanni Andrea Sirani's workshop she would have acted as a tutor in the training of her own teacher's brilliant daughter.
Massimo Pulini

3.23
Ginevra Cantofoli
Bologna, 1618 – Bologna, 1672
Allegory of Sincerity
c. 1650
Oil on canvas, 71 × 59 cm
Private collection

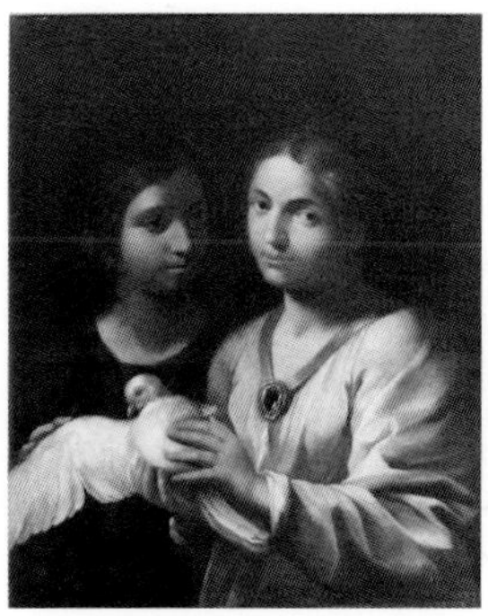

Half-length portraits of two girls dressed in simple tunics that recall the garments of the ancient vestals: midnight blue for the girl on the left, and white with a gold necklace bearing a large gem pendant for the younger girl on the right. In the simple scene that emerges from an impenetrable, shadowy space, the younger girl delicately holds a dove as she looks discreetly at the viewer, while the older girl regards her admiringly.
We the viewers are asked to grasp the allegorical reference emanating from this vision of purity of soul. The idealised soft physical shapeliness of the figures, far removed from the notion of portraiture, underscores the symbolic dimension of the painting and its a precise moral attribute of the dove.
Under the heading "sincerity" in Cesare Ripa's *Iconologia* is a description that fits the image: "Woman dressed in gold, who in her right hand holds a white dove, and with her left hand gracefully & beautifully offers a heart. It is pure sincerity without false appearance or any artifice". The absence of the heart is compensated for by the loving, open attitude of the girl, who "does not hide the intrinsic nature of her heart, but makes it clear to everyone".
Although current definitions might interpret it as a symbol of innocence, that precise iconographic canon, published in Rome in 1603, defines innocence as a "Virgin dressed in white wearing a garland of flowers on her head and carrying a lamb in her arms". In the case of sentiments close in kind, these descriptions constituted a recipe that artists could interpret while maintaining the substance of the original concepts, as did the artist of the painting in question, whom I consider to be Ginevra Cantofoli, several times. This work appears in the first collection devoted to the Ginevra (Pulini 2006, pp. 92–94) after it was auctioned at Christie's in South Kensington in December 2003, attributed to the Florentine Onorio Marinari.
No further comment is required: the painting bears a very close resemblance to the other canvases on display and also to the first paintings that enabled the renaissance of this virtually ignored artistic figure. In addition to the expressive forms and metaphorical references, also the delicate, nuanced pictorial style is consistent with a spirit that is constant in Ginevra's production, whose style, coincidentally, was not unlike those of Onorio Marinari, Giandomenico Cerrini and Luigi Gentile, who worked in classicist circles between Florence and Rome around the middle of the seventeenth century.
Although Malvasia describes her as rather insignificant in the few lines he adds in the margin of Elisabetta Sirani's life (Malvasia 1678, II, p. 407), in works such as this, Ginevra Cantofoli appears to us with her own personal expressive autonomy.
In the almost kinetic sequence of female faces that unfold in her catalogue, the *Allegory of Sincerity* constitutes a particular synthesis, precisely by virtue of the presence of the second girl in the background. This representation of a female couple returns on other occasions, such as in the Brera picture, but also in two fine paintings recently published by Riccardo Lattuada (2013).
Massimo Pulini

3.24
Ginevra Cantofoli
Bologna, 1618 – Bologna, 1672
Berenice
c. 1660
Oil on canvas, 76 × 59 cm
Rome, Galleria Borghese, inv. 99

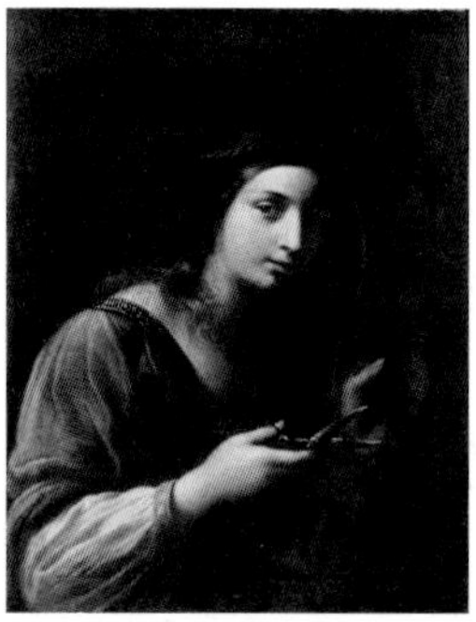

The best known literary or mythical figures represented holding scissors number only two. In the mythology of ancient Greece, Atropos, one of the three Moirai (or Roman "Fates"), had the power to sever the thread of human existence. Although she was the oldest of the triad of spinners and usually depicted as aged, in 1959 Paola Della Pergola interpreted the painting in the Galleria Borghese in this symbolic way, even before a restoration revealed the lock of hair that the young woman is about to cut.
Since then we have been obliged to see this enigmatic beauty as a version of Berenice of Cyrene at the moment she keeps her vow to sacrifice a lock of her hair once her husband, Ptolemy III Euergetes, king of Egypt, returned safely from the war fought against the Syrians in the year 245 BCE. In Callimachus's poem the *Lock of Berenice*, the hair placed on the altar of the temple mysteriously disappears, and Conon, the court astronomer, having discovered a new constellation on the same night, dedicates it to the sovereign, as if Berenice's hair had been stolen by the gods to be placed in heaven.
The young queen turns to us as she performs the act with a gaze that is pregnant with inextricable thoughts. A strip of fabric, twisted like a rope, is tied on her head and its midnight blue colour has been chosen to evoke the constellation. The extremely fine pictorial execution, which burnishes her complexion and lingers on every fibre, places the work among Ginevra Cantofoli's greatest achievements.
This *Berenice* is close in quality, physiognomy and pose to the *Sea Nymph* previously in the Luigi Koelliker collection in Milan, a masterpiece of invention and charm with which it also shares a possible dating to the early 1660s.
The distilled and highly cultivated style of these works presupposes a knowledge of the most refined Roman classicism. The styles of both Giandomenico Cerrini from Perugia and Flemish artist Luigi Gentile echo in the queen's sober figure as she emerges from the shadows, sensual and elusive like a momentary, dreamlike apparition.
A trip to Rome in the mid-1600s and contact with Domenichino's pupils, who formed a purist group of acolytes at the heart of the Baroque era, would explain the similarities just noted, but there are still no biographical documents or stylistic links to identify a forgotten female painter.
In the bequest of the painting to the Galleria Borghese, the name of Giovanni Francesco Romanelli was suggested as its author. Venturi later proposed Simon Vouet, whereas Roberto Longhi and Paola Della Pergola assigned *Berenice* to the followers of Guido Reni (Della Pergola 1955–1959, II, no. 111). It was only in 2004 that this writer (Pulini 2004, p. 140) proposed assigning it to the painter Ginevra Cantofoli, who had trained in the Bolognese workshop of Giovanni Andrea Sirani, a painter influenced by Reni.
Massimo Pulini

3.25
Elisabetta Sirani
Bologna, 1638 – Bologna, 1665
Self-Portrait as a Saint (Certosina)
1658
Oil on canvas, 50.5 × 38 cm
Bologna, Pinacoteca Nazionale, inv. 57

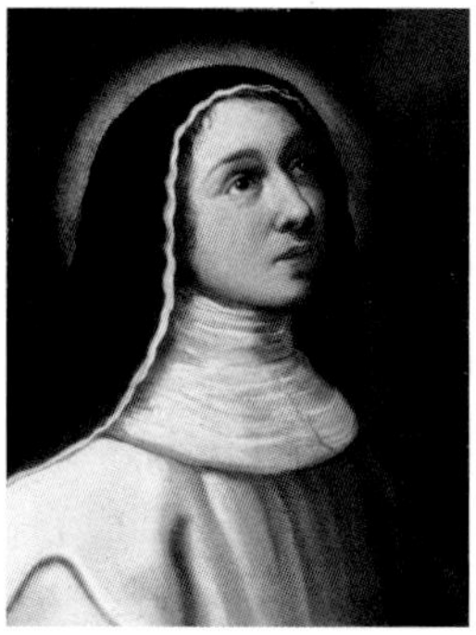

Elisabetta painted this self-portrait as a saint as a companion piece to another Certosina, the *Blessed Rosellina*, both originally located on either side of her large debut piece the *Baptism of Christ* at La Certosa di Bologna. In her *Nota delle pitture* the artist enters under the year 1658: "A very large painting for the Fathers of the Charterhouse, within which there is the Baptism of Christ in the River Jordan: the two female saints who accompany it in the lateral bands, and in one of these there is my portrait, the one who looks up to Heaven" (Malvasia 1678, ed. 1841, II, p. 394).
It is significant that Elisabetta included her self-image in this work, for the *Baptism* was an extremely important work, her first major public church commission in Bologna, and hence crucial to the development of her

career (Bohn 2004a, pp. 277–278).
Elisabetta's *Baptism* formed part of a large on-going narrative cycle of Christ's Life, commissioned by the prior of the Certosa Don Daniele Granchio from a number of major Bolognese painters, including Giovanni Andrea Sirani, Lorenzo Pasinelli, Francesco Gessi, and Domenica Maria Canuti.
Elisabetta was the only woman and the youngest of the group, having just turned 19 when she received the commission in February 1657 and she completed the altarpiece within one year, being paid the exorbitant amount of 1000 lire (Crespi 1772, pp. 20–22; Pellicciari 2003, pp. 179–180, 188–196).
The pair of *Female Saints*, originally over two metres high, was placed in a similar format to the two *Beati* flanking her father's *Feast in the House of the Pharisee* (1652) on the opposite wall of the chapel, as well as Domenico Maria Canuti's *Saint Beatrice* and *Saint Magdalene* on either side of his *Last Judgement* (1658).
Of Elisabetta's two lateral saints, only one, the *Blessed Rosellina*, is currently *in situ* next to the *Baptism*, the other replaced by the *Blessed Vincenzo Certosino* painted by padre Marco Veneziano (Brogi 1998, p. 70 note 43).
The second Certosina, that is Elisabetta's self-portrait, has been identified in the head of a nun now in the Pinacoteca Nazionale di Bologna, cut down in the nineteenth century from the full length damaged original, and largely repainted during its 1979 restoration. It had remained *in situ* at La Certosa, recorded there by Malvasia in 1686 (ed. 1969, p. 342, no. 17) and Marcello Oretti in the second half of the eighteenth century (Oretti 1760–1780, ms. B. 109, no. 135), until the Napoleonic suppressions at the turn of century, when it was removed to the Accademia di Belle Arti, and reduced to its present size within the next 50 years (prior to 1853). It is inscribed on a piece of wood on the verso in a nineteenth-century hand: "Portrait of Elisabetta Sirani painted by herself in the form of a Carthusian nun: remainder of a painting that was already much ruined by time, which now belongs to the Royal Picture Gallery in Bologna".
Elisabetta's features in this painting, with its fleshy lips and large nose, are extremely similar to her self-portrait drawing in the Weld-Blund collection now in the Walker Art Gallery, Liverpool (Brookes 1998, pp. 104–105, no. 52).
The portrait depicts Elisabetta's self-representation as a pious young woman, looking to the heavens for her guiding light (Ghirardi 2004, pp. 91–93; Ghirardi, in *Elisabetta Sirani* 2004, p. 166), thereby conforming to Counter-reformation ideals of perfect womanhood as passive spiritual beings. In this respect it is interesting to compare the artist's own humble comments reported by Malvasia regarding her talent being the gift of God: "[…] she said that she was no better than the others, nor more talented, that that virtue was not her own, but a gift from God, which just as it had touched her could touch all others" (Malvasia 1961, p. 101; see also Modesti 2014, p. 196 note 187, p. 238).
Adelina Modesti

3.26
Elisabetta Sirani
Bologna, 1638 – Bologna, 1665
The Holy Family, Saint Anne, Saint John the Baptist and an Angel
1660
Oil on canvas, 100.5 × 131 cm
Vercelli, Fondazione Museo Francesco Borgogna, inv. 1906, IV, 113

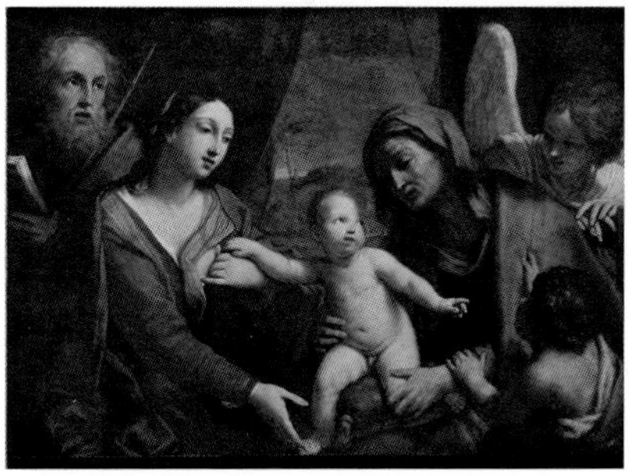

The painting, signed and dated "ELISA SIRANI / F. 1660" on the right-hand side of the back of the chair, was purchased by Antonio Borgogna for 2550 lire at the Gatterburg-Morosini auction in Venice in 1894 (*Vente à Venise* 1894, p. 50, no. 633). The home of lawyer and collector Antonio Borgogna (1822-1906) contained paintings, decorative art and furnishings purchased during his travels and at auctions and exhibitions in Italy and abroad. On his death in 1906, his house and eclectic collection were donated to the city of Vercelli with the objective of founding a public museum dedicated to his father, Francesco, which opened in 1908.
The purchase of a painting by a female painter reflects the character of Borgogna's collection, which also contains works by Angelica Kauffmann, Camilla Edle von Malheim Friedländer and Emilie Rouillon (Lacchia 2006; Lacchia 2016).
We do not know how the canvas by Elisabetta Sirani (Viale 1969, p. 82, no. 132, pl. 136) became part of the Gatterburg-Morosini collection (Tonini 2020, p. 137, fig. 8, p. 131), but in 1689 it was the most valuable work in the collection of the rich Bolognese goldsmith Orazio Ceschi (Morselli 1998a, pp. 161–162; Modesti 2014, pp. 267–268, no. 44; fig. 30, p. 267). In the inventory of her production, published by Carlo Cesare Malvasia in his *Felsina pittrice* from 1678, Sirani lists the painting among works made in 1660, but she does not indicate the nature of the commission: "An 'overdoor' half-figure with the Blessed Virgin, Saint Anna, Saint John, & an Angel. Saint Anna holds the infant Jesus in her lap & he indicates he wants to go to his Mother to take milk, which she is about to offer him, at the same time indicating to his mother-in-law [*sic*], that in exchange he is giving her another child, namely John the Baptist" (Malvasia 1678, II, p. 469).
The milieu in which Sirani was trained represented the true height of Baroque painting, which she achieved thanks to the example of her father, Andrea Sirani, a pupil of Guido Reni, developing a personal style sensitive to changes of light (Modesti 2004). From 1660 her style assumed the characteristics of a measured classicism and a composed, mellow gestural quality, expressed above all in chamber paintings of religious subjects and in portraits commissioned by Bolognese families as well as others (Frisoni 1989).
The work belongs to the last phase in which Reni's influence is still evident in the pearly complexions, the Virgin's heavy eyelids and the intensity of affections (Frisoni 1992a, p. 344). The worn surface and the domestic setting of the sacred family show the influence of both Francesco Gessi and Carlo Cignani (Frisoni 1978, pp. 4, 9, pl. 14; Frisoni, in *Elisabetta Sirani* 2004, p. 181, no. 21).
The composition is divided into two sections, with the Child in the centre between Saint Anne and Mary, to whom he turns seeking her breast. In the three peripheral corners are three onlookers: Saint Joseph, who turns, his hair moved by the wind, an angel, and Saint John the Baptist. The background is divided into two wings: to the right a wall, and to the left drapery that opens like a theatre curtain onto a landscape.
A full-bodied colour on a subtle base reveals Sirani's technical emancipation from her father. Bright colours are accompanied by shadows softened by half-tints, such as in the face of the angel, backlit but completely legible, and in the angel's foreshortened wing (Frisoni 2004, p. 83; Frisoni, in *Elisabetta Sirani* 2004, p. 181, no. 21).
Following the restoration by Barbara Rinetti carried out in Turin in 2004 for the Bologna exhibition "Elisabetta Sirani 'pittrice eroina'" 1638–1665, the presence of blue lapis lazuli emerged in the fabric, indicating the preciousness of the materials used. IR reflectography showed a first version with some alterations to the angel, which was previously further to the left, and to Saint Anne, initially in the centre next to Mary. The painting, which had already undergone previous restorations (*Opere d'arte a Vercelli* 1976, p. 142; Lacchia, Pozzato 2004), including a relining, has now been restored to complete legibility by removing the retouching and discoloured paint. The lower section, which had a large plastered gap, has been masked by a brown wooden strip.
Alessia Meglio

3.27
Elisabetta Sirani
Bologna, 1638 – Bologna, 1665
Timoclea Kills the Captain of Alexander the Great
1659

Oil on canvas, 228 × 174.5 cm
Inscriptions: signed and dated "ELISAB.TA SIRANI F. 1659."
Naples, Museo e Real Bosco di Capodimonte, inv. Q633

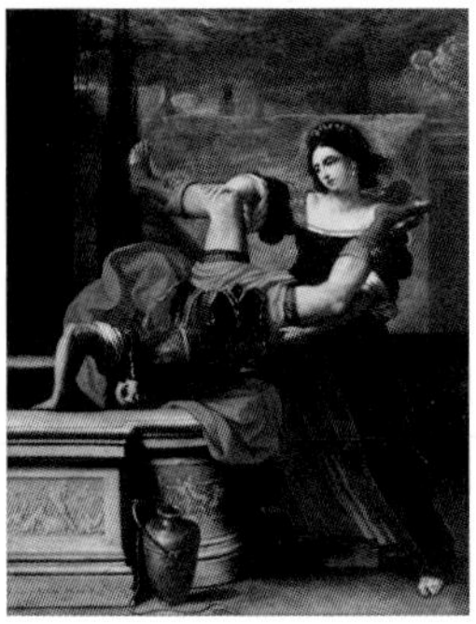

"A life-size Timoclea throwing the Captain down the well, for Sig. Andrea Catalani". This is how the artist herself described this painting in her *Nota delle pitture fatte da me Elisabetta Sirani*, under the year 1659 (Malvasia 1678, ed. 1841, II, p. 394). A striking example of the artist's painting of historical subject matter (*Istoria*), the *Timoclea* formed a companion piece to her *Judith Triumphant* (Stamford, Burghley House) produced the year before for the same patron, the wealthy Bolognese banker Andrea Cattalani. Both paintings explore heroic themes of political justice brought about by powerful women (*femmes fortes*), a subject dear to the artist's heart. Located together in what may have been Cattalani's commercial studio, the "Lower Room" of his palace in the parish of San Barbaziano, Bologna (as described in Cattalani's post-mortem inventory dated 1668; see Morselli 1998b, p. 155), the pair of life-size paintings would have made quite an impression on the banker's clients and visitors, as they gazed upon the virtuous deeds and noble actions of the women portrayed, one from biblical the other from classical history. They also would have been taken aback by the image of two murderous women, who nonetheless are presented by Elisabetta as *exempla iustitiae*, examples of civic and political virtue and social justice.
The theorist Giovanni Paolo Lomazzo had recommended that righteous images such as that of the biblical heroine Judith, who overcame the tyrant Holofernes, oppressor of the Israelites, be placed "In the places where justice is done [… where] examples are sought of the dead of dastardly men punished for their misdeeds".
(*Trattato*, 1584, book VI, chap. XXIV; see also Modesti 2004, pp. 234–248, p. 282 note 101).
The story of Timoclea is quite rare in the history of art, and is told in Plutarch's *Lives*, a text that Elisabetta could access in her father's library, rich with all manner of books from classical history and literature to the latest theoretical tracts and manuals on art (Sabbatini 1995; Modesti 2004, pp. 135–138). In his "Life of Alexander" (33, 12) Plutarch recounts how Timoclea, a matron of Thebes – the rebellious Greek city sacked by Alexander the Great, King of Macedonia (356–323 BC) – was raped by one of his generals. Timoclea avenged herself by claiming that her wealth was hidden at the bottom of a well in her garden, promptly pushing her rapist down as he peered over the edge and then killing him with stones. Artists traditionally approached the subject by showing Timoclea with her children, brought before the King, who recognizing a woman of noble dignity sets her free (e.g. Domenichino, *Alexander and Timoclea*, c. 1615, Louvre). Characteristically, Elisabetta chose not to represent this particular episode highlighting Alexander's clemency, but a prior moment of Plutarch's narrative, focusing instead on Timoclea's heroic actions, as she vindicates herself. Thus male magnanimity is superceded by female ingenuity and virtue. The artist highlights the heroine's superior moral character, intelligence, dignity, independence and courage, just as Plutarch had done in his historical account. Elisabetta achieves this contrast (*paragone*) in the formal composition of the painting. Timoclea stands tall and upright, with the captain literally head over heels with his gangly legs as she cartwheels him into the well. Note his startled expression and the look of horror on his face and in his eyes as he realizes the fate that awaits him. The Amazonian Timoclea by contrast remains noble and resolute, the only sign of emotion being the furrowed brow and flared nostrils to indicate her anger (*ira*), as had been outlined by Lomazzo in his theories of the emotions (*affetti*) in his painting treatise (book II, chap. XI), this text also located in the Sirani library which Elisabetta could consult freely. Note how the light falls diagonally across the painting from light to dark to light again: from good to evil and back again, highlighting Timoclea's face and bust (the brightest point of the picture), and throwing the general into deep shadow, except for the upper part of his face, whilst below him the light sculpts into the sarcophagus-like well (ready to entomb him) the *Story of the Lapiths and the Centaurs* and a *Triumph of Galatea*, further ancient attempted rape stories in which virtue trumps vice. It is also here at the bottom of the well that Elisabetta incises her signature, as if to claim that Timoclea's vindication is also hers as a successful female artist.
This specific Alexandrian episode has never before, nor since, been represented in easel painting, with Elisabetta responsible for introducing its unusual iconography into Italian art, evidence of her capacity for *invenzione*, considered the mark of true artistic genius. It is possible that she was aware of an illustration of the well scene by the Northern European artist Matthäus Merian the Elder which may have served as her visual source for it depicts common elements of Timoclea throwing an ungainly captain in a well set in a garden (Golahny 2011). Elisabetta's interpretation, nonetheless, remains the first large-scale representation of this particular episode. I know of only one later easel painting that depicts the well scene, by the French artist Henri-Antoine de Favanne (1668–1752), but which represents a different and rather less aggressive account by Plutarch from his *Mulierum Virtutis* (XXIV) (Modesti 2001b, pp. 201–205, and pl. 37). In this account and as seen in de Favanne's picture, the captain voluntarily enters the well in search of Timoclea's treasure, whilst the heroine and her maidens gently look on, ready to gather up the rocks placed conveniently around the base of the well. Elisabetta's version is a far more violent image of a powerful, active and defiant woman, singularly intent on her mission. The *Timoclea* proved to be very popular for a number of sonnets were written in its honour, when the painting was publicly exhibited before being consigned to its patron. Nicola Mellini also later produced a series of commercial etchings after the painting between 1801 and 1804 (Modesti 2001b, pp. 197–198, pls. 35, 36, 39, 40).
Elisabetta Sirani's *Timoclea* is a mature example of how the artist reworked existing artistic traditions and was innovative in her development of new and unusual subject matter with its unique iconography and narratives featuring female heroes from biblical and classical history, mythology or literature. Elisabetta specialised in these historical canvases, for which she prepared by studying the ancient texts and handbooks, and the visual sources in her father's library and art collection, with the artist depicting her heroines as independent political agents, who acted with intelligence, courage and dignity (Modesti 2001a, pp. 401–402), that is, with virtues usually associated with men (Bohn 2002; Graziani, in *Elisabetta Sirani* 2004, p. 212).
Adelina Modesti

3.28
Elisabetta Sirani
Bologna, 1638 – Bologna, 1665
Portia Wounding her Thigh
1664
Oil on canvas, 101 × 138 cm
Inscriptions: signed and dated "ELISAB.ᴬ SIRANI F. 1664"
Bologna, Collezione d'Arte e di Storia della Fondazione Cassa di Risparmio in Bologna, inv. M32228

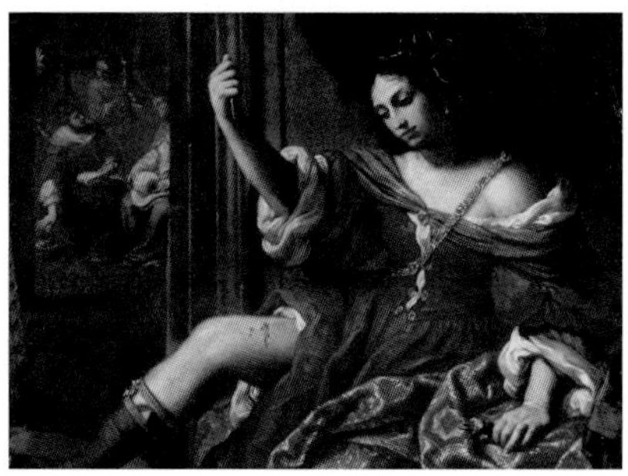

Elisabetta Sirani was an innovative artist who reworked existing artistic traditions and developed new and unusual subject matter with unique iconography and narratives, especially those featuring female heroes from biblical and classical history, mythology and literature, as we have seen with her *Timoclea* (cat. 3.27), *Cleopatra* (cat. 3.34), and *Circe* (cat. 3.33). Elisabetta specialised in these historical canvases (*Istoria*), and in her novel representations of these *femmes fortes* the artist developed an equally virile painterly manner which contemporaries gendered as masculine. Malvasia claimed that she painted "better than a man", drew "like a great master", and that her work "had something virile and great about it" (Malvasia 1678, ed. 1841, II, pp. 386, 402), while the Florentine painter Baldassare Franceschini (Il Volterrano) called her "the finest painter of her day in Bologna" (as reported by Ferdinando Cospi to Leopoldo de' Medici, Archivio di Stato di Firenze, Carteggio degli Artisti, XVI, fol. 348, letter dated 19 August 1662). Elisabetta thus can be considered one of the first women artists to be publicly acknowledged by colleagues and critics as a female *virtuoso* possessing artistic genius and *invenzione*, usually considered beyond the scope of women (Modesti 2001a, p. 400; Modesti 2017).
The *Portia*, first brought to scholarly attention by Ann Sutherland Harris (in *Women Artists* 1976, p. 150), is a perfect example of Elisabetta's inventive powers and her masterful bold virtuosity. Described by the artist in her *Nota delle pitture* as "A Portia in the act of wounding her thigh, when she yearned to know the conspiracy her husband was weaving; an overdoor painting, and far away in another bedroom, damsels working, for Sig. Simone Tassi" (Malvasia 1678, ed. 1841, II, p. 399), this impressive painting, with its extremely rare subject matter, is drawn from Plutarch's "Life of Brutus" (XIII, 18–26). Plutarch recounts how Portia, the daughter of Cato, noticing that something was seriously troubling her husband Marcus Brutus – he was conspiring the overthrow of Julius Caesar to establish the Roman Republic – asked that he confide in her, after she had proven her own bravery and constancy of character via an act of self-mutilation. *Portia* can be interpreted as an image of a strong-willed woman, inflicting a cruel wound to her body to test her courage and own strength of will to convince her husband that a woman can share in man's stoic virtue, and thus gain Brutus' political trust. Elisabetta highlights Portia's strength, presenting her as a virile politicized heroine, not as the Roman matron who commits suicide by ingesting hot coals, which was the more common iconography found in seventeenth-century painting (Bohn 2002, p. 68; Graziani, in *Elisabetta Sirani* 2004, p. 217).
Portia is placed in *primo piano*, her body, encased in a magnificent Baroque costume, taking up much of the pictorial space. Her bloodied thigh, in which she has just plunged the knife, occupies centre stage, whilst her lower leg is shod in a Roman style boot. Note also that Elisabetta has referenced the goddess Diana and the Amazons in the slipped blouse that almost exposes her breast, and chiton-like jewelled girdle that drapes over her naked left shoulder. She is physically separated from the women in the back room, who, oblivious of the scene that is taking place in the foreground, are busy with their domestic activities of sewing and lacemaking. As Plutarch recounts Portia "could not ask her husband what ailed him before she had made some proof by herself ", and so "causing her maids and women go out of her chamber, gave herself a great gash withal in her thigh, that he was straight all of a gore-blood" (XIII, 23). Elisabetta chose to represent the actual solitary act of Portia's self-mutilation and courage, with Brutus nowhere to be seen, and this work remains the only known representation of this particular event in the history of art (Modesti 2004, pp. 248–254).
The painting was commissioned by the wealthy silk merchant and collector Simone Tassi, apparently as a companion piece for an *Absalom Weighing his Hair*, by Giovanni Andrea Sirani (Malvasia 1961, p. 95 note 28), and may depict Tassi's wife, Isabella Bordani, in the guise of Portia. Given the seric profession of her patron Elisabetta especially concentrated on the luxuriousness of the fabrics, silk velvets and brocade, orchestrated in brilliant red and gold, giving the painting a rich and dramatic intensity. Tassi's collection, which included four other paintings by Elisabetta, including the *Saint Anthony Adoring the Christ Child* (Bologna, Pinacoteca Nazionale), was dispersed immediately by his heirs and wife's family after the merchant's death, his legal inventory being drawn up on 20 June 1671. The following month, another Sirani patron, the haberdashery merchant Lodovico Foschi, bought the *Portia* and its pendant from the Bordani. Foschi was to cede part of his art collection to Domenico Maria Riva in 1696 in exchange of a loan. The *Portia* and its companion piece may have been amongst these paintings, and therefore in the Riva collection prior to finding their way to the Bonfiglioli family in the mid-eighteenth century, when they were both attributed to Elisabetta. The painting then disappeared from the historical record until 1973 (Modesti 2014, pp. 337–338).
Adelina Modesti

3.29
Giovanni Andrea Sirani
Bologna, 1610 – Bologna, 1670
Venus and Cupid
c. 1645
Oil on canvas, 112 × 93 cm
Bologna, Collezione d'Arte e di Storia della Fondazione Cassa di Risparmio in Bologna, inv. F32243

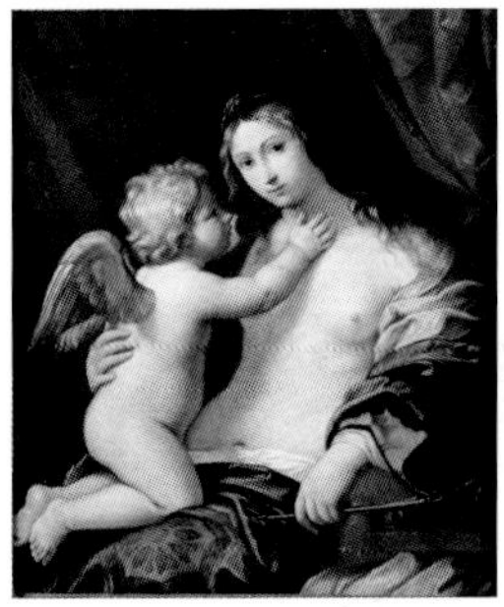

Giovanni Andrea Sirani, father of Elisabetta, has received less scholarly attention, probably due to being overshadowed by his more famous daughter. Fiorella Frisoni devoted an important essay to him in 1992 (Frisoni 1992b) whilst the present writer examined his contribution to his daughter's training (Modesti 2004, chap. 4) and the Sirani studio in Bologna (Modesti 2013). Babette Bohn has further analysed Sirani's reception in the seventeenth-century Bologna in the context of Reni's and Elisabetta's artistic success (Bohn 2011).
We know that Sirani trained with a number of minor artists, and after a short apprenticeship with Giacomo Cavedone he joined the studio of Guido Reni, becoming the *maestro*'s most trusted and loyal assistant. After Reni's death in 1642, Sirani opened his own *bottega*, firstly in various locations throughout the city, to settle definitively at his *casa-studio* in Via Urbana, in the parish of San Mammolo. The Sirani studio was one of the most important and successful in the city, and it was here that Giovanni Andrea taught a number of apprentices, including his three daughters, Elisabetta, Barbara and Anna Maria, who all became professional artists. Malvasia considered Sirani a masterful teacher, second to none in his ability to impart theoretical concepts, as well as the latest techniques in painting and printmaking (Malvasia 1678, ed. 1841, II, p. 407). In addition, Sirani was a successful art merchant and appraiser, as well as professor at Bologna's life drawing academies.
It is believed that Sirani's *Venus and Cupid* was painted in the middle of the 1640s, soon after his master's death, and relies on Renian prototypes such as the *Cupid Disarmed by Venus* in the Toledo Museum, Ohio (see Pepper 1973). Sirani was especially influenced by this painting in his treatment of Cupid, whose profile and outstretched right arm is identical to Reni's. We do not know for whom Sirani's painting was produced, but it is worth noting that "A Venus with Cupid [...] copy of a work by Sig. Guido painted by Sig. Gio. And.a Sirani" was located in the Bolognese collection of Giovanni Francesco Davia in 1689 (Mazza, in *Antico e Moderno* 2014, p. 88).
With regards to Sirani's production during this period, we can compare his *Rebecca and Eleazaro* at the Palazzo Pitti, Florence, or the *Ulysses and Circe* in the Musei Capitolini, Rome. All three paintings reveal a Renian

mise-en-scene, as well as brilliant lighting and chromatic range. Venus sits majestically in the centre of the composition, taking up most of the picture space, and framed by a red Baroque curtain as she gazes directly out at the viewer. Cupid sits upon the blue mantle on her lap, about to caress his mother. The goddess of Love has disarmed her son; she holds his arrow away from him in her left hand. Such allegories of love were popular in patrician circles, especially as marriage gifts. Having deprived Cupid of his arms, the allegory is clear, the recipient of the gift is to renounce all others in favour of their legitimate spouse (Frisoni, in *Elisabetta Sirani* 2004, p. 234).
In terms of its allegorical meaning, Sirani's mythological painting can be compared to the *Venus and Cupid* by his daughter Elisabetta, also on display in this exhibition (cat. 3.30).
Adelina Modesti

3.30
Elisabetta Sirani
Bologna, 1638 – Bologna, 1665
Venus and Cupid
1664
Oil on canvas, 101 × 85 cm
Inscriptions: signed and dated "ELIS.ª SIRANI F. 1664"
Private collection

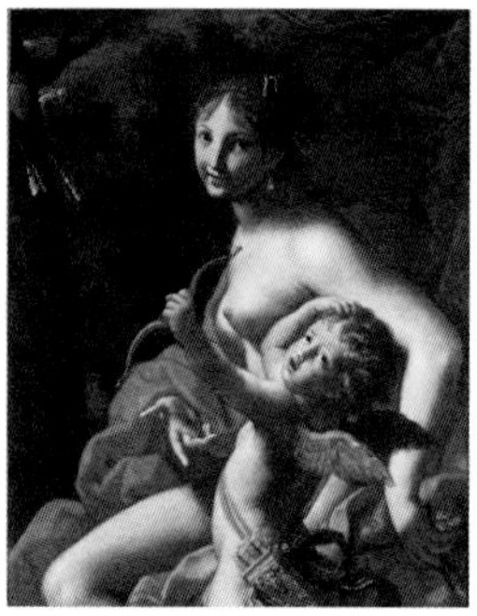

This beautiful signed painting, long considered lost (Frisoni 1992a, p. 350; Modesti 2003, p. 379 note 9), recently appeared on the international art market in 2007 (Bukowskis Stockholm; Adam Williams Fine Art New York) and again in 2018 (Sotheby's New York). It is a mythological allegory, representing Venus chastising Cupid for having failed to pierce a heart with his arrows — the heart and two missed arrows can be seen in the top left hand of the picture, hanging from a tree. It is a delightful and playful image, which is highlighted by Elisabetta in the cheeky expression she has given her Venus who smiles knowingly out to the viewer; we are made complicit in the "reprimanding" of her son. Cupid himself scratches his head in anguished disappointment and disbelief in his lack of marksmanship and inability to successfully accomplish his mission.
Elisabetta described the painting's subject in her *Nota delle pitture* under the year 1664: "A half-figure Venus, who laughing shows us indignant Cupid, for having failed in wanting to wound a heart, for the distinguished Sig. Co. Annibale Ranuzzi" (Malvasia 1678, ed. 1841, II, p. 399). The painting was commissioned by the nobleman and senator Count Annibale Ranuzzi, a major figure in Bologna's public chivalric events, private salons (known as *conversazioni*), and political circles (*Ranuzzi* 2000, pp. 45–48; see also pp. 315–330 for two essays by Carapelli). Together with his father-in-law Marquis Ferdinando Cospi, Ranuzzi was not only a committed Sirani patron, but also acted as Elisabetta's professional agent, especially in mediating commissions from the Medici of Florence (Goldberg 1983, chap. 2). He in particular was engaged by Cardinal Leopoldo de' Medici to supervise his 1663–1664 commission from Elisabetta of the *Allegory of Good Medici Government (Justice, Charity and Prudence)* (Vignola) for which the artist received a silver cross with 56 diamonds in recompense (Modesti 2003, pp. 371–372). Ranuzzi was to request another painting from the artist the following year, this time a combination of the sacred and profane: an allegorical portrait of his sister, Anna Maria Ranuzzi Marsigli, with her two sons, as Charity (cat. 3.36). Ranuzzi's son Vincenzo Ranuzzi Cospi, whose portrait Elisabetta had painted the previous year, inherited not only this *Venus* and *Charity* from his father, but also his grandfather Ferdinando Cospi's entire painting collection, which included the aforementioned portrait and the *Galatea* (cat. 3.32), as well as three other mythological paintings by Elisabetta.
The artist's paintings for the Ranuzzi-Cospi ended up in Girolamo Ranuzzi's collection in the second half of the eighteenth century, when the *Venus and Cupid* was described in his 1788 Probate inventory as "A painting representing a Venus, and little Cupid, life-sized half-figures, a work by Elisabetta Sirani [...] with ancient carved and gilded frame".
The painting was valued at 750 lire, quite a substantial amount, and indicative of the high value patrons and collectors placed on this woman artist's work. It was also located in the "Bedroom n° 6, which has two windows, which look onto the narrow road known as Ruini", of Casa Ranuzzi (Archivio di Stato di Bologna, Notarile, Egidio Teodori Zenobio, 13 March 1788) (Modesti 2014, pp. 342–343). Such a location was in keeping with the trend during this period, as advocated by Giulio Mancini in his *Considerazioni sulla pittura* written sometime between 1617 and 1621, to place painted allegories of love and erotic mythological scenes in bedrooms of married couples to incite amorous desire engendering beautiful progeny. In this respect the painting can be related to the *Venus and Cupid* by Elisabetta's father, Giovanni Andrea Sirani (cat. 3.29).
Note also the artist's unique use of her signature, which she wraps around the top of Cupid's quiver in bold capital letters.
Unlike male Bolognese artists who rarely signed their works, Elisabetta is known to have signed over 70% of her extant work in an age when women's signatures held little legal value (Bohn 2004c). In many of her works, Elisabetta's signature is inscribed in the very fabric of the painting, embroidered along cushion edges, tassels, necklines and cuffs, or inscribed in stone as in her *Timoclea* (cat. 3.27). The artist was self-consciously asserting her identity as both a woman and a professional painter, in an art world dominated by men. Elisabetta's signature became her trademark, a clever marketing strategy to promote herself and her work, drawing attention to the fact that she, and she alone, produced the paintings (Modesti 2004, pp. 20–22).
Stylistically, the painting's warm *impasto* reflects the neo-venetian influence of Flaminio Torri, as does the cross-hatched and fluid brushwork, typical of Elisabetta's work from this later period (see *Portia*, cat. 3.28). It also demonstrates the artist's knowledge of the female nude, which is painted with a naturalness and ease, belying the misguided opinion that women were not capable of doing so. Like Lavinia Fontana and Artemisia Gentileschi, Elisabetta successfully painted male and female nudes throughout her career.
Adelina Modesti

3.31
Elisabetta Sirani
Bologna, 1638 – Bologna, 1665
Triumphant Cupid (*Medici Cupid*)
1661
Oil on canvas, 89 × 70 cm
Bologna, private collection

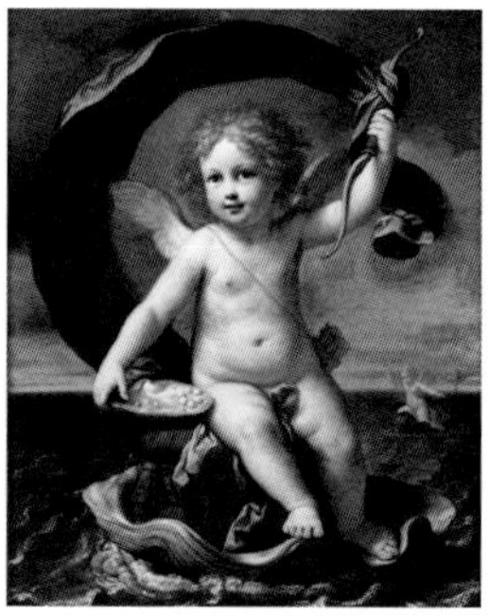

In 1661 Elisabetta recorded three paintings representing a triumphant cupid floating upon the sea, two of which were for Florentine patrons. The work on display can be identified with the artist's first recorded example, described in her *Nota delle pitture fatte da me Elisabetta Sirani* as "A Cupid in the Sea, for the great Princess Margherita, who with one hand makes a sail with a cloth folded into an arch, and with her right hand holds a mother-of-pearl with many pearls inside, including six very large pearls, which outline the bridegroom's coat of arms, and also allude to his name; and in the distance a dolphin straddled by another Cupid, who with the whip of a coral root encourages it along its path" (Malvasia 1678, ed. 1841, II, p. 395). The eventual recipient of this painting was Princess Marguerite Louise d'Orleans de Bourbon (1641–1721), the granddaughter of Queen Marie de' Medici, cousin to Louis XIV, and future Grand Duchess of Tuscany. The exquisite jewel of a painting, attributed to Elisabetta Sirani by Federico Zeri (Frisoni 1992a, p. 344), was intended as a wedding gift from Grand Duchess Vittoria della Rovere for the marriage of her son Grand Prince Cosimo de' Medici to the French Princess, the Florentine celebrations of which took place in June of 1661.

The marriage was a strategic political move by the Medici. In forging this union between the young Marguerite Louise and the crown Prince of Tuscany, the family was cementing these two ruling European dynasties, to ensure continuing peace between the Grand Duchy and France, the most important power in Europe. The Medici's longstanding political alliance with the French court was thus to have been secured further by this marriage and depended upon its positive outcome.

As Elisabetta's own description indicates, this union was visually symbolised by the iconography of her painting. The Cupid holds a large oyster shell in his right hand displaying the Medici coat of arms represented by six large "Margherita" Baroque pearls, alluding as well to the bride's name. A single pearl in an oyster shell (which can be seen at the left near Cupid's thumb) was also Vittoria della Rovere's own personal symbol, thereby the artist at the same time paid honour to her patron, the bearer of the wedding gift.

With this beautifully painted work, in which Elisabetta's rich painterly technique is masterfully highlighted, especially in the rendering of the putto's soft flesh, the artist was offering her best wishes to the young couple. For this reason she included the small putto riding on a dolphin in the right background holding some coral, which ùin the emblematic language of the period represented "the pleasing, friendly, loving soul" (Ripa 1593, ed. 1992, pp. 23–25), to augur a harmonious union. The marriage, however, was far from peaceful ending in an official separation, with Marguerite Louise eventually leaving her husband and three children in 1675 to return to Paris, taking the painting with her (Modesti 2014, p. 283).

Such artworks and luxury objects served as diplomatic gifts that circulated in the courts of Italy and Europe, aiding the establishment or consolidation of local and international political alliances. Elisabetta herself, aware of the importance of such diplomatic gift-giving for advancing her own career, wisely presented the painting first to Grand Duchess Vittoria della Rovere to give to her new daughter-in-law, as a letter of 1662 from her patron Marquis Ferdinando Cospi to Prince Leopoldo de' Medici (Vittoria's brother-in-law) reveals: "Your Highness should have seen that Cupid which I brought as a gift now of late when I was there with the distinguished Grand Duchess" (Mazza, in *Tesori ritrovati* 1998, pp. 136–137). Both Antonio di Paolo Masini in his *Bologna Perlustrata* of 1666, and Elisabetta's eulogist Giovanni Luigi Picinardi confirm that the painting was gifted by the artist to the Grand Duchess Vittoria di Toscana (Modesti 2020, p. 166).

The Bolognese poet Gasparo Bombaci wrote a sonnet celebrating the painting which Elisabetta included in her diary entry, whilst Picinardi was to refer to this *Amorino* as having been "traced by the hand of the graces with a ray of sunlight", perfectly summing up the brilliant luminosity of this piece, which glimmers iridescently like the symbolic pearls it depicts (Modesti 2014, pp. 283–284).

Adelina Modesti

3.32

Elisabetta Sirani

Bologna, 1638 – Bologna, 1665

Galatea

1664

Oil on canvas, 43 × 58.5 cm

Inscriptions: signed and dated "ELISAB.^ SIRANI F. 1664"

Modena, Museo Civico d'Arte, inv. Ser. 8

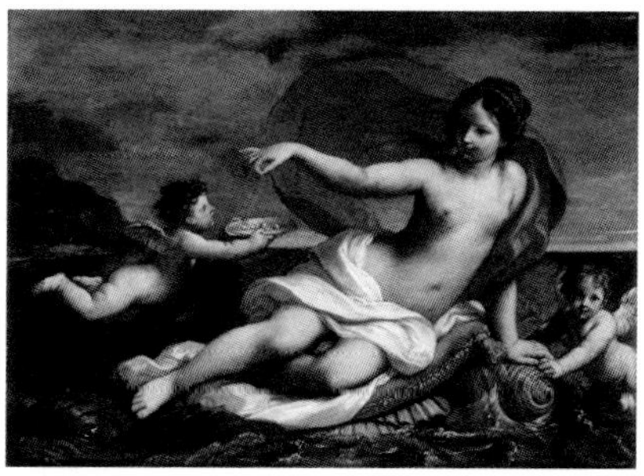

Elisabetta Sirani's characteristic *pastosità* and fluid brushwork is evident in this exquisite enamel-like painting depicting the triumph of the sea nymph Galatea, who escaped the amorous advances and jealous rage of Polyphemus (Ovid, *Metamorphosis*, XII), first brought to our attention by Fiorella Frisoni (1992a, pp. 345, 362) The artist's detailed description in her *Nota delle pitture fatte da me Elisabetta Sirani* (1664) reads "A little Galatea in the sea, led by two Dolphins, with two Cupids, one of whom clings onto the shells on which the aforementioned Galatea is reclining, and the other presents her with a mother-of-pearl open with various pearls, where she is in the act of lifting one of them up, for the distinguished Sig. Marquis, Senator, and Bailiff Ferdinando Cospi" (Malvasia 1678, ed. 1841, II, p. 399).

The nobleman Ferdinando Cospi was an avid collector and one of Bologna's elder statesmen, whose private museum of natural and scientific curiosities, the Museo Cospiano, was left to the city in 1660, annexed to the Museo Aldrovandi at the Palazzo Pubblico (Legati 1677: Elisabetta's *Galatea* is mentioned here on p. 516, together with three other paintings by the artist in the marquis' collection). Cospi also acted as Bolognese art agent for the Medici together with his son-in-law Count Annibale Ranuzzi, both staunch protectors of the young Elisabetta who actively promoted her work at the Florentine court (Goldberg 1983, pp. 34–53; Carapelli 1984; Carapelli 1988; Modesti 2003; Bohn 2013a).

Cospi was amongst Elisabetta's most committed patrons, and owned at least five works by the artist, including a *Madonna of the Girdle* dating from circa 1663, which he donated to the parish church of Santi Biagio e Giacomo, in Bagnarola di Budrio, near his country villa (Modesti 2014, pp. 317–318, cat. 94). Cospi's large art collection, including Elisabetta's *Galatea*, together with his entire estate, was inherited in 1686 by his grandson Vincenzo Ferdinando Ranuzzi Cospi, whose own portrait the artist painted for the marquis in 1663 when the child was about four years of age (now in Warsaw, National Museum). This allegorical portrait shows the young boy, a page at the Medici court, dressed in elegant courtly style complete with feathered hat, in the guise of Cupid armed with bow and arrows (Modesti 2014, pp. 312–313, cat. 90).

A year later, in 1664, Cospi commissioned from Elisabetta this small painting of Galatea, which was documented by Marcello Oretti in the latter half of the eighteenth century as being located in Palazzo Cospi in Strada Castiglione (Oretti 1760–1780, ms. B. 104, II, fol. 16). The painting still retains its original gilded frame, elaborately carved by Sirani family carpenter Domenico Angiolino Riva with dolphin and scallop shell motifs by which the artist clearly wanted to make reference to her patron's humanist interest in natural history (Modesti 2003, p. 387 note 95). The frame intentionally echoes the subject matter of Elisabetta's painting, in which the marine Nereid floats along on giant conch and scallop shells pulled by two dolphins, as she picks pearls from an oyster shell held by a flying putto. Another putto gently pushes Galatea along (Benati, in *Tesori ritrovati* 1998, pp. 134–135; Benati, in *La donazione Sernicoli* 2009, pp. 76–77). Elisabetta's naturalism is evident in the accuracy with which she represented the shells, most probably drawn from direct observation of the *naturalia* in Cospi's collection (Modesti 2004, pp. 134–135), or from the images contained in her father's copy of Pliny the Elder's *Naturalis Historia.*

The painting, with its subtle eroticism, depicts the young sea nymph enveloped by a red fluttering mantle that acts as a wind-filled sail aiding her movement through the waters, and reveals in its jewel-like colouring a neo-venetian influence filtered through the art of Flaminio Torre (Graziani, in *Elisabetta Sirani* 2004, p. 218). Elisabetta's *Galatea* is a delightful example of the kind of mythological works drawn directly from ancient sources (Ovid's *Metamorphosis*, together with other classical texts, was located in the Sirani family library) that this erudite female artist could produce with consummate skill and élan. An

ink wash preparatory study is in Hamburger Kunsthalle previously attributed to Francesco Trevisani and identified as a Venus (Pulini 2006, p. 48, fig. 48).
Adelina Modesti

3.33
Elisabetta Sirani
Bologna, 1638 – Bologna, 1665
Circe
c. 1664
Oil on canvas, 112 × 92 cm
Private collection

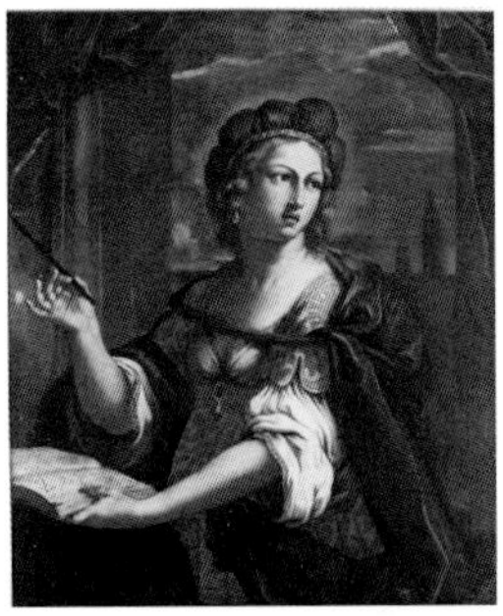

Queen Circe was a sorceress whom Ulysses encountered during his wanderings after the Trojan War (Homer, *Odyssey*, X). She was said to have access to supernatural powers that turned men into swine. Artists traditionally depicted Circe surrounded by animals and pigs, formerly Ulysses' men, as the hero arrives to save them (Ovid, *Metamorphoses*, XIV), as seen in Giovanni Andrea Sirani's *Ulysses and Circe* in the Musei Capitolini, Rome (reproduced Modesti 2004, fig. 153). Elisabetta chose to represent not this particular narrative event that defines Circe as a *femme fatale*, but rather, as the artist was often wont to do, she focuses on Circe's status as a queen, her regal power and extraordinary knowledge (*sapientia*) with her book of spells and wand to represent her mastery of the *ars magica*. This iconic single half-length image of the Queen in *primo piano*, dressed magnificently in an orientalising costume of velvets, brocade and turban, was typical of Elisabetta's interpretation of heroic, and even anti-heroic, women (see *Cleopatra*, cat. 3.34). By associating Circe's power with specialised female knowledge, Elisabetta was alluding to the Bolognese tradition of learned women, as well as to her own renowned erudition (Graziani, in *Elisabetta Sirani* 2004, p. 212; Modesti 2014, p. 353). It is documented that the artist studied the many books in her father's library to prepare for her canvases. Contemporaries referred to Elisabetta herself as a "Vigilant Sorceress, and great wise Painter" in poetry produced in her honour, for her ability to transform and transcend nature in her paintings (see *Alla Virtù della Signora Isabetta Sirani Dignissima Pittrice*, anonymous sonnet, Bologna 1658, in Modesti 2001b, pl. 16).
Whilst only registering "a Circe" as a companion piece to "a Ulisse" in her *Nota delle pitture* as part of a series of "various half-figures" representing classical mythological and biblical personages painted in 1657 for an unidentified patron (Malvasia 1678, ed. 1841, II, p. 394) Elisabetta is believed to have produced at least two versions of the subject, both of which should be considered self-portraits dating from after 1663.
The *Circe* here displayed is in all likelihood to be identified with the "Sorceress" by Elisabetta Sirani registered in the seventeenth-century collection of the Davia family, noted bankers and creditors, itself a companion piece to another "Sorceress" attributed to Carlo Cignani, both encased in gold frames. These two sorceresses were amongst a handful of the one hundred and thirty-seven works in the 1675 collection of Marcello Davia to be identified by its author, as was the "Alexander with gilded Frame by Sirana", evidence of their prestige (Modesti 2014, p. 353).
Sometime between 1684 and 1689 Elisabetta's *Circe* passed into the possession of the *causidico* Matteo Landi, in lieu of a loan, remaining with the creditor till 1715. Landi was the husband of the painter Elena Maria Panzacchi, a follower of our artist, and they were the maternal grandparents of Valerio Boschi, in whose collection Elisabetta's *Circe* was later found.
Elisabetta's painting formed a companion piece to a *Cleopatra* attributed to Simone Cantarini, and was located not in the Palazzo Boschi's noted Galleria, but in the private apartments of Signora Anna Orsi, Valerio Boschi's wife, and described in his probate inventory of 1777 as "A half-figure, life-size *Circe*, with carved, gilded frame, by La Sirani" (Modesti 2001b, pp. 183–186, notes 101–107). The painting was to remain with the Boschi family till 1858, after which the collection was dispersed.
Stylistically the work relates to Elisabetta's other paintings of heroines such as *Judith Triumphant* of 1658 or the *Beauty Triumphs over Time*, in which a similar model can be seen, perhaps Elisabetta herself. The shadowy Cignanesque brushwork and deep *chiaroscuro* of this work is typical of Sirani's later painterly style, and it also reveals the influence of Guercino's *macchio fondo*, dating this work to circa 1664. Elisabetta's *Circe* was to inspire Cesare Gennari's circa 1678 representation of the female classical philosopher and poet Ipparchia di Moranea that appeared recently on the international art market (Stenta 2019, fig. 8).
Adelina Modesti

3.34
Elisabetta Sirani
Bologna, 1638 – Bologna, 1665
Cleopatra
c. 1664
Oil on canvas, 110 × 91 cm
Private collection

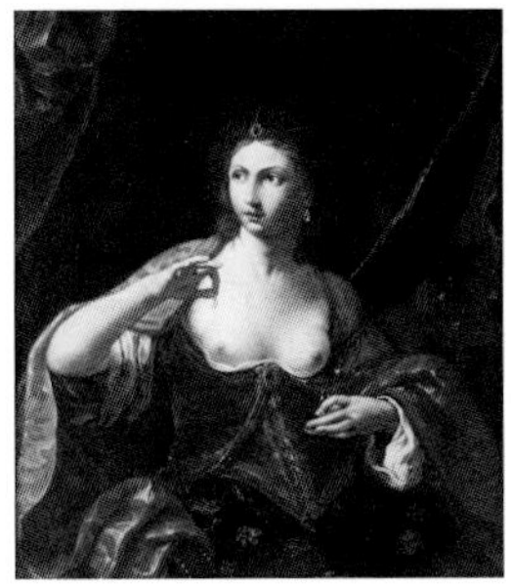

A recent addition to Elisabetta's oeuvre, the *Cleopatra* was first brought to my attention by Alex Cavallucci, and highlights the artist's virtuosity, her technical *bravura*, dramatic colour orchestration and use of strong chiaroscuro. The rich red, gold and ultramarine of the Queen of Egypt"s costume contrast with the dark crimson curtained background, the whole composed in a theatrical stage set. Elisabetta has carefully deployed the light to focus on Cleopatra's exposed flesh – breasts, arm, and face – as well as picking up the reflected light on the glass cup held in her left hand and on the vase in the right background. This demonstrates her mastery of the paint medium, being able to so successfully capture and portray the transparency of glass and its reflections. Cleopatra's hands are also beautifully and gracefully rendered in their elegant pose, as they hold the large Baroque pearl (one of her earrings) and cup of vinegar in which it is about to be dropped. Her right arm reveals a *pentimento*, showing how Elisabetta rethought and reworked her compositions directly on the canvas (Modesti 2018b, pp. 90–91).
The painting, which dates to about 1664, can be related stylistically to two other works by Elisabetta from the same period: *Portia* (see cat. 3.28), and the *Allegory of Justice, Charity and Prudence* (commissioned by Prince Leopoldo de' Medici; see Modesti 2014, pp. 334–336 and pl. 25), especially in the staging of the female figures and treatment of the drapery. Elisabetta was renowned for these images of powerful women, in which the artist gives prominence to the figure of the heroine, both thematically and visually, often excluding the male protagonist "hero" through whom these women's identity had come to be defined. Here Elisabetta represents Cleopatra without her lover the Roman general Mark Antony, choosing to depict the lone heroine in a single iconic image, in order to concentrate on the powerful queen herself. It is noteworthy that Elisabetta does not illustrate Cleopatra's suicide, which had been the more popular subject represented during the first half of the seventeenth century (such as those by Guido Reni or Guido Cagnacci). Rather she chooses the moment when the Queen demonstrates her wealth to Mark Antony, but, interestingly, does not represent the banquet scene in which this act usually takes place, which would put the lovers within the same pictorial space, as seen in the many

examples of the *Banquet of Cleopatra* by Tiepolo the following century. Elisabetta, always inventive in her choice of subject manner and their representation, reinterprets the banquet according to her knowledge of specific texts in her father's library: Pliny the Elder's *Natural History*, Plutarch's "Life of Mark Antony", and Giovanni Lomazzo's *Trattato della Pittura*. The artist foregoes staging the entire banquet that plays on the gendered power relationship between the Egyptian queen and her Roman lover. Instead Elisabetta focuses on a solitary image of the female protagonist, Cleopatra dropping her pearl earring in the vase of vinegar to demonstrate her apparent indifference to her wealth, sign of her political power, and thereby winning her bet with Mark Antony as to who of the two was the wealthiest.
Queen Cleopatra of Egypt was considered in her own time and culture "the most illustrious and wise among woman [...] great in herself and in her achievements in courage and strength", according to the Coptic Bishop John of Nukiu (Hughes-Hallett 1997, p. 95), famed for her "intellectual power", "clever conversation" and wit, "irresistible charm" and extraordinary political acumen, as Plutarch's account tells us, while Lomazzo wrote that Cleopatra "was grand and magnanimous". Elisabetta knew these sources, and combined these qualities with Cleopatra's seductive charm in an image that is far more sensuous than her other known representations of the queen (see Modesti 2014, pp. 162–164, and pp. 326–327, figs. 78–79).
Adelina Modesti

3.35
Elisabetta Sirani
Bologna, 1638 – Bologna, 1665
Penitent Mary Magdalene
1663
Oil on canvas, 113.5 × 94 cm
Paris, Musée du Louvre, in deposit in Besançon, Musée des Beaux-Arts et d'Archéologie, inv. D.864.1.3/569

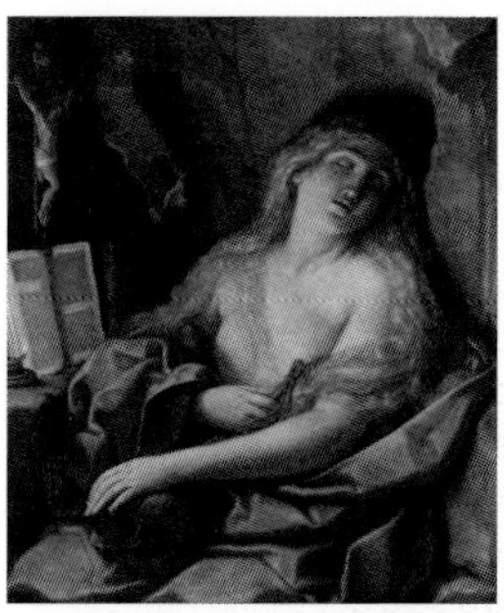

Elisabetta described the painting in her *Nota delle pitture* as "A penitent Mary Magdalene, half-figure, looking up to Heaven with a whip in her right hand, for Sig. Marquis Ferdinando Barbazzi" (Malvasia 1678, ed. 1841, II, p. 398). In this image of an ecstatic semi-nude Magdalene, who is depicted as both spiritually and physically transported in her penance, Elisabetta has successfully absorbed Guido Reni's erotic visual language of swooning saints and suicidal classical heroines (Spear 1997, pp. 179–180; Cottino 2003, pp. 17–18). There is an emotional intensity in Elisabetta's eroticized Magdalene, with its smooth almost pastel-like brushwork and its naturalistic treatment of the saint's skin reminiscent of Parmigianino and Correggio.
In this work she may have been influenced by a painting of the same subject by her father Giovanni Andrea Sirani, described by Malvasia as "A Mary Magdalene, half-figure, life-size, who, with bare shoulders, resting her left hand on her chest, with her right grasping small iron chains, beats herself before a Crucifix; beautiful air, beautiful hands, beautiful fabrics, with certain rosy flesh tones in the style of Parmigianino" (Malvasia 1961, p. 119).
Painted for the Bolognese nobleman Ferdinando Barbazza in 1663, Elisabetta's *Penitent Mary Magdalene* served as a companion piece for her *Madonna Lactans* (unidentified), as Marcello Oretti observed in the eighteenth century: "Barbazza House, a Blessed Virgin nursing the Child; a half-figure Saint Mary Magdalene penitent who looks up to Heaven with a whip in her hand, they are by La Sirani" (Oretti 1760–1790, ms. B. 104, II, no. 47, fol. 105). During the Counter-reformation images of saints, often paired together such as Mary Magdalene with Saint Jerome or Saint Sebastian, were intended as *exempla virtutis*, to invoke devotion, identification and repentance in the Christian viewer. This power of the visual image had been outlined in Archbishop Gabriele Paleotti's *Discorso intorno alle imagini sacre e profane* (1582), as well as promulgated via Ignatius Loyola's *Spiritual Exercises* (1652–1654), a series of Christian meditations, contemplations and prayers in which the Jesuit founder encouraged the faithful to visualize Christ's sufferings as their own. This could be achieved by reciting the exercises in front of a holy image, and we know that Elisabetta specialized in such devotional *quadretti da letto*, some of which were even used as printed images on prayer sheets (Modesti 2004, p. 87, fig. 45).
Elisabetta's interpretation of the Magdalene here presents the saint as a repentant sinner, in accordance with Cesare Ripa's description of *Purgazione de' peccati*: "Thin woman, who cries many tears from her eyes; with her right hand she holds a whip [...] to show her conscience not simulated but clear, with many signs, to purge the sins, which with sobs, tears and laments we regret things sadly and brutally committed". In this painting, the saint swoons as if in ecstasy or from a bout of self-flagellation. The scourge, so prominent here, reveals the Magdalene as an imitator of Christ's passion, through which she achieves forgiveness and salvation. Elisabetta has included the crucifix with a suffering Christ in front of the open scriptures, evidence of God's divine plan. The viewer, placed in front of the painting, likewise becomes actively involved in this process of Loyola's *imitatio*: through contemplation, daily meditation and prayer, examination of conscience (*interregatione*), and general and liturgical confession. These are the necessary preparations of the soul for partaking of the Holy Sacrament of the Eucharist, via which we participate in the passion, death and resurrection of Christ and commune with the Divine, providing spiritual consolation and eternal salvation (Modesti 2014, p. 314).
Elisabetta's *Penitent Mary Magdalene* remained in the Barbazza family collection until the late eighteenth century. It was next found in the private property of Giovanni Pietro Campana, Director of the Monte de' Pietà, Rome, who bequeathed his vast art collection to the French State in 1861, with the painting deposited at Besançon in 1864 (Sarti 2001, IX, no. 569).
Adelina Modesti

3.36
Elisabetta Sirani
Bologna, 1638 – Bologna, 1665
Anna Maria Ranuzzi Portrayed as Charity
1665
Oil on canvas, 96 × 78 cm
Inscriptions: signed and dated "ELISA.TA SIRANI F 1665"
Bologna, Collezione d'Arte e di Storia della Fondazione Cassa di Risparmio in Bologna, inv. M3085

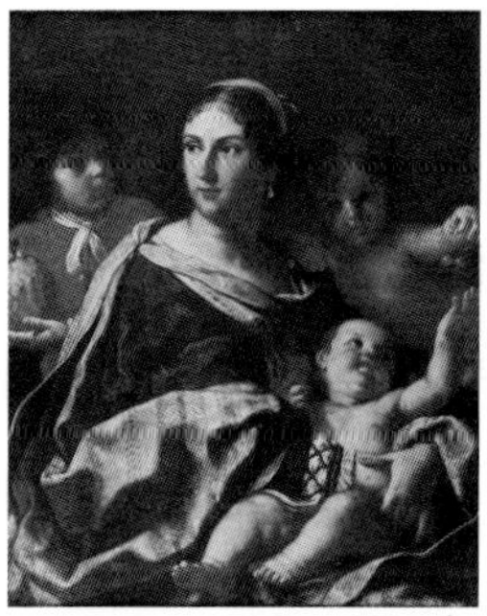

Elisabetta produced a number of society portraits of women, mainly half figures though she also painted two full-length pictures, most of which remain untraced. The present work perfectly exemplifies the genre of historiated portraiture by which the artist would place her sitters in allegorical situations (cf. *Ortensia Leoni Cordini as Saint Dorothy*, Madison, Chazen Museum of Art; and *Vincenzo Ferdinando Ranuzzi Cospi as Cupid*, Warsaw, National Museum).
Anna Maria Ranuzzi Portrayed as Charity was painted in early 1665 for the sitter's brother Count Annibale Ranuzzi, Bolognese agent for Prince Leopoldo de' Medici, and an assiduous supporter of the Sirani, whom he visited "almost every day" (as reported by Ferdinando Cospi to Leopoldo de' Medici on 29 August 1665, Archivio di Stato di Firenze, Mediceo del Principato 5532, row 35, fol. 327). Ranuzzi's sister, the noblewoman Anna

Maria Ranuzzi had married Cesare Marsigli ten years earlier on 8 June 1655 (*Ranuzzi* 2000, p. 113, no. 42). One of only two extant female portraits by the artist (she lists 8 in her work diary) this was one of the last completed paintings Elisabetta worked on before her early death in late August 1665. On completion the portrait was delivered to her patron Annibale Ranuzzi by the Sirani domestic Anna Maria Donnini on the evening of 13 August, according to the testimony of Giovanni Andrea Sirani (Manaresi 1975, p. 10). It must be noted that Sirani later accused another family retainer, Lucia Tolomelli of having poisoned his daughter Elisabetta; the young housemaid was brought to trial and later exonerated.
Elisabetta's own description of this work in her *Nota delle pitture* makes it quite clear that she takes credit for the idea (*concetto*) to represent the sitter in the allegorical guise of Charity: "A Charity, for which *I wanted* to depict Miss Anna Maria Ranuzzi Marsigli, as a beautiful Woman, and similarly her children Silvio, and Francesco Maria, the third having been added on a whim, and this for the most distinguished Count Annibale Ranuzzi, brother of the lady" (Malvasia 1678, ed. 1841, II, p. 400; my emphasis).
In terms of the painting's iconography, the figure of Charity is presented surrounded by three children, one usually at her breast (Ripa 1593, ed. 1992, pp. 48–49). As the artist herself notes, Anna Maria Ranuzzi Marsigli had only two children so she added the third child from her own invention "like a *capriccio*". This capricious child teasingly dangles some cherries for the baby Francesco Maria, safe in his mother's lap, to play with. The older Silvio Maria, behind his mother's right shoulder, holds a large citrus. The fruit represented was symbolic of good will, mercy and compassion, so the intimate family portrait can be understood as an allegory of virtue (Ghirardi, in *Elisabetta Sirani* 2004, pp. 204–205; Frisoni, in *Italian Women Artists* 2007, p. 252). This interpretation gains further credence when we consider that Elisabetta's portrait was placed on display in Palazzo Ranuzzi together with its companion piece, an *Immaculate Conception* by Lorenzo Pasinelli, the only two works documented in the room (most probably a bed chamber). Together these two paintings represented the divine and earthly virtue of motherhood and maternal love (Modesti 2014, p. 360).
Annibale Ranuzzi's post-mortem legal inventory, dated19 April 1698, also reveals that Elisabetta's painting was worth almost double that of Pasinelli; 530 lire compared to 225 lire (Campori 1870, p. 413), evidence of the high value her work attracted.
The portrait's fine passages of virtuoso brushwork, restrained palette of lilacs and dark brown, accentuated with the odd touch of red, the intimacy of this family group and its psychological insight of a mother proud of both her children and social status, make it a masterful example of Bolognese portraiture in the second half of the seventeenth century.
It remained in the Ranuzzi family till the late nineteenth century after which it entered the collection of Marquis Giuseppe Malvezzi de' Medici. The painting has been exhibited numerous times over the years, beginning with the 1911 "Mostra del Ritratto Italiano" in Florence, right up to the 2019 exhibition of Bolognese seventeenth-century painting from the collections of the Fondazione Cassa di Risparmio in Bologna, testament to its quality and lasting appeal. An identical autograph signed copy, with a lighter tonal range, is located in a US private collection.
The portrait on display here was the second painting of Charity that Elisabetta produced for the Ranuzzi-Marsigli. The year before in 1664 the artist recorded in her work diary "A Charity, half-figure, life-size, who with her right hand pressing her finger to her mouth, signals to one child to be quiet, the other shown sleeping while being nursed is supported with her left arm, and the third dressed in a blue garment shows an apple to the onlookers" (Malvasia 1678, ed. 1841, II, p. 399). Painted for the nobleman Cesare Marsigli alias Rossi, Anna Maria Ranuzzi's husband, the work has not yet come to light.
Adelina Modesti

3.37
Jacopo Robusti, known as Tintoretto
Venice, 1518 – Venice, 1594
Portrait of Jacopo Soranzo
c. 1550–1551
Oil on canvas, 75 × 60 cm
Milan, Castello Sforzesco, Pinacoteca, inv. 64

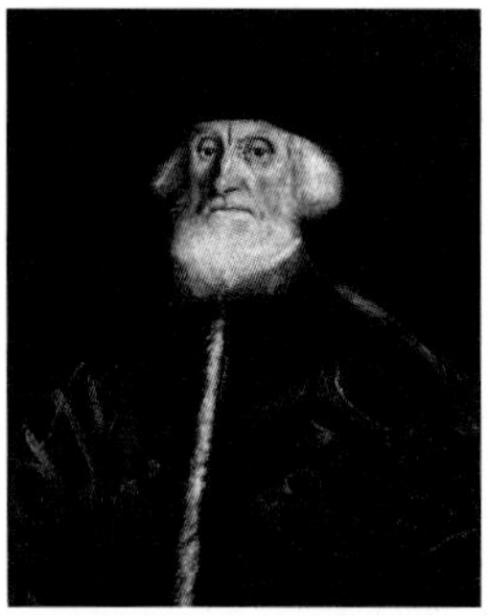

In the industry that was Tintoretto's workshop, portrait production immediately proved to be a sector of greatest and constant success. The young Jacopo soon became "a friend and family member of most of the Venetian Gentlemen; nor was there a man of letters or fine mind in that time who did not aspire to his practice, in which he mostly painted portraits" (Ridolfi 1642, p. 88). Among the members of the patriciate who turned to him was the wealthy Soranzo da San Polo family, who established lasting, trustful relationship with his workshop for at least three generations. This resulted in the portraits of Jacopo Soranzo jr (Venice, Gallerie dell'Accademia) and his brothers Lorenzo (1553, Vienna, Kunsthistorisches Museum), Benedetto (1563, Harewood House) and Zuanne (private collection), all of whom held prestigious public offices in the context of the Ottoman-Venetian War. They were ambassadors, galley captains and *provedditori* at the Arsenale. On display in the exhibition we see the remarkable portrait of the progenitor, procurator Jacopo senior (1467–1551), grandfather to the men mentioned above. Tintoretto painted him several times (a more official and standardised version of the portrait, destined for the offices of the Procuratie, is now in the Gallerie dell'Accademia). The work dates from about 1550 to 1551, and it has been suggested that it constituted the central part of the *Portrait of Fourteen Members of the Soranzo Family* today in the Castello Sforzesco, Milan. It is currently divided into two parts and lacks the key figure of the paterfamilias (Rossi, in *Jacopo Tintoretto* 1994, pp. 90–97, nos. 8–11). However, considering the remarkable quality of this single painting and the collective painting's lack of stylistic unity, Rearick (1995, p. 60) has suggested we consider this canvas as an autonomous, stand-alone work. Its dimensions do not fit within the gap between the two cut halves of the imposing *Family Portrait*, whereas they would be consistent with the approximately fifty portraits of senators and procurators that Tintoretto left us over the course of his long career. Moreover, the painting is characterised by an intense and refined psychological tone, decidedly incompatible with the mechanical seriality of a workshop product. The austere procurator emerges with patriarchal authority from the dark background, forcing us to meet his resolute yet veiled gaze, wisely wary and mindful of the many concerns engraved in the deep vertical wrinkle in his brow.
The expressive force of this face, outlined with a few essential brushstrokes, leads us to agree with Lanzi (1795–1796, II, p. 111) on the indisputable qualities of Tintoretto the portraitist: "especially in animating figures, he was the sovereign master".
Claudia Terribile

3.38
Marietta Robusti, known as Tintoretta (attributed)
Venice, c. 1554 – Venice, 1590
Self-Portrait (?)
Before 1590
Oil on canvas, 101 × 78 cm
Rome, Galleria Borghese, inv. 93

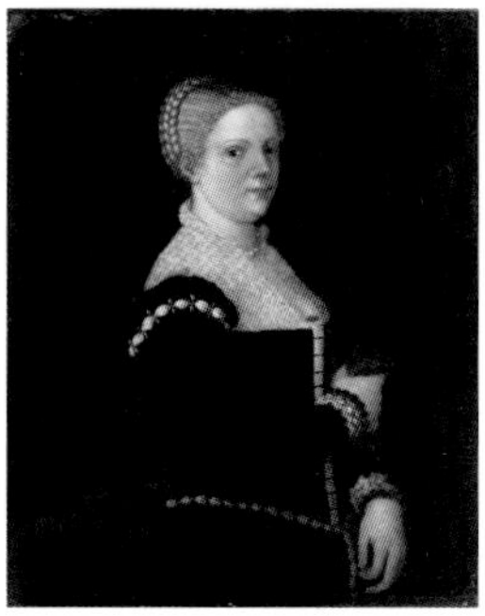

We have no certain knowledge about the identity of this young woman who looks us straight in the eye with the flower of her youth on her breast and the gloves of aristocratic lineage in her hands, even though there are at least three painted versions of this portrait in public collections. A fourth version, no longer traceable, was auctioned off in Vienna in 1920 (Ingersoll-Smouse 1927, p. 227), and there is also a late eighteenth-century engraving. In the 1955 catalogue of Galleria Borghese paintings, Della Pergola (1955–1959, I, p. 128, no. 232) listed this canvas as a replica of the one preserved in the Louvre today (D.1958.1). He attributed both works to Marietta Robusti, albeit with the benefit of the doubt, and classified them as self-portraits. In the past, the name of Irene da Spilimbergo was proposed for no apparent reason as the author of the painting in the Musei Civici, Padua (inv. 223), while in turn the French painting is considered to be a copy of the lost portrait of Elisabetta Querini, painted by Titian around 1545–1546. The link with Querini, a Venetian noblewoman, wife of Lorenzo Massolo and the muse of both Bembo and Giovanni Della Casa, is the only one to have any basis. The aforementioned Canale print, which unequivocally copies the painting, shows the woman's name and the Querini family coat of arms at the bottom of the image (Gallo 1935, p. 163).
Unfortunately, we do not know the origin of the engraving, but it still remains the only evidence we have that can be used to investigate further. The fame of a woman like Elisabetta Querini, celebrated by Titian's brush and eternalised by the verses of two of the greatest sixteenth-century poets, could have encouraged the request for copies of the portrait, and it would certainly justify the existence of the three replicas and engraving that have reached us.
Ridolfi tells us that Titian, "who was in the good graces of Monsignor della Casa, Nuncio of the Pontiff in Venice, who wished to have any record of his hand, made the portrait of a beautiful Venetian Lady, and afterwards he was celebrated by that melodious poet as follows: 'Now I see Titian in new forms'" (Ridolfi 1648, ed. 1835–1837, I, p. 224). This was how the portrait was recorded in the various printed editions of Della Casa's *Rime*, due to the two sonnets he composed about it. Gilles Ménage reminds us of this interesting detail in the mid-seventeenth century by commenting: "Today this painting is to be found in Rome, and a copy is in Venice at the Padovani Pittori [Paduan Painters]" (*Rime* 1667, pp. 90–91). This information is very promising for further investigations considering that both the French and the Paduan copies are attributed to Varotari. The provenance of these paintings needs to be established as firmly as possible, together with when they entered into their current collections. We also need to understand which canvas Canale may have used to make the engraving, and where; and we need to cross-reference the dates with the hereditary circumstances of Della Casa's assets. Only then we will be able to say with more certainty whether or not those were Elisabetta's graceful blond braids, which still today, "part between fresh roses and pure milk".
Claudia Terribile

3.39
Marietta Robusti, known as Tintoretta
Venice, c. 1554 – Venice, 1590
Self-Portrait with Madrigal
c. 1580
Oil on canvas, 93.5 × 91.5 cm
Florence, Gallerie degli Uffizi, 1890, inv. 1898

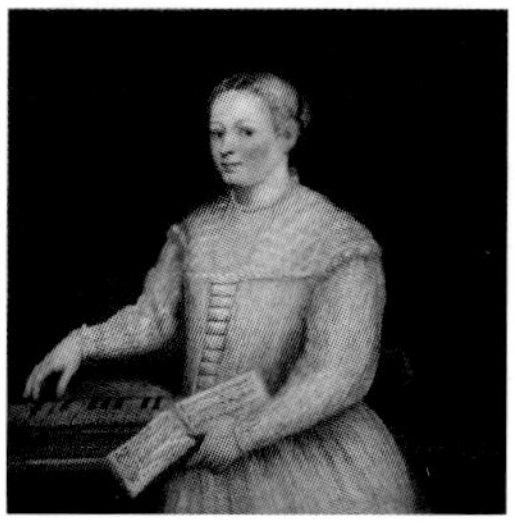

The Uffizi painting's attribution to Marietta is from 1675 and can be traced to the correspondence of Marco Boschini, commissioned by Cardinal Leopoldo de' Medici to purchase works of art from the Venetian collections. In the previous Régnier and Fontana collections, the painting was inventoried respectively as a work by Tintoretto and by Titian.
The canvas is not in excellent condition and appears to have been mishandled: the modelling of the face, but above all of the hands, has been compromised by drastic cleaning.
The young woman is depicted at half-length, standing in front of a spinet. Her right hand rests with intimate confidence on her instrument, almost as if she is about to embrace the spinet, while her left hand holds open a book of madrigals and she looks directly at the viewer with a secure, questioning look. The bituminous background contrasts with the completely white dress, the garment's crimped surface suggesting a very light, vaporous fabric, perhaps muslin, today somewhat spoiled by the peeling paint. The white clothes, the candour of the gaze and the pallid pearls display the dress code of a girl of marriageable age or of a new bride, and recall other paintings of young women in the ritual passage from virginal age to one of desire. Among these is Titian's *Portrait of a Lady in White* (c. 1561), now in the Gemäldegalerie Alte Meister, Dresden, who is also pictured wearing a white dress with a flush of rosiness in her cheeks. Marietta married in 1578 and, if it is a self-portrait, it could perhaps have been a personal gift or invitation to her husband in the form of a cultured musical metaphor. It has been noted that the musical score is open at the meticulously transcribed *cantus* of a madrigal by Philippe Verdelot: *Madonna per voi ardo* from the first book of the *Primo libro dei madrigali a quattro voci*, printed in Venice in 1533. The text is anonymous and rather banal in its longing for love from a woman who is reluctant to believe and reciprocate such love. However, the intention to present this specific musical reference and make its meaning perfectly intelligible is evident.
Philippe Verdelot's madrigals were extraordinarily successful in the sixteenth century and played a crucial role, together with those of Arcadelt, in the genesis and widespread diffusion of this new musical form. Even more than the astonishing fourteen reprints that were made between 1533 and 1566, the tangible echo of the fame of the first madrigals can be heard in figurative testimonies like this one, where we find a precisely cited musical edition from fifty years earlier (it happens again with Caravaggio's *Lute Player*, who is performing a piece by Arcadelt). The genre had evolved considerably since then, and from the 1580s until the end of the century, more topical references and authors were chosen and inserted. The anachronism is obviously deliberate and cannot be ascribed solely to past fashions or the client's taste for "vintage". The large-scale diffusion guaranteed by print offered wide-ranging performance opportunities for the earliest secular and poetic madrigal repertory, even in contexts beyond the court. Indeed, the music of Verdelot, Arcadelt and De Rore became a common cultural heritage widely shared by citizens throughout Europe; naturally, this resulted in raising their aspirations to a higher level of musical skill, drawing a boundary between those who were on one or the other side of such musical ability. It was music that managed above all to reach many women, allowing them to rise, at least in terms of artistic training, to the rank of a court lady. This important milestone was sufficient reason for a woman to present herself by exhibiting universally recognised musical skills. But in this painting Marietta, or whoever the woman was, plays an even more subtle game. To understand this fully, we need to remember that ancient printed musical scores were published in as many versions as there were voices envisaged by the composer. In the case of Verdelot's *Primo libro dei madrigali*, there were four: cantus, altus, tenor and bassus. Each publication was called a "part-book" because it contained only the melodic lines of the corresponding voice. In order to sing the piece, each of the four singers had to read from their own book, or they had to have an instrument that could play the harmony of the missing voices in order to accompany a soloist.
In the Uffizi portrait the woman is neither playing nor singing, but is showing the cantus, namely the part in her vocal register, and is explicitly urging her beloved to share in the performance. It is a secret, conscious and explicit invitation: the hand placed on the instrument not only metaphorically

guarantees her "virginal" chastity as a betrothed or new bride, but also denotes musical skills that could easily allow her to sit at the instrument and accompany herself. However, the pose, the score she exhibits and the direction of her gaze declare that she has chosen another path, that of seeking an harmonious and erotic pact with the privileged recipient of the painting.
Claudia Terribile

3.40
Guglielmo De Martino
Nicastro (Catanzaro), 1845 – Nicastro (Catanzaro), 1898
Tintoretto Portraying his Dying Daughter
Before 1881
Oil on canvas, 77.5 × 103.5 cm
Catanzaro, MARCA – Museo delle Arti di Catanzaro, inv. 0011345

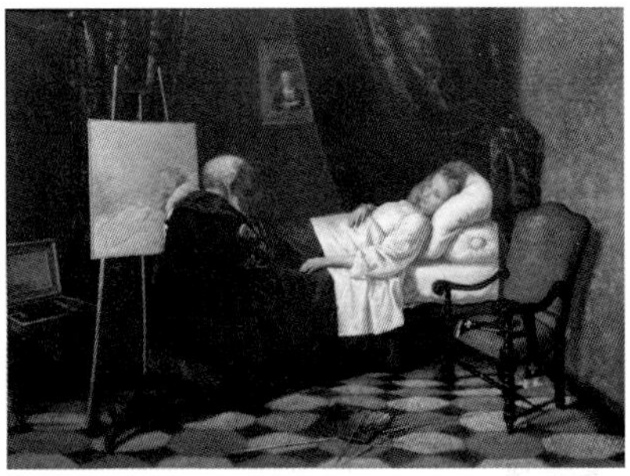

The painting is first recorded in documentary sources in 1881 under the title *Tintoretto Paints his Dead Daughter* (Caivano-Schipani 1881, p. 83), and constitutes one of Gugliemo De Martino's greatest efforts. The artist trained in the circle of Andrea Cefaly, a Garibaldian painter and later a parliamentary deputy of the Kingdom of Italy, the centre of gravity in an episode of political and artistic participation between Calabria and Naples that involved the major players in the process of uniting Italy, from Giuseppe Mazzini to Giuseppe Garibaldi, the Palizzi brothers and Domenico Morelli. From Cortale (Catanzaro), where Cefaly began a pedagogical experiment by founding a free school of painting, De Martino enrolled in the Royal Institute of Fine Arts in Naples in 1861 with a subsidy from the Provincial Deputation of Catanzaro. His production oscillates between genre scenes and Risorgimento themes. Among these, the painting *Tintoretto Portraying his Dying Daughter* demonstrates De Martino's interest in the pantheon of illustrious men of historical Romanticism, making his way through the repertoire of the famous lives of Venetian artists, whose main source was the *Meraviglie dell'arte* by Cesare Ridolfi (1648). His attention was focused on the episode of the untimely death of Marietta Robusti (c. 1554–1590), the daughter of Jacopo (known as Tintoretto), described in the *Meraviglie dell'arte*, republished in a successful edition (Padua 1832). This increased her literary fame during the nineteenth century, fuelled by texts such as Francesco Berlan's book dedicated to *Fanciulle celebri e l'infanzia delle donne illustri d'Italia* (Milan 1865). Marietta is described as having such an ability in the arts, as well as in music, that it amazed her contemporaries, as did her tendency as a young girl to dress as a boy. This fame – documented in life by Moderata Fonte in *Merito delle donne* (published posthumously in 1600; see Grosso 2017) – was interrupted by an early death aged about thirty, suffered "bitterly" by her father "as if it were part of his entrails" (Ridolfi 1648, p. 261). De Martino focused on this passage. The scene is set in an interior where a heavy curtain acts as a backdrop to the theatre of pain that opens against the back wall, where a painting is hanging – the counterpart of the one just sketched on canvas by Tintoretto as he portrays his dying daughter. Overwhelmed, he has just stopped working: the palette and brushes are scattered on the floor, the case of colours is open behind the easel. Tintoretto is seated next to the bed where Maria is reclining on large soft pillows, wrapped in a white robe, almost falling into a sweet sleep. Her arm, stretching out towards her father, now rests on the heavy green blanket. The uniformity of the earthy tones, which expertly outline the details of the painted space, is brightened by a red armchair on which a prayer book lies. Although the prototype of the subject is certainly *Tintoretto Portraying his Dead Daughter* (1843, Bordeaux, Musée des Beaux-Arts) by Léon Cogniet, the theme was also taken up in Italian painting by Giuseppe Giani, who in 1858 exhibited at the Turin promoter exhibition *Tintoretto Portraying his Dead Daughter*. And at the National Exhibition in Florence in 1861, Eleuterio Pagliano also presented *The Death of Tintoretto's Daughter* (1861, Milan, Galleria d'Arte Moderna), the year in which he hosted Domenico Morelli in his Milanese studio. In the same orbit of Neapolitan visual culture, Nicola Pitocchi presented *Tintoretto's Dead Daughter* at the fourth Naples promoter exhibition (1866). The small-format sketch of the painting is probably the one conserved in the Pinacoteca Patiniana.
De Martino took part in Neapolitan Promoter Society exhibitions with a certain regularity from 1870 to 1891, and also the "Exhibition of Fine Arts" held at the Palazzo di Brera in Milan (1873); the "National Exhibition of Naples" (1877); and the international exhibitions of Melbourne (1880) and Rome (1883) (see *Andrea Cefaly* 1998, pp. 95, 98–99; Le Pera 2008, p. 148; Silvano 2014–2015). A member of the Association of Scientists Writers and Artists, in 1875 De Martino obtained the qualification to teach drawing, and in 1878 he was in charge of starting and running "a drawing school in the village of Capodimonte" (Caivano-Schipani 1881, p. 83).
As part of the Neapolitan artistic system, De Martino was involved in the Galleria del Conservatorio di San Pietro at Majella, set up by Francesco Florimo, and received four commissions, including, around 1880 and 1881, historical portraits of Orlando di Lasso (1532–1594) and the Flemish composer Johannes Tinctoris (c. 1435 – before 1511). Among his other works are *Enjoy this special time, my dear girl / This is a joyful season (Leopardi)*, presented at the Naples promoter exhibition in 1873 (formerly in the Francia collection), an homage to *Sabato del Villaggio* (1829) by the poet who had spent the last years of his life in Naples (1833–1837). Also *A Future Raffaello* (1876, Naples, Provincial Administration); and *The Nicastro Castle Besieged by the Saracens* (1868, Lamezia Terme, City Hall).
The work was presented at the first Calabrian art exhibition, held in Catanzaro in 1912, indicated in the catalogue already in the patrimony of the Museo Provinciale, Catanzaro (Frangipane 1913, p. 74, no. 219; see *Catalogo* 1925, no. 96; Comanducci 1962, p. 593; Pelaggi 1976, p. 15, no. 125), where *The Wait* is also kept (Catanzaro, MARCA).
Maria Saveria Ruga

3.41
Chiara Varotari
Padua, 1584 – Venice, post 1663
Portrait of a Lady
c. 1620–1629
Oil on canvas, 205 × 120 cm
Padua, Museo d'Arte Medioevale e Moderna, legacy of Count Leonardo Emo Capodilista, 1864, inv. 138

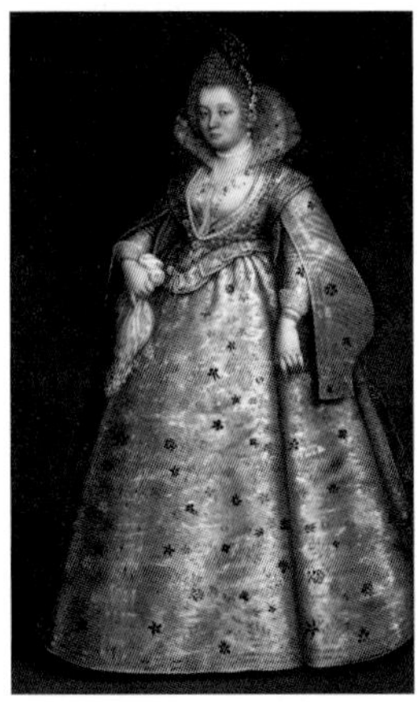

The painting was bequeathed to the Padua museum by Count Leonardo Emo Capodilista (1864).
The lady was identified by Botter (1967, pp. 25–26 note 28) as Pantasilea Dotto, wife of Pio Capodilista, who held the position of governor of arms in Palma, the fortress city built in 1593 by the Republic of Venice. The identification was rejected by Ballarin (1968 [actually 1969], p. 250), since it was based solely on the fact that the painting came from the Capodilista collection. Botter hypothesised that the other full-length female portrait signed by Chiara Varotari and also part of the Emo Capodilista bequest to the Padua museum (inv. 136) depicts a

daughter of Pio and Pantasilea, perhaps Piera.
The noblewoman portrayed here has a pointed hairstyle with her hair raised in the centre and probably lightened, according to a fashion that was very widespread among Venetian women in the sixteenth century (Francesco Sansovino, 1581, and Cesare Vecellio, 1590, mention this custom). Her collar, decorated with flowers and probably embroidered on a fine transparent veil, is a "Medici" model: raised at the back to outline the face, and with caning typical of ruffs. The bodice has a wide neckline that reveals another finely embroidered underbodice (or blouse) beneath. Flap-like attachments that open laterally form shaped fake sleeves decorated with woven gold braid stripes. The real sleeves, tight with lace cuffs, are also decorated with the same gold braid stripes, as is the skirt.
Elisa Masiero, an expert on fabric and costume, believes that the dress fabric may date to the first quarter of the seventeenth century. Its design is similar to a freer and more naturalistic version of mesh rhomboid patterns often found in fabrics for clothing and furnishings in the previous century, with pine cones or thistle flowers in the centre. The fabric seems to be lampas with a damask background, probably including silver thread and thrown wefts, and the presence of brocading is not excluded. The dating of the painting has varied between the first two decades of the seventeenth century (Prelli 1998, p. 13) and the 1630s (Fossaluzza 1977 [1994], pp. 133–134; Banzato, in *Malerei in Venetien* 1987, p. 111, cat. 32, p. 113; Banzato, in *La peinture vénitienne* 1991, pp. 82–83, cat. 24; Banzato, in *Pietro Damini* 1993, pp. 96–97, cat. 6; Rubbi, in *Italian Women Artists* 2007, pp. 190–191, cat. 41). As far as we know, Ericani (1996, pp. 69, 71–73, 75) was the first to analyse the garments more closely, proposing the late 1620s, followed by Banzato (2000, pp. 129, 136, fig. 161) and by Pellegrini (in *La donna* 2003, p. 163, cat. 1).
The lady sports a valuable belt, necklaces, bracelets and rings, which underscore her high social status. In one hand she holds a handkerchief with a needle lace (*punto in aria*) border, according to the fashions in vogue at the time.
Pallucchini (1981, I, p. 106) describes Chiara Varotari's portraiture as "stately and effective [...] entirely focused on highlighting in meticulous detail the quality of the textiles and the opulence of the jewels", and that it "reduces the characters to mere mannequins". Indeed the figure framed against the dark background does not stand out as a result of her psychological characteristics but because of her external appearance: every detail of the sumptuous dress and elaborate hairstyle make this work an example of status portraiture.
Elisabetta Gastaldi

3.42
Chiara Varotari
Padua, 1584 – Venice, post 1663
Portrait of a Girl
c. 1620–1629
Oil on canvas, 122 × 70 cm
Padua, Museo d'Arte Medioevale e Moderna, legacy of Count Leonardo Emo Capodilista, 1864, inv. 134

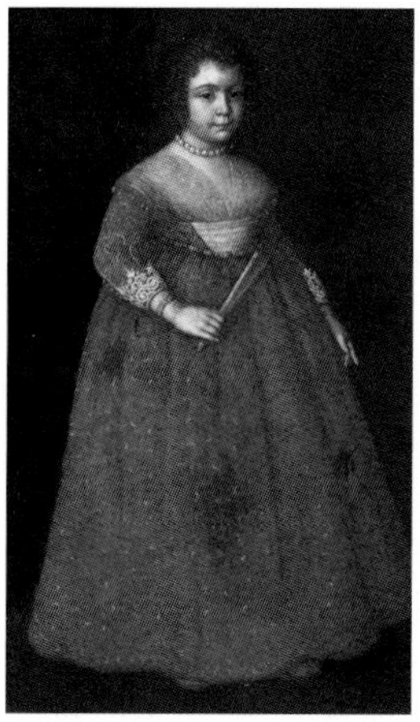

This work was bequeathed to the museum together with its pendant (inv. 140, cat. 3.43) by Count Leonardo Emo Capodilista (1864). Pier Luigi Fantelli (1973, p. 6) cautiously attributed it to Chiara Varotari "due to the difficulty of reading the poorly preserved canvas", whereas Davide Banzato (in *La Quadreria* 1988, pp. 114–115, cat. 174) considered this attribution certain, as was later confirmed by the critics.
The girl's hair is styled with curls arranged on her forehead and the sides of her head. She is dressed as an adult, wearing a slightly shaped high-waisted dress bodice bordered by a costly belt. The bodice is open at the front to reveal the blouse underneath and a tightly pleated fichu in a delicate fabric that softens the neckline (similar solutions can be seen in portraits from the mid-1500s). The bodice and sleeves are decorated with embroidery that simulates the presence of braid trimmings. As in the case of the young boy, the sleeves are tight fitting with removable Venetian needle lace (*punto in aria*) borders at the wrists. The sleeves are also detachable and connected to the bodice by ribbons with costly fasteners (the shoulder attachment is low). Along the underside of the forearm is a row of buttons similar to those in the portrait of the young boy. The skirt has a wide bell-shape, slightly gathered at the waist, and along the hem runs same embroidered decoration as on the bodice and sleeves.
The dress fabric is probably a satin or spun gold taffeta (see the half-moon motifs), but unlike the boy's outfit there is no red lining (our thanks to Elisa Masiero for this observation). The girl's pale leather shoes can just be seen.
The girl, a future lady, is depicted holding a fan, a fashion accessory from the second half of the sixteenth century, and is wearing a pearl necklace and two bracelets.
Giuliana Ericani (1996, p. 73) dates the painting to around the 1620s to 1630s; Valeria Rubbi (in *Italian Women Artists* 2007, pp. 192–193, cat. 42) proposes the 1640s, whereas Roberto Pancheri (2015, pp. 72–73) suggests around 1630. However, due to the style of the clothes, Elisa Masiero (communicated orally) proposes limiting the date to the 1620s.
Elisabetta Gastaldi

3.43
Chiara Varotari
Padua, 1584 – Venice, post 1663
Portrait of a Boy
c. 1620–1629
Oil on canvas, 122 × 70 cm
Padua, Museo d'Arte Medioevale e Moderna, legacy of Count Leonardo Emo Capodilista, 1864, inv. 140

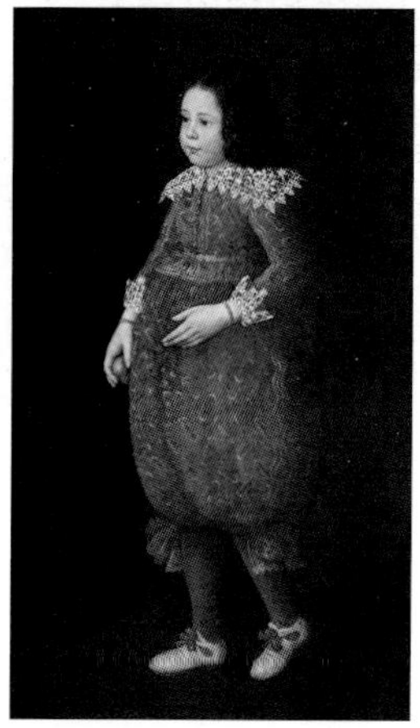

The painting, together with its pendant (inv. 134, cat. 3.42), entered the museum as the bequest of Count Leonardo Emo Capodilista (1864). It was first published in 1988 by Davide Banzato, who attributed it to Chiara Varotari (Banzato, in *La Quadreria* 1988, pp. 114–115, cat. 175).
The boy has a loose, natural hairstyle and is wearing a bodice with tight-fitting sleeves and a high waist, edged by shaped flaps. The ribbons knotted in bows have ornamental tips that were passed through holes in the bodice band to support the trousers. The upper part is fastened by a row of spherical buttons that are repeated along the forearms. The wide collar leaves and the cuffs are embellished with needle lace (*punto in aria*), typical of Venetian workmanship. These clothing accessories were removable and could be worn with a variety of outfits. The trousers are very wide and tied below the knee. Very simple gold thread trimmings, probably made on a loom, run along the sides and sleeves of the upper section and the sides of the trousers.
The boy is dressed like an adult, since in that era no differentiation was made between adult and children's fashion.
Elisa Masiero has commented that the fabric

is very interesting. As in the case of the portrait of the young girl, it is probably a satin or taffeta brocaded in spun gold (note the half-moon elements), with cuts arranged to form a decorative pattern that reveals the underlying red lining, which is the same as the cuffs and collar.
The fabric motifs are arranged *a mazze* (literally, "like maces"), a configuration already in vogue at the end of the 1500s. The stockings are well-fitting and the white leather shoes, tied with bows, were those reserved for elegant occasions.
Giuliana Ericani (1996, p. 73) dates the painting to around the 1620s to 1630s, followed by Davide Banzato (in *Lo spirito e il corpo* 2009, p. 66, fig. 38, p. 100, cat. 38). According to Alberto Prelli (1998, p. 48) and Elisa Masiero (communicated orally), the style of the costume style narrows the date to the 1620s.
Elisabetta Gastaldi

3.44
Fede Galizia
Milan?, 1574/1578 – Milan, post 21 June 1630
Pears and a Majolica Fruit Bowl with Grapes and Plums
c. 1610
Oil on panel, 27.5 × 38 cm
Private collection

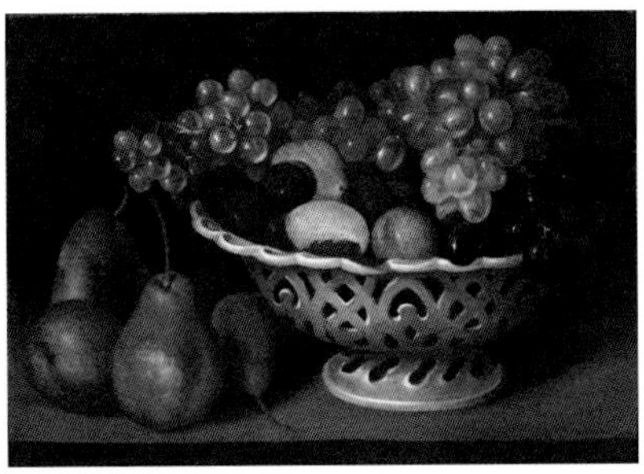

The composition presents a close-up view of a pale ceramic fruit bowl containing clusters of black and green grapes and various types of plums. On the table beside the bowl are four pears. The composition of the scene is simple and essential, with sharply defined light directed only on the foreground, leaving the surrounding area sunk in shadow. Moreover, the use of a wood panel support (frequent in Fede Galizia's work rather than canvas) enhances the effect of the glaze-like gloss on the fruit, which creates a powerful and melancholy contrast to the predominantly dark areas.
The circular perforated fruit bowl in majolica has a single foot and a thick milky white enamel glaze. Several examples are known and a particularly similar one was recently on sale at a Pandolfini auction (18 April 2018, no. 54). Even the latter's measurements were probably very close to those of the bowl in the painting, since a diameter of 27 cm and height of 15.6 cm are in perfect proportion to the fruits represented. Another similar bowl is the one bearing the coat of arms of Cardinal Pietro Crescenzi (Rome, 1572–1645, cardinal from 1611), conserved in the Musei del Bargello, Florence. As far as is known, majolica of this type was fairly classic of Faenza production at the beginning of the seventeenth century, therefore the date is consistent with the one considered most likely for the painting.
The depiction of the fruit is absolutely lifelike. The pears are particularly striking, perfectly resembling common fruits with a red-tinged skin, a quality that anticipates Williams pears, which are very similar to the ones shown here, but are a variety that has been produced in England only since the end of the eighteenth century. However, with the end of summer harvest between August and September, pears can accompany grapes in the autumn period. The three varieties of plums are also depicted with extreme fidelity: *Prunus domestica* or damsons (dark), greengages (light green), and Victoria (red outside and yellow inside). These are gathered between June and September, and thus help to date the execution of the painting to September.
An almost identical version of the fruit portrayed in the bowl, but with a greater number of pears on the table, was recently auctioned at Sotheby's, New York (1 February 2018, lot no. 20, 27.3 × 38.7 cm; together with a counterpart of the same size). A picture of our painting was published in the sales catalogue as a comparison to fig. 2, indicating its provenance as a Sotheby's London sale on 12 December 1984. On that occasion our painting was also accompanied by another counterpart, identical in size and with the same subject as the second painting of the 2018 sale (Frangi, in *The Lure of Still Life* 1995, pp. 50–55). From this we must suppose that Fede Galizia made two pairs of paintings almost identical to each other.
Scrupulous and almost scientific realism characterises many of the still life paintings during the late sixteenth and early seventeenth centuries, especially in the wake of the naturalistic collections that became fashionable in the latter half of the 1500s as an effect of the *Wunderkammern*, and before the spectacular settings that occurred towards the 1630s and 1640s, which included of curtains, carpets and numerous other items. Fede Galizia in particular shows acute sensitivity from her earliest works. She is at home in the Lombard style of painting from life, with the ability to render a humid, fertile, Po valley climate which is heightened by the "humbler" details in her paintings. Every aspect speaks this language: from the rough peel on the pears that absorb the light to the spots on the plums, or the irregular reflections of light on the grapes that conjure the slightly sticky sensation of the sugary surface.
Within her chronology, the painting can be confidently located around 1610 (as Francesco Solinas proposed in *De dames* 2018, pp. 110–111, no. 24). Fede Galizia, then fully mature at an age of about thirty-five, had progressed beyond the more painstaking, academic style of her early works to achieve these heights of meditation on the domestic condition of existence, confined in the narrow space of a moment, a penumbra, or the foggy countryside, which was a paradigm not only for the splendour of the human situation in general, but also its imminent decadence. It is worth recalling how inappropriate Flavio Caroli's comment was, when in the catalogue to the 2018 auction he described the "clear, astral and powerful" quality of the two paintings: in other words, everything they are not.
Giovanni Valagussa

3.45
Fede Galizia
Milan?, 1574/1578 – Milan, post 21 June 1630
Crystal Fruit Stand with Peaches, Quinces and Jasmine Flowers
c. 1607
Oil on poplar wood panel, 28.8 × 41 cm
Cremona, Museo Civico Ala Ponzone, inv. 217

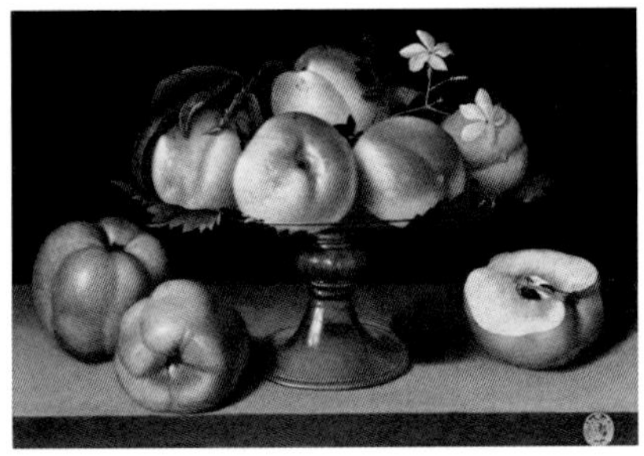

In the centre of the composition is a crystal fruit stand, whose foot reflects the light entering from a window. It holds six peaches arranged on vine leaves. Among them on the right is a sprig of jasmine with two flowers. The stand is placed on a surface seen from above, whose depth in shadow aligns with the base of the painting. Next to the stand are two quinces on the left and half a quince on the right, revealing its fleshy pulp with the core and seeds. The extreme naturalism and tactile qualities with which the objects are described illustrate the artist's sensitive approach and her keen eye for detail, even if, as has been recently pointed out, peaches and quinces ripen at different times (Solinas, in *De dames* 2018, p. 108).
The painting is one of Fede's most successful inventions and was already described with precision in 1635 by Antonio Mariani della Corgna in the inventory of the collection of Charles Emmanuel I, Duke of Savoy (1562–1630), despite the fact that he wrongly attributed it to Panfilo Nuvolone: "six peaches with jasmine on a dish, and 2 and a half quinces on the table" and "By Panfilo Cremonese. Good" (*Musei d'Arte* [1994], I, p. 23 no. 454). As a matter of fact, the Savoy collection must have contained two versions of this subject, given that the inventory also records a "Glass dish with peaches, and 2 ½

quinces" (see *Musei d'Arte* [1994], I, p. 33 no. 656, which differs from the former painting because there is no jasmine). Della Corgna's mistaken attribution was the source of subsequent misunderstandings about the invention of the subject (Morandotti, in *Fasto e rigore* 2000, pp. 136–137). Indeed, until 1938 the first known example of this composition (then in the Vitale Bloch collection) had already been attributed to Galizia by Curt Benedict after a comparison with the only still life she had signed and dated in 1602, which was formerly in the Anholt collection, Amsterdam (Benedict 1938, p. 309 note 1, and p. 313, fig. 14).
Regarding the painting in question, in the preparatory notes to the catalogue of the Cremonese Art Gallery of 1951, Alfredo Puerari credited Fede as the artist; yet, inexplicably, the work (and its twin, cat. 3.46) were not published (Marubbi, in *La Pinacoteca* 2007, pp. 38–39, see also for the different opinions on authorship). Only in 1998 was the question definitively resolved following the restoration of a panel painting with the same composition, at the time in the Metropolitan Museum of Art in New York (in 2015 it returned to a private collection). On the edge of the panel, the initials FG and the date 1607 were discovered, which therefore enabled the work and all other similar compositions to be attributed to Fede Galizia (Segal 1998).
To date, six versions are known, all autographed, but with slight variations that differentiate them, such as the presence or absence of a jasmine flower on the ground, which is absent in the Cremonese Art Gallery painting and also in another, which has a springing locust in its place and the two quinces placed on the left in different positions (reproduced in *Pittori della realtà* 2004, pp. 230–231). The four remaining versions are distinguished by the slightly changed position of the fallen jasmine, or by slight differences in the peaches. They can be identified as follows: the former Bloch version, later French & Company (reproduced in Caroli 1989a, pl. 11); the former Katz version, later in a private collection in Bassano (reproduced in Caroli 1989a, pl. 13); one signed and dated, now in a private collection (reproduced in *Pittori della realtà* 2004, pp. 228–229); and finally the one indicated by Flavio Caroli from a photograph belonging to the Witt Library in London, which – at least at first sight – does not seem to correspond to any of the others (Caroli 1989a, pl. 13). In addition, there is a parchment version with a snail in the place of the locust (Berra 2016, p. 86 note 113).
The question remains whether the example (or rather both) registered in the Savoyard collections is among the versions listed so far. The cautiously proposed hypothesis that it may be the painting now in Cremona (Marubbi, in *La Pinacoteca* 2007, p. 39) is so far not supported by documentary evidence. It is certainly odd that the Ala Ponzone collection contains two still lifes by Fede that correspond iconographically to the ones described in the Della Corgna inventory. Furthermore, the two panels are distinguished by a gold stamp with the epigraph "IOS[ephus] Mo ALA C[omes] PONZONUS" (namely, Marquis Giuseppe Sigismondo Ala Ponzone. See *La collezione* 2005, p. 177 no. IX.a 4 and fig. a, p. 178. This is therefore not a reference to the grandfather, Pietro Martire, as erroneously reported in *La Pinacoteca* 2007, p. 39). In the entire Ala Ponzone collection this epigraph appears only on the two still lifes by Fede (both on display) and on the panel *Goldfinch with Cherries and Pears* (inv. 1012), attributed to Orsola Maddalena Caccia (Paliaga, in *La Pinacoteca* 2007, pp. 44–45, no. 27; Cottino, in *Orsola* 2012, pp. 86–87), which is too weak an indication of a possible Piedmont origin for all three works. As for the date of the panel in question, it appears impossible to attempt a sequence within the series above, given the absence of documentary evidence. Centring on the example dated 1607, it would be more appropriate to use "circa" for the others, on the basis that the different replicas would have probably been made within a short time of one another, when the invention was still fresh and could be re-proposed almost by rote. Perhaps the Cremona panel could be considered the prototype, given that all the others have additional variants (the grasshopper or the fallen jasmine flower).
Mario Marubbi

3.46
Fede Galizia
Milan?, 1574/1578 – Milan, post 21 June 1630
Basket of Chestnuts with Apples and a Rabbit
c. 1607–1610
Oil on poplar wood panel, 28.8 × 41 cm
Cremona, Museo Civico Ala Ponzone, inv. 218

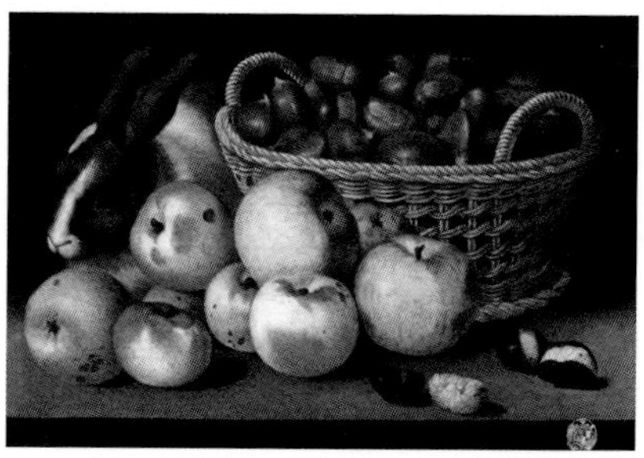

The painting is a pendant to the previous one (cat. 3.45). Not only does it share the same dimensions and probably the same course of historical events, but it also bears the same gold stamp as the *Crystal Fruit Stand with Peaches*. The same spatial structure has also been followed, with the objects aligned in a double row.
A rabbit crouches on the surface next to a wicker basket containing chestnuts. In the foreground are nine apples, the two behind barely visible; on the right side are two partially peeled chestnuts and one completely peeled with its skin beside it. This composition, if not this specific painting, also appears in the inventory of Charles Emmanuel I collection, compiled in 1635 by Antonio Mariani della Corgna and described as "a basket of chestnuts, apples and a rabbit", but without any reference to the artist (*Musei d'Arte* [1994], I, p. 25 no. 480). A few years later, in 1647, the same invention is described in the inventory of Pierre Bonnard's collection in Paris: "un petit tableau peint à l'huile sur bois, barré par derrière, ancien sur le quel sont peints des pommes, des marrons et un lapin d'Inde de la main de la Signora Fede, d'un pied 7 pouces delarges 30 livres, n. 59" (Faré 1974, p. 374). The two attestations document the success of the subject and, in the case of the Bonnard painting, also confirm the attribution to Fede, perhaps based on a signature or a caption. The precise indication of the existence of crosspieces applied to the back of the panel ("barré par derrière") confirms a recurring practice in preparing supports for Galizia's still lifes.
An element that played a significant role in evaluating the work was the identification of an inscription on the reverse (Paliaga 1997, p. 102), variously interpreted in the past, but which today can be definitively stated as "Rafael Sonctius fecit". Whatever the meaning may be – perhaps a promotional writing alluding to Raphael (but the second letter, unequivocally an "o", does not fit the *Sanctius* interpretation), or one of the Soreau painters (*Sorectius*, though the interpretation of the third letter as an "r" is not clear, in addition to the fact that no Raffaele Soreau is even documented) – doubts about the attribution must now be considered erased. Among the various opinions on the subject, two are worth recalling: that of Alessandro Morandotti (in *Fasto e rigore* 2000, p. 137), who notes the lower quality of this work compared to its pendant, yet supports the attribution to Fede, and Giacomo Berra (in *Vincenzo Campi* 2000, pp. 222–223) who remarks on its weakness and the simplistic development in execution. This writer thought that it might be a copy, precisely due to the cursory rendering of some parts, in particular the wicker basket, which is flat and empty of luminous vibrations when compared to the much more refined technique in the *Crystal Fruit Stand with Peaches* (Marubbi, in *La Pinacoteca* 2007, pp. 39–40).
The occasion of this exhibition enabled a reconsideration of the work, starting with the support, which on closer analysis revealed that the grain of the wood is completely consistent with that of the pendant. Both the *Crystal Fruit Stand with Peaches* and the *Basket of Chestnuts* were painted on wood from the same trunk, hence at the same time, and therefore, it must be concluded, in the same workshop. Further confirmation came when cleaning the painting (Gianmaria and Alberto Casella) which revealed the previously inappreciable luminous qualities. There still remains a certain mechanical aspect to the

construction of the basket, which is however consistent with the other versions of this subject. On the other hand, the exquisite naturalism of the painted chestnuts has re-emerged, a true example of realism painting, among the best in Fede Galizia's work.
The composition is also known from two other very similar versions. In the first, perhaps the prototype since it has the fewest elements, there is no chestnut on the edge of the surface, nor the apple in the background just below the basket; in the second, which is more complete, there is an extra fragment of chestnut skin compared to the Cremona painting (see both reproduced in Caroli 1989a, figs. 60 and 81).
Mario Marubbi

3.47
Fede Galizia
Milan?, 1574/1578 – Milan, post 21 June 1630
Saint Charles in a Penitential Robe with the Cross and the Holy Nail
c. 1615
Oil on canvas, 216 × 121 cm
Milan, Veneranda Fabbrica del Duomo di Milano, inv. D10

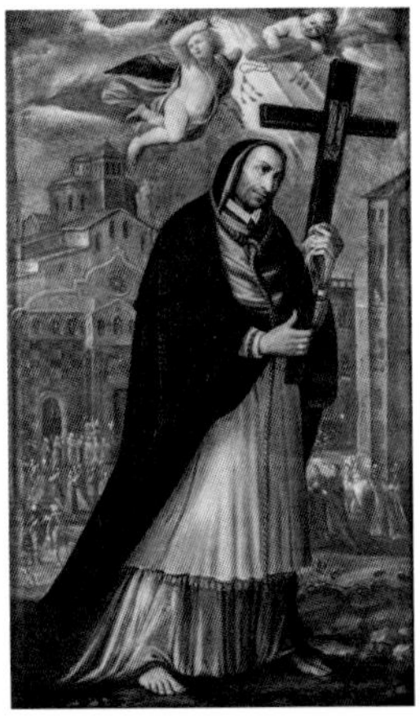

The painting entered its current location from the Milanese church of Sant'Antonio Abate in Porta Romana in 1918. Agostino Santagostino described it for the first time above the confessional near the cemetery door (Santagostino 1671, ed. 1980, p. 21 note 2). A few years later, Carlo Torre mentions it, this time next to the door itself: "Saint Charles, who supports the Sacred Nail within the Grand Cross, the work of Fede Galizia, a woman it is true, but a prodigious Amazon in Painting with no need to envy any painterly Master" (Torre 1674, p. 44). The canvas was mentioned again in subsequent Milan guides of the eighteenth and nineteenth centuries, always referring to Galizia. Only in the modern age did doubts arise regarding her authorship (Bottari 1965, pp. 14–15; Caroli 1989a, pp. 90–91), but they soon reverted to their former opinion (Bona Castellotti 1990, p. 350; Massimi 1998, p. 501; Terzaghi, in *Pittura a Milano* 1999, p. 239; Strada 2013, p. 49), probably due to the unusual pietist content that Galizia presents us with, perfectly aligned with the Borromean climate of reform in sacred images. With the theme of the exaltation of the holiness of Charles Borromeo, Fede embarked on a subject, promoted by the Milanese Church, that widely occupied Milan in the first thirty years of the seventeenth century. She had tackled the theme earlier in 1611, with an elaborate *Saint Charles in Ecstasy*, which Pietro Cortone from Bergamo donated in 1614 to the Neapolitan church of San Carlo alle Mortelle (Ruotolo 1968). The story referred to in the Museo del Duomo painting illustrates a moment connected to the penitential processions through the streets of Milan (3, 5 and 6 October 1576) that Charles Borromeo, Archbishop of Milan, announced in order to pray for an end to the plague. It was an episode that had great success among the saint's biographers (Bascapè 1592, pp. 141–143; Giussano 1610, pp. 267–271; Grattarola 1614, p. 150), and it was also highly influential in constructing the Carlian iconography, both in view of his beatification in 1602 and, later, his canonisation in 1610. Its developments can be followed starting from the *Procession with the Holy Nail* made by Gian Battista della Rovere for one of the *quadroni* ("great paintings") in Milan cathedral (1602). Next is the fresco by Domenico Pellegrino in the chapel of San Carlo in Arcivescovado, followed by the fresco by Cesare Nebbia in the Collegio Borromeo in Pavia (1603–1604), and finally the later altarpieces by Moncalvo in San Marco in Novara (1614), by Giulio Cesare Procaccini in Santa Maria Assunta in Orta (1616), and the one painted by Tanzio da Varallo in the parish church of Cellio in Valsesia (1628). All of these recall the 6 October 1576 procession in which Saint Charles walked barefoot from the cathedral to the Basilica of Santa Maria in San Celso, wearing penitential robes, a hood over his head and a rope around his neck, as was customary for the condemned, dragging the end on the ground and holding a crucifix in his hands "on which he kept his eyes fixed and full of tears" (Giussano 1610, p. 267), with the relic of the Holy Nail specially attached to it. In Fede's painting, however, attention is focused solely on the figure of the saint, isolated in the foreground, while in the distance the procession of a mass of indistinguishable figures wind their way as they return the cathedral. This apparently precise iconographic choice, certainly the decision of the Theatine commission, was intended to make a sort of devotional icon of the saint and exalt his proverbial zeal for prayer and penance. This is also confirmed by the two young angels, standard bearers of heavenly favour, who descend from the sky while a ray of sunshine breaks through the clouds. One of them bears the cardinal's galero, a reference to Borromeo's ecclesiastical dignity, while the other carries a palm and a sword facing upwards: an episode alluding to the apparition of Saint Michael to Pope Gregory the Great and the consequent end of the epidemic. Note that Pope Gregory is explicitly mentioned by Giussano as the inspirer of Carlian processions (Giussano 1610, p. 266). As a result of the powerful iconic value that the work embodied from the start, it became the object of particular devotion during the plague of 1630 (*Le chiese di Milano* 2006, p. 297; Bianchi Janetti, in *Milano* 2017, p. 295). In terms of iconographic content, the canvas is an interesting document of the outward form of Milan cathedral at that time; in fact the painting shows the cathedral bulk and the lantern still without the spire. In front is the ancient bell tower, which was only demolished in 1866, and the facade of the cathedral of Santa Maria Maggiore, still *in situ* to temporarily close the new church.
The canvas can be dated to after Borromeo's canonisation in 1610, due to the presence of the halo indicating his recent sanctity. It was probably painted before the mid-1610s, especially given its stylistic affinities with the 1616 *Noli Me Tangere* in the Pinacoteca di Brera.
Mario Marubbi

3.48
Fede Galizia
Milan?, 1574/1578 – Milan, post 21 June 1630
Judith with the Head of Holofernes
1601
Oil on canvas, 123 × 92 cm
Inscriptions: signed and dated on the edge of the basin "FEDE GALIZIA. F. 1601"
Rome, Galleria Borghese, inv. 165

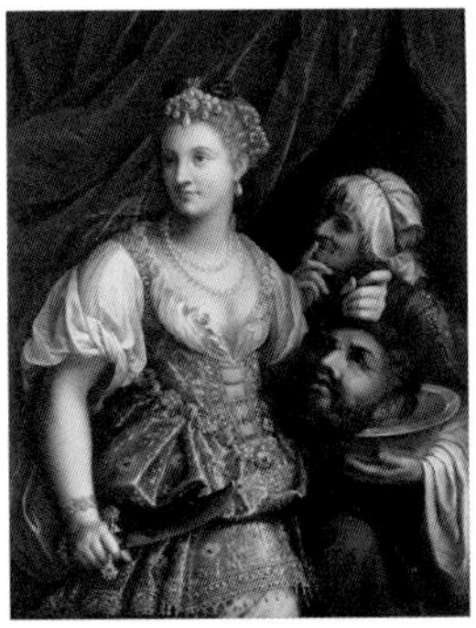

The biblical heroine Judith is the protagonist of the well-known story in which she frees the Israelites from the siege of the Assyrians through her impetuous action against General Holofernes. As a symbol of freedom against oppressors, the story of Judith has always been popular in Western art. However, unlike Artemisia Gentileschi, Fede did not depict the most dramatic moment of the action, namely the bloody act of beheading Holofernes, preferring instead the epilogue of the story (Judith 13, 9–10), when Judith comes out of the tent to offer the now severed and bleeding head of Holofernes to her handmaid, who places it in a basin. The biblical text refers to a saddlebag, as seen in Botticelli or Mantegna, not a metal basin, although Titian had already introduced it.

For invention and pictorial quality it is one of Fede Galizia's most famous works: courtly in layout and tragic in subject, strengthened by a Michelangeloesque monumentality, sumptuous in its colours, starting with the purple-red curtain (as described in the Book of Judith 10, 21), and explored with an algid naturalism whose optical effects surprise in the blade of the knife and in the mirror surface of the basin that reflects the maidservant's hand. The painting is further enhanced by the refined depiction of costume, based on the very high level of specialisation achieved by the Galizia workshop of father and daughter in producing not only theatrical costumes, but also elaborate ceremonial attire, both sacred and profane (Berra 1990, p. 58; Morandotti 2004–2005, pp. 217–218), expressed here in all its splendour in the embroidery of the dress. The level of the undertaking is equal to the heroic composure of Judith, whose face reveals no emotion and whose mind seems enraptured by the inscrutability of divine justice. Only the old servant betrays her shock with her finger to her mouth in a gesture of amazement.
The canvas entered the Borghese collection as a bequest from Cardinal Antonio Maria Salviati. It was registered in the 1612 inventory of his possessions as "a painting with Judith holding the head of Holofernes, with a servant who hands the head to her, without frame" (Della Pergola 1960, p. 195). Long considered the work of Artemisia Gentileschi (Della Pergola 1955–1959, II, pp. 27–28, no. 30), it was only recognised as that of Galizia in 1893, following a cleaning that revealed her signature (Venturi 1893, p. 109). Although it led to no further insight, it is worth mentioning that in 1958 the painting was sent to Zurich for an exhibition dedicated to female artists (*Die Frau als Künstlerin* 1958, p. 11, no. 18).
As was her custom with still lifes, Fede dealt with this same subject several times. The first example we know of is in a smaller format and still Mannerist in style. Judith is depicted half-length with the head of Holofernes in one hand, the sword turned upward in the other, while the handmaid watches wide-eyed (Ferro 2019, pp. 145–146). This was probably her first attempt at the subject, perhaps still dating from first half of the 1590s. Only later did she arrive at a definitive composition, known today through six examples, the oldest of which is believed to be the one in the Ringling Museum in Sarasota, Florida, signed and dated 1596. This is unless we suppose that the smaller version on wood (*La pittura lombarda* 1985, pl. 303; Caroli 1989a, pl. 4 and p. 82; Ginnaneschi, in *Il Cinquecento lombardo* 2000, p. 464) is in fact the prototype of the invention, later used for the various replicas, as Filippo Maria Ferro proposes in his recent hypothesis (2019, p. 145 note 7). Compared to the other versions, the Ringling painting is characterised by the intense red of the curtain and, moreover, it is the only one in which Judith wears a pearl hanging from her necklace, which conforms precisely to Fede's practice of varying details in the serial editions of her still lifes. Her presence at the Turin court alongside her father Nunzio (Baudi di Vesme, 1963–1982, II, p. 490) justifies the existence of two versions of a "Bejewelled Judith with the head of Holofernes in a basin" cited by the 1635 Savoy inventory by Antonio della Corgna (*Musei d'Arte* [1994], I, p. 24, no. 470 and p. 25, no. 488), one of which is still held in the collections of the Palazzo Reale (inv. 5478). Like the Sarasota painting, the Turin example does not show the pink underskirt on Judith's leg, which appears in all the other specimens, but in both cases, this could be due to a resizing of the canvas.
The Turin *Judith*, however, wears a ring on her left ring finger, a detail reproduced only in another version in a private collection (reproduced in Caroli 1989a, pl. 42 and p. 90), and perhaps for this reason is also referable to the final years of the sixteen century. The series may have ended with the example on display, dated 1601 (Longhi 1928, p. 193; Bottari 1965, pp. 12, 14, 28 note 14; Strada 2013, p. 50), and with the canvas in the Palacio Real de La Granja de San Ildefonso (Redín Michaus, in *De Caravaggio a Bernini* 2016, pp. 130–132). Both share the same pendant chain on the flounces of the overdress, which is totally absent in the other versions. The Spanish painting, formerly in the collection of Elisabetta Farnese, is perhaps chronologically a little later than the Borghese one, and is distinguished from it by a generally rosier toned skin and the purple coloured curtain. The Borghese example is noted for the exceptionally tactile rendering of the details and for the opalescent whiteness of Judith's arm and décolleté.
Mario Marubbi

3.49
Maddalena Natali
Cremona, 1654 – Cremona or Rome, documented until 1675
Portrait of a Prelate
1675
Oil on canvas, 69.5 × 57 cm
Inscriptions: "Magdalena de Natalibus Cremonensis annorum xviij pingebat / Romae Anno Iubilei M.D.C.LXXV mense Maij" (written in pen and black ink on a label glued to the *verso*)
Cremona, Museo Civico Ala Ponzone, inv. 1220

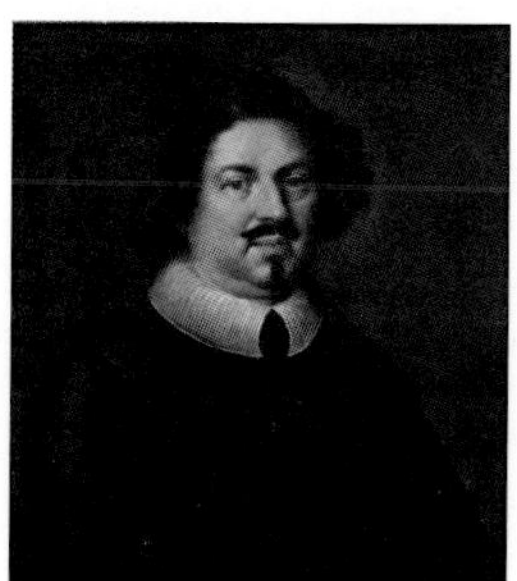

The inscription on the *verso* is the only element that enables an attribution of this work to Natali; it is also the only evidence available for reconstructing her artistic activity. The painting was first described by historian Giovanni Battista Zaist (1774, II, pp. 86–87), who remembered it from the collection of Antonio Simoni from Cremona (1723-1792): "in her picture is painted the portrait of a prelate, which is very beautiful, and judiciously interpreted". Zaist also reported the inscription, which is still visible today. The same information is repeated in the *Abecedario biografico* of Cremona artists (Grasselli 1827, pp. 185–186), but the author no longer knew the work's location. In all likelihood, the painting was by then in the collection of Marquis Giuseppe Sigismondo Ala Ponzone, whose bequest (1842) brought it to its current home. After being long forgotten, Anna Maccabelli was responsible for returning to it in the context of her studies on the Natali family, proposing once again the traditional reference to the ecclesiastical world, although the lack of defining elements of clothing or attributes certainly did not favour a definitive solution to its identification (Maccabelli, in *La Pinacoteca* 2007, pp. 223–225, cat. 223). The half-length figure, turned slightly to the right, is illuminated by a light source from the left. He wears a type of black doublet closed in front with a row of buttons to the neck from which the two leaves of a white collar emerge. The sobriety of the dress, devoid of Baroque ribbons or frills, remains the main cause of uncertainty about the secular or ecclesiastical status of the character, whereas the bushy hairstyle, short moustache and musket beard are consistent with the fashion of the day. The stylistic aspect closely resembles her father's production, visible in the comparison with the *Portrait of Carena the Physicist* in the same art gallery, but the execution is less precise, suggesting her attraction towards a more relaxed approach like that of Voet, who in those years was an obligatory reference for portraiture in Rome.
Mario Marubbi

3.50
Giuseppe Patania
Palermo, 1780 – Palermo, 1852
The Benedictine Fathers of Monreale Visit Pietro Novelli in his Studio
1835–1840
Pen, dark ink and grey watercolour on ivory paper, 290 × 450 mm
Inscriptions: below left "Patania"
Palermo, Galleria Regionale della Sicilia – Palazzo Abatellis, inv. S.L.M. Patania tav. 42

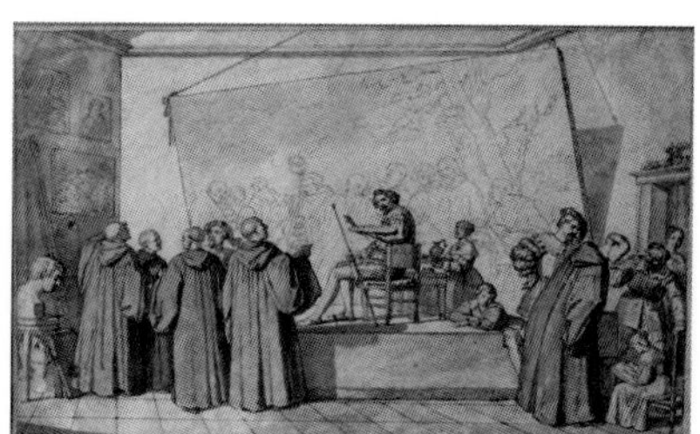

Pietro Novelli, a well-to-do painter as his clothing demonstrates, interrupts his work on a large canvas to converse with a group of friars, while on the right a man appears to be pointing out the skill of a young girl intent on drawing, to another elegantly dressed man and to a monk, who watch her approvingly. This depiction of history, which preserves all the freshness and immediacy of a genre scene, in keeping with a number of developments in nineteenth-century historicist painting, is a double homage: to the painter Pietro Novelli, the greatest seventeenth-century Sicilian painter, and to his daughter, Rosalia, whose artistic talent was noted from a very young age as she worked in her father's studio. The woman watching the group from the doorway with a satisfied expression is probably Costanza Adamo, wife of Pietro and mother of Rosalia. Pietro's studio is depicted as a large, elegant room, indicated by the ornate door frame and upholstered chair. Paintings decorate the walls, including the Salvator Mundi canvas for the oratory of the Compagnia Sant'Orsola, together with the inevitable busts and statues, all of which conjure the historically verifed image of an established artist of relatively high social status, also confirmed by the maid who is handing him a tray.

The episode depicted is an imaginary visit to Novelli's studio made by the Benedictine fathers of Monreale, the commissioners of the monumental canvas depicting *Saint Benedict Distributing Bread* (380 × 520 cm), which the artist is in the process of painting and is undoubtedly one of his most famous and celebrated works. The demanding artwork was completed around 1635 and Rosalia, born in 1628, is therefore correctly depicted as a girl of about seven years of age.

The artist who made the lively and expertly executed drawing is Giuseppe Patania, a prominent artist on the nineteenth-century scene and a great admirer of Novelli, whose work he reproduced in quantity. But as Gaetano Bongiovanni supposes (in *Pompa magna* 2008, p. 122, with previous bibliography), the drawing's singular and erudite subject was suggested by Agostino Gallo (1790–1874), a scholar, writer on many subjects, collector, connoisseur of art and Patania's friend, client and admirer. Gallo was the author of the first nineteenth-century monograph on Novelli, namely the *Elogio storico di Pietro Novelli da Monreale, famoso dipintore, architetto ed incisore*, published in three editions between 1821 and 1830, and in which Rosalia is also presented with an albeit questionable catalogue of her paintings.

This drawing, together with numerous others by Patania and other artists from Agostino Gallo's collection of drawings, entered the gallery after several earlier locations, as a bequest from Pietro Sgadari di Lo Monaco, who was the first to promote the drawing when it was still in his possession by publishing it in his 1940 monograph *Pittori e scultori siciliani*.

The association between Patania and Gallo is widely corroborated. In 1821 the scholar began commissioning the artist to make, among other things, many of the one hundred and fifty-two "portraits" of illustrious Sicilians that adorned the walls of his home-study in the Loggia district, and which were later bequeathed in his will to Palermo's municipal library. Among these were ones of Pietro and Rosalia Novelli. Indeed Pietro's features in this drawing are the same as those in the painting by Patania, and in the engraving, which though anonymous, was probably made from a drawing by Patania, which accompanies Gallo's aforementioned *Elogio storico*.

In the 1827 canvas, now in the municipal library, Rosalia, however, seems a replica of the woman in a turban from the painting of *Saint Benedict Distributes the Loaves*, which accords with a widespread tradition that she is believed to have been the model for that figure. But in the 1830 edition of the *Elogio storico* (Gallo 1830, p. 34 note 1) Gallo himself, having confirmed the date of the painting as 1635, made it clear that Rosalia, a child at the time, could not be considered, and that he had been mistaken "before knowing for sure the era of the canvas; so I convinced myself to make Patania copy that head".

This circumstance is further evidence of the *post quem* dating of the drawing in question, which, based on its style, Ivana Bruno assigns to 1835–1840 (Bruno 1993, p. 217), and the special attention Gallo reserved for Rosalia.

Valeria Sola

3.51

Rosalia Novelli

Palermo, 1628 – Palermo, documented until 1689

Saint Prassede

c. 1648–1667

Black pencil and grey watercolour on ivory paper, 270 × 220 mm

Inscriptions: in pencil on the *verso*: "D. Rosolea Bono"

Palermo, Galleria Regionale della Sicilia – Palazzo Abatellis, inv. 1565/1

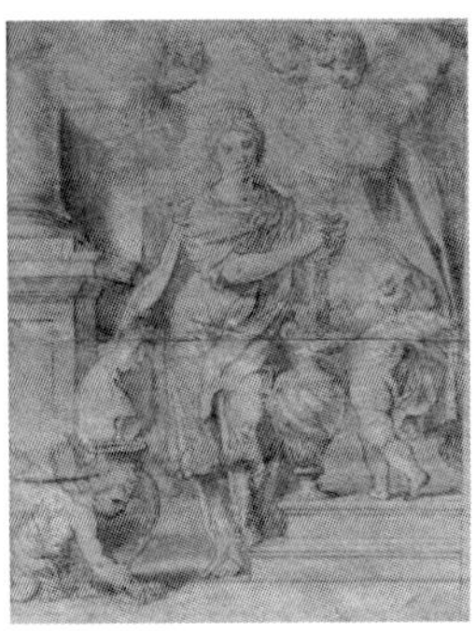

"A woman squeezing a sponge into a vase" is how the drawing is described in the edition of the complete works of Pietro Novelli, known as the Raphael of Sicily in the specific literary genre of "historical tribute" (Gallo 1830, p. XIII). The drawing was published for the first time in 1990 under the title *Allegorical Figure* in the large graphic section in the catalogue of the Pietro Novelli exhibition (Grasso 1990, pp. 370–371, fig. 1; pp. 405–406, fig. III.42). The inscription on the back bearing the name of Rosalia Bono gave rise to the hypothesis of attributing the drawing to Rosalia Novelli, while keeping in mind the evident characteristics of her father, Pietro's, work. Subsequently, the critical history of the work followed the sole direction of Rosalia Novelli, whose identity and artistic character is taking shape with increasing clarity due to the great effort and tenacity of Santina Grasso's studies (Grasso 2017, with previous bibliography).

The surname Bono on the inscription enables the work to be dated to the years of Rosalia's marriage to Don Diego Bono, from about 1648 to 1667. Comparison with other signatures by Rosalia on documents has provided positive results, and the stylistic analysis of the work further confirms that the name is her signature rather than merely a certificate of ownership of one of her father's drawings. In fact, the iconographic and compositional character that is pure Novelli – from the skilful standardised architectural setting to the typology and physical appearance of the figures, including the cherubs – is expressed in a different drawing style. Whereas Pietro Novelli has a rapid and concise approach, the drawing in question has been executed with a particular search for definition, from the shadows on the vase to the outline of the figures and geometry of the lines, which at the same time reveal a sure and practised hand. As Grasso suggests, it could be an idea of Pietro's executed by Rosalia, despite the late Mannerist character of the central figure with its twisting pose from bust to pelvis, swathed in late sixteenth-century style clothes. In this sense the references are to the courtly repertoire of the late sixteenth century, which in Palermo, city of the viceroys, had been portrayed by the artist Giuseppe Alvino.

Evelina De Castro

3.52

Pietro Novelli

Monreale (Palermo), 1603 – Palermo, 1647

Marriage of the Virgin

1647

Oil on canvas, 305 × 185 cm

Inscriptions: on the right at the base of the plinth "OPUS COMPONI FECIT / FRANCISCUS CRISPALDI / AN SAL / CIƆIƆCXLVII"

Palermo, Arcidiocesi di Palermo, church of San Matteo al Cassaro, inv. 7

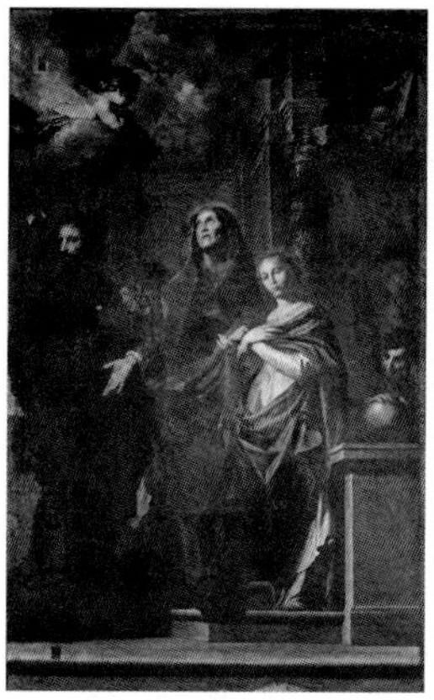

The *Marriage of the Virgin*, kept in the chapel dedicated to Saint Anne in the church of San Matteo al Cassaro, is unanimously attributed to Pietro Novelli for obvious stylistic reasons, albeit without documentary evidence. As we learn from the inscription at the base of the plinth, the painting was commissioned by Francesco Crispaldi, a wealthy former cobbler and a member of the Unione dei Miseremini di San Matteo, to which he donated all his possessions in his 1639 will. The work dates to the fateful year of 1647 when Novelli lost his life on 27 August following a wound suffered during Giuseppe d'Alesi's anti-Spanish revolt. The acquaintance between the two was probably due to an intermediary, the modeller Giancola Viviano (1590/1595–1668), Novelli's friend and companion, who in 1626 had served in the congregation of Jesus Mary and Joseph at the church of San Giuseppe dei Teatini as a "relative", whereas Crispaldi was superior. Crispaldi himself died on 15 October 1648 and the expenses for his funeral and the frame for the painting were paid.
The canvas is dominated by the figure of Saint Anne, who stands imposingly between the Virgin and Saint Joseph turning her gaze to the sky, symbolised by swollen clouds with angels peeping from them, as if invoking a blessing on the newlyweds. Whereas in the most common iconography the focus of the scene is the priest, here one barely sees him. He is presented from behind as he turns back towards the viewer before entering the mysterious shadow of the temple after officiating the ceremony. In a clear reversal of roles, Saint Anne, patron saint of the chapel, takes the part of lead figure, as if she were the protector and godmother of the spouses, while the priest who is moving away perhaps alludes to the Old Testament giving way to the New.
Among the other figures in the painting whose faces can be seen in the background, one young man may be a rejected suitor, whereas the young woman could be one of Mary Virgin's companions in the temple. Less easy to interpet is the young male whose face is illuminated by a diagonal ray of light as he leans forward against a sphere on the plinth that bears the inscription relating to the client. Although the the figure is undoubtedly important in the context of the painting, in some way he remains marginal and extraneous to the content of the scene and seems to be watching it almost secretly. His role is not clear; perhaps he was a contemporary of the period. Immersed in a silent, almost dreamlike aura, and in a certain sense cloaked in mystery, the characters are each absorbed in their own melancholy isolation where no gazes meet. Some are even caught in an attitude of disinterest as they leave, namely the two young people and the priest. Only Saint Anne conveys a certain communicative emphasis, albeit in a classical composition of gesture and expression. Indeed we are not witnessing the event, which has already been celebrated, but the more intimate and private moments immediately after.
The iconographic peculiarities, perhaps suggested by a learned theologian, are joined by compositional ones, which largely restrict the narration to the figures that tower in the foreground, relegating to the margin the architectural element of the temple, represented by the Solomonic spiral column. Generally, however, especially during the Renaissance, the symbolic construction was imposed in terms of size and centrality. This arrangement fully corresponds to the work's stylistic tone, in which the calm elegance of the classically inspired figures, enlivened by the soft modulation in colour derived from Flemish painting, emerges from the dark background, due to a vivid Caravaggio-inspired luminosity. The divine light, entering from the top left, illuminates the whole scene diagonally, dwelling with symbolic intensity on the figure of the Virgin. The unifying balance thus established makes this one of Pietro Novelli's most successful and mature works, executed at the end of his activity and his life: a very busy moment due to commitments and requests that nonethless did not prevent him from creating in this painting a meditated and complete synthesis of his art, in which the fundamental guiding principles of his entire figurative aesthetic are condensed.
Santina Grasso

3.53
Rosalia Novelli
Palermo, 1628 – Palermo, documented until 1689
The Immaculate Virgin Mary and Saint Francesco Borgia
1663
Oil on canvas, 200 × 160 cm
Palermo, church of the Gesù, Casa Professa – Direzione centrale degli Affari dei culti e per l'amministrazione del Fondo Edifici di Culto del Ministero dell'Interno

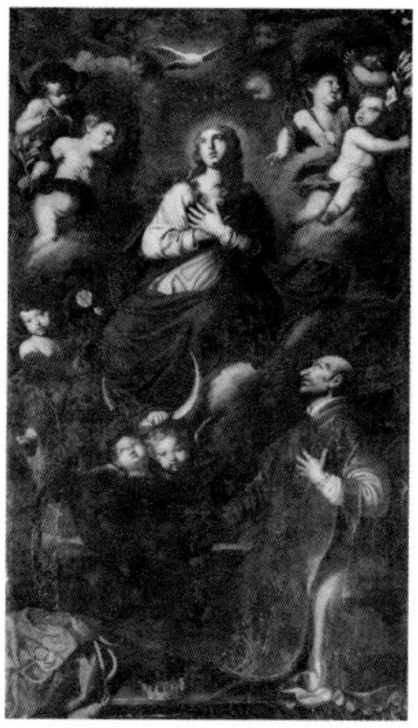

Located on the altar of the eponymous chapel in the church of the Gesù, Casa Professa, the canvas depicting the Immaculate Virgin Mary and Saint Francesco Borgia is the only documented work by Rosalia Novelli, daughter of the painter Pietro (1603–1647), known as Monrealese. Commissioned by the fathers of the Society of Jesus, it was carried out for the sum of forty onze, paid to Rosalia in various payments between 15 October 1662 and 10 June 1663.
It is presumed that the unusual choice of a female painter, mentioned in the Jesuit cash books with the respectful appellation of "Donna Rosalia Bono e Novelli" (which includes the surname of her second husband), arose from the consolidated relationship between the Jesuit order and Pietro Novelli, creator of numerous works for Jesuit churches, and with the father of Rosalia's first husband, Don Giovanni Paolo Durante Poerio, who was buried in this same church (1648) and left to it a legacy of ten onze in his will and a further six hundred onze for requiem masses for himself and various relatives, as well as other donations to the confraternity of the Santissima Annunziata, of which he was a member, and which was based in the same religious complex.
Rosalia was considered by eighteenth and nineteenth-century sources as a copyist, working in the style of her father and of the Flemish painter Anthony van Dyck. Therefore she was seen as the logical extension of her father's painting legacy, and the same expectations were applied to her, the "daughter of Monrealese", as she was already called by her contemporaries, when re-proposing his most successful inventions, even many years after his death.
The canvas in question amply justifies this vision, given that it is almost a collage of ideas taken from Pietro's work, from the Lanfranchian diagonal spatial construction, frequently used by Novelli, to the warm Vandyckian harmonies of colour and luminosity, including the indistinct background light. The figure of the Virgin is almost a copy of the *Immaculate Conception* in the Palermo church of Sant'Antonio da

Padova, painted by Novelli around 1635. Very similar, in fact, are the blue mantle that flutters on the clouds and the white robe, the position of the hands and, above all, the face, with a foreshortened forehead, a round chin, bright lips and flowing curly hair. Her attempt to reproduce the paternal model is also evident in the shading that clearly defines the Virgin's neck and round face. It is also apparent in the folds of her clothes that fall artificially, in a vain attempt to reproduce the natural softness of her father's drapery.
This female model recurs almost unchanged in works attributed to Pietro Novelli, but in Rosalia's version the dreamy spirit and poetic delicacy of execution of the original are missing.
On the other hand, due to the posture and liturgical vestments, the figure of Saint Francesco Borgia seems to be inspired by Saint Ignatius in the painting of *The Virgin and Child with Saints Ignatius and Francis Xavier* in the cathedral of Palermo, which Pietro Novelli perhaps made for the same Jesuits between 1632 and 1633. The saint's expression of suffering, however, is more closely related to the the more marked influences of Jusepe de Ribera in her father's work.
The work is completed by cherubs and angelic heads that flank the Virgin, an essential component of her father's works. Among these, the chubby face of the little angel with the pointed nose holding the palm, and the pair of angelic heads at the foot of the Virgin, are identical to those in two works also attributed to Rosalia, *Saint Rosalia with Saints Mary Magdalene and Francis* (datable to 1663) in the mother church of Piraino (Messina), and the *Vision of Saint Teresa* in the mother church of Castelvetrano (Trapani).
However, as is clear from the now vast *corpus* of works that have been attributed to her over the years, Rosalia's art is not exclusively an impersonal imitation of her father's paradigm, but at times goes beyond, realizing a composite classical-baroque model, above all when she abandons the more concise compositional schemes, with figures tightly packed in a space with little depth, in favour of paintings that are more spatially complex and dynamic, such as *Saint Agatha Professes her Faith before the Consul Quinziano*, located in the same chapel of the church and datable to the 1660s.
Santina Grasso

3.54
Vincenzo Volò,
known as Vincenzino dei fiori
Rémondans (France), 1620 – Milan, 1671
Two-Handled Metal Vase with Roses, Tulips, Lilies, Bluebells and Other Flowers
1667
Oil on panel, 36 × 33 cm
Cremona, Museo Civico Ala Ponzone, inv. 1038

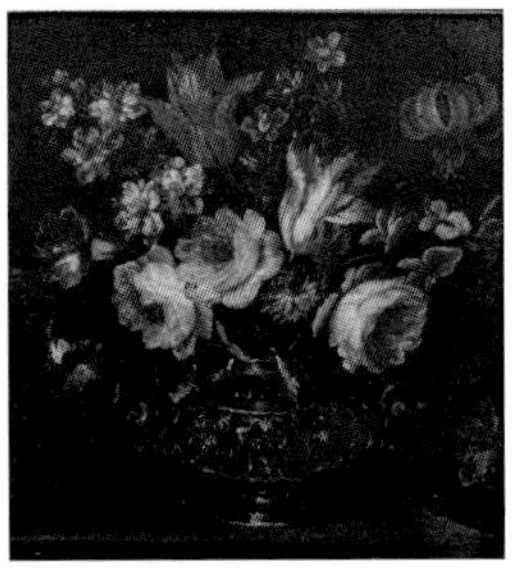

The execution of this painting depicting a *Two-Handled Metal Vase with Roses, Tulips, Lilies, Bluebells and Other Flowers* and its pendant (cat. 3.55) was made at the same time as a third still life depicting *Flowers, Fruits and Wild Animals*, located in the same civic museum and originally intended for the Ala Ponzone, one of most prominent aristocratic families in Cremona (G. Bocchi, U. Bocchi, in *Gilardo da Lodi* 2004, pp. 74–75, no. 8).
Whereas the pair of vases with flowers immediately helped realign the attributions of other similar paintings, the third panel is an excellent prototype for beginning to understanding Vincenzo Volò's range of expressive skills. For despite being remembered with the clinging epithet of "Vincenzino dei fiori", he was also an excellent painter of fruits, insects and birds, an accomplishment ably assimilated by his daughter Francesca.
Far from Milan and from the areas where he worked above all for Vitaliano VI Borromeo on Isola Bella, as can be seen from several examples of his paintings depicting vases of flowers still conserved in the palace (Bocchi 2015, pp. 52–54 figs. 2-6; Morandotti 2020, p. 61), Vincenzo had to relinquish his favourite supports in marble or slate and instead use the poplar wood panels more easily found in areas of the Po Valley.
The refined two-handled metal and blue glass container, perhaps Venetian, was Volò's favourite model and is found in similar small works that followed his first Milanese paintings, such as the two *Vases with Flowers* from the Borromeo collection, published in 2015 and probably made in the 1650s, and another from a private collection in Parma (Bocchi 2014, p. 71, figs. 6–8).
During the restoration of a still life attributed to Evaristo Baschenis – which depicts a surface with plucked poultry and other birds in the centre and a mortar and a plate with fruits on one side – a vase of flowers was discovered in the centre, previously obscured in an attempt to give greater credibility to the belief that the painting had been entirely made by the Bergamo priest. The insert, whose workmanship can be attributed unequivocally to Vincenzo Volò, contains once again the characteristic metal vase with blue glass, filled with the particular flora Volò preferred, thus proving his collaboration with the still life painter Baschenis (Ravelli 2012; Bocchi 2014, p. 75, fig. 14).
Vincenzo's masterly influence clearly emerges in the paintings of his three daughters, Margherita, Francesca and Giovanna, the only siblings whose age allowed them to frequent their father's workshop.
Margherita, an eclectic and talented painter, left Milan in 1667, aged nineteen, thus becoming independent of her father's teachings after having mainly learned from him the art of painting flowers, which she went on to develop with great success throughout the course of her flourishing career.
In contrast, Francesca and Giovanna remained in the Milan workshop alongside Vincenzo until his death in 1671, when Francesca was twenty-one and Giovanna nineteen. Under his tuition they had developed versatility in other fields of application in addition to painting flowers.
A number of plants, fruit and animal subjects painted by Vincenzo Volò were reused with meticulous precision by both Francesca and Giovanna. Only when the three sisters were once more brought together in Piacenza during the two-year period 1678–1679, did some specific Vincenzino dei fiori patterns begin to appear in Margherita's canvases, an evident consequence of a fruitful two-way exchange that also had positive effects on the work of the younger sisters.
All of Vincenzo Volò's children of both sexes, whether artists or not, gradually acquired the nickname Vicenzini, a tribute to the cultural legacy of undisputed distinction that also passed along the male line to spouses and to the following generation. This is confirmed by the documented report of a painter called Domenica Vicenzina, active at the beginning of the eighteenth century and probably the daughter or wife of another male family member, perhaps Giulio or Antonio. A number of her signed works were seen by Malvezzi (Malvezzi 1882, p. 258).
Gianluca Bocchi

3.55
Vincenzo Volò,
known as Vincenzino dei fiori
Rémondans (France), 1620 – Milan, 1671
Two-Handled Ceramic Vase with Anemones, Roses, Tulips, Jasmine and Other Flowers
1667
Oil on panel, 36.5 × 33 cm
Cremona, Museo Civico Ala Ponzone, inv. 1039

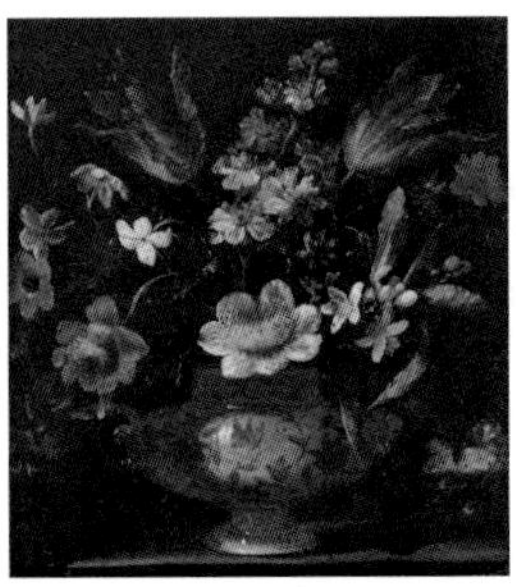

Until almost the end of the twentieth century Vincenzo Volò remained an artist little known

in critical literature, relegated to very few documents in Milan and Piacenza that did not always present him correctly. Even his daughter's 1710 death certificate, recorded in the Milan health registers, wrongly identifies her father as Francesco. Indeed, Vincenzo's own death certificate of 6 November 1671, registered in the parish of San Paolo in Compito, states his age as sixty-five and his year of birth as 1606, whereas the 7 November entry in the health registers documents him as eighty years old, and dates his birth to the previous century. Moreover, it has distorted his surname to the more common Della Valle.
Documentary investigations conducted in Italy and France have shown that he was born in Rémondans, a small village in the jurisdiction of Neuchâtel in Franche-Comté, where he was baptised on 5 July 1620 as Vincent Voulot in the parish of Dambelin, the son of the notary of that locality (Bocchi 2014).
Vincenzo emigrated from his birthplace during the bloody Ten Years War – a local war in Franche-Comté that was part of the Thirty Years War (1635–1644) – in order to escape the raids perpetrated by the Protestant troop factions. He took refuge in Catholic Milan during the first five years of the 1640s.
It is not known if before arriving in Lombardy he had the opportunity to spend time with some master artist in Switzerland or Piedmont to learn the basic rudiments of the profession, but he definitely arrived in a city with a particularly favourable and welcoming moment for a flower painter, since the major artists of the previous generation had all died.
This small composition and its pendant were restored in the laboratory of the Museo Civico Ala Ponzone in Cremona and identified in 1998 as works by Vincenzo Volò, thus definitively solving an anonymous attribution that at the time considered the only alternative to be the more famous Giuseppe Vicenzino, Vincenzo's son (G. Bocchi, U. Bocchi 1998a).
Starting from that initial intuition, it has been possible to gather around this wonderful pair of vases of flowers a nascent nucleus of similar subjects with an archaising appearance, almost always painted on stone, easily distinguishable from those of Francesca and Giovanna, his two painter daughters who worked closely with him and absorbed his teachings.
The progressive recognition of Vincenzo Volò's production has led to identifying his rudimentary study of several Flemish models by Frans Snyders (1579–1657), as well as German examples of the Hanau school, most significantly by exponents Peter Binoit (c. 1590–1632) and Franz Godin (c. 1590–post 1624), known in Italy as Francesco Codino. All reinterpreted in the light of Vincenzo's very strong artistic personality.
The description of two panels depicting birds with flowers, cherries and insects in the 1651 inventory of the Marquis Del Carpio's Madrid collection suggest that Vincenzo may have known the naturalistic production of Sister Orsola Maddalena Caccia (1596–1676) in Piedmont and may also have seen the ornithological depictions of Turin-born Carlo Battaglia, known as Paiola (recorded until 1644).
Since there is no evidence of Vincenzo receiving instruction from any flourishing top-level master, it would be correct to describe him as a substantially self-taught painter who was able to express a strongly characterised style, which influenced his own children and a proportion of Milan's still-life painters during the second half of the seventeenth century.
The two paintings in the Museo Civico Ala Ponzone can be dated to the final phase of his production, specifically the year 1667, when Vincenzo accompanied his daughter Margherita and son-in-law Ludovico to Cremona, residing for some time in the vicinity of San Donato, where Margherita's father-in-law, Carlo Caffi, also lived.
Volò's presence in Cremona is validated by a document drawn up on 29 October 1667 by notary Angelo Maria Penna, certifying the marriage in accordance with the rule of "double notification", namely in Milan, the bride's city, and in Cremona the groom's. In the deed, Margherita and Ludovico acknowledge receipt of the sum of "four thousand imperial lira as and for Margherita's dowry from Vincenzo Volò, son of Pietro".
Unlike the refined metal and glass vase, reproduced several times by Vincenzo Volò in his earliest work (cat. 3.54), the two-handled white ceramic vase decorated with plant motifs seems to be unique. Moreover, based on the examples in our possession so far, it did not become part of Volò's subsequent repertoire. Since it was painted during the short period of his stay in Cremona, Vincenzo may have kept the same structure of the metal and glass vase while changing it either to a model he saw in Cremona, or perhaps at the request of his client.
Gianluca Bocchi

3.56
Margherita Volò Caffi
Milan, 1648 – Milan, 1710
Vase with Flowers and a Garland of Flowers
1685
Oil on canvas, 116 × 106.5 cm
Inscriptions: signed "MARG.TA CAFFI"
Varallo (Vercelli), Palazzo dei Musei, Pinacoteca, inv. 3424-2014

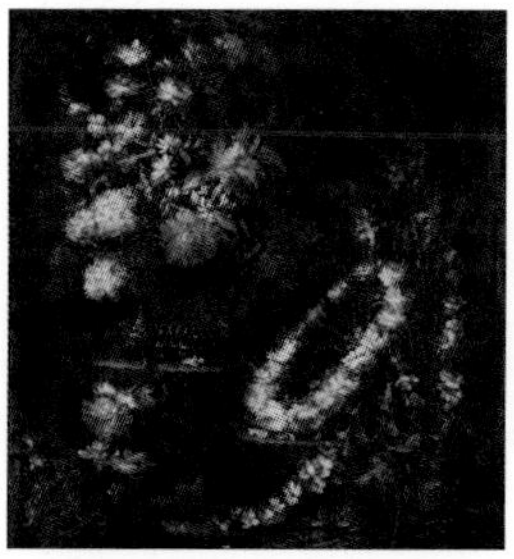

Margherita was the most famous of Vincenzo Volò's daughters and also the most gifted, even though she exclusively painted botanical subjects, whereas like their father, her sisters Francesca and Giovanna painted flowers, fruits and small animals. We do not have sufficient information to explain this choice, but it cannot be excluded that the marriage she contracted at nineteen with Ludovico Caffi and their immediate transfer to Cremona perhaps prevented a longer education that might also have included other fields of still life.
That said, there is no doubt that her decision to specialise was a deliberate and successful one, given that her virtuosity brought her a renown that rapidly extended throughout northern Italy, as far as the grand ducal court of Florence, the imperial court of Vienna and the royal court of Madrid.
Her success resulted from her natural artistic inclination, which led her to experiment with new forms and styles throughout her long career, but it was also due to her move from Milan, which enabled her to make herself known in areas other than the one where her siblings remained to work.
Research undertaken to gain a better knowledge of her life has revealed that after living for some time in Cremona, she moved to Piacenza, and from there to Modena and Bologna (Bocchi 2013). Archival investigations and information from historians have confirmed the success of her paintings, copiously listed in the inventories of families from Piacenza, Modena, Ferrara and Bologna.
During the period spent in Bologna (1672–1676), Margherita strengthened her relationship with her artist brother-in-law Francesco Caffi, who had moved to Venice in the interim. Although he continued to work as a painter, he also broadened his entrepreneurial activities by trading in various kinds of paintings. His role as a merchant and his promotion of his sister-in-law's paintings led to purchases of Margherita's work by Vittoria della Rovere and Grand Prince Ferdinando de' Medici during the second half of the 1680s. After about nine years spent in Piacenza and Cremona, Margherita returned to Milan for good (Bocchi 2012, pp. 102–103).
The painting in the Pinacoteca Civica in Varallo Sesia dates to her early days back in Milan, and was part of a series of three canvases formerly in the D'Adda collection. The paintings, all the same size, are signed identically "MARG.TA CAFFI", the characteristic wording with which she signed her name throughout the Emilian period. The naturalism and three-dimensional quality that distinguish her flowers are characteristics she developed and refined during the seven years of her second period in Piacenza and are still unaffected by subsequent developments in Milan during the 1690s.
We can probably date these paintings to 1685, given that the Caffi family was still in Cremona the year before and from 1686 she

began to sign herself "MARG.TA CAFFI VICENCINA", as can be seen of the pair of canvases from the Borromeo collection dated 1686 (G. Bocchi, U. Bocchi 1998b, p. 89, figs. 78–79). A comparison between these two paintings and the three in the Varallo art gallery highlights striking similarities, particularly evident in the example on display, thus confirming an almost identical date. All five are vertically conceived, with on the left vases containing cut flowers, or flowers placed on square stone surfaces, and on the right, groups of flowers arranged in a festoon, in a crown, and in a low container completely hidden by the botanical mass (the three from Varallo), or else lying delicately on the surface beside others rising from the ground (the two from the Borromeo collection).
Margherita first painted the crown of variously coloured roses in one of the canvases from the Piacenza cycle, made between 1678 and 1679 for Count Ranunzio Scotti di Agazzano's town house. The motif was then replicated in other Milanese canvases from the 1680s, among them one of the two large paintings made for the marquises Crivelli in 1687.
Although Margherita's use of the family name as her signature after 1685 is evidence of her definitive participation in the family workshop, it is also right to point out that maintaining the surname Caffi, successfully used for fifteen years throughout northern Italy, was an unequivocal and successful marketing decision, confirming at the same time her desire to acknowledge her cultural identity as an artist who was in every sense a true self-made woman.
Gianluca Bocchi

3.57
Margherita Volò Caffi
Milan, 1648 – Milan, 1710
Vase with Flowers Outdoors
1694
Oil on oval canvas, 63 × 83 cm
Inscriptions: signed "MARG.TA CAFFI VICENCINA F. 1694 MILANO"
Private collection

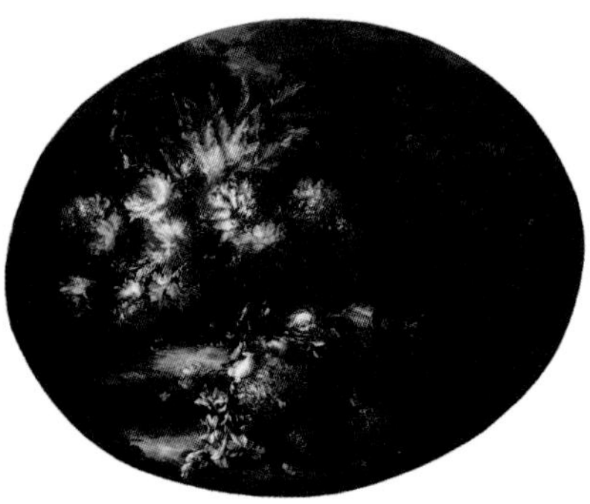

The painting is on public display for the first time in this exhibition, after being reproduced in an article about the Vicenzini family (Bocchi 2015, p. 64, fig. 19).
The signature clearly states Margherita's place of residence, namely Milan, whereas her now definitive affiliation to the family atelier is indicated by the addition of the family surname "Vicenzina", an appellation her sisters Francesca and Giovanna had already been using for about a quarter of a century since the death of their father in 1671.
When Caffi painted this canvas she had been a widow for three years since her husband died of liver disease. In a deed two years later, stipulated by the notary Ardizzini of Cremona and certifying the sale of a pew in the cathedral, formerly the property of her mother-in-law Agata Caffi, Margherita declared that she resided in the Milan parish of San Nazaro. After the death of her husband Ludovico in October 1691, she had probably left the house in the parish of Santa Maria Beltrade, where she previously lived with her family, to move to the house in Strada Pantano, close to where her elderly mother was living with her sisters and her brother Giuseppe.
By 1694 Margherita was living permanently in Milan and had interrupted her professional relations with Cremona, never completely severed until that moment, and had in fact still been intact the previous year. Indeed, the register of inhabitants in the Cremona parish of San Prospero attests that the Marquises Crotti occasionally hosted her in their city palace between 1690 and 1693.
Between the second half of 1693 and 1694, Margherita Caffi and her brother Giuseppe Vicenzino jointly took on the commission to decorate a room with small paintings in Giberto Borromeo's villa in Senago. The surviving works of that cycle (G. Bocchi, U. Bocchi 1998b, pp. 91–93, figs. 82–87) reveal a stylistic turning point that is clearly apparent in the oval painting of a *Vase with Flowers Outdoors* from 1694.
In this work, Caffi developed a three-part horizontal pattern already seen in other vertical ovals dating to ten and twenty years earlier. Here I am referring to the pair of canvases from 1674 in the Bolognese collection (Bocchi 2013, p. 95, figs. 49–50) and the 1684 painting in the Museo Civico Ala Ponzone in Cremona (G. Bocchi, U. Bocchi 1998b, p. 86, fig. 75). In all these paintings the flowers on the left are arranged on two levels, while on the right a flowering plant rises vertically from the ground. The latter is merely mentioned here, since the focus is on the rest of the painting.
In her paintings from the end of the century, Margherita Caffi displays a new level of virtuosity: her depiction of flora has become more delicate and vaporous and seem to emerge weightlessly from the darkness of the background with a lightness far removed from the solid Emilian representations in her first Milan works, such as the D'Adda paintings in Varallo. In reference to this new, unconstrained and extremely refined form of expression that Margherita reached at the peak of her Milan career, in 1998 Ulisse Bocchi and I coined the term "feathery style". Many examples of this phase exist and, like this painting, most of them are signed and dated, bearing both the appellation "Vicenzina" and the place of execution, "Milan". Among them is a still unpublished pair, painted for the Marquises Crivelli in 1687; a pair from 1696 that appeared on the Austrian market (Dorotheum, Vienna, 15 October 2013, lot 510); an undated canvas from a private collection in Cremona (Bocchi 2015, p. 64, fig. 18), and one dated 1698 in a private collection in Bergamo (G. Bocchi, U. Bocchi 1998b, p. 96, fig. 92).
I would like to mention yet another painting from the end of the century: a canvas with flowers in the Musée des Beaux-Arts in Dole, the Jura department, Franche-Comté. This painting, which I identified as a work by Volò Caffi several years ago, thereby removing its flattering but false attribution to the Rome painter Mario dei Fiori, shows remarkable similarities to the 1694 oval work. After an adequate cleaning, it revealed the incomplete but genuine presence of Margherita Caffi's signature.
Gianluca Bocchi

3.58
Margherita Volò Caffi
Milan, 1648 – Milan, 1710
Still Life with Flowers
1697
Oil on canvas, 72 × 98 cm
Inscriptions: "MARG.TA CAFFI VICENCINA F. 1697"
Milan, Castello Sforzesco, Pinacoteca, inv. 1010

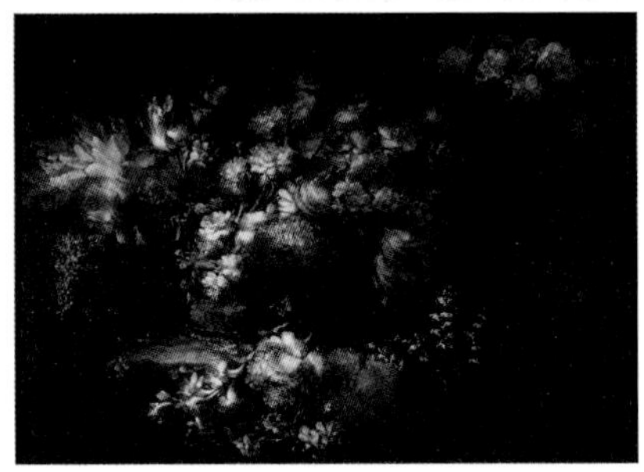

This painting, owned by the civic collections of Castello Sforzesco, was a 1945 bequest from Countess Morando and was destined for the permanent exhibition, together with its counterpart: a picture of identical size depicting flowers, some in a glass vase and some lying on a stone surface.
Previous reports and publications about the two paintings (Morandotti 1989, p. 255; De Marchi, in *Museo d'Arte Antica* 1999, p. 45, nos. 509–510) did not mention the presence of signatures or dates, which emerged only after an appropriate restoration, that also revealed a dazzling state of conservation.
The year of the painting's execution, 1697, assumes a very particular meaning in the life and career of Margherita Caffi. On 2 February the artist was admitted to the Accademia di San Luca in Milan, together with her sister Francesca and a certain Lucrezia Ferrari, a painter so far without any identified painting or document that could help in even

partially reconstructing her life.
In the acceptance document, the two sisters are named the same way, "Vicenzina Milanese Painter", a sign of their link to a single workshop, namely the Vicenzini, by then generally known in the city.
The event was the result of an exceptional amendment to the academy's statute, whose approval was not unrelated to the intervention of Francesca's brother-in-law, Federico Macagni, and the support of the designated "prince" of the academy for the following year, Andrea Lanzani, a collaborator of Margherita's in at least two paintings. Until that year academicians had been exclusively men, unlike the Rome institution of San Luca, where women had been granted access several years before.
The women painters' induction represented a great innovation in the life of the academy, bringing prestige and prominence to the three women, even if it is fair to say that they were granted very few prerogatives compared to their male colleagues, given that they were accepted as members, but ones without access to meetings or voting rights. The single concession made was that they were invited to attend the titular saint's celebrations. In the ten years that Margherita was an academy member, neither her presence nor that of the other two women went unnoticed, and somehow left its mark. In this regard, during the 1702 preparations for the celebration of the feast of San Luca, when Carlo Preda was head of the academy and Francesca Vicenzina had been dead for two years, there were displays in silk and paintings of flowers and fruit, which certainly involved the participation of Margherita Caffi, Lucrezia Ferrari and other guests, among whom it does not seem implausible to suggest the presence of her brother, Giuseppe Vicenzino (Bianchi Janetti 2017, p. 430).
In both of the Palazzo Morando paintings, created shortly after the 1694 oval canvas on show in this exhibition (cat. 3.57), the design follows a horizontal organisation on a rock surface, without the presence of plants emerging vertically from the ground. Cut flowers are arranged in elegant glass vases whose features are only vaguely suggested by skilfully painted glimmers of light, so that the containers emerge discreetly from the darkness of the background. In these canvases, the artistry of the flowers reaches levels of vibrant virtuosity, where not only are the vases eclipsed, but Margherita also decided to do without the stone supports, thus concentrating solely on her flower groups, which emerge from nowhere in all their delicacy and colour. Similar examples are the other pair in the civic collections of the Castello Sforzesco (see De Marchi, *Museo d'Arte Antica* 1999, p. 45, nos. 11–12), and the two floral bouquets in the Museo Civico Ala Ponzone in Cremona (G. Bocchi, U. Bocchi 1998b, p. 99, figs. 97–98).
These are the most striking results of the "feathery style" that Margherita Caffi developed at the peak of her career during the 1690s.
Gianluca Bocchi

3.59
Francesca Volò,
known as Francesca Vicenzina
Milan, 1650 – Milan?, 1700
Still Life Outdoors with Flowers and Grapes
1680–1685
Oil on canvas, 84.5 × 122.5 cm
Inscriptions: signed "FRANC.CA VICENZINA"
Private collection

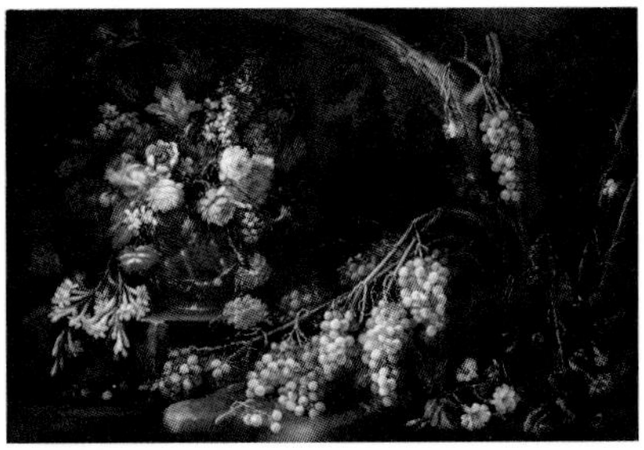

The art of Francesca Vicenzina was publicly recognised for the first time in 1998 through reproductions of several signed paintings presented on the antiques market and through other works with an unequivocally recognisable stylistic and iconographic similarity (G. Bocchi, U. Bocchi 1998c). All were signed "FRANC.CA VICENZINA", and even at first glance showed sufficient differences to identify a style that initially followed the characteristics of her brother Giuseppe, and later drew ever closer to the sensibilities of her sister Margherita. These first impressions, based on a fairly small sample of indisputable works, have been consolidated over time following the rediscovery of new signed paintings, which have expanded her catalogue to several dozen examples.
The paintings selected for this exhibition represent three different moments in her career and testify to the collaboration, or at least the reciprocal influences, established between Francesca Vicenzina, her brother Giuseppe and her older sister Margherita. Francesca began working alongside her father Vincenzo in the second half of the 1660s, but by the beginning of the following decade she found herself having to lead the family workshop herself due to his death. The 1670s were marked by her collaboration with her sister Giovanna, a professional partnership established between two young women who called themselves the "Vicenzine", thus characterising their art in a unique and unifying way. During this decade, both helped to train the young Giuseppe, and after Giovanna's death in 1680, he joined Francesca as her closest assistant.
The painting titled *Fruits and Flowers with a Tray and Ruins in a Landscape* was the prototype demonstration of Francesca's work in the first half of the 1680s. It was sold by Sotheby's in New York on 30 January 1987 and immediately noted for its resemblance to the known works of Giuseppe Vicenzino (G. Bocchi, U. Bocchi 1998c, p. 105, fig. 102). Painted on a long, narrow canvas (58 × 196.5 cm), the composition depicts three distinct still lifes: the one on the left shows clusters of white grapes resting on a square boulder, the central one has flowers cascading from a tray, and the one on the right depicts leaves of *Cordyline terminalis* "Tricolor", an ornamental plant native to the Pacific islands, used first by Vincenzo Volò and then by all his children. This *modus operandi* is found in compositions that are generally more than one metre tall or wide, and where two Volò family artists working together could each create their designs without interfering too much with the others.
The organisation of seventeenth-century painting workshops was substantially similar to other artisans' workshops, and it is not surprising that once they received an order they divided the work in an efficient way that enabled them to produce increasingly beautiful and innovative works.
The study of this painting depicting *Still Life Outdoors with Flowers and Grapes* leads to the same conclusions: there is no doubt that on discovering her brother's extraordinary skill in rendering bunches of white and black grapes on canvas, Francesca reserved the entire right side for him, allotting herself, as the recipient of the commission and therefore the only one who could sign the work, the sole portrayal of a vase of flowers. The result is certainly surprising: in a canvas signed in large letters by Francesca Vicenzina, it is Giuseppe who has the more spectacular and innovative section, comprised of bunches of grapes still on the vine: beautiful clusters that shine with their own light, one bunch hanging from a b ranch of a tree, a suggestive idea repeated a few years later in a famous painting signed by Vicenzino in the Dubini collection.
The structure and arrangement of the plants, consisting of a tree trunk rising to the left and decumbent vines of black and white grapes facing the same direction, create the optical illusion of a semicircle that circumscribes and focuses the gaze on the vase of flowers, giving it an unusual monumentality, effectively enhanced by the precious historiated container.
This still life painting, detailed five years ago in an article discussing the genealogical, historical and artistic distinction of all the members of the Volò family (Bocchi 2015, p. 61, fig. 14), is publicly exhibited here for the first time as a splendid example of art from the Vicenzini workshop.
Gianluca Bocchi

3.60
Francesca Volò,
known as Francesca Vicenzina
Milan, 1650 – Milan?, 1700
Still Life Outdoors with Flowers,
Fruit and Vegetables
1694–1696

Oil on canvas, 90 × 118 cm
Inscriptions: signed "[FRAN.[CA]] VICENZ [INA]"
Private collection

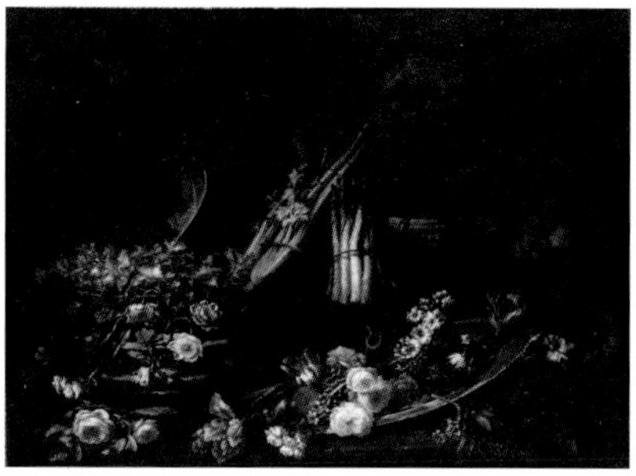

Of the three canvases signed by Francesca Vicenzina on display, this is the only one previously unpublished. Stylistically, it belongs to an intermediate phase around the mid-1690s, when Francesca no longer worked jointly with her younger brother Giuseppe and had developed a closer working relationship with her sister Margherita, with whom she was preparing her ambitious entry into Milan's Accademia di San Luca artists' association.
If we look at the biography of Francesca Vicenzina, who married in 1689 at the age of thirty-nine to a soldier named Nicolaus Miller of probable Swiss nationality, we can well imagine the operational changes that began to take place that year in the Vicenzini workshop.
Pregnant at forty, she gave birth to a daughter, Barbara Maria, on 27 June 1691. We should consider it highly likely that after having witnessed the death of her twenty-eight-years-old sister Giovanna in 1680 due to a postpartum infection, Francesca preferred to interrupt her professional work for some time and devote herself entirely to raising her only child. This appears to be confirmed by the fact that Francesca did not participate in an important commission at the Senago villa of Giberto IV Borromeo, completed by Giuseppe Vicenzino and his sister Margherita Caffi probably between 1693 e il 1694.
The second half of the 1680s also marked Giuseppe's definitive professional launch, now independent from his sister and already the recipient of a payment from Vitaliano VI Borromeo on 12 February 1685.
Between 1694 and 1695 Francesca returned to authoritatively resume her place in the Vicenzini atelier. Together with Margherita and the unknown Lucrezia Ferrari, she applied for membership to the Accademia di San Luca. In December that year the three women asked to participate in the presentation of oblations, an act that was a prelude to their candidature in 1696 and subsequent admission in February 1697.
We can date this signed canvas from a private collection to about that time. In this *Still Life Outdoors with Flowers, Fruit and Vegetables* Francesca displays a large part of her repertoire in a skilful composition of flowers, vessels, asparagus, celery, frisee salad, cherries and peaches. Francesca uses one of the best-tested family configurations, treated with consummate intelligence by her and Giuseppe in numerous compositions during those years, where elements arranged vertically contrast with others arranged diagonally in the foreground, almost always trays from which flowers cascade.
The frisee salad leaves with tiny blue flowers, placed on the ground or in this case scattered on a plate, are one of the most frequently recurring motifs in Francesca Vicenzina's production, an image derived from her father's examples. This is confirmed by the description of a painting he left to his wife Veronica to give to his daughter Margherita and son-in-law Ludovico Caffi, in which he expressly records "frisee salad with *borasa* [*sic*] flowers".
The celery stalks tied with string and placed diagonally on the left of the composition are also elements depicted by Vincenzo Volò (defined in the description of the same painting as "a pair of *sellari* [*sic*]"), subsequently rendered by his daughter in the signed work "FRAN.[CA] VOLÒ DETTA VICENCINA PINSE IN MILAN" (Bocchi 2015, p. 61, fig. 13), datable to between 1686 and 1688 due to the presence of her maiden name. The illustration of celery assumes increasing importance in the paintings of the last years of the 1600s, among them the canvas *Flowers, Fruits and Vegetables* in a private collection in Brescia (G. Bocchi, U. Bocchi 1998c, p. 109, fig. 107); the painting *Ceramic Fruit Bowl with Strawberries, Flowers, Endive, Celery and Oysters* (Christie's, Bologna, 4 June 1991, lot 244); and the painting depicting a *Ceramic Fruit Bowl with Strawberries, Flowers, Endive, Celery and Oysters*, held in the depository of the Kunsthistorisches Museum in Vienna (inv. GG 2870). It was formerly accredited to Margherita and definitively attributed to Francesca after the discovery of her first signed works (Bocchi 2004, p. 36). At the bottom right are artichokes, and higher up in background some half-hidden peaches, recurring elements in both Francesca's and Giuseppe's paintings.
The cluster of grapes in shade at the top left corner is the subdued repetition of a much more visually accentuated motif in the canvas *Bunches of Grapes, Bouquet of Flowers, Jasmine, a Peach and Three Birds* which was shown at Christie's in Milan on 26 November 2009 (lot 29), and in another painting from a private collection in Modena depicting a *Crystal Tureen with Flowers, a Tray with Jasmine, a Plate of Peaches and Bunches of Grapes*, both previously attributed erroneously to Giuseppe Vicenzino.
Gianluca Bocchi

3.61
Francesca Volò, known as Francesca Vicenzina
Milan, 1650 – Milan?, 1700
Still Life Outdoors with Flowers, Frisee Salad, Oysters and Strawberries in a Fruit Bowl
1697–1700
Oil on canvas, 88 × 111 cm
Private collection

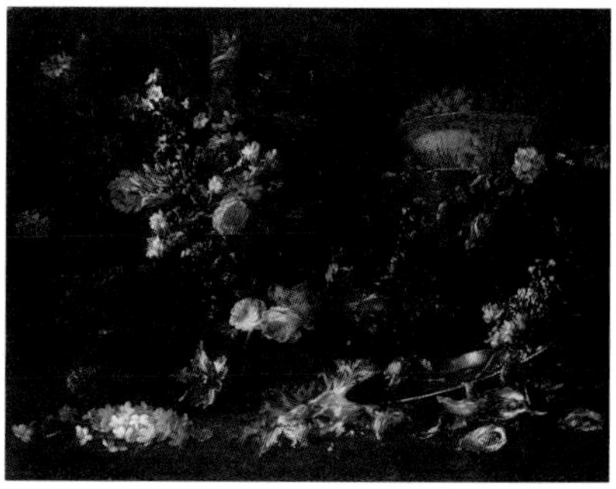

I saw a preview of this admirable example of Francesca Vicenzina's mature production in 2006, when Roman scholar Ludovica Trezzani brought it to my attention prior to its auction (Finarte, Milan, 14 November 2006, lot 31). Trezzani had brilliantly identified it in a private collection by comparing it with the signed paintings published in the first monographic essay devoted to Francesca Volò (G. Bocchi, U. Bocchi 1998c). Despite the age-old patina that covered it, it was at once clear that we were dealing with a more refined version of the *Ceramic Fruit Bowl with Strawberries, Flowers, Endive, Celery and Oysters* that had been sold on the antiques market in previous years with incorrect attributions: first assigned to Margherita Caffi (Christie's, Bologna, 4 June 1991, lot 244) and then to Giuseppe Vicenzino (Arosio, in *Natura morta* 1991, no. 9; *Nature morte* 2003, p. 32).
The restoration highlighted all the refinements that Francesca had interpreted so well in her paintings during the last years of the century, and whose exemplary prototypes included two pairs of canvases that Ferdinando Bologna wrote in 1973 he had seen in two separate homes, one in Rome and one in Naples, belonging to different branches of the same family. The common origin of the series and the presence of a real signature indicated for the first time the existence of this painter and provided the stimulus for a difficult course of research, which ended when the historian from L'Aquila was finally able to show them to me twenty-five years later. The four paintings were indispensable for the initial reconstruction of Francesca Vicenzina's catalogue and to identify at once her most mature work in a close comparison with other works that showed a more marked adherence to the style of her brother Giuseppe (G. Bocchi, U. Bocchi 1998c, pp. 106–107, figs. 103–106).
The work was presented to the public for the third time after being shown in two exhibitions (*I fiori di Francesca* 2007, p. 14; Cottino, in *Donne* 2020, pp. 106–107, cat. 44).
Francesca Volò's bibliography was completed by the inclusion of the painting among the works catalogued in an article that served to

definitively clarify the parental and professional relationships of Vincenzo Volò's children (Bocchi 2015, p. 61, fig. 14).
When contemplating the degree of virtuosity Francesca achieved – the powerful touch of the play of light on the main objects, and the small, scattered glints that embellish the shaded parts – one can clearly appreciate the artistic turn that Francesca Vicenzina took in the 1690s, greatly influenced by her ever closer association with her sister Margherita. Gone are the days when one could admire in her signed canvases the solid constructions of her brother Giuseppe. In these final works everything is lightness, light and colour. Considering the spirit that animates this canvas, it almost seems to be a different painter from the Francesca Vicenzina of the 1680s, were it not for the continued presence of her particular stylistic features and structural modules, true integral parts of her artistic identity.
The presence of the frisee salad with blue flowers, which immediately attracted my attention as the signature motif in many of her paintings because it derived from an idea of her father's (G. Bocchi, U. Bocchi 1998c, p. 108; Bocchi 2004, p. 36), has been definitively accepted as her undisputed stylistic feature, also by later commentators. The large metal vase of flowers, a motif Francesca Vicenzina repeated both in easel paintings and in complex compositions of larger dimensions, assumes also here a very specific value in the economy of the scene, even if its presence does not dominate as in other examples.
All the elements in this painting from a private collection contribute on an equal footing to the final result. The keep the eye continually moving, prompting it to investigate the most obscure meanders of the canvas in search of details concealed in the shadows, such as artichokes, illuminated by shimmering glimmers, or the earthenware vase of carnations, wrapped in a soft glow.
A careful analysis of the compositional form reveals the persistence of a scheme also used by Francesca and Giuseppe Vicenzino during the1680s. I refer to the semi-circular arrangement of the elements in the right portion of the painting, which creates a concavity intended to focus the viewer's attention on the vase of flowers on the left. Although in this painting the effect is mitigated by the equal representation of flowers, fruits, vegetables, pottery and oysters, a very different effect is obtained by this Vicenzini technique in the painting titled *Still Life Outdoors with Flowers and Grapes*, on display in this exhibition (cat. 3.59), and also in the aforementioned painting *Ceramic Fruit Bowl with Strawberries, Flowers, Endive, Celery and Oysters* sold by Christie's in 1991.
Gianluca Bocchi

3.62
Giovanna Volò, known as Giovanna Vicenzina
Milan, 1652 – Milan, 1680

Federico Bianchi
Masnago (Varese), ? – Milan, 1706
Garland of Flowers with a Religious Scene
1670–1675
Oil on canvas, 120 × 90 cm
Varese, Fondazione F.lli Paolo e Tito Molina

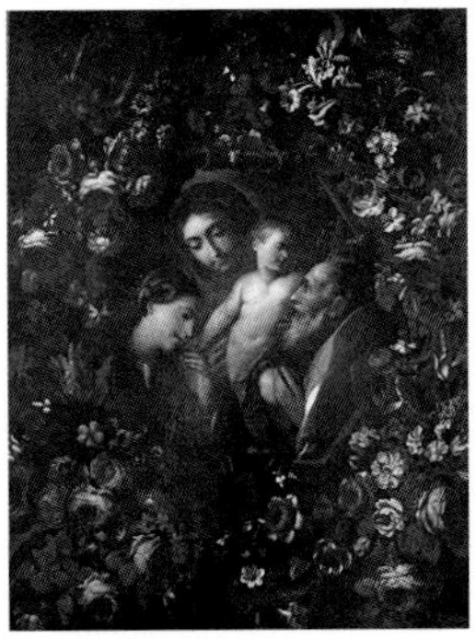

The painting, whose floral component is attributed to Giovanna Vicenzina for the first time in this exhibition, entered the Fondazione Molina as a bequest from Teresa Pedrelli Paradisi. Reproduced and discussed in 1998 in a publication promoted by the foundation (Bernardini, *La quadreria* 1998, pp. 22–24), the canvas was correctly recognised as a work of collaboration between a figure painter and a still life painter, identified respectively as Federico Bianchi and Giuseppe Vicenzino. Twenty-two years after that first proposal, Federico Bianchi's stylistic and chronological identification was confirmed as correct. The composition recalls models he followed in the 1670s when, still fresh from Antonio Busca's teaching, he expressed the assimilated aesthetic canons of Roman classicism, while also keeping up to date with Nuvolone's work in Milan.
Federico Bianchi's collaborations with still life painters interested both the Vicenzini atelier and Giovanni Saglier, an artist and close friend of the family. The 1690 inventory of the assets of Vitaliano VI Borromeo states that his collection contained two paintings by Federico Bianchi and Giovanni Saglier: *Venus Playing with Cupid* and the *Education of the Virgin*, the latter still is in the villa on Isola Bella.
Bianchi's work also includes a *Flora* in the Pinacoteca Ambrosiana, in which the botanical inserts were painted by Margherita Caffi shortly after her return to Milan in 1685 (Terzaghi, in *Pinacoteca Ambrosiana* 2007, pp. 30–31, no. 413), and a still unpublished pair of *Putti with Flowers* recently seen on the art market and datable to the end of the 1670s, in which the botanical sections are credited to Francesca and Giovanna.
Having clarified that Federico Bianchi's collaboration with flower painters lasted for at least fifteen years, we can confirm the date of the Fondazione Molina canvas to the beginning of the 1670s. The stylistic and iconographic elements in Bianchi's work contribute to this dating, as does the general setting modelled on known examples left by Vincenzo Volò and Francesco Cairo, which have to have been executed by 1665: *The Rest During the Flight into Egypt* in the picture gallery of the Archbishopric and the *Education of the Virgin* in Brescia's Spedali Civili (Bocchi 2014, p. 74, figs. 12–13).
In all three paintings the religious scene is contained within an octagonal frame with the flowers mainly distributed on the oblique sides, leaving the horizontal and vertical ones almost empty to reveal underlying baroque decorations, such as shells, scrolls and other ornamental elements. Such adherence to the two examples by Vincenzo Volò indicates the first half of the 1670s as the date of execution, thus excluding the possible intervention of Giuseppe Vicenzino, who was born in 1662 and was never a pupil of his father, who died in 1671. Giuseppe was taught instead by his sisters Francesca and Giovanna and began to produce work alongside Francesca during the 1680s.
The now well-established knowledge of Francesca's art, with three of her most representative works on display in this exhibition (cats. 3.59–61), excludes her as the artist and identifies Giovanna as the only possible author of these floral groups with unquestionable Vicenzini characteristics.
The attribution of the Molina painting to a collaboration between Federico Bianchi and Vincenzo Volò's third child enables us for the first time to focus attention on Giovanna Vicenzina's art in the literature, breaking the tradition established in the seventeenth-century Milanese documents, where the two sisters are remembered together under the unifying epithet "le Vicenzine".
Giovanna's professional career unfolded over scarcely a dozen years, given that she died aged 28 on 13 October 1680, a few days after giving birth to her first child. The importance of Giovanna Vicenzina and her husband Federico Macagni in the fortunes of the Vicenzini workshop has not been fully understood, and several commentators still confuse Giovanna, Vincenzo's third child (referred to as "la Macagna" in documents after the marriage) with Domenica Vicenzina, recorded by Luigi Malvezzi in 1882, despite the now confirmed familial and professional roles of all the Volò painters (Bocchi 2015).
The progressive recognition of Giovanna's works from those of her sister Francesca has made it possible to reconstruct a first *corpus* of autographed paintings and to develop a chronology, a complex operation that will be illustrated in detail in a book soon to be published.
Gianluca Bocchi

3.63
Anna Stanchi
Active in Rome in the mid-seventeenth century
Garland of Flowers with Venus and Adonis
1647
Oil on canvas, 125 × 111.5 cm
Inscriptions: signed and dated "Anna Stangui fecit Rome 1647"
Private collection

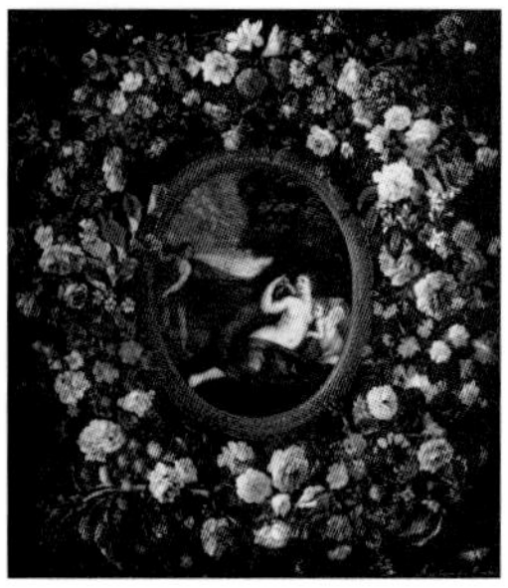

The discovery of Anna Stanchi, a flower painter in Rome in the mid-seventeenth century, is very recent and was made possible by the fortuitous discovery of a painting signed and dated "Anna Stangui fecit Rome 1643" illustrating a vase of flowers (Sotheby's, Amsterdam, 8 May 2007, lot 96). The restoration that followed the sale of the painting revealed that the crystal vase was not contemporary with the work but had been inserted later to hold the botanical component in order to give it the appearance of a finished work. When the painting reappeared on the market (Sotheby's, London, 24 April 2008, lot 405) it was observed that in addition to having erased the vase, the cleaning process had uncovered the edge of an oval frame at the top left. This relief confirmed that this canvas had also been designed to illustrate a garland of flowers, and the one visible with the inscription was merely the residual fragment corresponding to the lower right area of the original composition.
Despite its compromised state and the doubts of several art historians about the authenticity of the signature, for some years this fragment of a wreath represented the only example of Stanchi's work, a historical document whose rarity proved decisive for its acquisition by the Museum of Art at Middlebury College in Vermont when it reappeared on the market a third time (Christie's, New York, 26 October 2016, lot 90).
The discovery in 2013 of this stupendous *Garland of Flowers with Venus and Adonis* from a private collection, dazzling in its entirety and complete with an identical signature and the date 1647, situates it four years later (Crispo 2013, pp. 64, 68–70, fig. 2).
As already pointed out (Crispo, in *Donne* 2020, pp. 100–101, no. 44), the correct stylistic interpretation and meticulous comparison of the botanical prototypes found in this and other garlands poses the need for an essential revision of part of the production so far credited to Giovanni, thus raising Anna Stanchi to a level of quality equal to his and superior to that of the two younger brothers, Nicolò and Angelo.
A number of wreaths attributed by art critics to Giovanni Stanchi, generally ones of *tela da imperatore* size, and therefore the same as this one signed by Anna, have such close similarities that they suggest a common, contemporary origin. In particular, the painting in the Anhaltische Gemäldegalerie, Dessau, contains a depiction of Christ among the doctors surrounded by an identical oval frame with the same beaded motif.
In both cases, the religious and mythological scenes were created by the artists at the same time as the botanical element. Valid proof of this is the deliberate artifice of surmounting the frames with flowers and leaves in order to give depth to the composition. Indeed in this painting a leaf even covers the wrist and part of the forearm of the approaching Adonis. The study of the mythological scene has led to identifying Anna Stanchi's anonymous collaborator as a figurative painter who was a follower of Francesco Albani, and whose impressive production of scenes with cupids enjoyed a wide following in Rome and Bologna during the first half of the seventeenth century.
The figure of Adonis is taken from the one depicted in the painting of the same subject in the Gemäldegalerie in Kassel (inv. GK 1163), whose attribution was suggested by Richard Spear and accepted by later commentators.
The floral wreath was first invented in Rome by Daniel Seghers, who was present in the city in 1625 and author with Domenichino of the painting made for the Ludovisi collection *Garland of Flowers with the Chariot of Love*, now in the Musée du Louvre.
Numerous Baroque painters in Rome took up this iconographic motif, but only Giovanni and Anna Stanchi show that they have carefully studied Seghers' models, to the extent that they can be defined as the most Flemish of the Roman painters active in the first half of the seventeenth century.
Gianluca Bocchi

3.64
Elisabetta Marchioni
Active in Rovigo in the second half of the seventeenth century
Frontal for the Holy Eucharist
End of the seventeenth century
Oil on canvas, 94 × 234 cm
Rovigo, Pinacoteca dell'Accademia dei Concordi, inv. 387

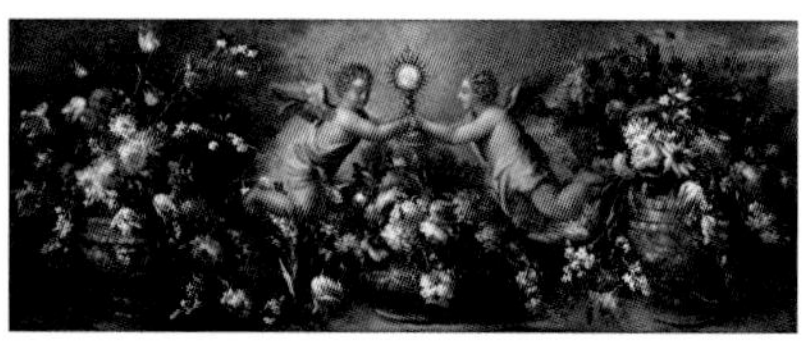

The *Frontal for the Holy Eucharist*, conserved in the Pinacoteca dell'Accademia dei Concordi was painted by Elisabetta Marchioni and donated personally by the painter to the Capuchin church of Rovigo, probably at the end of her career. The historian Francesco Bartoli recalls it with these words: "She reached old age and left a frontal to the P.P. Capuchin, which is seen exhibited on the High Altar during various functions, and in the centre she painted two little angels holding the monstrance" (Bartoli 1793, pp. 318–319). In the first half of the nineteenth century the work passed to the Venezze family, and it was Francesco Antonio, a family member and director of the Accademia dei Concordi, who donated it in 1848 to the prestigious Rovigo institution.
The very precise description of the painting made by Francesco Bartoli, together with the knowledge of its changes of ownership, confirm the certain identity of a work that has been used by all scholars as a valid basis for attributing Marchioni with other paintings that over the course of time have returned from the market and from private collections (Safarik, Bottari 1989; G. Bocchi, U. Bocchi 1998d).
Among the little information passed on by Bartoli concerning Marchioni's style of painting is this description: "Marchioni, celebrated Painter of Flowers [...] She had a graceful brush, and sought to imitate nature. The observer's eye remains so satisfied in seeing the freshness and verity of her paintings that it would never remove itself from her paintings [...] Beautiful vases painted by her, on which pyramids of her flowers rise in such variety that they actually enthral [...] The assortment of the various flowers is so elegantly and skilfully arranged that they do not create any confusion, but please and subtly enchant". In this large frontal Elisabetta Marchioni confirms Bartoli's opinion.
Particularly effective is her rendition and distribution of the floral masses contained in capacious, embossed metal vases. Her depiction of the two little angels is rather more awkward, perhaps because she received help from a less skilled local painter. Other paintings conserved *ab antiquo* in Rovigo should also be considered genuine prototypes by Marchioni. Two paintings, one of which is *Still Life of Flowers and Fruit*, still in the Accademia dei Concordi, and the other *Vase of Flowers* conserved in the Archiepiscopal Seminary in Rovigo, seem to have come from the Silvestri picture gallery. Whereas the former is clearly distinguishable by its subject, the second is identifiable by both the subject and measurements: it was located on the "facade opposite the entrance door", in the "Picture Gallery".
Francesco Bartoli recalls that several paintings by Marchioni hung in the Silvestri home: "Among the flower paintings are many by Marchioni from Rovigo, a painter who had a much fame in this kind of painting". The characteristics of the two abovementioned paintings, their exuberance and the floral richness, are such signature qualities of Marchioni's work that their attribution has never been in question. Another canvas from the Archiepiscopal Seminary, depicting a *Vase of Flowers*, was also considered her work and turned out to be the fragment of a larger painting adapted to complement the Silvestri one. In all likelihood, this painting also comes from the same collection, having been one of the four paintings that adorned "the room at the end of the corridor facing the theatre". As

evidence of the collecting tastes of the Silvestri family, it is worth recalling that the same collection also held several works by the eighteenth-century painter Francesco Duramano, the son of Madama Duramano, reported by Pietro Zani at the beginning of the nineteenth century (Zani 1817–1824, part I, vol. VIII, p. 30) and the main promoter of an art workshop specialising in floral paintings which dominated Venetian production in that sector for the entire first half of the eighteenth century. The most recent and accurate studies (Bocchi 2012) identify the atelier of Francesco Duramano as the workplace where these paintings were made, and which late twentieth-century literature grouped under the pseudonym "Master of the Guardeschi Flowers". Considering the compositional analogies between this eighteenth-century production and that of Elisabetta Marchioni, it is natural to wonder about the role played in the Venetian area by the mysterious Madama Duramano, and the connections and reciprocal influences that may have been established with Elisabetta in the second half of the seventeenth century. The Accademia dei Concordi frontal, created towards the end of her life from rich pictorial material and strong chromatic lighting, may help us understand how much the paintings of Margherita Caffi, who resided in nearby Bologna in the 1670s, and who throughout the 1680s sent paintings for her brother-in-law Francesco in Venice to sell, may have influenced a clear stylistic change in Elisabetta's work, given that most of the other works attributable to her are much less lively and more delicate.
Gianluca Bocchi

4.1
Diana Scultori, known as Diana Mantovana
Mantua, c. 1547 – Rome, 1612
Latona Giving Birth to Apollo and Diana on the Island of Delos
1565–1572
Burin, trimmed sheet 257 × 384 mm
Rome, Istituto centrale per la grafica, inv. FC50748 (property of the Accademia Nazionale dei Lincei)

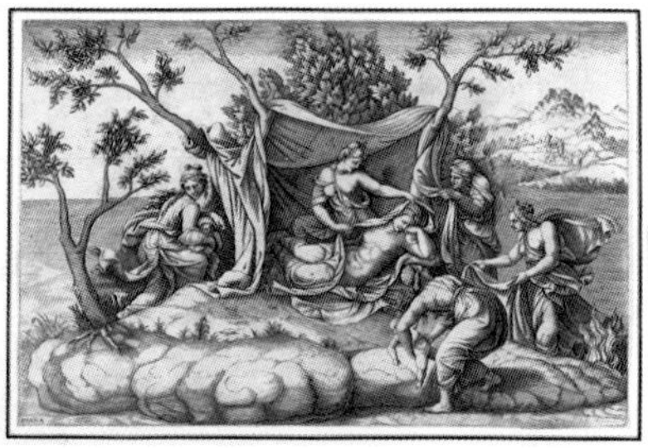

The engraving, a fifth state impression of which is on display here with all the inscriptions abraded (Bellini 1991, p. 174, no. 9), was made after an invention by Giulio Romano for an oil painting today preserved in the Royal Collection at Windsor (RCIN 482816, attributed to the workshop of Giulio Romano), a preparatory drawing for which is also known (Louvre, Cabinet des Dessins, inv. 3500, 304 × 446 mm, recently shown at the "Giulio Romano a Mantova. Con nuova e stravagante maniera" exhibition, Serra, in *Giulio Romano* 2019, p. 165, no. 59, dated circa 1533). In the engraving, the composition is reversed, an indication of its derivation from the original invention. The scene shows Latona's childbirth on the secluded and floating island of Delos, where the goddess hoped to elude the wrath of Juno; according to the myth (Ovid, *Metamorphosis*, VI), Juno banned the pregnant woman from giving birth anywhere on "mainland", and that Cycladic island, shrouded in fog and always moving, was the only shelter that would take her in.
The atmosphere of the composition is electric with tension: the just-born twins are cared for by nymphs who are wary and fearful of the threat of punishment, while Latona rests under a makeshift tent, draped over the tree branches. Diana's print faithfully copies the drawing, in particular the figures' postures, the emphatic expressions typical of Giulio Romano's style, and the barren rocks on the shore, but she adds details in the surrounding vegetation, as well as a coastal landscape in the distance with a cluster of houses, details also present in the painting. It is possible that this painting was made to decorate a room in the Palazzo Te, together with other subjects on the infancy of Jupiter and his family, not all identified, which were perhaps realised on the occasion of the birth of Francesco III around 1533 (Hartt 1958, I, p. 213). One of the other paintings, *Jupiter and the Goat Amalthea*, also attributed to Giulio Romano's workshop and dated around 1535, is located in Windsor (RCIN 402781), and the subject was engraved by Giulio Bonasone. From the same series is the *Infancy of Jupiter*, today in the London National Gallery, with provenance from the Gonzaga collection, then Charles I of England, then the Orléans collection, which has a very similar composition, being set on the island of Crete (for a reconstruction of the series dedicated to the infancy of Jupiter and of other gods, see Shearman 1983, pp. 129–130).
The painting came into the British royal collections with the acquisition of the Gonzaga collection in Mantua by Charles I of England; scholars tend to date the engraving to before 1572, that is, when Diana was still in Mantua and had the opportunity to see the painting, and perhaps even the drawing. Shearman considers the Louvre folio, from the Jabach collection, a copy of Giulio's preliminary sketch, identifying it as the model for an engraving preserved in Munich (Graphische Sammlung, inv. 21144, not found in the on-line collection).
In the collections of the Istituto Centrale per la Grafica, there are two other versions: FC50746 (fourth state, with the inscriptions of the editors Orazio Pacifico and Carlo Losi and the date 1733), and FC50747 (third state, with the inscriptions of the editors Giambattista de Rossi and Orazio Pacifico), located in the same volume 40H17 in the Corsini collection, bearing the inscription "Adamo e Diana Scultori stampe" on the spine. The plate, which in the first state shows the artist's name "DIANA", was probably used by the artist to pull prints on her own, and was later edited in succession by Orazio Pacifico (active in Rome in around 1580), Giambattista De Rossi "Il Milanese" (active in Rome between 1640 and 1642) and Carlo Losi (active between 1772 and 1774). The copperplate is not, in fact, listed in the *Indice delle stampe De Rossi* from 1735, nor is it in the Calcografia collection.
Rita Bernini

4.2
Diana Scultori, known as Diana Mantovana
Mantua, c. 1547 – Rome, 1612
Achilles Defuctus, Battle around the Body of Patroclus
c. 1570
Burin, sheet 456 × 654 mm, impression 244 × 398 mm
Inscriptions: lower left "Iulius Rom. In"; lower left margin "Achilles defuctus"
Rome, Istituto centrale per la grafica, inv. CL2452/746

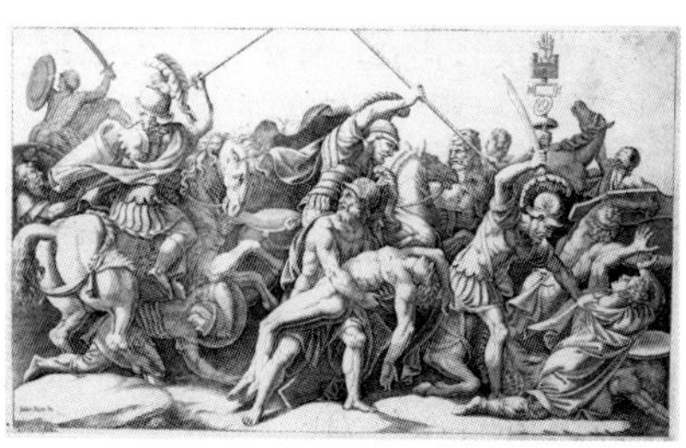

The subject is the *Battle around the Body of Patroclus*, after an invention by Giulio Romano, shown in the vault fresco in the Sala di Troia in the Palazzo Ducale in Mantua, made between 1536 and 1539 (Hartt 1958, I, p. 178; II, fig. 392). The scenes in the decorative cycle are taken from Book V of the Iliad, following an iconographic program conceived by the humanist Benedetto Lampridio (Talvacchia 1981, pp. 240–242). The model for this composition derives from the Roman relief depicting the Battle between Romans and Gauls, today on display in the Loggia delle Città in the Old Court of the Palazzo Ducale in Mantua (inv. 6579), also Giulio's source of inspiration for the *Battle of Constantine* in the Vatican. The relief was actually part of the collection of ancient works of art assembled by Raphael's pupil, which he took to Mantua when he moved there in 1524 at Marquis Federico II Gonzaga's invitation. The piece came from the collection of the Roman antiques dealer Giovanni Ciampolini. Part of the collection was purchased in Rome by Giulio Romano (through his father and administrator Pietro Pippi) and Giovanfrancesco Penni between 1510 and 1520 (Lanciani 1899, p. 108; Fusco, Corti 1991).
The relief is probably the one described as "a part of a frieze" in the list of the contents of one of the crates shipped to Mantua in March 1526 as Giulio's gift to the Marquis Federico II (*Giulio Romano* 1992, p. 134). A drawing of the frieze attributed to Amico Aspertini is preserved at the British Museum (https://www.britishmuseum.org/collection/object/P_1898-1123-3-11). The Sala di Troia was intended for official political meetings, and Federico had placed the works of classical art from his collection there. Only the central scene of the ancient frieze, with the figure of the dying Patroclus supported by Menelaus (or Telamonian Ajax, according to other interpretations, see Talvacchi 1981, pp. 150–152), as the battle rages on around them, was used by Giulio Romano for the fresco, while the rest of the composition is a sort of reconstruction of the missing parts, his way of recovering antiquity that shows his classical culture, certainly acquired in Rome in Raphael's workshop. The scene that Diana Scultori reproduced differs somewhat from the original frescoed one and the preparatory drawing, not identified (Hartt 1958 identifies only four preparatory drawings for the entire cycle of the Sala di Troia, nos. 232–235). An anonymous pen and brown ink drawing with watercolour strokes and whiting on paper made brownish by a deteriorated protective varnish, shows on the *verso* a barely-hinted-at detail of the episode of the construction of the Trojan horse, using the same technique; preserved in the Fondo Nazionale of the Istituto centrale per la grafica in Rome (FN 14722R; Serra, in *Giulio Romano* 2019, p. 174, no. 66), it refers, however, to the episode shown in the fresco, as is obvious from several details, and it bears a handwritten attribution to

Giorgio Vasari and the date 1550 in red chalk. Diana, instead, adds a series of figures in the background and to the sides of the composition, giving the scene a more crowded appearance that is well-suited to the fury of the battle, expanding the overall view of the setting.
The plate, inv. 643 Calcografia, identified as "Battle of the ancient Romans; engraved using a burin by Diana Mantovana, sideways royal format", is listed in the *Indice delle stampe De Rossi* of 1735, and was owned by the De Rossi family of publishers as early as 1677 (*Giulio Romano* 1993, p. 145). It was purchased by Pope Clement XII Corsini from the same family of publishers, along with the other five autograph plates by Diana, making the first nucleus of the Calcografia Camerale. Two other copies of the same engraving are preserved in the Instituto's collections (FN1079, vol. 9, Fondo Pio, III state, and FC71147, vol. 40H17, III state, in poor condition).
Rita Bernini

4.3
Diana Scultori, known as Diana Mantovana
Mantua, c. 1547 – Rome, 1612
The Continence of Scipio
Before 1575
Burin, sheet 370 × 478 mm,
impression 207 × 255 mm
Inscriptions: on the arch impost, left "DIA / NA"; right "IVLIVS. RO. INVE."; lower left "LIBERALITATIS ET / CONTINENTIAE / EXEMPLVM"
Stamps: "Sopraintendenza Camerale / 3ª prova"; "AR"
Rome, Istituto centrale per la grafica, inv. CL2452/752

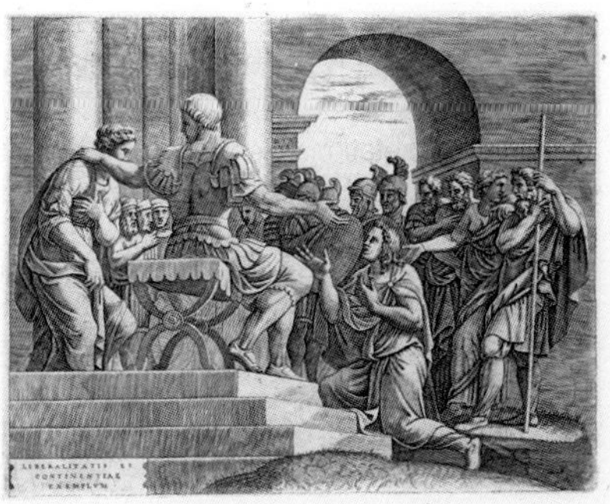

The print depicts Scipio Africanus's demonstration of magnanimity after the surrender of the fortress of *Nova Carthago*, or Cartagena, the Carthaginian colony in Spain, according to the narrative of, among others, Polybius, Livy, and Valerius Maximus. Scipio returned a beautiful, young prisoner, unharmed, endowing her with the gold offered by her family as ransom, in exchange only for the promise from her betrothed, the Celtiberian chieftain, to work toward reconciliation. The episode, later recalled by Petrarch and Machiavelli, took a central role in the Renaissance debate about the "perfect captain" – the *quaestio de ducibus*, so hotly debated in the second half of the sixteenth century and the early seventeenth – that identified in the figure of the Roman general the heroic model for modern men-at-arms and statesmen.
The composition is directly derived from the wall painting of the same name by Giulio Romano, enclosed in a medallion decorating the vault of the Sala degli Imperatori or dei Cesari, in Palazzo Te, which, with the parallel depiction of *Alexander the Great Safeguarding the Writings of Homer*, celebrates the moral tenor of the ancient generals. This decorative programme has been interpreted as a tribute to Emperor Charles V, who in 1530 had conferred on Federico Gonzaga the title of duke.
As Paolo Bellini has pointed out (1991, pp. 172–174), the engraving shows some differences with respect to Giulio Romano's preparatory drawing for the painting (Frankfurt, Städelsches Kunstinstitut, inv. 4342), and even more so compared to another drawing which is a first version of the theme (Milan, Biblioteca Ambrosiana, inv. F. 281, inf. no. 56). Comparison with the Frankfurt drawing makes it possible to correct a small compositional incongruity, that is, the apparent asymmetry of the arch in the background that shows a sort of capital in the left-hand impost and a simple cornice moulding in the one to the right, an incongruity due to a two-dimensional reduction of the composition in the painting and in the engraving compared to the first design.
The type of signature – with just the first name – and the style similar to that of Marcantonio Raimondi suggest that the engraving dates from the early period when the artist was still in Mantua, invalidating the earlier proposal of 1542, which arose from a misunderstanding in the course of the nineteenth century clearly contradicted by Diana's biographical details, definitively established by Valeria Pagani (1992).
The print is a second state pulled from the plate engraved by Diana that came into the Calcografia Camerale with the collection of the historical De Rossi printing press, acquired in 1738 from the Vatican to avoid its dispersal on the international market.
Ilaria Fiumi Sermattei

4.4
Diana Scultori, known as Diana Mantovana
Mantua, c. 1547 – Rome, 1612
Jesus Christ and the Adulteress
By 1575
Burin, sheet 610 × 871 mm,
impression 423 × 583 mm
Inscriptions: lower left "IVLIVS R. / INVENTOR / DIANA F."; centre: "Si stampano da Gio. Jacomo de Rossi alla Pace. Con privilegio DI PAPA [...] XIII / PER ANNI X, Diana Scultora Mantoana fece [...] Roma l'anno 1633"; to the right the dedication by Maurilio Bona to Pompeo Colonna whose coat of arms appears in the upper right.
Stamps: "Sopraintendenza Camerale / 3ª Prova"; "AR"
Rome, Istituto centrale per la grafica, inv. CL2452/744

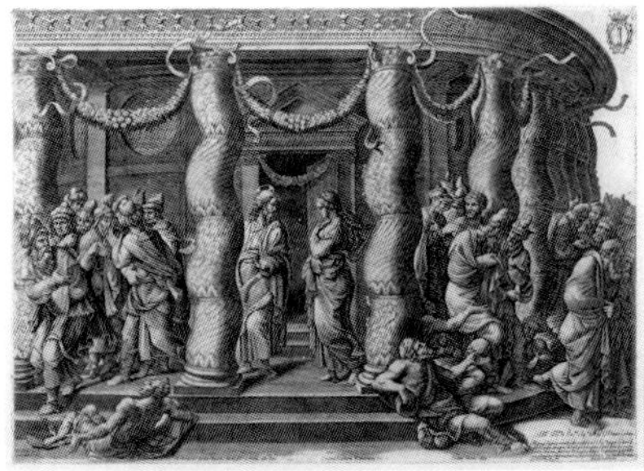

A work unanimously recognised by art historians as "capital" in the Mantuan artist's output, it shows Jesus pardoning the woman accused of adultery by the scribes and pharisees (John, 8, 2–11). The setting is in the portico of the Temple of Jerusalem, easily identified by the spiral columns that according to tradition distinguished the structure founded by King Solomon. At the centre, before the open door of the temple, Christ's calm gesture freeing the pregnant woman from censure sets off a flurry of movement that disperses and marginalises the crowd that had gathered to condemn her and who now react animatedly, to the point of nearly running over in their hasty flight some beggars sitting on the steps. The architecture of the background is part of this movement, thanks to the asymmetrical aspect of the composition, the twisting line of the columns, and the central plan of the building, noticeable in the curvature of the entablature, almost like a carousel turning, blowing the ribbons of the festoons hanging between the columns.
As Stefania Massari has pointed out (in *Giulio Romano* 1993, pp. 157–159), the invention can be traced to a drawing considered a copy from Giulio Romano (Musée du Louvre, inv. 3614 *recto*), reversed with respect to the engraving under examination. This lineage links the print to Diana's early period in Mantua, her birthplace, where she trained in the workshop of her father, Giovanni Battista, sculptor, plasterer, and engraver, who worked with Giulio Romano in the main construction sites there. In fact, the Gonzaga court with its fertile relationship with Rome was the political and cultural context for Diana's activity and for this engraving in particular. The artist's original dedication of the work was to Eleonora, Duchess of Mantua, with an inscription later abraded and by others replaced with the dedication to Pompeo Colonna, which we can read in this specimen, a fourth state also bearing the Colonna family coat of arms. The spiral columns also refer to Rome, where they decorated the *pergola* above Saint Peter's tomb in the old Constantinian basilica, and Mantua, where the same columns are the mark of Giulio Romano's work and his Raphaelesque pedigree, also recurring in the tapestry that shows *Saint Peter Healing the Cripple* from the series of the Acts of the Apostles, woven in Flanders and a copy of the one made for Pope Leo X based on Raphael's cartoons, purchased by Cardinal Ercole Gonzaga in the mid-sixteenth century, still

today conserved in the Palazzo Te.
The work is also mentioned in a document of crucial importance for the life of Diana and, more in general, for the history of the engraving. On 5 June 1575, Pope Gregory XIII wrote a "brief", a document of the papal chancellery drawn up in the form of a letter, assuring Diana of the protection of her engraving production, identified by the signature, reserving the exclusive right of sale for the following ten years. It is a unique privilege, preceded by rare measures that, however, concerned literary works, never images, and it bears witness to the considerable qualitative recognition achieved by the artist, also documented by Giorgio Vasari's testimony in the second edition of the *Lives*, and the solidity of her social relations, achieved also thanks to her marriage with the architect Francesco Capriani, of Volterra. Cited among the already executed prints that were subject to the protection of the papal government, *Jesus Christ and the Adulteress* thus has a sure *terminus ante quem* for its dating, still relevant to the Mantuan context or close to when she moved to Rome.
Ilaria Fiumi Sermattei

4.5
Diana Scultori, known as Diana Mantovana
Mantua, c. 1547 – Rome, 1612
Madonna and Child with the Archangels Michael, Gabriel and Raphael
Before 1572–1575
Burin, sheet 646 × 469 mm,
impression 361 × 272 mm
Inscriptions: lower left "DIANA" (the letter N reversed), right "R.V.I."; in the lower margin "REGINA ANGELORUM / CUM TRIBUS ARCHANGELIS, MICHAELE, GABRIELE, RAPHAELE.", below "Romae ex Calcographia Dominici de Ruberis Heredis Io. Jacobi de Rubeis ad Templum S. Mariae de Pace cum Priv. S. Pont."
Stamps: "Sopraintendenza Camerale / 3ª Prova"
Rome, Istituto centrale per la grafica,
inv. CL2496/2392

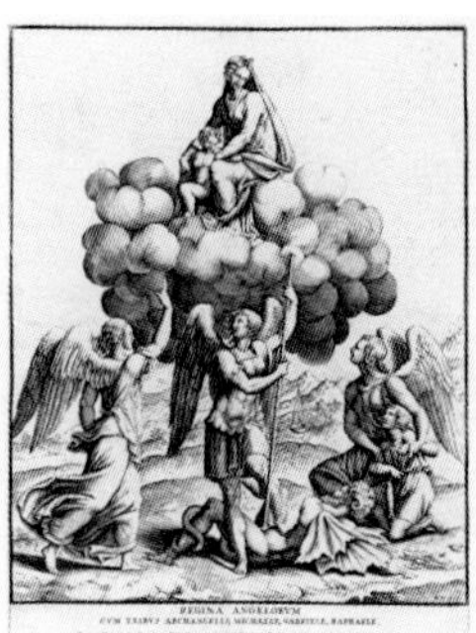

The composition shows, above, the Madonna in glory with the Child on a throne of clouds and below, in a pleasant hilly landscape, the three archangels: Gabriel, in the act of announcing the Incarnation, Michael, in arms, subduing the devil, and Raphael, kneeling with young Tobias whom he accompanied on a dangerous journey.
After centuries of mistrust and caution on the part of the Church, the worship of angels and archangels experienced a moment of particular revival in the mid-sixteenth century, thanks to the work of the priest Antonio del Duca, who, in 1561, obtained from Pope Pius IV Medici the dedication of the Basilica of Santa Maria degli Angeli inside the ruins of the Baths of Diocletian, which was to be built to a design by Michelangelo. Specifically, the iconographic source of Diana's print, as well as in a drawing by Francesco Primaticcio at the Louvre (RF 31874) and in a painting by Marco d'Oggiono in the Pinacoteca di Brera (inv. Nap. 2), was recognised by Stefania Pasti (2003) in the *Apocalypsis Nova*. Attributed to the Franciscan friar Amadeo Menez da Silva, who died in 1482, but probably written about twenty years later by another Franciscan, Juraj Dragišić, known as Giorgio Benigno Salviati, this theological text attributes great importance to the Virgin and the three archangels.
In the past, the invention for the print had been identified in a lost drawing by Raphael, based on the initials "R.V.I." – *Raphael Urb. Invenit* – and the pervasive Raphaelesque inspiration that clearly emerges, in particular in the figure of the Virgin that is a copy of the *Madonna of Foligno* in the Musei Vaticani, which Diana herself had already engraved. Actually, Raphael's initials had been added later to the plate, in the fourth state, which corresponds to when the Rossi printing press marketed the print in the eighteenth century. The invention of the *Regina Angelorum* instead probably derived from a lost drawing by Giulio Romano, formerly in the Gatteraux collection, as clearly demonstrated by the Giulian compositional style, though thoroughly steeped in the Raphaelesque culture (Bellini 1991, pp. 170–180).
The print in question is a fifth state, pulled from the engraved plate from the Rossi alla Pace printing press, a calcography collection acquired by the Vatican in 1738 and destined to the Calcografia Camerale for the purpose established. Previously, the print engraved by Diana appears in the *Indice* of the publisher and art dealer Antonio Lafrery, among the holy and devotional images, listed under the number 356, as the *Madonna of the Angels*. This listing allows the dating of the engraving to be anchored to the years 1572-1575, the chronological span of the *Indice*, therefore, still in the youthful, Mantuan period of Diana Scultori's activity, or close to when she moved to Rome.
Ilaria Fiumi Sermattei

4.6
Anna Maria Vaiani
Milan, c. 1604? – Rome, 1654
Saint Mary Magdalene
1627
Etching, sheet 252 × 203 mm,
impression 184 × 144 mm
Inscriptions: lower right "Anna Maria / Vaiani Sculp. / 1627"
Rome, Istituto centrale per la grafica,
inv. FC76527 (property of the Accademia Nazionale dei Lincei)

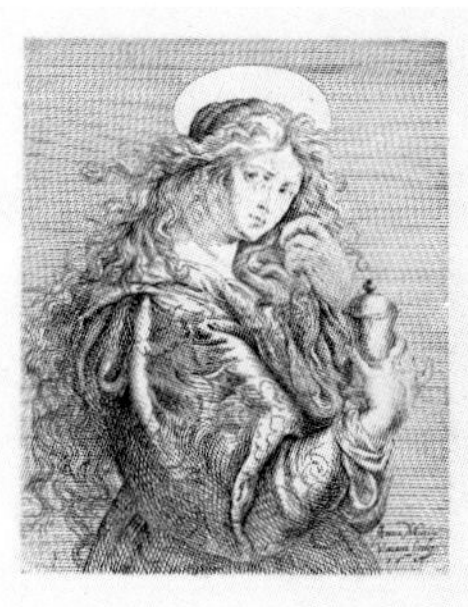

Mary Magdalene is portrayed with her bust almost in profile, while she turns her face to the observer. Her gaze is directed over her shoulder, outside of the visual field; her expression is concentrated, intrigued. The flowing mass of her hair is partly gathered at the nape of her neck, but most of it falls down her back, reaching past her waist, in long waves: it seems to be moving, as if affected by her gait, or the twisting of her figure, or by a sudden gust of wind, revealing her beautiful face. With her left hand, she takes a lock of hair at breast level and wraps it around her finger, while with her right hand she gracefully holds the unguent pot (TIB 1983, vol. 44, p. 336), one of the canonical attributes of the figure. The reference is to the episode of the Gospel where a repentant sinner – since the sixth century identified as Mary of Magdala – anointed Christ's feet after having wet them with her tears and dried them with her hair. The long, loose locks of her hair are one of the distinctive traits of the saint, whether she is standing and iconic – as in the medieval polyptychs – or shown penitent or in meditation in the desert. Magdalene is portrayed here elegantly attired, wearing an embroidered dress with wide sleeves, and a rolled-up scarf that falls from her shoulder onto her breast: but she is not a distraught prostitute, as in many contemporary paintings. Vaiani renders an image of a woman with a strong-willed and self-confident air; contributing to this impression is precisely the tumultuous hair, which enhances the feeling of seductive feminine power. The print is signed and dated 1627 and is the first known work by the artist, which shows, however, a certain inexperience in the anatomical rendering of non-negligible details: the left hand is rather disproportionate, with thick fingers, while the neck seems too robust for the face (Guerrieri Borsoi 2010, p. 247). The marked shading that climbs from her chin to her temple instead gives the impression of a mask on her face. Despite this, the overall perception is dynamic and fluid: the swift and free strokes defining the figure are at odds with the compact background, rendered with dense parallel lines, omitted only in the area corresponding to the halo. The inventories mention five engravings by Vaiani, the *Mary Magdalene*, a *Vase of Flowers* for Giovan Battista Ferrari's *De Florum Cultura* (1663), and three panels for the *Galleria Giustiniana* (1632–1633): *Pallas*, *Homer* and *Pindar*, and *Sappho* and *Young Cleopatra* (Nagler 1835–1853, XIX, pp. 292–293; Le Blanc

1854–1859, V, p. 80). If, for these last four prints, Bartsch's opinion seems rather harsh – the artist's burin is described as "thin", "clumsy, little practised" – the critic uses more nuanced tones for this engraving: although he doubts the authorship of the invention, he considers the drawing on the whole "accurate", with a sweeping, free etching technique (Bartsch 1803–1821, XX, pp. 126–127). In fact, the indication of the *sculpsit* alone could suggest that it is the invention of another, since Vaiani signs the other works differently, referring to its *invenit* as well. It is worth recalling, in this regard, that her brother Sebastiano engraved a *Repentant Mary Magdalene with the Angel* (1628), mentioning in his dedication its derivation from an invention of his father. The physiognomic features are similar to those of our etching, and even suggest that Anna Maria's model may have been a drawing or a painting by her father Alessandro. The print of the Istituto centrale per la grafica was conserved in the Corsini volume (vol. 47H14) dedicated to the etchings of the "Tuscan engravers" of the seventeenth and eighteenth centuries. After all, Anna Maria always boasted her "Florentine" family and cultural heritage: it suffices to recall the portrait of her that Claude Mellan passed on to us (1626–1627).
Isabella Rossi

4.7
Claude Mellan
Abbeville (France), 1598 – Paris, 1688
Portrait of Maddalena Corvina
1636
Burin, trimmed sheet 117 × 85 mm
Inscriptions: "MADALENA CORVINA PITRICE ET MINIATRICE ROMANA / *Mellan del et f. Romae 1636*."
Rome, Istituto centrale per la grafica, inv. FC32050 (property of the Accademia Nazionale dei Lincei)

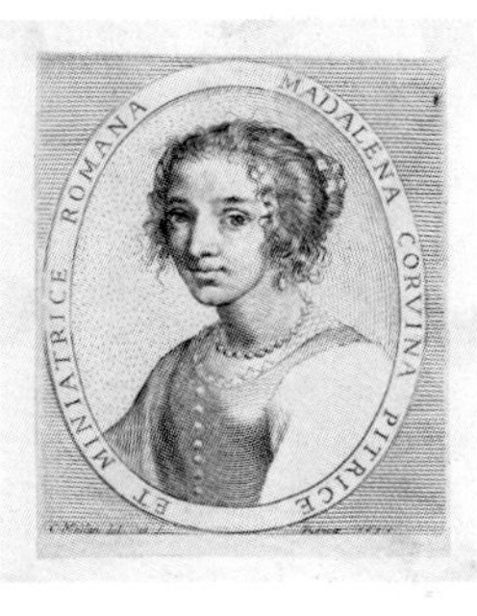

The incision depicts the Roman miniaturist Maddalena Corvina (1607–1664), half-length and slightly turned towards the observer. Claude Mellan had already used the same graphic scheme for two other portraits of artists taken from life: Virginia Vezzi and Anna Maria Vaiani. The image shows us a twenty-nine-year-old woman who, after completing her apprenticeship with Guido Reni and following in her family tradition of miniature painting – starting with her grandfather, Frans van de Casteele, and her uncle Michele Castello – lays claim to her profession. Like many woman artists of her time, she chose not to marry and specialised as a painter and illustrator of codices, making use of botanical drawing skills learned from her father Enrico Corvino (De Laurentiis 2010a, p. 44, fig. 42; Lollobrigida 2017a, pp. 19–21; Lollogrigida 2017b, p. 122, fig. 5). The date of execution, 1636, situates the portrait, together with that of Alphonse de Richelieu, cardinal of Lyon, among Mellan's last Roman works (Le Comte 1702, II, p. 317). The decade spent in the papal capital (1624–1636) during the years of the Baroque explosion was particularly fruitful for the definition of the French artist's graphic language. The "translations" from Simon Vouet's paintings, the engravings by Gian Lorenzo Bernini, the realisation of some illustrations for the *Galleria Giustiniana* and the *De Florum Cultura*, an undertaking to which Corvina herself may have contributed some images, all bear witness to fundamental moments in the evolution of a highly personal style, made distinctive by the almost exclusive use of parallel lines carved with a burin, modulated in depth in relation to the tonal values and the modelling sought.
In this portrait of Maddalena Corvina, the areas where the lines intersect are small, qualifying as spots that lend a certain mobility to the expression of the young woman's thin face, made magnetic by the large eyes. In the backdrop to the figure, touches of the burin tip, like a constellation of stars, are alternated with curved lines. The Städelsches Kunstinstitut collections in Frankfurt (inv. 1025; *Französische Zeichnungen* 1986, p. 18) conserves a black chalk drawing, the outlines reworked with a metallic tip, that is considered preparatory to the engraving, while the facial features of the miniaturist shown in a sheet in the Stockholm Nationalmuseum (VM 2622/1863; Snickare, in *Face to Face* 2001, pp. 269, 273, no. 373) do not offer a convincing likeness (Brejon de Lavergnée, in *Claude Mellan* 1989, p. 344, no. 119). In the second half of the eighteenth century, the copperplate was in Paris, as documented in a second state of the work, dating from 1755–1765, reused by Michel Odieuvre for the publication of *Europe illustre*. On that occasion, the following inscription was added: "A Paris chez Oudieuvre M. d d'Estampes Quai / de l'Ecole vis à vis le coté de la Samaritaine / à la belle Image C.P.R." (Préaud 1939, p. 20; Préaud 1988, p. 17, Mellan, no. 151; Ficacci, in *Claude Mellan* 1989, p. 345, cat. 120). The portrait of Maddalena Corvina is an example of the French engraver's ability to capture a person's soul in just a few strokes; however, even though it is a mature work, it does not mark a technical milestone in his long career. In 1649, Mellan would demonstrate incredible skill in his execution of the *Face of Christ*, a visionary rendering of the veil of Veronica, created from a single, continuous line.
The print published here is conserved in volume 34 I4 of the Fondo Corsini, from the collection of the Andreoli booksellers of Rome, entirely dedicated to portraits by Claude Mellan (Pezzini Bernini 2001, p. 80).
Gabriella Bocconi

4.8
Johannes Valdor II
(after Maddalena Corvina)
Liège (Belgium), 1616 – Liège (Belgium), 1675
Portrait of Enrico Corvino
1639–1640
Etching and burin, trimmed sheet
148 × 112 mm
Inscriptions: "ENRICVS CORVINVS DELPHICVS AETATIS SVE 82 // Vnicus Herbarum Vires Corvine tenebas, Vnicus aeternum Vivere Dignus eras. / Madalena Corvinua Pin. / I. Valdor F. Romae"
Rome, Istituto centrale per la grafica, inv. FC41062 (property of the Accademia Nazionale dei Lincei)

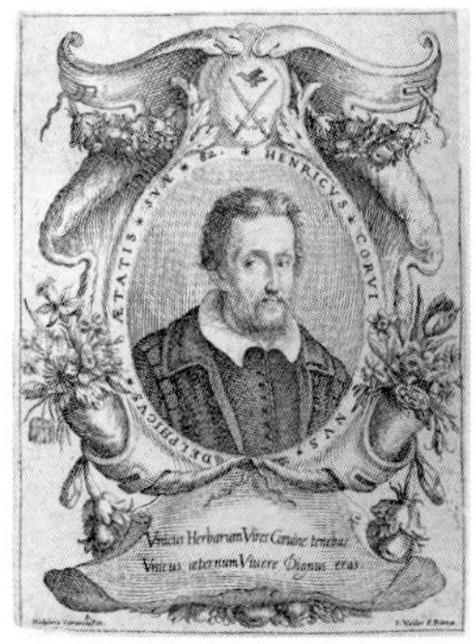

The person portrayed in this engraving by Johannes Valdor II is the Dutch apothecary Hendrik De Raef (Delft, c. 1565 – Rome, 1639), shown on the occasion of his death, based on a painting by his daughter Maddalena, as can be surmised from the details provided at the bottom of the image; to this day the painting has not been found (Luijten 1988, p. 116, no. 3; Petrucci 2008, p. 542; De Laurentiis 2010b, p. 67).
The man changed his original name to Enrico Corvino when he moved to Rome in around 1590. About five years later, he became the owner of the pharmacy marked by the sign of an eagle (Baldriga 2002, p. 233). In the course of his long life, he turned his attention to many fields of knowledge, participating in the cultural ferment of the Eternal City in those years. The Roman ruins and the catacombs, such as those of Domatilla, discovered by Antonio Bosio in 1593, fascinated him and became a destination for archaeological and scientific excursions. His richly stocked laboratory attracted a *bona fide* intellectual circle of literati, patrons of the arts, and artists – who also went there to buy their pigments –, men of science and of letters who for the most part belonged to the Batavian-Alemannic community in seventeenth-century Rome. Among the habitués were the Dutch painter and engraver Adam Elsheimer and the German Johannes Faber, a member of Accademia dei Lincei and doctor at the hospital of Santo Spirito in Sassia, as well as the director of the Papal

Botanical Garden and a follower of the Doctrine of Signatures (Belloni Speciale 1993).
It is widely believed that De Raef commissioned to the painter Giovanna Garzoni the plates for the *Piante varie* manuscript today conserved a Dumbarton Oaks, Washington D.C., dating of which is still debated (Barker 2020, p. 19). The *horto corviniano* – Corvino's botanical garden – in Vicolo de' Riari was considered one of the richest in the city. Giovan Pietro Bellori (1664, ed. 1976, pp. 27–28) was still singing its praises in 1664, mentioning the miniatures by Maddalena who was "renowned for this art" (Mazzetti di Pietralata 2010, p. 95). The Dutch apothecary's many interests found a certain correspondence with those of his erudite brother-in-law Pietro Castelli, son of the painter and miniaturist originally from Brussels, Frans van de Casteele, and the brother of Catherine, whom Corvino married in 1603 (Michel 1995, p. 401).
Before moving to Paris and receiving the appointment as the king's engraver in 1646, Johannes Valdor II was active in Rome between 1639 and 1640, and during his stay in Rome, he made the small portrait of Corvino. Fully in step with the graphic style of the time, he favoured the use of parallel lines and rather wide cross-hatchings, a method more suited to the use of the burin, a technique that he used in his work for the *Chalcographie du Roi*. The flowers overflowing from the cornucopias decorating the medallion with the herbalist's likeness stand out for their three-dimensionality, and clearly refer to the subject's botanical expertise and the extraordinary legacy of rare and precious plants he cultivated. The ornaments enclose, almost as if to form a coat of arms, two crossed swords surmounted by an eagle, an allusion to his pharmacy in Rome. Despite his advanced age, Enrico Corvino's face shows a keen gaze, a sign of his intellectual vitality, highlighted by the dense stippling of the flesh and the lines marking individual strands of hair animate the regular hatching, either parallel or crossed, of the background and the shading. The touching inscription, which repeats the word *unicus*, stresses Maddalena's ties with her father, who certainly played a role of primary importance in her activity as painter and miniaturist.
For the Corsini collection volume containing print published here, the hypothesis of a Medici provenance has been proposed (Pezzini Bernini 2001, p. 80).
Gabriella Bocconi

4.9
Maddalena Corvina
Rome, 1607 – Rome, 1664
Young Gentleman Holding Gloves
1639
Gouache on parchment, 140 × 110 mm
Inscriptions: in the lower endpaper, "Magdalena Corvina F. Roma 1639"
Fondazione Cavallini Sgarbi

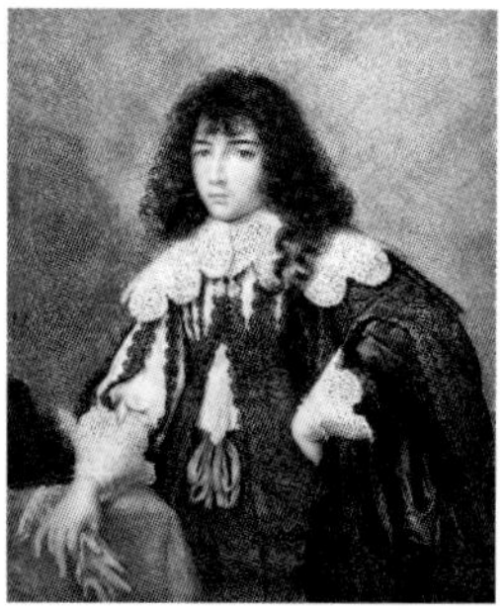

In this small format work, Maddalena Corvina portrays an elegant young man in three-quarters view, his right arm resting on a table. An air of sadness transpires from his eyes, a hint of a beard slightly darkens his complexion. The neutral background showcases the rendering, particularly realistic, of the fabrics, from the brocade to the velvets, the lustrous silk, the lacy collar completely covering the man's shoulders, in vogue at the time. The meticulous depiction of the attire highlights its preciousness and confers nobility on an almost idealised, extremely delicate physiognomy. The formal pose contrasts with the subject's expression as he gazes at the observer, as if to establish a more intimate and relaxed relationship, conveying the fragility of the moment in a man's life that marks his transition from youth to adulthood.
During the seventeenth century there was boom in the production of small format works, carried out on wood, paper, parchment, or oil on copper, primarily landscapes, still lifes, portraits, sacred or mythological subjects for decoration of the home, often commissioned by middle class buyers who had little space available for display. In the Netherlands, this "minor" painting sector had already become established in previous centuries, thanks to the influence of a burgeoning bourgeoisie. One of the painters who tried his luck with this sector in Rome was not coincidentally the Dutchman Adam Elsheimer (1578–1610), member of the same Batavian-Alemannic community to which Maddalena's father belonged.
Maddalena herself worked in the papal capital in a period that was particularly bountiful for European culture, and she brought with her the Flemish temperament linked to her family heritage, while assimilating the ideas of the Baroque aesthetics as they took shape within the context of the Barberini court's patronage (Lollobrigida 2017b, p. 123). Her miniature works fit in with an international trend that enjoyed greater success between Flanders and France, and only started to dwindle with the advent of photography. The *Young Gentleman Holding Gloves* may be added to the small body of works by the Roman artist currently identified (De Laurentiis 2010b, p. 67, fig. 101, p. 75 note 111). The attribution to Corvina is supported by the presence in the lower endpaper of the signature "Magdalena Corvina F. Roma 1639". It is part of the collection of the Fondazione Cavallini Sgarbi (*L'arte delle donne* 2007, pp. 93 and 341).
The drawing had been sold at a Christies's auction on 7 July 1998 (Olm Master Drawings, lot no. 128). It is chronologically positioned together with the lost drawing made on the occasion of her father Hendrik De Raef's death, preparatory for the engraving by Johannes Valdor (see cat. 4.8).
Gabriella Bocconi

4.10
Giovanna Garzoni
Ascoli Piceno, 1600 – Rome, 1670
Emmanuel Philibert of Savoy
c. 1632–1637
Tempera on parchment, 425 × 330 mm
Inscriptions: signed lower right "Giovanna Garzoni F."
Turin, Musei Reali – Palazzo Reale, inv. 1966, no. 5206

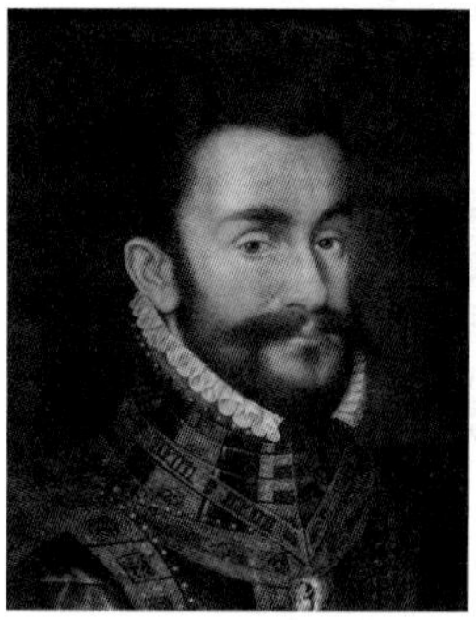

The portrait of Emmanuel Philibert, Duke of Savoy from 1553 to 1580, called "Iron Head" for his military stubbornness, is the twin to the one depicting his son Charles Emmanuel, both documented in the Palazzo Reale collection (Pettenati, in *Diana* 1989, p. 140, cat. 145). In this case as well, it is a posthumous portrait taken from an existing model: the artist was asked to turn her hand to official court portraiture, still based on Mannerist models.
The characteristic facial features are derived from the full-length portrait of the duke by Giacomo Vighi, called L'Argenta, conserved at the Galleria Sabauda in Turin, and from another half-length example, attributed to the same artist, now in the Geneva Musée d'Art et d'Histoire (Casale 1991, pp. 52–53, A 3). In the miniature here, Emmanuel Philibert is captured in three-quarters profile, dressed in finely chiselled armour, wearing the Collar of the Annunciation, the highest honour of the House of Savoy. Garzoni positioned her perfectly calligraphic signature to the right, just above the figure's shoulder. Her technical skill is exceedingly recognisable for its high pictorial quality and the fine rendering of the materials, distinctive characteristics of her style. This sample of decorative virtuosity in the armour goes along with the meticulous definition of the facial features and the refined execution of the subject's hair, beard and moustache, so fine as to seem silken threads

(Casale, in *Gli incanti* 1996, p. 38, cat. 6). The work is therefore part of an iconographic cycle dedicated to the main exponents of the ducal family, a series of small-format images, similar to those that would be commissioned to the artist by members of the French nobility and the Grand Dukes of Tuscany (Solinas, in *De dames* 2018, p. 182, cat. 46).
Matteo Procaccini

4.11
Giovanna Garzoni
Ascoli Piceno, 1600 – Rome, 1670
Charles Emmanuel I of Savoy
c. 1632–1637
Tempera on parchment, 430 × 330 mm
Inscriptions: signed lower left "Giovanna Garzoni F."
Turin, Musei Reali – Palazzo Reale, inv. 1966, no. 5246

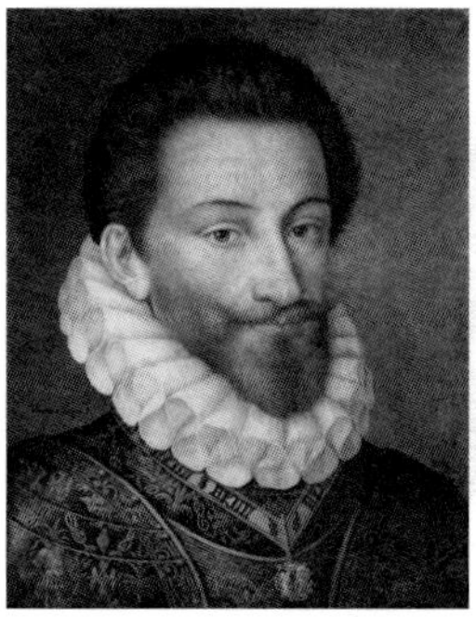

The portrait, signed to the lower left, just above the subject's shoulder, depicts Charles Emmanuel I, Duke of Savoy from 1580 to 1630, and is one of the finest works realised by Garzoni during her stay at the Savoy court, between 1632 and 1637. The miniaturist had been summoned to Turin by Christine of France through her intermediary in Rome, Count Ludovico d'Agliè (Baudi di Vesme 1963–1982, II, pp. 516–517). Explicitly mentioned in the surviving accounting documents as in the exclusive service of the duchess, who assigned her an annual stipend, Garzoni found at court a favourable view of the art of the miniature, both for the practice of portraiture and for the naturalistic representations, attested in the inventories of the ducal collections between the private rooms in Palazzo San Giovanni and the Castle of Valentino (Failla, in *La reggia* 2007, II, p. 41). The portrait of Charles Emmanuel I belongs to the series of four known works portraying the members of the Savoy dynasty: it is, in fact, paired with the other depicting his father Emmanuel Philibert, kept in the same Musei Reali collection in Turin – Palazzo Reale (inv. 5206; cat. 4.10), while the two parchments with the likenesses of his wife Catalina Micaela of Spain and his son Victor Amadeus I are in the Gallerie degli Uffizi (Galleria delle Statue e delle Pitture, inv. 1890, nos. 814, 817). Even though it is a portrait from memory, the painting shows Garzoni's refined drawing and elegant painting technique, with a remarkable realism in the rendering of the young duke's facial features (Solinas, in *De dames* 2018, p. 182, cat. 46). The portrait must have been made a few years after his death, borrowing the facial features from the numerous examples of official court portraits made by the Flemish painter Jan Kraeck, called Caracca (Panero, in *Le meraviglie* 2016, pp. 36–37, cat. 21). The *condottiero*'s vivid gaze is, moreover, highlighted by the showy collar in fine Flemish cloth, which leaves room for the collar of the Supreme Order of the Most Holy Annunciation, and the golden gleams of the precious armour he wears, richly adorned by the heraldic symbols of the House of Savoy.
Matteo Procaccini

4.12
Giovanna Garzoni
Ascoli Piceno, 1600 – Rome, 1670
Lapdog with Biscotti and a Chinese Cup
1648
Tempera on parchment, 275 × 395 mm
Inscriptions: signed in the lower righthand corner "Giovanna Garzoni F."
Florence, Gallerie degli Uffizi, inv. Pal. 4770

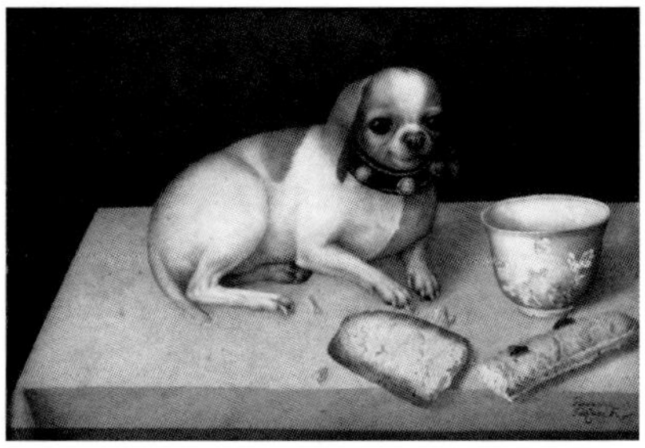

The parchment, signed on the lower right edge of the tablecloth, was certainly made as a gift to Vittoria Della Rovere, as we learn from a note by Garzoni herself in the *Fatture*: "Her ladyship has had a lapdog and two little pictures of flowers". In the Medici inventories, its early provenance from the Poggio Imperiale villa is also documented, described as hanging on the wall: "[…] a white and red small dog, lying on a small table covered with red velvet, with two slices of almond paste biscuits and a porcelain cup" (Casale 1991, p. 118). It is known that this was the favourite residence of the Grand Duchess of Tuscany, who was quite fond of surrounding herself with her pets. The little dog, portrayed life-sized, is a lapdog of the pug breed, a small animal popular with noblewomen and especially appreciated for the rarity of the white colour of its coat. This type of animal was part of an established diplomatic tradition of the exchange of gifts between the Medici duchy and the main courts of the time (Hogan, in *La grandezza* 2020, p. 162, cat. 24).
From a stylistic point of view, the miniature hinges on the contrast between the black ground and the red velvet tablecloth where the dog is curled up, where the very delicate pointillism used by Garzoni seems almost to allow the tablecloth to change colour based on the slant of the natural light. However, the portrait of the animal differs noticeably in tone from the official ones commissioned by Christine of Lorraine and Federico Ubaldo, respectively the grandmother and father of Grand Duchess Vittoria: the framing of the pose, the detail of the leather collar decorated with small jingle bells, and, in particular, the definition of the animal's sweet gaze are all intended to enhance its inherent qualities, making this a true study in psychology. Furthermore, the introduction of the still-life elements of the slice of bread, complete with crumbs, and the almond paste biscuit, freshly broken and beset by flies, stands out as a real exercise in virtuoso painting technique by Garzoni. The technical highpoint in the rendering of detail is reached, however, with the almost opalescent reflections of the cup glazed in pastel grey and blue hues, recently identified as one of the precious artefacts of Dehua porcelain pottery already present in the Medici collections since the early seventeenth century (Morena, in *La grandezza* 2020, p. 164, cat. 25).
Matteo Procaccini

4.13
Giovanna Garzoni
Ascoli Piceno, 1600 – Rome, 1670
Glass Vase with Flowers
1648
Tempera on parchment, 330 × 230 mm
Private collection, inv. 650

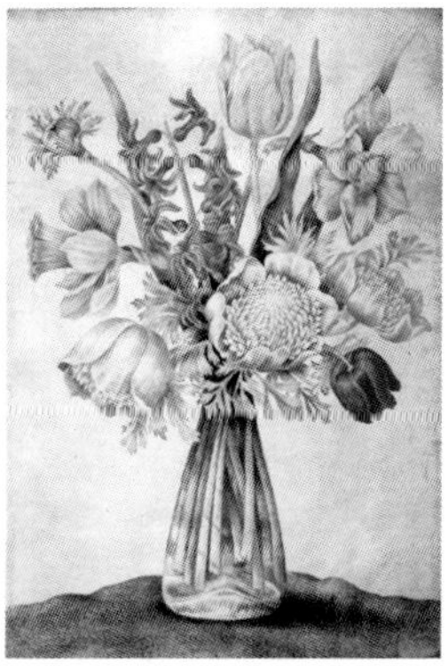

This miniature represents an example of the brilliance of Giovanna Garzoni who, with her usual descriptive precision, depicts a colourful bouquet submerged in a transparent glass carafe. The botanical species introduced in the composition are rather common: in fact, we can identify anemones, narcissi, hyacinths and tulips, shown at different stages of blooming, without any of them presenting signs of wilting (Tongiorgi Tomasi 2002, p. 87, cat. 53). The small vase, called *caraffina* (small carafe) in the seventeenth-century inventories of the Medici villa of Poggio Imperiale (Casale 1991, p. 97), looks much like the one depicted in a parchment in the Accademia di San Luca (c. 16), dating from the artist's years in Florence (Policicchio, in *De dames* 2018, p. 216, cat. 48.16), and another one conserved in the Gabinetto

Disegni e Stampe of the Uffizi (inv. 2138 Orn.), where she renders sophisticated effects of transparency and reflections of light. The stylistic affinities and the dimensions that this parchment shares with the latter confirm its identification as one of the two temperas conceived as a matching pair, made on commission for Vittoria Della Rovere and paid in full to Garzoni in 1648 (Meloni Trkulija 1986, p. 98). From the *Fatture*, it is possible to reconstruct the dispatch to the Duchess of "two small carafes of flowers" (Casale, in *Gli incanti* 1996, p. 56), together with the miniature showing the *Lapdog with Biscotti and a Chinese Cup* (cat. 4.12). The meticulous description of the different floral varieties does not at all inhibit the poetic vein of the composition, derived from the typologies of Nordic still lifes from the same period, especially Flemish ones, due to the modelling of the buds that stand out against the white ground of the support. Finally, the section showing the detail of the stems refracted, distorted on the surface of the vase, is demonstration of Garzoni's excellent knowledge of the contemporary scientific developments in the field of optics (Bliznukov, in *Donne* 2020, p. 96, cat. 39).
Matteo Procaccini

4.14
Giovanna Garzoni
Ascoli Piceno, 1600 – Rome, 1670
Still Life with Squash
c. 1650
Tempera on parchment, 222 × 343 mm
Private collection, inv. 488

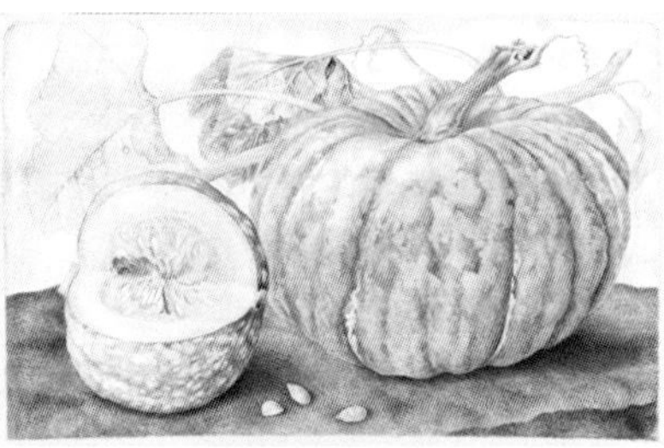

The parchment shows two different species of squash, a classic specimen of *Curcubita maxima*, which occupies the middle ground, and a *Curcubita pepo*, in the foreground to the left, both at centre stage of the composition, in keeping with an iconographic practice much in vogue at the Medici court between the seventeenth and eighteenth centuries (Tongiorgi Tomasi 2002, p. 83, cat. 52). The smaller specimen is shown upside down and cut open, deprived of a quarter of its pulp, a scenic device that allows Garzoni to show off not only the excellent quality of her brushwork, but also the didactic-academic purpose of this type of creation. In the background, framing the composition, is a branch cut from the same plant, highlighting the painter's mastery in rendering the typical downy surface of the large cucurbit leaves (Bliznukov, in *Donne* 2020, p. 98, cat. 40).

Although this miniature has always been paired with the one showing the *Muskmelon and Slice of Watermelon* from the Galleria Palatina in Florence (inv. 1890, no. 4771; Casale 1991, p. 80, A 27), an even more fitting comparison can be established with another version of *Still Life with Squash*, already pointed out in a private collection (Casale 1996, p. 17), confirming Garzoni's personal penchant for repeating the same subject several times, albeit with minimal variations. In this version, the accentuated foreshortening of the *Curcubita moschata*, seen sideways, makes the miniaturist's use of a convex mirror even more obvious; this tool served to facilitate projection of three-dimensional objects onto a plane (Spike 1983, p. 68): it is a technical device that makes it possible to define the picture on the surface, creating that peculiar effect of spatial abstraction characteristic of Garzoni's naturalistic compositions.
Matteo Procaccini

4.15
Giovanna Garzoni
Ascoli Piceno, 1600 – Rome, 1670
Figs with a Beetle
c. 1650
Tempera on parchment, 152 × 184 mm
Private collection, inv. 957

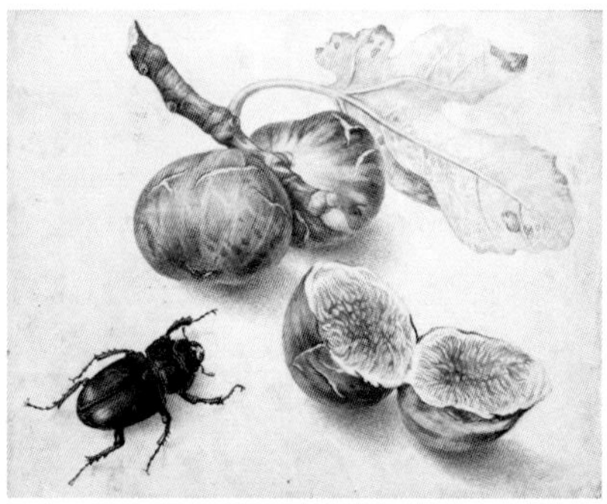

This small miniature shows a pair of ripe figs still attached to a piece of branch, along with a large, withered leaf, against a neutral backdrop; a little lower down, in the foreground to the right, is a detail of a fig split open, allowing Garzoni to show the inside, characterised by the small seeds and stringy, reddish pulp. This device, also used in a preparatory study for similar compositions (see Casale 1991, p. 85, A 31), demonstrates the didactic and academic intent of this typology of works, which become objects of botanical study. In fact, if a fundamental precedent can be identified in the naturalistic tables created by Jacopo Ligozzi for the Medici court, we cannot, however, deny the exquisitely aesthetic purposes assumed by compositions of this type: the miniaturist from Ascoli manages to render the idea of a very ripe fruit, minutely describing the cracks in the peel, thanks to compact and fluid brushstrokes that render the luminous surface of the fruits. On the left, there is a beetle (*Melolontha melolontha*), similar to the "Bark beetle" in a parchment that appeared briefly on the market with an attribution to the German scientific illustrator Sibylla Merian (Wannenes, 3 December 2013, lot 49). The stiffness of the position suggests that the beetle was not drawn "from life", as was Garzoni's usual practice, but rather copied from a model appearing in an *herbarium*. Although it has been hypothesised that this work, also in light of its very small dimensions, may have been an example for the decoration of some handheld fans created for Grand Duchess Vittoria Della Rovere (Tongiorgi Tomasi 2002, p. 85, cat. 51), the stylistic similarities with the miniatures contained in the Accademia di San Luca album support the idea that it came from some notebooks in which Garzoni had drawn many varieties of flowers, fruits, vegetables, animals and insects, in order to be free to compose her own still life pictures, regardless of the season.
Matteo Procaccini

4.16
Giovanna Garzoni
Ascoli Piceno, 1600 – Rome, 1670
Quince with a Lizard
c. 1650
Tempera on parchment, 154 × 187 mm
Private collection, inv. 956

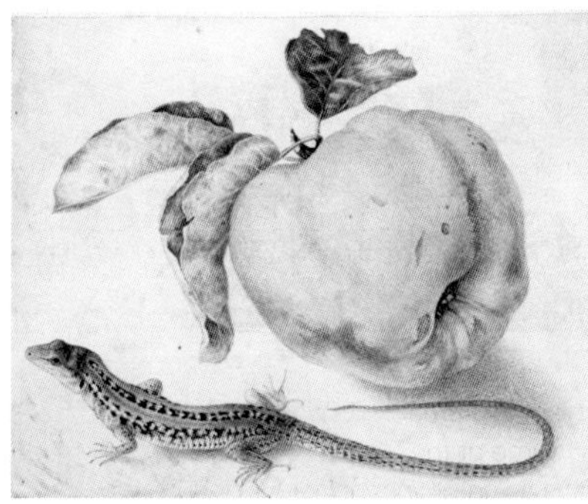

This small miniature shows, against a neutral backdrop, a quince that appears to have been picked several days earlier, given the clear signs of bruising and the large, withered leaves still attached to the stem of the fruit of the *Cydonia oblonga*. Depicted from the bottom, as if it had just fallen from the tree, it casts a shadow on the imaginary pictorial plane, away from which the lizard, slightly lower down, seems to have just darted. The reptile seems to be portrayed in a pose very different from that of other known examples by Garzoni, such as the one that enlivens the foreground of the miniature depicting a *Hyacinth Plant with Four Cherries, a Lizard and an Artichoke*, conserved in the Gabinetto Disegni e Stampe of Uffizi (Inv. 2147; Tongiorgi Tomasi 2020, p. 81, fig. 4), which, due to the unnatural position of the legs was considered derived from a dead specimen, in turn also present, reversed, in a parchment from the Accademia di San Luca album (c. 13; Casale 1991, p. 128, A 69). In fact, in the case shown here, the lizard is captured in a

vigilant pose with a much brighter gaze, in addition to the meticulous rendering of the highlights on the horny scales covering its body, making it quite like the one depicted in a miniature that was briefly on the antiques market with an attribution to Garzoni herself (Dorotheum, 22 October 2019, lot 53). Although, as with the parchment showing the *Figs with a Beetle* (cat. 4.15), it has been identified as an example for the decoration of some fans commissioned by Vittoria Della Rovere (Tongiorgi Tomasi 2002, p. 85, cat. 50), the most striking stylistic feature remains the artist's usual care in rendering the various surfaces of the individual elements making up this composition which, according to an allegorical analysis, could have an underlying moral message (Policicchio, in *De dames* 2018, p. 210, cat, 48.13).
Matteo Procaccini

4.17
Giovanna Garzoni
Ascoli Piceno, 1600 – Rome, 1670
Plate of Apricots with a Rose
c. 1655–1662
Tempera on parchment, 260 × 365 mm
Private collection, inv. 516

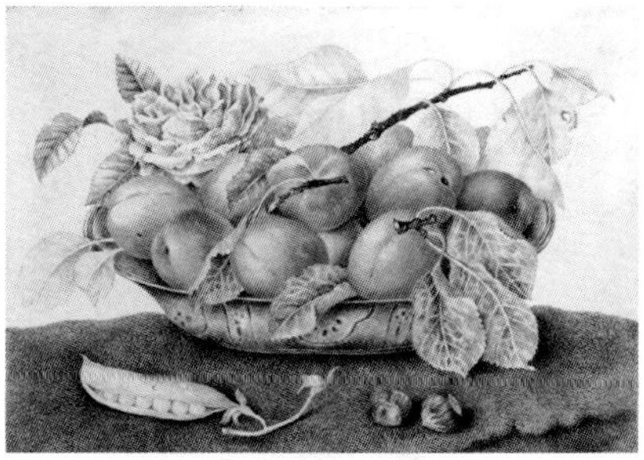

This miniature, exhibited to the public for the first time at the "Gli incanti dell'iride" exhibition (Casale, in *Gli incanti* 1996, pp. 88–89, cat. 31), has been linked to the series of over "twenty Little Pictures on Sheepskin" that at the close of the seventeenth century decorated the Stanza dell'Aurora in the villa of Poggio Imperiale, as can be seen in the Medici inventories (Casale 1991, p. 244). Commissioned to the Ascoli painter by Ferdinando II de' Medici, these "miniatures of fruits" must have been made over a rather long period of time, between the close of her Florentine stay and October 1662, when Garzoni wrote to the Grand Duke thanking him for the generosity shown in the payment for the series (Casale 1991, p. 208, D.I.13). The composition is indeed analogous, in size and in the subject of a naturalistic kind, to the homogeneous nucleus of miniatures still conserved at the Galleria Palatina in Florence (Barker, in *La grandezza* 2020, pp. 196–211, cats. 41–60). A Chinese Kraak porcelain dish, with the characteristic two-tone decoration in white and cobalt blue, very similar to ones kept in the very same setting by Ferdinando II's wife Vittoria Della Rovere (Focarile 2020), is filled with apricots, among which nestles an elegant and magnificent white rose. A newly split-open pea pod and two chestnuts rest on the rocky terrain, accessory elements that also appear in other compositions of the same series (see *Nature morte* 2000, pp. 45, 65). The atmosphere is delicate and subdued, almost rarefied, an effect that the yellow hue of the leafy branch closing off the view seems to heighten. But it is precisely in the depiction of the velvety surface of the apricots, the undisputed protagonists of the composition, that Garzoni provides proof of her very fine brush technique, especially in the rendering of the subtlest play of light, which varies depending on the angle of incidence on the plate and the ripeness of the fruit.
Matteo Procaccini

4.18
Giovanna Garzoni
Ascoli Piceno, 1600 – Rome, 1670
Still Life with Lemons
c. 1655–1662
Tempera on parchment, 225 × 335 mm
Private collection, inv. 550

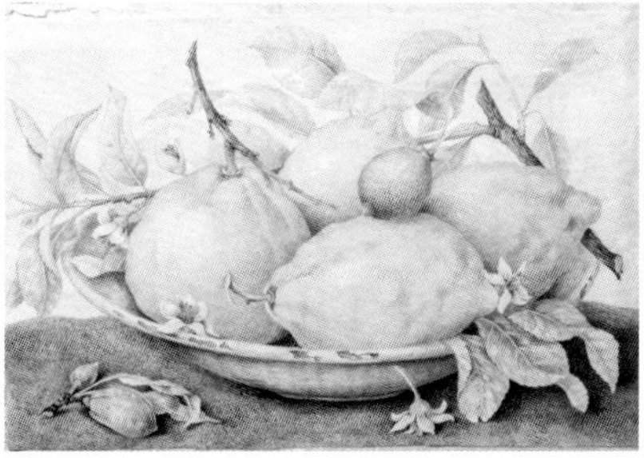

A white pottery bowl, worn on the surface and chipped along the edge, holds five large, ripe lemons and one unripe one, still attached to the leafy branch of the plant, which crosses the composition diagonally. In the parchment, exhibited for the first time in "Gli incanti dell'iride" exhibition (Casale, in *Gli incanti* 1996, pp. 90–91, cat. 32), Garzoni provides proof of her masterful technique in the minute rendering of the naturalistic details of the *Citrus limon*, so that we can recognise the exact *zagara bianca* variety, so-called for the pure white colour of its blossoms, which are shown in various stages of blooming, cadencing the composition. On the rugged foreground to the right, there is the detail of two smaller fruits still attached to a cut branch that, for this very reason, has withered leaves. Even though from a stylistic point of view this parchment can be included in the group of twenty miniatures made for the Grand Duke Ferdinando II, the existence of other digressions that Garzoni dedicated to the same botanical variety also merit consideration, among which are the *Still Life with Bowl of Citrons* conserved at the Getty Museum (inv. 2001.29), where we can still see the influence of the Flemish and Lombard artists in attendance in the Savoy court, and the parchment showing *Three Lemons with a Bumblebee*, already mentioned in the private collection (Tongiorgi Tomasi 2002, p. 88, cat. 55). This type of work helps to shed light on the miniaturist's painstaking technique, starting with the rapid outlining of the subject in black chalk directly on the support, then proceeding to fill in the forms with gouache tempera, applied with compact and very fine brushstrokes, or tiny dots made with the tip of the brush, depending on the details to be rendered, skilfully combining the different shades of colour, often achieving an effect of pointillism.
Matteo Procaccini

4.19
Giovanna Garzoni (attributed)
Ascoli Piceno, 1600 – Rome, 1670
Memento mori
c. 1665–1670
Tempera on parchment, 110 × 135 mm
Ascoli Piceno, Pinacoteca Civica, inv. 121

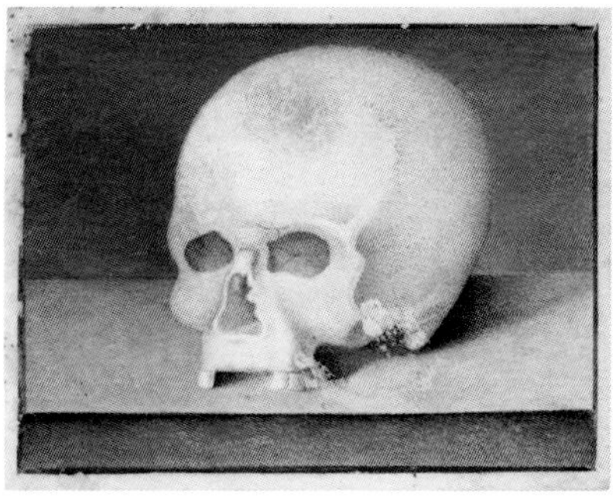

The attribution of the miniature can be traced back to a letter dated 4 May 1869 from Giulio Gabrielli to the mayor of Ascoli Piceno, now conserved in the city's Archivio di Stato (Casale 1991, p. 179). In the letter, we learn of Canon Francesco Bastoni's donation of a few paintings to the Pinacoteca, among which "a miniature parchment, representing a human skull, the work of Giovanna Garzoni, miniaturist from Ascoli" (Gagliardi 1988, p. 24). It is certainly the work shown here, which represents, in the centre, a skull that casts its shadow onto a grey surface, standing out against the azure backdrop. The parchment, characterized by its small dimensions that might suggest it is a clipping, is enriched by a gold border. The attribution of this work to Garzoni has been questioned in the past due to the not-optimal state of conservation of the paint layer, together with a homogeneous nucleus of *vanitas* conserved in the Collezione Lodi in Campione d'Italia (*Natura morta* 1984, p. 106, nos. 43-46). As has been correctly pointed out, the moralising intent is never clearly expressed in Garzoni's compositions, although *vanitas* motifs can be identified in the insertions of withered flowers or overripe fruit. The miniature under examination may well be the most explicit outcome of a profound reflection matured by the artist in her declining years on the transience of life and earthly goods, just before her total loss of sight and physical health put an end to her intense activity as miniaturist.
Matteo Procaccini

4.20
Carlo Maratti
Camerano (Ancona), 1625 – Rome, 1713
Portrait of Giovanna Garzoni
c. 1665
Oil on canvas, 64 × 49 cm
Ascoli Piceno, Pinacoteca Civica, inv. 364

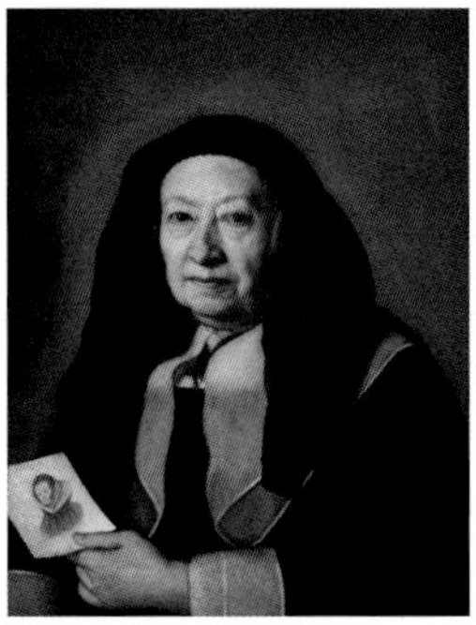

The evocative portrait of the miniaturist Giovanna Garzoni in old age, discovered by Giulio Cantalamessa (1923) and still conserved in the Pinacoteca Civica of Ascoli Piceno, her birthplace, was made by Carlo Maratti at the height of his career, around 1665, after the painter was elected *principe* of the Accademia di San Luca (Solinas, in *De dames* 2018, p. 184, cat. 47). Garzoni herself was intimately linked to the Roman congregation of artists and made regular donations starting in 1654; she also bequeathed to the institution her considerable estate gained from her prolific activity, even though, as a woman, she had never been able to participate in the Academy meetings and lectures (Lukehart 2020).
The painting was initially attributed to Pier Leone Ghezzi, often confused with his father Giuseppe, the author of a copy conserved in the Academy collections (inv. 622); a third copy was stolen from the chapel that Garzoni had requested to be built inside the church of the artists, dedicated to Saints Luke and Martina. The subject's deep and magnetic gaze looms out from the oval of her face, carved from the black veil and made heavy by time's mark on her features. The elegant dress worn by Garzoni is refined and austere, almost monastic, and it announces her condition as widow, following the suicide of the Venetian portraitist Tiberio Tinelli, to whom she had been joined in matrimony between 1622 and 1624 (Bottacin 1998, p. 142). In her left hand, the artist seems to show to the observer a small portrait of a young woman in travelling clothes, a sort of pictorial *vanitas* that recalls Garzoni's moment of greatest success, when she was summoned to the most important courts of Europe (Barker 2020).
After her initial training in Venice at Giacomo Rogni's school of calligraphy, the artist was able to develop her own personal style during her first stay in Florence, thanks to an early familiarity with Jacopo Ligozzi's naturalistic representations, and later in Rome, under the influence of the scientific studies promoted by the Accademia dei Lincei, when she was introduced there by the scholar and collector Cassiano dal Pozzo. After her formative stays between the Savoy court, England, and the court of Louis XII of France, Garzoni returned into the service of the Grand Duchy of the Medici between 1642 and 1651, the year in which she decided to return to Rome, where she remained until her death.
Matteo Procaccini

4.21
Claude Mellan
Abbeville (France), 1598 – Paris, 1688
Portrait of Virginia Vezzi
1626
Burin, 113 × 78 mm
Inscriptions: on the oval frame "VIRGINIA DE VEZZO DA VELLETRI PITTRICE"; in the lower margin "Qui saggia mano ha di Virginia accolto / Gli occhi. la fronte. il crin co i tratti suoi; / Ma. se l'arte. e lo spirto ammirar vuoi, / Mira le tele sue, piu ch. il suo. volto. / Cl Mellan franc. F. – Rom. 1626"
Rome, Istituto centrale per la grafica, Gabinetto Stampe, inv. FC32049 (property of the Accademia Nazionale dei Lincei)

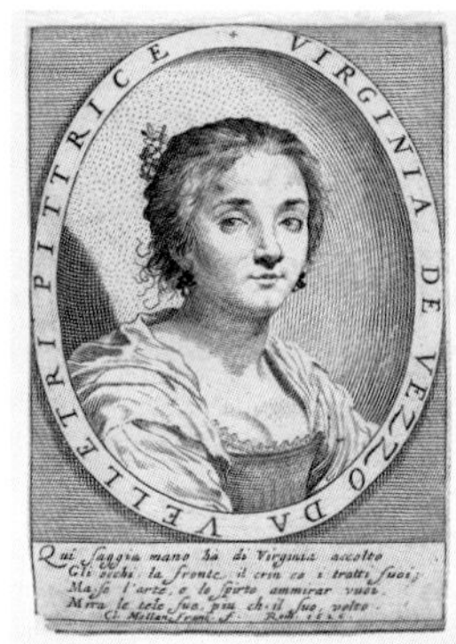

The Velletri-born painter is shown in three-quarters view, as she looks to the side, her hair gathered in the back with some flowers, a dimple in her chin, a dress with a tight-fitting bodice and wide, flowing sleeves. The engraving was made in the year of her marriage to Vouet – the flowers in her hair could be orange blossoms –, when she was already a member of the Accademia di San Luca and she was also the muse and model of the French painter (*Simon Vouet* 2008, p. 201). During those years, Virginia worked in full partnership with her husband, who had already established a family workshop in Rome. Her works soon began to be confused with those of the celebrated Vouet (Tersenghi 1926, p. 59).
She was in any case an esteemed painter, if in that same year, 1626, the poet Marcello Giovannetti published a collection of poems that included a sonnet entitled *Per una Danae, Dipinta dalla Sig. Virginia Vezzi*, dedicated to a painting by Virginia. The verse speaks about love and painting and refers to the female hand that created the painting, and Virginia's talent is praised on a par with that of her male colleagues (Crelly 1992, p. 180).
Claude Mellan arrived in Rome in 1624, and the following year he was living in the same house as Vouet, where he was registered as "Claudio engraver" (Bousquet 1952, p. 298). In contact with Vouet, he perfected his technique, and before engraving Virginia's portrait he also made a reversed engraving of a drawing (Städel Museum, Frankfurt), in which the painter's features and face make up the basis of this work. The artist made some thirty portraits of friends and colleagues, but only about ten of them were realised in print form (*Claude Mellan* 1989, p. 208).
In the Frankfurt drawing, the painter's face is rendered in a simple manner, while in the engraving, the shadows and highlights of the face are not accentuated, but the simplicity of the lines maintains the grace of the face and the beauty of the figure.
The oval of the face, the dimple on the chin, and the hair gathered at the nape are recurring features in the drawings of Vouet, who portrayed Virginia, known not only for her talent as a painter, but also for her extraordinary beauty (Crilly 1992, p. 184). The engravings realised for the couple's works bear witness to the close relationship between the three artists; in 1627, Mellan would become the godfather of Francesca Vouet, the couple's firstborn and the only one of the children to be born in Italy (Bousquet 1952, p. 299).
Even as *principe* of the Accademia di San Luca, Vouet often dedicated his attention to the teaching of drawing from life; in France, always alongside his wife, he would continue this practice, producing numerous studies of details (in charcoal with white heightening) and overall (in charcoal or lavis over a charcoal or red chalk sketch) (Brejon de Lavergnée 1991, p. 229). Even if we know that his output of portraits during his period in Italy was prolific, today many have gone missing, and some are only known through the engravings of them (in the years in Rome, by Mellan; in France, the ones that Vouet himself made and owned), while others that had once been found are now no longer available (Brejon de Lavergnée 2011, p. 245).
In Paris, Virginia continued to make portraits and drawings, and she handled the teaching of women, including,"among others, one of the daughters of *sieur* Metheseau, architect to the King, and the young lady Stabre" (Félibien 1705, III, p. 306); at the time, in fact, young women were not allowed to apprentice with a painter of the male sex and the only ones who could be oriented towards painting were daughters or sisters of painters – thus their education was all in the family – or princesses or noblewomen who could take on a private instructor (Thuillier 1991b, p. 37).
The Rennes Musée des Beaux-Arts conserves the drawing of a *Half-Length Figure of a Young Woman*, which, according to the description, was made by Marie Metézeau, a copy of one of Vezzi's drawings of 1636 (Brejon de Lavergnée 1991, p. 229).
Sara Bruno

4.22
Claude Mellan (after Virginia Vezzi)
Abbeville (France), 1598 – Paris, 1688
Judith with the Head of Holofernes
c. 1626
Burin, 163 × 114 mm
Inscriptions: on the lower margin "Pudica vincit impudicum dextera, / Pia impium necat, ebriosum sobria"; to the left "Virginia da Vezzo pinx"; to the right "Cl. Mellan Gall.(us)f. Roma."
Rome, Istituto centrale per la grafica, inv. FC43866 (property of the Accademia Nazionale dei Lincei)

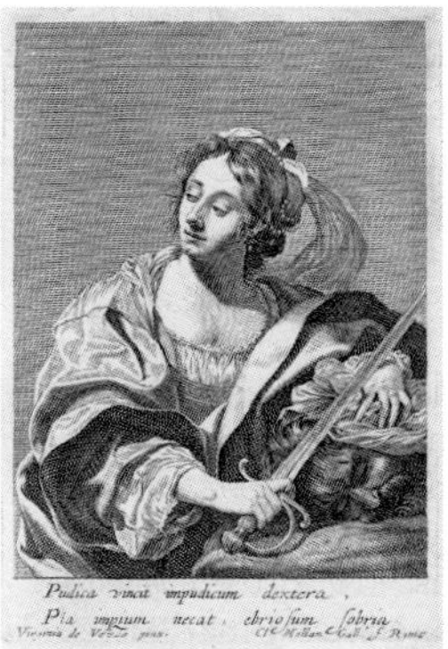

Mellan's engraving depicts the only work ascribed with certainty to the artist, and it was of fundamental importance in the attribution to her of the Nantes Musée des Beaux-Arts *Judith*, a recognition first made by Olivier Michel (1992, p. 127).

The Nantes *Judith* is an oil on canvas (98 × 74.4 cm), formerly in the Busiri-Vici collection; it was part of the Galleri W. Apolloni collection in Rome until 2009, when it was purchased by the Nantes Musée des Beaux-Arts (*Simon Vouet* 2008, p. 200).

Mellan's engraving, later accurately copied by Charles David as well, was made before 1627, the year of Virginia's departure for Paris, since Mellan stayed in Rome and would not have seen the work after that date (*Claude Mellan* 1989, p. 218); it probably dates from 1626, because most of the engravings made of the couple's works were from that year, while the canvas may have been earlier, possibly painted in 1624 as Vezzi's presentation tableau for admittance to the Accademia di San Luca (Michel 1992, p. 127).

Judith is a frequent subject in the work of all the women painters we know of: champion and protectress of the Israelites, the violence of her act was justified for the purpose of liberating the Jewish people.

In Vezzi's *Judith*, however, the murderous act is secondary, and the paladin is shown in a moment of reflection afterwards (*Simon Vouet* 2008, p. 200). The voluminous drapery of her robes attenuates the presence of the sword and Holoferne's head, which is in a secondary plane, almost covered by Judith's arm. It can be assumed, as in the case of Artemisia Gentileschi's *Allegory of Painting*, that the face of the paladin is a self-portrait of the artist in the role of Judith.

The face is round and there is a dimple on the chin, also visible in the portrait of Virginia engraved by Claude Mellan (cat. 4.21); furthermore, the facial features seem like those of the female figures in the works of Vouet for which we know that she posed as a model.

Virginia appears as an established painter and, even though in general her style shows Vouet's influence (Judith's profile and nose, her long fingers, and the colours of the robes are similar to Simon's works from the final years in Rome), the contours are sharper, and the drawing is more incisive (*Simon Vouet* 2008, p. 200).

The same pose that characterises Vezzi's *Judith* can be found in another canvas on the same subject, now at the Alte Pinakothek in Munich, which is very similar in the robes and the layout of the painting.

After the two artists married, also in light of the many commissions that Simon received, it appears that Virginia's role was mainly that of model and collaborator, in addition to drawing teacher, and she was perhaps dedicated to the realisation of easel paintings. Since Vezzi's *Judith* does not seem to have been an isolated case and, given the numerous commissions to Simon's workshop between 1624 and 1627, it is possible that most of the half-length figures and similar compositions known as Vouet's works may have been done by his wife (Thuillier 1991b, p. 34).

The engraving of the *Judith* is consistent with Simon Vouet's decision to have his printed works reproduced starting in the 1620s; later, the same artist, who owned the copperplates and press, and who shortly after Virginia's death had forty engraved plates and nearly four thousand engraved sheets in his studio (Thullier 1991c, pp. 57–58), began to print and sell his engravings; it is possible that Virginia also worked alongside her husband in this kind of activity.
Sara Bruno

4.23
Simon Vouet
Paris, 1590 – Paris, 1649
Madonna and Child
(*Madonna of the Basket*)
1625–1626
Oil on panel, 132 × 98 cm
Florence, Gallerie degli Uffizi, inv. 1890, no. 984

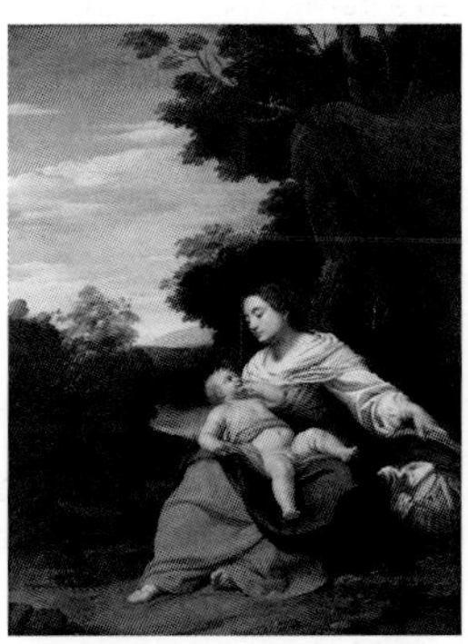

The painter situates the composition in a landscape, where the Virgin wearing flowing mantle and robes holds the Child in her lap while she opens the basket with her left hand. The Child is plump and smiling, and the Virgin, in her graceful pose, is one of the artist's variations on female heads with perfectly oval faces, a heavy chignon and downcast eyes, in this case, in three-quarters view. The Virgin's face seems to be one of the many portraits of Virginia Vezzi, whose husband often used her as a muse and a model in the creation of female subjects. The painting was long attributed to La Hyre, until the restoration in the 1970s, when Pierre Rosemberg ascribed it with certainty to Simon Vouet, placing it chronologically in the late Roman years, based on comparisons of the artist's work from that time, such as the *Virgin with Saints Elizabeth, John the Baptist and Catherine* in the Prado, and the *Rest on the Flight into Egypt* in San Francisco; the similarities are above all with the latter, made in 1626 for Cardinal Francesco Barberini, also on wood panel (*Pittura francese* 1977, p. 159). Also from the same period is the Berlin *Annunciation* from the Giustiniani collection, lost, almost always seen in connection with the Prado painting (Loire 2011, p. 196), outstanding for the figure of the Virgin, the drapery, the basket in the foreground with more drapery and the simplicity of the setting.

The painting shows how Vouet, before his return to France in 1627, had changed his style and had taken on a brighter, more elegant, and refined manner. This was the period when Simon and Virginia began to collaborate very closely, attending the Accademia di San Luca (of which Virginia was a member and Simon was *principe*, often holding meetings in their home), and they were prominent figures on the Roman art scene (Michel 1992, p. 125).

In this painting in the Uffizi, the execution seems particularly painstaking, both in the rendering of the Virgin and Child, and for the importance of the landscape (Loire 2011, p. 204).

The contact with Lanfranco and the painting of the Carraccis, together with the shift towards a clearer and brighter style that would later characterize the French manner, seems particularly evident; the execution is nimbler, and the chromatic refinement recalls the Emilian manner and the Carracci use of colour.

Upon his arrival in Italy, Vouet was interested in naturalism and the realistic representation of the human figure "in flesh and blood", as well as in the Venetian use of colour and Tintoretto's chiaroscuro (Thuillier 1991a, p. 22). Over time, he grew away from Caravaggism as he gradually developed an increasingly complex style that was more cultured and more attentive to classical references; there were numerous contacts and reciprocal exchanges, including the likes of Reni and Lanfranco, whose elegant and

refined style – Baroque, classicist, and almost neo-Correggesque – the French painter appreciated (Schleier 1992, pp. 209–210). Vezzi's painting, too, seems to have significant points of contact with Lanfranco himself, as well as with Guercino, who was in Rome 1621–1623.
Simon Vouet appreciated the works of the Carraccis, Annibale in particular, and had purchased a *Madonna and Child* of his, which the couple took to France and which appears in the inventory of the painter's possessions upon his death (Collange 2008, p. 33).
Upon his return to France, Vouet continued to consider drawing the foundation of his teaching and the style of the atelier, to which Virginia also contributed, was based on the study of anatomy using models and on the observation of nature (Brejon de Lavergnée 1991, p. 229).
His period in Italy appears as a phase of study and experimentation, aiming at the elaboration of a personal style of high quality, attentive to design and execution, that, upon his return to France, culminated in lucrative commissions and his appointment as *Premier peintre du Roi*. The artist's brilliant style, under the influence of Reni, Lanfranco and the Venetian painters first Tintoretto, then Veronese – led him to develop the luminous style that dominated French painting for nearly twenty-five years (Temperini 1999, p. 247).
Sara Bruno

4.24
Simon Vouet
Paris, 1590 – Paris, 1649
with the collaboration of Virginia Vezzi
Velletri (Rome), 1600 – Paris, 1638
Angel with Tunic and Dice
1627
Oil on canvas, 104 × 77 cm
Naples, Museo e Real Bosco di Capodimonte, inv. Q1141

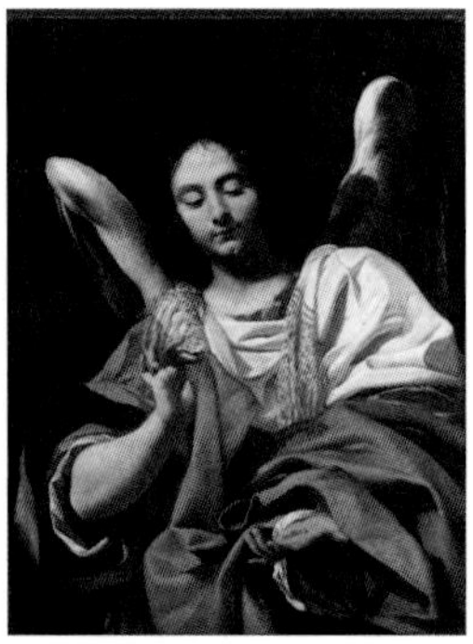

4.25
Simon Vouet
Paris, 1590 – Paris, 1649
Angel with Sponge and Spear
1627
Oil on canvas, 105 × 80 cm
Naples, Museo e Real Bosco di Capodimonte, inv. Q1142

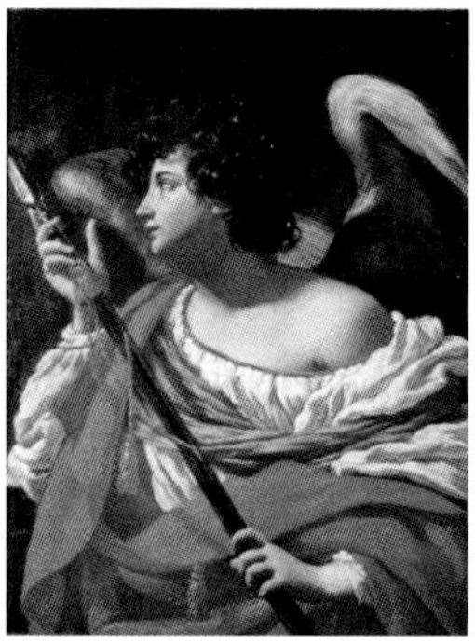

The two canvases are part of a series of twelve paintings commissioned to Simon Vouet by Cardinal Filomarino, mentioned in the inventory of 1700 of his nephew Duke Alfonso Della Torre as "Twelve pictures measuring about three spans by four ish with twelve Angels depicting the Mysteries of the Passion, by Monsù Vouet, with a turquoise-coloured frame with gilt highlights" (Ruotolo 1977, p. 80).
For a long time, only the two figures in the Museo di Capodimonte were known from this pictorial cycle: the *Angel with Tunic and Dice* and the *Angel with Sponge and Spear*, which, among other things, reported different dating, one from the mid-teens of the seventeenth century, and the other from the following decade. In 1969, the Minneapolis Institute of Art purchased two canvases from a Neapolitan private collection showing an *Angel Holding the Vessel and Towel for Washing the Hands of Pontius Pilate* and an *Angel Holding the Superscription from the Cross*, clearly traceable to the Vouet series; following new contributions, it has been possible to trace two other paintings in private collections to the series, an *Angel Holding Judas's Purse with Thirty Pieces of Silver and his Noose* and an *Angel with the Ladder of the Cross* (Fiorillo 1983, p. 208 and *Vouet* 1991, pp. 133–134). An identical copy of the latter subject can be found at the Brindisi Museo Diocesano (Galante, in *Per la storia della chiesa* 1991, pp. 5–9); due to its smaller dimensions, it had been mistakenly believed that the French artist had created two identical series. The smaller size, however, was actually the result of a later modification.
Thus, we know six of the twelve subjects in the series that was made and conserved in Naples, and first mentioned at the start of the eighteenth century as a series of the Apostles in an inventory of Palazzo Filomarino Della Rocca, coming from the estate of Marcantonio Filomarino Della Rocca. Cardinal Ascanio Filomarino, Marcantonio's relative as well as his legal representative, who at the time lived in Rome in Vicolo dell'Osteria Torretta, near the church of San Lorenzo in Lucina and Vouet's residence, had commissioned it directly to the artist. This was not his first commission, because already in 1620 Filomarino had paid him the outstanding balance of 30 scudi on the total bill of 120 "for a painting of 8 spans with many figures that he will have to deliver to him, so it can be sent to Signor Marco Antonio Filomarino" (Lorizzo 2006, p. 116). On 4 May 1623, the cardinal paid the artist the balance of 100 scudi on a total of 250 for the purchase of fifteen paintings depicting the Apostles, a Christ, a Virgin and a Saint John the Baptist (Di Mauro 2008, p. 215) and on 5 June 1627 he paid him another 120 scudi "final payment of the price of 12 Angels he made in 12 paintings" (Lorizzo 2006, p. 117). In 1634 a inventory was drawn up of Vouet's works in the Filomarino collection, among which are listed a *Saint Catherine*, a *Circumcision*, a *Visitation*, and "fourteen paintings of Christ with the Apostles" (the twelve angels), a *Christ*, and a *Saint John* (Lorizzo 2006, p. 15).
Ascanio Filomarino was very close to Vouet and the pro-French milieu of the Barberini family, and the commission had arrived when the painter, by then having reached his maturity in terms of style, had received his most prestigious commissions, shortly before leaving Rome to return to France (*Simon Vouet* 2008, pp. 93–98).
The detailed description of the twelve angels with the Instruments of the Passion admired in Palazzo Filomarino della Rocca – which in the past century became the residence of Benedetto Croce – was provided by the engraver and art critic Charles Nicolas Cochin, who visited Naples together with Madame de Pompadour's brother in 1751 (Cochin 1756, I, p. 191).
The presence of Vouet's angels in Palazzo Filomarino dell Rocca was again attested in 1776, when the Marquis de Sade saw them during his tour of Italy and expressed an unflattering opinion about the collection (De Sade ed. 1996, pp. 257–258).
The canvases inherited by the descendants of Filomarino della Rocca remained there until 1799, and then the collection was dispersed; the two Capodimonte angels were purchased in 1829 from the Oberto collection for the Real Museo Borbonico (*Il Secolo d'Oro* 1994, pp. 34–35 and 72–73).
The iconographic theme of the angels with the symbols of the Passion had medieval origins, but returned in vogue during the Counter-Reformation and in the first half of the seventeenth century; in Rome, contemporary examples substantiating this are the series of six angels in Galleria Pallavicini, erroneously attributed to Vouet, and Bernini's ten sculptures of angels on the Ponte Sant'Angelo (*Vouet* 1991, p. 134).
The Neapolitan series may have been inspired by the *Apostles* painted for Giovan Carlo Doria by Giulio Cesare Procaccini, whose Milanese workshop Vouet visited in 1621, and the title of the cycle is probably also due to this connection (Lorizzo 2006, p. 19).
The theme should also be seen in relation to the most prestigious commissions that Vouet received during his Roman period: the request to fresco the chapel of the Canons in Basilica of San Pietro and to decorate the wall above Michelangelo's *Pietà*. Thus, it

coincides with the final years in Rome, when Simon and Virginia Vezzi, who became his wife in 1626, were members of the Accademia di San Luca and worked together (*Simon Vouet* 2008, pp. 93–98).
The twelve half-length figures created for Filomarino are similar in subject to the details of the fresco made for Saint Peter's, but they are static angels, portrayed frontally or in profile, and they are very beautiful youths, almost in an attitude of reflection.
The commission is also closely linked in terms of chronology and subject to that of the Alaleoni chapel in San Lorenzo in Lucina, where the artist painted angels on the ceiling that recall those under examination in their poses and attitudes (*Simon Vouet* 2008, p. 94).
To honour the many commissions received in these years, Vouet took advantage of the workshop in which his wife, Virginia, and his brother Aubin were active contributors (*Vouet* 1991, pp. 32–34). For the easel works, considering his wife's talent, we can imagine her involvement: the figures of some angels, for the material rendering of the fabrics, and the refined workmanship in the contours of the faces and hands, recall the painter's *Judith* now conserved at Nantes, her only certain work, but which certainly cannot be considered an isolated case (*Vouet* 1991, pp. 32–34).
It is possible that the cycle was carried out jointly, given the number of canvases to finish before returning to France, concomitant with the paintings for San Lorenzo in Lucina. That Vouet had some help from the workshop finds confirmation in the fact that the angels have often been attributed to Mellin or other collaborators (the colours of the Minneapolis pictures are, for example, considered too bright for the artist's painting in the Roman years). In the *Angel with Tunic and Dice*, the collaboration with his wife is more evident, while the *Angel with Sponge and Spear* suggests collaboration with Charles Mellin (Brejon de Lavernée, in *Le collezioni borboniche* 2016, pp. 112–113, no. 220, and pp. 114–116, no. 225); however, the solid forms, the colour ranges and the well-defined contours make the group a coherent series, the overall design of which can be directly attributed to the French artist (Loire 2011, p. 213).
To be sure, the variation of the figures – in the faces and in the rendering of the hands and the drapery – showcases a remarkable, virtuoso flair; the clearly defined contours demonstrate how Vouet's overall vision was well thought out: each figure is characterised and made different from the others in a series that otherwise, given the number of paintings, could have turned out boring.
Sara Bruno

4.26
Plautilla Bricci (execution)
Rome, 1616 – Rome, post 1690
Elpidio Benedetti (concept)
Rome or Poggio Mirteto (Rieti), 1609 – Rome, 1690
Design of the Funeral Monument of Cardinal Giulio Mazzarino
1657
Pen and brown ink, grey watercolour on light-coloured paper, 512 × 391 mm
Inscriptions: on the *recto*, autograph of Elpidio Benedetti, "ISOLATO", and of Plautilla Bricci; in the shield "S.R.E. CARDINALIS MAZARINVS"; in the cartouche "VIVIT ADVC MORTVVS", in the commemorative plaque "IVLIVS M...". Below, in Benedetti's hand: "La base di bianco e nero, li bassi rilievi di marmo, / l'armi di metallo dorato, la morte di metallo, / il libro di [pietra di] paragone, le statue di marmo bianco / rappresentano queste la Giustizia, la Fama e l'Immortalità, questa / sgrida la morte, che vogli registrare il nome del Signor Cardinale / nel libro de' morti, avertendola che se ben morto viverà / immortale il nome di Sua Eminenza come gli mostra notato nel / suo simbolo dell'eternità. / L'urna di nero, o bianco e nero con i gigli, e modelloni [*sic*, medalloni] di / metallo dorato. / Li due angelini di marmo bianco, il ritratto simile / et il festone di metallo dorato"
Turin, Biblioteca Nazionale Universitaria, *Album Valperga*, q.I.65, nos. 155–156

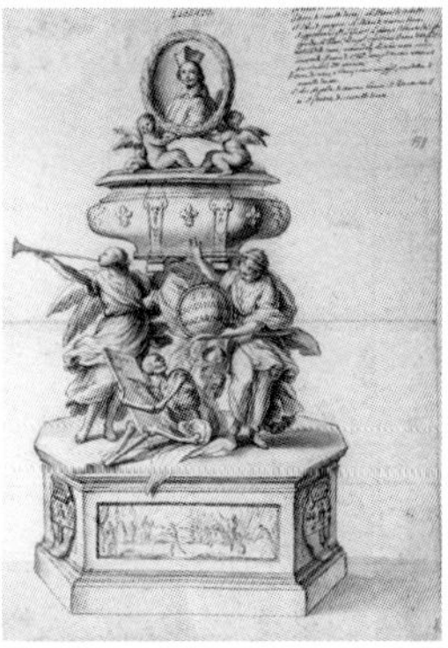

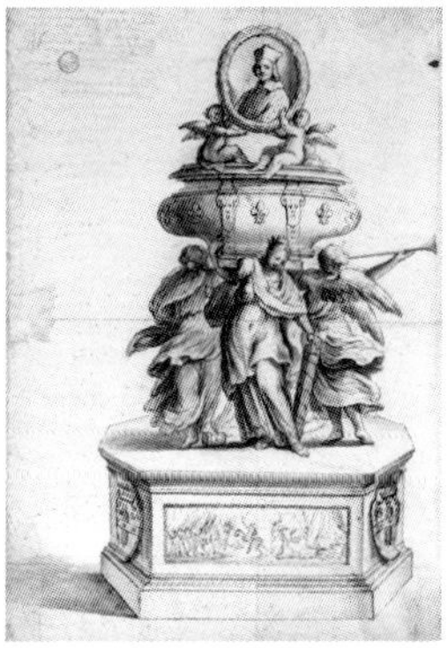

Between 1656 and 1657, Cardinal Giulio Mazzarino envisioned leaving a tangible sign of himself in the city of Paris, in celebration of his glorious accomplishments, so he went about hiring Italian architects for the construction of the Collège des Quatre-Nations, a sort of *ville mazarine* facing the Île de la Cité, comprising a vast palace, a library, and a church with a magnificent mausoleum. It was there that he wished to be buried, similarly to what his predecessor Richelieu had done at the Sorbonne.
After Bernini declined to participate in this undertaking, the prelate had his Roman agent, Abbot Elpidio Benedetti, deliver "a tin tube holding 4 drawings of ideas for the sepulchre" as well as two plans for two distinct funerary monuments, one "placed against the wall" and the other "free-standing". The latter shows a massive octagonal base bearing the Mazarin coat of arms on the short sides while on the long sides are commemorative reliefs of the military triumphs Mazzarino accomplished in Monferrato and during the Thirty Years War. Above, three graceful female allegories support a monumental *imago clipeata* of the cardinal. There is no doubt that the "ideas" for the two tombs were formulated by Benedetti, who wrote in his own hand detailed annotations on the back of the drawings and personally arranged for their dispatch to France. However, he was not the one who actually carried out the projects, which have recently been ascribed by the present writer to an artist from the abbot's inner circle: the painter Plautilla Bricci, debuting here as architect (see Primarosa 2018, to which the reader is referred for the bibliography). In the two drawings, there are abundant references to Bernini's poetics, not by chance: while the medallion portraits recall the funerary monument of the Sister Maria Raggi in Santa Maria sopra Minerva, or that of Alessandro Valtrini in San Lorenzo in Damaso, Death writing the name of Mazzarino in the book is an explicit reference to the tomb of Urban VIII in San Pietro's, while the sculptures supporting the "free-standing" sarcophagus rework the idea of the *Cathedra Petri* in the Vatican, then under construction.
Yuri Primarosa

5.1
Orazio Lomi Gentileschi
Pisa, 1562 – London, 1639
Saint Cecilia Playing the Spinet
1615–1620
Oil on canvas, 90 × 105 cm
Perugia, Galleria Nazionale dell'Umbria, inv. 1083

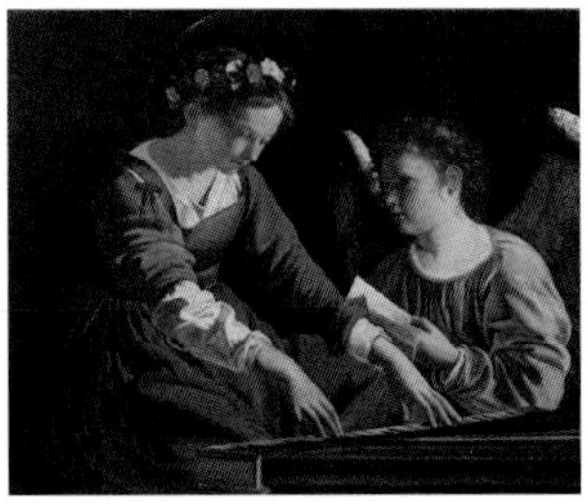

The painting was rediscovered in 1973 by Francesco Santi in the monastery of San Francesco al Borgo in Todi. Acquired in 1976 for the Galleria Nazionale dell'Umbria, it was published by Santi that year and deemed to be a work by Orazio Gentileschi (Santi 1976). Santi compared the painting in Perugia with the version that is in Washington (National Gallery of Art, Kress collection), highlighting the similarities and differences between the two works: the garland and the halo on the saint's head that appears only on the Perugia version; the different colours in the angel's wings; and a spinet in the Perugian painting and an organ in the Washington version. According to Erich Schleier and Diane de Grazia, who published the documentation that assigned the heads to Orazio and the rest of the Washington *Saint Cecilia* to Giovanni Lanfranco, this latter work is datable to around 1620–1621 (de Grazia, Schleier 1994). In the two versions of the *Saint Cecilia*, the drawing of the saint and that of the angel are based, respectively, on the figures of Mary and the angel in a masterpiece by Orazio: the *Virgin Presenting the Child to Frances of Rome* previously in the church of Santa Caterina martire in Fabriano and now in Urbino, Galleria Nazionale delle Marche (see now Bernardini, in *La luce e i silenzi* 2019, pp. 124–125, no. 5, with previous bibliography). Subsequent interventions on the Perugia painting proposed attributions wholly or partially to Giovan Francesco Guerrieri, who was thought to have collaborated or interacted with Orazio in the period that he spent in the Marche (1613–1620); but the prevailing opinion today is that the work was created exclusively by Orazio, who was well-known to engage in the (now much discussed) use of cartoons and transparencies for individual figures and even for entire compositions (for essays on Orazio's methods in relation to some of his most significant works – including the two versions of the *Saint Cecilia* – see Pierluigi Carofano and Raymond Ward Bissell, in *Un capolavoro* 2018, respectively on pp. 11–18 and 31–40; 19-30 and 49–54). This method, of which Orazio would make ever-increasing use, becoming increasingly classical in his approach once he moved to England, also underpinned the working methods of his daughter Artemisia, who would often deploy cartoons and transparencies to produce replicas of her compositions or to make astute changes to them.
The Perugia painting must then be situated between 1615 and 1620, during what was a particularly happy time in Orazio's career. During this period, the Pisan master had distilled once and for all his synthesis of the Florentine tradition of accurate drawing in support of the painting, as well as the use of a terse, objective light, which confers upon the forms a crystalline aspect, and these characteristics can be seen fully also in the Perugia painting, despite its imperfect conservation (particularly visible in the angel's hair).
We can then observe a painstaking calculation in the narrative choices: the face of the young woman is looking downwards to the instrument; her head is already surrounded by the halo of sanctity and is crowned by the diadem of flowers that symbolises divine grace; her eyes are half-closed as she listens intently to a music that miraculously reaches her brain through the communication of the angel on her left. Her hands resting lightly on the keyboard speak of an intimate mysticism bound up with the interior sphere, as if during the playing of a piece the young woman were awaiting some form of connection with her instrument. This mode of recounting the impact with sanctity is aligned with the practices of private ascesis codified in the *Spiritual Exercises* of Ignatius of Loyala, and must have been particularly suited to Orazio, a brutal, violent man but one capable of exceptional visual sensitivity in relation to sacred themes.
Riccardo Lattuada

5.2
Artemisia Gentileschi (attributed)
Rome, 1593 – Naples, after August 1654
Nursing Madonna
1617–1620
Oil on canvas, 123.5 × 86 cm
Private collection

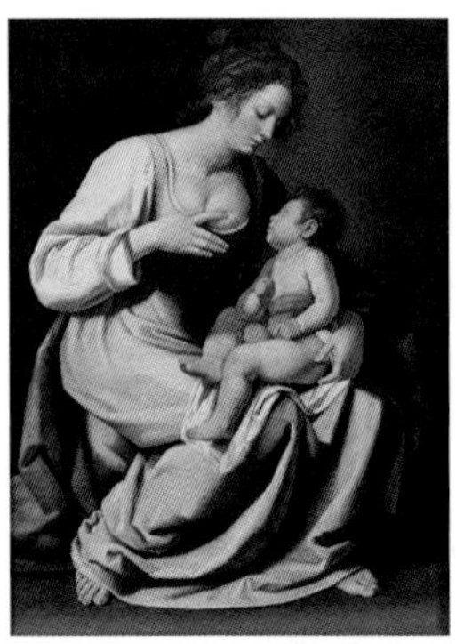

Forming part of the inheritance of an affluent Nivernais family, this *Nursing Madonna* returned to the public eye at a Parisian auction held by Métayer in November 2015, at which it was given a cautious attribution to Artemisia Gentileschi. The entry stressed the evident similarities to the *Madonna and Child* created by the painter for Grand Duke Cosimo II (reg. 1609–1621) around 1616 and today held at the Galleria Palatina in Palazzo Pitti (inv. 1890, no. 2129; c. 1616–1618).
After around one year, in the thick of the preparations for the exhibition entitled "Les Dames du Baroque" at the Museum of Fine Arts in Ghent (*Des dames* 2018), I finally went to examine the painting, and I found it rather interesting. The dimensions of the Norman *Madonna* coincide perfectly with those of the Grand Duke's painting, especially in terms of the figures, which are true to life, and in the poses of Mary and the Child. At first sight, the two paintings seemed to me to have been based on a single cartoon, and to have both been made in Florence, in that house-cum-studio in Piazza Frescobaldi, in the Oltrarno quarter, to which Artemisia had moved around 1616, thanks to her friend Francesco Maria Maringhi (Florence, 1593 – Naples?, after 1654) (*Le lettere*, forthcoming). I wondered if I had not been influenced by my work on the letters of the painter and her husband Pierantonio Stiattesi, in which, time and again, there are allusions to the use of cartoons and preparatory sketches, as well as references to how Artemisia would work on the drawing of models right through to her old age (Contini, in *Artemisia* 2013; Contini 2020; *Le lettere*, forthcoming). In the studios of the painters in those days – especially in Tuscany – a cartoon (a large drawing on thick paper often with perforated edges) was used to create a charcoal outline of a composition, and could be used multiple times, even in a fragmentary fashion. Artemisia, like her father Orazio – who was known to use cartoons in the opposite direction, so to speak – would often repeat her inventions in more or less similar drafts, using drawings and cartoons prepared in advance. As we learn from the documents themselves, during her time in Florence (1613–1620), the painter received assistance, and not only from her husband Pierantonio, on "making stretchers and preparing paints" and canvases; she was also helped by brilliant artists such as Cristofano Allori, the advocate of her rise to the artistic empire of the Gran Duchy. In Florence, Artemisia was aided by less celebrated but nevertheless capable artists, such as the well-travelled Alessandro Bardelli (Uzzano, 1583 – Bologna, 1633), a close collaborator of Allori, who in return for a few sizeable tips would help her in the studio and so have access to her drawings, cartoons and models (*Le lettere*, forthcoming). As has been confirmed by reflectographic analyses carried out in 2018 by Cinzia Pasquali at the time of the conscientious restoration of the painting now in Normandy, we are almost entirely convinced that the cartoon used to trace out the drawing for it was the same as that used for the Grand Duke's painting. Viewed in the flesh, the composition of the painting appeared to me to be verging on the phenomenal: the life-size figures, vanishing in the darkness of the background, seemed to me even more monumental and, at the same time, essential with respect to those in the Grand Duke's painting. The colours are the same as those used by the young artist in her early Roman works and in the canvases of the

Florentine years (1613–1620), as is confirmed by the detailed chromatic analysis conducted in 2018, again by Pasquali. Rose madder mixed with white lead to achieve the various, ever-changing nuances of clear pink (*rosino*) was a typical technique used by Artemisia, as were the accomplished variations of blue, from sky-blue to the deep blue of the Virgin's cloak. And vis-à-vis blue, I asked myself if I were actually looking at the famous "ultra-marine" of precious Afghan lapis lazuli, the exorbitant cost of which was paid separately, over and above the price of the paintings, by the artist's well-heeled clientele (see *Le lettere*, forthcoming). And while the material struck me as rich and pasty, like that used by Artemisia in her Florentine period, the ancient cracks included tiny, repeated horizontal creases, indicating that the canvas, once painted, had been rolled up, but not cut, like many of those removed or stolen by the Napoleonic troops. The selvages are intact.
Compared to the works painted in Florence between 1613 and the early months of 1620, just before her rushed return to Rome in the April of that year, the *Nursing Madonna* presented here is an extremely singular work. With the old repainted sections removed, and the original crack repaired, the canvas displays parts that are not entirely finished; at the time of the restoration of the pictorial surface, a number of areas were discovered to have been left incomplete – albeit well-prepared and as if awaiting further applications of paint and washes – details that had been covered by old, non-original repaintings. The painting was probably "finished" at the time of its *rintelo*, in the early nineteenth century. There are myriad disguised *pentimenti*, and the parts of the face and body of the Christ Child that were little more than sketched are clearly concealed; the dressing around his waist is only hinted at, and the white cloth that envelopes him in the Medicean painting is here a simple handkerchief. The blonde Virgin has lost the transparent organza veil that falls on the chest with the abundant brunette coiffure of the Madonna in the Pitti Palace, but the magnificent face of the blonde Virgin is more than finished, redolent of pure beauty and Florentine tradition, perhaps even more elegant than that of the Grand Duke's Madonna. The hairstyle is simplified and reinstates a certain normality, in comparison with the extravagant hairstyles seen in the other versions – an equally voluminous bun of dark blonde hair that stands out against the magnificent abyss of the velvet backdrop, uncovered thanks to the careful cleaning by Pasquali. The seated figure of the Virgin is dressed in fine woollen clothes that wrap her in wonderfully rendered folds, in the usual colours reinvented using ancient recipes. The white linen blouse, with its beautiful turned-up sleeve, is covered by the chamois garment in light, ever-changing clear pink, tending towards the magnificent red of the rose madder applied over the violet preparation. The cloak is rich, stunning, perfectly intact under the oxidised coatings, because it was painted with the mixture carefully produced by Artemisia, based on Afghan lapis lazuli powder, which has since been expertly analysed by Pasquali in her chromatic investigations. The ultramarine created using that precious powder is an exceptionally deep, intense blue that has not oxidised over the centuries, despite Artemisia having lightened it, eking it out and carefully blending it with white lead.
Unfinished, this *Nursing Madonna* is, in our opinion, a second version of the *Grand Duke's Madonna* currently at Palazzo Pitti. The canvas was in all probability painted by Artemisia in Florence between 1617 and the early months of 1620, with plentiful resources and subsidies to cover the cost of the ultramarine.
At the time of her precipitous flight from the Gran Ducal capital, heading first for Prato and then for Rome, in February 1620, the artist left the painting unfinished, and also left behind dozens of other works and pieces of furniture in her house-cum-studio in Piazza Frescobaldi. Four hundred years ago, the entire contents of the artist's house was seized by the Grand Ducal authorities; the canvas in question may have been amongst the sketched-out works or unfinished paintings of various sizes, on a range of different surfaces, described alongside the furniture and furnishings in a note drafted for the painter by Francesco Conti. Around a year later, for the substantial sum of 165 ducats, the nobleman Francesco Maria Maringhi – the painter's smitten lover and future second husband – purchased the assets and works belonging to Artemisia that had remained in Florence (*Le lettere*, forthcoming).
On completion of the restoration, in the Autumn of 2018, the painting was displayed for the first time at the exhibition "Les Dames du Baroque", at the Museum voor Schone Kunsten in Ghent, in Flanders.
Francesco Solinas

5.3
Artemisia Gentileschi
Rome, 1593 – Naples, after August 1654
Cleopatra
c. 1620
Oil on canvas, 97.5 × 71.5 cm
Fondazione Cavallini Sgarbi, inv. 215

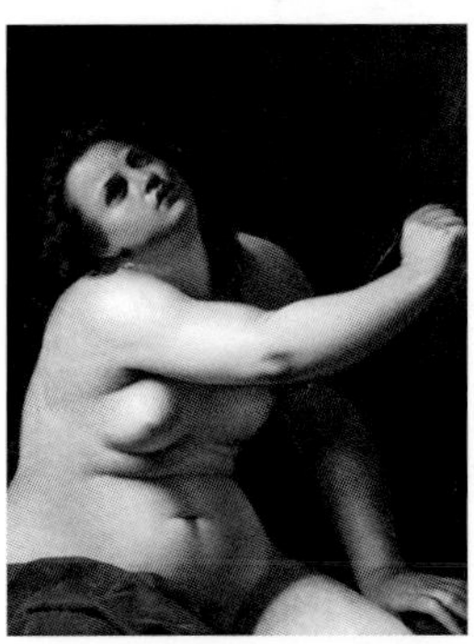

In 1994, the painting – traditionally attributed to Guido Cagnacci – was ascribed to Artemisia Gentileschi by Gianni Papi on the basis of a photograph held at the Fondazione Longhi (Papi 1994, p. 197). Rediscovered and acquired by Vittorio Sgarbi in the early 1990s, once cleaned it was added permanently to the painter's catalogue (see Sgarbi, in *La Collezione* 2018, pp. 176–177, no. 57, with previous bibliography).
The current opinion is that this *Cleopatra* – which is not the only version of that subject matter produced by Artemisia – was created around 1620, shortly before or shortly after the painter's move from Florence to Rome. The compact pictorial *ductus*, rigorously anchored to the design of the composition, would seem to confirm this dating, even if on Artemisia's artistic journey we witness sudden moments of disconnection and returns to previous methods of making art – a practice in which she engaged not infrequently, even with gaps of many years in between.
Sgarbi rightly compares the female modelling and identical posture of the *Cleopatra* to the *Lucretia* previously in Genoa in the Pagano collection and today in the Etro collection (on which see, for example, Treves, in *Artemisia* 2020, pp. 170–173, no. 21). Again it is Sgarbi who observes that in this painting "the […] realism is absolute, imminent, without the slightest lyrical or intimist concession. […] Rarely has a nude renounced every external agreeableness in its forms and pose. With this Cleopatra, we can smell her odour, her sweat, her stench. […] She is a Cleopatra who has never been less regal. She is just a woman, the body taking precedence over the soul, her existence over her essence" (Sgarbi, in *La Collezione* 2018, p. 176).
The decision to embody the Queen of Egypt in a monumental nude, often Junoesque and therefore substantially heroic, was not entirely innovative: leaving aside the examples provided by Giampietrino, Leonardo da Pistola, Lanfranco, Guercino and Cagnacci, amongst others, we can already see this type of depiction in the *Cleopatra* by Denys Calvaert in Cesena – which was in the Borghese collection and may have been viewed in Rome by Artemisia – and in many other Nordic prints.
Since the idea has been posited that the same *Lucretia* now in the Etro collection may have been carried out by Artemisia in the mirror – and therefore that it is a self-portrait, produced at a time in which she had put on weight, as she herself wrote on 21 March 1621 to Francesco Maria Maringhi (see Cavazzini 2015, p. 133; p. 143, no. 13 and *passim*; and Treves, in *Artemisia* 2020, pp. 170–173, no. 21) – then perhaps also the Sgarbi *Cleopatra* may be a self-portrait, or at least an image based on sessions during which the painter was posing in front of the mirror.
However, for me the layout of this dramatic *Cleopatra* seems to arise from a more complex process of pure "absolute realism", which is profoundly striking to us: the woman seated and almost entirely nude, with her head facing upwards and her bust leaning slightly downwards, is not only indebted to the so-called Ariadne, aka Arianna del Belvedere, in the Musei Vaticani, and to the noted figure derived from her in Titian's *Andrians*, but seems almost to be arranged as a diptych with the *Cleopatra* by Rosso Fiorentino today in

Braunschweig, at the Herzog-Anton-Ulrich-Museum. It is a painting for which it is practically impossible to list all of the copies, which came to be scattered right across Italy and throughout Europe in the sixteenth and seventeenth centuries.
In short, as is almost always the case in Orazio's oeuvre, and even more so in that of Artemisia, so in the Sgarbi *Cleopatra* we see a combination of the dignified models of the grand sixteenth-century Manner and the need to give living flesh to these canons, viewed as cornerstones of seventeenth-century modernity. It is here, in my opinion, that Artemisia exerts her greatest fascination: the underlying structure of her images is cultured and far more astute than may be assumed at first sight, while the evidence may be so realistic as to approach brutality.
Riccardo Lattuada

5.4
Artemisia Gentileschi
Rome, 1593 – Naples, after August 1654
Mary Magdalene in Meditation
c. 1630–1631
Oil on canvas, 100 × 73 cm
Sorrento (Naples), Museo Correale di Terranova, inv. 2925

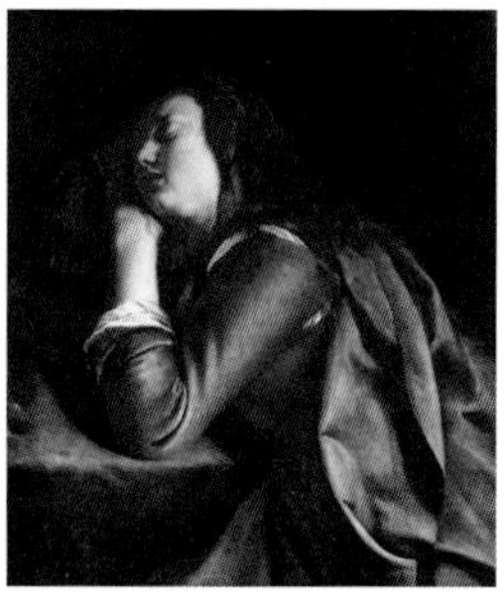

It was Roberto Contini (in *Artemisia* 1991), who – basing his conjecture on an old black-and-white photo – formulated the hypothesis that this *Mary Magdalene*, previously attributed to Massimo Stanzione, should in fact be ascribed to the hand of Artemisia; subsequently, and again on the basis of that same photograph, an attribution to Antiveduto Gramatica (Ward Bissell 1999, pp. 339–340, no. X–34, fig. 236) was put forward.
In 2001, I rediscovered the painting in the Museo Correale di Terranova in Sorrento, where it was attributed to Stanzione (Lattuada, in Lattuada, Nappi 2005, pp. 81–82, fig. 3). I reassigned the work to Artemisia and I convinced the management of the museum to do so, too. The reinstatement of Artemisia's authorship did not meet with any opposition, and was confirmed by Contini himself (see Contini, in *Artemisia* 2011, pp. 196–197, no. 27).
The work should be situated between the end of the painter's second Roman period and the beginning of her Neapolitan period (c. 1630–1631). The pink-crimson and green-ochre shades glisten thanks to the silk reflections of the fabrics in the half-light, in a similar way to those in the works that had made Orazio Gentileschi's name in Rome and in the Marche. The woman's red hair is spread across her shoulder like almost-transparent filaments (a phenomenon due, in part, to time-worn surface losses), as had already happened to the *Mary Magdalene* by Orazio in the church of the same name in Fabriano. It seems possible to trace even the physical typology of Mary Magdalene back to the same figure in Orazio's *Way to Calvary*, at the Kunsthistorisches Museum in Vienna. But Artemisia, who depicted Mary Magdalene time and again, here finds a different thread than that used in other, later versions. The woman, with her full, oval visage and small, recessed chin, has the left side of her face illuminated; a large shaded area conceals her chin and neck; a subtle half-light falls on the area from the corner of her mouth to her half-closed eyelids. Her expression is not one of penitence but of meditation; her head is leaning on her clasped hands, delicately resting on a skull, sitting on a book. The surface losses on the shaded parts of her forehead prevent us from establishing with any certainty whether her brow is at all furrowed, but a light languor can be detected on her ever-so-slightly open, fleshy lips.
The *Mary Magdalene* in the Museo Correale is one of the finest encapsulations of Artemisia's ability to go beyond the stereotypes of a given subject – even one that was amongst the most widely referenced in the painting of her time. Her visual exploration of this figure of the young woman offers up a depth of introspection and empathic engagement that can withstand comparison to practically any of the most highly acclaimed examples to be found in the art of the seventeenth century. Having taken refuge in a cave, kneeling before a block of stone, Mary Magdalene is bathed in the semi-darkness lacerated by a sudden light. Engrossed in contemplation, in her mind the woman is already far-removed from the luxurious garments she still wears, and which are what remains of the first part of her life – a period that came to an end following her meeting with Christ. But the beam of light that illuminates her does not distract her from her trance-like state; she has begun her journey towards the transcendent sphere.
Riccardo Lattuada

5.5
Artemisia Gentileschi
Rome, 1593 – Naples, after August 1654
David with the Head of Goliath
1630–1631
Oil on canvas, 203.5 × 152 cm
Private collection

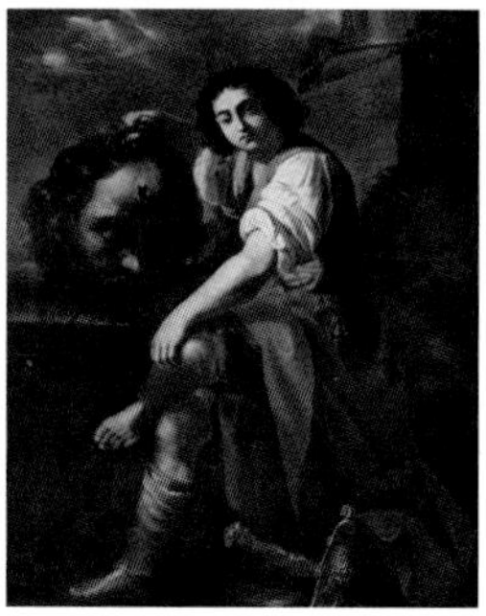

I attributed the painting to Artemisia Gentileschi – as did, independently, Roberto Contini and Nicola Spinosa (Solinas, in *Artemisia* 2013, pp. 46–49, no. 4, with a brief summary of Artemisia's versions of *David*) – and it was then included in an essay on the painter's output while in Naples (Lattuada 2017, p. 193; pp. 194–195, figs. 14–15). All of the evidence indicates that this was the work seen in 1631 by Joachim von Sandrart in Artemisia's Neapolitan home (Sandrart 1675, ed. 1925, p. 290: "The most beautiful life-size representation of David holding the enormous, terrible head of Goliath in his hands"), and then cited in a 1638 inventory of the collection of Marquis Giustiniani in Rome: "a full figure of David who holds in his hand the head of the giant Goliath" (Danesi Squarzina 2003, p. 289).
A second version of the painting, signed on David's sword and dated 163[?], just slightly smaller in size (202 × 137 cm), was traded on the market in London in 1975 and was rightly attributed to Artemisia in 1996 by Gianni Papi. This version, which re-emerged recently at a Hampel auction in Munich (Papi, Chaplin, Gillespie 2020), displays a fundamental variant: Goliath's head is at David's feet, and as such David's hand rests on the hilt of the sword. Courtesy of Simon Gillespie, who at the request of the current owner allowed me to study this second *David* while it was being restored, I was able to compare a transparency featuring the outline of the figure with that of the *David* in question. Leaving aside my report on that comparison for some future time, it can be stated that the two versions are based on the same cartoon. The variations between them betray an equal level of authorial input: the painting on show here has a more elaborate backdrop, with the plinth and the column behind David; in the other version, the background is a wooded slope, constructed in the manner of Micco Spadaro. The detail of Goliath's large head held in David's hand is impressive – equally potent, albeit of a different physical type, is the same head in the other painting, where it appears at the hero's feet.
I have already highlighted the existence of multiple versions of works by Artemisia based on a single cartoon – a practice already used repeatedly by Orazio (Lattuada 2017, pp. 203–205; for Orazio's methods, see Lattuada 2016, Lattuada 2017 and Lattuada 2018 and now Morselli 2019). Personally, I am unable to share Gianni Papi's doubts on the full authorship of the painting being discussed here, nor do I agree with Simon Gillespie's observation that the "less subtle layering and the application of paint is so precise that there is actually a gap between certain areas, with almost no overlapping of different colours". It is also important to overturn the thesis whereby the painting on show here is deemed to be deficient in the "three-dimensional effect [of the former Hampel version] whereas the Dorotheum picture lacks this higher finish and [is] therefore flatter". In reality, as Papi states, in the former Hampel version "some problems in its state of conservation have been gently mitigated, but not hidden", and this situation can clearly be

seen with the naked eye. The more tormented *chiaroscuro* of the former Hampel version has been intensified due to the fact that very aggressive cleaning operations have led to the surfacing throughout of a greyish tone that affects the entire image; the yellow shade of the cloak has also undergone this impoverishment, and the face is in even worse condition.
In contrast, the painting exhibited here shows the plastic relief found in so many of Artemisia's Neapolitan works; the brilliance of the orange tones of the cloak and the bright light colouring of the blouse can be compared to all of the works considered by Gianni Papi for the former Hampel version, and there is vigour in the objective rendering and the quality of the pictorial handling of details such as the wound on Goliath's forehead and the catapult on the stone surface. While the painting formerly in Hampel may be signed, the version discussed here is no less important because, as already indicated, it is the only one in which, as Sandrart states, David holds "the terrible head of Goliath in his hands" or, as the Giustiniani inventory puts it, the hero "holds the head of the giant Goliath". Gianni Papi has compared the composition of the former Hampel *David* with the *David* by Domenico Fetti in Dresden's Gemäldegalerie, renowned for the innumerable other versions produced by the artist and his studio. But in the comparison with our painting, this applies only to the fact that the hero is seated and stares at the viewer. In reality, the physical type of David's face looks similar to that of the *David* by Nicolas Régnier in the Musée des Beaux-Arts in Dijon; in Artemisia's painting, the imposing seated *David*, holding the decapitated head of Goliath by the hair, is depicted with crossed legs, resting after vanquishing the giant. This cocky pose, very unusual in the iconographic tradition of the victorious David and very rare in itself, seems to find its antecedent in *Day* and *Twilight* by Michelangelo on the tombs of Giuliano and Lorenzo de' Medici in the New Sacristy of the Basilica di San Lorenzo (Florence): works known everywhere through the etchings of Cornelis Cort (1570), which have been studied and cited in disparate cultural areas (for example, for the case of Francesco Rustici see Carofano 2020). And it is perhaps from this model that the true precedent of Artemisia's *David* draws its inspiration – Jusepe de Ribera's *Hercules at Rest*, previously in the collection of Barbara Piasecka Johnson and then in London, at Fergus Hall. This work, datable to 1630, must have provided Artemisia with the impetus to reset Michelangelo's invention in a different iconographic and narrative context, but one that is no less intense or significant; and the painter knew how to make excellent use of the resources to which she had access, constructing an image with great visual and emotional impact.
Riccardo Lattuada

5.6
Artemisia Gentileschi
Rome, 1593 – Naples, after August 1654
Mary Magdalene
1630–1631
Oil on canvas, 102 × 118 cm
Beirut, Sursock Palace Collection

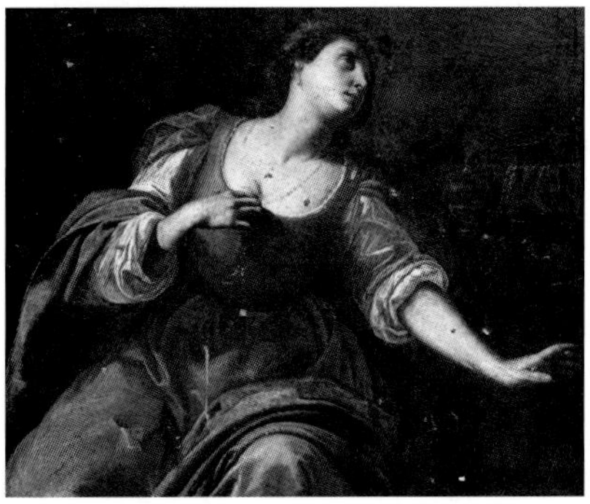

Damaged by the explosion at the port of Beirut on 4 August 2020, weighed down by dirt and marred by old touch-ups and stucco infills – none of which have succeeded in quelling its visual impact – this *Mary Magdalene* demonstrates all of the stylish, highly visual storytelling that was a feature of Artemisia Gentileschi's output from the start of her Neapolitan years (1630–1631). The work has not been seen before; the attribution to Artemisia was made by Dr Gregory Buchakjian, who informs us that he posited the idea in his PhD thesis submitted in 1996 at the Sorbonne. The work was exhibited in its current state not only because it constitutes a crucial addition to Artemisia's catalogue, but also to show the scale of the *vulnus* inflicted on Beirut, its inhabitants and its artistic heritage by the explosion of 2020.
The attribution to Artemisia is given valid support through comparisons with the figures (seated or kneeling in a transversal posture) and the compositions (in which a table on the right shows the attributes of the female character) of works such as the later *Cleopatra* in a private collection (see Lattuada, in Lattuada, Nappi 2005, pp. 84–85, fig. 10; Lattuada, in *Artemisia* 2016, pp. 228–229, no. 70) or the *Mary Magdalene* in Oslo (Nasjonalgalleriet), correctly ascribed to Artemisia by Raymond Ward Bissell (1999, pp. 275–276, no. 43, figs. 177–178) and by Federico Zeri. This even applies to paintings with subjects that have nothing to do with Mary Magdalene, such as the two versions – tangibly divergent in terms of palette and date of creation – of *Lucretia*: that sold in Paris at Artcurial in 2019 and now at the Matthiesen Gallery in London, which may date from the painter's Venetian sojourn (1627-c. 1630) (*Artemisia Gentileschi* 2020); and that auctioned in 2018 by Dorotheum in Vienna (23 October 2018, lot 56), which quite obviously dates from the first Neapolitan period. The true inventor of this mode of laying out the figures was Simon Vouet, whose *Lucretia* in the Národní galerie in Prague (also known for a wonderful engraving by Claude Mellan), produced in the mid-1730s, provided the basic impetus not only for the inventions of Artemisia – who was presumably bound by a genuine, mutual friendship with the French master – but of others, too.
The unmistakable tones of dark golden-yellow and ultramarine, against which the whiteness of the blouse stands out, are emphasised by the power of the chiaroscuro, which does not prevent the illuminated parts from achieving a clear, effective radiance even in the transitions towards the forms in the half-light – this being a particular feature of Artemisia's Neapolitan period.
While it may be easy to affirm the attribution of the Beirut *Mary Magdalene* to Artemisia in both stylistic and formal terms, it is equally clear that here, as in all of her best works, the painter succeeds in capturing the emotional essence of the painted subject: the saint, whose ecstatic gaze transmits her gratification for the shift to a new life underpinned by faith, seems to enter into a mental dialogue with the divine, while behind her the jewels and the vase of ointments are positioned almost as if to underline her abandonment of her previous existence.
Also from the Sursock Palace Collection in Beirut there is another, immense canvas depicting *Heracles and Omphale*. This unseen work – which itself has never been displayed in public and was, tragically, even more badly damaged in the explosion of 4 August 2020 – shows in the figures of Heracles, Omphale and the maidservant in the foreground on the left, all of the properties of Artemisia's painting, as already claimed by Gregory Buchakjian. But in the erote resting on Heracles' knee and in the figure in the background at the upper left corner, it seems possible to discern the presence of Bernardo Cavallino, who for his part produced other versions of *Heracles and Omphale*, such as that, sadly in a poor state of conservation, at the Museo Civico di Castel Nuovo, in Naples.
If, after the restoration, this hypothesis were to be confirmed, we would be dealing with the first case of a collaboration between the two artists. I have referred to the case of the *Susanna* already sold at auction in London (Sotheby's, London, 6 December, 1995, lot 53), in that passage attributed to Artemisia, Domenico Gargiulo and Viviano Codazzi. In my opinion, it should be reattributed to Artemisia, Cavallino, Codazzi and Gargiulo (see Lattuada, in Lattuada, Nappi 2005, pp. -88-89, fig. 18), an idea already posited cautiously by Ward Bissell (1999, pp. 266–67, no. 38). Returning to *Heracles and Omphale*, the re-emergence of this work is perhaps the most important recent rediscovery of a testament to Artemisia's Neapolitan phase; it can be dated to some time around 1640 and embodies her deep immersion in the city's art scene.
Riccardo Lattuada

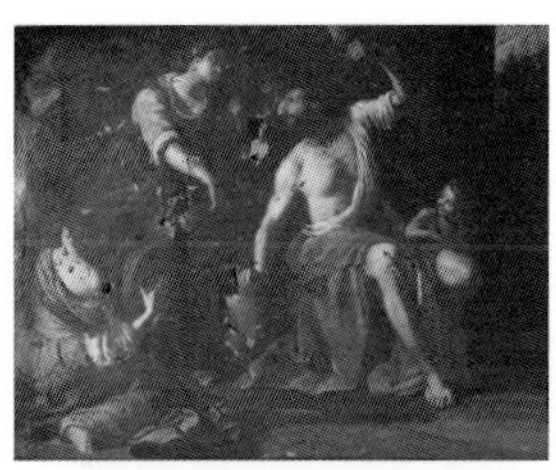

Artemisia Gentileschi and Bernardo Cavallino
Heracles and Omphale, c. 1640
Beirut, Sursock Palace Collection

BIBLIOGRAPHY

Before 1327
D'Ascoli C., *L'Acerba*, before 1327 (ed. 2011 edited by A. Crespi, Milan).

1469
Bembo I., *Specchio di illuminazione*, 1469 (ed. 2001 edited by S. Mostaccio, Florence).

c. 1475
Incomenza uno libretto composto da una beata religiosa del Corpo de Cristo sore Caterina da Bologna, n.d. [Bologna, c. 1475].

1480–1489
Ficino M., *De triplici vita*, Florence, 1480–1489 (ed. consulted *Sulla vita*, edited by A. Tarabochia Canavero, Milan, 1995).

c. 1500
Altieri M. A., *Li Nuptiali*, c. 1500 (ed. consulted Rome, 1873).

1502
Leonardi C., *Speculum lapidum*, Venice, 1502 (ed. consulted Venice, 1516).

1549
Domenichi L., *La nobiltà delle donne*, Venice.

1550
Vasari G., *Le vite de' più eccellenti architetti, pittori, et scultori italiani, da Cimabue insino a' tempi nostri*, Florence, 1550 (ed. 1986 edited by L. Bellosi, A. Rossi, Turin; English ed. *The Lives of the Artists*, Translated with an Introduction and Notes by J. Conaway Bondanella and P. Bondanella, Oxford-New York, 1998).

1561
Atanagi D., "Vita della Signora Irene", in *Rime di diversi nobilissimi et eccellentissimi autori in morte della Signora Irene delle Signore di Spilimbergo*, Venice, 1561 (ed. 1839 in P. Giordani, "In omaggio 'A Madama Adelaide Calderara Butti'", in *Fiori d'arti e di lettere italiane per l'anno 1839*, edited by F. Ambrosoli, Milan, pp. 128–153).

1565
Dolce L., *Delle diverse sorti delle gemme*, Venice.

1567
Guicciardini L., *Descrittione di tutti i Paesi Bassi*, Antwerp, 1567.

1568
Vasari G., *Le vite de' più eccellenti pittori, scultori, e architettori*, Florence, 1568 (ed. 1878–1885 edited by G. Milanesi, 9 vols., Florence; ed. 1966–1987 text edited by R. Bettarini, comment by P. Barocchi, 6 vols., Florence; ed. 1967 edited by P. Della Pergola, L. Grassi, G. Previtali, 9 vols., Novara; English ed. *Lives of The Most Eminent Painters Sculptors & Architects*, translated by G. du C. De Vere, 10 vols., Macmillian, London, 1912–1915; *The lives of the painters sculptors and architects v. 1–4*, translated by A.B. Hinds, edited by W. Gaunt, London-New York, 1963).

1569
Zava F., *Orationes IV, Epistolae libri VIII et Carmina Libri III*, Cremona, 1569.

1574–1575
Caro A., *De le lettere familiari del Commendatore Annibal Caro*, 2 vols., Venice, 1574–1575.

1581
Sansovino F., *Venetia città nobilissima, et singolare, descritta in XIII Libri da M. Francesco Sansovino [...]*, Venice, 1581.

1584
Borghini R., *Il riposo in cui della pittura e della scultura si favella, dei più illustri pittori, e scultori, e delle più famose opere loro si fa menzione; E le cose principali appartenenti a dette arti si insegnano*, Florence, 1584.
Lamo A., *Discorso intorno alla scoltura, et pittura, dove ragiona della Vita, & Opere in molti luoghi, & à diversi Prencipi e Personaggi fatte dall'Eccell. & Nobile M. Bernardino Campo pittore cremonese*, Cremona, 1584 (appendix to G. B. Zaist, *Notizie istoriche de' pittori, cultori, ed architetti cremonesi*, Cremona, 1774, II).
Lomazzo G. P., *Trattato dell'arte della pittura, scultura et architettura*, Milan, 1584.

1585
Campi A., *Cremona fidelissima città, et nobilissima clonia de' Romani, rappresentata in disegno col suo contado, et illustrata d'una breve historia delle cose più notabili appartenenti ad essa...*, Cremona, 1585.

1587
Lomazzo G. P., *Rime [...] divise in sette libri: nelle quali ad imitazione de' i Grotteschi usati da' Pittori, ha cantato le lodi di Dio ec. e quelle dei Pittori, scultori, architetti...*, Milan, 1587.

1590
Lomazzo G. P., *Idea del tempio della pittura [...] nella quale egli discorre dell'origine, & fondamento delle cose contenute nel suo trattato dell'arte della pittura*, Milan, 1590.
Vecellio C., *Degli habiti antichi, et moderni di diverse parti del mondo libri due*, Venice, 1590.

1592
Bascapè C., *De vita et rebus gestis Caroli S.R.E cardinalis, tituli S. Praxedis archiepiscopi Mediolani libri septem*, Ingolstadt, 1592.
Borgogni G., *Nuova scielta di rime*, Bergamo, 1592.
Morigia P., *Historia dell'antichità di Milano*, Venice, 1592.

1593
Ripa C., *Iconologia*, Rome, 1593 (ed. 1992 edited by P. Buscaroli, Milan).

1595
Morigia P., *La Nobiltà di Milano*, Milan, 1595.

1598
Borgogni G., *La Fonte del Diporto. Dialogo [...] nel quale si raccontano alcuni bellissimi, e morali avvenimenti, e si leggono nuove, e diverse poesie, et altre materie curiose*, Bergamo, 1598.
Rinaldi C., *Delle Rime di Cesare Rinaldi Bolognese*, Bologna, 1598.

1602
Sigüenza J. de, *La fundación del monasterio de El Escorial*, 1602 (ed. consulted Madrid, 1988).

1609
De Ribera P. P., *Le Glorie immortali de' Trionfi, et heroiche imprese d'ottocento quarantacinque Donne illustri, antiche & moderne dotate di varie Scienza, e conditione segnalate. Cioè in sacra Scrittura, Teologia, Profetia, Filosofia, Greco, Rettorica, Gramatica, Medicina, Astrologia, Leggi civili, Pittura, Musica, Armi [...]*, Venice, 1609.

1610
Giussano G. P., *Vita di S. Carlo Borromeo*, Rome, 1640.

1614
Grattarola M. A., *Successi meravigliosi della venerazione di S. Carlo Cardinale di S. Prassede e Arcivescovo di Milano*, Milan, 1614.
Sandero A., *Flandria Illustrata*, Cologne, 1641.

1615–1620
Bronzini C., *Della dignità et della nobiltà delle donne*, Biblioteca Nazionale Centrale di Firenze, Magl. Cl. VIII, 1525, I (1615–1620) (published in Barker S., "The First Biography of Artemisia Gentileschi: Self-Fashioning and Proto-Feminist Art History in Cristofano Bronzini's Notes on Women Artists", in *Mitteilungen Kunsthistorischen Institutes in Florenz*, LX, 3, 2018b, pp. 405–435).

1618
Ripa C., *Iconologia*, Padua, 1618 (ed. 1986 edited by P. Buscaroli, preface by M. Praz, 2 vols., Turin).

1620
Marino G. B., *La Galeria del cavalier Marino distinta in pitture & sculture*, Ancona 1620.
Rossi O., *Elogi historici di bresciani illustri, Theatro*, Brescia, 1620.

1633
Agnelli S., *Mariale o Dell'interna croce della Madre di Dio...*, Venice, 1633.

1636
Gratiano G. C., *Di Orlando Santo vita, et morte con venti mila Christiani uccisi in Roncisvalle Cavata dal Catalogo de Santi*, Ascoli, 1636 (ed. 1997 in F. Jacobs, *Defining the Renaissance "Virtuosa": Women Artists and the Language of Art History and Criticism*, Cambridge, pp. 175–177).

1642
Baglione G., *Le Vite de' Pittori scvltori et architetti. Dal pontificato di Gregorio XIII del 1572. In fino a' tempi di Papa Vrbano Ottauo nel 1642*, Rome, 1642.
Ridolfi C., *Vita di Giacopo Robusti detto il Tintoretto*, Venice, 1642.

1648
Ridolfi C., *Le maraviglie dell'arte, overo le vite de gl'illustri pittori veneti, e dello Stato [...]*, Venice, 1648 (ed. 1835–1837, 2 vols., Padua).

1649
Pacheco F., *El arte de la pintura*, 1649 (ed. 1990 edited by B. Bassegoda, Madrid).

1650
Manilli G., *Villa Borghese fuori di Porta Pinciana, Guardaroba di detta villa*, Rome, 1650.

1653
Picinelli F., *Mondo Simbolico*, Venice, 1653 (ed. consulted Milan, 1669).

1657
Della Lengueglia G. A., *Ritratti della prosapia et heroi Moncadi nella Sicilia*, Vicenza, 1657.

1660
Boschini M., *La carta del navegar pitoresco. Dialogo tra un Senator venetian deletante, e un professor de Pitura [...]*, Venice, 1660.

1663
Sansovino F., Martinioni G., *Venetia città nobilissima, et singolare, descritta in XIII Libri da M. Francesco Sansovino [...] con aggiunta di tutte le Cose Notabili della stessa Città, fatte, & occorse dall'Anno 1580 sino al presente 1663 da D. Giustiniano Martinioni [...]*, Venice, 1663.

1664
Bellori G. P., *Nota delli musei, librerie, gallerie & ornamenti di statue, e pitture, ne' palazzi, nelle case e ne' giardini di Roma*, Rome, 1664 (ed. 1976 edited by E. Zocca, Rome).
Terzago P. M., *Musaeum septalianum*, Milan, 1664.

1666
Masini Antonio di Paolo, *Bologna Perlustrata*, Bologna, 1666.

1667
Rime di monsignor Giovanni Della Casa con le annotazioni del signor Egidio Menagio, Paris, 1667.

1671
Santagostino A., *L'immortalità e gloria del pennello. Catalogo delle pitture insigni che stanno esposte al pubblico nella città di Milano*, 1671 (ed. 1980 edited by M. Bona Castellotti, Milan).

1674
Soprani R., *Le vite de' pittori, scoltori et architetti genovesi*, Genoa, 1674.
Tornamira P. A., *Relatione della presa di due galere della squadra di Sicilia*, Palermo, 1674.
Torre C., *Il Ritratto di Milano*, Milan, 1674.

1675
Sandrart J. von, *Teutsche Academie der Elden Bau-, Bild- und Mahlerey Künste*, Neremberg, 1675 (ed. 1925 edited by R.A. Peltzer, Munich).

1677
Benedetti E. [alias M. Mayer], *Villa Benedetta descritta da Matteo Mayer e dal medesimo dedicata al serenissimo prencipe Ludouico Landgrauio d'Hassia...*, Rome, 1677.
Legati L., *Museo Cospiano, annesso a quello del famoso Ulisse Aldrovandi e donato alla sua patria dall'Illustrissimo Ferdinando Cospi, Patrizio di Bologna e Senatore*, Bologna,1677.

1678
Malvasia C. C., *Felsina pittrice. Vite de' pittori bolognesi*, 2 vols., Bologna, 1678 (ed. 1841 edited by G. Zanotti, 2 vols., Bologna).

1681–1728
Baldinucci F., *Notizie dei professori del disegno da Cimabue in qua*, 6 vols., Florence, 1681–1728 (ed. 1767–1774 with new annotations by D. M. Manni, 21 vols., Florence; ed. 1768–1820, with various dissertations, notes and supplements by G. Piacenza, 6 vols., Turin; ed. 1845–1847, edited by F. Ranalli, 5 vols., Florence).

1682
Bullart I., *Académie des Sciences et des Arts, Contenant les Vies, & les Eloges Historiques des Hommes Illustres, Qui ont excellé en ces Professions depuis environ quatre Siècles parmy diverses Nations de l'Europe*, Paris, 1682.

1686
Malvasia C. C., *Le pitture di Bologna*, Bologna, 1686 (ed. 1969 edited by A. Emiliani, Bologna).

1695
Du Fresnoy C. A., *De Arte Graphica. The Art of Painting* (1668), London, 1695.

1702
Le Comte F., *Cabinet des singularitez d'architecture, peinture, sculpture, et graveure ou Introduction à la connoissance des plus beaux arts, figurés sous les tableaux, les statues & les estampes*, Brussels, 1702.

1702–1706
Arisi F., *Cremona literata*, 2 vols., Parma, 1702–1706.

1704
Orlandi P. A., *Abcedario pittorico nel quale compendiosamente sono descritte le patrie, i maestri, ed i tempi [...]*, Bologna, 1704.

1705
Félibien A., *Entretiens sur les vies et sur les ouvrages des plus excellens peintres anciens et modernes*, 4. vols., Paris, 1705.

1715–1720
Arisi D., *Accademia de' pittori cremonesi con alcuni scultori ed architetti pur cremonesi*, 1715–1720, ms. Getty Research Institute.

1719
Orlandi P. A., *L'Abecedario pittorico dell'autore ristampato, corretto et accresciuto di molti professori e di altre notizie spettanti alla pittura*, Bologna, 1719.

1723
Joannis Georgii Graevii Thesaurus Antiquitatum et Historiarum Italiae, Lugduni Batavorum, 1723.

Before 1730
Ghiselli A. F., *Memorie antiche manoscritte di Bologna*, before 1730, LXVII, Bologna, Biblioteca Universitaria.

1736
Pascoli L., *Vite de' Pittori, Scultori, ed Architetti moderni*, II, Rome, 1736.

1739
Zanotti G., *Storia dell'Accademia Clementina*, 2 vols., Bologna, 1739.

1750
Roisecco G., *Roma antica e moderna o sia nuova descrizione di tutti gl'edifici antichi et moderni...*, 3 vols., Rome, 1750.

1753
Orlandi P. A., *Abecedario pittorico del m.r.p. Pellegrino Antonio Orlandi bolognese contenente le notizie de' professori di pittura, scoltura, ed architettura in questa edizione corretto e notabilmente di nuove notizie accresciuto da Pietro Guarienti*, Venice, 1753.

1754
Bottari G., *Raccolta di Lettere sulla Pittura, Scultura, ed Architettura*, I, Rome, 1754.

1756
Cochin C. N., *Voyage d'Italie, ou recueil de Notes sur les Ouvrages de Peinture et de Sculpture, qu'on voit dans les principales villes d'Italie*, Paris, 1756.

1758
Richa G., *Notizie istoriche delle chiese fiorentine, tomo settimo del quartiere di San Giovanni*, Florence, 1758.

1760–1780
Oretti M., *Le Pitture che si ammirano nelli Palaggi e Case de' Nobili della Città di Bologna e di altri edificii in d.a Città*, 1760–1780, Biblioteca Comunale dell'Archiginnasio, Bologna, ms. B. 104.
Oretti M., *Indice delli Ritratti de Pittori scultori e Architetti in dipinto ed in scultura è dove ritrovansi in pubblico ed in privato nella città di Bologna*, 1760–1780, Biblioteca Comunale dell'Archiginnasio, Bologna, ms. B. 109.
Oretti M., *Notizie de' Professori del Dissegno, cioè Pittori, Scultori ed Architetti bolognesi e de' Forestieri di sua scuola*, 1760–1780, Bologna, Biblioteca Comunale dell'Archiginnasio, mss. B. 123–135.

1762
Panni A. M., *Distinto rapporto delle dipinture, che trovansi nelle Chiese della Città, e sobborghi di Cremona*, Cremona, 1762.

1763
Cadioli G., *Descrizione delle pitture, sculture ed architetture che si osservano nella città di Mantova, e ne' suoi contorni*, Mantua, 1763.

1772
Crespi L., *La Certosa di Bologna descritta nelle sue pitture*, Bologna, 1772.
Passeri G. B., *Vite de' pittori, scultori ed architetti che hanno lavorato in Roma, e che son morti dal 1641 al 1673*, Bologna, 1772.

1774
Zaist G. B., *Notizie istoriche de' pittori, scultori ed architetti cremonesi*, 2 vols., Cremona, 1774.

1780
Calvi J. A., *Versi e prose sopra una serie di eccellenti pitture posseduta dal Signor Marchese Filippo Hercolani, principe del S. R. I.*, Bologna, 1780.
Rossetti G., *Descrizione delle pitture, sculture ed architetture di Padova, Con alcune Osservazioni intorno ad esse, ed altre curiose Notizie*, Padua, 1780.

1793
Bartoli F., *Le pitture, sculture e architetture della città di Rovigo*, Venice, 1793.

1795–1796
Lanzi L., *Storia pittorica della Italia*, 2 vols., Bassano, 1795–1796.

1803–1821
Bartsch A., *Le peintre graveur*, 21 vols., Paris, 1803–1821.

1809
Lanzi L., *Storia pittorica della Italia dal risorgimento delle Belle Arti fin presso al fine del XVIII secolo*, Florence, 1809 (ed. 1968–1974 edited by M. Capucci, 3 vols., Florence).

1815–1817
Lanzi L., *Storia pittorica dell'Italia*, 6 vols., Pisa, 1815–1817.

1817–1824
Zani P., *Enciclopedia metodica critico-ragionata delle belle arti dell'abate d. Pietro Zani fidentino*, part I 9 vols., part II 19 vols., Parma, 1817–1824.

1819
Di Maniago F., *Storia delle Belle Arti friulane*, Venice, 1819.

1821
Varchi B., *Sonetti per la infermità e guarigione di Cosimo I, dei Medici: pubblicati per la prima volta in occasione della recuperata salute di S.A.I., ER. il granduca di Toscana Ferdinando III*, Florence, 1821.

1822–1825
Bottari G. G., Ticozzi S., *Raccolta di lettere sulla pittura, scultura ed architettura scritte da' più celebri personaggi dei secoli XV, XVI e XVII, pubblicata da M. Gio. Bottari e continuata fino ai nostri giorni da Stefano Ticozzi*, 8 vols., Milan, 1822–1825.

1823
Cantalamessa G., "Ritratto della miniatrice Garzoni dipinto da Carlo Maratti", in *Roma*, 1.6, 1823, pp. 245–247.
Landon C. P., *Choix de tableaux modernes de la Galerie de son Altesse Royale M.me la Duchesse de Berry*, Paris, 1823.
Lanzi L., *Storia pittorica della Italia dal risorgimento delle belle arti fin presso al fine del XVIII secolo. Sesta edizione*, 6 vols., Milan, 1823.

1826
Moschini G., *Della origine e delle vicende della pittura in Padova. Memoria*, Padua, 1826.

1827
Grasselli G., *Abecedario biografico dei pittori, scultori ed architetti cremonesi*, Milan, 1827.

1828
Hemans F., *Records of Woman: With Other Poems*, Edinburgh-London, 1828.

1830
Cantalamessa Carboni G., *Memorie intorno i letterati e gli artisti della città di Ascoli nel Piceno*, Ascoli Piceno, 1830.
Gallo A., *Elogio Storico di Pietro Novelli da Morreale in Sicilia, pittore, architetto ed incisore*, Palermo, 1830.

1834
Ricci A., *Memorie storiche delle arti e degli artisti della marca di Ancona*, Macerata, 1834.

1835–1853
Nagler G. K., *Neues allgemeines Künstler-Lexicon oder Nachrichten von dem Leben und den Werken der Maler, Bildhauer, Baumeister, Kupferstecher, Formschneider, Lithographen, Zeichner, Medailleure, Elfenbeinarbeiter, etc.*, 22 vols., Munich, 1835–1853.

1840
"Royal Academy Exhibition", in *Blackwood's Edinburgh Magazine*, XLVIII, CCXCIX, 1840, pp. 374–386.

1842
Meneghelli A., *Breve ragguaglio delle collezioni sacre alle glorie patrie ed alle belle arti presso l'avv. Antonio Piazza di Padova*, Padua, 1842.

1853
Cappi A., *Luca Longhi illustrato*, Ravenna, 1853.
Odorici F., *Guida di Brescia in rapporto alle arti ed ai monumenti antichi e moderni*, Brescia, 1853.
Pietrucci N., *Delle illustri donne padovane. Cenni biografici. Seconda edizione con note ed aggiunte dell'autore*, Padua, 1853.

1854–1890
Le Blanc C., *Manuel de l'amateur d'estampes*, 4 vols., Paris, 1854–1890.

1858
Guhl E., *Die Frauen in der Kunstgeschichte*, Berlin, 1858.
Pietrucci N., *Biografia degli artisti padovani*, Padua, 1858.

1859
Fries Lummis Ellet E., *Women Artists in All Ages and Countries*, London, 1859.

1860
Odorici F., "Dello spirito di associazione di alcune città lombarde nel medio evo", in *Archivio Storico Italiano*, XI, I, 21, 1860, pp. 73–108.

1868
Mazzoni Toselli O., *Racconti storici estratti dall'Archivio Criminale di Bologna*, 3 vols., Bologna, 1868.

1869
Bonturini G., *Elogio delle pittrici veneziane Irene di Spilimbergo e Maria Tintoretto. Letto nella Regia Accademia delle Belle Arti in Venezia*, Venice, 1869.

1870
Campori G., *Raccolta di cataloghi ed inventarii inediti di quadri, statue, disegni, bronzi, dorerie, smalti, medaglie, avorii, ecc. dal secolo XV al secolo XIX*, Modena, 1870.

1872
Rondoni F., *Guida del R. Museo Fiorentino di S. Marco con aggiunta di brevi notizie sulla chiesa annessa*, Florence, 1872.
Sacchi F., *Notizie pittoriche cremonesi*, Cremona, 1872.

1875
Magni B., "Notizie di Virginia Vezzi pittrice", in Id., *Prose d'Arte*, Rome, 1875, pp. 110–111.

1877
Crowe J. A., Cavalcaselle G.B., *Titian: His Life and Times*, 2 vols., London, 1877.
Minghetti M., *Le donne italiane nelle Belle Arti al secolo XV e XVI*, Florence, 1877.

1881
Caivano-Schipani F., *Dizionario biografico de' soci dell'Accademia Pittagorica*, Naples, 1881.

1882
J. A., "La première exposition de L'Union des Femmes peintres et sculpteurs", in *La Gazette des Femmes*, 10 February 1882, pp. 1–3.
Malvezzi L., *Le glorie dell'arte lombarda, ossia illustrazione storica delle più belle opere che produssero i Lombardi in pittura, scultura ed architettura dal 590 al 1850*, Milan, 1882.
"Union des Femmes peintres et sculpteurs", in *La Gazette des Femmes*, 25 January 1882, p. 1.

1884
De Nolhac P., "Les collections de Fulvio Orsini. Galerie de peinture au XVI siècle", in *Gazette des Beaux Arts*, XXIX, 1884, pp. 427–436.

1885
De Vit V., *Opuscoli letterari*, Milan, 1885.
Venturi A., "Zur Geschichte der Kunstsammlungen Kaiser Rudolf II", in *Repertorium für Kunstwissenschaft*, VIII, Berlin-Stuttgart, 1885, pp. 20–21.

1893
Henrotin E. M., "An Outsider's View of the Woman's Exhibit", in *The Cosmopolitan*, XV, 5, 1893, pp. 560–566.
Howe Elliott M., *Art and Handicraft in the Woman's Building of the World's Columbian Exposition*, Paris-New York, 1893.
Official Catalogue of Exhibits. World's Columbian Exposition. Woman's Building, Chicago, 1893.
Vachon M., *La Femme dans l'Art*, Paris, 1893.
Venturi A., *Il Museo e la Galleria Borghese*, Rome, 1893.

1894
Vente à Venise par suite du décès de Mme la Comtesse Lauredana Gatterburg-Morosini, objets d'art et d'ameublement, Diamants, Perles, Orfèvrerie, Tableaux, Guipures, Dentelles, Étoffes, Palais Morosini (Piazza Francesco Morosini già San Stefano), Venice, 1894.

1895
Intra G., *Il Monastero di Santa Orsola in Mantova*, Milan, 1895.
Martelli D., "A Silvestro Lega", in *Corriere Italiano*, 269–270, 26–27 September 1895.

1897
Baudi di Vesme A., "La Regia Pinacoteca di Torino", in *Le Gallerie Nazionali Italiane*, Rome, 1897, III, pp. 3–68.

1898
Fogolari G., "Artisti trentini a Milano: Nunzio e Fede Galizia (1573-1630)", in *Tridentum*, I, 1898, pp. 293–318.

1899
Lanciani R., "La raccolta antiquaria di Giovanni Ciampolini", in *Bullettino della Commissione archaeologica communale di Roma*, V, XXVII, 1899, pp. 101–115.

1900
Schweitzer E., "La scuola pittorica cremonese (ricordo dell'esposizione d'arte sacra in Cremona)", in *L'Arte*, III, file I–IV, 1900, pp. 41–71.

1901
Carotti G., *Capi d'arte appartenenti a S.E. la duchessa Joséphine Melzi d'Eril Barbò*, Bergamo, 1901.

1902
Cust L., *A Description of the Sketch-book by Sir Anthony van Dyck, Used by Him in Italy, 1621 – 1627 and Preserved in the Collection of the Duke of Devonshire in Chatsworth*, London, 1902.

1904
Catalogo degli oggetti di sommo pregio, Rome, 1904.
Erskine Clement Waters C., *Women in the Fine Arts*, Boston-New York, 1904.

1905
Shaw Sparrow W., *Women Painters of the World*, London, 1905.

1908
Auquier P., *Catalogue des peintures, sculptures, pastels et dessins*, Marseille, 1908.

1909
Justi C., *"Philip II als Kunstfreund"*, in Id., *Miscellaneen aus drei Jahrhunderten spanischen Kunstlebens*, II, Berlin, 1909, pp. 1–30.

1910
Ulm O., "I ritratti d'Irene ed Emilia di Spilimbergo erroneamente attribuiti a Tiziano", in *Emporium*, XXXI, 182, 1910, pp. 126–135.

1911
Millunzi G., "Memorie originali dei pittori monrealesi Pietro Antonio Novelli e Pietro Novelli suo figlio", in *Archivio Storico Siciliano*, XXXVI, 1911, pp. 313–395.

1912
Nievo I., *Canti del Friuli*, Udine, 1912.

1913
Frangipane A., *La Prima Mostra d'Arte Calabrese dell'Ottocento*, Bergamo, 1913.

1914
Bernicoli S., "Documenti sui Longhi", in *Felix Ravenna*, 1914, pp. 634–639.
D'Ancona P., *La miniatura fiorentina II. Secoli XV-XVI*, Florence, 1914.
Supino I. B., *Le sculture delle porte di San Petronio in Bologna illustrate con documenti inediti*, Florence, 1914.
Zotti R., *Irene da Spilimbergo*, Udine, 1914.

1916
Ruffo V., "Galleria Ruffo nel secolo XVII in Messina (con lettere di pittori e altri documenti inediti)", in *Bollettino d'Arte*, X, I, I–II, 1916, pp. 165–192.

1922
Borenius T., "A Portrait by L. Fontana", in *The Burlington Magazine*, XLI, 232, 1922, pp. 41–42.
Ronchi O., *Guida storico-artistica di Padova e dintorni*, Padua, 1922.

1925
Catalogo dei quadri conservati nel Museo Provinciale di Catanzaro, 14 January 1925, ms., Catanzaro, Biblioteca Provinciale "Chimirri".

1926
Tarchiani N., "Silvestro Lega alla mostra di Modigliana", in *Emporium*, LXIV, 381, 1926, pp. 197–204.
Tersenghi A., "Un po' più di luce intorno alla pittrice veliterna Virginia Vezzi", in *Bollettino dell'Associazione veliterna di archeologia, storia ed arte*, I, 1926, pp. 59–64.
Venturi L., *La collezione Gualino*, Rome-Turin, 1926.

1927
Ingersoll-Smouse F., "L'œuvre paint de Paul Véronèse en France", in *Gazette des Beaux-Arts*, 2nd semester, 1927, pp. 211–235.
[Nicodemi G.], *La Pinacoteca Tosio Martinengo*, Bologna, 1927.

1928
Bonetti C., "Nel Centenario di Sofonisba Anguissola", in *Archivio Storico Lombardo*, 6/3, 1928, pp. 285–306.
Hildebrandt H., *Die Frau als Künstlerin*, Berlin, 1928.
Longhi R., *Precisioni nelle gallerie italiane. I. R. Galleria Borghese*, Rome, 1928.

1929
Ricci C., "Ritratti "tizianeschi" di G. Paolo Pace", in *Rivista del Reale Istituto d'Archeologia e Storia dell'Arte di Roma*, I, II, 1929, pp. 249–265.

1931
Vaes M., "Appunti di Carel van Mander su vari pittori italiani, suoi contemporanei", in *Roma. Rivista di Studi e di Vita romana*, IX, 1, 1931, pp. 193–208, 341–356.

1933
Besta B., "Alcune notizie per una storia degli artisti milanesi del Seicento", in *Archivio Storico Lombardo*, LX, 1933, pp. 447–471.
Venturi A., *Storia dell'Arte Italiana*, IX, part VI, Milan, 1933.

1934
Tietze-Conrat E., "Marietta, fille du Tintoret, peintre de portraits", in *Gazette des Beaux-Arts*, 862, 1934, pp. 258–262.

1935
Gallo R., "Per il San Lorenzo martire di Tiziano", in *Rivista di Venezia*, 4, 1935, pp. 155–174.

1936
Gronau G., *Documenti artistici urbinati*, Florence, 1936.
Mauceri E., "Nella pittura bolognese: Lavinia Fontana", in *Bologna. Rivista mensile del Comune*, XXIII, 1936, pp. 15–17.

1938
Benedict C., "Un peintre oublié de natures mortes – Osias Beert", in *L'amour de l'art*, XIX, 8, 1938, pp. 307–314.

1939
Centanni L., "Le rapine d'opere d'arte fatte alle Romagne sotto il primo Regno italico", in *Melozzo da Forlì. Rassegna d'arte romagnola*, 6, 1939, pp. 317–320.
Préaud M., *Inventaire du fonds français. Graveurs du XVIIe siècle*, Paris, 1939.

1940
Galli R., *Lavinia Fontana pittrice 1552-1614*, Imola, 1940.
Sgadari di Lo Monaco G., *Pittori e scultori siciliani dal Seicento al Primo Ottocento*, Palermo, 1940.
Thieme U., Becker F., *Allgemeines Lexikon der Bildenden Künstler von der Antike bis zur Gegenwart*, XXXIV, Leipzig, 1940.

1943
Croce B., "Scrittori del pieno e del tardo Rinascimento. XIX, Irene di Spilimbergo", in *La Critica*, 41, 1943, pp. 123–131.

1949
Il Castello del Valentino, edited by M. Bernardi, Turin, 1949.
Ozzòla L., *La galleria di Mantova*, Mantua, 1949.

1951
Puerari A., *La Pinacoteca di Cremona*, Cremona, 1951.

1952
Bousquet J., "Documents sur le séjour de Simon Vouet à Rome", in *Mélanges de l'école française de Rome*, LXIV, 1952, pp. 287–300.

1953
Lettere dei Macchiaioli, edited by L. Vitali, Turin, 1953.
Tietze H., Tietze-Conrat E., "I ritratti Spilimbergo a Washington", in *Emporium*, CXVII, 699, 1953, pp. 99–107.

1954
Della Pergola P., "Contributi per la Galleria Borghese", in *Bollettino d'Arte*, XXXIX, IV, II, 1954, pp. 134–140.
Zeri F., *La Galleria Spada in Roma*, Florence, 1954.

1955
Fiocco G., "Una decorazione floreale di Francesco Guardi", in *Arte Veneta*, IX, 1955, pp. 204–210.

1955–1959
Della Pergola P., *Galleria Borghese. I dipinti*, 2 vols., Rome, 1955–1959.

1957
Zeri F., *Pittura e Controriforma. L'arte senza tempo di Scipione da Gaeta*, Turin, 1957.

1958
Baldi G., *La farmacia nella breve mortale malattia della pittrice bolognese Elisabetta Sirani: 1638-1665*, Pisa, 1958 (abstract from *Atti del II Congresso internazionale di storia della farmacia*, Padua-Venice, 1958).
Die Frau als Künstlerin. Werke aus vier Jahrhunderten, exhibition catalogue (Zürich, Helmhaus, 2 July – 31 August 1958), Zürich, 1958.
Hartt F., *Giulio Romano*, 2 vols., New Haven, 1958.

1959–1967
Prodi P., *Il cardinale Gabriele Paleotti (1522-1597)*, 2 vols., Rome, 1959–1967.

1960
Della Pergola P., "Gli Inventari Salviati (I)", in *Arte Antica e Moderna*, 10, 1960, pp. 193–200.

1961
Malvasia C. C., *Vite dei pittori bolognesi: appunti inediti*, edited by A. Arfelli, Bologna, 1961.

1962
Comanducci A. M., *Dizionario illustrato dei pittori, disegnatori e incisori italiani moderni e contemporanei*, Milan, 1962.

1963
Griseri A., "La pittura", in *Mostra del Barocco piemontese*, exhibition catalogue (Turin, Palazzo Madama, Palazzo Reale, Palazzina di Stupinigi, 22 June – 10 November 1963), edited by V. Viale, 3 vols., Turin, 1963, III, pp. 1–128.

Mostra del Barocco piemontese, exhibition catalogue (Turin, Palazzo Madama, Palazzo Reale, Palazzina di Stupinigi, 22 June – 10 November 1963), edited by V. Viale, 3 vols., Turin, 1963.

1963–1982

Baudi di Vesme A., *Schede Vesme. L'arte in Piemonte dal XVI al XVIII secolo*, 4 vols., Turin, 1963–1982.

1965

Bottari S., *Fede Galizia pittrice (1578-1630)*, Trento, 1965.

Procacci L., Procacci U., "Il carteggio di Marco Boschini con il cardinale Leopolodo de' Medici", in *Saggi e memorie di storia dell'arte*, 4, 1965, pp. 85–114.

1966

Chastel A., "Diane de Poitiers: 'l'Eros de la beauté froide'", in *Friendship's Garland. Essays Presented to Mario Praz on his Seventieth Birthday*, edited by V. Gabrieli, Rome, 1966, I, pp. 95–104.

Griseri A., "Giovenale Boetto incisore", in N. Carboneri, A. Griseri, C. Morra, *Giovenale Boetto. Architetto e incisore*, Fossano, 1966, pp. 33–62.

Mariani L. M., *Santuari mariani di Sicilia*, Milan, 1966.

1967

Botter M., *La villa Capodilista di Dario Varotari a Montecchia*, Treviso, 1967.

Donzelli C., Pilo G. M., *I pittori del Seicento veneto*, Florence, 1967.

1968

Ballarin A., "Pittura veneziana nei Musei di Budapest, Dresda, Praga e Varsavia", in *Arte Veneta*, XXII, 1968 [1969], pp. 237–255.

Ruotolo R., "Un dipinto ignoto di Fede Galizia", in *Paragone*, 215, 1968, pp. 65–67.

1969

Millar O., "Notes on Three Pictures by van Dyck", in *The Burlington Magazine*, CXI, 769, 1969, pp. 414–418.

Viale V., *Civico Museo Francesco Borgogna, Vercelli. I Dipinti*, Vercelli, 1969.

1970

Romano G., *Casalesi del Cinquecento. L'avvento del manierismo in una città padana*, Turin, 1970.

1971

Bora G., *Disegni di manieristi lombardi*, Vicenza, 1971.

Valsecchi M., "Nuove aggiunte al Peterzano", in *Studi di storia dell'arte in onore di Antonio Morassi*, Venice, 1971, pp. 172–183.

1972

Daneu Lattanzi A., "I manoscritti e incunaboli miniati italiani della Biblioteca Bodleiana di Oxford nel catalogo di O. Pächt e J. J. G. Alexander", in *Bollettino d'Arte*, LVII, V, I, 1972, pp. 46–56.

Gualdo jr. G., *1650. Giardino di Chà Gualdo*, edited by L. Puppi, Florence, 1972.

Michel O., "Bricci, Plautilla", in *Dizionario Biografico degli Italiani*, 14, Rome, 1972, pp. 223–224.

Romano G., "Caccia, Orsola Maddalena", in *Dizionario Biografico degli Italiani*, 15, Rome, 1972, pp. 762–763.

1973

Bucci M., Bencini R., *Palazzi di Firenze. Quartiere di Santa Maria Novella*, Florence, 1973.

Caroli F., "Per Lucia Anguissola", in *Paragone*, 283, 1973, pp. 69–73.

Fantelli P. L., "Chiara Varotari (sorella del Padovanino) e i suoi dipinti al Museo Civico", abstract of "Padova e la sua Provincia", no. 1, January 1973, pp. 2–7.

Pepper D. S., "Guido Reni's 'Il Diamante': A New Masterpiece for Toledo", in *The Burlington Magazine*, CXV, 847, 1973, pp. 630–639.

1974

Faré M., *Le grand siècle de la nature morte en France. Le XVIIe siècle*, Freiburg-Paris, 1974.

Marini M., "L'opera di Simon Vouet nella cappella Alaleoni in San Lorenzo in Lucina", in *Arte Illustrata*, 58, 1974, pp. 197–203.

1975

Manaresi A., *Il processo di avvelenamento fatto nel 1665-66 in Bologna contro Lucia Tolomelli per la morte di Elisabetta Sirani* (1904), Bologna, 1975.

1976

Askew P., "Lucrina Fetti", in *Women Artists 1550-1950*, exhibition catalogue (Los Angeles, County Museum of Art, 21 December 1976 – 13 March 1977; Austin, University Art Museum, 12 April – 12 June 1977; Pittsburgh, Museum of Art, 14 July – 4 September 1977; Brooklyn, City Museum, 8 October – 27 November 1977), New York, 1976, pp. 127–128.

Cipriani A., "Giovanna Garzoni miniatrice", in *Ricerche di Storia dell'Arte*, I, 1–2, 1976, pp. 241–254.

Dizionario enciclopedico dei pittori e degli incisori italiani dall'XI al XX secolo, XI, Turin, 1976.

Godi G., *Nicolò dell'Abate e la presunta attività del Parmigianino a Soragna*, Parma, 1976.

Omaggio a Leopoldo de' Medici, part II: *Ritrattini*, exhibition catalogue (Florence, Gabinetto Disegni e Stampe degli Uffizi, February–April 1976), edited by A. Forlani Tempesti, A. M. Petroli Tofani, S. Meloni Trkulja, Florence, 1976.

Opere d'arte a Vercelli e nella sua provincia. Recuperi e restauri 1900-1970, exhibition catalogue (Vercelli, Museo Borgogna, June–September 1976), Turin, 1976.

Pelaggi A., *Catalogo delle opere in pittura con note illustrative*, s.l. [Chiaravalle], 1976.

Santi F., "Una tela di Orazio Gentileschi in Umbria", in *Bollettino d'Arte*, LXI, V, I-II, 1976, pp. 43–44.

Strocchi M. L., "Ricerche d'Archivio. Il Gabinetto d'opere in piccolo del Gran Principe Ferdinando a Poggio a Caiano", in *Paragone*, 27, 311, 1976, pp. 83–116.

Vils U., "A Tribute to Women Artists", in *Los Angeles Times*, 27 December 1976, pp. IV/1, 6.

Weil Carr A., "Women Artists in the Middle Ages", in *The Feminist Art Journal*, 5, 1, 1976, pp. 5–9, 26.

Women Artists 1550-1950, exhibition catalogue (Los Angeles, County Museum of Art, 21 December 1976 – 13 March 1977; Austin, University Art Museum, 12 April – 12 June 1977; Pittsburgh, Museum of Art, 14 July – 4 September 1977; Brooklyn, City Museum, 8 October – 27 November 1977), New York, 1976.

1977

Fossaluzza G., "Schede su Pietro Damini", in *Pietro Damini 1592-1631. Pittura e Controriforma*, proceedings of the study day (Padua, 29 September 1993), edited by D. Banzato, P. L. Fantelli, in *Bollettino del Museo Civico di Padova*, LXVI, 1977 [1994], pp. 123–154.

Pittura francese nelle collezioni pubbliche fiorentine, exhibition catalogue (Florence, Palazzo Pitti, 24 April – 30 June 1977), edited by P. Rosenberg with S. Meloni Trkulja, I. Julia, N. Reynaud, Florence, 1977.

Ruotolo R., "Aspetti del collezionismo napoletano: il cardinale Filomarino", in *Antologia di Belle Arti*, March 1977, pp. 71–82.

1978

Bona Castellotti M., "Due aggiunte al catalogo di Fede Galizia", in *Arte Lombarda*, 49, 1978, pp. 30–32.

Colombo C., *Virginia Vezzi: una pittrice veliterna alla corte di Luigi XIII*, s.l., 1978, pp. 92–94.

Di Giampaolo M., "Camillo Boccaccino: A Painting and a Drawing", in *The Burlington Magazine*, CXX, 899, 1978, pp. 82–85.

Frisoni F., "La vera Sirani", in *Paragone*, 335, 1978, pp. 3–18.

1979

Bandera S., "Un corrispondente cremonese di Leopoldo de' Medici: Giovanni Battista Natali e la provenienza dei disegni cremonesi degli Uffizi", in *Paragone*, 347, 1979, pp. 34–55 and 92–106.

Meloni Trkulja S., "Le miniature degli Uffizi", in *Gli Uffizi. Catalogo generale*, Florence, 1979, pp. 1167–1172.

Spanò Martinelli S., "Caterina Vigri, santa", in *Dizionario Biografico degli Italiani*, 22, Rome, 1979, pp. 381–383.

Sutherland Harris A., "Introduzione", in A. Sutherland Harris, L. Nochlin, *Le grandi pittrici 1550-1950*, Milan, 1979, pp. 15–42.

Sutherland Harris A., Nochlin L., *Le grandi pittrici 1550-1950*, Milan, 1979.

1980

Garrard M. D., "Artemisia Gentileschi's Self-Portrait as the Allegory of Painting", in *The Art Bulletin*, LXII, 1, 1980, pp. 97–112.

Larsen E., *L'opera completa di Van Dyck 1613-1626*, Milan, 1980.

Mostra di opere restaurate. Secoli XIV-XIX, exhibition catalogue (Modena, December 1980 – January 1981), edited by C. Volpe, G. Guandalini, Modena, 1980.

1981

Artemisia Gentileschi / Agostino Tassi. Atti di un processo per stupro, edited by E. Menzio, Milan, 1981.

Fortunati Pietrantonio V., "Per una storia della presenza femminile nella vita artistica del Cinquecento bolognese: Properzia de' Rossi 'schultrice'", in *Il Carrobbio*, VII, 1981, pp. 168–177.

Marchetti V., "Chizzola, Ippolito", in *Dizionario Biografico degli Italiani*, 25, Rome, 1981, pp. 68–72.

Pallucchini R., *La pittura veneziana del Seicento*, 2 vols., Milan, 1981.

Splendours of the Gonzaga, exhibition catalogue (London, Victoria and Albert Museum, 4 November 1981 – 31 January 1982), edited by D. S. Chambers, J. Martineau, Cinisello Balsamo, 1981.

Talvacchia B., *Giulio Romano's Sala di Troia: A Synthesis of Epic Narrative and Emblematic Imagery*, ph. Diss., Stanford University, Ann Arbor, 1981.

Tanzi M., "Inediti campeschi tra 'vero' e 'maniera'", in *Itinerari. Contributi alla storia dell'arte in memoria di M.L. Ferrari*, II, 1981, pp. 67–77.
Weimann J. M., *The Fair Women. The Story of The Woman's Building World's Columbian Exposition Chicago 1893*, Chicago, 1981.

1982
Feminism and Art History. Questioning the Litany, edited by N. Broude, M. D. Garrard, New York, 1982.
Fortunati Pietrantonio V., "L'immaginario degli artisti bolognesi tra Maniera e Controriforma: Prospero Fontana (1512-1597)", in *Le arti a Bologna e in Emilia dal XVI al XVII secolo*, proceedings of the 24th Congress of C.I.H.A. (Bologna, 10–18 September 1979), edited by A. Emiliani, Bologna, 1982, pp. 97–111.
Garrard M. D., "Artemisia and Susanna", in *Feminism and Art History. Questioning the Litany*, edited by N. Broude, M. D. Garrard, New York, 1982, pp. 146–171.
Haskell F., *Riscoperte nell'arte. Aspetti del gusto, della moda e del collezionismo*, Milan, 1982.
Levi Momigliano L., "Per la storia delle collezioni sabaude: due inventari del 1822", in *Conoscere la Galleria Sabauda. Documenti sulla storia delle sue collezioni*, Turin, 1982, pp. 87–100.
Romano G., "Le origini dell'armeria sabauda e la Grande Galleria di Carlo Emanuele I", in *L'Armeria Reale di Torino*, edited by F. Mazzini, Busto Arsizio, 1982, pp. 15–30.

1983
Fiorillo C., "Francesco de Maria (I)", in *Napoli Nobilissima*, XXII, 1983, pp. 183–209.
Goldberg E., *Patterns in Late Medici Art Patronage*, Princeton, 1983.
Meloni Trkulja S., "Corvini, Maddalena", in *Dizionario Biografico degli Italiani*, 29, Rome, 1983a (on-line).
Meloni Trkulja S., "Giovanna Garzoni miniatora medicea", in *FMR*, 15, 1983b, pp. 77–96.
Shearman J., *The Pictures in the Collection of Her Majesty The Queen. The Early Italian Pictures*, Cambridge (Mass.) - London, 1983.
Spike J. T., *Italian Still Life Paintings from Three Centuries*, Florence, 1983.
The Illustrated Bartsch. Italian Masters of the Seventeenth Century, edited by P. Bellini, M. Carter Leach, XLIV, New York, 1983.

1984
Brugnoli M. V., "Le porte minori", in *La basilica di San Petronio in Bologna*, Cinisello Balsamo, 1984, II, pp. 61–94.
Carapelli R., "Annibale Ranuzzi e i suoi rapporti con la Firenze medicea del Seicento", in *Il Carrobbio*, X, 1984, pp. 69–79.
Comelli G., "Irene di Spilimbergo in una prestigiosa edizione del Cinquecento con un carme latino di Tiziano", in *Spilimbèrc*, edited by N. Cantarutti, C. Bergamini, Udine, 1984, pp. 233–236.
Ghirardi A., "Una pittrice bolognese nella Roma del primo Seicento: Lavinia Fontana", in *Il Carrobbio*, X, 1984, pp. 148–161.
Natura morta italiana. Tre secoli di natura morta italiana. La raccolta Silvano Lodi, exhibition catalogue (Munich, Pinakothek der Moderne, 27 November 1984 –22 February 1985), edited by L. Salerno, Florence, 1984.
Rosci M., *Giovanna Garzoni dal Palazzo Reale di Torino a Superga*, in *Scritti di Storia dell'Arte in onore di Federico Zeri*, 2 vols., Milan, 1984, II, pp. 565–567.
Vittori F., "Cotta, Paolo Michele, detto Catellano", in *Dizionario Biografico degli Italiani*, 30, Rome, 1984, pp. 464–465.

1985
I Campi e la cultura artistica cremonese del Cinquecento, exhibition catalogue (Cremona, various venues, 27 April – 24 July), edited by M. Gregori, Milan, 1985.
Forma vera. Contributi a una storia della natura morta italiana, exhibition catalogue (Bergamo, Galleria Lorenzelli, 1985), edited by P. Lorenzelli, A. Veca, Bergamo, 1985.
Griseri A., "Ritratti sabaudi di Giovanna Garzoni", in *Studi Piemontesi*, XIV, 2, 1985, pp. 355–357.
La pittura lombarda del '600, edited by M. Bona Castellotti, Milan, 1985.
Rosci M., "Octavianus Monfort e la miniatura su pergamena nel XVII secolo", in P. Chiapatti, M. Rosci, *Octavianus Monfort*, Turin, 1985, pp. 7–35.
Santa Caterina Vegri, *Le Sette armi spirituali*, edited by C. Foletti, Padua, 1985.

1986
Nell'età di Correggio e dei Carracci. Pittura in Emilia dei secoli XVI e XVII, exhibition catalogue (Bologna, Pinacoteca Nazionale e Accademia di Belle Arti, Museo Civico Archeologico, 10 September – 10 November 1986; Washington, National Gallery of Art, 19 December 1986 – 16 February 1987; New York, The Metropolitan Museum of Art, 26 March – 24 May 1987), Bologna, 1986.
Fortunati Pietrantonio V., "Lavinia Fontana", in *Pittura bolognese del '500*, edited by V. Fortunati Pietrantonio, 2 vols., Bologna, 1986, II, pp. 727–775.
Französische Zeichnungen im Städelschen Kunstinstitut, 1550 bis 1800, exhibition catalogue (Frankfurt, Städtische Galerie im Städelschen Kunstinstitut, 14 November 1986 – 1 March 1987), edited by H. Bauereisen, M. Stuffmann, Frankfurt am Main, 1986.
Meloni Trkulja S., "Garzoni Giovanna", in *Il Seicento fiorentino: arte a Firenze da Ferdinando I a Cosimo III*, exhibition catalogue (Florence, Palazzo Strozzi, 21 December 1986 – 4 May 1987), edited by G. Guidi, D. Marcucci, 3 vols., Florence, 1986, III, pp. 97–99.
Winkelmann J., "Orazio Samacchini", in *Pittura bolognese del '500*, edited by V. Fortunati Pietrantonio, 2 vols., Bologna, 1986, II, pp. 631–682.
Zeri F., Rossi F., *La raccolta Morelli dell'Accademia Carrara*, Bergamo, 1986.

1987
Bertini G., *La Galleria del Duca di Parma. Storia di una collezione*, Parma, 1987.
Degli Angeli A. M., "Il mito della donna artista nella Bologna del Seicento", in *Il Carrobbio*, XIII, 1987, pp. 120–128.
Malerei in Venetien. Pittura nel Veneto. 1500-1800. 50 Werke aus dem Museo Civico in Padua. 50 opere dal Museo Civico di Padova, exhibition catalogue (Freiburg im Breisgau, Augustinermuseum, 2 October – 29 November 1987), Freiburg im Breisgau, 1987.

1988
Dall'avanguardia dei Carracci al secolo barocco (1580-1600), exhibition catalogue (Bologna, Museo Civico Archeologico, 7 July – 30 August 1988), edited by A. Emiliani, Bologna, 1988.
Carapelli R., "Un importante collezionista bolognese del Seicento: Ferdinando Cospi i suoi rapporti con la Firenze medicea", in *Il Carrobbio*, XIV, 1988, pp. 99–114.
Di Macco M., "Quadreria di Palazzo e pittori di corte. Le scelte ducali dal 1630 al 1684", in *Figure del Barocco in Piemonte. La corte, la città, i cantieri, le province*, edited by G. Romano, Turin, 1988, pp. 41–138.
Gagliardi G., *La Pinacoteca di Ascoli Piceno*, Ascoli Piceno, 1988.
Griseri A., *Il Diamante. La villa di Madama Reale Cristina di Francia*, Turin, 1988.
Larsen E., *The Paintings of Anthony van Dyck*, 2 vols., Freren, 1988.
Leonardi L., "Caterina Vegri", in *Scrittrici mistiche italiane*, edited by G. Pozzi, C. Leonardi, Genoa, 1988, pp. 261–286.
Luijten G., "Johannes Valdor, Corvinus Henricus", in *Hollstein's Dutch & Flemish Etchings Engravings and Woodcuts CA. 1450 – 1700. Petrus Valck to Petrus Esaias Van de Velde*, XXXII, Roosendaal, 1988.
Préaud M., *Inventaire du fonds français: Graveurs du XVII*e *siècle*, Paris, 1988.
La Quadreria Emo Capodilista. 543 dipinti dal '400 al '700, exhibition catalogue (Padua, Palazzo della Ragione, 7 May – 25 September 1988), edited by D. Banzato, Rome, 1988.
Sacchi R., "Documenti per Sofonisba Anguissola", in *Paragone*, 457, 1988, pp. 73–89.
Scalon C., *La biblioteca di Adriano di Spilimbergo (1542)*, Spilimbergo, 1988.

1989
Berra G., "Alcune puntualizzazioni sulla pittrice Fede Galizia attraverso le testimonianze del letterato Gherardo Borgogni", in *Paragone*, 469, 1989, pp. 14–29.
Biffi G., *Memorie per servire alla storia degli artisti cremonesi*, edited by L. Bandera Gregori, Cremona, 1989.
Cantaro M. T., *Lavinia Fontana bolognese "pittora singolare" 1552-1614*, Milan-Rome, 1989.
Caroli F., *Fede Galizia*, Turin, 1989a.
Caroli F., "Aggiunte a Sofonisba Anguissola", in *Arte Documento*, 3, 1989b, pp. 138–141.
Claude Mellan, gli anni romani. Un incisore tra Vouet e Bernini, exhibition catalogue (Rome, Galleria Nazionale d'Arte Antica, 24 October 1989 – 8 January 1990), edited by L. Ficacci, Rome, 1989.
Di Macco M., "Il ritratto e l'omaggio simbolico", in *Diana trionfatrice. Arte di Corte nel Piemonte del Seicento*, exhibition catalogue (Turin, 27 May – 24 September 1989), edited by M. Di Macco, G. Romano, Turin, 1989, pp. 18–19.
Diana trionfatrice. Arte di Corte nel Piemonte del Seicento, exhibition catalogue (Turin, 27 May – 24 September 1989), edited by M. Di Macco, G. Romano, Turin, 1989.
Frisoni F., "Elisabetta Sirani", in *La pittura in Italia. Il Seicento*, edited by M. Gregori, E. Schleier, 2 vols., Milan, 1989, II, p. 888.
Fumagalli E., "Giovanna Garzoni", in *La natura morta in Italia*, edited by F. Porzio, F. Zeri, 2 vols., Milan, 1989, II, pp. 568–571.
Garrard M. D., *Artemisia Gentileschi: The Image of the Female Hero in Italian Baroque Art*, Princeton, 1989.
Kusche M., "Sofonisba Anguissola en España retratista en la corte de Felipe II junto a Alonso Sánchez Coello y Jorge de la Rua", in *Archivo Español de Arte*, LXII, 248, 1989, pp. 391–420.
Morandotti A., "Margherita Caffi", in *La natura morta in Italia*, edited by F. Porzio, F. Zeri, 2 vols., Milan, 1989, I, pp. 254–259.
Piglione C., "Giovanna Garzoni", in *La pittura in Italia. Il Seicento*, edited by M. Gregori, E. Schleier, 2 vols., Milan, 1989, II, pp. 754–755.

Safarik E., Bottari F., "Elisabetta Marchioni", in *La natura morta in Italia*, edited by F. Porzio, F. Zeri, 2 vols., Milan, 1989, I, pp. 329–333.
Zerbi Fanna M., "Lucrina Fetti pittrice", in *Civiltà Mantovana*, 23, 1989, pp. 35–53.

1990
Berra G., "La natura morta nella bottega di Fede Galizia", in *Osservatorio delle Arti*, V, 1990, pp. 55–62.
Bona Castellotti M., "Uno studio recente su Fede Galizia", in *Arte cristiana*, LXXVIII, 1990, pp. 347–350.
Grasso S., "Appunti sui disegni figurativi di Pietro Novelli", in *Pietro Novelli e il suo ambiente*, exhibition catalogue (Palermo, Albergo dei Poveri, 10 June – 30 October 1990), Palermo, 1990, pp. 370–455.
Guazzoni V., "Dopo i Campi", in *Pittura a Cremona dal Romanico al Settecento*, edited by M. Gregori, Milan, 1990, pp. 49–58.
Pietro Novelli e il suo ambiente, exhibition catalogue (Palermo, Albergo dei Poveri, 10 June – 30 October 1990), Palermo, 1990.
Pittura a Cremona dal Romanico al Settecento, edited by M. Gregori, Milan, 1990.
Zarri G., *Le "sante vive". Profezie di corte e devozione femminile fra '400 e '500*, Turin, 1990.

1991
Artemisia, exhibition catalogue (Florence, Casa Buonarroti, 18 June – 4 November 1991), edited by R. Contini, G. Papi, Rome, 1991.
Bellini P., *L'opera incisa di Adamo e Diana Scultori*, Milan, 1991.
Bona Castellotti M., *Collezionisti a Milano nel '700. Giovanni Battista Visconti, Gian Matteo Pertusati, Giuseppe Pozzobonelli*, Florence, 1991.
Brejon de Lavergnée B., "Simon Vouet e il disegno", in *Vouet*, exhibition catalogue (Rome, Palazzo delle Esposizioni, 6 March – 28 April 1991), edited by J. Thuillier, B. Brejon de Lavergnée, D. Lavalle, Rome, 1991, pp. 229–231.
Casale G., *Giovanna Garzoni, "insigne miniatrice" 1600-1670*, Milan-Rome, 1991.
Fusco L., Corti G., "Giovanni Ciampolini (d. 1505), a Renaissance Dealer in Rome and His Collection of Antiquities", in *Xenia*, 21, 1991, pp. 1–46.
Merz J. M., *Pietro da Cortona. Der Aufstieg zum führenden Maler im barocken Rom*, Tübingen, 1991.
Natura morta italiana del secolo XVII. Una raccolta di dipinti inediti, exhibition catalogue (Milan, Le Quinte di via dell'Orso, 26 October – 16 November 1991), edited by C. Arosio, Milan, 1991.
Pagani V., "A Lunario for the Years 1584-1585 by Francesco da Volterra and Diana Mantovana", in *Print Quarterly*, VIII, 2, 1991, pp. 140–145.
La peinture vénitienne 1600-1800. 65 peintures des collections des musées de la ville de Padoue, exhibition catalogue (Nancy, Musée des Beaux-Arts, 27 June – 23 September 1991), edited by D. Banzato, F. Pellegrini, Nancy, 1991.
Per la storia della chiesa di Santa Teresa a Brindisi. Il restauro dell'angelo con il simbolo della passione, Brindisi, 1991.
Pinacoteca di Brera. Scuola emiliana, scientific direction F. Zeri, Milan, 1991.
Schutte Jacobson A., "Irene di Spilimbergo: The Image of a Creative Woman in Late Renaissance Italy", in *Renaissance Quarterly*, XLIV, 1, 1991, pp. 42–61.
Thuillier J., "Chi era Simon Vouet", in *Vouet*, exhibition catalogue (Rome, Palazzo delle Esposizioni, 6 March – 28 April 1991), edited by J. Thuillier, B. Brejon de Lavergnée, D. Lavalle, Rome, 1991a, pp. 17–24.
Thuillier J., "Vouet e il suo atelier", in *Vouet*, exhibition catalogue (Rome, Palazzo delle Esposizioni, 6 March – 28 April 1991), edited by J. Thuillier, B. Brejon de Lavergnée, D. Lavalle, Rome, 1991b, pp. 25–56.
Thuillier J., "Vouet e l'incisione", in *Vouet*, exhibition catalogue (Rome, Palazzo delle Esposizioni, 6 March – 28 April 1991), edited by J. Thuillier, B. Brejon de Lavergnée, D. Lavalle, Rome, 1991c, pp. 57–78.
Vouet, exhibition catalogue (Rome, Palazzo delle Esposizioni, 6 March – 28 April 1991), edited by J. Thuillier, B. Brejon de Lavergnée, D. Lavalle, Rome, 1991.

1992
Berra G., "Appunti per Fede Galizia", in *Arte cristiana*, 748, 1992, pp. 37–44.
Crelly W. R., "Marcello Giovannetti: sonnets et tableaux", in *Simon Vouet*, proceedings of the International Conference (Paris, Galeries Nationales du Grand Palais, 5–6–7 February 1991), edited by S. Loire, Paris, 1992, pp. 169–191.
Frisoni F., "Elisabetta Sirani", in *La scuola di Guido Reni*, edited by E. Negro, M. Pirondini, Modena, 1992a, pp. 343–364.
Frisoni F., "Giovanni Andrea Sirani", in *La scuola di Guido Reni*, edited by E. Negro, M. Pirondini, Modena, 1992b, pp. 365–381.
Ghirardi A., "Una ricerca iconografica nel cenacolo delle Anguissola: i ritratti di Minerva", in *Paragone*, 509–511, 1992, pp. 35–43.
Giulio Romano. Repertorio di fonti documentarie, edited by D. Ferrari, Rome, 1992.
Kusche M., "Sofonisba Anguissola retratista de la corte española", in *Paragone*, 509–511, 1992, pp. 3–34.
Michel O., "Virginia Vezzi et l'entourage de Simon Vouet à Rome", in *Simon Vouet*, proceedings of the International Conference (Paris, Galeries Nationales du Grand Palais, 5–6–7 February 1991), edited by S. Loire, Paris, 1992, pp. 123–131.
Pagani V., "Adamo Scultori and Diana Mantovana", in *Print Quarterly*, IX, 1, 1992, pp. 72–87.
Perlingieri I. S., *Sofonisba Anguissola: The First Great Woman Artist of the Renaissance*, New York, 1992.
Schleier E., "Lanfranco, Perrier, Simon et Aubin Vouet: quelques points de contact", in *Simon Vouet*, proceedings of the International Conference (Paris, Galeries Nationales du Grand Palais, 5–6–7 February 1991), edited by S. Loire, Paris, 1992, pp. 209–224.
Tellini Perina C., "Documenti inediti riguardanti Sofonisba Anguissola", in *Paragone*, 509–511, 1992, pp. 97–98.

1993
Belloni Speciale G., "Faber, Giovanni", in *Dizionario Biografico degli Italiani*, 43, Rome, 1993 (on-line).
Bruno I., *Giuseppe Patania pittore dell'Ottocento*, Palermo, 1993.
Cantaro M. T., "Aggiornamenti e precisazioni sul catalogo di Lavinia Fontana", in *Bollettino d'Arte*, LXXVIII, VI, 79, 1993, pp. 85–102.
Ceroni N., *Pinacoteca Comunale di Ravenna*, Rome, 1993.
Cuccia A., "Novelli Rosalia", in L. Sarullo, *Dizionario degli Artisti siciliani*, II: *Pittura*, edited by M. A. Spadaro, Palermo, 1993, p. 379.
Fredericksen B. F., *The Index of Paintings Sold in the British Isles during Nineteenth Century*, 3.1, London-Munich, 1993.
Giulio Romano pinxit et delineavit. Opere grafiche autografe di collaborazione e bottega, exhibition catalogue (Rome, Istituto nazionale per la grafica, 11 February –10 April 1993), edited by S. Massari, Rome, 1993.
Grönwoldt R., *Stickereien von der Vorzeit bis zur Gegenwart*, Munich, 1993.
Kliemann J., *Gesta dipinte. La grande decorazione nelle dimore italiane dal Quattrocento al Seicento*, Cinisello Balsamo, 1993.
Laureati L., Trezzani L., *Il patrimonio artistico del Quirinale. Pittura antica. La quadreria*, Rome-Milan, 1993.
Noè E., *Pinacoteca di Brera. Due dipinti bolognesi restaurati*, Milan, 1993.
Pietro Damini 1592-1631. Pittura e Controriforma, exhibition catalogue (Padua, Palazzo della Ragione, 15 May – 30 September 1993), edited by D. Banzato, P. L. Fantelli, Milan, 1993.

1993–1994
Ghirardi A., "Exempla per l'iconografia dell'infanzia nel secondo Cinquecento padano", in *Il Carrobbio*, XIX–XX, 1993–1994, pp. 123–139.

1994
Binaghi M. T., "I ricamatori milanesi tra Rinascimento e Barocco", in *I tessili nell'età di Carlo Bascapè vescovo di Novara (1593-1615)*, exhibition catalogue (Novara, Palazzo dei Vescovi, 19 November 1994 – 19 February 1995), edited by P. Venturoli, Novara, 1994, pp. 96–123.
Bora G., "Sofonisba Anguissola e la sua formazione cremonese: il ruolo del disegno", in *Sofonisba Anguissola e le sue sorelle*, exhibition catalogue (Cremona, Centro culturale "Città di Cremona" – Santa Maria della Pietà, 17 September – 11 December 1994; Vienna, Kunsthistorisches Museum, January–March 1995; Washington, The National Museum of Women in the Arts, April–June 1995), Milan, 1994, pp. 79–88.
Casale G., "Sul rapporto 'Arte-Scienza' nel sec. XVII: Giovanna Garzoni Pittrice Ascolana (1600-1670)", in *Il Seicento nelle Marche. Profilo di una civiltà*, edited by C. Costanza, M. Massa, Ancona, 1994, pp. 234–256.
De Grazia D., Schleier E., "St. Cecilia and an Angel. The Heads by Orazio Gentileschi, the Rest by Lanfranco", in *The Burlington Magazine*, CXXXVI, 1091, 1994, pp. 73–78.
Fortunati V., "Lavinia Fontana. Una pittrice nell'autunno del Rinascimento", in *Lavinia Fontana 1552-1614*, exhibition catalogue (Bologna, Museo Civico Archeologico, 1 October – 4 December 1994), edited by V. Fortunati, Milan, 1994, pp. 11–36.
Garrard M. D., "Here's Looking at Me: Sofonisba Anguissola and the Problem of the Woman Artist", in *Renaissance Quarterly*, XLVII, 3, 1994, pp. 556–622.
Ghirardi A., "Lavinia Fontana allo specchio. Pittrici e autoritratto nel secondo Cinquecento", in *Lavinia Fontana 1552-1614*, exhibition catalogue (Bologna, Museo Civico Archeologico, 1 October – 4 December 1994), edited by V. Fortunati, Milan, 1994a, pp. 37–51.
Ghirardi A., "Ritratto e scena di genere. Arte, scienza, collezionismo nell'autunno del Rinascimento", in *La pittura in Emilia e in*

Romagna. Il Cinquecento. Un'avventura artistica tra natura e idea, edited by V. Fortunati, Bologna 1994b, I, pp. 148–183.
Ghirardi A., "Per Bernardino Campi ritrattista", in *Quaderni di Palazzo Te*, 1, 1994c, pp. 79–87.
Gilardi A., "Le sorelle di Sofonisba", in *Sofonisba Anguissola e le sue sorelle*, exhibition catalogue (Cremona, Centro culturale "Città di Cremona" – Santa Maria della Pietà, 17 September - 11 December 1994; Vienna, Kunsthistorisches Museum, January–March 1995; Washington, The National Museum of Women in the Arts, April–June 1995), Milan, 1994, pp. 75–78.
Graziani I., "La leggenda dell'artista donna", in *La pittura in Emilia e in Romagna. Il Cinquecento. Un'avventura artistica tra natura e idea*, edited by V. Fortunati, Bologna, 1994, I, pp. 129–147.
Gregori M., "Fama e oblio di Sofonisba Anguissola", in *Sofonisba Anguissola e le sue sorelle*, exhibition catalogue (Cremona, Centro culturale "Città di Cremona" – Santa Maria della Pietà, 17 September – 11 December 1994; Vienna, Kunsthistorisches Museum, January–March 1995; Washington, The National Museum of Women in the Arts, April–June 1995), Milan, 1994, pp. 11–44.
Guazzoni V., "Donna, pittrice e gentildonna. La nascita di un mito femminile del Cinquecento", in *Sofonisba Anguissola e le sue sorelle*, exhibition catalogue (Cremona, Centro culturale "Città di Cremona" – Santa Maria della Pietà, 17 September – 11 December 1994; Vienna, Kunsthistorisches Museum, January–March 1995; Washington, The National Museum of Women in the Arts, April–June 1995), Milan, 1994, pp. 57–70.
Jacopo Tintoretto. Ritratti, exhibition catalogue (Venice, Gallerie dell'Accademia, 25 March – 10 July 1994; Vienna, Kunsthistorishes Museum, Gemäldegalerie, 31 July – 30 October 1994), edited by P. Rossi, Milan, 1994.
Kusche M., "Sofonisba Anguissola al servizio dei re di Spagna", in *Sofonisba Anguissola e le sue sorelle*, exhibition catalogue (Cremona, Centro culturale "Città di Cremona" – Santa Maria della Pietà, 17 September – 11 December 1994; Vienna, Kunsthistorisches Museum, January–March 1995; Washington, The National Museum of Women in the Arts, April–June 1995), Milan, 1994a, pp. 89–116.
Kusche M., "Sofonisba e il ritratto di rappresentanza ufficiale nella corte spagnola", in *Sofonisba Anguissola e le sue sorelle*, exhibition catalogue (Cremona, Centro culturale "Città di Cremona" – Santa Maria della Pietà, 17 September – 11 December 1994; Vienna, Kunsthistorisches Museum, January–March 1995; Washington, The National Museum of Women in the Arts, April–June 1995), Milan, 1994b, pp. 117–152.
Lavinia Fontana 1552-1614, exhibition catalogue (Bologna, Museo Civico Archeologico, 1 October – 4 December 1994), edited by V. Fortunati, Milan, 1994.
Musei d'Arte a Torino. Cataloghi e inventari delle collezioni sabaude, edited by S. Pinto, 7 files, n.d. [1994].
Papi G., "Artemisia, senza dimora conosciuta", in *Paragone*, 45, 529/533, 1994, pp. 197–202.
Sacchi R., "Sofonisba Anguissola", in *Sofonisba Anguissola e le sue sorelle*, exhibition catalogue (Cremona, Centro culturale "Città di Cremona" – Santa Maria della Pietà, 17 September – 11 December 1994; Vienna, Kunsthistorisches Museum, January–March 1995; Washington, The National Museum of Women in the Arts, April–June 1995), Milan, 1994a, pp. 71–74.
Sacchi R., "Tra la Sicilia e Genova: Sofonisba Anguissola Moncada e poi Lomellini", in *Sofonisba Anguissola e le sue sorelle*, exhibition catalogue (Cremona, Centro culturale "Città di Cremona" – Santa Maria della Pietà, 17 September – 11 December 1994; Vienna, Kunsthistorisches Museum, January–March 1995; Washington, The National Museum of Women in the Arts, April–June 1995), Milan, 1994b, pp. 153–169.
Sacchi R., "Intorno agli Anguissola", in *Sofonisba Anguissola e le sue sorelle*, exhibition catalogue (Cremona, Centro culturale "Città di Cremona" – Santa Maria della Pietà, 17 September – 11 December 1994; Vienna, Kunsthistorisches Museum, January–March 1995; Washington, The National Museum of Women in the Arts, April–June 1995), Milan, 1994c, pp. 345–360.
Sacchi R. (edited by), *Regesto dei documenti*, in *Sofonisba Anguissola e le sue sorelle*, exhibition catalogue (Cremona, Centro culturale "Città di Cremona" – Santa Maria della Pietà, 17 September – 11 December 1994; Vienna, Kunsthistorisches Museum, January–March 1995; Washington, The National Museum of Women in the Arts, April–June 1995), Milan, 1994d, pp. 361–402.
Sacchi R., "Fonti a stampa e letterarie 1550-1625", in *Sofonisba Anguissola e le sue sorelle*, exhibition catalogue (Cremona, Centro culturale "Città di Cremona" – Santa Maria della Pietà, 17 September – 11 December 1994; Vienna, Kunsthistorisches Museum, January–March 1995; Washington, The National Museum of Women in the Arts, April–June 1995), Milan, 1994e, pp. 403–411.
Il Secolo d'Oro della Pittura Napoletana: da Battistello a Luca Giordano, pittori del Seicento nei musei di Napoli, exhibition catalogue (Naples, Castel Sant'Elmo, Autumn 1994 – Spring 1995), edited by N. Spinosa, Naples, 1994.
Sofonisba Anguissola e le sue sorelle, exhibition catalogue (Cremona, Centro culturale "Città di Cremona" – Santa Maria della Pietà, 17 September – 11 December 1994; Vienna, Kunsthistorisches Museum, January–March 1995; Washington, The National Museum of Women in the Arts, April–June 1995), Milan, 1994.

1995

Bava A. M., "La collezione di pittura e i grandi progetti decorativi", in *Le collezioni di Carlo Emanuele I di Savoia*, edited by G. Romano, Turin, 1995a, pp. 211–252.
Bava A. M., "La collezione di oggetti preziosi", in *Le collezioni di Carlo Emanuele I di Savoia*, edited by G. Romano, Turin, 1995b, pp. 266–332.
Le collezioni del Museo Civico di Casale. Catalogo delle opere esposte, edited by G. Mazza, C. E. Spantigati, Casale Monferrato, 1995.
Le collezioni di Carlo Emanuele I di Savoia, edited by G. Romano, Turin, 1995.
Dardanello G., "Memoria professionale nei disegni degli Album Valperga. Allestimenti decorativi e collezionismo di mestiere", in *Le collezioni di Carlo Emanuele I di Savoia*, edited by G. Romano, Turin, 1995, pp. 63–134.
Dickey S. S., "'Met een wenende ziel ... doch droge ogen': Women holding handkerchiefs in seventeenth-century Dutch portraits", in *Nederlands Kunsthistorisch Jaarboek (NKJ) / Netherlands Yearbook for History of Art*, XLVI, 1995, pp. 332–367.
Epifani M., "La collezione di armi di Carlo Emanuele I", in *Le collezioni di Carlo Emanuele I di Savoia*, edited by G. Romano, Turin, 1995, pp. 321–323.
Ericani G., "Un rinascimento per le donne? La donna ritratta e la donna artista tra Cinque e Seicento", in *Tracciati del femminile a Padova. Immagini e Storie di Donne*, exhibition catalogue (Padua, Palazzo della Ragione, 5 March – 30 April 1995), edited by C. Limentani Virdis, M. Cisotto Nalon, Padua, 1995, pp. 71–76.
Fallica S., *Paternò: scopre in casa un capolavoro del '500*, in "Giornale di Sicilia", 26 April 1995, p. 23.
King C., "Looking a Sight: Sixteenth-Century Portraits of Woman Artists", in *Zeitschrift für Kunstgeschichte*, 58, 3, 1995, pp. 381–406.
The Lure of Still Life, edited by J. Lorenzelli, E. Lingenauber, Bergamo, 1995.
Mamino S., "Reimagining the Grande Galleria of Carlo Emanuele I of Savoy", in *Res, Anthropology and Aesthetics*, 27, 1995, pp. 70–88.
Michel O., "Maddalena Corvina e i suoi", in *Strenna dei Romanisti*, 1995, pp. 399–407.
Modesti A., "Elisabetta Sirani "Pittrice Eroina": A Portrait of the Artist as a Young Woman", in *Identità e Appartenenza: donne e relazioni di genere dal mondo classico all'età contemporanea*, edited by M. Palazzi, 3 vols., Bologna, 1995, III, pp. 745–768.
Rearick W. R., "Reflections on Tintoretto as a Portraitist", in *Artibus et Historiae*, XVI, 31, 1995, pp. 51–68.
Romano G., "Artisti alla corte di Carlo Emanuele I: la costruzione di una nuova tradizione figurativa", in *Le collezioni di Carlo Emanuele I di Savoia*, edited by G. Romano, Turin, 1995, pp. 535–544.
Sabbatini S., "Per una storia delle donne pittrici bolognesi: Anna Maria Sirani e Ginevra Cantofoli", in *Schede umanistiche*, 2, 1995, pp. 83–101.

1996

Casale G., "Giovanna Garzoni e l'arte del suo tempo. Alcuni aspetti della natura morta fiorentina del Seicento", in *Gli incanti dell'iride. Giovanna Garzoni pittrice nel Seicento*, exhibition catalogue (San Severino Marche, Palazzo di Città, 29 June – 31 August 1996), edited by G. Casale, Cinisello Balsamo, 1996, pp. 13–26.
De Sade, D. A. F., *Viaggio in Italia ovvero Dissertazioni critiche, storiche e filosofiche sulle città di Firenze, Roma, Napoli e Loreto, e sulle strade adiacenti a queste quattro città*, Turin, 1996.
Ericani G., "Chiara Varotari", in *Le tele svelate. Antologia di pittrici venete dal Cinquecento al Novecento*, edited by C. Limentani Virdis, Mirano, 1996, pp. 64–75.
Gli incanti dell'iride. Giovanna Garzoni pittrice nel Seicento, exhibition catalogue (San Severino Marche, Palazzo di Città, 29 June – 31 August 1996), edited by G. Casale, Cinisello Balsamo, 1996.
Murphy C. P., "Lavinia Fontana and "Le Dame della città": Understanding Female Artistic Patronage in Late Sixteenth-Century Bologna", in *Renaissance Studies*, X, 2, 1996, pp. 190–208.
Safarik E., *Collezione dei dipinti Colonna: inventari 1611-1795*, Berlin, 1996.

1997

Anderson J., *Judith*, Paris, 1997.
Bava A. M., "Guglielmo Caccia detto il Moncalvo

– Una biografia", in *Guglielmo Caccia detto il Moncalvo (1568-1625). Dipinti e disegni*, exhibition catalogue (Casale Monferrato, Museo Civico, 1997), edited by G. Romano, C. E. Spantigati, Casale Monferrato, 1997, pp. 17–25.
Fortunati V., "Fontana, Lavinia", in *Dizionario Biografico degli Italiani*, 48, Rome, 1997, pp. 694–695.
Fumagalli E., "Il granducato di Ferdinando II (1628-1670). Il cardinale Leopoldo (1617-1675)", in *Il Giardino del Granduca. Natura morta nelle collezioni medicee*, edited by M. Chiarini, Turin, 1997, pp. 141–153.
Hughes-Hallett L., *Cleopatra. Histories, Dreams and Distortions*, London, 1997.
Jacobs F. H., *Defining the Renaissance* Virtuosa. *Women Artists and the Language of Art History and Criticism*, Cambridge, 1997.
Paliaga F., "Le nature morte", in *La Pinacoteca. Origine e Collezioni*, edited by V. Guazzoni, Cremona, 1997, pp. 101–103.
Spear R. E., *The "Divine" Guido. Religion, Sex, Money and Art in the World of Guido Reni*, New Haven-London, 1997.

1998
Andrea Cefaly e la scuola di Cortale, exhibition catalogue (Catanzaro, Complesso Monumentale del San Giovanni, 18 December 1998 – 31 January 1999), edited by T. Sicoli, I. Valente, Catanzaro, 1998.
Baron J. H., "Paintress, Princess and Physician's Paramour: Poison or Perforation?", in *Journal of the Royal Society of Medicine*, 91, 1998, pp. 213–216.
Blu, rosso e oro. Segni e colori dell'araldica in carte, codici e oggetti d'arte, exhibition catalogue (Turin, Archivio di Stato, 29 September – 30 November 1998), edited by I. Massabò Ricci, M. Carassi, L. C. Gentile, Milan, 1998.
Bocchi G., Bocchi U., "Vincenzo Volò detto Vincenzino dei fiori", in *Naturaliter. Nuovi contributi alla natura morta in Italia settentrionale e Toscana fra XVII e XVIII secolo*, edited by G. Bocchi, U. Bocchi, Calenzano, 1998a, pp. 66–71.
Bocchi G., Bocchi U., "Margherita Volò Caffi detta Vicencina o Vicenzina o Vicenia", in *Naturaliter. Nuovi contributi alla natura morta in Italia settentrionale e Toscana fra XVII e XVIII secolo*, edited by G. Bocchi, U. Bocchi, Calenzano, 1998b, pp. 78–101.
Bocchi G., Bocchi U., "Francesca Volò Smiller detta Francesca Vicenzina", in *Naturaliter. Nuovi contributi alla natura morta in Italia settentrionale e Toscana fra XVII e XVIII secolo*, edited by G. Bocchi, U. Bocchi, Calenzano, 1998c, pp. 104–111.
Bocchi G., Bocchi U., "Elisabetta Marchioni", in *Naturaliter. Nuovi contributi alla natura morta in Italia settentrionale e Toscana fra XVII e XVIII secolo*, edited by G. Bocchi, U. Bocchi, Calenzano, 1998d, pp. 417–434.
Bottacin F., "Appunti per il soggiorno veneziano di Giovanna Garzoni: documenti inediti", in *Arte Veneta*, 52, 1998, pp. 141–147.
Brogi A., "Il patrimonio d'arte e del monastero. Dall'età dei Carracci all'arrivo dei Francesi", in *La Certosa di Bologna. Immortalità della memoria*, edited by G. Pesci, Bologna, 1998, pp. 56–71.
Brookes X., *Mantegna to Rubens. The Weld-Blundell Drawings Collection*, London, 1998.
Corsaro A., "Dionigi Atanagi e la silloge per Irene di Spilimbergo (Intorno alla formazione del giovane Tasso)", in *Italica*, 75, 1, 1998, pp. 41–61.
Fortunati V., "Lavinia Fontana: A Woman Artist in the Age of the Counter-Reformation", in *Lavinia Fontana of Bologna 1552-1614*, exhibition catalogue (Washington, The National Museum of Women in the Arts, 5 February – 7 June 1998), edited by V. Fortunati, Milan, 1998, pp. 13–31.
Galleria Colonna in Roma. Dipinti, edited by E. Safarik, Rome, 1998.
Galleria Nazionale di Parma. Catalogo delle opere del Cinquecento e iconografia farnesiana, edited by L. Fornari Schianchi, Milan, 1998.
Ghirardi A., "Women Artists of Bologna: The Self-Portrait and the Legend from Caterina Vigri to Anna Morandi Manzolini (1413-1774)", in *Lavinia Fontana of Bologna 1552-1614*, exhibition catalogue (Washington, The National Museum of Women in the Arts, 5 February – 7 June 1998), edited by V. Fortunati, Milan, 1998, pp. 32–47.
Lavinia Fontana of Bologna 1552-1614, exhibition catalogue (Washington, The National Museum of Women in the Arts, 5 February – 7 June 1998), edited by V. Fortunati, Milan, 1998.
Massimi M. E., "Galizia, Fede", in *Dizionario Biografico degli Italiani*, 51, Rome, 1998, pp. 499–502.
Morselli R., "Orazio Ceschi 1689", in *Collezioni e quadrerie nella Bologna del Seicento. Inventari 1640-1707*, edited by A. Cera Sones, Los Angeles, 1998a, pp. 161–163.
Morselli R., "Andrea Cattalani", in *Collezioni e quadrerie nella Bologna del Seicento. Inventari 1640-1707*, edited by A. Cera Sones, Los Angeles, 1998b, pp. 153–158.
Pinessi O., *Sofonisba Anguissola. Un "pittore" alla corte di Filippo II*, Milan, 1998.
Prelli A., *Vestirsi in provincia nel '600. L'abbigliamento in Terra Ferma. Il caso emblematico di Palma*, Palmanova, 1998.
La quadreria dell'Istituto Molina: un secolo e mezzo di storia, exhibition catalogue (Varese, Quadreria dell'Istituto Geriatrico Fratelli Molina, 28 November – 8 December 1998), Varese, 1998.
Rabisch. Il grottesco nell'arte del Cinquecento. L'Accademia della Val di Blenio, Lomazzo e l'ambiente milanese, exhibition catalogue (Lugano, Museo Cantonale d'Arte, 28 March – 21 June 1998), edited by G. Bora, M. Kahn-Rossi, F. Porzio, Milan, 1998.
Segal S., "An Early Still life by Fede Galizia", in *The Burlington Magazine*, CXL, 1140, 1998, pp. 164–171.
Spanò Martinelli S., "Caterina da Bologna", in *Il grande libro dei santi. Dizionario enciclopedico*, supervision by C. Leonardi, A. Riccardi, G. Zarri, edited by E. Guerriero, D. Toniz, 3 vols., Cinisello Balsamo, 1998, I, pp. 383–385.
Tesori ritrovati. La pittura del ducato estense nel collezionismo privato, edited by D. Benati, Milan, 1998.

1999
Benati D., "Lorenzo Sabbatini: 'quadri con donne nude'", in *Scritti di storia dell'arte in onore di Jürgen Winkelmann*, edited by S. Béguin, M. Di Giampaolo, P. Narcisi, Naples, 1999, pp. 51–63.
Bénézit E., "Dictionnaire des Peintres Sculpteurs Dessinateurs et Graveurs", edited by E. H. Zeiger-Viallet, J. Busse, Paris, 1999, III, p. 926.
Kliemann J., "Federico Zuccari e la Grande Galleria di Torino", in *Der Maler Federico Zuccari*, proceedings of the international congress of the Bibliotheca Hertziana (Rome-Florence, 23–26 February 1993), edited by M. Winner, D. Heikamp ("Romisches Jahrbuch der Bibliotheca Hertziana", 32), Munich, 1999, pp. 317–346.
Mamino S., "La Grande Galleria come 'Tipocosmo". Interessi naturalistici e enciclopedismo in Carlo Emanuele I', in *Le magnificenze del XVII-XVIII secolo alla Biblioteca Reale di Torino*, exhibition catalogue (Turin, Biblioteca Reale, 28 October – 15 December 1999), edited by G. Giacobello Bernard, A. Griseri, Milan-Turin, 1999a, pp. 47–67.
Mamino S., "Quarantotto immagini naturalistiche per la "Grande Galleria" di Carlo Emanuele I di Savoia", in *Politica e cultura nell'età di Carlo Emanuele I. Torino, Parigi, Madrid*, proceedings of the conference (Turin, 1995), edited by M. Masoero, S. Mamino, C. Rosso, Turin, 1999b, pp. 289–309.
Marubbi M., "Bernardino Campi e un nuovo ritratto di Vespasiano Gonzaga", in *Vespasiano Gonzaga 1531-1591. L'Uomo e le Opere*, proceedings of the conference (Sabbioneta, Teatro Olimpico, 5 June 1999), Viadana, 1999, pp. 39–50.
Museo d'Arte Antica del Castello Sforzesco. Pinacoteca, III, Milan, 1999.
Passerin d'Entrèves P., "Album di pesci, molluschi, crostacei, rettili e cetacei", in *Le magnificenze del XVII-XVIII secolo alla Biblioteca Reale di Torino*, exhibition catalogue (Turin, Biblioteca Reale, 28 October – 15 December 1999), edited by G. Giacobello Bernard, A. Griseri, Milan-Turin, 1999a, pp. 69–71.
Passerin d'Entrèves P., "Atlante degli uccelli", in *Le magnificenze del XVII-XVIII secolo alla Biblioteca Reale di Torino*, exhibition catalogue (Turin, Biblioteca Reale, 28 October – 15 December 1999), edited by G. Giacobello Bernard, A. Griseri, Milan-Turin, 1999b, pp. 71–72.
Pittura a Milano dal Seicento al Neoclassicismo, edited by M. Gregori, Milan, 1999.
Pozzi G., "Introduzione. Lettere ad Agnese", in Chiara d'Assisi, *Lettere ad Agnese; La visione dello specchio*, edited by G. Pozzi, B. Rima, Milan, 1999, pp. 13–57.
Safarik E., *Palazzo Colonna*, with contributions by M. G. Picozzi, R. Valeriani, Rome, 1999.
Simoni S., "Appunti intorno a Barbara Longhi (1562-1638)", in *Romagna arte e storia*, 19, 55, 1999, pp. 59–72.
Temperini R., "Tra barocco e classicismo", in *La pittura in Europa. La pittura francese*, edited by P. Rosenberg, Milan, 1999, pp. 246–247.
Ward Bissell R., *Artemisia Gentileschi and the Authority of Art. Critical Reading and Catalogue Raisonné*, State College, 1999.

2000
Acquisizioni e restauri. 1992-2000, exhibition catalogue (Asti, Palazzo Mazzetti, 2000), edited by E. Ragusa, Asti, 2000.
Banzato D., "Padova 1600-1650", in *La pittura nel Veneto. Il Seicento*, edited by M. Lucco, Milan, 2000, I, pp. 120–154.
Bonfait O., *Les Tableaux et les Pinceaux: la naissance de L'École Bolonaise (1680-1780)*, Rome, 2000.
Cammarota G. P., *Le origini della Pinacoteca Nazionale di Bologna. Una raccolta di fonti*, III: *La Collezione Zambeccari*, Bologna, 2000.
Il Cinquecento lombardo. Da Leonardo a Caravaggio, exhibition catalogue (Milan, Palazzo Reale, 4 October 2000 – 25 February 2001), edited by F. Caroli, Milan, 2000.

Fasto e rigore. La Natura Morta nell'Italia settentrionale dal XVI al XVIII secolo, exhibition catalogue (Reggia di Colorno, 20 April – 25 June 2000), edited by G. Godi, Milan, 2000.
Fumagalli E., "Giovanna Garzoni in Paris", in *Nature morte. Giovanna Garzoni*, edited by S. Meloni Trkulja, E. Fumagalli, Paris, 2000, pp. 11–12.
Lafranconi M., "Da Vouet a Poussin: la comunità artistica francese nell'Accademia di San Luca", in *L'idéal classique. Les échanges artistiques entre Rome et Paris au temps de Bellori, 1640-1700*, proceedings of the conference "Il Bello Ideale e le Accademie. Relazioni artistiche tra Roma e Parigi nell'età di Bellori" (Rome, Villa Medici, 7–9 June 2000), edited by O. Bonfait, A.-L. Desmas Rome, 2000, pp. 211–222.
Lincoln E., *The Invention of the Italian Renaissance Printmaker*, New Haven, CT 2000.
Nature morte. Giovanna Garzoni, edited by S. Meloni Trkulja, E. Fumagalli, Paris, 2000.
Ranuzzi. Storia genealogia e iconografia, edited by G. Malvezzi Campeggi, Bologna, 2000.
Rosci M., *Il Cerano*, Milan, 2000.
I segreti di un collezionista. Le straordinarie raccolte di Cassiano dal Pozzo 1588-1657, exhibition catalogue (Rome, Galleria Nazionale d'Arte Antica, Palazzo Barberini, 29 September – 26 November 2000), edited by F. Solinas, Rome, 2000.
Simoni S., "Barbara Longhi", in *Donne nella storia: nel territorio di Ravenna, Faenza e Lugo dal Medioevo al XX secolo*, edited by C. Bassi Angelini, Ravenna, 2000, pp. 209–214.
Solinas F., *L'Uccelliera: un libro di arte e di scienza nella Roma dei primi Lincei*, Florence, 2000.
Suor Plautilla Nelli (1523-1588). The First Woman Painter of Florence, proceedings of the conference (Fiesole, 27 May 1998), edited by J. Nelson, Fiesole, 2000.
Vigri C., *Laudi, trattati e lettere*, critical edition by S. Serventi, Florence, 2000a.
Vigri C., *Le Sette armi spirituali*, critical edition by A. Degl'Innocenti, Florence, 2000b.
Vincenzo Campi. Scene del quotidiano, exhibition catalogue (Cremona, Museo Civico Ala Ponzone, 2 December 2000 – 18 March 2001), Milan, 2000.
Viroli G., *I Longhi. Luca, Francesco, Barbara pittori ravennati (sec. XVI-XVII)*, Ravenna, 2000.

2001
Banzato D., "Varotari Chiara", in *La pittura nel Veneto. Il Seicento*, edited by M. Lucco, Milan, 2001, II, p. 884.
Cifani A., Monetti F., "'L'illustrissimo cugino': Cassiano e Amedeo dal Pozzo. Le relazioni artistiche del Marchese di Voghera e la storia della sua quadreria", in *I segreti di un collezionista. Le straordinarie raccolte di Cassiano dal Pozzo (1588-1657)*, exhibition catalogue (Biella, Museo del Territorio Biellese, 16 December 2001 – 16 March 2002), edited by F. Solinas, Rome, 2001, pp. 29–52.
De Girolami Cheney L., "Lavinia Fontana: A Woman Collector of Antiquity", in *Aurora. The Journal of the History of Art*, 2, 2001, pp. 22–42.
Face to Face. Portraits from Five Centuries, exhibition catalogue (Stoccolma, Nationalmuseum, 4 October 2001 – 27 January 2002), edited by G. Cavalli-Björkman, E.-L. Karlsson, Stockholm 2001.
Garrard M. D., *Artemisia Gentileschi Around 1622. The Shaping and Reshaping of an Artistic Identity*, Berkeley, 2001.
I Giustiniani e l'antico, exhibition catalogue (Rome, Palazzo Fontana di Trevi, 26 October 2001 – 27 January 2002), edited by G. Fusconi, Rome, 2001.
Melasecchi O., "Ginnasi, Caterina", in *Dizionario Biografico degli Italiani*, 55, Rome, 2001, pp. 770–774.
Miller D. C., *Marcantonio Franceschini*, Turin, 2001.
Modesti A., "The Making of a Cultural Heroine: Elisabetta Sirani 'Pittrice Celebrissima' di Bologna", in *Per l'Arte. Da Venezia all'Europa. Studi in onore di Giuseppe Maria Pilo*, edited by M. Piantoni, L. De Rossi, 2 vols., Monfalcone, 2001a, II, pp. 399–404.
Modesti A., "Alcune riflessioni sulle opere grafiche di Elisabetta Sirani nelle raccolte dell'Archiginnasio", in *L'Archiginnasio*, 94, 2001b, pp. 151–215.
Orazio e Artemisia Gentileschi, exhibition catalogue (Rome, Palazzo Venezia, 20 October 2001 – 20 January 2002; New York, The Metropolitan Museum of Art, 14 February – 12 May 2002; Saint Louis, The Saint Louis Art Museum, 15 June – 15 September 2002), edited by K. Christiansen, J. W. Mann, Milan, 2001.
Pezzini Bernini G., "La collezione di disegni e stampe Corsini nell'ambito del collezionismo di grafica del XVIII secolo", in *Il Gabinetto nazionale delle Stampe. Storia e collezioni*, edited by G. Mariani, Rome, 2001, pp. 65–87.
Pinacoteca comunale di Ravenna. La Collezione Antica, edited by N. Ceroni, Ravenna, 2001.
Rizzini M., "'Essendo che sono cose che restano a perpetua memoria'. Due ricami milanesi del primo Seicento", in *Il ricamo in Italia dal XVI al XVIII secolo*, proceedings of the study days (Novara, 21–22 November 1998), edited by F. Fiori, M. Zanetta Accornero, Novara, 2001, pp. 74–143.
Sarti S., *Giovanni Pietro Campana 1808-1880, the Man and his Collection*, Oxford, 2001.
Zama R., "Un'inedita Santa Caterina siglata Barbara Longhi", in *Romagna arte e storia*, 65, 2001, pp. 79–84.

2002
Amor è vivo. Due dipinti erotici di Lavinia Fontana, exhibition catalogue (Milan, Galleria Marco Riccomini, April 2002), Milan, 2002.
Baldriga I., *L'occhio della lince. I primi lincei tra arte, scienza e collezionismo (1603-1630)*, Rome, 2002.
Biancani S., "La leggenda di un'artista monaca: Caterina Vigri", in *Vita artistica nel monastero femminile. Exempla*, edited by V. Fortunati, Bologna, 2002, pp. 203–219.
Bohn B., "The Antique Heroines of Elisabetta Sirani", in *Renaissance Studies*, XVI, 1, 2002, pp. 52–79.
Cottino A., "Storie di donne e di pittura", in *Il genio e la grazia. La Donna nella pittura italiana del Sei e Settecento*, edited by A. Cottino, Turin, 2003, pp. 15–32.
D'Apuzzo M. G., "Le monache di Savonarola tra arte e committenza", in *Vita artistica nel monastero femminile. Exempla*, edited by V. Fortunati, Bologna, 2002, pp. 131–145.
De Fanti L., "Il 'Pittore della Santa': Marcantonio Franceschini e la decorazione nella chiesa del Corpus Domini di Bologna", in *Vita artistica nel monastero femminile. Exempla*, edited by V. Fortunati, Bologna, 2002, pp. 265–289.
Di Macco M., "'Critica occhiuta': la cultura figurativa (1630-1678)", in *Storia di Torino*, IV: *La città fra crisi e ripresa (1630-1730)*, edited by G. Ricuperati, Turin, 2002, pp. 337–430.
I dipinti della Galleria Nuova, edited by G. Rodella, Mantua, 2002.
Fortunati V., "Ruolo e funzione dell'immagine nei monasteri femminili", in *Vita artistica nel monastero femminile. Exempla*, edited by V. Fortunati, Bologna, 2002, pp. 11–42.
Ghirardi A., "Dipingere in lode del Cielo: suor Orsola Maddalena Caccia e la vocazione artistica delle Orsoline di Moncalvo", in *Vita artistica nel monastero femminile. Exempla*, edited by V. Fortunati, Bologna, 2002, pp. 115–129.
Graziani I., "L'iconografia di Caterina Vigri: dalla clausura alla città", in *Vita artistica nel monastero femminile. Exempla*, edited by V. Fortunati, Bologna, 2002, pp. 220–241.
Marotta Rizzo F., "Il dubbio sciolto. La storia di un quadro ritrovato", in *Scena illustrata*, 12, 2002, pp. 27–28.
Mazza A., "Da Parma a Bologna con Nicolò dell'Abate: le grandi vedute della campagna bolognese della giovane Lavinia Fontana", in *Parmigianino e il manierismo europeo*, proceedings of the international study conference (Parma, 13–15 June 2002), edited by L. Fornari Schianchi, Milan, 2002, pp. 392–398.
Percorsi nell'arte dal XVI al XVIII secolo, exhibition catalogue (Bologna, Fondantico, 26 October – 24 December 2002), edited by D. Benati, Bologna, 2002.
Rebecchini G., "Sculture e scultori nella Mantova di Giulio Romano. 1. Bernardino Germani e il sepolcro di Pietro Strozzi (con il cognome di Giovan Battista Scultori)", in *Prospettiva*, 108, 2002, pp. 65–79.
Il ritratto in Lombardia da Moroni a Ceruti, exhibition catalogue (Varese, Castello di Masnago, 21 April – 14 July 2002), edited by F. Frangi, A. Morandotti, Milan, 2002.
Tongiorgi Tomasi L., "The Flowering of Florence: Botanical Art for the Medici", in *The Flowering of Florence. Botanical Art for the Medici*, exhibition catalogue (Washington, National Gallery of Art, 3 March – 27 May 2002), edited by L. Tongiorgi Tomasi, G. Hirschauer, Washington-London, 2002, pp. 15–107.
Vita artistica nel monastero femminile. Exempla, edited by V. Fortunati, Bologna, 2002.
Weaver E. B., *Convent Theatre in Early Modern Italy: Spiritual Fun and Learning for Women*, Cambridge, 2002.

2003
Chiodo A., "Orsola Maddalena Caccia: note in margine alla vita e alle opere di una monaca pittrice", in *Archivi e storia*, 21–22, 2003, pp. 153–202.
Danesi Squarzina S., *La collezione Giustiniani*, Turin, 2003.
La donna nella pittura italiana del Seicento e Settecento. Il Genio e la Grazia, exhibition catalogue (Turin, Museo Pietro Accorsi, 28 March – 27 July 2003), edited by A. Cottino, Turin, 2003.
Ghirardi A., "Strategie dell'apparire. Ritratti d'amore e di morte nell'Italia moderna", in *Storia d'Italia. Annali 19*, *La moda*, edited by C. M. Belfanti, F. Giusberti, Turin, 2003, pp. 149–183.
Kusche M., *Retratos y retratadores. Alonso Sánchez Coello y sus competidores Sofonisba Anguissola, Jorge de la Rua y Rolan Moys*, Madrid, 2003.
Modesti A., "Patrons as Agents and Artists as Dealers in Seicento Bologna", in *The Art Market in Italy 15th-17th Centuries / Il Mercato dell'Arte in Italia secc. XV-XVII*, edited by M. Fantoni, L. C. Matthew, S. F. Matthews-Grieco, Modena, 2003, pp. 367–388.

Murphy C. P., *Lavinia Fontana. A Painter and her Patrons in Sixteenth-Century Bologna*, Cambridge, 2003.

Nature morte lombarde del XVII e XVIII secolo, exhibition catalogue (Milan, Galleria Lampronti-Lebole, 7 April – 20 May 2003), edited by M. C. Bagolan, Milan, 2003.

Pasti S., "La Vierge, reine des anges: les sources d'un dessin de Primatice (1504-1570) conservé au musée du Louvre", in *La revue des musées de France*, 63, 5, 2003, pp. 38–47.

Pedrocco F., "Le pittrici a Venezia tra Seicento e Settecento", in *La donna nella pittura italiana del Seicento e Settecento. Il Genio e la Grazia*, exhibition catalogue (Turin, Museo Pietro Accorsi, 28 March – 27 July 2003), edited by A. Cottino, Turin, 2003, pp. 75–82.

Pellicciari A., "Due dipinti di Giovan Andrea ed Elisabetta Sirani per S. Girolamo della Certosa", in *Il Carrobbio*, XXIX, 2003, pp. 179–196.

Piccinelli R., *Le collezioni Gonzaga. Il carteggio tra Milano e Mantova (1563-1634)*, Cinisello Balsamo, 2003.

La Pinacoteca Ala Ponzone. Il Cinquecento, edited by M. Marubbi, Cinisello Balsamo, 2003.

Il processo di canonizzazione di Caterina Vigri (1586-1712), critical edition by S. Spanò Martinelli, Florence, 2003.

2003–2004

Serafini C., *Arte, scienza e diletto nella Roma di Urbano VIII: il trattato 'De Florum Cultura' di Giovanni Battista Ferrari S.I. (1583-1655). Una fonte per il giardino italiano*, thesis, Università degli Studi di Roma "La Sapienza", Literature and Philosophy Department, History of Art Institute, 2003–2004.

2004

Abbate V., "Van Dyck a Palermo", in *Anton van Dyck. Riflessi italiani*, exhibition catalogue (Milan, Palazzo Reale, 19 February – 4 July 2004), edited by M. G. Bernardini, Milan, 2004, pp. 69–81.

Anselmi A., *Il diario del viaggio in Spagna del cardinale Francesco Barberini scritto da Cassiano dal Pozzo*, Aranjuez (Madrid), 2004.

Artemisia Gentileschi. Lettere precedute da Atti di un processo per stupro, edited by E. Menzio, with an essay by A. Boetti and a text by R. Barthes, Milan, 2004.

Bocchi G., "La famiglia Volò, Ludovico Caffi e Gilardo da Lodi", in *Gilardo da Lodi e la pittura d'uva in Lombardia nel Seicento e nel Settecento*, exhibition catalogue (Lodi, church of San Cristoforo, 24 April – 6 June 2004), edited by T. Gipponi, Milan, 2004, pp. 33–41.

Bohn B., "Female Self-portraiture in Early Modern Bologna", in *Renaissance Studies*, XVIII, 2, 2004a, pp. 239–286.

Bohn B., "Elisabetta Sirani and Drawing Practices in Early Modern Bologna", in *Master Drawings*, XLII, 2004b, pp. 207–236.

Bohn B., "Il fenomeno della firma: Elisabetta Sirani e le firme dei pittori a Bologna", in *Elisabetta Sirani "pittrice eroina" 1638-1665*, exhibition catalogue (Bologna, Museo Civico Archeologico, 4 December 2004 – 27 February 2005), edited by J. Bentini, V. Fortunati, Bologna, 2004c, pp. 107–117.

Bottacin F., *Tiberio Tinelli "Pittore e Cavaliere"*, Mariano del Friuli, 2004a.

Bottacin F., "Giovanna Garzoni pittrice di ritratti 'amorevoli': una proposta per il soggiorno veneziano", in *Donne a Venezia: vicende femminili fra Trecento e Settecento*, edited by S. Winter, Rome, 2004b, pp. 71–83.

Checa Cremades F., "El marqués del Carpio (1629-1687) y la pintura veneciana del Renacimiento. Negociaciones de Antonio Saurer", in *Anales de Historia del Arte*, 14, 2004, pp. 193–212.

Cléopâtre dans le miroir de l'art occidental, exhibition catalogue (Ginevra, Musée Rath, 25 March – 1 August 2004), edited by C. Ritschard, A. Morehead, Milan, 2004.

Corelli Grappadelli I., "Il cosiddetto stemma della famiglia Grassi e la scultrice Properzia de' Rossi", in *Atti e memorie. Deputazione di Storia Patria per le Province di Romagna*, 2004, pp. 315–333.

Elisabetta Sirani "pittrice eroina" 1638-1665, exhibition catalogue (Bologna, Museo Civico Archeologico, 4 December 2004 – 27 February 2005), edited by J. Bentini, V. Fortunati, Bologna, 2004.

Fortunati V., "Frammenti di un dialogo nel tempo: Elisabetta Sirani e le donne artiste", in *Elisabetta Sirani "pittrice eroina" 1638-1665*, exhibition catalogue (Bologna, Museo Civico Archeologico, 4 December 2004 – 27 February 2005), edited by J. Bentini, V. Fortunati, Bologna, 2004a, pp. 19–39.

Fortunati V., "Pregare con le immagini. Le miniature di Caterina Vigri nel suo breviario", in *Pregare con le immagini. Il breviario di Caterina Vigri*, edited by V. Fortunati, C. Leonardi, Florence, 2004b, pp. 43–81.

Frisoni F., "Una Sirani ancora più vera", in *Elisabetta Sirani "pittrice eroina" 1638-1665*, exhibition catalogue (Bologna, Museo Civico Archeologico, 4 December 2004 – 27 February 2005), edited by J. Bentini, V. Fortunati, Bologna, 2004, pp. 77–89.

Ghirardi A., "Con gli occhi al cielo. Elisabetta Sirani e il ritratto", in *Elisabetta Sirani "pittrice eroina" 1638-1665*, exhibition catalogue (Bologna, Museo Civico Archeologico, 4 December 2004 – 27 February 2005), edited by J. Bentini, V. Fortunati, Bologna, 2004, pp. 91–105.

Gilardo da Lodi e la pittura d'uva in Lombardia nel Seicento e nel Settecento, exhibition catalogue (Lodi, church of San Cristoforo, 24 April – 6 June 2004), edited by T. Gipponi, Milan, 2004.

Gozzano N., *La quadreria di Lorenzo Onofrio Colonna. Prestigio nobiliare e collezionismo nella Roma barocca*, Rome, 2004.

Graziani I., "Il Cenacolo di Elisabetta Sirani", in *Elisabetta Sirani "pittrice eroina" 1638-1665*, exhibition catalogue (Bologna, Museo Civico Archeologico, 4 December 2004 – 27 February 2005), edited by J. Bentini, V. Fortunati, Bologna, 2004a, pp. 119–133.

Graziani I., "L'icona della monaca artista e le fonti storiografiche sul Breviario di Caterina Vigri", in *Pregare con le immagini. Il breviario di Caterina Vigri*, edited by V. Fortunati, C. Leonardi, Florence, 2004b, pp. 29–42.

L'Occaso S., "Pitture dell'epoca del duca Ferdinando", in *Atti e memorie dell'Accademia Nazionale Virgiliana*, LXXI, 2003 (2004), pp. 53–68.

Lacchia C., Pozzato R., conservative sheet and historical-artistic report on Elisabetta Sirani's painting, *Sacra Famiglia con sant'Anna, san Giovannino e un angelo*, Vercelli, Archivio Museo Borgogna, 2004.

Leonardi C., "Le glosse di Caterina Vigri al suo breviario", in *Pregare con le immagini. Il breviario di Caterina Vigri*, edited by V. Fortunati, C. Leonardi, Florence, 2004, pp. 9–27.

Modesti A., *Elisabetta Sirani. Una virtuosa del Seicento bolognese*, Bologna, 2004.

Pittori della realtà. Le ragioni di una rivoluzione da Foppa e Leonardo a Caravaggio e Ceruti, exhibition catalogue (Cremona, Museo Civico Ala Ponzone, 14 February – 2 May 2004), edited by M. Gregori, A. Bayer, Milan, 2004.

Pregare con le immagini. Il breviario di Caterina Vigri, edited by V. Fortunati, C. Leonardi, Florence, 2004.

Pulini M., "1656. Ritratto di Ginevra Cantofoli pittrice", in *Elisabetta Sirani "pittrice eroina" 1638-1665*, exhibition catalogue (Bologna, Museo Civico Archeologico, 4 December 2004 – 27 February 2005), edited by J. Bentini, V. Fortunati, Bologna, 2004, pp. 134–141.

Roncuzzi Roversi-Monaco V., "Il 'personaggio' Elisabetta Sirani nella produzione editoriale bolognese dell'Ottocento", in *Elisabetta Sirani "pittrice eroina" 1638-1665*, exhibition catalogue (Bologna, Museo Civico Archeologico, 4 December 2004 – 27 February 2005), edited by J. Bentini, V. Fortunati, Bologna, 2004, pp. 153–163.

Witcombe C. L. C. E., *Copyright in the Renaissance. Prints and the* privilegio *in Sixteenth-century Venice and Rome*, Leiden-Boston ,2004.

2004–2005

Morandotti A., "Inventare una famiglia. Un pezzo di bravura nella Milano di Federico Borromeo", in *Nuovi Studi*, 11, 2004–2005, pp. 213–224.

2005

Astrua P., "Gli anni di Emanuele Filiberto", in *"Il nostro pittore fiamengo". Giovanni Caracca alla corte dei Savoia (1568-1607)*, exhibition catalogue (Turin, Galleria Sabauda, 21 September 2005 – 8 January 2006), edited by P. Astrua, A. M. Bava, C. E. Spantigati, Turin, 2005, pp. 9–26.

Atti dell'Accademia Clementina (1710-1764) Verbali consiliari, edited by S. Questioli, transcript by D. Magnolo, S. Questioli, I, Bologna, 2005.

Bava A. M., "Giovanni Caracca alla corte dei Savoia", in *"Il nostro pittore fiamengo". Giovanni Caracca alla corte dei Savoia (1568-1607)*, exhibition catalogue (Turin, Galleria Sabauda, 21 September 2005 – 8 January 2006), edited by P. Astrua, A. M. Bava, C. E. Spantigati, Turin, 2005, pp. 27–44.

Il Cerano 1573-1632. Protagonista del Seicento lombardo, exhibition catalogue (Milan, Palazzo Reale, 24 February – 5 June 2005), edited by M. Rosci, Milan, 2005.

La collezione di sigilli Ala Ponzone, edited by A. Foglia, Cinisello Balsamo, 2005.

Dabbs J. K., "Sex, Lies and Anecdotes: Gender Relations in the Life Stories of Italian Women Artists, 1550-1800", in *Aurora: the Journal of the History of Art*, 6, 2005, pp. 17–37.

Failla M. B., "L'immagine della Corte sabauda: taccuini di disegni e ritratti incisi", in *"Il nostro pittore fiamengo". Giovanni Caracca alla corte dei Savoia (1568-1607)*, exhibition catalogue (Turin, Galleria Sabauda, 21 September 2005 – 8 January 2006), edited by P. Astrua, A. M. Bava, C. E. Spantigati, Turin, 2005, pp. 57–68.

Gladen C. A., "Suor Lucrina Fetti: pittrice in una corte monastica seicentesca", in *I monasteri femminili come centri di cultura fra Rinascimento e Barocco*, proceedings of the international historical conference (Bologna, 8–10 December 2000), edited by G. Pomata, G. Zarri, Rome, 2005, pp. 123–141.

Lattuada R., Nappi E., "New Documents and Some Remarks on Artemisia's Production in Naples and Elsewhere", in *Artemisia Gentileschi: Taking Stock*, edited by J. W. Mann, Turnhout, 2005, pp. 79–98.
Morandotti A., *Milano profana nell'età dei Borromeo*, Milan, 2005.
"Il nostro pittore fiamengo". Giovanni Caracca alla corte dei Savoia (1568-1607), exhibition catalogue (Turin, Galleria Sabauda, 21 September 2005 – 8 January 2006), edited by P. Astrua, A. M. Bava, C. E. Spantigati, Turin, 2005.
Proni M. S., "La famiglia Stanchi", in *Pittori di natura morta a Roma. Artisti italiani 1630-1750*, edited by G. Bocchi, U. Bocchi, Viadana, 2005, pp. 244–323.
Ravelli L., *Stanchi dei fiori*, Bergamo, 2005.
Viroli G., "Longhi, Barbara", in *Dizionario Biografico degli Italiani*, 65, Rome, 2005, pp. 638–640.

2006
Le chiese di Milano, edited by M. T. Fiorio, Milan, 2006.
La gloria della pittura, edited by D. Benati, Bologna, 2006.
Lacchia C., "Orientamenti di gusto nel collezionismo privato a Vercelli: Antonio Borgogna e la formazione delle raccolte d'arte moderna", in *Arti figurative a Biella e a Vercelli. L'Ottocento*, edited by V. Natale, Biella, 2006, pp. 129–142.
Lorizzo L., *La collezione del cardinale Ascanio Filomarino. Pittura, scultura e mercato dell'arte tra Roma e Napoli nel Seicento con una nota sulla vendita dei beni del cardinale Del Monte*, Naples, 2006.
Maccabelli A., "'Casa Natali'. La famiglia si allarga", in *La scuola classica di Cremona*, XIV, 2006, pp. 251–261.
Pinacoteca Ambrosiana, II: *Dipinti dalla metà del Cinquecento alla metà del Seicento*, Milan, 2006.
Pinacoteca Nazionale di Bologna. Catalogo generale. 2. Da Raffaello ai Carracci, edited by J. Bentini, G. P. Cammarota, Venice, 2006.
Pulini M., *Ginevra Cantofoli. La nuova nascita di una pittrice nella Bologna del Seicento*, Bologna, 2006.

2007
L'arte delle donne. Dal Rinascimento al Surrealismo, exhibition catalogue (Milan, Palazzo Reale, 5 December 2007 – 9 March 2008), edited by V. Sgarbi, H. A. Peters, B. Buscaroli, Milan, 2007.
Benocci C., *Villa Il Vascello*, Rome, 2007.
Ceroni N., "Barbara Longhi", in *Italian Women Artists from Renaissance to Baroque*, exhibition catalogue (Washington, The National Museum of Women in the Arts, 16 March – 15 July 2007), edited by V. Fortunati, J. Pomeroy, C. Strinati, Milan, 2007, p. 167.
Chiodo A., "La produzione artistica di Orsola Maddalena Caccia nel vercellese", in *Bollettino Storico Vercellese*, 67, 2007, pp. 13–46.
Di Macco M., "Duchi, Madame Reali e Re sabaudi: forme d'arte di corte a Torino dal Cinquecento al Settecento", in *La reggia di Venaria e i Savoia. Arte, magnificenza e storia di una corte europea*, exhibition catalogue (Venaria Reale, Reggia, 12 October 2007 – 30 March 2008), edited by E. Castelnuovo, 2 vols., Turin, 2007, I, pp. 237–270.
I fiori di Francesca. Nature morte di Francesca Vicenzina nella Milano del Seicento, exhibition catalogue (Legnano, Galleria Romigioli, 20 October – 11 November 2007), edited by A. Cottino, Legnano, 2007.
Fortunati V., "Towards a History of Women Artists in Bologna between the Renaissance and the Baroque: Additions and Clarifications", in *Italian Women Artists from Renaissance to Baroque*, exhibition catalogue (Washington, The National Museum of Women in the Arts, 16 March – 15 July 2007), edited by V. Fortunati, J. Pomeroy, C. Strinati, Milan, 2007, pp. 41–48.
Italian Women Artists from Renaissance to Baroque, exhibition catalogue (Washington, The National Museum of Women in the Arts, 16 March – 16 July 2007), edited by V. Fortunati, J. Pomeroy, C. Strinati, Milan, 2007.
La Pinacoteca Ala Ponzone. Il Seicento, edited by M. Marubbi, Cinisello Balsamo, 2007.
Pinacoteca Ambrosiana, III: *Dipinti dalla metà del Seicento alla fine del Settecento*, edited by M. Rossi, A. Rovetta, Milan, 2007.
La raccolta Mario Scaglia. Dipinti e sculture, medaglie e placchette da Pisanello a Ceruti, exhibition catalogue (Milan, Museo Poldi Pezzoli, 30 October 2007 – 30 March 2008), edited by A. Di Lorenzo, F. Frangi, Cinisello Balsamo, 2007.
La reggia di Venaria e i Savoia. Arte, magnificenza e storia di una corte europea, exhibition catalogue (Venaria Reale, Reggia, 12 October 2007 – 30 March 2008), edited by E. Castelnuovo, 2 vols., Turin, 2007.
Rubbi V., "Chiara Varotari", in *Italian Women Artists from Renaissance to Baroque*, exhibition catalogue (Washington, The National Museum of Women in the Arts, 16 March – 15 July 2007), edited by V. Fortunati, J. Pomeroy, C. Strinati, Milan, 2007, p. 189.

2008
Chiodo A., "Problemi aperti sul rapporto fra il giovane Guglielmo Caccia detto il Moncalvo e la realtà artistica del Piemonte orientale sul finire del Cinquecento", in *Monferrato. Arte e Storia*, 20, 2008, pp. 81–115.
Collange A., "Du Caravage au Bernin, parcours dans la Rome de Simon Vouet (1613-1627)", in *Simon Vouet (les années italiennes 1613/1627)*, exhibition catalogue (Nantes, Musée des Beaux-Arts, 21 November 2008 – 23 February 2009; Besançon, Musée des Beaux-Arts, 27 March – 29 July 2009), edited by B. Chavanne, D. Jacquot, A. Collange, Paris, 2008, pp. 22–28.
Di Mauro M., "Palazzo Filomarino della Rocca", in *Studi di Storia dell'Arte*, 19, 2008, pp. 207–232.
Fortunati V., "'Capriccioso e destrissimo ingegno' (Vasari): Properzia de' Rossi dalla leggenda alla storia", in V. Fortunati, I. Graziani, *Properzia de' Rossi. Una scultrice a Bologna nell'età di Carlo V*, Bologna, 2008, pp. 9–27.
Fortunati V., Graziani I., *Properzia de' Rossi. Una scultrice a Bologna nell'età di Carlo V*, Bologna, 2008.
Garrard M. D., *Artemisia Gentileschi*, Princeton, 2008.
Graziani I., "Ritratto di Madonna Properzia de' Rossi, scultrice", in V. Fortunati, I. Graziani, *Properzia de' Rossi. Una scultrice a Bologna nell'età di Carlo V*, Bologna, 2008a, pp. 29–43.
Graziani I., "Properzia de' Rossi e la scultura in miniatura", in V. Fortunati, I. Graziani, *Properzia de' Rossi. Una scultrice a Bologna nell'età di Carlo V*, Bologna, 2008b, pp. 45–58.
Le Pera E., *Enciclopedia dell'arte di Calabria. Ottocento e Novecento*, Soveria Mannelli, 2008.
Muzzi A., "The Artistic Training and Savonarola's Ideas of Plautilla Nelli", in *Plautilla Nelli (1524-1588). The Painter-Prioress of Renaissance Florence*, edited by J. K. Nelson, Florence, 2008, pp. 28–44.
Petrucci F., *Pittura di ritratto a Roma. Il Seicento. Repertorio*, III, Rome, 2008.
Plautilla Nelli (1524-1588). The Painter-Prioress of Renaissance Florence, edited by J. K. Nelson, Florence, 2008.
Pompa magna. Pietro Novelli e l'ambiente monrealese, exhibition catalogue (Monreale, Palazzo Arcivescovile, 26 April – 26 June 2006), edited by G. Davi, G. Mendola, Palermo, 2008.
Sacchi R., "Caterina Bianca Stampa Petra e poi Lodrone", in *Donne di potere nel Rinascimento*, edited by L. Arcangeli, S. Peyronel, Florence, 2008, pp. 655–667.
Simon Vouet (les années italiennes 1613/1627), exhibition catalogue (Nantes, Musée des Beaux-Arts, 21 November 2008 – 23 February 2009; Besançon, Musée des Beaux-Arts, 27 March – 29 July 2009), edited by B. Chavanne, D. Jacquot, A. Collange, Paris, 2008.
Tessuti, ricami, merletti. Opere scelte, edited by G. L. Bovenzi, C. Maritano, Savigliano, 2008.
Tomasi Tongiorgi L., "'La femminil pazienza': Women Painters and Natural History in the Seventeenth and Early Eighteenth Centuries", in *The Art of Natural History: Illustrated Treatised and Botanical Paintings, 1400-1850*, proceedings of the symposium (Washington, 3–4 May 2002), edited by T. O'Malley, A. R. W. Meyers, Washington, 2008, pp. 159–185.
Turrill C., "Appendix 2. Paintings Attributed to Plautilla Nelli", in *Plautilla Nelli (1524-1588). The Painter-Prioress of Renaissance Florence*, edited by J. K. Nelson, Florence, 2008, pp. 118–130.

2009
Arti figurative a Biella: San Sebastiano, edited by V. Natale, Candelo, 2009.
Benati D., "Un 'quadro grande con donne nude' da Joachim Wtewael a Lorenzo Sabbatini", in *Il più dolce lavorare che sia. Mélanges en l'honneur de Mauro Natale*, edited by F. Eldig, N. Etienne, G. Extermann, Cinisello Balsamo, 2009, pp. 115–121.
Bourne M., "From Court to Cloister and Back Again: Margherita Gonzaga, Caterina de' Medici and Lucrina Fetti at the Convent of Sant'Orsola in Mantua", in *Domestic institutional Interiors in Early Modern Europe*, edited by S. Cavallo, S. Evangelisti, Farnham, 2009, pp. 153–179.
Domestic Institutional Interiors in Early Modern Europe, edited by S. Cavallo, S. Evangelisti, Farnham, 2009.
La donazione Sernicoli: dipinti e argenti, edited by F. Piccinini, C. Stefani, Modena, 2009.
Herklotz I., "Alfonso Chacón e le gallerie dei ritratti nell'età della Controriforma", in *Arte e committenza nel Lazio nell'età di Cesare Baronio*, proceedings of the International Conference (Frosinone, Sora, 16–18 May 2007), edited by P. Tosini, Rome, 2009, pp. 111–142.
Kusche M., "Comentarios sobre las atribuciones a Sofonisba Anguissola por el Doctor Alfio Nicotra", in *Archivo Español de Arte*, LXXXII, 327, 2009, pp. 285–295.
Lo spirito e il corpo. 1550-1560. Cento anni di ritratti a Padova nell'età di Galileo, exhibition catalogue (Padova, Musei Civici agli Eremitani, 28 February – 15 July 2009), edited by D. Banzato, F. Pellegrini, Milan, 2009.
De Van Dyck à Bellotto. Splendeurs à la cour de Savoie, exhibition catalogue (Brussels, Palais des Beaux-Arts, 20 February – 24 May 2009), edited by P. Astrua, A. M. Bava, S. Damiano, C. E. Spantigati, Turin, 2009.

2010

Colonna P., *I Colonna*, Rome, 2010.

De Laurentiis E., "The Liturgical Codex of Seventeenth Century Papal Court and the Illuminated Manuscripts of Pope Urbano VIII in Toledo (Spain)", in *The Lost Manuscripts from the Sistine Chapel: An Epic Journey from Rome to Toledo*, exhibition catalogue (Dallas, Meadows Museum, 23 January – 23 April 2011), edited by E. De Laurentiis, E. A. Talamo, Madrid-Dallas 2010a, pp. 29–56.

De Laurentiis E., "Biographical Notes on the Illuminators and Copyists of Pope Urban VIII", in *The Lost Manuscripts from the Sistine Chapel: An Epic Journey from Rome to Toledo*, exhibition catalogue (Dallas, Meadows Museum, 23 January – 23 April 2011), edited by E. De Laurentiis, E. A. Talamo, Madrid-Dallas 2010b, pp. 57–75.

Guerrieri Borsoi M. B., "Novità su Alessandro e Anna Maria Vaiani", in *Bollettino dei Monumenti, Musei e Gallerie Pontificie*, 27, 2010, pp. 241–264.

The Lost Manuscripts from the Sistine Chapel: An Epic Journey from Rome to Toledo, exhibition catalogue (Dallas, Meadows Museum, 23 January – 23 April 2011), edited by E. De Laurentiis, E. A. Talamo, Madrid-Dallas 2010.

Mazzetti di Pietralata C., "Il mestiere del giardiniere", in *Giardini storici. Artificiose nature a Roma e nel Lazio*, Rome, 2010, pp. 91–100.

2011

Artemisia. Storia di una passione, exhibition catalogue (Milan, Palazzo Reale, 22 September 2011 – 30 January 2012), edited by R. Contini, F. Solinas, Milan, 2011.

Bohn B., "The Construction of Artistic Reputation in Seicento Bologna: Guido Reni and the Sirani", in *Renaissance Studies*, XXV, 4, 2011, pp. 511–537.

Bovenzi G. L., "Ricami in seta", in *Seta Oro Incarnadino. Lusso e devozione nella Lombardia spagnola*, edited by C. Buss, Cesano Maderno, 2011a, pp. 113–157.

Bovenzi G. L., "Note sui tessuti dipinti nella tela di Santa Agata, Caterina e Apollonia di Orsola Maddalena Caccia", in *I dipinti e le sculture lignee delle chiese di Lu*, edited by L. Palmieri, Casale Monferrato, 2011b, pp. 73–78.

Brejon de Lavergnée A., "Portraits de Simon Vouet", in *Simon Vouet en Italie*, edited by O. Bonfait, H. Rousteau-Chambon, Rennes, 2011, pp. 245–248.

De Laurentiis E., "Los códices de la Sacristía Sixtina en Toledo. Historia de un descubrimiento", in *Códices de la Capilla Sixtina en la Biblioteca Capitular de Toledo*, exhibition catalogue (Toledo, Capilla de Reyes Nuevos de la Catedral, 25 June – 30 September 2011), edited by Á. Fernández Collado, Toledo, 2011, pp. 33–43.

Fabbri A., *Museo d'Arte della Città di Ravenna*, Ravenna, 2011.

Golahny A., "Elisabetta Sirani's Timoclea and Visual Precedent", in *Source: Notes in the History of Art*, 30, 2011, pp. 37–42.

L'Occaso S., *Museo di Palazzo Ducale di Mantova. Catalogo generale delle collezioni inventariate. Dipinti fino al XIX secolo*, Mantua, 2011.

Lettere di Artemisia, edited by F. Solinas, Rome, 2011.

Loire S., "Simon Vouet en Italie (1613-1627)", in *Simon Vouet en Italie*, edited by O. Bonfait, H. Rousteau-Chambon, Rennes, 2011, pp. 183–233.

Meijer B. W., Sluiter G., Squellati Brizio P., *Repertory of Dutch and Flemish Paintings in Italian Public Collections. III Piedmont and Valle d'Aosta*, 2 vols., Florence, 2011.

Merkel K., "Elisabetta Sirani und Guido Reni", in *Kunstlergrabmaler: Genese – Typologie – Intention – Metamorphosen*, edited by B. U. Münch, M. W. Herzog, A. Tacke, Petersberg, 2011, pp. 137–150.

Osimo A., "Le Pellegrine, due ricamatrici", in *Seta Oro Incarnadino. Lusso e devozione nella Lombardia spagnola*, edited by C. Buss, Cesano Maderno, 2011, pp. 22–24.

Palmieri L., "Il patrimonio pittorico e le sculture lignee delle chiese di Lu Monferrato", in *I dipinti e le sculture lignee delle chiese di Lu*, edited by L. Palmieri, Casale Monferrato, 2011, pp. 7–71.

Pecchenini F., "Una santa a corte. Annotazioni sulle vesti di Santa Caterina d'Alessandria nel dipinto di Orsola Maddalena Caccia", in *I dipinti e le sculture lignee delle chiese di Lu*, edited by L. Palmieri, Casale Monferrato, 2011, pp. 79–82.

Pinacoteca Nazionale di Bologna. Catalogo generale, IV: *Seicento e Settecento*, edited by J. Bentini, G. P. Cammarota, A. Mazza, D. Scaglietti Kelescian, A. Stanzani, Venice, 2011.

Simoni S., "Ritratti e autoritratti del Cinquecento ravennate. Barbara Longhi e la donna artista", in *Romagna arte e storia*, 31, 92–93, 2011, pp. 5–22.

Todorov T., *L'arte o la vita! Il caso Rembrandt*, Rome, 2011.

Varallo F., "Dal Theatro alla Grande Galleria. La biblioteca ducale tra Cinque e Seicento", in *Il Teatro di tutte le scienze e le arti. Raccogliere libri per coltivare idee in una capitale di età moderna. Torino 1559-1861*, exhibition catalogue (Turin, Archivio di Stato, 22 November 2011 – 27 February 2012), edited by M. Carassi, I. Massabò Ricci, S. Pettenati, Turin, 2011, pp. 25–34.

Volti svelati. Antico e passione per l'antico, exhibition catalogue (Florence, Gallerie degli Uffizi, Sala delle Reali Poste, 15 December 2011 – 29 January 2012), edited by V. Conticelli, F. Paolucci, Livorno, 2011.

Webb H., "'Lacrime cordiali', Catherine of Siena and the Value of Tears", in *A Companion to Catherine of Siena*, edited by C. Muessig, G. Ferzoco, B. Kienzle, Leiden, 2011, pp. 99–112.

2012

Bocchi G., "I pittori di fiori a Venezia nel Seicento", in *Francesco Guardi nella terra degli avi. Dipinti di figura e capricci floreali*, exhibition catalogue (Trento, Castello del Buonconsiglio, 6 October 2012 – 6 January 2013), edited by E. Mich, Trento, 2012, pp. 95–114.

Chiodo A., review of the exhibition "Orsola Maddalena Caccia. Storia singolare di una monaca pittrice", in *Monferrato Arte e Storia*, 24, 2012, pp. 99–104.

Cottino A., "Metafore dipinte: le nature morte 'devote' di Orsola Maddalena Caccia", in *Orsola Maddalena Caccia*, exhibition catalogue (San Secondo di Pinerolo, Castello di Miradolo, 3 March – 29 July 2012), edited by P. Caretta, D. Magnetti, Savigliano, 2012, pp. 37–46.

D'Albo O., "Una 'Sant'Orsola' e altre proposte per la 'Reverenda Madre' Caccia", in *Paragone*, 751, 2012, pp. 45–50.

Di mano donnesca. Donne artiste dal XVI al XVII secolo, exhibition catalogue (Rome, Palazzo Venezia, 4–14 October 2012edited by C. Lollobrigida, Rome, 2012.

Ferro F. M., "Le 'preghiere dipinte' di Orsola Maddalena Caccia: aggiunte e riflessioni", in *Arte Cristiana*, 868, 2012, pp. 49–56.

Iozzia A. M., "Documenti di archivio su Sofonisba Anguissola", in *Data News*, 10, 2012, pp. 12–16.

Orsola Maddalena Caccia, exhibition catalogue (San Secondo di Pinerolo, Castello di Miradolo, 3 March – 29 July 2012), edited by P. Caretta, D. Magnetti, Savigliano, 2012.

Porcella M. F., "Iconografia e culto di Nostra Signora d'Itria nella Sardegna spagnola", in *Ricerca e confronti*, preceedings of archeology and history of art study days twenty years after the establishment of the Archeological and Historical-Artistic Sciences Department of Università di Cagliari (Cagliari, 1–5 March 2010), in *ArcheoArte. Rivista elettronica di Archeologia e Arte*, insert, 2012, pp. 687–701.

Primarosa Y., "La committenza artistica della Compagnia della Misericordia di Poggio Mirteto tra Sei e Settecento: Plautilla Bricci, Michelangelo Cerruti, Gaspare Serenario, Alessandro Specchi", in *Palazzi, chiese, arredi e pittura, II*, edited by E. Debenedetti, Rome, 2012, pp. 135–164.

Le raccolte del principe Eugenio condottiero e intellettuale. Collezionismo tra Vienna, Parigi e Torino nel primo Settecento, exhibition catalogue (Reggia di Venaria, 5 April – 9 September 2012), edited by C. E. Spantigati, Cinisello Balsamo, 2012.

Ravelli L., "A proposito di un dipinto di Evaristo Baschenis", in *La Rivista di Bergamo*, 69, 2012, pp. 64–67.

Tapié A., afterword, in *Artemisia 1593-1654. Pouvoir, gloire et passions d'une femme peintre*, exhibition catalogue (Paris, Musée Maillol, 14 March – 15 July 2012), edited by R. Contini, F. Solinas, Paris, 2012, p. 223.

Van Dyck in Sicily. 1624-1625 Painting and The Plague, exhibition catalogue (London, Dulwich Picture Gallery, 15 February – 27 May 2012), edited by X. F. Salomon, Cinisello Balsamo, 2012.

2013

Artemisia. La musa Clio e gli anni napoletani, exhibition catalogue (Pisa, Palazzo Blu, 23 March – 30 June 2013), edited by R. Contini, F. Solinas, Rome, 2013.

Binaghi Olivari M. T., "I ricami dell'Infanta", in *L'Infanta. Caterina d'Austria, duchessa di Savoia (1567-1597)*, edited by B. A. Raviola, F. Varallo, Rome, 2013, pp. 359–369.

Bocchi G., "Il soggiorno bolognese di Ludovico e Margherita Caffi", in *Strenna piacentina 2013*, 2013, pp. 92–101.

Bohn B., "Elisabetta Sirani and the Marchese Ferdinando Cospi: Humanism, Natural History, and Art Collecting in Early Modern Bologna", in *I Tatti Studies in Honor of Joseph Connors*, edited by M. Israëls, L. A. Waldman, Cambridge, 2013a, pp. 577–582, 945–996.

Bohn B., "Patronizing *pittrici* in Early Modern Bologna", in *Bologna. Cultural Crossroads from the Medieval to the Baroque: Recent Anglo-American Scholarship*, edited by G. M. Anselmi, A. De Benedictis, N. Terpstra, Bologna, 2013b, pp. 113–126.

Chiodo A., "Il collezionismo di opere di Guglielmo Caccia detto il Moncalvo e della figlia Orsola Maddalena: il caso della collezione Dal Pozzo", in *Annali di storia moderna e contemporanea*, n. s., 1, 2013, pp. 297–322.

Crispo A., "Pietro Paolo Cennini e la bottega degli Stanchi", in *Parma per l'Arte*, n. s., XIX, 2013, pp. 63–95.

D'Orazio C., *Caravaggio segreto. I misteri nascosti nei suoi capolavori*, Milan, 2013.
Daniele G., "Un dipinto di Luca Longhi a Castel Sant'Angelo: ritratto di Giulia Farnese?", in *Storia dell'arte*, 135, 2013a, pp. 8–17.
Daniele G., "Luca Longhi inedito: una Madonna con il Bambino, sant'Anna e san Giovannino ed altri dipinti", in *Romagna arte e storia*, 98, 2013b, pp. 63–74.
Failla M. B., "Il 'cahier' delle dame di Caterina Micaela", in *L'infanta Caterina d'Austria, duchessa di Savoia (1567-1597)*, edited by B. A. Raviola, F. Varallo, Rome, 2013, pp. 329–340.
Ghirardi A., *Ritrattisti in Emilia-Romagna. Una traccia*, Bologna, 2013.
L'infanta Caterina d'Austria, duchessa di Savoia (1567-1597), edited by B. A. Raviola, F. Varallo, Rome, 2013.
Kleopatra. Die ewige Diva, exhibition catalogue (Bonn, Bundeskunsthalle, 28 June – 6 October 2013), edited by E. Bronfen, A. Lulińska, Munich, 2013.
Lamon R., *Le Donne nella storia di Padova*, Padua, 2013.
Lattuada R., "Due coppie rare e inedite: una di Ginevra Cantofoli e una di Giovanni Antonio Burrini", in *Valori tattili*, 2, 2013, pp. 110–129.
Modesti A., "'A Casa con i Sirani': A Successful Family Business and Household in Early Modern Bologna", in *The Early Modern Domestic Interior 1400-1700: Objects, Spaces, Domesticities*, edited by E. J. Campbell, E. Consavari, S. Miller, Farnham, 2013, pp. 47–66.
Seicento lombardo a Brera. Capolavori e riscoperte, exhibition catalogue (Milan, Pinacoteca di Brera, 8 October 2013 – 12 January 2014), edited by S. Coppa, P. Strada, Milan, 2013.
Strada P., "Madonna Fede Galizia. Il *Noli me tangere* di Brera", in *Il Seicento lombardo a Brera. Capolavori e riscoperte*, exhibition catalogue (Milan, Pinacoteca di Brera, 8 October 2013 – 12 January 2014), edited by S. Coppa, P. Strada, Milan, 2013, pp. 45–53.
Verdon T., "Moncalvo, i Caccia e la pittura della Controriforma", in *Fede e cultura nel Monferrato di Guglielmo e Orsola Caccia*, edited by T. Verdon, A. Longhi, Savigliano, 2013, pp. 11–45.
Il Visibile Narrare, exhibition catalogue (Cesena, Galleria Comunale d'Arte, 1 December 2013 – 26 January 2014), edited by A. Giovanardi, Cesena, 2013.
Wadsworth S., Wiegand W. A., *Right Here I See My Own Books. The Woman's Building Library at the World's Columbian Exposition*, Amherst, 2013.

2014

Antico e Moderno. Acquisizioni e donazioni per la storia di Bologna (2001-2013), edited by A. Mazza, Bologna, 2014.
Barker S., "A New Document Concerning Artemisia Gentileschi's Marriage", in *The Burlington Magazine*, CLVI, 1341, 2014, pp. 803–804.
Bava A. M., Goria C., "Artists Working for the House of Savoy in the Seventeenth Century", in *The Court Artist in Seventeenth-Century Italy*, edited by E. Fumagalli, R. Morselli, Rome, 2014, pp. 199–235.
Bocchi G., "Vincenzo Volò pittore di nature morte: le origini borgognone e alcuni aspetti della sua attività milanese", in *Arte Lombarda*, 170–171, 1–2, 2014, pp. 62–75.
Cantaro M. T., "Lavinia Fontana: il primo 'Autoritratto alla spinetta' ritrovato e una breve disamina sugli autoritratti della pittrice", in *Bollettino d'Arte*, XCIX, VII, 24, 2014, pp. 99–110.
Cerboni Baiardi A., "La frutta è servita: noccioli intagliati dalla collezione Bonamini Pepoli. Note su Properzia de' Rossi e Filippo Santacroce", in *Riflessi del collezionismo, tra bilanci critici e nuovi contributi*, proceedings of the conference (Urbino, Palazzo Albani, aula Clemente XI, 3–5 October 2013), edited by G. Perini Folesani, A. M. Ambrosini Massari, Florence, 2014, pp. 103–123.
Failla M. B., "Les commandes de Christine et Victor-Amédée pour la renovation des palais ducaux", in *De Paris à Turin. Christine de France Duchesse de Savoie*, edited by G. Ferretti, Paris, 2014, pp. 157–165.
Modesti A., *Elisabetta Sirani "Virtuosa". Women's Cultural Production in Early Modern Bologna*, Turnhout, 2014.
Primarosa Y., "Nuova luce su Plautilla Bricci pittrice e 'architettrice'", in *Studi di Storia dell'Arte*, 25, 2014, pp. 145–160.

2014–2015

Silvano V., *Guglielmo Martino e la scuola di Cortale*, thesis, Università della Calabria, academic year 2014–2015.

2015

Artiste nel chiostro. Produzione artistica nei monasteri femminili in età moderna ("Memorie domenicane", 46), edited by S. Barker with L. Cinelli, Florence, 2015.
Baldassari F., *Carlo Dolci. Complete Catalogue of the Paintings*, Florence, 2015.
Barker S., "Painting and Humanism in Early Modern Florentine Convents", in *Artiste nel chiostro. Produzione artistica nei monasteri femminili in età moderna* ("Memorie domenicane", 46), edited by S. Barker with L. Cinelli, Florence, 2015, pp. 105–139.
Bocchi G., "Ricerche genealogiche e indagini storico-artistiche intorno a una famiglia di pittori milanesi del XVII secolo: i Vicenzini", in *Arte Lombarda*, 175, 3, 2015, pp. 47–69.
Caretta P., "Orizzonti figurativi e riferimenti culturali nell'opera di Orsola Maddalena Caccia", in *Artiste nel chiostro. Produzione artistica nei monasteri femminili in età moderna* ("Memorie domenicane", 46), edited by S. Barker with L. Cinelli, Florence, 2015, pp. 179–189, 315–319.
Cavazzini P., "'Queste lascive immagini… sono altari dell'Inferno': dipinti provocanti nelle dimore romane del primo Seicento", in *I pittori del dissenso. Giovanni Benedetto Castiglione, Andrea de Leone, Pier Francesco Mola, Pietro Testa, Salvator Rosa*, edited by S. Albl, A. V. Sganzerla, G. M. Weston, Rome, 2015, pp. 131–145.
Chiodo A., "Biografie di Guglielmo e Orsola Maddalena Caccia", in A. Monti, G. Bertola, G. Vaglio, *Le chiese di Moncalvo e i capolavori di Guglielmo e Orsola Maddalena Caccia. Alla scoperta di un tesoro di fede, di storia e di arte*, Asti, 2015, pp. 8–14.
Da Cimabue a Morandi. Felsina pittrice, exhibition catalogue (Bologna, Palazzo Fava, Palazzo delle Esposizioni, Pinacoteca Nazionale, 14 February – 17 May 2015), edited by V. Sgarbi, Bologna, 2015.
De Girolami Cheney L., "Lavinia Fontana's Nude Minervas", in *Woman's Art Journal*, 36, 2, 2015, pp. 30–40.
Lacas M., *Des femmes peintres, du XVe à l'aube du XIXe siècle*, Paris, 2015.
Lozano J. S., "Entre publicidad y virtud. Sofonisba Anguissola, autorretratista", in *Me veo luego existo. Mujeres que representan, mujeres representadas*, proceedings of the International Conference (Valencia, Universitat de València, 5–7 November 2013), edited by E. Alba Pagán, L. Pérez Ochando, Madrid, 2015, pp. 523–537.
Maccabelli A., "Giovanni Battista Natali. Estrato Ramemorativo, osia anotacioni (ms. Vat. Lat. 10305). Memoria e saperi di un artista lombardo del Seicento tra Cremona e Roma", in *Annali della Biblioteca Statale e Libreria Civica di Cremona*, LXI (2012–2014), Cremona-Rome, 2015.
Mausoli S., "Caterina Cantoni e l'iconografia del drappo di Torino: un'ipotesi interpretativa", in *Il Seicento a Ricamo. Dipingere con l'ago: stendardi, drappi da arredo, paramenti liturgici*, edited by F. Fiori, M. Accornero Zaneta, Sr. M. L. Ferrari, s.l. 2015, pp. 18–35.
Me veo luego existo. Mujeres que representan, mujeres representadas, proceedings of the International Conference (Valencia, Universitat de València, 5–7 November 2013), edited by E. Alba Pagán, L. Pérez Ochando, Madrid, 2015.
Monti A., Bertola G., Vaglio G., *Le chiese di Moncalvo e i capolavori di Guglielmo e Orsola Maddalena Caccia. Alla scoperta di un tesoro di fede, di storia e di arte*, Asti, 2015.
Morandotti A., "Natura morta lombarda (e piemontese) delle origini. Alcuni spunti nella Fototeca Zeri", in *La natura morta di Federico Zeri*, edited by A. Bacchi, F. Mambelli, E. Sambo, Bologna, 2015, pp. 57–69.
Navarro F., "'I sospiri mi sono cibo, e le lagrime beveraggio…'. Suor Plautilla Nelli per Santa Caterina da Siena", in *Artiste nel chiostro. Produzione artistica nei monasteri femminili in età moderna* ("Memorie domenicane", 46), edited by S. Barker with L. Cinelli, Florence, 2015, pp. 141–154.
Pancheri R., "L'età favolosa. Ritratti di bambini nella pittura dell'Italia settentrionale dal Cinquecento al Settecento", in *Il sogno della vita che verrà. La ritrattistica infantile dal 1500 a oggi*, exhibition catalogue (Castel Tirolo, Museo storico-culturale della Provincia di Bolzano, 4 July – 22 November 2015), edited by L. Andergassen, Castel Tirolo, 2015, pp. 66–77.
Sarchi A., "Una nuova proposta attributiva per Properzia de' Rossi", in *Una vita per l'arte. Studi in onore di Andrea Emiliani*, edited by M. Baldassari, P. Carofano, in *Valori tattili*, 5/6, 2015, pp. 91–98.
Spanò Martinelli S., Graziani I., "Caterina de' Vigri between Manuscript and Print: Text, Image and Gender", in *The Saint between Manuscript and Print. Italy 1400-1600*, Toronto, 2015, pp. 351–378 (Irene Graziani: pp. 360–367).
Strocchia S. T., "Knowing Hands: Nuns and the Needle Arts in Renaissance Italy", in *Artiste nel chiostro. Produzione artistica nei monasteri femminili in età moderna* ("Memorie domenicane", 46), edited by S. Barker with L. Cinelli, Florence, 2015, pp. 31–52, 279–280.
Tassinari M., "Ricamatori e ricami lombardi fra Cinque e Seicento a Roma e la pianeta Farnese del Gesù, con una proposta per Camillo Procaccini", in *Il Seicento a Ricamo. Dipingere con l'ago: stendardi, drappi da arredo, paramenti liturgici*, edited by F. Fiori, M. Accornero Zaneta, Sr. M. L. Ferrari, s.l. 2015, pp. 108–134.
Turrill C., "'Il Frate''s Follower. Classifying and Collecting the Work of Plautilla Nelli in the 1800s", in *Artiste nel chiostro. Produzione artistica nei monasteri femminili in età moderna* ("Memorie domenicane", 46), edited by

S. Barker with L. Cinelli, Florence, 2015, pp. 155–178.
Zarri G., "Culture nel chiostro. Tra arte e vita", in *Artiste nel chiostro. Produzione artistica nei monasteri femminili in età moderna* ("Memorie domenicane", 46), edited by S. Barker with L. Cinelli, Florence, 2015, pp. 19–29.

2016

Artemisia Gentileschi e il suo tempo, exhibition catalogue (Rome, Palazzo Braschi, 30 November 2016 – 7 May 2017), edited by F. Baldassari, J. W. Mann, N. Spinosa, Milan, 2016.
Barker S., "Lucrezia Quistelli (1541-94), a Woman Artist in Vasari's Florence", in *Women Artists in Early Modern Italy. Careers, Fame, and, Collectors*, edited by S. Barker, Turnhout, 2016, pp. 47–80.
Bava A. M., "Pittura e scultura: scelte figurative e committenze di corte", in *Le meraviglie del mondo. Le collezioni di Carlo Emanuele I di Savoia*, exhibition catalogue (Turin, Musei Reali, 16 December 2016 – 2 April 2017), edited by A. M. Bava, E. Pagella, Genoa, 2016, pp. 257–267.
Berra G., "I pionieri lombardi della natura morta italiana", in *L'origine della natura morta in Italia. Caravaggio e il Maestro di Hartford*, exhibition catalogue (Rome, Galleria Borghese, 16 November 2016 – 19 February 2017), edited by A. Coliva, D. Dotti, Milan, 2016, pp. 47–87.
Bovenzi G. L., "Ricami e ricamatori fra Torino e Milano nel Seicento", in *Scambi artistici tra Torino e Milano 1580-1714. Cantiere di studio*, proceedings of the conference (Turin, 28–29 May 2015), edited by A. Morandotti, G. Spione, Milan, 2016, pp. 278–295.
Le collezioni borboniche e postunitarie. Dipinti del XVII e XVIII secolo. Scuole italiane ed europee, edited by O. Agrillo, N. Spinosa, Milan, 2016.
De Caravaggio a Bernini. Obras maestras del Seicento italiano en las Colleciones Reales, exhibition catalogue (Madrid, Palacio Real, 7 June–16 October 2016), edited by G. Redín Michaus, Madrid, 2016.
Di Lorenzo A., Cantaro M. T., "Ancora sugli autoritratti alla spinetta di Lavinia Fontana", in *Bollettino d'Arte*, CI, VII, 32, 2016, pp. 129–132.
Failla M. B., "L'immagine del duca: ritratti e strategie di rappresentazione di una corte europea", in *Le meraviglie del mondo. Le collezioni di Carlo Emanuele I di Savoia*, exhibition catalogue (Turin, Musei Reali, 16 December 2016 – 2 April 2017), edited by A. M. Bava, E. Pagella, Genoa, 2016, pp. 25–29.
Failla M. B., Cornaglia P., "Il palazzo di San Giovanni per i duchi Vittorio Amedeo di Savoia e Cristina di Francia", in *Carlo e Amedeo di Castellamonte 1571-1683. Ingegneri e architetti per i Duchi di Savoia*, proceedings of the conference (Venaria, Turin, 2013), edited by A. Merlotti, Rome, 2016, pp. 97–115.
Gamberini C., "Sofonisba Anguissola at the Court of Philip II", in *Women Artists in Early Modern Italy. Careers, Fame, and Collectors,* edited by S. Barker, Turnhout 2016, pp. 29–38.
Garrard M. D., "The Cloister and the Square: Gender Dynamics in Renaissance Florence", in *Early Modern Women*, 11, 1, 2016, pp. 5–44.
Graziani I., "La visione della Notte di Natale di Caterina Vigri: due pale d'altare e la diffusione del culto della Santa dopo il processo di canonizzazione", in *Archivio italiano per la storia della pietà*, XXIX, 2016, pp. 205–220.
Lacchia C., "Antonio Borgogna, un 'imprenditore' vercellese della cultura tra filantropia e arte", in *Vercellesi illustri. Uomini di Scienza e di Cultura*, edited by A. Ruffino, Vercelli, 2016, pp. 173–205.
Lattuada R., "A new Annunciation and a *Fall of the Rebel Angels* on alabaster by Orazio Gentileschi, and some observations on the visual sources of the two versions of the Annunciation in Turin and Genoa", in *Valori tattili*, 7, 2016, pp. 14–29, 188.
Leoncini M., *Natura simbolica del gioco degli scacchi*, s.l. 2016.
Maritano C., "Filiberto Pingone e la storia dinastica di Casa Savoia", in *Le meraviglie del mondo. Le collezioni di Carlo Emanuele I di Savoia*, exhibition catalogue (Turin, Musei Reali, 16 December 2016 – 2 April 2017), edited by A. M. Bava, E. Pagella, Genoa, 2016, pp. 75–77.
Le meraviglie del mondo. Le collezioni di Carlo Emanuele I di Savoia, exhibition catalogue (Turin, Musei Reali, 16 December 2016 – 2 April 2017), edited by A. M. Bava, E. Pagella, Genoa, 2016.
Olivato L., "Pittrici sorelle: un dipinto di Europa Anguissola", in *Uno sguardo verso Nord. Scritti in onore di Caterina Virdis Limentani*, edited by M. Pietrogiovanna, Padua, 2016, pp. 305–310.
Passerin d'Entrèves P., "Le meraviglie della natura", in *Le meraviglie del mondo. Le collezioni di Carlo Emanuele I di Savoia*, exhibition catalogue (Turin, Musei Reali, 16 December 2016 – 2 April 2017), edited by A. M. Bava, E. Pagella, Genoa, 2016, pp. 129–135.
Sotheby's, European Decorative Arts from Caramoor Center for Music and the Arts, auction catalogue, New York, 12 April 2016.
Tosini P., "La Grande Galleria di Federico Zuccari a Torino: il capolavoro mancato", in *Le meraviglie del mondo. Le collezioni di Carlo Emanuele I di Savoia*, exhibition catalogue (Turin, Musei Reali, 16 December 2016 – 2 April 2017), edited by A. M. Bava, E. Pagella, Genoa, 2016, pp. 65–73.
Tramelli B., "'Pittora de Natura': A Page from Van Dyck's Italian Sketchbook", in *Women Artists in Early Modern Italy. Careers, Fame, and Collectors*, edited by S. Barker, Turnhout, 2016, pp. 39–45.
Varallo F., "Il luogo del sapere: la Grande Galleria di Carlo Emanuele I", in *Le meraviglie del mondo. Le collezioni di Carlo Emanuele I di Savoia*, exhibition catalogue (Turin, Musei Reali, 16 December 2016 – 2 April 2017), edited by A. M. Bava, E. Pagella, Genoa, 2016, pp. 117–127.
Women Artists in Early Modern Italy. Careers, Fame, and Collectors, edited by S. Barker, Turnhout, 2016.
Zanchi M., "Il gesto delle corna. Magico, sacrale, scaramantico", in *Art e Dossier*, 328, 2016, pp. 58–63.

2017

Artemisia Gentileschi in a Changing Light, edited by S. Barker, Turnhout, 2017.
Bianchi Janetti E., "L'Accademia di San Luca. Organizzazione, orientamenti e aspirazioni", in *Le arti nella Lombardia asburgica durante il Settecento. Novità e aperture*, proceedings of the conference (Milan, 5–6 June 2014), edited by E. Bianchi, A. Rovetta, A. Squizzato, Milan, 2017, pp. 425–441.
Bruno S., *Virginia Vezzi (1600-1638)*, Rome, 2017.
Garrard M. D., "Identifying Artemisia: The Archive and the Eye", in *Artemisia Gentileschi in a Changing Light*, edited by S. Barker, Turnhout, 2017, pp. 11–40.
Giansante M., "Rossi, Properzia de'", in *Dizionario Biografico degli Italiani*, 88, Rome, 2017, pp. 715–719.
Grasso S., "L'arte gentile. Profilo biografico e artistico di Rosalia Novelli", in S. Grasso, M. C. Gulisano, M. I. Randazzo, D. Vullo, *Voci d'artiste. Sofonisba Anguissola, Rosalia Novelli, Anna Fortino*, Palermo, 2017, pp. 37–63.
Grosso M., "Robusti, Maria (Marietta), detta Tintoretta", in *Dizionario Biografico degli Italiani*, 88, Rome, 2017 (on-line).
Kessel E. van, "A Martyr of Painting: Irene di Spilimbergo, Titian, and Venetian Portraiture between Life and Death", in *The Lives of Paintings: Presence, Agency and Likeness in Venetian Art of the Sixteenth Century*, Boston-Berlin, 2017, pp. 131–179.
Lari R., "Note sui restauri e sulla tecnica di Plautilla Nelli", in *Plautilla Nelli. Arte e devozione sulle orme di Savonarola / Art and Devotion in Savonarola's Footsteps*, exhibition catalogue (Florence, Gallerie degli Uffizi, 8 March – 4 June 2017), edited by F. Navarro, Livorno, 2017, pp. 60–69.
Lattuada R., "Unknown Paintings by Artemisia in Naples, and New Points Regarding her Daily Life and *Bottega*", in *Artemisia Gentileschi in a Changing Light*, edited by S. Barker, Turnhout, 2017, pp. 187–216.
Locker J., "Artemisia Gentileschi: The Literary Formation of an Unlearned Artist", in *Artemisia Gentileschi in a Changing Light*, edited by S. Barker, Turnhout, 2017, pp. 89–102.
Lollobrigida C., *Plautilla Bricci. Pictura et Architectura Celebris. L'architettrice del Barocco Romano*, 2017a.
Lollobrigida C., "Women Artists in Casa Barberini: Plautilla Bricci, Maddalena Corvini, Artemisia Gentileschi, Anna Maria Vaiani, and Virginia da Vezzo", in *Artemisia Gentileschi in a Changing Light*, edited by S. Barker, Turnhout, 2017b, pp. 119–130.
Matthiews-Grieco S. F., "Self-portraits, self-fashioning and the language of things: Sofonisba Anguissola & Lavinia Fontana", in *Archetipi del femminile. Rappresentazioni di genere, identità e ruoli sociali nell'arte dalle origini a oggi*, edited by A. Buccheri, G. Ingarao, E. Valenza, Milan-Udine, 2017, pp. 23–39.
Milano. Museo e Tesoro del Duomo. Catalogo generale, edited by G. Benati, Cinisello Balsamo, 2017.
Modesti A., "'Il pennello virile': Elisabetta Sirani and Artemisia Gentileschi as Masculanized Painters?", in *Artemisia Gentileschi in a Changing Light*, edited by S. Barker, Turnhout, 2017, pp. 131–146.
Navarro F., "'Semplice lecto, semplice studio, semplici figure': Suor Plautilla Nelli 'dipintora' per Santa Caterina de' Ricci tra Firenze e Prato", in *Plautilla Nelli. Arte e devozione sulle orme di Savonarola / Art and Devotion in Savonarola's Footsteps*, exhibition catalogue (Florence, Gallerie degli Uffizi, 8 March – 4 June 2017), edited by F. Navarro, Livorno, 2017, pp. 34–59.
Plautilla Nelli. Arte e devozione sulle orme di Savonarola / Art and Devotion in Savonarola's Footsteps, exhibition catalogue (Florence, Gallerie degli Uffizi, 8 March – 4 June 2017), edited by F. Navarro, Livorno, 2017.
Rocco P., *The Devout Hand. Women, Virtue, and Visual Culture in Early Modern Italy*, Montreal, 2017.
Tanzi B., "Sofonisba sotto l'ala di Colombino", in *Studi in onore di Fabrizio Lemme*, edited by F. Baldassarri, A. Agresti, Rome, 2017, pp. 73–79.
Turrill C., "Biografia e fortuna critica di Plautilla Nelli: una rilettura", in *Plautilla Nelli. Arte e devozione sulle orme di Savonarola / Art*

and Devotion in Savonarola's Footsteps, exhibition catalogue (Florence, Gallerie degli Uffizi, 8 March – 4 June 2017), edited by F. Navarro, Livorno, 2017, pp. 19–33.

2018

Barker S., "'Marvellousy Gifted': Giovanna Garzoni's First Visit to the Medici Court", in *The Burlington Magazine*, CLX, 1385, 2018a, pp. 654–659.

Barker S., "The First Biography of Artemisia Gentileschi: Self-Fashioning and Proto-Feminist Art History in Cristofano Bronzini's Notes on Women Artists", in *Mitteilungen Kunsthistorischen Institutes in Florenz*, LX, 3, 2018b, pp. 405–435.

Bava A. M., Failla M. B., "Antoon Van Dyck e i Savoia", in *Van Dyck pittore di corte*, exhibition catalogue (Turin, Galleria Sabauda, 16 November 2018 – 3 March 2019), edited by A. M. Bava, M. G. Bernardini, Rome, 2018, pp. 61–67.

Un capolavoro ritrovato di Orazio Gentileschi. La Madonna in adorazione del Bambino, exhibition catalogue (Pisa, Museo delle Sinopie, 19 July – 19 September 2018), edited by P. Carofano, Pisa, 2018.

La Collezione Cavallini Sgarbi. Da Niccolò dell'Arca a Gaetano Previati. Tesori d'arte per Ferrara, exhibition catalogue (Ferrara, Castello Estense, 3 February – 3 June 2018), edited by P. Di Natale, Milan, 2018.

De dames van de barok. Vrouwelijke schilders in het Italië van de 16de en 17de eeuw / Les dames du baroque. Femmes peintres dans l'Italie du XVIe et XVIIe siècle, exhibition catalogue (Ghent, Museum voor Schone Kunsten, 20 October 2018 – 20 January 2019), edited by V. De Beir, F. Solinas, A. Tapié, Ghent, 2018.

De Girolami Cheney L., "Lavinia Fontana's Cleopatra the Alchemist", in *Journal of Literature and Art Studies*, VIII, 8, 2018, pp. 1–22.

Ferro F. M., "Il lume interiore di Fede Galizia: riflessioni in margine ad una nuova natura morta, a due tavolette poco note e ad un'altra inedita", in *Valori tattili*, 10/11, 2018, pp. 74–84.

Furlotti B., "Scultori, Diana", in *Dizionario Biografico degli Italiani*, 91, Rome, 2018 (on-line).

Gamberini C., "Sofonisba Anguissola", in *Autographa*, II.1: *Donne, sante e madonne (da Matilde di Canossa ad Artemisia Gentileschi)*, edited by G. Murano, Imola 2018, pp. 193–200.

Ghirardi A., "Carbonarola 1648-1649: la beata Osanna dipinta da suor Orsola e gli altari della fondazione", in *Osanna e Orsola. Arte, storia e fede nel Seicento tra Mantova e il Monferrato*, exhibition catalogue (Mantua, Museo Diocesano, 22 September 2018 – 6 January 2019), edited by A. Ghirardi, R. Golinelli Berto, Mantua, 2018, pp. 21–53.

Lattuada R., "Disegno latente. Esempi e metodi eterodossi di progettare immagini tra Cinquecento e Settecento", in *Libri e album di disegni 1550-1800*, edited by V. Segreto, Rome, 2018, pp. 119–126.

Lavenia V., "Sigonio, Carlo", in *Dizionario Biografico degli Italiani*, 92, Rome, 2018 (on-line).

Lollobrigida C., "Artiste a Roma tra Controriforma e Barocco", in Ead., *Plautilla Bricci. Pictura et Architectura Celebris. L'architettrice del Barocco Romano*, Rome, 2018, pp. 30–38.

Lorenzoni A. M., "La verità della storia: i documenti", in *Osanna e Orsola. Arte, storia e fede nel Seicento tra Mantova e il Monferrato*, exhibition catalogue (Mantua, Museo Diocesano, 22 September 2018 – 6 January 2019), edited by A. Ghirardi, R. Golinelli Berto, Mantua, 2018, pp. 167–271.

Modesti A., "Sirani, Elisabetta", in *Dizionario Biografico degli Italiani*, 92, Rome, 2018a, pp. 816–819.

Modesti A., "Maestra Elisabetta Sirani: 'Virtuosa del pennello'", in *Imagines, il Magazine delle Gallerie degli Uffizi*, II, 2018b, pp. 84–97.

Nigrelli G., "Il vescovo Scipione Agnelli (1593-1653) committente e feudatario a Carbonarola", in *Osanna e Orsola: arte, storia e fede nel Seicento tra Mantova e il Monferrato*, exhibition catalogue (Mantua, Museo Diocesano, 22 September 2018 – 6 January 2019), edited by A. Ghirardi, R. Golinelli Berto, Mantua, 2018, pp. 89–115.

Osanna e Orsola. Arte, storia e fede nel Seicento tra Mantova e il Monferrato, exhibition catalogue (Mantua, Museo Diocesano, 22 September 2018 – 6 January 2019), edited by A. Ghirardi, R. Golinelli Berto, Mantua 2018.

Policicchio G., "Het album met miniaturen en tekeningen van Giovanna Garzoni uit de Accademia di San Luca / L'Album de miniatures et dessins de Giovanna Garzoni à l'Accademia di San Luca", in *De dames van de barok. Vrouwelijke schilders in het Italië van de 16de en 17de eeuw / Les dames du baroque. Femmes peintres dans l'Italie du XVIe et XVIIe siècle*, exhibition catalogue (Ghent, Museum voor Schone Kunsten, 20 October 2018 – 20 January 2019), edited by V. De Beir, F. Solinas, A. Tapié, Ghent, 2018, pp. 188–197.

Primarosa Y., *Elpidio Benedetti (1609-1690). Committenza e relazioni artistiche di un agente del re di Francia nella Roma del Seicento*, Turin, 2018.

Riga P. G., "Spilimbergo, Irene di", in *Dizionario Biografico degli Italiani*, 93, Rome, 2018, pp. 605–607.

Serventi S., "Caterina Vigri (1413-1463). 'Chaterina poverella'", in *Autographa*, II.1: *Donne, sante e madonne (da Matilde di Canossa ad Artemisia Gentileschi)*, edited by G. Murano, Imola, 2018, pp. 64–69.

Simoni S., "Da una tombola alla collezione Pio di Ravenna", in *Collezionismo d'arte in Romagna in età moderna*, edited by B. Ghelfi, O. Orsi, Bologna, 2018, pp. 103–119.

Tanzi M., "Due esercitazioni lombarde. Bernardino Campi e Giulio Cesare Procaccini", in *Storia dell'Arte*, 149, 1, 2018, pp. 9–30.

Tapié A., "Giovanna Garzoni (Ascoli Piceno 1600 – Rome 1670)", in *De dames van de barok. Vrouwelijke schilders in het Italië van de 16de en 17de eeuw / Les dames du baroque. Femmes peintres dans l'Italie du XVIe et XVIIe siècle*, exhibition catalogue (Ghent, Museum voor Schone Kunsten, 20 October 2018 – 20 January 2019), edited by V. De Beir, F. Solinas, A. Tapié, Ghent 2018, pp. 176–178.

Van Dyck pittore di corte, exhibition catalogue (Turin, Galleria Sabauda, 16 November 2018 – 3 March 2019), edited by A. M. Bava, M. G. Bernardini, Rome, 2018.

2019

Barone G., "Sofonisba Anguissola e Orazio Lomellino. Pittura, politica ed economia da Genova a Palermo (1580-1625)", in *Archivio storico per la Sicilia orientale*, III, 2, 2019, pp. 135–146.

Bava A. M., "Riccardo Gualino e la Galleria Sabauda", in *I mondi di Riccardo Gualino collezionista e imprenditore*, edited by A. M. Bava, G. Bertolino, Turin, 2019, pp. 90–109.

Bohn B., "Collecting Women's Art in Early Modern Bologna: Myth and Reality", in *Reframing Seventeenth-Century Bolognese Art. Archival Discoveries*, edited by B. Bohn, R. Morselli, Amsterdam, 2019, pp. 73–93.

Bredekamp H., *Galileo's Thinking Hand: Mannerism, Anti-Mannerism and the Virtue of Drawing in the Foundation of Early Modern Science* (2014), Berlin-Boston, 2019.

Cole M. W., *Sofonisba's Lesson. A Renaissance Artist and her Work*, Princeton, 2019a.

Cole M. W., "Artes hermanas", in *Historia de dos pintoras: Sofonisba Anguissola y Lavinia Fontana*, exhibition catalogue (Madrid, Museo Nacional del Prado, 22 October 2019 – 2 February 2020), edited by L. Ruiz Gómez, Madrid, 2019b, pp. 39–51.

Dal Pozzolo E. M., *Un apice erotico di Lavinia Fontana e la rinascita della Callipigia nel Cinquecento italiano*, Treviso, 2019.

Ferro F. M., "Un'inedita *Giuditta e Oloferne* di Fede Galizia", in *Arte Lombarda*, 186–187, 2–3, 2019, pp. 145–148.

Fra Bartolomeo 1517, proceedings of the conference (Florence, 26–28 October 2017), edited by A. Assonitis, L. Cinelli, M. Tamassia, Florence, 2019.

Ghirardi A., *Ritratto e iconografia. Amore morte e ricordo tra l'Italia e l'Europa*, Bologna, 2019a.

Ghirardi A., "Bartolomeo Passerotti e Lavinia Fontana, ritrattisti nell'età del papa Boncompagni: rileggendo l'Ignazio Danti di Brest e il Carlo Sigonio di Modena", in *Gregorio XIII Boncompagni. Un quadro nel quadro. "Per speculum et in aenigmate"*, proceedings of the study day (Frascati, Villa Sora, 19 January 2018), edited by F. Bertini, D. Delle Fave, Rome, 2019b, pp. 241–251.

Giovannini Luca A., "Femmes fortes e cultura del ritratto nell'epoca delle Reggenti", in *Madame Reali. Cultura e potere da Parigi a Torino. Cristina di Francia e Giovanna Battista di Savoia Nemours*, exhibition catalogue (Turin, Palazzo Madama, 20 December 2018 – 6 May 2019), edited by C. Arnaldi di Balme, M. P. Ruffino, Genoa, 2019, pp. 51–57.

Giulio Romano a Mantova. "Con nuova e stravagante maniera", exhibition catalogue (Mantua, Palazzo Ducale, 6 October 2019 – 6 January 2020), edited by L. Angelucci, R. Serra, P. Assmann, P. Bertelli, Milan, 2019.

Goria C., Spione G., "Cultura figurativa nell'età delle Madame Reali", in *Madame Reali. Cultura e potere da Parigi a Torino. Cristina di Francia e Giovanna Battista di Savoia Nemours*, exhibition catalogue (Turin, Palazzo Madama, 20 December 2018 – 6 May 2019), edited by C. Arnaldi di Balme, M. P. Ruffino, Genoa, 2019, pp. 67–85.

Griseri A., "Cristina di Francia e Filippo d'Aglié. La scacchiera del Potere", in *Madame Reali. Cultura e potere da Parigi a Torino. Cristina di Francia e Giovanna Battista di Savoia Nemours*, exhibition catalogue (Turin, Palazzo Madama, 20 December 2018 – 6 May 2019), edited by C. Arnaldi di Balme, M. P. Ruffino, Genoa, 2019, pp. 15–23.

Historia de dos pintoras: Sofonisba Anguissola y Lavinia Fontana, exhibition catalogue (Madrid, Museo Nacional del Prado, 22 October 2019 – 2 February 2020), edited by L. Ruiz Gómez, Madrid, 2019.

Iozzia A. M., "Da Madrid a Paternò. I documenti dell'Archivio di Stato di Catania (1573-1579)", in *Archivio Storico per la Sicilia Orientale*, III, 2, 2019, pp. 94–104.

Jover de Celis M., Gayo García M. D., Alba Carcelén L., "Sofonisba Anguissola en el

Museo del Prado. Una aproximación a su técnica", in *Historia de dos pintoras: Sofonisba Anguissola y Lavinia Fontana*, exhibition catalogue (Madrid, Museo Nacional del Prado, 22 October 2019 – 2 February 2020), edited by L. Ruiz Gómez, Madrid, 2019, pp. 71–88.
Lozano J.S., "'Quella Cremonese che dipinge': Sofonisba Anguissola in Spagna", in *Sofonisba Anguissola*, proceedings of the international studies day (Catania, Università degli Studi di Catania, 13 October 2019), *Archivio Storico per la Sicilia Orientale*, III, 2, 2019, pp. 67–74.
La luce e i silenzi. Orazio Gentileschi e la pittura caravaggesca nelle Marche del Seicento, exhibition catalogue (Fabriano, Pinacoteca Civica Bruno Molajoli, 2 August – 8 December 2019), edited by A. Delpriori, A. M. Ambrosini Massari, Ancona, 2019.
Madame Reali. Cultura e potere da Parigi a Torino. Cristina di Francia e Giovanna Battista di Savoia Nemours, exhibition catalogue (Turin, Palazzo Madama, 20 December 2018 – 6 May 2019), edited by C. Arnaldi di Balme, M. P. Ruffino, Genoa, 2019.
Mazzucco M. G., *L'architettrice*, Turin, 2019.
Miscioscia A., "Le sorelle Anguissola: cinque 'virtuose' delle arti in cerca di affermazione", in *Archivio Storico per la Sicilia Orientale*, III, 2, 2019, pp. 25–46.
Montanari A. M., *Cleopatra in Italian and English Renaissance Drama*, Amsterdam, 2019.
Morselli R., "Opere multiple. La pratica della serialità nell'impresa dei Gentileschi", in *La luce e i silenzi. Orazio Gentileschi e la pittura caravaggesca nelle Marche del Seicento*, exhibition catalogue (Fabriano, Pinacoteca Civica Bruno Molajoli, 2 August – 8 December 2019), edited by A. Delpriori, A. M. Ambrosini Massari, Ancona, 2019, pp. 284–299.
Nicotra A., "Venticinque anni di ricerche e attribuzioni", in *Archivio Storico per la Sicilia orientale*, III, 2, 2019, pp. 11–24.
Palazzo Colonna. Appartamento Principessa Isabelle. Catalogo dei dipinti, edited by M. Natale, in collaboration with P. Piergiovanni, Rome, 2019.
Pérez de Tudela A., "Sofonisba Anguissola en la corte de Felipe II", in *Historia de dos pintoras: Sofonisba Anguissola y Lavinia Fontana*, exhibition catalogue (Madrid, Museo Nacional del Prado, 22 October 2019 – 2 February 2020), edited by L. Ruiz Gómez, Madrid, 2019, pp. 53–69.
Prosperi C., *Artisti e maestranze in Monferrato nei secoli XVI e XVII. Ricerche d'archivio*, Acqui Terme, 2019.
Ruiz Gómez L., *Historia de dos pintoras: Sofonisba Anguissola y Lavinia Fontana*, in *Historia de dos pintoras: Sofonisba Anguissola y Lavinia Fontana*, exhibition catalogue (Madrid, Museo Nacional del Prado, 22 October 2019 – 2 February 2020), edited by L. Ruiz Gómez, Madrid, 2019, pp. 15–37.
Scalisi L., "Sofonisba Anguissola alla corte dei Moncada. Tra potere, arte e cultura", in *Sofonisba Anguissola*, proceedings of the international studies day (Catania, Università degli Studi di Catania, 13 October 2019), *Archivio Storico per la Sicilia Orientale*, III, 2, 2019, pp. 105–117.
Sofonisba Anguissola, proceedings of the international studies day (Catania, Università degli Studi di Catania, 13 October 2019), *Archivio Storico per la Sicilia Orientale*, III, 2, 2019.
Stenta P., "Cesare Gennari pittore di 'sommo studio'. La maturità, le influenze artistiche e un nuovo quadro con l'*Ipparchia di Maronea*", in *MuseoinVita*, 9–10, 2019 (available on https://www.museoinvita.it/stenta-gennari/).

2020

Artemisia, exhibition catalogue (London, National Gallery, 3 October 2020 – 24 January 2021), edited by L. Treves, London, 2020.
Artemisia Gentileschi. 'A Venetian Lucretia', London, 2020.
Barker S., "L'universo di Giovanna Garzoni. L'arte, i viaggi e un immaginario geografico senza confini", in *"La grandezza dell'universo" nell'arte di Giovanna Garzoni*, exhibition catalogue (Florence, Gallerie degli Uffizi – Palazzo Pitti, 10 March – 24 May 2020), edited by S. Barker, Livorno, 2020, pp. 16–29.
Brigstocke H., D'Albo O., *Giulio Cesare Procaccini. Life and Work*, Turin, 2020.
Carofano P., "Considerazioni sul soggiorno romano di Francesco Rustici detto 'Il Rustichino'" (2017), in *A Tale of Two Cities, Rome and Siena in the Early Modern Period (1550-1750)*, edited by S. Sperindei, G. Martina Weston, P. Carofano, Pisa, 2020, pp. 163–187.
Contini R., "Gentileschi patrigno e figliastra", in *Predella. Journal of Visual Arts*, 45–46, 2020, pp. 27–33.
Cosgrove A., "'E scrittrice, e pittrice': Giovanna Garzoni e l'arte della calligrafia", in *"La grandezza dell'universo" nell'arte di Giovanna Garzoni*, exhibition catalogue (Florence, Gallerie degli Uffizi – Palazzo Pitti, 10 March – 24 May 2020), edited by S. Barker, Livorno, 2020, pp. 30–35.
De Girolami Cheney L., *Lavinia Fontana's Mythological Paintings: Art, Beauty and Wisdom*, Cambridge, 2020a.
De Girolami Cheney L., "Lavinia Fontana's 'Galatea': Personification of Fortune and Venus", in *Journal of Literature and Art Studies*, X, 1, 2020b, pp. 42–59.
Donne nell'arte. Da Tiziano a Boldini, exhibition catalogue (Brescia, Palazzo Martinengo Cesaresco, 18 January – 7 June 2020), edited by D. Dotti, Cinisello Balsamo 2020.
Ffolliott S., "'La Miniatrice di Madama Reale': Giovanna Garzoni in Savoia", in *"La grandezza dell'universo" nell'arte di Giovanna Garzoni*, exhibition catalogue (Florence, Gallerie degli Uffizi – Palazzo Pitti, 10 March – 24 May 2020), edited by S. Barker, Livorno, 2020, pp. 46–53.
Focarile P., "L'omaggio di Vittoria della Rovere a Giovanna Garzoni: la Stanza dell'Aurora nella Villa del Poggio Imperiale", in *"La grandezza dell'universo" nell'arte di Giovanna Garzoni*, exhibition catalogue (Florence, Gallerie degli Uffizi – Palazzo Pitti, 10 March – 24 May 2020), edited by S. Barker, Livorno, 2020, pp. 106–115.
Fumagalli E., "Miniatrici e miniatori alla corte dei Medici nel Seicento", in *"La grandezza dell'universo" nell'artea di Giovanna Garzoni*, exhibition catalogue (Florence, Gallerie degli Uffizi – Palazzo Pitti, 10 March – 24 May 2020), edited by S. Barker, Livorno, 2020, pp. 54–60.
Gago B., *Galere perdute. Verdadera relación de la pérdida de la Galera Capitana de Palermo en que venía el Ilustrísimo duque de Terranova de Palermo a Nápoles el mes de abril 1578*, edited by E. Lodi, Milan, 2020.
Garrard M. D., *Artemisia Gentileschi and Feminism in Early Modern Europe*, London, 2020a.
Garrard M. D., "Le nature 'non proprio morte' di Giovanna Garzoni", in *"La grandezza dell'universo" nell'arte di Giovanna Garzoni*, exhibition catalogue (Florence, Gallerie degli Uffizi – Palazzo Pitti, 10 March – 24 May 2020), edited by S. Barker, Livorno, 2020b, pp. 62–77.
"La grandezza dell'universo" nell'arte di Giovanna Garzoni, exhibition catalogue (Florence, Gallerie degli Uffizi – Palazzo Pitti, 10 March – 24 May 2020), edited by S. Barker, Livorno 2020.
Lukehart P. M., "Giovanna Garzoni, 'Accademica'", in *"La grandezza dell'universo" nell'arte di Giovanna Garzoni*, exhibition catalogue (Florence, Gallerie degli Uffizi – Palazzo Pitti, 10 March – 24 May 2020), edited by S. Barker, Livorno, 2020, pp. 96–105.
Mausoli S., "'De la gran Cantona i chiari honori': Caterina Cantoni, Lomazzo, and the Accademia della Val di Blenio", in *Lomazzo's Aesthetic Principles Reflected in the Art of his Time*, edited by L. Tantardini, R. Norris, Boston, 2020, pp. 109–130.
Modesti A., *Women's Patronage and Gendered Cultural Networks in Early Modern Italy*, London-New York, 2020.
Morandotti A., "La ricchezza degli interni. 1. I criteri di allestimento e il ruolo della pittura", in *Vitaliano VI Borromeo. L'invenzione dell'Isola Bella*, exhibition catalogue (Isola Bella, Palazzo Borromeo, 20 March – 2 September 2020), edited by A. Morandotti, M. Natale, Milan, 2020, pp. 44–63.
Morena F., "Una *liaison* esotica. La Cina, i Medici e Giovanna Garzoni", in *"La grandezza dell'universo" nell'arte di Giovanna Garzoni*, exhibition catalogue (Florence, Gallerie degli Uffizi – Palazzo Pitti, 10 March – 24 May 2020), edited by S. Barker, Livorno 2020, pp. 88–95.
Papi G., Chaplin T. D., Gillespie S., "A 'David and Goliath' by Artemisia Gentileschi Rediscovered", in *The Burlington Magazine*, CLXII, 1404, 2020, pp. 188–195.
Pennini A., "Verrua, Filiberto Amedeo Scaglia di", in *Dizionario Biografico degli Italiani*, 99, Rome, 2020 (on-line).
Solinas F., "'Bella, pulita, e senza macchia': Artemisia and Her Letters", in *Artemisia*, exhibition catalogue (London, National Gallery, 3 October 2020 – 24 January 2021), edited by L. Treves, London, 2020, pp. 46–63.
Tongiorgi Tomasi L., "Giovanna Garzoni tra arte e scienza: il panorama floroglo/floristico del suo tempo", in *"La grandezza dell'universo" nell'arte di Giovanna Garzoni*, exhibition catalogue (Florence, Gallerie degli Uffizi – Palazzo Pitti, 10 March – 24 May 2020), edited by S. Barker, Livorno, 2020, pp. 78–87.
Tonini C., "I Morosini dalla Sbarra e il palazzo di santo Stefano nell'Ottocento", in *Palazzo Morosini a Venezia. La dimora dell'ultimo eroe della Serenissima*, edited by V. Mancini, S. Guerriero, Venice, 2020, pp. 125–143.
Tosini P., "Ottaviano Rabasco, un letterato dimenticato nella Roma di Caravaggio, e *La Pallade ignuda* di Lavinia Fontana per Marco Sittico Altemps IV", in *Caravaggio e i letterati*, edited by S. Ebert-Schifferer, L. Tezza, Todi, 2020, pp. 125–140.

Forthcoming

Butchart D., "Sons and Daughters of Florence: the Baptismal Records of Alessandro Striggio's Children", in *Il saggiatore musicale*, forthcoming.
Chiodo A., *Orsola Maddalena Caccia e la virtù pittorica della pittrice monaca*, forthcoming.
Le lettere di Artemisia. Nuova edizione critica e annotata, edited by F. Solinas, Rome, forthcoming.

PHOTOGRAPHIC CREDITS

© Accademia Nazionale di San Luca, Rome: p. 60, cat. 3.3
© Bnf, Paris: p. 31
© Marco Gargano, Dipartimento di Fisica, Università degli Studi di Milano: pp. 84–89
© Matteo Interlenghi, Istituto di Bioimmagini e Fisiologia Molecolare – Consiglio Nazionale delle Ricerche (IBFM-CNR): pp. 81, 83
© The John and Mable Ringling Museum of Art: p. 56
© MiBACT – Musei Reali, Galleria Sabauda: pp. 2–3, cats. 1.4, 1.11, 2.7
© MiBACT – Musei Reali, Palazzo Reale: cats. 4.10, 4.11
© Musée des Beaux-Arts de Limoges, cl. C. Bourgouin: p. 43
© Musée des Beaux-Arts et d'Archéologie, Besançon – Photographie Chipault & Soligny: cat. 3.35
© National Gallery of Art, Washington: p. 29
© Philip Mould & Company: p. 76
© Pinacoteca di Brera, Milan: cats. 1.10, 3.6, 3.19
© The Trustees of the British Museum: fig. 1 p. 26
© Ville de Marseille, Dist. RMN–Grand Palais / Gérard Bonnet-Magellan - Rmn distr. Alinari: cat. 3.9
2021 © MAR – Museo d'Arte della città di Ravenna / ph. Degli Esposti e Nicoletti per Equipe Fotostudio, Bologna: cat. 3.18
Archivio di Stato di Torino: fig. 3 p. 69
Archivio fotografico Civici Musei di Brescia – Fotostudio Rapuzzi: cat. 1.6
Archivio fotografico del Museo Civico, Modena. Photo Paolo Terzi: cats. 3.4, 3.32
Archivio Iconografico del Comune di Ascoli Piceno. Photo Domenico Oddi, Ascoli Piceno: cats. 4.19, 4.20
Biblioteca Angelica. Photo Mario Setter: cat. 1.3
Biblioteca Comunale Ariostea di Ferrara: cats. 2.2, 2.3
Bridgeman Images: p. 27
Barbara Cavalcoli: cat. 4.9
CISM, Udine: p. 45
Collezione d'Arte e di Storia della Fondazione Cassa di Risparmio in Bologna: cats. 3.28, 3.29, 3.36
Collection Musée Savoisien. Savoie. Photo Solenne Paul: fig. 5 p. 70
Courtesy of Cantore Galleria Antiquaria: cat. 3.21
Equipe Fotostudio di Marco Degli Esposti, Bologna: cat. 3.13
Già Fondantico di Tiziana Sassoli, Bologna: cat. 3.15
Fotostudio Rapuzzi: cats. 1.12, 3.8
Fototeca della Veneranda Fabbrica del Duomo di Milano: cats. 1.19, 3.47
Galleria Regionale della Sicilia – Palazzo Abatellis: cats. 3.50, 3.51
Istituto centrale per la grafica, Rome. Courtesy of Ministero per i Beni e le Attività Culturali e per il Turismo: cats. 4.1–4.8, 4.21, 4.22
Istituto per la storia del Risorgimento italiano, Rome: p. 37
Federica Lazzarini: p. 1, cats. 1.5, 3.17, 3.20, 3.45, 3.46, 3.49, 3.54, 3.55
MARCA – Museo delle Arti di Catanzaro. Photi Giulio Archinà: cat. 3.40
Ministero per i Beni e le Attività Culturali e per il Turismo – Galleria Borghese: cover, p. 57, cats. 3.7, 3.11, 3.24, 3.38, 3.48
Museo Civico Casa Cavassa, Saluzzo: fig. 4 p. 70
Museo Civico Medievale, Bologna: cat. 1.1
Museo Correale di Terranova, Sorrento: cat. 5.4
Museo di San Marco, Florence: cats. 2.5, 2.6
Nuova Arte Fotografica, Rome: cat. 1.7
ÖNB/Wien, Cod. 1923, fol. 89*r*: p. 32
Andrea Parisi: cat. 3.23
Photo AD studio Iliana Boccardo: cat. 3.56
Photo Davide Casazza, Vercelli: cat. 3.26
Photo © Luigino Bonato: cat. 2.8
Pinacoteca dell'Accademia dei Concordi, Rovigo: cat. 3.64
Pinacoteca del Castello Sforzesco, Milan. Copyright Comune di Milano, all rigths reserved. Photo Anelli, 1997: cats. 1.13, 1.14
Pinacoteca del Castello Sforzesco, Milan. Copyright Comune di Milano, all rigths reserved. Photo Anelli, 2001: cat. 3.37
Pinacoteca del Castello Sforzesco, Milan. Copyright Comune di Milano, all rigths reserved. Photo Saporetti, 2005: cat. 3.58
Property of Fondazione Pisa/Palazzo Blu: p. 41
Property of Accademia Virgiliana di Mantova, Palazzo Ducale, Mantua. Courtesy Ministero per i Beni e le Attività Culturali e per il Turismo. Photo Michelotti: cat. 2.17
Raczyński Foundation – National Museum in Poznań: pp. 4–5, cat. 1.8
Mauro Ranzani: cat. 1.2
Royal Collection Trust © Her Majesty Queen Elizabeth II, 2021 / Bridgeman Images: p. 40
Andrea Samaritani: pp. 6–7, cat. 5.3
Segretariato Generale della Presidenza della Repubblica: pp. 71, 74
Soprintendenza Speciale per il Patrimonio Storico Artistico ed Etnoantropologico e per il Polo Museale della città di Firenze, Gabinetto fotografico delle Gallerie degli Uffizi, Florence. Courtesy of Ministero per i Beni e le Attività Culturali e per il Turismo: pp. 62, 68, cats. 3.1, 3.39, 4.12, 4.23
Courtesy of Ministero per i Beni e le Attività Culturali e per il Turismo, Biblioteca Nazionale Universitaria di Torino: p. 73, cat. 4.26
Courtesy of Ministero per i Beni e le Attività Culturali e per il Turismo, Direzione Regionale Musei dell'Emilia-Romagna, Pinacoteca Nazionale di Bologna. Under copyright and civil law they cannot be reproduced or copied by any means: cats. 2.1, 3.5, 3.16, 3.25
Courtesy of Ministero per i Beni e le Attività Culturali e per il Turismo, Galleria Nazionale dell'Umbria, Perugia: cats. 2.4, 5.1
Courtesy of Ministero per i Beni e le Attività Culturali e per il Turismo, Museo e Real Bosco di Capodimonte. Under copyright and civil law they cannot be reproduced or copied by any means: fig. 2 p. 26, cats. 3.27, 4.24, 4.25
Courtesy of Ministero per i Beni e le Attività Culturali e per il Turismo, Musei Reali – Biblioteca Reale, Turin: p. 72
Courtesy of Fondazione Accademia Carrara, Bergamo: cat. 1.9
Courtesy of Comune di Padova – Assessorato alla Cultura: p. 8, cats. 3.22, 3.41, 3.42, 3.43
Courtesy of Direzione Musei Statali della città di Roma, Galleria Spada: cat. 3.12
Carlo Vannini: cat. 3.14